2014 Scholarship Handbook

2014 Scholarship Handbook

Seventeenth Edition

The College Board, New York

About the College Board

The College Board is a mission-driven not-for-profit organization that connects students to college success and opportunity. Founded in 1900, the College Board was created to expand access to higher education. Today, the membership association is made up of over 6,000 of the world's leading educational institutions and is dedicated to promoting excellence and equity in education. Each year, the College Board helps more than seven million students prepare for a successful transition to college through programs and services in college readiness and college success — including the SAT® and the Advanced Placement Program®. The organization also serves the education community through research and advocacy on behalf of students, educators and schools.

For further information, visit www.collegeboard.org.

Editorial inquiries concerning this book should be directed to Guidance Publications, The College Board, 45 Columbus Avenue, New York, NY 10023-6992; or telephone 800-323-7155.

Copies of this book are available from your local bookseller or may be ordered from College Board Publications, P.O. Box 4699, Mount Vernon, IL 62864. The book may also be ordered online through the College Board Store at www.collegeboard.org. The price is $29.99.

ISBN: 978-1-4573-0020-2

Printed in the United States of America

Distributed by Macmillan. For information on bulk purchases please contact Macmillan Corporate and Premium Sales Department at (800) 221-7945 x5442.

The College Board is committed to publishing in a manner that both respects the environment and helps preserve its resources. We seek to achieve this through eco-friendly practices, including the use of soy inks, FSC and recycled paper, and biodegradable materials. When you see this symbol, be assured that we are working to reduce our ecological footprint.

Contents

Preface vii

How to Use This Book 1

Understanding Financial Aid 5

Finding and Applying for Scholarships 11

Sources of Information About State Grant Programs 18

Glossary 21

Eligibility Indexes

- Corporate/Employer 27
- Disabilities 27
- Field of Study/Intended Career 27
- Gender 50
- International Student 51
- Military Participation 51
- Minority Status 53
- National/Ethnic Background 58
- Organization/Civic Affiliation 58
- Religious Affiliation 60
- Returning Adult 60
- State of Residence 60
- Study Abroad 77

Scholarships 79

Internships 549

Loans 593

Sponsor Index 605

Program Index 611

Preface

Searching for scholarships has often been described as looking for a needle in a haystack. There are thousands of award programs available, but the typical student can expect to qualify for only a small number of them. This book is designed to point you toward programs that match your own personal and academic qualifications.

Compiled within this book are detailed descriptions of national and state-level award programs for undergraduate students. All are portable to more than one college or university. Most are available to all undergraduates, but some are restricted to entering freshmen, and others are only for continuing students — sophomores, juniors or seniors. Most awards are only available to U.S. citizens or permanent residents, but some are also available to students in other countries who plan to come to the United States for college.

Not included in this book are scholarships that colleges award directly to their own students, as these are generally awarded upon admission rather than by separate application. Such "inside" scholarships can be found listed in the college profiles in the College Board book *Getting Financial Aid 2014*.

The award program descriptions are based on information provided by the sponsors themselves, in response to the College Board's Annual Survey of Financial Aid Programs, conducted in the spring of 2013. A staff of editors verified the facts for every award program. While every effort was made to ensure that the information is correct and up to date, we urge you to confirm facts, especially deadline information, with the programs themselves. The award programs' websites are the best sources for current information.

We'd like to thank those who worked so hard to bring the *Scholarship Handbook 2014* to press: editors Elizabeth Blue, Kelly Borgeson, Lisa Herring, and Rachael Mason, who compiled the data under the direction of project manager Andy Costello. In addition, we would like to thank the team of programmers and composers at DataStream Content Solutions, LLC, who converted the database into readable pages.

Tom Vanderberg
Senior Editor, Guidance Publications

How to Use This Book

You may be tempted to go directly to the program descriptions and start browsing, but to get the most out of this book, start by reading the information and advice in the opening pages. They'll help you get a realistic perspective on financial aid and give you useful guidelines for understanding and taking advantage of your college funding options.

Your next step should be to complete the "Personal Characteristics Checklist" on page 13. This will help you think about all the ways you might qualify for scholarships and give you an idea of where you might start looking for awards you can apply for.

Using the eligibility indexes

After your checklist is complete, use the eligibility indexes beginning on page 27 to find the award programs that correspond to your qualifications. You can also use the scholarship search program on www.collegeboard.org. This user-friendly program enables you to search with more criteria and with much greater speed than is possible with print indexes.

Please keep in mind that the eligibility indexes show programs for which *one* of the criteria is covered by the index. Most of these programs have additional requirements, such as financial need (as demonstrated on the FAFSA or CSS/Financial Aid PROFILE®), standardized test scores or GPA.

Corporate/Employer: Listed here are the many companies and businesses that offer scholarships to employees and/or employees' family members. You should check out any company that employs a member of your immediate family.

Disabilities: This category covers students with hearing or visual impairments, physical handicaps or learning disabilities.

Field of Study/Intended Career: This category, by far the longest, identifies broad major and career areas. If you don't see your specific area of interest, look for a more general area into which it might fit. In many cases, these awards require applicants to be already enrolled in college and to have declared a major in the relevant field.

KNOW THE LINGO

You'll find sidebars like this throughout the first part of this book highlighting and defining key terms. There's also a comprehensive glossary beginning on page 21.

Gender: Although the vast majority of awards are not gender-specific, there are more than 95 awards in this book exclusively for women, and more than 20 for men only.

International Students: Most awards in this book are available only to U.S. citizens or permanent residents. The programs in this category, however, are open to students from outside the United States.

Military Participation: Many of the awards in this category are for the children, descendants or spouses of members of the military, including the Reserves and National Guard, going back as far as the Civil War.

Minority Status: There are eight groups within this category, representing a wide range of awards.

National/Ethnic Background: The national/ethnic groups in this category are determined by the sponsoring organizations that responded to our annual survey.

Organization/Civic Affiliation: Many membership organizations and civic associations have generous higher education funding programs that are available for their members and/or their members' dependents or relatives. Check to see if any apply to your family.

Religious Affiliation: The 10 denominations in this category represent a broad range but, like the national/ethnic category, are determined by the respondents to our annual survey.

Returning Adult: This category includes awards for undergraduate, graduate and nondegree study. The age qualification varies, but most often is for students 25 years or older.

State of Residence: Each state has several award programs exclusively for state residents. Be sure to examine closely all those listed under your state.

Study Abroad: While most award programs for study abroad are for graduate students, a few are geared for undergraduates, and you will find them listed here.

KEEP IN MIND

This book does not describe local award programs that are restricted to a single community or school. For information about local programs for which you might qualify, talk to your school counselor or contact your local chamber of commerce.

Also not included in this are scholarships offered by colleges to their own students. For these "inside" awards, you should consult the financial aid offices at the colleges you are considering. Detailed financial aid information for more than 3,000 colleges can also be found in the College Board book *Getting Financial Aid 2014*.

What's in the program descriptions?

The scholarship programs in this book are organized alphabetically by sponsor within three sections.

The scholarships section covers public and private scholarships and research grants for undergraduates. To be included, a scholarship program must grant at least $250 for the purpose of financing some aspect of higher education: tuition and fees, research, study abroad, travel expenses or other educational endeavors.

PLANNING AHEAD

Even if you qualify for a scholarship, you won't get it if you don't **apply on time**! Use the **planning worksheet on page 17** to keep track of deadlines, application requirements and notification dates for the programs you've selected.

The internships section covers public and private internships, providing opportunities either to earn money for education or to gain academic credit. To be included, paid internships must pay at least $100 per week and provide a viable path toward a future career. (The ESPN internship is an example of this; the Oscar Mayer Wienermobile is not.)

The loans section covers public and private education loan programs. Many have loan forgiveness options, usually in exchange for public or community service for a certain period of time.

Each program description contains all of the information provided by the sponsor and verified for accuracy by a staff of editors at the College Board. A typical description includes:

GOOD TO KNOW

In addition to the eligibility indexes preceding the scholarship descriptions, there are two general indexes in the back of the book that list award programs by sponsor name and program name.

Type of award: Whether the award is a scholarship, grant, internship or loan; and whether it's renewable.

Intended use: Tells you the range and limitations of the award, such as level of study, full time or part time, at what kind of institution, and whether in the United States or abroad.

Eligibility: Indicates the characteristics you must have to be considered for an award — for example, U.S. citizenship, specific state of residence, disability, membership in a particular organization or minority status.

Basis for selection: May include major or career interest; personal qualities such as seriousness of purpose, high academic achievement or depth of character; or financial need.

KNOW THE LINGO

Academic internship — An internship where you are not paid for your work, but rather earn college credit.

Paid internship — An internship where you are paid for your work.

Application requirements: Outlines what you must provide in support of your application, such as recommendations, essay, transcript, interview, proof of eligibility, a résumé or references.

Additional information: Gives you any facts or requirements not covered in the categories above — for example, which test scores to submit, GPA required, whether a particular type of student is given special consideration, when application forms are available, etc.

Amount of award: A single figure generally means the standard amount, but may indicate the maximum of a range of amounts. If a program awards different amounts, the range is provided.

Number of awards: Tells you how many awards are granted by the sponsor.

Number of applicants: Tells you how many students applied the previous year.

Application deadline: The date by which your application must be submitted; some scholarships have two deadlines for considering applications. Note: This information was obtained in spring 2013. Deadlines may have passed or changed. Check the sponsor's website for current deadlines.

Notification begins: The earliest date that an award notification is sent; in some cases, all go out on the same date; in others, notification is on a rolling basis. If there are two application deadlines, there are usually two notification dates.

Total amount awarded: Tells you how much money is disbursed in the current award year, including renewable awards.

Contact: Gives you all available information on where to get application forms and further information. Where the contact name and address are identical for several different scholarship programs sponsored by the same organization, this information will appear at the end of the last scholarship in that group.

While some descriptions don't include all these details because they were either not applicable or not supplied by the sponsor, in every case all essential information is provided. Readers are urged to verify all information (the sponsor's website is the best source) before submitting applications.

Understanding Financial Aid

You shouldn't count on "outside scholarships" and summer internships like the ones in this book to pay for college. Rather, you should treat them as one possible source of aid, along with federal student aid and the scholarships and work-study jobs offered by colleges. In fact, outside scholarships account for only 4 percent of total student financial aid each year.

In order to get the most out of this book, you should first understand how to apply for the other 96 percent of total aid.

What Is Financial Aid?

Financial aid is money given or loaned to you to help you pay for college. Different forms have different rules. The vast majority of aid comes from the federal government, and most of it consists of loans that you must pay back. However, some aid does not require repayment — which makes it the best kind.

If you qualify for financial aid, your college will put together an aid "package," usually with different types of aid bundled together. Most students qualify for some form of financial aid, so it makes sense to apply for it.

You'll apply for financial aid either at the same time or soon after you apply for admission. You may have to fill out more than one application. At the very least you will fill out the FAFSA, or federal government form, available on the Web at www.fafsa.ed.gov. You may also fill out another form, the CSS/Financial Aid PROFILE, which many colleges require. Some colleges and state aid agencies require their own financial aid forms, too. The colleges to which you apply will use the forms to figure out what your family can afford to pay and what your "need" is — that is, the difference between what you can pay and what the college actually costs. If the school wants you as a student but sees that you can't handle the whole bill, it will make you a financial aid offer to help you meet your need. If you accept, that financial aid package is your award.

KNOW THE LINGO

Merit aid — Aid awarded on the basis of academics, character or talent.

Need-based aid — Aid awarded on the basis of a family's inability to pay the full cost of attending a particular college.

Non-need-based aid — Aid awarded on some basis other than need or merit, such as grants with eligibility requirements related to field of study or state residence.

You will need to apply for financial aid every year that you are in college, mainly because your family's financial situation changes yearly. As a result, your financial aid package will probably be somewhat different from year to year.

Financial aid is a helping hand, not a free pass. In the United States, everyone has a right to a free public school education, but not to a free college education. The federal government and most colleges agree that students and their parents are the ones most responsible for paying for college. "The primary responsibility of paying for the student's education lies with the student and his or her parents," says Forrest M. Stuart, the director of financial aid at Furman University in Greenville, S.C. "Financial aid comes in to fill that gap, if you will, between what they can afford and what the college costs."

GOOD TO KNOW

For a more thorough explanation of student financial aid, read the College Board book *Getting Financial Aid 2014*, or read the "Pay for College" articles in BigFuture™ on www.collegeboard.org.

Types of Aid

Financial aid may come in many forms. However, all forms can be grouped into two major categories: gift aid and self-help aid.

Gift Aid

Gift aid is free money, money that you don't have to pay back or work for. Naturally, this is the kind of aid most people want. It can take the form of grants or scholarships.

The terms "grant" and "scholarship" are often used interchangeably to mean free money. But here's the difference: A grant is usually given only on the basis of need, or your family's inability to pay the full cost of college. Scholarships are usually awarded only to those who have "merit," such as proven ability in academics, the arts or athletics. Once you're in college, you may have to maintain a minimum GPA or take certain courses to continue receiving a scholarship.

Self-Help Aid

Self-help aid is money that requires a contribution from you. That can mean paying back the money (if the aid is a loan) or working for the money (if the aid is a work-study job).

The most common form of self-help aid is a loan. A loan is money that you have to pay back with interest. In light of that, you might not consider this aid at all. But it is — a loan means you don't have to pay the full price of college all at once: You can stretch the payments over time, as you would when buying a house or a car. Furthermore, some student loans are subsidized by the federal government, which means you don't have to pay the interest that comes due while you're in college.

Subsidized loans, which are awarded based on need and administered by the college, are the best kind. But you can also take out unsubsidized student loans and parent loans, which are not packaged by most colleges. However, be careful not to take on more debt than necessary. No matter what kind of loan you take out, you will have to pay it back.

Another form of self-help is work-study. This is financial aid in the form of a job. Since you earn the money through your work, this too may not seem like aid. But it is, because the federal work-study program pays most of your wages. And work-study jobs are usually available right on campus, with limits on your hours so that you won't be unduly distracted from studying.

Who Gets Aid?

Grants and loans are not just for the poorest of the poor, nor are scholarships only for the smartest of the smart. The truth about who gets financial aid is somewhat different from what many people think.

Those Who Need It

Most financial aid is based on need, not merit. There is money for merit, but most colleges in the United States focus their financial aid packages on meeting financial need.

However, there is a lot of confusion about what "need" means. "A lot of people think that they either have to be on welfare or Social Security — really poor — to get financial aid, and that's not correct," says Mary San Agustin, director of financial aid and scholarships at Palomar College in San Marcos, Calif. On the other hand, some wealthy families mistakenly think they are needy because their high living expenses leave them little money for college. "It's this expectation of, I pay my taxes, so my kid should be entitled to some federal financial aid regardless of how much money I make," says San Agustin.

Need simply means that your family can't afford to pay the full cost of a particular college. The *amount* of your need will vary from college to college, because it depends on the cost of attending an individual college. Whether your family has need is determined not by whether you think you are rich or poor, but by the financial aid forms you fill out.

Those Who Don't

Despite the overall emphasis on need, many colleges do give away money on the basis of merit. They do this to attract the students they want most, and they may award this money even if it is more than the student needs. However, in many cases, the student both needs the money and has earned it on the basis of merit.

Don't think that only geniuses get merit aid. At many colleges a B average can put you in the running for merit money. Sometimes a separate application for merit aid is required to put you into consideration; sometimes your application for admission is enough. In either case, don't count yourself out by not applying; apply and let the college decide.

Grants are sometimes awarded based on neither need nor merit. For example, you may get a grant if you are in a certain field of study, are a resident of the state, or are a student from the same town as the college.

KNOW THE LINGO

EFC (Expected Family Contribution) — How much money a family is expected to pay for college, based on the family's ability to pay.

Need — The difference between your EFC and the cost of attending a particular college you've chosen. Financial aid is designed to meet your need, not your EFC.

Gap — The difference (if any) between the financial aid you need and the amount offered by a particular college.

Part-Time Students

Some kinds of aid are only available to students enrolled in college full time — usually 12 or more credit hours of courses per semester. But part-time students are eligible for some financial aid. For example, federal loan programs require only that students be enrolled at least half time. Also, some employers offer tuition reimbursement benefits to students who work full time and go to college part time.

Where the Money Comes From

Financial aid comes from three basic sources: governments (both federal and state), colleges and outside benefactors.

From the Government

The lion's share of total financial aid awarded to undergraduates comes from the federal government. Fully 74 percent of all such aid is sent from Washington. For undergraduates, the largest chunk of that aid consists of federal loans, which total $70 billion a year and represent 39 percent of all student aid. The loans take multiple shapes. Perkins loans are subsidized, with the lowest interest rate of any education loan. Stafford loans may be subsidized or unsubsidized. Both Perkins and Stafford loans are for students, but parents may take out a PLUS loan, which is not subsidized, to help pay for their children's education.

The federal government also offers grants, such as the Pell Grant and the Supplemental Educational Opportunity Grant (SEOG). These grants are strictly need based, with no academic criteria. The government also funds the federal work-study program, which provides part-time employment (usually on-campus) and is also strictly need-based.

A much smaller piece of the financial aid pie (5 percent) comes from individual state governments. This is available in the form of grants, scholarships and loans. Most of this aid is for use only at colleges within the state, though a few states offer "portable" aid, which state residents can take with them to a college in another state.

From the College

A great deal of financial aid comes from individual colleges, using their own "institutional" funds. In fact, colleges award nearly half of all grants. Many, though not all, award merit scholarships as well as need-based grants. They may also offer on-campus job opportunities and loans.

Private colleges give more financial aid than public ones, but their tuition is usually higher as well. Public colleges award less aid, but taxpayer support keeps their tuition lower.

Outside Grants and Scholarships

Outside grants and scholarships (what you will find in this book) come from sources other than the college. These sources may include corporations like Coca-Cola or community groups like the Elks Club. Some are well known, such as National Merit Scholarship Corporation, but altogether they are the smallest piece of the financial aid pie: Only 4 percent of all student aid comes from outside sources. Pursue them, but don't expect them to outweigh the other aid you will get.

Bear in mind also that an outside scholarship is unlikely to expand the total aid you receive. If a college has already "met your full need" — that is, offered an aid package that covers the entire difference between what the college costs and what your family is expected to pay — it will not add an outside scholarship to that aid package. Rather, it will use your scholarship to substitute for some other piece of aid in the package. Think of your financial aid package as a barrel: When the barrel is full, no more can be added unless something is taken away. The last thing colleges will take away is whatever sum of money your family is expected to contribute.

How Outside Awards Can Help

Even though outside scholarships rarely decrease the amount that your family is expected to pay out of pocket, it's still very worthwhile to pursue them. Why? Simply put, they expand your options for where you can go to college.

At some colleges, the first things taken away from a full-need package to make room for an outside scholarship are loans. Since that reduces the total amount you will have to pay back later, it makes that college more affordable. (Colleges vary in their policies on how they adjust packages for outside scholarships; you should call or e-mail the financial aid offices at the colleges you're considering to learn about their policies.)

There are also colleges that can't afford to offer every admitted student a financial aid package that meets the student's full need. If, for example, your need is $25,000 at a particular university, and the university's aid office can only offer you a combined total of $23,000 in grants, scholarships, work-study and subsidized federal loans, then there is a $2,000 "gap" in your aid package. Outside scholarships can help fill that gap.

Finally, there may be colleges where you don't have any financial need. For example, if your family's expected contribution to your college costs is $10,000, a state university that costs $10,000 a year to attend couldn't offer you any need-based aid. An outside merit scholarship, in this case, could decrease what your family pays below their expected contribution.

FINANCIAL AID APPLICATION CALENDAR

SOPHOMORE/JUNIOR YEARS

- Talk to your parents about college costs. Have realistic expectations, but understand how financial aid can expand your options.
- Take the PSAT/NMSQT® in October of each year. If you take it as a junior and meet other requirements, you will be entered into National Merit Scholarship Corporation competitions.
- Think about colleges you might want to apply to. If possible, visit some campuses in the spring of your junior year.
- Take the SAT® in the spring of your junior year.
- If you have a job, do your taxes each year (ask your parents for help). Knowing about tax forms and documents will be helpful when you have to fill out financial aid applications.
- Think about taking SAT Subject Tests™ near the end of courses in the subject areas you are studying.

SENIOR YEAR

SEPTEMBER

- Create a list of colleges you want to apply to. Start a checklist of their financial aid requirements and deadlines.
- If you're thinking about applying Early Decision to a college, ask whether it offers an early estimate of financial aid eligibility, and if so, what forms are required to receive one.
- Begin searching for outside scholarship programs available to seniors. Ask your school counselor about local scholarships offered by groups and businesses in your community.

OCTOBER

- Ask your school counselor if there will be a family financial aid night at your school or elsewhere in your area this fall. If there is, be sure to attend; the event may be your single best source of information.
- Use the online calculators at **www.collegeboard.org** to estimate your family's Expected Family Contribution (EFC).
- If you need to fill out the CSS/Financial Aid PROFILE, you can do so on the PROFILE Online Web site starting Oct. 1.

NOVEMBER

- Finalize the list of colleges that you'll apply to regular decision. Make sure you have all the financial aid forms you need.
- Starting Nov. 1, you can visit the FAFSA on the Web and get a sense of how the site works and what the application will ask for. But remember, you can't file the FAFSA until Jan. 1.

DECEMBER

- You and your parents should save all end-of-year pay stubs for the year. You can use these to estimate income on aid forms.
- Apply for scholarships in time to meet application deadlines.
- Get PINs for the FAFSA for both yourself and one of your parents from **www.pin.ed.gov**.

JANUARY

- You can file the FAFSA starting Jan. 1.
- If any colleges you're applying to have a financial aid priority date of Feb. 1, fill out the FAFSA (and PROFILE, if necessary) using estimated income information from your end-of-year pay stubs and last year's tax returns.
- Submit any other financial aid forms that may be required. Keep copies.

FEBRUARY

- If you didn't file the FAFSA and other aid forms in January, do so now, using drafts of your family's income tax returns.
- Use the IRS Data Retrieval Tool (available through FAFSA on the Web) to update your FAFSA after your family's tax returns have been processed by the IRS (about three weeks after filing the return online, eight weeks if filed by mail.)
- You and your parents should consider filing your income tax returns early this year. Some colleges will want to verify the information on your family's returns before finalizing offers.

MARCH

- If necessary, write to colleges alerting them to special circumstances that affect your family's ability to pay for college.
- As you begin to receive letters of acceptance, check with aid offices to see if additional documentation (such as tax forms) must be submitted.

APRIL

- Compare your financial aid award letters using the online tools at **www.collegeboard.org**.
- Write, e-mail or call the colleges that have offered you aid if you have any questions about the packages they've offered you.
- If you don't get enough aid to be able to attend a college, consider your options, which include appealing the award.

MAY

- Be sure to accept the aid package from the college you want to attend by May 1.
- Be sure also to let other schools know you won't be attending.
- Plan now how you will cover your family's out-of-pocket expenses.
- Apply for loans if necessary.

Finding and Applying for Scholarships

While you're researching and applying for colleges, you should also use this book to find scholarships that you qualify for and apply for them. In this chapter you'll find advice, as well as a calendar and worksheets to help keep you on track.

When to Start Looking

It's never too early to start looking for scholarships. There are several programs that are open only to high school freshmen and sophomores, and some that are open only to juniors. There are other programs where you begin the work of applying up to a year before the final determination is made. For example, National Merit Scholarship Corporation competitions begin when students take the PSAT/NMSQT® in October of their junior year, and the competitions proceed in several rounds until fall of their senior year. If you're already a senior, though, don't despair — there are plenty of programs for entering freshmen that you can apply for during your senior year.

No matter what grade level you're in, the best time of the year to research programs is in the summer or early fall. That way you can be sure to find programs before their deadlines have passed, and with enough advance time to prepare a complete, competitive application. Remember that many scholarship programs require you to submit an essay as part of your application, and essays take time to write. Many programs also require recommendations; as a general rule, you should ask for recommendations at least four weeks in advance, and preferably more. Some programs even require you to perform additional academic work outside of school, such as writing a research paper or competing in a science fair.

You should let your school counselor know as early as possible that you're interested in applying for scholarships. He or she can help you think about your strengths as a student, which will make it easier to narrow down your scholarship search. Your counselor will also be able to recommend some programs you should apply for. (See "Thinking Locally" on page 14.)

PLANNING AHEAD

If you haven't already started looking for scholarships, start now. Today. Use this book to find a program you qualify for, and make a note of its application deadline and requirements. Then go to the program's website and download an application.

Playing Catch-Up

If it's already the middle of your senior year, you've probably missed a lot of opportunities to apply for scholarships with October, November and December deadlines. But don't give up yet; there are plenty of scholarships with January, February and March deadlines.

The key to playing catch-up is to start working now, today. Find scholarships where the deadline hasn't passed. Get applications from the sponsors' websites. Talk to your school counselor immediately. The longer you wait, the less likely you are to win any awards.

The good news: Since you're already far into the college application process, you're now a pro at describing yourself to admission committees and scholarship review boards. You also have personal essays, academic writing samples and teacher recommendations ready to go.

Choosing Where to Apply

There are so many scholarships, grants, fellowships, internships, fee waivers, work-study jobs and low-interest loans available for college-level study that just looking at the options can be daunting. (This book alone describes 2,100 national and state-level programs.) Fortunately, there are some easy ways to narrow the field of potential programs down to the ones where you have a good chance of winning an award.

The personal characteristics checklist on the next page highlights some of the common eligibility criteria for scholarship programs. You're not likely to find a scholarship that's targeted to every one of your characteristics, but you can use your answers on the checklist as a starting point for finding programs. The eligibility indexes on pages 27 to 69 will help you quickly match your characteristics to programs.

You'll probably find a few scholarship programs that match your characteristics. If you find a lot, you should consider narrowing your search — applying for scholarships is a lot of work! It's far better to send in four high-quality applications to programs that closely match your characteristics and interests than to send 16 hurried applications to a wide variety of programs.

PERSONAL CHARACTERISTICS CHECKLIST

Are you **male** or **female**?

What is your **state of residence**?

Do you have a **learning or physical disability**? Many scholarships are offered to those who are disabled in any way, but some are for those with a specific disability.

Military service is the basis of many scholarships. Many of these awards are not just for those who have worn a uniform, but also for their spouses and children, or even descendants of a veteran. Talk to your family about its military history (was Grandpa in the Korean War?) Be sure to find out what branch of the military your family members served in, and, if possible, which unit(s) they served in.

List any family history of military service here:

You'll find scholarships for students with **minority status**, (e.g., African American, Alaska Native), and also for students with a particular **nationality or ethnic background** (e.g., Chinese, Greek).

If you belong to a minority, list it here:

List your ethnic and/or national origin(s) here:

What, if any, is your **religious affiliation**?

Are you an **international student** (a citizen of a foreign country, including Canada, seeking to study in the United States)?

The largest category of scholarships and internships is for students planning to study a particular college major (e.g., math, English, a foreign language) or prepare for a particular career (e.g., law, education, aviation). Even if you are "undecided" at this point, you should list all the **majors/careers** you are leaning toward.

☐ Do you want to **study abroad**? There are scholarships to help you pay for it — check here to remind yourself to seek them out.

"**Returning adult**" refers to students who have been out of high school a year or more before entering college. If that's you, look for scholarships designed to encourage your pursuit.

Years out of high school:

Your age:

Do you or any members of your family belong to a **national or local organization** or **civic association** (e.g., Kiwanis, Rotary, Elks Club)? Many such groups offer scholarships to members and/or their families. List here any that apply:

Employers and corporations often offer scholarship benefits to employees and/or their families. List the companies that you or someone in your family works for here:

Narrowing Your Search

If you're having trouble narrowing down your scholarship search, consider the following:

How many applicants are there each year? Some of the better-known programs (such as the Coca-Cola Scholars Program) see hundreds of applicants for every award they give out! It can't hurt to apply for these programs, but you shouldn't invest so much effort in applying for them that you miss out on smaller programs where your chances may be better.

Is this really for me? If you couldn't get through *Atlas Shrugged* the first time, don't force yourself to read it and write an essay on its philosophical meaning for the Ayn Rand Institute contest — even if you're a great English student. Focus instead on programs that appeal to you or sound like fun.

Can I live with the strings attached? Many scholarship and internship programs have service requirements. Most notably, the Reserve Officers Training Corps (ROTC) program requires cadets to become military reserve officers upon graduation. And some summer internships will require you to move to another city.

KEEP IN MIND

Don't let your scholarship search overshadow your other responsibilities and application requirements. You still need to do well in school, get your college applications in on time, and submit the FAFSA and other financial aid forms by your colleges' priority dates.

Thinking Locally

This book contains national and statewide financial aid programs offered by government agencies, charitable foundations and major corporations. But there are also thousands of small scholarship programs offered on a local level by civic clubs, parishes, memorial foundations and small businesses.

In many cases, these programs award just a few hundred dollars — enough to buy a semester's worth of textbooks. But since they are offered on a local level, your chances of receiving an award are much higher than they are for the big national competitions. So it pays to look for local scholarships.

Your school counselor may have files of local scholarship programs. There may even be a scholarship designated for graduates of your high school — you'll never know until you ask. You should also check with employers (either your parents' or your own); your church, temple or mosque; and any civic clubs that your family members are involved in.

Avoiding Scholarship Scams

The Federal Trade Commission (FTC) developed Project $cholar$cam to alert students and families about potential scams and how to recognize them. Here are the FTC's seven basic warning signs:

- "This scholarship is guaranteed or your money back."
- "You can't get this information anywhere else."
- "May I have your credit card/bank account number to hold this scholarship?"
- "We'll do all the work for you."

GOOD TO KNOW

For more information about Project $cholar$cam, visit the FTC's website at **www.ftc.gov**.

- "The scholarship will cost some money."
- "You've been selected by a national foundation to receive a scholarship."
- "You're a finalist" in a competition you never entered.

Remember that no one can guarantee that you'll receive a grant or scholarship, and that you will have to do the work of submitting applications to be considered. Don't pay money for a service without a written document saying what you'll get for your money and what the company's refund policies are. And never, ever give your credit card number, Social Security number or bank account information to someone who called you unsolicited.

Applying for Scholarships

This may mean not only filling out a form but also compiling supporting documents, such as transcripts, recommendations and an essay. Or you might need to provide evidence of leadership, patriotism, depth of character, desire to serve, or financial need. Get to know the requirements of each scholarship as early as possible so you can do any necessary extra work on time.

A few pointers to remember:

Apply early! Apply as early as possible to scholarship programs. If you can, do it in the fall of your senior year, even if the deadlines aren't until February or March. Very often, scholarship programs will have awarded all their funds for the year on a first-come, first-served basis before their stated deadline.

Follow directions. Read instructions carefully and do what they say. Scholarship programs receive hundreds and even thousands of applications. Don't lose out because of failure to submit a typewritten essay versus a handwritten one if required, or to provide appropriate recommendations. If you have a question about your eligibility for a particular scholarship or how to complete the application, contact the scholarship sponsors.

Be organized. It's a good idea to create a separate file for each scholarship and sort them by their due dates. Track application deadlines and requirements. Store in one place the different supporting documents you may need, such as transcripts, standardized test scores and letters of recommendation.

Check your work. Proofread your applications for spelling or grammar errors, fill in all blanks and make sure your handwriting is legible.

Keep copies of everything. If application materials get lost, having copies on file will make it easier to resend the application quickly.

Reapply. Some programs only offer money for the first year of college, but others must be renewed each subsequent year.

SCHOLARSHIP APPLICATION PLANNER

	PROGRAM 1	PROGRAM 2	PROGRAM 3
PROGRAM/SPONSOR	*WyzAnt Scholarship*	*Young Epidemiology Scholars*	*First Bank*
ELIGIBILITY REQUIREMENTS	*Essay contest*	*Academic merit*	*Need, local residency*
TYPE OF AWARD	*Scholarship*	*Scholarship*	*Internship*
AMOUNT OF AWARD	*$2,000–$5,000*	*$1,000 or more*	*$2,500*
CAN BE USED FOR	*Any expense*	*Any expense*	*Any expense*
CAN BE USED AT	*Any 4-yr college*	*Any college*	*In-state colleges*
DEADLINE	*April 1*	*Feb. 1*	*April 1*
FORMS REQUIRED	*Online application*	*Web form*	*Application (includes need analysis)*
TEST SCORES REQUIRED	*None*	*None*	*SAT*
ESSAY OR ACADEMIC SAMPLE	*300-word essay*	*Essay, research project*	*None required*
RECOMMENDATIONS	*None*	*None*	*One teacher (Mr. Filmer), Local branch manager*
NOTIFICATION BEGINS	*May 15*	*Not sure*	*May 15*
REQUIREMENTS TO KEEP AFTER FRESHMAN YEAR	*One-time payment only*	*One-time payment only*	*Based on performance during internship*

For a blank version of this worksheet that you can photocopy for your own use, see the next page.

SCHOLARSHIP APPLICATION PLANNER

	PROGRAM 1	PROGRAM 2	PROGRAM 3
PROGRAM/SPONSOR			
ELIGIBILITY REQUIREMENTS			
TYPE OF AWARD			
AMOUNT OF AWARD			
CAN BE USED FOR			
CAN BE USED AT			
DEADLINE			
FORMS REQUIRED			
TEST SCORES REQUIRED			
ESSAY OR ACADEMIC SAMPLE			
RECOMMENDATIONS			
NOTIFICATION BEGINS			
REQUIREMENTS TO KEEP AFTER FRESHMAN YEAR			

Sources of Information About State Grant Programs

Alabama
Alabama Commission on Higher Education
P.O. Box 302000
Montgomery, AL 36130-2000
334-242-1998
www.ache.state.al.us

Alaska
Alaska Commission on Postsecondary Education
P.O. Box 110510
Juneau, AK 99811-0510
800-441-2962
www.acpe.alaska.gov

Arizona
Arizona Department of Education
1535 West Jefferson Street
Phoenix, AZ 85007
800-352-4558
www.azed.gov

Arkansas
Arkansas Department of Higher Education
23 Main Street, Ste. 400
Little Rock, AR 72201
501-371-2050
www.adhe.edu

California
California Student Aid Commission
P.O. Box 419026
Rancho Cordova, CA 95741-9026
888-224-7268
www.csac.ca.gov

Colorado
Colorado Department of Education
201 East Colfax Avenue
Denver, CO 80203-1799
303-866-6600
www.cde.state.co.us

Connecticut
Connecticut Office of Higher Education
61 Woodland Street
Hartford, CT 06105-2326
860-947-1800
www.ctohe.org

Delaware
Delaware Higher Education Office
John G. Townsend Bldg.
401 Federal St., Ste. 2
Dover, DE 19901
800-292-7935
www.doe.k12.de.us/dheo

District of Columbia
Office of the State Superintendent of Education
810 First Street, NE, 9th Floor
Washington, DC 20002
202-727-6436
www.seo.dc.gov

Florida
Florida Department of Education
Office of Student Financial Assistance
325 W. Gaines Street, Suite 1314
Tallahassee, FL 32399-0400
888-827-2004
www.floridastudentfinancialaid.org

Georgia
Georgia Student Finance Commission
2082 East Exchange Place
Tucker, GA 30084
800-505-4732
www.gsfc.org

Hawaii
Hawaii State Department of Education
P.O. Box 2360
Honolulu, HI 96804
808-586-3230
www.doe.k12.hi.us

Idaho
Idaho State Department of Education
650 West State Street
P.O. Box 83720
Boise, ID 83720-0027
800-432-4601
www.sde.idaho.gov

Illinois
Illinois Student Assistance Commission
1755 Lake Cook Road
Deerfield, IL 60015-5209
800-899-4722
www.isac.org

Indiana
State Student Assistance Commission of Indiana
W462 Indiana Government Center South
402 West Washington Street
Indianapolis, IN 46204
888-528-4719
www.in.gov/ssaci

Iowa
Iowa College Student Aid Commission
603 E. 12th Street, FL 5th
Des Moines, IA 50319
877-272-4456
www.iowacollegeaid.gov

Kansas
Kansas Board of Regents
1000 SW Jackson Street, Suite 520
Topeka, KS 66612-1368
785-296-3421
www.kansasregents.org

Kentucky
KHEAA Student Aid Branch
100 Airport Road
Frankfort, KY 40602
800-928-8926
www.kheaa.com

Louisiana
Louisiana Office of Student Financial Assistance
602 North 5th Street
Baton Rouge, LA 70802
800-259-5626
www.osfa.la.gov

Maine
Finance Authority of Maine
Education Assistance Division
P.O. Box 949
5 Community Drive
Augusta, ME 04332-0949
800-228-3734
www.famemaine.com

Maryland
Maryland Higher Education Commission
Office of Student Financial Assistance
6 N. Liberty St.
Baltimore, MD 21201
800-974-0203
www.mhec.state.md.us

Massachusetts
Massachusetts Department of Higher Education
Office of Student Financial Assistance
454 Broadway, Suite 200
Revere, MA 02151-3034
617-727-9420
www.osfa.mass.edu

Michigan
Michigan Higher Education Assistance Authority
Office of Scholarships and Grants
P.O. Box 30462
Lansing, MI 48909-7962
888-447-2687
www.michigan.gov/mistudentaid

Minnesota
Minnesota Office of Higher Education
1450 Energy Park Drive, Suite 350
St. Paul, MN 55108-5227
800-657-3866
www.ohe.state.mn.us

Mississippi
Mississippi Office of Student Financial Aid
3825 Ridgewood Road
Jackson, MS 39211-6453
800-327-2980
www.mississippi.edu/riseupms

Missouri
Missouri Department of Higher Education
205 Jefferson Street
P.O. Box 1469
Jefferson City, MO 65102-1469
800-473-6757
www.dhe.mo.gov

Montana
Montana Board of Regents
P.O. Box 203201
2500 Broadway Street
Helena, MT 59620-3201
406-444-6570
http://mus.edu/board

Nebraska
Coordinating Commission for Postsecondary Education
P.O. Box 95005
Lincoln, NE 68509-5005
402-471-2847
www.ccpe.state.ne.us

Nevada
Nevada Department of Education
700 East Fifth Street
Carson City, NV 89701
775-687-9220
www.doe.nv.gov

New Hampshire
New Hampshire Postsecondary Education Commission
101 Pleasant Street
Concord, NH 03301-3494
888-747-2382, ext. 119
www.education.nh.gov/highered

New Jersey
HESAA Grants & Scholarships
P.O. Box 540
Trenton, NJ 08625-0540
800-792-8670
www.hesaa.org

New Mexico
New Mexico Higher Education Department
2048 Galisteo Street
Santa Fe, NM 87505
505-476-8400
www.hed.state.nm.us

New York
New York State Higher Education Services Corporation
99 Washington Avenue
Albany, NY 12255
888-697-4372
www.hesc.ny.gov

North Carolina
North Carolina State Education Assistance Authority
P.O. Box 14103
Research Triangle Park, NC 27709
919-549-8614
www.ncseaa.edu

North Dakota
North Dakota University System
10th Floor, State Capitol
600 East Boulevard Ave, Dept. 215
Bismarck, ND 58505-0230
701-328-2960
www.ndus.edu

Ohio
Ohio Board of Regents
25 South Front Street
Columbus, OH 43215
614-466-6000
www.ohiohighered.org

Oklahoma
Oklahoma State Regents for Higher Education
Tuition Aid Grant Program
655 Research Parkway, Suite 200
Oklahoma City, OK 73104
405-225-9100
www.okhighered.org

Oregon
Oregon Student Assistance Commission
1500 Valley River Drive, Suite 100
Eugene, OR 97401
800-452-8807
www.oregonstudentaid.gov

Pennsylvania
Pennsylvania Higher Education Assistance Agency
1200 North Seventh Street
Harrisburg, PA 17102-1444
800-233-0557
www.pheaa.org

Puerto Rico
Departmento de Educacion
P.O. Box 190759
San Juan, PR 00919-0759
787-773-3475
www.de.gobierno.pr

Rhode Island
Rhode Island Higher Education Assistance Authority
560 Jefferson Boulevard, Suite 100
Warwick, RI 02886-1304
800-922-9855
www.riheaa.org

South Carolina
South Carolina Commission on Higher Education
1122 Lady Street, Suite 300
Columbia, SC 29201
803-737-2260
www.che.sc.gov

South Dakota
South Dakota Department of Education
Office of Finance and Management
800 Governors Drive
Pierre, SD 57501
605-773-3134
www.doe.sd.gov

Tennessee
Tennessee Student Assistance Corporation
404 James Robertson Parkway, Suite 1510, Parkway Towers
Nashville, TN 37243-0820
800-342-1663
www.state.tn.us/tsac

Texas
Texas Higher Education Coordinating Board
Student Loan Programs
P.O. Box 12788
Austin, TX 78711-2788
800-242-3062
www.hhloans.com

Utah
Utah Higher Education Assistance Authority
P.O. Box 145110
Salt Lake City, UT 84114-5112
877-336-7378
www.uheaa.org

Vermont
Vermont Student Assistance Corporation
P.O. Box 999
Winooski, VT 05404
800-798-8722
www.vsac.org

Virginia
State Council of Higher Education for Virginia
James Monroe Building
101 North 14th Street, 10th Fl.
Richmond, VA 23219
804-225-2600
www.schev.edu

Washington
Washington Higher Education Coordinating Board
P.O. Box 43430
Olympia, WA 98504-3430
360-753-7800
www.hecb.wa.gov

West Virginia
West Virginia Higher Education Policy Commission
Central Office, Higher Education Grant Program
1018 Kanawha Boulevard East, Suite 700
Charleston, WV 25301-2800
304-558-4614
wvhepcnew.wvnet.edu/

Wisconsin
Wisconsin Higher Educational Aids Board
P. O. Box 7885
Madison, WI 53707-7885
608-267-2206
www.heab.state.wi.us

Wyoming
Wyoming Department of Education
2300 Capitol Avenue
Hathaway Building, Second Floor
Cheyenne, WY 82002-0050
307-777-7690
www.edu.wyoming.gov

Guam
University of Guam
Student Financial Aid Office
UOG Station
Mangilao, GU 96923
www.uog.edu

Virgin Islands
Financial Aid Office, Virgin Islands Board of Education
P.O. Box 11900
St. Thomas, VI 00801
340-774-4546
www.myviboe.com

Glossary

ACT. A college admission test given at test centers on specified dates. Please visit the organization's website for further information.

Advanced Placement Program® (AP®). An academic program of the College Board that provides high school students with the opportunity to study and learn at the college level. AP offers courses in 34 subjects, each culminating in a rigorous exam. High schools offer the courses and administer the exams to interested students. Most colleges and universities accept qualifying AP Exam scores for credit, advanced placement, or both.

Bachelor's, or baccalaureate, degree. A degree received after the satisfactory completion of a four- or five-year, full-time program of study (or its part-time equivalent) at a college or university. The bachelor of arts (B.A.), bachelor of science (B.S.), and bachelor of fine arts (B.F.A.) are the most common bachelor's degrees. Policies concerning their award vary from college to college.

College Scholarship Service (CSS). A unit of the College Board that assists postsecondary institutions, state scholarship programs and private scholarship organizations in the equitable and efficient distribution of student financial aid funds, mainly through its stewardship of the CSS/Financial Aid PROFILE.

Community/junior college. A two-year college. Community colleges are public, whereas junior colleges are private. Both usually offer vocational programs as well as the first two years of a four-year program.

Competition. An award based upon superior performance in relation to others in the competition. This book lists competitions based upon artistic talent, writing ability and other demonstrable talents.

Cooperative education (co-op). A career-oriented program in which students alternate between class attendance and employment in business, industry or government. Co-op students usually receive both academic credit and payment for their work. Under a cooperative plan, five years are normally required for completion of a bachelor's degree, but graduates have the advantage of about a year's practical work experience in addition to their studies.

CSS code. A four-digit College Board number that students use to designate colleges or scholarship programs to receive their CSS/Financial Aid PROFILE information. A complete list of all CSS codes can be viewed at the CSS/Financial Aid PROFILE section on collegeboard.org.

CSS/Financial Aid PROFILE®. A Web-based application service offered by the College Board and used by some colleges, universities and private scholarship programs to award their private financial aid funds. Students register for and complete the PROFILE on collegeboard.org. The PROFILE is not a federal form and may not be used to apply for federal student aid.

Curriculum Vitae (CV). A type of résumé, from the Latin for "the course of one's life." Typically, a CV is used by applicants for fellowships or grants, or jobs in higher education, the sciences, or in a research capacity. The CV is typically longer than a résumé, and provides details about papers published, research conducted and more.

Dependents. Generally speaking, people who are dependent upon others (parents, relatives, a spouse) for food, clothing, shelter, and other basics. For purposes of getting federal financial aid, students must meet strict criteria in order to be defined as dependents; in the view of federal aid programs, the family is the primary source of support for college. College students may have dependents (children dependent on them), and this too is taken into account by the federal government. Federal forms ask a series of questions about age, marital status, etc., to determine whether applicants are dependent on others or independent.

Direct Loan Program. *See* Federal Direct Loan Program.

Expected Family Contribution (EFC). The total amount students and their families are expected to pay toward college costs from their income and assets for one academic year.

FAFSA. *See* Free Application for Federal Student Aid.

Federal code number. A six-digit number that identifies a specific college to which students want their Free Application for Federal Student Aid form submitted. Also known as the Title IV number.

Federal Parent Loan for Undergraduate Students (PLUS). A program that permits parents of undergraduate students to borrow up to the full cost of education, less any other financial aid the student may have received.

Federal Pell Grant Program. A federally sponsored and administered program that provides need-based grants to undergraduate students. Eligibility for Pell Grants is based on a student's expected family contribution, the total cost of attendance at the college, and whether the student is attending the college full time or part time.

Federal Perkins Loan Program. A federally funded campus-based program that provides low-interest loans, based on need, for undergraduate study. The combined cumulative total of loan funds available to an individual for undergraduate study is $27,500. Repayment need not begin until completion of the student's education, and may be deferred for limited periods of service in the military, Peace Corps or approved comparable organizations. The total debt may be forgiven by the federal government if the recipient enters a career of service as a public health nurse, law enforcement officer, public school teacher or social worker.

Federal Stafford Loan. A program that allows students to borrow money for education expenses from banks and other lending institutions (and sometimes from the colleges themselves). Subsidized Stafford loans are offered by colleges based on need. The federal government pays the interest on subsidized loans while the borrower is in college. Unsubsidized Stafford loans are non-need-based; anyone may apply for one, regardless of their ability to pay for college. The interest on unsubsidized loans begins accumulating immediately. For both programs, the amounts that may be borrowed depend on the student's year in school.

Federal student aid. A number of programs sponsored by the federal government that award students loans, grants or work-study jobs for the purpose of meeting their financial need. To receive any federal student aid, a student must demonstrate financial need by filing the Free Application for Federal Student Aid, be enrolled in college at least half time, and meet certain other eligibility requirements.

Federal Supplemental Educational Opportunity Grant Program (SEOG). A federal campus-based program that provides need-based grants for undergraduate study. Each college is given a certain total amount of SEOG money each year to distribute among its financial aid applicants, and each determines the amount to which the student is entitled.

Federal Work-Study Program. A campus-based financial aid program that allows students to meet some of their financial need by working on or off campus while attending school. The wages earned are used to help pay the student's education costs for the academic year. Job opportunities vary from campus to campus. The time commitment for a work-study job is usually between 10 and 15 hours each week.

Financial aid. Money awarded to students to help them pay for college. Financial aid comes in the form of gifts (scholarships and grants) and self-help aid (loans and work-study opportunities). Most aid is awarded on the basis of financial need, but some awards are non-need-based. Both need-based and non-need-based aid may be offered on the additional basis of merit.

Financial aid award letter. *See* award letter.

Financial aid package. The total financial aid offered to a student by a college, including all loans, grants, scholarships and work-study opportunities.

Financial Aid PROFILE. *See* CSS/Financial Aid PROFILE.

Financial need. The difference between the total cost of attending a college and a student's expected family contribution (EFC). Financial aid grants, loans and work-study will be offered by each college to fill the student's need.

Free Application for Federal Student Aid (FAFSA). A form completed by all applicants for federal student aid. The FAFSA is available on the Web at www.fafsa.ed.gov. In many states, completion of the FAFSA is also sufficient to establish eligibility for state-sponsored aid programs. There is no charge to students for completing the FAFSA. The FAFSA may be filed any time after Jan. 1 of the year for which one is seeking aid (e.g., after Jan. 1, 2014, for the academic year 2014-15).

Full-time status. Enrollment at a college or university for 12 or more credit hours per semester. Students must be enrolled full time to qualify for the maximum award available to them from federal grant programs.

General Educational Development (GED). A series of tests that individuals who did not complete high school may take through their state education system to qualify for a high school equivalency certificate.

Gift. Financial aid in the form of scholarships or grants that do not have to be repaid.

Grade Point Average (GPA). A system used by many schools for evaluating the overall scholastic performance of students. Grade points are determined by first multiplying the number of hours given for a course by the numerical value of the grade and then dividing the sum of all grade points by the total number of hours carried. The most common system of numerical values for grades is A = 4, B = 3, C = 2, D = 1, and E or F = 0.

Graduate study. A program leading to a master's degree or doctoral degree; advanced study generally following a bachelor's degree.

Grant. A financial aid award that is given to a student and does not have to be paid back. The terms "grant" and "scholarship" are often used interchangeably to refer to gift aid, but often grants are awarded solely on the basis of financial need, while scholarships may require the student to demonstrate merit.

Half-time status. Enrollment at a college or university for at least six credit hours per semester, but less than the 12 credit hours required to qualify as full time. Students must be enrolled at least half time to qualify for federal student aid loan programs.

High school transcript. A formal document that shows all classes taken and grades earned in high school. It needs to be sent from the school to the scholarship sponsor, not from the applicant.

Independent student. For federal financial aid purposes, the status that generally includes students who are either 24 years old, married, a veteran or an orphan, a ward of the court, certified as homeless or have legal dependents (not including spouse). Independent students do not need to provide parental information to be considered for federal financial aid programs. However, private institutions may require independent students to provide parental information on their institutional forms in order to be considered for nonfederal sources of funding.

Internship. Any short-term, supervised work, usually related to a student's major, for which academic credit is earned. The work can be full or part time, on or off campus, paid or unpaid. Some majors require the student to complete an internship.

IRS Data Retrieval Tool. Accessible from FAFSA on the Web, this tool allows students and parents to access the IRS tax return information needed to complete the FAFSA, and transfer the data directly into their FAFSA. Students or parents who filed their tax returns electronically within the last three weeks, or through the mail within the last eight weeks, might need to either enter their tax return information manually or return to the FAFSA at a later date, as their tax return information might not be available for transfer from the IRS.

Loan. Money lent with interest for a specified period of time. This book includes several loan programs; some forgive the loan in exchange for public service, such as teaching in a rural area.

Major. The subject area in which students concentrate during their undergraduate study. At most colleges, students take a third to a half of their courses in the major; the rest of their course work is devoted to core requirements and electives. In liberal arts majors, students generally take a third of their courses in their chosen field. In career-related programs, such as nursing or engineering, students may take up to half of their courses in their major.

Merit aid. Financial aid awarded on the basis of academic qualifications, artistic or athletic talent, leadership or similar qualities. Most merit aid comes in the form of scholarships. Merit aid may be non-need based, or the merit criteria may be in addition to a requirement that the student demonstrate financial need.

Need-based aid. Financial aid (scholarships, grants, loans or work-study opportunities) given to students who have demonstrated financial need, calculated by subtracting the student's expected family contribution from a college's total cost of attendance. The largest source of need-based aid is the federal government, but colleges, states and private foundations also award need-based aid to eligible students.

Nomination. Being named as a candidate for an award or scholarship. Some scholarship programs require that a teacher or principal nominate students as applicants, and do not invite applications from students.

Non-need-based aid. Financial aid awarded without regard to the student's demonstrated ability to pay for college. Unsubsidized loans and scholarships awarded solely on the basis of merit are both non-need based. Some financial aid sponsors also offer non-need-based grants that are not tied to merit, but rather to other qualities, such as state of residence or participation in ROTC.

Outside resources. Student financial aid granted by a source other than the college that the college must take into account when assembling an aid package. Examples of common outside resources include scholarships from private foundations, employer tuition assistance and veterans' educational benefits.

Parents' contribution. The amount a student's parents are expected to pay toward college costs from their income and assets. It is derived from need analysis of the parents' overall financial situation. The parents' contribution and the student's contribution together constitute the total expected family contribution (EFC).

Part-time status. Enrollment at a college or university for 11 or fewer credit hours per semester.

Pell Grant. *See* Federal Pell Grant Program.

Perkins Loan. *See* Federal Perkins Loan Program.

Permanent resident. A non-U.S. citizen who has been given permission to make his or her permanent home in the United States. All permanent residents hold a "green card," and all holders of a green card are permanent residents. Permanent residents are eligible for numerous award programs.

PLUS Loan. *See* Federal Parent Loan for Undergraduate Students.

Portfolio. A collection of a student's work that demonstrates skills and accomplishments. Portfolios may be physical or electronic. There are academic portfolios that include student-written papers and projects, and also portfolios that include created objects — art, photography, fashion illustrations and more. Some scholarship programs request a portfolio.

PROFILE. *See* CSS/Financial Aid PROFILE®.

PSAT/NMSQT® (Preliminary SAT/ National Merit Scholarship Qualifying Test). A comprehensive program that helps schools put students on the path to college. The PSAT/NMSQT is administered by high schools to sophomores and juniors each year in October and serves as the qualifying test for scholarships awarded by the National Merit Scholarship Corporation.

Renewable. A scholarship or loan that can be renewed after the first award. Typically students have to apply annually in order to receive the funds after the first year.

Renewal FAFSA. A simplified reapplication form for continuing students. The Renewal FAFSA allows the student to update the financial information and other items that have changed from the prior year's FAFSA, rather than completing the entire FAFSA for each award year.

Reserve Officers' Training Corps (ROTC). Programs conducted by certain colleges in cooperation with the United States Air Force, Army and Navy reserves. Participating students may receive a merit scholarship while they are in college, and will enter the reserves of their service branch as an officer upon graduation. Navy ROTC includes the Marine Corps. (The Coast Guard and Merchant Marine do not sponsor ROTC programs.) Local recruiting offices of the services themselves can supply detailed information about these programs, as can participating colleges.

Residency requirements. The minimum amount of time a student is required to have lived in a particular state or community in order to be eligible for scholarship, internship or loan programs offered to such residents. Can also refer to the minimum amount of time a student is required to have lived in a state to be eligible for in-state tuition at a public college or university.

SAT®. A college entrance exam that tests critical reading, writing and mathematics skills that is given on specified dates throughout the year at test centers in the United States and other countries. The SAT is used by most colleges and sponsors of financial aid programs.

SAT Subject Tests™. Admission tests in specific subjects that are given at test centers in the United States and other countries on specified dates throughout the year. The tests are used by colleges for help in both evaluating applicants for admission and determining course placement and exemption of enrolled first-year students.

Scholarship. A type of financial aid that doesn't have to be repaid. Grants are often based on financial need. Scholarships may be based on need, on need combined with merit, or solely on the basis of merit or some other qualification, such as minority status.

Section 529 plans. State-sponsored college savings programs commonly referred to as "529 plans" after the section of the Internal Revenue Code that provides the plan's tax breaks. There are two kinds: Section 529 college savings plans and Section 529 prepaid tuition plans.

Self-help aid. Student financial aid, such as loans and jobs, that requires repayment or employment.

SEOG. *See* Federal Supplemental Educational Opportunity Grant Program.

Stafford Loan. *See* Federal Stafford Loan.

Student expense budget. A calculation of the annual cost of attending college that is used to determine your financial need. Student expense budgets usually include tuition and fees, books and supplies, room and board, personal expenses and transportation. Sometimes additional expenses are included for students with special education needs, students who have a disability, or students who are married or have children.

Student's contribution. The amount you are expected to pay toward college costs from your income and assets. The amount is derived from need analysis of your resources. Your contribution and your parents' contribution together add up to the total expected family contribution.

Subsidized Federal Stafford Loan. *See* Federal Stafford Loan.

Subsidized loan. A loan awarded to a student on the basis of financial need. The federal government or the state awarding the loan pays the borrower's interest while the student is in college at least half time, thereby subsidizing the loan.

Supplemental Educational Opportunity Grant. *See* Federal Supplemental Educational Opportunity Grant Program.

Transcript. A copy of a student's official academic record listing all courses taken and grades received.

Tuition. The price of instruction at a college. Tuition may be charged per term or per credit hour.

Two-year college. *See* Community/junior college.

Undergraduate. A college student in the freshman, sophomore, junior or senior year of study, as opposed to a graduate student who has earned an undergraduate degree and is pursuing a master's, doctoral or professional degree.

Unmet need. The difference between a specific student's total available resources and the total cost for the student's attendance at a specific institution.

Unsubsidized Federal Stafford Loan. *See* Federal Stafford Loan.

Unsubsidized loan. An education loan that is non-need based and therefore not subsidized by the federal government; the borrower is responsible for accrued interest throughout the life of the loan.

Verification. A procedure whereby a school checks the information that the student reported on the FAFSA, usually by requesting a copy of the tax returns filed by the student and, if applicable, the student's spouse and parent(s). Colleges are required by federal regulations to verify a minimum percentage of financial aid applications.

Vocational program. An education program designed to prepare students for immediate employment. These programs usually can be completed in less than four years beyond high school and are available in most community colleges, career colleges, and vocational-technical institutes.

Work-Study. An arrangement by which a student combines employment and college study. The employment may be an integral part of the academic program (as in cooperative education and internships) or simply a means of paying for college (as in the need-based Federal Work-Study Program).

Eligibility Indexes

Corporate/Employer

Aviation industry, 88
Federal/U.S. Government, 261
Footwear/Leather Industry, 519
Wal-Mart Stores, Inc., 536
West Pharmaceutical Services, Inc., 539

Disabilities

Hearing impaired

AG Bell College Scholarship Awards, 92
Blind or Deaf Beneficiary Grant Program, 452
Courage Center Scholarship for People with Disabilities, 248
New York State Readers Aid Program, 428
Sertoma Scholarships for Students Who are Hard of Hearing or Deaf, 471
Students With Disabilities Endowed Scholarship Honoring Elizabeth Daley Jeffords, 534
Texas Tuition Exemption for Blind or Deaf Students, 510
Wisconsin Hearing & Visually Handicapped Student Grant, 543

Learning disabled

The Challenge Met Scholarship, 181
Marion Huber Learning Through Listening Award, 369
North Carolina Vocational Rehabilitation Award, 431
Students With Disabilities Endowed Scholarship Honoring Elizabeth Daley Jeffords, 534
The Tommy Tranchin Award, 250

Physically challenged

Courage Center Scholarship for People with Disabilities, 248
National ChairScholars Scholarship, 237
New Mexico Teacher's Loan-for-Service, 598
New York Metropolitan Area Scholarship Program, 237
North Carolina Vocational Rehabilitation Award, 431
RehabGYM Scholarship, 533
Students With Disabilities Endowed Scholarship Honoring Elizabeth Daley Jeffords, 534
The Tommy Tranchin Award, 250

Visually impaired

Alabama Scholarship for Dependents of Blind Parents, 497
Arthur and Helen Copeland Scholarship, 523
Arthur E. Copeland Scholarship, 524
Blind or Deaf Beneficiary Grant Program, 452
Charles E. Leonard Memorial Scholarship, 532
Christian Record Services Scholarship, 239
Courage Center Scholarship for People with Disabilities, 248
Delta Gamma Foundation Florence Margaret Harvey Memorial Scholarship, 106
Ferdinand Torres Scholarship, 107
Floyd Qualls Memorial Scholarship, 101
The Gladys C. Anderson Memorial Scholarship, 107
Jewish Guild Scholar Program, 357
Lighthouse College-Bound Award, 370
Lighthouse Undergraduate Award, 371
Mary P. Oenslager Scholastic Achievement Award, 369
National Federation of the Blind Scholarships, 413
New York State Readers Aid Program, 428
The Paul and Helen Ruckes Scholarship, 107
R.L. Gillette Scholarship, 107
The Rudolph Dillman Memorial Scholarship, 107
Students With Disabilities Endowed Scholarship Honoring Elizabeth Daley Jeffords, 534
Texas Tuition Exemption for Blind or Deaf Students, 510
Wisconsin Hearing & Visually Handicapped Student Grant, 543

Field of Study/Intended Career

Agricultural science, business, and natural resources conservation

Abbie Sargent Memorial Scholarship, 80
AGCO Scholarships, 268
Agricredit Acceptance LLC Scholarship, 268
Agrium U.S. Inc. Scholarship, 268
Alpha Gamma Rho Educational Foundation Scholarship, 268
American Chemical Society Scholars Program, 97
American Florists' Exchange Scholarship, 102
American Society for Enology and Viticulture Scholarship Program, 193
American Veterinary Medical Association Scholarship, 269
Ameriprise Financial and AGSTAR Financial Services, Inc. Scholarship, 269
AMHI Educational Scholarships, 172
AMHI van Schaik Dressage Scholarship, 173
Amtrol Scholarship, 108
Anadarko/SEG Scholarship, 482
The Andersons, Inc. Scholarship, 269
Animal Health International Scholarship, 270
Annie's Homegrown Sustainable Agriculture Scholarships, 205
ANS Decommissioning, Decontamination and Reutilization Scholarship, 174
Arabian Horse Association (Region 14) Scholarship, 270
Arboriculture Internship, 568
Archer Daniels Midland Company Scholarships, 270
Arthur K. Gilkey Memorial/Bedayn Research Grants, 95
Arysta LifeScience North America Scholarship, 270
A.T. Anderson Memorial Scholarship, 114
Ball Horticultural Company Scholarship, 103
Baroid Scholarship, 108
Beck's Hybrids Scholarship, 270
Behlen Mfg. Co./Walter and Ruby Behlen Memorial Scholarship, 271
Birdsong Peanuts Scholarship, 271

Blain's Farm & Feet Scholarship, 271
BNSF Railway Company Scholarship, 271
Booker T. Washington Scholarship, 272
Bridgestone Scholarship, 272
Brown and Caldwell Minority Scholarship Program, 229
Bryan A. Champion Scholarship, 336
Bud Olman Memorial Scholarship, 103
Bunge North America Scholarship, 272
California Farm Bureau Scholarship, 231
Caroline Thorn Kissel Summer Environmental Studies Scholarship, 286
Carville M. Akehurst Memorial Scholarship, 337
Casey's General Stores, Inc. Scholarship, 272
Charles P. Lake - Rain For Rent Scholarship, 272
Charles (Tommy) Thomas Memorial Scholarship, 175
Chief Industries Scholarship, 273
Church & Dwight Company, Inc. Scholarship, 273
Clara Carter Higgins Scholarship and GCA Awards for Summer Environmental Studies, 286
CNH Capital Scholarship, 273
Cooperative Resources International Scholarship, 273
Corliss Knapp Engle Scholarship in Horticulture, 287
CSX Scholarship, 274
Dairy Student Recognition Program, 410
Dallas Geophysical Society Scholarship, 482
Dan & Pauline Lutkenhouse & Hawaii Tropical Botanical Garden Scholarship, 299
Darling International, Inc. Scholarship, 274
Dean Foods Company Scholarship, 274
Department of Energy Community College Institute at Oak Ridge National Laboratory, 575
DGS/Karen Kellogg Shaw Memorial Scholarship, 482
DHS Summer Faculty and Student Research Team Program for Minority Serving Institutions, 576
Disney Theme Parks & Resorts Professional Internships, 591
DMI Milk Marketing Scholarships, 410
DOE Faculty and Student Teams Program at Oak Ridge National Laboratory, 576
DOE Science Undergraduate Laboratory Internships at Oak Ridge National Laboratory, 576
Donald A. Williams Soil Conservation Scholarship, 489
Donald and Nancy Frye Scholarship, 482
Dr. W. Wes Eckenfelder Jr. Scholarship, 230
Dupont Pioneer Scholarships, 274
Earl Dedman Memorial Scholarship, 103
Earl R. Sorensen Memorial Scholarships, 274
Ecotrust Native American Scholarship, 111
Elizabeth Gardner Norweb Summer Environmental Studies Scholarship, 287
Environmental Management Participation at the U.S. Army Environmental Command (USAEC), 577
EPA Greater Research Opportunities Undergraduate Student Fellowships, 527
EPA National Network for Environmental Management Studies Fellowship, 528
Excel Geophysical Services Scholarship, 483
Farm Credit Services of Mid-America Scholarship, 275
Farmers Mutual Hail Insurance Company of Iowa Scholarship, 275
Fastline Publications Scholarship, 275
Filoli Garden Internships and Apprenticeships, 561
Foundation for Environmental Agriculture Scholarship, 276
Fran Johnson Non-Traditional Scholarship, 104
The Francis Walton Memorial Scholarship, 183
Garden Club Federation of Massachusetts, 286
GCA Award in Desert Studies, 287
GCA Internship in Garden History and Design, 562
GCA Zone VI Fellowship in Urban Forestry, 288
Geophysical Society of Alaska Scholarship, 483
George Washington Carver Internship, 592
Good Eats Scholarship Fund, 304
Grange Denise Scholarship, 425
GSH/Hugh Hardy Scholarship, 483
G.W. Hohmann Memorial Scholarship, 483
Harold Bettinger Memorial Scholarship, 104
Higher Education Research Experiences at Oak Ridge National Laboratory for Students, 577
Hoard's Dairyman Scholarship, 276
Hormel Foods Corporation Scholarship, 277
Horticultural Research Institute Spring Meadow Scholarship, 337
Iager Dairy Scholarship, 411
ILC Resources Scholarship, 277
Iowa Interstate Railroad, Ltd. Scholarship, 277
Irrigation Foundation Scholarship, 277
Jacob Van Namen Marketing Scholarship, 104
James Bridenbaugh Memorial Scholarship, 104
J.K. Rathmell, Jr. Memorial Scholarship for Work/Study Abroad, 104
Joan K. Hunt and Rachel M. Hunt Summer Scholarship in Field Botany, 288
John and Amy Rakestraw Scholarship, 277
John L. Tomasovic, Sr. Scholarship, 105
Katharine M. Grosscup Scholarships in Horticulture, 288
KenAG Scholarship, 278
Kent Nutrition Group, Inc. Scholarship, 278
KeyBank Scholarship, 278
Kikkoman Foods, Inc. Scholarship, 278
Kildee Scholarship, 411
King Ranch Scholarship, 279
Klussendorf Scholarship, 411
Limi Boosters National Educational Grant, 430
Lindbergh Grant, 238
Long Island Flower Grower Association (LIFGA) Scholarship, 105
Louisiana Rockefeller Wildlife Scholarship, 372
The Loy McCandless Marks Scholarship in Tropical Horticulture, 288
Mahindra USA Women in Ag Scholarship, 279
Markham-Colegrave International Scholarship, 105
Marshall E. McCullough Undergraduate Scholarship, 411
Mary T. Carothers Environmental Studies Scholarship, 288
Masonic Range Science Scholarship, 481
Melville H. Cohee Student Leader Conservation Scholarship, 490
MetLife Foundation Scholarship, 279
Mike and Flo Novovesky Scholarship, 106
Mills Fleet Farm Scholarship, 280
Minority and Underrepresented Environmental Literacy Program, 391
Morris Arboretum Education Internship, 569
Morris Arboretum Horticulture Internship, 569
MTA Doug Slifka Memorial Scholarship, 393
Muggets Scholarship, 337
NAPA Auto Parts Scholarship, 280

NASA Space Grant South Carolina Undergraduate Student Research Fellowship, 403
National Dairy Shrine Maurice E. Core Scholarship, 412
National Energy Technology Laboratory Professional Internship Program, 577
The National FFA Alumni Association Scholarship, 280
The National FFA Scholarship Funded by National FFA Staff, Board and Individual Contributors, 280
National Greenhouse Manufacturing Association (NGMA) Scholarship, 106
National Mastis Council Scholarship, 280
National Wild Turkey Federation Scholarship, 281
NEHA/AAS Scholarship, 412
Norfolk Southern Foundation Scholarship, 281
NPFDA Scholarship, 416
Oak Ridge National Laboratory Undergraduate Student Cooperative Education Program, 578
Oak Ridge Science Semester, 578
Oregon Dungeness Crab Commission, 446
Oregon Foundation for Blacktail Deer Scholarship, 446
Owens Corning Internships, 583
Paradigm Scholarship, 484
Pennsylvania Targeted Industry Program (PA-TIP), 453
Penton Media Scholarship, 281
Peterson Family Scholarship, 282
Phipps Conservatory and Botanical Gardens Internships, 583
PLANET Academic Excellence Foundation Scholarship, 282
Plant Propagation Internship, 569
Plant Protection Internship, 569
Rabo Agrifinance Scholarship, 282
Rain Bird Intelligent Use of Water Scholarship, 367
Research Participation at the Centers for Disease Control and Prevention/Agency for Toxic Substances and Disease Registry, 578
Research Participation Program for the U.S. Air Force Research Laboratory (USAFRL), Wright Patterson Air Force Base, 580
Research Participation Program for the U.S. Air Force School of Aerospace Medicine (USAFSAM), 580
Research Participation Program for the U.S. Army Public Health Command, 580
Research Participation Program for the U.S. Army Research Institute for Environmental Medicine (USARIEM), 581
Rose Acre Farms Scholarship, 283
Rose and Flower Garden Internship, 570
SCA Conservation Internships, 587
Seed Companies Scholarship, 106
SEG Foundation/Apache Scholarship, 484
SEG/Denver Geophysical Society Scholarship, 481
SEG/Gary and Lorene Servos Scholarship, 484
Seneca Foods Corporation Scholarship, 283
Siemens Competition in Math, Science and Technology, 473
Smithsonian Environmental Research Center Internship Program, 585
Smithsonian Minority Internship, 585
Society of Exploration Geophysicists Scholarship, 485
South Dakota Ardell Bjugstad Scholarship, 494
Southern Nursery Organization Sidney B. Meadows Scholarship, 472
Southface Internship, 587
Student Internship Program at the U.S. Army Center for Health Promotion and Preventive Medicine, 581
Student Research at the U.S. Army Edgewood Chemical Biological Center, 581
Susie & Bruce Usrey Scholarship, 337
Theisen's Home Farm Auto Scholarship, 284
Thomas M. Stetson Scholarship, 108
Timothy and Palmer W. Bigelow, Jr. Scholarship, 337
Truman D. Picard Scholarship, 347
Tyrholm Big R Stores Scholarship, 284
Tyson Foods Inc. Scholarship, 284
Tyson Foods Intern Program, 588
United Dairymen of Idaho Scholarship, 284
Universal Lubricants Scholarship, 285
Urban Forestry Internship, 570
U.S. National Arboretum Horticultural Internship, 590
U.S. National Arboretum National Herb Garden Year-Long Internship, 590
USDA/1890 National Scholars Program, 526
Virgil Eihusen Foundation Scholarship, 285
Vocational (Bettinger, Holden and Perry) Memorial Scholarship, 106
Water Companies (NJ Chapter) Scholarship, 409
Wells Fargo Scholarship, 285
Wilbur-Ellis Company High School Scholarship, 285

Architecture and design

AIA New Jersey Scholarship Foundation, 117
AIA/AAF Minority/Disadvantaged Scholarship, 117
Alfred T. Granger Student Art Fund Scholarship, 531
American Society of Interior Designers Legacy Scholarship for Undergraduates, 198
Arboriculture Internship, 568
ASHRAE Region IV Benny Bootle Scholarship, 196
BIA Cares of San Diego Scholarship, 230
Black & Veatch Summer Internship Program, 556
Bryan A. Champion Scholarship, 336
Carville M. Akehurst Memorial Scholarship, 337
CBC Scholarship, 243
Center for Architecture Design Scholarship, 236
Courtland Paul Scholarship, 366
Dallas Architectural Foundation - Swank Travelling Fellowship, 249
David Barrett Memorial Scholarship, 198
Disney Theme Parks & Resorts Professional Internships, 591
The EDSA Minority Scholarship, 366
Eleanor Allwork Scholarship, 236
Elizabeth Dow Ltd. Internships, 555
Filoli Garden Internships and Apprenticeships, 561
Florence Lemcke Memorial Scholarship, 166
Gabriel Prize, 541
Garden Club Federation of Massachusetts, 286
GCA Award in Desert Studies, 287
GCA Internship in Garden History and Design, 562
GCSAA Scholars Competition, 258
GCSAA Student Essay Contest, 258
Green/Sustainable Design Scholarship, 346
Hawaii Chapter/David T. Woolsey Scholarship, 366
Hawaii Community Scholarship Fund, 305
Horticultural Research Institute Spring Meadow Scholarship, 337
IFDA Leaders Commemorative Scholarship, 346
International Furnishings and Design Association Educational Foundation Part-Time Student Scholarship, 346
International Furnishings and Design Association Student Member Scholarships, 346
Irene Winifred Eno Grant, 198
Irrigation Foundation Scholarship, 277
J. Paul Getty Multicultural Undergraduate Summer Internships at the Getty Center, 564
J.K. Rathmell, Jr. Memorial Scholarship for Work/Study Abroad, 104
Joel Polsky Academic Achievement Award, 199

Joel Polsky Prize, 199
Kohler Company Scholarship, 279
Landscape Forms Design for People Scholarship, 367
The Loy McCandless Marks Scholarship in Tropical Horticulture, 288
Muggets Scholarship, 337
NASA Space Grant Wisconsin Consortium Undergraduate Research Program, 405
NAWIC Founders' Undergraduate Scholarship, 409
Peridian International Inc./Rae L. Price FASLA Scholarship, 367
Phipps Conservatory and Botanical Gardens Internships, 583
PLANET Academic Excellence Foundation Scholarship, 282
Rain Bird Intelligent Use of Water Scholarship, 367
Raymond F. Cain Scholarship Fund, 318
Southface Internship, 587
Steven G. King Play Environments Scholarship, 367
Susie & Bruce Usrey Scholarship, 337
Timothy and Palmer W. Bigelow, Jr. Scholarship, 337
Urban Forestry Internship, 570
U.S. National Arboretum Horticultural Internship, 590
Wilbur-Ellis Company High School Scholarship, 285
Women in Architecture Scholarship, 221

Area and ethnic studies

Adele Filene Student Presenter Grant, 246
AFSCMA/UNCF Union Scholars Program, 550
Blossom Kalama Evans Memorial Scholarship, 297
Harriet Irsay Scholarship, 118
Jennifer C. Groot Fellowship, 97
Jerry Clark Memorial Scholarship, 102
Joseph S. Adams Senior Scholarship, 481
King Olav V Norwegian-American Heritage Fund, 491
Kosciuszko Foundation Year Abroad Program, 364
Smithsonian Native American Internship, 585

Arts, visual and performing

Abe Voron Scholarship, 228
Academy of Television Arts & Sciences Student Internship Program, 549
Adele Filene Student Presenter Grant, 246
Alexander M. Tanger Scholarship, 228
Alfred T. Granger Student Art Fund Scholarship, 531
American Conservatory Theater Production Fellowships, 550
American Institute of Graphic Arts (AIGA) Honolulu Chapter Scholarship Fund, 296
American Legion Kansas Music Scholarship, 133
American Legion Maryland Auxiliary Scholarship, 138
Americans for the Arts Arts & Business Council of New York Internship, 551
Americans for the Arts Arts Marketing Internship, 552
Americans for the Arts Arts Policy Internship, 552
Americans for the Arts Development Internship, 552
Americans for the Arts Government and Public Affairs Internship, 553
Americans for the Arts Leadership Alliances Internship, 553
Americans for the Arts Local Arts Advancement Services Internship, 553
Americans for the Arts Membership Internship, 554
Americans for the Arts Private-Sector Initiatives Internship, 554
Americans for the Arts Research Services Internship, 554
Anna K. Meredith Fund Scholarship, 499
Anthropology Internship Program, 551
Applied Arts Internships, 554
APTRA-Clete Roberts/Kathryn Dettman Memorial Journalism Scholarship, 220
Armenian General Benevolent Union Performing Arts Fellowships, 209
Artistic and Administrative Fellowships, 550
Audria M. Edwards Scholarship Fund, 451
BEA Founders Award, 228
Bernard B. Jacobs Internship Program, 574
BMI Student Composer Awards, 226
Broadcast News Grants, 211
Carole Fielding Video Grant, 525
Carole Simpson Scholarship, 407, 461
The CBC Spouses Heineken USA Performing Arts Scholarship Program, 242
The CBC Spouses Visual Arts Scholarship, 242
Center for Architecture Design Scholarship, 236
Charles & Lucille King Family Foundation Scholarships, 238
Clare Brett Smith Scholarship, 499
The Cloisters Summer Internship Program, 567
Davidson Fellows Scholarship, 251
DOE Scholars Program, 576
Doris & Clarence Glick Classical Music Scholarship, 299
Dr. Alma S. Adams Scholarship for Outreach and Health Communications to Reduce Tobacco Use Among Priority Populations, 118
Eastman Kodak Cooperative Internship Programs, 559
Ed Bradley Scholarship, 461
Elizabeth A. Sackler Museum Educational Trust, 499
Elizabeth Dow Ltd. Internships, 555
The Elizabeth Greenshields Grant, 256
Ellen Hamada Fashion Design Scholarship, 301
Endowment Fund For Education (EFFE), 225
ESPN Internship, 560
Essence Summer Internship, 560
Esther Kanagawa Memorial Art Scholarship, 302
Eugene Bennet Visual Arts Scholarship, 443
Eugenia Vellner Fischer Award for the Performing Arts, 389
Fisher Broadcasting Company Scholarship for Minorities, 262
Florence Lemcke Memorial Scholarship, 166
Florence Travel Stipend, 499
GCA Internship in Garden History and Design, 562
The George Foreman Tribute to Lyndon B. Johnson Scholarship, 461
George Washington Carver Internship, 592
Gerrit R. Ludwig Scholarship, 304
The Gillian Award, 499
The Gladys C. Anderson Memorial Scholarship, 107
Guggenheim Museum Internship, 586
Harriet Irsay Scholarship, 118
Harry & Lorraine Ausprich Endowed Scholarship for the Arts, 454
Hawaii Community Scholarship Fund, 305
Hearst Journalism Award, 541
Hon Chew Hee Scholarship Fund, 308
IFDA Leaders Commemorative Scholarship, 346
International Incentive Awards, 500
J. Paul Getty Multicultural Undergraduate Summer Internships at the Getty Center, 564
John Bayliss Scholarship Award, 229
John Lennon Scholarships, 227
Jules Maidoff Scholarship, 500
Kennedy Library Archival Internship, 565
Lee A. Lyman Memorial Music Scholarship, 532
Lele Cassin Scholarship, 500
Leonard M. Perryman Communications Scholarship for Ethnic Minority Students, 522

Lou and Carole Prato Sports Reporting Scholarship, 462
MCC Theater Internships, 567
Metropolitan Museum of Art Six-Month Internship, 567
Metropolitan Museum of Art Summer Internship Program, 568
Mike Reynolds Scholarship, 462
Mister Rogers Memorial Scholarship, 81
Morton Gould Young Composer Awards, 210
Museum Coca-Cola Internship, 573
NABJ Internships, 572
National Guild of Piano Teachers $200 Scholarship, 98
National Museum of the American Indian Internship, 572
New York American Legion Press Association Scholarship, 155
The Orlando HamCation Scholarship, 188
peermusic Latin Scholarship, 227
Peggy Guggenheim Internship, 586
Pete Wilson Journalism Scholarship, 462
PGA Tour Diversity Intern Program, 583
PGSF Annual Scholarship Competition, 460
Presidents Scholarships, 462
Princess Grace Award for Dance, 459
Princess Grace Award For Film, 459
Princess Grace Award For Playwriting, 459
Princess Grace Award For Theater, 459
Randy Pausch Scholarship Fund, 80
Ray Yoshida Kauai Fine Arts Scholarship, 318
Research Participation Program for the Johns Hopkins University Applied Physics Laboratory, 579
Research Participation Program for the U.S. Army Aeromedical Research Laboratory (USAARL), 580
Research Participation Program for the U.S. Army Public Health Command, 580
Richard Eaton Foundation Award, 229
Richie M. Gregory Fund, 319
R.L. Gillette Scholarship, 107
Roosevelt Archival Internships, 562
Rudolf Nissim Prize, 211
Ruth Clark Furniture Design Scholarship, 347
SACI Alumni Heritage Scholarship, 500
SACI Consortium Scholarship, 500
Scholastic Art Portfolio Gold Award, 93
Scholastic Art Portfolio Silver With Distinction Award, 93
Scholastic Photography Portfolio Silver Award, 93
Scholastic Writing Portfolio Gold Award, 94
Sculpture Society Scholarship, 418
Seattle Professional Chapter Scholarship, 222
Smithsonian Minority Internship, 585
Sony Credited Internship, 586
Southern California Council Endowed Internship, 573
Southface Internship, 587
Spoleto Festival USA Apprenticeship Program, 587
Stanfield and D'Orlando Art Scholarships, 521
Stella Blum Student Research Grant, 246
TAG Education Collaborative Web Challenge Contest, 502
Time Inc. Internship Program, 588
Two Ten Footwear Design Scholarship, 519
United States Holocaust Memorial Museum Internship, 588
Virgin Islands Music Scholarship, 535
Virginia Museum of Fine Arts Visual Arts and Art History Fellowship, 536
Walter S. Patterson Scholarship, 229
Wolf Trap Foundation for the Performing Arts Internship, 592
Worldstudio AIGA Scholarship, 546

Biological and biomedical sciences

American Legion Maryland Auxiliary Scholarship, 138
Endowment Fund For Education (EFFE), 225
Lindbergh Grant, 238
Research Participation Program for the U.S. Air Force School of Aerospace Medicine (USAFSAM), 580

Biological and physical sciences

Accelerator Applications Division Scholarship, 173
Adler Science and Math Scholarship, 137
Aerospace Undergraduate STEM Research Scholarship Program, 404
AFCEA Military Personnel & Dependents Scholarship, 207
AFCEA ROTC Scholarship, 207
AFCEA Scholarship for Underserved Students (HBCU), 208
AFCEA War Veterans/Disabled War Veterans Scholarship, 208
AfterCollege Science Student Scholarship, 86
AIAA Foundation Undergraduate Scholarship, 116
Air Force Research Laboratory, 711 Human Performance Wing, 575
The Allen and Bertha Watson Memorial Scholarship, 179
American Chemical Society Scholars Program, 97
American Legion Maryland Auxiliary Scholarship, 138
American Meteorological Society Freshman Undergraduate Scholarship Program, 171
American Meteorological Society Named Undergraduate Scholarship, 171
American Meteorological Society/Industry Minority Scholarship, 172
American Nuclear Society Operations and Power Division Scholarship, 174
American Society for Microbiology Undergraduate Research Fellowship (URF), 193
American Veterinary Medical Association Scholarship, 269
Amtrol Scholarship, 108
Anadarko/SEG Scholarship, 482
Angelo S. Bisesti Scholarship, 174
ANS Decommissioning, Decontamination and Reutilization Scholarship, 174
ANS Undergraduate Scholarships, 174
Applied Materials Internship and Co-op Program, 555
Arizona Public Service Navajo Scholars Program, 111
The ARRL Northwestern Division Scholarship Fund, 180
Arthur and Doreen Parrett Scholarship, 210
Arthur K. Gilkey Memorial/Bedayn Research Grants, 95
Arysta LifeScience North America Scholarship, 270
ASNE Scholarship, 199
A.T. Anderson Memorial Scholarship, 114
Baroid Scholarship, 108
Barry M. Goldwater Scholarship, 225
Behlen Mfg. Co./Walter and Ruby Behlen Memorial Scholarship, 271
Boeing Internships, 556
Brown and Caldwell Minority Scholarship Program, 229
Bunge North America Scholarship, 272
Burlington Northern Santa Fe Foundation Scholarship, 115
Casey's General Stores, Inc. Scholarship, 272
Castle & Cooke Mililani Technology Park Scholarship Fund, 298
Charles and Annette Hill Scholarship, 133
Charles (Tommy) Thomas Memorial Scholarship, 175
Clara Carter Higgins Scholarship and GCA Awards for Summer Environmental Studies, 286
ConocoPhillips Scholarships, 245
Dallas Geophysical Society Scholarship, 482

Dan & Pauline Lutkenhouse & Hawaii Tropical Botanical Garden Scholarship, 299
Davidson Fellows Scholarship, 251
DEED Student Research Grants, 178
Delaware Space Grant Undergraduate Summer Research Internship, 571
Delaware Space Grant Undergraduate Tuition Scholarship, 396
Delayed Education Scholarship for Women, 175
Department of Energy Community College Institute at Oak Ridge National Laboratory, 575
DGS/Karen Kellogg Shaw Memorial Scholarship, 482
DHS HS-STEM Summer Internship Program, 576
DHS Summer Faculty and Student Research Team Program for Minority Serving Institutions, 576
DOE Faculty and Student Teams Program at Oak Ridge National Laboratory, 576
DOE Scholars Program, 576
DOE Science Undergraduate Laboratory Internships at Oak Ridge National Laboratory, 576
Donald and Nancy Frye Scholarship, 482
Dr. W. Wes Eckenfelder Jr. Scholarship, 230
DuPont Co-ops, 559
Dupont Pioneer Scholarships, 274
Eastman Kodak Cooperative Internship Programs, 559
Endowment Fund For Education (EFFE), 225
The Entomological Foundation BioQuip Undergraduate Scholarship, 257
Environmental Management Participation at the U.S. Army Environmental Command (USAEC), 577
EPA Greater Research Opportunities Undergraduate Student Fellowships, 527
Excel Geophysical Services Scholarship, 483
Explorers Club Youth Activity Fund, 261
Extrusion Division/Lew Erwin Memorial Scholarship, 486
Father James B. Macelwane Annual Award, 172
Filoli Garden Internships and Apprenticeships, 561
Fleming/Blaszcak Scholarship, 486
Foth Production Solutions, LLC Scholarship, 276
Foundation for Environmental Agriculture Scholarship, 276
Frances M. Peacock Native Bird Habitat Scholarship, 287
Garden Club Federation of Massachusetts, 286
Gary J. Miller Undergraduate Prizes for Cancer and Cancer-Related Biomedical Research, 96
GCA Award in Desert Studies, 287
GCA Internship in Garden History and Design, 562
GCA Summer Scholarship in Field Botany, 287
GE Hispanic Forum Scholarship, 327
Genentech, Inc. Internship Program, 562
Geophysical Society of Alaska Scholarship, 483
Geophysical Society of Tulsa Scholarship, 483
George A. Hall/Harold F. Mayfield Award, 542
George Washington Carver Internship, 592
GSH/Hugh Hardy Scholarship, 483
Gulf Coast Hurricane Scholarships, 486
G.W. Hohmann Memorial Scholarship, 483
HENAAC Scholars Program, 294
The Henry Broughton, K2AE, Memorial Scholarship, 184
Herbert Levy Memorial Endowment Fund Scholarship, 485
Hershey Company Tribal Scholarship, 112
Higher Education Research Experiences at Oak Ridge National Laboratory for Students, 577
Hoffman-La Roche Inc. Student Internship, 563
Hoku Scholarship Fund, 307
Horizons Scholarship, 545
Ida M. Pope Memorial Scholarship, 308
James K. Vogt Radiochemistry Scholarship, 176
Jennifer Ritzmann Scholarship for Studies in Tropical Biology, 247
Joan K. Hunt and Rachel M. Hunt Summer Scholarship in Field Botany, 288
John and Muriel Landis Scholarship, 176
John R. Lamarsh Scholarship, 176
Joseph R. Dietrich Scholarship, 176
K. K. Wang Scholarship, 487
KeyBank Scholarship, 278
Laboratory Technology Program, 577
Lockheed Martin American Heroes Scholarship, 329
Louisiana Rockefeller Wildlife Scholarship, 372
The Loy McCandless Marks Scholarship in Tropical Horticulture, 288
Marathon Oil Corporation College Scholarship, 329
Massachusetts Math and Science Teachers Scholarship, 381
Math And Science Teachers Loan Forgiveness Program, 600
McAlinden Divers Scholarship, 420
MESBEC Scholarships, 234
Mickey Leland Energy Fellowship Program, 577
Microscopy Society of America Undergraduate Research Scholarship, 385
Microsoft General Scholarship, 386
Minority and Underrepresented Environmental Literacy Program, 391
Morgan Stanley Foundation Scholarship, 330
Morris Arboretum Education Internship, 569
MSGC Undergraduate Underrepresented Minority Fellowship Program, 398
MTA Doug Slifka Memorial Scholarship, 393
Nancy Lorraine Jensen Memorial Scholarship, 491
NASA Academy Internship, 572
NASA Connecticut Space Grant Undergraduate Fellowship, 395
NASA Idaho Space Grant Undergraduate Scholarship, 397
NASA Minnesota Space Grant Consortium Wide Scholarship, 398
NASA Missouri State Space Grant Undergraduate Scholarship, 399
NASA New Jersey Space Grant Consortium Undergraduate Summer Fellowships in Engineering and Science, 571
NASA North Carolina Space Grant Consortium Undergraduate Research Scholarship, 400
NASA North Carolina Space Grant Consortium Undergraduate Scholarship Program, 400
NASA Ohio Space Grant Junior/Senior Scholarship Program, 401
NASA Pennsylvania Space Grant Undergraduate Scholarship, 402
NASA Rhode Island Space Grant Summer Undergraduate Scholarship, 402
NASA Space Grant Arizona Undergraduate Research Internship, 571
NASA Space Grant Georgia Fellowship Program, 396
NASA Space Grant Hawaii Undergraduate Fellowship Program, 396
NASA Space Grant Illinois Undergraduate Scholarship, 397
NASA Space Grant Kentucky Undergraduate Scholarship, 397
NASA Space Grant Maine Consortium Annual Scholarship and Fellowship Program, 397
NASA Space Grant Michigan Undergraduate Fellowship, 398
NASA Space Grant Montana Undergraduate Scholarship Program, 399

NASA Space Grant Nevada Undergraduate Scholarship, 399
NASA Space Grant New Mexico Undergraduate Scholarship, 400
NASA Space Grant North Dakota Consortium Lillian Goettler Scholarship, 401
NASA Space Grant North Dakota Undergraduate Scholarship, 401
NASA Space Grant Oregon Undergraduate Scholarship, 402
NASA Space Grant Rhode Island Undergraduate Research Scholarship, 402
NASA Space Grant South Carolina Undergraduate Student Research Fellowship, 403
NASA Space Grant Undergraduate Scholarship, 395
NASA Space Grant Vermont Consortium Undergraduate Scholarships, 404
NASA Space Grant Virginia Community College STEM Scholarship, 404
NASA Space Grant Wisconsin Consortium Undergraduate Research Program, 405
NASA Space Grant Wisconsin Consortium Undergraduate Scholarship, 405
NASA Utah Space Grant Consortium Undergraduate Scholarship, 403
NASA West Virginia Space Grant Undergraduate Research Fellowship, 405
National Energy Technology Laboratory Professional Internship Program, 577
National Greenhouse Manufacturing Association (NGMA) Scholarship, 106
New York State Math and Science Teaching Incentive Program, 427
Nick Van Pernis Scholarship, 316
Norfolk Southern Foundation Scholarship, 281
Nuclear Regulatory Commission Historically Black Colleges and Universities Student Research Participation, 578
Oak Ridge National Laboratory Undergraduate Student Cooperative Education Program, 578
Oak Ridge Nuclear Engineering Science Laboratory Synthesis, 578
Oak Ridge Science Semester, 578
Oregon Foundation for Blacktail Deer Scholarship, 446
Pacific Gas and Electric Summer Intern Program, 583
Paradigm Scholarship, 484
Paul A. Stewart Award, 542
The Paul and Helen Ruckes Scholarship, 107
Payzer Scholarship, 261
Pearl I. Young Scholarship, 401
Peggy Dixon Two-Year Scholarship, 485
Pennsylvania Targeted Industry Program (PA-TIP), 453
Peterson Family Scholarship, 282
Phipps Conservatory and Botanical Gardens Internships, 583
Pittsburgh Local Section Scholarship, 176
Pittsburgh Scholarship, 487
Plant Propagation Internship, 569
Plant Protection Internship, 569
Plasma Physics National Undergraduate Fellowship Program, 584
Plastics Pioneers Scholarships, 487
Procter & Gamble - Orgullosa Scholarship, 331
Rabo Agrifinance Scholarship, 282
Raymond DiSalvo Scholarship, 177
RCMI Technical/Trade School Scholarship, 464
Research Experiences for Undergraduates - Maria Mitchell Observatory, 573
Research Experiences for Undergraduates in the Physical Sciences, 551
Research Participation at the Centers for Disease Control and Prevention/Agency for Toxic Substances and Disease Registry, 578
Research Participation at the National Center for Toxicological Research, 579
Research Participation at the U.S. Food and Drug Administration, 579
Research Participation Program for the Combat Casualty Care Research Program (CCCRP), 579
Research Participation Program for the Johns Hopkins University Applied Physics Laboratory, 579
Research Participation Program for the U.S. Air Force Research Laboratory (USAFRL), Wright Patterson Air Force Base, 580
Research Participation Program for the U.S. Air Force School of Aerospace Medicine (USAFSAM), 580
Research Participation Program for the U.S. Army Aeromedical Research Laboratory (USAARL), 580
Research Participation Program for the U.S. Army Medical Research Institute of Chemical Defense, 580
Research Participation Program for the U.S. Army Public Health Command, 580
Research Participation Program for the U.S. Army Research Institute for Environmental Medicine (USARIEM), 581
Research Participation Program for the U.S. Army Research Laboratory, 581
Robert G. Lacy Scholarship, 177
Robert T. (Bob) Liner Scholarship, 177
Rocky Mountain Coal Mining Institute Scholarship, 464
Rodney Cottrell Scholarship, 484
SCA Conservation Internships, 587
Scholarship for Minority Undergraduate Physics Majors, 177
SEG Foundation/Apache Scholarship, 484
SEG/Denver Geophysical Society Scholarship, 481
SEG/Gary and Lorene Servos Scholarship, 484
SEG/Marvin and Jene Hewitt Scholarship, 484
SEG/P.C. Havens/Seismic Exchange Inc. Scholarship, 484
Seneca Foods Corporation Scholarship, 283
Shuichi, Katsu and Itsuyo Suga Scholarship, 321
Siemens Competition in Math, Science and Technology, 473
Smithsonian Environmental Research Center Internship Program, 585
Smithsonian Minority Internship, 585
Society of Exploration Geophysicists Scholarship, 485
Society of Physics Students Future Teacher Scholarship, 485
Society of Physics Students Leadership Scholarship, 485
Society of Physics Students Summer Internship Program, 586
Society of Plastics Engineers General Scholarships, 487
SPIE Optics and Photonics Education Scholarships, 496
Stan Beck Fellowship, 257
STEM Bridge Scholarship, 405
STEM Columbia Crew Memorial Scholarship, 403
STEM Majors Scholarship, 208
Student Internship Program at the U.S. Army Center for Health Promotion and Preventive Medicine, 581
Student Research at the U.S. Army Edgewood Chemical Biological Center, 581
Technical Minority Scholarship, 546
Thermoforming Division Memorial Scholarship, 488
Thermoset Division/James I. MacKenzie Memorial Scholarship, 488
Thomas J. Bardos Science Education Awards for Undergraduate Students, 96
Thomas M. Stetson Scholarship, 108
Toshiba/NSTA ExploraVision Award, 418
Tyson Foods Intern Program, 588

UNCF Merck Science Initiative, 523
Urban Forestry Internship, 570
U.S. Air Force Medial Support Agency, 581
U.S. Army Natick Soldier Research Development & Engineering Center, 582
U.S. Department of State Internship, 589
U.S. National Arboretum Horticultural Internship, 590
U.S. National Arboretum National Herb Garden Year-Long Internship, 590
USDA/1890 National Scholars Program, 526
Water Companies (NJ Chapter) Scholarship, 409
The Wayne Nelson, KB4UT, Memorial Scholarship, 191
West Virginia Engineering, Science, and Technology Scholarship, 540
Western Plastics Pioneers Scholarship, 488
Wilbur-Ellis Company High School Scholarship, 285
William James & Dorothy Bading Lanquist Fund, 323
The William R. Goldfarb Memorial Scholarship, 191
Women Soar Scholarship for Innovation, 261
The Yasme Foundation Scholarship, 191
Zeller Summer Scholarship in Medicinal Botany, 289

Business/management/administration

Accountemps Student Scholarship, 117
Actuarial Diversity Scholarships, 81
Actuary of Tomorrow Stuart A. Robertson Memorial Scholarship, 82
Advertising Internship, 556
AFSCMA/UNCF Union Scholars Program, 550
AfterCollege Business Student Scholarship, 85
AGCO Scholarships, 268
Agrium U.S. Inc. Scholarship, 268
AICP Heartland Chapter Jim Latteman Scholarship, 223
AICP Scholarship, 223
Al Schulman Ecolab First-Time Freshmen Entrepeneurial Scholarship, 417
Allstate Internships, 549
ALPFA Scholarship, 326
Alpha Beta Gamma National Scholarship, 94
American Bar Foundation Summer Research Diversity Fellowships in Law and Social Sciences for Undergraduate Students, 550
American Express Scholarship Competition, 109
American Hotel & Lodging Educational Foundation Incoming Freshman Scholarship Competition, 109
American Institute of Certified Public Accountants Scholarship for Minority Accounting Students, 118
American Legion Maryland Auxiliary Scholarship, 138
American Society of International Law Internships, 551
Americans for the Arts Arts Action Fund Internship, 552
Americans for the Arts Arts & Business Council of New York Internship, 551
Americans for the Arts Arts Marketing Internship, 552
Americans for the Arts Arts Policy Internship, 552
Americans for the Arts Development Internship, 552
Americans for the Arts Government and Public Affairs Internship, 553
Americans for the Arts Leadership Alliances Internship, 553
Americans for the Arts Local Arts Advancement Services Internship, 553
Americans for the Arts Marketing and Communications Internship, 553
Americans for the Arts Meetings and Events/Executive Office Internship, 553
Americans for the Arts Membership Internship, 554
Americans for the Arts Private-Sector Initiatives Internship, 554
Americans for the Arts Research Services Internship, 554
Applied Arts Internships, 554
Applied Materials Internship and Co-op Program, 555
Arabian Horse Association (Region 14) Scholarship, 270
The ARRL Northwestern Division Scholarship Fund, 180
Artistic and Administrative Fellowships, 550
Arts and Business Council of New York Multicultural Arts Management Internship Program, 555
Arysta LifeScience North America Scholarship, 270
Aspiring Sports Journalist Internship, 587
ASTA Alaska Airlines Scholarship, 512
ASTA American Express Travel Scholarship, 512
ASTA Northern California Chapter - Richard Epping Scholarship, 513
ASTA Pacific Northwest Chapter/William Hunt Scholarship, 513
ASTA Princess Cruises Scholarship, 513
Award of Excellence Scholarship, 344
Bern Laxer Memorial Scholarship, 351
Bernard B. Jacobs Internship Program, 574
Best Teen Chef Culinary Scholarship Competition, 210
BIA Cares of San Diego Scholarship, 230
Bick Bickson Scholarship, 297
Black & Veatch Summer Internship Program, 556
BNSF Railway Company Scholarship, 271
Bob Zappatelli Memorial Scholarship, 352
Boeing Internships, 556
Burlington Northern Santa Fe Foundation Scholarship, 115
Candon, Todd, & Seabolt Scholarship Fund, 298
C.A.R. Scholarship, 231
Casey's General Stores, Inc. Scholarship, 272
CBC Scholarship, 243
Charles and Annette Hill Scholarship, 133
Chefs of Louisiana Cookery Scholarship, 352
CI Construction Engineering Student Scholarship, 245
CIA Undergraduate Scholarship Program, 237
Citizens for Global Solutions Internship, 557
CNH Capital Scholarship, 273
Colorado Society of CPAs General Scholarship, 241
Congressional Institute Internships, 557
ConocoPhillips Scholarships, 245
Cooperative Resources International Scholarship, 273
Dairy Student Recognition Program, 410
Delta Faucet Company Scholarship, 456
Denver Rescue Mission Center for Mission Studies Internships, 558
Discover Scholarship, 327
Disney Theme Parks & Resorts Professional Internships, 591
DOE Scholars Program, 576
Dow Jones Business Reporting Intern Program, 558
Dr. Alvin and Monica Saake Scholarship, 299
DuPont Co-ops, 559
DuPont Internships, 559
Eastman Kodak Cooperative Internship Programs, 559
Ecolab Scholarship Competition, 110
Economic Research Division Project Internships, 556
Elizabeth Dow Ltd. Internships, 555

Entergy Jumpstart Co-ops and Internships, 560
EPA National Network for Environmental Management Studies Fellowship, 528
ESPN Internship, 560
Essence Summer Internship, 560
Farm Credit Services of Mid-America Scholarship, 275
Federal Reserve Bank of New York Undergraduate Summer Internship, 560
Financial Women International Scholarship, 302
Fisher Broadcasting Company Scholarship for Minorities, 262
Ford Motor Company Tribal College Scholarship, 112
GE Foundation/LULAC Scholarship Program, 368
GE Hispanic Forum Scholarship, 327
Genentech, Inc. Internship Program, 562
George and Donna Nigh Public Service Scholarship, 438
George Mason Business Scholarship Fund, 303
George Washington Carver Internship, 592
Guggenheim Museum Internship, 586
Harold Bettinger Memorial Scholarship, 104
Harriet Irsay Scholarship, 118
Hawaii Society of Certified Public Accountants Scholarship Fund, 306
Henry A. Zuberano Scholarship, 306
Hershey Company Tribal Scholarship, 112
Hoffman-La Roche Inc. Student Internship, 563
Honda Scholarship, 328
Horizons Scholarship, 545
Hormel Foods Corporation Scholarship, 277
House Member Internships, 589
Hudner Medal of Honor Scholarship, 260
The Hyatt Hotels Fund for Minority Lodging Management Students Competition, 110
IATAN Ronald A. Santana Memorial Scholarship, 514
IBM Co-op and Intern Program, 563
IEHA Educational Foundation Scholarship, 345
INROADS Internship, 564
ISFA Education Foundation College Scholarship, 344
J. Paul Getty Multicultural Undergraduate Summer Internships at the Getty Center, 564
Jacob Van Namen Marketing Scholarship, 104
James A. Turner, Jr. Memorial Scholarship, 202
James E. Webb Internship Program for Minority Undergraduate Seniors and Graduate Students in Business and Public Administration, 585
Jedidiah Zabrosky Scholarship, 532
John L. Mendez Business Scholarship, 383
John Wiley and Sons, Inc. Internship Program, 565
Johnson Controls Co-op and Internship Programs, 566
Kennedy Center Arts Management Internship, 565
KeyBank Scholarship, 278
Kittredge Coddington Memorial Scholarship, 532
Lagrant Scholarships, 365
Letitia B. Carter Scholarship, 463
Lou and Carole Prato Sports Reporting Scholarship, 462
Louis Carr Summer Internship, 566
Maine Innkeepers Association Scholarship, 374
Makovsky & Company Inc. Public Relations Internship, 567
Marathon Oil Corporation College Scholarship, 329
Marathon Petroleum Corporation College Scholarship, 330
Marcia S. Harris Legacy Fund Scholarship, 463
Mark Beaumont Scholarship Fund, 80
Mark J. Smith Scholarship, 241
Markham-Colegrave International Scholarship, 105
Marriott Scholars Program, 326
Marsh Scholarship, 344
MCC Theater Internships, 567
MESBEC Scholarships, 234
MetLife Foundation Scholarship, 279
Metropolitan Museum of Art Summer Internship Program, 568
Mills Fleet Farm Scholarship, 280
Morgan Stanley Foundation Scholarship, 330
Morgan Stanley Richard B. Fisher Scholarship Program, 394
Morgan Stanley Scholars Program, 112
Museum Coca-Cola Internship, 573
NABA National Scholarship Program, 406
NASA Space Grant Wisconsin Consortium Undergraduate Research Program, 405
NASCAR/Wendell Scott Sr. Award, 325
National Mastis Council Scholarship, 280
National Society of Accountants Scholarship, 419
NAWIC Founders' Construction Trades Scholarship, 409
NAWIC Founders' Undergraduate Scholarship, 409
NCR Summer Internships, 573
NEEBC Scholarship, 421
NextEra Energy Internship Program, 575
Nissan North America, Inc. Scholarship Program, 330
Norfolk Southern Foundation Scholarship, 281
NTA Canada Scholarship, 514
NTA Connecticut Scholarship, 514
NTA Florida Scholarship, 514
NTA LaMacchia Family Scholarship, 515
NTA Massachusetts Scholarship, 515
NTA New Horizons - Kathy LeTarte Scholarship, 515
NTA New Jersey Scholarship, 515
NTA New York Scholarship, 515
NTA North America Scholarship, 516
NTA Ohio Scholarship, 516
NTA Pat & Jim Host Scholarship, 516
NTA Rene Campbell - Ruth McKinney Scholarship, 516
NTA Utah Keith Griffall Scholarship, 517
Oscar and Rosetta Fish Fund, 317
Owens Corning Internships, 583
Pacific Gas and Electric Summer Intern Program, 583
Penton Media Scholarship, 281
Peterson Family Scholarship, 282
PGA Tour Diversity Intern Program, 583
PHCC Educational Foundation Scholarships, 457
Philip and Alice Angell Eastern Star Scholarship, 533
PRSA-Hawaii/Roy Leffingwell Public Relations Scholarship, 318
Rabo Agrifinance Scholarship, 282
Rhode Island State Government Internship Program, 584
Ritchie-Jennings Memorial Scholarship, 81
Roller Skating Foundation College Scholarship, 465
Scarlett Family Foundation Scholarship, 469
Scholarship for Foodservice Communication Careers, 345
Seattle Professional Chapter Scholarship, 222
Seneca Foods Corporation Scholarship, 283
Shirley McKown Scholarship Fund, 320
Sony Credited Internship, 586
Southern California Council Endowed Internship, 573
Southface Internship, 587
Spoleto Festival USA Apprenticeship Program, 587
Texas Fifth-Year Accounting Student Scholarship Program, 509
Theisen's Home Farm Auto Scholarship, 284
Thomas R. Pickering Foreign Affairs Fellowship, 545
Time Inc. Internship Program, 588
Traditional CITE Scholarship, 245

Travelers Foundation Scholarship, 113
Travelers Scholarship, 325
Tribal Business Management Scholarship, 235
Tri-State Surveying & Photogrammetry Kris M. Kunze Scholarship, 100
Tyson Foods Intern Program, 588
U.S. Department of State Internship, 589
U.S. National Arboretum National Herb Garden Year-Long Internship, 590
U.S. Senate Member Internships, 589
Washington Crossing Foundation Scholarship, 537
Water Companies (NJ Chapter) Scholarship, 409
Wells Fargo Scholarship, 285
Wells Fargo Undergraduate Internships, 591
The William R. Goldfarb Memorial Scholarship, 191
Wilma D. Hoyal/Maxine Chilton Memorial Scholarship, 121
Wolf Trap Foundation for the Performing Arts Internship, 592
Wooddy Scholarship, 82

Communications

AAJA Texas Student Scholarship, 212
AAJA/NBC Summer Partnership, 555
AdOhio Advertising Internship, 582
Advertising Internship, 556
AfterCollege Business Student Scholarship, 85
AGCO Scholarships, 268
Allison E. Fisher Scholarship, 407
American Association of Advertising Agencies Multicultural Advertising Intern Program, 549
American Society of International Law Internships, 551
Americans for the Arts Local Arts Advancement Services Internship, 553
Americans for the Arts Marketing and Communications Internship, 553
Americans for the Arts Meetings and Events/Executive Office Internship, 553
APTRA-Clete Roberts/Kathryn Dettman Memorial Journalism Scholarship, 220
Arabian Horse Association (Region 14) Scholarship, 270
ARRL Foundation PHD Scholarship, 180
Asian American Journalists Association Print & Online News Grants, 211
Aspiring Sports Journalist Internship, 587
BIA Cares of San Diego Scholarship, 230
Boston Globe Summer Internship, 556
Broadcast News Grants, 211
Bunge North America Scholarship, 272
Carole Simpson Scholarship, 407, 461
CCNMA Scholarships, 235
Charles & Lucille King Family Foundation Scholarships, 238
The Charles Clarke Cordle Memorial Scholarship, 181
The Charles N. Fisher Memorial Scholarship, 182
CIC/Anna Chennault Scholarship, 212
Citizens for Global Solutions Internship, 557
CNH Capital Scholarship, 273
Congressional Institute Internships, 557
Cooperative Resources International Scholarship, 273
CSX Scholarship, 274
The Dallas Morning New Journalism Scholarship, 249
Dana Campbell Memorial Scholarship, 353
David E. Rosenbaum Reporting Internship in Washington, D.C., 575
DeWayne Wickham Founder's High School Scholarship, 407
Disney Theme Parks & Resorts Professional Internships, 591
DOE Scholars Program, 576
Dow Jones Business Reporting Intern Program, 558
Dow Jones Digital Intern Program, 558
Dow Jones News Editing Intern Program, 558
Dow Jones Sports Editing Intern Program, 559
Dr. Alma S. Adams Scholarship for Outreach and Health Communications to Reduce Tobacco Use Among Priority Populations, 118
The Dr. James L. Lawson Memorial Scholarship, 183
Ed Bradley Scholarship, 461
Edward J. Nell Memorial Scholarship, 461
Edward Payson and Bernice Pi'ilani Irwin Scholarship Trust Fund, 301
Endowment Fund For Education (EFFE), 225
EPA National Network for Environmental Management Studies Fellowship, 528
ESPN Internship, 560
Essence Summer Internship, 560
The Eugene "Gene" Sallee, W4YFR, Memorial Scholarship, 183
Fisher Broadcasting Company Scholarship for Minorities, 262
The Francis Walton Memorial Scholarship, 183
The Fred R. McDaniel Memorial Scholarship, 184
The George Foreman Tribute to Lyndon B. Johnson Scholarship, 461
George Washington Carver Internship, 592
Guggenheim Museum Internship, 586
Harold K. Douthit Scholarship, 437
Harriet Irsay Scholarship, 118
Hearst Journalism Award, 541
House Member Internships, 589
INROADS Internship, 564
International Radio and Television Society Foundation Summer Fellowship Program, 564
The Irving W. Cook WA0CGS Scholarship, 185
J. Paul Getty Multicultural Undergraduate Summer Internships at the Getty Center, 564
Jackson Foundation Journalism Scholarship, 444
The Jake McClain Driver KC5WXA Scholarship Fund, 185
Jerry Clark Memorial Scholarship, 102
John Wiley and Sons, Inc. Internship Program, 565
Kennedy Library Archival Internship, 565
KeyBank Scholarship, 278
The L. Phil and Alice J. Wicker Scholarship, 186
Lagrant Scholarships, 365
Larry Whiteside Scholarship, 407
Leonard M. Perryman Communications Scholarship for Ethnic Minority Students, 522
Lou and Carole Prato Sports Reporting Scholarship, 462
Louis Carr Summer Internship, 566
The Magnolia DX Association Scholarship, 186
Makovsky & Company Inc. Public Relations Internship, 567
Marshall E. McCullough Undergraduate Scholarship, 411
MetLife Foundation Scholarship, 279
Mike Reynolds Scholarship, 462
The Mississippi Scholarship, 187
Mother Jones Ben Bagdikian Fellowship Program, 570
Museum Coca-Cola Internship, 573
NABJ Internships, 572
NABJ Scholarship, 408
NABJ Visual Task Force (VTF) Scholarship, 408
NASA Space Grant Arizona Undergraduate Research Internship, 571
National Mastis Council Scholarship, 280
The New Republic Internships, 574
New York American Legion Press Association Scholarship, 155
New York Times James Reston Reporting Fellowships, 575
New York Women in Communications Foundation Scholarship, 428
Nissan North America, Inc. Scholarship Program, 330

Norfolk Southern Foundation Scholarship, 281
NPPF Scholarship, 417
Ohio Newspaper Association Publications/Public Relations Internship, 582
Ohio Newspapers Minority Scholarship, 437
Ohio Newspapers Women's Scholarship, 437
The Orlando HamCation Scholarship, 188
The Paul and Helen L. Grauer Scholarship, 188
Pennsylvania Women's Press Association Scholarship, 456
Penton Media Scholarship, 281
Pete Wilson Journalism Scholarship, 462
Peterson Family Scholarship, 282
PGA Tour Diversity Intern Program, 583
PGSF Annual Scholarship Competition, 460
Presidents Scholarships, 462
PRSA-Hawaii/Roy Leffingwell Public Relations Scholarship, 318
Pulliam Journalism Fellowship, 563
Rabo Agrifinance Scholarship, 282
Research Participation Program for the Johns Hopkins University Applied Physics Laboratory, 579
Research Participation Program for the U.S. Army Aeromedical Research Laboratory (USAARL), 580
Research Participation Program for the U.S. Army Public Health Command, 580
SCA Conservation Internships, 587
Scholarship for Foodservice Communication Careers, 345
Scholastic Photography Portfolio Silver Award, 93
Scholastic Writing Portfolio Gold Award, 94
Seattle Professional Chapter Scholarship, 222
Shirley McKown Scholarship Fund, 320
Simon and Schuster Internship Program, 584
Sony Credited Internship, 586
Stanford Chen Internship Grant, 212
Thomas R. Pickering Foreign Affairs Fellowship, 545
Time Inc. Internship Program, 588
Traditional CITE Scholarship, 245
United States Holocaust Memorial Museum Internship, 588
University Journalism Scholarship, 437
U.S. Department of State Internship, 589
U.S. Senate Member Internships, 589
The Wall Street Journal Asia Internship, 590
The Wall Street Journal Europe Internship, 590
The Wall Street Journal Journalism Internship, 590
Water Companies (NJ Chapter) Scholarship, 409
William D. Greenlee Scholarship, 455

Computer and information sciences

Aerospace Undergraduate STEM Research Scholarship Program, 404
AFCEA Intelligence Scholarship, 207
AFCEA Military Personnel & Dependents Scholarship, 207
AFCEA ROTC Scholarship, 207
AFCEA Scholarship for Underserved Students (HBCU), 208
AFCEA War Veterans/Disabled War Veterans Scholarship, 208
AfterCollege Computer Science & Engineering Student Scholarship, 85
AHIMA Student Merit Scholarships, 87
Air Force Research Laboratory, 711 Human Performance Wing, 575
AISES Google Scholarship, 114
Albert E. Wischmeyer Memorial Scholarship Award, 474
The Allen and Bertha Watson Memorial Scholarship, 179
Allen and Loureena Weber Scholarship, 474
Allstate Internships, 549
ALPFA Scholarship, 326
Alpha Beta Gamma National Scholarship, 94
Alvin and June Sabroff Manufacturing Engineering Scholarship, 474
Androscoggin Amateur Radio Club Scholarship, 179
Applied Materials Internship and Co-op Program, 555
Arizona Public Service Navajo Scholars Program, 111
ARRL Foundation PHD Scholarship, 180
Arthur and Gladys Cervenka Scholarship, 475
A.T. Anderson Memorial Scholarship, 114
Black & Veatch Summer Internship Program, 556
BMW/SAE Engineering Scholarships, 466
Boeing Internships, 556
Buick Achievers Scholarship Program, 289
Burlington Northern Santa Fe Foundation Scholarship, 115
Castle & Cooke Mililani Technology Park Scholarship Fund, 298
The CBC General Mills Health Scholarship, 242
Chapter 17 - St. Louis Scholarship, 475
Chapter 198 - Downriver Detroit Scholarship, 475
Chapter 52 - Wichita Scholarship, 476
Chapter 6 - Fairfield County Scholarship, 476
Chapter 67 - Phoenix Scholarship, 476
CIA Undergraduate Scholarship Program, 237
Citizens for Global Solutions Internship, 557
Clinton J. Helton Manufacturing Scholarship Award, 477
Connie and Robert T. Gunter Scholarship, 478
Cyber Security Scholarships, 208
Davidson Fellows Scholarship, 251
Delaware Space Grant Undergraduate Summer Research Internship, 571
Delaware Space Grant Undergraduate Tuition Scholarship, 396
Denver Rescue Mission Center for Mission Studies Internships, 558
Department of Energy Community College Institute at Oak Ridge National Laboratory, 575
DHS HS-STEM Summer Internship Program, 576
DHS Summer Faculty and Student Research Team Program for Minority Serving Institutions, 576
Discover Scholarship, 327
Disney Theme Parks & Resorts Professional Internships, 591
DOE Faculty and Student Teams Program at Oak Ridge National Laboratory, 576
DOE Science Undergraduate Laboratory Internships at Oak Ridge National Laboratory, 576
DPMA/PC Scholarship, 251
DuPont Internships, 559
E. Wayne Kay Community College Scholarship, 478
E. Wayne Kay Co-op Scholarship, 478
E. Wayne Kay High School Scholarship, 478
Eastman Kodak Cooperative Internship Programs, 559
Economic Research Division Project Internships, 556
Entergy Jumpstart Co-ops and Internships, 560
Environmental Management Participation at the U.S. Army Environmental Command (USAEC), 577
EPA Greater Research Opportunities Undergraduate Student Fellowships, 527
EPA National Network for Environmental Management Studies Fellowship, 528
ESPN Internship, 560
Federal Reserve Bank of New York Undergraduate Summer Internship, 560

Ford Motor Company Tribal College Scholarship, 112
Foth Production Solutions, LLC Scholarship, 276
GE Hispanic Forum Scholarship, 327
Genentech, Inc. Internship Program, 562
Giuliano Mazzetti Scholarship, 479
Google Hispanic College Fund Scholarship Program, 325
HENAAC Scholars Program, 294
Hershey Company Tribal Scholarship, 112
High Technology Scholar/Intern Tuition Waiver Program, 379
Higher Education Research Experiences at Oak Ridge National Laboratory for Students, 577
Hoffman-La Roche Inc. Student Internship, 563
Hoku Scholarship Fund, 307
Horizons Scholarship, 545
IBM Co-op and Intern Program, 563
The Indianapolis Amateur Radio Association Fund, 184
INROADS Internship, 564
Intel Scholarship, 115
The Jake McClain Driver KC5WXA Scholarship Fund, 185
John Wiley and Sons, Inc. Internship Program, 565
Kawasaki-McGaha Scholarship Fund, 312
Lockheed Martin American Heroes Scholarship, 329
The Magnolia DX Association Scholarship, 186
Marathon Petroleum Corporation College Scholarship, 330
Marble-Boyle Award, 222
MESBEC Scholarships, 234
Mickey Leland Energy Fellowship Program, 577
Microsoft General Scholarship, 386
Morgan Stanley Foundation Scholarship, 330
Morgan Stanley Richard B. Fisher Scholarship Program, 394
Morgan Stanley Scholars Program, 112
NABA National Scholarship Program, 406
NASA New Jersey Space Grant Consortium Undergraduate Summer Fellowships in Engineering and Science, 571
NASA North Carolina Space Grant Consortium Undergraduate Research Scholarship, 400
NASA North Carolina Space Grant Consortium Undergraduate Scholarship Program, 400
NASA Space Grant Georgia Fellowship Program, 396
NASA Space Grant Montana Undergraduate Scholarship Program, 399
NASA Space Grant Nevada Undergraduate Scholarship, 399
NASA Space Grant New Mexico Undergraduate Scholarship, 400
NASA Space Grant North Dakota Undergraduate Scholarship, 401
NASA Space Grant Oregon Undergraduate Scholarship, 402
NASA Space Grant Virginia Community College STEM Scholarship, 404
NASA Utah Space Grant Consortium Undergraduate Scholarship, 403
NASCAR/Wendell Scott Sr. Award, 325
National Energy Technology Laboratory Professional Internship Program, 577
National Security Agency Stokes Educational Scholarship Program, 418
NCR Summer Internships, 573
NextEra Energy Internship Program, 575
The North Fulton Amateur Radio League Scholarship Fund, 187
Nuclear Regulatory Commission Historically Black Colleges and Universities Student Research Participation, 578
Oak Ridge National Laboratory Undergraduate Student Cooperative Education Program, 578
Oak Ridge Science Semester, 578
Oracle Product Development Summer Internship Program, 582
Owens Corning Internships, 583
Pacific Gas and Electric Summer Intern Program, 583
The Paul and Helen Ruckes Scholarship, 107
Pearl I. Young Scholarship, 401
PGA Tour Diversity Intern Program, 583
Plasma Physics National Undergraduate Fellowship Program, 584
Procter & Gamble - Orgullosa Scholarship, 331
Rabo Agrifinance Scholarship, 282
The Ray, NØRP, & Katie, WØKTE, Pautz Scholarship, 189
Research Participation at the National Center for Toxicological Research, 579
Research Participation Program for the Combat Casualty Care Research Program (CCCRP), 579
Research Participation Program for the Johns Hopkins University Applied Physics Laboratory, 579
Research Participation Program for the U.S. Air Force School of Aerospace Medicine (USAFSAM), 580
Research Participation Program for the U.S. Army Aeromedical Research Laboratory (USAARL), 580
Research Participation Program for the U.S. Army Public Health Command, 580
Research Participation Program for the U.S. Army Research Institute for Environmental Medicine (USARIEM), 581
Research Participation Program for the U.S. Army Research Laboratory, 581
Rodney E. Powell Memorial Scholarship, 431
Roosevelt Archival Internships, 562
SAE Detroit Section Technical Scholarship, 467
Seneca Foods Corporation Scholarship, 283
Shuichi, Katsu and Itsuyo Suga Scholarship, 321
Siemens Competition in Math, Science and Technology, 473
SME-FF Future Leaders of Manufacturing Scholarships, 480
Sony Credited Internship, 586
STEM Bridge Scholarship, 405
STEM Columbia Crew Memorial Scholarship, 403
STEM Majors Scholarship, 208
Student Research at the U.S. Army Edgewood Chemical Biological Center, 581
TAG Education Collaborative Web Challenge Contest, 502
Technical Minority Scholarship, 546
Time Inc. Internship Program, 588
Traditional CITE Scholarship, 245
Travelers Foundation Scholarship, 113
Travelers Scholarship, 325
Tyson Foods Intern Program, 588
U.S. Air Force Medial Support Agency, 581
U.S. Army Natick Soldier Research Development & Engineering Center, 582
U.S. Department of State Internship, 589
Washington Internships for Students of Engineering, 591
Water Companies (NJ Chapter) Scholarship, 409
The Wayne Nelson, KB4UT, Memorial Scholarship, 191
West Virginia Engineering, Science, and Technology Scholarship, 540
William E. Weisel Scholarship, 480
The William R. Goldfarb Memorial Scholarship, 191
Women Soar Scholarship for Innovation, 261

Education

AFCEA Military Personnel & Dependents Scholarship, 207

AFCEA ROTC Scholarship, 207
AFCEA War Veterans/Disabled War Veterans Scholarship, 208
AGCO Scholarships, 268
Alma White-Delta Kappa Gamma Scholarship, 296
American Legion Illinois Auxiliary Special Education Teaching Scholarships, 129
American Legion Maryland Auxiliary Scholarship, 138
American Legion Nebraska Auxiliary Graduate Scholarship, 148
Americans for the Arts Government and Public Affairs Internship, 553
Applied Arts Internships, 554
Arabian Horse Association (Region 14) Scholarship, 270
Arthur Patch McKinlay Scholarship, 97
Averyl Elaine Keriakedes Memorial Scholarship, 149
Burlington Northern Santa Fe Foundation Scholarship, 115
California Child Development Grant Program, 232
California Teachers Association Martin Luther King, Jr., Memorial Scholarship, 233
Christa McAuliffe Memorial Scholarship, 151
Christa McAuliffe Teacher Incentive Program, 594
CNH Capital Scholarship, 273
Connecticut Minority Teacher Incentive Grant, 244
Critical Needs Teacher Loan/Scholarship, 596
CTA Scholarship for Dependent Children, 233
CTA Scholarships for Members, 233
Cushman School Internship, 557
David Family Scholarship, 443
Delta Gamma Foundation Florence Margaret Harvey Memorial Scholarship, 106
DMI Milk Marketing Scholarships, 410
Dr. Alma S. Adams Scholarship for Outreach and Health Communications to Reduce Tobacco Use Among Priority Populations, 118
Dr. Hannah K. Vuolo Memorial Scholarship, 154
Dr. Hans & Clara Zimmerman Foundation Education Scholarship, 300
Eight and Forty Lung and Respiratory Disease Nursing Scholarship, 146
Erman W. Taylor Memorial Scholarship, 142
George Washington Carver Internship, 592
Golden Apple Scholars of Illinois Program, 291
Golden Key Undergraduate Achievement Scholarship, 293
Grow Your Own Teacher Scholarship Program, 339
Guggenheim Museum Internship, 586
Harriet Hoffman Memorial Scholarship, 132
Harriet Irsay Scholarship, 118
Hawaii Community Scholarship Fund, 305
Henry and Dorothy Castle Memorial Scholarship, 306
Hokuli'a Foundation Scholarship Fund, 307
Ichiro & Masako Hirata Scholarship, 308
Ida M. Pope Memorial Scholarship, 308
Illinois Special Education Teacher Tuition Waiver, 342
Incentive Program for Aspiring Teachers, 379
Indiana Minority Teacher & Special Education Services Scholarship, 497
Isemoto Contracting Co., Ltd. Scholarship Fund, 308
James Carlson Memorial Scholarship, 445
Jedidiah Zabrosky Scholarship, 532
Kansas Teacher Service Scholarship, 361
Kentucky Early Childhood Development Scholarship, 362
Kentucky Teacher Scholarship, 363
KeyBank Scholarship, 278
L. Gordon Bittle Memorial Scholarship for SCTA, 234
Latin Honor Society Scholarship, 415
Lindbergh Grant, 238
Lutheran Student Scholastic and Service Scholarship, 225
Massachusetts Early Childhood Educators Scholarship, 380
Massachusetts Math and Science Teachers Scholarship, 381
Math And Science Teachers Loan Forgiveness Program, 600
Maureen V. O'Donnell/Eunice C. Kraft Teacher Training Scholarships, 97
MESBEC Scholarships, 234
MetLife Foundation Scholarship, 279
Minority Teacher Education Scholarship Program/Florida Fund for Minority Teachers, Inc., 265
Minority Teachers of Illinois Scholarship, 343
Minority Teaching Scholarship, 391
Mississippi William Winter Teacher Scholar Loan Program, 597
Mister Rogers Memorial Scholarship, 81
Morris Arboretum Education Internship, 569
Museum Coca-Cola Internship, 573
NASA Pennsylvania Space Grant Undergraduate Scholarship, 402
NASA Space Grant Arizona Undergraduate Research Internship, 571
NASA Space Grant Georgia Fellowship Program, 396
NASA Space Grant Kentucky Undergraduate Scholarship, 397
NASA Space Grant Oregon Undergraduate Scholarship, 402
National Junior Classical League Scholarship, 415
National Mastis Council Scholarship, 280
Native American Leadership in Education Scholarship, 235
New Mexico Teacher's Loan-for-Service, 598
New York State Math and Science Teaching Incentive Program, 427
Nick Van Pernis Scholarship, 316
Norfolk Southern Foundation Scholarship, 281
Oklahoma Future Teachers Scholarship, 439
Oregon Alpha Delta Kappa Scholarship, 446
PAGE Foundation Scholarships, 460
Peggy Guggenheim Internship, 586
Peterson Family Scholarship, 282
Philip and Alice Angell Eastern Star Scholarship, 533
Rabo Agrifinance Scholarship, 282
Ron Bright Scholarship, 319
Roosevelt Archival Internships, 562
The Rudolph Dillman Memorial Scholarship, 107
Sarah Rosenberg Teacher Education Scholarship, 320
SCA Conservation Internships, 587
Seneca Foods Corporation Scholarship, 283
Smithsonian Environmental Research Center Internship Program, 585
Society of Physics Students Future Teacher Scholarship, 485
Society of Sponsors Scholarship Program, 421
South Carolina Teacher Loans, 599
South Dakota Annis I. Fowler/Kaden Scholarship, 494
South Dakota Haines Memorial Scholarship, 495
STEM Teacher Scholarships, 209
Teacher Education Assistance for College and Higher Education (TEACH) Grant, 453
Tennessee Minority Teaching Fellows Program, 600
Tennessee Teaching Scholars Program, 600
United Health Foundation Scholarship, 113
U.S. National Arboretum National Herb Garden Year-Long Internship, 590
Utah Career Teaching Scholarship/T.H. Bell Teaching Incentive Loan, 602

Weisman Scholarship, 245
West Virginia Underwood-Smith Teacher Scholarship, 540
Wilma D. Hoyal/Maxine Chilton Memorial Scholarship, 121
Wisconsin Minority Teacher Loan Program, 602

Engineering and engineering technology

Accelerator Applications Division Scholarship, 173
ACEC Scholarship, 101
ACSM Fellows Scholarship, 98
Aerospace Undergraduate STEM Research Scholarship Program, 404
AFCEA Intelligence Scholarship, 207
AFCEA Military Personnel & Dependents Scholarship, 207
AFCEA ROTC Scholarship, 207
AFCEA Scholarship for Underserved Students (HBCU), 208
AFCEA War Veterans/Disabled War Veterans Scholarship, 208
AfterCollege Electrical Engineering Student Scholarship, 85
AfterCollege Engineering Scholarship, 85
AGC Education and Research Undergraduate Scholarship, 219
AGCO Scholarships, 268
Agnes Malakate Kezios Scholarship, 214
Agrium U.S. Inc. Scholarship, 268
AIAA Foundation Undergraduate Scholarship, 116
Air Force Research Laboratory, 711 Human Performance Wing, 575
AISES Google Scholarship, 114
Albert E. Wischmeyer Memorial Scholarship Award, 474
The Alfred E. Friend, Jr., W4CF Memorial Scholarship, 179
The Allen and Bertha Watson Memorial Scholarship, 179
Allen and Loureena Weber Scholarship, 474
Allen J. Baldwin Scholarship, 214
Allen Rhodes Memorial Scholarship, 215
Alvin and June Sabroff Manufacturing Engineering Scholarship, 474
Alwin B. Newton Scholarship, 195
American Chemical Society Scholars Program, 97
American Electric Power Scholarship, 215
American Meteorological Society Freshman Undergraduate Scholarship Program, 171
American Meteorological Society Named Undergraduate Scholarship, 171
American Meteorological Society/Industry Minority Scholarship, 172
American Nuclear Society Operations and Power Division Scholarship, 174
Amtrol Scholarship, 108
Androscoggin Amateur Radio Club Scholarship, 179
Angelo S. Bisesti Scholarship, 174
ANS Decommissioning, Decontamination and Reutilization Scholarship, 174
ANS Incoming Freshman Scholarship, 174
ANS Undergraduate Scholarships, 174
ANS Washington, D.C. Section Undergraduate Scholarship, 175
Applied Materials Internship and Co-op Program, 555
Arabian Horse Association (Region 14) Scholarship, 270
Arizona Chapter Vertical Flight Engineering Scholarship, 108
Arizona Public Service Navajo Scholars Program, 111
The ARRL Earl I. Anderson Scholarship, 179
ARRL Foundation PHD Scholarship, 180
The ARRL Northwestern Division Scholarship Fund, 180
Arthur and Doreen Parrett Scholarship, 210
Arthur and Gladys Cervenka Scholarship, 475
ASDSO Undergraduate Scholarship, 223
ASHRAE Engineering Technology Scholarships, 196
ASHRAE General Scholarships, 196
ASHRAE Memorial Scholarship, 196
ASHRAE Region IV Benny Bootle Scholarship, 196
ASHRAE Region VIII Scholarship, 196
ASM Outstanding Scholars Awards, 212
ASME Auxiliary Student Loan Fund, 593
ASME Auxiliary/FIRST Clarke Scholarship, 216
The ASME Foundation Hanley Scholarship, 216
ASME Foundation Scholarships, 216
ASME Metropolitan Section John Rice Memorial Scholarship, 216
ASME Power Division Scholarship, 217
ASME Student Loan Program, 593
ASNE Scholarship, 199
A.T. Anderson Memorial Scholarship, 114
B. Charles Tiney Memorial ASCE Student Chapter Scholarship, 194
Baroid Scholarship, 108
Barry K. Wendt Commitment Award and Scholarship, 420
Barry M. Goldwater Scholarship, 225
Berna Lou Cartwright Scholarship, 215
Berntsen International Scholarship in Surveying Technology, 99
The Betty Weatherford, KQ6RE, Memorial Scholarship, 180
BIA Cares of San Diego Scholarship, 230
Bill Sanderson Aviation Maintenance Technician Scholarship Award, 323
Black & Veatch Summer Internship Program, 556
BMW/SAE Engineering Scholarships, 466
Boeing Internships, 556
Brown and Caldwell Minority Scholarship Program, 229
Buick Achievers Scholarship Program, 289
Bunge North America Scholarship, 272
Burlington Northern Santa Fe Foundation Scholarship, 115
Cady McDonnell Memorial Scholarship, 99
California Farm Bureau Scholarship, 231
Casey's General Stores, Inc. Scholarship, 272
Castle & Cooke Mililani Technology Park Scholarship Fund, 298
The CBC General Mills Health Scholarship, 242
CBC Scholarship, 243
Center for Architecture Design Scholarship, 236
Chapter 17 - St. Louis Scholarship, 475
Chapter 198 - Downriver Detroit Scholarship, 475
Chapter 311 - Tri City Scholarship, 475
Chapter 4 - Lawrence A. Wacker Memorial Scholarship, 476
Chapter 52 - Wichita Scholarship, 476
Chapter 56 - Fort Wayne Scholarship, 476
Chapter 6 - Fairfield County Scholarship, 476
Chapter 67 - Phoenix Scholarship, 476
Chapter 93 - Albuquerque Scholarship, 477
Chapter One - Detroit Founding Chapter Scholarship Award, 477
Charles and Annette Hill Scholarship, 133
Charles B. Scharp Scholarship, 215
Charles P. Lake - Rain For Rent Scholarship, 272
Charles (Tommy) Thomas Memorial Scholarship, 175
Church & Dwight Company, Inc. Scholarship, 273
CI Construction Engineering Student Scholarship, 245
CIA Undergraduate Scholarship Program, 237
Clarence & Josephine Myers Scholarship, 477

Clinton J. Helton Manufacturing Scholarship Award, 477
Connie and Robert T. Gunter Scholarship, 478
ConocoPhillips Scholarships, 245
Cyber Security Scholarships, 208
D. Fred and Mariam L. Bovie Scholarship, 201
David Alan Quick Scholarship, 259
David Arver Memorial Scholarship, 88
David Mineck Memorial Scholarship, 260
Davidson Fellows Scholarship, 251
DEED Student Research Grants, 178
Delaware Space Grant Undergraduate Summer Research Internship, 571
Delaware Space Grant Undergraduate Tuition Scholarship, 396
Delayed Education Scholarship for Women, 175
Delta Faucet Company Scholarship, 456
Department of Energy Community College Institute at Oak Ridge National Laboratory, 575
DHS HS-STEM Summer Internship Program, 576
DHS Summer Faculty and Student Research Team Program for Minority Serving Institutions, 576
Disney Theme Parks & Resorts Professional Internships, 591
DOE Faculty and Student Teams Program at Oak Ridge National Laboratory, 576
DOE Scholars Program, 576
DOE Science Undergraduate Laboratory Internships at Oak Ridge National Laboratory, 576
Dr. W. Wes Eckenfelder Jr. Scholarship, 230
Duane Hanson Scholarship, 197
DuPont Co-ops, 559
Dutch and Ginger Arver Scholarship, 89
E. Wayne Kay Co-op Scholarship, 478
E. Wayne Kay High School Scholarship, 478
E. Wayne Kay Scholarship, 478
Eastman Kodak Cooperative Internship Programs, 559
The Edmond A. Metzger Scholarship, 183
Edward D. Hendrickson/SAE Engineering Scholarship, 466
Edward J. Brady Memorial Scholarship, 202
Edward J. Dulis Scholarship, 213
Edward S. Roth Manufacturing Engineering Scholarship, 479
Ellison Onizuka Memorial Scholarship, 302
Engineers Foundation of Ohio Scholarships, 257
Entergy Jumpstart Co-ops and Internships, 560
Environmental Management Participation at the U.S. Army Environmental Command (USAEC), 577
EPA Greater Research Opportunities Undergraduate Student Fellowships, 527
Eugene C. Figg Jr. Civil Engineering Scholarship, 194
Extrusion Division/Lew Erwin Memorial Scholarship, 486
ExxonMobil Scholarship, 327
Father James B. Macelwane Annual Award, 172
Field Aviation Co. Inc. Scholarship, 89
Fleming/Blaszcak Scholarship, 486
Ford Motor Company Tribal College Scholarship, 112
Foth Production Solutions, LLC Scholarship, 276
Frank and Dorothy Miller ASME Auxiliary Scholarships, 217
Frank M. Coda Scholarship, 197
Fred M. Young, Sr./SAE Engineering Scholarship, 466
Freeman Fellowship, 194
F.W. "Beich" Beichley Scholarship, 217
Garland Duncan Scholarships, 217
Garmin Scholarship, 89
Gary J. Miller Undergraduate Prizes for Cancer and Cancer-Related Biomedical Research, 96
The Gary Wagner, K3OMI, Scholarship, 184
GE Foundation/LULAC Scholarship Program, 368
GE Hispanic Forum Scholarship, 327
Genentech, Inc. Internship Program, 562
George A. Roberts Scholarships, 213
Giuliano Mazzetti Scholarship, 479
Google Hispanic College Fund Scholarship Program, 325
Gulf Coast Hurricane Scholarships, 486
Hansen Scholarship, 260
Helicopter Association International Maintenance Technician Certificate Scholarship, 324
HENAAC Scholars Program, 294
Henry Adams Scholarship, 197
The Henry Broughton, K2AE, Memorial Scholarship, 184
Hershey Company Tribal Scholarship, 112
High Technology Scholar/Intern Tuition Waiver Program, 379
Higher Education Research Experiences at Oak Ridge National Laboratory for Students, 577
Hoffman-La Roche Inc. Student Internship, 563
Hoku Scholarship Fund, 307
Honda Scholarship, 328
Horizons Scholarship, 545
Human Factors, Instrumentation and Controls Division (HFICD) Nuclear Power Scholarship, 175
IBM Co-op and Intern Program, 563
The Indianapolis Amateur Radio Association Fund, 184
Industrial Automation Engineering College Scholarships, 211
INROADS Internship, 564
Intel Scholarship, 115
Isemoto Contracting Co., Ltd. Scholarship Fund, 308
J. Richard Mehalick Scholarship, 197
James L. Allhands Essay Competition, 220
Jeffrey Alan Scoggins Memorial Scholarship, 445
Jere W. Thompson, Jr. Scholarship Fund, 250
John & Elsa Gracik Scholarships, 217
John and Muriel Landis Scholarship, 176
John Lenard Civil Engineering Scholarship, 194
John M. Haniak Scholarship, 213
John R. Lamarsh Scholarship, 176
Johnny Davis Memorial Scholarship, 89
Johnson Controls Co-op and Internship Programs, 566
Joseph R. Dietrich Scholarship, 176
Josephine and Robert B.B. Moorman Scholarship, 195
Julio C. Mendez Engineering Scholarship, 383
K. K. Wang Scholarship, 487
Kate Gleason Scholarship, 218
Kenneth Andrew Roe Mechanical Engineering Scholarship, 218
KeyBank Scholarship, 278
L-3 Avionics Systems Scholarship, 89
Laboratory Technology Program, 577
Ladish Co. Foundation Scholarships, 213
Lawrence W. and Francis W. Cox Scholarship, 195
Lee Tarbox Memorial Scholarship, 90
Lockheed Martin American Heroes Scholarship, 329
Lowell Gaylor Memorial Scholarship, 90
Lucile B. Kaufman Women's Scholarship, 479
Lucille & Charles A. Wert Scholarship, 213
Lynn G. Bellenger Scholarship, 197
The Magnolia DX Association Scholarship, 186
Maine Metal Products Association Scholarship, 374
Maine Society of Professional Engineers Scholarship Program, 375
Marathon Oil Corporation College Scholarship, 329

Marathon Petroleum Corporation College Scholarship, 330
Matsuo Bridge Company Ltd. of Japan Scholarship, 203
Melvin R. Green Scholarships, 218
MESBEC Scholarships, 234
MetLife Foundation Scholarship, 279
Michigan Society of Professional Engineers Scholarships for High School Seniors, 385
Mickey Leland Energy Fellowship Program, 577
Microscopy Society of America Undergraduate Research Scholarship, 385
Microsoft General Scholarship, 386
Mid-Continent Instrument Scholarship, 90
Mills Fleet Farm Scholarship, 280
Minority and Underrepresented Environmental Literacy Program, 391
Morgan Stanley Foundation Scholarship, 330
MSGC Undergraduate Underrepresented Minority Fellowship Program, 398
Myrtle and Earl Walker Scholarship, 479
Nancy Lorraine Jensen Memorial Scholarship, 491
NANT Educational Assistance Program, 406
NASA Academy Internship, 572
NASA Connecticut Space Grant Undergraduate Fellowship, 395
NASA Idaho Space Grant Undergraduate Scholarship, 397
NASA Minnesota Space Grant Consortium Wide Scholarship, 398
NASA Missouri State Space Grant Undergraduate Scholarship, 399
NASA New Jersey Space Grant Consortium Undergraduate Summer Fellowships in Engineering and Science, 571
NASA North Carolina Space Grant Consortium Undergraduate Research Scholarship, 400
NASA North Carolina Space Grant Consortium Undergraduate Scholarship Program, 400
NASA Ohio Space Grant Junior/Senior Scholarship Program, 401
NASA Pennsylvania Space Grant Undergraduate Scholarship, 402
NASA Rhode Island Space Grant Summer Undergraduate Scholarship, 402
NASA Space Grant Arizona Undergraduate Research Internship, 571
NASA Space Grant Georgia Fellowship Program, 396
NASA Space Grant Hawaii Undergraduate Fellowship Program, 396
NASA Space Grant Illinois Undergraduate Scholarship, 397
NASA Space Grant Kentucky Undergraduate Scholarship, 397
NASA Space Grant Maine Consortium Annual Scholarship and Fellowship Program, 397
NASA Space Grant Michigan Undergraduate Fellowship, 398
NASA Space Grant Montana Undergraduate Scholarship Program, 399
NASA Space Grant Nevada Undergraduate Scholarship, 399
NASA Space Grant New Mexico Undergraduate Scholarship, 400
NASA Space Grant North Dakota Consortium Lillian Goettler Scholarship, 401
NASA Space Grant North Dakota Undergraduate Scholarship, 401
NASA Space Grant Oregon Undergraduate Scholarship, 402
NASA Space Grant Rhode Island Undergraduate Research Scholarship, 402
NASA Space Grant South Carolina Undergraduate Student Research Fellowship, 403
NASA Space Grant Undergraduate Scholarship, 395
NASA Space Grant Vermont Consortium Undergraduate Scholarships, 404
NASA Space Grant Virginia Community College STEM Scholarship, 404
NASA Space Grant Wisconsin Consortium Undergraduate Research Program, 405
NASA Space Grant Wisconsin Consortium Undergraduate Scholarship, 405
NASA Utah Space Grant Consortium Undergraduate Scholarship, 403
NASA West Virginia Space Grant Undergraduate Research Fellowship, 405
NASCAR/Wendell Scott Sr. Award, 325
National Energy Technology Laboratory Professional Internship Program, 577
National Geographic Society Geography Students Internship, 572
National Security Agency Stokes Educational Scholarship Program, 418
NAWIC Founders' Undergraduate Scholarship, 409
NCR Summer Internships, 573
NextEra Energy Internship Program, 575
Nissan North America, Inc. Scholarship Program, 330
Norfolk Southern Foundation Scholarship, 281
North Central Region Scholarship, 479
The North Fulton Amateur Radio League Scholarship Fund, 187
Nuclear Engineering Division (NED) Scholarship, 218
Nuclear Regulatory Commission Historically Black Colleges and Universities Student Research Participation, 578
Oak Ridge National Laboratory Undergraduate Student Cooperative Education Program, 578
Oak Ridge Nuclear Engineering Science Laboratory Synthesis, 578
Oak Ridge Science Semester, 578
Oklahoma Engineering Foundation Scholarship, 438
Owens Corning Internships, 583
Pacific Gas and Electric Summer Intern Program, 583
Past Presidents Scholarship, 203
The Paul and Helen Ruckes Scholarship, 107
Payzer Scholarship, 261
Pearl I. Young Scholarship, 401
Pennsylvania Targeted Industry Program (PA-TIP), 453
Peterson Family Scholarship, 282
PHCC Educational Foundation Scholarships, 457
Pittsburgh Local Section Scholarship, 176
Pittsburgh Scholarship, 487
Plasma Physics National Undergraduate Fellowship Program, 584
Plastics Pioneers Scholarships, 487
Procter & Gamble - Orgullosa Scholarship, 331
Rain Bird Intelligent Use of Water Scholarship, 367
Ralph K. Hillquist Honorary SAE Scholarship, 467
Raymond DiSalvo Scholarship, 177
RCMI Technical/Trade School Scholarship, 464
Research Participation at the U.S. Food and Drug Administration, 579
Research Participation Program for the Combat Casualty Care Research Program (CCCRP), 579
Research Participation Program for the Johns Hopkins University Applied Physics Laboratory, 579
Research Participation Program for the U.S. Air Force Research Laboratory, Tyndall Air Force Base (AFRL-TYNDALL), 580
Research Participation Program for the U.S. Air Force Research Laboratory (USAFRL), Wright Patterson Air Force Base, 580
Research Participation Program for the U.S. Air Force School of Aerospace Medicine (USAFSAM), 580

Research Participation Program for the U.S. Army Aeromedical Research Laboratory (USAARL), 580
Research Participation Program for the U.S. Army Research Institute for Environmental Medicine (USARIEM), 581
Research Participation Program for the U.S. Army Research Laboratory, 581
Reuben Trane Scholarship, 198
Robert G. Lacy Scholarship, 177
Robert T. (Bob) Liner Scholarship, 177
Rocky Mountain Coal Mining Institute Scholarship, 464
Rodney E. Powell Memorial Scholarship, 431
RWMA Scholarship, 204
SAE Detroit Section Technical Scholarship, 467
SAE Long-Term Member Sponsored Scholarship, 467
SAE Women Engineers Committee Scholarship, 467
SAE/David Hermance Hybird Technologies Scholarship, 467
SAE/Ford Partnership for Advanced Studies Scholarship, 468
Samuel Fletcher Tapman ASCE Student Chapter Scholarship, 195
Seneca Foods Corporation Scholarship, 283
Siemens Competition in Math, Science and Technology, 473
SME Education Foundation Family Scholarship, 480
SME-FF Future Leaders of Manufacturing Scholarships, 480
Society of Plastics Engineers General Scholarships, 487
Southface Internship, 587
The SPE Foundation Blow Molding Division Memorial Scholarships, 488
Spence Reese Scholarship, 227
SPIE Optics and Photonics Education Scholarships, 496
STEM Bridge Scholarship, 405
STEM Columbia Crew Memorial Scholarship, 403
STEM Majors Scholarship, 208
Stephen T. Kugle Scholarship, 219
Student Internship Program at the U.S. Army Center for Health Promotion and Preventive Medicine, 581
Student Research at the U.S. Army Edgewood Chemical Biological Center, 581
SWE Scholarships, 489
Sylvia W. Farny Scholarship, 215
Tau Beta Pi/SAE Engineering Scholarship, 468
Technical Minority Scholarship, 546
TeeJet Technologies Scholarship, 283
Theisen's Home Farm Auto Scholarship, 284
Thermoforming Division Memorial Scholarship, 488
Thermoset Division/James I. MacKenzie Memorial Scholarship, 488
TMC/SAE Donald D. Dawson Technical Scholarship, 468
Toyota Motor Sales, U.S.A. Inc. Scholarship, 284
Traditional CITE Scholarship, 245
Travelers Foundation Scholarship, 113
Travelers Scholarship, 325
Tyson Foods Intern Program, 588
UNCF Merck Science Initiative, 523
U.S. Army Natick Soldier Research Development & Engineering Center, 582
Vertical Flight Foundation Scholarship, 109
The Victor Poor W5SMM Memorial Scholarship Fund, 190
Walt Bartram Memorial Education Award (Region 12 and Chapter 119), 480
Washington Internships for Students of Engineering, 591
Water Companies (NJ Chapter) Scholarship, 409
The Wayne Nelson, KB4UT, Memorial Scholarship, 191
West Virginia Engineering, Science, and Technology Scholarship, 540
Western Plastics Pioneers Scholarship, 488
William & Mary Dyrkacz Scholarships, 214
William E. Weisel Scholarship, 480
William J. and Marijane E. Adams, Jr. Scholarship, 219
William Park Woodside Founder's Scholarship, 214
William R. and Mila Kimel Scholarship, 177
The William R. Goldfarb Memorial Scholarship, 191
Willis F. Thompson Memorial Scholarship, 219
Willis H. Carrier Scholarship, 198
Wix Filters Scholarship, 286
Women in Architecture Scholarship, 221
Women Soar Scholarship for Innovation, 261
Yanmar/SAE Scholarship, 468
The Yasme Foundation Scholarship, 191
Y.C. Yang Civil Engineering Scholarship, 195

English and literature

Ahmad-Sehar Saleha Ahmad and Abrahim Ekramullah Zafar Foundation, 441
Arthur Patch McKinlay Scholarship, 97
Artistic and Administrative Fellowships, 550
Aspiring Sports Journalist Internship, 587
Davidson Fellows Scholarship, 251
Florence Lemcke Memorial Scholarship, 166
Gerrit R. Ludwig Scholarship, 304
Kennedy Library Archival Internship, 565
Latin Honor Society Scholarship, 415
Makovsky & Company Inc. Public Relations Internship, 567
Maureen V. O'Donnell/Eunice C. Kraft Teacher Training Scholarships, 97
Morgan Stanley Foundation Scholarship, 330
National Junior Classical League Scholarship, 415
R.L. Gillette Scholarship, 107
Scholastic Photography Portfolio Silver Award, 93
Scholastic Writing Portfolio Gold Award, 94
Signet Classic Student Scholarship Essay Contest, 451
United States Holocaust Memorial Museum Internship, 588

Foreign languages

AFCEA Military Personnel & Dependents Scholarship, 207
AFCEA ROTC Scholarship, 207
Alpha Mu Gamma Scholarships, 94
CIA Undergraduate Scholarship Program, 237
Joseph S. Adams Senior Scholarship, 481
Sant'Anna Institute-Sorrento Lingue Scholarship, 490
Sons of Italy Italian Language Scholarship, 490
Thomas R. Pickering Foreign Affairs Fellowship, 545
United States Holocaust Memorial Museum Internship, 588
U.S. Department of State Internship, 589

Health professions and allied services

ADHA Institute for Oral Health Scholarship for Academic Excellence, 82
AETNA Nursing Scholarship, 324
AfterCollege Pharmacy Student Scholarship, 86
AfterCollege Speech Language Pathology Student Scholarship, 86
AfterCollege/AACN Nursing Student Scholarships, 86
AHIMA Student Merit Scholarships, 87
Aiea General Hospital Association Scholarship, 296

Allan Eldin & Agnes Sutorik Geiger Scholarship Fund, 296
Allman Medical Scholarships, 389
Aloha Scholarship, 144
AMBUCS Scholars-Scholarship for Therapists, 95
American Legion Arizona Auxiliary Health Care Occupation Scholarship, 121
American Legion Arizona Auxiliary Nurses' Scholarship, 121
American Legion Colorado Auxiliary Past Presidents Parley Nurse's Scholarship, 124
American Legion Delaware Auxiliary Past Presidents Parley Nursing Scholarship, 125
American Legion Georgia Auxiliary Past Presidents Parley Nurses Scholarship, 127
American Legion Idaho Auxiliary Nurse's Scholarship, 128
American Legion Illinois Auxiliary Student Nurse Scholarship, 129
American Legion Indiana Auxiliary Past Presidents Parley Nursing Scholarship, 131
American Legion Maine Auxiliary Presidents Parley Nursing Scholarship, 136
American Legion Maryland Auxiliary Past Presidents Parley Scholarship, 138
American Legion Maryland Auxiliary Scholarship, 138
American Legion Massachusetts Auxiliary Past Presidents Parley Scholarship, 139
American Legion Michigan Auxiliary Medical Career Scholarships, 140
American Legion Minnesota Auxiliary Past Presidents Parley Health Care Scholarship, 141
American Legion Missouri Auxiliary Past Presidents Parley Scholarship, 144
American Legion Nebraska Auxiliary Nurse Gift Tuition Scholarships, 148
American Legion Nebraska Auxiliary Practical Nursing Scholarship, 148
American Legion Nevada Auxiliary Past Presidents Parley Nurses' Scholarship, 149
American Legion New Hampshire Auxiliary Past Presidents Parley Nurses' Scholarship, 152
American Legion New Jersey Auxiliary Past Presidents Parley Nurses' Scholarship, 153
American Legion New Mexico Auxiliary Past President's Parley Scholarship for Nurses, 154
American Legion New York Auxiliary Past Presidents Parley Student Scholarship in Medical Field, 155
American Legion North Dakota Auxiliary Past Presidents Parley Scholarship, 157
American Legion Ohio Auxiliary Past Presidents Parley Nurse's Scholarship, 158
American Legion Oregon Auxiliary Department Nurses Scholarship, 158
American Legion Puerto Rico Auxiliary Nursing Scholarships, 160
American Legion Texas Past Presidents Parley Scholarship, 163
American Legion Virginia Auxiliary Past Presidents Parley Nurse's Scholarship, 165
American Legion Wisconsin Auxiliary Past Presidents Parley R.N. Scholarship, 169
American Legion Wyoming Auxiliary Past Presidents Parley Scholarship, 170
American Medical Technologists Student Scholarship, 171
American Veterinary Medical Association Scholarship, 269
The ARRL Northwestern Division Scholarship Fund, 180
Arthur and Doreen Parrett Scholarship, 210
A.T. Anderson Memorial Scholarship, 114
Athletic Trainers' Entry Level Scholarship, 409
Behavioral Sciences Student Fellowship, 258
Bertha P. Singer Scholarship, 442
Black Nurses Scholarship, 410
Burlington Northern Santa Fe Foundation Scholarship, 115
California Farm Bureau Scholarship, 231
Carol Bauhs Benson Scholarship, 82
The Carole J. Streeter, KB9JBR, Scholarship, 181
Caroline Kark Scholarship, 425
The CBC General Mills Health Scholarship, 242
Charles W. Riley Fire and Emergency Medical Services Tuition Reimbursement Program, 375
Chester Haddan Scholarship Program, 449
CIGNA Foundation Tribal Scholars Healthcare, 111
Clark-Phelps Scholarship, 442
Colgate "Bright Smiles, Bright Futures" Minority Scholarships, 82
Colon Furr Nursing Scholarship, 156
Cooperative Resources International Scholarship, 273
Cora Aguda Manayan Fund, 298
Crest Oral-B Dental Hygiene Scholarship, 83
The Cynthia E. Morgan Memorial Scholarship Fund, 248
Cystic Fibrosis Student Traineeship, 249
Dairy Student Recognition Program, 410
Dan & Pauline Lutkenhouse & Hawaii Tropical Botanical Garden Scholarship, 299
Dan McKeever Scholarship Program, 449
David Family Scholarship, 443
Dean Foods Company Scholarship, 274
Delaware Nursing Incentive Program, 594
Delta Gamma Foundation Florence Margaret Harvey Memorial Scholarship, 106
Denver Rescue Mission Center for Mission Studies Internships, 558
DHS Summer Faculty and Student Research Team Program for Minority Serving Institutions, 576
DOE Faculty and Student Teams Program at Oak Ridge National Laboratory, 576
Dr. Alma S. Adams Scholarship for Outreach and Health Communications to Reduce Tobacco Use Among Priority Populations, 118
Dr. Alvin and Monica Saake Scholarship, 299
Dr. Esther Wilkins Scholarship, 83
Dr. Hans and Clara Zimmerman Foundation Health Scholarship, 300
Ecotrust Native American Scholarship, 111
Edward J. and Norma Doty Scholarship, 301
Eight and Forty Lung and Respiratory Disease Nursing Scholarship, 146
Filipino Nurses' Organization of Hawaii Scholarship, 302
Foundation for Surgical Technology Student Scholarship, 266
Gary J. Miller Undergraduate Prizes for Cancer and Cancer-Related Biomedical Research, 96
Genentech, Inc. Internship Program, 562
George & Lucille Cushnie Scholarship, 303
Georgina S. Mendez Pharmacology Scholarship, 383
The Grotto Scholarships, 501
Hannaford Internships, 562
Hawaii Pacific Gerontological Society Nursing Scholarship Fund, 305
Health Career Scholarship, 347
Higher Education Research Experiences at Oak Ridge National Laboratory for Students, 577
Hoffman-La Roche Inc. Student Internship, 563
Hokuli'a Foundation Scholarship Fund, 307
Hu-Friedy/Esther Wilkins Instrument Scholarships, 83

Ida M. Pope Memorial Scholarship, 308
Indiana Minority Teacher & Special Education Services Scholarship, 497
Indiana Nursing Scholarship, 498
INROADS Internship, 564
Isemoto Contracting Co., Ltd. Scholarship Fund, 308
Jimmy A. Young Memorial Education Recognition Award, 192
John and Geraldine Hobble Licensed Practical Nursing Scholarship, 134
John Dawe Dental Education Fund, 310
Juliette A. Southard/Oral-B Laboratories Scholarship, 101
June Gill Nursing Scholarship, 425
Kansas Nursing Service Scholarship, 360
Karla Girts Memorial Community Outreach Scholarship, 83
Kathleen McDermott Scholarship, 247
Ken Chagnon Scholarship, 449
Kildee Scholarship, 411
Laura N. Dowsett Fund, 314
Laurence R. Foster Memorial Scholarship, 445
Lillian B. Reynolds Scholarship, 314
Lindbergh Grant, 238
Louis Stokes Health Scholars, 242
Lutheran Student Scholastic and Service Scholarship, 225
Margaret Jones Memorial Nursing Scholarship, 315
Marguerite McAlpin Nurse's Scholarship, 167
Mary Marshall Nursing RN Scholarship, 535
Mary Marshall Nursing Scholarship Program (LPN), 536
Mary Virginia Macrea Memorial Scholarship, 132
Maryland Tuition Reduction for Non-Resident Nursing Students, 377
Massachusetts Gilbert Matching Student Grant, 380
McFarland Charitable Foundation Scholarship, 295
M.D. Jack Murphy Memorial Nurses Training Fund, 143
MESBEC Scholarships, 234
Mississippi Health Care Professions Loan/Scholarship, 596
Missouri League for Nursing Scholarship, 392
Momentum, Inc. Healthcare Scholarship, 454
Morton B. Duggan, Jr. Memorial Education Recognition Award, 192
NASA Space Grant Maine Consortium Annual Scholarship and Fellowship Program, 397
NASA Space Grant Wisconsin Consortium Undergraduate Research Program, 405
National Amateur Baseball Federation Scholarship, 406
National Health Service Corps Scholarship, 527
National Mastis Council Scholarship, 280
National Student Nurses Association Scholarship, 266
NBRC/AMP Robert M. Lawrence, MD Education Recognition Award, 193
NBRC/AMP William W. Burgin, Jr. MD Education Recognition Award, 193
NEEBC Scholarship, 421
NEHA/AAS Scholarship, 412
New Leader Scholarship, 79
New Mexico Allied Health Student Loan-for-Service Program, 597
New Mexico Nursing Student Loan-for-Service, 598
Nick Van Pernis Scholarship, 316
Nuclear Regulatory Commission Historically Black Colleges and Universities Student Research Participation, 578
Oak Ridge Science Semester, 578
Ohio Nurse Education Assistance Loan Program, 598
OMNE/Nursing Leaders of Maine Scholarship, 440
ONS Foundation Bachelor's Scholarships, 440
Patrick and Judith McHugh Scholarship, 533
Paulina L. Sorg Scholarship, 317
Philippine Nurses' Association Scholarship, 318
Raymond K. Conley Memorial Scholarship, 151
Research Participation at the Centers for Disease Control and Prevention/Agency for Toxic Substances and Disease Registry, 578
Research Participation at the National Center for Toxicological Research, 579
Research Participation at the U.S. Food and Drug Administration, 579
Research Participation Program for the Combat Casualty Care Research Program (CCCRP), 579
Research Participation Program for the U.S. Air Force Research Laboratory (USAFRL), Wright Patterson Air Force Base, 580
Research Participation Program for the U.S. Air Force School of Aerospace Medicine (USAFSAM), 580
Research Participation Program for the U.S. Army Aeromedical Research Laboratory (USAARL), 580
Research Participation Program for the U.S. Army Medical Research Institute of Chemical Defense, 580
Research Participation Program for the U.S. Army Public Health Command, 580
Research Participation Program for the U.S. Army Research Institute for Environmental Medicine (USARIEM), 581
Research Participation Program for the U.S. Army Research Laboratory, 581
Rich Meiers Health Administration Fund, 319
Robanna Fund, 319
ROTC/Navy Nurse Corps Scholarship Program, 528
The Rudolph Dillman Memorial Scholarship, 107
Siemens Competition in Math, Science and Technology, 473
Sigma Phi Alpha Certificate/Associate Scholarship, 84
Sigma Phi Alpha Undergraduate Scholarship, 84
Spence Reese Scholarship, 227
Student Internship Program at the U.S. Army Center for Health Promotion and Preventive Medicine, 581
Thomas J. Bardos Science Education Awards for Undergraduate Students, 96
Thz Fo Farm Fund, 321
Tyson Foods Intern Program, 588
United Health Foundation Scholarship, 113
United Health/Hispanic Association of Colleges and Universities Scholarship, 325
U.S. Air Force Medial Support Agency, 581
U.S. Army Natick Soldier Research Development & Engineering Center, 582
U.S. Army/ROTC Nursing Scholarship, 523
Virginia Tuition Assistance Grant, 497
Virginia's Nurse Practitioner Nurse Midwife Scholarship, 536
Walter and Marie Schmidt Scholarship, 448
The William R. Goldfarb Memorial Scholarship, 191
Wilma Motley Memorial California Merit Scholarship, 84

Home economics

Academy of Nutrition and Dietetics Graduate, Baccalaureate or Coordinated Program Scholarships, 80
Al Schulman Ecolab First-Time Freshmen Entrepeneurial Scholarship, 417
American Chemical Society Scholars Program, 97

American Society for Enology and Viticulture Scholarship Program, 193
Arabian Horse Association (Region 14) Scholarship, 270
Bern Laxer Memorial Scholarship, 351
Bob Zappatelli Memorial Scholarship, 352
Chefs of Louisiana Cookery Scholarship, 352
Christian Wolffer Scholarship, 352
Clay Triplette Scholarship, 352
The Cynthia E. Morgan Memorial Scholarship Fund, 248
Dairy Student Recognition Program, 410
Dean Foods Company Scholarship, 274
Deseo at the Westin Scholarship, 353
DMI Milk Marketing Scholarships, 410
Foth Production Solutions, LLC Scholarship, 276
Foundation for Environmental Agriculture Scholarship, 276
Hormel Foods Corporation Scholarship, 277
Iager Dairy Scholarship, 411
Institute of Food Technologists Freshman Scholarship, 343
Institute of Food Technologists Undergraduate Scholarship, 344
Kikkoman Foods, Inc. Scholarship, 278
Kildee Scholarship, 411
Marcia S. Harris Legacy Fund Scholarship, 463
New Mexico Allied Health Student Loan-for-Service Program, 597
NPFDA Scholarship, 416
Paradise Tomato Kitchens Scholarship, 281
The Peter Cameron/Housewares Charity Foundation Scholarship, 354
Peter Kump Memorial Scholarship, 355
Research Participation at the U.S. Food and Drug Administration, 579
Rose Acre Farms Scholarship, 283
Scholarship for Foodservice Communication Careers, 345
Tyson Foods Intern Program, 588
USDA/1890 National Scholars Program, 526
Wells Fargo Scholarship, 285

Law

American Bar Foundation Summer Research Diversity Fellowships in Law and Social Sciences for Undergraduate Students, 550
American Society of International Law Internships, 551
Bick Bickson Scholarship, 297
Congressional Institute Internships, 557
Dairy Student Recognition Program, 410
EPA National Network for Environmental Management Studies Fellowship, 528
Genentech, Inc. Internship Program, 562
Horizons Scholarship, 545
Johnson Controls Co-op and Internship Programs, 566
NASA Space Grant Wisconsin Consortium Undergraduate Research Program, 405
New Leader Scholarship, 79
Sony Credited Internship, 586
Spence Reese Scholarship, 227
Tyson Foods Intern Program, 588
U.S. Senate Member Internships, 589
Water Companies (NJ Chapter) Scholarship, 409

Liberal arts and interdisciplinary studies

AFSCMA/UNCF Union Scholars Program, 550
American Bar Foundation Summer Research Diversity Fellowships in Law and Social Sciences for Undergraduate Students, 550
Charles L. Hebner Memorial Scholarship, 252
Feminism & Leadership Internship, 561
Harriet Irsay Scholarship, 118
Hawaii Community Scholarship Fund, 305
J. Paul Getty Multicultural Undergraduate Summer Internships at the Getty Center, 564
National Federation of the Blind Scholarships, 413
National Junior Classical League Scholarship, 415
Pulliam Journalism Fellowship, 563

Library science

ALISE Bohdan S. Wynar Research Paper Competition, 220
ALISE Research Grant, 221
ALISE/Dialog Methodology Paper Competition, 221
Guggenheim Museum Internship, 586
Kennedy Library Archival Internship, 565
Museum Coca-Cola Internship, 573
Roosevelt Archival Internships, 562

Mathematics

Actuarial Diversity Scholarships, 81
Actuary of Tomorrow Stuart A. Robertson Memorial Scholarship, 82
Adler Science and Math Scholarship, 137
Aerospace Undergraduate STEM Research Scholarship Program, 404
AFCEA Military Personnel & Dependents Scholarship, 207
AFCEA ROTC Scholarship, 207
AFCEA Scholarship for Underserved Students (HBCU), 208
AFCEA War Veterans/Disabled War Veterans Scholarship, 208
AfterCollege Computer Science & Engineering Student Scholarship, 85
AIAA Foundation Undergraduate Scholarship, 116
AICP Heartland Chapter Jim Latteman Scholarship, 223
AICP Scholarship, 223
Air Force Research Laboratory, 711 Human Performance Wing, 575
Allstate Internships, 549
Arizona Public Service Navajo Scholars Program, 111
A.T. Anderson Memorial Scholarship, 114
Barry M. Goldwater Scholarship, 225
Boeing Internships, 556
Burlington Northern Santa Fe Foundation Scholarship, 115
Chapter 198 - Downriver Detroit Scholarship, 475
Davidson Fellows Scholarship, 251
Delaware Space Grant Undergraduate Summer Research Internship, 571
Delaware Space Grant Undergraduate Tuition Scholarship, 396
Department of Energy Community College Institute at Oak Ridge National Laboratory, 575
DHS HS-STEM Summer Internship Program, 576
DHS Summer Faculty and Student Research Team Program for Minority Serving Institutions, 576
DOE Faculty and Student Teams Program at Oak Ridge National Laboratory, 576
DOE Scholars Program, 576
DOE Science Undergraduate Laboratory Internships at Oak Ridge National Laboratory, 576
Economic Research Division Project Internships, 556
EPA Greater Research Opportunities Undergraduate Student Fellowships, 527
ESPN Internship, 560
GE Hispanic Forum Scholarship, 327
HENAAC Scholars Program, 294
Hershey Company Tribal Scholarship, 112
Higher Education Research Experiences at Oak Ridge National Laboratory for Students, 577
Hoku Scholarship Fund, 307
Horizons Scholarship, 545

Lockheed Martin American Heroes Scholarship, 329
Massachusetts Math and Science Teachers Scholarship, 381
Math And Science Teachers Loan Forgiveness Program, 600
MESBEC Scholarships, 234
Mickey Leland Energy Fellowship Program, 577
Microsoft General Scholarship, 386
Morgan Stanley Foundation Scholarship, 330
MSGC Undergraduate Underrepresented Minority Fellowship Program, 398
NASA Academy Internship, 572
NASA Idaho Space Grant Undergraduate Scholarship, 397
NASA Minnesota Space Grant Consortium Wide Scholarship, 398
NASA Missouri State Space Grant Undergraduate Scholarship, 399
NASA North Carolina Space Grant Consortium Undergraduate Research Scholarship, 400
NASA North Carolina Space Grant Consortium Undergraduate Scholarship Program, 400
NASA Ohio Space Grant Junior/Senior Scholarship Program, 401
NASA Pennsylvania Space Grant Undergraduate Scholarship, 402
NASA Space Grant Michigan Undergraduate Fellowship, 398
NASA Space Grant Nevada Undergraduate Scholarship, 399
NASA Space Grant New Mexico Undergraduate Scholarship, 400
NASA Space Grant North Dakota Consortium Lillian Goettler Scholarship, 401
NASA Space Grant North Dakota Undergraduate Scholarship, 401
NASA Space Grant Oregon Undergraduate Scholarship, 402
NASA Space Grant South Carolina Undergraduate Student Research Fellowship, 403
NASA Space Grant Vermont Consortium Undergraduate Scholarships, 404
NASA Space Grant Virginia Community College STEM Scholarship, 404
NASA Utah Space Grant Consortium Undergraduate Scholarship, 403
NASA West Virginia Space Grant Undergraduate Research Fellowship, 405
National Energy Technology Laboratory Professional Internship Program, 577
New York State Math and Science Teaching Incentive Program, 427
Nuclear Regulatory Commission Historically Black Colleges and Universities Student Research Participation, 578
Oak Ridge National Laboratory Undergraduate Student Cooperative Education Program, 578
Oak Ridge Science Semester, 578
Pacific Gas and Electric Summer Intern Program, 583
Payzer Scholarship, 261
Pearl I. Young Scholarship, 401
Plasma Physics National Undergraduate Fellowship Program, 584
Procter & Gamble - Orgullosa Scholarship, 331
Research Participation at the National Center for Toxicological Research, 579
Research Participation Program for the Combat Casualty Care Research Program (CCCRP), 579
Research Participation Program for the Johns Hopkins University Applied Physics Laboratory, 579
Research Participation Program for the U.S. Air Force Research Laboratory (USAFRL), Wright Patterson Air Force Base, 580
Research Participation Program for the U.S. Army Aeromedical Research Laboratory (USAARL), 580
Research Participation Program for the U.S. Army Public Health Command, 580
Research Participation Program for the U.S. Army Research Institute for Environmental Medicine (USARIEM), 581
Shuichi, Katsu and Itsuyo Suga Scholarship, 321
Siemens Competition in Math, Science and Technology, 473
Smithsonian Environmental Research Center Internship Program, 585
STEM Bridge Scholarship, 405
STEM Columbia Crew Memorial Scholarship, 403
STEM Majors Scholarship, 208
Student Research at the U.S. Army Edgewood Chemical Biological Center, 581
Traditional CITE Scholarship, 245
Travelers Foundation Scholarship, 113
U.S. Air Force Medial Support Agency, 581
U.S. Army Natick Soldier Research Development & Engineering Center, 582

Military science

Hudner Medal of Honor Scholarship, 260
Research Participation Program for the Joint POW/MIA Accounting Command/Central Identification Laboratory (JPAC-CIL), 579
United States Army/ROTC Four-Year Scholarship, 523
U.S. Army/ROTC Nursing Scholarship, 523

Mortuary science

American Board of Funeral Service Education National Scholarship, 96

Philosophy, religion, and theology

Calvin Coolidge Memorial Foundation Scholarship, 531
Davidson Fellows Scholarship, 251
Denver Rescue Mission Center for Mission Studies Internships, 558
Leonard M. Perryman Communications Scholarship for Ethnic Minority Students, 522

Protective services

American Bar Foundation Summer Research Diversity Fellowships in Law and Social Sciences for Undergraduate Students, 550
Calvin Coolidge Memorial Foundation Scholarship, 531
Captain James J. Regan Memorial Scholarship, 369
Charles W. Riley Fire and Emergency Medical Services Tuition Reimbursement Program, 375
NC Sheriff's Association Criminal Justice Scholarship, 433
Ritchie-Jennings Memorial Scholarship, 81
Sheryl A. Horak Law Enforcement Explorer Scholarship, 370

Social sciences and history

Adele Filene Student Presenter Grant, 246
AFCEA ROTC Scholarship, 207
AFSCMA/UNCF Union Scholars Program, 550
AfterCollege Business Student Scholarship, 85
AGCO Scholarships, 268
AICP Heartland Chapter Jim Latteman Scholarship, 223
AICP Scholarship, 223
Air Force Research Laboratory, 711 Human Performance Wing, 575
ALPFA Scholarship, 326
American Bar Foundation Summer Research Diversity Fellowships in Law and Social Sciences for Undergraduate Students, 550
American Society of International Law Internships, 551

Americans for the Arts Arts Action Fund Internship, 552
Americans for the Arts Government and Public Affairs Internship, 553
Anne U. White Fund, 222
Anthropology Internship Program, 551
Averyl Elaine Keriakedes Memorial Scholarship, 149
Behavioral Sciences Student Fellowship, 258
Boeing Internships, 556
Calvin Coolidge Memorial Foundation Scholarship, 531
Casey's General Stores, Inc. Scholarship, 272
Charles L. Hebner Memorial Scholarship, 252
CIA Undergraduate Scholarship Program, 237
Citizens for Global Solutions Internship, 557
The Cloisters Summer Internship Program, 567
CNH Capital Scholarship, 273
Congressional Institute Internships, 557
Darrel Hess Community College Geography Scholarship, 222
Delaware Space Grant Undergraduate Summer Research Internship, 571
Delaware Space Grant Undergraduate Tuition Scholarship, 396
Denver Rescue Mission Center for Mission Studies Internships, 558
DHS Summer Faculty and Student Research Team Program for Minority Serving Institutions, 576
The Don Riebhoff Memorial Scholarship, 182
Dr. Alma S. Adams Scholarship for Outreach and Health Communications to Reduce Tobacco Use Among Priority Populations, 118
Economic Research Division Project Internships, 556
Ecotrust Native American Scholarship, 111
Environmental Management Participation at the U.S. Army Environmental Command (USAEC), 577
EPA Greater Research Opportunities Undergraduate Student Fellowships, 527
Farm Credit Services of Mid-America Scholarship, 275
Federal Reserve Bank of New York Undergraduate Summer Internship, 560
Feminism & Leadership Internship, 561
The Francis Walton Memorial Scholarship, 183
GE Hispanic Forum Scholarship, 327
George Washington Carver Internship, 592
Harriet Irsay Scholarship, 118
Hawaii Community Scholarship Fund, 305
Henry A. Zuberano Scholarship, 306
Hokuli'a Foundation Scholarship Fund, 307
Horizons Scholarship, 545
Hormel Foods Corporation Scholarship, 277
House Member Internships, 589
Jennifer C. Groot Fellowship, 97
Jerry Clark Memorial Scholarship, 102
Kawasaki-McGaha Scholarship Fund, 312
Kennedy Library Archival Internship, 565
Lambda Alpha National Collegiate Honors Society Senior Scholarship, 365
Lutheran Student Scholastic and Service Scholarship, 225
Makovsky & Company Inc. Public Relations Internship, 567
Marble-Boyle Award, 222
The Merchants Exchange Scholarship Fund, 384
MetLife Foundation Scholarship, 279
Metropolitan Museum of Art Six-Month Internship, 567
Mississippi Health Care Professions Loan/Scholarship, 596
Morgan Stanley Foundation Scholarship, 330
Mother Jones Ben Bagdikian Fellowship Program, 570
NASA Space Grant Hawaii Undergraduate Fellowship Program, 396
National Geographic Society Geography Students Internship, 572
New Leader Scholarship, 79
Nissan North America, Inc. Scholarship Program, 330
Pacific Gas and Electric Summer Intern Program, 583
Patrick and Judith McHugh Scholarship, 533
Rain Bird Intelligent Use of Water Scholarship, 367
Research Participation at the Centers for Disease Control and Prevention/Agency for Toxic Substances and Disease Registry, 578
Research Participation Program for the Combat Casualty Care Research Program (CCCRP), 579
Research Participation Program for the Joint POW/MIA Accounting Command/Central Identification Laboratory (JPAC-CIL), 579
Research Participation Program for the U.S. Air Force Research Laboratory (USAFRL), Wright Patterson Air Force Base, 580
Research Participation Program for the U.S. Army Aeromedical Research Laboratory (USAARL), 580
Research Participation Program for the U.S. Army Public Health Command, 580
Research Participation Program for the U.S. Army Research Institute for Environmental Medicine (USARIEM), 581
Rhode Island State Government Internship Program, 584
Roosevelt Archival Internships, 562
SCA Conservation Internships, 587
Smithsonian Minority Internship, 585
Southface Internship, 587
Spence Reese Scholarship, 227
Stella Blum Student Research Grant, 246
Theisen's Home Farm Auto Scholarship, 284
Thomas R. Pickering Foreign Affairs Fellowship, 545
Tribal Business Management Scholarship, 235
United Health/Hispanic Association of Colleges and Universities Scholarship, 325
United States Holocaust Memorial Museum Internship, 588
U.S. Air Force Medial Support Agency, 581
U.S. Department of State Internship, 589
U.S. Senate Member Internships, 589
Washington Crossing Foundation Scholarship, 537
Wells Fargo Scholarship, 285
Wells Fargo Undergraduate Internships, 591
William D. Greenlee Scholarship, 455
Wilma D. Hoyal/Maxine Chilton Memorial Scholarship, 121
Women in Architecture Scholarship, 221

Trade and industry

AAGS Joseph F. Dracup Scholarship Award, 98
ACSM Fellows Scholarship, 98
AFCEA ROTC Scholarship, 207
AGC Education and Research Undergraduate Scholarship, 219
AGC of Maine Scholarship Program, 220
AGCO Scholarships, 268
Air Traffic Control Full-Time Employee Student Scholarship, 88
Air Traffic Control Non-Employee Student Scholarship, 88
Airgas-Jerry Baker Scholarship, 200
Airgas-Terry Jarvis Memorial Scholarship, 200
AIWF Culinary Scholarship, 531

Al Schulman Ecolab First-Time Freshmen Entrepeneurial Scholarship, 417
Al Schuman Ecolab Undergraduate Entrepeneurial Scholarship, 417
Albert E. Wischmeyer Memorial Scholarship Award, 474
Alice Glaisyer Warfield Memorial Scholarship, 517
Allen and Loureena Weber Scholarship, 474
Allen Susser Scholarship, 351
Alvin and June Sabroff Manufacturing Engineering Scholarship, 474
Alwin B. Newton Scholarship, 195
American Restaurant Scholarship, 351
American Welding Society District Scholarship Program, 200
Androscoggin Amateur Radio Club Scholarship, 179
Arizona Chapter Vertical Flight Engineering Scholarship, 108
Arsham Amirikian Engineering Scholarship, 200
Arthur and Gladys Cervenka Scholarship, 475
ASHRAE Engineering Technology Scholarships, 196
ASHRAE General Scholarships, 196
ASHRAE Memorial Scholarship, 196
ASHRAE Region IV Benny Bootle Scholarship, 196
ASHRAE Region VIII Scholarship, 196
ASTA Alaska Airlines Scholarship, 512
ASTA American Express Travel Scholarship, 512
ASTA Arizona Scholarship, 513
ASTA Northern California Chapter - Richard Epping Scholarship, 513
ASTA Pacific Northwest Chapter/William Hunt Scholarship, 513
ASTA Princess Cruises Scholarship, 513
Bern Laxer Memorial Scholarship, 351
Berntsen International Scholarship in Surveying, 99
Berntsen International Scholarship in Surveying Technology, 99
Best Teen Chef Culinary Scholarship Competition, 210
BIA Cares of San Diego Scholarship, 230
Bick Bickson Scholarship, 297
Bill Ramsey/Craig Noone Memorial Scholarship, 352
Bob Zappatelli Memorial Scholarship, 352
Boeing Internships, 556
Buckingham Memorial Scholarship, 88
Buick Achievers Scholarship Program, 289
Cady McDonnell Memorial Scholarship, 99
Casey's General Stores, Inc. Scholarship, 272
CBC Scholarship, 243
Champlain Valley Street Rodders Scholarship, 531
Chapter 17 - St. Louis Scholarship, 475
Chapter 198 - Downriver Detroit Scholarship, 475
Chapter 23 - Quad Cities Iowa/Illinois Scholarship, 475
Chapter 311 - Tri City Scholarship, 475
Chapter 4 - Lawrence A. Wacker Memorial Scholarship, 476
Chapter 52 - Wichita Scholarship, 476
Chapter 6 - Fairfield County Scholarship, 476
Chapter 67 - Phoenix Scholarship, 476
Chapter One - Detroit Founding Chapter Scholarship Award, 477
The Charles Clarke Cordle Memorial Scholarship, 181
The Charles N. Fisher Memorial Scholarship, 182
Charlotte Woods Memorial Scholarship, 517
Chefs of Louisiana Cookery Scholarship, 352
Christian Wolffer Scholarship, 352
Clarence & Josephine Myers Scholarship, 477
Clay Triplette Scholarship, 352
Clinton J. Helton Manufacturing Scholarship Award, 477
Connie and Robert T. Gunter Scholarship, 478
CSX Scholarship, 274
D. Fred and Mariam L. Bovie Scholarship, 201
D. Fred and Mariam L. Bovie Technical Scholarship, 201
Dairy Student Recognition Program, 410
Dana Campbell Memorial Scholarship, 353
David Arver Memorial Scholarship, 88
DEED Student Research Grants, 178
Delta Faucet Company Scholarship, 456
Denny Lydic Scholarship, 517
Deseo at the Westin Scholarship, 353
Donald and Shirley Hastings National Scholarship, 201
Donald F. Hastings Scholarship, 201
The Dr. James L. Lawson Memorial Scholarship, 183
Duane Hanson Scholarship, 197
Dutch and Ginger Arver Scholarship, 89
E. Wayne Kay Community College Scholarship, 478
E. Wayne Kay Co-op Scholarship, 478
E. Wayne Kay High School Scholarship, 478
E. Wayne Kay Scholarship, 478
Eastman Kodak Cooperative Internship Programs, 559
Edward J. Brady Memorial Scholarship, 202
Edward S. Roth Manufacturing Engineering Scholarship, 479
The Elkes Family Culinary Scholarship, 353
The Eugene "Gene" Sallee, W4YFR, Memorial Scholarship, 183
Field Aviation Co. Inc. Scholarship, 89
The Food Network Scholarship for Immigrants in the Kitchen, 353
The Francis Walton Memorial Scholarship, 183
Frank M. Coda Scholarship, 197
The Fred R. McDaniel Memorial Scholarship, 184
Gabe A. Hartl Scholarship, 88
Garmin Scholarship, 89
GE Hispanic Forum Scholarship, 327
Ginger and Fred Deines Canada Scholarship, 517
Ginger and Fred Deines Mexico Scholarship, 518
Giuliano Mazzetti Scholarship, 479
Good Eats Scholarship Fund, 304
Hansen Scholarship, 260
Harry E. Arcamuzi Aviation Scholarship, 260
Helicopter Association International Commercial Helicopter Rating Scholarship, 324
Henry Adams Scholarship, 197
Hooper Memorial Scholarship, 518
Hormel Foods Corporation Scholarship, 277
Howard E. and Wilma J. Adkins Memorial Scholarship, 202
H.P. "Bud" Milligan Aviation Scholarship, 260
Hudner Medal of Honor Scholarship, 260
Iager Dairy Scholarship, 411
IATAN Ronald A. Santana Memorial Scholarship, 514
INROADS Internship, 564
IRARC Memorial, Joseph P. Rubino, WA4MMD, Scholarship, 185
The Irving W. Cook WA0CGS Scholarship, 185
J. Richard Mehalick Scholarship, 197
Jack R. Barckhoff Welding Management Scholarship, 202
The Jake McClain Driver KC5WXA Scholarship Fund, 185
James A. Turner, Jr. Memorial Scholarship, 202
James Beard Foundation School Scholarships, 353
James L. Allhands Essay Competition, 220
John C. Lincoln Memorial Scholarship, 202
Johnny Davis Memorial Scholarship, 89

Johnson Controls Co-op and Internship Programs, 566
Jose and Victoria Martinez Maison Blanche Scholarship, 353
Kikkoman Foods, Inc. Scholarship, 278
Kildee Scholarship, 411
Kurt W. Schneider Memorial Scholarship Fund, 314
The L. Phil and Alice J. Wicker Scholarship, 186
L-3 Avionics Systems Scholarship, 89
La Toque Scholarship in Wine Studies, 354
Lacroix at the Rittenhouse Scholarship, 354
Lee Tarbox Memorial Scholarship, 90
Lemaire Restaurant at the Jefferson Hotel Scholarship, 354
Lindbergh Grant, 238
Lowell Gaylor Memorial Scholarship, 90
The Lowell H. and Dorothy Loving Undergraduate Scholarship, 99
Lucile B. Kaufman Women's Scholarship, 479
Lynn G. Bellenger Scholarship, 197
The Magnolia DX Association Scholarship, 186
Maine Innkeepers Association Scholarship, 374
Maine Metal Products Association Scholarship, 374
Marcia S. Harris Legacy Fund Scholarship, 463
Marriott Scholars Program, 326
Mary Macey Scholarship, 545
Matsuo Bridge Company Ltd. of Japan Scholarship, 203
Mid-Continent Instrument Scholarship, 90
Miller Electric Manufacturing Company Ivic Scholarship, 203
Miller Electric Mfg. Co. Scholarship, 203
The Mississippi Scholarship, 187
Museum Coca-Cola Internship, 573
Myrtle and Earl Walker Scholarship, 479
NASA Space Grant Virginia Community College STEM Scholarship, 404
NAWIC Founders' Construction Trades Scholarship, 409
NAWIC Founders' Undergraduate Scholarship, 409
Nettie Dracup Memorial Scholarship, 100
New England Hadassah Scholarship, 354
North Carolina State Board of Refrigeration Examiners Scholarship, 431
North Central Region Scholarship, 479
NSPS Board of Governors Scholarship, 100
NSPS Scholarships, 100
NTA Canada Scholarship, 514
NTA Connecticut Scholarship, 514
NTA Florida Scholarship, 514
NTA LaMacchia Family Scholarship, 515
NTA Massachusetts Scholarship, 515
NTA New Horizons - Kathy LeTarte Scholarship, 515
NTA New Jersey Scholarship, 515
NTA New York Scholarship, 515
NTA North America Scholarship, 516
NTA Ohio Scholarship, 516
NTA Pat & Jim Host Scholarship, 516
NTA Rene Campbell - Ruth McKinney Scholarship, 516
NTA Utah Keith Griffall Scholarship, 517
Omaha Steaks Scholarship, 354
Past Presidents Scholarship, 203
The Paul and Helen L. Grauer Scholarship, 188
Payzer Scholarship, 261
The Peter Cameron/Housewares Charity Foundation Scholarship, 354
Peter Kump Memorial Scholarship, 355
PGSF Annual Scholarship Competition, 460
PHCC Educational Foundation Scholarships, 457
Praxair International Scholarship, 203
Professional Land Surveyors of Oregon Scholarship, 447
The Ranch House at Devil's Thumb Scholarship, 355
The Ray, NØRP, & Katie, WØKTE, Pautz Scholarship, 189
Research Participation Program for the U.S. Air Force Research Laboratory, Tyndall Air Force Base (AFRL-TYNDALL), 580
Restaurant at Sunset Marquis Scholarship, 355
Reuben Trane Scholarship, 198
Richard Lee Vernon Aviation Scholarship, 261
Robert L. Peaslee Brazing Scholarship, 204
Rodney E. Powell Memorial Scholarship, 431
Roller Skating Foundation College Scholarship, 465
Rose Acre Farms Scholarship, 283
RWMA Scholarship, 204
Schnitzer Steel "Racing to Stop Hunger" Scholarship, 355
Scholarship for Foodservice Communication Careers, 345
Schonstedt Scholarships in Surveying, 100
Seneca Foods Corporation Scholarship, 283
SME Directors Scholarship, 480
SME Education Foundation Family Scholarship, 480
SME-FF Future Leaders of Manufacturing Scholarships, 480
STEM Majors Scholarship, 208
Steven Scher Memorial Scholarship for Aspiring Restaurateurs, 355
Studio at the Montage Resort & Spa Scholarship, 355
Sunday Supper South Atlanta Scholarship, 356
Texas Transportation Scholarship, 518
Tri-State Surveying & Photogrammetry Kris M. Kunze Scholarship, 100
Tyson Foods Intern Program, 588
Vertical Flight Foundation Scholarship, 109
Vicki Willder Scholarship Fund, 322
Walt Bartram Memorial Education Award (Region 12 and Chapter 119), 480
The Wayne Nelson, KB4UT, Memorial Scholarship, 191
William A. and Ann M. Brothers Scholarship, 204
William B. Howell Memorial Scholarship, 204
William E. Weisel Scholarship, 480
Willis H. Carrier Scholarship, 198
Zov's Bistro Scholarship, 356

Gender

Female

Ahmad-Sehar Saleha Ahmad and Abrahim Ekramullah Zafar Foundation, 441
Allman Medical Scholarships, 389
Alumnae Panhellenic Association Women's Scholarship, 94
American Legion Indiana Auxiliary Past Presidents Parley Nursing Scholarship, 131
American Legion Kentucky Auxiliary Mary Barrett Marshall Scholarship, 135
American Legion Maryland Auxiliary Past Presidents Parley Scholarship, 138
American Legion Maryland Auxiliary Scholarship, 138
American Legion Michigan Auxiliary Memorial Scholarship, 140
Arthur and Helen Copeland Scholarship, 523
Averyl Elaine Keriakedes Memorial Scholarship, 149
Cady McDonnell Memorial Scholarship, 99
California's Distinguished Young Woman Competition, 253

Clorox Suena Sin Limites Mother Scholarship, 327
Delayed Education Scholarship for Women, 175
Distinguished Young Women Scholarship, 254
Dorothy Campbell Memorial Scholarship, 443
Elizabeth A. Sackler Museum Educational Trust, 499
Eugenia Vellner Fischer Award for the Performing Arts, 389
Financial Women International Scholarship, 302
The Gillian Award, 499
The Gladys C. Anderson Memorial Scholarship, 107
Grace S. High Memorial Child Welfare Scholarship Fund, 152
The Grotto Scholarships, 501
Horizons Scholarship, 545
Ida M. Pope Memorial Scholarship, 308
Jean Fitzgerald Scholarship Fund, 309
Jeanette Rankin Foundation Scholarship, 357
Ka'iulani Home for Girls Trust Scholarship, 311
Kate Gleason Scholarship, 218
Lillie Lois Ford Girls' Scholarship, 143
Lucile B. Kaufman Women's Scholarship, 479
Lynn G. Bellenger Scholarship, 197
Mahindra USA Women in Ag Scholarship, 279
Mary Barrett Marshall Student Loan Fund, 593
Miss America Competition Awards, 389
Nancy Lorraine Jensen Memorial Scholarship, 491
NASA Space Grant North Dakota Consortium Lillian Goettler Scholarship, 401
New England Hadassah Scholarship, 354
Pearl I. Young Scholarship, 401
R.L. Gillette Scholarship, 107
SAE Women Engineers Committee Scholarship, 467
San Jose Local Scholarships for Women, 96
Shannon Scholarship, 519
Society of Daughters of United States Army Scholarship Program, 481
Student Aid Foundation Loan, 599
Supreme Guardian Council, International Order of Job's Daughters Scholarship, 501
Susan Burdett Scholarship, 167
Susie Holmes Memorial Scholarship, 501
SWE Scholarships, 489
Top 10 College Women Competition, 291
Women in Architecture Scholarship, 221
Women's Self Worth Foundation Scholarship, 114
Women's Western Golf Foundation Scholarship, 545

Male

Alpha Gamma Rho Educational Foundation Scholarship, 268
American Legion Eagle Scout of the Year, 146
American Legion Florida Eagle Scout of the Year, 125
American Legion Iowa Boy Scout of the Year Scholarship, 131
American Legion Iowa Outstanding Citizen of Boys State Scholarship, 132
American Legion Maryland Boys State Scholarship, 137
American Legion New Hampshire Boys State Scholarship, 150
American Legion Tennessee Eagle Scout of the Year Scholarship, 162
American Legion Vermont Eagle Scout of the Year, 164
American Legion Wisconsin Eagle Scout of the Year Scholarship, 168
Arthur E. Copeland Scholarship, 524
Arthur M. and Berdena King Eagle Scout Scholarship, 419
Chester M. Vernon Memorial Eagle Scout Scholarship, 414
Dr. Click Cowger Scholarship, 134
Dr. Dan J. and Patricia S. Pickard Scholarship, 249
Frank D. Visceglia Memorial Scholarship, 227
Frank L. Weil Memorial Eagle Scout Scholarship, 415
Hall/McElwain Merit Scholarship, 412
John A. High Child Welfare Scholarship, 151
John McKee Scholarship, 383
Lillie Lois Ford Boys' Scholarship, 143
NESA Academic Scholarships, 412
Spence Reese Scholarship, 227

International Student

Academy of Television Arts & Sciences Student Internship Program, 549
Actuarial Diversity Scholarships, 81
Adele Filene Student Presenter Grant, 246
AGBU International Scholarships, 209
Allison E. Fisher Scholarship, 407
Angie Houtz Scholarship, 205
Carole Simpson Scholarship, 407
Dow Jones Business Reporting Intern Program, 558
Dow Jones Digital Intern Program, 558
Dow Jones News Editing Intern Program, 558
Dow Jones Sports Editing Intern Program, 559
Eleanor Allwork Scholarship, 236
ExxonMobil Scholarship, 327
The Food Network Scholarship for Immigrants in the Kitchen, 353
Ford Blue Oval Scholarship, 325
GE Hispanic Forum Scholarship, 327
HACEMOS Scholarship, 328
Hannaford Internships, 562
Helicopter Association International Commercial Helicopter Rating Scholarship, 324
Helicopter Association International Maintenance Technician Certificate Scholarship, 324
Hoover-Lee Scholars Program, 522
Houston Livestock Show and Rodeo School Art Scholarships, 339
Human Factors, Instrumentation and Controls Division (HFICD) Nuclear Power Scholarship, 175
Metropolitan Museum of Art Six-Month Internship, 567
Metropolitan Museum of Art Summer Internship Program, 568
Museum of Modern Art Internship, 570
Rubincam Youth Award, 413
Southface Internship, 587
Stella Blum Student Research Grant, 246
Texas Competitive Scholarship Waiver, 507
United States Holocaust Memorial Museum Internship, 588
Wolf Trap Foundation for the Performing Arts Internship, 592

Military Participation

Air Force

AFCEA War Veterans/Disabled War Veterans Scholarship, 208
Air Force Sergeants Association Scholarship, Airmen Memorial Foundation, and Chief Master Sergeants of the Air Force Scholarship Programs, 84
American Legion Missouri Commander's Scholarship Fund, 142
Arkansas Military Dependents Scholarship Program, 206
Darlene Hooley for Oregon Veterans Scholarship, 443

Erman W. Taylor Memorial Scholarship, 142
General Henry H. Arnold Education Grant, 87
Helping Heroes Grant, 503
Joseph J. Frank Scholarship, 143
Kansas Military Service Scholarship, 360
Kathern F. Gruber Scholarship Program, 226
Korean War Veteran's Children's Scholarship, 313
Lillie Lois Ford Boys' Scholarship, 143
Lillie Lois Ford Girls' Scholarship, 143
Lockheed Martin American Heroes Scholarship, 329
Maria C. Jackson-General George A. White Scholarship, 445
M.D. Jack Murphy Memorial Nurses Training Fund, 143
Minnesota GI Bill, 387
MOAA Interest-Free Loan and Grant Program, 595
North Carolina Scholarships for Children of War Veterans, 431
Shane Dean Voyles Memorial Scholarship, 144
Thomas H. Miller Scholarship, 226
West Virginia War Orphans Educational Assistance, 539

Army

AFCEA War Veterans/Disabled War Veterans Scholarship, 208
American Legion Missouri Commander's Scholarship Fund, 142
Arkansas Military Dependents Scholarship Program, 206
Darlene Hooley for Oregon Veterans Scholarship, 443
Erman W. Taylor Memorial Scholarship, 142
Helping Heroes Grant, 503
Joseph J. Frank Scholarship, 143
Kansas Military Service Scholarship, 360
Kathern F. Gruber Scholarship Program, 226
Korean War Veteran's Children's Scholarship, 313
Lillie Lois Ford Boys' Scholarship, 143
Lillie Lois Ford Girls' Scholarship, 143
Lockheed Martin American Heroes Scholarship, 329
Maria C. Jackson-General George A. White Scholarship, 445
Maryland Edward T. Conroy Memorial Scholarship Program, 376
M.D. Jack Murphy Memorial Nurses Training Fund, 143
MG James Ursano Scholarship Program, 209
Minnesota GI Bill, 387
MOAA Interest-Free Loan and Grant Program, 595
Montgomery GI Bill (MGIB), 525
Montgomery GI Bill (MGIB) "Kicker", 525
North Carolina Scholarships for Children of War Veterans, 431
Selected Reserve Montgomery GI Bill, 525
Shane Dean Voyles Memorial Scholarship, 144
Thomas H. Miller Scholarship, 226
U.S. Army Recruiting Command Student Loan Repayment Program, 526
West Virginia War Orphans Educational Assistance, 539

Coast Guard

AFCEA War Veterans/Disabled War Veterans Scholarship, 208
American Legion Missouri Commander's Scholarship Fund, 142
Arkansas Military Dependents Scholarship Program, 206
Darlene Hooley for Oregon Veterans Scholarship, 443
Erman W. Taylor Memorial Scholarship, 142
Joseph J. Frank Scholarship, 143
Kathern F. Gruber Scholarship Program, 226
Lillie Lois Ford Boys' Scholarship, 143
Lillie Lois Ford Girls' Scholarship, 143
Maria C. Jackson-General George A. White Scholarship, 445
M.D. Jack Murphy Memorial Nurses Training Fund, 143
Minnesota GI Bill, 387
MOAA Interest-Free Loan and Grant Program, 595
North Carolina Scholarships for Children of War Veterans, 431
Shane Dean Voyles Memorial Scholarship, 144
Thomas H. Miller Scholarship, 226
West Virginia War Orphans Educational Assistance, 539

Marines

1st Marine Division Association Scholarship, 79
AFCEA War Veterans/Disabled War Veterans Scholarship, 208
American Legion Missouri Commander's Scholarship Fund, 142
Arkansas Military Dependents Scholarship Program, 206
Darlene Hooley for Oregon Veterans Scholarship, 443
Erman W. Taylor Memorial Scholarship, 142
Gold Star Scholarship Program, 420
Helping Heroes Grant, 503
Joseph J. Frank Scholarship, 143
Kansas Military Service Scholarship, 360
Kathern F. Gruber Scholarship Program, 226
Korean War Veteran's Children's Scholarship, 313
Lillie Lois Ford Boys' Scholarship, 143
Lillie Lois Ford Girls' Scholarship, 143
Lockheed Martin American Heroes Scholarship, 329
Maria C. Jackson-General George A. White Scholarship, 445
Marine Corps Scholarship, 375
M.D. Jack Murphy Memorial Nurses Training Fund, 143
Minnesota GI Bill, 387
MOAA Interest-Free Loan and Grant Program, 595
North Carolina Scholarships for Children of War Veterans, 431
Second Marine Division Association Scholarship Fund, 470
Shane Dean Voyles Memorial Scholarship, 144
Society of Sponsors Scholarship Program, 421
Thomas H. Miller Scholarship, 226
Vice Admiral E.P. Travers Loan, 597
West Virginia War Orphans Educational Assistance, 539

Navy

AFCEA War Veterans/Disabled War Veterans Scholarship, 208
American Legion Missouri Commander's Scholarship Fund, 142
Arkansas Military Dependents Scholarship Program, 206
Darlene Hooley for Oregon Veterans Scholarship, 443
Erman W. Taylor Memorial Scholarship, 142
Gold Star Scholarship Program, 420
Helping Heroes Grant, 503
Joseph J. Frank Scholarship, 143
Kansas Military Service Scholarship, 360
Kathern F. Gruber Scholarship Program, 226
Korean War Veteran's Children's Scholarship, 313
Lillie Lois Ford Boys' Scholarship, 143
Lillie Lois Ford Girls' Scholarship, 143
Lockheed Martin American Heroes Scholarship, 329
Maria C. Jackson-General George A. White Scholarship, 445
M.D. Jack Murphy Memorial Nurses Training Fund, 143

Minnesota GI Bill, 387
MOAA Interest-Free Loan and Grant Program, 595
Navy Supply Corps Foundation Scholarship, 420
North Carolina Scholarships for Children of War Veterans, 431
Seabee Memorial Scholarship, 470
Shane Dean Voyles Memorial Scholarship, 144
Society of Sponsors Scholarship Program, 421
Thomas H. Miller Scholarship, 226
Vice Admiral E.P. Travers Loan, 597
West Virginia War Orphans Educational Assistance, 539

Reserves/National Guard

AFCEA War Veterans/Disabled War Veterans Scholarship, 208
Alabama National Guard Educational Assistance Program, 90
Arkansas Military Dependents Scholarship Program, 206
Darlene Hooley for Oregon Veterans Scholarship, 443
Helping Heroes Grant, 503
Illinois National Guard Grant, 342
Indiana National Guard Supplemental Grant, 498
Iowa National Guard Educational Assistance Program, 348
Minnesota GI Bill, 387
MOAA Interest-Free Loan and Grant Program, 595
National Guard Educational Assistance Program, 361
National Guard Tuition Waiver, 438
Ohio National Guard Scholarship Program, 436
Selected Reserve Montgomery GI Bill, 525
Texas Armed Services Scholarship Program, 507
Texas National Guard Tuition Assistance Program, 509
West Virginia War Orphans Educational Assistance, 539

Minority Status

African American

Actuarial Diversity Scholarships, 81
AFSCMA/UNCF Union Scholars Program, 550
American Association of Advertising Agencies Multicultural Advertising Intern Program, 549
American Chemical Society Scholars Program, 97
American Institute of Certified Public Accountants Scholarship for Minority Accounting Students, 118
American Meteorological Society/Industry Minority Scholarship, 172
Black Nurses Scholarship, 410
Booker T. Washington Scholarship, 272
Brown and Caldwell Minority Scholarship Program, 229
California Teachers Association Martin Luther King, Jr., Memorial Scholarship, 233
Carole Simpson Scholarship, 407
The Chesapeake Energy Scholarship, 249
Colgate "Bright Smiles, Bright Futures" Minority Scholarships, 82
Connecticut Minority Teacher Incentive Grant, 244
Diversity Internship Program, 588
Dr. Dan J. and Patricia S. Pickard Scholarship, 249
The EDSA Minority Scholarship, 366
Fifth Third Bank of Central Indiana Scholarship, 275
Fisher Broadcasting Company Scholarship for Minorities, 262
Gates Millennium Scholars Program, 289
GE Foundation/LULAC Scholarship Program, 368
Herbert Lehman Educational Fund, 395
The Hyatt Hotels Fund for Minority Lodging Management Students Competition, 110
Indiana Minority Teacher & Special Education Services Scholarship, 497
INROADS Internship, 564
J. Paul Getty Multicultural Undergraduate Summer Internships at the Getty Center, 564
Jackie Robinson Foundation Mentoring and Leadership Curriculum, 351
James E. Webb Internship Program for Minority Undergraduate Seniors and Graduate Students in Business and Public Administration, 585
Kansas Ethnic Minority Scholarship, 360
Lagrant Scholarships, 365
Larry Whiteside Scholarship, 407
Leonard M. Perryman Communications Scholarship for Ethnic Minority Students, 522
Louis Carr Summer Internship, 566
Marathon Oil Corporation College Scholarship, 329
Mildred Towle Scholarship for African-Americans, 316
Minority Teacher Education Scholarship Program/Florida Fund for Minority Teachers, Inc., 265
Minority Teachers of Illinois Scholarship, 343
Minority Teaching Scholarship, 391
Morgan Stanley Richard B. Fisher Scholarship Program, 394
MSGC Undergraduate Underrepresented Minority Fellowship Program, 398
NABA National Scholarship Program, 406
NABJ Internships, 572
NABJ Visual Task Force (VTF) Scholarship, 408
NAFEO (National Association for Equal Opportunity in Higher Education) Scholarships, 116
National Achievement Scholarships, 416
Ohio Newspapers Minority Scholarship, 437
Ron Brown Scholar Program, 465
Sachs Foundation Undergraduate Grant, 466
Scholarship for Minority Undergraduate Physics Majors, 177
STEM Bridge Scholarship, 405
Technical Minority Scholarship, 546
Tennessee Minority Teaching Fellows Program, 600
Traditional CITE Scholarship, 245
UNCF Merck Science Initiative, 523
Weisman Scholarship, 245
Wisconsin Minority Teacher Loan Program, 602
Wisconsin Minority Undergraduate Retention Grant, 544

Alaskan native

Actuarial Diversity Scholarships, 81
AFSCMA/UNCF Union Scholars Program, 550
AISES Google Scholarship, 114
American Institute of Certified Public Accountants Scholarship for Minority Accounting Students, 118
American Meteorological Society/Industry Minority Scholarship, 172
Anonymous Foundation Scholarship, 110
Anthony A. Welmas Scholarship, 110
Arizona Public Service Navajo Scholars Program, 111
A.T. Anderson Memorial Scholarship, 114
Booker T. Washington Scholarship, 272
Brown and Caldwell Minority Scholarship Program, 229
Burlington Northern Santa Fe Foundation Scholarship, 115
California Teachers Association Martin Luther King, Jr., Memorial Scholarship, 233
The Chesapeake Energy Scholarship, 249
CIGNA Foundation Tribal Scholars Healthcare, 111
Connecticut Minority Teacher Incentive Grant, 244

Eligibility Indexes

Diversity Internship Program, 588
Ecotrust Native American Scholarship, 111
The EDSA Minority Scholarship, 366
Fifth Third Bank of Central Indiana Scholarship, 275
Fisher Broadcasting Company Scholarship for Minorities, 262
Ford Motor Company Tribal College Scholarship, 112
Gates Millennium Scholars Program, 289
GE Foundation/LULAC Scholarship Program, 368
Helen K. and Arthur E. Johnson Foundation Scholarship, 112
Hershey Company Tribal Scholarship, 112
The Hyatt Hotels Fund for Minority Lodging Management Students Competition, 110
INROADS Internship, 564
Intel Scholarship, 115
Jackie Robinson Foundation Mentoring and Leadership Curriculum, 351
James E. Webb Internship Program for Minority Undergraduate Seniors and Graduate Students in Business and Public Administration, 585
Kansas Ethnic Minority Scholarship, 360
Lagrant Scholarships, 365
Leonard M. Perryman Communications Scholarship for Ethnic Minority Students, 522
Marathon Oil Corporation College Scholarship, 329
MESBEC Scholarships, 234
Minority Teacher Education Scholarship Program/Florida Fund for Minority Teachers, Inc., 265
Minority Teachers of Illinois Scholarship, 343
Morgan Stanley Scholars Program, 112
NABA National Scholarship Program, 406
Native American Education Grant, 458
Nissan North America, Inc. Scholarship, 112
San Manuel Band of Missions Indians Tribal Scholarship, 113
Smithsonian Native American Internship, 585
Sovereign Nations Scholarship, 113
STEM Bridge Scholarship, 405
Technical Minority Scholarship, 546
Tennessee Minority Teaching Fellows Program, 600
Travelers Foundation Scholarship, 113
Tribal Business Management Scholarship, 235
Truman D. Picard Scholarship, 347
United Health Foundation Scholarship, 113
Weisman Scholarship, 245
Women's Self Worth Foundation Scholarship, 114

American Indian

Actuarial Diversity Scholarships, 81
AFSCMA/UNCF Union Scholars Program, 550
AISES Google Scholarship, 114
American Association of Advertising Agencies Multicultural Advertising Intern Program, 549
American Chemical Society Scholars Program, 97
American Institute of Certified Public Accountants Scholarship for Minority Accounting Students, 118
American Meteorological Society/Industry Minority Scholarship, 172
Anonymous Foundation Scholarship, 110
Anthony A. Welmas Scholarship, 110
Arizona Public Service Navajo Scholars Program, 111
A.T. Anderson Memorial Scholarship, 114
Austin Family Scholarship Endowment, 111
Booker T. Washington Scholarship, 272
Brown and Caldwell Minority Scholarship Program, 229
Bureau of Indian Education Higher Education Grant Program, 230
Burlington Northern Santa Fe Foundation Scholarship, 115
California Teachers Association Martin Luther King, Jr., Memorial Scholarship, 233
The Chesapeake Energy Scholarship, 249
Choctaw Nation Higher Education Program, 238
CIGNA Foundation Tribal Scholars Healthcare, 111
Colgate "Bright Smiles, Bright Futures" Minority Scholarships, 82
Connecticut Minority Teacher Incentive Grant, 244
Diversity Internship Program, 588
Ecotrust Native American Scholarship, 111
The EDSA Minority Scholarship, 366
Fifth Third Bank of Central Indiana Scholarship, 275
Fisher Broadcasting Company Scholarship for Minorities, 262
Ford Motor Company Tribal College Scholarship, 112
Gates Millennium Scholars Program, 289
GE Foundation/LULAC Scholarship Program, 368
Helen K. and Arthur E. Johnson Foundation Scholarship, 112
Hershey Company Tribal Scholarship, 112
Hopi BIA Higher Education Grant, 331
Hopi Education Award, 332
Hopi Tribal Priority Award, 332
The Hyatt Hotels Fund for Minority Lodging Management Students Competition, 110
INROADS Internship, 564
Intel Scholarship, 115
J. Paul Getty Multicultural Undergraduate Summer Internships at the Getty Center, 564
Jackie Robinson Foundation Mentoring and Leadership Curriculum, 351
James E. Webb Internship Program for Minority Undergraduate Seniors and Graduate Students in Business and Public Administration, 585
Kansas Ethnic Minority Scholarship, 360
Lagrant Scholarships, 365
Leonard M. Perryman Communications Scholarship for Ethnic Minority Students, 522
Louis Carr Summer Internship, 566
Marathon Oil Corporation College Scholarship, 329
Menominee Adult Vocational Training Grant, 383
Menominee Higher Education Grant, 384
MESBEC Scholarships, 234
Minnesota Indian Scholarship Program, 388
Minority Teacher Education Scholarship Program/Florida Fund for Minority Teachers, Inc., 265
Minority Teachers of Illinois Scholarship, 343
Minority Teaching Scholarship, 391
Morgan Stanley Richard B. Fisher Scholarship Program, 394
Morgan Stanley Scholars Program, 112
MSGC Undergraduate Underrepresented Minority Fellowship Program, 398
NABA National Scholarship Program, 406
Native American Education Grant, 458
Native American Leadership in Education Scholarship, 235
Nissan North America, Inc. Scholarship, 112
North American Indian Scholarship, 347
North Dakota Indian Scholarship Program, 434
Northern Cheyenne Higher Education Program, 435
Ohio Newspapers Minority Scholarship, 437
Osage Tribal Education Committee Award, 230
Osage Tribal Education Scholarship, 450

San Manuel Band of Missions Indians Tribal Scholarship, 113
Scholarship for Minority Undergraduate Physics Majors, 177
Seneca Nation Higher Education Program, 471
Shoshone Tribal Scholarship, 472
Silver Eagle Indian Scholarship, 150
Smithsonian Native American Internship, 585
South Dakota Ardell Bjugstad Scholarship, 494
Sovereign Nations Scholarship, 113
STEM Bridge Scholarship, 405
Technical Minority Scholarship, 546
Tennessee Minority Teaching Fellows Program, 600
Travelers Foundation Scholarship, 113
Tribal Business Management Scholarship, 235
Truman D. Picard Scholarship, 347
United Health Foundation Scholarship, 113
Weisman Scholarship, 245
Wisconsin Indian Student Assistance Grant, 544
Wisconsin Minority Teacher Loan Program, 602
Wisconsin Minority Undergraduate Retention Grant, 544
Women's Self Worth Foundation Scholarship, 114

Asian American

AFSCMA/UNCF Union Scholars Program, 550
American Association of Advertising Agencies Multicultural Advertising Intern Program, 549
American Institute of Certified Public Accountants Scholarship for Minority Accounting Students, 118
American Meteorological Society/Industry Minority Scholarship, 172
Booker T. Washington Scholarship, 272
Brown and Caldwell Minority Scholarship Program, 229
California Teachers Association Martin Luther King, Jr., Memorial Scholarship, 233
The Chesapeake Energy Scholarship, 249
Colgate "Bright Smiles, Bright Futures" Minority Scholarships, 82
Connecticut Minority Teacher Incentive Grant, 244
Diversity Internship Program, 588
The EDSA Minority Scholarship, 366
Fifth Third Bank of Central Indiana Scholarship, 275
Fisher Broadcasting Company Scholarship for Minorities, 262
Gates Millennium Scholars Program, 289
GE Foundation/LULAC Scholarship Program, 368
The Hyatt Hotels Fund for Minority Lodging Management Students Competition, 110
Indian American Scholarship, 525
INROADS Internship, 564
J. Paul Getty Multicultural Undergraduate Summer Internships at the Getty Center, 564
Jackie Robinson Foundation Mentoring and Leadership Curriculum, 351
James E. Webb Internship Program for Minority Undergraduate Seniors and Graduate Students in Business and Public Administration, 585
Kansas Ethnic Minority Scholarship, 360
Leonard M. Perryman Communications Scholarship for Ethnic Minority Students, 522
Louis Carr Summer Internship, 566
Minority Teacher Education Scholarship Program/Florida Fund for Minority Teachers, Inc., 265
Minority Teachers of Illinois Scholarship, 343
Minority Teaching Scholarship, 391
NABA National Scholarship Program, 406
OCA-AXA Achievement Scholarships, 435
OCA/UPS Foundation Gold Mountain College Scholarship, 436
Ohio Newspapers Minority Scholarship, 437
STEM Bridge Scholarship, 405
Technical Minority Scholarship, 546
Tennessee Minority Teaching Fellows Program, 600
Weisman Scholarship, 245
Wisconsin Minority Teacher Loan Program, 602
Wisconsin Minority Undergraduate Retention Grant, 544

Hispanic American

Actuarial Diversity Scholarships, 81
AFSCMA/UNCF Union Scholars Program, 550
ALPFA Scholarship, 326
American Association of Advertising Agencies Multicultural Advertising Intern Program, 549
American Chemical Society Scholars Program, 97
American Institute of Certified Public Accountants Scholarship for Minority Accounting Students, 118
American Meteorological Society/Industry Minority Scholarship, 172
AT&T Foundation Scholarship, 326
Booker T. Washington Scholarship, 272
Brown and Caldwell Minority Scholarship Program, 229
California Teachers Association Martin Luther King, Jr., Memorial Scholarship, 233
CCNMA Scholarships, 235
The Chesapeake Energy Scholarship, 249
Clorox Suena Sin Limites Mother Scholarship, 327
Coca-Cola Live Positively Publix Supermarkets Scholarship, 327
Colgate "Bright Smiles, Bright Futures" Minority Scholarships, 82
Connecticut Minority Teacher Incentive Grant, 244
Discover Scholarship, 327
Diversity Internship Program, 588
The EDSA Minority Scholarship, 366
ExxonMobil Scholarship, 327
Fifth Third Bank of Central Indiana Scholarship, 275
Fisher Broadcasting Company Scholarship for Minorities, 262
Ford Blue Oval Scholarship, 325
Gates Millennium Scholars Program, 289
GE Foundation/LULAC Scholarship Program, 368
GE Hispanic Forum Scholarship, 327
Google Hispanic College Fund Scholarship Program, 325
Goya Scholarship, 328
HACEMOS Scholarship, 328
HACU (Hispanic Association of Colleges and Universities) Scholarships, 115
HENAAC Scholars Program, 294
Hispanic Heritage Youth Awards Program, 326
Honda Scholarship, 328
HSF Achievement Scholarship, 328
HSF General College Scholarship, 329
The Hyatt Hotels Fund for Minority Lodging Management Students Competition, 110
Indiana Minority Teacher & Special Education Services Scholarship, 497
INROADS Internship, 564
J. Paul Getty Multicultural Undergraduate Summer Internships at the Getty Center, 564
Jackie Robinson Foundation Mentoring and Leadership Curriculum, 351
James E. Webb Internship Program for Minority Undergraduate Seniors and Graduate Students in Business and Public Administration, 585
Jose Marti Scholarship Challenge Grant Fund, 264
Kansas Ethnic Minority Scholarship, 360
Lagrant Scholarships, 365
Latin American Educational Scholarship, 368

Latino Diamante Scholarship Fund, 433
Leonard M. Perryman Communications Scholarship for Ethnic Minority Students, 522
Lockheed Martin American Heroes Scholarship, 329
Los Padres Foundation College Tuition Assistance Program, 371
Los Padres Foundation Second Chance Program, 371
Louis Carr Summer Internship, 566
Macy's College Scholarship Program, 329
Marathon Oil Corporation College Scholarship, 329
Marathon Petroleum Corporation College Scholarship, 330
Marriott Scholars Program, 326
Minority Teacher Education Scholarship Program/Florida Fund for Minority Teachers, Inc., 265
Minority Teachers of Illinois Scholarship, 343
Minority Teaching Scholarship, 391
Morgan Stanley Foundation Scholarship, 330
Morgan Stanley Richard B. Fisher Scholarship Program, 394
MSGC Undergraduate Underrepresented Minority Fellowship Program, 398
NABA National Scholarship Program, 406
Nissan North America, Inc. Scholarship Program, 330
Northwest Arkansas Bilingual Teacher Scholarship, 331
Ohio Newspapers Minority Scholarship, 437
Procter & Gamble - Orgullosa Scholarship, 331
Scholarship for Minority Undergraduate Physics Majors, 177
STEM Bridge Scholarship, 405
Technical Minority Scholarship, 546
Tennessee Minority Teaching Fellows Program, 600
USHCC-Wells Fargo Scholarship, 331
VAMOS Scholarship, 331
Weisman Scholarship, 245
Wisconsin Minority Teacher Loan Program, 602
Wisconsin Minority Undergraduate Retention Grant, 544

Mexican American

Actuarial Diversity Scholarships, 81
AFSCMA/UNCF Union Scholars Program, 550
ALPFA Scholarship, 326
American Association of Advertising Agencies Multicultural Advertising Intern Program, 549
American Chemical Society Scholars Program, 97
American Institute of Certified Public Accountants Scholarship for Minority Accounting Students, 118
American Meteorological Society/Industry Minority Scholarship, 172
AT&T Foundation Scholarship, 326
Booker T. Washington Scholarship, 272
Brown and Caldwell Minority Scholarship Program, 229
California Teachers Association Martin Luther King, Jr., Memorial Scholarship, 233
CCNMA Scholarships, 235
The Chesapeake Energy Scholarship, 249
Clorox Suena Sin Limites Mother Scholarship, 327
Coca-Cola Live Positively Publix Supermarkets Scholarship, 327
Colgate "Bright Smiles, Bright Futures" Minority Scholarships, 82
Connecticut Minority Teacher Incentive Grant, 244
Discover Scholarship, 327
Diversity Internship Program, 588
The EDSA Minority Scholarship, 366
ExxonMobil Scholarship, 327
Fifth Third Bank of Central Indiana Scholarship, 275
Fisher Broadcasting Company Scholarship for Minorities, 262
Fleming/Blaszcak Scholarship, 486
Ford Blue Oval Scholarship, 325
Gates Millennium Scholars Program, 289
GE Foundation/LULAC Scholarship Program, 368
GE Hispanic Forum Scholarship, 327
Goya Scholarship, 328
HACEMOS Scholarship, 328
HACU (Hispanic Association of Colleges and Universities) Scholarships, 115
Honda Scholarship, 328
HSF Achievement Scholarship, 328
HSF General College Scholarship, 329
The Hyatt Hotels Fund for Minority Lodging Management Students Competition, 110
Indiana Minority Teacher & Special Education Services Scholarship, 497
INROADS Internship, 564
J. Paul Getty Multicultural Undergraduate Summer Internships at the Getty Center, 564
Jackie Robinson Foundation Mentoring and Leadership Curriculum, 351
James E. Webb Internship Program for Minority Undergraduate Seniors and Graduate Students in Business and Public Administration, 585
Jose Marti Scholarship Challenge Grant Fund, 264
Kansas Ethnic Minority Scholarship, 360
Lagrant Scholarships, 365
Latin American Educational Scholarship, 368
Leonard M. Perryman Communications Scholarship for Ethnic Minority Students, 522
Lockheed Martin American Heroes Scholarship, 329
Los Padres Foundation College Tuition Assistance Program, 371
Los Padres Foundation Second Chance Program, 371
Louis Carr Summer Internship, 566
Macy's College Scholarship Program, 329
Marathon Petroleum Corporation College Scholarship, 330
Marriott Scholars Program, 326
Minority Teacher Education Scholarship Program/Florida Fund for Minority Teachers, Inc., 265
Minority Teachers of Illinois Scholarship, 343
Morgan Stanley Foundation Scholarship, 330
Morgan Stanley Richard B. Fisher Scholarship Program, 394
NABA National Scholarship Program, 406
Nissan North America, Inc. Scholarship Program, 330
Northwest Arkansas Bilingual Teacher Scholarship, 331
Procter & Gamble - Orgullosa Scholarship, 331
Scholarship for Minority Undergraduate Physics Majors, 177
STEM Bridge Scholarship, 405
Technical Minority Scholarship, 546
USHCC-Wells Fargo Scholarship, 331
VAMOS Scholarship, 331
Weisman Scholarship, 245
Wisconsin Minority Teacher Loan Program, 602
Wisconsin Minority Undergraduate Retention Grant, 544

Native Hawaiian/Pacific Islander

Actuarial Diversity Scholarships, 81
AFSCMA/UNCF Union Scholars Program, 550
AISES Google Scholarship, 114
Ambassador Minerva Jean Falcon Hawaii Scholarship, 296
American Association of Advertising Agencies Multicultural Advertising Intern Program, 549
American Institute of Certified Public Accountants Scholarship for Minority Accounting Students, 118
American Meteorological Society/Industry Minority Scholarship, 172

A.T. Anderson Memorial Scholarship, 114
Blossom Kalama Evans Memorial Scholarship, 297
Booker T. Washington Scholarship, 272
Brown and Caldwell Minority Scholarship Program, 229
Burlington Northern Santa Fe Foundation Scholarship, 115
California Teachers Association Martin Luther King, Jr., Memorial Scholarship, 233
The Chesapeake Energy Scholarship, 249
Connecticut Minority Teacher Incentive Grant, 244
Diversity Internship Program, 588
The EDSA Minority Scholarship, 366
Fifth Third Bank of Central Indiana Scholarship, 275
Fisher Broadcasting Company Scholarship for Minorities, 262
Gates Millennium Scholars Program, 289
GE Foundation/LULAC Scholarship Program, 368
Helen K. and Arthur E. Johnson Foundation Scholarship, 112
The Hyatt Hotels Fund for Minority Lodging Management Students Competition, 110
Ida M. Pope Memorial Scholarship, 308
INROADS Internship, 564
Intel Scholarship, 115
J. Paul Getty Multicultural Undergraduate Summer Internships at the Getty Center, 564
Jackie Robinson Foundation Mentoring and Leadership Curriculum, 351
James E. Webb Internship Program for Minority Undergraduate Seniors and Graduate Students in Business and Public Administration, 585
Ka'iulani Home for Girls Trust Scholarship, 311
Kansas Ethnic Minority Scholarship, 360
Lagrant Scholarships, 365
Leonard M. Perryman Communications Scholarship for Ethnic Minority Students, 522
Louis Carr Summer Internship, 566
Marathon Oil Corporation College Scholarship, 329
Minority Teacher Education Scholarship Program/Florida Fund for Minority Teachers, Inc., 265
Minority Teachers of Illinois Scholarship, 343
MSGC Undergraduate Underrepresented Minority Fellowship Program, 398
NABA National Scholarship Program, 406
Nissan North America, Inc. Scholarship, 112
OCA-AXA Achievement Scholarships, 435
OCA/UPS Foundation Gold Mountain College Scholarship, 436
Office of Hawaiian Affairs Scholarship Fund, 317
Philippine Nurses' Association Scholarship, 318
Rosemary & Nellie Ebrie Fund, 320
San Manuel Band of Missions Indians Tribal Scholarship, 113
STEM Bridge Scholarship, 405
Technical Minority Scholarship, 546
Tennessee Minority Teaching Fellows Program, 600
Weisman Scholarship, 245

Puerto Rican

Actuarial Diversity Scholarships, 81
AFSCMA/UNCF Union Scholars Program, 550
ALPFA Scholarship, 326
American Association of Advertising Agencies Multicultural Advertising Intern Program, 549
American Chemical Society Scholars Program, 97
American Institute of Certified Public Accountants Scholarship for Minority Accounting Students, 118
American Meteorological Society/Industry Minority Scholarship, 172
AT&T Foundation Scholarship, 326
Booker T. Washington Scholarship, 272
Brown and Caldwell Minority Scholarship Program, 229
California Teachers Association Martin Luther King, Jr., Memorial Scholarship, 233
CCNMA Scholarships, 235
The Chesapeake Energy Scholarship, 249
Clorox Suena Sin Limites Mother Scholarship, 327
Coca-Cola Live Positively Publix Supermarkets Scholarship, 327
Colgate "Bright Smiles, Bright Futures" Minority Scholarships, 82
Connecticut Minority Teacher Incentive Grant, 244
Discover Scholarship, 327
Diversity Internship Program, 588
The EDSA Minority Scholarship, 366
ExxonMobil Scholarship, 327
Fifth Third Bank of Central Indiana Scholarship, 275
Fisher Broadcasting Company Scholarship for Minorities, 262
Ford Blue Oval Scholarship, 325
Gates Millennium Scholars Program, 289
GE Foundation/LULAC Scholarship Program, 368
GE Hispanic Forum Scholarship, 327
Goya Scholarship, 328
HACEMOS Scholarship, 328
HACU (Hispanic Association of Colleges and Universities) Scholarships, 115
Honda Scholarship, 328
HSF Achievement Scholarship, 328
HSF General College Scholarship, 329
The Hyatt Hotels Fund for Minority Lodging Management Students Competition, 110
Indiana Minority Teacher & Special Education Services Scholarship, 497
INROADS Internship, 564
J. Paul Getty Multicultural Undergraduate Summer Internships at the Getty Center, 564
Jackie Robinson Foundation Mentoring and Leadership Curriculum, 351
James E. Webb Internship Program for Minority Undergraduate Seniors and Graduate Students in Business and Public Administration, 585
Jose Marti Scholarship Challenge Grant Fund, 264
Kansas Ethnic Minority Scholarship, 360
Lagrant Scholarships, 365
Latin American Educational Scholarship, 368
Leonard M. Perryman Communications Scholarship for Ethnic Minority Students, 522
Lockheed Martin American Heroes Scholarship, 329
Los Padres Foundation College Tuition Assistance Program, 371
Los Padres Foundation Second Chance Program, 371
Louis Carr Summer Internship, 566
Macy's College Scholarship Program, 329
Marathon Petroleum Corporation College Scholarship, 330
Marriott Scholars Program, 326
Minority Teacher Education Scholarship Program/Florida Fund for Minority Teachers, Inc., 265
Minority Teachers of Illinois Scholarship, 343
Morgan Stanley Foundation Scholarship, 330
Morgan Stanley Richard B. Fisher Scholarship Program, 394
NABA National Scholarship Program, 406
Nissan North America, Inc. Scholarship Program, 330
Northwest Arkansas Bilingual Teacher Scholarship, 331
Procter & Gamble - Orgullosa Scholarship, 331
Scholarship for Minority Undergraduate Physics Majors, 177

STEM Bridge Scholarship, 405
Technical Minority Scholarship, 546
USHCC-Wells Fargo Scholarship, 331
VAMOS Scholarship, 331
Weisman Scholarship, 245
Wisconsin Minority Teacher Loan Program, 602
Wisconsin Minority Undergraduate Retention Grant, 544

National/ethnic background

Armenian

AGBU International Scholarships, 209
Armenian General Benevolent Union Performing Arts Fellowships, 209

Chinese

Thz Fo Farm Fund, 321

Italian

Alphonse A. Miele Scholarship, 520
College Scholarship Program, 241
Henry Salvatori Scholarship, 490
Italian Catholic Federation Scholarship, 349
Major Don S. Gentile Scholarship, 520
Sant'Anna Institute-Sorrento Lingue Scholarship, 490
Sons of Italy General Scholarship, 490
Sons of Italy Italian Language Scholarship, 490
Sons of Italy National Leadership Grant, 491
Theodore Mazza Scholarship, 520
William C. Davini Scholarship, 520

Japanese

Ventura County Japanese-American Citizens League Scholarships, 530

Jewish

Jewish War Veterans of the United States of America Bernard Rotberg Memorial Scholarship, 358
Robert and Rebecca Memorial Grant, 358
Seymour and Phyllis Shore Memorial Grant, 358

Polish

Massachusetts Federation of Polish Women's Clubs Scholarships, 364
The Polish American Club of North Jersey Scholarships, 364
The Polish National Alliance of Brooklyn, USA, Inc. Scholarships, 365

Swiss

Sonia Streuli Maguire Outstanding Scholastic Achievement Award, 502
Swiss Benevolent Society Medicus Student Exchange, 502
Swiss Benevolent Society Pellegrini Scholarship, 502

Welsh

Welsh Heritage Scholarship, 538
Welsh Society of Philadelphia Undergraduate Scholarship, 538

Organization/civic affiliation

American Indian Science & Engineering Society

AISES Google Scholarship, 114
A.T. Anderson Memorial Scholarship, 114
Burlington Northern Santa Fe Foundation Scholarship, 115
Intel Scholarship, 115

American Legion

Alaska Boys State Scholarship, 120
Albert M. Lappin Scholarship, 133
Albert T. Marcoux Memorial Scholarship, 150
American Legion Alabama Oratorical Contest, 119
American Legion Alabama Scholarship, 119
American Legion Alaska Oratorical Contest, 120
American Legion Arizona Oratorical Contest, 120
American Legion Arkansas Oratorical Contest, 121
American Legion Coudret Trust Scholarship, 122
American Legion Florida Eagle Scout of the Year, 125
American Legion Florida General Scholarship, 126
American Legion Florida High School Oratorical Contest, 126
American Legion Georgia Oratorical Contest, 127
American Legion Idaho Scholarships, 128
American Legion Illinois Scholarships, 128
American Legion Indiana Eagle Scout of the Year Scholarship, 130
American Legion Indiana Family Scholarship, 130
American Legion Maine Children and Youth Scholarship, 136
American Legion Massachusetts General and Nursing Scholarships, 138
American Legion Minnesota Legionnaire Insurance Trust Scholarship, 140
American Legion Minnesota Memorial Scholarship, 141
American Legion Nebraska Oratorical Contest, 147
American Legion New Hampshire Department Vocational Scholarship, 150
American Legion New Jersey Department of New Jersey Scholarship, 153
American Legion New York Oratorical Contest, 154
American Legion Ohio Department Oratorical Awards, 157
American Legion Ohio Scholarships, 157
American Legion Washington Children and Youth Scholarship Fund, 166
American Legion Western District Postsecondary Scholarship, 120
American Legion Wyoming E.A. Blackmore Memorial Scholarship, 170
Charles and Annette Hill Scholarship, 133
Charles L. Bacon Memorial Scholarship, 142
Department of New Hampshire Scholarship, 151
Dr. Hannah K. Vuolo Memorial Scholarship, 154
Edgar J. Boschult Memorial Scholarship, 147
Hugh A. Smith Scholarship, 134
James F. Mulholland American Legion Scholarship, 154
James V. Day Scholarship, 136
Joseph J. Frank Scholarship, 143
Joseph P. Gavenonis Scholarship, 159
Maynard Jensen American Legion Memorial Scholarship, 147
New York American Legion Press Association Scholarship, 155
Rosedale Post 346 Scholarship, 134
Samsung American Legion Scholarship, 147
Schneider-Emanuel American Legion Scholarships, 168
Ted and Nora Anderson Scholarship, 134

American Legion Auxiliary

Adrienne Alix Scholarship, 152
Aloha Scholarship, 144

American Legion Alabama Auxiliary Scholarship, 119
American Legion Alaska Auxiliary Scholarship, 120
American Legion Alaska Auxiliary Western District Scholarship, 120
American Legion Arizona Auxiliary Health Care Occupation Scholarship, 121
American Legion Arizona Auxiliary Nurses' Scholarship, 121
American Legion Arkansas Auxiliary Scholarships, 122
American Legion Auxiliary National Presidents Scholarship, 145
American Legion Auxiliary Spirit of Youth Scholarship for Junior Members, 145
American Legion California Auxiliary General Scholarships, 123
American Legion Colorado Auxiliary Department President's Scholarship, 123
American Legion Colorado Auxiliary Department President's Scholarship for Junior Auxiliary Members, 124
American Legion Colorado Auxiliary Past Presidents Parley Nurse's Scholarship, 124
American Legion Connecticut Auxiliary Memorial Education Grant, 124
American Legion Connecticut Auxiliary Past Presidents Parley Education Grant, 125
American Legion Delaware Auxiliary Past Presidents Parley Nursing Scholarship, 125
American Legion Florida Auxiliary Department Scholarships, 126
American Legion Florida Auxiliary Memorial Scholarship, 126
American Legion Georgia Auxiliary Past Presidents Parley Nurses Scholarship, 127
American Legion Georgia Scholarship, 127
American Legion Indiana Auxiliary Past Presidents Parley Nursing Scholarship, 131
American Legion Kentucky Auxiliary Mary Barrett Marshall Scholarship, 135
American Legion Minnesota Auxiliary Department Scholarship, 141
American Legion Minnesota Auxiliary Past Presidents Parley Health Care Scholarship, 141
American Legion Missouri Auxiliary National President's Scholarship, 144
American Legion New Hampshire Auxiliary Past Presidents Parley Nurses' Scholarship, 152
American Legion North Dakota Auxiliary Past Presidents Parley Scholarship, 157
American Legion Ohio Auxiliary Department President's Scholarship, 157
American Legion Ohio Auxiliary Past Presidents Parley Nurse's Scholarship, 158
American Legion Oregon Auxiliary National President's Scholarship, 158
American Legion Rhode Island Auxiliary Book Award, 160
American Legion Scholarship for Non-Traditional Students, 146
American Legion South Carolina Auxiliary Scholarship, 161
American Legion South Dakota Auxiliary Scholarships, 161
American Legion South Dakota Auxiliary Senior Member Scholarship, 161
American Legion Wisconsin Auxiliary Department President's Scholarship, 169
American Legion Wisconsin Auxiliary H.S. and Angeline Lewis Scholarships, 169
American Legion Wisconsin Auxiliary Merit and Memorial Scholarship, 169
American Legion Wisconsin Auxiliary Past Presidents Parley R.N. Scholarship, 169
Anna Gear Junior Scholarship, 165
Children of Warriors National President's Scholarship, 165
Della Van Deuren Memorial Scholarship, 170
Dr. Kate Waller Barrett Grant, 165
Edna M. Barcus Memorial Scholarship and Hoosier Scholarship, 131
Elsie B. Brown Scholarship Fund, 152
Florence Lemcke Memorial Scholarship, 166
Grace S. High Memorial Child Welfare Scholarship Fund, 152
Laura Blackburn Memorial Scholarship, 135
Lucille Ganey Memorial Scholarship, 123
Marguerite McAlpin Nurse's Scholarship, 167
Marion J. Bagley Scholarship, 152
Mary Barrett Marshall Student Loan Fund, 593
Nannie W. Norfleet Scholarship, 156
Ruby Paul Campaign Fund Scholarship, 149
Spirit of Youth Scholarship, 159
Susan Burdett Scholarship, 167
Thelma Foster Junior American Legion Auxiliary Members Scholarship, 162
Thelma Foster Senior American Legion Auxiliary Member Scholarship, 162
Violet Morrow Education Scholarship, 124
Wilma D. Hoyal/Maxine Chilton Memorial Scholarship, 121

American Legion, Boys State

American Legion Iowa Outstanding Citizen of Boys State Scholarship, 132
American Legion Maryland Boys State Scholarship, 137
American Legion New Hampshire Boys State Scholarship, 150
Lillie Lois Ford Boys' Scholarship, 143

American Legion/Boys Scouts of America

American Legion Wisconsin Eagle Scout of the Year Scholarship, 168

Boy Scouts of America

American Legion Illinois Boy Scout Scholarship, 128

Boy Scouts of America, Eagle Scouts

American Legion Eagle Scout of the Year, 146
American Legion Iowa Boy Scout of the Year Scholarship, 131
American Legion Tennessee Eagle Scout of the Year Scholarship, 162
American Legion Vermont Eagle Scout of the Year, 164

First Catholic Slovak Ladies Association

First Catholic Slovak Ladies Association Scholarship Program, 262

Harness Racing Industry

Harness Tracks of America Scholarship Fund, 294

International Union of EESMF Workers, AFL-CIO

Bruce van Ess Scholarship, 349
James B. Carey Scholarship, 349
Sal Ingrassia Scholarship, 350
Willie Rudd Scholarship, 350

Jaycees

Charles R. Ford Scholarship, 356
Jaycee War Memorial Scholarship, 357
Thomas Wood Baldridge Scholarship, 357

Learning for Life

Captain James J. Regan Memorial Scholarship, 369

Sheryl A. Horak Law Enforcement Explorer Scholarship, 370

New York State Grange

Caroline Kark Scholarship, 425
Grange Denise Scholarship, 425
Grange Student Loan Fund, 598
Grange Susan W. Freestone Education Award, 425
June Gill Nursing Scholarship, 425

Polish National Alliance of Brooklyn

The Polish National Alliance of Brooklyn, USA, Inc. Scholarships, 365

Reserve Officers Training Corps (ROTC)

Kansas ROTC Service Scholarship, 360

Screen Actor's Guild

John L. Dales Standard Scholarship, 469
John L. Dales Transitional Scholarship, 470

Society of Physics Students

Herbert Levy Memorial Endowment Fund Scholarship, 485
Peggy Dixon Two-Year Scholarship, 485
Society of Physics Students Future Teacher Scholarship, 485
Society of Physics Students Leadership Scholarship, 485
Society of Physics Students Summer Internship Program, 586

Society of Women Engineers

SWE Scholarships, 489

Soil and Water Conservation Society

Donald A. Williams Soil Conservation Scholarship, 489
Melville H. Cohee Student Leader Conservation Scholarship, 490

Sons of Norway

Astrid G. Cates Scholarship Fund and Myrtle Beinhauer Scholarship, 491
King Olav V Norwegian-American Heritage Fund, 491
Nancy Lorraine Jensen Memorial Scholarship, 491

Transportation Clubs International

Alice Glaisyer Warfield Memorial Scholarship, 517
Charlotte Woods Memorial Scholarship, 517
Denny Lydic Scholarship, 517
Ginger and Fred Deines Canada Scholarship, 517
Ginger and Fred Deines Mexico Scholarship, 518
Hooper Memorial Scholarship, 518
Texas Transportation Scholarship, 518

United Food and Commerical Workers

United Food and Commercial Workers International Union Plus Scholarship Program, 521

United Transportation Union

United Transportation Union Insurance Association Scholarship, 524

Religious Affiliation

Eastern Orthodox

Boy and Girl Scouts Scholarship, 255

Episcopal

Shannon Scholarship, 519

Jewish

Chester M. Vernon Memorial Eagle Scout Scholarship, 414
Frank L. Weil Memorial Eagle Scout Scholarship, 415
Jewish Vocational Service Scholarship Fund, 357
JFCS Scholarship Fund, 595
Taglit-Birthright Israel Gift, 503

Lutheran

Lutheran Student Scholastic and Service Scholarship, 225

Presbyterian

National Presbyterian College Scholarship, 458
Presbyterian Student Opportunity Scholarship, 458
Presbyterian Undergraduate and Graduate Loan, 599
Samuel Robinson Award, 458

Protestant

Juliette M. Atherton Scholarship - Minister's Sons and Daughters, 311

Roman Catholic

Italian Catholic Federation Scholarship, 349

Unitarian Universalist

Stanfield and D'Orlando Art Scholarships, 521

United Methodist

Hoover-Lee Scholars Program, 522
Leonard M. Perryman Communications Scholarship for Ethnic Minority Students, 522
September 11 Memorial Scholarship, 522
United Methodist Loan Program, 601
United Methodist Scholarships, 522

Returning Adult

Adrienne Alix Scholarship, 152
Air Traffic Control Full-Time Employee Student Scholarship, 88
American Legion Alaska Auxiliary Western District Scholarship, 120
Arkansas Second Effort Scholarship, 206
Arkansas Workforce Improvement Grant, 207
Charles R. Ford Scholarship, 356
Connecticut Tuition Waiver for Senior Citizens, 244
Delayed Education Scholarship for Women, 175
Eight and Forty Lung and Respiratory Disease Nursing Scholarship, 146
Fran Johnson Non-Traditional Scholarship, 104
Minority Teaching Scholarship, 391
NASA North Carolina Space Grant Consortium Undergraduate Research Scholarship, 400
New York State Veterans Tuition Award, 428
Texas Senior Citizen, 65 or Older, Free Tuition for Up to 6 Credit Hours, 510
West Virginia Higher Education Adult Part-time Student (HEAPS) Grant Program, 540

State of Residence

ACEC Scholarship, 101
Agrium U.S. Inc. Scholarship, 268

Allen Susser Scholarship, 351
Alumnae Panhellenic Association Women's Scholarship, 94
American Legion Vermont Scholarship, 164
Azurea at One Ocean Resort Hotel & Spa Scholarship, 351
College Scholarship Program, 241
The Dayton Amateur Radio Association Scholarships, 182
Hudner Medal of Honor Scholarship, 260
Idaho GEAR UP Scholarship, 340
Jose and Victoria Martinez Maison Blanche Scholarship, 353
Kansas Comprehensive Grant, 359
Kansas Ethnic Minority Scholarship, 360
Kansas Nursing Service Scholarship, 360
Kansas Teacher Service Scholarship, 361
L. Gordon Bittle Memorial Scholarship for SCTA, 234
The L.B. Cebik, W4RNL, and Jean Cebik, N4TZP, Memorial Scholarship, 186
Massachusetts MASSgrant Program, 381
Minnesota GI Bill, 387
Missouri Department of Higher Education Vietnam Veteran's Survivor Grant Program, 392
Morgan Stanley Foundation Scholarship, 330
NASA Space Grant Oregon Undergraduate Scholarship, 402
National Co-op Scholarship, 410
The Northern California DX Foundation Scholarship, 187
Omaha Steaks Scholarship, 354
The Ranch House at Devil's Thumb Scholarship, 355
The Richard W. Bendicksen, N7ZL, Memorial Scholarship, 189
United Health Foundation Scholarship, 113
Wilbur-Ellis Company High School Scholarship, 285
Wilma Motley Memorial California Merit Scholarship, 84
The Zachary Taylor Stevens Scholarship, 192

Alabama

Alabama National Guard Educational Assistance Program, 90
Alabama Scholarship for Dependents of Blind Parents, 497
Alabama Student Assistance Program, 91
Alabama Student Grant Program, 91
American Legion Alabama Auxiliary Scholarship, 119
American Legion Alabama Oratorical Contest, 119
American Legion Alabama Scholarship, 119
The Andersons, Inc. Scholarship, 269
Animal Health International Scholarship, 270
Birdsong Peanuts Scholarship, 271
The Charles Clarke Cordle Memorial Scholarship, 181
Dana Campbell Memorial Scholarship, 353
Fastline Publications Scholarship, 275
Gulf Coast Hurricane Scholarships, 486
Mahindra USA Women in Ag Scholarship, 279
MetLife Foundation Scholarship, 279
Moody's Mega Math "M3" Challenge, 394
NASA Space Grant Undergraduate Scholarship, 395
The North Fulton Amateur Radio League Scholarship Fund, 187
Police/Firefighters' Survivors Educational Assistance Program, 91
Southern Nursery Organization Sidney B. Meadows Scholarship, 472
Toyota Motor Sales, U.S.A. Inc. Scholarship, 284

Alaska

Alaska Boys State Scholarship, 120
Alaska Performance Scholarship, 92
AlaskAdvantage Education Grant, 92
American Legion Alaska Auxiliary Scholarship, 120
American Legion Alaska Auxiliary Western District Scholarship, 120
American Legion Alaska Oratorical Contest, 120
American Legion Western District Postsecondary Scholarship, 120
The ARRL Northwestern Division Scholarship Fund, 180
ASTA Pacific Northwest Chapter/William Hunt Scholarship, 513
Cady McDonnell Memorial Scholarship, 99
Carl N. & Margaret Karcher Founders' Scholarship, 234
Clark-Phelps Scholarship, 442
Geophysical Society of Alaska Scholarship, 483
The Mary Lou Brown Scholarship, 186

Arizona

American Legion Arizona Auxiliary Health Care Occupation Scholarship, 121
American Legion Arizona Auxiliary Nurses' Scholarship, 121
American Legion Arizona Oratorical Contest, 120
Animal Health International Scholarship, 270
Arysta LifeScience North America Scholarship, 270
Burlington Northern Santa Fe Foundation Scholarship, 115
Cady McDonnell Memorial Scholarship, 99
Carl N. & Margaret Karcher Founders' Scholarship, 234
The Central Arizona DX Association Scholarship, 181
Chapter 67 - Phoenix Scholarship, 476
The Charles N. Fisher Memorial Scholarship, 182
Charles P. Lake - Rain For Rent Scholarship, 272
Deseo at the Westin Scholarship, 353
HACEMOS Scholarship, 328
Horatio Alger Arizona Scholarship, 332
Italian Catholic Federation Scholarship, 349
Mahindra USA Women in Ag Scholarship, 279
NASA Space Grant Arizona Undergraduate Research Internship, 571
Nissan North America, Inc. Scholarship Program, 330
RCMI Technical/Trade School Scholarship, 464
Rocky Mountain Coal Mining Institute Scholarship, 464
Travelers Foundation Scholarship, 113
Wilbur-Ellis Company High School Scholarship, 285
Wilma D. Hoyal/Maxine Chilton Memorial Scholarship, 121

Arkansas

American Legion Arkansas Auxiliary Scholarships, 122
American Legion Arkansas Oratorical Contest, 121
American Legion Coudret Trust Scholarship, 122
Animal Health International Scholarship, 270
Arkansas Academic Challenge Scholarship, 205
Arkansas Governor's Scholars Program, 206
Arkansas Law Enforcement Officers' Dependents Scholarship, 206
Arkansas Military Dependents Scholarship Program, 206
Arkansas Second Effort Scholarship, 206
Arkansas Workforce Improvement Grant, 207
ASHRAE Region VIII Scholarship, 196
Dana Campbell Memorial Scholarship, 353
Farmers Mutual Hail Insurance Company of Iowa Scholarship, 275
Fastline Publications Scholarship, 275

The Fred R. McDaniel Memorial Scholarship, 184
The Jake McClain Driver KC5WXA Scholarship Fund, 185
Mahindra USA Women in Ag Scholarship, 279
MetLife Foundation Scholarship, 279
Southern Nursery Organization Sidney B. Meadows Scholarship, 472

California

10,000 Degrees Undergraduate Scholarships, 79
American Legion California Auxiliary General Scholarships, 123
American Legion California Oratorical Contest, 122
Animal Health International Scholarship, 270
Arysta LifeScience North America Scholarship, 270
ASTA Northern California Chapter - Richard Epping Scholarship, 513
BIA Cares of San Diego Scholarship, 230
BNSF Railway Company Scholarship, 271
Burlington Northern Santa Fe Foundation Scholarship, 115
Cady McDonnell Memorial Scholarship, 99
Cal Grant A & B Entitlement Award Program, 231
Cal Grant A and B Competitive Awards, 231
Cal Grant C Award, 232
California Child Development Grant Program, 232
California Farm Bureau Scholarship, 231
California Law Enforcement Personnel Dependents (LEPD) Grant Program, 232
California Teachers Association Martin Luther King, Jr., Memorial Scholarship, 233
California's Distinguished Young Woman Competition, 253
C.A.R. Scholarship, 231
Carl N. & Margaret Karcher Founders' Scholarship, 234
The Charles N. Fisher Memorial Scholarship, 182
Charles P. Lake - Rain For Rent Scholarship, 272
CTA Scholarship for Dependent Children, 233
CTA Scholarships for Members, 233
Epilepsy Foundation of San Diego County Scholarship, 258
Grange Insurance Scholarship, 293
HACEMOS Scholarship, 328
Horatio Alger California (Northern) Scholarship Program, 333
Italian Catholic Federation Scholarship, 349
Jewish Vocational Service Scholarship Fund, 357
JFCS Scholarship Fund, 595
Lucille Ganey Memorial Scholarship, 123
Mahindra USA Women in Ag Scholarship, 279
MetLife Foundation Scholarship, 279
Muggets Scholarship, 337
New Leader Scholarship, 79
Nissan North America, Inc. Scholarship Program, 330
Pete Wilson Journalism Scholarship, 462
San Jose Local Scholarships for Women, 96
Southern California Council Endowed Internship, 573
Toyota Motor Sales, U.S.A. Inc. Scholarship, 284
Travelers Foundation Scholarship, 113
Ventura County Japanese-American Citizens League Scholarships, 530
Wells Fargo Scholarship, 285
Wilbur-Ellis Company High School Scholarship, 285
William J. and Marijane E. Adams, Jr. Scholarship, 219

Colorado

American Legion Colorado Auxiliary Department President's Scholarship, 123
American Legion Colorado Auxiliary Department President's Scholarship for Junior Auxiliary Members, 124
American Legion Colorado Auxiliary Past Presidents Parley Nurse's Scholarship, 124
American Legion Colorado National High School Oratorical Contest, 123
Animal Health International Scholarship, 270
Burlington Northern Santa Fe Foundation Scholarship, 115
Cady McDonnell Memorial Scholarship, 99
Carl N. & Margaret Karcher Founders' Scholarship, 234
Clinton J. Helton Manufacturing Scholarship Award, 477
Colorado Council Volunteerism and Community Service Scholarship, 240
Colorado Masons Scholarship, 240
Colorado Society of CPAs General Scholarship, 241
Colorado Student Grant, 240
Colorado Work-Study Program, 240
The Daniels Scholarship, 251
Farmers Mutual Hail Insurance Company of Iowa Scholarship, 275
Grange Insurance Scholarship, 293
Greenhouse Scholars Program, 294
Helen K. and Arthur E. Johnson Foundation Scholarship, 112
HSF Achievement Scholarship, 328
John and Amy Rakestraw Scholarship, 277
Latin American Educational Scholarship, 368
Legacy of Hope, 498
Mark J. Smith Scholarship, 241
MetLife Foundation Scholarship, 279
RCMI Technical/Trade School Scholarship, 464
Rocky Mountain Coal Mining Institute Scholarship, 464
The Rocky Mountain Division Scholarship, 189
Sachs Foundation Undergraduate Grant, 466
Travelers Foundation Scholarship, 113
Violet Morrow Education Scholarship, 124
Wilbur-Ellis Company High School Scholarship, 285

Connecticut

American Legion Connecticut National High School Oratorical Contest, 124
Androscoggin Amateur Radio Club Scholarship, 179
The Byron Blanchard, N1EKV Memorial Scholarship Fund, 181
CBC Scholarship, 243
Connecticut Aid for Public College Students, 243
Connecticut Aid to Dependents of Deceased/POW/MIA Veterans, 243
Connecticut Capitol Scholarship Program, 244
Connecticut Independent College Student Grant, 244
Connecticut Minority Teacher Incentive Grant, 244
Connecticut Tuition Waiver for Senior Citizens, 244
Connecticut Tuition Waiver for Veterans, 244
Connecticut Tuition Waiver for Vietnam MIA/POW Dependents, 245
The Dr. James L. Lawson Memorial Scholarship, 183
HACEMOS Scholarship, 328
Kent Nutrition Group, Inc. Scholarship, 278
Lighthouse College-Bound Award, 370
Lighthouse Undergraduate Award, 371
Mahindra USA Women in Ag Scholarship, 279
Milton Fisher Scholarship for Innovation and Creativity, 463
Moody's Mega Math "M3" Challenge, 394
NEBHE's Tuition Break Regional Student Program, 421
The New England FEMARA Scholarship, 187
NTA Connecticut Scholarship, 514

Sonia Streuli Maguire Outstanding Scholastic Achievement Award, 502
Swiss Benevolent Society Pellegrini Scholarship, 502
Timothy and Palmer W. Bigelow, Jr. Scholarship, 337
Travelers Foundation Scholarship, 113
Weisman Scholarship, 245
Yankee Clipper Contest Club Youth Scholarship, 191

Delaware

American Legion Delaware Auxiliary Past Presidents Parley Nursing Scholarship, 125
B. Bradford Barnes Scholarship, 252
Charles L. Hebner Memorial Scholarship, 252
Christa McAuliffe Teacher Incentive Program, 594
Dana Campbell Memorial Scholarship, 353
Delaware Educational Benefits for Children of Deceased Veterans and Others, 253
Delaware Nursing Incentive Program, 594
Delaware Scholarship Incentive Program, 253
Diamond State Scholarship, 253
Herman M. Holloway, Sr. Memorial Scholarship, 253
Horatio Alger Delaware Scholarship Program, 333
Kent Nutrition Group, Inc. Scholarship, 278
Lighthouse College-Bound Award, 370
Lighthouse Undergraduate Award, 371
Moody's Mega Math "M3" Challenge, 394
Sonia Streuli Maguire Outstanding Scholastic Achievement Award, 502
Swiss Benevolent Society Pellegrini Scholarship, 502
Welsh Society of Philadelphia Undergraduate Scholarship, 538

District of Columbia

American Legion District of Columbia National High School Oratorical Contest, 125
DC Tuition Assistance Grant Program (DCTAG), 254
HACEMOS Scholarship, 328
Horatio Alger District of Columbia, Maryland and Virginia Scholarship Program, 333
Lighthouse College-Bound Award, 370
Lighthouse Undergraduate Award, 371
Moody's Mega Math "M3" Challenge, 394

Florida

Access to Better Learning and Education (ABLE) Grant Program, 263
American Legion Florida Auxiliary Department Scholarships, 126
American Legion Florida Auxiliary Memorial Scholarship, 126
American Legion Florida Eagle Scout of the Year, 125
American Legion Florida General Scholarship, 126
American Legion Florida High School Oratorical Contest, 126
The Andersons, Inc. Scholarship, 269
Animal Health International Scholarship, 270
The ARRL Earl I. Anderson Scholarship, 179
Bern Laxer Memorial Scholarship, 351
Birdsong Peanuts Scholarship, 271
Children of Florida UPS Employees Scholarship, 359
Coca-Cola Live Positively Publix Supermarkets Scholarship, 327
CSX Scholarship, 274
Dana Campbell Memorial Scholarship, 353
Fastline Publications Scholarship, 275
Florida Academic Scholars Award, 263
Florida Bright Futures Scholarship Program, 263
Florida First Generation Matching Grant Program, 263
Florida Gold Seal Vocational Scholars Award, 263
Florida Medallion Scholars Award, 264
Florida Public Postsecondary Career Education Student Assistance Grant Program, 264
Florida Scholarships for Children and Spouses of Deceased or Disabled Veterans, 264
Florida Student Assistance Grant (FSAG) Program, 264
Florida Work Experience Program, 561
Gulf Coast Hurricane Scholarships, 486
HACEMOS Scholarship, 328
IRARC Memorial, Joseph P. Rubino, WA4MMD, Scholarship, 185
Jose Marti Scholarship Challenge Grant Fund, 264
Lighthouse College-Bound Award, 370
Lighthouse Undergraduate Award, 371
Mahindra USA Women in Ag Scholarship, 279
Mary McLeod Bethune Scholarship, 265
MetLife Foundation Scholarship, 279
Minority Teacher Education Scholarship Program/Florida Fund for Minority Teachers, Inc., 265
Moody's Mega Math "M3" Challenge, 394
The North Fulton Amateur Radio League Scholarship Fund, 187
NTA Florida Scholarship, 514
The Orlando HamCation Scholarship, 188
Salute to Education Scholarship, 469
Southern Nursery Organization Sidney B. Meadows Scholarship, 472
State University System of Florida Theodore R. and Vivian M. Johnson Scholarship, 359
Travelers Foundation Scholarship, 113
The Wayne Nelson, KB4UT, Memorial Scholarship, 191
William L. Boyd, IV, Florida Resident Access Grant (FRAG) Program, 265

Georgia

Accel Program Grant, 289
American Legion Georgia Auxiliary Past Presidents Parley Nurses Scholarship, 127
American Legion Georgia Oratorical Contest, 127
American Legion Georgia Scholarship, 127
Animal Health International Scholarship, 270
ASHRAE Region IV Benny Bootle Scholarship, 196
Birdsong Peanuts Scholarship, 271
The Charles Clarke Cordle Memorial Scholarship, 181
CSX Scholarship, 274
Dana Campbell Memorial Scholarship, 353
The Eugene "Gene" Sallee, W4YFR, Memorial Scholarship, 183
Fastline Publications Scholarship, 275
Georgia Hope Grant - GED Recipient, 290
Georgia Hope Grant - Public Technical Institution, 290
Georgia Hope Scholarship - Private Institution, 290
Georgia Hope Scholarship - Public College or University, 290
Georgia Student Finance Commission Public Safety Memorial Grant, 291
Georgia Tuition Equalization Grant, 291
The Gwinnett Amateur Radio Society Scholarship, 184
HACEMOS Scholarship, 328
Horatio Alger Georgia Scholarship Program, 333
Horatio Alger Ronald C. Waranch Scholarship Program, 335
Lighthouse College-Bound Award, 370
Lighthouse Undergraduate Award, 371

Eligibility Indexes

Mahindra USA Women in Ag Scholarship, 279
MetLife Foundation Scholarship, 279
Moody's Mega Math "M3" Challenge, 394
NASA Space Grant Georgia Fellowship Program, 396
The North Fulton Amateur Radio League Scholarship Fund, 187
PAGE Foundation Scholarships, 460
Rose Acre Farms Scholarship, 283
The Southeastern DX Club Scholarship Fund, 190
Southern Nursery Organization Sidney B. Meadows Scholarship, 472
Student Aid Foundation Loan, 599
TAG Education Collaborative Web Challenge Contest, 502

Hawaii

A & B Ohana Scholarship, 295
ABC Stores Jumpstart Scholarship, 295
Aiea General Hospital Association Scholarship, 296
Allan Eldin & Agnes Sutorik Geiger Scholarship Fund, 296
Alma White-Delta Kappa Gamma Scholarship, 296
Ambassador Minerva Jean Falcon Hawaii Scholarship, 296
American Institute of Graphic Arts (AIGA) Honolulu Chapter Scholarship Fund, 296
American Legion Hawaii Oratorical Contest, 127
Arthur Jackman Memorial Scholarship, 297
Bal Dasa Scholarship Fund, 297
Bick Bickson Scholarship, 297
Blossom Kalama Evans Memorial Scholarship, 297
Booz Allen Scholarship, 297
Cady McDonnell Memorial Scholarship, 99
Camille C. Chidiac Fund, 297
Candon, Todd, & Seabolt Scholarship Fund, 298
Carl N. & Margaret Karcher Founders' Scholarship, 234
Castle & Cooke Mililani Technology Park Scholarship Fund, 298
Castle & Cooke W. Y. Yim Scholarship Fund, 298
Cora Aguda Manayan Fund, 298
CPB Works For You Scholarship, 298
Dan & Pauline Lutkenhouse & Hawaii Tropical Botanical Garden Scholarship, 299
David L. Irons Memorial Scholarship Fund, 299
Dolly Ching Scholarship Fund, 299
Doris & Clarence Glick Classical Music Scholarship, 299
Dr. Alvin and Monica Saake Scholarship, 299
Dr. and Mrs. Moon Park Scholarship, 300
Dr. Edison and Sallie Miyawaki Scholarship, 300
Dr. Hans & Clara Zimmerman Foundation Education Scholarship, 300
Dr. Hans and Clara Zimmerman Foundation Health Scholarship, 300
Eastside & Northshore Kauai Scholarship Fund, 300
Edward J. and Norma Doty Scholarship, 301
Edward Payson and Bernice Pi'ilani Irwin Scholarship Trust Fund, 301
E.E. Black Scholarship, 301
Elena Albano "Maka'alohilohi" Scholarship Fund, 301
Ellen Hamada Fashion Design Scholarship, 301
Ellison Onizuka Memorial Scholarship, 302
Esther Kanagawa Memorial Art Scholarship, 302
F. Koehnen Ltd. Scholarship Fund, 302
Filipino Nurses' Organization of Hawaii Scholarship, 302
Financial Women International Scholarship, 302
Fletcher & Fritzi Hoffmann Education Fund, 303
Frances S. Watanabe Memorial Scholarship, 303
George & Augusta Rapozo Kama'aina Scholarship Fund, 303
George & Lucille Cushnie Scholarship, 303
George Mason Business Scholarship Fund, 303
Gerrit R. Ludwig Scholarship, 304
Good Eats Scholarship Fund, 304
Grace Pacific Outstanding Scholars Fund, 304
Guy Marshall Scholarship Fund, 304
Haseko Training Fund, 305
Hawaii Chapter/David T. Woolsey Scholarship, 366
Hawaii Community Scholarship Fund, 305
Hawaii GEAR UP Scholars Program, 305
Hawaii Pacific Gerontological Society Nursing Scholarship Fund, 305
Hawaii Pizza Hut Scholarship Fund, 305
Hawaii Society of Certified Public Accountants Scholarship Fund, 306
H.C. Shipman Vocational Scholarship Fund, 306
Henry A. Zuberano Scholarship, 306
Henry and Dorothy Castle Memorial Scholarship, 306
Herbert & Ollie Brook Fund, 306
Hew-Shinn Scholarship Fund, 307
Hideko & Zenzo Matsuyama Scholarship Fund, 307
Hilo Chinese School Scholarship, 307
Hoku Scholarship Fund, 307
Hokulani Hawaii Fund, 307
Hokuli'a Foundation Scholarship Fund, 307
Hon Chew Hee Scholarship Fund, 308
Ho'omaka Hou - A New Beginning Fund, 308
Ian Doane Smith Scholarship Fund, 308
Ichiro & Masako Hirata Scholarship, 308
Ida M. Pope Memorial Scholarship, 308
Isemoto Contracting Co., Ltd. Scholarship Fund, 308
Iwamoto Family Scholarship, 309
Iwamoto Family Vocational Scholarship, 309
Jean Estes Epstein Charitable Foundation Scholarship, 309
Jean Fitzgerald Scholarship Fund, 309
Jean Ileialoha Beniamina Scholarship for Ni'ihau Students Fund, 309
Johanna Drew Cluney Scholarship, 310
John & Anne Clifton Scholarship Fund, 310
John Dawe Dental Education Fund, 310
John M. Ross Foundation Scholarship, 310
Joseph & Alice Duarte Memorial Fund, 310
Juliette M. Atherton Scholarship - Minister's Sons and Daughters, 311
Kahala Nui Residents Scholarship Fund, 311
Kalihi Education Coalition Scholarship Fund, 311
Ka'iulani Home for Girls Trust Scholarship, 311
Kapolei Business & Community Scholarship, 311
Ka'a'awa Community Fund, 311
Kawasaki-McGaha Scholarship Fund, 312
Kazuma and Ichiko Hisanaga Scholarship Fund, 312
Kenneth Makinney & David T. Pietsch Familes Scholarship Fund, 312
King Kekaulike High School Scholarship, 312
K.M. Hatano Scholarship, 313
Kohala Ditch Education Fund, 313
Koloa Scholarship, 313
Korean University Club Scholarship Fund, 313
Korean War Veteran's Children's Scholarship, 313
Kurt W. Schneider Memorial Scholarship Fund, 314
Laura N. Dowsett Fund, 314
Laura Rowe Burdick Scholarship Fund, 314
Lillian B. Reynolds Scholarship, 314
Logan Nainoa Fujimoto Memorial Scholarship, 314

March Taylor Educational Fund Scholarship, 315
Margaret Follett Haskins Hawaii Scholarship, 315
Margaret Follett Haskins (Maui) Scholarship, 315
Margaret Jones Memorial Nursing Scholarship, 315
Marion Maccarrell Scott Scholarship, 315
Mary Josephine Bloder Scholarship, 316
Mildred Towle Scholarship - Study Abroad, 316
Mitsuo Shito Public Housing Scholarship, 316
Nick Van Pernis Scholarship, 316
Oscar and Rosetta Fish Fund, 317
Ouida Mundy Hill Memorial Fund, 317
Paulina L. Sorg Scholarship, 317
Perry & Sally Sorenson Scholarship for Dependents of Hospitality Workers, 317
Perry & Sally Sorenson Scholarship for Foster Youth, 318
Peter R. Papworth Scholarship, 318
Philippine Nurses' Association Scholarship, 318
PRSA-Hawaii/Roy Leffingwell Public Relations Scholarship, 318
Ray Yoshida Kauai Fine Arts Scholarship, 318
Raymond F. Cain Scholarship Fund, 318
Rich Meiers Health Administration Fund, 319
Richard Smart Scholarship, 319
Richie M. Gregory Fund, 319
Rise Up Scholarship, 319
Robanna Fund, 319
Ron Bright Scholarship, 319
Rosemary & Nellie Ebrie Fund, 320
Safeway Foundation Hawaii Scholarship Fund, 320
Sarah Rosenberg Teacher Education Scholarship, 320
Senator Richard M. & Dr. Ruth Matsuura Scholarship Fund, 320
Shirley McKown Scholarship Fund, 320
Shuichi, Katsu and Itsuyo Suga Scholarship, 321
Takehiko Hasegawa Academic Scholarship, 321
Takehiko Hasegawa Kaua'i Community College Scholarship, 321
Thz Fo Farm Fund, 321
Times Supermarket Shop & Score Scholarship, 321
Tommy Lee Memorial Scholarship Fund, 322
Tongan Cultural Society Scholarship, 322
Toraji & Toki Yoshinaga Scholarship, 322
Troy Barboza Educational Fund Scholarship, 322
Vicki Willder Scholarship Fund, 322
Victoria S. and Bradley L. Geist Foundation Scholarship, 323
Will J. Henderson Scholarship Fund in Hawaii, 323
William J. and Marijane E. Adams, Jr. Scholarship, 219
William James & Dorothy Bading Lanquist Fund, 323

Idaho

American Legion Idaho Auxiliary Nurse's Scholarship, 128
American Legion Idaho Oratorical Contest, 127
American Legion Idaho Scholarships, 128
Animal Health International Scholarship, 270
The ARRL Northwestern Division Scholarship Fund, 180
ASTA Pacific Northwest Chapter/William Hunt Scholarship, 513
Cady McDonnell Memorial Scholarship, 99
Carl N. & Margaret Karcher Founders' Scholarship, 234
Charles P. Lake - Rain For Rent Scholarship, 272
Earl Dedman Memorial Scholarship, 103
Fastline Publications Scholarship, 275
Grange Insurance Scholarship, 293
Grow Your Own Teacher Scholarship Program, 339
Idaho Freedom Scholarship, 339
Idaho Governor's Cup Scholarship, 340
Idaho Opportunity Scholarship, 340
Idaho State Board of Education Public Safety Officer Dependent Scholarship, 340
KeyBank Scholarship, 278
Mahindra USA Women in Ag Scholarship, 279
The Mary Lou Brown Scholarship, 186
MetLife Foundation Scholarship, 279
Robert R. Lee Promise Category A Scholarship, 340
Robert R. Lee Promise Category B Scholarship, 341
Treacy Foundation Scholarship, 518
United Dairymen of Idaho Scholarship, 284
Wilbur-Ellis Company High School Scholarship, 285

Illinois

American Legion Illinois Auxiliary Ada Mucklestone Memorial Scholarship, 129
American Legion Illinois Auxiliary Special Education Teaching Scholarships, 129
American Legion Illinois Auxiliary Student Nurse Scholarship, 129
American Legion Illinois Boy Scout Scholarship, 128
American Legion Illinois Oratorical Contest, 128
American Legion Illinois Scholarships, 128
Americanism Essay Contest Scholarship, 129
The Andersons, Inc. Scholarship, 269
The ARRL Earl I. Anderson Scholarship, 179
Arysta LifeScience North America Scholarship, 270
Beck's Hybrids Scholarship, 270
Blain's Farm & Feet Scholarship, 271
BNSF Railway Company Scholarship, 271
Casey's General Stores, Inc. Scholarship, 272
The Chicago FM Club Scholarship, 182
CSX Scholarship, 274
David Arver Memorial Scholarship, 88
The Edmond A. Metzger Scholarship, 183
Farmers Mutual Hail Insurance Company of Iowa Scholarship, 275
Fastline Publications Scholarship, 275
The Francis Walton Memorial Scholarship, 183
Golden Apple Scholars of Illinois Program, 291
Greenhouse Scholars Program, 294
HACEMOS Scholarship, 328
Horatio Alger Illinois Scholarship Program, 333
Hormel Foods Corporation Scholarship, 277
ILC Resources Scholarship, 277
Illinois Monetary Award Program (MAP), 342
Illinois National Guard Grant, 342
Illinois Special Education Teacher Tuition Waiver, 342
Illinois Veteran Grant (IVG) Program, 342
The Indianapolis Amateur Radio Association Fund, 184
Italian Catholic Federation Scholarship, 349
Kent Nutrition Group, Inc. Scholarship, 278
Mahindra USA Women in Ag Scholarship, 279
Marie Sheehe Trade School Scholarship, 129
MetLife Foundation Scholarship, 279
Midwest Student Exchange Program, 386
Mildred R. Knoles Scholarship, 130
Minority Teachers of Illinois Scholarship, 343

Moody's Mega Math "M3" Challenge, 394
The Peoria Area Amateur Radio Club Scholarship, 188
Rose Acre Farms Scholarship, 283
The Six Meter Club of Chicago Scholarship, 189
Travelers Foundation Scholarship, 113

Indiana

American Legion Indiana Americanism and Government Test, 130
American Legion Indiana Auxiliary Past Presidents Parley Nursing Scholarship, 131
American Legion Indiana Eagle Scout of the Year Scholarship, 130
American Legion Indiana Family Scholarship, 130
American Legion Indiana Oratorical Contest, 130
American Legion Legacy Scholarship, 146
The Andersons, Inc. Scholarship, 269
The ARRL Earl I. Anderson Scholarship, 179
Beck's Hybrids Scholarship, 270
Casey's General Stores, Inc. Scholarship, 272
Chapter 56 - Fort Wayne Scholarship, 476
The Chicago FM Club Scholarship, 182
Chief Industries Scholarship, 273
David Arver Memorial Scholarship, 88
The Edmond A. Metzger Scholarship, 183
Edna M. Barcus Memorial Scholarship and Hoosier Scholarship, 131
Farmers Mutual Hail Insurance Company of Iowa Scholarship, 275
Fastline Publications Scholarship, 275
Fifth Third Bank of Central Indiana Scholarship, 275
The Francis Walton Memorial Scholarship, 183
Frank O'Bannon Grant, 497
Hormel Foods Corporation Scholarship, 277
Indiana Minority Teacher & Special Education Services Scholarship, 497
Indiana National Guard Supplemental Grant, 498
Indiana Nursing Scholarship, 498
Indiana Twenty-First Century Scholars Program, 498
The Indianapolis Amateur Radio Association Fund, 184
Kent Nutrition Group, Inc. Scholarship, 278
MetLife Foundation Scholarship, 279
Midwest Student Exchange Program, 386
The Mitch Daniels Early Graduation Scholarship, 498
Moody's Mega Math "M3" Challenge, 394
Paradise Tomato Kitchens Scholarship, 281
Rose Acre Farms Scholarship, 283
The Six Meter Club of Chicago Scholarship, 189
Toyota Motor Sales, U.S.A. Inc. Scholarship, 284

Iowa

Agricredit Acceptance LLC Scholarship, 268
AICP Heartland Chapter Jim Latteman Scholarship, 223
All Iowa Opportunity Scholarship, 348
American Legion Department of Iowa Scholarships, 132
American Legion Iowa Auxiliary Past President's Scholarship, 132
American Legion Iowa Boy Scout of the Year Scholarship, 131
American Legion Iowa Oratorical Contest, 131
American Legion Iowa Outstanding Citizen of Boys State Scholarship, 132
The Andersons, Inc. Scholarship, 269
Animal Health International Scholarship, 270
ARRL Foundation PHD Scholarship, 180
Arysta LifeScience North America Scholarship, 270
Blain's Farm & Feet Scholarship, 271
BNSF Railway Company Scholarship, 271
Casey's General Stores, Inc. Scholarship, 272
David Arver Memorial Scholarship, 88
Earl R. Sorensen Memorial Scholarships, 274
Farmers Mutual Hail Insurance Company of Iowa Scholarship, 275
Fastline Publications Scholarship, 275
Governor Terry E. Branstad Iowa State Fair Scholarship, 348
Harriet Hoffman Memorial Scholarship, 132
Horatio Alger Ak-Sar-Ben Scholarship Program, 332
Hormel Foods Corporation Scholarship, 277
ILC Resources Scholarship, 277
Iowa Grant, 348
Iowa Interstate Railroad, Ltd. Scholarship, 277
Iowa National Guard Educational Assistance Program, 348
Iowa Tuition Grant, 348
Iowa Vocational-Technical Tuition Grant, 349
Kent Nutrition Group, Inc. Scholarship, 278
Mahindra USA Women in Ag Scholarship, 279
Mary Virginia Macrea Memorial Scholarship, 132
MetLife Foundation Scholarship, 279
Mills Fleet Farm Scholarship, 280
North Central Region Scholarship, 479
The Paul and Helen L. Grauer Scholarship, 188
The Ray, NØRP, & Katie, WØKTE, Pautz Scholarship, 189
Robert D. Blue Scholarship, 349
Rose Acre Farms Scholarship, 283
Theisen's Home Farm Auto Scholarship, 284

Kansas

AICP Heartland Chapter Jim Latteman Scholarship, 223
Albert M. Lappin Scholarship, 133
American Legion Kansas Auxiliary Department Scholarships, 135
American Legion Kansas Music Scholarship, 133
American Legion Kansas Oratorical Contest, 133
Animal Health International Scholarship, 270
ARRL Foundation PHD Scholarship, 180
Arysta LifeScience North America Scholarship, 270
BNSF Railway Company Scholarship, 271
Burlington Northern Santa Fe Foundation Scholarship, 115
Career Technical Workforce Grant, 359
Casey's General Stores, Inc. Scholarship, 272
Chapter 52 - Wichita Scholarship, 476
Charles and Annette Hill Scholarship, 133
David Arver Memorial Scholarship, 88
Dr. Click Cowger Scholarship, 134
Farmers Mutual Hail Insurance Company of Iowa Scholarship, 275
Fastline Publications Scholarship, 275
Hormel Foods Corporation Scholarship, 277
Hugh A. Smith Scholarship, 134
ILC Resources Scholarship, 277
The Irving W. Cook WA0CGS Scholarship, 185
John and Geraldine Hobble Licensed Practical Nursing Scholarship, 134
Kansas Military Service Scholarship, 360
Kansas ROTC Service Scholarship, 360
Kansas State Scholarship, 360
Kansas Vocational Education Scholarship, 361

Kent Nutrition Group, Inc. Scholarship, 278
Mahindra USA Women in Ag Scholarship, 279
MetLife Foundation Scholarship, 279
Midwest Student Exchange Program, 386
National Guard Educational Assistance Program, 361
The Paul and Helen L. Grauer Scholarship, 188
The Ray, NØRP, & Katie, WØKTE, Pautz Scholarship, 189
Rosedale Post 346 Scholarship, 134
Ted and Nora Anderson Scholarship, 134
Travelers Foundation Scholarship, 113
Universal Lubricants Scholarship, 285
Wilbur-Ellis Company High School Scholarship, 285

Kentucky

Allen and Loureena Weber Scholarship, 474
American Legion Kentucky Auxiliary Mary Barrett Marshall Scholarship, 135
American Legion Kentucky Department Oratorical Awards, 135
Beck's Hybrids Scholarship, 270
CSX Scholarship, 274
Dana Campbell Memorial Scholarship, 353
Farm Credit Services of Mid-America Scholarship, 275
Fastline Publications Scholarship, 275
Kent Nutrition Group, Inc. Scholarship, 278
Kentucky College Access Program Grant (CAP), 362
Kentucky Early Childhood Development Scholarship, 362
Kentucky Educational Excellence Scholarship (KEES), 362
Kentucky Go Higher Grant, 363
Kentucky Mary Jo Young Scholarship, 363
Kentucky Teacher Scholarship, 363
Kentucky Tuition Grant, 363
Kentucky Work-Study Program, 566
Laura Blackburn Memorial Scholarship, 135
Mahindra USA Women in Ag Scholarship, 279
Mary Barrett Marshall Student Loan Fund, 593
MetLife Foundation Scholarship, 279
Moody's Mega Math "M3" Challenge, 394
NTA Pat & Jim Host Scholarship, 516
Paradise Tomato Kitchens Scholarship, 281
Southern Nursery Organization Sidney B. Meadows Scholarship, 472
Toyota Motor Sales, U.S.A. Inc. Scholarship, 284

Louisiana

Animal Health International Scholarship, 270
ASHRAE Region VIII Scholarship, 196
Chafee Educational and Training Voucher, 372
Chefs of Louisiana Cookery Scholarship, 352
Dana Campbell Memorial Scholarship, 353
Fastline Publications Scholarship, 275
The Fred R. McDaniel Memorial Scholarship, 184
Gulf Coast Hurricane Scholarships, 486
Horatio Alger Louisiana Scholarship Program, 334
The Jake McClain Driver KC5WXA Scholarship Fund, 185
Louisiana Go Grants, 372
Louisiana Rockefeller Wildlife Scholarship, 372
Louisiana Taylor Opportunity Program for Students (TOPS) Award, 372
Louisiana TOPS Tech Early Start Program, 373
Louisiana Tops Tech Program, 373
Louisiana Veterans Affairs Survivors and Dependents Education Program, 371
Mahindra USA Women in Ag Scholarship, 279
MetLife Foundation Scholarship, 279
Moody's Mega Math "M3" Challenge, 394
Southern Nursery Organization Sidney B. Meadows Scholarship, 472

Maine

AGC of Maine Scholarship Program, 220
American Legion Maine Auxiliary Presidents Parley Nursing Scholarship, 136
American Legion Maine Auxiliary Scholarship, 136
American Legion Maine Children and Youth Scholarship, 136
Androscoggin Amateur Radio Club Scholarship, 179
The Byron Blanchard, N1EKV Memorial Scholarship Fund, 181
Daniel E. Lambert Memorial Scholarship, 136
The Dr. James L. Lawson Memorial Scholarship, 183
James V. Day Scholarship, 136
The Joel Abromson Memorial Scholarship, 259
Kent Nutrition Group, Inc. Scholarship, 278
Lighthouse College-Bound Award, 370
Lighthouse Undergraduate Award, 371
Mahindra USA Women in Ag Scholarship, 279
Maine Innkeepers Association Scholarship, 374
The Maine Loan, 595
Maine Metal Products Association Scholarship, 374
Maine Society of Professional Engineers Scholarship Program, 375
Maine Veterans Services Dependents Educational Benefits, 374
Moody's Mega Math "M3" Challenge, 394
NEBHE's Tuition Break Regional Student Program, 421
The New England FEMARA Scholarship, 187
OMNE/Nursing Leaders of Maine Scholarship, 440
Senator George J. Mitchell Scholarship, 471
Timothy and Palmer W. Bigelow, Jr. Scholarship, 337
Yankee Clipper Contest Club Youth Scholarship, 191

Maryland

Adler Science and Math Scholarship, 137
American Legion Maryland Auxiliary Past Presidents Parley Scholarship, 138
American Legion Maryland Auxiliary Scholarship, 138
American Legion Maryland Boys State Scholarship, 137
American Legion Maryland Oratorical Contest, 137
American Legion Maryland Scholarship, 137
Carville M. Akehurst Memorial Scholarship, 337
Charles W. Riley Fire and Emergency Medical Services Tuition Reimbursement Program, 375
The Cynthia E. Morgan Memorial Scholarship Fund, 248
Dana Campbell Memorial Scholarship, 353
The Gary Wagner, K3OMI, Scholarship, 184
Horatio Alger District of Columbia, Maryland and Virginia Scholarship Program, 333
Howard P. Rawlings Guaranteed Access Grant, 376
Kent Nutrition Group, Inc. Scholarship, 278
Letitia B. Carter Scholarship, 463
Lighthouse College-Bound Award, 370
Lighthouse Undergraduate Award, 371
Mahindra USA Women in Ag Scholarship, 279
Marcia S. Harris Legacy Fund Scholarship, 463
Maryland Delegate Scholarship, 376

Maryland Educational Assistance Grant, 376
Maryland Edward T. Conroy Memorial Scholarship Program, 376
Maryland Jack F. Tolbert Memorial Grant, 377
Maryland Part-Time Grant Program, 377
Maryland Senatorial Scholarship, 377
Maryland Tuition Waiver for Foster Care Recipients, 378
Moody's Mega Math "M3" Challenge, 394
Southern Nursery Organization Sidney B. Meadows Scholarship, 472
Welsh Society of Philadelphia Undergraduate Scholarship, 538

Massachusetts

Agnes M. Lindsey Scholarship, 378
American Legion Department of Massachusetts Oratorical Contest, 138
American Legion Massachusetts Auxiliary Past Presidents Parley Scholarship, 139
American Legion Massachusetts Auxiliary Scholarship, 139
American Legion Massachusetts General and Nursing Scholarships, 138
Androscoggin Amateur Radio Club Scholarship, 179
The Byron Blanchard, N1EKV Memorial Scholarship Fund, 181
Categorical Tuition Waiver, 378
DCF Foster Child Tuition Waiver and Fee Assistance Program, 378
The Dr. James L. Lawson Memorial Scholarship, 183
Foster Child Grant Program, 378
Garden Club Federation of Massachusetts, 286
Gear Up Scholarship Program, 379
High Technology Scholar/Intern Tuition Waiver Program, 379
Incentive Program for Aspiring Teachers, 379
John and Abigail Adams Scholarship, 379
Kent Nutrition Group, Inc. Scholarship, 278
Lighthouse College-Bound Award, 370
Lighthouse Undergraduate Award, 371
Mahindra USA Women in Ag Scholarship, 279
Massachusetts Cash Grant Program, 380
Massachusetts Christian A. Herter Memorial Scholarship Program, 380
Massachusetts Early Childhood Educators Scholarship, 380
Massachusetts Educational Rewards Grant Program, 380
Massachusetts Gilbert Matching Student Grant, 380
Massachusetts MASSgrant Program, 381
Massachusetts Math and Science Teachers Scholarship, 381
Massachusetts No Interest Loan, 595
Massachusetts Paraprofessional Teacher Preparation Grant Program, 381
Massachusetts Part-Time Grant Program, 381
Massachusetts Public Service Grant Program, 382
Moody's Mega Math "M3" Challenge, 394
NEBHE's Tuition Break Regional Student Program, 421
The New England FEMARA Scholarship, 187
NTA Massachusetts Scholarship, 515
One Family Scholars Program, 440
Paul Tsongas Scholarship Program, 382
PHCC of Massachusetts Auxiliary Scholarship, 457
September 11, 2001 Tragedy Tuition Waiver Program, 382
Stanley Z. Koplik Certificate of Mastery Tuition Waiver Program, 382
Timothy and Palmer W. Bigelow, Jr. Scholarship, 337
Valedictorial Tuition Waiver Program, 382
Yankee Clipper Contest Club Youth Scholarship, 191

Michigan

American Legion Michigan Auxiliary Medical Career Scholarships, 140
American Legion Michigan Auxiliary Memorial Scholarship, 140
American Legion Michigan Auxiliary National President's Scholarship, 140
American Legion Michigan Oratorical Contest, 139
The Andersons, Inc. Scholarship, 269
The ARRL Earl I. Anderson Scholarship, 179
Beck's Hybrids Scholarship, 270
Children of Veterans Tuition Grant, 384
David Arver Memorial Scholarship, 88
Earl R. Sorensen Memorial Scholarships, 274
Farmers Mutual Hail Insurance Company of Iowa Scholarship, 275
Fastline Publications Scholarship, 275
Guy M. Wilson Scholarship, 139
HACEMOS Scholarship, 328
Hormel Foods Corporation Scholarship, 277
Kent Nutrition Group, Inc. Scholarship, 278
Mahindra USA Women in Ag Scholarship, 279
MetLife Foundation Scholarship, 279
Michigan Competitive Scholarship, 385
Michigan Society of Professional Engineers Scholarships for High School Seniors, 385
Michigan Tuition Grant, 385
Michigan Tuition Incentive Program, 385
Midwest Student Exchange Program, 386
Moody's Mega Math "M3" Challenge, 394
MSGC Undergraduate Underrepresented Minority Fellowship Program, 398
Nissan North America, Inc. Scholarship Program, 330
North Central Region Scholarship, 479
NTA New Horizons - Kathy LeTarte Scholarship, 515
Toyota Motor Sales, U.S.A. Inc. Scholarship, 284
Wilbur-Ellis Company High School Scholarship, 285
William D. & Jewell W. Brewer Scholarship Trusts, 139

Minnesota

AICP Heartland Chapter Jim Latteman Scholarship, 223
American Family Insurance Scholarship, 269
American Legion Minnesota Auxiliary Department Scholarship, 141
American Legion Minnesota Auxiliary Past Presidents Parley Health Care Scholarship, 141
American Legion Minnesota Legionnaire Insurance Trust Scholarship, 140
American Legion Minnesota Memorial Scholarship, 141
American Legion Minnesota Oratorical Contest, 141
The Andersons, Inc. Scholarship, 269
Animal Health International Scholarship, 270
BNSF Railway Company Scholarship, 271
Burlington Northern Santa Fe Foundation Scholarship, 115
Carol Bauhs Benson Scholarship, 82
Casey's General Stores, Inc. Scholarship, 272
Courage Center Scholarship for People with Disabilities, 248
David Arver Memorial Scholarship, 88
Farmers Mutual Hail Insurance Company of Iowa Scholarship, 275
Fastline Publications Scholarship, 275
Hormel Foods Corporation Scholarship, 277
ILC Resources Scholarship, 277
MetLife Foundation Scholarship, 279

Midwest Student Exchange Program, 386
Mills Fleet Farm Scholarship, 280
Minnesota Educational Assistance for Veterans, 387
Minnesota Indian Scholarship Program, 388
Minnesota Post-Secondary Child Care Grant, 388
Minnesota Public Safety Officers Survivors Program, 388
Minnesota State Grant Program, 388
Minnesota Work-Study Program, 568
Moody's Mega Math "M3" Challenge, 394
North Central Region Scholarship, 479
Travelers Foundation Scholarship, 113
Wilbur-Ellis Company High School Scholarship, 285

Mississippi

American Legion Mississippi Auxiliary Scholarship, 141
Animal Health International Scholarship, 270
Critical Needs Teacher Loan/Scholarship, 596
Dana Campbell Memorial Scholarship, 353
Fastline Publications Scholarship, 275
The Fred R. McDaniel Memorial Scholarship, 184
Gulf Coast Hurricane Scholarships, 486
The Jake McClain Driver KC5WXA Scholarship Fund, 185
John and Amy Rakestraw Scholarship, 277
Leveraging Educational Assistance Partnership Program (LEAP), 389
The Magnolia DX Association Scholarship, 186
Mahindra USA Women in Ag Scholarship, 279
MetLife Foundation Scholarship, 279
Mississippi Eminent Scholars Grant, 389
Mississippi Health Care Professions Loan/Scholarship, 596
Mississippi Higher Education Legislative Plan, 390
Mississippi Resident Tuition Assistance Grant, 390
The Mississippi Scholarship, 187
Mississippi William Winter Teacher Scholar Loan Program, 597
Moody's Mega Math "M3" Challenge, 394
Nissan North America, Inc. Scholarship Program, 330
Nissan Scholarship, 390
Southern Nursery Organization Sidney B. Meadows Scholarship, 472
Toyota Motor Sales, U.S.A. Inc. Scholarship, 284

Missouri

Access Missouri Financial Assistance Program, 391
AICP Heartland Chapter Jim Latteman Scholarship, 223
American Family Insurance Scholarship, 269
American Legion Missouri Auxiliary National President's Scholarship, 144
American Legion Missouri Auxiliary Past Presidents Parley Scholarship, 144
American Legion Missouri Auxiliary Scholarship, 144
American Legion Missouri Commander's Scholarship Fund, 142
American Legion Missouri Oratorical Contest, 142
Animal Health International Scholarship, 270
ARRL Foundation PHD Scholarship, 180
Casey's General Stores, Inc. Scholarship, 272
Charles L. Bacon Memorial Scholarship, 142
CSX Scholarship, 274
Dana Campbell Memorial Scholarship, 353
David Arver Memorial Scholarship, 88
Erman W. Taylor Memorial Scholarship, 142
Farmers Mutual Hail Insurance Company of Iowa Scholarship, 275
Fastline Publications Scholarship, 275
HACEMOS Scholarship, 328
Horatio Alger Missouri Scholarship Program, 334
Hormel Foods Corporation Scholarship, 277
ILC Resources Scholarship, 277
Joseph J. Frank Scholarship, 143
Kent Nutrition Group, Inc. Scholarship, 278
Lillie Lois Ford Boys' Scholarship, 143
Lillie Lois Ford Girls' Scholarship, 143
Mahindra USA Women in Ag Scholarship, 279
Marguerite Ross Barnett Memorial Scholarship, 391
M.D. Jack Murphy Memorial Nurses Training Fund, 143
MetLife Foundation Scholarship, 279
Midwest Student Exchange Program, 386
Minority and Underrepresented Environmental Literacy Program, 391
Minority Teaching Scholarship, 391
Missouri Higher Education "Bright Flight" Academic Scholarship, 392
Missouri League for Nursing Scholarship, 392
NASA Missouri State Space Grant Undergraduate Scholarship, 399
The Paul and Helen L. Grauer Scholarship, 188
Public Safety Officer or Employee's Child Survivor Grant, 392
The Ray, NØRP, & Katie, WØKTE, Pautz Scholarship, 189
Rose Acre Farms Scholarship, 283
Shane Dean Voyles Memorial Scholarship, 144
Southern Nursery Organization Sidney B. Meadows Scholarship, 472
Toyota Motor Sales, U.S.A. Inc. Scholarship, 284

Montana

Aloha Scholarship, 144
American Legion Montana Auxiliary Scholarships (1), 145
American Legion Montana Auxiliary Scholarships (2), 145
Animal Health International Scholarship, 270
The ARRL Northwestern Division Scholarship Fund, 180
ASTA Pacific Northwest Chapter/William Hunt Scholarship, 513
BNSF Railway Company Scholarship, 271
Burlington Northern Santa Fe Foundation Scholarship, 115
Cady McDonnell Memorial Scholarship, 99
Earl Dedman Memorial Scholarship, 103
Horatio Alger Montana Scholarship Program, 334
Legacy of Hope, 498
The Mary Lou Brown Scholarship, 186
MetLife Foundation Scholarship, 279
Montana Governor's Best and Brightest Merit Scholarship, 393
Montana Governor's Best and Brightest Merit-at-Large Scholarship, 393
Montana Governor's Best and Brightest Need Based Scholarship, 393
Montana Higher Education Grant, 394
Montana Honorably Discharged Veteran Fee Waiver, 394
Montana University System Honor Scholarship, 394
Peterson Family Scholarship, 282
RCMI Technical/Trade School Scholarship, 464
Rocky Mountain Coal Mining Institute Scholarship, 464
Treacy Foundation Scholarship, 518
Wilbur-Ellis Company High School Scholarship, 285

Nebraska

AICP Heartland Chapter Jim Latteman Scholarship, 223
American Legion Nebraska Auxiliary Graduate Scholarship, 148
American Legion Nebraska Auxiliary Junior Member Scholarship, 148
American Legion Nebraska Auxiliary Nurse Gift Tuition Scholarships, 148
American Legion Nebraska Auxiliary Practical Nursing Scholarship, 148
American Legion Nebraska Auxiliary Student Aid Grant or Vocational Technical Scholarship, 148
American Legion Nebraska Oratorical Contest, 147
American Legion Nebraska President's Scholarship, 148
The Andersons, Inc. Scholarship, 269
Animal Health International Scholarship, 270
ARRL Foundation PHD Scholarship, 180
Averyl Elaine Keriakedes Memorial Scholarship, 149
Behlen Mfg. Co./Walter and Ruby Behlen Memorial Scholarship, 271
BNSF Railway Company Scholarship, 271
Casey's General Stores, Inc. Scholarship, 272
Chief Industries Scholarship, 273
David Arver Memorial Scholarship, 88
Edgar J. Boschult Memorial Scholarship, 147
Farmers Mutual Hail Insurance Company of Iowa Scholarship, 275
Fastline Publications Scholarship, 275
Horatio Alger Ak-Sar-Ben Scholarship Program, 332
Hormel Foods Corporation Scholarship, 277
ILC Resources Scholarship, 277
Kent Nutrition Group, Inc. Scholarship, 278
Maynard Jensen American Legion Memorial Scholarship, 147
MetLife Foundation Scholarship, 279
Midwest Student Exchange Program, 386
Nebraska Opportunity Grant, 421
North Central Region Scholarship, 479
The Paul and Helen L. Grauer Scholarship, 188
The Ray, NØRP, & Katie, WØKTE, Pautz Scholarship, 189
Roberta Marie Stretch Memorial Scholarship, 149
Ruby Paul Campaign Fund Scholarship, 149
Virgil Eihusen Foundation Scholarship, 285
Wilbur-Ellis Company High School Scholarship, 285

Nevada

ABC Stores Jumpstart Scholarship, 295
American Legion Nevada Auxiliary Past Presidents Parley Nurses' Scholarship, 149
American Legion Nevada Auxiliary President's Scholarship, 150
American Legion Nevada Oratorical Contest, 149
Animal Health International Scholarship, 270
Cady McDonnell Memorial Scholarship, 99
Carl N. & Margaret Karcher Founders' Scholarship, 234
Italian Catholic Federation Scholarship, 349
Mahindra USA Women in Ag Scholarship, 279
Silver Eagle Indian Scholarship, 150
William J. and Marijane E. Adams, Jr. Scholarship, 219

New Hampshire

Abbie Sargent Memorial Scholarship, 80
Adrienne Alix Scholarship, 152
Albert T. Marcoux Memorial Scholarship, 150
American Legion New Hampshire Auxiliary Past Presidents Parley Nurses' Scholarship, 152
American Legion New Hampshire Boys State Scholarship, 150
American Legion New Hampshire Department Vocational Scholarship, 150
American Legion New Hampshire Oratorical Contest, 150
Androscoggin Amateur Radio Club Scholarship, 179
The Byron Blanchard, N1EKV Memorial Scholarship Fund, 181
Christa McAuliffe Memorial Scholarship, 151
Department of New Hampshire Scholarship, 151
The Dr. James L. Lawson Memorial Scholarship, 183
Elsie B. Brown Scholarship Fund, 152
Grace S. High Memorial Child Welfare Scholarship Fund, 152
John A. High Child Welfare Scholarship, 151
Kent Nutrition Group, Inc. Scholarship, 278
Lighthouse College-Bound Award, 370
Lighthouse Undergraduate Award, 371
Mahindra USA Women in Ag Scholarship, 279
Marion J. Bagley Scholarship, 152
Moody's Mega Math "M3" Challenge, 394
NEBHE's Tuition Break Regional Student Program, 421
The New England FEMARA Scholarship, 187
Raymond K. Conley Memorial Scholarship, 151
Timothy and Palmer W. Bigelow, Jr. Scholarship, 337
Yankee Clipper Contest Club Youth Scholarship, 191

New Jersey

AIA New Jersey Scholarship Foundation, 117
American Legion New Jersey Auxiliary Department Scholarships, 153
American Legion New Jersey Auxiliary Past Presidents Parley Nurses' Scholarship, 153
American Legion New Jersey Department of New Jersey Scholarship, 153
American Legion New Jersey Oratorical Contest, 153
Caroline Thorn Kissel Summer Environmental Studies Scholarship, 286
Claire Oliphant Memorial Scholarship, 153
Frank D. Visceglia Memorial Scholarship, 227
HACEMOS Scholarship, 328
Kent Nutrition Group, Inc. Scholarship, 278
Lighthouse College-Bound Award, 370
Lighthouse Undergraduate Award, 371
Los Padres Foundation College Tuition Assistance Program, 371
Los Padres Foundation Second Chance Program, 371
Mahindra USA Women in Ag Scholarship, 279
Moody's Mega Math "M3" Challenge, 394
New Jersey Educational Opportunity Fund Grant, 422
New Jersey Law Enforcement Officer Memorial Scholarship, 422
New Jersey Part-Time Tuition Aid Grant for County Colleges, 422
New Jersey STARS II, 422
New Jersey Student Tuition Assistance Reward Scholarship (NJSTARS), 423
New Jersey Tuition Aid Grants (TAG), 423
New Jersey World Trade Center Scholarship, 423
NTA New Jersey Scholarship, 515
Rainbow Scholarship and Queer Student of the Year Scholarship, 459
Sonia Streuli Maguire Outstanding Scholastic Achievement Award, 502
Swiss Benevolent Society Pellegrini Scholarship, 502

Water Companies (NJ Chapter) Scholarship, 409
Welsh Society of Philadelphia Undergraduate Scholarship, 538
Yankee Clipper Contest Club Youth Scholarship, 191

New Mexico

American Legion New Mexico Auxiliary National Presidents Scholarship, 154
American Legion New Mexico Auxiliary Past President's Parley Scholarship for Nurses, 154
Animal Health International Scholarship, 270
Arysta LifeScience North America Scholarship, 270
Burlington Northern Santa Fe Foundation Scholarship, 115
Cady McDonnell Memorial Scholarship, 99
Carl N. & Margaret Karcher Founders' Scholarship, 234
The Daniels Scholarship, 251
The Fred R. McDaniel Memorial Scholarship, 184
Mahindra USA Women in Ag Scholarship, 279
New Mexico Allied Health Student Loan-for-Service Program, 597
New Mexico Legislative Endowment Program, 424
New Mexico Legislative Lottery Scholarship, 424
New Mexico Nursing Student Loan-for-Service, 598
New Mexico Scholars Program, 424
New Mexico Student Choice Grant, 424
New Mexico Student Incentive Grant, 424
New Mexico Teacher's Loan-for-Service, 598
New Mexico Work-Study Program, 574
RCMI Technical/Trade School Scholarship, 464
Rocky Mountain Coal Mining Institute Scholarship, 464
The Rocky Mountain Division Scholarship, 189
Wilbur-Ellis Company High School Scholarship, 285

New York

Albert E. Wischmeyer Memorial Scholarship Award, 474
Albert Shanker College Scholarship Fund, 521
American Legion New York Auxiliary Past Presidents Parley Student Scholarship in Medical Field, 155
American Legion New York Auxiliary Scholarship, 155
American Legion New York Oratorical Contest, 154
Caroline Kark Scholarship, 425
Christian Wolffer Scholarship, 352
City University SEEK/College Discovery Program, 426
CSX Scholarship, 274
The Dr. James L. Lawson Memorial Scholarship, 183
Eleanor Allwork Scholarship, 236
Fastline Publications Scholarship, 275
Flight 587 Memorial Scholarships, 426
Grange Denise Scholarship, 425
Grange Student Loan Fund, 598
Grange Susan W. Freestone Education Award, 425
HACEMOS Scholarship, 328
The Henry Broughton, K2AE, Memorial Scholarship, 184
James F. Mulholland American Legion Scholarship, 154
June Gill Nursing Scholarship, 425
Kent Nutrition Group, Inc. Scholarship, 278
Lighthouse College-Bound Award, 370
Lighthouse Undergraduate Award, 371
Los Padres Foundation College Tuition Assistance Program, 371
Los Padres Foundation Second Chance Program, 371
Mahindra USA Women in Ag Scholarship, 279
MCC Theater Internships, 567
Milton Fisher Scholarship for Innovation and Creativity, 463
Moody's Mega Math "M3" Challenge, 394
New York American Legion Press Association Scholarship, 155
New York Military Service Recognition Scholarship (MSRS), 426
New York State Aid for Part-Time Study Program, 426
New York State Arthur O. Eve Higher Education Opportunity Program (HEOP), 425
New York State Memorial Scholarship for Families of Deceased Police/Volunteer Firefighters/Peace Officers and Emergency Medical Service Workers, 427
New York State Readers Aid Program, 428
New York State Regents Awards for Children of Deceased and Disabled Veterans, 427
New York State Tuition Assistance Program, 427
New York State Veterans Tuition Award, 428
The Norman E. Strohmeier, W2VRS, Memorial Scholarship, 187
NTA New York Scholarship, 515
Sonia Streuli Maguire Outstanding Scholastic Achievement Award, 502
Swiss Benevolent Society Pellegrini Scholarship, 502
Wilbur-Ellis Company High School Scholarship, 285
Yankee Clipper Contest Club Youth Scholarship, 191

North Carolina

American Legion North Carolina Oratorical Contest, 155
ASHRAE Region IV Benny Bootle Scholarship, 196
Colon Furr Nursing Scholarship, 156
Dana Campbell Memorial Scholarship, 353
Fastline Publications Scholarship, 275
The Gary Wagner, K3OMI, Scholarship, 184
GlaxoSmithKline Opportunity Scholarship, 432
Golden LEAF Scholars Program - Two-Year Colleges, 432
Golden LEAF Scholarship - Four-Year University Program, 432
HACEMOS Scholarship, 328
Jagannathan Scholarship, 432
The L. Phil and Alice J. Wicker Scholarship, 186
Latino Diamante Scholarship Fund, 433
Lighthouse College-Bound Award, 370
Lighthouse Undergraduate Award, 371
Mahindra USA Women in Ag Scholarship, 279
MetLife Foundation Scholarship, 279
Moody's Mega Math "M3" Challenge, 394
Nannie W. Norfleet Scholarship, 156
NC Sheriff's Association Criminal Justice Scholarship, 433
North Carolina Aubrey Lee Brooks Scholarship, 433
North Carolina Community Colleges Wells Fargo Technical Scholarship, 431
North Carolina Education Lottery Scholarship, 240
North Carolina Scholarships for Children of War Veterans, 431
North Carolina State Board of Refrigeration Examiners Scholarship, 431
North Carolina Vocational Rehabilitation Award, 431
NTA Rene Campbell - Ruth McKinney Scholarship, 516
The Outdoor Hams Scholarship, 188
Rodney E. Powell Memorial Scholarship, 431
Rose Acre Farms Scholarship, 283
Southern Nursery Organization Sidney B. Meadows Scholarship, 472

North Dakota

AICP Heartland Chapter Jim Latteman Scholarship, 223

American Legion North Dakota Auxiliary Past Presidents Parley Scholarship, 157
American Legion North Dakota Auxiliary Scholarships, 157
American Legion North Dakota Oratorical Contest, 156
Animal Health International Scholarship, 270
Arysta LifeScience North America Scholarship, 270
BNSF Railway Company Scholarship, 271
Burlington Northern Santa Fe Foundation Scholarship, 115
Carol Bauhs Benson Scholarship, 82
David Arver Memorial Scholarship, 88
Farmers Mutual Hail Insurance Company of Iowa Scholarship, 275
Fastline Publications Scholarship, 275
Hattie Tedrow Memorial Fund Scholarship, 156
Horatio Alger North Dakota Scholarship Program, 335
Hormel Foods Corporation Scholarship, 277
ILC Resources Scholarship, 277
MetLife Foundation Scholarship, 279
Midwest Student Exchange Program, 386
Mills Fleet Farm Scholarship, 280
North Central Region Scholarship, 479
North Dakota Academic Scholarships, 433
North Dakota Career & Technical Education Scholarships, 434
North Dakota Indian Scholarship Program, 434
North Dakota Scholars Program, 434
North Dakota State Student Incentive Grant, 434
RCMI Technical/Trade School Scholarship, 464
Rocky Mountain Coal Mining Institute Scholarship, 464
South Dakota Ardell Bjugstad Scholarship, 494
Treacy Foundation Scholarship, 518
Wilbur-Ellis Company High School Scholarship, 285

Ohio

AdOhio Advertising Internship, 582
American Legion Ohio Auxiliary Department President's Scholarship, 157
American Legion Ohio Auxiliary Past Presidents Parley Nurse's Scholarship, 158
American Legion Ohio Department Oratorical Awards, 157
The Andersons, Inc. Scholarship, 269
Beck's Hybrids Scholarship, 270
CSX Scholarship, 274
Engineers Foundation of Ohio Scholarships, 257
Farm Credit Services of Mid-America Scholarship, 275
Farmers Mutual Hail Insurance Company of Iowa Scholarship, 275
Fastline Publications Scholarship, 275
Harold K. Douthit Scholarship, 437
Kent Nutrition Group, Inc. Scholarship, 278
Mahindra USA Women in Ag Scholarship, 279
MetLife Foundation Scholarship, 279
Moody's Mega Math "M3" Challenge, 394
NMIA Ohio Scholarship Program, 429
NTA Ohio Scholarship, 516
Ohio College Opportunity Grant, 436
Ohio Newspaper Association Publications/Public Relations Internship, 582
Ohio Newspapers Minority Scholarship, 437
Ohio Newspapers Women's Scholarship, 437
Ohio Nurse Education Assistance Loan Program, 598
Ohio Safety Officers College Memorial Fund, 436
Ohio War Orphans Scholarship, 436
Paradise Tomato Kitchens Scholarship, 281
The Thomas W. Porter, W8KYZ, Scholarship Honoring Michael Daugherty, W8LSE, 190
University Journalism Scholarship, 437
Wilbur-Ellis Company High School Scholarship, 285

Oklahoma

Animal Health International Scholarship, 270
ASHRAE Region VIII Scholarship, 196
Austin Family Scholarship Endowment, 111
Burlington Northern Santa Fe Foundation Scholarship, 115
Carl N. & Margaret Karcher Founders' Scholarship, 234
Dana Campbell Memorial Scholarship, 353
Farmers Mutual Hail Insurance Company of Iowa Scholarship, 275
Fastline Publications Scholarship, 275
The Fred R. McDaniel Memorial Scholarship, 184
George and Donna Nigh Public Service Scholarship, 438
HACEMOS Scholarship, 328
Independent Living Act (Department of Human Services Tuition Waiver), 438
Mahindra USA Women in Ag Scholarship, 279
MetLife Foundation Scholarship, 279
National Guard Tuition Waiver, 438
Oklahoma Academic Scholars Program, 439
Oklahoma Engineering Foundation Scholarship, 438
Oklahoma Future Teachers Scholarship, 439
Oklahoma Tuition Aid Grant, 439
Oklahoma's Promise - Oklahoma Higher Learning Access Program, 439
Regional University Baccalaureate Scholarship, 439
Southern Nursery Organization Sidney B. Meadows Scholarship, 472
SREB Academic Common Market, 440
The Tom and Judith Comstock Scholarship, 190

Oregon

Ahmad-Sehar Saleha Ahmad and Abrahim Ekramullah Zafar Foundation, 441
Allcott/Hunt Share It Now II Scholarship, 441
American Legion Department Oratorical Contest, 158
American Legion Oregon Auxiliary Department Nurses Scholarship, 158
American Legion Oregon Auxiliary National President's Scholarship, 158
Animal Health International Scholarship, 270
The ARRL Northwestern Division Scholarship Fund, 180
Arysta LifeScience North America Scholarship, 270
ASTA Pacific Northwest Chapter/William Hunt Scholarship, 513
Audria M. Edwards Scholarship Fund, 451
Bandon Submarine Cable Council Scholarship, 441
Ben Selling Scholarship, 442
Benjamin Franklin/Edith Green Scholarship, 442
Bertha P. Singer Scholarship, 442
Burlington Northern Santa Fe Foundation Scholarship, 115
Cady McDonnell Memorial Scholarship, 99
Carl N. & Margaret Karcher Founders' Scholarship, 234
Chafee Education and Training Grant, 442
Clark-Phelps Scholarship, 442
Darlene Hooley for Oregon Veterans Scholarship, 443
David Family Scholarship, 443
Dorothy Campbell Memorial Scholarship, 443
DPMA/PC Scholarship, 251

Earl Dedman Memorial Scholarship, 103
Eugene Bennet Visual Arts Scholarship, 443
Fastline Publications Scholarship, 275
Ford Opportunity Program, 443
Ford Scholars Program, 444
Frank Stenzel M.D. and Kathryn Stenzel II Scholarship, 444
Glenn Jackson Scholars, 444
Grange Insurance Scholarship, 293
Ida M. Crawford Scholarship, 444
Jackson Foundation Journalism Scholarship, 444
James Carlson Memorial Scholarship, 445
Jeffrey Alan Scoggins Memorial Scholarship, 445
Jerome B. Steinbach Scholarship, 445
Laurence R. Foster Memorial Scholarship, 445
Mahindra USA Women in Ag Scholarship, 279
Maria C. Jackson-General George A. White Scholarship, 445
The Mary Lou Brown Scholarship, 186
Northwest Danish Association Scholarship, 435
One World Scholarship Essay, 446
Oregon Alpha Delta Kappa Scholarship, 446
Oregon Dungeness Crab Commission, 446
Oregon Foundation for Blacktail Deer Scholarship, 446
Oregon Occupational Safety and Health Division Workers Memorial Scholarship, 446
Oregon Scholarship Fund Community College Student Award Programs, 447
Pepsi-Cola Bottling of Eastern Oregon Scholarship, 282
Professional Land Surveyors of Oregon Scholarship, 447
Spirit of Youth Scholarship, 159
Teamsters Clyde C. Crosby/Joseph M. Edgar Memorial Scholarship, 448
Teamsters Council #37 Federal Credit Union Scholarship, 448
Walter and Marie Schmidt Scholarship, 448
Wilbur-Ellis Company High School Scholarship, 285

Pennsylvania

American Legion Pennsylvania High School Oratorical Contest, 119
Blind or Deaf Beneficiary Grant Program, 452
Chafee Education and Training Grant (ETG) Program, 452
Dr. & Mrs. Arthur William Phillips Scholarship, 454
Fastline Publications Scholarship, 275
HACEMOS Scholarship, 328
Horatio Alger Pennsylvania Scholarship Program, 335
John McKee Scholarship, 383
Joseph P. Gavenonis Scholarship, 159
Kent Nutrition Group, Inc. Scholarship, 278
Lacroix at the Rittenhouse Scholarship, 354
Lighthouse College-Bound Award, 370
Lighthouse Undergraduate Award, 371
M & T Bank Scholarship, 454
Mahindra USA Women in Ag Scholarship, 279
Moody's Mega Math "M3" Challenge, 394
NASA Academy Internship, 572
Pennsylvania GEAR UP Scholarship, 452
Pennsylvania Higher Education Assistance Agency Partnership for Access to Higher Education (PATH), 452
Pennsylvania Higher Education Assistance Agency Postsecondary Educational Gratuity Program, 452
Pennsylvania State Grant Program, 453
Pennsylvania Women's Press Association Scholarship, 456
Pennsylvania Work-Study Program, 453
Pittsburgh Scholarship, 487
Quida and Anna Pichini Merit Scholarships, 455
Rainbow Scholarship and Queer Student of the Year Scholarship, 459
Robert W. Valimont Endowment Fund Scholarship, 159
Scholarship for Children of Deceased or Totally Disabled Veterans, 159
Scholarship for Children of Living Veterans, 159
Shannon Scholarship, 519
Sonia Streuli Maguire Outstanding Scholastic Achievement Award, 502
Swiss Benevolent Society Pellegrini Scholarship, 502
Welsh Society of Philadelphia Undergraduate Scholarship, 538
Yankee Clipper Contest Club Youth Scholarship, 191
The You've Got a Friend in Pennsylvania Scholarship, 192

Puerto Rico

American Legion Puerto Rico Auxiliary Nursing Scholarships, 160
HACEMOS Scholarship, 328
Los Padres Foundation Second Chance Program, 371
The North Fulton Amateur Radio League Scholarship Fund, 187

Rhode Island

American Legion Rhode Island Auxiliary Book Award, 160
American Legion Rhode Island Oratorical Contest, 160
Androscoggin Amateur Radio Club Scholarship, 179
The Byron Blanchard, N1EKV Memorial Scholarship Fund, 181
College Bound Fund Academic Promise Scholarship, 464
The Dr. James L. Lawson Memorial Scholarship, 183
Kent Nutrition Group, Inc. Scholarship, 278
Lighthouse College-Bound Award, 370
Lighthouse Undergraduate Award, 371
Moody's Mega Math "M3" Challenge, 394
NEBHE's Tuition Break Regional Student Program, 421
The New England FEMARA Scholarship, 187
Rhode Island State Government Internship Program, 584
Rhode Island State Grant, 464
Timothy and Palmer W. Bigelow, Jr. Scholarship, 337
Yankee Clipper Contest Club Youth Scholarship, 191

South Carolina

American Legion South Carolina Auxiliary Scholarship, 161
American Legion South Carolina Department Oratorical Contest, 160
ASHRAE Region IV Benny Bootle Scholarship, 196
C.G. Fuller Foundation Scholarship, 237
Charleston Women in International Trade Scholarship, 238
CSX Scholarship, 274
Dana Campbell Memorial Scholarship, 353
Fastline Publications Scholarship, 275
James F. Byrnes Scholarship, 356
The L. Phil and Alice J. Wicker Scholarship, 186
Lighthouse College-Bound Award, 370
Lighthouse Undergraduate Award, 371
Mahindra USA Women in Ag Scholarship, 279
MetLife Foundation Scholarship, 279
Moody's Mega Math "M3" Challenge, 394
Palmetto Fellows Scholarship Program, 492
South Carolina Dayco Scholarship Program, 492
South Carolina HOPE Scholarships, 492
South Carolina LIFE Scholarship Program, 493

South Carolina Lottery Tuition Assistance Program, 493
South Carolina Need-Based Grants Program, 493
South Carolina Teacher Loans, 599
South Carolina Tuition Grants, 493
Southern Nursery Organization Sidney B. Meadows Scholarship, 472

South Dakota

AICP Heartland Chapter Jim Latteman Scholarship, 223
American Legion South Dakota Auxiliary Scholarships, 161
American Legion South Dakota Auxiliary Senior Member Scholarship, 161
American Legion South Dakota Educational Loan, 593
American Legion South Dakota Oratorical Contest, 161
Animal Health International Scholarship, 270
Arysta LifeScience North America Scholarship, 270
BNSF Railway Company Scholarship, 271
Burlington Northern Santa Fe Foundation Scholarship, 115
Carol Bauhs Benson Scholarship, 82
Casey's General Stores, Inc. Scholarship, 272
David Arver Memorial Scholarship, 88
Farmers Mutual Hail Insurance Company of Iowa Scholarship, 275
Fastline Publications Scholarship, 275
Horatio Alger South Dakota Scholarship Program, 335
Hormel Foods Corporation Scholarship, 277
ILC Resources Scholarship, 277
Jump Start Scholarship Program, 494
MetLife Foundation Scholarship, 279
North Central Region Scholarship, 479
South Dakota Annis I. Fowler/Kaden Scholarship, 494
South Dakota Ardell Bjugstad Scholarship, 494
South Dakota Haines Memorial Scholarship, 495
South Dakota Marlin R. Scarborough Memorial Scholarship, 495
South Dakota Opportunity Scholarship Program, 495
Thelma Foster Junior American Legion Auxiliary Members Scholarship, 162
Thelma Foster Senior American Legion Auxiliary Member Scholarship, 162
Wilbur-Ellis Company High School Scholarship, 285

Tennessee

American Legion Tennessee Eagle Scout of the Year Scholarship, 162
American Legion Tennessee Oratorical Contest, 162
CSX Scholarship, 274
Fastline Publications Scholarship, 275
The Gary Wagner, K3OMI, Scholarship, 184
HACEMOS Scholarship, 328
Helping Heroes Grant, 503
Hope Foster Child Tuition Grant, 503
HOPE-Aspire Award, 503
Hope-General Assembly Merit Scholarship, 504
The Jake McClain Driver KC5WXA Scholarship Fund, 185
Laboratory Technology Program, 577
Mahindra USA Women in Ag Scholarship, 279
Math And Science Teachers Loan Forgiveness Program, 600
MetLife Foundation Scholarship, 279
Moody's Mega Math "M3" Challenge, 394
Nissan North America, Inc. Scholarship Program, 330
Scarlett Family Foundation Scholarship, 469
Southern Nursery Organization Sidney B. Meadows Scholarship, 472
Tennessee Dependent Children Scholarship Program, 504
Tennessee Dual Enrollment Grant, 504
Tennessee HOPE Access Grant, 504
Tennessee HOPE Scholarship, 505
Tennessee Minority Teaching Fellows Program, 600
Tennessee Ned McWherter Scholars Program, 505
Tennessee Student Assistance Award Program, 505
Tennessee Teaching Scholars Program, 600
Vara Gray Scholarship Fund, 163
Wilder-Naifeh Technical Skills Grant, 505

Texas

American Legion Texas Auxiliary General Education Scholarship, 163
American Legion Texas Oratorical Contest, 163
American Legion Texas Past Presidents Parley Scholarship, 163
Animal Health International Scholarship, 270
Area Go Texan Scholarships, 338
ASHRAE Region VIII Scholarship, 196
Blue Bell Scholarship, 506
BNSF Railway Company Scholarship, 271
Burlington Northern Santa Fe Foundation Scholarship, 115
C. J. Davidson Scholarship, 506
Carl N. & Margaret Karcher Founders' Scholarship, 234
The Chesapeake Energy Scholarship, 249
Dallas Architectural Foundation - Swank Travelling Fellowship, 249
Dallas Geophysical Society Scholarship, 482
The Dallas Morning New Journalism Scholarship, 249
Dana Campbell Memorial Scholarship, 353
Dr. Dan J. and Patricia S. Pickard Scholarship, 249
Dr. Don and Rose Marie Benton Scholarship, 250
Fastline Publications Scholarship, 275
FFA Scholarships, 507
The Fred R. McDaniel Memorial Scholarship, 184
The George Foreman Tribute to Lyndon B. Johnson Scholarship, 461
Greater Houston Retailers and Coca-Cola Live Positively Scholarship, 328
Gulf Coast Hurricane Scholarships, 486
HACEMOS Scholarship, 328
Horatio Alger John Hardin Hudiburg Scholarship Program, 334
Horatio Alger Texas Scholarship Program, 336
Houston Livestock Show and Rodeo Metropolitan Scholarships, 338
Houston Livestock Show and Rodeo Opportunity Scholarship, 338
Houston Livestock Show and Rodeo Scholarships, 506
Houston Livestock Show and Rodeo School Art Scholarships, 339
HSF Achievement Scholarship, 328
Jere W. Thompson, Jr. Scholarship Fund, 250
Mahindra USA Women in Ag Scholarship, 279
MetLife Foundation Scholarship, 279
Nissan North America, Inc. Scholarship Program, 330
PHCC Auxiliary of Texas Scholarship, 457
RCMI Technical/Trade School Scholarship, 464
Rocky Mountain Coal Mining Institute Scholarship, 464
Southern Nursery Organization Sidney B. Meadows Scholarship, 472
Texas 4-H Opportunity Scholarships, 505
Texas Armed Services Scholarship Program, 507
Texas College Access Loan (CAL), 601
Texas Competitive Scholarship Waiver, 507
Texas Concurrent Enrollment Waiver (Enrollment in Two Texas Community Colleges), 507

Texas Exemption for Peace Officers Disabled in the Line of Duty, 508
Texas Exemption for Students Under Conservatorship of the Dept. of Family & Protective Services, 508
Texas Exemption for the Surviving Spouse and Dependent Children of Certain Deceased Public Servants (Employees), 508
Texas Exemptions for Texas Veterans (Hazelwood Exemption), 508
Texas Farm Bureau Scholarship, 506
Texas Fifth-Year Accounting Student Scholarship Program, 509
TEXAS Grant (Toward Excellence, Access, and Success), 509
Texas National Guard Tuition Assistance Program, 509
Texas Reduction in Tuition Charges for Students Taking 15 or More Semester Credit Hours Per Term, 510
Texas Senior Citizen, 65 or Older, Free Tuition for Up to 6 Credit Hours, 510
Texas Tuition Equalization Grant (TEG), 510
Texas Tuition Exemption for Blind or Deaf Students, 510
Texas Tuition Exemption for Children of Disabled or Deceased Firefighters, Peace Officers, Game Wardens, and Employees of Correctional Institutions, 511
Texas Tuition Rebate for Certain Undergraduates, 511
The Tom and Judith Comstock Scholarship, 190
The Tommy Tranchin Award, 250
Toyota Motor Sales, U.S.A. Inc. Scholarship, 284
Travelers Foundation Scholarship, 113
Tuition Exemption for Children of U.S. Military POW/MIAs from Texas, 511
Wilbur-Ellis Company High School Scholarship, 285

Utah

American Legion Utah Auxiliary National President's Scholarship, 164
Animal Health International Scholarship, 270
Cady McDonnell Memorial Scholarship, 99
Carl N. & Margaret Karcher Founders' Scholarship, 234
The Daniels Scholarship, 251
Higher Education Success Stipend Program, 529
Horatio Alger Utah Scholarship Program, 336
Mahindra USA Women in Ag Scholarship, 279
NTA Utah Keith Griffall Scholarship, 517
RCMI Technical/Trade School Scholarship, 464
Rocky Mountain Coal Mining Institute Scholarship, 464
The Rocky Mountain Division Scholarship, 189
Utah Career Teaching Scholarship/T.H. Bell Teaching Incentive Loan, 602

Vermont

AIWF Culinary Scholarship, 531
Alfred T. Granger Student Art Fund Scholarship, 531
American Legion Vermont Eagle Scout of the Year, 164
American Legion Vermont National High School Oratorical Contest, 164
Androscoggin Amateur Radio Club Scholarship, 179
The Byron Blanchard, N1EKV Memorial Scholarship Fund, 181
Calvin Coolidge Memorial Foundation Scholarship, 531
Champlain Valley Street Rodders Scholarship, 531
Charles E. Leonard Memorial Scholarship, 532
The Dr. James L. Lawson Memorial Scholarship, 183
Emily Lester Vermont Opportunity Scholarship, 532
Jedidiah Zabrosky Scholarship, 532
Kent Nutrition Group, Inc. Scholarship, 278
Kittredge Coddington Memorial Scholarship, 532
Lee A. Lyman Memorial Music Scholarship, 532
Lighthouse College-Bound Award, 370
Lighthouse Undergraduate Award, 371
Mahindra USA Women in Ag Scholarship, 279
Moody's Mega Math "M3" Challenge, 394
NASA Space Grant Vermont Consortium Undergraduate Scholarships, 404
NEBHE's Tuition Break Regional Student Program, 421
The New England FEMARA Scholarship, 187
Patrick and Judith McHugh Scholarship, 533
People's United Bank Scholarship, 533
Philip and Alice Angell Eastern Star Scholarship, 533
RehabGYM Scholarship, 533
Samara Foundation of Vermont Scholarship, 533
Students With Disabilities Endowed Scholarship Honoring Elizabeth Daley Jeffords, 534
Timothy and Palmer W. Bigelow, Jr. Scholarship, 337
Vermont Golf Association Scholarship, 530
Vermont Incentive Grant, 534
Vermont John H. Chafee Education and Training Scholarship, 534
Vermont Non-Degree Program, 534
Vermont Part-Time Grant, 534
Yankee Clipper Contest Club Youth Scholarship, 191

Virgin Islands

The North Fulton Amateur Radio League Scholarship Fund, 187
Virgin Islands Music Scholarship, 535
Virgin Islands Territorial Grants/Loans Program, 602

Virginia

American Legion Virginia Auxiliary Past Presidents Parley Nurse's Scholarship, 165
American Legion Virginia Oratorical Contest, 164
Anna Gear Junior Scholarship, 165
Carville M. Akehurst Memorial Scholarship, 337
Children of Warriors National President's Scholarship, 165
Dana Campbell Memorial Scholarship, 353
Dr. Kate Waller Barrett Grant, 165
Fastline Publications Scholarship, 275
The Gary Wagner, K3OMI, Scholarship, 184
Horatio Alger District of Columbia, Maryland and Virginia Scholarship Program, 333
Kent Nutrition Group, Inc. Scholarship, 278
The L. Phil and Alice J. Wicker Scholarship, 186
Lighthouse College-Bound Award, 370
Lighthouse Undergraduate Award, 371
Mahindra USA Women in Ag Scholarship, 279
Mary Marshall Nursing RN Scholarship, 535
Moody's Mega Math "M3" Challenge, 394
Southern Nursery Organization Sidney B. Meadows Scholarship, 472
Virginia Academic Common Market, 496
Virginia Lee-Jackson Scholarship, 535
Virginia Museum of Fine Arts Visual Arts and Art History Fellowship, 536
Virginia Tuition Assistance Grant, 497

Washington

American Legion Washington Auxiliary Scholarships, 166

American Legion Washington Children and Youth Scholarship Fund, 166
American Legion Washington Department Oratorical Contest, 166
Animal Health International Scholarship, 270
The ARRL Northwestern Division Scholarship Fund, 180
Arthur and Doreen Parrett Scholarship, 210
Arysta LifeScience North America Scholarship, 270
ASTA Pacific Northwest Chapter/William Hunt Scholarship, 513
Audria M. Edwards Scholarship Fund, 451
Burlington Northern Santa Fe Foundation Scholarship, 115
Cady McDonnell Memorial Scholarship, 99
Carl N. & Margaret Karcher Founders' Scholarship, 234
Dayle and Frances Pieper Scholarship, 166
DPMA/PC Scholarship, 251
Earl Dedman Memorial Scholarship, 103
Edmund F. Maxwell Foundation Scholarship, 255
Florence Lemcke Memorial Scholarship, 166
Fred G. Zahn Scholarship Fund, 267
Grange Insurance Scholarship, 293
Mahindra USA Women in Ag Scholarship, 279
Marguerite McAlpin Nurse's Scholarship, 167
The Mary Lou Brown Scholarship, 186
MetLife Foundation Scholarship, 279
Northwest Danish Association Scholarship, 435
Seattle Professional Chapter Scholarship, 222
Susan Burdett Scholarship, 167
Travelers Foundation Scholarship, 113
Washington State American Indian Endowed Scholarship, 114
Washington State Need Grant, 537
Washington State Scholarship Program, 538
Wilbur-Ellis Company High School Scholarship, 285

West Virginia

The Albert H. Hix, W8AH, Memorial Scholarship, 178
American Legion West Virginia Auxiliary Scholarship, 168
American Legion West Virginia Oratorical Contest, 167
Carville M. Akehurst Memorial Scholarship, 337
CSX Scholarship, 274
Dana Campbell Memorial Scholarship, 353
Fastline Publications Scholarship, 275
The Gary Wagner, K3OMI, Scholarship, 184
Greater Kanawha Valley Scholarship Program, 294
Kent Nutrition Group, Inc. Scholarship, 278
The L. Phil and Alice J. Wicker Scholarship, 186
Lighthouse College-Bound Award, 370
Lighthouse Undergraduate Award, 371
Mahindra USA Women in Ag Scholarship, 279
Moody's Mega Math "M3" Challenge, 394
PROMISE Scholarship, 539
Sons of the American Legion Scholarship, 167
Southern Nursery Organization Sidney B. Meadows Scholarship, 472
The Thomas W. Porter, W8KYZ, Scholarship Honoring Michael Daugherty, W8LSE, 190
Toyota Motor Sales, U.S.A. Inc. Scholarship, 284
West Virginia Engineering, Science, and Technology Scholarship, 540
West Virginia Higher Education Adult Part-time Student (HEAPS) Grant Program, 540
West Virginia Higher Education Grant, 540
West Virginia Underwood-Smith Teacher Scholarship, 540
West Virginia War Orphans Educational Assistance, 539

Wisconsin

American Family Insurance Scholarship, 269
American Legion Wisconsin Auxiliary Department President's Scholarship, 169
American Legion Wisconsin Auxiliary H.S. and Angeline Lewis Scholarships, 169
American Legion Wisconsin Auxiliary Merit and Memorial Scholarship, 169
American Legion Wisconsin Auxiliary Past Presidents Parley R.N. Scholarship, 169
American Legion Wisconsin Baseball Scholarship, 168
American Legion Wisconsin Eagle Scout of the Year Scholarship, 168
American Legion Wisconsin Oratorical Contest Scholarships, 168
The Andersons, Inc. Scholarship, 269
Carol Bauhs Benson Scholarship, 82
Casey's General Stores, Inc. Scholarship, 272
The Chicago FM Club Scholarship, 182
David Arver Memorial Scholarship, 88
Della Van Deuren Memorial Scholarship, 170
The Edmond A. Metzger Scholarship, 183
Farmers Mutual Hail Insurance Company of Iowa Scholarship, 275
Fastline Publications Scholarship, 275
Foth Production Solutions, LLC Scholarship, 276
The Francis Walton Memorial Scholarship, 183
Hormel Foods Corporation Scholarship, 277
The Indianapolis Amateur Radio Association Fund, 184
Kikkoman Foods, Inc. Scholarship, 278
Ladish Co. Foundation Scholarships, 213
Mahindra USA Women in Ag Scholarship, 279
MetLife Foundation Scholarship, 279
Midwest Student Exchange Program, 386
Mills Fleet Farm Scholarship, 280
Moody's Mega Math "M3" Challenge, 394
North Central Region Scholarship, 479
Schneider-Emanuel American Legion Scholarships, 168
The Six Meter Club of Chicago Scholarship, 189
Wisconsin Academic Excellence Scholarship, 543
Wisconsin Hearing & Visually Handicapped Student Grant, 543
Wisconsin Higher Education Grant, 543
Wisconsin Indian Student Assistance Grant, 544
Wisconsin Minority Teacher Loan Program, 602
Wisconsin Minority Undergraduate Retention Grant, 544
Wisconsin Talent Incentive Program Grant, 544
Wisconsin Tuition Grant, 544
Wisconsin Veterans Affairs Retraining Grant, 542
Wisconsin Veterans Education GI Bill Tuition Remission Program, 543

Wyoming

American Legion Wyoming E.A. Blackmore Memorial Scholarship, 170
American Legion Wyoming Oratorical Contest, 170
Animal Health International Scholarship, 270
Cady McDonnell Memorial Scholarship, 99

The Daniels Scholarship, 251
Davis-Roberts Scholarship, 252
Earl Dedman Memorial Scholarship, 103
Grange Insurance Scholarship, 293
Horatio Alger Wyoming Scholarship Program, 336
MetLife Foundation Scholarship, 279
RCMI Technical/Trade School Scholarship, 464
Rocky Mountain Coal Mining Institute Scholarship, 464
The Rocky Mountain Division Scholarship, 189

Study Abroad

Anna K. Meredith Fund Scholarship, 499
Clare Brett Smith Scholarship, 499
Diversity Abroad Achievement Scholarship, 115
Elizabeth A. Sackler Museum Educational Trust, 499
HACU (Hispanic Association of Colleges and Universities) Scholarships, 115
International Incentive Awards, 500
International Semester Scholarship, 116
Jules Maidoff Scholarship, 500
Kosciuszko Foundation Year Abroad Program, 364
Lele Cassin Scholarship, 500
NAFEO (National Association for Equal Opportunity in Higher Education) Scholarships, 116
SACI Alumni Heritage Scholarship, 500
SACI Consortium Scholarship, 500
Swiss Benevolent Society Medicus Student Exchange, 502

Scholarships

10,000 Degrees

10,000 Degrees Undergraduate Scholarships

Type of award: Scholarship, renewable.
Intended use: For full-time undergraduate study at accredited 2-year or 4-year institution in United States.
Eligibility: Applicant must be residing in California.
Basis for selection: Applicant must demonstrate financial need.
Application requirements: Essay. FAFSA.
Additional information: Must be resident of Marin, Sonoma, Vallejo, Richmond, or Ringgold counties. Must be enrolled for minimum of twelve units per term. Applicants automatically considered for six other scholarships ranging from $500-$5,000. Students seeking teaching credentials with an interest in working with children over 5 years old also eligible. Awards and amounts may vary. Visit Website for more information.

Amount of award:	$500-$5,000
Number of awards:	20

Contact:
10,000 Degrees
781 Lincoln Avenue
Suite 140
San Rafael, CA 94901
Phone: 415-451-4002
Fax: 415-459-0527
Web: www.10000degrees.org/students/scholarships/undergraduate-scholarships

New Leader Scholarship

Type of award: Scholarship.
Intended use: For full-time sophomore, junior, senior or graduate study at postsecondary institution. Designated institutions: University of California, Berkeley; California State University East Bay; San Francisco State University; San Jose State University; Sonoma State University.
Eligibility: Applicant must be residing in California.
Basis for selection: Major/career interest in economics; health sciences; law; medicine; psychology; social work or sociology. Applicant must demonstrate financial need, high academic achievement, leadership and service orientation.
Application requirements: Interview, recommendations, essay, transcript. Financial statement.
Additional information: Preference given to recent immigrants and students of color. Applicants do not need to be Marin County residents to apply. Applicants should demonstrate commitment to giving back to their communities and plan to pursue career in public, legal, psychological, health, or social services. Graduate students may be considered if they have received scholarship as undergraduate and are attending California public universities. See Website (www.goldmanfamilyfund.com) for more information. Minimum 3.5 GPA. Consideration will be given to students with a GPA of 3.2 - 3.49 under special circumstances. Awards and amounts may vary.

Amount of award:	$8,000
Application deadline:	March 15

Contact:
10,000 Degrees
New Leader Scholarship
781 Lincoln Avenue, Suite 140
San Rafael, CA 94901
Phone: 415-459-4240
Fax: 415-459-0527
Web: www.newleaderscholarship.org, www.10000degrees.org

1199SEIU Benefit Funds

Joseph Tauber Scholarship

Type of award: Scholarship, renewable.
Intended use: For full-time undergraduate or non-degree study at accredited vocational, 2-year or 4-year institution in or outside United States.
Basis for selection: Applicant must demonstrate financial need.
Application requirements: Proof of eligibility. CSS profile.
Additional information: Applicant must be dependent of eligible member of 1199SEIU. Minimum award is $750 each year for full-time students. Must be receiving family coverage (Wage or Eligibility Class One) through benefit fund. Apply for pre-screening by deadline date; applications sent to qualified candidates. Visit Website for updates. Must apply for renewal. Amount of award varies.

Amount of award:	$750
Number of awards:	3,000
Number of applicants:	6,000
Application deadline:	January 31
Notification begins:	November 1
Total amount awarded:	$4,500,000

Contact:
1199SEIU Child Care Funds Joseph Tauber Scholarship Program
330 West 42nd Street, 18th Floor
New York, NY 10036-6977
Phone: 646-473-8999
Fax: 646-473-6949
Web: www.1199seiubenefits.org

1st Marine Division Association

1st Marine Division Association Scholarship

Type of award: Scholarship, renewable.
Intended use: For full-time undergraduate study at accredited vocational, 2-year or 4-year institution in United States.

Eligibility: Applicant must be U.S. citizen. Applicant must be dependent of disabled veteran or deceased veteran who served in the Marines. Must have served specifically in any unit part of, attached to, or in support of 1st Marine Division.
Basis for selection: Applicant must demonstrate depth of character and seriousness of purpose.
Application requirements: Essay, proof of eligibility. Veteran sponsor's DD214 if available (if not, applicant must complete Standard Form 180). Death certificate or affidavit proving veteran's 100 percent and permanent disability. Copy of applicant's birth certificate. Photograph. See Website for other required information.
Additional information: Number of awards varies. Visit Website for application deadline and details.

Amount of award:	$1,750
Total amount awarded:	$40,250

Contact:
1st Marine Division Association
403 North Freeman St.
Oceanside, CA 92054
Phone: 760-967-8561
Fax: 760-967-8567
Web: www.1stmarinedivisionassociation.org/Scholarships.html

Abbie Sargent Memorial Scholarship Fund

Abbie Sargent Memorial Scholarship

Type of award: Scholarship, renewable.
Intended use: For undergraduate or graduate study at postsecondary institution.
Eligibility: Applicant must be residing in New Hampshire.
Basis for selection: Major/career interest in agriculture. Applicant must demonstrate financial need, high academic achievement and depth of character.
Application requirements: Recommendations, essay, transcript. Recent photo.
Additional information: Recipient may attend out-of-state university. Send SASE for application or download from Website. Number of awards varies.

Amount of award:	$400-$1,000
Number of applicants:	8
Application deadline:	March 15
Notification begins:	June 1

Contact:
Abbie Sargent Memorial Scholarship
Attn: Diane Clary, Treasurer
295 Sheep Davis Road
Concord, NH 03301
Phone: 603-224-1934
Web: www.nhfarmbureau.org

Academy of Interactive Arts & Sciences

Mark Beaumont Scholarship Fund

Type of award: Scholarship.
Intended use: For full-time sophomore, junior, senior or graduate study in United States.
Basis for selection: Major/career interest in business. Applicant must demonstrate financial need, depth of character, leadership and service orientation.
Application requirements: Recommendations, transcript, proof of eligibility. Verification of enrollment. Two-page letter including information about your studies and how they will benefit the game industry and statement addressing service, leadership, character, and financial need.
Additional information: Minimum 3.3 GPA. Must intend to enter game industry in the area of business. Possible career paths include, but are not limited to: executive leadership, law, marketing, public relations, business development. Deadline in summer. Notifications begin in August.

Amount of award:	$2,500
Number of awards:	2
Total amount awarded:	$5,000

Contact:
Academy of Interactive Arts & Sciences
Web: www.interactive.org/foundation/scholarships.asp

Randy Pausch Scholarship Fund

Type of award: Scholarship.
Intended use: For full-time sophomore, junior, senior or graduate study at accredited postsecondary institution in United States.
Basis for selection: Major/career interest in music; arts, general or computer graphics. Applicant must demonstrate financial need, depth of character, leadership and service orientation.
Application requirements: Recommendations, transcript, proof of eligibility. Two-page letter including information about your studies and how they will benefit the game industry and statement addressing service, leadership, character, and financial need.
Additional information: Minimum 3.3 GPA. Must intend to enter game industry as developer of interactive entertainment. Possible career paths include, but are not limited to: art, animation, programming, engineering, game direction, game design, sound design, music composition. Deadline in summer. Notifications begin in August.

Amount of award:	$2,500
Number of awards:	2
Total amount awarded:	$5,000

Contact:
Academy of Interactive Arts & Sciences
Web: www.interactive.org/foundation/scholarships.asp

Academy of Nutrition and Dietetics

Academy of Nutrition and Dietetics Graduate, Baccalaureate or Coordinated Program Scholarships

Type of award: Scholarship, renewable.
Intended use: For full-time junior, senior or graduate study at accredited 4-year or graduate institution. Designated institutions: ACEND-accredited/approved dietetics education programs.
Eligibility: Applicant must be U.S. citizen or permanent resident.

Basis for selection: Major/career interest in dietetics/nutrition. Applicant must demonstrate high academic achievement and seriousness of purpose.
Application requirements: Recommendations, proof of eligibility. GPA documentation signed by academic advisor.
Additional information: Applicant must be a member of the Academy of Nutrition and Dietetics. Number and amount of awards varies. Minority status considered. Must demonstrate or show promise of being a valuable, contributing member of the profession. See Website for more information and application.

Amount of award:	$500-$3,000
Number of applicants:	500
Total amount awarded:	$264,000

Contact:
Academy of Nutrition and Dietetics
Education Programs
120 South Riverside Plaza, Suite 2000
Chicago, IL 60606-6995
Web: www.eatright.org/students/careers/aid.aspx

Academy of Television Arts & Sciences Foundation

Mister Rogers Memorial Scholarship

Type of award: Scholarship.
Intended use: For undergraduate or graduate study at accredited postsecondary institution.
Basis for selection: Major/career interest in education, early childhood; film/video; music or radio/television/film.
Application requirements: Recommendations, essay. Project plan and budget.
Additional information: Applicant must have ultimate goal of working in children's media and must have studied or have experience in at least two of the following fields: early childhood education, child development/child psychology, film/television production, music, or animation. Must be currently enrolled in college. Deadline in February. Download application from Website.

Amount of award:	$10,000
Number of awards:	4
Number of applicants:	100
Total amount awarded:	$40,000

Contact:
Academy of Television Arts & Sciences Foundation
Attn: Nancy Robinson
5220 Lankershim Boulevard
North Hollywood, CA 91601-3109
Phone: 818-754-2802
Web: www.emmysfoundation.org

ACFE Foundation

Ritchie-Jennings Memorial Scholarship

Type of award: Scholarship.
Intended use: For full-time undergraduate or graduate study at accredited 4-year institution.
Basis for selection: Major/career interest in criminal justice/law enforcement; accounting; business or finance/banking.
Application requirements: Recommendations, essay, transcript. Applicant must include three letters of recommendation, preferably one from a certified fraud examiner.
Additional information: Award includes one-year ACFE Student Associate membership. Deadline in early February. Notifications of awards begin in end of April. Visit Website for additional information.

Amount of award:	$1,000-$10,000
Number of awards:	30
Number of applicants:	150
Notification begins:	April 15
Total amount awarded:	$53,000

Contact:
ACFE Foundation Scholarships Program Coordinator
The Gregor Building
716 West Avenue
Austin, TX 78701-2727
Phone: 800-245-3321
Fax: 512-276-8127
Web: www.acfe.com/scholarship.aspx

The Actuarial Foundation

Actuarial Diversity Scholarships

Type of award: Scholarship, renewable.
Intended use: For full-time undergraduate or graduate study at accredited 2-year, 4-year or graduate institution.
Eligibility: Applicant must be Alaskan native, African American, Mexican American, Hispanic American, Puerto Rican, American Indian or Native Hawaiian/Pacific Islander. Applicant must be U.S. citizen, permanent resident or international student.
Basis for selection: Major/career interest in insurance/actuarial science or mathematics. Applicant must demonstrate high academic achievement.
Application requirements: Recommendations, essay, transcript, proof of eligibility. SAT/ACT scores.
Additional information: Must have at least one birth parent who is Black/African American, Hispanic, or Native American. Applicant must be admitted to institution offering actuarial science program or courses that will prepare student for actuarial career. Minimum 3.0 GPA. Minimum 28 ACT math score or 600 SAT math score. International students must have F1 visa. Visit Website for application, deadline, and more information.

Amount of award:	$1,000-$3,000
Number of awards:	30
Application deadline:	May 2
Notification begins:	August 5

Contact:
The Actuarial Foundation
Actuarial Diversity Scholarship
475 North Martingale Road, Suite 600
Schaumburg, IL 60173-2226
Phone: 847-706-3535
Fax: 847-706-3599
Web: www.actuarialfoundation.org/programs/actuarial/scholarships.shtml

Actuary of Tomorrow Stuart A. Robertson Memorial Scholarship

Type of award: Scholarship.
Intended use: For full-time sophomore, junior or senior study at accredited 4-year institution in United States.
Basis for selection: Major/career interest in accounting; mathematics or statistics. Applicant must demonstrate high academic achievement.
Application requirements: Recommendations, essay, transcript.
Additional information: Minimum 3.0 GPA. Must have successfully completed two actuarial exams. Must pursue course of study leading to career in actuarial science. Visit Website for essay topic and application.

Amount of award:	$7,500
Number of awards:	1
Application deadline:	June 1
Notification begins:	August 1
Total amount awarded:	$7,500

Contact:
The Actuarial Foundation
Attn: Actuary of Tomorrow Scholarship
475 N. Martingale Road, Suite 600
Schaumburg, IL 60173-2226
Phone: 847-706-3535
Fax: 847-706-3599
Web: www.actuarialfoundation.org/programs/actuarial/scholarships.shtml

Wooddy Scholarship

Type of award: Scholarship.
Intended use: For full-time senior study at 4-year institution.
Eligibility: Applicant must be U.S. citizen or permanent resident.
Basis for selection: Major/career interest in insurance/actuarial science. Applicant must demonstrate high academic achievement and leadership.
Application requirements: Recommendations, essay, transcript, nomination by professor.
Additional information: Applicant must have passed at least one actuarial examination and must rank in the top quarter of class. Application is available on Website. Immediate relatives of members of the Board of Trustees of the Actuarial Foundation or boards of affiliated organizations are not eligible to apply. Limit one application per school.

Amount of award:	$2,000
Number of awards:	14
Application deadline:	June 19
Notification begins:	August 22
Total amount awarded:	$26,000

Contact:
The Actuarial Foundation
Attn: John Culver Wooddy Scholarship
475 N. Martingale Road, Suite 600
Schaumburg, IL 60173-2226
Phone: 847-706-3535
Fax: 847-706-3599
Web: www.actuarialfoundation.org/programs/actuarial/scholarships.shtml

ADHA Institute for Oral Health

ADHA Institute for Oral Health Scholarship for Academic Excellence

Type of award: Scholarship.
Intended use: For full-time sophomore, junior or senior study at accredited 2-year or 4-year institution in United States.
Basis for selection: Major/career interest in dental hygiene.
Additional information: Applicant must have completed minimum one year dental hygiene curriculum; may apply during first year. Minimum 3.5 GPA in dental hygiene. Must be member of ADHA or Student ADHA.

Amount of award:	$1,000
Number of awards:	5
Application deadline:	February 1
Notification begins:	July 1

Contact:
ADHA Institute for Oral Health
Scholarship Award Program
444 N. Michigan Ave., Suite 3400
Chicago, IL 60611
Phone: 312-440-8900
Web: www.adha.org/scholarships-and-grants

Carol Bauhs Benson Scholarship

Type of award: Scholarship.
Intended use: For full-time undergraduate certificate, sophomore, junior, senior or post-bachelor's certificate study at accredited 2-year institution in United States.
Eligibility: Applicant must be residing in Wisconsin, South Dakota, Minnesota or North Dakota.
Basis for selection: Major/career interest in dental hygiene. Applicant must demonstrate financial need and high academic achievement.
Application requirements: Recommendations, essay. FAFSA.
Additional information: Must have completed one year in a dental hygiene curriculum by award year; may apply during first year. Must be active ADHA or Student ADHA member with minimum 3.5 GPA in dental hygiene. Download application from Website. All applications must be typed. Applying to more than one scholarship may void application.

Amount of award:	$1,000
Number of awards:	1
Application deadline:	February 1
Notification begins:	July 1

Contact:
ADHA Institute for Oral Health
Scholarship Award Program
444 N. Michigan Ave., Ste. 3400
Chicago, IL 60611-3980
Phone: 312-440-8900
Web: www.adha.org/scholarships-and-grants

Colgate "Bright Smiles, Bright Futures" Minority Scholarships

Type of award: Scholarship, renewable.
Intended use: For full-time undergraduate certificate, sophomore, junior or senior study in United States.

Eligibility: Applicant must be Asian American, African American, Mexican American, Hispanic American, Puerto Rican or American Indian.
Basis for selection: Major/career interest in dental hygiene. Applicant must demonstrate financial need and high academic achievement.
Application requirements: Recommendations, essay. FAFSA.
Additional information: Applicant must be member of ADHA or Student ADHA. Men considered a minority in this field and encouraged to apply. Applicant must have completed at least one year of certificate-level dental hygiene program; may apply during first year. Minimum 3.5 dental hygiene GPA. Download application from Website. All applications must be typed. Applying to more than one scholarship may void application.

Amount of award:	$1,250
Number of awards:	2
Application deadline:	February 1
Notification begins:	July 1

Contact:
ADHA Institute for Oral Health
Scholarship Award Program
444 N. Michigan Ave., Suite 3400
Chicago, IL 60611-3980
Phone: 312-440-8900
Web: www.adha.org/scholarships-and-grants

Crest Oral-B Dental Hygiene Scholarship

Type of award: Scholarship.
Intended use: For full-time sophomore, junior or senior study at accredited 4-year institution in United States.
Basis for selection: Major/career interest in dental hygiene. Applicant must demonstrate financial need, high academic achievement and seriousness of purpose.
Application requirements: Recommendations, essay. FAFSA.
Additional information: Applicant must have completed minimum one year dental hygiene curriculum; may apply during first year. Minimum 3.5 GPA in dental hygiene. Must demonstrate intent to encourage professional excellence and scholarship, promote quality research, and support dental hygiene through public and private education. Must be member of ADHA or Student ADHA. Download application from Website. All applications must be typed. Applying to more than one scholarship may void application. Amount of award varies.

Amount of award:	$1,000
Number of awards:	2
Application deadline:	February 1
Notification begins:	July 1

Contact:
ADHA Institute for Oral Health
Scholarship Award Program
444 N. Michigan Ave., Suite 3400
Chicago, IL 60611-3980
Phone: 312-440-8900
Web: www.adha.org/scholarships-and-grants

Dr. Esther Wilkins Scholarship

Type of award: Scholarship.
Intended use: For full-time sophomore, junior, senior or post-bachelor's certificate study at accredited 2-year or 4-year institution in United States.
Basis for selection: Major/career interest in dental hygiene. Applicant must demonstrate financial need and high academic achievement.
Application requirements: Essay. FAFSA.
Additional information: Awarded to applicants pursuing additional degree necessary for career in dental hygiene education. Applicants must have completed an entry-level dental hygiene program. Must be active ADHA or Student ADHA member with minimum 3.5 GPA. Download application from Website. All applications must be typed. Applying to more than one scholarship may void application. Amount of award varies.

Amount of award:	$1,000
Number of awards:	1
Application deadline:	February 1
Notification begins:	July 1

Contact:
ADHA Institute for Oral Health
Scholarship Award Program
444 N. Michigan Ave., Ste. 3400
Chicago, IL 60611-3980
Phone: 312-440-8900
Web: www.adha.org/scholarships-and-grants

Hu-Friedy/Esther Wilkins Instrument Scholarships

Type of award: Scholarship.
Intended use: For full-time undergraduate certificate, sophomore, junior or senior study at accredited 2-year or 4-year institution in United States.
Basis for selection: Major/career interest in dental hygiene. Applicant must demonstrate financial need and high academic achievement.
Application requirements: FAFSA.
Additional information: Must have completed one year of dental hygiene curriculum by award year; may apply during first year. Must be active ADHA or Student ADHA member with minimum 3.5 dental hygiene GPA. Download application from Website. Award given as $1,000 worth of Hu-Friedy dental hygiene instruments. All applications must be typed. Applying to more than one scholarship may void application.

Amount of award:	$1,000
Number of awards:	5
Application deadline:	February 1
Notification begins:	July 1

Contact:
ADHA Institute for Oral Health
Scholarship Award Program
444 N. Michigan Avenue, Suite 3400
Chicago, IL 60611-3980
Phone: 312-440-8900
Web: www.adha.org/scholarships-and-grants

Karla Girts Memorial Community Outreach Scholarship

Type of award: Scholarship.
Intended use: For full-time undergraduate certificate, sophomore, junior or senior study at accredited 2-year or 4-year institution in United States.
Basis for selection: Major/career interest in dental hygiene. Applicant must demonstrate financial need and high academic achievement.
Application requirements: Recommendations, essay. FAFSA. Additional essay required.
Additional information: Applicants must display a commitment to improving oral health within the geriatric population. Must have completed one year in a dental hygiene curriculum by award year; may apply during first year. Must be active ADHA or Student ADHA member with minimum 3.0

dental hygiene GPA. Download application from Website. All applications must be typed. Applying to more than one scholarship may void application. Amount of award varies.

Amount of award: $2,000
Number of awards: 2
Application deadline: February 1
Notification begins: July 1

Contact:
ADHA Institute for Oral Health
Scholarship Award Program
444 N. Michigan Avenue, Suite 3400
Chicago, IL 60611-3980
Phone: 312-440-8900
Web: www.adha.org/scholarships-and-grants

Sigma Phi Alpha Certificate/ Associate Scholarship

Type of award: Scholarship.
Intended use: For full-time sophomore, junior, senior or post-bachelor's certificate study at accredited vocational or 2-year institution in United States.
Basis for selection: Major/career interest in dental hygiene.
Additional information: Applicant must have completed minimum one year dental hygiene curriculum; may apply during first year. Minimum 3.5 GPA in dental hygiene. Must be member of ADHA or Student ADHA. Applicant's school must have active chapter of the Sigma Phi Alpha Dental Hygiene Honor Society.

Amount of award: $1,000
Number of awards: 1
Application deadline: February 1
Notification begins: July 1

Contact:
ADHA Institute for Oral Health
Scholarship Award Program
444 N. Michigan Ave., Suite 3400
Chicago, IL 60611
Phone: 312-440-8900
Web: www.adha.org/scholarships-and-grants

Sigma Phi Alpha Undergraduate Scholarship

Type of award: Scholarship.
Intended use: For full-time undergraduate certificate, sophomore, junior or senior study at accredited 2-year or 4-year institution in United States. Designated institutions: Schools with active chapter of Sigma Phi Alpha Dental Hygiene Honor Society.
Basis for selection: Major/career interest in dental hygiene. Applicant must demonstrate financial need and high academic achievement.
Application requirements: Recommendations, essay. FAFSA.
Additional information: Must be member of Sigma Phi Alpha. Minimum 3.5 GPA in dental hygiene. Must be member of ADHA or Student ADHA. Must have completed at least one year of dental hygiene program. Visit Website for application. All applications must be typed. Applying to more than one scholarship may void application. Amount of award varies.

Amount of award: $1,000
Number of awards: 1
Application deadline: February 1
Notification begins: July 1

Contact:
ADHA Institute for Oral Health
Scholarship Award Program
444 N. Michigan Avenue, Suite 3400
Chicago, IL 60611-3980
Phone: 312-440-8900
Web: www.adha.org/scholarships-and-grants

Wilma Motley Memorial California Merit Scholarship

Type of award: Scholarship.
Intended use: For full-time sophomore, junior, senior or graduate study at accredited 2-year, 4-year or graduate institution in United States.
Basis for selection: Major/career interest in dental hygiene. Applicant must demonstrate high academic achievement and leadership.
Application requirements: Recommendations, essay.
Additional information: Awarded to individuals pursuing associate/certificate in dental hygiene, baccalaureate degree, degree completion in dental hygiene, Registered Dental Hygienist in Alternative Practice (RDHAP), master's or doctorate degree in dental hygiene or related field. Applicants must either be a resident of California or attending a dental hygiene program in California. Must have completed one year in a dental hygiene curriculum by award year; may apply during first year. Must be active ADHA or Student ADHA member with minimum 3.5 GPA. Download application from Website. All applications must be typed. Applying to more than one scholarship may void application. Amount of award varies.

Amount of award: $2,000
Number of awards: 3
Application deadline: February 1
Notification begins: July 1

Contact:
ADHA Institute for Oral Health
Scholarship Award Program
444 N. Michigan Ave., Ste. 3400
Chicago, IL 60611-3980
Phone: 312-440-8900
Web: www.adha.org/scholarships-and-grants

AFSA Scholarship Programs

Air Force Sergeants Association Scholarship, Airmen Memorial Foundation, and Chief Master Sergeants of the Air Force Scholarship Programs

Type of award: Scholarship.
Intended use: For full-time undergraduate study at accredited postsecondary institution in United States.
Eligibility: Applicant must be single, no older than 23. Applicant must be dependent of active service person or veteran in the Air Force. May be dependent of retired member as well. Dependents of members of the Air National Guard or Air Force Reserve also eligible.
Basis for selection: Applicant must demonstrate high academic achievement, depth of character and leadership.

Application requirements: Recommendations, essay, transcript, proof of eligibility.
Additional information: Applicant must be under 23 years of age as of August 1 of award year. Applications available January 1 to March 31. Amount of award varies. See Website for application and eligibility requirements.

Amount of award:	$1,000-$3,000
Number of awards:	46
Number of applicants:	287
Application deadline:	March 31
Notification begins:	July 1
Total amount awarded:	$74,000

Contact:
AFSA Scholarship Programs
Attn: Brandon Alsobrooks, Scholarship Coord.
5211 Auth Road
Suitland, MD 20746
Phone: 301-899-3500 ext. 230
Web: www.hqafsa.org

AfterCollege

AfterCollege Business Student Scholarship

Type of award: Scholarship, renewable.
Intended use: For full-time undergraduate study at accredited 2-year or 4-year institution.
Basis for selection: Major/career interest in business; accounting; economics; business/management/administration; human resources; public relations; advertising or finance/banking. Applicant must demonstrate high academic achievement.
Application requirements: Recommendations, transcript.
Additional information: Minimum 3.0 GPA. Quarterly deadlines: 3/31; 6/30; 9/30; 12/31. Winners notified 30 days after scholarship deadline. Scholarship award is divided over 4 quarters.

Amount of award:	$2,000
Number of awards:	1
Number of applicants:	453
Application deadline:	March 31, June 30
Total amount awarded:	$2,000

Contact:
AfterCollege
98 Battery Street
Suite 502
San Francisco, CA 94111
Phone: 415-263-1300
Web: acdc.mx/acschools

AfterCollege Computer Science & Engineering Student Scholarship

Type of award: Scholarship.
Intended use: For full-time undergraduate study at accredited 2-year or 4-year institution.
Basis for selection: Major/career interest in computer/information sciences or mathematics. Applicant must demonstrate high academic achievement.
Application requirements: Recommendations, transcript.
Additional information: Computer engineering majors also eligible. Minimum 3.0 GPA. Quarterly deadlines: 3/31; 6/30; 9/30; 12/31. Winners notified 30 days after scholarship deadline. Scholarship award is divided over 4 quarters.

Amount of award:	$2,000
Number of awards:	1
Number of applicants:	357
Application deadline:	March 31, June 30
Total amount awarded:	$2,000

Contact:
AfterCollege
98 Battery Street
Suite 502
San Francisco, CA 94111
Phone: 415-263-1300
Web: acdc.mx/acschools

AfterCollege Electrical Engineering Student Scholarship

Type of award: Scholarship, renewable.
Intended use: For full-time undergraduate study at accredited 2-year or 4-year institution.
Basis for selection: Major/career interest in engineering, electrical/electronic. Applicant must demonstrate high academic achievement.
Application requirements: Recommendations, transcript.
Additional information: Minimum 3.0 GPA. Quarterly deadlines: 3/31; 6/30; 9/30; 12/31. Winners notified 30 days after scholarship deadline.

Amount of award:	$2,000
Number of awards:	1
Number of applicants:	264
Application deadline:	March 31, June 30
Total amount awarded:	$2,000

Contact:
AfterCollege
98 Battery Street
Suite 502
San Francisco, CA 94111
Phone: 415-263-1300
Web: acdc.mx/acschools

AfterCollege Engineering Scholarship

Type of award: Scholarship, renewable.
Intended use: For full-time undergraduate study at accredited 2-year or 4-year institution.
Basis for selection: Major/career interest in engineering. Applicant must demonstrate high academic achievement.
Application requirements: Recommendations, transcript.
Additional information: Minimum 3.0 GPA. Quarterly deadlines: 3/31; 6/30; 9/30; 12/31. Winners notified 30 days after scholarship deadline. Scholarship award is divided over 4 quarters.

Amount of award:	$2,000
Number of awards:	1
Number of applicants:	1,334
Application deadline:	March 31, June 30
Total amount awarded:	$2,000

Contact:
AfterCollege
98 Battery Street
Suite 502
San Francisco, CA 94111
Phone: 415-263-1300
Web: acdc.mx/acschools

AfterCollege Medical Technologist & Clinical Lab Scientist Student Scholarship

Type of award: Scholarship, renewable.
Intended use: For full-time undergraduate or graduate study at accredited 4-year or graduate institution.
Basis for selection: Applicant must demonstrate high academic achievement.
Application requirements: Recommendations, transcript.
Additional information: Must be current student in good standing studying Medical Technology or Clinical Laboratory Science. Minimum 3.0 GPA. Quarterly deadlines: 3/31; 6/30; 9/30; 12/31. Winners notified 30 days after scholarship deadline. Scholarship award is divided over 4 quarters.

Amount of award:	$2,000
Number of awards:	1
Number of applicants:	139
Application deadline:	March 31, June 30
Total amount awarded:	$2,000

Contact:
AfterCollege
98 Battery Street
Suite 502
San Francisco, CA 94111
Phone: 415-263-1300
Web: acdc.mx/acschools

AfterCollege Pharmacy Student Scholarship

Type of award: Scholarship, renewable.
Intended use: For full-time undergraduate or graduate study at accredited 4-year or graduate institution.
Basis for selection: Major/career interest in pharmacy/pharmaceutics/pharmacology. Applicant must demonstrate high academic achievement.
Application requirements: Recommendations, transcript.
Additional information: Must be studying to be a pharmacy technician, pharmacologist or doctor of pharmacy. Minimum 3.0 GPA. Quarterly deadlines: 3/31; 6/30; 9/30; 12/31. Winners notified 30 days after scholarship deadline. Scholarship award is divided over 4 quarters.

Amount of award:	$2,000
Number of awards:	1
Number of applicants:	712
Application deadline:	March 31, June 30
Total amount awarded:	$2,000

Contact:
AfterCollege
98 Battery Street
Suite 502
San Francisco, CA 94111
Phone: 415-263-1300
Web: acdc.mx/acschools

AfterCollege Science Student Scholarship

Type of award: Scholarship, renewable.
Intended use: For full-time undergraduate study at accredited 2-year or 4-year institution.
Basis for selection: Major/career interest in science, general. Applicant must demonstrate high academic achievement.
Application requirements: Recommendations, transcript.
Additional information: Minimum 3.0 GPA. Quarterly deadlines: 3/31; 6/30; 9/30; 12/31. Winners notified 30 days after scholarship deadline. Scholarship award is divided over 4 quarters.

Amount of award:	$2,000
Number of awards:	1
Number of applicants:	599
Application deadline:	March 31, June 30
Total amount awarded:	$2,000

Contact:
AfterCollege
98 Battery Street
Suite 502
San Francisco, CA 94111
Phone: 415-263-1300
Web: acdc.mx/acschools

AfterCollege Speech Language Pathology Student Scholarship

Type of award: Scholarship, renewable.
Intended use: For full-time undergraduate or graduate study at accredited 4-year or graduate institution.
Basis for selection: Major/career interest in speech pathology/audiology. Applicant must demonstrate high academic achievement.
Application requirements: Recommendations, transcript.
Additional information: Communication sciences majors also eligible. Minimum 3.0 GPA. Quarterly deadlines: 3/31; 6/30; 9/30; 12/31. Winners notified 30 days after scholarship deadline. Scholarship award is divided over 4 quarters.

Amount of award:	$2,000
Number of awards:	1
Number of applicants:	219
Application deadline:	March 31, June 30
Total amount awarded:	$2,000

Contact:
AfterCollege
98 Battery Street
Suite 502
San Francisco, CA 94111
Phone: 415-263-1300
Web: acdc.mx/acschools

AfterCollege/AACN Nursing Student Scholarships

Type of award: Scholarship.
Intended use: For full-time undergraduate or graduate study at accredited 4-year or graduate institution.
Basis for selection: Major/career interest in nursing. Applicant must demonstrate high academic achievement.
Application requirements: Recommendations, transcript.
Additional information: Minimum 3.0 GPA. Quarterly deadlines: 3/31; 6/30; 9/30; 12/31. Winners notified 30 days after scholarship deadline. Scholarship award is divided over 4 quarters.

Amount of award:	$10,000
Number of awards:	2
Application deadline:	March 31, June 30
Total amount awarded:	$20,000

Contact:
AfterCollege
98 Battery Street
Suite 502
San Francisco, CA 94111
Phone: 415-263-1300
Web: acdc.mx/acschools

AHIMA Foundation

AHIMA Student Merit Scholarships

Type of award: Scholarship.
Intended use: For full-time undergraduate or graduate study at accredited 2-year, 4-year or graduate institution.
Basis for selection: Major/career interest in information systems; health services administration or health-related professions. Applicant must demonstrate high academic achievement, seriousness of purpose and service orientation.
Application requirements: Recommendations, transcript. Enrollment verification form.
Additional information: Applicant must be member of AHIMA and enrolled in an undergraduate CAHIIM-accredited health information administration or health information technology program or a national accredited graduate level program. Minimum 3.5 GPA. Applicants must be actively enrolled in a minimum of six credit hours. Must have completed twenty-four credit hours toward a degree (graduate applicants can include undergraduate credit hours), and have at least six credit hours remaining after award date. Award is $1,000 for associate's degree, $1,500 for bachelor's degrees, $2,000 for master's degrees, and $2,500 for doctoral degrees. Apply online.

Amount of award:	$1,000-$2,500
Number of awards:	58
Number of applicants:	215
Application deadline:	September 30
Notification begins:	November 30
Total amount awarded:	$91,500

Contact:
AHIMA Foundation
233 North Michigan Avenue, 21st Floor
Chicago, IL 60601-5809
Phone: 312-233-1585
Web: www.ahimafoundation.org/Scholarships/MeritScholarships.aspx

Air Force Aid Society

General Henry H. Arnold Education Grant

Type of award: Scholarship.
Intended use: For full-time undergraduate study at accredited vocational, 2-year or 4-year institution in or outside United States.
Eligibility: Applicant must be spouse of active service person or deceased veteran who serves or served in the Air Force. Applicant may also be dependent child of active, retired or deceased Air Force service member. Veteran status alone not eligible. Sponsoring member must be active duty, retired due to length of service, retired Reserve with 20-plus qualifying years of service, or deceased while on active duty or in retired status. Dependent children of Title 32 AGR performing full-time active duty service are also eligible.
Basis for selection: Applicant must demonstrate financial need and high academic achievement.
Application requirements: Proof of eligibility.
Additional information: Minimum 2.0 GPA.

Amount of award:	$2,000
Number of awards:	3,000
Number of applicants:	4,300
Application deadline:	March 14
Notification begins:	June 1
Total amount awarded:	$6,000,000

Contact:
Air Force Aid Society
Education Assistance Department
241 18th Street South, Suite 202
Arlington, VA 22202
Phone: 800-429-9475
Web: www.afas.org

Air Force/ROTC

Air Force/ROTC Four-Year Scholarship (Types 1, 2, and 7)

Type of award: Scholarship.
Intended use: For freshman study at accredited 4-year institution in United States.
Eligibility: Applicant must be at least 17, no older than 30, high school senior. Applicant must be U.S. citizen.
Basis for selection: Applicant must demonstrate high academic achievement and leadership.
Application requirements: Interview, recommendations, transcript. SAT/ACT scores, physical fitness assessment, resume.
Additional information: Recipients agree to serve four years' active duty. Minimum 3.0 GPA. At least 24 ACT or 1100 SAT excluding writing tests. Opportunities available in any major. Applicants must not be enrolled in college full-time prior to application. Type 1 provides full tuition, most fees, $900 for textbooks, and is awarded mostly to technical fields. Type 2 provides tuition, most fees up to $18,000, $900 for textbooks per year. Type 7 provides tuition and fees up to the equivalent of the in-state rate, $900 for books. Scholarship board decides which type is offered. For all scholarships, amount of stipend is based on student's academic year. Apply online.

Amount of award:	Full tuition
Application deadline:	December 1

Contact:
Air Force/ROTC
High School Scholarship Section
551 E. Maxwell Blvd.
Maxwell AFB, AL 36112-5917
Phone: 866-423-7682
Web: www.afrotc.com

Scholarships

Air Traffic Control Association, Inc.

Air Traffic Control Full-Time Employee Student Scholarship

Type of award: Scholarship.
Intended use: For freshman, sophomore, junior, graduate or non-degree study at accredited postsecondary institution.
Eligibility: Applicant or parent must be employed by Aviation industry. Applicant must be returning adult student.
Basis for selection: Major/career interest in aviation. Applicant must demonstrate financial need.
Application requirements: Recommendations, essay, transcript.
Additional information: Applicant must work full-time in aviation-related field and be enrolled in coursework designed to enhance air traffic control or aviation skills. Must have minimum 30 semester or 45 quarter hours still to be completed before graduation. Award amount determined by ATCA Scholarship Program Board of Directors. Visit Website for application.

Number of awards: 1
Application deadline: May 1

Contact:
Air Traffic Control Association, Inc.
Attn: Scholarship Fund
1101 King Street, Suite 300
Alexandria, VA 22314
Phone: 703-299-2430
Fax: 703-299-2437
Web: www.atca.org

Air Traffic Control Non-Employee Student Scholarship

Type of award: Scholarship.
Intended use: For freshman, sophomore, junior or graduate study at accredited 4-year or graduate institution.
Basis for selection: Major/career interest in aviation. Applicant must demonstrate financial need.
Application requirements: Recommendations, essay, transcript.
Additional information: Must have minimum 30 semester hours or 45 quarter hours still to be completed before graduation. Number of awards varies based on funding. Visit Website for application.

Application deadline: May 1

Contact:
Air Traffic Control Association, Inc.
Attn: Scholarship Fund
1101 King Street, Suite 300
Alexandria, VA 22314
Phone: 703-299-2430
Fax: 703-299-2437
Web: www.atca.org

Buckingham Memorial Scholarship

Type of award: Scholarship, renewable.
Intended use: For freshman, sophomore, junior or graduate study at accredited 4-year or graduate institution in United States.
Eligibility: Applicant or parent must be employed by Aviation industry. Applicant must be U.S. citizen.
Basis for selection: Major/career interest in aviation. Applicant must demonstrate financial need.
Application requirements: Recommendations, essay, transcript.
Additional information: Must be child of a person serving, or having served, as an air traffic control specialist. Must have minimum of 30 semester or 45 quarter hours to be completed before graduation. Number of awards varies based on funding. Visit Website for application.

Application deadline: May 1

Contact:
Air Traffic Control Association, Inc.
Attn: Scholarship Fund
1101 King Street, Suite 300
Alexandria, VA 22314
Phone: 703-299-2430
Fax: 703-299-2437
Web: www.atca.org

Gabe A. Hartl Scholarship

Type of award: Scholarship.
Intended use: For freshman, sophomore, junior or graduate study at accredited 2-year, 4-year or graduate institution. Designated institutions: FAA-approved institutions.
Basis for selection: Major/career interest in aviation. Applicant must demonstrate financial need.
Application requirements: Recommendations, essay, transcript.
Additional information: Must have minimum of 30 semester or 45 quarter hours to be completed before graduation. Must be enrolled in air traffic control curriculum. Number of awards varies based on funding. Visit Website for application.

Application deadline: May 1

Contact:
Air Traffic Control Association, Inc.
Attn: Scholarship Fund
1101 King Street, Suite 300
Alexandria, VA 22314
Phone: 703-299-2430
Fax: 703-299-2437
Web: www.atca.org

Aircraft Electronics Association Educational Foundation

David Arver Memorial Scholarship

Type of award: Scholarship, renewable.
Intended use: For full-time undergraduate study at accredited vocational or 2-year institution.
Eligibility: Applicant must be residing in Wisconsin, Michigan, Iowa, South Dakota, Minnesota, Kansas, Indiana, Nebraska, Illinois, North Dakota or Missouri.
Basis for selection: Major/career interest in aviation; aviation repair or electronics. Applicant must demonstrate high academic achievement, depth of character and seriousness of purpose.
Application requirements: Recommendations, essay, transcript, proof of eligibility.

Additional information: Minimum 2.5 GPA. Awards are announced at AEA Annual Convention and Trade Show each spring. Visit Website for more information.

Amount of award:	$1,000
Number of awards:	1
Application deadline:	February 15
Notification begins:	April 1
Total amount awarded:	$1,000

Contact:
Aircraft Electronics Association Educational Foundation
3570 NE Ralph Powell Road
Lee's Summit, MO 64064
Phone: 816-347-8400
Fax: 816-347-8405
Web: www.aea.net/educationalfoundation

Dutch and Ginger Arver Scholarship

Type of award: Scholarship, renewable.
Intended use: For full-time undergraduate study at accredited vocational, 2-year or 4-year institution.
Basis for selection: Major/career interest in aviation; electronics or aviation repair. Applicant must demonstrate high academic achievement, depth of character and seriousness of purpose.
Application requirements: Recommendations, essay, transcript, proof of eligibility.
Additional information: Minimum 2.5 GPA. Awards are announced at AEA Annual Convention and Trade Show each spring. Visit Website for more information.

Amount of award:	$1,000
Number of awards:	1
Application deadline:	February 15
Notification begins:	April 1
Total amount awarded:	$1,000

Contact:
Aircraft Electronics Association Educational Foundation
3570 NE Ralph Powell Road
Lee's Summit, MO 64064
Phone: 816-347-8400
Fax: 816-347-8405
Web: www.aea.net/educationalfoundation

Field Aviation Co. Inc. Scholarship

Type of award: Scholarship, renewable.
Intended use: For full-time undergraduate study at accredited vocational, 2-year or 4-year institution.
Basis for selection: Major/career interest in aviation; aviation repair or electronics. Applicant must demonstrate high academic achievement, depth of character and seriousness of purpose.
Application requirements: Recommendations, essay, transcript, proof of eligibility.
Additional information: Minimum 2.5 GPA. Awards are announced at AEA Annual Convention and Trade Show each spring. Visit Website for more information.

Amount of award:	$1,000
Number of awards:	1
Application deadline:	February 15
Notification begins:	April 1

Contact:
Aircraft Electronics Association Educational Foundation
3570 NE Ralph Powell Road
Lee's Summit, MO 64064
Phone: 816-347-8400
Fax: 816-347-8405
Web: www.aea.net/educationalfoundation

Garmin Scholarship

Type of award: Scholarship, renewable.
Intended use: For full-time undergraduate study at accredited vocational, 2-year or 4-year institution.
Basis for selection: Major/career interest in aviation; aviation repair or electronics. Applicant must demonstrate high academic achievement, depth of character and seriousness of purpose.
Application requirements: Recommendations, essay, transcript, proof of eligibility.
Additional information: Minimum 2.5 GPA. Awards are announced at AEA Annual Convention and Trade Show each spring. For more information, visit Website.

Amount of award:	$2,000
Number of awards:	1
Application deadline:	February 15
Notification begins:	April 1
Total amount awarded:	$2,000

Contact:
Aircraft Electronics Association Educational Foundation
3570 NE Ralph Powell Road
Lee's Summit, MO 64064
Phone: 816-347-8400
Fax: 816-347-8405
Web: www.aea.net/educationalfoundation

Johnny Davis Memorial Scholarship

Type of award: Scholarship, renewable.
Intended use: For full-time undergraduate study at accredited vocational, 2-year or 4-year institution.
Basis for selection: Major/career interest in aviation; aviation repair or electronics. Applicant must demonstrate high academic achievement, depth of character and seriousness of purpose.
Application requirements: Recommendations, essay, transcript, proof of eligibility.
Additional information: Minimum 2.5 GPA. Awards are announced at AEA Annual Convention and Trade Show each spring. Visit Website for additional information.

Amount of award:	$1,000
Number of awards:	1
Application deadline:	February 15
Notification begins:	April 1
Total amount awarded:	$1,000

Contact:
Aircraft Electronics Association Educational Foundation
3570 NE Ralph Powell Road
Lee's Summit, MO 64064
Phone: 816-347-8400
Fax: 816-347-8405
Web: www.aea.net/educationalfoundation

L-3 Avionics Systems Scholarship

Type of award: Scholarship, renewable.
Intended use: For full-time undergraduate study at accredited vocational, 2-year or 4-year institution.

Basis for selection: Major/career interest in aviation; aviation repair or electronics. Applicant must demonstrate high academic achievement, depth of character and seriousness of purpose.
Application requirements: Recommendations, essay, transcript, proof of eligibility.
Additional information: Applicant may be high school senior. Minimum 2.5 GPA. Awards are announced at AEA Annual Convention and Trade Show each spring. Visit Website for more information.

Amount of award:	$2,500
Number of awards:	1
Application deadline:	February 15
Notification begins:	April 1
Total amount awarded:	$2,500

Contact:
Aircraft Electronics Association Educational Foundation
3570 NE Ralph Powell Road
Lee's Summit, MO 64064
Phone: 816-347-8400
Fax: 816-347-8405
Web: www.aea.net/educationalfoundation

Lee Tarbox Memorial Scholarship

Type of award: Scholarship, renewable.
Intended use: For full-time undergraduate study at accredited vocational, 2-year or 4-year institution.
Basis for selection: Major/career interest in aviation; aviation repair or electronics. Applicant must demonstrate high academic achievement, depth of character and seriousness of purpose.
Application requirements: Recommendations, essay, transcript, proof of eligibility.
Additional information: Minimum 2.5 GPA. Awards are announced at AEA Annual Convention and Trade Show each spring. Visit Website for additional information.

Amount of award:	$2,500
Number of awards:	1
Application deadline:	February 15
Notification begins:	April 1
Total amount awarded:	$2,500

Contact:
Aircraft Electronics Association Educational Foundation
3570 NE Ralph Powell Road
Lee's Summit, MO 64064
Phone: 816-347-8400
Fax: 816-347-8405
Web: www.aea.net/educationalfoundation

Lowell Gaylor Memorial Scholarship

Type of award: Scholarship, renewable.
Intended use: For full-time undergraduate study at accredited vocational, 2-year or 4-year institution.
Basis for selection: Major/career interest in aviation; aviation repair or electronics. Applicant must demonstrate high academic achievement, depth of character and seriousness of purpose.
Application requirements: Recommendations, essay, transcript, proof of eligibility.
Additional information: Minimum 2.5 GPA. Awards are announced at AEA Annual Convention and Trade Show each spring. Visit Website for more information.

Amount of award:	$1,000
Number of awards:	1
Application deadline:	February 15
Notification begins:	April 1

Contact:
Aircraft Electronics Association Educational Foundation
3570 NE Ralph Powell Road
Lee's Summit, MO 64064
Phone: 816-347-8400
Fax: 816-347-8405
Web: www.aea.net/educationalfoundation

Mid-Continent Instrument Scholarship

Type of award: Scholarship, renewable.
Intended use: For full-time undergraduate study at accredited vocational, 2-year or 4-year institution.
Basis for selection: Major/career interest in aviation; electronics or aviation repair. Applicant must demonstrate high academic achievement, depth of character and seriousness of purpose.
Application requirements: Recommendations, essay, transcript, proof of eligibility.
Additional information: Minimum 2.5 GPA. Awards are announced at AEA Annual Convention and Trade Show each spring. Visit Website for more information.

Amount of award:	$1,000
Number of awards:	1
Application deadline:	February 15
Notification begins:	April 1
Total amount awarded:	$1,000

Contact:
Aircraft Electronics Association Educational Foundation
3570 NE Ralph Powell Road
Lee's Summit, MO 64064
Phone: 816-347-8400
Fax: 816-347-8405
Web: www.aea.net/educationalfoundation

Alabama Commission on Higher Education

Alabama National Guard Educational Assistance Program

Type of award: Scholarship, renewable.
Intended use: For undergraduate or graduate study at postsecondary institution. Designated institutions: Public institutions in Alabama.
Eligibility: Applicant must be U.S. citizen residing in Alabama. Applicant must be in military service in the Reserves/National Guard. Must be active member in good standing with federally recognized unit of Alabama National Guard.
Application requirements: Proof of eligibility.
Additional information: Award to be used for tuition, books, fees, and supplies (minus any federal veterans benefits). Applications available from Alabama National Guard units. Funds are limited; apply early.

Amount of award:	$25-$1,000
Number of applicants:	653
Total amount awarded:	$404,119

Contact:
Alabama Commission on Higher Education
Phone: 334-242-2273
Fax: 334-242-2269
Web: www.ache.alabama.gov

Alabama Student Assistance Program

Type of award: Scholarship, renewable.
Intended use: For full-time undergraduate study. Designated institutions: Eligible Alabama institutions.
Eligibility: Applicant must be residing in Alabama.
Basis for selection: Applicant must demonstrate financial need.
Application requirements: Proof of eligibility. FAFSA.
Additional information: Students urged to apply early. Applications available at college financial aid office.

Amount of award:	$300-$5,000
Number of applicants:	8,261
Total amount awarded:	$5,610,418

Contact:
Alabama Commission on Higher Education
Phone: 334-242-2273
Fax: 334-242-2269
Web: www.ache.alabama.gov

Alabama Student Grant Program

Type of award: Scholarship, renewable.
Intended use: For undergraduate study at 2-year or 4-year institution. Designated institutions: Private institutions: Amridge University, Birmingham-Southern College, Concordia College, Faulkner University, Huntingdon College, Judson College, Miles College, Oakwood University, Samford University, South University, Spring Hill College, Stillman College, United States Sports Academy, University of Mobile.
Eligibility: Applicant must be residing in Alabama.
Application requirements: Proof of eligibility.
Additional information: For use at private institutions. For more information, contact financial aid office of participating colleges.

Amount of award:	$1,200
Number of applicants:	6,908
Application deadline:	February 15, September 15
Total amount awarded:	$16,235,000

Contact:
Alabama Commission on Higher Education
Phone: 334-242-2273
Fax: 334-242-2269
Web: www.ache.alabama.gov

Police/Firefighters' Survivors Educational Assistance Program

Type of award: Scholarship, renewable.
Intended use: For undergraduate study at vocational, 2-year or 4-year institution. Designated institutions: Public institutions.
Eligibility: Applicant must be residing in Alabama. Applicant's parent must have been killed or disabled in work-related accident as firefighter or police officer.
Application requirements: Proof of eligibility.
Additional information: Grant covers full tuition, mandatory fees, books, and supplies. Also available to eligible spouses.

Amount of award:	Full tuition
Number of applicants:	14
Total amount awarded:	$107,550

Contact:
Alabama Commission on Higher Education
P.O. Box 302000
Montgomery, AL 36130-2000
Phone: 334-242-2273
Fax: 334-242-2269
Web: www.ache.alabama.gov

Alabama Department of Postsecondary Education

Alabama Institutional Scholarship Waivers

Type of award: Scholarship, renewable.
Intended use: For freshman or sophomore study at accredited 2-year institution. Designated institutions: Alabama public 2-year community or technical colleges.
Eligibility: Applicant must be U.S. citizen or permanent resident.
Basis for selection: Applicant must demonstrate high academic achievement.
Additional information: Focus of scholarship is determined by each institution. Application deadlines printed on application forms. Award may be renewed if student demonstrates academic excellence. Contact individual institutions for scholarship/waiver requirements. Number and amount of awards vary. Visit Website for participating institutions.
Contact:
Department of Postsecondary Education
P.O. Box 302130
Montgomery, AL 36130-2130
Phone: 334-293-4557
Fax: 334-293-4559
Web: www.accs.cc

Alabama Junior/Community College Athletic Scholarship

Type of award: Scholarship, renewable.
Intended use: For freshman or sophomore study at 2-year institution. Designated institutions: Alabama public 2-year community colleges.
Eligibility: Applicant must be U.S. citizen or permanent resident.
Basis for selection: Competition/talent/interest in athletics/sports, based on athletic ability determined through tryouts.
Additional information: Renewal dependent on continued athletic participation. Contact individual institutions for specific requirements and amount of awards. Number of awards available varies by sport. Visit Website for participating institutions.
Contact:
Department of Postsecondary Education
P.O. Box 302130
Montgomery, AL 36130-2130
Phone: 334-293-4557
Fax: 334-293-4559
Web: www.accs.cc

Alabama Department of Veterans Affairs

Alabama G.I. Dependents' Scholarship Program

Type of award: Scholarship, renewable.
Intended use: For undergraduate or graduate study at postsecondary institution. Designated institutions: Alabama public institutions.
Eligibility: Applicant must be dependent of disabled veteran, deceased veteran or POW/MIA; or spouse of disabled veteran, deceased veteran or POW/MIA. Veteran must have served for at least 90 days continuous active federal duty during a wartime period, be rated with at least a 20% service-connected disability and must have resided in the state of Alabama for at least one year prior to enlistment or be rated with a 100% service connected disability and be a permanent resident of the State of Alabama for at least 5 years immediately prior to application for program.
Application requirements: Proof of eligibility.
Additional information: Children of veterans must submit application before their 26th birthday. Spouses of veterans have no age limit, but must not be remarried. Award for five academic years for children and three academic years for spouses (or part-time equivalent); covers tuition, textbooks, and laboratory fees. Unlimited number of awards available; no application deadline.

Amount of award:	Full tuition
Number of applicants:	3,126
Total amount awarded:	$30,094,787

Contact:
Alabama Department of Veterans Affairs
P.O. Box 1509
Montgomery, AL 36102-1509
Phone: 334-242-5077
Fax: 334-353-4078
Web: www.va.alabama.gov/scholarship.htm

Alaska Commission on Postsecondary Education

Alaska Performance Scholarship

Type of award: Scholarship.
Intended use: For undergraduate study at postsecondary institution in United States.
Eligibility: Applicant must be high school senior. Applicant must be residing in Alaska.
Basis for selection: Applicant must demonstrate financial need and high academic achievement.
Application requirements: FAFSA.
Additional information: Application is the Free Application for Federal Student Aid (FAFSA). Complete FAFSA as early as possible after January 1 of the year you plan to attend school. Minimum 2.5 GPA. Award amount dependent upon academic performance, ACT and/or SAT scores, and WorkKeys scores. Visit Website for eligibility requirements and additional information,

Amount of award:	$2,378-$4,755
Application deadline:	June 30

Contact:
Alaska Commission on Postsecondary Education
P.O. Box 110505
Juneau, AK 99811-0505
Phone: 907-465-2962
Fax: 907-465-5316
Web: www.alaskadvantage.state.ak.us

AlaskAdvantage Education Grant

Type of award: Scholarship.
Intended use: For undergraduate study at vocational, 2-year or 4-year institution in United States. Designated institutions: Alaska institutions.
Eligibility: Applicant must be U.S. citizen or permanent resident residing in Alaska.
Basis for selection: Applicant must demonstrate financial need.
Application requirements: FAFSA.
Additional information: Applicants must be eligible for federal Title IV aid. To apply, student must complete FAFSA between January 1 and June 30 each year.

Amount of award:	$500-$2,000
Application deadline:	June 30

Contact:
Alaska Commission on Postsecondary Education
P.O. Box 110505
Juneau, AK 99811-0505
Phone: 907-465-2962
Fax: 907-465-5316
Web: www.alaskadvantage.state.ak.us

Alexander Graham Bell Association for the Deaf and Hard of Hearing

AG Bell College Scholarship Awards

Type of award: Scholarship.
Intended use: For full-time undergraduate or graduate study at accredited 4-year or graduate institution in or outside United States.
Eligibility: Applicant must be hearing impaired.
Basis for selection: Applicant must demonstrate high academic achievement.
Application requirements: Recommendations, essay, transcript, proof of eligibility. Audiogram or CI programming report.
Additional information: Applicant must have bilateral hearing loss in the moderate to profound range, diagnosed before the fourth birthday. Must use listening and spoken language as primary form of communication, and be accepted or enrolled in mainstream college/university. Number of awards granted varies. Visit Website for additional eligibility criteria and application.

Amount of award:	$1,000-$10,000
Number of awards:	20
Number of applicants:	141
Application deadline:	March 15
Total amount awarded:	$100,000

Contact:
AG Bell College Scholarship Program
3417 Volta Place, NW
Washington, DC 20007-2778
Phone: 202-337-5220
Web: www.agbell.org

Alexia Foundation

Alexia Foundation Grant and Scholarship

Type of award: Scholarship.
Intended use: For full-time undergraduate or graduate study in or outside United States or Canada.
Basis for selection: Competition/talent/interest in photography.
Application requirements: Essay. 750-word proposal and 25-word summary, resume, portfolio of 10 to 20 photographs.
Additional information: Awards and amounts may vary yearly. Students who have completed more than three internships or who have a year of full-time professional experience are not eligible. Application must be submitted online. Check Website for number of awards available and additional information.

Amount of award:	$2,100-$16,000
Number of awards:	5
Application deadline:	February 1

Contact:
David Sutherland/The Alexia Competition
S.I. Newhouse School of Communications
215 University Place
Syracuse, NY 13244-2100
Phone: 315-443-3370
Web: www.alexiafoundation.org

Alliance for Young Artists and Writers

Scholastic Art Portfolio Gold Award

Type of award: Scholarship.
Intended use: For undergraduate study at postsecondary institution.
Eligibility: Applicant must be high school senior.
Basis for selection: Competition/talent/interest in visual arts, based on originality, level of technical proficiency, and emergence of personal style or vision. Major/career interest in arts, general.
Application requirements: Portfolio, essay. Signed registration form, artist's statement. Portfolio must contain eight digital works uploaded online.
Additional information: Deadline varies by region. Contact sponsor or visit Website for more information.

Amount of award:	$10,000
Number of applicants:	4,500

Contact:
Alliance for Young Artists & Writers
The Scholastic Art & Writing Awards
557 Broadway
New York, NY 10012
Phone: 212-343-7729
Fax: 212-389-3939
Web: www.artandwriting.org

Scholastic Art Portfolio Silver With Distinction Award

Type of award: Scholarship.
Intended use: For undergraduate study at postsecondary institution.
Eligibility: Applicant must be high school senior.
Basis for selection: Competition/talent/interest in visual arts, based on originality, level of technical proficiency, and emergence of personal style or vision. Major/career interest in arts, general.
Application requirements: Portfolio, essay. Signed registration form, artist's statement. Portfolio must contain eight digital works uploaded online.
Additional information: Students nominated for scholarships offered by participating higher education institutions. Deadline varies by region. Contact sponsor or visit Website for more information.

Amount of award:	$1,000
Number of applicants:	4,500

Contact:
Alliance for Young Artists & Writers
The Scholastic Art & Writing Awards
557 Broadway
New York, NY 10012
Phone: 212-343-7729
Fax: 212-389-3939
Web: www.artandwriting.org

Scholastic Photography Portfolio Silver Award

Type of award: Scholarship.
Intended use: For undergraduate study at postsecondary institution.
Eligibility: Applicant must be high school senior.
Basis for selection: Competition/talent/interest in writing/journalism, based on originality, level of technical proficiency, and emergence of personal style or vision. Major/career interest in arts, general; journalism; literature; theater arts or English.
Application requirements: Portfolio. Signed registration form. For writing, writer's statement. Portfolio must contain three to eight works. Excerpts from longer works permitted. Entry form must be signed by student's parent and teacher, counselor, or principal.
Additional information: Students nominated for scholarships offered by participating higher education institutions. Deadline varies by region. Application fee varies by location and may be waived. Contact sponsor or visit Website for more information.

Amount of award:	$1,000
Number of applicants:	900

Contact:
Alliance for Young Artists & Writers
The Scholastic Art & Writing Awards
557 Broadway
New York, NY 10012
Phone: 212-343-7729
Fax: 212-389-3939
Web: www.artandwriting.org

Scholastic Writing Portfolio Gold Award

Type of award: Scholarship.
Intended use: For undergraduate study at postsecondary institution.
Eligibility: Applicant must be high school senior.
Basis for selection: Competition/talent/interest in writing/journalism, based on originality, level of technical proficiency, and emergence of personal voice or style. Major/career interest in English; journalism; literature or theater arts.
Application requirements: Portfolio. Writer's statement. Portfolio must contain three to eight works in any category demonstrating diversity and talent. Excerpts from longer works permitted. Entry form must be signed by student's parent and teacher, counselor, or principal.
Additional information: Deadline varies by region. Application fee varies by location and may be waived. Contact sponsor or visit Website for more information.

Amount of award:	$10,000
Number of applicants:	900

Contact:
Alliance for Young Artists & Writers
The Scholastic Art & Writing Awards
557 Broadway
New York, NY 10012
Phone: 212-343-7729
Fax: 212-389-3939
Web: www.artandwriting.org

Alpha Beta Gamma International Business Honor Society

Alpha Beta Gamma National Scholarship

Type of award: Scholarship.
Intended use: For full-time junior or senior study at accredited 4-year institution. Designated institutions: Participating four-year colleges.
Basis for selection: Major/career interest in business; business, international; business/management/administration; accounting or computer/information sciences. Applicant must demonstrate high academic achievement and leadership.
Application requirements: Recommendations. Copy of ABG diploma.
Additional information: Must be initiated member of Alpha Beta Gamma. Awarded to enrollees of two-year schools who have been accepted at four-year schools to pursue baccalaureate degree in business or related professions. Some colleges have minimum GPA requirement. Amount of award varies by institution.

Amount of award:	$500-$8,100
Number of awards:	300
Number of applicants:	400
Total amount awarded:	$600,000

Contact:
Alpha Beta Gamma Scholarship Committee
75 Grasslands Road
Valhalla, NY 10595
Web: www.abg.org

Alpha Mu Gamma, the National Collegiate Foreign Language Honor Society

Alpha Mu Gamma Scholarships

Type of award: Scholarship.
Intended use: For full-time undergraduate, graduate or postgraduate study at 2-year, 4-year or graduate institution.
Basis for selection: Major/career interest in foreign languages. Applicant must demonstrate high academic achievement and seriousness of purpose.
Application requirements: Recommendations, essay, transcript. Photocopy of applicant's AMG full member certificate.
Additional information: Applicant must be full member of Alpha Mu Gamma. Three $1,000 awards granted for study of any foreign language; one $400 award for study of Esperanto or Spanish. May apply unlimited number of times. National office will not send out applications; forms must be requested from advisor of local AMG chapter.

Amount of award:	$400-$1,000
Number of awards:	4
Number of applicants:	25
Application deadline:	February 1
Notification begins:	April 1
Total amount awarded:	$3,400

Contact:
Advisor of local Alpha Mu Gamma chapter.
Web: www.lacitycollege.edu/academic/honor/amg/homepage.html

Alumnae Panhellenic Association of Washington, D.C.

Alumnae Panhellenic Association Women's Scholarship

Type of award: Scholarship, renewable.
Intended use: For sophomore, junior, senior or graduate study at 4-year or graduate institution.
Eligibility: Applicant must be female.
Basis for selection: Based on sorority involvement. Applicant must demonstrate high academic achievement and service orientation.
Application requirements: Recommendations, essay, transcript.

Additional information: Applicant must be member in good standing of sorority of National Panhellenic Conference and live or attend school in Washington, D.C., metro area. Send email for application request. Deadline in February or March. Amount and number of awards varies.

Number of awards:	3
Number of applicants:	20
Total amount awarded:	$2,550

Contact:
Alumnae Panhellenic Association of Washington, DC
Nancy Carman, Vice President
20621 Plum Creek Court
Gaithersburg, MD 20882
Web: www.dcalumnaepanhellenic.shutterfly.com

Alzheimer's Foundation of America

AFA Teens for Alzheimer's Awareness College Scholarship

Type of award: Scholarship.
Intended use: For freshman study at accredited 4-year institution.
Eligibility: Applicant must be high school senior. Applicant must be U.S. citizen or permanent resident.
Application requirements: Essay, proof of eligibility. 200-word or less autobiography. Two copies of 1,200 to 1,500 word essay based on topic on Website. Entire submission fastened with paper clip.
Additional information: Must be current high school junior or senior planning to enter college. First place: $5,000; second place: $500; third place: $250. Winners must agree to have name and city published, have essay published on AFA Teens Website, provide AFA with photo for publicity purposes, and be available for interviews with media. Proof of college registration and U.S. citizenship required upon selection.

Amount of award:	$250-$5,000
Number of awards:	3
Number of applicants:	3
Application deadline:	February 15
Notification begins:	April 15
Total amount awarded:	$5,750

Contact:
Alzheimer's Foundation of America
Attn: AFA Teens College Scholarship
322 Eighth Avenue, 7th Floor
New York, NY 10001
Phone: 866-232-8484
Web: www.afateens.org

AMBUCS

AMBUCS Scholars-Scholarship for Therapists

Type of award: Scholarship.
Intended use: For full-time junior, senior or master's study at accredited 4-year or graduate institution in United States. Designated institutions: Schools with programs accredited by appropriate health therapy association.
Eligibility: Applicant must be U.S. citizen.
Basis for selection: Major/career interest in occupational therapy; physical therapy or speech pathology/audiology. Applicant must demonstrate financial need, depth of character and service orientation.
Additional information: Award amount typically maximum $1,500, but one additional two-year award of $6,000 offered. Students must apply online; no paper applications accepted. Applicants may print online enrollment certificate. Additional documentation, including prior year's 1040 tax form, requested if applicant is selected as semifinalist.

Amount of award:	$500-$6,000
Number of applicants:	1,267
Application deadline:	April 15
Notification begins:	June 20
Total amount awarded:	$150,000

Contact:
AMBUCS Resource Center
P.O. Box 5127
High Point, NC 27262
Phone: 336-852-0052
Fax: 336-852-6830
Web: www.ambucs.org

American Alpine Club

Arthur K. Gilkey Memorial/Bedayn Research Grants

Type of award: Research grant.
Intended use: For undergraduate or graduate study.
Basis for selection: Major/career interest in science, general; biology; environmental science; forestry or atmospheric sciences/meteorology.
Application requirements: Research proposal. Curriculum vitae with biographical information.
Additional information: Research proposals evaluated on scientific or technical quality and contribution to scientific endeavor germane to mountain regions. Research focus may vary yearly; contact organization before applying. Applications available from Website; must be submitted via email. Number of awards varies.

Amount of award:	$500-$2,000
Number of applicants:	18
Application deadline:	March 1
Notification begins:	May 1
Total amount awarded:	$10,000

Contact:
American Alpine Club
710 Tenth Street
Suite 100
Golden, CO 80401
Phone: 303-384-0110
Fax: 303-384-0111
Web: www.americanalpineclub.org/grants

Scholarships

American Association for Cancer Research

Gary J. Miller Undergraduate Prizes for Cancer and Cancer-Related Biomedical Research

Type of award: Scholarship.
Intended use: For full-time undergraduate study at 4-year institution.
Basis for selection: Competition/talent/interest in science project. Major/career interest in biochemistry; biology; chemistry; pharmacy/pharmaceutics/pharmacology; microbiology; engineering, chemical; epidemiology; oncology or science, general.
Additional information: Applicants compete in the annual Undergraduate Student Caucus and Poster Competition, where applicants exhibit a scientific poster concerning cancer or cancer-related biomedical research. First prize receives $1,500 in funding to support cost of participation in the next AACR Annual Meeting. Second place receives $300; third place receives $200. All applicants receive complimentary registration to the AACR Annual Meeting, where the competition takes place. Application deadline and Abstract submission deadlines in March. Visit Website for dates and details.

Amount of award:	$200-$1,500
Number of awards:	5
Number of applicants:	85

Contact:
American Association for Cancer Research
615 Chestnut Street, 17th Floor
Philadelphia, PA 19106-4404
Phone: 215-440-9300
Fax: 215-440-9412
Web: www.aacr.org/USCPC

Thomas J. Bardos Science Education Awards for Undergraduate Students

Type of award: Research grant.
Intended use: For full-time junior study at 4-year institution.
Basis for selection: Major/career interest in biochemistry; biology; chemistry; pharmacy/pharmaceutics/pharmacology; microbiology; science, general; epidemiology or oncology. Applicant must demonstrate high academic achievement.
Application requirements: Recommendations, essay.
Additional information: Two-year award consists of $1,500 per year for travel expenses and registration fee waiver for AACR annual meeting. Selection based on qualifications and interest in research, mentor references, and selection committee's evaluation of potential professional benefit. Applicants not yet committed to cancer research welcome; those studying molecular biology and genetics or pathology also eligible. Awardees must attend scientific sessions at AACR meeting for at least four days and participate in required activities. Must submit two comprehensive reports each year. Contact AACR or visit Website for more information.

Amount of award:	$3,000
Number of awards:	17
Number of applicants:	66
Application deadline:	November 30

Contact:
American Association for Cancer Research
615 Chestnut Street, 17th Floor
Philadelphia, PA 19106-4404
Phone: 215-440-9300
Fax: 215-440-9412
Web: www.aacr.org/Bardos

American Association of University Women San Jose

San Jose Local Scholarships for Women

Type of award: Scholarship, renewable.
Intended use: For junior or senior study at accredited 4-year institution in United States.
Eligibility: Applicant must be female. Applicant must be U.S. citizen or permanent resident residing in California.
Basis for selection: Applicant must demonstrate high academic achievement.
Additional information: Minimum 3.0 GPA. Must have a permanent home address in Campbell, Milpitas, San Jose, or Santa Clara, California. Number and amount of scholarships awarded depends upon funds available. Eligibility includes completion of two full years at an accredited college or university. Deadline in late March. Visit Website for specific dates.

Amount of award:	$1,000-$2,500
Number of awards:	8
Number of applicants:	21
Application deadline:	April 15
Notification begins:	May 1
Total amount awarded:	$15,000

Contact:
American Association of University Women San Jose
Grace O'Leary
1128 Sterling Gate Drive
San Jose, CA 95120-4246
Phone: 408-268-0798 or 408-314-2928
Fax: 408-323-9050
Web: www.aauwsanjose.org

American Board of Funeral Service Education

American Board of Funeral Service Education National Scholarship

Type of award: Scholarship.
Intended use: For full-time undergraduate study at 2-year or 4-year institution in United States.
Eligibility: Applicant must be U.S. citizen or permanent resident.
Basis for selection: Major/career interest in mortuary science. Applicant must demonstrate financial need, high academic achievement, depth of character, leadership and seriousness of purpose.
Application requirements: Recommendations, essay.

Additional information: Student must have completed at least one semester (or quarter) of study in funeral service or mortuary science at an education program accredited by American Board of Funeral Service Education. Visit Website for more information and application. Extracurricular activities are considered for eligibility. Number of awards varies.

Amount of award:	$250-$1,000
Number of applicants:	200
Application deadline:	March 1, September 1
Notification begins:	May 1, November 1
Total amount awarded:	$25,000

Contact:
American Board of Funeral Service Education
Attn: Scholarship Committee
3414 Ashland, Suite G
St. Joseph, MO 64506
Phone: 816-233-3747
Fax: 816-233-3793
Web: www.abfse.org

American Center of Oriental Research

Jennifer C. Groot Fellowship

Type of award: Research grant.
Intended use: For undergraduate or graduate study.
Eligibility: Applicant must be U.S. citizen or Canadian citizen.
Basis for selection: Major/career interest in archaeology; Middle Eastern studies; ancient Near Eastern studies or ethnic/cultural studies.
Application requirements: Proof of acceptance on archaeological fieldwork in Jordan.
Additional information: Applicant must be accepted as staff member on archaeological project in Jordan with ASOR/CAP affiliation. Award used only for travel to project site in Jordan.

Amount of award:	$1,800
Number of awards:	2
Number of applicants:	15
Application deadline:	February 1
Notification begins:	April 15
Total amount awarded:	$5,400

Contact:
American Center of Oriental Research
Fellowship Committee
656 Beacon Street
Boston, MA 02215-2010
Phone: 617-353-6571
Fax: 617-353-6575
Web: www.bu.edu/acor

American Chemical Society

American Chemical Society Scholars Program

Type of award: Scholarship, renewable.
Intended use: For full-time undergraduate study at accredited 2-year or 4-year institution in United States.
Eligibility: Applicant must be African American, Mexican American, Hispanic American, Puerto Rican or American Indian. Applicant must be U.S. citizen or permanent resident.
Basis for selection: Major/career interest in chemistry; biochemistry; engineering, chemical; materials science; environmental science; forensics or food science/technology. Applicant must demonstrate financial need, high academic achievement, leadership, seriousness of purpose and service orientation.
Application requirements: Recommendations, transcript. SAR. ACT/SAT scores (for high school applicants).
Additional information: Other chemically-related majors also eligible. Minimum 3.0 GPA. Must be planning career in chemical sciences (pre-med, pharmacy, nursing, dentistry, veterinary medicine programs not eligible).

Amount of award:	$1,000-$5,000
Number of awards:	100
Number of applicants:	480
Application deadline:	March 1
Notification begins:	November 1
Total amount awarded:	$1,000,000

Contact:
ACS Scholars Program
1155 16th Street, NW
Washington, DC 20036
Phone: 800-227-5558 ext. 6250
Fax: 202-872-4361
Web: www.acs.org/scholars

American Classical League

Arthur Patch McKinlay Scholarship

Type of award: Scholarship.
Intended use: For non-degree study.
Basis for selection: Major/career interest in classics or education. Applicant must demonstrate financial need.
Application requirements: Recommendations. Study program proposal, including budget.
Additional information: Must be current member of American Classical League and for three years preceding application. Must be planning to teach classics in elementary or secondary school in upcoming school year. May apply for independent study program funding or support to attend American Classical League Institute for first time. Number of awards varies year to year.

Amount of award:	$1,500
Number of applicants:	14
Application deadline:	January 15

Contact:
American Classical League Scholarship Awards
Miami University
422 Wells Mill Drive
Oxford, OH 45056
Phone: 513-529-7741
Fax: 513-529-7742
Web: www.aclclassics.org

Maureen V. O'Donnell/Eunice C. Kraft Teacher Training Scholarships

Type of award: Scholarship.
Intended use: For junior, senior or graduate study at 4-year or graduate institution.

Scholarships

Basis for selection: Major/career interest in education or classics.
Application requirements: Recommendations.
Additional information: Must be member of ACL. Must be training for certification to teach Latin and have completed a substantial number of these courses. Must wait at least three years before reapplying. Number of awards varies.

Amount of award:	$1,000
Number of applicants:	14
Application deadline:	January 15

Contact:
The American Classical League
Miami University
422 Wells Mill Drive
Oxford, OH 45056
Phone: 513-529-7741
Fax: 513-529-7742
Web: www.aclclassics.org

American College of Musicians

National Guild of Piano Teachers $200 Scholarship

Type of award: Scholarship.
Intended use: For undergraduate, graduate or non-degree study.
Basis for selection: Major/career interest in music.
Application requirements: Nomination by piano teacher, who must be member of National Guild of Piano Teachers. Copies of ten inner report cards and stubs.
Additional information: Award to be used for piano study. Student must have been national winner for ten years, Paderewski Medal winner, and Guild High School Diploma recipient.

Amount of award:	$200
Number of awards:	150
Application deadline:	September 15
Notification begins:	October 1

Contact:
American College of Musicians
Scholarship Committee
P.O. Box 1807
Austin, TX 78767-1807
Phone: 512-478-5775
Web: www.pianoguild.com

National Guild of Piano Teachers Composition Contest

Type of award: Scholarship.
Intended use: For undergraduate, graduate or non-degree study.
Basis for selection: Competition/talent/interest in music performance/composition, based on composition for solo keyboard and keyboard ensemble.
Application requirements: Manuscript of composition.
Additional information: Teacher must be member of National Guild of Piano Teachers. Compositions rated on imagination, originality, and skill. Entry fees vary according to classification of student and length of composition. See Website for specific details.

Amount of award:	$50-$150
Number of awards:	14
Application deadline:	November 8

Contact:
American College of Musicians
P.O. Box 1807
Austin, TX 78767-1807
Phone: 512-478-5775
Web: www.pianoguild.com

American Congress on Surveying and Mapping

AAGS Joseph F. Dracup Scholarship Award

Type of award: Scholarship, renewable.
Intended use: For undergraduate study at 4-year institution.
Basis for selection: Major/career interest in surveying/mapping. Applicant must demonstrate high academic achievement and seriousness of purpose.
Application requirements: Recommendations, essay, transcript, proof of eligibility.
Additional information: Applicant must be member of American Congress on Surveying and Mapping. Preference will be given to applicants with significant focus on geodetic surveying. Students may also be enrolled in degree program related to surveying, such as geomatics or survey engineering. Visit Website for deadlines and additional information.

Amount of award:	$2,000
Number of awards:	1
Total amount awarded:	$2,000

Contact:
NSPS and AAGS Scholarships
5119 Pegasus Court
Suite Q
Frederick, MD 21704
Phone: 240-439-4615
Fax: 240-439-4952
Web: www.acsm.net

ACSM Fellows Scholarship

Type of award: Scholarship.
Intended use: For junior or senior study at 4-year institution.
Basis for selection: Major/career interest in surveying/mapping or cartography. Applicant must demonstrate high academic achievement and seriousness of purpose.
Application requirements: Recommendations, essay, transcript, proof of eligibility.
Additional information: Applicant must be an ACSM member and be student in one of ACSM disciplines: surveying, mapping, geographic land sciences, or cartography. Student may also study related disciplines including geomatics or surveying engineering. Visit Website for deadlines and additional information.

Amount of award:	$2,000
Number of awards:	1
Total amount awarded:	$2,000

Contact:
NSPS and AAGS Scholarships
5119 Pegasus Court
Suite Q
Frederick, MD 21704
Phone: 240-439-4615
Fax: 240-439-4952
Web: www.acsm.net

Berntsen International Scholarship in Surveying

Type of award: Scholarship, renewable.
Intended use: For undergraduate study at 4-year institution.
Basis for selection: Major/career interest in surveying/mapping. Applicant must demonstrate high academic achievement and seriousness of purpose.
Application requirements: Recommendations, essay, transcript, proof of eligibility.
Additional information: Applicant must be member of ACSM. Open to students in surveying or closely related programs such as geomatics or surveying engineering. Degree of financial need will be used, if necessary, to break ties after the primary criteria have been considered. Funded by Berntsen International Inc. of Madison, Wisconsin. Visit Website for deadlines and additional information.

Amount of award:	$2,000
Number of awards:	1
Total amount awarded:	$2,000

Contact:
NSPS and AAGS Scholarships
5119 Pegasus Court
Suite Q
Frederick, MD 21704
Phone: 240-439-4615
Fax: 240-439-4952
Web: www.acsm.net

Berntsen International Scholarship in Surveying Technology

Type of award: Scholarship, renewable.
Intended use: For undergraduate certificate study at 2-year institution.
Basis for selection: Major/career interest in surveying/mapping or cartography. Applicant must demonstrate high academic achievement and seriousness of purpose.
Application requirements: Recommendations, essay, transcript, proof of eligibility.
Additional information: Applicant must be member of ACSM. Funded by Berntsen International Inc. of Madison, Wisconsin. Visit Website for deadlines and additional information.

Amount of award:	$1,000
Number of awards:	1
Total amount awarded:	$1,000

Contact:
NSPS and AAGS Scholarships
5119 Pegasus Court
Suite Q
Frederick, MD 21704
Phone: 240-439-4615
Fax: 240-439-4952
Web: www.acsm.net

Cady McDonnell Memorial Scholarship

Type of award: Scholarship, renewable.
Intended use: For undergraduate study at 2-year or 4-year institution.
Eligibility: Applicant must be female. Applicant must be residing in Utah, Alaska, Washington, Arizona, Nevada, Wyoming, California, Montana, Oregon, New Mexico, Idaho, Colorado or Hawaii.
Basis for selection: Major/career interest in surveying/mapping or cartography. Applicant must demonstrate high academic achievement and seriousness of purpose.
Application requirements: Recommendations, essay, transcript, proof of eligibility. Proof of legal home residence.
Additional information: Applicant must be member of American Congress on Surveying and Mapping. Degree of financial need will be used, if necessary, to break ties after the primary criteria have been considered. Visit Website for deadlines and additional information.

Amount of award:	$1,000
Number of awards:	1
Total amount awarded:	$1,000

Contact:
NSPS and AAGS Scholarships
5119 Pegasus Court
Suite Q
Frederick, MD 21704
Phone: 240-439-4615
Fax: 240-439-4952
Web: www.acsm.net

The Lowell H. and Dorothy Loving Undergraduate Scholarship

Type of award: Scholarship.
Intended use: For junior or senior study at accredited postsecondary institution in United States.
Basis for selection: Major/career interest in surveying/mapping. Applicant must demonstrate high academic achievement and seriousness of purpose.
Application requirements: Recommendations, essay, transcript, proof of eligibility.
Additional information: Applicant must be ACSM member. In addition to basic surveying, applicant must take courses in at least two of the following: land surveying, geometric geodesy, photogrammetry/remote sensing; or analysis and design of spatial measurement. Visit Website for deadlines and additional information.

Amount of award:	$2,500
Number of awards:	1
Total amount awarded:	$2,500

Contact:
NSPS and AAGS Scholarships
5119 Pegasus Court
Suite Q
Frederick, MD 21704
Phone: 240-439-4615
Fax: 240-439-4952
Web: www.acsm.net

Nettie Dracup Memorial Scholarship

Type of award: Scholarship, renewable.
Intended use: For undergraduate study at accredited 4-year institution. Designated institutions: ABET-accredited colleges and universities.
Eligibility: Applicant must be U.S. citizen.
Basis for selection: Major/career interest in surveying/mapping. Applicant must demonstrate high academic achievement and seriousness of purpose.
Application requirements: Recommendations, essay, transcript, proof of eligibility.
Additional information: Applicant must be member of American Congress on Surveying and Mapping and enrolled in geodetic surveying program. Degree of financial need will be used, if necessary, to break ties after primary criteria have been considered. Visit Website for deadlines and additional information.

Amount of award:	$2,000
Number of awards:	2
Total amount awarded:	$4,000

Contact:
NSPS and AAGS Scholarships
5119 Pegasus Court
Suite Q
Frederick, MD 21704
Phone: 240-439-4615
Fax: 240-439-4952
Web: www.acsm.net

NSPS Board of Governors Scholarship

Type of award: Scholarship, renewable.
Intended use: For junior study at 4-year institution.
Basis for selection: Major/career interest in surveying/mapping. Applicant must demonstrate high academic achievement and seriousness of purpose.
Application requirements: Recommendations, essay, transcript, proof of eligibility.
Additional information: Applicant must be member of American Congress on Surveying and Mapping. Minimum 3.0 GPA. Degree of financial need will be used, if necessary, to break ties after the primary criteria have been considered. Visit Website for deadlines and additional information.

Amount of award:	$1,000
Number of awards:	1
Total amount awarded:	$1,000

Contact:
NSPS and AAGS Scholarships
5119 Pegasus Court
Suite Q
Frederick, MD 21704
Phone: 240-439-4615
Fax: 240-439-4952
Web: www.acsm.net

NSPS Scholarships

Type of award: Scholarship, renewable.
Intended use: For full-time undergraduate study at 4-year institution.
Basis for selection: Major/career interest in surveying/mapping. Applicant must demonstrate high academic achievement and seriousness of purpose.
Application requirements: Recommendations, essay, transcript, proof of eligibility.
Additional information: Applicant must be member of American Congress on Surveying and Mapping. Students may also be enrolled in related degree program such as geomatics or surveying engineering. Degree of financial need will be used, if necessary, to break ties after the primary criteria have been considered. Awarded by National Society of Professional Surveyors. Visit Website for deadlines and additional information.

Amount of award:	$1,000
Number of awards:	2
Total amount awarded:	$2,000

Contact:
NSPS and AAGS Scholarships
5119 Pegasus Court
Suite Q
Frederick, MD 21704
Phone: 240-439-4615
Fax: 240-439-4952
Web: www.acsm.net

Schonstedt Scholarships in Surveying

Type of award: Scholarship, renewable.
Intended use: For undergraduate study at 4-year institution.
Basis for selection: Major/career interest in surveying/mapping. Applicant must demonstrate high academic achievement and seriousness of purpose.
Application requirements: Recommendations, essay, transcript, proof of eligibility.
Additional information: Applicant must be member of American Congress on Surveying and Mapping. Preference given to applicants with junior or senior standing. Degree of financial need will be used, if necessary, to break ties after primary criteria have been considered. Funded by Schonstedt Instrument Company of Kearneysville, West Virginia. Schonstedt donates magnetic locator to surveying program at each recipient's school. Visit Website for deadlines and additional information.

Amount of award:	$1,500
Number of awards:	2
Total amount awarded:	$3,000

Contact:
NSPS and AAGS Scholarships
5119 Pegasus Court
Suite Q
Frederick, MD 21704
Phone: 240-439-4615
Fax: 240-439-4952
Web: www.acsm.net

Tri-State Surveying & Photogrammetry Kris M. Kunze Scholarship

Type of award: Scholarship.
Intended use: For undergraduate study at postsecondary institution in United States.
Basis for selection: Major/career interest in business; business/management/administration or surveying/mapping. Applicant must demonstrate high academic achievement and seriousness of purpose.
Additional information: Applicant must be ACSM member. First priority: licensed professional land surveyors or certified photogrammetrists taking college business administration or

management courses. Second priority: certified land survey interns taking college business administration or management courses. Third priority: full-time students in two or four-year surveying and mapping degree programs taking business administration or management courses. Visit Website for deadlines and additional information.

Amount of award: $1,000
Number of awards: 1
Total amount awarded: $1,000

Contact:
NSPS and AAGS Scholarships
5119 Pegasus Court
Suite Q
Frederick, MD 21704
Phone: 240-439-4615
Fax: 240-439-4952
Web: www.acsm.net

American Council of Engineering Companies

ACEC Scholarship

Type of award: Scholarship, renewable.
Intended use: For junior, senior, master's or doctoral study at 4-year or graduate institution. Designated institutions: ABET-accredited engineering programs.
Eligibility: Applicant must be U.S. citizen.
Basis for selection: Major/career interest in engineering. Applicant must demonstrate high academic achievement and seriousness of purpose.
Application requirements: Recommendations, essay.
Additional information: Applicants may also be seeking a degree from an accredited land-surveying program. Submit application through respective state member organization. Deadline date, number and amount of awards varies. Visit Website for deadlines and more information.

Number of applicants: 19

Contact:
American Council of Engineering Companies
1015 15th Street, NW
8th Floor
Washington, DC 20005-2605
Phone: 202-347-7474
Fax: 202-898-0068
Web: www.acec.org/getinvolved/scholarships.cfm

American Council of the Blind

Floyd Qualls Memorial Scholarship

Type of award: Scholarship, renewable.
Intended use: For full-time undergraduate or graduate study at accredited postsecondary institution in United States.
Eligibility: Applicant must be visually impaired.
Basis for selection: Applicant must demonstrate high academic achievement, depth of character and leadership.
Application requirements: Interview, recommendations, essay, transcript, proof of eligibility.
Additional information: Applicant must be legally blind in both eyes. One award each for an entering freshman, other undergraduate, graduate, and vocational student, plus one discretionary award. Number of awards may vary.

Amount of award: $3,000
Number of awards: 5
Number of applicants: 200
Application deadline: March 1
Notification begins: May 15
Total amount awarded: $28,250

Contact:
American Council of the Blind
6300 Shingle Creek Parkway
Suite 195
Brooklyn Center, MN 55430
Phone: 612-332-3242
Fax: 763-432-7562
Web: www.acb.org

American Dental Assistants Association

Juliette A. Southard/Oral-B Laboratories Scholarship

Type of award: Scholarship.
Intended use: For undergraduate study.
Basis for selection: Major/career interest in dental assistant. Applicant must demonstrate high academic achievement.
Application requirements: Recommendations, essay, transcript, proof of eligibility.
Additional information: Scholarships open to high school graduates and GED certificate holders. Must be ADAA member. Applicants must be enrolled in dental assisting program or be taking courses applicable to furthering career in dental assisting. Visit Website for application. All forms must be submitted via email.

Amount of award: $750
Number of awards: 10
Number of applicants: 30
Application deadline: March 15
Total amount awarded: $7,500

Contact:
American Dental Assistants Association
35 East Wacker Drive
Suite 1730
Chicago, IL 60601-2211
Phone: 312-541-1550
Fax: 312-541-1496
Web: www.dentalassistant.org

American Federation of State, County and Municipal Employees

AFSCME Family Scholarship

Type of award: Scholarship, renewable.
Intended use: For full-time undergraduate study at accredited 4-year institution.

Eligibility: Applicant must be high school senior.
Application requirements: Recommendations, essay, transcript, proof of eligibility. SAT or ACT scores.
Additional information: Scholarships open to children and financially dependent grandchildren of active or retired full dues-paying AFSCME members.

Amount of award:	$2,000
Number of awards:	10
Number of applicants:	650
Application deadline:	December 31
Notification begins:	March 31
Total amount awarded:	$20,000

Contact:
AFSCME Family Scholarship Program
Attn: AFSCME Advantage
1625 L Street, NW
Washington, DC 20036-5687
Phone: 202-429-5066
Web: www.afscme.org/family

Jerry Clark Memorial Scholarship

Type of award: Scholarship, renewable.
Intended use: For full-time junior study at accredited 4-year institution.
Basis for selection: Major/career interest in political science/ government; sociology; communications or ethnic/cultural studies. Applicant must demonstrate high academic achievement.
Application requirements: Transcript, proof of eligibility.
Additional information: Scholarships open to children and financially dependent grandchildren of AFSCME members. Applicant must be a current college sophomore. Winners given opportunity to intern at International Union headquarters in Political Action department. Minimum 2.5 GPA.

Amount of award:	$5,000
Number of awards:	2
Number of applicants:	30
Application deadline:	April 30
Notification begins:	August 1
Total amount awarded:	$10,000

Contact:
Jerry Clark Memorial Scholarship Program
AFSCME, Attn: Department of Education
1625 L Street, NW
Washington, DC 20036-5687
Phone: 202-429-1250
Web: www.afscme.org

American Fire Sprinkler Association

AFSA $20,000 High School Scholarship Contest

Type of award: Scholarship.
Intended use: For freshman study at vocational or 4-year institution in United States.
Eligibility: Applicant must be high school senior. Applicant must be U.S. citizen or permanent resident.
Additional information: Applicant is to read essay on Website, fill out registration information, and take ten-question multiple choice open book test. For each question answered correctly, applicant receives one entry into drawing for $2,000 scholarship. Scholarship payable to winner's college, university, or certified trade school. Relatives of AFSA staff or board members not eligible. Visit Website for more information and to enter. No phone calls or emails.

Amount of award:	$2,000
Number of awards:	10
Number of applicants:	85,000
Application deadline:	April 2
Notification begins:	April 16
Total amount awarded:	$20,000

Contact:
American Fire Sprinkler Association
Web: www.afsascholarship.org

AFSA $5,000 Second Chance Scholarship Contest

Type of award: Scholarship.
Intended use: For undergraduate or graduate study at accredited vocational, 2-year, 4-year or graduate institution in United States.
Eligibility: Applicant must be U.S. citizen or permanent resident.
Additional information: Must have high school diploma, GED, or equivalent. Applicant must read essay on Website, complete registration page, and take ten-question open book multiple choice test. For each question answered correctly, applicant gets one entry into drawing for one of five $1,000 scholarships. Relatives of AFSA staff or board members not eligible. Visit Website for more information and to enter. No phone calls or emails.

Amount of award:	$1,000
Number of awards:	5
Number of applicants:	35,589
Application deadline:	August 27
Total amount awarded:	$3,000

Contact:
American Fire Sprinkler Association
Web: www.afsascholarship.org

American Floral Endowment

American Florists' Exchange Scholarship

Type of award: Scholarship, renewable.
Intended use: For junior or senior study at 4-year institution.
Basis for selection: Major/career interest in agriculture. Applicant must demonstrate high academic achievement.
Additional information: Minimum 3.0 GPA. Must be resident or attending college in California and majoring in agriculture with an emphasis on a future in floriculture. Visit Website for additional information.

Amount of award:	$500-$2,000
Number of awards:	1
Number of applicants:	1
Application deadline:	May 1

Contact:
American Floral Endowment
Attn: AFE Scholarship Applications
1601 Duke Street
Alexandria, VA 22314
Phone: 703-838-5211
Fax: 703-838-5212
Web: www.endowment.org

Ball Horticultural Company Scholarship

Type of award: Scholarship.
Intended use: For junior or senior study at accredited 4-year institution in United States.
Eligibility: Applicant must be U.S. citizen or permanent resident.
Basis for selection: Major/career interest in horticulture. Applicant must demonstrate high academic achievement.
Application requirements: Recommendations, transcript.
Additional information: Intended for students pursuing career in commercial floriculture. Submit transcript and letters of recommendation via e-mail. Submit applications on the Website.

Amount of award:	$500-$800
Number of awards:	1
Number of applicants:	1
Application deadline:	May 1
Notification begins:	January 1
Total amount awarded:	$600

Contact:
American Floral Endowment
Attn: AFE Scholarship Applications
1601 Duke Street
Alexandria, VA 22314
Phone: 703-838-5211
Fax: 703-838-5212
Web: www.endowment.org

Bioworks/IPM Sustainable Practices Scholarship

Type of award: Scholarship, renewable.
Intended use: For sophomore, junior or senior study at 2-year or 4-year institution.
Eligibility: Applicant must be U.S. citizen or permanent resident.
Basis for selection: Applicant must demonstrate high academic achievement.
Application requirements: Recommendations, transcript.
Additional information: Applicant should major or show a career interest in floriculture, specifically in furthering the use of Integrated Pest Management (IPM) or sustainable practices. Minimum 3.0 GPA. E-mail is preferred method for submitting transcript and letters of recommendation. Submit applications via the Website.

Amount of award:	$1,000-$1,200
Number of awards:	1
Number of applicants:	1
Application deadline:	May 1
Notification begins:	January 1
Total amount awarded:	$1,150

Contact:
American Floral Endowment
1601 Duke Street
Alexandria, VA 22314
Phone: 703-838-5211
Fax: 703-838-5212
Web: www.endowment.org

Bud Olman Memorial Scholarship

Type of award: Scholarship, renewable.
Intended use: For sophomore, junior or senior study at accredited postsecondary institution in United States.
Eligibility: Applicant must be U.S. citizen or permanent resident.
Basis for selection: Major/career interest in horticulture. Applicant must demonstrate high academic achievement.
Application requirements: Recommendations, transcript.
Additional information: For students pursuing a career in growing bedding plants. Minimum 3.0 GPA. E-mail is preferred method for submitting transcript and letters of recommendation. Submit applications via the Website.

Amount of award:	$500
Number of awards:	1
Number of applicants:	1
Application deadline:	May 1
Notification begins:	January 1
Total amount awarded:	$500

Contact:
American Floral Endowment
1601 Duke Street
Alexandria, VA 22314
Phone: 703-838-5211
Fax: 703-838-5212
Web: www.endowment.org

Earl Dedman Memorial Scholarship

Type of award: Scholarship.
Intended use: For full-time sophomore, junior or senior study at accredited 4-year institution in United States.
Eligibility: Applicant must be U.S. citizen or permanent resident residing in Wyoming, Oregon, Montana, Idaho or Washington.
Basis for selection: Major/career interest in horticulture. Applicant must demonstrate high academic achievement.
Application requirements: Recommendations, transcript.
Additional information: Minimum 3.0 GPA. Career interest in becoming a greenhouse grower required. To apply for this scholarship, applicant must have interest in greenhouse production and potted plants. Applicant must be from the Northwestern area of the U.S. Number and amount of scholarships vary. Submit applications via the Website.

Amount of award:	$1,500-$2,000
Number of awards:	1
Number of applicants:	1
Application deadline:	May 1
Notification begins:	January 1
Total amount awarded:	$1,850

Contact:
American Floral Endowment
1601 Duke Street
Alexandria, VA 22314
Phone: 703-838-5211
Fax: 703-838-5212
Web: www.endowment.org

Fran Johnson Non-Traditional Scholarship

Type of award: Scholarship.
Intended use: For full-time undergraduate or graduate study at accredited 4-year or graduate institution in United States.
Eligibility: Applicant must be returning adult student. Applicant must be U.S. citizen or permanent resident.
Basis for selection: Major/career interest in horticulture. Applicant must demonstrate financial need and high academic achievement.
Application requirements: Recommendations, transcript.
Additional information: Specific interest in bedding plants or floral crops required. Must be re-entering school after a minimum three-year absence. Number and amount of awards vary. Submit applications via the Website.

Amount of award:	$800-$1,200
Number of awards:	1
Number of applicants:	1
Application deadline:	May 1
Notification begins:	January 1
Total amount awarded:	$1,050

Contact:
American Floral Endowment
1601 Duke Street
Alexandria, VA 22314
Phone: 703-838-5211
Fax: 703-838-5212
Web: www.endowment.org

Harold Bettinger Memorial Scholarship

Type of award: Scholarship.
Intended use: For full-time sophomore, junior or senior study at accredited 4-year institution in United States.
Eligibility: Applicant must be U.S. citizen or permanent resident.
Basis for selection: Major/career interest in horticulture; business or marketing. Applicant must demonstrate financial need and high academic achievement.
Application requirements: Recommendations, transcript.
Additional information: Minimum 3.0 GPA. To apply for this scholarship, applicant's major or minor must be in business and/or marketing with intent to apply it to a horticulture-related business. Amount of award varies. Submit applications via the Website.

Amount of award:	$1,500-$2,000
Number of awards:	1
Number of applicants:	1
Application deadline:	May 1
Notification begins:	January 1
Total amount awarded:	$1,875

Contact:
American Floral Endowment
1601 Duke Street
Alexandria, VA 22314
Phone: 703-838-5211
Fax: 703-838-5212
Web: www.endowment.org

Jacob Van Namen Marketing Scholarship

Type of award: Scholarship.
Intended use: For sophomore, junior or senior study at accredited 2-year or 4-year institution in United States.
Eligibility: Applicant must be U.S. citizen or permanent resident.
Basis for selection: Major/career interest in marketing or agribusiness. Applicant must demonstrate financial need and high academic achievement.
Application requirements: Recommendations, transcript.
Additional information: Minimum 3.0 GPA. Applicant must have interest in agribusiness marketing and distribution of floral products. Number and amount of awards vary.

Amount of award:	$800-$1,200
Number of awards:	1
Number of applicants:	1
Application deadline:	May 1
Notification begins:	January 1
Total amount awarded:	$1,025

Contact:
American Floral Endowment
1601 Duke Street
Alexandria, VA 22314
Phone: 703-838-5211
Fax: 703-838-5212
Web: www.endowment.org

James Bridenbaugh Memorial Scholarship

Type of award: Scholarship.
Intended use: For sophomore, junior or senior study at accredited postsecondary institution.
Eligibility: Applicant must be U.S. citizen or permanent resident.
Basis for selection: Major/career interest in horticulture. Applicant must demonstrate high academic achievement.
Application requirements: Recommendations, transcript.
Additional information: For students pursuing career in floral design and marketing of fresh flowers and plants. Minimum 3.0 GPA. E-mail is preferred method for submitting transcripts and letters of recommendation. Submit applications via the Website.

Amount of award:	$500
Number of awards:	1
Number of applicants:	1
Application deadline:	May 1
Notification begins:	January 1
Total amount awarded:	$425

Contact:
American Floral Endowment
Attn: AFE Scholarship Applications
1601 Duke Street
Alexandria, VA 22314
Phone: 703-838-5211
Fax: 703-838-5212
Web: www.endowment.org

J.K. Rathmell, Jr. Memorial Scholarship for Work/Study Abroad

Type of award: Scholarship.
Intended use: For full-time junior, senior or graduate study at accredited 4-year or graduate institution outside United States.
Eligibility: Applicant must be U.S. citizen or permanent resident.
Basis for selection: Competition/talent/interest in study abroad. Major/career interest in horticulture or landscape architecture. Applicant must demonstrate financial need, high academic achievement, depth of character and seriousness of purpose.

Application requirements: Recommendations, transcript. Letter of invitation from host institution abroad.
Additional information: Minimum 3.0 GPA. Applicants must plan work/study abroad and submit specific plan for such. Preference given to those planning to work or study for six months or longer. Must have interest in floriculture, ornamental horticulture, or landscape architecture. Number and amount of awards vary.

Amount of award:	$2,500-$3,500
Number of awards:	1
Number of applicants:	1
Application deadline:	May 1
Notification begins:	January 1
Total amount awarded:	$3,100

Contact:
American Floral Endowment
1601 Duke Street
Alexandria, VA 22314
Phone: 703-838-5211
Fax: 703-838-5212
Web: www.endowment.org

John L. Tomasovic, Sr. Scholarship

Type of award: Scholarship, renewable.
Intended use: For sophomore, junior or senior study at accredited postsecondary institution.
Eligibility: Applicant must be U.S. citizen or permanent resident.
Basis for selection: Major/career interest in horticulture. Applicant must demonstrate financial need and high academic achievement.
Application requirements: Recommendations, transcript.
Additional information: For horticulture students with financial need. 3.0-3.5 GPA required. Email is preferred method for submitting transcript and letters of recommendation. Submit applications via the Website.

Amount of award:	$500-$1,000
Number of awards:	1
Number of applicants:	1
Application deadline:	May 1
Notification begins:	January 1
Total amount awarded:	$825

Contact:
American Floral Endowment
1601 Duke Street
Alexandria, VA 22314
Phone: 703-838-5211
Fax: 703-838-5212
Web: www.endowment.org

Julio and Sarah Armellini Scholarship

Type of award: Scholarship, renewable.
Intended use: For sophomore, junior or senior study at 4-year institution.
Additional information: Must have an interest in the marketing or distribution of floral products. Visit Website for additional information.

Amount of award:	$500-$2,000
Number of awards:	1
Number of applicants:	1
Application deadline:	May 1

Contact:
American Floral Endowment
Attn: AFE Scholarship Applications
1601 Duke Street
Alexandria, VA 22314
Phone: 703-838-5211
Fax: 703-838-5212
Web: www.endowment.org

Long Island Flower Grower Association (LIFGA) Scholarship

Type of award: Scholarship, renewable.
Intended use: For sophomore, junior or senior study at 2-year or 4-year institution. Designated institutions: Institutions in the Long Island/New York area.
Basis for selection: Major/career interest in horticulture. Applicant must demonstrate high academic achievement.
Application requirements: Recommendations, transcript.
Additional information: For students pursuing a career in ornamental horticulture. Minimum 3.0 GPA. Email is preferred method for submitting transcript and letters of recommendation. Submit applications via the Website.

Amount of award:	$1,000-$1,500
Number of awards:	1
Number of applicants:	1
Application deadline:	May 1
Notification begins:	January 1
Total amount awarded:	$1,200

Contact:
American Floral Endowment
1601 Duke Street
Alexandria, VA 22314
Phone: 703-838-5211
Fax: 703-838-5212
Web: www.endowment.org

Markham-Colegrave International Scholarship

Type of award: Scholarship.
Intended use: For sophomore, junior, senior or graduate study at accredited 2-year, 4-year or graduate institution in United States or Canada.
Eligibility: Applicant must be U.S. citizen, permanent resident or Canadian citizen.
Basis for selection: Major/career interest in horticulture or marketing. Applicant must demonstrate financial need and high academic achievement.
Application requirements: Recommendations, transcript.
Additional information: Minimum 3.0 GPA. Must have interest in studying horticulture marketing through international travel. Operates in conjunction with the David Colegrave Foundation in London, England. Scholarship is part of annual exchange of students between U.S. and Europe, alternating between the two countries. U.S. students should apply in even number years (i.e. 2012, 2014, etc.). Number and amount of awards vary. Submit applications via the Website.

Amount of award:	$3,000-$4,000
Number of awards:	1
Number of applicants:	1
Application deadline:	May 1
Notification begins:	January 1
Total amount awarded:	$3,500

Contact:
American Floral Endowment
1601 Duke Street
Alexandria, VA 22314
Phone: 703-838-5211
Fax: 703-838-5212
Web: www.endowment.org

Mike and Flo Novovesky Scholarship

Type of award: Scholarship, renewable.
Intended use: For sophomore, junior or senior study at accredited postsecondary institution.
Eligibility: Applicant must be U.S. citizen or permanent resident.
Basis for selection: Major/career interest in horticulture. Applicant must demonstrate financial need and high academic achievement.
Application requirements: Recommendations, transcript.
Additional information: For married students with financial need. Minimum 2.5 GPA. E-mail is preferred method for submitting transcript and letters of recommendation.

Amount of award:	$1,000-$1,500
Number of awards:	1
Number of applicants:	1
Application deadline:	May 1
Total amount awarded:	$1,150

Contact:
American Floral Endowment
1601 Duke Street
Alexandria, VA 22314
Phone: 703-838-5211
Fax: 703-838-5212
Web: www.endowment.org

National Greenhouse Manufacturing Association (NGMA) Scholarship

Type of award: Scholarship, renewable.
Intended use: For sophomore, junior or senior study at accredited 4-year institution.
Eligibility: Applicant must be U.S. citizen or permanent resident.
Basis for selection: Major/career interest in horticulture or bioengineering. Applicant must demonstrate high academic achievement.
Application requirements: Recommendations, transcript.
Additional information: Minimum 3.0 GPA. E-mail is preferred method for submitting transcript and letters of recommendation. Submit applications via the Website.

Amount of award:	$500-$750
Number of awards:	1
Number of applicants:	1
Application deadline:	May 1
Notification begins:	January 1
Total amount awarded:	$550

Contact:
American Floral Endowment
1601 Duke Street
Alexandria, VA 22314
Phone: 703-838-5211
Fax: 703-838-5212
Web: www.endowment.org

Seed Companies Scholarship

Type of award: Scholarship, renewable.
Intended use: For junior or senior study at accredited postsecondary institution.
Eligibility: Applicant must be U.S. citizen or permanent resident.
Basis for selection: Major/career interest in horticulture. Applicant must demonstrate high academic achievement.
Application requirements: Recommendations, transcript.
Additional information: For students pursuing a career in the seed industry. Minimum 3.0 GPA. E-mail is preferred method for submitting transcript and letters of recommendation.

Amount of award:	$2,000-$2,500
Number of awards:	1
Number of applicants:	1
Application deadline:	May 1
Notification begins:	January 1
Total amount awarded:	$2,300

Contact:
American Floral Endowment
1601 Duke Street
Alexandria, VA 22314
Phone: 703-838-5211
Fax: 703-838-5212
Web: www.endowment.org

Vocational (Bettinger, Holden and Perry) Memorial Scholarship

Type of award: Scholarship.
Intended use: For full-time undergraduate certificate, freshman, sophomore or non-degree study at accredited vocational or 2-year institution in United States.
Eligibility: Applicant must be U.S. citizen or permanent resident.
Basis for selection: Major/career interest in horticulture. Applicant must demonstrate financial need and high academic achievement.
Application requirements: Recommendations, transcript.
Additional information: Minimum 3.0 GPA. Must intend to become floriculture grower or greenhouse manager. Number and amount of awards vary.

Amount of award:	$1,000-$1,500
Number of awards:	1
Number of applicants:	1
Application deadline:	May 1
Notification begins:	January 1
Total amount awarded:	$1,325

Contact:
American Floral Endowment
1601 Duke Street
Alexandria, VA 22314
Phone: 703-838-5211
Fax: 703-838-5212
Web: www.endowment.org

American Foundation for the Blind

Delta Gamma Foundation Florence Margaret Harvey Memorial Scholarship

Type of award: Scholarship.
Intended use: For undergraduate or graduate study at accredited postsecondary institution in United States.

Eligibility: Applicant must be visually impaired.
Basis for selection: Major/career interest in education, special or rehabilitation/therapeutic services.
Application requirements: Recommendations, essay, transcript, proof of eligibility.
Additional information: Applicant must be legally blind and studying in field of rehabilitation and/or education of blind or visually impaired persons.

Amount of award:	$1,000
Number of awards:	1
Application deadline:	April 30
Total amount awarded:	$1,000

Contact:
American Foundation for the Blind Scholarship Committee
Attn: Tara Annis
1000 5th Avenue, Suite 350
Huntington, WV 25701
Phone: 800-232-5463
Web: www.afb.org/scholarships.asp

Ferdinand Torres Scholarship

Type of award: Scholarship.
Intended use: For full-time undergraduate or graduate study at postsecondary institution in United States.
Eligibility: Applicant must be visually impaired. Applicant must be permanent resident.
Basis for selection: Applicant must demonstrate financial need.
Application requirements: Recommendations, essay, transcript, proof of eligibility.
Additional information: Applicant must be legally blind. Preference given to residents of New York City metropolitan area and new immigrants to the United States.

Amount of award:	$3,500
Number of awards:	1
Application deadline:	April 30

Contact:
American Foundation for the Blind Scholarship Committee
Attn: Tara Annis
1000 5th Avenue, Suite 350
Huntington, WV 25701
Phone: 800-232-5463
Web: www.afb.org/scholarships.asp

The Gladys C. Anderson Memorial Scholarship

Type of award: Scholarship.
Intended use: For undergraduate or graduate study at 2-year, 4-year or graduate institution.
Eligibility: Applicant must be visually impaired. Applicant must be female.
Basis for selection: Competition/talent/interest in music performance/composition. Major/career interest in music.
Application requirements: Recommendations, essay, transcript, proof of eligibility. Music performance on CD.
Additional information: Applicant must be legally blind and studying classical or religious music.

Amount of award:	$1,000
Number of awards:	1
Application deadline:	April 30

Contact:
American Foundation for the Blind
Attn: Tara Annis
1000 5th Avenue, Suite 350
Huntington, WV 25701
Phone: 800-232-5463
Web: www.afb.org/scholarships.asp

The Paul and Helen Ruckes Scholarship

Type of award: Scholarship, renewable.
Intended use: For full-time undergraduate or graduate study at accredited postsecondary institution in United States.
Eligibility: Applicant must be visually impaired.
Basis for selection: Major/career interest in engineering; computer/information sciences; physical sciences or life sciences.
Application requirements: Recommendations, essay, transcript, proof of eligibility.
Additional information: Applicant must be legally blind.

Amount of award:	$1,000
Number of awards:	1
Application deadline:	April 30
Total amount awarded:	$1,000

Contact:
American Foundation for the Blind Scholarship Committee
Attn: Tara Annis
1000 5th Avenue, Suite 350
Huntington, WV 25701
Phone: 800-232-5463
Web: www.afb.org/scholarships.asp

R.L. Gillette Scholarship

Type of award: Scholarship, renewable.
Intended use: For full-time undergraduate study at accredited 4-year institution in United States.
Eligibility: Applicant must be visually impaired. Applicant must be female.
Basis for selection: Major/career interest in literature or music.
Application requirements: Recommendations, essay, transcript, proof of eligibility. Creative writing sample or performance tape/CD not to exceed 30 minutes.
Additional information: Applicant must be legally blind.

Amount of award:	$1,000
Number of awards:	2
Application deadline:	April 30
Total amount awarded:	$2,000

Contact:
American Foundation for the Blind Scholarship Committee
Attn: Tara Annis
1000 5th Avenue, Suite 350
Huntington, WV 25701
Phone: 800-232-5463
Web: www.afb.org/scholarships.asp

The Rudolph Dillman Memorial Scholarship

Type of award: Scholarship.
Intended use: For full-time undergraduate or graduate study at accredited postsecondary institution in United States.
Eligibility: Applicant must be visually impaired.
Basis for selection: Major/career interest in education, special or rehabilitation/therapeutic services.

Application requirements: Recommendations, essay, transcript, proof of eligibility.
Additional information: Applicant must be legally blind and studying in field of rehabilitation and/or education of blind or visually impaired persons.

Amount of award:	$2,500
Number of awards:	4
Application deadline:	April 30
Total amount awarded:	$10,000

Contact:
American Foundation for the Blind Scholarship Committee
Attn: Tara Annis
1000 5th Avenue, Suite 350
Huntington, WV 25701
Phone: 800-232-5463
Web: www.afb.org/scholarships.asp

American Ground Water Trust

Amtrol Scholarship

Type of award: Scholarship.
Intended use: For full-time freshman study at 4-year institution.
Eligibility: Applicant must be high school senior. Applicant must be U.S. citizen or permanent resident.
Basis for selection: Major/career interest in geology/earth sciences; engineering, environmental; environmental science; natural resources/conservation or hydrology. Applicant must demonstrate high academic achievement, leadership, seriousness of purpose and service orientation.
Application requirements: Recommendations, essay, transcript. Description of completed high school science project involving ground water resources or of non-school work experience related to environment and natural resources.
Additional information: Applicant must be entering field related to ground water, e.g., geology, hydrology, environmental science, or hydrogeology. Minimum 3.0 GPA required. Visit Website for application procedure and forms.

Amount of award:	$1,500
Number of awards:	2
Number of applicants:	40
Application deadline:	June 1
Notification begins:	August 15
Total amount awarded:	$3,000

Contact:
American Ground Water Trust Scholarship
50 Pleasant Street, Suite 2
Concord, NH 03301-4073
Phone: 603-228-5444
Fax: 603-228-6557
Web: www.agwt.org

Baroid Scholarship

Type of award: Scholarship.
Intended use: For full-time freshman study at accredited 4-year institution.
Eligibility: Applicant must be high school senior. Applicant must be U.S. citizen or permanent resident.
Basis for selection: Major/career interest in engineering, environmental; geology/earth sciences; environmental science or natural resources/conservation. Applicant must demonstrate high academic achievement, leadership, seriousness of purpose and service orientation.
Application requirements: Recommendations, essay, transcript. Description of previously completed high school science project involving ground water resources or of non-school work experience related to environment and natural resources.
Additional information: Must be entering field related to ground water, e.g., hydrology or hydrogeology. Minimum 3.0 GPA. Visit Website for application procedure and forms.

Amount of award:	$2,000
Number of awards:	1
Number of applicants:	40
Application deadline:	June 1
Notification begins:	August 15
Total amount awarded:	$2,000

Contact:
American Ground Water Trust Scholarship
50 Pleasant Street, Suite 2
Concord, NH 03301-4073
Phone: 603-228-5444
Fax: 603-228-6557
Web: www.agwt.org

Thomas M. Stetson Scholarship

Type of award: Scholarship.
Intended use: For full-time undergraduate study at accredited 4-year institution in United States. Designated institutions: Colleges and universities located west of the Mississippi River.
Eligibility: Applicant must be high school senior. Applicant must be U.S. citizen or permanent resident.
Basis for selection: Major/career interest in environmental science; natural resources/conservation or science, general. Applicant must demonstrate high academic achievement.
Application requirements: Recommendations, essay.
Additional information: Applicant must intend to pursue career in ground water related field. Minimum 3.0 GPA. Visit Website for application procedure and forms.

Amount of award:	$2,000
Number of awards:	1
Number of applicants:	40
Application deadline:	June 1
Notification begins:	August 15
Total amount awarded:	$2,000

Contact:
American Ground Water Trust
50 Pleasant Street
Concord, NH 03301
Phone: 603-228-5444
Fax: 603-228-6557
Web: www.agwt.org

American Helicopter Society

Arizona Chapter Vertical Flight Engineering Scholarship

Type of award: Scholarship.
Intended use: For full-time undergraduate or graduate study. Designated institutions: Schools of engineering in Arizona.

Basis for selection: Major/career interest in aviation or engineering. Applicant must demonstrate high academic achievement.
Application requirements: Recommendations, transcript. Resume.
Additional information: Award for students who demonstrate an interest in pursuing engineering careers in the fixed wing, rotorcraft, or VTOL aircraft industry. Recipients also receive one-year membership in AHS.

Amount of award:	$1,500-$2,500
Number of awards:	1
Application deadline:	October 10
Notification begins:	November 26

Contact:
Ms. Pam Howard
The Boeing Company
Mail Stop M530-B111, 5000 East McDowell Road
Mesa, AZ 85215-9797
Phone: 480-891-5475
Web: www.vtol.org

Vertical Flight Foundation Scholarship

Type of award: Scholarship.
Intended use: For full-time junior, senior, master's or doctoral study at accredited postsecondary institution.
Basis for selection: Major/career interest in aerospace; aviation or engineering. Applicant must demonstrate high academic achievement, depth of character and seriousness of purpose.
Application requirements: Recommendations, essay, transcript. Resume.
Additional information: Must demonstrate career interest in vertical flight engineering. Minimum 3.0 GPA required, 3.5 recommended. Number of awards varies based on funding.

Amount of award:	$1,000-$5,000
Number of applicants:	62
Application deadline:	February 1
Notification begins:	April 15
Total amount awarded:	$50,000

Contact:
The Vertical Flight Foundation
217 North Washington Street
Alexandria, VA 22314-2538
Phone: 703-684-6777
Fax: 703-739-9279
Web: www.vtol.org/education/vertical-flight-foundation-scholarships

American Hellenic Educational Progressive Association Educational Foundation

AHEPA Educational Foundation Scholarships

Type of award: Scholarship.
Intended use: For full-time undergraduate or graduate study at accredited postsecondary institution.
Basis for selection: Applicant must demonstrate high academic achievement and service orientation.
Application requirements: Recommendations, transcript. Photo, financial information (when applicable).
Additional information: Applicant must be of Greek descent, or member/child of member (in good standing) of AHEPA, Daughters of Penelope, Sons of Pericles, or Maids of Athena. Minimum 3.0 GPA. High school seniors eligible to apply. Visit Website for details and application.

Amount of award:	$2,000
Application deadline:	March 31

Contact:
AHEPA Educational Foundation
1909 Q Street N.W., Suite 500
Washington, DC 20009
Phone: 202-232-6300
Fax: 202-232-2140
Web: www.ahepa.org

American Hotel & Lodging Educational Foundation

American Express Scholarship Competition

Type of award: Scholarship, renewable.
Intended use: For undergraduate study at accredited 2-year or 4-year institution.
Basis for selection: Major/career interest in hotel/restaurant management or hospitality administration/management.
Application requirements: Essay, transcript.
Additional information: Must work a minimum of 20 hours a week at hotel and have 12 months of hotel experience. Hotel must be member of American Hotel & Lodging Association. Dependents of hotel employees may also apply. Award must be used in hospitality management degree program. Visit Website to download application or apply online.

Amount of award:	$500-$2,000
Number of applicants:	20
Application deadline:	May 1
Notification begins:	July 15
Total amount awarded:	$11,000

Contact:
American Hotel & Lodging Educational Foundation
1201 New York Avenue, NW
Suite 600
Washington, DC 20005-3931
Phone: 202-289-3100
Fax: 202-289-3199
Web: www.ahlef.org

American Hotel & Lodging Educational Foundation Incoming Freshman Scholarship Competition

Type of award: Scholarship.
Intended use: For full-time freshman study at 2-year or 4-year institution.
Eligibility: Applicant must be U.S. citizen or permanent resident.
Basis for selection: Major/career interest in hotel/restaurant management or hospitality administration/management. Applicant must demonstrate high academic achievement.
Additional information: Award must be used in hospitality management program. Minimum 2.0 GPA. $1,000 awards go to

Associate majors, $2,000 to Baccalaureate majors. Preference will be given to high school graduates of the Hospitality and Tourism Management Program (HTMP) or the Lodging Management Program (LMP). Visit Website to download application or apply online.

Amount of award: $1,000-$2,000
Number of applicants: 158
Application deadline: May 1
Notification begins: July 15
Total amount awarded: $19,000

Contact:
American Hotel & Lodging Educational Foundation
1201 New York Avenue, NW
Suite 600
Washington, DC 20005-3931
Phone: 202-289-3100
Fax: 202-289-3199
Web: www.ahlef.org

Ecolab Scholarship Competition

Type of award: Scholarship.
Intended use: For full-time undergraduate study at 2-year or 4-year institution in United States.
Basis for selection: Major/career interest in hotel/restaurant management or hospitality administration/management.
Application requirements: Essay, transcript.
Additional information: Award must be used in hospitality management program. Applicant must maintain minimum 12 credit hours. Visit Website to download application or apply online.

Amount of award: $1,000-$2,000
Number of applicants: 620
Application deadline: May 1
Notification begins: July 15
Total amount awarded: $26,000

Contact:
American Hotel & Lodging Educational Foundation
1201 New York Avenue, NW
Suite 600
Washington, DC 20005-3931
Phone: 202-289-3100
Fax: 202-289-3199
Web: www.ahlef.org

The Hyatt Hotels Fund for Minority Lodging Management Students Competition

Type of award: Scholarship, renewable.
Intended use: For junior or senior study at 4-year institution.
Eligibility: Applicant must be Alaskan native, Asian American, African American, Mexican American, Hispanic American, Puerto Rican, American Indian or Native Hawaiian/Pacific Islander. Applicant must be U.S. citizen or permanent resident.
Basis for selection: Major/career interest in hotel/restaurant management or hospitality administration/management.
Application requirements: Essay, transcript.
Additional information: Award must be used in hospitality management program. Must be enrolled in at least 12 credit hours for upcoming fall and spring semesters, or just fall semester if graduating in December. Visit Website to download application or apply online.

Amount of award: $2,000
Number of applicants: 102
Application deadline: May 1
Notification begins: July 15
Total amount awarded: $38,000

Contact:
American Hotel & Lodging Educational Foundation
1201 New York Avenue, NW
Suite 600
Washington, DC 20005
Phone: 202-289-3100
Fax: 202-289-3199
Web: www.ahlef.org

American Indian College Fund

Anonymous Foundation Scholarship

Type of award: Scholarship.
Intended use: For full-time undergraduate study at postsecondary institution.
Eligibility: Applicant must be Alaskan native or American Indian. Applicant must be U.S. citizen.
Basis for selection: Applicant must demonstrate financial need and high academic achievement.
Application requirements: Essay, transcript, proof of eligibility. Photo, proof of tribal enrollment or tribal ancestry, financial needs analysis (FNA) form.
Additional information: Minimum 2.0 GPA. Not for use at tribal college. Must be registered member of tribe or descendant of at least one grandparent who is enrolled tribe member. Must be permanent resident of California or member of California based tribe. Visit Website for additional information.

Amount of award: $5,500
Application deadline: May 31

Contact:
American Indian College Fund
Anonymous Foundation Scholarship
8333 Greenwood Blvd.
Denver, CO 80221
Phone: 800-776-3863
Web: www.collegefund.org

Anthony A. Welmas Scholarship

Type of award: Scholarship.
Intended use: For full-time undergraduate study at 2-year or 4-year institution.
Eligibility: Applicant must be Alaskan native or American Indian. Applicant must be U.S. citizen.
Basis for selection: Applicant must demonstrate financial need and high academic achievement.
Application requirements: Essay, transcript, proof of eligibility. Photo, proof of tribal enrollment or ancestry, financial needs analysis (FNA) form.
Additional information: Minimum 3.0 GPA. Not for use at tribal college. Must be enrolled member in a federally recognized tribe. Visit Website for additional information.

Amount of award: $1,000
Application deadline: May 31

Contact:
American Indian College Fund
Anthony A. Welmas Scholarship
8333 Greenwood Blvd.
Denver, CO 80221
Phone: 800-776-3863
Web: www.collegefund.org

Arizona Public Service Navajo Scholars Program

Type of award: Scholarship.
Intended use: For full-time undergraduate study at 2-year or 4-year institution in United States. Designated institutions: Institutions in Arizona or New Mexico.
Eligibility: Applicant must be Alaskan native or American Indian. Applicant must be U.S. citizen.
Basis for selection: Major/career interest in mathematics; science, general; engineering or technology. Applicant must demonstrate financial need, high academic achievement and service orientation.
Application requirements: Essay, transcript, proof of eligibility. Photo, proof of tribal enrollment, financial needs analysis (FNA) form.
Additional information: Minimum 3.0 GPA. Not for use at tribal college. Must be a Navajo Nation tribal member with membership in the Nenahnezad, San Juan, Burnham, Hogback or Upper Fruitland chapters. Must have an interest in interning or working for Arizona Public Service and be willing to attend the AIHEC Student Congress Summer Leadership Training (all expenses paid). Visit Website for additional information.

Amount of award:	$10,000
Application deadline:	May 31

Contact:
American Indian College Fund
AZ Public Service Navajo Scholars Program
8333 Greenwood Blvd.
Denver, CO 80221
Phone: 800-776-3863
Web: www.collegefund.org

Austin Family Scholarship Endowment

Type of award: Scholarship, renewable.
Intended use: For full-time undergraduate study at 2-year or 4-year institution in United States. Designated institutions: University of Oklahoma (OU), Southeastern Oklahoma State University (SOSU), or an Oklahoma public two-year college.
Eligibility: Applicant must be American Indian. Applicant must be U.S. citizen residing in Oklahoma.
Basis for selection: Applicant must demonstrate financial need and high academic achievement.
Application requirements: Essay, transcript, proof of eligibility. Recent photo, proof of tribal enrollment or ancestry, financial needs analysis (FNA) form.
Additional information: Minimum 2.0 GPA. Not for use at tribal college. Must be a member or descendant of a tribe in Oklahoma. Must have proof of American Indian/Alaskan Native enrollment or descent. Visit Website for additional information.

Amount of award:	$1,000
Application deadline:	May 31

Contact:
American Indian College Fund
Austin Family Scholarship Endowment
8333 Greenwood Blvd.
Denver, CO 80221
Phone: 800-776-3863
Web: www.collegefund.org

CIGNA Foundation Tribal Scholars Healthcare

Type of award: Scholarship.
Intended use: For full-time junior or senior study at 4-year institution in United States. Designated institutions: Institutions in Arizona, Colorado, Washington, or California.
Eligibility: Applicant must be Alaskan native or American Indian. Applicant must be U.S. citizen.
Basis for selection: Major/career interest in medicine; pharmacy/pharmaceutics/pharmacology; nursing; dentistry; health sciences or health-related professions. Applicant must demonstrate financial need and high academic achievement.
Application requirements: Essay, transcript, proof of eligibility. Photo, proof of tribal affiliation, financial needs analysis (FNA) form.
Additional information: Minimum 3.0 GPA. Not for use at tribal college. Must be registered member of tribe or descendant of at least one grandparent who is enrolled tribe member. Visit Website for additional information.

Amount of award:	$2,666
Application deadline:	May 31

Contact:
American Indian College Fund
CIGNA Foundation Tribal Scholars Healthcare
8333 Greenwood Blvd.
Denver, CO 80221
Phone: 800-776-3863
Web: www.collegefund.org

Ecotrust Native American Scholarship

Type of award: Scholarship.
Intended use: For full-time undergraduate study at postsecondary institution in United States. Designated institutions: Institutions in California or Oregon.
Eligibility: Applicant must be Alaskan native or American Indian. Applicant must be U.S. citizen.
Basis for selection: Major/career interest in natural resources/conservation; environmental science; public health; economics or social/behavioral sciences. Applicant must demonstrate financial need, high academic achievement and leadership.
Application requirements: Essay, transcript, proof of eligibility. Photo, proof of tribal enrollment or ancestry, financial needs analysis (FNA) form.
Additional information: Minimum 2.5 GPA. Not for use at tribal college. Must be registered member of tribe or descendant of at least one grandparent who is enrolled tribe member. Visit Website for additional information.

Amount of award:	$3,000
Application deadline:	May 31

Contact:
American Indian College Fund
Ecotrust Native American Scholarship
8333 Greenwood Blvd.
Denver, CO 80221
Phone: 800-776-3863
Web: www.collegefund.org

Scholarships

Ford Motor Company Tribal College Scholarship

Type of award: Scholarship.
Intended use: For full-time undergraduate study at 4-year institution.
Eligibility: Applicant must be Alaskan native or American Indian. Must have proof of tribal enrollment or ancestry. Applicant must be U.S. citizen.
Basis for selection: Major/career interest in accounting; computer/information sciences; finance/banking; business/management/administration; engineering or marketing. Applicant must demonstrate financial need, high academic achievement, depth of character and leadership.
Application requirements: Essay, transcript, proof of eligibility. Small color photo, financial needs analysis (FNA) form.
Additional information: Minimum 3.0 GPA. For use at mainstream institution, not tribal college. Must have proof of American Indian/Alaskan Native enrollment or descent. Preference given to students attending a Michigan college. Visit Website for additional information.

Amount of award:	$3,000
Application deadline:	May 31
Notification begins:	September 30

Contact:
American Indian College Fund
Corporate Scholars Program
8333 Greenwood Blvd.
Denver, CO 80221
Phone: 800-776-3863
Fax: 303-426-1200
Web: www.collegefund.org

Helen K. and Arthur E. Johnson Foundation Scholarship

Type of award: Scholarship.
Intended use: For undergraduate study at 4-year institution. Designated institutions: Non-tribal institutions.
Eligibility: Applicant must be Alaskan native, American Indian or Native Hawaiian/Pacific Islander. Applicant must be U.S. citizen residing in Colorado.
Application requirements: Proof of eligibility.
Additional information: Minimum 2.0 GPA. Must be registered as member of a federal or state-recognized tribe, or a descendant of at least one grandparent or parent who is an enrolled tribal member. Must be Colorado resident or member of Southern Ute tribe or Mountain Ute tribe.

Amount of award:	$2,400
Application deadline:	May 31

Contact:
American Indian College Fund
8333 Greenwood Blvd.
Denver, CO 80221
Phone: 800-776-3863
Web: www.collegefund.org

Hershey Company Tribal Scholarship

Type of award: Scholarship.
Intended use: For full-time undergraduate study at postsecondary institution in United States.
Eligibility: Applicant must be Alaskan native or American Indian. Applicant must be U.S. citizen.
Basis for selection: Major/career interest in mathematics; technology; science, general; engineering or business. Applicant must demonstrate financial need and high academic achievement.
Application requirements: Essay, transcript, proof of eligibility. Photo, proof of tribal enrollment or ancestry, financial needs analysis (FNA) form.
Additional information: Minimum 3.0 GPA. Not for use at tribal college. Must be registered member of tribe or descendant of at least one grandparent who is enrolled tribe member. Priority given to students residing or studying at schools in Pennsylvania, Tennessee, Virginia, or Illinois. Recipients are strongly encouraged to apply for the Hershey Company's internship program. Visit Website for additional information.

Amount of award:	$2,500
Application deadline:	May 31

Contact:
American Indian College Fund
Hershey Company Tribal Scholarship
8333 Greenwood Blvd.
Denver, CO 80221
Phone: 800-776-3863
Web: www.collegefund.org

Morgan Stanley Scholars Program

Type of award: Scholarship, renewable.
Intended use: For full-time undergraduate study at 4-year institution.
Eligibility: Applicant must be Alaskan native or American Indian. Must have proof of tribal enrollment or ancestry. Applicant must be U.S. citizen.
Basis for selection: Major/career interest in business; finance/banking; information systems; marketing or accounting. Applicant must demonstrate high academic achievement.
Application requirements: Essay, transcript, proof of eligibility. Fall class schedule (when available), small color photograph, financial needs analysis (FNA) form. Personal Statement describing background and career/academic goals.
Additional information: Minimum 3.0 GPA. For use at mainstream institution, not tribal college. Must have proof of American Indian/Alaskan Native enrollment or descent. Visit Website for additional information.

Amount of award:	$5,000
Application deadline:	May 31
Notification begins:	September 30

Contact:
American Indian College Fund
8333 Greenwood Blvd.
Denver, CO 80221
Phone: 800-776-3863
Web: www.collegefund.org

Nissan North America, Inc. Scholarship

Type of award: Scholarship.
Intended use: For undergraduate study at 4-year institution. Designated institutions: Non-tribal institutions.
Eligibility: Applicant must be Alaskan native, American Indian or Native Hawaiian/Pacific Islander. Applicant must be U.S. citizen.
Basis for selection: Applicant must demonstrate leadership and service orientation.
Application requirements: Proof of eligibility.
Additional information: Minimum 2.5 GPA. Must have commitment to American Indian community. Must be

registered as a member of a federal or state recognized tribe, or a descendant of at least one grandparent or parent who is an enrolled tribal member.

Amount of award: $3,000
Application deadline: May 31

Contact:
American Indian College Fund
8333 Greenwood Blvd.
Denver, CO 80211
Phone: 800-776-3863
Web: www.collegefund.org

San Manuel Band of Missions Indians Tribal Scholarship

Type of award: Scholarship.
Intended use: For undergraduate study at 4-year institution. Designated institutions: Non-tribal institutions.
Eligibility: Applicant must be Alaskan native, American Indian or Native Hawaiian/Pacific Islander. Applicant must be U.S. citizen.
Application requirements: Proof of eligibility.
Additional information: Minimum 2.0 GPA. Must be registered as a member of a federal or state recognized tribe, or a descendant of at least one grandparent or parent who is an enrolled tribal member.

Amount of award: $1,000
Application deadline: May 31

Contact:
American Indian College Fund
8333 Greenwood Blvd.
Denver, CO 80221
Phone: 800-776-3863
Web: www.collegefund.org

Sovereign Nations Scholarship

Type of award: Scholarship.
Intended use: For full-time undergraduate study at 4-year or graduate institution.
Eligibility: Applicant must be Alaskan native or American Indian. Must have proof of tribal enrollment or ancestry. Applicant must be U.S. citizen.
Basis for selection: Applicant must demonstrate financial need and high academic achievement.
Application requirements: Essay, transcript, proof of eligibility. Two short essays, fall class schedule (when available), small color photograph, financial needs analysis (FNA) form, proof of American Indian or Alaskan Native tribal enrollment or ancestry.
Additional information: Minimum 2.0 GPA. For use at mainstream institution, not tribal college. Must have proof of American Indian/Alaskan Native enrollment or descent. Visit Website for additional information.

Amount of award: $2,000
Application deadline: May 31
Notification begins: September 30

Contact:
American Indian College Fund
8333 Greenwood Blvd.
Denver, CO 80221
Phone: 800-776-3863
Web: www.collegefund.org

Travelers Foundation Scholarship

Type of award: Scholarship.
Intended use: For full-time sophomore, junior or senior study in United States.
Eligibility: Applicant must be Alaskan native or American Indian. Must have proof of tribal enrollment or ancestry. Applicant must be U.S. citizen residing in Texas, Minnesota, Washington, Kansas, Arizona, Florida, California, Connecticut, Colorado or Illinois.
Basis for selection: Major/career interest in accounting; business; computer/information sciences; engineering or mathematics. Applicant must demonstrate financial need and high academic achievement.
Application requirements: Essay, transcript, proof of eligibility. Recent photo, financial needs analysis (FNA) form.
Additional information: Minimum 3.0 GPA. May also major in computer technology. Preference given to juniors and seniors. For use at mainstream institution, not tribal college. Must have proof of American Indian/Alaskan Native enrollment or descent. Eligible areas of study vary by applicants' location. Visit Website for additional information.

Amount of award: $4,000
Application deadline: May 31

Contact:
American Indian College Fund
Travelers Foundation
8333 Greenwood Blvd.
Denver, CO 80221
Phone: 800-776-3863
Web: www.collegefund.org

United Health Foundation Scholarship

Type of award: Scholarship, renewable.
Intended use: For full-time undergraduate study at 4-year institution. Designated institutions: Arizona State University, Northern Arizona University, San Juan College-Farmington, University of Arizona, University of New Mexico-Albuquerque, Western New Mexico University.
Eligibility: Applicant must be Alaskan native or American Indian. Must have proof of tribal enrollment or ancestry. Applicant must be U.S. citizen.
Basis for selection: Major/career interest in health-related professions; health education; health sciences or health services administration. Applicant must demonstrate financial need, high academic achievement and service orientation.
Application requirements: Recommendations, essay, transcript, proof of eligibility. Two short essays, fall class schedule (when available), and small color photograph. Proof of American Indian/Alaskan Native tribal enrollment or ancestry.
Additional information: Minimum 3.0 GPA. For use at mainstream institution, not tribal college. Must have proof of American Indian/Alaskan Native enrollment or descent. Visit Website for additional information.

Amount of award: $5,000
Application deadline: May 31
Notification begins: September 30
Total amount awarded: $20,000

Contact:
American Indian College Fund
8333 Greenwood Blvd.
Denver, CO 80221
Phone: 800-776-3863
Web: www.collegefund.org

Women's Self Worth Foundation Scholarship

Type of award: Scholarship, renewable.
Intended use: For full-time undergraduate study at 4-year institution.
Eligibility: Applicant must be Alaskan native or American Indian. Must have proof of tribal enrollment or ancestry. Applicant must be female. Applicant must be U.S. citizen.
Basis for selection: Applicant must demonstrate financial need, high academic achievement and service orientation.
Application requirements: Essay, transcript, proof of eligibility. Recent photo, financial needs analysis (FNA) form.
Additional information: Minimum 2.5 GPA. Applicant must commit to volunteering 12 hours/year, submitting end-of-year confirmation of volunteer efforts, and completing degree within timeframe. For use at mainstream institution, not tribal college. Must have proof of American Indian/Alaskan Native enrollment or descent. Visit Website for additional information.

Amount of award:	$8,000
Application deadline:	May 31

Contact:
American Indian College Fund
8333 Greenwood Blvd.
Denver, CO 80221-4488
Phone: 800-776-3863
Web: www.collegefund.org

American Indian Endowed Scholarship Program

Washington State American Indian Endowed Scholarship

Type of award: Scholarship, renewable.
Intended use: For full-time undergraduate or graduate study at accredited vocational, 2-year, 4-year or graduate institution. Designated institutions: Washington colleges and universities.
Eligibility: Applicant must be U.S. citizen residing in Washington.
Basis for selection: Applicant must demonstrate financial need, high academic achievement and service orientation.
Application requirements: Recommendations, essay, transcript, proof of eligibility. FAFSA.
Additional information: Must have close social and cultural ties to American Indian community within Washington State and strong commitment to return service to state's American Indian community. Awards and amounts may vary. Applicants pursuing degree in theology not eligible.

Amount of award:	$500-$2,000
Application deadline:	February 1
Notification begins:	March 1

Contact:
American Indian Endowed Scholarship Program
Washington Student Achievement Council
917 Lakeridge Way
Olympia, WA 98502
Phone: 360-753-7843
Fax: 360-704-6243
Web: www.hecb.wa.gov

American Indian Science & Engineering Society

AISES Google Scholarship

Type of award: Scholarship.
Intended use: For full-time junior, senior or graduate study at accredited 2-year, 4-year or graduate institution.
Eligibility: Applicant or parent must be member/participant of American Indian Science & Engineering Society. Applicant must be Alaskan native, American Indian or Native Hawaiian/Pacific Islander. Must be member of American Indian tribe or be at least 1/4 American Indian/Alaskan Native blood.
Basis for selection: Major/career interest in computer/information sciences or engineering, computer. Applicant must demonstrate high academic achievement.
Application requirements: Recommendations, essay, transcript, proof of eligibility. Resume, proof of tribal enrollment or ancestry.
Additional information: People of First Nations from Canada also eligible. Must be AISES member. Minimum 3.0 GPA. Award amount for Canadian students: $5,000 CAD; amount for US students: $10,000 USD. Winners also receive invite to Google Scholars' Retreat (all expenses paid). Deadline is in late winter or early spring. Students enrolled at a 2-year college must demonstrate transition plan to 4-year college or university. Membership and scholarship applications available on Website.

Amount of award:	$5,000-$10,000

Contact:
American Indian Science & Engineering Society
Scholarship Coordinator
P.O. Box 9828
Albuquerque, NM 87119-9828
Phone: 505-765-1052
Fax: 505-765-5608
Web: www.aises.org

A.T. Anderson Memorial Scholarship

Type of award: Scholarship.
Intended use: For full-time undergraduate or graduate study at accredited 2-year, 4-year or graduate institution in United States.
Eligibility: Applicant or parent must be member/participant of American Indian Science & Engineering Society. Applicant must be Alaskan native, American Indian or Native Hawaiian/Pacific Islander. Must be member of American Indian tribe or be at least 1/4 American Indian/Alaskan Native blood.
Basis for selection: Major/career interest in science, general; engineering; medicine; natural resources/conservation; mathematics; physical sciences or technology. Applicant must demonstrate high academic achievement, depth of character, leadership, seriousness of purpose and service orientation.
Application requirements: Recommendations, essay, transcript, proof of eligibility. Resume, proof of tribal enrollment or ancestry.
Additional information: Must be AISES member. Minimum 3.0 GPA. Undergraduate student award $1,000; graduate student award $2,000. Deadline is in mid-June. Membership and scholarship applications available on Website.

Amount of award:	$1,000-$2,000
Notification begins:	October 1

Contact:
AISES Scholarships
P.O. Box 9828
Albuquerque, NM 87119-9828
Phone: 505-765-1052
Fax: 505-765-5608
Web: www.aises.org

Burlington Northern Santa Fe Foundation Scholarship

Type of award: Scholarship, renewable.
Intended use: For full-time freshman study at accredited 4-year institution in United States.
Eligibility: Applicant or parent must be member/participant of American Indian Science & Engineering Society. Applicant must be Alaskan native, American Indian or Native Hawaiian/Pacific Islander. Must be member of American Indian tribe or be at least 1/4 American Indian/Alaskan Native blood. Applicant must be high school senior. Applicant must be U.S. citizen residing in South Dakota, Texas, Minnesota, Kansas, Washington, Arizona, California, Oklahoma, Montana, Oregon, New Mexico, Colorado or North Dakota.
Basis for selection: Major/career interest in science, general; engineering; mathematics; physical sciences; medicine; natural sciences; business; health services administration; technology or education. Applicant must demonstrate financial need, high academic achievement, depth of character, leadership, seriousness of purpose and service orientation.
Application requirements: Recommendations, essay, transcript, proof of eligibility. Resume, proof of tribal enrollment or ancestry.
Additional information: Applicant must be AISES member. Minimum 2.0 GPA. Award is renewable for four years (eight semesters) or until degree obtained, whichever comes first, assuming eligibility maintained. Deadline is in mid-April. Membership and scholarship applications available on Website.

Amount of award:	$2,500
Number of awards:	5
Notification begins:	October 1

Contact:
AISES Scholarships
P.O. Box 9828
Albuquerque, NM 87119-9828
Phone: 505-765-1052
Fax: 505-765-5608
Web: www.aises.org

Intel Scholarship

Type of award: Scholarship.
Intended use: For full-time undergraduate or graduate study at accredited 2-year, 4-year or graduate institution.
Eligibility: Applicant or parent must be member/participant of American Indian Science & Engineering Society. Applicant must be Alaskan native, American Indian or Native Hawaiian/Pacific Islander.
Basis for selection: Major/career interest in computer/information sciences; engineering, computer; engineering, electrical/electronic; engineering, chemical or materials science. Applicant must demonstrate high academic achievement.
Application requirements: Recommendations, essay, transcript, proof of eligibility. Certificate of Indian Blood or proof of tribal enrollment document. Resume.
Additional information: Minimum 3.0 GPA. Must be a member of an American Indian tribe or be considered American Indian by the tribe which affiliation is claimed or have at least 1/4 American Indian blood; or be at least 1/4 Alaskan Native or considered to be an Alaskan Native by an Alaskan Native group to which affiliation is claimed. Must be a member of AISES. To obtain an AISES membership, visit Website. Deadline is in mid-June. Award is $5,000 for undergraduates; $10,000 for graduates.

Amount of award:	$5,000-$10,000
Notification begins:	October 1

Contact:
AISES Scholarships
P.O. Box 9828
Albuquerque, NM 87119-9828
Phone: 505-765-1052
Fax: 505-765-5608
Web: www.aises.org

American Institute for Foreign Study

Diversity Abroad Achievement Scholarship

Type of award: Scholarship.
Intended use: For undergraduate study at postsecondary institution in Argentina, Australia, Austria, Botswana, Chile, China, Costa Rica, Czech Republic, England, France, Greece, India, Ireland, Italy, New Zealand, Russia, South Africa, Spain, Turkey. Designated institutions: AIFS programs.
Basis for selection: Competition/talent/interest in study abroad. Applicant must demonstrate high academic achievement and leadership.
Application requirements: Recommendations, essay, transcript. Disciplinary clearance.
Additional information: Minimum 3.0 GPA. Must be involved in multicultural/international activities. Scholarship offered to student from under represented group. Number of awards varies. Application deadlines are April 15 for fall and September 15 for spring.

Amount of award:	$1,000
Number of applicants:	50
Application deadline:	September 15, April 15
Notification begins:	November 1, May 15
Total amount awarded:	$20,000

Contact:
AIFS College Division
9 West Broad Street
Stamford, CT 06902-3788
Phone: 800-727-2437
Fax: 203-399-5597
Web: www.aifsabroad.com

HACU (Hispanic Association of Colleges and Universities) Scholarships

Type of award: Scholarship.
Intended use: For undergraduate study in Argentina, Australia, Austria, Botswana, Brazil, Chile, China, Costa Rica, Czech Republic, England, France, Germany, Greece, India, Ireland, Italy, New Zealand, Russia, South Africa, Spain, Turkey. Designated institutions: HACU member institutions.
Eligibility: Applicant must be Mexican American, Hispanic American or Puerto Rican.

Basis for selection: Competition/talent/interest in study abroad. Applicant must demonstrate high academic achievement and leadership.
Application requirements: Recommendations, essay, transcript. Disciplinary clearance.
Additional information: Scholarship intended for use at AIFS programs. Applicant must be involved in multicultural/ international activities. Deadlines are March 1 for summer, April 15 for fall, and September 15 for spring. Award amount is up to half of the AIFS all-inclusive program fee for summer and semester programs.

Number of awards:	3
Number of applicants:	40
Application deadline:	April 15
Notification begins:	April 1, May 15
Total amount awarded:	$25,000

Contact:
AIFS College Division
9 West Broad Street
Stamford, CT 06902-3788
Phone: 800-727-2437
Fax: 203-399-5597
Web: www.aifsabroad.com

International Semester Scholarship

Type of award: Scholarship.
Intended use: For undergraduate study in Argentina, Australia, Austria, Botswana, Brazil, Chile, China, Costa Rica, Czech Republic, England, France, Germany, Greece, India, Ireland, Italy, New Zealand, Russia, South Africa, Spain, Turkey. Designated institutions: AIFS programs.
Basis for selection: Competition/talent/interest in study abroad. Applicant must demonstrate high academic achievement and leadership.
Application requirements: Recommendations, essay, transcript. Disciplinary clearance.
Additional information: Minimum 3.0 GPA. Must be involved in multicultural/international activities. Award amount is $500 for summer and $1,000 for semester program. Number of awards varies. Application deadlines are March 1 for summer, April 15 for fall, and September 15 for spring.

Amount of award:	$500-$1,000
Number of awards:	130
Number of applicants:	500
Application deadline:	September 15, April 15
Notification begins:	November 1, May 15
Total amount awarded:	$105,000

Contact:
AIFS College Division
9 West Broad Street
Stamford, CT 06902-3788
Phone: 800-727-2437
Fax: 203-399-5597
Web: www.aifsabroad.com

NAFEO (National Association for Equal Opportunity in Higher Education) Scholarships

Type of award: Scholarship.
Intended use: For undergraduate study in Argentina, Australia, Austria, Botswana, Chile, Costa Rica, Czech Republic, England, France, Greece, India, Ireland, Italy, New Zealand, Russia, South Africa, Spain, Turkey. Designated institutions: HCBUs or PBIs.
Eligibility: Applicant must be African American.
Basis for selection: Competition/talent/interest in study abroad. Applicant must demonstrate high academic achievement and leadership.
Application requirements: Recommendations, essay, transcript. Disciplinary clearance.
Additional information: Scholarship intended for use at AIFS programs. Applicant must be involved in multicultural/ international activities. Deadlines are April 15 for fall and September 15 for spring. Award amount is up to half of the AIFS all-inclusive program fee for semester programs.

Number of awards:	2
Number of applicants:	25
Application deadline:	April 15, September 15
Notification begins:	May 15, November 1
Total amount awarded:	$20,000

Contact:
AIFS College Division
9 West Broad Street
Stamford, CT 06902-3788
Phone: 800-727-2437
Fax: 203-399-5597
Web: www.aifsabroad.com

American Institute of Aeronautics and Astronautics

AIAA Foundation Undergraduate Scholarship

Type of award: Scholarship, renewable.
Intended use: For full-time sophomore, junior or senior study in United States.
Basis for selection: Major/career interest in aerospace; engineering; mathematics or science, general. Applicant must demonstrate high academic achievement.
Application requirements: Recommendations, essay, transcript.
Additional information: Minimum 3.3 GPA. Must be AIAA member to apply. Not open to members of any AIAA national committees or subcommittees. Applicants must reapply for renewal.

Amount of award:	$2,500
Number of awards:	11
Number of applicants:	58
Application deadline:	January 31
Notification begins:	June 15
Total amount awarded:	$17,500

Contact:
AIAA Student Programs - Scholarships
1801 Alexander Bell Drive
Suite 500
Reston, VA 20191-4344
Phone: 703-264-7500
Web: www.aiaa.org

American Institute of Architects

AIA/AAF Minority/Disadvantaged Scholarship

Type of award: Scholarship, renewable.
Intended use: For full-time freshman or sophomore study at accredited postsecondary institution in United States. Designated institutions: NAAB-accredited institutions.
Eligibility: Applicant must be high school senior. Applicant must be U.S. citizen or permanent resident.
Basis for selection: Major/career interest in architecture. Applicant must demonstrate financial need.
Application requirements: Recommendations, essay, transcript, proof of eligibility, nomination by high school guidance counselor, architect, or other individual who can speak to student's aptitude for architecture. Drawing.
Additional information: Check Website for deadline. Open to high school seniors, community college students and college freshmen who plan to enter programs leading to professional degree in architecture. Students who have completed full year of undergraduate course work not eligible. Renewable up to two years. Visit Website for deadlines and additional information.

Amount of award:	$3,000-$4,000
Number of awards:	5
Number of applicants:	120
Application deadline:	March 15
Total amount awarded:	$20,000

Contact:
The American Institute of Architects
1735 New York Avenue, NW
Washington, DC 20006-5292
Phone: 202-626-7529
Fax: 202-626-7399
Web: www.aia.org/education/AIAB081881

American Institute of Architects New Jersey

AIA New Jersey Scholarship Foundation

Type of award: Scholarship, renewable.
Intended use: For full-time sophomore, junior, senior, master's or first professional study at accredited postsecondary institution. Designated institutions: Architectural schools.
Eligibility: Applicant must be residing in New Jersey.
Basis for selection: Major/career interest in architecture. Applicant must demonstrate financial need, high academic achievement, depth of character and seriousness of purpose.
Application requirements: $5 application fee. Portfolio, essay, transcript. FAFSA.
Additional information: Non-New Jersey residents attending architecture school in New Jersey also eligible. Applicant must have completed at least one year of architectural school at an accredited architecture program. Number of awards may vary. Deadline late May. Visit Website for more information.

Amount of award:	$2,500-$5,000
Number of awards:	3
Number of applicants:	35
Notification begins:	August 1
Total amount awarded:	$10,000

Contact:
AIA New Jersey Scholarship Foundation, Inc.
Attn: Cris Miseo
205 Mt. Pleasant Avenue
East Hanover, NJ 07936
Phone: 908-725-7800 or 973-533-0002
Fax: 908-725-7957
Web: www.aia-nj.org/about/scholarship.shtml

American Institute of Certified Public Accountants

Accountemps Student Scholarship

Type of award: Scholarship.
Intended use: For full-time sophomore, junior, senior or graduate study at postsecondary institution in United States. Designated institutions: AACSB- and/or ACBSP-accredited institutions.
Eligibility: Applicant must be U.S. citizen or permanent resident.
Basis for selection: Major/career interest in accounting. Applicant must demonstrate financial need, high academic achievement, leadership and service orientation.
Application requirements: Recommendations, essay, transcript. Resume.
Additional information: Minimum 3.0 GPA. Must be AICPA student affiliate member. Applicants may also study accounting-related fields, and must exhibit strong commitment to becoming a licensed CPA professional. Applicants must have completed at least thirty semester hours, including at least six hours in accounting. Students selected to advance to second round selections notified in May. Award recipients must commit to performing eight hours of CPA-related community service per semester. AICPA and RHI/Accountemps staff and family members are ineligible.

Amount of award:	$2,500
Number of awards:	10
Number of applicants:	400
Application deadline:	April 1
Notification begins:	August 1
Total amount awarded:	$25,000

Contact:
AICPA/ Accountemps Student Scholarship
Samantha Mitchell
220 Leigh Farm Road
Durham, NC 27707
Phone: 919-402-2161
Fax: 919-419-4705
Web: www.thiswaytocpa.com/accountemps

American Institute of Certified Public Accountants Scholarship for Minority Accounting Students

Type of award: Scholarship, renewable.
Intended use: For full-time undergraduate or graduate study at postsecondary institution.
Eligibility: Applicant must be Alaskan native, Asian American, African American, Mexican American, Hispanic American, Puerto Rican, American Indian or Native Hawaiian/Pacific Islander. Applicant must be U.S. citizen or permanent resident.
Basis for selection: Major/career interest in accounting. Applicant must demonstrate high academic achievement, leadership and seriousness of purpose.
Application requirements: Recommendations, essay, transcript, proof of eligibility. Resume.
Additional information: Applicants must have completed at least 30 semester hours or equivalent of college work, with at least six hours in accounting. Minimum 3.0 GPA. Applicants must be enrolled as accounting major, taxation major, finance major, or other related field and must exhibit strong commitment to becoming a licensed CPA professional. Application must be submitted online. Recipients must complete eight hours of community service per semester.

Amount of award:	$5,000
Number of awards:	80
Number of applicants:	300
Application deadline:	April 1
Notification begins:	August 1
Total amount awarded:	$240,000

Contact:
AICPA Minority Scholarship Program
Samantha Mitchell
220 Leigh Farm Road
Durham, NC 27707
Phone: 919-402-2161
Fax: 919-419-4705
Web: www.thiswaytocpa.com/minorityscholarship

American Institute of Polish Culture

Harriet Irsay Scholarship

Type of award: Scholarship.
Intended use: For full-time undergraduate or graduate study in United States.
Eligibility: Applicant must be U.S. citizen or permanent resident.
Basis for selection: Major/career interest in communications; education; film/video; history; humanities/liberal arts; international relations; journalism; polish language/studies; public relations or music. Applicant must demonstrate high academic achievement.
Application requirements: $10 application fee. Recommendations, essay, transcript. Detailed resume or CV, 700-word article on any subject about Poland.
Additional information: Send SASE with application request or download from Website. Preference given to American students of Polish heritage.

Amount of award:	$1,000
Number of awards:	5
Application deadline:	June 28
Notification begins:	August 9

Contact:
The American Institute of Polish Culture Scholarship Applications
1440 79th Street Causeway
Suite 117
Miami, FL 33141-3555
Phone: 305-864-2349
Fax: 305-865-5150
Web: www.ampolinstitute.org

American Legacy Foundation

Dr. Alma S. Adams Scholarship for Outreach and Health Communications to Reduce Tobacco Use Among Priority Populations

Type of award: Scholarship.
Intended use: For undergraduate or graduate study at accredited 4-year or graduate institution in United States.
Basis for selection: Major/career interest in public health; communications; social work; education or arts, general. Applicant must demonstrate financial need, high academic achievement and service orientation.
Application requirements: Recommendations, essay, transcript. Must provide evidence of community service activities in an underserved community setting. Must submit sample of applicant's originally developed health communication material.
Additional information: Minimum 3.0 GPA. Must submit the Student Aid Report received as result of filing FAFSA. Awards primarily granted based on student's commitment to community service in an underserved community, preferably related to tobacco prevention; and the best use of visual arts, media, creative writing, or other creative endeavor to convey health messages aimed at raising tobacco awareness. Number of awards varies.

Amount of award:	$10,000-$15,000
Number of awards:	4
Number of applicants:	85
Application deadline:	April 30
Notification begins:	June 30
Total amount awarded:	$17,000

Contact:
American Legacy Foundation
Attn: Dr. Alma S. Adams Scholarship Fund
1724 Massachusetts Ave., NW
Washington, DC 20036
Phone: 202-454-5920
Fax: 202-454-5775
Web: www.legacyforhealth.org/adamsscholarship

American Legion

American Legion Pennsylvania High School Oratorical Contest

Type of award: Scholarship.
Intended use: For undergraduate study at postsecondary institution.
Eligibility: Applicant must be enrolled in high school. Applicant must be U.S. citizen or permanent resident residing in Pennsylvania.
Basis for selection: Competition/talent/interest in oratory/debate, based on language style, voice, diction, delivery, originality, logic, breadth of knowledge, application of knowledge about topic, and skill in selecting examples and analogies.
Additional information: Awards: First place, $7,500; second place, $5,000; third place, $4,000. Contact local American Legion Post for details and application.

Amount of award:	$4,000-$7,500
Number of awards:	3
Application deadline:	January 1
Total amount awarded:	$16,500

Contact:
American Legion Pennsylvania
Scholarship Secretary
P.O. Box 2324
Harrisburg, PA 17105-2324
Phone: 717-730-9100
Web: www.pa-legion.com

American Legion Alabama

American Legion Alabama Oratorical Contest

Type of award: Scholarship.
Intended use: For undergraduate study at postsecondary institution.
Eligibility: Applicant or parent must be member/participant of American Legion. Applicant must be enrolled in high school. Applicant must be U.S. citizen residing in Alabama.
Basis for selection: Competition/talent/interest in oratory/debate, based on language style, voice, diction, delivery, originality, logic, breadth of knowledge, application of knowledge about topic, and skill in selecting examples and analogies.
Application requirements: Proof of eligibility.
Additional information: First place, $3,000; second place, $2,000; third place, $1,000. State finals held in March. Send business-size SASE for application.

Amount of award:	$1,000-$3,000
Number of awards:	3
Total amount awarded:	$6,000

Contact:
The American Legion, Department of Alabama
P.O. Box 1069
Montgomery, AL 36101-1069
Phone: 334-262-6638
Web: www.americanlegionalabama.org

American Legion Alabama Scholarship

Type of award: Scholarship, renewable.
Intended use: For undergraduate study at postsecondary institution.
Eligibility: Applicant or parent must be member/participant of American Legion. Applicant must be U.S. citizen or permanent resident residing in Alabama. Applicant must be descendant of veteran; or dependent of veteran during Korean War, Persian Gulf War, WW I, WW II or Vietnam.
Application requirements: Recommendations, transcript, proof of eligibility. SAT/ACT scores.
Additional information: Four-year scholarships at Alabama colleges. Children and grandchildren of U.S. military veterans may apply. Send business-size SASE for application or download online.

Amount of award:	$850
Number of awards:	130
Application deadline:	April 1
Total amount awarded:	$110,500

Contact:
The American Legion, Department of Alabama
P.O. Box 1069
Montgomery, AL 36101-1069
Phone: 334-262-6638
Web: www.americanlegionalabama.org

American Legion Alabama Auxiliary

American Legion Alabama Auxiliary Scholarship

Type of award: Scholarship, renewable.
Intended use: For undergraduate study at postsecondary institution. Designated institutions: Alabama state-supported colleges.
Eligibility: Applicant or parent must be member/participant of American Legion Auxiliary. Applicant must be U.S. citizen or permanent resident residing in Alabama. Applicant must be descendant of veteran; or dependent of veteran during Grenada conflict, Korean War, Lebanon conflict, Panama conflict, Persian Gulf War, WW I, WW II or Vietnam.
Application requirements: Proof of eligibility.
Additional information: Four-year scholarships at Alabama colleges. Previous one-year scholarship recipients can reapply. Grandchildren of veterans also eligible. Also applicable for descendents/dependents of veterans of Operation Desert Shield/Storm. Send SASE for application.

Amount of award:	$850
Number of awards:	40
Application deadline:	April 1
Total amount awarded:	$34,000

Contact:
American Legion Auxiliary, Department of Alabama
120 North Jackson Street
Montgomery, AL 36104
Phone: 334-262-1176

Scholarships

American Legion Alaska

Alaska Boys State Scholarship

Type of award: Scholarship.
Eligibility: Applicant or parent must be member/participant of American Legion. Applicant must be residing in Alaska.
Additional information: Winner selected by the counselors.
Amount of award: $1,500
Contact:
Web: www.alaskalegion.org

American Legion Alaska Oratorical Contest

Type of award: Scholarship.
Intended use: For undergraduate study at postsecondary institution.
Eligibility: Applicant or parent must be member/participant of American Legion. Applicant must be enrolled in high school. Applicant must be U.S. citizen or permanent resident residing in Alaska.
Basis for selection: Competition/talent/interest in oratory/debate, based on language style, voice, diction, delivery, originality, logic, breadth of knowledge, application of knowledge about topic, and skill in selecting examples and analogies.
Application requirements: Proof of eligibility.
Additional information: Awards: First place, $3,000; second place, $2,000; third and fourth place, $1,000. Must be high school student attending Alaska accredited institution. Must participate in local speech contests. Contest begins in November.
Amount of award: $1,000-$3,000
Number of awards: 4
Total amount awarded: $7,000
Contact:
American Legion, Department of Alaska
Department Adjutant
1550 Charter Circle
Anchorage, AK 99508
Phone: 907-278-8598
Fax: 907-278-0041
Web: www.alaskalegion.org

American Legion Western District Postsecondary Scholarship

Type of award: Scholarship.
Intended use: For undergraduate study at vocational, 2-year or 4-year institution.
Eligibility: Applicant or parent must be member/participant of American Legion. Applicant must be high school senior. Applicant must be residing in Alaska.
Basis for selection: Applicant must demonstrate financial need, high academic achievement, seriousness of purpose and service orientation.
Application requirements: Recommendations, essay, transcript.
Additional information: Minimum 2.0 GPA.
Amount of award: $1,000
Application deadline: February 15
Contact:
American Legion Western District Postsecondary Scholarship
Attn: Jim Scott
1124 Holmes Road
North Pole, AK 99705
Phone: 907-488-5310
Web: www.alaskalegion.org

American Legion Alaska Auxiliary

American Legion Alaska Auxiliary Scholarship

Type of award: Scholarship.
Intended use: For freshman study at postsecondary institution.
Eligibility: Applicant or parent must be member/participant of American Legion Auxiliary. Applicant must be at least 17, no older than 24, high school senior. Applicant must be U.S. citizen or permanent resident residing in Alaska. Applicant must be dependent of veteran during Grenada conflict, Korean War, Lebanon conflict, Panama conflict, Persian Gulf War, WW I, WW II or Vietnam.
Application requirements: Proof of eligibility.
Additional information: Scholarship to apply toward tuition, laboratory, or similar fees. Must not have attended institution of higher education.
Amount of award: $1,500
Application deadline: March 15
Contact:
American Legion Auxiliary, Department of Alaska
P.O. Box 670750
Chugiak, AK 99567
Web: www.alaskalegionauxiliary.org

American Legion Alaska Auxiliary Western District Scholarship

Type of award: Scholarship.
Intended use: For undergraduate study at accredited vocational, 2-year, 4-year or graduate institution.
Eligibility: Applicant or parent must be member/participant of American Legion Auxiliary. Applicant must be returning adult student. Applicant must be residing in Alaska.
Additional information: For continuing education students who are furthering their education to enhance work skills for entry or re-entry into the work field.
Amount of award: $1,000
Contact:
American Legion Auxiliary, Department of Alaska
P.O. Box 670750
Chugiak, AK 99567
Web: www.alaskalegionauxiliary.org

American Legion Arizona

American Legion Arizona Oratorical Contest

Type of award: Scholarship.
Intended use: For undergraduate study at postsecondary institution.

Eligibility: Applicant or parent must be member/participant of American Legion. Applicant must be enrolled in high school. Applicant must be U.S. citizen or permanent resident residing in Arizona.
Basis for selection: Competition/talent/interest in oratory/debate, based on language style, voice, diction, delivery, originality, logic, breadth of knowledge, application of knowledge about topic, and skill in selecting examples and analogies.
Additional information: Awards: First place, $1,500; second place, $800; third place, $500. For students enrolled in accredited Arizona high schools.

Amount of award:	$500-$1,500
Number of awards:	3
Application deadline:	January 15
Total amount awarded:	$2,800

Contact:
American Legion Arizona, Oratorical Contest
4701 North 19th Avenue, Suite 200
Phoenix, AZ 85015-3799
Phone: 602-264-7706
Fax: 602-264-0029
Web: www.azlegion.org

American Legion Arizona Auxiliary

American Legion Arizona Auxiliary Health Care Occupation Scholarship

Type of award: Scholarship.
Intended use: For undergraduate or post-bachelor's certificate study at accredited vocational, 2-year or 4-year institution. Designated institutions: Arizona tax-supported institutions.
Eligibility: Applicant or parent must be member/participant of American Legion Auxiliary. Applicant must be U.S. citizen residing in Arizona.
Basis for selection: Major/career interest in health-related professions; health sciences or physical therapy. Applicant must demonstrate financial need, high academic achievement, depth of character and seriousness of purpose.
Application requirements: Recommendations, essay, transcript. Photograph of self.
Additional information: Must be resident of Arizona at least one year. Preference given to immediate family members of veterans.

Amount of award:	$500
Application deadline:	May 15

Contact:
American Legion Auxiliary, Department of Arizona
4701 North 19th Avenue, Suite 100
Phoenix, AZ 85015-3727
Phone: 602-241-1080
Fax: 602-604-9640
Web: www.aladeptaz.org

American Legion Arizona Auxiliary Nurses' Scholarship

Type of award: Scholarship.
Intended use: For sophomore study. Designated institutions: Arizona institutions.
Eligibility: Applicant or parent must be member/participant of American Legion Auxiliary. Applicant must be U.S. citizen residing in Arizona.
Basis for selection: Major/career interest in nursing.
Application requirements: Recommendations, essay, transcript. Photograph of self.
Additional information: Must be pursuing RN degree. Must be Arizona resident for at least one year. Preference given to immediate family members of veterans.

Amount of award:	$600
Application deadline:	May 15

Contact:
American Legion Auxiliary, Department of Arizona
4701 North 19th Avenue, Suite 100
Phoenix, AZ 85015-3727
Phone: 602-241-1080
Fax: 602-604-9640
Web: www.aladeptaz.org

Wilma D. Hoyal/Maxine Chilton Memorial Scholarship

Type of award: Scholarship.
Intended use: For full-time sophomore, junior or senior study. Designated institutions: University of Arizona, Arizona State University, Northern Arizona University.
Eligibility: Applicant or parent must be member/participant of American Legion Auxiliary. Applicant must be U.S. citizen residing in Arizona.
Basis for selection: Major/career interest in political science/government; education, special or public administration/service. Applicant must demonstrate financial need, high academic achievement, depth of character and seriousness of purpose.
Application requirements: Recommendations, transcript. Resume.
Additional information: For second-year or upper-division full-time students. Three $1,000 awards payable to three designated institutions in Arizona. Applicant must be state resident at least one year. Preference given to immediate family members of veterans.

Amount of award:	$3,000
Number of awards:	3
Application deadline:	May 15

Contact:
American Legion Auxiliary, Department of Arizona
4701 North 19th Avenue, Suite 100
Phoenix, AZ 85015-3727
Phone: 602-241-1080
Fax: 602-604-9640
Web: www.aladeptaz.org

American Legion Arkansas

American Legion Arkansas Oratorical Contest

Type of award: Scholarship.
Intended use: For undergraduate study at postsecondary institution.
Eligibility: Applicant or parent must be member/participant of American Legion. Applicant must be high school sophomore, junior or senior. Applicant must be U.S. citizen or permanent resident residing in Arkansas.

Basis for selection: Competition/talent/interest in oratory/debate, based on language style, voice, diction, delivery, originality, logic, breadth of knowledge, application of knowledge about topic, and skill in selecting examples and analogies.
Application requirements: Proof of eligibility.
Additional information: Oratorical Contest, State Division: first place, $2,000; second place, $1,500; third place, $1,000. Must apply to local Post.

Amount of award:	$1,000-$2,000
Number of awards:	3
Application deadline:	January 1
Total amount awarded:	$4,500

Contact:
American Legion Arkansas
Department Adjutant
P.O. Box 3280
Little Rock, AR 72203
Phone: 501-375-1104
Fax: 501-375-4236
Web: www.arlegion.org

American Legion Coudret Trust Scholarship

Type of award: Scholarship.
Intended use: For undergraduate study at postsecondary institution.
Eligibility: Applicant or parent must be member/participant of American Legion. Applicant must be residing in Arkansas.
Basis for selection: Applicant must demonstrate depth of character, patriotism and seriousness of purpose.
Application requirements: Recommendations, essay, transcript, proof of eligibility. Photograph.
Additional information: Must be child, grandchild, or great-grandchild of American Legion member. Must have either received high school diploma or be graduate of two-year AR institution by time of award.

Amount of award:	$2,000
Number of awards:	4
Application deadline:	March 15
Total amount awarded:	$8,000

Contact:
American Legion Arkansas
Department Adjutant
P.O. Box 3280
Little Rock, AR 72203
Phone: 501-375-1104
Fax: 501-375-4236
Web: www.arlegion.org

American Legion Arkansas Auxiliary

American Legion Arkansas Auxiliary Scholarships

Type of award: Scholarship.
Intended use: For undergraduate study at postsecondary institution.
Eligibility: Applicant or parent must be member/participant of American Legion Auxiliary. Applicant must be high school senior. Applicant must be U.S. citizen residing in Arkansas. Applicant must be descendant of veteran; or dependent of veteran during Grenada conflict, Korean War, Lebanon conflict, Panama conflict, Persian Gulf War, WW I, WW II or Vietnam.
Basis for selection: Applicant must demonstrate financial need, high academic achievement, depth of character, leadership and patriotism.
Application requirements: Recommendations, essay, transcript, proof of eligibility. SAT/ACT scores.
Additional information: Academic Scholarship: one $1,000; Nurse Scholarship: one $500. Awards paid half first semester, half second semester. Student must be Arkansas resident attending Arkansas school. Include name of high school and SASE with application request.

Amount of award:	$500-$1,000
Number of awards:	2
Application deadline:	March 1
Total amount awarded:	$1,500

Contact:
American Legion Auxiliary, Department of Arkansas
Department Secretary
1415 West 7th St.
Little Rock, AR 72201
Phone: 501-374-5836
Web: www.auxiliary.arlegion.org

American Legion California

American Legion California Oratorical Contest

Type of award: Scholarship.
Intended use: For undergraduate study at postsecondary institution.
Eligibility: Applicant must be enrolled in high school. Applicant must be U.S. citizen or permanent resident residing in California.
Basis for selection: Competition/talent/interest in oratory/debate, based on language style, voice, diction, delivery, originality, logic, breadth of knowledge, application of knowledge about topic, and skill in selecting examples and analogies.
Additional information: Students selected by schools to participate in district contests, followed by area and departmental finals. Awards: First place, $1,200; second place, $1,000; third to sixth place, $700 each. Contact local Post for entry.

Amount of award:	$700-$1,200
Number of awards:	6
Total amount awarded:	$5,000

Contact:
American Legion California
401 Van Ness Avenue, Room 117
San Francisco, CA 94102-4587
Phone: 415-431-2400
Fax: 415-255-1571
Web: www.calegion.org

American Legion California Auxiliary

American Legion California Auxiliary General Scholarships

Type of award: Scholarship.
Intended use: For freshman study at postsecondary institution. Designated institutions: California colleges and universities.
Eligibility: Applicant or parent must be member/participant of American Legion Auxiliary. Applicant must be residing in California. Applicant must be dependent of veteran.
Basis for selection: Applicant must demonstrate financial need.
Application requirements: Recommendations, transcript, proof of eligibility. Cover letter.
Additional information: One $2,000 scholarship; four $1,000 scholarships; three $500 scholarships. Applications must be submitted to local Unit. Applicant may also be Girl Scout, or child of American Legion member or Sons of Legion member.

Amount of award:	$500-$2,000
Number of awards:	8
Total amount awarded:	$7,500

Contact:
American Legion Auxiliary, Department of California
War Memorial Building
401 Van Ness Avenue, Room 113
San Francisco, CA 94102-4586
Phone: 415-861-5092
Fax: 415-861-8365
Web: www.calegionaux.org

Lucille Ganey Memorial Scholarship

Type of award: Scholarship.
Intended use: For undergraduate study. Designated institutions: Stephens College, Missouri.
Eligibility: Applicant or parent must be member/participant of American Legion Auxiliary. Applicant must be high school senior. Applicant must be residing in California. Applicant must be dependent of active service person or veteran during Grenada conflict, Korean War, Lebanon conflict, Panama conflict, Persian Gulf War, WW I, WW II or Vietnam.
Additional information: Awarded annually to California high school senior who will attend Stephens College in Missouri. California students already attending Stephens College in Missouri also eligible. See Website for application. Applications must be submitted to local Unit.

Amount of award:	$500
Number of awards:	1
Application deadline:	March 16
Total amount awarded:	$500

Contact:
American Legion Auxiliary, Department of California
War Memorial Building
401 Van Ness Avenue, Room 113
San Francisco, CA 94102
Phone: 415-861-5092
Fax: 415-861-8365
Web: www.calegionaux.org

American Legion Colorado

American Legion Colorado National High School Oratorical Contest

Type of award: Scholarship.
Intended use: For undergraduate study at postsecondary institution.
Eligibility: Applicant must be enrolled in high school. Applicant must be residing in Colorado.
Basis for selection: Competition/talent/interest in oratory/debate, based on language style, voice, diction, delivery, originality, logic, breadth of knowledge, application of knowledge about topic, and skill in selecting examples and analogies.
Additional information: Awards: First place, $1,250; second place, $750; third place, $500. Apply at local Post.

Amount of award:	$500-$1,250
Number of awards:	3
Total amount awarded:	$2,500

Contact:
American Legion, Department of Colorado
7465 East First Avenue, Suite D
Denver, CO 80230
Web: www.coloradolegion.org

American Legion Colorado Auxiliary

American Legion Colorado Auxiliary Department President's Scholarship

Type of award: Scholarship.
Intended use: For undergraduate study at postsecondary institution.
Eligibility: Applicant or parent must be member/participant of American Legion Auxiliary. Applicant must be high school senior. Applicant must be residing in Colorado. Applicant must be dependent of veteran during Grenada conflict, Korean War, Lebanon conflict, Panama conflict, Persian Gulf War, WW I, WW II or Vietnam.
Additional information: One $1,000 award and two $500 awards.

Amount of award:	$500-$1,000
Number of awards:	3
Application deadline:	March 11
Total amount awarded:	$2,000

Contact:
American Legion Auxiliary, Department of Colorado
7465 East First Avenue, Suite D
Denver, CO 80230
Web: www.alacolorado.com

American Legion Colorado Auxiliary Department President's Scholarship for Junior Auxiliary Members

Type of award: Scholarship.
Intended use: For undergraduate study at postsecondary institution.
Eligibility: Applicant or parent must be member/participant of American Legion Auxiliary. Applicant must be high school senior. Applicant must be residing in Colorado. Applicant must be Colorado Junior Auxiliary member.

Amount of award:	$1,000
Number of awards:	1
Application deadline:	March 11
Total amount awarded:	$1,000

Contact:
American Legion Auxiliary, Department of Colorado
7465 East First Avenue, Suite D
Denver, CO 80230
Web: www.alacolorado.com

American Legion Colorado Auxiliary Past Presidents Parley Nurse's Scholarship

Type of award: Scholarship.
Intended use: For undergraduate study at accredited 2-year or 4-year institution.
Eligibility: Applicant or parent must be member/participant of American Legion Auxiliary. Applicant must be residing in Colorado. Applicant must be veteran; or dependent of veteran; or spouse of veteran during Grenada conflict, Korean War, Lebanon conflict, Panama conflict, Persian Gulf War, WW I, WW II or Vietnam.
Basis for selection: Major/career interest in nursing.
Additional information: Number and amount of awards vary.

Amount of award:	$500-$1,000
Application deadline:	April 15

Contact:
American Legion Auxiliary, Department of Colorado
7465 East First Avenue, Suite D
Denver, CO 80230

Violet Morrow Education Scholarship

Type of award: Scholarship.
Intended use: For undergraduate study at postsecondary institution.
Eligibility: Applicant or parent must be member/participant of American Legion Auxiliary. Applicant must be high school senior. Applicant must be residing in Colorado.
Basis for selection: Applicant must demonstrate depth of character and leadership.
Application requirements: Recommendations, essay, transcript.
Additional information: Applicant must be relative of veteran who served in Armed Forces. Applicant must be senior in high school or in the first four years of college. Forms available online; mail completed application to Violet Morrow Educational Scholarship Committee, 5934 S. Yank Court, Littleton, CO 80127.

Amount of award:	$500
Number of awards:	1
Application deadline:	March 11
Total amount awarded:	$500

Contact:
American Legion Auxiliary, Department Headquarters
7465 East First Ave
Suite D
Denver, CO 80230
Web: www.alacolorado.com

American Legion Connecticut

American Legion Connecticut National High School Oratorical Contest

Type of award: Scholarship.
Intended use: For undergraduate study at postsecondary institution.
Eligibility: Applicant must be no older than 19, enrolled in high school. Applicant must be residing in Connecticut.
Basis for selection: Competition/talent/interest in oratory/debate, based on language style, voice, diction, delivery, originality, logic, breadth of knowledge, application of knowledge about topic, and skill in selecting examples and analogies.
Additional information: Awards: First place, $1,500; second, $1,000; third to seventh place, $500. Contest open only to students attending Connecticut high schools. Contact high school for more information.

Amount of award:	$500-$1,500
Number of awards:	7
Total amount awarded:	$5,000

Contact:
American Legion, Department of Connecticut
Department Oratorical Chairman
P.O. Box 208
Rocky Hill, CT 06067
Phone: 860-436-9986
Web: www.ct.legion.org

American Legion Connecticut Auxiliary

American Legion Connecticut Auxiliary Memorial Education Grant

Type of award: Scholarship.
Intended use: For undergraduate study at vocational, 2-year or 4-year institution.
Eligibility: Applicant or parent must be member/participant of American Legion Auxiliary. Applicant must be at least 16, no older than 23.
Basis for selection: Applicant must demonstrate financial need.

Application requirements: Recommendations, essay, transcript, proof of eligibility.
Additional information: Candidate must be Connecticut resident and child of veteran; child/grandchild of Connecticut American Legion or American Legion Auxiliary member (no residency required); or member of Connecticut ALA or Sons of the American Legion (no residency required).

Amount of award:	$500
Number of awards:	4
Application deadline:	March 1
Total amount awarded:	$2,000

Contact:
American Legion Auxiliary, Department of Connecticut
P.O. Box 266
Rocky Hill, CT 06067-0266
Phone: 860-616-2343
Fax: 860-616-2342
Web: www.ct.legion.org

American Legion Connecticut Auxiliary Past Presidents Parley Education Grant

Type of award: Scholarship, renewable.
Intended use: For undergraduate study at vocational, 2-year or 4-year institution.
Eligibility: Applicant or parent must be member/participant of American Legion Auxiliary. Applicant must be at least 16, no older than 23.
Basis for selection: Applicant must demonstrate financial need.
Application requirements: Recommendations, essay, transcript, proof of eligibility.
Additional information: Preference given to child or grandchild of ex-servicewoman who is a CT American Legion or American Legion Auxiliary member of at least three years or who was a member for the three years prior to her death. Second preference to child or grandchild of CT American Legion, American Legion Auxiliary, or Sons of American Legion member of at least three years, or who was a member for three years prior to death.

Amount of award:	$500
Number of awards:	4
Application deadline:	March 1
Total amount awarded:	$2,000

Contact:
American Legion Auxiliary, Department of Connecticut
P.O. Box 266
Rocky Hill, CT 06067-0266
Phone: 860-616-2343
Fax: 860-616-2342
Web: www.ct.legion.org

American Legion Delaware Auxiliary

American Legion Delaware Auxiliary Past Presidents Parley Nursing Scholarship

Type of award: Scholarship.
Intended use: For undergraduate study at postsecondary institution.
Eligibility: Applicant or parent must be member/participant of American Legion Auxiliary. Applicant must be residing in Delaware. Applicant must be dependent of veteran.
Basis for selection: Major/career interest in nursing.

Amount of award:	$300
Number of awards:	1
Application deadline:	February 28
Total amount awarded:	$300

Contact:
American Legion Auxiliary, Department of Delaware
Attn: Tina Washington
25109 Prettyman Rd.
Georgetown, DE 19947

American Legion District of Columbia

American Legion District of Columbia National High School Oratorical Contest

Type of award: Scholarship.
Intended use: For undergraduate study at postsecondary institution.
Eligibility: Applicant must be no older than 19, enrolled in high school. Applicant must be U.S. citizen or permanent resident residing in District of Columbia.
Basis for selection: Competition/talent/interest in oratory/debate, based on language style, voice, diction, delivery, originality, logic, breadth of knowledge, application of knowledge about topic, and skill in selecting examples and analogies.
Application requirements: Proof of eligibility.
Additional information: Awards: First place, $1,500; second place, $500; third place, $300; fourth place, $100.

Amount of award:	$100-$800
Number of awards:	4
Total amount awarded:	$1,600

Contact:
The American Legion, Department of DC
1325 D St. SE
Suite 202
Washington, DC 20003
Phone: 202-362-9151
Fax: 202-362-9152

American Legion Florida

American Legion Florida Eagle Scout of the Year

Type of award: Scholarship.
Intended use: For undergraduate study at accredited postsecondary institution in United States.
Eligibility: Applicant or parent must be member/participant of American Legion. Applicant must be male, enrolled in high school. Applicant must be residing in Florida.
Application requirements: Transcript, proof of eligibility.

Scholarships

Additional information: Applicant must have earned Eagle Award and religious emblem, must be a high school student and Florida resident, must be in a troop chartered to an American Legion Post or the son/grandson of a Legion Member or parent eligible to join the American Legion Department of Florida. Awards: First place, $2,500; second place, $1,500; third place, $1,000; fourth place, $500.

Amount of award:	$500-$2,500
Number of awards:	4
Application deadline:	March 1
Total amount awarded:	$5,500

Contact:
American Legion Florida, Department Headquarters
P.O. Box 547859
Orlando, FL 32854-7859
Phone: 407-295-2631
Web: www.floridalegion.org

American Legion Florida General Scholarship

Type of award: Scholarship.
Intended use: For undergraduate study at accredited postsecondary institution in United States.
Eligibility: Applicant or parent must be member/participant of American Legion. Applicant must be high school senior. Applicant must be residing in Florida. Must be child, grandchild, great-grandchild, or legally adopted child of member in good standing of American Legion Florida, or of a deceased U.S. veteran who would have been eligible for membership.
Application requirements: Proof of eligibility.
Additional information: Awards: First place, $2,500; second place, $1,500; third place, $1,000; fourth to seventh place, $500. Student must be senior attending Florida high school. Parents must be Florida residents.

Amount of award:	$500-$2,500
Number of awards:	7
Application deadline:	March 1
Total amount awarded:	$7,000

Contact:
American Legion Florida, Department Headquarters
P.O. Box 547859
Orlando, FL 32854-7859
Phone: 407-295-2631
Web: www.floridalegion.org

American Legion Florida High School Oratorical Contest

Type of award: Scholarship.
Intended use: For undergraduate study at postsecondary institution.
Eligibility: Applicant or parent must be member/participant of American Legion. Applicant must be enrolled in high school. Applicant must be residing in Florida.
Basis for selection: Competition/talent/interest in oratory/debate, based on language style, voice, diction, delivery, originality, logic, breadth of knowledge, application of knowledge about topic, and skill in selecting examples and analogies.
Additional information: Awards: First place, $2,500; second place, $1,500; third place, $1,000; fourth to sixth place, $500. Parents must be Florida residents.

Amount of award:	$500-$2,500
Number of awards:	6
Application deadline:	December 1
Total amount awarded:	$6,500

Contact:
American Legion Florida, Department Headquarters
P.O. Box 547859
Orlando, FL 32854-7859
Phone: 407-295-2631
Web: www.floridalegion.org

American Legion Florida Auxiliary

American Legion Florida Auxiliary Department Scholarships

Type of award: Scholarship, renewable.
Intended use: For undergraduate study at vocational, 2-year or 4-year institution.
Eligibility: Applicant or parent must be member/participant of American Legion Auxiliary. Applicant must be residing in Florida. Must be child or stepchild of honorably discharged U.S. military veteran and sponsored by local Auxiliary Unit.
Basis for selection: Applicant must demonstrate high academic achievement.
Application requirements: Recommendations, essay, transcript, proof of eligibility. Income tax forms.
Additional information: Up to $2,000 for four-year university; $1000 for junior colleges and vocational schools. Must maintain minimum 2.5 GPA.

Amount of award:	$1,000-$2,000

Contact:
American Legion Auxiliary, Department of Florida
Department Secretary
P.O. Box 547917
Orlando, FL 32854
Fax: 407-293-7411
Web: www.alafl.org

American Legion Florida Auxiliary Memorial Scholarship

Type of award: Scholarship, renewable.
Intended use: For full-time undergraduate study at vocational, 2-year or 4-year institution.
Eligibility: Applicant or parent must be member/participant of American Legion Auxiliary. Applicant must be residing in Florida. Must be member or daughter/granddaughter of member with at least three years' membership in FL unit.
Basis for selection: Applicant must demonstrate high academic achievement.
Application requirements: Recommendations, essay, transcript, proof of eligibility. Income tax forms.
Additional information: Up to $2,000 for four-year university; $1,000 for junior colleges and vocational schools. Must maintain minimum 2.5 GPA.

Amount of award:	$1,000-$2,000
Application deadline:	February 1

Contact:
American Legion Auxiliary, Department of Florida
Department Secretary
P.O. Box 547917
Orlando, FL 32854
Fax: 407-293-7411
Web: www.alafl.org

American Legion Georgia

American Legion Georgia Oratorical Contest

Type of award: Scholarship.
Eligibility: Applicant or parent must be member/participant of American Legion. Applicant must be residing in Georgia.
Additional information: Awards: First place, $1,300; second place, $900; third place, $650; fourth place, $450.

Amount of award:	$450-$1,300
Number of awards:	4

Contact:
American Legion, Department of Georgia
3035 Mt. Zion Rd
Stockbridge, GA 30281-4101
Phone: 678-289-8883
Web: www.galegion.org

American Legion Georgia Scholarship

Type of award: Scholarship.
Intended use: For undergraduate study at postsecondary institution.
Eligibility: Applicant or parent must be member/participant of American Legion Auxiliary. Applicant must be high school senior. Applicant must be residing in Georgia. Applicant must be dependent of veteran or deceased veteran.
Additional information: Applicant must be outstanding student endorsed by post and high school principal. Must be child or grandchild of veteran member of Georgia Legion.

Amount of award:	$1,000
Number of awards:	6
Total amount awarded:	$6,000

Contact:
American Legion Georgia, Department Headquarters
3035 Mt. Zion Road
Stockbridge, GA 30281-4101
Phone: 678-289-8883
Web: www.galegion.org

American Legion Georgia Auxiliary

American Legion Georgia Auxiliary Past Presidents Parley Nurses Scholarship

Type of award: Scholarship.
Intended use: For undergraduate study at 2-year or 4-year institution.
Eligibility: Applicant or parent must be member/participant of American Legion Auxiliary. Applicant must be residing in Georgia. Applicant must be dependent of veteran or deceased veteran. Must be sponsored by local Auxiliary Unit.
Basis for selection: Major/career interest in nursing.
Application requirements: Proof of eligibility.
Additional information: Number and amount of scholarships determined by available funds.

Application deadline:	June 1

Contact:
American Legion Georgia Auxiliary, Department Headquarters
3035 Mt. Zion Road
Stockbridge, GA 30281-4101
Phone: 678-289-8446
Web: www.galegionaux.org

American Legion Hawaii

American Legion Hawaii Oratorical Contest

Type of award: Scholarship.
Intended use: For undergraduate study at postsecondary institution.
Eligibility: Applicant must be enrolled in high school. Applicant must be residing in Hawaii.
Basis for selection: Competition/talent/interest in oratory/debate, based on language style, voice, diction, delivery, originality, logic, breadth of knowledge, application of knowledge about topic, and skill in selecting examples and analogies.
Additional information: Awards: First place, $1,000; second place, $500; third place, $100; fourth place, $50. Contest normally held in February.

Amount of award:	$50-$1,000
Number of awards:	4
Total amount awarded:	$1,650

Contact:
American Legion Hawaii, Department Headquarters
612 McCully Street
Honolulu, HI 96826
Phone: 808-946-6383
Fax: 808-947-3957
Web: www.americanlegionhawaii.org

American Legion Idaho

American Legion Idaho Oratorical Contest

Type of award: Scholarship.
Intended use: For undergraduate study at postsecondary institution.
Eligibility: Applicant must be enrolled in high school. Applicant must be residing in Idaho.
Basis for selection: Competition/talent/interest in oratory/debate, based on language style, voice, diction, delivery, originality, logic, breadth of knowledge, application of knowledge about topic, and skill in selecting examples and analogies.

Scholarships

Additional information: Awards: First place, $750; second place, $500; third place, $250; fourth place, $100. Visit Website for more information.

Amount of award:	$100-$750
Number of awards:	4
Total amount awarded:	$1,600

Contact:
American Legion Idaho, Department Headquarters
901 Warren Street
Boise, ID 83706
Phone: 208-342-7061
Fax: 208-342-1964
Web: idlegion.home.mindspring.com

American Legion Idaho Scholarships

Type of award: Scholarship.
Intended use: For undergraduate study at postsecondary institution.
Eligibility: Applicant or parent must be member/participant of American Legion. Applicant must be residing in Idaho.
Application requirements: Proof of eligibility.
Additional information: Grandchildren of American Legion members and children/grandchildren of American Legion Auxiliary members in Idaho also eligible. Scholarships determined annually. See Website for more information.

Application deadline:	July 1

Contact:
American Legion Idaho, Department Headquarters
901 Warren Street
Boise, ID 83706
Phone: 208-342-7061
Fax: 208-342-1964
Web: idlegion.home.mindspring.com

American Legion Idaho Auxiliary

American Legion Idaho Auxiliary Nurse's Scholarship

Type of award: Scholarship.
Intended use: For undergraduate study at 2-year or 4-year institution.
Eligibility: Applicant must be at least 17, no older than 35. Applicant must be residing in Idaho. Applicant must be veteran; or dependent of veteran.
Basis for selection: Major/career interest in nursing.
Application requirements: Recommendations, transcript, proof of eligibility. Financial statement, photograph.
Additional information: Grandchildren of veterans also eligible. Submit application to local Auxiliary Unit.

Amount of award:	$1,000
Application deadline:	May 15

Contact:
American Legion Idaho Auxiliary, Department Headquarters
905 Warren Street
Boise, ID 83706-3825
Phone: 208-342-7066
Web: www.idahoala.org

American Legion Illinois

American Legion Illinois Boy Scout Scholarship

Type of award: Scholarship.
Intended use: For undergraduate study at postsecondary institution.
Eligibility: Applicant or parent must be member/participant of Boy Scouts of America. Applicant must be high school senior. Applicant must be residing in Illinois.
Basis for selection: Competition/talent/interest in writing/journalism.
Application requirements: Proof of eligibility. 500-word essay on American Legion, Americanism, and Boy Scout programs.
Additional information: Boy Scout Scholarship: $700. Runner-up awards: $200. Contact American Legion Department of Illinois, Post, County, District, or Division for application.

Amount of award:	$200-$700
Number of awards:	3
Application deadline:	April 30

Contact:
American Legion, Department of Illinois
c/o Boy Scout Committee
2720 E. Lincoln St.
Bloomington, IL 61704
Web: www.illegion.org

American Legion Illinois Oratorical Contest

Type of award: Scholarship.
Intended use: For undergraduate study at vocational, 2-year or 4-year institution.
Eligibility: Applicant must be enrolled in high school. Applicant must be U.S. citizen or permanent resident residing in Illinois.
Basis for selection: Competition/talent/interest in oratory/debate, based on language style, voice, diction, delivery, originality, logic, breadth of knowledge, application of knowledge about topic, and skill in selecting examples and analogies.
Application requirements: Proof of eligibility.
Additional information: Contest begins in January and starts at Post level, continuing to District level, to Division level, to Department level. Awards: First place, $2,000; second place, $1,500; third place, $1,200; fourth and fifth place, $1,000. First place winner of Department will proceed to national competition. Contact local Post or Department Headquarters.

Amount of award:	$1,000-$2,000
Number of awards:	5
Application deadline:	February 1
Total amount awarded:	$6,700

Contact:
American Legion, Department of Illinois
2720 E. Lincoln St.
Bloomington, IL 61704
Web: www.illegion.org

American Legion Illinois Scholarships

Type of award: Scholarship.
Intended use: For undergraduate study at accredited vocational, 2-year or 4-year institution.

Eligibility: Applicant or parent must be member/participant of American Legion. Applicant must be high school senior. Applicant must be residing in Illinois.
Basis for selection: Applicant must demonstrate financial need and high academic achievement.
Application requirements: Proof of eligibility.
Additional information: Grandchildren of American Legion members also eligible.

Amount of award:	$1,000
Application deadline:	March 15

Contact:
American Legion, Department of Illinois
2720 E. Lincoln St.
Bloomington, IL 61704
Web: www.illegion.org

American Legion Illinois Auxiliary

American Legion Illinois Auxiliary Ada Mucklestone Memorial Scholarship

Type of award: Scholarship.
Intended use: For undergraduate study at postsecondary institution.
Eligibility: Applicant must be residing in Illinois. Applicant must be descendant of veteran; or dependent of veteran during Grenada conflict, Korean War, Lebanon conflict, Panama conflict, Persian Gulf War, WW I, WW II or Vietnam.
Basis for selection: Applicant must demonstrate financial need, high academic achievement, depth of character and leadership.
Application requirements: Recommendations, essay, transcript, proof of eligibility. Copy of parents' most recent federal income tax return.
Additional information: Must be a high school senior or graduate of accredited high school. For first time post-secondary education only. May also be a grandchild or great-grandchild of eligible veteran. Must be a resident of Illinois or a member in good standing of The American Legion Family, Department of Illinois. Nursing majors not eligible. Unit sponsorship required. Contact local Unit for application.

Amount of award:	$1,000
Application deadline:	March 15

Contact:
American Legion Auxiliary, Department of Illinois
2720 E. Lincoln St.
Bloomington, IL 61704
Phone: 309-663-9366
Web: www.ilala.org

American Legion Illinois Auxiliary Special Education Teaching Scholarships

Type of award: Scholarship.
Intended use: For sophomore or junior study at 4-year institution.
Eligibility: Applicant must be residing in Illinois. Applicant must be veteran or descendant of veteran; or dependent of veteran during Grenada conflict, Korean War, Lebanon conflict, Panama conflict, Persian Gulf War, WW I, WW II or Vietnam.
Basis for selection: Major/career interest in education, special. Applicant must demonstrate financial need.
Application requirements: Proof of eligibility.
Additional information: Unit sponsorship required. Contact local Unit for application.

Amount of award:	$1,000
Application deadline:	March 15
Total amount awarded:	$1,000

Contact:
American Legion Auxiliary, Department of Illinois
2720 E. Lincoln St.
Bloomington, IL 61704
Phone: 309-663-9366
Web: www.ilala.org

American Legion Illinois Auxiliary Student Nurse Scholarship

Type of award: Scholarship.
Intended use: For undergraduate study at 2-year or 4-year institution.
Eligibility: Applicant must be residing in Illinois.
Basis for selection: Major/career interest in nursing.
Application requirements: Proof of eligibility.
Additional information: Unit sponsorship required. Contact local Unit for application.

Amount of award:	$1,000
Number of awards:	1
Application deadline:	March 15
Total amount awarded:	$1,000

Contact:
American Legion Auxiliary, Department of Illinois
2720 E. Lincoln St.
Bloomington, IL 61704
Phone: 309-663-9366
Web: www.ilala.org

Americanism Essay Contest Scholarship

Type of award: Scholarship.
Intended use: For undergraduate study at postsecondary institution.
Eligibility: Applicant must be enrolled in high school. Applicant must be residing in Illinois.
Application requirements: 500-word essay on selected topic.
Additional information: Award amount depends on placement and grade level. Open to students grade 7-12 enrolled at accredited Illinois junior high and high schools or home schooled. Deadline is first Friday in February. Submit essay to local American Legion Post, Auxiliary Unit, or Sons of American Legion Squadron.

Amount of award:	$100-$1,200

Contact:
American Legion Illinois Auxiliary
2720 E. Lincoln St.
Bloomington, IL 61704
Web: www.illegion.org

Marie Sheehe Trade School Scholarship

Type of award: Scholarship.
Intended use: For undergraduate study at vocational institution.

Eligibility: Applicant must be residing in Illinois. Applicant must be descendant of veteran; or dependent of veteran during Grenada conflict, Korean War, Lebanon conflict, Panama conflict, Persian Gulf War, WW I, WW II or Vietnam.
Basis for selection: Applicant must demonstrate financial need, high academic achievement, depth of character and leadership.
Application requirements: Recommendations, essay, transcript, proof of eligibility. Copy of parents' most recent federal income tax return.
Additional information: May also be grandchild of eligible veteran. Must be Illinois resident or member in good standing of American Legion Family, Department of Illinois. Unit sponsorship required. Contact local Unit for application.

Amount of award:	$800
Number of awards:	1
Application deadline:	March 15
Total amount awarded:	$800

Contact:
American Legion Auxiliary, Department of Illinois
2720 E. Lincoln St.
Bloomington, IL 61704
Phone: 309-663-9366
Web: www.ilala.org

Scholarships

Mildred R. Knoles Scholarship

Type of award: Scholarship.
Intended use: For sophomore, junior or senior study at postsecondary institution.
Eligibility: Applicant must be residing in Illinois. Applicant must be veteran or descendant of veteran; or dependent of veteran during Grenada conflict, Korean War, Lebanon conflict, Panama conflict, Persian Gulf War, WW I, WW II or Vietnam.
Basis for selection: Applicant must demonstrate financial need, high academic achievement, depth of character and leadership.
Application requirements: Recommendations, essay, transcript, proof of eligibility. Copy of most recent federal income tax return.
Additional information: Must be resident of Illinois or member in good standing of the American Legion Family, Department of Illinois. Awards: one $1,200; several $800. Unit sponsorship required. Contact local Unit for application. Nursing students not eligible.

Amount of award:	$1,000
Application deadline:	March 15

Contact:
American Legion Auxiliary, Department of Illinois
2720 E. Lincoln St.
Bloomington, IL 61704
Phone: 309-663-9366
Web: www.ilala.org

American Legion Indiana

American Legion Indiana Americanism and Government Test

Type of award: Scholarship.
Intended use: For undergraduate study at postsecondary institution.
Eligibility: Applicant must be high school sophomore, junior or senior. Applicant must be residing in Indiana.
Additional information: Six state winners chosen annually (one male, one female in each grade). Test given during American Education Week in November. Visit Website for local chairperson's contact information.

Amount of award:	$1,000
Number of awards:	6
Total amount awarded:	$6,000

Contact:
American Legion Indiana, Department Headquarters
Americanism Office
777 North Meridian Street
Indianapolis, IN 46204
Phone: 317-630-1300
Web: www.indlegion.org

American Legion Indiana Eagle Scout of the Year Scholarship

Type of award: Scholarship.
Intended use: For at postsecondary institution in United States.
Eligibility: Applicant or parent must be member/participant of American Legion. Applicant must be residing in Indiana.
Additional information: Eagle Scout of the Year winner from IN submitted to the National Organization. Indiana awards the state winner a $1,000 scholarship and district winners receive a $200 scholarship. Applicant must attend U.S. postsecondary education institution for advance education beyond high school. Check website for details.

Amount of award:	$200-$1,000
Application deadline:	March 1

Contact:
Phone: 317-630-1300
Web: www.indlegion.org

American Legion Indiana Family Scholarship

Type of award: Scholarship.
Intended use: For undergraduate study at accredited vocational, 2-year or 4-year institution in United States.
Eligibility: Applicant or parent must be member/participant of American Legion. Applicant must be residing in Indiana. Applicant must be child or grandchild of current or deceased member of The American Legion Indiana, American Legion Indiana Auxiliary, or Sons of The American Legion.
Application requirements: Essay, transcript, proof of eligibility.
Additional information: Five $1,500 awards.

Amount of award:	$1,500
Number of awards:	5
Application deadline:	April 1

Contact:
American Legion Indiana, Department Headquarters
Americanism Office
777 North Meridian Street
Indianapolis, IN 46204
Phone: 317-630-1300
Web: www.indlegion.org

American Legion Indiana Oratorical Contest

Type of award: Scholarship.
Intended use: For undergraduate study at postsecondary institution.

Eligibility: Applicant must be no older than 19, enrolled in high school. Applicant must be residing in Indiana.
Basis for selection: Competition/talent/interest in oratory/debate, based on language style, voice, diction, delivery, originality, logic, breadth of knowledge, application of knowledge about topic, and skill in selecting examples and analogies.
Application requirements: Proof of eligibility.
Additional information: State awards: First place, $3,400; second to fourth place, $1,000. Zone awards: four winners receive $800 each; 7 participants receive $200 each. Must participate in local contests. Competition begins in December.

Amount of award:	$200-$3,400
Number of awards:	15
Total amount awarded:	$11,000

Contact:
American Legion Indiana, Department Headquarters
Americanism Office
777 North Meridian Street
Indianapolis, IN 46204
Phone: 317-630-1300
Web: www.indlegion.org

American Legion Indiana Auxiliary

American Legion Indiana Auxiliary Past Presidents Parley Nursing Scholarship

Type of award: Scholarship.
Intended use: For undergraduate study.
Eligibility: Applicant or parent must be member/participant of American Legion Auxiliary. Applicant must be female. Applicant must be residing in Indiana.
Basis for selection: Major/career interest in nursing.
Application requirements: Send SASE for application.

Amount of award:	$500
Total amount awarded:	$500

Contact:
American Legion Auxiliary, Department of Indiana
Department Secretary
777 North Meridian Street, Room 107
Indianapolis, IN 46204
Phone: 317-630-1390
Fax: 317-630-1277
Web: www.amlegauxin.org

Edna M. Barcus Memorial Scholarship and Hoosier Scholarship

Type of award: Scholarship.
Intended use: For undergraduate study at postsecondary institution. Designated institutions: Indiana institutions.
Eligibility: Applicant or parent must be member/participant of American Legion Auxiliary. Applicant must be residing in Indiana. Applicant must be dependent of veteran.
Basis for selection: Applicant must demonstrate high academic achievement.
Application requirements: Send SASE for application.

Amount of award:	$500
Application deadline:	April 1

Contact:
American Legion Auxiliary, Department of Indiana
Department Secretary
777 North Meridian Street, Room 107
Indianapolis, IN 46204
Phone: 317-630-1390
Fax: 317-630-1277
Web: www.amlegauxin.org

American Legion Iowa

American Legion Iowa Boy Scout of the Year Scholarship

Type of award: Scholarship.
Intended use: For undergraduate study at postsecondary institution.
Eligibility: Applicant or parent must be member/participant of Boy Scouts of America, Eagle Scouts. Applicant must be male, at least 15. Applicant must be residing in Iowa.
Basis for selection: Applicant must demonstrate service orientation.
Application requirements: Recommendations, transcript, proof of eligibility.
Additional information: Must be registered, active member of Boy Scout Troop, Varsity Scout Team, or Venturing Crew chartered to American Legion Post, Auxiliary Unit, or Sons of American Legion Squadron; or be a registered, active member of Boy Scout Troop, Varsity Scout Team, or Venturing Crew and the son or grandson of an American Legion or Sons of American Legion member. Awards: First place, $2,000; second place, $1,500; third place, $1,000. Awarded on recommendation of Boy Scout Committee to Boy Scout who demonstrates outstanding service to religious institution, school, and community. Must have received Eagle Scout Award.

Amount of award:	$1,000-$2,000
Number of awards:	3
Application deadline:	February 1
Total amount awarded:	$4,500

Contact:
American Legion Iowa, Department Headquarters
720 Lyon Street
Des Moines, IA 50309
Phone: 515-282-5068
Fax: 515-282-7583
Web: www.ialegion.org

American Legion Iowa Oratorical Contest

Type of award: Scholarship.
Intended use: For undergraduate study at postsecondary institution.
Eligibility: Applicant must be enrolled in high school. Applicant must be U.S. citizen or permanent resident residing in Iowa.
Basis for selection: Competition/talent/interest in oratory/debate, based on language style, voice, diction, delivery, originality, logic, breadth of knowledge, application of knowledge about topic, and skill in selecting examples and analogies.
Application requirements: Proof of eligibility.

Additional information: Awards: First place, $2,000; second place, $1,500; third place, $1,000. Must enter Oratorical Contest at local level in September.

Amount of award:	$1,000-$2,000
Number of awards:	3
Total amount awarded:	$4,500

Contact:
American Legion Iowa, Department Headquarters
720 Lyon Street
Des Moines, IA 50309
Phone: 515-282-5068
Fax: 515-282-7583
Web: www.ialegion.org

American Legion Iowa Outstanding Citizen of Boys State Scholarship

Type of award: Scholarship.
Intended use: For undergraduate study at postsecondary institution. Designated institutions: Eligible colleges and universities in Iowa.
Eligibility: Applicant or parent must be member/participant of American Legion, Boys State. Applicant must be male, high school senior. Applicant must be residing in Iowa.
Application requirements: Recommendations.
Additional information: Must have completed junior year in high school to attend Boys State. Awarded on recommendation of Boys State.

Amount of award:	$5,000
Number of awards:	1

Contact:
American Legion Iowa, Department Headquarters
720 Lyon Street
Des Moines, IA 50309
Phone: 515-282-5068
Fax: 515-282-7583
Web: www.ialegion.org

American Legion Iowa Auxiliary

American Legion Department of Iowa Scholarships

Type of award: Scholarship.
Intended use: For undergraduate study at postsecondary institution. Designated institutions: Eligible Iowa postsecondary institutions.
Eligibility: Applicant must be residing in Iowa. Applicant must be veteran or descendant of veteran; or dependent of veteran or deceased veteran; or spouse of veteran or deceased veteran.
Application requirements: Recommendations, essay, transcript, proof of eligibility. Photo of self.

Amount of award:	$300
Number of awards:	10
Application deadline:	May 20
Total amount awarded:	$3,000

Contact:
American Legion Auxiliary, Department of Iowa
Attn: Education Chair
720 Lyon Street
Des Moines, IA 50309
Phone: 515-282-7987
Fax: 515-282-7583
Web: www.ialegion.org/ala

American Legion Iowa Auxiliary Past President's Scholarship

Type of award: Scholarship.
Intended use: For undergraduate study at postsecondary institution.
Eligibility: Applicant must be residing in Iowa. Applicant must be veteran or descendant of veteran; or dependent of veteran or deceased veteran; or spouse of veteran or deceased veteran.
Application requirements: Recommendations, essay, transcript, proof of eligibility. Photo of self.
Additional information: Amount of award varies.

Application deadline:	May 20

Contact:
American Legion Iowa Auxiliary
Attn: Education Chair
720 Lyon Street
Des Moines, IA 50309
Phone: 515-282-7987
Fax: 515-282-7583
Web: www.ialegion.org/ala/

Harriet Hoffman Memorial Scholarship

Type of award: Scholarship.
Intended use: For undergraduate study at postsecondary institution. Designated institutions: Eligible Iowa postsecondary institutions.
Eligibility: Applicant must be residing in Iowa. Applicant must be veteran or descendant of veteran; or dependent of veteran or deceased veteran; or spouse of veteran or deceased veteran.
Basis for selection: Major/career interest in education or education, teacher.
Application requirements: Recommendations, essay, transcript, proof of eligibility. Photo of self.

Amount of award:	$400
Number of awards:	1
Application deadline:	May 20
Total amount awarded:	$400

Contact:
American Legion Auxiliary, Department of Iowa
Attn: Education Chair
720 Lyon Street
Des Moines, IA 50309
Phone: 515-282-7987
Fax: 515-282-7583
Web: www.ialegion.org/ala

Mary Virginia Macrea Memorial Scholarship

Type of award: Scholarship.
Intended use: For undergraduate study at postsecondary institution. Designated institutions: Eligible Iowa postsecondary institutions.

Eligibility: Applicant must be residing in Iowa. Applicant must be veteran or descendant of veteran; or dependent of veteran or deceased veteran; or spouse of veteran or deceased veteran.
Basis for selection: Major/career interest in nursing.
Application requirements: Recommendations, essay, transcript, proof of eligibility. Photo of self.

Amount of award:	$400
Number of awards:	1
Application deadline:	May 20
Total amount awarded:	$400

Contact:
American Legion Auxiliary, Department of Iowa
Attn: Education Chair
720 Lyon Street
Des Moines, IA 50309
Phone: 515-282-7987
Fax: 515-282-7583
Web: www.ialegion.org/ala

American Legion Kansas

Albert M. Lappin Scholarship

Type of award: Scholarship.
Intended use: For freshman or sophomore study at accredited vocational, 2-year or 4-year institution. Designated institutions: Eligible colleges, universities, and trade schools in Kansas.
Eligibility: Applicant or parent must be member/participant of American Legion. Applicant must be residing in Kansas.
Application requirements: Recommendations, essay, transcript, proof of eligibility. Income tax forms. Photo of self.
Additional information: High school seniors may also apply. Must be child of member of American Legion Kansas or American Legion Kansas Auxiliary whose parent has been a member for the past three years; or be a child of deceased member of either organization whose dues were paid-up at time of death.

Amount of award:	$1,000
Number of awards:	1
Application deadline:	February 15
Total amount awarded:	$1,000

Contact:
American Legion Kansas
1314 Southwest Topeka Boulevard
Topeka, KS 66612-1886
Phone: 785-232-9315
Web: www.ksamlegion.org

American Legion Kansas Music Scholarship

Type of award: Scholarship.
Intended use: For freshman or sophomore study at accredited vocational, 2-year or 4-year institution. Designated institutions: Eligible Kansas colleges and universities.
Eligibility: Applicant must be residing in Kansas.
Basis for selection: Major/career interest in music. Applicant must demonstrate financial need.
Application requirements: Recommendations, transcript, proof of eligibility. Income tax forms. Photo of self.
Additional information: High school seniors may also apply.

Amount of award:	$1,000
Number of awards:	1
Application deadline:	February 15
Total amount awarded:	$1,000

Contact:
American Legion Kansas
1314 Southwest Topeka Boulevard
Topeka, KS 66612-1886
Phone: 785-232-9315
Web: www.ksamlegion.org

American Legion Kansas Oratorical Contest

Type of award: Scholarship.
Intended use: For undergraduate study at postsecondary institution.
Eligibility: Applicant must be enrolled in high school. Applicant must be residing in Kansas.
Basis for selection: Competition/talent/interest in oratory/debate, based on language style, voice, diction, delivery, originality, logic, breadth of knowledge, application of knowledge about topic, and skill in selecting examples and analogies.
Additional information: State awards: First place, $1,500; second place, $500; third place, $250; and fourth place, $150. Many Posts, County Councils, and Districts also provide scholarships.

Amount of award:	$150-$1,500
Number of awards:	4
Total amount awarded:	$2,400

Contact:
American Legion Kansas
1314 Southwest Topeka Boulevard
Topeka, KS 66612-1886
Phone: 785-232-9315
Web: www.ksamlegion.org

Charles and Annette Hill Scholarship

Type of award: Scholarship.
Intended use: For freshman, sophomore or junior study at postsecondary institution.
Eligibility: Applicant or parent must be member/participant of American Legion. Applicant must be residing in Kansas. Must be descendent of member of American Legion Kansas who has been a member for the past three years; or be descendent of deceased member whose dues were paid-up at time of death.
Basis for selection: Major/career interest in science, general; engineering or business/management/administration. Applicant must demonstrate high academic achievement.
Application requirements: Recommendations, essay, transcript, proof of eligibility. Income tax forms. Photo of self.
Additional information: Minimum 3.0 GPA. High school seniors may also apply.

Amount of award:	$1,000
Number of awards:	1
Application deadline:	February 15
Total amount awarded:	$1,000

Contact:
American Legion Kansas
1314 Southwest Topeka Blvd.
Topeka, KS 66612-1886
Phone: 785-232-9315
Web: www.ksamlegion.org

Scholarships

Dr. Click Cowger Scholarship

Type of award: Scholarship.
Intended use: For freshman or sophomore study at accredited vocational, 2-year or 4-year institution. Designated institutions: Eligible Kansas colleges, universities, and trade schools.
Eligibility: Applicant must be male. Applicant must be residing in Kansas.
Basis for selection: Competition/talent/interest in athletics/sports.
Application requirements: Recommendations, essay, transcript, proof of eligibility. Income tax forms.
Additional information: For current players or those who have played in Kansas American Legion Baseball. High school seniors may also apply.

Amount of award:	$500
Number of awards:	1
Application deadline:	July 15
Total amount awarded:	$500

Contact:
American Legion Kansas
1314 Southwest Topeka Boulevard
Topeka, KS 66612-1886
Phone: 785-232-9315
Web: www.ksamlegion.org

Hugh A. Smith Scholarship

Type of award: Scholarship.
Intended use: For freshman or sophomore study at accredited vocational, 2-year or 4-year institution. Designated institutions: Eligible Kansas colleges, universities, and trade schools.
Eligibility: Applicant or parent must be member/participant of American Legion. Applicant must be residing in Kansas. Applicant must be dependent of veteran or deceased veteran.
Application requirements: Recommendations, essay, transcript, proof of eligibility. Income tax forms. Photo of self.
Additional information: Must be child of member of American Legion Kansas or American Legion Kansas Auxiliary whose parent has been a member for the past three years; or be a child of deceased member of either organization whose dues were paid up at time of death.

Amount of award:	$500
Number of awards:	1
Application deadline:	February 15
Total amount awarded:	$500

Contact:
American Legion Kansas
1314 Southwest Topeka Boulevard
Topeka, KS 66612-1886
Phone: 785-232-9315
Web: www.ksamlegion.org

John and Geraldine Hobble Licensed Practical Nursing Scholarship

Type of award: Scholarship.
Intended use: For freshman study at accredited postsecondary institution. Designated institutions: Kansas accredited schools that award LPN diplomas.
Eligibility: Applicant must be at least 18. Applicant must be residing in Kansas.
Basis for selection: Major/career interest in nursing. Applicant must demonstrate financial need.
Application requirements: Recommendations, transcript, proof of eligibility. Income tax forms, photo of self.
Additional information: One-time award of $300.

Amount of award:	$300
Number of awards:	1
Application deadline:	February 15
Total amount awarded:	$300

Contact:
American Legion Kansas
1314 Southwest Topeka Boulevard
Topeka, KS 66612-1886
Phone: 785-232-9315
Web: www.ksamlegion.org

Rosedale Post 346 Scholarship

Type of award: Scholarship.
Intended use: For freshman or sophomore study at vocational, 2-year or 4-year institution.
Eligibility: Applicant or parent must be member/participant of American Legion. Applicant must be high school senior. Applicant must be residing in Kansas. Applicant must be dependent of veteran or deceased veteran. Must be child of member of American Legion Kansas or American Legion Kansas Auxiliary whose parent has been a member for the past three years; or be a child of deceased member of either organization whose dues were paid up at time of death.
Application requirements: Recommendations, essay, transcript, proof of eligibility. Income tax forms. Photo of self.
Additional information: High school seniors may also apply.

Amount of award:	$1,500
Number of awards:	2
Application deadline:	February 15
Total amount awarded:	$3,000

Contact:
American Legion Kansas
1314 Southwest Topeka Blvd.
Topeka, KS 66612-1886
Phone: 785-232-9315
Web: www.ksamlegion.org

Ted and Nora Anderson Scholarship

Type of award: Scholarship.
Intended use: For freshman or sophomore study at accredited vocational, 2-year or 4-year institution. Designated institutions: Eligible colleges, universities, and trade schools in Kansas.
Eligibility: Applicant or parent must be member/participant of American Legion. Applicant must be residing in Kansas. Applicant must be dependent of veteran or deceased veteran. Must be child of member of American Legion Kansas or American Legion Kansas Auxiliary whose parent has been a member for the past three years; or be a child of deceased member of either organization whose dues were paid up at time of death.
Basis for selection: Applicant must demonstrate financial need.
Application requirements: Recommendations, essay, transcript, proof of eligibility. Photo of self.
Additional information: High school seniors may also apply.

Amount of award:	$500
Number of awards:	4
Application deadline:	February 15
Total amount awarded:	$2,000

Contact:
American Legion Kansas
1314 Southwest Topeka Boulevard
Topeka, KS 66612-1886
Phone: 785-232-9315
Web: www.ksamlegion.org

American Legion Kansas Auxiliary

American Legion Kansas Auxiliary Department Scholarships

Type of award: Scholarship.
Intended use: For full-time freshman study at postsecondary institution. Designated institutions: Kansas institutions.
Eligibility: Applicant must be residing in Kansas. Applicant must be descendant of veteran; or dependent of veteran; or spouse of veteran or deceased veteran.
Application requirements: Recommendations, transcript. SAT/ACT scores.
Additional information: Eight two-year scholarships of $500, payable at $250 per year for two years. Applicants must be entering college for the first time. Spouses of deceased veterans must not be remarried.

Amount of award:	$500
Number of awards:	8
Application deadline:	April 1
Total amount awarded:	$4,000

Contact:
American Legion Kansas Auxiliary
Department Secretary
1314-B Southwest Topeka Boulevard
Topeka, KS 66612-1886
Phone: 785-232-1396
Web: www.kslegionaux.org

American Legion Kentucky

American Legion Kentucky Department Oratorical Awards

Type of award: Scholarship.
Intended use: For undergraduate study at postsecondary institution.
Eligibility: Applicant must be enrolled in high school. Applicant must be residing in Kentucky.
Basis for selection: Competition/talent/interest in oratory/debate, based on language style, voice, diction, delivery, originality, logic, breadth of knowledge, application of knowledge about topic, and skill in selecting examples and analogies.
Additional information: Awards: First place, $2,000; second place, $1,500; third place, $1,000. District winners (11) each receive $200.

Amount of award:	$200-$2,000
Number of awards:	14
Total amount awarded:	$5,800

Contact:
American Legion Kentucky, Department Headquarters
P.O. Box 2123
Louisville, KY 40201
Phone: 502-587-1414
Fax: 502-587-6356
Web: www.kylegion.org

American Legion Kentucky Auxiliary

American Legion Kentucky Auxiliary Mary Barrett Marshall Scholarship

Type of award: Scholarship.
Intended use: For undergraduate study at vocational, 2-year or 4-year institution. Designated institutions: Eligible postsecondary institutions in Kentucky.
Eligibility: Applicant or parent must be member/participant of American Legion Auxiliary. Applicant must be female. Applicant must be residing in Kentucky. Applicant must be descendant of veteran; or dependent of veteran; or spouse of veteran or deceased veteran during Grenada conflict, Korean War, Lebanon conflict, Panama conflict, Persian Gulf War, WW I, WW II or Vietnam.
Application requirements: Proof of eligibility. SASE.

Amount of award:	$1,000
Number of awards:	1
Application deadline:	April 1
Total amount awarded:	$1,000

Contact:
American Legion Auxiliary, Department of Kentucky
P.O. Box 5435
Frankfort, KY 40602
Phone: 502-352-2380
Fax: 502-352-2381
Web: www.kyamlegionaux.org

Laura Blackburn Memorial Scholarship

Type of award: Scholarship.
Intended use: For undergraduate study at postsecondary institution.
Eligibility: Applicant or parent must be member/participant of American Legion Auxiliary. Applicant must be high school senior. Applicant must be residing in Kentucky. Applicant must be descendant of veteran; or dependent of veteran during Grenada conflict, Korean War, Lebanon conflict, Panama conflict, Persian Gulf War, WW I, WW II or Vietnam.
Application requirements: Recommendations, essay, transcript, proof of eligibility. SAT/ACT scores.
Additional information: Must submit application to local American Legion Auxiliary Unit president.

Amount of award:	$1,000
Number of awards:	1
Application deadline:	March 31
Total amount awarded:	$1,000

Contact:
American Legion Auxiliary, Department of Kentucky
P.O. Box 5435
Frankfort, KY 40602
Phone: 502-352-2380
Fax: 502-352-2381
Web: www.kyamlegionaux.org

Scholarships

American Legion Maine

American Legion Maine Children and Youth Scholarship

Type of award: Scholarship.
Intended use: For undergraduate study at accredited postsecondary institution.
Eligibility: Applicant or parent must be member/participant of American Legion. Applicant must be high school senior. Applicant must be residing in Maine.
Basis for selection: Applicant must demonstrate financial need and depth of character.
Application requirements: Recommendations, essay, transcript.
Additional information: High school seniors, college students, and veterans eligible. Students with GED may also apply.

Amount of award:	$500
Number of awards:	7
Number of applicants:	300
Application deadline:	May 1
Total amount awarded:	$3,500

Contact:
American Legion Maine
Department Adjutant, State Headquarters
P.O. Box 900
Waterville, ME 04903-0900
Phone: 207-873-3229
Fax: 207-872-0501
Web: www.mainelegion.org

Daniel E. Lambert Memorial Scholarship

Type of award: Scholarship.
Intended use: For undergraduate study at accredited vocational, 2-year or 4-year institution.
Eligibility: Applicant must be high school senior. Applicant must be U.S. citizen residing in Maine. Applicant must be descendant of veteran; or dependent of veteran.
Basis for selection: Applicant must demonstrate financial need and depth of character.
Application requirements: Recommendations, proof of eligibility.
Additional information: Must be child or grandchild of veteran.

Amount of award:	$1,000
Number of awards:	2
Application deadline:	May 1
Total amount awarded:	$2,000

Contact:
American Legion Maine
Department Adjutant, State Headquarters
P.O. Box 900
Waterville, ME 04903-0900
Phone: 207-873-3229
Fax: 207-872-0501
Web: www.mainelegion.org

James V. Day Scholarship

Type of award: Scholarship.
Intended use: For undergraduate study at vocational, 2-year or 4-year institution.
Eligibility: Applicant or parent must be member/participant of American Legion. Applicant must be high school senior. Applicant must be U.S. citizen residing in Maine.
Basis for selection: Applicant must demonstrate financial need, high academic achievement and depth of character.
Application requirements: Recommendations, essay, proof of eligibility.
Additional information: Must be in top half of graduating class. Grandchildren of current American Legion Post in Maine also eligible.

Amount of award:	$500
Number of awards:	2
Application deadline:	May 1
Total amount awarded:	$1,000

Contact:
American Legion Maine
Department Adjutant, State Headquarters
P.O. Box 900
Waterville, ME 04903-0900
Phone: 207-873-3229
Fax: 207-872-0501
Web: www.mainelegion.org

American Legion Maine Auxiliary

American Legion Maine Auxiliary Presidents Parley Nursing Scholarship

Type of award: Scholarship.
Intended use: For undergraduate study.
Eligibility: Applicant must be residing in Maine. Applicant must be descendant of veteran; or dependent of veteran during WW I or WW II.
Basis for selection: Major/career interest in nursing.
Application requirements: Proof of eligibility.
Additional information: Must be graduate of accredited high school.

Amount of award:	$300
Number of awards:	1
Total amount awarded:	$300

Contact:
American Legion Auxiliary, Department of Maine
Department Secretary
886B Kennedy Memorial Drive
Oakland, ME 04963
Phone: 207-465-4966
Fax: 207-465-4967
Web: www.mainelegion.org

American Legion Maine Auxiliary Scholarship

Type of award: Scholarship.
Intended use: For undergraduate study at vocational, 2-year or 4-year institution.
Eligibility: Applicant must be high school senior. Applicant must be residing in Maine. Applicant must be dependent of veteran.
Basis for selection: Applicant must demonstrate financial need.

Scholarships

Application requirements: Send SASE with application request.

Amount of award:	$300
Number of awards:	2
Application deadline:	April 5
Total amount awarded:	$600

Contact:
American Legion Auxiliary, Department of Maine
Department Secretary
886B Kennedy Memorial Drive
Oakland, ME 04963
Phone: 207-465-4966
Fax: 207-465-4967
Web: www.mainelegion.org

American Legion Maryland

Adler Science and Math Scholarship

Type of award: Scholarship.
Intended use: For full-time undergraduate study at postsecondary institution.
Eligibility: Applicant must be at least 16, no older than 19. Applicant must be residing in Maryland. Applicant must be dependent of veteran.
Basis for selection: Major/career interest in science, general or mathematics.
Application requirements: Recommendations, essay, transcript.

Amount of award:	$500
Number of awards:	1
Application deadline:	April 5
Total amount awarded:	$500

Contact:
American Legion Maryland
Attn: Department Adjutant
101 N. Gay St.
Baltimore, MD 21202
Phone: 410-752-1405
Fax: 410-752-3822
Web: www.mdlegion.org

American Legion Maryland Boys State Scholarship

Type of award: Scholarship.
Intended use: For undergraduate study at postsecondary institution.
Eligibility: Applicant or parent must be member/participant of American Legion, Boys State. Applicant must be male, at least 16, no older than 19. Applicant must be residing in Maryland.
Application requirements: Recommendations, transcript.
Additional information: Applicant must be Maryland Boys State graduate.

Amount of award:	$500
Number of awards:	5
Application deadline:	May 1
Total amount awarded:	$2,500

Contact:
American Legion Maryland
Attn: Department Adjutant
101 N. Gay St.
Baltimore, MD 21202-1405
Phone: 410-752-1405
Fax: 410-752-3822
Web: www.mdlegion.org

American Legion Maryland Oratorical Contest

Type of award: Scholarship.
Intended use: For undergraduate study at postsecondary institution.
Eligibility: Applicant must be at least 16, no older than 19. Applicant must be U.S. citizen or permanent resident residing in Maryland.
Basis for selection: Competition/talent/interest in oratory/debate, based on language style, voice, diction, delivery, originality, logic, breadth of knowledge, application of knowledge about topic, and skill in selecting examples and analogies.
Additional information: Awards: First place, $2,500; second place, $1,000; third through seventh place, $500 each. Apply to nearest American Legion Post.

Amount of award:	$500-$2,500
Number of awards:	7
Application deadline:	October 1
Total amount awarded:	$6,000

Contact:
American Legion Maryland
Attn: Department Adjutant
101 N. Gay St.
Baltimore, MD 21202-1405
Phone: 410-752-1405
Fax: 410-752-3822
Web: www.mdlegion.org

American Legion Maryland Scholarship

Type of award: Scholarship.
Intended use: For undergraduate study at postsecondary institution.
Eligibility: Applicant must be at least 16, no older than 19. Applicant must be residing in Maryland. Applicant must be dependent of veteran.
Application requirements: Recommendations, essay, transcript.
Additional information: Applicant must not have reached 20th birthday by January 1 of calendar year application is filed.

Amount of award:	$500
Number of awards:	11
Application deadline:	April 15
Total amount awarded:	$5,500

Contact:
American Legion Maryland
Attn: Department Adjutant
101 N. Gay St.
Baltimore, MD 21202-1405
Phone: 410-752-1405
Fax: 410-752-3822
Web: www.mdlegion.org

American Legion Maryland Auxiliary

American Legion Maryland Auxiliary Past Presidents Parley Scholarship

Type of award: Scholarship.
Intended use: For undergraduate study at 2-year or 4-year institution.
Eligibility: Applicant must be female, at least 16, no older than 22. Applicant must be residing in Maryland. Must be daughter/step-daughter, granddaughter/step-granddaughter, great-granddaughter/step-great-granddaughter of ex-servicewoman or ex-serviceman.
Basis for selection: Major/career interest in nursing. Applicant must demonstrate financial need.
Application requirements: Recommendations.
Additional information: For RN degree only.

Amount of award:	$2,000
Number of awards:	1
Application deadline:	May 1
Total amount awarded:	$2,000

Contact:
American Legion Maryland Auxiliary
Chairman, Past President's Parley Scholarship
1589 Sulphur Spring Road, Suite 105
Baltimore, MD 21227
Phone: 410-242-9519
Fax: 410-242-9553
Web: www.alamd.org

American Legion Maryland Auxiliary Scholarship

Type of award: Scholarship, renewable.
Intended use: For undergraduate study at 2-year or 4-year institution.
Eligibility: Applicant must be female, high school senior. Applicant must be residing in Maryland. Applicant must be dependent of veteran.
Basis for selection: Major/career interest in arts, general; biomedical; business; education; health-related professions; health sciences; physical therapy; physician assistant; public administration/service or science, general. Applicant must demonstrate financial need, depth of character and leadership.
Additional information: Other medical majors eligible. Nursing students not eligible.

Amount of award:	$2,000
Number of awards:	1
Application deadline:	May 1
Total amount awarded:	$2,000

Contact:
American Legion Auxiliary, Department of Maryland
Department Secretary
1589 Sulphur Spring Road, Suite 105
Baltimore, MD 21227
Phone: 410-242-9519
Fax: 410-242-9553
Web: www.alamd.org

American Legion Massachusetts

American Legion Department of Massachusetts Oratorical Contest

Type of award: Scholarship.
Intended use: For undergraduate study at postsecondary institution.
Eligibility: Applicant must be no older than 19. Applicant must be residing in Massachusetts.
Basis for selection: Competition/talent/interest in oratory/debate, based on language style, voice, diction, delivery, originality, logic, breadth of knowledge, application of knowledge about topic, and skill in selecting examples and analogies.
Application requirements: Proof of eligibility.
Additional information: Awards: First place, $1,000; second place, $800; third place, $700; fourth place, $600.

Amount of award:	$600-$1,000
Number of awards:	4
Application deadline:	December 15
Total amount awarded:	$3,100

Contact:
American Legion Massachusetts
Department Oratorical Chair
State House, Room 546-2
Boston, MA 02133-1044
Phone: 617-727-2966
Fax: 617-727-2960
Web: www.masslegion.org

American Legion Massachusetts General and Nursing Scholarships

Type of award: Scholarship.
Intended use: For freshman study at 2-year or 4-year institution.
Eligibility: Applicant or parent must be member/participant of American Legion. Applicant must be residing in Massachusetts. Applicant must be descendant of veteran; or dependent of veteran.
Application requirements: Recommendations, transcript, proof of eligibility.
Additional information: Grandchildren of American Legion Department of Massachusetts members also eligible. General Scholarships: Nine $1,000 awards; ten $500 awards. Nursing Scholarship: One $1,000 award.

Amount of award:	$500-$1,000
Number of awards:	20
Application deadline:	April 1
Total amount awarded:	$15,000

Contact:
American Legion Massachusetts
Department Adjutant
State House, Room 546-2
Boston, MA 02133-1044
Phone: 617-727-2966
Fax: 617-727-2969
Web: www.masslegion.org

American Legion Massachusetts Auxiliary

American Legion Massachusetts Auxiliary Past Presidents Parley Scholarship

Type of award: Scholarship.
Intended use: For undergraduate study at postsecondary institution.
Eligibility: Applicant must be residing in Massachusetts. Applicant must be dependent of veteran or deceased veteran.
Basis for selection: Major/career interest in nursing.
Additional information: Must be child of living or deceased veteran not eligible for Federal or Commonwealth scholarships.

Amount of award:	$200
Number of awards:	1
Total amount awarded:	$200

Contact:
American Legion Massachusetts Auxiliary
Department Secretary
State House, Room 546-2
Boston, MA 02133-1044
Phone: 617-727-2958
Fax: 617-727-0741
Web: www.masslegion-aux.org

American Legion Massachusetts Auxiliary Scholarship

Type of award: Scholarship.
Intended use: For undergraduate study at vocational, 2-year or 4-year institution.
Eligibility: Applicant must be at least 16, no older than 22. Applicant must be residing in Massachusetts. Applicant must be descendant of veteran; or dependent of veteran or deceased veteran during Grenada conflict, Korean War, Lebanon conflict, Panama conflict, Persian Gulf War, WW I, WW II or Vietnam.
Additional information: One $750 award; ten $200 awards.

Amount of award:	$200-$750
Number of awards:	11
Application deadline:	March 1
Total amount awarded:	$2,750

Contact:
American Legion Auxiliary, Department of Massachusetts
Department Secretary
State House, Room 546-2
Boston, MA 02133-1044
Phone: 617-727-2958
Fax: 617-727-0741
Web: www.masslegion-aux.org

American Legion Michigan

American Legion Michigan Oratorical Contest

Type of award: Scholarship.
Intended use: For undergraduate study at postsecondary institution.
Eligibility: Applicant must be no older than 19, enrolled in high school. Applicant must be U.S. citizen or permanent resident residing in Michigan.
Basis for selection: Competition/talent/interest in oratory/debate, based on ability to deliver an 8- to 10-minute speech on the U.S. Constitution.
Additional information: Awards: First place, $1,500; second place, $1,000; third place, $800. Local contest in early February. Contact local American Legion Post for more information.

Amount of award:	$800-$1,500
Number of awards:	3
Total amount awarded:	$3,300

Contact:
Deanna Clark American Legion Michigan
212 North Verlinden Avenue
Ste A
Lansing, MI 48915
Phone: 517-371-4720 ext. 11
Fax: 517-371-2401
Web: www.michiganlegion.org

Guy M. Wilson Scholarship

Type of award: Scholarship.
Intended use: For undergraduate study at 2-year or 4-year institution. Designated institutions: Michigan institutions.
Eligibility: Applicant must be enrolled in high school. Applicant must be residing in Michigan. Applicant must be descendant of veteran; or dependent of veteran or deceased veteran.
Basis for selection: Applicant must demonstrate financial need and high academic achievement.
Application requirements: Transcript, proof of eligibility.
Additional information: Minimum 2.5 GPA. Application should be filed at local American Legion Post. Deadline in mid-January.

Amount of award:	$500
Application deadline:	January 14

Contact:
Deanna Clark American Legion Michigan
212 North Verlinden Avenue
Ste A
Lansing, MI 48915
Phone: 517-371-4720 ext. 11
Fax: 517-371-2401
Web: www.michiganlegion.org

William D. & Jewell W. Brewer Scholarship Trusts

Type of award: Scholarship.
Intended use: For undergraduate study at 2-year or 4-year institution.
Eligibility: Applicant must be residing in Michigan. Applicant must be descendant of veteran; or dependent of veteran or deceased veteran.
Basis for selection: Applicant must demonstrate financial need and high academic achievement.
Application requirements: Transcript, proof of eligibility.
Additional information: Minimum 2.5 GPA. Application should be filed at local American Legion Post. Deadline in mid-January.

Amount of award:	$500
Application deadline:	January 14

Contact:
Deanna Clark American Legion Michigan
212 North Verlinden Avenue
Ste A
Lansing, MI 48915
Phone: 517-371-4720 ext. 11
Fax: 517-371-2401
Web: www.michiganlegion.org

American Legion Michigan Auxiliary

American Legion Michigan Auxiliary Medical Career Scholarships

Type of award: Scholarship.
Intended use: For freshman study at postsecondary institution. Designated institutions: Michigan institutions.
Eligibility: Applicant must be high school senior. Applicant must be residing in Michigan. Applicant must be descendant of veteran; or dependent of veteran or deceased veteran; or spouse of veteran or deceased veteran during Grenada conflict, Korean War, Lebanon conflict, Panama conflict, Persian Gulf War, WW I, WW II or Vietnam. Applicant must be child, grandchild, great-grandchild, wife, or spouse of honorably discharged or deceased veteran.
Basis for selection: Major/career interest in medicine; physical therapy; respiratory therapy or nursing. Applicant must demonstrate financial need and high academic achievement.
Application requirements: Recommendations, transcript, proof of eligibility. FAFSA or copy of income tax form.
Additional information: Applicants must be pursuing education in medical field. Applications available after November 15. Visit Website for details and application.

Amount of award:	$500
Application deadline:	March 15

Contact:
American Legion Auxiliary, Department of Michigan
212 North Verlinden Avenue
Lansing, MI 48915
Phone: 517-267-8809 ext. 22
Fax: 517-371-2401
Web: www.michalaux.org

American Legion Michigan Auxiliary Memorial Scholarship

Type of award: Scholarship, renewable.
Intended use: For undergraduate study at postsecondary institution. Designated institutions: Michigan institutions.
Eligibility: Applicant must be female, at least 16, no older than 21. Applicant must be residing in Michigan. Applicant must be descendant of veteran; or dependent of veteran or deceased veteran during Grenada conflict, Korean War, Lebanon conflict, Panama conflict, Persian Gulf War, WW I, WW II or Vietnam. Applicant must be daughter, granddaughter, or great-granddaughter of honorably discharged or deceased veteran.
Basis for selection: Applicant must demonstrate financial need and high academic achievement.
Application requirements: Recommendations, transcript, proof of eligibility. FAFSA or copy of parents' income tax forms.
Additional information: Must be Michigan resident for at least one year. Visit Website for details and application.

Amount of award:	$500
Application deadline:	March 15

Contact:
American Legion Auxiliary, Department of Michigan
212 North Verlinden Avenue
Lansing, MI 48915
Phone: 517-267-8809 ext. 22
Fax: 517-371-2401
Web: www.michalaux.org

American Legion Michigan Auxiliary National President's Scholarship

Type of award: Scholarship.
Intended use: For undergraduate study at postsecondary institution.
Eligibility: Applicant must be high school senior. Applicant must be residing in Michigan. Applicant must be descendant of veteran; or dependent of veteran during Grenada conflict, Korean War, Middle East War, Lebanon conflict, Panama conflict, Persian Gulf War, WW I, WW II or Vietnam.
Application requirements: Applicant must have completed 50 hours of community service during high school.

Amount of award:	$2,500-$3,500
Number of awards:	1
Application deadline:	March 1

Contact:
American Legion Auxiliary, Department of Michigan
212 North Verlinden Avenue
Lansing, MI 48915
Phone: 517-267-8809 ext. 22
Fax: 517-371-2401
Web: www.michalaux.org

American Legion Minnesota

American Legion Minnesota Legionnaire Insurance Trust Scholarship

Type of award: Scholarship.
Intended use: For undergraduate study at accredited vocational, 2-year or 4-year institution. Designated institutions: Minnesota colleges and universities and institutions in neighboring states with reciprocating agreements.
Eligibility: Applicant or parent must be member/participant of American Legion. Applicant must be U.S. citizen residing in Minnesota. Applicant must be veteran or descendant of veteran; or dependent of veteran.
Basis for selection: Applicant must demonstrate financial need and high academic achievement.
Application requirements: Recommendations, essay, transcript, proof of eligibility.

Amount of award:	$500
Number of awards:	3
Application deadline:	April 1
Total amount awarded:	$1,500

Contact:
American Legion Minnesota
Education Committee
20 West 12th Street, Room 300A
St. Paul, MN 55155-2000
Phone: 866-259-9163
Web: www.mnlegion.org

American Legion Minnesota Memorial Scholarship

Type of award: Scholarship.
Intended use: For undergraduate study at accredited postsecondary institution. Designated institutions: Minnesota colleges and universities and institutions in neighboring states with reciprocating agreement.
Eligibility: Applicant or parent must be member/participant of American Legion. Applicant must be residing in Minnesota.
Basis for selection: Applicant must demonstrate financial need.
Application requirements: Recommendations, essay, transcript, proof of eligibility.
Additional information: Grandchildren of American Legion or American Legion Auxiliary members also eligible.

Amount of award:	$500
Number of awards:	6
Application deadline:	April 1
Total amount awarded:	$3,000

Contact:
American Legion Minnesota
Education Committee
20 West 12th Street, Room 300A
St. Paul, MN 55155-2000
Phone: 866-259-9163
Web: www.mnlegion.org

American Legion Minnesota Oratorical Contest

Type of award: Scholarship.
Intended use: For undergraduate study at accredited postsecondary institution.
Eligibility: Applicant must be enrolled in high school. Applicant must be U.S. citizen or permanent resident residing in Minnesota.
Basis for selection: Competition/talent/interest in oratory/debate, based on language style, voice, diction, delivery, originality, logic, breadth of knowledge, application of knowledge about topic, and skill in selecting examples and analogies.
Additional information: Awards: First place, $1,500; second place, $1000; third place, $700; fourth place, $500.

Amount of award:	$500-$1,500
Number of awards:	4
Application deadline:	December 15
Total amount awarded:	$3,700

Contact:
American Legion Minnesota
Education Committee
20 West 12th Street, Room 300A
St. Paul, MN 55155-2000
Phone: 866-259-9163
Web: www.mnlegion.org

American Legion Minnesota Auxiliary

American Legion Minnesota Auxiliary Department Scholarship

Type of award: Scholarship.
Intended use: For undergraduate study at accredited postsecondary institution.
Eligibility: Applicant or parent must be member/participant of American Legion Auxiliary. Applicant must be residing in Minnesota. Applicant must be descendant of veteran; or dependent of veteran.
Application requirements: Recommendations, essay, transcript.

Amount of award:	$1,000
Number of awards:	7
Application deadline:	March 15
Total amount awarded:	$7,000

Contact:
American Legion Auxiliary, Department of Minnesota
State Veterans Service Building
20 W 12th Street, Room 314
St. Paul, MN 55155-2069
Phone: 651-224-7634
Fax: 651-224-5243
Web: www.mnala.org

American Legion Minnesota Auxiliary Past Presidents Parley Health Care Scholarship

Type of award: Scholarship.
Intended use: For undergraduate study at accredited postsecondary institution.
Eligibility: Applicant or parent must be member/participant of American Legion Auxiliary. Applicant must be residing in Minnesota.
Basis for selection: Major/career interest in health-related professions.

Amount of award:	$1,000
Number of awards:	10
Application deadline:	March 15
Total amount awarded:	$10,000

Contact:
American Legion Auxiliary, Department of Minnesota
State Veterans Service Building
20 W. 12th Street, Room 314
St. Paul, MN 55155-2069
Phone: 651-224-7634
Fax: 651-224-5243
Web: www.mnala.org

American Legion Mississippi Auxiliary

American Legion Mississippi Auxiliary Scholarship

Type of award: Scholarship.
Intended use: For undergraduate study at accredited postsecondary institution.

Eligibility: Applicant must be high school senior. Applicant must be residing in Mississippi. Applicant must be descendant of veteran; or dependent of veteran during Korean War, Lebanon conflict, Panama conflict, Persian Gulf War, WW I, WW II or Vietnam.
Basis for selection: Applicant must demonstrate financial need.

Amount of award:	$500
Number of awards:	1
Application deadline:	March 1
Total amount awarded:	$500

Contact:
American Legion Mississippi Auxiliary, Department Headquarters
P.O. Box 1382
Jackson, MS 39215-1382
Phone: 601-353-3681
Fax: 601-353-3682
Web: www.missala.com

American Legion Missouri

American Legion Missouri Commander's Scholarship Fund

Type of award: Scholarship.
Intended use: For full-time undergraduate study at postsecondary institution. Designated institutions: Vocational/technical colleges or universities in Missouri.
Eligibility: Applicant must be residing in Missouri. Applicant must be veteran who served in the Army, Air Force, Marines, Navy or Coast Guard. Applicant must have served in one of the U.S. Armed Forces branches for a minimum of 90 days and received honorable discharge.
Application requirements: Proof of eligibility. Letter of acceptance from college or university.
Additional information: Membership in The American Legion not required.

Amount of award:	$1,000
Number of awards:	2
Application deadline:	April 20
Total amount awarded:	$2,000

Contact:
American Legion Missouri
Attn: Education and Scholarship Committee
P.O. Box 179
Jefferson City, MO 65102-0179
Phone: 800-846-9023
Web: www.missourilegion.org

American Legion Missouri Oratorical Contest

Type of award: Scholarship.
Intended use: For undergraduate study at postsecondary institution.
Eligibility: Applicant must be enrolled in high school. Applicant must be residing in Missouri.
Basis for selection: Competition/talent/interest in oratory/debate, based on language style, voice, diction, delivery, originality, logic, breadth of knowledge, application of knowledge about topic, and skill in selecting examples and analogies.
Application requirements: Proof of eligibility.
Additional information: Awards: First place, $2,000; second place, $1,800; third place, $1,600; and fourth place, $1,400. Awards to be used to defray expenses of higher education.

Amount of award:	$1,400-$2,000
Number of awards:	4
Total amount awarded:	$6,800

Contact:
American Legion Missouri
Department Headquarters
P.O. Box 179
Jefferson City, MO 65102-0179
Phone: 800-846-9023
Web: www.missourilegion.org

Charles L. Bacon Memorial Scholarship

Type of award: Scholarship.
Intended use: For full-time undergraduate study at accredited 2-year or 4-year institution.
Eligibility: Applicant or parent must be member/participant of American Legion. Applicant must be single, no older than 20. Applicant must be U.S. citizen residing in Missouri.
Basis for selection: Applicant must demonstrate financial need.
Additional information: Applicants must be current member of American Legion, American Legion Auxiliary or the Sons of the American Legion, or descendent of any member.

Amount of award:	$500
Number of awards:	2
Application deadline:	April 20
Notification begins:	July 1
Total amount awarded:	$1,000

Contact:
American Legion Missouri
Attn: Education and Scholarship Committee
P.O. Box 179
Jefferson City, MO 65102-0179
Phone: 800-846-9023
Web: www.missourilegion.org

Erman W. Taylor Memorial Scholarship

Type of award: Scholarship.
Intended use: For full-time undergraduate study at accredited 2-year or 4-year institution.
Eligibility: Applicant must be single, no older than 20. Applicant must be U.S. citizen residing in Missouri. Applicant must be descendant of veteran who served in the Army, Air Force, Marines, Navy or Coast Guard. Must be child, grandchild, or great-grandchild of veteran who served 90 or more days of active duty in the Army, Navy, Air Force, Marines, or Coast Guard and has an honorable discharge.
Basis for selection: Major/career interest in education.
Application requirements: Proof of eligibility. Copy of discharge certificate for veteran parent, grandparent; essay on selected topic.

Amount of award:	$500
Number of awards:	2
Application deadline:	April 20
Notification begins:	July 1
Total amount awarded:	$1,000

Contact:
American Legion Missouri
Attn: Education and Scholarship Committee
P.O. Box 179
Jefferson City, MO 65102-0179
Phone: 800-846-9023
Web: www.missourilegion.org

Joseph J. Frank Scholarship

Type of award: Scholarship.
Intended use: For full-time freshman study at accredited postsecondary institution.
Eligibility: Applicant or parent must be member/participant of American Legion. Applicant must be single, no older than 20. Applicant must be residing in Missouri. Applicant must be veteran or descendant of veteran; or dependent of veteran who served in the Army, Air Force, Marines, Navy or Coast Guard. Applicant must have served in one of the U.S. Armed Forces branches for a minimum of 90 days and received honorable discharge.
Application requirements: Proof of eligibility.
Additional information: Applicant must have attended a full session of the American Legion Boys State or Auxiliary Girls State program.

Amount of award:	$500
Number of awards:	5
Application deadline:	April 20
Total amount awarded:	$2,500

Contact:
American Legion Missouri
Attn: Education and Scholarship Committee
P.O. Box 179
Jefferson City, MO 65102-0179
Phone: 800-846-9023
Web: www.missourilegion.org

Lillie Lois Ford Boys' Scholarship

Type of award: Scholarship.
Intended use: For full-time undergraduate study at accredited postsecondary institution.
Eligibility: Applicant or parent must be member/participant of American Legion, Boys State. Applicant must be single, male, no older than 20. Applicant must be residing in Missouri. Applicant must be descendant of veteran who served in the Army, Air Force, Marines, Navy or Coast Guard. Must be child, grandchild, or great-grandchild of veteran who served at least 90 days active duty in Army, Navy, Air Force, Marines, or Coast Guard, and was honorably discharged.
Basis for selection: Applicant must demonstrate financial need.
Application requirements: Proof of eligibility.
Additional information: Must have attended complete session of American Legion Boys State or American Legion Department of Missouri Cadet Patrol Academy.

Amount of award:	$1,000
Number of awards:	1
Application deadline:	April 20
Notification begins:	July 1
Total amount awarded:	$1,000

Contact:
American Legion Missouri
Attn: Education and Scholarship Committee
P.O. Box 179
Jefferson City, MO 65102-0179
Phone: 800-846-9023
Web: www.missourilegion.org

Lillie Lois Ford Girls' Scholarship

Type of award: Scholarship.
Intended use: For full-time undergraduate study at accredited postsecondary institution.
Eligibility: Applicant must be single, female, no older than 20. Applicant must be residing in Missouri. Applicant must be descendant of veteran who served in the Army, Air Force, Marines, Navy or Coast Guard. Must be child, grandchild, or great-grandchild of veteran who served at least 90 days active duty in Army, Navy, Air Force, Marines, or Coast Guard, and was honorably discharged.
Basis for selection: Applicant must demonstrate financial need.
Application requirements: Proof of eligibility.
Additional information: Must have attended complete session of American Legion Auxiliary Girls State or American Legion Department of Missouri Cadet Patrol Academy.

Amount of award:	$1,000
Number of awards:	1
Application deadline:	April 20
Notification begins:	July 1
Total amount awarded:	$1,000

Contact:
American Legion Missouri
Attn: Education and Scholarship Committee
P.O. Box 179
Jefferson City, MO 65102
Phone: 800-846-9023
Web: www.missourilegion.org

M.D. Jack Murphy Memorial Nurses Training Fund

Type of award: Scholarship, renewable.
Intended use: For full-time undergraduate study at 2-year or 4-year institution.
Eligibility: Applicant must be single, no older than 20. Applicant must be residing in Missouri. Applicant must be descendant of veteran who served in the Army, Air Force, Marines, Navy or Coast Guard. Must be child, grandchild, or great-grandchild of veteran who served at least 90 days active duty in Army, Navy, Air Force, Marines, or Coast Guard, and was honorably discharged.
Basis for selection: Major/career interest in nursing. Applicant must demonstrate financial need.
Application requirements: Proof of eligibility.
Additional information: Available to students training to be registered nurses. Applicant must have graduated in top 40% of high school class or have minimum "C" or equivalent standing from last college semester prior to applying for award.

Amount of award:	$750
Number of awards:	1
Application deadline:	April 20
Notification begins:	July 1
Total amount awarded:	$750

Contact:
American Legion Missouri
Attn: Education and Scholarship Committee
P.O. Box 179
Jefferson City, MO 65102-0179
Phone: 800-846-9023
Web: www.missourilegion.org

Shane Dean Voyles Memorial Scholarship

Type of award: Scholarship.
Intended use: For full-time freshman study at accredited postsecondary institution.
Eligibility: Applicant must be single, no older than 20, high school senior. Applicant must be residing in Missouri. Applicant must be descendant of veteran; or dependent of veteran who served in the Army, Air Force, Marines, Navy or Coast Guard. Applicant must have served in one of the U.S. Armed Forces branches for a minimum of 90 days and received honorable discharge.
Basis for selection: Applicant must demonstrate high academic achievement, leadership and service orientation.
Application requirements: Nomination by high school.
Additional information: Each school in Missouri may nominate one student for the award. Nominee selected based on leadership, athletic, and scholastic abilities.

Amount of award:	$500
Number of awards:	1
Application deadline:	April 20
Total amount awarded:	$500

Contact:
American Legion Missouri
Attn: Education and Scholarship Committee
P.O. Box 179
Jefferson City, MO 65102-0179
Phone: 800-846-9023
Web: www.missourilegion.org

American Legion Missouri Auxiliary

American Legion Missouri Auxiliary National President's Scholarship

Type of award: Scholarship.
Eligibility: Applicant or parent must be member/participant of American Legion Auxiliary. Applicant must be residing in Missouri. Applicant must be dependent of veteran.
Additional information: Applicant must be child of veteran who served in the Armed Forces during the eligibility dates of the American Legion. Applicant must complete 50 hours of community service during student's high school years.

Amount of award:	$500
Number of awards:	1
Total amount awarded:	$500

Contact:
American Legion Missouri Auxiliary
600 Ellis Blvd
Jefferson City, MO 65101-2204
Phone: 573-636-9133
Fax: 573-635-3467
Web: www.deptmoala.org

American Legion Missouri Auxiliary Past Presidents Parley Scholarship

Type of award: Scholarship.
Intended use: For undergraduate study at 2-year or 4-year institution.
Eligibility: Applicant must be residing in Missouri. Applicant must be descendant of veteran; or dependent of veteran.
Basis for selection: Major/career interest in nursing.
Application requirements: Recommendations.
Additional information: Applicant must not have previously attended institution of higher learning.

Amount of award:	$500
Number of awards:	2

Contact:
American Legion Missouri Auxiliary
Department Secretary
600 Ellis Blvd
Jefferson City, MO 65101-2204
Phone: 573-636-9133
Fax: 573-635-3467
Web: www.deptmoala.org

American Legion Missouri Auxiliary Scholarship

Type of award: Scholarship.
Intended use: For undergraduate study at postsecondary institution.
Eligibility: Applicant must be high school senior. Applicant must be residing in Missouri. Applicant must be descendant of veteran; or dependent of veteran during Korean War, Lebanon conflict, Panama conflict, Persian Gulf War, WW I, WW II or Vietnam.
Additional information: Applicant must not have previously attended institution of higher learning.

Amount of award:	$500
Number of awards:	2
Application deadline:	March 1
Total amount awarded:	$1,000

Contact:
American Legion Missouri Auxiliary
Department Secretary
600 Ellis Blvd.
Jefferson City, MO 65101-2204
Phone: 573-636-9133
Fax: 573-635-3467
Web: www.deptmoala.org

American Legion Montana Auxiliary

Aloha Scholarship

Type of award: Scholarship.
Intended use: For freshman study at postsecondary institution. Designated institutions: Accredited nursing schools.
Eligibility: Applicant or parent must be member/participant of American Legion Auxiliary. Applicant must be residing in Montana.
Basis for selection: Major/career interest in nursing. Applicant must demonstrate depth of character and leadership.

Application requirements: Recommendations, essay, transcript, proof of eligibility.
Additional information: Grandchildren of Auxiliary members also eligible.

Amount of award: $400
Number of awards: 1
Application deadline: April 1

Contact:
American Legion Montana Auxiliary
Department Secretary
P.O. Box 17318
Missoula, MT 59808
Phone: 406-541-8425
Web: www.mtlegion.org/auxiliary

American Legion Montana Auxiliary Scholarships (1)

Type of award: Scholarship.
Intended use: For undergraduate study at postsecondary institution.
Eligibility: Applicant must be high school senior. Applicant must be residing in Montana. Applicant must be dependent of veteran.
Basis for selection: Applicant must demonstrate financial need.
Application requirements: Essay, proof of eligibility. 500-word essay on any topic.
Additional information: Applicant must be high school senior or graduate who has not attended college. Must be state resident for at least two years.

Amount of award: $500
Number of awards: 2
Application deadline: March 15
Total amount awarded: $1,000

Contact:
American Legion Montana Auxiliary
Department Secretary
P.O. Box 17318
Missoula, MT 59808
Phone: 406-266-4566
Web: www.mtlegion.org/auxiliary

American Legion Montana Auxiliary Scholarships (2)

Type of award: Scholarship.
Intended use: For junior study at postsecondary institution.
Eligibility: Applicant must be residing in Montana. Applicant must be dependent of veteran.
Application requirements: Proof of eligibility. Essay stating interest in issues relating to children and youth.
Additional information: Must have completed sophomore year in college and be going into field relating to children and youth.

Amount of award: $500
Number of awards: 2
Application deadline: June 1
Total amount awarded: $1,000

Contact:
American Legion Montana Auxiliary
Department Secretary
P.O. Box 17318
Missoula, MT 59808
Phone: 406-266-4566
Web: www.mtlegion.org/auxiliary

American Legion National Headquarters

American Legion Auxiliary National Presidents Scholarship

Type of award: Scholarship.
Intended use: For undergraduate study at postsecondary institution.
Eligibility: Applicant or parent must be member/participant of American Legion Auxiliary. Applicant must be high school senior. Applicant must be dependent of veteran during Grenada conflict, Korean War, Lebanon conflict, Panama conflict, Persian Gulf War, WW I, WW II or Vietnam.
Basis for selection: Applicant must demonstrate financial need, high academic achievement, depth of character, leadership, patriotism and service orientation.
Additional information: Scholarships awarded annually: five-$3,500; five-$3,000; five-$2,500. Applications available online, from Unit President of Auxiliary in local community, from Department Secretary, or from National Headquarters. See Website for details.

Amount of award: $2,500-$3,500
Number of awards: 15
Application deadline: March 1
Total amount awarded: $45,000

Contact:
American Legion Auxiliary
8945 North Meridian Street
Indianapolis, IN 46260-1189
Phone: 317-569-4500
Fax: 317-569-4502
Web: www.legion-aux.org

American Legion Auxiliary Spirit of Youth Scholarship for Junior Members

Type of award: Scholarship.
Intended use: For undergraduate study at postsecondary institution.
Eligibility: Applicant or parent must be member/participant of American Legion Auxiliary. Applicant must be high school senior. Applicant must be U.S. citizen.
Basis for selection: Applicant must demonstrate financial need, high academic achievement, depth of character, leadership and patriotism.
Application requirements: Proof of eligibility.
Additional information: Must be Junior member of three years' standing, holding current membership card. Applications available online, from Unit President of Auxiliary in local community, from Department Secretary, or from National Headquarters. See Website for details.

Amount of award: $5,000
Number of awards: 5
Application deadline: March 1
Total amount awarded: $25,000

Contact:
American Legion Auxiliary
8945 North Meridian Street
Indianapolis, IN 46260
Phone: 317-569-4500
Fax: 317-569-4502
Web: www.legion-aux.org

Scholarships

American Legion Eagle Scout of the Year

Type of award: Scholarship.
Intended use: For undergraduate study at accredited postsecondary institution in United States.
Eligibility: Applicant or parent must be member/participant of Boy Scouts of America, Eagle Scouts. Applicant must be male, enrolled in high school. Applicant must be U.S. citizen.
Basis for selection: Applicant must demonstrate depth of character, leadership, patriotism and service orientation.
Application requirements: Recommendations, transcript, proof of eligibility, nomination.
Additional information: Applicant must be registered, active member of Boy Scout Troop, Varsity Scout Team or Venturing Crew AND either (1) chartered to American Legion Post/ Auxiliary Unit or (2) son or grandson of American Legion or Auxiliary member. Awards: One $10,000 Eagle Scout of the Year; three runners-up get $2,500. Scholarships available upon graduation from accredited high school and must be used within four years of graduation date. Request application from State Department Headquarters.

Amount of award:	$2,500-$10,000
Number of awards:	4
Total amount awarded:	$17,500

Contact:
American Legion National Headquarters
Eagle Scout of the Year
P.O. Box 1055
Indianapolis, IN 46206-1055
Phone: 317-630-1200
Fax: 317-630-1223
Web: www.legion.org

American Legion Legacy Scholarship

Type of award: Scholarship, renewable.
Intended use: For undergraduate study at postsecondary institution in United States.
Eligibility: Applicant must be high school senior. Applicant must be residing in Indiana. Applicant must be child (dependent, legally adopted, or from a spouse of prior marriage) of active duty personnel of the U.S. military or National Guard or military reservists who were federalized and died on active duty on or after September 11, 2001.
Application requirements: Transcript, proof of eligibility.
Additional information: Amount and number of awards vary. Previous scholarship recipients may reapply. Visit Website for details.

Application deadline:	April 15

Contact:
American Legion National Headquarters
Education Programs Chair
P.O. Box 1055
Indianapolis, IN 46206-1055
Phone: 317-630-1200
Fax: 317-630-1223
Web: www.legion.org

American Legion National High School Oratorical Contest

Type of award: Scholarship.
Intended use: For undergraduate study at postsecondary institution.
Eligibility: Applicant must be no older than 19, enrolled in high school. Applicant must be U.S. citizen or permanent resident.
Basis for selection: Competition/talent/interest in oratory/ debate, based on language style, voice, diction, delivery, originality, logic, breadth of knowledge, application of knowledge about topic, and skill in selecting examples and analogies.
Additional information: Awards: Finalists win $18,000 (first place), $16,000 (runner-up), and $14,000 (third place). Other certified participants who advance beyond first round receive $1,500; those who make it past second round receive additional $1,500. Obtain oratorical contest rules from local Legion Post or state Department Headquarters.

Amount of award:	$1,500-$18,000
Number of awards:	54

Contact:
American Legion National Headquarters
Education Programs Chair
P.O. Box 1055
Indianapolis, IN 46206-1055
Phone: 317-630-1200
Fax: 317-630-1223
Web: www.legion.org

American Legion Scholarship for Non-Traditional Students

Type of award: Scholarship.
Eligibility: Applicant or parent must be member/participant of American Legion Auxiliary.
Basis for selection: Applicant must demonstrate financial need, depth of character and leadership.
Additional information: Applicant must be a non-traditional student returning to school after some period in which his or her formal education was interrupted or who is just beginning his or her education at a later point in life.

Amount of award:	$2,000
Number of awards:	5
Application deadline:	March 1
Total amount awarded:	$10,000

Contact:
American Legion Auxiliary
8945 North Meridian Street
Indianapolis, IN 46260
Phone: 317-569-4500
Fax: 317-569-4502
Web: www.legion-aux.org

Eight and Forty Lung and Respiratory Disease Nursing Scholarship

Type of award: Scholarship.
Intended use: For undergraduate, graduate or non-degree study.
Eligibility: Applicant must be returning adult student.
Basis for selection: Major/career interest in health education; health services administration or nursing.
Application requirements: Proof of eligibility.
Additional information: Applicant must be registered nurse. Program assists registered nurses with advanced preparation for positions in supervision, administration, or teaching. On completion of education, must have full-time employment prospects related to pediatric lung and respiratory control in hospitals, clinics, or health departments. Contact Eight and

Forty Scholarship Chairman or the American Legion Education Program for application. Number of awards varies.

Amount of award: $5,000
Application deadline: May 15
Notification begins: July 1

Contact:
American Legion National Headquarters
Eight and Forty Scholarships
P.O. Box 1055
Indianapolis, IN 46206-1055
Phone: 317-630-1200
Fax: 317-630-1223
Web: www.legion.org

Samsung American Legion Scholarship

Type of award: Scholarship.
Intended use: For undergraduate study at postsecondary institution in United States.
Eligibility: Applicant or parent must be member/participant of American Legion. Applicant must be high school junior. Applicant must be descendant of veteran; or dependent of veteran.
Basis for selection: Applicant must demonstrate financial need, high academic achievement and service orientation.
Application requirements: Essay, proof of eligibility.
Additional information: Applicant must have completed American Legion Boys State or Girls State program. Amount and number of awards vary. In 2010, 10 $20,000 and 90 $1,000 scholarships awarded. Visit Website for details.
Contact:
American Legion National Headquarters
Education Programs Chair
P.O. Box 1055
Indianapolis, IN 46206-1055
Phone: 317-630-1200
Fax: 317-630-1223
Web: www.legion.org

American Legion Nebraska

American Legion Nebraska Oratorical Contest

Type of award: Scholarship.
Intended use: For undergraduate study at postsecondary institution.
Eligibility: Applicant or parent must be member/participant of American Legion. Applicant must be enrolled in high school. Applicant must be residing in Nebraska.
Basis for selection: Competition/talent/interest in oratory/debate, based on language style, voice, diction, delivery, originality, logic, breadth of knowledge, application of knowledge about topic, and skill in selecting examples and analogies.
Application requirements: Proof of eligibility.
Additional information: Awards: First place, $1,000; second place, $600; third place, $400; and fourth place, $200. Contact local American Legion post for more information.

Amount of award: $200-$1,000
Application deadline: November 1

Contact:
American Legion Nebraska, Department Headquarters
P.O. Box 5205
Lincoln, NE 68505-0205
Phone: 402-464-6338
Fax: 402-464-6330
Web: www.nebraskalegion.net

Edgar J. Boschult Memorial Scholarship

Type of award: Scholarship.
Intended use: For full-time undergraduate study. Designated institutions: University of Nebraska.
Eligibility: Applicant or parent must be member/participant of American Legion. Applicant must be residing in Nebraska.
Basis for selection: Applicant must demonstrate financial need and high academic achievement.
Additional information: Must be student at University of Nebraska with high academic and ROTC standing, or military veteran attending University of Nebraska with financial need and acceptable scholastic standing.

Amount of award: $500
Number of awards: 4
Application deadline: March 1

Contact:
American Legion Nebraska, Department Headquarters
P.O. Box 5205
Lincoln, NE 68505-0205
Phone: 402-464-6338
Fax: 402-464-6330
Web: www.nebraskalegion.net

Maynard Jensen American Legion Memorial Scholarship

Type of award: Scholarship.
Intended use: For full-time undergraduate study at vocational, 2-year or 4-year institution. Designated institutions: Nebraska institutions.
Eligibility: Applicant or parent must be member/participant of American Legion. Applicant must be residing in Nebraska. Applicant must be descendant of veteran; or dependent of veteran, deceased veteran or POW/MIA.
Basis for selection: Applicant must demonstrate financial need and high academic achievement.

Amount of award: $500
Number of awards: 10
Application deadline: March 1
Total amount awarded: $5,000

Contact:
American Legion Nebraska, Department Headquarters
P.O. Box 5205
Lincoln, NE 68505-0205
Phone: 402-464-6338
Fax: 402-464-6330
Web: www.nebraskalegion.net

American Legion Nebraska Auxiliary

American Legion Nebraska Auxiliary Graduate Scholarship

Type of award: Scholarship.
Intended use: For graduate study.
Eligibility: Applicant must be residing in Nebraska. Applicant must be descendant of veteran; or dependent of veteran; or spouse of veteran.
Basis for selection: Major/career interest in education, special.
Amount of award: $200
Contact:
American Legion Nebraska Auxiliary, Department Headquarters
P.O. Box 5227
Lincoln, NE 68505-0227
Phone: 402-466-1808
Web: www.nebraskalegionaux.net

American Legion Nebraska Auxiliary Junior Member Scholarship

Type of award: Scholarship.
Intended use: For undergraduate study at postsecondary institution.
Eligibility: Applicant must be residing in Nebraska.
Additional information: Given to Nebraska's entry for Spirit of Youth Scholarship for Junior member, in event applicant does not win same.
Amount of award: $200
Application deadline: March 1
Contact:
American Legion Nebraska Auxiliary
Department Education Chairman
P.O. Box 5227
Lincoln, NE 68505-0227
Phone: 402-466-1808
Web: www.nebraskalegionaux.net

American Legion Nebraska Auxiliary Nurse Gift Tuition Scholarships

Type of award: Scholarship.
Intended use: For undergraduate study.
Eligibility: Applicant must be residing in Nebraska. Applicant must be descendant of veteran; or dependent of veteran; or spouse of veteran.
Basis for selection: Major/career interest in nursing. Applicant must demonstrate financial need.
Application requirements: Recommendations, essay, transcript, proof of eligibility.
Additional information: Awards given as funds permit.
Amount of award: $200-$400
Application deadline: March 1
Contact:
American Legion Nebraska Auxiliary, Department Headquarters
P.O. Box 5227
Lincoln, NE 68505-0227
Phone: 402-466-1808
Web: www.nebraskalegionaux.net

American Legion Nebraska Auxiliary Practical Nursing Scholarship

Type of award: Scholarship.
Intended use: For undergraduate study at 2-year or 4-year institution. Designated institutions: Schools of practical nursing.
Eligibility: Applicant must be residing in Nebraska. Applicant must be veteran or descendant of veteran; or dependent of veteran; or spouse of veteran.
Basis for selection: Major/career interest in nursing. Applicant must demonstrate financial need.
Application requirements: Recommendations, transcript, proof of eligibility.
Additional information: Must be Nebraska resident for at least three years, be accepted at school of practical nursing, and be veteran-connected.
Amount of award: $300
Contact:
American Legion Nebraska Auxiliary, Department Headquarters
P.O. Box 5227
Lincoln, NE 68505-0227
Phone: 402-466-1808
Web: www.nebraskalegionaux.net

American Legion Nebraska Auxiliary Student Aid Grant or Vocational Technical Scholarship

Type of award: Scholarship.
Intended use: For undergraduate study at vocational or 2-year institution in United States.
Eligibility: Applicant must be residing in Nebraska. Applicant must be descendant of veteran; or dependent of veteran; or spouse of veteran.
Application requirements: Recommendations, transcript, proof of eligibility.
Additional information: Nursing students not eligible.
Amount of award: $200-$300
Application deadline: March 1
Contact:
American Legion Nebraska Auxiliary, Department Headquarters
P.O. Box 5227
Lincoln, NE 68505-0227
Phone: 402-466-1808
Web: www.nebraskalegionaux.net

American Legion Nebraska President's Scholarship

Type of award: Scholarship.
Intended use: For undergraduate study at postsecondary institution.
Eligibility: Applicant must be residing in Nebraska.
Additional information: Given to Nebraska's entry for National President's Scholarship in event applicant does not win same.
Amount of award: $200
Application deadline: March 1
Contact:
American Legion Nebraska Auxiliary, Department Headquarters
P.O. Box 5227
Lincoln, NE 68505-0227
Phone: 402-466-1808
Web: www.nebraskalegionaux.net

Averyl Elaine Keriakedes Memorial Scholarship

Type of award: Scholarship.
Intended use: For undergraduate study. Designated institutions: University of Nebraska-Lincoln.
Eligibility: Applicant must be female. Applicant must be residing in Nebraska. Applicant must be descendant of veteran; or dependent of veteran; or spouse of veteran.
Basis for selection: Major/career interest in education or social/behavioral sciences.
Application requirements: Recommendations, transcript, proof of eligibility.
Additional information: Applicant must plan to teach middle or junior high school social studies. Awards given as funds permit.

Amount of award:	$200-$400

Contact:
American Legion Nebraska Auxiliary, Department Headquarters
P.O. Box 5227
Lincoln, NE 68505-0227
Phone: 402-466-1808
Web: www.nebraskalegionaux.net

Roberta Marie Stretch Memorial Scholarship

Type of award: Scholarship.
Intended use: For undergraduate or master's study at 4-year institution.
Eligibility: Applicant must be residing in Nebraska. Applicant must be descendant of veteran; or dependent of veteran; or spouse of veteran.
Application requirements: Recommendations, transcript, proof of eligibility.
Additional information: Preference given to former Nebraska Girls State citizens.

Amount of award:	$400
Application deadline:	March 1

Contact:
American Legion Nebraska Auxiliary, Department Headquarters
P.O. Box 5227
Lincoln, NE 68505-0227
Phone: 402-466-1808
Web: www.nebraskalegionaux.net

Ruby Paul Campaign Fund Scholarship

Type of award: Scholarship.
Intended use: For freshman study at accredited 2-year or 4-year institution.
Eligibility: Applicant or parent must be member/participant of American Legion Auxiliary. Applicant must be high school senior. Applicant must be residing in Nebraska. Must be Legion member, ALA member, Sons of the American Legion member of two years' standing, or child, grandchild, or great-grandchild of American Legion or ALA member of two years' standing.
Basis for selection: Applicant must demonstrate high academic achievement.
Application requirements: Recommendations, essay, transcript, proof of eligibility.
Additional information: Award varies with availability of funds. Applicant must be state resident for three years. Must have maintained "B" or better during last two semesters of high school. Must be accepted for fall term at college or university. Scholarships exclude applicants enrolled in nursing.

Amount of award:	$100-$300
Application deadline:	March 1

Contact:
American Legion Nebraska Auxiliary, Department Headquarters
P.O. Box 5227
Lincoln, NE 68505-0227
Phone: 402-466-1808
Web: www.nebraskalegionaux.net

American Legion Nevada

American Legion Nevada Oratorical Contest

Type of award: Scholarship.
Intended use: For undergraduate study at postsecondary institution.
Eligibility: Applicant must be enrolled in high school. Applicant must be U.S. citizen or permanent resident residing in Nevada.
Basis for selection: Competition/talent/interest in oratory/debate, based on language style, voice, diction, delivery, originality, logic, breadth of knowledge, application of knowledge about topic, and skill in selecting examples and analogies.
Additional information: Awards: First place, $500; second place, $300; and third place, $200.

Amount of award:	$200-$500
Number of awards:	3
Application deadline:	January 15
Total amount awarded:	$1,000

Contact:
American Legion Nevada Oratorical Contest
737 Veterans Memorial Drive
Las Vegas, NV 89101
Web: www.nevadalegion.org

American Legion Nevada Auxiliary

American Legion Nevada Auxiliary Past Presidents Parley Nurses' Scholarship

Type of award: Scholarship.
Intended use: For junior study at postsecondary institution.
Eligibility: Applicant must be residing in Nevada. Applicant must be veteran; or dependent of veteran.
Basis for selection: Major/career interest in nursing.
Additional information: $150 for each university. Applicant must have completed first two years of training.

Amount of award:	$150

Contact:
American Legion Nevada Auxiliary
4030 Bobolink Cir.
Reno, 89
Phone: 775-224-0073
Web: www.nevadaauxiliary.com

American Legion Nevada Auxiliary President's Scholarship

Type of award: Scholarship.
Intended use: For undergraduate study at postsecondary institution.
Eligibility: Applicant must be residing in Nevada.
Additional information: President's Scholarship: $300 for winner of Department competition.

Amount of award:	$300
Number of awards:	1

Contact:
American Legion Nevada Auxiliary, Department Secretary
4030 Bobolink Cir.
Reno, NV 89508
Phone: 775-224-0073
Web: www.nevadaauxiliary.com

Silver Eagle Indian Scholarship

Type of award: Scholarship.
Intended use: For undergraduate study at postsecondary institution.
Eligibility: Applicant must be American Indian. Applicant must be U.S. citizen residing in Nevada. Applicant must be child or grandchild of American Indian veteran.

Amount of award:	$200

Contact:
American Legion Nevada Auxiliary, Department Secretary
4030 Bobolink Cir.
Reno, NV 89508
Phone: 775-224-0073
Web: www.nevadaauxiliary.com

American Legion New Hampshire

Albert T. Marcoux Memorial Scholarship

Type of award: Scholarship.
Intended use: For freshman study at accredited postsecondary institution.
Eligibility: Applicant or parent must be member/participant of American Legion. Applicant must be residing in New Hampshire. Must be child of living or deceased New Hampshire American Legion or New Hampshire American Legion Auxiliary member.
Basis for selection: Applicant must demonstrate high academic achievement.
Application requirements: Recommendations, essay, transcript, proof of eligibility. Resume.
Additional information: Must be child of living or deceased New Hampshire Legionnaire or Auxiliary member. Must be graduate of New Hampshire high school and state resident for three years.

Amount of award:	$2,000
Number of awards:	1
Application deadline:	May 1
Total amount awarded:	$2,000

Contact:
American Legion New Hampshire
State House Annex
25 Capitol Street, Room 431
Concord, NH 03301-6312
Phone: 603-271-2211
Web: www.nhlegion.org

American Legion New Hampshire Boys State Scholarship

Type of award: Scholarship.
Intended use: For undergraduate study at postsecondary institution.
Eligibility: Applicant or parent must be member/participant of American Legion, Boys State. Applicant must be male. Applicant must be residing in New Hampshire.
Additional information: Award given to participants of Boys State during Boys State graduation. Award amount varies. Apply during Boys State session.
Contact:
American Legion New Hampshire
State House Annex
25 Capitol Street, Room 431
Concord, NH 03301-6312
Phone: 603-271-2211
Web: www.nhlegion.org

American Legion New Hampshire Department Vocational Scholarship

Type of award: Scholarship.
Intended use: For freshman study at vocational or 2-year institution.
Eligibility: Applicant or parent must be member/participant of American Legion. Applicant must be enrolled in high school. Applicant must be residing in New Hampshire.
Basis for selection: Applicant must demonstrate high academic achievement.
Application requirements: Recommendations, essay, transcript, proof of eligibility.
Additional information: Must be high school student or graduate from New Hampshire school entering first year of higher education in specific vocation; state resident for at least three years.

Amount of award:	$2,000
Number of awards:	1
Application deadline:	May 1
Total amount awarded:	$2,000

Contact:
American Legion New Hampshire
State House Annex
25 Capitol Street, Room 431
Concord, NH 03301-6312
Phone: 603-271-2211
Web: www.nhlegion.org

American Legion New Hampshire Oratorical Contest

Type of award: Scholarship.
Intended use: For undergraduate study at postsecondary institution.

Eligibility: Applicant must be enrolled in high school. Applicant must be residing in New Hampshire.
Basis for selection: Competition/talent/interest in oratory/debate, based on language style, voice, diction, delivery, originality, logic, breadth of knowledge, application of knowledge about topic, and skill in selecting examples and analogies.
Application requirements: Proof of eligibility.
Additional information: Awards: First place, $1,000; second place, $750; third place, $500; fourth place, $250; and four $100 awards.

Amount of award:	$100-$1,000
Number of awards:	8
Total amount awarded:	$2,900

Contact:
American Legion New Hampshire
State House Annex
25 Capitol Street, Room 431
Concord, NH 03301-6312
Phone: 603-271-2211
Web: www.nhlegion.org

Christa McAuliffe Memorial Scholarship

Type of award: Scholarship.
Intended use: For freshman study at accredited 4-year institution.
Eligibility: Applicant must be residing in New Hampshire.
Basis for selection: Major/career interest in education. Applicant must demonstrate high academic achievement.
Application requirements: Recommendations, essay, transcript. Resume.
Additional information: Must be high school student or recent graduate of New Hampshire school entering first year of higher education; state resident for at least three years.

Amount of award:	$2,000
Number of awards:	1
Application deadline:	May 1
Total amount awarded:	$2,000

Contact:
American Legion New Hampshire
State House Annex
25 Capitol Street, Room 431
Concord, NH 03301-6312
Phone: 603-271-2211
Web: www.nhlegion.org

Department of New Hampshire Scholarship

Type of award: Scholarship.
Intended use: For freshman study at accredited 4-year institution.
Eligibility: Applicant or parent must be member/participant of American Legion. Applicant must be enrolled in high school. Applicant must be residing in New Hampshire.
Basis for selection: Applicant must demonstrate high academic achievement.
Application requirements: Recommendations, essay, transcript. Resume.
Additional information: Must be high school student or graduate from New Hampshire school entering first year of higher education; state resident for at least three years.

Amount of award:	$2,000
Number of awards:	2
Application deadline:	May 1
Total amount awarded:	$4,000

Contact:
American Legion New Hampshire
State House Annex
25 Capitol Street, Room 431
Concord, NH 03301-6312
Phone: 603-271-2211
Web: www.nhlegion.org

John A. High Child Welfare Scholarship

Type of award: Scholarship.
Intended use: For freshman study at postsecondary institution.
Eligibility: Applicant must be male, high school senior. Applicant must be residing in New Hampshire.
Basis for selection: Applicant must demonstrate financial need, high academic achievement, depth of character and patriotism.
Application requirements: Recommendations, essay, transcript.
Additional information: Parent must be member of American Legion New Hampshire or American Legion New Hampshire Auxiliary for three consecutive years.

Amount of award:	$2,000
Number of awards:	1
Application deadline:	May 1
Total amount awarded:	$2,000

Contact:
American Legion New Hampshire
State House Annex
25 Capitol Street, Room 431
Concord, NH 03301-6312
Phone: 603-271-2211
Web: www.nhlegion.org

Raymond K. Conley Memorial Scholarship

Type of award: Scholarship.
Intended use: For freshman study at vocational, 2-year or 4-year institution.
Eligibility: Applicant must be high school senior. Applicant must be residing in New Hampshire.
Basis for selection: Major/career interest in rehabilitation/therapeutic services. Applicant must demonstrate high academic achievement.
Application requirements: Recommendations, essay, transcript.
Additional information: Three-year state residency required. Must have at least a "B" average.

Amount of award:	$2,000
Number of awards:	1
Application deadline:	May 1
Total amount awarded:	$2,000

Contact:
American Legion New Hampshire
State House Annex
25 Capitol Street, Room 431
Concord, NH 03301-6312
Phone: 603-271-2211
Web: www.nhlegion.org

American Legion New Hampshire Auxiliary

Adrienne Alix Scholarship

Type of award: Scholarship.
Intended use: For undergraduate study at postsecondary institution.
Eligibility: Applicant or parent must be member/participant of American Legion Auxiliary. Applicant must be returning adult student. Applicant must be residing in New Hampshire.
Application requirements: Recommendations, essay.
Additional information: Must be one of the following: Re-entering work force or upgrading skills; displaced from work force; or recently honorably discharged from military. Scholarship must be used for a refresher course or to advance applicant's knowledge of techniques needed in today's work force.

Amount of award:	$1,000
Number of awards:	1
Application deadline:	May 1
Total amount awarded:	$1,000

Contact:
American Legion New Hampshire Auxiliary
Department Secretary
25 Capitol Street, Room 432
Concord, NH 03301-6312
Web: www.nhlegion.org

American Legion New Hampshire Auxiliary Past Presidents Parley Nurses' Scholarship

Type of award: Scholarship.
Intended use: For undergraduate study at postsecondary institution.
Eligibility: Applicant or parent must be member/participant of American Legion Auxiliary. Applicant must be residing in New Hampshire.
Basis for selection: Major/career interest in nursing. Applicant must demonstrate financial need.
Application requirements: Recommendations, essay, transcript.
Additional information: Applicant must be high school graduate. Children of veteran given preference. One award to Registered Nurse study and one to Licensed Practical Nurse study.

Number of awards:	2
Application deadline:	May 1

Contact:
American Legion Auxiliary, Department of New Hampshire
Department Secretary
25 Capitol Street, Room 432
Concord, NH 03301-6312
Web: www.nhlegion.org

Elsie B. Brown Scholarship Fund

Type of award: Scholarship.
Intended use: For freshman study at postsecondary institution.
Eligibility: Applicant or parent must be member/participant of American Legion Auxiliary. Applicant must be residing in New Hampshire. Applicant must be dependent of deceased veteran.
Application requirements: Recommendations, essay, transcript.

Amount of award:	$150
Number of awards:	1
Application deadline:	May 1
Total amount awarded:	$150

Contact:
American Legion New Hampshire Auxiliary
Department Secretary
25 Capitol Street, Room 432
Concord, NH 03301-6312
Web: www.nhlegion.org

Grace S. High Memorial Child Welfare Scholarship Fund

Type of award: Scholarship.
Intended use: For undergraduate study at postsecondary institution.
Eligibility: Applicant or parent must be member/participant of American Legion Auxiliary. Applicant must be female. Applicant must be residing in New Hampshire. Daughters of deceased veterans also eligible.
Basis for selection: Applicant must demonstrate financial need.
Application requirements: Recommendations, essay, transcript, proof of eligibility.
Additional information: Applicant must be high school graduate and daughter of Legion or Auxiliary member. Parent must be member of American Legion New Hampshire or American Legion New Hampshire Auxiliary for at least three years.

Amount of award:	$300
Number of awards:	2
Application deadline:	May 1
Total amount awarded:	$600

Contact:
American Legion Auxiliary, Department of New Hampshire
Department Secretary
25 Capitol Street, Room 432
Concord, NH 03301-6312
Web: www.nhlegion.org

Marion J. Bagley Scholarship

Type of award: Scholarship.
Intended use: For undergraduate study at accredited postsecondary institution.
Eligibility: Applicant or parent must be member/participant of American Legion Auxiliary. Applicant must be residing in New Hampshire.
Application requirements: Recommendations, essay, transcript.
Additional information: Applicant must be high school graduate (or equivalent) or attending school of higher learning.

Amount of award:	$1,000
Number of awards:	1
Application deadline:	May 1
Total amount awarded:	$1,000

Contact:
American Legion Auxiliary, Department of New Hampshire
Department Secretary
25 Capitol Street, Room 432
Concord, NH 03301-6312
Web: www.nhlegion.org

American Legion New Jersey

American Legion New Jersey Department of New Jersey Scholarship

Type of award: Scholarship.
Intended use: For undergraduate study at 4-year institution.
Eligibility: Applicant or parent must be member/participant of American Legion. Applicant must be high school senior. Applicant must be residing in New Jersey.
Basis for selection: Applicant must demonstrate financial need, high academic achievement, depth of character, leadership and seriousness of purpose.
Application requirements: Recommendations, essay, transcript, proof of eligibility.
Additional information: Two $4,000 awards; four $2,000 awards; and two $1,000 awards. Applicant must be natural or adopted child of American Legion, Department of New Jersey member, or of a deceased member if parent was member at time of death. Contact local Post for application.

Amount of award:	$1,000-$4,000
Number of awards:	8
Application deadline:	February 15

Contact:
American Legion, Department of New Jersey
Department Adjutant
135 West Hanover Street
Trenton, NJ 08618
Phone: 609-695-5418
Web: www.njamericanlegion.org

American Legion New Jersey Oratorical Contest

Type of award: Scholarship.
Intended use: For undergraduate study at postsecondary institution.
Eligibility: Applicant must be enrolled in high school. Applicant must be residing in New Jersey.
Basis for selection: Competition/talent/interest in oratory/debate, based on language style, voice, diction, delivery, originality, logic, breadth of knowledge, application of knowledge about topic, and skill in selecting examples and analogies.
Application requirements: Proof of eligibility.
Additional information: Awards: First place, $4,000; second place, $2,500; third place, $2,000; fourth place, $1000; fifth place, $1000. See high school counselor for application.

Amount of award:	$1,000-$4,000
Number of awards:	5
Total amount awarded:	$10,500

Contact:
American Legion New Jersey
135 West Hanover Street
Trenton, NJ 08618
Phone: 609-695-5418
Web: www.njamericanlegion.org

American Legion New Jersey Auxiliary

American Legion New Jersey Auxiliary Department Scholarships

Type of award: Scholarship.
Intended use: For freshman study at 2-year or 4-year institution.
Eligibility: Applicant must be high school senior. Applicant must be residing in New Jersey. Must be child or grandchild of honorably discharged veteran of U.S. Armed Forces.
Additional information: Amount and number of awards vary. Must be New Jersey resident for at least two years.
Contact:
American Legion Auxiliary, Department of New Jersey
Department Secretary
1540 Kuser Road, Suite A-8
Hamilton, NJ 08619
Phone: 609-581-9580
Fax: 609-581-8429
Web: www.alanj.org

American Legion New Jersey Auxiliary Past Presidents Parley Nurses' Scholarship

Type of award: Scholarship.
Intended use: For freshman study at 2-year or 4-year institution.
Eligibility: Applicant must be high school senior. Applicant must be residing in New Jersey. Must be child or grandchild of honorably discharged veteran of U.S. Armed Forces.
Basis for selection: Major/career interest in nursing.
Additional information: Applicant must be enrolled in nursing program. Must be New Jersey resident for at least two years. Award amount varies.
Contact:
American Legion Auxiliary, Department of New Jersey
Department Secretary
1540 Kuser Road, Suite A-8
Hamilton, NJ 08619
Phone: 609-581-9580
Fax: 609-581-8429
Web: www.alanj.org

Claire Oliphant Memorial Scholarship

Type of award: Scholarship.
Intended use: For freshman study at 2-year or 4-year institution.
Eligibility: Applicant must be high school senior. Applicant must be residing in New Jersey. Must be child of honorably discharged veteran of U.S. Armed Forces.
Additional information: Must be New Jersey resident for at least two years. Rules and applications distributed to all New Jersey high school guidance departments.

Amount of award:	$1,800
Number of awards:	1
Application deadline:	April 15
Total amount awarded:	$1,800

Contact:
American Legion Auxiliary, Department of New Jersey
Department Secretary
1540 Kuser Road, Suite A-8
Hamilton, NJ 08619
Phone: 609-581-9580
Fax: 609-581-8429
Web: www.alanj.org

American Legion New Mexico Auxiliary

American Legion New Mexico Auxiliary National Presidents Scholarship

Type of award: Scholarship.
Intended use: For undergraduate study at postsecondary institution.
Eligibility: Applicant must be residing in New Mexico.
Additional information: Awarded to Department winner of National President's Scholarship, if candidate does not win in Division. If candidate does, it will be given to second-place winner in Department.

Amount of award:	$150
Number of awards:	1
Application deadline:	April 1
Total amount awarded:	$150

Contact:
American Legion New Mexico Auxiliary
Attn: National President's Scholarship
1215 Mountain Road, NE
Albuquerque, NM 87102
Phone: 505-247-0400
Web: www.nmlegion.org

American Legion New Mexico Auxiliary Past President's Parley Scholarship for Nurses

Type of award: Scholarship.
Intended use: For undergraduate study at postsecondary institution.
Eligibility: Applicant must be residing in New Mexico.
Basis for selection: Major/career interest in health-related professions; nursing or medicine.
Application requirements: Copy of school registration and letter of request for assistance.

Application deadline:	May 1

Contact:
American Legion Auxiliary, Department of New Mexico
Attn: Nurses Scholarship
1215 Mountain Road, NE
Albuquerque, NM 87102
Phone: 505-247-0400
Web: www.nmlegion.org

American Legion New York

American Legion New York Oratorical Contest

Type of award: Scholarship.
Intended use: For undergraduate study at postsecondary institution.
Eligibility: Applicant or parent must be member/participant of American Legion. Applicant must be no older than 19, enrolled in high school. Applicant must be residing in New York.
Basis for selection: Competition/talent/interest in oratory/debate, based on language style, voice, diction, delivery, originality, logic, breadth of knowledge, application of knowledge about topic, and skill in selecting examples and analogies.
Application requirements: Proof of eligibility.
Additional information: Awards: First place, $6,000; second place, $4,000; third place, $2,500; fourth and fifth place, $2,000. Scholarship payments are made directly to student's college and are awarded over a four-year period. Contact local Post for more information.

Amount of award:	$2,000-$6,000
Number of awards:	5
Total amount awarded:	$16,500

Contact:
American Legion, Department of New York
Department Adjutant
112 State Street, Suite 1300
Albany, NY 12207
Phone: 518-463-2215
Web: www.ny.legion.org

Dr. Hannah K. Vuolo Memorial Scholarship

Type of award: Scholarship.
Intended use: For freshman study at accredited 2-year or 4-year institution.
Eligibility: Applicant or parent must be member/participant of American Legion. Applicant must be no older than 20, high school senior. Applicant must be descendant of veteran.
Basis for selection: Major/career interest in education, teacher.
Additional information: Applicant must be natural or adopted direct descendant of member or deceased member of American Legion, Department of New York.

Amount of award:	$1,000
Number of awards:	1
Application deadline:	May 1
Total amount awarded:	$1,000

Contact:
American Legion, Department of New York
Department Adjutant
112 State Street, Suite 1300
Albany, NY 12207
Phone: 518-463-2215
Web: www.ny.legion.org

James F. Mulholland American Legion Scholarship

Type of award: Scholarship.
Intended use: For freshman study at postsecondary institution.
Eligibility: Applicant or parent must be member/participant of American Legion. Applicant must be high school senior.

Applicant must be residing in New York. Applicant must be dependent of veteran.
Basis for selection: Applicant must demonstrate financial need and high academic achievement.

Amount of award: $500
Number of awards: 2
Application deadline: May 1
Total amount awarded: $1,000

Contact:
American Legion, Department of New York
Department Adjutant
112 State Street, Suite 1300
Albany, NY 12207
Phone: 518-463-2215
Web: www.ny.legion.org

New York American Legion Press Association Scholarship

Type of award: Scholarship.
Intended use: For full-time undergraduate study at accredited 4-year institution.
Eligibility: Applicant or parent must be member/participant of American Legion. Applicant must be residing in New York.
Basis for selection: Major/career interest in communications; journalism; graphic arts/design; film/video or radio/television/film.
Additional information: Applicant must be child of New York Legion or Auxiliary member; Sons of American Legion or American Legion Auxiliary Junior member; or graduate of New York American Legion Boys State or Girls State.

Amount of award: $1,000
Number of awards: 1
Application deadline: April 15

Contact:
New York American Legion Press Association
Scholarship Chairman
P.O. Box 650
East Aurora, NY 14052
Web: www.ny.legion.org

American Legion New York Auxiliary

American Legion New York Auxiliary Past Presidents Parley Student Scholarship in Medical Field

Type of award: Scholarship.
Intended use: For undergraduate study at 2-year or 4-year institution.
Eligibility: Applicant must be no older than 19, high school senior. Applicant must be U.S. citizen residing in New York. Applicant must be descendant of veteran; or dependent of veteran during Grenada conflict, Korean War, Lebanon conflict, Panama conflict, Persian Gulf War, WW I, WW II or Vietnam.
Basis for selection: Major/career interest in health-related professions. Applicant must demonstrate financial need, high academic achievement, depth of character, leadership and patriotism.
Application requirements: Essay, transcript.
Additional information: Visit Website for application.

Amount of award: $1,000
Number of awards: 2
Application deadline: March 1

Contact:
American Legion New York Auxiliary
112 State Street, Suite 1310
Albany, NY 12207-0003
Phone: 518-463-1162
Web: www.deptny.org

American Legion New York Auxiliary Scholarship

Type of award: Scholarship.
Intended use: For undergraduate study at postsecondary institution.
Eligibility: Applicant must be U.S. citizen residing in New York. Applicant must be descendant of veteran; or dependent of veteran or deceased veteran during Grenada conflict, Korean War, Lebanon conflict, Panama conflict, Persian Gulf War, WW I, WW II or Vietnam.
Basis for selection: Applicant must demonstrate financial need, high academic achievement, depth of character, leadership and patriotism.
Application requirements: Essay, transcript.
Additional information: May use other scholarships. Visit Website for application.

Amount of award: $1,000
Number of awards: 1
Application deadline: March 1
Total amount awarded: $1,000

Contact:
American Legion New York Auxiliary
112 State Street, Suite 1310
Albany, NY 12207-0003
Phone: 518-463-1162
Web: www.deptny.org

American Legion North Carolina

American Legion North Carolina Oratorical Contest

Type of award: Scholarship.
Intended use: For undergraduate study at postsecondary institution.
Eligibility: Applicant must be enrolled in high school. Applicant must be U.S. citizen or permanent resident residing in North Carolina.
Basis for selection: Competition/talent/interest in oratory/debate, based on language style, voice, diction, delivery, originality, logic, breadth of knowledge, application of knowledge about topic, and skill in selecting examples and analogies.
Additional information: Awards: First place, $2,000; second place, $750; third, fourth, and fifth place, $500. Visit Website for more information.

Amount of award: $500-$2,000
Number of awards: 5
Total amount awarded: $4,250

Contact:
American Legion North Carolina
Oratorical Contest
P.O. Box 26657
Raleigh, NC 27611-6657
Phone: 919-832-7506
Web: www.nclegion.org

Colon Furr Nursing Scholarship

Type of award: Scholarship.
Intended use: For undergraduate study at 2-year or 4-year institution. Designated institutions: North Carolina schools granting LPN or RN degree.
Eligibility: Applicant must be residing in North Carolina.
Basis for selection: Major/career interest in nursing.
Application requirements: Recommendations, transcript, nomination by North Carolina American Legion Post.
Additional information: Applicant must be accepted or enrolled in a one-year LPN program or a two, three, or four-year RN program. Contact local Post for application.

Amount of award:	$600
Number of awards:	1
Total amount awarded:	$600

Contact:
American Legion North Carolina
P.O. Box 26657
Raleigh, NC 27611-6657
Phone: 919-832-7506
Web: www.nclegion.org

American Legion North Carolina Auxiliary

Nannie W. Norfleet Scholarship

Type of award: Scholarship.
Intended use: For undergraduate study at postsecondary institution.
Eligibility: Applicant or parent must be member/participant of American Legion Auxiliary. Applicant must be high school senior. Applicant must be residing in North Carolina.
Basis for selection: Applicant must demonstrate financial need.
Additional information: Preference given to children of American Legion Auxiliary members.

Amount of award:	$1,000
Number of awards:	1
Total amount awarded:	$1,000

Contact:
American Legion North Carolina Auxiliary, Department Headquarters
P.O. Box 25726
Raleigh, NC 27611
Phone: 919-832-4051
Web: www.nclegion.org

American Legion North Dakota

American Legion North Dakota Oratorical Contest

Type of award: Scholarship.
Intended use: For undergraduate study at postsecondary institution.
Eligibility: Applicant must be high school freshman, sophomore, junior or senior. Applicant must be residing in North Dakota.
Basis for selection: Competition/talent/interest in oratory/debate, based on language style, voice, diction, delivery, originality, logic, breadth of knowledge, application of knowledge about topic, and skill in selecting examples and analogies.
Application requirements: Proof of eligibility. For application, contact local American Legion Post or Department Headquarters after start of school year.
Additional information: State awards: First place, $400; second place, $300; third place, $200; and fourth place, $100. Local contests begin in the fall.

Amount of award:	$100-$400

Contact:
American Legion North Dakota, Department Headquarters
P.O. Box 5057
West Fargo, ND 58078-2666
Phone: 701-293-3120
Fax: 701-293-9951
Web: www.ndlegion.org

Hattie Tedrow Memorial Fund Scholarship

Type of award: Scholarship.
Intended use: For undergraduate study at vocational, 2-year or 4-year institution.
Eligibility: Applicant must be high school senior. Applicant must be residing in North Dakota. Applicant must be descendant of veteran; or dependent of veteran.
Basis for selection: Applicant must demonstrate high academic achievement.
Application requirements: Essay, proof of eligibility. SASE.
Additional information: Number and amount of awards based on availability of funds.

Amount of award:	$2,000
Application deadline:	April 1

Contact:
American Legion North Dakota
Hattie Tedrow Memorial Fund Scholarship
P.O. Box 1055
Indianapolis, IN 46206
Phone: 701-293-3120
Fax: 701-293-9951
Web: www.ndlegion.org

American Legion North Dakota Auxiliary

American Legion North Dakota Auxiliary Past Presidents Parley Scholarship

Type of award: Scholarship.
Intended use: For undergraduate study at 2-year or 4-year institution. Designated institutions: North Dakota hospital and nursing schools.
Eligibility: Applicant or parent must be member/participant of American Legion Auxiliary. Applicant must be residing in North Dakota.
Basis for selection: Major/career interest in nursing.
Additional information: Children, grandchildren or great-grandchildren of American Legion or Auxiliary member in good standing. Must be graduate of North Dakota high school. Apply to local American Legion Auxiliary Unit.

Amount of award:	$350
Application deadline:	May 15

Contact:
American Legion Auxiliary, Department of North Dakota
Chair of Dept. Parley Scholarship Committee
P.O. Box 1060
Jamestown, ND 58402-1060
Phone: 701-253-5992
Web: www.ndlegion-aux.org

American Legion North Dakota Auxiliary Scholarships

Type of award: Scholarship.
Intended use: For undergraduate study at postsecondary institution. Designated institutions: North Dakota institutions.
Eligibility: Applicant must be residing in North Dakota.
Basis for selection: Applicant must demonstrate financial need.
Additional information: Obtain application from local American Legion Auxiliary Unit.

Amount of award:	$500
Number of awards:	4
Application deadline:	January 15

Contact:
American Legion North Dakota Auxiliary
Department Education Chairman
P.O. Box 1060
Jamestown, ND 58402-1060
Phone: 701-253-5992
Web: www.ndlegion-aux.org

American Legion Ohio

American Legion Ohio Department Oratorical Awards

Type of award: Scholarship.
Intended use: For undergraduate study at postsecondary institution.
Eligibility: Applicant or parent must be member/participant of American Legion. Applicant must be enrolled in high school. Applicant must be residing in Ohio.
Basis for selection: Competition/talent/interest in oratory/debate, based on language style, voice, diction, delivery, originality, logic, breadth of knowledge, application of knowledge about topic, and skill in selecting examples and analogies.
Additional information: Awards: First place, $2,000; second place, $1000. Additional smaller awards based on number of overall participants.
Contact:
American Legion Ohio
Department Scholarship Committee
P.O. Box 8007
Delaware, OH 43015-8007
Phone: 740-362-7478
Fax: 740-362-1429
Web: www.ohiolegion.com

American Legion Ohio Scholarships

Type of award: Scholarship.
Intended use: For undergraduate study at postsecondary institution.
Eligibility: Applicant or parent must be member/participant of American Legion. For Legion members; direct descendants of Legionnaires in good standing; direct descendants of deceased Legionnaires; spouses or children of deceased U.S. military persons who died on active duty or of injuries received on active duty.
Additional information: Number and amount of awards vary. Contact sponsor or visit Website for more information.

Application deadline:	April 15

Contact:
American Legion, Department of Ohio
Department Scholarship Committee
P.O. Box 8007
Delaware, OH 43015-8007
Phone: 740-362-7478
Fax: 740-362-1429
Web: www.ohiolegion.com

American Legion Ohio Auxiliary

American Legion Ohio Auxiliary Department President's Scholarship

Type of award: Scholarship.
Intended use: For freshman study at postsecondary institution.
Eligibility: Applicant or parent must be member/participant of American Legion Auxiliary. Applicant must be high school senior. Applicant must be residing in Ohio. Applicant must be descendant of veteran; or dependent of veteran or deceased veteran during Grenada conflict, Korean War, Lebanon conflict, Persian Gulf War, WW I, WW II or Vietnam.
Additional information: Awards: one $1,500 and one $1,000.

Amount of award:	$1,000-$1,500
Number of awards:	2
Application deadline:	March 1
Total amount awarded:	$2,500

Scholarships

Contact:
American Legion Ohio Auxiliary
Department Secretary
1100 Brandywine Blvd., Suite D
Zanesville, OH 43702-2760
Phone: 740-452-8245
Fax: 740-452-2620
Web: www.alaohio.org

American Legion Ohio Auxiliary Past Presidents Parley Nurse's Scholarship

Type of award: Scholarship.
Intended use: For undergraduate study at 2-year or 4-year institution.
Eligibility: Applicant or parent must be member/participant of American Legion Auxiliary. Applicant must be residing in Ohio. Applicant must be descendant of veteran; or dependent of veteran; or spouse of veteran.
Basis for selection: Major/career interest in nursing. Applicant must demonstrate financial need, high academic achievement, depth of character, leadership, patriotism and seriousness of purpose.
Application requirements: Recommendations, essay, transcript.
Additional information: Number and amount of awards varies annually.

Application deadline:	May 1

Contact:
American Legion Ohio Auxiliary
Department Secretary
1100 Brandywine Blvd., Suite D
Zanesville, OH 43702-2760
Phone: 740-452-8245
Fax: 740-452-2620
Web: www.alaohio.org

American Legion Oregon

American Legion Department Oratorical Contest

Type of award: Scholarship.
Intended use: For undergraduate study at postsecondary institution.
Eligibility: Applicant must be enrolled in high school. Applicant must be U.S. citizen or permanent resident residing in Oregon.
Basis for selection: Competition/talent/interest in oratory/debate, based on language style, voice, diction, delivery, originality, logic, breadth of knowledge, application of knowledge about topic, and skill in selecting examples and analogies.
Application requirements: Proof of eligibility.
Additional information: Awards available for first place through fourth place. Applications available at local high schools.

Amount of award:	$200-$500
Number of awards:	4
Application deadline:	December 1
Total amount awarded:	$1,400

Contact:
American Legion Oregon
P.O. Box 1730
Wilsonville, OR 97070-1730
Phone: 503-685-5006
Fax: 503-685-5008
Web: www.orlegion.org

American Legion Oregon Auxiliary

American Legion Oregon Auxiliary Department Nurses Scholarship

Type of award: Scholarship.
Intended use: For undergraduate study at accredited 2-year or 4-year institution.
Eligibility: Applicant must be residing in Oregon. Applicant must be dependent of disabled veteran or deceased veteran; or spouse of disabled veteran or deceased veteran.
Basis for selection: Major/career interest in nursing. Applicant must demonstrate financial need, high academic achievement, depth of character, seriousness of purpose and service orientation.
Application requirements: Proof of eligibility.

Amount of award:	$1,500
Number of awards:	1
Application deadline:	May 15
Total amount awarded:	$1,500

Contact:
American Legion Auxiliary, Department of Oregon
Chairman of Education
P.O. Box 1730
Wilsonville, OR 97070-1730
Phone: 503-682-3162
Fax: 503-685-5008
Web: www.alaoregon.org

American Legion Oregon Auxiliary National President's Scholarship

Type of award: Scholarship.
Intended use: For undergraduate study at postsecondary institution.
Eligibility: Applicant or parent must be member/participant of American Legion Auxiliary. Applicant must be high school senior. Applicant must be residing in Oregon. Applicant must be dependent of veteran during Grenada conflict, Korean War, Lebanon conflict, Panama conflict, Persian Gulf War, WW I, WW II or Vietnam.
Additional information: Three awards in each division of American Legion Auxiliary: First place, $2,500; second place, $2,000; and third place, $1,000.

Amount of award:	$1,000-$2,500
Number of awards:	15
Application deadline:	March 1

Contact:
American Legion Auxiliary, Department of Oregon
Chairman of Education
P.O. Box 1730
Wilsonville, OR 97070-1730
Phone: 503-682-3162
Fax: 503-685-5008
Web: www.alaoregon.org

Spirit of Youth Scholarship

Type of award: Scholarship.
Intended use: For undergraduate study at accredited vocational, 2-year or 4-year institution.
Eligibility: Applicant or parent must be member/participant of American Legion Auxiliary. Applicant must be residing in Oregon. Applicant must be dependent of deceased veteran; or spouse of disabled veteran or deceased veteran.
Additional information: Must be Junior member of the American Legion Auxiliary for past three years and hold current membership.

Amount of award:	$1,000
Application deadline:	March 1

Contact:
American Legion Auxiliary, Department of Oregon
Chairman of Education
P.O. Box 1730
Wilsonville, OR 97070-1730
Phone: 503-682-3162
Fax: 503-685-5008
Web: www.alaoregon.org

American Legion Pennsylvania

Joseph P. Gavenonis Scholarship

Type of award: Scholarship, renewable.
Intended use: For full-time undergraduate study at 4-year institution. Designated institutions: Pennsylvania colleges and universities.
Eligibility: Applicant or parent must be member/participant of American Legion. Applicant must be high school senior. Applicant must be residing in Pennsylvania. Applicant must be child of living member in good standing of Pennsylvania American Legion, or child of deceased Pennsylvania American Legion member.
Basis for selection: Applicant must demonstrate financial need and high academic achievement.
Application requirements: Transcript, proof of eligibility.
Additional information: Award is $1,000 per year for four years; renewal based on grades. Minimum GPA 2.5.

Amount of award:	$1,000
Number of awards:	1
Application deadline:	May 30
Total amount awarded:	$4,000

Contact:
American Legion Pennsylvania
Scholarship Secretary
P.O. Box 2324
Harrisburg, PA 17105-2324
Phone: 717-730-9100
Web: www.pa-legion.com

Robert W. Valimont Endowment Fund Scholarship

Type of award: Scholarship, renewable.
Intended use: For full-time undergraduate study at vocational or 2-year institution.
Eligibility: Applicant must be residing in Pennsylvania. Applicant must be dependent of active service person, veteran or deceased veteran.
Basis for selection: Applicant must demonstrate financial need and high academic achievement.
Application requirements: Proof of eligibility.
Additional information: Parent must be member of American Legion, Pennsylvania. Award is $600 for first year; must reapply for second year. Minimum 2.5 GPA.

Amount of award:	$600
Application deadline:	May 30
Total amount awarded:	$600

Contact:
American Legion Pennsylvania
Scholarship Secretary
P.O. Box 2324
Harrisburg, PA 17105-2324
Phone: 717-730-9100
Web: www.pa-legion.com

American Legion Pennsylvania Auxiliary

Scholarship for Children of Deceased or Totally Disabled Veterans

Type of award: Scholarship, renewable.
Intended use: For undergraduate study at postsecondary institution.
Eligibility: Applicant must be high school senior. Applicant must be residing in Pennsylvania. Applicant must be dependent of disabled veteran or deceased veteran.
Basis for selection: Applicant must demonstrate financial need.
Additional information: Award is $600 per year, renewable for four years.

Amount of award:	$600
Number of awards:	1
Application deadline:	March 15
Total amount awarded:	$2,400

Contact:
American Legion Auxiliary, Department of Pennsylvania
Department Education Chairman
P.O. Box 1285
Camp Hill, PA 17001
Phone: 717-763-7545
Web: www.ala.pa-legion.com

Scholarship for Children of Living Veterans

Type of award: Scholarship, renewable.
Intended use: For undergraduate study at postsecondary institution.

Eligibility: Applicant must be high school senior. Applicant must be residing in Pennsylvania. Applicant must be dependent of veteran.
Basis for selection: Applicant must demonstrate financial need.
Additional information: Award: $600 per year, renewable for four years.

Amount of award:	$600
Number of awards:	1
Application deadline:	March 15
Total amount awarded:	$2,400

Contact:
American Legion Auxiliary, Department of Pennsylvania
Department Education Chairman
P.O. Box 1285
Camp Hill, PA 17001
Phone: 717-763-7545
Web: www.ala.pa-legion.com

Scholarships

American Legion Puerto Rico Auxiliary

American Legion Puerto Rico Auxiliary Nursing Scholarships

Type of award: Scholarship.
Intended use: For undergraduate study at 2-year or 4-year institution. Designated institutions: Eligible institutions in Puerto Rico.
Eligibility: Applicant must be residing in Puerto Rico.
Basis for selection: Major/career interest in nursing.
Application requirements: Interview.
Additional information: Two $250 awards for two consecutive years.

Amount of award:	$250
Number of awards:	2
Application deadline:	March 15

Contact:
American Legion Auxiliary, Department of Puerto Rico
Education Chairman
P.O. Box 11424
Caparra Heights Station, PR 00922-1424

American Legion Rhode Island

American Legion Rhode Island Oratorical Contest

Type of award: Scholarship.
Eligibility: Applicant must be enrolled in high school. Applicant must be U.S. citizen or permanent resident residing in Rhode Island.
Basis for selection: Competition/talent/interest in oratory/debate, based on language style, voice, diction, delivery, originality, logic, breadth of knowledge, application of knowledge about topic, and skill in selecting examples and analogies.
Additional information: Awards: First place, $500; second place, $250; third place, $100; fourth place, $50.

Amount of award:	$50-$500
Number of awards:	4
Total amount awarded:	$900

Contact:
American Legion of Rhode Island, Oratorical Contest
1005 Charles Street
North Providence, RI 02904
Phone: 401-726-2126
Fax: 401-726-2464
Web: www.legionri.org

American Legion Rhode Island Auxiliary

American Legion Rhode Island Auxiliary Book Award

Type of award: Scholarship.
Intended use: For undergraduate study at postsecondary institution.
Eligibility: Applicant or parent must be member/participant of American Legion Auxiliary. Applicant must be residing in Rhode Island. Applicant must be descendant of veteran; or dependent of veteran.
Additional information: Award: $500. Must be child or grandchild of veteran.

Amount of award:	$500
Number of awards:	1
Application deadline:	April 1
Total amount awarded:	$500

Contact:
American Legion Auxiliary, Department of Rhode Island
Department Secretary
55 Algonquin Dr.
Warwick, RI 02888
Phone: 401-369-7998
Web: www.rialaux.com

American Legion South Carolina

American Legion South Carolina Department Oratorical Contest

Type of award: Scholarship.
Intended use: For undergraduate study at postsecondary institution.
Eligibility: Applicant must be enrolled in high school. Applicant must be residing in South Carolina.
Basis for selection: Competition/talent/interest in oratory/debate, based on language style, voice, diction, delivery, originality, logic, breadth of knowledge, application of knowledge about topic, and skill in selecting examples and analogies.
Additional information: Awards: First place, $3,500; second place, $2,000; third and fourth place, $500. Distributed over four-year period. Zone Contest winners: four $100 awards.

Amount of award: $100-$3,500
Number of awards: 8
Application deadline: January 28
Total amount awarded: $6,900

Contact:
American Legion South Carolina, Department Adjutant
P.O. Box 3309
Irmo, SC 29063
Phone: 803-612-1171
Fax: 803-213-9902
Web: www.scarolinalegion.org

American Legion South Carolina Auxiliary

American Legion South Carolina Auxiliary Scholarship

Type of award: Scholarship.
Intended use: For undergraduate study at postsecondary institution.
Eligibility: Applicant or parent must be member/participant of American Legion Auxiliary. Applicant must be high school senior. Applicant must be residing in South Carolina.
Additional information: Must be American Legion Auxiliary junior or senior member with at least three consecutive years' membership at time of application. Must have current membership card.

Amount of award: $500
Number of awards: 2
Application deadline: April 15
Total amount awarded: $1,000

Contact:
American Legion Auxiliary, Department of South Carolina
Department Secretary
107 A Legion Plaza Rd.
Columbia, SC 29210
Phone: 803-772-6366
Fax: 803-772-6284
Web: www.aladsc.org

American Legion South Dakota

American Legion South Dakota Oratorical Contest

Type of award: Scholarship.
Intended use: For undergraduate study at postsecondary institution.
Eligibility: Applicant must be enrolled in high school. Applicant must be residing in South Dakota.
Basis for selection: Competition/talent/interest in oratory/debate, based on language style, voice, diction, delivery, originality, logic, breadth of knowledge, application of knowledge about topic, and skill in selecting examples and analogies.
Application requirements: Proof of eligibility.
Additional information: Awards: First place, $1,000; second place, $500; third place, $300; fourth through eighth place, $100. Redeemable within five years of date of award.

Amount of award: $100-$1,000
Number of awards: 8
Total amount awarded: $2,300

Contact:
American Legion, Department of South Dakota
Department Adjutant
P.O. Box 67
Watertown, SD 57201-0067
Phone: 605-886-3604
Web: www.sdlegion.org

American Legion South Dakota Auxiliary

American Legion South Dakota Auxiliary Scholarships

Type of award: Scholarship.
Intended use: For undergraduate study at vocational, 2-year or 4-year institution.
Eligibility: Applicant or parent must be member/participant of American Legion Auxiliary. Applicant must be at least 16, no older than 22. Applicant must be residing in South Dakota. Applicant must be dependent of veteran.
Basis for selection: Applicant must demonstrate financial need, high academic achievement, depth of character, leadership and patriotism.
Application requirements: Recommendations, essay, transcript.
Additional information: College scholarships: two $500; vocational scholarships: two $500.

Amount of award: $500
Number of awards: 4
Application deadline: March 1
Total amount awarded: $2,000

Contact:
American Legion South Dakota Auxiliary
P.O. Box 1819
Sioux Falls, SD 57101
Phone: 605-338-9774
Fax: 605-332-3032
Web: www.sdlegion-aux.org

American Legion South Dakota Auxiliary Senior Member Scholarship

Type of award: Scholarship.
Intended use: For undergraduate study at vocational, 2-year or 4-year institution.
Eligibility: Applicant or parent must be member/participant of American Legion Auxiliary. Applicant must be residing in South Dakota.
Basis for selection: Applicant must demonstrate financial need, high academic achievement, depth of character, leadership and patriotism.
Application requirements: Recommendations, essay, transcript. Resume.

Additional information: Applicant must have been senior South Dakota American Legion Auxiliary member for three consecutive years including current year.

Amount of award:	$400
Number of awards:	1
Application deadline:	March 1
Total amount awarded:	$400

Contact:
American Legion South Dakota Auxiliary
P.O. Box 1819
Sioux Falls, SD 57101
Phone: 605-338-9774
Fax: 605-332-3032
Web: www.sdlegion-aux.org

Thelma Foster Junior American Legion Auxiliary Members Scholarship

Type of award: Scholarship.
Intended use: For undergraduate study at postsecondary institution.
Eligibility: Applicant or parent must be member/participant of American Legion Auxiliary. Applicant must be residing in South Dakota. Must be Junior American Legion member for at least three years, including current year.
Basis for selection: Applicant must demonstrate financial need, high academic achievement, depth of character, leadership and patriotism.
Application requirements: Recommendations, essay, transcript.
Additional information: Must be high school senior or graduate of accredited high school.

Amount of award:	$300
Number of awards:	1
Application deadline:	March 1

Contact:
American Legion South Dakota Auxiliary
P.O. Box 1819
Sioux Falls, SD 57101
Phone: 605-338-9774
Fax: 605-332-3032
Web: www.sdlegion-aux.org

Thelma Foster Senior American Legion Auxiliary Member Scholarship

Type of award: Scholarship.
Intended use: For undergraduate study at postsecondary institution.
Eligibility: Applicant or parent must be member/participant of American Legion Auxiliary. Applicant must be residing in South Dakota. Must be senior South Dakota American Legion Auxiliary member for past three years, including current year.
Basis for selection: Applicant must demonstrate financial need, depth of character, leadership and patriotism.
Application requirements: Recommendations, essay.

Amount of award:	$300
Number of awards:	1
Application deadline:	March 1
Total amount awarded:	$300

Contact:
American Legion South Dakota Auxiliary
P.O. Box 1819
Sioux Falls, SD 57101
Phone: 605-338-9774
Fax: 605-332-3032
Web: www.sdlegion-aux.org

American Legion Tennessee

American Legion Tennessee Eagle Scout of the Year Scholarship

Type of award: Scholarship.
Intended use: For undergraduate study at postsecondary institution in United States.
Eligibility: Applicant or parent must be member/participant of Boy Scouts of America, Eagle Scouts. Applicant must be male, at least 15, no older than 18, enrolled in high school. Applicant must be residing in Tennessee.
Application requirements: Nomination by Tennessee American Legion.
Additional information: Must be registered, active member of Boy Scout Troop, Varsity Scout Team, or Venturing Crew and either chartered to an American Legion Post, Auxiliary Unit or Sons of American Legion Squadron, or be son or grandson of American Legion or American Legion Auxiliary member.

Amount of award:	$3,000
Number of awards:	1
Total amount awarded:	$3,000

Contact:
American Legion Tennessee
318 Donelson Pike
Nashville, TN 37214
Phone: 615-391-5088
Web: www.tennesseelegion.org

American Legion Tennessee Oratorical Contest

Type of award: Scholarship, renewable.
Intended use: For undergraduate study at vocational, 2-year or 4-year institution in United States.
Eligibility: Applicant must be enrolled in high school. Applicant must be residing in Tennessee.
Basis for selection: Competition/talent/interest in oratory/debate, based on language style, voice, diction, delivery, originality, logic, breadth of knowledge, application of knowledge about topic, and skill in selecting examples and analogies.
Application requirements: Proof of eligibility.
Additional information: Awards: First place, $3,000; second place, $2,000; third place, $1,000. Enter contest through local high school participating in Tennessee Oratorical Contest.

Amount of award:	$1,000-$3,000
Number of awards:	3
Application deadline:	January 1
Total amount awarded:	$6,000

Contact:
American Legion Tennessee
318 Donelson Pike
Nashville, TN 37214
Phone: 615-391-5088
Web: www.tennesseelegion.org

American Legion Tennessee Auxiliary

Vara Gray Scholarship Fund

Type of award: Scholarship.
Intended use: For undergraduate study at vocational, 2-year or 4-year institution.
Eligibility: Applicant must be high school senior. Applicant must be residing in Tennessee. Applicant must be dependent of veteran.
Application requirements: Recommendations, essay, nomination by local American Legion Auxiliary Unit.
Additional information: Call for more information.

Amount of award:	$500
Number of awards:	3
Application deadline:	March 1
Total amount awarded:	$1,500

Contact:
American Legion Tennessee Auxiliary, Department Headquarters
104 Point East Drive
Nashville, TN 37216
Phone: 615-226-8648
Fax: 615-226-8649

American Legion Texas

American Legion Texas Oratorical Contest

Type of award: Scholarship.
Intended use: For undergraduate study at postsecondary institution.
Eligibility: Applicant must be no older than 18, enrolled in high school. Applicant must be residing in Texas.
Basis for selection: Competition/talent/interest in oratory/debate, based on language style, voice, diction, delivery, originality, logic, breadth of knowledge, application of knowledge about topic, and skill in selecting examples and analogies. Applicant must demonstrate patriotism.
Application requirements: Proof of eligibility.
Additional information: Awards: First place, $2,000; second place, $1,500; third place, $1,000; fourth place, $500. First place winner eligible to enter national contest.

Amount of award:	$500-$2,000
Number of awards:	4
Application deadline:	August 31
Total amount awarded:	$5,000

Contact:
American Legion, Department of Texas
P.O. Box 140527
Austin, TX 78714-0527
Phone: 512-472-4138
Fax: 512-472-0603
Web: www.txlegion.org

American Legion Texas Auxiliary

American Legion Texas Auxiliary General Education Scholarship

Type of award: Scholarship.
Intended use: For undergraduate study at postsecondary institution.
Eligibility: Applicant must be residing in Texas. Applicant must be descendant of veteran; or dependent of veteran during Grenada conflict, Korean War, Lebanon conflict, Panama conflict, Persian Gulf War, WW I, WW II or Vietnam.
Basis for selection: Applicant must demonstrate financial need and depth of character.
Application requirements: Recommendations, transcript. Resume listing statements of financial support from all their sources not listed on the application, extracurricular activities, and honors and awards received.
Additional information: Obtain application from local Unit. Unit sponsorship required.

Amount of award:	$500
Application deadline:	April 1

Contact:
American Legion Auxiliary, Department of Texas
P.O. Box 140407
Austin, TX 78721-0407
Phone: 512-476-7278
Web: www.alatexas.org

American Legion Texas Past Presidents Parley Scholarship

Type of award: Scholarship.
Intended use: For undergraduate study at postsecondary institution.
Eligibility: Applicant must be residing in Texas. Applicant must be descendant of veteran; or dependent of veteran during Grenada conflict, Korean War, Lebanon conflict, Panama conflict, Persian Gulf War, WW I, WW II or Vietnam.
Basis for selection: Major/career interest in medicine; health sciences; health-related professions; medical assistant or nursing. Applicant must demonstrate depth of character and seriousness of purpose.
Application requirements: Recommendations, essay, transcript, proof of eligibility.
Additional information: Applicant must be pursuing career in medical field. Obtain application from local Unit.

Amount of award:	$1,000
Application deadline:	May 1

Contact:
American Legion Auxiliary, Department of Texas
P.O. Box 140407
Austin, TX 78721-0407
Phone: 512-476-7278
Web: www.alatexas.org

American Legion Utah Auxiliary

American Legion Utah Auxiliary National President's Scholarship

Type of award: Scholarship.
Intended use: For undergraduate study at postsecondary institution.
Eligibility: Applicant must be high school senior. Applicant must be residing in Utah. Applicant must be descendant of veteran; or dependent of veteran during Grenada conflict, Korean War, Lebanon conflict, Panama conflict, Persian Gulf War, WW I, WW II or Vietnam.

Amount of award:	$1,500
Number of awards:	1
Application deadline:	February 15
Total amount awarded:	$1,500

Contact:
American Legion Utah Auxiliary
Department Secretary
P.O. Box 148000
Salt Lake City, UT 84114-8000
Phone: 801-539-1011
Web: www.utlegion.org

American Legion Vermont

American Legion Vermont Eagle Scout of the Year

Type of award: Scholarship.
Intended use: For undergraduate study.
Eligibility: Applicant or parent must be member/participant of Boy Scouts of America, Eagle Scouts. Applicant must be male, at least 15, no older than 18, enrolled in high school. Applicant must be residing in Vermont.
Application requirements: Recommendations.
Additional information: Must be registered, active member of Boy Scout Troop, Varsity Scout Troop, or Explorer Post. Awarded for outstanding service to school and community. Applicant must have received Eagle Scout Award.

Amount of award:	$1,000
Number of awards:	1
Application deadline:	March 1
Total amount awarded:	$1,000

Contact:
American Legion of Vermont
Education and Scholarship Committee
P.O. Box 396
Montpelier, VT 05601
Phone: 802-223-7131
Fax: 802-223-0318
Web: www.vtlegion.org

American Legion Vermont National High School Oratorical Contest

Type of award: Scholarship.
Intended use: For undergraduate study at postsecondary institution.
Eligibility: Applicant must be enrolled in high school. Applicant must be U.S. citizen or permanent resident residing in Vermont.
Basis for selection: Competition/talent/interest in oratory/debate, based on language style, voice, diction, delivery, originality, logic, breadth of knowledge, application of knowledge about topic, and skill in selecting examples and analogies.
Additional information: Winner receives $2,000; runners-up, $100. Selection based on prepared oration. Request rules by January 1.

Amount of award:	$100-$2,000

Contact:
American Legion of Vermont
Education and Scholarship Committee
P.O. Box 396
Montpelier, VT 05601-0396
Phone: 802-223-7131
Fax: 802-223-0318
Web: www.vtlegion.org

American Legion Vermont Scholarship

Type of award: Scholarship.
Intended use: For undergraduate study at postsecondary institution.
Eligibility: Applicant must be high school senior. Applicant must be U.S. citizen or permanent resident.
Application requirements: Recommendations, transcript.
Additional information: Awards: Charles Barber, one $1,000 award; Ray Greenwood, one $1,500 award and ten $500 awards. Applicant must be senior at Vermont secondary school; senior from adjacent state whose parents are legal Vermont residents; or senior from adjacent state attending Vermont school.

Amount of award:	$500-$1,500
Number of awards:	12
Application deadline:	April 1
Total amount awarded:	$7,500

Contact:
American Legion of Vermont
Education and Scholarship Committee
P.O. Box 396
Montpelier, VT 05601
Phone: 802-223-7131
Fax: 802-223-0318
Web: www.vtlegion.org

American Legion Virginia

American Legion Virginia Oratorical Contest

Type of award: Scholarship.
Intended use: For undergraduate study at postsecondary institution.
Eligibility: Applicant must be enrolled in high school. Applicant must be residing in Virginia.
Basis for selection: Competition/talent/interest in oratory/debate, based on language style, voice, diction, delivery, originality, logic, breadth of knowledge, application of knowledge about topic, and skill in selecting examples and analogies.

Application requirements: Proof of eligibility.
Additional information: Awards given to first-, second-, and third-place finishers.

Number of awards: 3
Application deadline: December 1

Contact:
American Legion Virginia
Department Adjutant
1708 Commonwealth Ave.
Richmond, VA 23230
Phone: 804-353-6606
Fax: 804-358-1940
Web: www.valegion.org

American Legion Virginia Auxiliary

American Legion Virginia Auxiliary Past Presidents Parley Nurse's Scholarship

Type of award: Scholarship.
Intended use: For at postsecondary institution.
Eligibility: Applicant must be U.S. citizen residing in Virginia. Applicant must be descendant of veteran; or dependent of veteran.
Basis for selection: Major/career interest in nursing.
Application requirements: Recommendations, essay, transcript, proof of eligibility.
Additional information: Applicants may be seniors in or graduates of high school, but may not have attended institute of higher education. Previous recipients not eligible.

Amount of award: $1,000
Application deadline: April 1

Contact:
American Legion Virginia Auxiliary
Donna J. Ellis, Past President Parleys Chair
328 South 14th Avenue
Hopewell, VA 23860
Phone: 804-355-6410
Web: www.vaauxiliary.org

Anna Gear Junior Scholarship

Type of award: Scholarship.
Intended use: For undergraduate study at postsecondary institution.
Eligibility: Applicant or parent must be member/participant of American Legion Auxiliary. Applicant must be high school senior. Applicant must be residing in Virginia. Must be Junior member of American Legion Auxiliary for three years.
Basis for selection: Applicant must demonstrate leadership and service orientation.
Application requirements: Recommendations, essay.

Amount of award: $1,000
Number of awards: 1
Application deadline: May 1
Total amount awarded: $1,000

Contact:
American Legion Auxiliary, Department of Virginia
Education Chairman
1708 Commonwealth Avenue
Richmond, VA 23230
Phone: 804-355-6410
Web: www.vaauxiliary.org

Children of Warriors National President's Scholarship

Type of award: Scholarship.
Intended use: For at postsecondary institution.
Eligibility: Applicant or parent must be member/participant of American Legion Auxiliary. Applicant must be high school senior. Applicant must be U.S. citizen residing in Virginia. Applicant must be descendant of veteran; or dependent of veteran.
Basis for selection: Applicant must demonstrate financial need, high academic achievement and depth of character.
Application requirements: Recommendations, essay, transcript, proof of eligibility. SAT/ACT scores, FAFSA, verification of 50 hours of voluntary service.
Additional information: One $1,500, $2,000, and $2,500 scholarship awarded. Previous scholarship recipients not eligible.

Amount of award: $1,500-$2,500
Number of awards: 15
Application deadline: March 1
Total amount awarded: $6,000

Contact:
American Legion Virginia Auxiliary
1708 Commonwealth Avenue
Richmond, VA 23230
Phone: 804-355-6410
Web: www.vaauxiliary.org

Dr. Kate Waller Barrett Grant

Type of award: Scholarship.
Intended use: For undergraduate study at accredited vocational, 2-year or 4-year institution.
Eligibility: Applicant or parent must be member/participant of American Legion Auxiliary. Applicant must be high school senior. Applicant must be residing in Virginia. Applicant must be dependent of veteran.
Basis for selection: Applicant must demonstrate financial need, high academic achievement, leadership and service orientation.
Application requirements: Recommendations, essay, transcript.

Amount of award: $1,000
Number of awards: 1
Application deadline: March 15
Total amount awarded: $1,000

Contact:
American Legion Auxiliary, Department of Virginia
Education Chairman
1708 Commonwealth Avenue
Richmond, VA 23230
Phone: 804-355-6410
Web: www.vaauxiliary.org

American Legion Washington

American Legion Washington Children and Youth Scholarship Fund

Type of award: Scholarship.
Intended use: For undergraduate study at accredited vocational, 2-year or 4-year institution. Designated institutions: Eligible institutions in Washington State.
Eligibility: Applicant or parent must be member/participant of American Legion. Applicant must be high school senior. Applicant must be residing in Washington.
Basis for selection: Applicant must demonstrate financial need, leadership and seriousness of purpose.
Application requirements: Recommendations.
Additional information: Must be child of living or deceased member of American Legion Department of Wisconsin or its auxiliary. One $2,500 award and one $1,500 award.

Amount of award:	$1,500-$2,500
Number of awards:	2
Application deadline:	April 1
Total amount awarded:	$4,000

Contact:
American Legion Washington
Chairman, Department of Child Welfare
P.O. Box 3917
Lacey, WA 98503
Phone: 360-491-4373
Fax: 360-491-7442
Web: www.walegion.org

American Legion Washington Department Oratorical Contest

Type of award: Scholarship.
Intended use: For undergraduate study at postsecondary institution.
Eligibility: Applicant must be enrolled in high school. Applicant must be residing in Washington.
Basis for selection: Competition/talent/interest in oratory/debate, based on language style, voice, diction, delivery, originality, logic, breadth of knowledge, application of knowledge about topic, and skill in selecting examples and analogies.
Additional information: State winner receives $2,000 scholarship. Runners-up also receive awards.

Application deadline:	December 15
Total amount awarded:	$5,000

Contact:
American Legion Washington
Chairman, Department of Child Welfare
P.O. Box 3917
Lacey, WA 98503
Phone: 360-491-4373
Fax: 360-491-7442
Web: www.walegion.org

American Legion Washington Auxiliary

American Legion Washington Auxiliary Scholarships

Type of award: Scholarship.
Intended use: For undergraduate study at postsecondary institution.
Eligibility: Applicant must be high school senior. Applicant must be residing in Washington. Applicant must be dependent of disabled veteran or deceased veteran.
Basis for selection: Applicant must demonstrate financial need.
Application requirements: Recommendations, essay, transcript, proof of eligibility.
Additional information: Must be high school senior or high school graduate who has not attended institution of higher learning. Must submit application to Unit chairman.

Amount of award:	$400
Number of awards:	2
Application deadline:	March 1

Contact:
American Legion Washington Auxiliary
P.O. Box 5867
Lacey, WA 98503
Phone: 360-456-5995
Fax: 360-491-7442
Web: www.walegion-aux.org

Dayle and Frances Pieper Scholarship

Type of award: Scholarship.
Intended use: For undergraduate study at postsecondary institution.
Eligibility: Applicant must be residing in Washington. Applicant must be dependent of veteran, disabled veteran or deceased veteran.
Basis for selection: Applicant must demonstrate financial need, high academic achievement, depth of character and leadership.
Application requirements: Recommendations, essay, transcript, proof of eligibility.
Additional information: Must be a dependant of veteran.

Amount of award:	$1,000
Number of awards:	1
Application deadline:	March 15
Total amount awarded:	$1,000

Contact:
American Legion Auxiliary, Department of Washington
P.O. Box 5867
Lacey, WA 98503
Phone: 360-456-5995
Fax: 360-491-7442
Web: www.walegion-aux.org

Florence Lemcke Memorial Scholarship

Type of award: Scholarship.
Intended use: For undergraduate study at 2-year or 4-year institution.

Eligibility: Applicant or parent must be member/participant of American Legion Auxiliary. Applicant must be high school senior. Applicant must be residing in Washington. Applicant must be dependent of veteran or deceased veteran.
Basis for selection: Major/career interest in arts, general; art/art history; architecture; dance; literature; music or theater arts. Applicant must demonstrate financial need and depth of character.
Application requirements: Recommendations, essay, transcript, proof of eligibility.
Additional information: For use in field of fine arts.

Amount of award:	$1,000
Number of awards:	1
Application deadline:	April 25
Total amount awarded:	$1,000

Contact:
American Legion Washington Auxiliary
P.O. Box 5867
Lacey, WA 98503
Phone: 360-456-5995
Fax: 360-491-7442
Web: www.walegion-aux.org

Marguerite McAlpin Nurse's Scholarship

Type of award: Scholarship.
Intended use: For undergraduate or graduate study at postsecondary institution.
Eligibility: Applicant or parent must be member/participant of American Legion Auxiliary. Applicant must be residing in Washington. Applicant must be dependent of veteran, disabled veteran or deceased veteran. Grandchildren of veterans also eligible.
Basis for selection: Major/career interest in nursing. Applicant must demonstrate financial need, high academic achievement and depth of character.
Application requirements: Recommendations, essay, transcript, proof of eligibility.
Additional information: Must submit application to local Unit chairman.

Amount of award:	$1,000
Number of awards:	1
Application deadline:	April 25
Total amount awarded:	$1,000

Contact:
American Legion Washington Auxiliary
P.O. Box 5867
Lacey, WA 98503
Phone: 360-456-5995
Fax: 360-491-7442
Web: www.walegion-aux.org

Susan Burdett Scholarship

Type of award: Scholarship.
Intended use: For undergraduate study at postsecondary institution.
Eligibility: Applicant or parent must be member/participant of American Legion Auxiliary. Applicant must be female. Applicant must be residing in Washington. Applicant must be dependent of veteran, disabled veteran or deceased veteran. Grandchildren of veterans also eligible.
Basis for selection: Applicant must demonstrate financial need, high academic achievement, depth of character and leadership.
Application requirements: Recommendations, essay, transcript, proof of eligibility.
Additional information: Applicant must be former citizen of Evergreen Girls State (WA). Must submit application to local Unit chairman.

Amount of award:	$1,000
Number of awards:	1
Application deadline:	April 25
Total amount awarded:	$1,000

Contact:
American Legion Washington Auxiliary
Education Scholarships
P.O. Box 5867
Lacey, WA 98503
Phone: 360-456-5995
Fax: 360-491-7442
Web: www.walegion-aux.org

American Legion West Virginia

American Legion West Virginia Oratorical Contest

Type of award: Scholarship.
Intended use: For undergraduate study at postsecondary institution.
Eligibility: Applicant must be enrolled in high school. Applicant must be residing in West Virginia.
Basis for selection: Competition/talent/interest in oratory/debate, based on language style, voice, diction, delivery, originality, logic, breadth of knowledge, application of knowledge about topic, and skill in selecting examples and analogies.
Additional information: State winner receives $500 and four-year scholarship to West Virginia University or other eligible state college. Nine district awards of $200; three section awards of $300. Contest is held in January and February. Information may be obtained from local high school or American Legion Post.

Amount of award:	$200-$500

Contact:
American Legion West Virginia
State Adjutant
Box 3191
Charleston, WV 25332-3191
Phone: 304-343-7591
Fax: 304-343-7592
Web: www.wvlegion.org

Sons of the American Legion Scholarship

Type of award: Scholarship.
Intended use: For full-time freshman study at postsecondary institution.
Eligibility: Applicant must be residing in West Virginia.
Application requirements: Essay, transcript. Must submit copy of transcript from first college semester to receive award.
Additional information: First place winner: $1,000; second place: $500.

Amount of award:	$500-$1,000
Number of awards:	1
Application deadline:	May 15
Total amount awarded:	$1,000

Scholarships

Contact:
American Legion, Department of West Virginia
State Adjutant
Box 3191
Charleston, WV 25332-3191
Phone: 304-343-7591
Fax: 304-343-7592
Web: www.wvlegion.org

American Legion West Virginia Auxiliary

American Legion West Virginia Auxiliary Scholarship

Type of award: Scholarship.
Intended use: For undergraduate study at postsecondary institution. Designated institutions: West Virginia institutions.
Eligibility: Applicant must be no older than 21. Applicant must be residing in West Virginia. Applicant must be dependent of veteran.
Application requirements: Proof of eligibility.
Additional information: Number and amount of awards varies.

Application deadline:	March 1

Contact:
American Legion West Virginia Auxiliary
HC 60 Box 17
New Martinsville, WV 26155
Phone: 888-604-2242
Web: www.wvaux.org

American Legion Wisconsin

American Legion Wisconsin Baseball Scholarship

Type of award: Scholarship.
Intended use: For undergraduate study at vocational, 2-year or 4-year institution.
Eligibility: Applicant must be residing in Wisconsin.
Basis for selection: Competition/talent/interest in athletics/sports. Applicant must demonstrate financial need.
Application requirements: Nomination by Wisconsin American Baseball Board of Directors.
Additional information: Applicant must be current member of Wisconsin American Legion baseball team. Award rotates yearly from region to region and is awarded at State Convention.

Amount of award:	$500
Number of awards:	1
Total amount awarded:	$500

Contact:
American Legion Wisconsin
Program Secretary
P.O. Box 388
Portage, WI 53901
Phone: 608-745-1090
Fax: 608-745-0179
Web: www.wilegion.org

American Legion Wisconsin Eagle Scout of the Year Scholarship

Type of award: Scholarship.
Intended use: For undergraduate study at postsecondary institution.
Eligibility: Applicant or parent must be member/participant of American Legion/Boys Scouts of America. Applicant must be male, high school senior. Applicant must be residing in Wisconsin.
Basis for selection: Applicant must demonstrate high academic achievement.
Additional information: Applicant must be Boy Scout, Varsity Scout or Explorer. Applicant's group must be sponsored by Legion, Auxiliary, or Sons of American Legion, applicant's father or grandfather must be Legion or Auxiliary member.

Amount of award:	$1,000
Number of awards:	1
Application deadline:	March 1
Total amount awarded:	$1,000

Contact:
American Legion Wisconsin
Program Secretary
P.O. Box 388
Portage, WI 53901
Phone: 608-745-1090
Fax: 608-745-0179
Web: www.wilegion.org

American Legion Wisconsin Oratorical Contest Scholarships

Type of award: Scholarship.
Intended use: For undergraduate study at postsecondary institution.
Eligibility: Applicant must be enrolled in high school. Applicant must be residing in Wisconsin.
Basis for selection: Competition/talent/interest in oratory/debate, based on language style, voice, diction, delivery, originality, logic, breadth of knowledge, application of knowledge about topic, and skill in selecting examples and analogies.
Additional information: Awards: First place, $2,000; second place, $1,500; third place, $1,000. Regional winners receive $1,000; regional participants win $600 each.

Amount of award:	$600-$2,000

Contact:
American Legion, Department of Wisconsin
Program Secretary
P.O. Box 388
Portage, WI 53901
Phone: 608-745-1090
Fax: 608-745-0179
Web: www.wilegion.org

Schneider-Emanuel American Legion Scholarships

Type of award: Scholarship.
Intended use: For undergraduate study at 4-year institution in United States.
Eligibility: Applicant or parent must be member/participant of American Legion. Applicant must be residing in Wisconsin. Applicant must be veteran; or dependent of veteran.
Basis for selection: Applicant must demonstrate financial need, high academic achievement and depth of character.

Application requirements: Recommendations, transcript. ACT scores.
Additional information: Must be current member or child/grandchild of current member of American Legion, Auxiliary/Junior Auxiliary, or Sons of the American Legion, and have membership card at time of application.

Amount of award:	$1,000
Number of awards:	3
Application deadline:	March 1
Total amount awarded:	$3,000

Contact:
American Legion, Department of Wisconsin
Program Secretary
P.O. Box 388
Portage, WI 53901
Phone: 608-745-1090
Fax: 608-745-0179
Web: www.wilegion.org

American Legion Wisconsin Auxiliary

American Legion Wisconsin Auxiliary Department President's Scholarship

Type of award: Scholarship.
Intended use: For undergraduate study at accredited postsecondary institution.
Eligibility: Applicant or parent must be member/participant of American Legion Auxiliary. Applicant must be residing in Wisconsin. Applicant must be descendant of veteran; or dependent of veteran; or spouse of veteran or deceased veteran. Mother of applicant or applicant must be Auxiliary member. Grandchildren and great-grandchildren of veterans eligible if Auxiliary members.
Basis for selection: Applicant must demonstrate financial need and high academic achievement.
Application requirements: Recommendations, essay, transcript, proof of eligibility.
Additional information: Minimum 3.5 GPA.

Amount of award:	$1,000
Number of awards:	3
Application deadline:	March 15
Total amount awarded:	$3,000

Contact:
American Legion Wisconsin Auxiliary
Department Secretary
P.O. Box 140
Portage, WI 53901-0140
Phone: 608-745-0124
Fax: 608-745-1947
Web: www.amlegionauxwi.org

American Legion Wisconsin Auxiliary H.S. and Angeline Lewis Scholarships

Type of award: Scholarship.
Intended use: For undergraduate or graduate study at accredited postsecondary institution.
Eligibility: Applicant or parent must be member/participant of American Legion Auxiliary. Applicant must be residing in Wisconsin. Applicant must be descendant of veteran; or dependent of veteran; or spouse of veteran or deceased veteran. Grandchildren and great-grandchildren of veterans eligible if members of Auxiliary.
Basis for selection: Applicant must demonstrate financial need and high academic achievement.
Application requirements: Recommendations, essay, transcript, proof of eligibility.
Additional information: Minimum 3.5 GPA. One award for graduate study; five awards for undergraduate study.

Amount of award:	$1,000
Number of awards:	6
Application deadline:	March 15
Total amount awarded:	$6,000

Contact:
American Legion Wisconsin Auxiliary
Department Secretary
P.O. Box 140
Portage, WI 53901-0140
Phone: 608-745-0124
Fax: 608-745-1947
Web: www.amlegionauxwi.org

American Legion Wisconsin Auxiliary Merit and Memorial Scholarship

Type of award: Scholarship.
Intended use: For undergraduate study.
Eligibility: Applicant or parent must be member/participant of American Legion Auxiliary. Applicant must be residing in Wisconsin. Applicant must be descendant of veteran; or dependent of veteran; or spouse of veteran or deceased veteran. Grandchildren and great-grandchildren of veterans eligible if members of Auxiliary.
Basis for selection: Applicant must demonstrate financial need and high academic achievement.
Application requirements: Recommendations, essay, transcript, proof of eligibility.
Additional information: Minimum 3.5 GPA.

Amount of award:	$1,000
Number of awards:	7
Application deadline:	March 15
Total amount awarded:	$7,000

Contact:
American Legion Wisconsin Auxiliary
Department Secretary
P.O. Box 140
Portage, WI 53901-0140
Phone: 608-745-0124
Fax: 608-745-1947
Web: www.amlegionauxwi.org

American Legion Wisconsin Auxiliary Past Presidents Parley R.N. Scholarship

Type of award: Scholarship.
Intended use: For undergraduate study at accredited vocational, 2-year or 4-year institution.
Eligibility: Applicant or parent must be member/participant of American Legion Auxiliary. Applicant must be residing in Wisconsin. Applicant must be descendant of veteran; or dependent of veteran or deceased veteran; or spouse of veteran.

or deceased veteran. Grandchildren or great-grandchildren of veterans eligible if Auxiliary member.
Basis for selection: Major/career interest in nursing. Applicant must demonstrate financial need and high academic achievement.
Application requirements: Recommendations, essay, transcript, proof of eligibility.
Additional information: Minimum 3.5 GPA. Must be in or accepted to accredited school of nursing, accredited hospital, or university registered nursing program. Hospital, university, or technical school program acceptable.

Amount of award:	$1,000
Number of awards:	2
Application deadline:	March 15

Contact:
American Legion Wisconsin Auxiliary
Department Secretary
P.O. Box 140
Portage, WI 53901-0140
Phone: 608-745-0124
Fax: 608-745-1947
Web: www.amlegionauxwi.org

Della Van Deuren Memorial Scholarship

Type of award: Scholarship.
Intended use: For undergraduate study.
Eligibility: Applicant or parent must be member/participant of American Legion Auxiliary. Applicant must be residing in Wisconsin. Applicant must be descendant of veteran; or dependent of veteran; or spouse of veteran or deceased veteran.
Basis for selection: Applicant must demonstrate financial need and high academic achievement.
Application requirements: Recommendations, essay, transcript, proof of eligibility.
Additional information: Applicant's mother or applicant must be member of American Legion Auxiliary. Grandchildren and great-grandchildren of veterans are eligible if they are members of American Legion Auxiliary. Minimum 3.5 GPA. Applicant's school need not be in Wisconsin.

Amount of award:	$1,000
Number of awards:	2
Application deadline:	March 15
Total amount awarded:	$2,000

Contact:
American Legion Wisconsin Auxiliary
Department Secretary
P.O. Box 140
Portage, WI 53901-0140
Phone: 608-745-0124
Fax: 608-745-1947
Web: www.amlegionauxwi.org

American Legion Wyoming

American Legion Wyoming E.A. Blackmore Memorial Scholarship

Type of award: Scholarship.
Intended use: For undergraduate study at postsecondary institution.
Eligibility: Applicant or parent must be member/participant of American Legion. Applicant must be residing in Wyoming. Applicant must be dependent of veteran.
Basis for selection: Applicant must demonstrate financial need and high academic achievement.
Application requirements: Recommendations, transcript, proof of eligibility. Resume. Photo.
Additional information: Must be child or grandchild of American Legion member in good standing, or child or grandchild of deceased American Legion member who was in good standing. Must rank in upper 20 percent of high school class.

Amount of award:	$1,000
Number of awards:	1
Application deadline:	May 15
Total amount awarded:	$1,000

Contact:
American Legion Wyoming
Department Adjutant
1320 Hugur Ave.
Cheyenne, WY 82001
Phone: 307-634-3035
Fax: 307-635-7093
Web: www.wylegion.org

American Legion Wyoming Oratorical Contest

Type of award: Scholarship.
Intended use: For undergraduate study at postsecondary institution.
Eligibility: Applicant must be enrolled in high school. Applicant must be U.S. citizen or permanent resident residing in Wyoming.
Basis for selection: Competition/talent/interest in oratory/debate, based on language style, voice, diction, delivery, originality, logic, breadth of knowledge, application of knowledge about topic, and skill in selecting examples and analogies.
Application requirements: Proof of eligibility.
Additional information: State awards: First place, $500; second place, $400; and third place, $200. District winners also receive awards.

Number of awards:	3
Application deadline:	May 15
Total amount awarded:	$1,450

Contact:
American Legion Wyoming
Department Adjutant
1320 Hugur Ave.
Cheyenne, WY 82001
Phone: 307-634-3035
Fax: 307-635-7093
Web: www.wylegion.org

American Legion Wyoming Auxiliary

American Legion Wyoming Auxiliary Past Presidents Parley Scholarship

Type of award: Scholarship, renewable.
Intended use: For full-time sophomore study at accredited 2-year or 4-year institution. Designated institutions: University of Wyoming or one of Wyoming community colleges.

Eligibility: Preference given to nursing students who are children of veterans.
Basis for selection: Major/career interest in health-related professions; medicine; nursing; occupational therapy; pharmacy/pharmaceutics/pharmacology; physical therapy; respiratory therapy or speech pathology/audiology. Applicant must demonstrate financial need and high academic achievement.
Application requirements: Recommendations.
Additional information: Must have completed one year or two semesters of study. Minimum 3.0 GPA. Preference given to Wyoming residents.

Amount of award:	$300
Number of awards:	1
Application deadline:	June 1

Contact:
American Legion Wyoming Auxiliary
Department Secretary
P.O. Box 2198
Gillette, WY 82717-2198
Phone: 307-686-7137
Web: www.wylegionaux.org

American Medical Technologists

American Medical Technologists Student Scholarship

Type of award: Scholarship.
Intended use: For full-time undergraduate study at accredited postsecondary institution in United States.
Eligibility: Applicant must be U.S. citizen or permanent resident.
Basis for selection: Major/career interest in medical assistant or dental assistant. Applicant must demonstrate financial need.
Application requirements: Recommendations, essay, transcript. W-2 current tax form.
Additional information: Scholarship is available only to high school seniors and graduates studying to become one of the following: medical assistant, dental assistant, medical administrative specialist, medical technologist, medical laboratory technician, medical laboratory assistant, allied health instructor, clinical laboratory consultant, or phlebotomy technician. Award amount may vary. Visit Website for application.

Amount of award:	$500
Number of awards:	5
Number of applicants:	76
Application deadline:	April 1
Total amount awarded:	$2,500

Contact:
American Medical Technologists
10700 West Higgins Road, Suite 150
Rosemont, IL 60018
Phone: 847-823-5169
Fax: 847-823-0458
Web: www.americanmedtech.org

American Meteorological Society

American Meteorological Society Freshman Undergraduate Scholarship Program

Type of award: Scholarship, renewable.
Intended use: For full-time freshman study at accredited 4-year institution in United States.
Eligibility: Applicant must be high school senior. Applicant must be U.S. citizen or permanent resident.
Basis for selection: Major/career interest in atmospheric sciences/meteorology; oceanography/marine studies or hydrology. Applicant must demonstrate high academic achievement.
Application requirements: Recommendations, essay, transcript. SAT/ACT scores.
Additional information: Scholarships are renewable for the sophomore year, providing recipient plans to continue studies in the AMS-related sciences. Marine biology majors not eligible. Minimum 3.0 GPA. Award is $2,500 each for freshman and sophomore years.

Amount of award:	$2,500
Number of awards:	14
Number of applicants:	159
Application deadline:	February 14
Notification begins:	May 1

Contact:
American Meteorological Society
Fellowship/Scholarship Program
45 Beacon Street
Boston, MA 02108-3693
Phone: 617-226-3907
Fax: 617-742-8718
Web: www.ametsoc.org

American Meteorological Society Named Undergraduate Scholarship

Type of award: Scholarship.
Intended use: For full-time senior study at accredited 4-year institution in United States.
Eligibility: Applicant must be U.S. citizen or permanent resident.
Basis for selection: Major/career interest in atmospheric sciences/meteorology; oceanography/marine studies or hydrology. Applicant must demonstrate high academic achievement and seriousness of purpose.
Application requirements: Recommendations, transcript.
Additional information: Minimum 3.25 GPA. Marine biology majors not eligible. Must be a junior at the time of application. Visit Website for more information and to download application. Number and amount of scholarships vary. Applicants must demonstrate financial need to be eligible for the Schroeder Scholarship. The Murphy Scholarship is awarded to students who, through curricular or extracurricular activities, have shown interest in weather forecasting or in the value and utilization of forecasts. The Glahn Scholarship is for a student who has shown strong interest in statistical meteorology. The Crow Scholarship is for a student who has shown strong interest in applied meteorology. Number and amount of awards varies.

Scholarships

Application deadline: February 14
Notification begins: May 1

Contact:
American Meteorological Society
Fellowship/Scholarship Program
45 Beacon Street
Boston, MA 02108-3693
Phone: 617-226-3907
Fax: 617-742-8718
Web: www.ametsoc.org

American Meteorological Society/ Industry Minority Scholarship

Type of award: Scholarship.
Intended use: For full-time freshman study at accredited 4-year institution in United States.
Eligibility: Applicant must be Alaskan native, Asian American, African American, Mexican American, Hispanic American, Puerto Rican, American Indian or Native Hawaiian/Pacific Islander. Applicant must be high school senior. Applicant must be U.S. citizen or permanent resident.
Basis for selection: Major/career interest in atmospheric sciences/meteorology; oceanography/marine studies or hydrology. Applicant must demonstrate high academic achievement.
Application requirements: Recommendations, essay, transcript. SAT or ACT scores.
Additional information: Minimum 3.0 GPA. Award is $3,000 per year for freshman and sophomore years. Award is for minority students who have traditionally been underrepresented in the sciences, especially Hispanic, Native American, and African-American students. Marine biology majors ineligible. Number of awards varies. Visit Website to download application.

Amount of award: $6,000
Number of applicants: 40
Application deadline: February 14
Notification begins: May 1
Total amount awarded: $3,000

Contact:
American Meteorological Society
Fellowship/Scholarship Program
45 Beacon Street
Boston, MA 02108-3693
Phone: 617-226-3907
Fax: 617-742-8718
Web: www.ametsoc.org

Father James B. Macelwane Annual Award

Type of award: Scholarship.
Intended use: For undergraduate study.
Eligibility: Applicant must be U.S. citizen or permanent resident.
Basis for selection: Major/career interest in atmospheric sciences/meteorology; oceanography/marine studies or hydrology.
Application requirements: Essay, transcript, proof of eligibility. Original paper plus four photocopies. Letter of application including contact information and stating paper's title and name of university where paper was written. Letter from university faculty stating author was undergraduate when paper was written and indicating elements of paper that are original contributions by the student. Abstract of maximum 250 words describing paper.
Additional information: Award intended to stimulate interest in meteorology among college students through submission of original papers concerned with some phase of atmospheric sciences. Student must have been undergraduate when paper was written. Submissions from women, minorities and disabled students who are traditionally underrepresented in atmospheric and related oceanic and hydrologic sciences encouraged. No more than two students from any one institution may enter papers in any one contest. Visit Website for application and additional information.

Amount of award: $1,000
Number of awards: 1
Application deadline: June 13
Notification begins: September 1
Total amount awarded: $1,000

Contact:
American Meteorological Society
Macelwane Award
45 Beacon Street
Boston, MA 02108-3693
Phone: 617-226-3907
Fax: 617-742-8718
Web: www.ametsoc.org

American Military Retirees Association

Sergeant Major Douglas R. Drum Memorial Scholarship

Type of award: Scholarship, renewable.
Intended use: For full-time undergraduate study at accredited 2-year or 4-year institution.
Additional information: Must be member or spouse, dependent child, or grandchild of member of American Military Retirees Association. Applications must be submitted electronically via fax or email to scholarship@amra1973.org.

Amount of award: $1,000-$5,000
Number of awards: 24
Number of applicants: 93
Application deadline: March 1
Total amount awarded: $35,000

Contact:
American Military Retirees Association
5436 Peru Street, Suite 1
Plattsburgh, NY 12901
Phone: 800-424-2969
Fax: 518-324-5204
Web: www.amra1973.org

American Morgan Horse Institute

AMHI Educational Scholarships

Type of award: Scholarship.
Intended use: For undergraduate or non-degree study at vocational, 2-year or 4-year institution.
Eligibility: Applicant must be high school senior.

Scholarships

Basis for selection: Major/career interest in equestrian/equine studies. Applicant must demonstrate financial need, depth of character, leadership, seriousness of purpose and service orientation.
Application requirements: Recommendations, essay, transcript. List of horse-related activities, photo.
Additional information: Applicant must meet at least one of the following criteria: involvement in the AMHA Horsemastership Program; involvement in a 4H/FFA program; won a USA Equestrian and/or awarded AMHA medal for equestrian; or placed in the top two in the junior division or the top four in the adult division of an open competition program. Send SASE or visit Website for application.

Amount of award:	$3,000
Number of awards:	5
Number of applicants:	45
Application deadline:	March 1
Notification begins:	June 15
Total amount awarded:	$15,000

Contact:
AMHI Scholarships
6120 Cedar Creek Lane
Lexington, KY 40515
Phone: 859-543-2387
Web: www.morganhorseinstitute.com

AMHI van Schaik Dressage Scholarship

Type of award: Scholarship.
Intended use: For non-degree study.
Basis for selection: Major/career interest in dressage or equestrian/equine studies. Applicant must demonstrate seriousness of purpose.
Application requirements: Recommendations, essay. Photo (optional).
Additional information: Must be dressage rider using a registered Morgan horse and interested in advancing from lower levels of dressage to Fourth Level and above. Preference given to applicants who have competed their Morgan at First Level Test 4 or above and scored 60 percent or higher at recognized competition. Visit Website for application.

Amount of award:	$1,000
Number of awards:	1
Number of applicants:	2
Application deadline:	November 30
Notification begins:	March 31
Total amount awarded:	$1,000

Contact:
AMHI Scholarship
Attn: AMHI van Schaik Dressage Scholarship
6120 Cedar Creek Lane
Lexington, KY 40515
Phone: 859-543-2387
Web: www.morganhorseinstitute.com

American Museum of Natural History

Young Naturalist Awards

Type of award: Scholarship, renewable.
Intended use: For freshman study.
Basis for selection: Competition/talent/interest in science project.
Application requirements: Essay. Original artwork/ photographs.
Additional information: For students grades 7-12 in the U.S and Canada to plan and conduct scientific investigations and report them in an illustrated essay. Children of Alcoa Corporation or American Museum of Natural History employees or consultants are ineligible. Two winners per grade level receive the following: 7th grade, $500; 8th grade, $750; 9th grade, $1,000; 10th grade, $1,500; 11th grade, $2,000; 12th grade, $2,500. Up to 36 additional finalists receive $50 prize. Deadline in early March. Visit Website for exact date.

Amount of award:	$50-$2,500
Number of awards:	48
Application deadline:	March 1

Contact:
Young Naturalist Awards Administrator
American Museum of Natural History
Central Park West at 79th Street
New York, NY 10024-5192
Phone: 212-496-3498
Web: www.amnh.org/learn-teach/young-naturalist-awards

American Nuclear Society

Accelerator Applications Division Scholarship

Type of award: Scholarship.
Intended use: For full-time junior study at accredited 4-year institution in United States.
Eligibility: Applicant must be U.S. citizen or permanent resident.
Basis for selection: Major/career interest in physics; engineering or materials science. Applicant must demonstrate financial need and high academic achievement.
Application requirements: Recommendations, essay, transcript.
Additional information: Applicant must be an ANS student member. Must be sponsored by ANS organization. Visit Website for application. One request/application covers all Graduate and Undergraduate scholarships; check appropriate boxes on application form. Number of awards varies. Additional consideration given to applicants who are members of an under-represented class (female/minority), and have a record of service to ANS. Recipients will receive $1,000 for their junior year and $1,000 for their senior year for a total award of $2000 over a two-year period.

Amount of award:	$2,000
Application deadline:	February 1

Contact:
American Nuclear Society
555 North Kensington Avenue
La Grange Park, IL 60526
Phone: 708-352-6611
Fax: 708-352-0499
Web: www.ans.org

American Nuclear Society Operations and Power Division Scholarship

Type of award: Scholarship.
Intended use: For full-time junior, senior or graduate study at accredited 4-year or graduate institution in United States.
Eligibility: Applicant must be U.S. citizen or permanent resident.
Basis for selection: Major/career interest in nuclear science or engineering, nuclear.
Application requirements: Recommendations, transcript.
Additional information: Applicant must be an ANS student member enrolled in a program leading to a degree in nuclear science, nuclear engineering or a nuclear related field. Must be sponsored by ANS organization. Must have completed at least two full academic years of four-year nuclear science or engineering program. Visit Website for application. One request/application covers all Graduate and Undergraduate scholarships; check appropriate boxes on application form.

Amount of award:	$2,500
Number of awards:	1
Application deadline:	February 1

Contact:
American Nuclear Society
555 North Kensington Avenue
La Grange Park, IL 60526
Phone: 708-352-6611
Fax: 708-352-0499
Web: www.ans.org

Angelo S. Bisesti Scholarship

Type of award: Scholarship.
Intended use: For full-time junior or senior study at accredited 4-year institution in United States.
Eligibility: Applicant must be U.S. citizen or permanent resident.
Basis for selection: Major/career interest in nuclear science or engineering, nuclear.
Application requirements: Recommendations, transcript.
Additional information: Applicant must be an ANS student member enrolled in a program leading to a degree in nuclear science, nuclear engineering or a nuclear related field. Must be sponsored by ANS organization. Visit Website for application. One request/application covers all Graduate and Undergraduate scholarships; check appropriate boxes on application form.

Amount of award:	$2,000
Number of awards:	1
Application deadline:	February 1
Total amount awarded:	$2,000

Contact:
American Nuclear Society
555 North Kensington Avenue
La Grange Park, IL 60526
Phone: 708-352-6611
Fax: 708-352-0499
Web: www.ans.org

ANS Decommissioning, Decontamination and Reutilization Scholarship

Type of award: Scholarship.
Intended use: For junior or senior study at accredited 4-year institution in United States.
Eligibility: Applicant must be U.S. citizen.
Basis for selection: Major/career interest in engineering, nuclear; environmental science; engineering, environmental or nuclear science.
Application requirements: Recommendations, essay, transcript.
Additional information: Applicant must be enrolled in curriculum of engineering or science associated with decommissioning/decontamination of nuclear facilities, management/characterization of nuclear waste, restoration of environment, or nuclear engineering. If awarded scholarship, student must join ANS and designate DDR Division as one professional division. Awardee must also provide support to DDR Division at next ANS meeting after receiving award (funding provided for travel to meeting, food, and lodging). Visit Website for application.

Amount of award:	$2,000
Number of awards:	1
Application deadline:	February 1

Contact:
American Nuclear Society
555 North Kensington Avenue
La Grange Park, IL 60526
Phone: 708-352-6611
Fax: 708-352-0499
Web: www.ans.org

ANS Incoming Freshman Scholarship

Type of award: Scholarship.
Intended use: For full-time freshman study at accredited postsecondary institution in United States.
Eligibility: Applicant must be high school senior. Applicant must be U.S. citizen or permanent resident.
Basis for selection: Major/career interest in engineering, nuclear. Applicant must demonstrate high academic achievement.
Application requirements: Recommendations, transcript, proof of eligibility. 500-word essay.
Additional information: For graduating high school seniors who have enrolled in college courses and are pursuing a degree in nuclear engineering or have the intent to pursue a degree in nuclear engineering.

Amount of award:	$1,000
Number of awards:	4
Application deadline:	April 1

Contact:
American Nuclear Society
555 North Kensington Avenue
La Grange Park, IL 60526
Phone: 708-352-6611
Fax: 708-352-0499
Web: www.ans.org

ANS Undergraduate Scholarships

Type of award: Scholarship.
Intended use: For sophomore, junior or senior study at accredited 4-year institution in United States.
Eligibility: Applicant must be U.S. citizen or permanent resident.
Basis for selection: Major/career interest in nuclear science or engineering, nuclear.
Application requirements: Recommendations, transcript.
Additional information: Maximum of four scholarships for entering sophomores in study leading to degree in nuclear science, nuclear engineering, or nuclear-related field; maximum

of 21 scholarships for students who will be entering junior or senior year. Applicant must be an ANS student member and must be sponsored by ANS organization. Visit Website for application. One request/application covers all Graduate and Undergraduate scholarships; check appropriate boxes on application form.

Amount of award: $2,000
Application deadline: February 1

Contact:
American Nuclear Society
555 North Kensington Avenue
La Grange Park, IL 60526
Phone: 708-352-6611
Fax: 708-352-0499
Web: www.ans.org

ANS Washington, D.C. Section Undergraduate Scholarship

Type of award: Scholarship.
Intended use: For full-time junior or senior study at accredited 4-year institution in United States.
Eligibility: Applicant must be U.S. citizen or permanent resident.
Basis for selection: Major/career interest in engineering, nuclear.
Application requirements: Recommendations, transcript.
Additional information: Permanent address must be within 100 miles of Washington, DC. Applicant must be an ANS student member enrolled in a program leading to a degree in nuclear engineering, health physics, or nuclear-related studies. Must be sponsored by ANS organization. Visit Website for application. One request/application covers all Graduate and Undergraduate scholarships; check appropriate boxes on application form.

Amount of award: $2,500
Number of awards: 1
Application deadline: February 1

Contact:
American Nuclear Society
555 North Kensington Avenue
La Grange Park, IL 60526
Phone: 708-352-6611
Fax: 708-352-0499
Web: www.ans.org

Charles (Tommy) Thomas Memorial Scholarship

Type of award: Scholarship.
Intended use: For full-time junior or senior study at accredited 4-year institution in United States.
Basis for selection: Major/career interest in nuclear science; engineering, nuclear; environmental science; engineering, environmental; ecology or natural resources/conservation.
Application requirements: Recommendations, transcript.
Additional information: Applicant must be an ANS student member enrolled in a program leading to a degree in nuclear science, nuclear engineering or a nuclear related field. Must be sponsored by ANS organization. Visit Website for application. One request/application covers all Graduate and Undergraduate scholarships; check appropriate boxes on application form.

Amount of award: $3,000
Number of awards: 1
Application deadline: February 1

Contact:
American Nuclear Society
555 North Kensington Avenue
La Grange Park, IL 60526
Phone: 708-352-6611
Fax: 708-352-0499
Web: www.ans.org

Delayed Education Scholarship for Women

Type of award: Scholarship.
Intended use: For undergraduate study at accredited 4-year institution in United States.
Eligibility: Applicant must be female, returning adult student. Applicant must be U.S. citizen or permanent resident.
Basis for selection: Major/career interest in nuclear science or engineering, nuclear. Applicant must demonstrate financial need and high academic achievement.
Application requirements: Recommendations, transcript.
Additional information: Must be a mature woman whose undergraduate studies in nuclear science, nuclear engineering, or a nuclear-related field have been delayed. Applicants must check the appropriate box on the Landis Scholarship form. For more information please call the American Nuclear Society scholarship coordinator.

Amount of award: $5,000
Number of awards: 1
Application deadline: February 1

Contact:
American Nuclear Society
555 North Kensington Avenue
La Grange Park, IL 60526
Phone: 708-352-6611
Fax: 708-352-0499
Web: www.ans.org

Human Factors, Instrumentation and Controls Division (HFICD) Nuclear Power Scholarship

Type of award: Scholarship.
Intended use: For undergraduate study at accredited 4-year institution in United States.
Eligibility: Applicant must be U.S. citizen or international student.
Basis for selection: Major/career interest in engineering, nuclear.
Application requirements: Recommendations, transcript. Letter of sponsorship.
Additional information: Must be ANS student member. Scholarship to be used to study technical disciplines involved in nuclear plant instrumentation, controls, and human-machine interface technologies in the context of nuclear power or other nuclear engineering specific applications.

Amount of award: $2,000
Number of awards: 1
Application deadline: February 1

Contact:
American Nuclear Society
555 North Kensington Avenue
La Grange Park, IL 60526
Phone: 708-352-6611
Fax: 708-352-0499
Web: www.ans.org

James K. Vogt Radiochemistry Scholarship

Type of award: Scholarship.
Intended use: For full-time junior, senior or graduate study at accredited 4-year or graduate institution in United States.
Eligibility: Applicant must be U.S. citizen or permanent resident.
Basis for selection: Major/career interest in chemistry or nuclear science.
Application requirements: Recommendations, essay, transcript.
Additional information: Applicants must be engaged in proposing to undertake graduate or undergraduate research in radioanalytical chemistry or its applications of nuclear science. Applicant must be an ANS student member and must be sponsored by ANS organization. Visit Website for application and requirements. One request/application covers all Graduate and Undergraduate scholarships; check appropriate boxes on application form.

Amount of award:	$3,000
Number of awards:	1
Application deadline:	February 1

Contact:
American Nuclear Society
555 North Kensington Avenue
La Grange Park, IL 60526
Phone: 708-352-6611
Fax: 708-352-0499
Web: www.ans.org

John and Muriel Landis Scholarship

Type of award: Scholarship.
Intended use: For undergraduate or graduate study at accredited 4-year or graduate institution in United States.
Eligibility: Applicant must be U.S. citizen or permanent resident.
Basis for selection: Major/career interest in nuclear science or engineering, nuclear. Applicant must demonstrate financial need.
Application requirements: Recommendations, transcript.
Additional information: Awarded to students with greater than average financial need. Consideration given to conditions or experiences that render student disadvantaged (poor high school/undergraduate preparation, etc.). Applicants should be planning career in nuclear science or nuclear engineering. Qualified high school seniors eligible to apply. Number of awards varies. Visit Website for application and requirements. Applicants must check the appropriate box on the Landis Scholarship form.

Amount of award:	$5,000
Number of awards:	9
Application deadline:	February 1

Contact:
American Nuclear Society
555 North Kensington Avenue
La Grange Park, IL 60526
Phone: 708-352-6611
Fax: 708-352-0499
Web: www.ans.org

John R. Lamarsh Scholarship

Type of award: Scholarship.
Intended use: For full-time junior or senior study at accredited 4-year institution in United States.
Eligibility: Applicant must be U.S. citizen or permanent resident.
Basis for selection: Major/career interest in nuclear science or engineering, nuclear.
Application requirements: Recommendations, transcript.
Additional information: Applicant must be an ANS student member enrolled in a program leading to a degree in nuclear science, nuclear engineering or a nuclear related field. Must be sponsored by ANS organization. Visit Website for application. One request/application covers all Graduate and Undergraduate scholarships; check appropriate boxes on application form.

Amount of award:	$2,000
Number of awards:	1
Application deadline:	February 1

Contact:
American Nuclear Society
555 North Kensington Avenue
La Grange Park, IL 60526
Phone: 708-352-6611
Fax: 708-352-0499
Web: www.ans.org

Joseph R. Dietrich Scholarship

Type of award: Scholarship.
Intended use: For full-time junior or senior study at accredited 4-year institution in United States.
Eligibility: Applicant must be U.S. citizen or permanent resident.
Basis for selection: Major/career interest in nuclear science; engineering, nuclear; chemistry or physics.
Application requirements: Recommendations, transcript.
Additional information: Applicant must be an ANS student member enrolled in a program leading to a degree in nuclear science, nuclear engineering or a nuclear related field. Must be sponsored by ANS organization. Visit Website for application. One request/application covers all Graduate and Undergraduate scholarships; check appropriate boxes on application form.

Amount of award:	$2,000
Number of awards:	1
Application deadline:	February 1

Contact:
American Nuclear Society
555 North Kensington Avenue
La Grange Park, IL 60526
Phone: 708-352-6611
Fax: 708-352-0499
Web: www.ans.org

Pittsburgh Local Section Scholarship

Type of award: Scholarship.
Intended use: For full-time junior, senior or graduate study at accredited 4-year or graduate institution in United States.
Basis for selection: Major/career interest in nuclear science or engineering, nuclear.
Application requirements: Recommendations, transcript.
Additional information: Applicant must either attend school in Western Pennsylvania or have some affiliation with the region. Awards are $2,000 for undergraduates and $3,500 for graduate students. Applicant must be an ANS student member enrolled in a program leading to a degree in nuclear science, nuclear engineering or a nuclear related field. Must be sponsored by ANS organization. Visit Website for application. One request/application covers all Graduate and Undergraduate scholarships; check appropriate boxes on application form.

Amount of award: $2,000-$3,500
Number of awards: 2
Application deadline: February 1
Contact:
American Nuclear Society
555 North Kensington Avenue
La Grange Park, IL 60526
Phone: 708-352-6611
Fax: 708-352-0499
Web: www.ans.org

Raymond DiSalvo Scholarship

Type of award: Scholarship.
Intended use: For full-time junior or senior study at accredited 4-year institution in United States.
Eligibility: Applicant must be U.S. citizen or permanent resident.
Basis for selection: Major/career interest in nuclear science or engineering, nuclear.
Application requirements: Recommendations, transcript.
Additional information: Applicant must be an ANS student member enrolled in a program leading to a degree in nuclear science, nuclear engineering or a nuclear related field. Must be sponsored by ANS organization. Visit Website for application. One request/application covers all Graduate and Undergraduate scholarships; check appropriate boxes on application form.
Amount of award: $2,000
Number of awards: 1
Application deadline: February 1
Contact:
American Nuclear Society
555 North Kensington Avenue
La Grange Park, IL 60526
Phone: 708-352-6611
Fax: 708-352-0499
Web: www.ans.org

Robert G. Lacy Scholarship

Type of award: Scholarship.
Intended use: For full-time junior or senior study at accredited 4-year institution in United States.
Eligibility: Applicant must be U.S. citizen or permanent resident.
Basis for selection: Major/career interest in nuclear science or engineering, nuclear.
Application requirements: Recommendations, transcript.
Additional information: Applicant must be an ANS student member enrolled in a program leading to a degree in nuclear science, nuclear engineering or a nuclear related field. Must be sponsored by ANS organization. Visit Website for application. One request/application covers all Graduate and Undergraduate scholarships; check appropriate boxes on application form.
Amount of award: $2,000
Number of awards: 1
Application deadline: February 1
Contact:
American Nuclear Society
555 North Kensington Avenue
La Grange Park, IL 60526
Phone: 708-352-6611
Fax: 708-352-0499
Web: www.ans.org

Robert T. (Bob) Liner Scholarship

Type of award: Scholarship.
Intended use: For full-time junior or senior study at accredited 4-year institution in United States.
Eligibility: Applicant must be U.S. citizen or permanent resident.
Basis for selection: Major/career interest in nuclear science or engineering, nuclear.
Application requirements: Recommendations, transcript.
Additional information: Applicant must be an ANS student member enrolled in a program leading to a degree in nuclear science, nuclear engineering or a nuclear related field. Must be sponsored by ANS organization. Visit Website for application. One request/application covers all Graduate and Undergraduate scholarships; check appropriate boxes on application form.
Amount of award: $2,000
Number of awards: 1
Application deadline: February 1
Contact:
American Nuclear Society
555 North Kensington Avenue
La Grange Park, IL 60526
Phone: 708-352-6611
Fax: 708-352-0499
Web: www.ans.org

William R. and Mila Kimel Scholarship

Type of award: Scholarship.
Intended use: For full-time junior or senior study at accredited 4-year institution in United States.
Eligibility: Applicant must be U.S. citizen or permanent resident.
Basis for selection: Major/career interest in engineering, nuclear.
Application requirements: Recommendations, transcript.
Additional information: Applicant must be an ANS student member enrolled in a program leading to a degree in nuclear science, nuclear engineering or a nuclear related field. Must be sponsored by ANS organization. Visit Website for application. One request/application covers all Graduate and Undergraduate scholarships; check appropriate boxes on application form. Number of awards varies.
Amount of award: $2,000
Application deadline: February 1
Contact:
American Nuclear Society
555 North Kensington Avenue
La Grange Park, IL 60526
Phone: 708-352-6611
Fax: 708-352-0499
Web: www.ans.org

American Physical Society

Scholarship for Minority Undergraduate Physics Majors

Type of award: Scholarship, renewable.
Intended use: For full-time freshman, sophomore or junior study at 2-year or 4-year institution in United States.

Designated institutions: Institutions with physics departments or provisions for procurement of physics degrees.
Eligibility: Applicant must be African American, Mexican American, Hispanic American, Puerto Rican or American Indian. Applicant must be U.S. citizen or permanent resident.
Basis for selection: Major/career interest in physics. Applicant must demonstrate high academic achievement.
Application requirements: Recommendations, essay, transcript, proof of eligibility. ACT/SAT scores.
Additional information: Must be high school senior or college freshman or sophomore to apply. Applications available early November. Visit Website for more information.

Amount of award:	$2,000-$3,000
Number of awards:	25
Number of applicants:	100
Application deadline:	February 1
Notification begins:	May 15
Total amount awarded:	$70,000

Contact:
American Physical Society
Minority Undergraduate Physics Scholarship
One Physics Ellipse
College Park, MD 20740
Phone: 301-209-3232
Fax: 301-209-3357
Web: www.aps.org/programs/minorities/honors/scholarship

American Public Power Association

DEED Student Research Grants

Type of award: Research grant.
Intended use: For undergraduate or graduate study at accredited 2-year, 4-year or graduate institution in United States or Canada.
Basis for selection: Major/career interest in electronics; engineering, electrical/electronic; engineering, mechanical or energy research.
Application requirements: Transcript.
Additional information: Applicants must complete energy-related research project and be sponsored by DEED member utility.

Amount of award:	$4,000
Number of awards:	10
Application deadline:	February 15, October 15
Total amount awarded:	$40,000

Contact:
American Public Power Association
Attn: DEED Administrator
1875 Connecticut Avenue, NW, Suite 1200
Washington, DC 20009-5715
Phone: 202-467-2960
Fax: 202-467-2910
Web: www.publicpower.org

American Quarter Horse Foundation

American Quarter Horse Foundation Scholarships

Type of award: Scholarship, renewable.
Intended use: For full-time undergraduate or first professional study in United States or Canada.
Eligibility: Applicant must be at least 17.
Basis for selection: Applicant must demonstrate financial need and high academic achievement.
Application requirements: Recommendations, transcript, proof of eligibility.
Additional information: Number of scholarships varies. Active membership in either the American Quarter Horse Youth Association or American Quarter Horse Association may be required. Number of awards given varies. Visit Website for requirements, deadline, and scholarship criteria.

Amount of award:	$500-$25,000
Number of applicants:	200
Application deadline:	December 1
Notification begins:	May 1
Total amount awarded:	$275,000

Contact:
American Quarter Horse Foundation
Scholarship Office
2601 I-40 East
Amarillo, TX 79104
Phone: 806-378-5029
Fax: 806-376-1005
Web: www.aqha.com/foundation

American Radio Relay League (ARRL) Foundation, Inc.

The Albert H. Hix, W8AH, Memorial Scholarship

Type of award: Scholarship.
Intended use: For at accredited postsecondary institution. Designated institutions: West Virginia institutions.
Eligibility: Applicant must be residing in West Virginia.
Basis for selection: Competition/talent/interest in amateur radio. Applicant must demonstrate high academic achievement.
Application requirements: Transcript. FAFSA.
Additional information: Minimum 3.0 GPA. Must be amateur radio operator with active General Class license or higher. High school seniors are eligible to apply. Residents of West Virginia Section and school attendance in the West Virginia Section preferred. Visit Website for application.

Amount of award:	$500
Number of awards:	1
Application deadline:	February 1

Contact:
American Radio Relay League (ARRL) Foundation, Inc.
225 Main Street
Newington, CT 06111
Phone: 860-594-0397
Fax: 860-594-0259
Web: www.arrlf.org

The Alfred E. Friend, Jr., W4CF Memorial Scholarship

Type of award: Scholarship.
Intended use: For undergraduate study at postsecondary institution.
Basis for selection: Competition/talent/interest in amateur radio. Major/career interest in engineering.
Application requirements: Transcript. FAFSA.
Additional information: Must be amateur radio operator with any class of active Amateur Radio license. Visit Website for application.

Amount of award:	$5,000
Number of awards:	1
Application deadline:	February 1

Contact:
American Radio Relay League (ARRL) Foundation, Inc.
225 Main Street
Newington, CT 06111
Phone: 860-594-0397
Fax: 860-594-0259
Web: www.arrlf.org

The Allen and Bertha Watson Memorial Scholarship

Type of award: Scholarship.
Intended use: For undergraduate study at 4-year institution.
Basis for selection: Competition/talent/interest in amateur radio. Major/career interest in science, general; technology or engineering.
Application requirements: Transcript. FAFSA.
Additional information: Must be amateur radio operator with any class of active Amateur Radio license and reside or attend a college or university in Oklahoma. If no qualified applicant is identified, preference will be awarded to applicants residing or attending a college or university in the ARRL Gulf Division (Texas and Oklahoma). Visit Website for application.

Amount of award:	$500
Number of awards:	1
Application deadline:	February 1

Contact:
American Radio Relay League (ARRL) Foundation, Inc.
225 Main Street
Newington, CT 06111
Phone: 860-594-0397
Fax: 860-594-0259
Web: www.arrlf.org

Androscoggin Amateur Radio Club Scholarship

Type of award: Scholarship.
Intended use: For undergraduate study at 2-year or 4-year institution.
Eligibility: Applicant must be residing in Vermont, Connecticut, New Hampshire, Maine, Massachusetts or Rhode Island.
Basis for selection: Competition/talent/interest in amateur radio. Major/career interest in computer/information sciences; electronics or engineering, electrical/electronic.
Application requirements: Transcript. FAFSA.
Additional information: Must be amateur radio operator with active Technician Class license or higher. High school seniors are eligible to apply. Offered as either $1,000 award for a 4-year college student or two awards of $500 each for 2-year college students. Related majors also eligible. Regional preference given to applicants in the Maine or New England Division, including Maine, New Hampshire, Vermont, Rhode Island, Massachusetts or Connecticut. Visit Website for application.

Amount of award:	$500-$1,000
Application deadline:	February 1

Contact:
American Radio Relay League (ARRL) Foundation, Inc.
225 Main Street
Newington, CT 06111
Phone: 860-594-0397
Fax: 860-594-0259
Web: www.arrlf.org

The ARRL Earl I. Anderson Scholarship

Type of award: Scholarship.
Intended use: For undergraduate or graduate study at accredited postsecondary institution in United States.
Eligibility: Applicant must be residing in Michigan, Indiana, Illinois or Florida.
Basis for selection: Competition/talent/interest in amateur radio. Major/career interest in engineering, electrical/electronic.
Application requirements: Transcript. FAFSA.
Additional information: Must be amateur radio operator holding any class license. Must be ARRL member. Major may be in other related technical field. Must be attending classes in Illinois, Indiana, Michigan, or Florida. High school seniors eligible to apply. Application may be obtained on Website, and will only be accepted via email.

Amount of award:	$1,250
Number of awards:	3
Application deadline:	February 1

Contact:
The ARRL Foundation, Inc. Scholarship Program
225 Main Street
Newington, CT 06111
Phone: 860-594-0397
Fax: 860-594-0259
Web: www.arrlf.org

ARRL Foundation General Fund Scholarship

Type of award: Scholarship.
Intended use: For undergraduate or graduate study at postsecondary institution.
Basis for selection: Competition/talent/interest in amateur radio.
Application requirements: Transcript. FAFSA.
Additional information: Must hold active Amateur Radio license. Number of awards varies. High school seniors eligible to apply. Application may be obtained on Website, and will only be accepted via email.

Amount of award:	$2,000
Application deadline:	February 1

Contact:
The ARRL Foundation, Inc. Scholarship Program
225 Main Street
Newington, CT 06111
Phone: 860-594-0397
Fax: 860-594-0259
Web: www.arrlf.org

ARRL Foundation PHD Scholarship

Type of award: Scholarship.
Intended use: For undergraduate, graduate or non-degree study at postsecondary institution in United States.
Eligibility: Applicant must be residing in Iowa, Nebraska, Kansas or Missouri.
Basis for selection: Competition/talent/interest in amateur radio. Major/career interest in journalism; computer/information sciences or engineering, electrical/electronic.
Application requirements: Transcript. FAFSA.
Additional information: Must hold active Amateur Radio license. May be child of deceased radio amateur. High school seniors eligible to apply. Application may be obtained on Website, and will only be accepted via email.

Amount of award:	$1,000
Number of awards:	1
Application deadline:	February 1
Total amount awarded:	$1,000

Contact:
The ARRL Foundation, Inc. Scholarship Program
225 Main Street
Newington, CT 06111
Phone: 860-594-0397
Fax: 860-594-0259
Web: www.arrlf.org

The ARRL Northwestern Division Scholarship Fund

Type of award: Scholarship.
Intended use: For undergraduate study at postsecondary institution.
Eligibility: Applicant must be residing in Oregon, Montana, Alaska, Idaho or Washington.
Basis for selection: Competition/talent/interest in amateur radio. Major/career interest in engineering; medicine; science, general or business.
Application requirements: Transcript. FAFSA.
Additional information: Must be amateur radio operator with active General Class Amateur Radio License or higher and reside in the ARRL Northwestern Division. Preference given to applicants with a 3.0 GPA or higher for the academic year immediately prior to application. Visit Website for application.

Amount of award:	$1,000
Number of awards:	1
Application deadline:	February 1

Contact:
American Radio Relay League (ARRL) Foundation, Inc.
225 Main Street
Newington, CT 06111
Phone: 860-594-0397
Fax: 860-594-0259
Web: www.arrlf.org

The ARRL Scholarship to Honor Barry Goldwater, K7UGA

Type of award: Scholarship.
Intended use: For undergraduate or graduate study at accredited 4-year or graduate institution in United States.
Basis for selection: Competition/talent/interest in amateur radio.
Application requirements: Transcript. FAFSA.
Additional information: Must hold active Amateur Radio license in any class. High school seniors are eligible to apply. Application may be obtained on Website, and will only be accepted via email.

Amount of award:	$5,000
Number of awards:	1
Application deadline:	February 1
Total amount awarded:	$5,000

Contact:
The ARRL Foundation, Inc. Scholarship Program
225 Main Street
Newington, CT 06111
Phone: 860-594-0397
Fax: 860-594-0259
Web: www.arrlf.org

The Betty Weatherford, KQ6RE, Memorial Scholarship

Type of award: Scholarship.
Intended use: For undergraduate study at postsecondary institution.
Basis for selection: Competition/talent/interest in amateur radio. Major/career interest in engineering, electrical/electronic.
Application requirements: Transcript. FAFSA.
Additional information: Must be amateur radio operator with any class of active Amateur Radio license. Applicants studying communications engineering also eligible. Visit Website for application.

Amount of award:	$1,000
Number of awards:	1
Application deadline:	February 1

Contact:
American Radio Relay League (ARRL) Foundation, Inc.
225 Main Street
Newington, CT 06111
Phone: 860-594-0397
Fax: 860-594-0259
Web: www.arrlf.org

The Bill, W2ONV, and Ann Salerno Memorial Scholarship

Type of award: Scholarship.
Intended use: For undergraduate study at accredited 4-year institution.
Basis for selection: Competition/talent/interest in amateur radio. Applicant must demonstrate financial need and high academic achievement.
Application requirements: Transcript. FAFSA.
Additional information: Minimum 3.7 GPA. Must be amateur radio operator with active Amateur Radio license. High school seniors are eligible to apply. Aggregate income of family household must be no greater than $100,000 per year. Visit Website for application.

Amount of award:	$1,000
Number of awards:	2
Application deadline:	February 1

Contact:
American Radio Relay League (ARRL) Foundation, Inc.
225 Main Street
Newington, CT 06111
Phone: 860-594-0397
Fax: 860-594-0259
Web: www.arrlf.org

The Byron Blanchard, N1EKV Memorial Scholarship Fund

Type of award: Scholarship.
Intended use: For undergraduate study at postsecondary institution.
Eligibility: Applicant must be residing in Vermont, Connecticut, New Hampshire, Maine, Massachusetts or Rhode Island.
Basis for selection: Competition/talent/interest in amateur radio.
Application requirements: Transcript. FAFSA.
Additional information: Must be amateur radio operator with any class of active Amateur Radio license and reside in ARRL New England Division. Visit Website for application.

Amount of award:	$500
Number of awards:	1
Application deadline:	February 1

Contact:
American Radio Relay League (ARRL) Foundation, Inc.
225 Main Street
Newington, CT 06111
Phone: 860-594-0397
Fax: 860-594-0259
Web: www.arrlf.org

The Carole J. Streeter, KB9JBR, Scholarship

Type of award: Scholarship.
Intended use: For undergraduate study at accredited postsecondary institution.
Eligibility: Applicant must be U.S. citizen.
Basis for selection: Competition/talent/interest in amateur radio. Major/career interest in medicine.
Application requirements: Transcript. FAFSA.
Additional information: Must be amateur radio operator with any class of active Amateur Radio license with preference for basic Morse code capability. High school seniors are eligible to apply. Applicants should study medicine or related majors. Visit Website for application.

Amount of award:	$750
Number of awards:	1
Application deadline:	February 1

Contact:
American Radio Relay League (ARRL) Foundation, Inc.
225 Main Street
Newington, CT 06111
Phone: 860-594-0397
Fax: 860-594-0259
Web: www.arrlf.org

The Central Arizona DX Association Scholarship

Type of award: Scholarship.
Intended use: For undergraduate study at postsecondary institution.
Eligibility: Applicant must be residing in Arizona.
Basis for selection: Competition/talent/interest in amateur radio. Applicant must demonstrate high academic achievement.
Application requirements: Transcript. FAFSA.
Additional information: Minimum 3.2 GPA. Must be amateur radio operator with active Technician Class or higher license. High school seniors are eligible to apply. Graduating high school students will be considered before current college students. Visit Website for application.

Amount of award:	$1,000
Number of awards:	1
Application deadline:	February 1

Contact:
American Radio Relay League (ARRL) Foundation, Inc.
225 Main Street
Newington, CT 06111
Phone: 860-594-0397
Fax: 860-594-0259
Web: www.arrlf.org

The Challenge Met Scholarship

Type of award: Scholarship.
Intended use: For undergraduate study at accredited vocational, 2-year or 4-year institution.
Eligibility: Applicant must be learning disabled.
Basis for selection: Competition/talent/interest in amateur radio.
Application requirements: Transcript, proof of eligibility. Documentation of learning disability by physician or school. FAFSA.
Additional information: Must be amateur radio operator holding any class license. Preference given to those with documented learning disabilities that put forth effort regardless of resulting grades. High school seniors are eligible to apply. Application may be obtained on Website, and will only be accepted via email. Number of awards varies.

Amount of award:	$500
Application deadline:	February 1

Contact:
The ARRL Foundation, Inc. Scholarship Program
225 Main Street
Newington, CT 06111
Phone: 860-594-0347
Fax: 860-594-0259
Web: www.arrlf.org

The Charles Clarke Cordle Memorial Scholarship

Type of award: Scholarship.
Intended use: For undergraduate or graduate study at postsecondary institution in United States. Designated institutions: Institutions in Alabama or Georgia.
Eligibility: Applicant must be residing in Alabama or Georgia.
Basis for selection: Competition/talent/interest in amateur radio. Major/career interest in electronics or communications. Applicant must demonstrate high academic achievement.
Application requirements: Transcript. FAFSA.
Additional information: Minimum 2.5 GPA. Must hold active Amateur Radio license. Preference to students of majors listed or other related fields. High school seniors are eligible to apply. Application may be obtained from Website, and will only be accepted via email.

Amount of award:	$1,000
Number of awards:	1
Application deadline:	February 1
Total amount awarded:	$1,000

Contact:
The ARRL Foundation, Inc. Scholarship Program
225 Main Street
Newington, CT 06111
Phone: 860-594-0397
Fax: 860-594-0259
Web: www.arrlf.org

The Charles N. Fisher Memorial Scholarship

Type of award: Scholarship.
Intended use: For undergraduate or graduate study at accredited postsecondary institution in United States.
Eligibility: Applicant must be residing in California or Arizona.
Basis for selection: Competition/talent/interest in amateur radio. Major/career interest in communications or electronics.
Application requirements: Transcript. FAFSA.
Additional information: Must hold active Amateur Radio license. Major may be in other fields related to those listed. California candidates must reside in Los Angeles, Orange County, San Diego, or Santa Barbara. High school seniors eligible to apply. Application may be obtained on Website, and will only be accepted via email.

Amount of award:	$1,000
Number of awards:	1
Application deadline:	February 1
Total amount awarded:	$1,000

Contact:
The ARRL Foundation, Inc. Scholarship Program
225 Main Street
Newington, CT 06111
Phone: 860-594-0397
Fax: 860-594-0259
Web: www.arrlf.org

The Chicago FM Club Scholarship

Type of award: Scholarship.
Intended use: For undergraduate study at accredited vocational, 2-year or 4-year institution in United States.
Eligibility: Applicant must be U.S. citizen residing in Wisconsin, Indiana or Illinois.
Basis for selection: Competition/talent/interest in amateur radio.
Application requirements: Transcript. FAFSA.
Additional information: Student also eligible if within three months of becoming U.S. citizen. Must be amateur radio operator with Technician Class license or higher. Number of awards varies. High school seniors eligible to apply. Application may be obtained on Website, and will only be accepted via email.

Amount of award:	$500
Application deadline:	February 1

Contact:
The ARRL Foundation, Inc. Scholarship Program
225 Main Street
Newington, CT 06111
Phone: 860-594-0397
Fax: 860-594-0259
Web: www.arrlf.org

The David Knaus Memorial Scholarship

Type of award: Scholarship.
Intended use: For undergraduate study at 2-year or 4-year institution.
Basis for selection: Competition/talent/interest in amateur radio.
Application requirements: Transcript. FAFSA.
Additional information: Must be amateur radio operator with active Amateur Radio license, any class. Preference to resident of Wisconsin. If no applicant identified, preference will be given to applicant from the ARRL Central Division (Illinois, Indiana, Wisconsin). Visit Website for application.

Amount of award:	$1,500
Number of awards:	1
Application deadline:	February 1

Contact:
American Radio Relay League (ARRL) Foundation, Inc.
225 Main Street
Newington, CT 06111
Phone: 860-594-0397
Fax: 860-594-0259
Web: www.arrlf.org

The Dayton Amateur Radio Association Scholarships

Type of award: Scholarship.
Intended use: For undergraduate study at accredited 4-year institution in United States.
Basis for selection: Competition/talent/interest in amateur radio.
Application requirements: Transcript. FAFSA.
Additional information: Must be amateur radio operator holding any class license. High school seniors are eligible to apply. Application may be obtained on Website, and will only be accepted via email.

Amount of award:	$1,000
Number of awards:	4
Application deadline:	February 1

Contact:
The ARRL Foundation, Inc. Scholarship Program
225 Main Street
Newington, CT 06111
Phone: 860-594-0347
Fax: 860-594-0259
Web: www.arrlf.org

The Don Riebhoff Memorial Scholarship

Type of award: Scholarship.
Intended use: For undergraduate or graduate study at accredited 2-year, 4-year or graduate institution in United States.
Basis for selection: Competition/talent/interest in amateur radio. Major/career interest in international relations. Applicant must demonstrate financial need and high academic achievement.
Application requirements: Transcript. FAFSA.
Additional information: Must be amateur radio operator with Active Technician class license or higher. Preference given to ARRL members and candidates seeking baccalaureate degree or higher. High school seniors are eligible to apply. Application may be obtained on Website, and will only be accepted via email.

Amount of award: $1,000
Number of awards: 1
Application deadline: February 1

Contact:
The ARRL Foundation, Inc. Scholarship Program
225 Main Street
Newington, CT 06111
Phone: 860-594-0397
Fax: 860-594-0259
Web: www.arrlf.org

The Dr. James L. Lawson Memorial Scholarship

Type of award: Scholarship.
Intended use: For undergraduate or graduate study at 4-year or graduate institution in United States. Designated institutions: Any institution in New England or New York State.
Eligibility: Applicant must be residing in Vermont, Connecticut, New York, New Hampshire, Maine, Massachusetts or Rhode Island.
Basis for selection: Competition/talent/interest in amateur radio. Major/career interest in communications or electronics.
Application requirements: Transcript. FAFSA.
Additional information: Must be amateur radio operator holding a General Class license or higher. Major may be in other fields related to those listed. High school seniors eligible to apply. Application may be obtained on Website, and will only be accepted via email.

Amount of award: $500
Number of awards: 1
Application deadline: February 1
Total amount awarded: $500

Contact:
The ARRL Foundation, Inc. Scholarship Program
225 Main Street
Newington, CT 06111
Phone: 860-594-0397
Fax: 860-594-0259
Web: www.arrlf.org

The Edmond A. Metzger Scholarship

Type of award: Scholarship.
Intended use: For undergraduate, graduate or non-degree study at 4-year or graduate institution in United States. Designated institutions: Schools in ARRL Central Division (Illinois, Indiana, Wisconsin).
Eligibility: Applicant must be residing in Wisconsin, Indiana or Illinois.
Basis for selection: Competition/talent/interest in amateur radio. Major/career interest in engineering, electrical/electronic.
Application requirements: Transcript. FAFSA.
Additional information: Must be amateur radio operator with active license in any class. Must be American Radio Relay League member. High school seniors eligible to apply. Application may be obtained on Website, and will only be accepted via email.

Amount of award: $500
Number of awards: 1
Application deadline: February 1
Total amount awarded: $500

Contact:
The ARRL Foundation, Inc. Scholarship Program
225 Main Street
Newington, CT 06111
Phone: 860-594-0397
Fax: 860-594-0259
Web: www.arrlf.org

The Eugene "Gene" Sallee, W4YFR, Memorial Scholarship

Type of award: Scholarship.
Intended use: For undergraduate or graduate study at accredited postsecondary institution in United States.
Eligibility: Applicant must be residing in Georgia.
Basis for selection: Competition/talent/interest in amateur radio. Major/career interest in electronics or communications. Applicant must demonstrate financial need and high academic achievement.
Application requirements: Transcript. FAFSA.
Additional information: Must be amateur radio operator with active Technician Plus or higher class license. Preference given to students with a minimum 3.0 GPA. Major may be in a related field. High school seniors are eligible to apply. Application may be obtained on Website, and will only be accepted via email.

Amount of award: $500
Number of awards: 1
Application deadline: February 1
Total amount awarded: $500

Contact:
The ARRL Foundation, Inc. Scholarship Program
225 Main Street
Newington, CT 06111
Phone: 860-594-0397
Fax: 860-594-0259
Web: www.arrlf.org

The Francis Walton Memorial Scholarship

Type of award: Scholarship.
Intended use: For undergraduate or graduate study at 4-year or graduate institution.
Eligibility: Applicant must be residing in Wisconsin, Indiana or Illinois.
Basis for selection: Competition/talent/interest in amateur radio. Major/career interest in agriculture; electronics; history or communications. Applicant must demonstrate financial need and high academic achievement.
Application requirements: Transcript. FAFSA.
Additional information: Must be amateur radio operator with any active Amateur Radio license class, with preference to applicants that provide documentation of CW proficiency of more than 5 wpm. High school seniors are eligible to apply. Other majors also eligible. Applicant should demonstrate interest in promoting Amateur Radio. Visit Website for application.

Amount of award: $500
Number of awards: 1
Application deadline: February 1

Contact:
American Radio Relay League (ARRL) Foundation, Inc.
225 Main Street
Newington, CT 06111
Phone: 860-594-0397
Fax: 860-594-0259
Web: www.arrlf.org

The Fred R. McDaniel Memorial Scholarship

Type of award: Scholarship.
Intended use: For undergraduate or graduate study at 4-year or graduate institution in United States. Designated institutions: Any colleges or universities in FCC fifth call district (Texas, Oklahoma, Arkansas, Louisiana, Mississippi, New Mexico).
Eligibility: Applicant must be residing in Oklahoma, Texas, Mississippi, Arkansas, New Mexico or Louisiana.
Basis for selection: Competition/talent/interest in amateur radio. Major/career interest in electronics or communications. Applicant must demonstrate high academic achievement.
Application requirements: Transcript. FAFSA.
Additional information: Preference for students with minimum 3.0 GPA. Must be amateur radio operator holding General Class license or higher. Major may be in other fields related to those listed. High school students eligible to apply. Application may be obtained from Website, and will only be accepted via email.

Amount of award:	$500
Number of awards:	1
Application deadline:	February 1
Total amount awarded:	$500

Contact:
The ARRL Foundation, Inc. Scholarship Program
225 Main Street
Newington, CT 06111
Phone: 860-594-0397
Fax: 860-594-0259
Web: www.arrlf.org

The Gary Wagner, K3OMI, Scholarship

Type of award: Scholarship.
Intended use: For undergraduate study at accredited 4-year institution.
Eligibility: Applicant must be U.S. citizen residing in Virginia, Tennessee, West Virginia, Maryland or North Carolina.
Basis for selection: Competition/talent/interest in amateur radio. Major/career interest in engineering. Applicant must demonstrate financial need.
Application requirements: Transcript. FAFSA.
Additional information: Must be amateur radio operator with an active Novice Class Amateur Radio License or higher. High school seniors are eligible to apply. Visit Website for application.

Amount of award:	$1,000
Number of awards:	1
Application deadline:	February 1

Contact:
American Radio Relay League (ARRL) Foundation, Inc.
225 Main Street
Newington, CT 06111
Phone: 860-594-0397
Fax: 860-594-0259
Web: www.arrlf.org

The Gwinnett Amateur Radio Society Scholarship

Type of award: Scholarship.
Intended use: For undergraduate study at 4-year institution.
Eligibility: Applicant must be residing in Georgia.
Basis for selection: Competition/talent/interest in amateur radio.
Application requirements: Transcript. FAFSA.
Additional information: Must be amateur radio operator with active Amateur Radio license, any class. Applicants must be residents of Gwinnett County, GA or the state of GA. High school seniors are eligible to apply. Visit Website for application.

Amount of award:	$500
Number of awards:	1
Application deadline:	February 1

Contact:
American Radio Relay League (ARRL) Foundation, Inc.
225 Main Street
Newington, CT 06111
Phone: 860-594-0397
Fax: 860-594-0259
Web: www.arrlf.org

The Henry Broughton, K2AE, Memorial Scholarship

Type of award: Scholarship.
Intended use: For undergraduate or graduate study at accredited 4-year or graduate institution in United States.
Eligibility: Applicant must be residing in New York.
Basis for selection: Competition/talent/interest in amateur radio. Major/career interest in engineering or science, general.
Application requirements: Transcript. FAFSA.
Additional information: Must be amateur radio operator with General Class license. Major may be in other fields similar to those listed. High school seniors are eligible to apply. Applicants must live within 70 miles of Schenectady, New York. May offer additional awards if funding permits. Application may be obtained on Website, and will only be accepted via email.

Amount of award:	$1,000
Number of awards:	1
Application deadline:	February 1

Contact:
The ARRL Foundation, Inc. Scholarship Program
225 Main Street
Newington, CT 06111
Phone: 860-594-0397
Fax: 860-594-0259
Web: www.arrlf.org

The Indianapolis Amateur Radio Association Fund

Type of award: Scholarship.
Intended use: For undergraduate study at postsecondary institution.
Eligibility: Applicant must be residing in Wisconsin, Indiana or Illinois.
Basis for selection: Competition/talent/interest in amateur radio. Major/career interest in engineering, electrical/electronic or computer/information sciences.
Application requirements: Transcript. FAFSA.

Additional information: Must be amateur radio operator with any class of active Amateur Radio license and reside in ARRL Central Division. Visit Website for application.

Amount of award: $1,000
Number of awards: 1
Application deadline: February 1

Contact:
American Radio Relay League (ARRL) Foundation, Inc.
225 Main Street
Newington, CT 06111
Phone: 860-594-0397
Fax: 860-594-0259
Web: www.arrlf.org

IRARC Memorial, Joseph P. Rubino, WA4MMD, Scholarship

Type of award: Scholarship.
Intended use: For undergraduate or post-bachelor's certificate study at accredited vocational or 4-year institution.
Eligibility: Applicant must be residing in Florida.
Basis for selection: Competition/talent/interest in amateur radio. Major/career interest in electronics. Applicant must demonstrate financial need and high academic achievement.
Application requirements: Transcript. FAFSA.
Additional information: Minimum 2.5 GPA. Must be amateur radio operator with any active Amateur Radio license class. High school seniors are eligible to apply. Number of awards varies. Visit Website for application. Preference given to residents of Brevard County, FL, or any Florida resident. Students enrolled in an electronic technician certification program also eligible.

Amount of award: $750
Application deadline: February 1

Contact:
American Radio Relay League (ARRL) Foundation, Inc.
225 Main Street
Newington, CT 06111
Phone: 860-594-0397
Fax: 860-594-0259
Web: www.arrlf.org

The Irving W. Cook WA0CGS Scholarship

Type of award: Scholarship.
Intended use: For undergraduate or graduate study at 4-year or graduate institution.
Eligibility: Applicant must be residing in Kansas.
Basis for selection: Competition/talent/interest in amateur radio. Major/career interest in communications or electronics.
Application requirements: Transcript. FAFSA.
Additional information: Must hold active Amateur Radio license. Major may be in other fields related to those listed. High school seniors eligible to apply. Application may be obtained on Website, and will only be accepted via email.

Amount of award: $1,000
Number of awards: 1
Application deadline: February 1
Total amount awarded: $1,000

Contact:
The ARRL Foundation, Inc. Scholarship Program
225 Main Street
Newington, CT 06111
Phone: 860-594-0397
Fax: 860-594-0259
Web: www.arrlf.org

The Jackson County ARA Scholarship

Type of award: Scholarship.
Intended use: For undergraduate or graduate study at postsecondary institution.
Basis for selection: Competition/talent/interest in amateur radio.
Application requirements: Transcript. FAFSA.
Additional information: Must be amateur radio operator with active Amateur Radio license, any class. Preference given to applicants from Mississippi. If no applicant is identified, preference will be given to an applicant from the ARRL Delta Division (Arkansas, Louisiana, Mississippi, and Tennessee). Visit Website for application.

Amount of award: $500
Number of awards: 1
Application deadline: February 1

Contact:
American Radio Relay League (ARRL) Foundation, Inc.
225 Main Street
Newington, CT 06111
Phone: 860-594-0397
Fax: 860-594-0259
Web: www.arrlf.org

The Jake McClain Driver KC5WXA Scholarship Fund

Type of award: Scholarship.
Intended use: For undergraduate study at postsecondary institution.
Eligibility: Applicant must be residing in Tennessee, Mississippi, Arkansas or Louisiana.
Basis for selection: Competition/talent/interest in amateur radio. Major/career interest in electronics; computer/information sciences or journalism.
Application requirements: Transcript. FAFSA.
Additional information: Must be amateur radio operator with active Technician Class Amateur Radio License or higher and can provide at least one QLSL card received within the past twelve months. Must reside in the ARRL Delta Division. Visit Website for application.

Amount of award: $1,000
Number of awards: 1
Application deadline: February 1

Contact:
American Radio Relay League (ARRL) Foundation, Inc.
225 Main Street
Newington, CT 06111
Phone: 860-594-0397
Fax: 860-594-0259
Web: www.arrlf.org

The K2TEO Martin J. Green, Sr. Memorial Scholarship

Type of award: Scholarship.
Intended use: For undergraduate or graduate study at postsecondary institution.
Basis for selection: Competition/talent/interest in amateur radio.
Application requirements: Transcript. FAFSA.
Additional information: Must be amateur radio operator with General Class license or higher. Preference given to student from family of ham operators. High school seniors are eligible

Scholarships

to apply. Application may be obtained on Website, and will only be accepted via email.

Amount of award: $1,000
Number of awards: 1
Application deadline: February 1
Total amount awarded: $1,000

Contact:
The ARRL Foundation, Inc. Scholarship Program
225 Main Street
Newington, CT 06111
Phone: 860-594-0397
Fax: 860-594-0259
Web: www.arrlf.org

The L. Phil and Alice J. Wicker Scholarship

Type of award: Scholarship.
Intended use: For undergraduate, graduate or non-degree study at 4-year or graduate institution in United States. Designated institutions: Schools in ARRL Roanoke Division (NC, SC, VA, WV).
Eligibility: Applicant must be residing in Virginia, West Virginia, North Carolina or South Carolina.
Basis for selection: Competition/talent/interest in amateur radio. Major/career interest in communications or electronics.
Application requirements: Transcript. FAFSA.
Additional information: Must be amateur radio operator holding a General Class license or higher. Major may be in other fields related to those listed. High school seniors eligible to apply. Application may be obtained on Website, and will only be accepted via email.

Amount of award: $500
Number of awards: 1
Application deadline: February 1

Contact:
The ARRL Foundation, Inc. Scholarship Program
225 Main Street
Newington, CT 06111
Phone: 860-594-0397
Fax: 860-594-0259
Web: www.arrlf.org

The L.B. Cebik, W4RNL, and Jean Cebik, N4TZP, Memorial Scholarship

Type of award: Scholarship.
Intended use: For undergraduate study at 4-year institution in United States.
Basis for selection: Competition/talent/interest in amateur radio.
Application requirements: Transcript. FAFSA.
Additional information: Must be amateur radio operator holding Technician Class license or higher. High school seniors are eligible to apply. Application may be obtained on Website, and will only be accepted via email.

Amount of award: $1,000
Number of awards: 1
Application deadline: February 1

Contact:
The ARRL Foundation, Inc. Scholarship Program
225 Main Street
Newington, CT 06111
Phone: 860-594-0397
Fax: 860-594-0259
Web: www.arrlf.org

The Louisiana Memorial Scholarship

Type of award: Scholarship.
Intended use: For undergraduate study at 4-year or graduate institution in United States.
Basis for selection: Competition/talent/interest in amateur radio. Applicant must demonstrate high academic achievement.
Application requirements: Transcript. FAFSA.
Additional information: Must be resident of or student in Louisiana. Minimum 3.0 GPA. Must be amateur radio operator holding Technician Class license or higher. High school seniors eligible to apply. Application may be obtained on Website, and will only be accepted via email.

Amount of award: $750
Number of awards: 1
Application deadline: February 1

Contact:
The ARRL Foundation, Inc. Scholarship Program
225 Main Street
Newington, CT 06111
Phone: 860-594-0397
Fax: 860-594-0259
Web: www.arrlf.org

The Magnolia DX Association Scholarship

Type of award: Scholarship.
Intended use: For undergraduate study at vocational, 2-year or 4-year institution. Designated institutions: Mississippi institutions.
Eligibility: Applicant must be high school senior. Applicant must be residing in Mississippi.
Basis for selection: Competition/talent/interest in amateur radio. Major/career interest in electronics; communications; computer/information sciences or engineering.
Application requirements: Transcript. FAFSA.
Additional information: Must be amateur radio operator with active Technician Class license or higher. Preference given to graduating high school seniors in Mississippi or Delta Division (Arkansas, Louisiana, Mississippi, and Tennessee) for use at a Mississippi institution. Visit Website for application.

Amount of award: $500
Number of awards: 1
Application deadline: February 1

Contact:
American Radio Relay League (ARRL) Foundation, Inc.
225 Main Street
Newington, CT 06111
Phone: 860-594-0397
Fax: 860-594-0259
Web: www.arrlf.org

The Mary Lou Brown Scholarship

Type of award: Scholarship.
Intended use: For undergraduate or graduate study at 4-year institution in United States.
Eligibility: Applicant must be residing in Oregon, Montana, Alaska, Idaho or Washington.
Basis for selection: Competition/talent/interest in amateur radio. Applicant must demonstrate high academic achievement.
Application requirements: Transcript. FAFSA.
Additional information: Minimum 3.0 GPA and demonstrated interest in promoting Amateur Radio Service. Must be amateur radio operator with General Class license. Number of awards

varies based on funding. High school seniors eligible to apply. Application may be obtained on Website, and will only be accepted via email.

Amount of award: $2,500
Application deadline: February 1

Contact:
The ARRL Foundation, Inc. Scholarship Program
225 Main Street
Newington, CT 06111
Phone: 860-594-0397
Fax: 860-594-0259
Web: www.arrlf.org

The Mississippi Scholarship

Type of award: Scholarship.
Intended use: For undergraduate or graduate study at 4-year or graduate institution in United States. Designated institutions: Schools in Mississippi.
Eligibility: Applicant must be no older than 30. Applicant must be residing in Mississippi.
Basis for selection: Competition/talent/interest in amateur radio. Major/career interest in communications or electronics.
Application requirements: Transcript. FAFSA.
Additional information: Must hold active Amateur Radio license. Major may be in other fields related to those listed. High school seniors eligible to apply. Application may be obtained on Website, and will only be accepted via email.

Amount of award: $500
Number of awards: 1
Application deadline: February 1
Total amount awarded: $500

Contact:
The ARRL Foundation, Inc. Scholarship Program
225 Main Street
Newington, CT 06111
Phone: 860-594-0397
Fax: 860-594-0259
Web: www.arrlf.org

The New England FEMARA Scholarship

Type of award: Scholarship.
Intended use: For undergraduate, graduate or non-degree study at postsecondary institution.
Eligibility: Applicant must be residing in Vermont, Connecticut, New Hampshire, Maine, Massachusetts or Rhode Island.
Basis for selection: Competition/talent/interest in amateur radio.
Application requirements: Transcript. FAFSA.
Additional information: Must be amateur radio operator holding Technical Class license or higher. Number of awards varies based on funding. High school seniors eligible to apply. Application may be obtained on Website, and will only be accepted via email.

Amount of award: $1,000
Application deadline: February 1

Contact:
The ARRL Foundation, Inc. Scholarship Program
225 Main Street
Newington, CT 06111
Phone: 860-594-0397
Fax: 860-594-0259
Web: www.arrlf.org

The Norman E. Strohmeier, W2VRS, Memorial Scholarship

Type of award: Scholarship.
Intended use: For undergraduate study at postsecondary institution.
Eligibility: Applicant must be residing in New York.
Basis for selection: Competition/talent/interest in amateur radio. Applicant must demonstrate high academic achievement.
Application requirements: Transcript. FAFSA.
Additional information: Minimum 3.2 GPA. Must be amateur radio operator with active Technician Class Amateur Radio License or higher. Preference given to Western New York resident. High school seniors are eligible to apply. Preference to high school senior. Applicant must provide documentation of Amateur Radio activities and achievements and any honor from community service. Visit Website for application.

Amount of award: $500
Number of awards: 1
Application deadline: February 1

Contact:
American Radio Relay League (ARRL) Foundation, Inc.
225 Main Street
Newington, CT 06111
Phone: 860-594-0397
Fax: 860-594-0259
Web: www.arrlf.org

The North Fulton Amateur Radio League Scholarship Fund

Type of award: Scholarship.
Intended use: For undergraduate study at postsecondary institution.
Eligibility: Applicant must be residing in Puerto Rico, Virgin Islands, Alabama, Georgia or Florida.
Basis for selection: Competition/talent/interest in amateur radio. Major/career interest in engineering or computer/information sciences.
Application requirements: Transcript. FAFSA.
Additional information: Must be a member of ARRL. If no qualified applicant in Georgia, preference will be awarded to applicants from the ARRL Southeastern Division (Alabama, Florida, Georgia, Puerto Rico, and the U.S. Virgin Islands). Award given to applicants regardless of field of study if there are no other qualified applicants.

Amount of award: $900
Number of awards: 1
Application deadline: February 1

Contact:
American Radio Relay League (ARRL) Foundation, Inc.
225 Main Street
Newington, CT 06111
Phone: 860-594-0397
Fax: 860-594-0259
Web: www.arrlf.org

The Northern California DX Foundation Scholarship

Type of award: Scholarship.
Intended use: For undergraduate study at accredited vocational, 2-year or 4-year institution in United States.
Basis for selection: Competition/talent/interest in amateur radio.
Application requirements: Transcript. FAFSA.

Additional information: Must be amateur radio operator holding Technician Class license or higher. Applicant must demonstrate interest and activity in DXing. High school seniors eligible to apply. Application may be obtained on Website, and will only be accepted via email.

Amount of award:	$1,500
Number of awards:	2
Application deadline:	February 1
Total amount awarded:	$3,000

Contact:
The ARRL Foundation, Inc. Scholarship Program
225 Main Street
Newington, CT 06111
Phone: 860-594-0397
Fax: 860-594-0259
Web: www.arrlf.org

The Orlando HamCation Scholarship

Type of award: Scholarship.
Intended use: For undergraduate study at accredited 4-year institution.
Eligibility: Applicant must be U.S. citizen residing in Florida.
Basis for selection: Competition/talent/interest in amateur radio. Major/career interest in radio/television/film or communications.
Application requirements: Transcript. FAFSA.
Additional information: Must be amateur radio operator with any class of active Amateur Radio license. High school seniors are eligible to apply. Preference given to residents of Central Florida (Orange, Seminole, Osceola, Lake, Volusia, Brevard and Polk counties); if no suitable applicant, resident of the State of Florida. Applicant should study a technical field that supports the radio arts. Visit Website for application.

Amount of award:	$1,000
Number of awards:	1
Application deadline:	February 1

Contact:
American Radio Relay League (ARRL) Foundation, Inc.
225 Main Street
Newington, CT 06111
Phone: 860-594-0397
Fax: 860-594-0259
Web: www.arrlf.org

The Outdoor Hams Scholarship

Type of award: Scholarship.
Intended use: For undergraduate study at accredited 2-year or 4-year institution.
Eligibility: Applicant must be residing in North Carolina.
Basis for selection: Competition/talent/interest in amateur radio.
Application requirements: Transcript. FAFSA.
Additional information: One $1,000 award given for a 4-year college or two $500 awards given for a 2-year college. Must be in technical field of study. Must be amateur radio operator with any class of active Amateur Radio license. Preference given to amateur radio operators that incorporate amateur radio into outdoor activities. Visit Website for application.

Amount of award:	$500-$1,000
Application deadline:	February 1

Contact:
American Radio Relay League (ARRL) Foundation, Inc.
225 Main Street
Newington, CT 06111
Phone: 860-594-0397
Fax: 860-594-0259
Web: www.arrlf.org

The Paul and Helen L. Grauer Scholarship

Type of award: Scholarship.
Intended use: For undergraduate or graduate study at 4-year or graduate institution in United States. Designated institutions: Schools in Midwest Division (Iowa, Kansas, Missouri, Nebraska).
Eligibility: Applicant must be residing in Iowa, Nebraska, Kansas or Missouri.
Basis for selection: Competition/talent/interest in amateur radio. Major/career interest in communications or electronics.
Application requirements: Transcript. FAFSA.
Additional information: Must hold active Amateur Radio license in any class. Major may be in other fields related to those listed. High school seniors are eligible to apply. Application may be obtained on Website, and will only be accepted via email.

Amount of award:	$1,000
Number of awards:	1
Application deadline:	February 1
Total amount awarded:	$1,000

Contact:
The ARRL Foundation, Inc. Scholarship Program
225 Main Street
Newington, CT 06111
Phone: 860-594-0397
Fax: 860-594-0259
Web: www.arrlf.org

The Peoria Area Amateur Radio Club Scholarship

Type of award: Scholarship.
Intended use: For undergraduate study at accredited 2-year or 4-year institution.
Eligibility: Applicant must be residing in Illinois.
Basis for selection: Competition/talent/interest in amateur radio.
Application requirements: Transcript. FAFSA.
Additional information: Must be amateur radio operator with active Technician Class license or higher. High school seniors are eligible to apply. Preference given to a resident of Central Illinois in one of the following counties: Peoria, Tazewell, Woodford, Knox, McLean, Fulton, Logan, Marshall or Stark. Visit Website for application.

Amount of award:	$500
Number of awards:	1
Application deadline:	February 1

Contact:
American Radio Relay League (ARRL) Foundation, Inc.
225 Main Street
Newington, CT 06111
Phone: 860-594-0397
Fax: 860-594-0259
Web: www.arrlf.org

The Ray, NØRP, & Katie, WØKTE, Pautz Scholarship

Type of award: Scholarship.
Intended use: For undergraduate study at accredited 4-year institution.
Eligibility: Applicant must be residing in Iowa, Nebraska, Kansas or Missouri.
Basis for selection: Competition/talent/interest in amateur radio. Major/career interest in electronics or computer/information sciences. Applicant must demonstrate financial need.
Application requirements: Transcript. FAFSA.
Additional information: Must be an ARRL member, and an amateur radio operator with active General Class or higher license. High school seniors are eligible to apply. Applicant should be majoring in electronics, computer science or related field. Visit Website for application.

Amount of award:	$500-$1,000
Number of awards:	1
Application deadline:	February 1

Contact:
American Radio Relay League (ARRL) Foundation, Inc.
225 Main Street
Newington, CT 06111
Phone: 860-594-0397
Fax: 860-594-0259
Web: www.arrlf.org

The Richard W. Bendicksen, N7ZL, Memorial Scholarship

Type of award: Scholarship.
Intended use: For undergraduate study at 4-year institution in United States.
Basis for selection: Competition/talent/interest in amateur radio.
Application requirements: Transcript. FAFSA.
Additional information: Must hold active Amateur Radio license. High school seniors eligible to apply. Application may be obtained on Website, and will only be accepted via email.

Amount of award:	$2,000
Number of awards:	1
Application deadline:	February 1

Contact:
The ARRL Foundation, Inc. Scholarship Program
225 Main Street
Newington, CT 06111
Phone: 860-594-0397
Fax: 860-594-0259
Web: www.arrlf.org

The Rocky Mountain Division Scholarship

Type of award: Scholarship.
Intended use: For undergraduate study at accredited 4-year institution in United States.
Eligibility: Applicant must be U.S. citizen residing in Wyoming, Utah, New Mexico or Colorado.
Basis for selection: Competition/talent/interest in amateur radio.
Application requirements: Recommendations, transcript. FAFSA.
Additional information: Winner also receives one-year ARRL membership if nominee is not an ARRL member. Must be amateur radio operator with active Amateur Radio license, any class. Visit Website for application.

Amount of award:	$500
Number of awards:	1
Application deadline:	February 1

Contact:
American Radio Relay League (ARRL) Foundation, Inc.
225 Main Street
Newington, CT 06111
Phone: 860-594-0397
Fax: 860-594-0259
Web: www.arrlf.org

The Scholarship of the Morris Radio Club of New Jersey

Type of award: Scholarship.
Intended use: For undergraduate study at 4-year institution.
Basis for selection: Competition/talent/interest in amateur radio.
Application requirements: Transcript. FAFSA.
Additional information: Must be amateur radio operator with active Technician Class or higher license. High school seniors are eligible to apply. Visit Website for application.

Amount of award:	$1,000
Number of awards:	1
Application deadline:	February 1

Contact:
American Radio Relay League (ARRL) Foundation, Inc.
225 Main Street
Newington, CT 06111
Phone: 860-594-0397
Fax: 860-594-0259
Web: www.arrlf.org

The Six Meter Club of Chicago Scholarship

Type of award: Scholarship.
Intended use: For undergraduate study at accredited postsecondary institution in United States. Designated institutions: Schools in Illinois, Indiana or Wisconsin.
Eligibility: Applicant must be residing in Wisconsin, Indiana or Illinois.
Basis for selection: Competition/talent/interest in amateur radio. Applicant must demonstrate high academic achievement.
Application requirements: Transcript. FAFSA.
Additional information: Must hold active Amateur Radio license. Preference given to applicants with minimum 2.5 GPA. High school seniors eligible to apply. Application may be obtained on Website, and will only be accepted via email.

Amount of award:	$500
Number of awards:	1
Application deadline:	February 1
Total amount awarded:	$500

Contact:
The ARRL Foundation, Inc. Scholarship Program
225 Main Street
Newington, CT 06111
Phone: 860-594-0397
Fax: 860-594-0259
Web: www.arrlf.org

The Southeastern DX Club Scholarship Fund

Type of award: Scholarship.
Intended use: For undergraduate study at postsecondary institution.
Eligibility: Applicant must be residing in Georgia.
Basis for selection: Competition/talent/interest in amateur radio.
Application requirements: Transcript. FAFSA.
Additional information: Must be an active member of an amateur radio club affiliated with the ARRL. If no qualified applicant in Georgia, preference will be awarded to applicants from the ARRL Southeastern Division (Alabama, Florida, Georgia, Puerto Rico, and the U.S. Virgin Islands). Preference given to applicants pursuing engineering or computer science. Visit Website for application.

Amount of award:	$500
Number of awards:	1
Application deadline:	February 1

Contact:
American Radio Relay League (ARRL) Foundation, Inc.
225 Main Street
Newington, CT 06111
Phone: 860-594-0397
Fax: 860-594-0259
Web: www.arrlf.org

The Ted, W4VHF, and Itice, K4LVV, Goldthorpe Scholarship

Type of award: Scholarship.
Intended use: For undergraduate study at 4-year institution.
Basis for selection: Competition/talent/interest in amateur radio. Applicant must demonstrate financial need and service orientation.
Application requirements: Transcript. FAFSA.
Additional information: Must be amateur radio operator with any active Amateur Radio license class. High school seniors are eligible to apply. Visit Website for application.

Amount of award:	$500
Number of awards:	1
Application deadline:	February 1

Contact:
American Radio Relay League (ARRL) Foundation, Inc.
225 Main Street
Newington, CT 06111
Phone: 860-594-0397
Fax: 860-594-0259
Web: www.arrlf.org

The Thomas W. Porter, W8KYZ, Scholarship Honoring Michael Daugherty, W8LSE

Type of award: Scholarship.
Intended use: For undergraduate study at accredited vocational, 2-year or 4-year institution.
Eligibility: Applicant must be residing in Ohio or West Virginia.
Basis for selection: Competition/talent/interest in amateur radio.
Application requirements: Transcript. FAFSA.
Additional information: Must be amateur radio operator with active Amateur Radio License of Technician Class or higher. High school seniors are eligible to apply. Visit Website for application.

Amount of award:	$1,000
Number of awards:	1
Application deadline:	February 1

Contact:
American Radio Relay League (ARRL) Foundation, Inc.
225 Main Street
Newington, CT 06111
Phone: 860-594-0397
Fax: 860-594-0259
Web: www.arrlf.org

The Tom and Judith Comstock Scholarship

Type of award: Scholarship.
Intended use: For freshman study at 2-year or 4-year institution in United States.
Eligibility: Applicant must be high school senior. Applicant must be residing in Oklahoma or Texas.
Basis for selection: Competition/talent/interest in amateur radio.
Application requirements: Transcript. FAFSA.
Additional information: Must hold active Amateur Radio license. Application may be obtained on Website, and will only be accepted via email.

Amount of award:	$2,000
Number of awards:	1
Application deadline:	February 1
Total amount awarded:	$2,000

Contact:
The ARRL Foundation, Inc. Scholarship Program
225 Main Street
Newington, CT 06111
Phone: 860-594-0397
Fax: 860-594-0259
Web: www.arrlf.org

The Victor Poor W5SMM Memorial Scholarship Fund

Type of award: Scholarship.
Intended use: For undergraduate study at postsecondary institution.
Basis for selection: Competition/talent/interest in amateur radio. Major/career interest in engineering, electrical/electronic.
Application requirements: Transcript. FAFSA.
Additional information: Must be amateur radio operator with active Technician Class Amateur Radio License or higher. Preference given to applicants with a concentration in digital communications. Visit Website for application.

Amount of award:	$2,500
Number of awards:	1
Application deadline:	February 1

Contact:
American Radio Relay League (ARRL) Foundation, Inc.
225 Main Street
Newington, CT 06111
Phone: 860-594-0397
Fax: 860-594-0259
Web: www.arrlf.org

The Wayne Nelson, KB4UT, Memorial Scholarship

Type of award: Scholarship.
Intended use: For undergraduate study at accredited 4-year institution.
Eligibility: Applicant must be U.S. citizen residing in Florida.
Basis for selection: Competition/talent/interest in amateur radio. Major/career interest in engineering; technology; science, general or electronics. Applicant must demonstrate high academic achievement.
Application requirements: Transcript. FAFSA.
Additional information: Minimum 3.0 GPA. Must be amateur radio operator with any class of active Amateur Radio license. High school seniors are eligible to apply. Preference given to residents of Central Florida (Orange, Seminole, Osceola, Lake, Volusia, Brevard and Polk counties); if no suitable applicant, resident of the State of Florida. Visit Website for application.

Amount of award:	$1,000
Number of awards:	1
Application deadline:	February 1

Contact:
American Radio Relay League (ARRL) Foundation, Inc.
225 Main Street
Newington, CT 06111
Phone: 860-594-0397
Fax: 860-594-0259
Web: www.arrlf.org

The William Bennett, W7PHO, Memorial Scholarship

Type of award: Scholarship.
Intended use: For undergraduate study at 4-year institution.
Basis for selection: Competition/talent/interest in amateur radio. Applicant must demonstrate high academic achievement.
Application requirements: Transcript. FAFSA.
Additional information: Minimum 3.0 GPA. Must be amateur radio operator with active General Class license or higher. High school seniors are eligible to apply. Applicants should be residents of the ARRL's Northwest, Pacific or Southwest Divisions. Visit Website for application.

Amount of award:	$500
Number of awards:	1
Application deadline:	February 1

Contact:
American Radio Relay League (ARRL) Foundation, Inc.
225 Main Street
Newington, CT 06111
Phone: 860-594-0397
Fax: 860-594-0259
Web: www.arrlf.org

The William R. Goldfarb Memorial Scholarship

Type of award: Scholarship, renewable.
Intended use: For freshman study at accredited 4-year institution in United States. Designated institutions: Regionally accredited institution.
Eligibility: Applicant must be high school senior.
Basis for selection: Competition/talent/interest in amateur radio. Major/career interest in business; engineering; science, general; computer/information sciences; medicine or nursing. Applicant must demonstrate financial need.
Application requirements: Recommendations, transcript. FAFSA or Student Aid Report.
Additional information: Must hold active Amateur Radio license. Award amount varies based on applicant's qualifications, need, and other funding; $10,000 is the minimum award. Application may be obtained on Website, and will only be accepted via email.

Amount of award:	$10,000
Number of awards:	1
Application deadline:	February 1

Contact:
The ARRL Foundation, Inc. Scholarship Program
225 Main Street
Newington, CT 06111
Phone: 860-594-0397
Fax: 860-594-0259
Web: www.arrlf.org

Yankee Clipper Contest Club Youth Scholarship

Type of award: Scholarship.
Intended use: For undergraduate study at accredited 2-year or 4-year institution in United States.
Eligibility: Applicant must be residing in Vermont, New York, Maine, Pennsylvania, Massachusetts, Connecticut, New Hampshire, New Jersey or Rhode Island.
Basis for selection: Competition/talent/interest in amateur radio.
Application requirements: Transcript. FAFSA.
Additional information: Must be amateur radio operator holding active General Class license or higher. Must be resident of or college/university student in area within 175-mile radius of YCCC Center in Erving, MA. This includes MA; RI; CT; Long Island, NY; and some of VT, NH, ME, PA, and NJ. High school seniors are eligible to apply. Application may be obtained on Website, and will only be accepted via email.

Amount of award:	$1,200
Number of awards:	1
Application deadline:	February 1

Contact:
The ARRL Foundation, Inc. Scholarship Program
225 Main Street
Newington, CT 06111
Phone: 860-594-0397
Fax: 860-594-0259
Web: www.arrlf.org

The Yasme Foundation Scholarship

Type of award: Scholarship, renewable.
Intended use: For undergraduate study at accredited 4-year institution in United States.
Basis for selection: Competition/talent/interest in amateur radio. Major/career interest in science, general or engineering. Applicant must demonstrate high academic achievement and service orientation.
Application requirements: Transcript. FAFSA.
Additional information: Must hold active amateur radio license Technician Class or higher. Preference given to high school applicants in top five to ten percent of class or college students in top ten percent of class. Participation in local amateur radio club and community service strongly preferred. Previous YASME winners must submit new application and transcript each year. Number of awards varies. Application may be obtained on Website, and will only be accepted via email.

Amount of award:	$2,000
Application deadline:	February 1

Scholarships

Contact:
The ARRL Foundation, Inc. Scholarship Program
225 Main Street
Newington, CT 06111
Phone: 860-594-0397
Fax: 860-594-0259
Web: www.arrlf.org

The You've Got a Friend in Pennsylvania Scholarship

Type of award: Scholarship.
Intended use: For undergraduate, graduate or non-degree study at postsecondary institution in United States.
Eligibility: Applicant must be residing in Pennsylvania.
Basis for selection: Competition/talent/interest in amateur radio. Applicant must demonstrate high academic achievement.
Application requirements: Transcript. FAFSA.
Additional information: Must be amateur radio operator with a General Class or Extra Class license. Must be member of American Radio Relay League and maintain an "A" equivalent GPA. High school seniors eligible to apply. Application may be obtained from Website, and will only be accepted via email.

Amount of award:	$2,000
Number of awards:	2
Application deadline:	February 1
Total amount awarded:	$4,000

Contact:
The ARRL Foundation, Inc. Scholarship Program
225 Main Street
Newington, CT 06111
Phone: 860-594-0397
Fax: 860-594-0259
Web: www.arrlf.org

The Zachary Taylor Stevens Scholarship

Type of award: Scholarship.
Intended use: For undergraduate study at accredited vocational, 2-year or 4-year institution in United States.
Basis for selection: Competition/talent/interest in amateur radio.
Application requirements: Transcript. FAFSA.
Additional information: Must be amateur radio operator holding Technician Class license or higher. High school seniors eligible to apply. Application may be obtained on Website, and will only be accepted via email.

Amount of award:	$750
Number of awards:	1
Application deadline:	February 1

Contact:
The ARRL Foundation, Inc. Scholarship Program
225 Main Street
Newington, CT 06111
Phone: 860-594-0397
Fax: 860-594-0259
Web: www.arrlf.org

American Respiratory Care Foundation

Jimmy A. Young Memorial Education Recognition Award

Type of award: Scholarship, renewable.
Intended use: For undergraduate study at accredited postsecondary institution.
Basis for selection: Competition/talent/interest in research paper. Major/career interest in respiratory therapy. Applicant must demonstrate high academic achievement.
Application requirements: Recommendations, transcript, proof of eligibility, nomination by school or program representative. Student may initiate request for sponsorship in absence of nomination. Original referenced paper on some aspect of respiratory care.
Additional information: Minimum 3.0 GPA. Award includes coach airfare, one night lodging, and registration for AARC Congress. Preference given to applicants of minority origin. Application available on Website.

Amount of award:	$1,000
Number of awards:	1
Application deadline:	June 15
Total amount awarded:	$1,000

Contact:
American Respiratory Care Foundation
Attn: Education Recognition Award
9425 N. MacArthur Blvd., Suite 100
Irving, TX 75063-4706
Phone: 972-243-2272
Fax: 972-484-2720
Web: www.arcfoundation.org/awards

Morton B. Duggan, Jr. Memorial Education Recognition Award

Type of award: Scholarship, renewable.
Intended use: For undergraduate study at accredited postsecondary institution.
Basis for selection: Competition/talent/interest in research paper. Major/career interest in respiratory therapy. Applicant must demonstrate high academic achievement.
Application requirements: Recommendations, transcript, proof of eligibility. Research paper on some aspect of respiratory care.
Additional information: Applicants accepted from all states, but preference given to applicants from Georgia and South Carolina. Minimum 3.0 GPA. Award includes airfare, one night lodging, and registration for the AARC Congress. Application available on Website.

Amount of award:	$1,000
Number of awards:	1
Application deadline:	June 15

Contact:
American Respiratory Care Foundation
Attn: Education Recogniton Award
9425 N. MacArthur Blvd., Suite 100
Irving, TX 75063-4706
Phone: 972-243-2272
Fax: 972-484-2720
Web: www.arcfoundation.org/awards

NBRC/AMP Robert M. Lawrence, MD Education Recognition Award

Type of award: Scholarship.
Intended use: For junior or senior study at accredited 4-year institution.
Basis for selection: Competition/talent/interest in research paper. Major/career interest in respiratory therapy. Applicant must demonstrate high academic achievement.
Application requirements: Recommendations, essay, transcript, proof of eligibility. Original referenced paper on some aspect of respiratory care.
Additional information: Minimum 3.0 GPA. Award includes coach airfare, one night lodging, and registration for AARC Congress. Application available on Website.

Amount of award:	$2,500
Number of awards:	1
Application deadline:	June 15

Contact:
American Respiratory Care Foundation
Attn: Education Recognition Award
9425 N. MacArthur Blvd., Suite 100
Irving, TX 75063-4706
Phone: 972-243-2272
Fax: 972-484-2720
Web: www.arcfoundation.org/awards

NBRC/AMP William W. Burgin, Jr. MD Education Recognition Award

Type of award: Scholarship.
Intended use: For sophomore study at accredited 2-year institution.
Basis for selection: Competition/talent/interest in research paper. Major/career interest in respiratory therapy. Applicant must demonstrate high academic achievement.
Application requirements: Recommendations, essay, transcript, proof of eligibility, nomination by school or educational program (or may apply directly). Original referenced paper on some aspect of respiratory care.
Additional information: Must be student in respiratory therapy associate's degree program. Minimum 3.0 GPA. Award includes coach airfare, one night lodging, and registration for AARC Congress. Application available on Website.

Amount of award:	$2,500
Number of awards:	1
Application deadline:	June 15

Contact:
American Respiratory Care Foundation
Attn: Education Recognition Award
9425 N. MacArthur Blvd., Suite 100
Irving, TX 75063-4706
Phone: 972-243-2272
Fax: 972-484-2720
Web: www.arcfoundation.org/awards

American Society for Enology and Viticulture

American Society for Enology and Viticulture Scholarship Program

Type of award: Scholarship, renewable.
Intended use: For full-time junior, senior or graduate study at accredited 4-year or graduate institution.
Eligibility: Applicant must be Resident of Canada or Mexico.
Basis for selection: Major/career interest in agriculture; food science/technology or horticulture. Applicant must demonstrate high academic achievement.
Application requirements: Recommendations, essay, transcript. Student questionnaire, statement of intent, list of planned courses for upcoming year.
Additional information: Minimum 3.0 overall GPA for undergraduates, 3.2 overall GPA for graduate students. Must reside in North America (Canada, Mexico, or U.S.A.). Applicants must be enrolled in major or graduate program emphasizing enology or viticulture, or in curriculum emphasizing science basic to wine and grape industry. Awards vary.

Number of applicants:	21
Application deadline:	March 1

Contact:
ASEV Scholarship Committee
P.O. Box 1855
Davis, CA 95617-1855
Phone: 530-753-3142
Fax: 530-753-3318
Web: www.asev.org/scholarship-program

American Society for Microbiology

American Society for Microbiology Undergraduate Research Fellowship (URF)

Type of award: Research grant.
Intended use: For full-time undergraduate study in United States.
Eligibility: Applicant must be U.S. citizen or permanent resident.
Basis for selection: Major/career interest in microbiology. Applicant must demonstrate high academic achievement and seriousness of purpose.
Application requirements: Recommendations, transcript.
Additional information: Applicant must demonstrate strong interest in pursuing graduate career (Ph.D. or M.D./Ph.D.) in microbiology. Students conduct research for a minimum of ten weeks in summer and present results at ASM General Meeting the following year. Fellowship offers up to $4,000 stipend and up to $1,000 to travel to ASM General Meeting (if abstract is accepted). Applicant must have ASM member at home institution willing to serve as faculty mentor. Students may not receive financial support for research from other scientific organizations during fellowship. Faculty member's department chair or dean must endorse research project. Number of awards varies. See Website for application.

Amount of award:	$5,000
Number of applicants:	81
Application deadline:	February 1
Notification begins:	April 15

Contact:
American Society for Microbiology
ASM Undergraduate Research Fellowship Program
1752 N Street, NW
Washington, DC 20036
Phone: 202-942-9283
Fax: 202-942-9329
Web: www.asm.org/students

American Society of Civil Engineers

B. Charles Tiney Memorial ASCE Student Chapter Scholarship

Type of award: Scholarship.
Intended use: For undergraduate study at accredited 4-year institution.
Basis for selection: Major/career interest in engineering, civil. Applicant must demonstrate financial need, high academic achievement and leadership.
Application requirements: Recommendations, essay, transcript. One-page resume, detailed financial plan.
Additional information: Must be American Society of Civil Engineers member in good standing and be enrolled in ABET-accredited program. Awards and amounts determined annually. Visit Website for deadline and awards.
Contact:
American Society of Civil Engineers
Attn: Honors and Awards Program
1801 Alexander Bell Drive
Reston, VA 20191-4400
Phone: 800-548-2723 ext. 6106
Fax: 703-295-6222
Web: www.asce.org

Eugene C. Figg Jr. Civil Engineering Scholarship

Type of award: Scholarship.
Intended use: For junior or senior study.
Eligibility: Applicant must be U.S. citizen.
Basis for selection: Major/career interest in engineering, civil. Applicant must demonstrate financial need, high academic achievement and leadership.
Application requirements: Recommendations, essay, transcript. One-page resume, detailed financial plan.
Additional information: Must be American Society of Civil Engineers member in good standing, be enrolled in ABET-accredited program, and have passion for bridges. Recipient eligible to interview for internship opportunity with Figg Engineering Group.

Amount of award:	$3,000
Number of awards:	1
Application deadline:	February 10
Total amount awarded:	$3,000

Contact:
American Society of Civil Engineers
Attn: Honors and Awards Program
1801 Alexander Bell Drive
Reston, VA 20191-4400
Phone: 800-548-2723 ext. 6106
Fax: 703-295-6222
Web: www.asce.org

Freeman Fellowship

Type of award: Research grant.
Intended use: For undergraduate or graduate study.
Basis for selection: Major/career interest in engineering, civil.
Application requirements: Recommendations, essay, transcript, research proposal. One- to two-page resume. Detailed financial statement indicating how fellowship will finance applicant's research. Statement from institution where research will be conducted.
Additional information: Applicant must be American Society of Civil Engineers member in good standing. Grants are made toward expenses for experiments, observations, and compilations to discover new and accurate data that will be useful in engineering. Grant may be in form of prize for most useful paper relating to science/art of hydraulic construction. Travel grants available to ASCE members under 45, in recognition of achievement or promise. Visit Website for application and more information.

Amount of award:	$2,000-$5,000
Application deadline:	February 10

Contact:
American Society of Civil Engineers
Attn: Honors and Awards Program
1801 Alexander Bell Drive
Reston, VA 20191-4440
Phone: 800-548-2723 ext. 6106
Fax: 703-295-6222
Web: www.asce.org

John Lenard Civil Engineering Scholarship

Type of award: Scholarship.
Intended use: For junior or senior study at accredited 4-year institution.
Basis for selection: Major/career interest in engineering, civil or engineering, environmental. Applicant must demonstrate financial need, high academic achievement and leadership.
Application requirements: Recommendations, essay, transcript. One-page resume, detailed financial plan.
Additional information: Must be American Society of Civil Engineers member in good standing, be enrolled in ABET-accredited program, and have demonstrated commitment to either water supply and/or environmental engineering. Awards may vary based on available funds.

Amount of award:	$2,000
Number of awards:	2
Application deadline:	February 10

Contact:
American Society of Civil Engineers
Attn: Honors and Awards Program
1801 Alexander Bell Drive
Reston, VA 20191-4400
Phone: 800-548-2723 ext. 6106
Fax: 703-295-6222
Web: www.asce.org

Josephine and Robert B.B. Moorman Scholarship

Type of award: Scholarship.
Intended use: For undergraduate study at accredited 4-year institution. Designated institutions: ABET-accredited schools.
Basis for selection: Major/career interest in engineering, civil. Applicant must demonstrate financial need, high academic achievement and leadership.
Application requirements: Recommendations, essay, transcript. One-page resume, detailed financial plan.
Additional information: Must be American Society of Civil Engineers member in good standing and be enrolled in ABET-accredited program. Awards may vary based on available funds.

Amount of award:	$2,000
Number of awards:	1
Application deadline:	February 10

Contact:
American Society of Civil Engineers
Attn: Honors and Awards Program
1801 Alexander Bell Drive
Reston, VA 20191-4400
Phone: 800-548-2723 ext. 6106
Fax: 703-295-6222
Web: www.asce.org

Lawrence W. and Francis W. Cox Scholarship

Type of award: Scholarship.
Intended use: For undergraduate study at accredited 4-year institution.
Basis for selection: Major/career interest in engineering, civil. Applicant must demonstrate financial need, high academic achievement and leadership.
Application requirements: Recommendations, essay, transcript. One-page resume, detailed annual budget.
Additional information: Must be American Society of Civil Engineers member in good standing and be enrolled in ABET-accredited program. Awards and amounts may vary based on available funding.

Amount of award:	$5,000
Number of awards:	
Application deadline:	February 10

Contact:
American Society of Civil Engineers
Attn: Honors and Awards Program
1801 Alexander Bell Drive
Reston, VA 20191-4400
Phone: 800-548-2723 ext. 6106
Fax: 703-295-6222
Web: www.asce.org

Samuel Fletcher Tapman ASCE Student Chapter Scholarship

Type of award: Scholarship, renewable.
Intended use: For undergraduate study at accredited postsecondary institution.
Basis for selection: Major/career interest in engineering, civil. Applicant must demonstrate financial need, high academic achievement and leadership.
Application requirements: Recommendations, essay, transcript. One-page resume, detailed annual budget.
Additional information: Applicant must be enrolled in ABET-accredited program and be member in good standing of local American Society of Civil Engineers student chapter and national society. Membership applications may be submitted with scholarship application. One submission per student chapter. Visit Website for application and more information.

Amount of award:	$3,000
Number of awards:	12
Application deadline:	February 10

Contact:
American Society of Civil Engineers
Attn: Honors and Awards Program
1801 Alexander Bell Drive
Reston, VA 20191-4440
Phone: 800-548-2723 ext. 6106
Fax: 703-295-6222
Web: www.asce.org

Y.C. Yang Civil Engineering Scholarship

Type of award: Scholarship.
Intended use: For junior or senior study.
Basis for selection: Major/career interest in engineering, civil or engineering, structural. Applicant must demonstrate financial need, high academic achievement and leadership.
Application requirements: Recommendations, essay, transcript. One-page resume, detailed financial plan.
Additional information: Must be student at ABET-accredited institution, an ASCE student member in good standing, and have interest in structural engineering. Awards may vary based on funding.

Amount of award:	$2,000
Number of awards:	2
Application deadline:	February 10

Contact:
American Society of Civil Engineers
Attn: Honors and Awards Program
1801 Alexander Bell Drive
Reston, VA 20191-4400
Phone: 800-548-2723 ext. 6106
Fax: 703-295-6222
Web: www.asce.org

American Society of Heating, Refrigerating, and Air-Conditioning Engineers, Inc.

Alwin B. Newton Scholarship

Type of award: Scholarship.
Intended use: For full-time undergraduate study at accredited 4-year institution in or outside United States. Designated institutions: Schools with ABET-accredited programs.
Basis for selection: Major/career interest in engineering or air conditioning/heating/refrigeration technology. Applicant must demonstrate financial need, high academic achievement, depth of character and leadership.
Application requirements: Recommendations, transcript.
Additional information: For engineering students considering service to heating/ventilation/air-conditioning (HVAC) and/or refrigeration profession. Minimum 3.0 GPA.

Amount of award: $3,000
Number of awards: 1
Application deadline: December 1
Contact:
ASHRAE, Inc. - Scholarship Administrator
1791 Tullie Circle, NE
Atlanta, GA 30329-2305
Phone: 404-636-8400
Fax: 404-321-5478
Web: www.ashrae.org/students/page/1271

ASHRAE Engineering Technology Scholarships

Type of award: Scholarship.
Intended use: For full-time undergraduate study at accredited 2-year or 4-year institution. Designated institutions: PAHRA accredited educational organizations with ABET-accredited engineering technology programs.
Basis for selection: Major/career interest in engineering or air conditioning/heating/refrigeration technology. Applicant must demonstrate financial need, high academic achievement, depth of character and leadership.
Application requirements: Recommendations, transcript.
Additional information: For students pursuing bachelor's or associate's degree in engineering technology and intending to pursue career in heating/ventilation/air-conditioning (HVAC) and/or refrigeration profession. Minimum 3.0 GPA.
Amount of award: $3,000
Number of awards: 3
Application deadline: May 1
Contact:
ASHRAE, Inc. - Scholarship Administrator
1791 Tullie Circle, NE
Atlanta, GA 30329-2305
Phone: 404-636-8400
Fax: 404-321-5478
Web: www.ashrae.org/students/page/1271

ASHRAE General Scholarships

Type of award: Scholarship.
Intended use: For full-time undergraduate study at accredited 4-year institution in or outside United States. Designated institutions: Schools with ABET-accredited programs.
Basis for selection: Major/career interest in engineering or air conditioning/heating/refrigeration technology. Applicant must demonstrate financial need, high academic achievement, depth of character and leadership.
Application requirements: Recommendations, transcript.
Additional information: For engineering students considering service to heating/ventilation/air-conditioning (HVAC) and/or refrigeration profession. Minimum 3.0 GPA.
Amount of award: $5,000
Number of awards: 2
Application deadline: December 1
Contact:
ASHRAE, Inc. - Scholarship Administrator
1791 Tullie Circle, NE
Atlanta, GA 30329-2305
Phone: 404-636-8400
Fax: 404-321-5478
Web: www.ashrae.org/students/page/1271

ASHRAE Memorial Scholarship

Type of award: Scholarship.
Intended use: For full-time undergraduate study at accredited 4-year institution in or outside United States. Designated institutions: Schools with ABET-accredited programs.
Basis for selection: Major/career interest in engineering or air conditioning/heating/refrigeration technology. Applicant must demonstrate financial need, high academic achievement, depth of character and leadership.
Application requirements: Recommendations, transcript.
Additional information: For engineering students considering service to heating/ventilation/air-conditioning (HVAC) and/or refrigeration profession. Minimum 3.0 GPA.
Amount of award: $5,000
Number of awards: 1
Application deadline: December 1
Contact:
ASHRAE, Inc. - Scholarship Administrator
1791 Tullie Circle, NE
Atlanta, GA 30329-2305
Phone: 404-636-8400
Fax: 404-321-5478
Web: www.ashrae.org/students/page/1271

ASHRAE Region IV Benny Bootle Scholarship

Type of award: Scholarship.
Intended use: For full-time undergraduate study at accredited 4-year institution. Designated institutions: Schools with NAAB or ABET-accredited program located within the geographic boundaries of ASHRAE's Region IV (North Carolina, South Carolina, Georgia).
Eligibility: Applicant must be residing in North Carolina, Georgia or South Carolina.
Basis for selection: Major/career interest in air conditioning/heating/refrigeration technology; architecture or engineering. Applicant must demonstrate financial need, high academic achievement, depth of character and leadership.
Application requirements: Recommendations, transcript.
Additional information: Minimum 3.0 GPA. For engineering or architecture students considering service to heating/ventilation/air-conditioning (HVAC) and/or refrigeration profession. Visit www.abet.org and www.naab.org for list of ABET- and NAAB-accredited programs within Region IV.
Amount of award: $3,000
Number of awards: 1
Application deadline: December 1
Contact:
ASHRAE, Inc. - Scholarship Administrator
1791 Tullie Circle, NE
Atlanta, GA 30329-2305
Phone: 404-636-8400
Fax: 404-321-5478
Web: www.ashrae.org/students/page/1271

ASHRAE Region VIII Scholarship

Type of award: Scholarship.
Intended use: For full-time undergraduate study in or outside United States. Designated institutions: Schools with ABET-accredited programs located within the geographic boundaries of ASHRAE's Region VIII (Arkansas, Oklahoma, Mexico, and parts of Louisiana and Texas).
Eligibility: Applicant must be residing in Oklahoma, Texas, Arkansas or Louisiana.

Basis for selection: Major/career interest in engineering or air conditioning/heating/refrigeration technology. Applicant must demonstrate financial need, high academic achievement, depth of character and leadership.
Application requirements: Recommendations, transcript.
Additional information: Minimum 3.0 GPA. For engineering students considering service to heating/ventilation/air-conditioning (HVAC) and/or refrigeration profession. Contact ASHRAE for information regarding Region VIII. Visit www.abet.org for ABET-accredited programs within the region.

Amount of award:	$3,000
Number of awards:	1
Application deadline:	December 1

Contact:
ASHRAE, Inc. - Scholarship Administrator
1791 Tullie Circle, NE
Atlanta, GA 30329-2305
Phone: 404-636-8400
Fax: 404-321-5478
Web: www.ashrae.org/students/page/1271

Duane Hanson Scholarship

Type of award: Scholarship.
Intended use: For full-time undergraduate study at accredited 4-year institution in or outside United States. Designated institutions: Schools with ABET-accredited programs.
Basis for selection: Major/career interest in engineering or air conditioning/heating/refrigeration technology. Applicant must demonstrate financial need, high academic achievement, depth of character and leadership.
Application requirements: Recommendations, transcript.
Additional information: For engineering students considering service to heating/ventilation/air-conditioning (HVAC) and/or refrigeration profession. Minimum 3.0 GPA.

Amount of award:	$3,000
Number of awards:	1
Application deadline:	December 1

Contact:
ASHRAE, Inc. - Scholarship Administrator
1791 Tullie Circle, NE
Atlanta, GA 30329-2305
Phone: 404-636-8400
Fax: 404-321-5478
Web: www.ashrae.org/students/page/1271

Frank M. Coda Scholarship

Type of award: Scholarship.
Intended use: For full-time undergraduate study at accredited 4-year institution in or outside United States. Designated institutions: Schools with ABET-accredited programs.
Basis for selection: Major/career interest in engineering or air conditioning/heating/refrigeration technology. Applicant must demonstrate financial need, high academic achievement, depth of character and leadership.
Application requirements: Recommendations, transcript.
Additional information: For engineering students considering service to heating/ventilation/air-conditioning (HVAC) and/or refrigeration profession. Minimum 3.0 GPA.

Amount of award:	$5,000
Number of awards:	1
Application deadline:	December 1

Contact:
ASHRAE, Inc. - Scholarship Administrator
1791 Tullie Circle, NE
Atlanta, GA 30329-2305
Phone: 404-636-8400
Fax: 404-321-5478
Web: www.ashrae.org/students/page/1271

Henry Adams Scholarship

Type of award: Scholarship.
Intended use: For full-time undergraduate study at accredited 4-year institution in or outside United States. Designated institutions: Schools with ABET-accredited programs.
Basis for selection: Major/career interest in engineering or air conditioning/heating/refrigeration technology. Applicant must demonstrate financial need, high academic achievement, depth of character and leadership.
Application requirements: Recommendations, transcript.
Additional information: For engineering students considering service to heating/ventilation/air-conditioning (HVAC) and/or refrigeration profession. Minimum 3.0 GPA.

Amount of award:	$3,000
Number of awards:	1
Application deadline:	December 1

Contact:
ASHRAE, Inc. - Scholarship Administrator
1791 Tullie Circle, NE
Atlanta, GA 30329-2305
Phone: 404-636-8400
Fax: 404-321-5478
Web: www.ashrae.org/students/page/1271

J. Richard Mehalick Scholarship

Type of award: Scholarship.
Intended use: For full-time undergraduate study at accredited 4-year institution in United States. Designated institutions: University of Pittsburgh.
Basis for selection: Major/career interest in engineering, mechanical or air conditioning/heating/refrigeration technology. Applicant must demonstrate financial need, high academic achievement, depth of character and leadership.
Application requirements: Recommendations, transcript.
Additional information: Must have minimum 3.0 GPA. For mechanical engineering students considering service to heating/ventilation/air-conditioning (HVAC) and/or refrigeration profession.

Amount of award:	$3,000
Number of awards:	1
Application deadline:	December 1

Contact:
ASHRAE, Inc. - Scholarship Administrator
1791 Tullie Circle, NE
Atlanta, GA 30329
Phone: 404-636-8400
Fax: 404-321-5478
Web: www.ashrae.org/students/page/1271

Lynn G. Bellenger Scholarship

Type of award: Scholarship.
Intended use: For full-time undergraduate study at accredited 4-year institution.
Eligibility: Applicant must be female.
Basis for selection: Major/career interest in engineering or air conditioning/heating/refrigeration technology. Applicant must

demonstrate financial need, high academic achievement, depth of character and leadership.
Application requirements: Recommendations, transcript.
Additional information: Must have minimum 3.0 GPA and/or a class ranking of no less than 30%. For mechanical engineering students considering service to heating/ventilation/air-conditioning (HVAC) and/or refrigeration profession.

Amount of award:	$5,000
Application deadline:	December 1

Contact:
ASHRAE, Inc. - Scholarship Administrator
1791 Tullie Circle, NE
Atlanta, GA 30329
Phone: 404-636-8400
Fax: 404-321-5478
Web: www.ashrae.org/students/page/1271

Reuben Trane Scholarship

Type of award: Scholarship.
Intended use: For full-time undergraduate study at accredited 4-year institution in or outside United States. Designated institutions: Schools with ABET-accredited programs.
Basis for selection: Major/career interest in air conditioning/heating/refrigeration technology or engineering. Applicant must demonstrate financial need, high academic achievement, depth of character and leadership.
Application requirements: Recommendations, transcript.
Additional information: Minimum 3.0 GPA. Award is for two years; $5,000 given at beginning of each year. Must be considering service to heating/ventilation/air-conditioning (HVAC) and/or refrigeration profession.

Amount of award:	$10,000
Number of awards:	4
Application deadline:	December 1

Contact:
ASHRAE, Inc. - Scholarship Administrator
1791 Tullie Circle, NE
Atlanta, GA 30329-2305
Phone: 404-636-8400
Fax: 404-321-5478
Web: www.ashrae.org/students/page/1271

Willis H. Carrier Scholarship

Type of award: Scholarship.
Intended use: For full-time undergraduate study at accredited 4-year institution in or outside United States. Designated institutions: ABET-accredited institutions.
Basis for selection: Major/career interest in engineering or air conditioning/heating/refrigeration technology. Applicant must demonstrate financial need, high academic achievement, depth of character and leadership.
Application requirements: Recommendations, transcript.
Additional information: For engineering students considering service to heating/ventilation/air-conditioning (HVAC) and/or refrigeration profession. Minimum 3.0 GPA.

Amount of award:	$10,000
Number of awards:	2
Application deadline:	December 1

Contact:
ASHRAE, Inc. - Scholarship Administrator
1791 Tullie Circle, NE
Atlanta, GA 30329-2305
Phone: 404-636-8400
Fax: 404-321-5478
Web: www.ashrae.org/students/page/1271

American Society of Interior Designers Foundation, Inc.

American Society of Interior Designers Legacy Scholarship for Undergraduates

Type of award: Scholarship.
Intended use: For junior or senior study at 4-year institution.
Basis for selection: Major/career interest in interior design.
Application requirements: Recommendations, essay, transcript. Portfolio, portfolio description (max. 250 words), list of portfolio components, personal statement with career goals, biographical statement (max. 100 words) and headshot.
Additional information: Deadline in April; visit Website for exact date and additional information.

Amount of award:	$4,000
Number of awards:	1

Contact:
American Society of Interior Designers Foundation, Inc.
Legacy Scholarship for Undergraduates
608 Massachusetts Avenue, NE
Washington, DC 20002-6006
Phone: 202-546-3480
Fax: 202-546-3240
Web: www.asidfoundation.org/ASID_FOUNDATION/SCHOLARSHIPS_and_AWARDS.html

David Barrett Memorial Scholarship

Type of award: Scholarship.
Intended use: For undergraduate or graduate study at 4-year or graduate institution.
Basis for selection: Major/career interest in interior design.
Application requirements: Portfolio, recommendations, essay. Design portfolio containing 8-12 design components with a written description detailing how classical designs and traditional materials are used in each design component.
Additional information: Visit Website for deadline and additional details.

Amount of award:	$12,000
Number of awards:	1
Application deadline:	December 1

Contact:
American Society of Interior Designers Foundation, Inc.
David Barret Memorial Scholarship
608 Massachusetts Avenue, NE
Washington, DC 20002-6006
Phone: 202-546-3480
Fax: 202-546-3240
Web: www.asidfoundation.org/ASID_FOUNDATION/SCHOLARSHIPS_and_AWARDS.html

Irene Winifred Eno Grant

Type of award: Research grant.
Intended use: For undergraduate or graduate study at 4-year or graduate institution.
Basis for selection: Major/career interest in interior design.
Application requirements: Abstract (max. 250 words), explanation of how you intend to use funds (max. 500 words), promotion plan (max. 1000 words), biographical statement and headshot.
Additional information: Awarded to individuals or groups engaged in the creation of an education program(s) or an

interior design research project dedicated to health, safety, and welfare. Open to students, educators, interior design practitioners, institutions or other interior-design related groups. Deadline in April; visit Website for exact date and additional information.

Amount of award: $5,000

Contact:
American Society of Interior Designers Foundation, Inc.
Irene Winifred Eno Grant
608 Massachusetts Avenue, NE
Washington, DC 20002-6006
Phone: 202-546-3480
Fax: 202-546-3240
Web: www.asidfoundation.org/ASID_FOUNDATION/SCHOLARSHIPS_and_AWARDS.html

Joel Polsky Academic Achievement Award

Type of award: Scholarship.
Intended use: For undergraduate or graduate study at postsecondary institution.
Basis for selection: Competition/talent/interest in research paper, based on content, breadth of material, comprehensive coverage of topic, innovative subject matter, bibliography, and references. Major/career interest in interior design.
Application requirements: Photo. Abstract (max. 250 words). Biographical statement. Thesis, dissertation, or research project.
Additional information: Award to recognize outstanding interior design research or thesis project addressing topics such as educational research, behavioral science, business practice, design process, theory, or other technical subjects. Deadline in April; visit Website for exact date.

Amount of award: $5,000
Number of awards: 1

Contact:
American Society of Interior Designers Foundation, Inc.
Joel Polsky Academic Achievement Award
608 Massachusetts Avenue, NE
Washington, DC 20002-6006
Phone: 202-546-3480
Fax: 202-546-3240
Web: www.asidfoundation.org/ASID_FOUNDATION/SCHOLARSHIPS_and_AWARDS.html

Joel Polsky Prize

Type of award: Scholarship.
Intended use: For undergraduate or graduate study at 4-year or graduate institution.
Basis for selection: Major/career interest in interior design.
Application requirements: Copy of publication or visual communication, description of publication or visual communication (max. 250 words), biographical statement and headshot.
Additional information: Different from the Joel Polsky Academic Achievement Award. Entries should address the needs of the public, designers and students on such topics as educational research, behavioral science, business practice, design process, theory or other technical subjects. Deadline in April; visit Website for exact date and additional information.

Amount of award: $5,000

Contact:
American Society of Interior Designers Foundation, Inc.
Joel Polsky Prize
608 Massachusetts Avenue, NE
Washington, DC 20002-6006
Phone: 202-546-3480
Fax: 202-546-3240
Web: www.asidfoundation.org/ASID_FOUNDATION/SCHOLARSHIPS_and_AWARDS.html

American Society of Naval Engineers

ASNE Scholarship

Type of award: Scholarship.
Intended use: For full-time senior or graduate study at accredited 4-year or graduate institution.
Eligibility: Applicant must be U.S. citizen.
Basis for selection: Major/career interest in engineering; engineering, civil; engineering, electrical/electronic; engineering, environmental; engineering, marine; engineering, mechanical; engineering, nuclear; engineering, structural or physical sciences. Applicant must demonstrate high academic achievement and seriousness of purpose.
Application requirements: Recommendations, essay, transcript.
Additional information: Graduate applicants must be members of American Society of Naval Engineers. Applicants' major/career interests may also include naval architecture, applied mathematics, aeronautical and ocean engineering, or other programs leading to careers with relevant military and civilian organizations. Financial need may be considered. Award also includes one-year honorary student membership to Society.

Amount of award: $3,000-$4,000
Number of awards: 25
Number of applicants: 55
Application deadline: February 28
Notification begins: May 1
Total amount awarded: $66,000

Contact:
American Society of Naval Engineers
1452 Duke Street
Alexandria, VA 22314-3458
Phone: 703-836-6727
Fax: 703-836-7491
Web: www.navalengineers.org/scholarships

American Water Ski Educational Foundation

American Water Ski Educational Foundation Scholarship

Type of award: Scholarship, renewable.
Intended use: For full-time sophomore, junior or senior study at 2-year or 4-year institution.
Eligibility: Applicant must be U.S. citizen.

Scholarships

Basis for selection: Applicant must demonstrate financial need, high academic achievement, depth of character, leadership and seriousness of purpose.
Application requirements: Recommendations, essay, transcript. College freshmen should include both college and high school transcripts. Visit Website for current essay topic.
Additional information: Must be member of USA Water Ski Association.

Amount of award:	$1,500-$3,000
Number of awards:	6
Number of applicants:	25
Application deadline:	March 1
Notification begins:	July 1
Total amount awarded:	$11,000

Contact:
American Water Ski Educational Foundation
1251 Holy Cow Road
Polk City, FL 33868-8200
Phone: 863-324-2472
Fax: 863-324-3996
Web: www.waterskihalloffame.com

American Welding Society Foundation, Inc.

Airgas-Jerry Baker Scholarship

Type of award: Scholarship, renewable.
Intended use: For full-time undergraduate study at postsecondary institution.
Eligibility: Applicant must be at least 18. Applicant must be U.S. citizen or Canadian citizen.
Basis for selection: Major/career interest in welding. Applicant must demonstrate high academic achievement.
Application requirements: Essay.
Additional information: Applicants must have minimum 2.8 overall GPA with 3.0 GPA in engineering courses. Priority given to individuals residing or attending school in Alabama, Georgia, or Florida. Applicant must show interest in welding engineering or welding engineering technology.

Amount of award:	$2,500
Number of awards:	1
Number of applicants:	8
Application deadline:	February 15
Notification begins:	April 1
Total amount awarded:	$2,500

Contact:
American Welding Society Foundation, Inc.
Attn: Scholarships
8669 Doral Boulevard, Suite 130
Doral, FL 33166
Phone: 800-443-9353 ext. 461
Web: www.aws.org/foundation/scholarships

Airgas-Terry Jarvis Memorial Scholarship

Type of award: Scholarship.
Intended use: For full-time sophomore, junior or senior study at 4-year institution in United States or Canada.
Eligibility: Applicant must be at least 18. Applicant must be U.S. citizen or Canadian citizen.
Basis for selection: Major/career interest in welding. Applicant must demonstrate high academic achievement.
Application requirements: Recommendations, essay, transcript, proof of eligibility.
Additional information: Must have interest in pursuing a minimum four-year degree in welding engineering or welding engineering technology. Minimum 2.8 GPA overall, with 3.0 GPA in engineering courses. Priority given to residents of Florida, Alabama, and Georgia. Applicant does not have to be a member of the American Welding Society.

Amount of award:	$2,500
Number of awards:	1
Number of applicants:	8
Application deadline:	February 15
Notification begins:	April 1
Total amount awarded:	$2,500

Contact:
American Welding Society Foundation, Inc.
Attn: Scholarships
8669 Doral Boulevard, Suite 130
Doral, FL 33166
Phone: 800-443-9353
Web: www.aws.org/foundation/scholarships

American Welding Society District Scholarship Program

Type of award: Scholarship.
Intended use: For undergraduate study at accredited vocational, 2-year or 4-year institution in United States.
Eligibility: Applicant must be U.S. citizen.
Basis for selection: Major/career interest in welding. Applicant must demonstrate financial need, high academic achievement, depth of character, leadership and seriousness of purpose.
Application requirements: Recommendations, transcript, proof of eligibility. Personal statement, biography, and photo.

Amount of award:	$200-$3,500
Number of awards:	189
Number of applicants:	436
Application deadline:	March 1
Notification begins:	July 1
Total amount awarded:	$165,000

Contact:
American Welding Society Foundation, Inc.
Attn: Scholarships
8669 Doral Boulevard, Suite 130
Doral, FL 33166
Phone: 800-443-9353
Web: www.aws.org/foundation/scholarships

Arsham Amirikian Engineering Scholarship

Type of award: Scholarship, renewable.
Intended use: For undergraduate study at accredited 4-year institution.
Eligibility: Applicant must be at least 18. Applicant must be U.S. citizen.
Basis for selection: Major/career interest in welding. Applicant must demonstrate financial need and high academic achievement.
Additional information: Minimum 3.0 GPA. Must show interest in pursuing career in the application of the art of welding in civil and structural engineering.

Amount of award: $2,500
Number of awards: 1
Number of applicants: 21
Application deadline: February 15
Notification begins: April 1
Total amount awarded: $2,500

Contact:
American Welding Society Foundation, Inc.
Attn: Scholarships
8669 Doral Boulevard, Suite 130
Doral, FL 33166
Phone: 800-443-9353
Web: www.aws.org/foundation/scholarships

D. Fred and Mariam L. Bovie Scholarship

Type of award: Scholarship, renewable.
Intended use: For full-time at 4-year institution. Designated institutions: The Ohio State University.
Eligibility: Applicant must be U.S. citizen.
Basis for selection: Major/career interest in welding or engineering, electrical/electronic.
Application requirements: Recommendations, essay, transcript, proof of eligibility. Statement of Unmet Financial Need.
Additional information: Award may be renewed for a maximum of four years. Membership in the American Welding Society is not required. Electrical engineering candidates will be considered if there are no qualified welding engineering candidates.

Amount of award: $3,000
Number of awards: 1
Number of applicants: 9
Application deadline: February 15

Contact:
American Welding Society Foundation, Inc.
Attn: Scholarships
8669 Doral Boulevard, Suite 130
Doral, FL 33166
Phone: 800-443-9353
Web: www.aws.org/foundation/scholarships

D. Fred and Mariam L. Bovie Technical Scholarship

Type of award: Scholarship, renewable.
Intended use: For undergraduate study at postsecondary institution.
Basis for selection: Major/career interest in welding. Applicant must demonstrate financial need and high academic achievement.
Application requirements: Recommendations, essay, transcript, proof of eligibility. Statement of Unmet Financial Need.
Additional information: Minimum 2.8 GPA. Applicant must be pursuing an associate's degree in welding, with a minimum of a two-year program. Award may be renewed for a maximum of four years. Membership in the American Welding Society is not required.

Amount of award: $2,000
Number of awards: 1
Number of applicants: 9
Application deadline: February 15
Total amount awarded: $2,000

Contact:
American Welding Society Foundation, Inc.
Attn: Scholarships
8669 Doral Boulevard, Suite 130
Doral, FL 33166
Phone: 800-443-9353 ext. 250
Web: www.aws.org/foundation/scholarships

Donald and Shirley Hastings National Scholarship

Type of award: Scholarship, renewable.
Intended use: For undergraduate study at 4-year institution in United States.
Eligibility: Applicant must be at least 18. Applicant must be U.S. citizen.
Basis for selection: Major/career interest in welding. Applicant must demonstrate financial need and high academic achievement.
Additional information: Minimum 2.5 GPA. Must show interest in welding engineering or welding engineering technology. Priority given to Iowa, Ohio, or California residents.

Amount of award: $2,500
Number of awards: 1
Number of applicants: 21
Application deadline: February 15
Notification begins: April 1
Total amount awarded: $2,500

Contact:
American Welding Society Foundation, Inc.
Attn: Scholarships
8669 Doral Boulevard, Suite 130
Doral, FL 33166
Phone: 800-443-9353
Web: www.aws.org/foundation/scholarships

Donald F. Hastings Scholarship

Type of award: Scholarship, renewable.
Intended use: For sophomore, junior or senior study at 4-year institution in United States.
Eligibility: Applicant must be at least 18. Applicant must be U.S. citizen.
Basis for selection: Major/career interest in welding. Applicant must demonstrate financial need, high academic achievement and seriousness of purpose.
Application requirements: Recommendations, transcript, proof of eligibility.
Additional information: Priority given to residents of Ohio and California. Minimum 2.5 GPA.

Amount of award: $2,500
Number of awards: 1
Number of applicants: 20
Application deadline: February 15
Notification begins: April 1
Total amount awarded: $2,500

Contact:
American Welding Society Foundation, Inc.
Attn: Scholarships
8669 Doral Boulevard, Suite 130
Doral, FL 33166
Phone: 800-443-9353
Web: www.aws.org/foundation/scholarships

Edward J. Brady Memorial Scholarship

Type of award: Scholarship, renewable.
Intended use: For sophomore, junior or senior study at 4-year institution.
Eligibility: Applicant must be at least 18. Applicant must be U.S. citizen or Canadian citizen.
Basis for selection: Major/career interest in welding or engineering. Applicant must demonstrate financial need, high academic achievement and seriousness of purpose.
Application requirements: Recommendations, essay, transcript, proof of eligibility. Proposed curriculum; brief biography; proof of hands-on welding experience.
Additional information: Interest in pursuing minimum four-year degree in welding engineering or welding engineering technology. Minimum 2.5 GPA.

Amount of award:	$2,500
Number of awards:	1
Number of applicants:	17
Application deadline:	February 15
Notification begins:	April 1
Total amount awarded:	$2,500

Contact:
American Welding Society Foundation, Inc.
Attn: Scholarships
8669 Doral Boulevard, Suite 130
Doral, FL 33166
Phone: 800-443-9353
Web: www.aws.org/foundation/scholarships

Howard E. and Wilma J. Adkins Memorial Scholarship

Type of award: Scholarship, renewable.
Intended use: For full-time junior or senior study at 4-year institution.
Eligibility: Applicant must be at least 18. Applicant must be U.S. citizen.
Basis for selection: Major/career interest in welding. Applicant must demonstrate high academic achievement and seriousness of purpose.
Application requirements: Recommendations, transcript, proof of eligibility.
Additional information: Applicant should have interest in pursuing four-year degree in welding engineering or welding engineering technology. Priority given to residents of Kentucky and Wisconsin. Minimum 3.2 GPA in engineering, scientific, and technical subjects; minimum overall 2.8 GPA.

Amount of award:	$2,500
Number of awards:	1
Number of applicants:	16
Application deadline:	February 15
Notification begins:	April 1
Total amount awarded:	$2,500

Contact:
American Welding Society Foundation Inc.
Attn: Scholarships
8669 Doral Boulevard, Suite 130
Doral, FL 33166
Phone: 800-443-9353
Web: www.aws.org/foundation/scholarships

Jack R. Barckhoff Welding Management Scholarship

Type of award: Scholarship.
Intended use: For junior study at 4-year institution. Designated institutions: Ohio State University.
Eligibility: Applicant must be U.S. citizen.
Basis for selection: Major/career interest in welding. Applicant must demonstrate high academic achievement.
Application requirements: Essay. 300- to 500-word essay.
Additional information: Minimum 2.5 GPA.

Amount of award:	$2,500
Number of awards:	2
Number of applicants:	5
Application deadline:	February 15
Notification begins:	April 1
Total amount awarded:	$5,000

Contact:
American Welding Society Foundation
Attn: Scholarships
8669 Doral Boulevard, Suite 130
Doral, FL 33166
Phone: 800-443-9353
Web: www.aws.org/foundation/scholarships

James A. Turner, Jr. Memorial Scholarship

Type of award: Scholarship, renewable.
Intended use: For full-time sophomore, junior or senior study at accredited 4-year institution.
Eligibility: Applicant must be at least 18. Applicant must be U.S. citizen.
Basis for selection: Major/career interest in welding or business/management/administration. Applicant must demonstrate financial need and seriousness of purpose.
Application requirements: Recommendations, transcript, proof of eligibility. Verification of employment, brief biography, financial aid report, proposed curriculum.
Additional information: Must have interest in pursuing management career in welding. Must work minimum ten hours per week at welding store.

Amount of award:	$3,500
Number of awards:	1
Number of applicants:	1
Application deadline:	February 15
Notification begins:	April 1
Total amount awarded:	$3,500

Contact:
American Welding Society Foundation, Inc.
Attn: Scholarships
8669 Doral Boulevard, Suite 130
Doral, FL 33166
Phone: 800-443-9353
Web: www.aws.org/foundation/scholarships

John C. Lincoln Memorial Scholarship

Type of award: Scholarship, renewable.
Intended use: For sophomore, junior or senior study at 4-year institution.
Eligibility: Applicant must be at least 18. Applicant must be U.S. citizen.
Basis for selection: Major/career interest in welding. Applicant must demonstrate financial need, high academic achievement and seriousness of purpose.

Application requirements: Recommendations, transcript, proof of eligibility.
Additional information: Minimum 2.5 GPA. Priority will be given to those individuals residing or attending school in Ohio or Arizona.

Amount of award:	$3,500
Number of awards:	1
Number of applicants:	22
Application deadline:	February 15
Notification begins:	April 1
Total amount awarded:	$3,500

Contact:
American Welding Society Foundation, Inc.
Attn: Scholarships
8669 Doral Boulevard, Suite 130
Doral, FL 33166
Phone: 800-443-9353
Web: www.aws.org/foundation/scholarships

Matsuo Bridge Company Ltd. of Japan Scholarship

Type of award: Scholarship.
Intended use: For junior, senior or graduate study at accredited 4-year or graduate institution in United States.
Eligibility: Applicant must be at least 18.
Basis for selection: Major/career interest in welding or engineering, civil. Applicant must demonstrate high academic achievement.
Application requirements: Recommendations, transcript, proof of eligibility.
Additional information: For students interested in pursuing career in civil engineering, welding engineering, or welding engineering technology. Priority given to applicants residing in California, Texas, Oregon, or Washington. Applicant does not have to be member of American Welding Society but must agree to participate in AWS Foundation or Matsuo Bridge Company sponsored publicity. Minimum 3.0 GPA.

Amount of award:	$2,500
Number of awards:	1
Number of applicants:	21
Application deadline:	February 15
Notification begins:	April 1
Total amount awarded:	$2,500

Contact:
American Welding Society Foundation, Inc.
Attn: Scholarships
8669 Doral Boulevard, Suite 130
Doral, FL 33166
Phone: 800-443-9353
Web: www.aws.org/foundation/scholarships

Miller Electric Manufacturing Company Ivic Scholarship

Type of award: Scholarship, renewable.
Intended use: For undergraduate study at accredited vocational, 2-year or 4-year institution in United States.
Eligibility: Applicant must be U.S. citizen.
Basis for selection: Major/career interest in welding. Applicant must demonstrate depth of character, leadership and seriousness of purpose.
Additional information: Competition based on AWS National Welding Trials and World Skills Competition.

Amount of award:	$10,000
Number of awards:	1

Contact:
American Welding Society Foundation, Inc.
Attn: Scholarships
8669 Doral Boulevard, Suite 130
Doral, FL 33166
Phone: 800-443-9353
Web: www.aws.org/foundation/scholarships

Miller Electric Mfg. Co. Scholarship

Type of award: Scholarship, renewable.
Intended use: For senior study at 4-year institution.
Eligibility: Applicant must be at least 18. Applicant must be U.S. citizen.
Basis for selection: Major/career interest in welding. Applicant must demonstrate high academic achievement.
Additional information: Applicant must show interest in welding engineering or welding engineering technology, and have work experience in the welding equipment field. Applicant must have minimum 3.0 GPA.

Amount of award:	$3,000
Number of awards:	2
Number of applicants:	20
Application deadline:	February 15
Notification begins:	April 1
Total amount awarded:	$6,000

Contact:
American Welding Society Foundation, Inc.
Attn: Scholarships
8669 Doral Boulevard, Suite 130
Doral, FL 33166
Phone: 800-443-9353
Web: www.aws.org/foundation/scholarships

Past Presidents Scholarship

Type of award: Scholarship.
Intended use: For junior, senior, master's or doctoral study at 4-year or graduate institution.
Basis for selection: Major/career interest in welding or engineering. Applicant must demonstrate financial need.
Application requirements: Essay. Essay should be 300-500 words.

Amount of award:	$2,500
Number of awards:	1
Number of applicants:	8
Application deadline:	February 15
Notification begins:	April 1
Total amount awarded:	$2,500

Contact:
American Welding Society Foundation, Inc.
Attn: Scholarships
8669 Doral Boulevard, Suite 130
Doral, FL 33166
Phone: 800-443-9353
Web: www.aws.org/foundation/scholarships

Praxair International Scholarship

Type of award: Scholarship, renewable.
Intended use: For full-time sophomore, junior or senior study at 4-year institution.
Eligibility: Applicant must be at least 18. Applicant must be U.S. citizen or Canadian citizen.
Basis for selection: Major/career interest in welding. Applicant must demonstrate financial need, high academic achievement, leadership and service orientation.

Application requirements: Recommendations, transcript, proof of eligibility.
Additional information: Applicant must have interest in pursuing minimum four-year degree in welding engineering or welding engineering technology. Minimum 2.5 GPA.

Amount of award:	$2,500
Number of awards:	1
Number of applicants:	22
Application deadline:	February 15
Notification begins:	April 1
Total amount awarded:	$2,500

Contact:
American Welding Society Foundation, Inc.
Attn: Praxair Scholarship
8669 Doral Boulevard, Suite 130
Doral, FL 33166
Phone: 800-443-9353
Web: www.aws.org/foundation/scholarships

Scholarships

Robert L. Peaslee Brazing Scholarship

Type of award: Scholarship, renewable.
Intended use: For junior or senior study at 4-year institution.
Eligibility: Applicant must be at least 18. Applicant must be U.S. citizen.
Basis for selection: Major/career interest in welding. Applicant must demonstrate high academic achievement.
Application requirements: Recommendations, essay, transcript.
Additional information: Applicant must have 3.0 GPA in engineering courses. Must show interest in pursuing degree in welding engineering or welding technology with emphasis on brazing applications.

Amount of award:	$2,500
Number of awards:	1
Number of applicants:	6
Application deadline:	February 15
Notification begins:	April 1
Total amount awarded:	$2,500

Contact:
American Welding Society Foundation, Inc.
Attn: Scholarships
8669 Doral Boulevard, Suite 130
Doral, FL 33166
Phone: 800-443-9353
Web: www.aws.org/foundation/scholarships

RWMA Scholarship

Type of award: Scholarship.
Intended use: For full-time junior study at 4-year institution.
Eligibility: Applicant must be U.S. citizen or Canadian citizens.
Basis for selection: Major/career interest in welding or engineering. Applicant must demonstrate high academic achievement.
Application requirements: Essay. 500-word or less essay.
Additional information: Minimum 3.0 GPA.

Amount of award:	$2,500
Number of awards:	1
Number of applicants:	3
Application deadline:	February 15
Notification begins:	April 1

Contact:
American Welding Society Foundation, Inc.
Attn: Scholarships
8669 Doral Boulevard, Suite 130
Doral, FL 33166
Phone: 800-443-9353
Web: www.aws.org/foundation/scholarships

William A. and Ann M. Brothers Scholarship

Type of award: Scholarship, renewable.
Intended use: For full-time undergraduate study at accredited 4-year institution.
Eligibility: Applicant must be at least 18. Applicant must be U.S. citizen.
Basis for selection: Major/career interest in welding. Applicant must demonstrate financial need and high academic achievement.
Additional information: Applicant must have minimum 2.5 GPA. Priority will be given to those individuals residing or attending schools in Ohio.

Amount of award:	$3,500
Number of awards:	1
Number of applicants:	23
Application deadline:	February 15
Notification begins:	April 1
Total amount awarded:	$3,500

Contact:
American Welding Society Foundation
Attn: Scholarships
8669 Doral Boulevard, Suite 130
Doral, FL 33166
Phone: 800-443-9353 ext. 461
Web: www.aws.org/foundation/scholarships

William B. Howell Memorial Scholarship

Type of award: Scholarship, renewable.
Intended use: For full-time undergraduate study at accredited 4-year institution in United States.
Eligibility: Applicant must be at least 18. Applicant must be U.S. citizen.
Basis for selection: Major/career interest in welding. Applicant must demonstrate financial need and high academic achievement.
Application requirements: Recommendations, transcript, proof of eligibility.
Additional information: Minimum 2.5 GPA required. Priority given to residents of Florida, Michigan, and Ohio. Applicant does not have to be a member of the American Welding Society.

Amount of award:	$2,500
Number of awards:	1
Number of applicants:	26
Application deadline:	February 15
Notification begins:	April 1
Total amount awarded:	$2,500

Contact:
American Welding Society Foundation, Inc.
Attn: Scholarships
8669 Doral Boulevard, Suite 130
Doral, FL 33166
Phone: 800-443-9353
Web: www.aws.org/foundation/scholarships

Angie Houtz Memorial Fund

Angie Houtz Scholarship

Type of award: Scholarship.
Intended use: For full-time undergraduate study at 2-year or 4-year institution in United States. Designated institutions: Maryland public institutions.
Eligibility: Applicant must be U.S. citizen, permanent resident or international student.
Basis for selection: Applicant must demonstrate high academic achievement and service orientation.
Application requirements: Recommendations, essay, transcript. List of extracurricular activities, detailed community service information.
Additional information: Minimum 3.0 GPA. Award based on GPA, amount and nature of community service, strength of letters of recommendation, and essay quality. Must have participated in at least 200 hours of community service in the last five years. Must not be related to any member of the Board of Directors. Award amount may vary. Applicant does not have to be a Maryland resident; international students encouraged to apply.

Amount of award:	$3,000
Number of awards:	3
Number of applicants:	100
Application deadline:	April 30
Total amount awarded:	$8,000

Contact:
Angie Houtz Memorial Fund
1450 Mercantile Lane
Suite 207C
Largo, MD 20774
Phone: 240-770-6688
Web: www.theangiefund.com/Scholarship.html

Annie's Homegrown

Annie's Homegrown Sustainable Agriculture Scholarships

Type of award: Scholarship.
Intended use: For full-time undergraduate or graduate study at accredited 2-year, 4-year or graduate institution in United States.
Basis for selection: Major/career interest in agriculture. Applicant must demonstrate high academic achievement.
Application requirements: Recommendations, essay, transcript.
Additional information: Award amount varies. Application and more information available on Website.

Amount of award:	$2,500-$10,000
Number of awards:	16
Application deadline:	December 15
Total amount awarded:	$100,000

Contact:
Annie's Homegrown Scholarship
Web: www.annies.com/our-practices/farming/agricultural-scholarships

Appaloosa Youth Foundation

Appaloosa Youth Foundation Educational Scholarships

Type of award: Scholarship, renewable.
Intended use: For full-time undergraduate or graduate study at accredited postsecondary institution in United States.
Eligibility: Applicant must be U.S. citizen or permanent resident.
Basis for selection: Applicant must demonstrate high academic achievement, leadership and service orientation.
Application requirements: Recommendations, essay, transcript, proof of eligibility. Photo. SAT/ACT scores optional.
Additional information: Applicant must be member of Appaloosa Horse Club or Appaloosa Youth Association. Must be involved in the Appaloosa industry and have general knowledge and accomplishments in horsemanship. GPA of 3.5 for one scholarship, GPA of 2.5 for other scholarships. Application available online.

Amount of award:	$1,000-$2,000
Number of awards:	7
Number of applicants:	25
Application deadline:	March 21
Notification begins:	June 1

Contact:
Appaloosa Youth Foundation Scholarship Committee
2720 Pullman Road
Moscow, ID 83843
Phone: 208-882-5578 ext. 245
Fax: 208-882-8150
Web: www.appaloosa.com

Arkansas Department of Higher Education

Arkansas Academic Challenge Scholarship

Type of award: Scholarship, renewable.
Intended use: For undergraduate study at postsecondary institution in United States. Designated institutions: Approved Arkansas colleges and universities.
Eligibility: Applicant must be high school senior. Applicant must be U.S. citizen or permanent resident residing in Arkansas.
Basis for selection: Applicant must demonstrate financial need and high academic achievement.
Application requirements: Transcript. ACT scores and FAFSA.
Additional information: Award is renewable up to four years. Eligibility requirements vary and are based on three student categories: Traditional (Incoming Freshman), Current Achievers, and Nontraditional Students. Visit Website for requirements. Applications available online or from the Department of Higher Education.

Amount of award:	$2,250-$4,500
Application deadline:	June 1

Scholarships

Contact:
Arkansas Department of Higher Education
423 Main Street
Suite 400
Little Rock, AR 72201
Phone: 501-371-2050
Web: www.adhe.edu

Arkansas Governor's Scholars Program

Type of award: Scholarship, renewable.
Intended use: For full-time undergraduate study at postsecondary institution. Designated institutions: Approved Arkansas colleges and universities.
Eligibility: Applicant must be high school senior. Applicant must be U.S. citizen or permanent resident residing in Arkansas.
Basis for selection: Applicant must demonstrate high academic achievement and leadership.
Additional information: Governor's Distinguished Scholars must have at least 32 ACT or 1410 SAT and minimum 3.5 GPA or have been selected as National Merit or National Achievement Finalist. Governor's Distinguished Scholars receive award equal to tuition, fees, room, and board up to $10,000 per year. One Governor's Scholarship award per county given to applicants who do not meet Governor's Distinguished Scholars criteria. Governor's Scholars must have minimum 3.5 GPA or 27 ACT or 1220 SAT and receive award of $4,000. Awards renewable up to four years if Distinguished Scholars maintain minimum 3.25 GPA and Governor's Scholars maintain minimum 3.0 GPA and at least 30 credit hours per year. Visit Website for more information.

Amount of award:	$4,000-$10,000
Number of awards:	375
Application deadline:	February 1

Contact:
Arkansas Department of Higher Education
Attn: Governor's Scholars Program
423 Main Street, Suite 400
Little Rock, AR 72201
Phone: 501-371-2050
Web: www.adhe.edu

Arkansas Law Enforcement Officers' Dependents Scholarship

Type of award: Scholarship, renewable.
Intended use: For undergraduate study at accredited vocational, 2-year or 4-year institution in United States. Designated institutions: Public schools in Arkansas.
Eligibility: Applicant must be U.S. citizen or permanent resident residing in Arkansas.
Basis for selection: Applicant must demonstrate high academic achievement.
Application requirements: Proof of eligibility.
Additional information: Applicant must be dependent or spouse of one of the following who was killed or permanently disabled in line of duty: law enforcement officer; firefighter; sheriff; constable; game warden; certain state highway, forestry, correction, or park employees; EMT; Department of Community Punishment employee. Dependent child applicant may be no older than 23; no age restriction for spouse, but must not be remarried. Award is for tuition, fees, and room and is for up to eight semesters. Must maintain 2.0 GPA. Visit Website for more information and application.

Amount of award:	Full tuition
Application deadline:	June 1

Contact:
Arkansas Department of Higher Education
423 Main Street
Suite 400
Little Rock, AR 72201
Phone: 501-371-2050
Web: www.adhe.edu

Arkansas Military Dependents Scholarship Program

Type of award: Scholarship, renewable.
Intended use: For full-time undergraduate study at vocational, 2-year or 4-year institution in United States. Designated institutions: Public schools in Arkansas.
Eligibility: Applicant must be U.S. citizen or permanent resident residing in Arkansas. Applicant must be dependent of disabled veteran or POW/MIA; or spouse of disabled veteran or POW/MIA who served in the Army, Air Force, Marines, Navy, Coast Guard or Reserves/National Guard. Parent/spouse may also have been killed in action or killed on ordinance delivery. All incidents must have occurred while on active duty after 1/1/60. Parent/spouse must be AR resident or must have been at time of enlistment. Dependent must have been born, adopted, or in legal custody of veteran under whom he/she is applying.
Basis for selection: Applicant must demonstrate high academic achievement.
Application requirements: Proof of eligibility.
Additional information: Award for tuition, fees, room, and board. Renewable up to four years. Must maintain 2.0 GPA and complete a minimum 24 semester hours per academic year. Visit Website for more information and application.

Amount of award:	Full tuition
Application deadline:	June 1

Contact:
Arkansas Department of Higher Education
Attn: Military Dependents Scholarship Program
423 Main Street, Suite 400
Little Rock, AR 72201
Phone: 501-371-2050
Web: www.adhe.edu

Arkansas Second Effort Scholarship

Type of award: Scholarship, renewable.
Intended use: For undergraduate study at postsecondary institution.
Eligibility: Applicant must be at least 18, returning adult student. Applicant must be U.S. citizen or permanent resident residing in Arkansas.
Basis for selection: Applicant must demonstrate high academic achievement.
Additional information: Applicant must not have graduated from high school. Must have scored in top ten on GED test in previous calendar year. Students do not apply for this award; top ten scorers are contacted directly by Arkansas Department of Higher Education. Award renewable up to four years (or equivalent if student is enrolled part-time), provided student maintains minimum 2.5 GPA.

Amount of award:	$1,000
Number of awards:	10

Contact:
Arkansas Department of Higher Education
423 Main Street
Suite 400
Little Rock, AR 72201
Phone: 501-371-2050
Web: www.adhe.edu

Arkansas Workforce Improvement Grant

Type of award: Scholarship.
Intended use: For undergraduate study at postsecondary institution. Designated institutions: Not-for-profit institutions in Arkansas.
Eligibility: Applicant must be at least 24, returning adult student. Applicant must be U.S. citizen or permanent resident residing in Arkansas.
Basis for selection: Applicant must demonstrate financial need.
Application requirements: FAFSA.
Additional information: Must be Arkansas resident at least six months before applying. Students enrolled part time will have grants prorated. Must have unmet need after any Pell Grant awarded. Application deadline determined by each institution for its students. Students apply by completing FAFSA. Must have graduated high school or have GED.

Amount of award:	$2,000

Contact:
Arkansas Department of Higher Education
423 Main Street
Suite 400
Little Rock, AR 72201
Phone: 501-371-2050
Web: www.adhe.edu

Armed Forces Communications and Electronics Association

AFCEA Intelligence Scholarship

Type of award: Scholarship.
Intended use: For full-time undergraduate or graduate study at accredited 2-year, 4-year or graduate institution in United States.
Eligibility: Applicant must be U.S. citizen.
Basis for selection: Major/career interest in computer/information sciences; information systems or engineering, computer. Applicant must demonstrate high academic achievement.
Application requirements: Recommendations, transcript.
Additional information: Minimum 3.0 GPA. Candidates must major in a field directly related to the support of U.S. cyber enterprises, U.S. Intelligence, and/or homeland security with relevance to the mission of AFCEA, such as cyber security, cyber attack, computer science, information technology, electronic engineering, and/or foreign language. Award amount is $2250 for undergraduate students and $5000 for graduate students. Distance-learning programs are eligible. Visit Website for application and details.

Amount of award:	$2,250-$5,000
Application deadline:	November 15

Contact:
Armed Forces Communications and Electronics Association
Attn: Mr. Fred H. Rainbow
4400 Fair Lakes Court
Fairfax, VA 22033-3899
Phone: 703-631-6149
Fax: 703-631-4693
Web: www.afcea.org

AFCEA Military Personnel & Dependents Scholarship

Type of award: Scholarship.
Intended use: For full-time sophomore or junior study at accredited 4-year institution in United States.
Eligibility: Applicant must be U.S. citizen. Applicant must be in military service, veteran or disabled while on active duty; or dependent of active service person or veteran; or spouse of active service person or veteran.
Basis for selection: Major/career interest in aerospace; computer/information sciences; engineering, chemical; physics; mathematics; engineering, electrical/electronic; education; technology; information systems or foreign languages. Applicant must demonstrate high academic achievement, depth of character, leadership, patriotism, seriousness of purpose and service orientation.
Application requirements: Recommendations, transcript, proof of eligibility. Copy of discharge form DD214, certificate of service, or facsimile of applicant's current DOD or Coast Guard identification card.
Additional information: Veterans enrolled as freshmen eligible to apply, but all other applicants must be in at least their sophomore year. Must have minimum 3.0 GPA. Majors directly related to support of U.S. intelligence enterprises or national security with relevance to the mission of AFCEA also eligible. Visit Website for application and deadline.

Amount of award:	$2,000
Number of awards:	10
Application deadline:	November 1
Notification begins:	June 1
Total amount awarded:	$20,000

Contact:
AFCEA Educational Foundation
Attn: Mr. Fred H. Rainbow
4400 Fair Lakes Court
Fairfax, VA 22033-3899
Phone: 703-631-6149
Fax: 703-631-4693
Web: www.afcea.org/scholarships

AFCEA ROTC Scholarship

Type of award: Scholarship.
Intended use: For full-time sophomore or junior study at accredited 4-year institution in United States.
Eligibility: Applicant must be U.S. citizen.
Basis for selection: Major/career interest in aerospace; engineering; computer/information sciences; education; physics; mathematics; technology; electronics; foreign languages or international studies. Applicant must demonstrate financial need, high academic achievement, depth of character, leadership, patriotism, seriousness of purpose and service orientation.
Application requirements: Recommendations, transcript, nomination by professor of military science, naval science, or aerospace studies or designated commanding officer.

Additional information: Applicant must be enrolled in ROTC. Majors directly related to support of U.S. national security enterprises with relevance to mission of AFCEA also eligible.

Amount of award: $2,000
Number of awards: 50
Application deadline: February 15
Notification begins: June 1
Total amount awarded: $112,000

Contact:
Armed Forces Communications and Electronics Association
Mr. Fred H. Rainbow
4400 Fair Lakes Court
Fairfax, VA 22033-3899
Phone: 703-631-6149
Fax: 703-631-4693
Web: www.afcea.org/scholarships

AFCEA Scholarship for Underserved Students (HBCU)

Type of award: Scholarship.
Intended use: For sophomore or junior study at accredited 2-year or 4-year institution in United States. Designated institutions: Historically black colleges and universities.
Basis for selection: Major/career interest in aerospace; engineering, electrical/electronic; engineering, computer; information systems; computer/information sciences; physics or mathematics. Applicant must demonstrate financial need, high academic achievement and leadership.
Application requirements: Recommendations, transcript.
Additional information: Distance-learning or online programs affiliated with HCBUs are eligible. Majors directly related to the support of U.S. intelligence or homeland security enterprises with relevance to the mission of AFCEA are also eligible. Special consideration given to military-enlisted candidates/military veterans.

Amount of award: $5,000
Number of awards: 2
Application deadline: May 15

Contact:
AFCEA Educational Foundation
Mr. Fred H. Rainbow
4400 Fair Lakes Court
Fairfax, VA 22033-3899
Phone: 703-631-6149
Fax: 703-631-4693
Web: www.afcea.org/scholarships

AFCEA War Veterans/Disabled War Veterans Scholarship

Type of award: Scholarship.
Intended use: For undergraduate study at 2-year or 4-year institution in United States.
Eligibility: Applicant must be U.S. citizen. Applicant must be in military service or veteran in the Army, Air Force, Marines, Navy, Coast Guard or Reserves/National Guard.
Basis for selection: Major/career interest in aerospace; engineering, computer; engineering, electrical/electronic; information systems; technology; computer/information sciences; physics; mathematics or education.
Application requirements: Recommendations, transcript. Certificate of Service, Discharge Form DD214, or facsimile of candidate's current DoD or Coast Guard Identification Card. Please black out your Social Security Number when submitting.
Additional information: For honorably discharged U.S. military veterans and disabled veterans of the Enduring Freedom (Afghanistan) or Iraqi Freedom operations. Majors directly related to the support of U.S. intelligence or national security enterprises with relevance to the mission of AFCEA are also eligible. Distance-learning or online programs affiliated with a major U.S. institution are eligible.

Amount of award: $2,500
Number of awards: 8
Application deadline: May 1, November 1

Contact:
Armed Forces Communications and Electronics Association
Mr. Fred H. Rainbow
4400 Fair Lakes Court
Fairfax, VA 22033-3899
Phone: 703-631-6138
Fax: 703-631-4693
Web: www.afcea.org/scholarships

Cyber Security Scholarships

Type of award: Scholarship, renewable.
Intended use: For sophomore, junior or graduate study at accredited 2-year, 4-year or graduate institution in United States.
Eligibility: Applicant must be U.S. citizen.
Basis for selection: Major/career interest in computer/information sciences or engineering, electrical/electronic. Applicant must demonstrate financial need, high academic achievement and leadership.
Application requirements: Recommendations, transcript.
Additional information: Minimum 3.0 GPA. Must be pursuing academic degree in cyber security, cyber attack, computer science, information technology, digital forensics, or electronic engineering.

Amount of award: $5,000
Application deadline: November 15

Contact:
Armed Forces Communications and Electronics Association
Attn: Mr. Fred Rainbow
4400 Fair Lakes Court
Fairfax, VA 22033
Phone: 800-336-4583
Web: www.afcea.org

STEM Majors Scholarship

Type of award: Scholarship, renewable.
Intended use: For undergraduate or graduate study at vocational, 4-year or graduate institution.
Eligibility: Applicant must be U.S. citizen.
Basis for selection: Major/career interest in electronics; computer/information sciences; engineering, chemical; technology; information systems; physics or mathematics. Applicant must demonstrate high academic achievement.
Application requirements: Recommendations, transcript.
Additional information: Minimum 3.4 GPA. Must be studying STEM major: Science, Technology, Engineering, or Math. Visit Website for more details.

Application deadline: May 1

Contact:
Armed Forces Communications and Electronics Association
Attn: Mr. Fred Rainbow
4400 Fair Lakes Court
Fairfax, VA 22033
Phone: 800-336-4583
Web: www.afcea.org

STEM Teacher Scholarships

Type of award: Scholarship.
Intended use: For full-time junior, senior or graduate study at accredited postsecondary institution in United States.
Eligibility: Applicant must be U.S. citizen.
Basis for selection: Major/career interest in education. Applicant must demonstrate high academic achievement.
Application requirements: Recommendations, transcript.
Additional information: Minimum 3.0 GPA. Intended for students pursuing an education degree for the purpose of teaching science, technology, engineering or mathematics at a U.S. middle or secondary school. Each graduating recipient receives a $1,000 AFCEA Science Teaching Tools grant per year for 3 years, on the condition they remain teaching a STEM subject.

Amount of award:	$5,000
Number of awards:	50
Application deadline:	April 1

Contact:
AFCEA Educational Foundation
Mr. Fred H. Rainbow
4400 Fair Lakes Court
Fairfax, VA 22033-3899
Phone: 703-631-6149
Fax: 703-631-4693
Web: www.afcea.org/scholarships

Armenian General Benevolent Union (AGBU)

AGBU International Scholarships

Type of award: Scholarship, renewable.
Intended use: For full-time undergraduate or graduate study at postsecondary institution outside United States or Canada.
Eligibility: Applicant must be Armenian. Applicant must be international student.
Basis for selection: Applicant must demonstrate financial need, high academic achievement and service orientation.
Application requirements: Recommendations, essay, transcript, proof of eligibility. Resume, passport-size photograph. Copy of Bursar's receipt, copy of financial award letter.
Additional information: Minimum 3.5 GPA. Awarded to students of Armenian descent enrolled in institutions in their countries of residence. Some selected fields of graduate study may also be considered. Excludes Armenian citizens studying in Armenia. Deadline is May 31 for study in all countries except Syria and France. Deadline for study in Syria and France is October 15. Number of awards varies. Not for use in the U.S.

Amount of award:	$500-$3,000
Number of applicants:	443
Application deadline:	May 31, October 15
Total amount awarded:	$445,000

Contact:
Armenian General Benevolent Union (AGBU)
55 East 59th Street
7th Floor
New York, NY 10022
Phone: 212-319-6383
Fax: 212-319-6507
Web: www.agbu-scholarship.org

Armenian General Benevolent Union Performing Arts Fellowships

Type of award: Scholarship, renewable.
Intended use: For full-time undergraduate or graduate study in or outside United States.
Eligibility: Applicant must be Armenian.
Basis for selection: Competition/talent/interest in performing arts. Major/career interest in performing arts. Applicant must demonstrate financial need, high academic achievement and service orientation.
Application requirements: Recommendations, essay, transcript, proof of eligibility. Resume, one passport-size photograph, enrollment verification/acceptance letter, bursar's receipt, financial award letter, CD of or link to most current recording (if applicable).
Additional information: Minimum 3.5 GPA. Number of awards varies based on funding. Applicants may be of Armenian descent. Excludes Armenian citizens studying in Armenia. Number of awards varies. Visit Website for more information.

Amount of award:	$2,500-$7,500
Number of applicants:	77
Application deadline:	May 15
Notification begins:	July 31
Total amount awarded:	$132,150

Contact:
Armenian General Benevolent Union
Attn: Scholarship Program
55 E. 59th Street, 7th Floor
New York, NY 10022-1112
Phone: 212-319-6383
Fax: 212-319-6507
Web: www.agbu-scholarship.org

ARMY Emergency Relief

MG James Ursano Scholarship Program

Type of award: Scholarship, renewable.
Intended use: For full-time undergraduate study at accredited postsecondary institution.
Eligibility: Applicant must be single, no older than 23. Applicant must be dependent of active service person, veteran or deceased veteran who serves or served in the Army.
Basis for selection: Applicant must demonstrate financial need, high academic achievement and leadership.
Application requirements: Transcript, proof of eligibility. Student Aid Report (SAR).
Additional information: Applicant must be registered in DEERS. Student Aid Report deadline 5/1. Must maintain 2.0 GPA. Amount of award and number of recipients vary. Application must be submitted via Website; supporting documentation should be emailed.

Amount of award:	$500-$3,500
Number of applicants:	5,300
Application deadline:	May 1
Notification begins:	June 1
Total amount awarded:	$6,000,000

Contact:
ARMY Emergency Relief
MG James Ursano Scholarship Program
200 Stovall Street
Alexandria, VA 22332-0600
Phone: 703-428-0035
Fax: 703-325-7183
Web: www.aerhq.org

The Art Institutes

Best Teen Chef Culinary Scholarship Competition

Type of award: Scholarship.
Intended use: For undergraduate study at 2-year or 4-year institution in United States. Designated institutions: Art Institute schools offering culinary arts programs.
Eligibility: Applicant must be high school senior. Applicant must be U.S. citizen, Canadian citizen (excluding Quebec).
Basis for selection: Competition/talent/interest in culinary arts, based on meal preparation ability and originality. Major/career interest in culinary arts or hotel/restaurant management. Applicant must demonstrate high academic achievement.
Application requirements: Essay, transcript. Recipe.
Additional information: Award amount varies depending on placement in competition. First-place winner will compete in national event slated for April. Minimum high school GPA of 2.0. Visit Website for deadline and application.

Amount of award:	$1,000-$4,000
Number of awards:	2
Number of applicants:	265
Total amount awarded:	$5,000

Contact:
The Art Institutes
210 Sixth Avenue, 33rd Floor
Pittsburgh, PA 15222-2603
Phone: 888-624-0300
Web: www.artinstitutes.edu

Arthur and Doreen Parrett Scholarship Trust Fund

Arthur and Doreen Parrett Scholarship

Type of award: Scholarship, renewable.
Intended use: For full-time sophomore, junior, senior, master's, doctoral or first professional study at accredited postsecondary institution.
Eligibility: Applicant must be residing in Washington.
Basis for selection: Major/career interest in science, general; engineering; dentistry or medicine. Applicant must demonstrate financial need and high academic achievement.
Application requirements: Recommendations, transcript.
Additional information: Applicants must have completed first year of college. Include SASE with inquiries, and information will be forwarded.

Amount of award:	$2,500-$3,600
Number of awards:	10
Number of applicants:	50
Application deadline:	January 31

Contact:
Arthur and Doreen Parrett Scholarship Trust Fund
c/o U.S. Bank - Trust Dept.
1420 5th Avenue, Suite 2100
Seattle, WA 98101

The ASCAP Foundation

The Herb Alpert Young Jazz Composer Awards

Type of award: Scholarship.
Intended use: For undergraduate study at postsecondary institution.
Eligibility: Applicant must be no older than 29. Applicant must be U.S. citizen or permanent resident.
Basis for selection: Competition/talent/interest in music performance/composition.
Application requirements: Notated score and CD or cassette of one composition. Biographical information listing music studies, background, and experience. SASE.
Additional information: Number of awards and award amounts vary. Must be under age 30 as of Dec. 31.

Amount of award:	$500-$2,000
Number of awards:	30
Number of applicants:	350
Application deadline:	December 1
Notification begins:	February 15
Total amount awarded:	$30,000

Contact:
Cia Toscanini, The ASCAP Foundation
Young JAZZ Composer Awards
One Lincoln Plaza
New York, NY 10023
Web: www.ascapfoundation.org

Morton Gould Young Composer Awards

Type of award: Scholarship, renewable.
Intended use: For non-degree study.
Eligibility: Applicant must be no older than 29.
Basis for selection: Competition/talent/interest in music performance/composition. Major/career interest in music.
Application requirements: Reproduction of original score, biographical and educational information, list of compositions to date, SASE, CD of composition (if available).
Additional information: Number of awards varies. Applicant must not have reached 30th birthday by January 1 and may submit only one composition. International applicants must have student visa.

Amount of award:	$750-$2,500
Number of applicants:	750
Application deadline:	February 15
Notification begins:	April 1
Total amount awarded:	$45,000

Contact:
The ASCAP Foundation Morton Gould Young Composer Awards
c/o Cia Toscanini
One Lincoln Plaza
New York, NY 10023
Phone: 212-621-6329
Web: www.ascapfoundation.org

Rudolf Nissim Prize

Type of award: Scholarship.
Intended use: For non-degree study.
Basis for selection: Competition/talent/interest in music performance/composition. Major/career interest in music.
Application requirements: Bound copy of score of one original concert work, composer biography, SASE.
Additional information: Award for work requiring a conductor that has not been performed professionally. Applicant must be concert composer member of ASCAP. Visit Website for specific application requirements and details.

Amount of award:	$5,000
Number of awards:	1
Number of applicants:	230
Application deadline:	November 15
Notification begins:	January 15
Total amount awarded:	$5,000

Contact:
Cia Toscanini
c/o The ASCAP Foundation/Rudolf Nissim Prize
One Lincoln Plaza
New York, NY 10023
Phone: 212-621-6329
Web: www.ascapfoundation.org

ASCO Numatics

Industrial Automation Engineering College Scholarships

Type of award: Scholarship.
Intended use: For full-time junior, senior or graduate study at accredited 4-year or graduate institution in United States.
Eligibility: Applicant must be U.S. citizen or permanent resident.
Basis for selection: Major/career interest in engineering; engineering, electrical/electronic or engineering, mechanical. Applicant must demonstrate high academic achievement and leadership.
Additional information: For students planning to pursue careers in industrial automation-related disciplines. Minimum 3.2 GPA. ASCO Numatics employees and their families are ineligible. Notification begins mid-June. Application details and forms available on Website.

Amount of award:	$5,000
Number of awards:	2
Application deadline:	May 23
Total amount awarded:	$10,000

Contact:
ASCO Numatics
50 Hanover Road
Florham Park, NJ 07932
Phone: 973-966-2000
Fax: 973-966-2628
Web: www.asconumatics.com/scholarship

Asian American Journalists Association

Asian American Journalists Association Print & Online News Grants

Type of award: Scholarship.
Intended use: For full-time undergraduate study.
Eligibility: Applicant must be at least 18.
Basis for selection: Major/career interest in journalism. Applicant must demonstrate financial need and seriousness of purpose.
Application requirements: Recommendations, essay. Resume, proof of age, statement of financial need, and internship verification. Submit original plus three copies of all material.
Additional information: Applicant may also be recent college graduate. Must have already secured summer internship at print or online company before applying. Must be committed to AAJA's mission. AAJA membership encouraged for all applicants and required for selected interns. Deadline mid-May; notification begins February. Visit Website for specific dates. Apply online.

Amount of award:	$1,000
Number of awards:	1

Contact:
Asian American Journalists Association
Print & Online News Grants
5 Third Street, Suite 1108
San Francisco, CA 94103
Phone: 415-346-2051 ext. 102
Fax: 415-346-6343
Web: www.aaja.org

Broadcast News Grants

Type of award: Scholarship.
Intended use: For full-time undergraduate study at 4-year institution.
Eligibility: Applicant must be at least 18.
Basis for selection: Major/career interest in journalism or radio/television/film. Applicant must demonstrate financial need.
Application requirements: Recommendations, essay. Resume, proof of age, statement of financial need, and internship verification. Submit original plus three copies of all materials.
Additional information: Applicant must have already secured summer broadcast internship at TV or radio network, and must be committed to AAJA's mission. AAJA membership encouraged for all applicants and required for awardees. Recent college graduates also eligible. Deadline mid-May; notification begins February. Visit Website for specific dates. Apply online.

Amount of award:	$1,000-$2,500
Number of awards:	2

Contact:
Asian American Journalists Association
Broadcast News Grants
5 Third Street, Suite 1108
San Francisco, CA 94103
Phone: 415-346-2051 ext. 102
Fax: 415-346-6343
Web: www.aaja.org

CIC/Anna Chennault Scholarship

Type of award: Scholarship.
Intended use: For sophomore study at 4-year institution.
Basis for selection: Major/career interest in journalism. Applicant must demonstrate high academic achievement.
Additional information: Award includes $3900 for student's college education and $1100 for travel, lodging, and registration costs for student to attend AAJA's annual national convention. Recipients must become AAJA student members. Applicant must demonstrate journalistic ability, commitment to the field of journalism, and sensitivity to Asian American and Pacific Islander issues. Deadline in May.

Amount of award:	$5,000

Contact:
Asian American Journalists Association
CIC/Anna Chennault Scholarship
5 Third Street, Suite 1108
San Francisco, CA 94103
Phone: 415-346-2051 ext. 102
Fax: 415-346-6343
Web: www.aaja.org

Stanford Chen Internship Grant

Type of award: Scholarship.
Intended use: For junior, senior or graduate study at 4-year or graduate institution.
Basis for selection: Major/career interest in journalism. Applicant must demonstrate financial need and seriousness of purpose.
Application requirements: Recommendations, essay, proof of eligibility. Resume, statement of financial need, and internship verification. Original plus three copies of all application materials.
Additional information: Applicant must have already secured internship with small- to medium-size media company (print companies with daily circulation under 100,000 and broadcast markets smaller than top 50). Application may be downloaded from Website. AAJA membership is encouraged for all applicants and required for selected recipients. Deadline varies. Visit Website for specific dates.

Amount of award:	$1,750
Number of awards:	1
Total amount awarded:	$1,750

Contact:
Asian American Journalists Association
Stanford Chen Internship Grant
5 Third Street, Suite 1108
San Francisco, CA 94103
Phone: 415-346-2051 ext. 102
Fax: 415-346-6343
Web: www.aaja.org

Asian American Journalists Association, Texas Chapter

AAJA Texas Student Scholarship

Type of award: Scholarship.
Intended use: For undergraduate or graduate study at accredited 4-year or graduate institution.
Basis for selection: Major/career interest in journalism. Applicant must demonstrate high academic achievement and seriousness of purpose.
Application requirements: Recommendations, essay, transcript. Resume, work samples.
Additional information: Applicant must be resident of or attending school in Texas, Arkansas, Louisiana, Oklahoma, or New Mexico. High school seniors also eligible to apply. Must display commitment to journalism and awareness of Asian-American issues. Visit Website for application.

Amount of award:	$1,000
Number of awards:	2
Application deadline:	May 31
Notification begins:	June 30
Total amount awarded:	$2,000

Contact:
Scott Nishimura Fort Worth Star-Telegram
P.O. Box 1870
Fort Worth, TX 76101
Phone: 817-390-7808
Web: www.aajatexas.org

ASM Materials Education Foundation

ASM Outstanding Scholars Awards

Type of award: Scholarship, renewable.
Intended use: For full-time sophomore, junior or senior study at accredited 4-year institution in or outside United States.
Basis for selection: Major/career interest in engineering, materials or materials science. Applicant must demonstrate high academic achievement.
Application requirements: Recommendations, essay, transcript. Photograph. Resume optional.
Additional information: May also major in metallurgy or related science or engineering disciplines if applicant demonstrates strong interest in materials science. Must be student member of Material Advantage. International student members may apply. Visit Website for application and full details.

Amount of award:	$2,000
Number of awards:	3
Application deadline:	May 1
Notification begins:	July 15
Total amount awarded:	$6,000

Contact:
ASM Materials Education Foundation
Undergraduate Scholarship Program
9639 Kinsman Road
Materials Park, OH 44073-0002
Phone: 440-338-5151
Fax: 440-338-4634
Web: www.asmfoundation.org

Edward J. Dulis Scholarship

Type of award: Scholarship, renewable.
Intended use: For junior or senior study at accredited 4-year institution in United States or Canada.
Basis for selection: Major/career interest in engineering, materials or materials science. Applicant must demonstrate financial need and high academic achievement.
Application requirements: Recommendations, essay, transcript. Photograph. Resume optional.
Additional information: Applicant may also major in metallurgy or related science or engineering field if interested in materials science. Must be student member of Material Advantage. Visit Website for application and full details.

Amount of award:	$1,500
Number of awards:	1
Application deadline:	May 1
Notification begins:	July 15

Contact:
ASM Materials Education Foundation
Undergraduate Scholarship Program
9639 Kinsman Road
Materials Park, OH 44073-0002
Phone: 440-338-5151
Fax: 440-338-4634
Web: www.asmfoundation.org

George A. Roberts Scholarships

Type of award: Scholarship, renewable.
Intended use: For junior or senior study at accredited 4-year institution in United States or Canada.
Basis for selection: Major/career interest in engineering, materials or materials science. Applicant must demonstrate financial need and high academic achievement.
Application requirements: Recommendations, essay, transcript. Photograph, resume optional.
Additional information: Applicant may also major in metallurgy or related science or engineering field if interested in materials science. Must be student member of Material Advantage. Visit Website for application and full details.

Amount of award:	$6,000
Number of awards:	7
Application deadline:	May 1
Notification begins:	July 15
Total amount awarded:	$42,000

Contact:
ASM Materials Education Foundation
Undergraduate Scholarship Program
9639 Kinsman Road
Materials Park, OH 44073-0002
Phone: 440-338-5151
Fax: 440-338-4634
Web: www.asmfoundation.org

John M. Haniak Scholarship

Type of award: Scholarship, renewable.
Intended use: For junior or senior study at accredited 4-year institution in United States or Canada.
Basis for selection: Major/career interest in engineering, materials or materials science. Applicant must demonstrate financial need and high academic achievement.
Application requirements: Recommendations, essay, transcript. Photograph. Resume optional.
Additional information: Applicant may also major in metallurgy or related science or engineering field if interested in materials science. Must be student member of Material Advantage. Visit Website for application and full details.

Amount of award:	$1,500
Number of awards:	1
Application deadline:	May 1
Notification begins:	July 15

Contact:
ASM Materials Education Foundation
Undergraduate Scholarship Program
9639 Kinsman Road
Materials Park, OH 44073-0002
Phone: 440-338-5151
Fax: 440-338-4634
Web: www.asmfoundation.org

Ladish Co. Foundation Scholarships

Type of award: Scholarship.
Intended use: For sophomore, junior or senior study at accredited 4-year institution. Designated institutions: Wisconsin institutions.
Eligibility: Applicant must be residing in Wisconsin.
Basis for selection: Major/career interest in engineering or materials science. Applicant must demonstrate high academic achievement, depth of character and seriousness of purpose.
Application requirements: Recommendations, essay, transcript. Photograph, resume optional.
Additional information: Applicant must be a Material Advantage student member, and must have intended or declared major in metallurgy, materials science engineering, or related science or engineering disciplines. Visit Website for application and details.

Amount of award:	$2,500
Number of awards:	2
Application deadline:	May 1
Notification begins:	July 15

Contact:
ASM Materials Education Foundation
Undergraduate Scholarship Program
9639 Kinsman Road
Materials Park, OH 44073-0002
Phone: 440-338-5151
Fax: 440-338-4634
Web: www.asmfoundation.org

Lucille & Charles A. Wert Scholarship

Type of award: Scholarship, renewable.
Intended use: For junior or senior study at accredited 4-year institution in United States or Canada.
Basis for selection: Major/career interest in engineering, materials or materials science. Applicant must demonstrate financial need and high academic achievement.
Application requirements: Recommendations, essay, transcript. Photograph, resume optional.

Additional information: Applicant may also major in metallurgy or related science or engineering field if interested in materials science. Must be student member of Material Advantage. Scholarship provides recipient with one-year full tuition up to $10,000. Visit Website for application and full details.

Amount of award: $10,000
Number of awards: 1
Application deadline: May 1
Notification begins: July 15

Contact:
ASM Materials Education Foundation
Undergraduate Scholarship Program
9639 Kinsman Road
Materials Park, OH 44073-0002
Phone: 440-338-5151
Fax: 440-338-4634
Web: www.asmfoundation.org

William & Mary Dyrkacz Scholarships

Type of award: Scholarship.
Intended use: For sophomore, junior or senior study at accredited 4-year institution.
Basis for selection: Major/career interest in engineering or materials science. Applicant must demonstrate high academic achievement, depth of character and seriousness of purpose.
Application requirements: Recommendations, essay, transcript. Photograph, resume optional.
Additional information: Applicant must be a Material Advantage student member, and must have intended or declared major in metallurgy, materials science engineering, or related science or engineering disciplines. Visit Website for application and details.

Amount of award: $6,000
Number of awards: 4
Application deadline: May 1
Notification begins: July 15

Contact:
ASM Materials Education Foundation
Undergraduate Scholarship Program
9639 Kinsman Road
Materials Park, OH 44073-0002
Phone: 440-338-5151
Fax: 440-338-4634
Web: www.asmfoundation.org

William Park Woodside Founder's Scholarship

Type of award: Scholarship, renewable.
Intended use: For junior or senior study at accredited 4-year institution in United States or Canada.
Basis for selection: Major/career interest in engineering, materials or materials science. Applicant must demonstrate financial need and high academic achievement.
Application requirements: Recommendations, essay, transcript. Photograph. Resume optional.
Additional information: May also have major in metallurgy or related science or engineering discipline if applicant demonstrates strong interest in materials science. Must be Material Advantage student member. Scholarship provides recipient with one-year full tuition, up to $10,000. Visit Website for application and full details.

Amount of award: $10,000
Number of awards: 1
Application deadline: May 1
Notification begins: July 15
Total amount awarded: $10,000

Contact:
ASM Materials Education Foundation
Undergraduate Scholarship Program
9639 Kinsman Road
Materials Park, OH 44073-0002
Phone: 440-338-5151
Fax: 440-338-4634
Web: www.asmfoundation.org

ASME Auxiliary, Inc.

Agnes Malakate Kezios Scholarship

Type of award: Scholarship.
Intended use: For full-time senior study at 4-year institution in United States. Designated institutions: Schools with ABET-accredited mechanical engineering programs.
Eligibility: Applicant must be U.S. citizen.
Basis for selection: Major/career interest in engineering, mechanical. Applicant must demonstrate financial need, high academic achievement and depth of character.
Application requirements: Recommendations, transcript.
Additional information: For student in final year of undergraduate program in mechanical engineering. Must be ASME student member. Download application from Website or send SASE or e-mail to request application.

Amount of award: $2,000
Number of awards: 1
Application deadline: March 15

Contact:
Sara Sahay
ASME Auxiliary - Undergraduate Scholarships
170 East Opel Drive
Glastonbury, CT 06033
Web: www.asme.org/about-asme/scholarship-and-loans/about-asme-scholarships

Allen J. Baldwin Scholarship

Type of award: Scholarship.
Intended use: For full-time senior study at 4-year institution in United States. Designated institutions: Schools with ABET-accredited mechanical engineering programs.
Eligibility: Applicant must be U.S. citizen.
Basis for selection: Major/career interest in engineering, mechanical. Applicant must demonstrate financial need, high academic achievement and depth of character.
Application requirements: Recommendations, transcript.
Additional information: For student in final year of undergraduate study in mechanical engineering. Must be ASME student member. Download application from Website or send SASE or e-mail to request application.

Amount of award: $2,000
Number of awards: 1
Application deadline: March 15

Contact:
Sara Sahay
ASME Auxiliary - Undergraduate Scholarships
170 East Opel Drive
Glastonbury, CT 06033
Web: www.asme.org/about-asme/scholarship-and-loans/about-asme-scholarships

Berna Lou Cartwright Scholarship

Type of award: Scholarship.
Intended use: For full-time senior study at 4-year institution in United States. Designated institutions: Schools with ABET-accredited mechanical engineering programs.
Eligibility: Applicant must be U.S. citizen.
Basis for selection: Major/career interest in engineering, mechanical. Applicant must demonstrate financial need, high academic achievement and depth of character.
Application requirements: Recommendations, transcript.
Additional information: For student in final year of undergraduate program in mechanical engineering. Must be ASME student member. Download application from Website or send SASE or email to request application.

Amount of award:	$2,000
Number of awards:	1
Application deadline:	March 15

Contact:
Sara Sahay
ASME Auxiliary - Undergraduate Scholarships
170 East Opel Drive
Glastonbury, CT 06033
Web: www.asme.org/about-asme/scholarship-and-loans/about-asme-scholarships

Charles B. Scharp Scholarship

Type of award: Scholarship.
Intended use: For full-time senior study at 4-year institution in United States. Designated institutions: Schools with ABET-accredited mechanical engineering programs.
Eligibility: Applicant must be U.S. citizen.
Basis for selection: Major/career interest in engineering, mechanical. Applicant must demonstrate financial need, high academic achievement and depth of character.
Application requirements: Recommendations, transcript.
Additional information: For student in final year of undergraduate program in mechanical engineering. Must be ASME student member. Download application from Website or send SASE or email to request application.

Amount of award:	$2,000
Number of awards:	1
Application deadline:	March 15

Contact:
Sara Sahay
ASME Auxiliary - Undergraduate Scholarships
170 East Opel Drive
Glastonbury, CT 06033
Web: www.asme.org/about-asme/scholarship-and-loans/about-asme-scholarships

Sylvia W. Farny Scholarship

Type of award: Scholarship.
Intended use: For full-time senior study at 4-year institution in United States. Designated institutions: Schools with ABET-accredited mechanical engineering programs.
Eligibility: Applicant must be U.S. citizen.
Basis for selection: Major/career interest in engineering, mechanical. Applicant must demonstrate financial need, high academic achievement and depth of character.
Application requirements: Recommendations, transcript.
Additional information: For student in final year of undergraduate study in mechanical engineering. Must be ASME student member. Download application from Website or send SASE or email to request application.

Amount of award:	$2,000
Number of awards:	1
Application deadline:	March 15

Contact:
Sara Sahay
ASME Auxiliary - Undergraduate Scholarships
170 East Opel Drive
Glastonbury, CT 06033
Web: www.asme.org/about-asme/scholarship-and-loans/about-asme-scholarships

ASME Foundation

Allen Rhodes Memorial Scholarship

Type of award: Scholarship.
Intended use: For full-time junior or senior study at accredited 4-year institution. Designated institutions: Schools with ABET-accredited programs.
Basis for selection: Major/career interest in engineering, mechanical. Applicant must demonstrate high academic achievement.
Application requirements: Recommendations, essay, transcript.
Additional information: For student with specific interest in oil and gas industry. Preference given to students enrolled at Villanova University. Applicant must be ASME student member in good standing. Mechanical engineering technology and other related majors also eligible. Apply online.

Amount of award:	$1,500
Number of awards:	1
Application deadline:	March 1
Notification begins:	June 30
Total amount awarded:	$1,500

Contact:
ASME
Attn: Beth Lefever
2 Park Avenue
New York, NY 10016-5990
Phone: 800-843-2763
Web: www.asme.org/about-asme/scholarship-and-loans/about-asme-scholarships

American Electric Power Scholarship

Type of award: Scholarship.
Intended use: For full-time junior or senior study at accredited 4-year institution. Designated institutions: Schools with ABET-accredited programs.
Basis for selection: Major/career interest in engineering, mechanical. Applicant must demonstrate high academic achievement.
Application requirements: Recommendations, essay, transcript.

Additional information: Applicant must be American Society of Mechanical Engineers student member in good standing. Preference given to students interested in power engineering or who reside or attend school in American Electric Power service area of Arkansas, Indiana, Kentucky, Louisiana, Michigan, Ohio, Oklahoma, Tennessee, Texas, Virginia, and West Virginia. Apply online.

Amount of award:	$3,000
Number of awards:	1
Application deadline:	March 1
Notification begins:	June 30
Total amount awarded:	$3,000

Contact:
ASME
Attn: Beth Lefever
2 Park Avenue
New York, NY 10016-5990
Phone: 800-843-2763
Web: www.asme.org/about-asme/scholarship-and-loans/about-asme-scholarships

ASME Auxiliary/FIRST Clarke Scholarship

Type of award: Scholarship.
Intended use: For full-time freshman study at accredited 4-year institution. Designated institutions: Schools with ABET-accredited programs.
Eligibility: Applicant must be high school senior.
Basis for selection: Major/career interest in engineering, mechanical. Applicant must demonstrate financial need, high academic achievement and leadership.
Application requirements: Transcript, nomination by ASME member, ASME Auxiliary member, or student member active with FIRST. Financial data worksheet, letter of support, resume.
Additional information: Applicant must be active on FIRST team. One nomination per member. Applicant may also enroll in mechanical engineering technology program. Recipient announced at FIRST National Championship. Visit Website for more information and to download forms.

Amount of award:	$5,000
Number of awards:	7
Application deadline:	March 15

Contact:
ASME
Attn: RuthAnn Bigley
3416 Washington Commons Avenue
Kennesaw, GA 30144
Phone: 212-591-7650
Fax: 770-917-8508
Web: www.asme.org/about-asme/scholarship-and-loans/about-asme-scholarships

The ASME Foundation Hanley Scholarship

Type of award: Scholarship.
Intended use: For full-time sophomore, junior or senior study at accredited 4-year institution. Designated institutions: Schools with ABET-accredited programs.
Basis for selection: Major/career interest in engineering, mechanical. Applicant must demonstrate financial need and high academic achievement.
Application requirements: Recommendations, essay, transcript.
Additional information: Must be American Society of Mechanical Engineers student member in good standing. Apply online.

Amount of award:	$2,500
Number of awards:	1
Application deadline:	March 1
Notification begins:	June 30

Contact:
ASME
Attn: Beth Lefever
2 Park Avenue
New York, NY 10016-5990
Phone: 800-843-2763
Web: www.asme.org/about-asme/scholarship-and-loans/about-asme-scholarships

ASME Foundation Scholarships

Type of award: Scholarship.
Intended use: For sophomore, junior or senior study at accredited 4-year institution. Designated institutions: Schools with ABET-accredited programs.
Basis for selection: Major/career interest in engineering, mechanical. Applicant must demonstrate high academic achievement.
Application requirements: Recommendations, essay, transcript.
Additional information: Applicant must be student member of American Society of Mechanical Engineers. Apply online.

Application deadline:	March 1
Notification begins:	June 15

Contact:
ASME
Attn: Beth Lefever
2 Park Avenue, 22nd Floor
New York, NY 10016-5990
Phone: 800-843-2763
Web: www.asme.org/about-asme/scholarship-and-loans/about-asme-scholarships

ASME Metropolitan Section John Rice Memorial Scholarship

Type of award: Scholarship.
Intended use: For full-time junior or senior study at 4-year institution. Designated institutions: City College/CUNY, College of Staten Island, Columbia University, Cooper Union, Manhattan College, NYC Technology College of City University, Polytechnic Institute of New York University (Brooklyn), SUNY/Maritime College.
Basis for selection: Major/career interest in engineering, mechanical. Applicant must demonstrate high academic achievement, depth of character, leadership and seriousness of purpose.
Application requirements: Recommendations, essay, transcript.
Additional information: Applicant must be a current ASME student member in good standing. Awarded to student attending a school within ASME Met Section. Apply online.

Amount of award:	$2,000
Number of awards:	1
Application deadline:	March 1
Notification begins:	June 30
Total amount awarded:	$2,000

Contact:
ASME
Attn: Beth Lefever
2 Park Avenue
New York, NY 10016-5990
Phone: 800-843-2763
Web: www.asme.org/about-asme/scholarship-and-loans/about-asme-scholarships

ASME Power Division Scholarship

Type of award: Scholarship.
Intended use: For full-time sophomore, junior or senior study at accredited 4-year institution. Designated institutions: Schools with ABET-accredited programs.
Basis for selection: Major/career interest in engineering, mechanical. Applicant must demonstrate financial need and high academic achievement.
Application requirements: Recommendations, essay, transcript.
Additional information: Applicant must be American Society of Mechanical Engineers student member in good standing and demonstrate special interest in area of fuels, combustion, or the power industry. Apply online.

Amount of award:	$3,000
Number of awards:	1
Application deadline:	March 1
Notification begins:	June 30
Total amount awarded:	$3,000

Contact:
ASME
Attn: Beth Lefever
2 Park Avenue
New York, NY 10016-5990
Phone: 800-843-2763
Web: www.asme.org/about-asme/scholarship-and-loans/about-asme-scholarships

Frank and Dorothy Miller ASME Auxiliary Scholarships

Type of award: Scholarship.
Intended use: For full-time sophomore, junior or senior study at accredited 4-year institution in United States. Designated institutions: Schools with ABET-accredited programs.
Eligibility: Applicant must be U.S. citizen, permanent resident or resident of Canada or Mexico.
Basis for selection: Major/career interest in engineering, mechanical. Applicant must demonstrate high academic achievement, depth of character and leadership.
Application requirements: Recommendations, essay, transcript.
Additional information: Applicant must be student member of American Society of Mechanical Engineers. Apply online.

Amount of award:	$2,000
Number of awards:	2
Number of applicants:	138
Application deadline:	March 1
Notification begins:	June 30

Contact:
ASME
Attn: Beth Lefever
2 Park Avenue
New York, NY 10016-5990
Phone: 800-843-2763
Web: www.asme.org/about-asme/scholarship-and-loans/about-asme-scholarships

F.W. "Beich" Beichley Scholarship

Type of award: Scholarship.
Intended use: For full-time junior or senior study at accredited 4-year institution in United States. Designated institutions: Schools with ABET-accredited programs.
Basis for selection: Major/career interest in engineering, mechanical. Applicant must demonstrate financial need, high academic achievement, depth of character and leadership.
Application requirements: Recommendations, essay, transcript.
Additional information: Applicant must be member of American Society of Mechanical Engineers. Apply online.

Amount of award:	$2,500
Number of awards:	1
Application deadline:	March 1
Notification begins:	June 30

Contact:
ASME
Attn: Beth Lefever
2 Park Avenue
New York, NY 10016-5990
Phone: 800-843-2763
Web: www.asme.org/about-asme/scholarship-and-loans/about-asme-scholarships

Garland Duncan Scholarships

Type of award: Scholarship.
Intended use: For full-time junior or senior study at accredited 4-year institution. Designated institutions: Schools with ABET-accredited programs.
Basis for selection: Major/career interest in engineering, mechanical. Applicant must demonstrate financial need, high academic achievement and leadership.
Application requirements: Recommendations, essay, transcript.
Additional information: Applicant must be member of American Society of Mechanical Engineers. Apply online.

Amount of award:	$5,000
Number of awards:	2
Number of applicants:	138
Application deadline:	March 1
Notification begins:	June 30
Total amount awarded:	$10,000

Contact:
ASME
Attn: Beth Lefever
2 Park Avenue
New York, NY 10016-5990
Phone: 800-843-2763
Web: www.asme.org/about-asme/scholarship-and-loans/about-asme-scholarships

John & Elsa Gracik Scholarships

Type of award: Scholarship.
Intended use: For full-time sophomore, junior or senior study at accredited 4-year institution in United States. Designated institutions: Schools with ABET-accredited programs.
Eligibility: Applicant must be U.S. citizen.
Basis for selection: Major/career interest in engineering, mechanical. Applicant must demonstrate financial need, high academic achievement, depth of character and leadership.
Application requirements: Recommendations, essay, transcript.
Additional information: Applicant must be member of American Society of Mechanical Engineers. Apply online.

Amount of award:	$2,000
Number of awards:	15
Number of applicants:	138
Application deadline:	March 1
Notification begins:	June 30

Contact:
ASME
Attn: Beth Lefever
2 Park Avenue
New York, NY 10016-5990
Phone: 800-843-2763
Web: www.asme.org/about-asme/scholarship-and-loans/about-asme-scholarships

Kate Gleason Scholarship

Type of award: Scholarship.
Intended use: For full-time sophomore, junior, senior or graduate study at accredited 4-year institution in United States. Designated institutions: Schools with ABET-accredited programs.
Eligibility: Applicant must be female.
Basis for selection: Major/career interest in engineering. Applicant must demonstrate financial need.
Application requirements: Recommendations, essay, transcript.
Additional information: Applicant must be American Society of Mechanical Engineers student member in good standing. Visit Website for additional information.

Amount of award:	$3,000
Number of awards:	1
Application deadline:	March 1
Notification begins:	June 30

Contact:
ASME Foundation
Attn: Beth Lefever
2 Park Avenue
New York, NY 10016-5990
Phone: 800-843-2763
Web: www.asme.org/about-asme/scholarship-and-loans/about-asme-scholarships

Kenneth Andrew Roe Mechanical Engineering Scholarship

Type of award: Scholarship.
Intended use: For full-time junior or senior study at accredited 4-year institution in United States. Designated institutions: Schools with ABET-accredited programs or equivalent.
Eligibility: Applicant must be U.S. citizen, permanent resident or resident of Canada or Mexico.
Basis for selection: Major/career interest in engineering, mechanical. Applicant must demonstrate high academic achievement, depth of character and leadership.
Application requirements: Recommendations, essay, transcript.
Additional information: Applicant must be member of American Society of Mechanical Engineers. Apply online.

Amount of award:	$12,500
Number of awards:	1
Number of applicants:	138
Application deadline:	March 1
Notification begins:	June 30
Total amount awarded:	$10,000

Contact:
ASME
Attn: Beth Lefever
2 Park Avenue
New York, NY 10016-5990
Phone: 800-843-2763
Web: www.asme.org/about-asme/scholarship-and-loans/about-asme-scholarships

Melvin R. Green Scholarships

Type of award: Scholarship.
Intended use: For full-time junior or senior study at accredited 4-year institution. Designated institutions: Schools with ABET-accredited programs.
Basis for selection: Major/career interest in engineering, mechanical. Applicant must demonstrate financial need, high academic achievement and leadership.
Application requirements: Recommendations, essay, transcript.
Additional information: Applicant must be student member of American Society of Mechanical Engineers. Apply online.

Amount of award:	$4,000
Number of awards:	2
Application deadline:	March 1
Notification begins:	June 30
Total amount awarded:	$8,000

Contact:
ASME
Attn: Beth Lefever
2 Park Avenue
New York, NY 10016-5990
Phone: 800-843-2763
Web: www.asme.org/about-asme/scholarship-and-loans/about-asme-scholarships

Nuclear Engineering Division (NED) Scholarship

Type of award: Scholarship.
Intended use: For full-time junior or senior study at accredited 4-year institution. Designated institutions: ABET-accredited organizations.
Basis for selection: Based on potential contribution to the nuclear engineering profession. Major/career interest in engineering, nuclear. Applicant must demonstrate financial need, high academic achievement, depth of character, leadership and seriousness of purpose.
Application requirements: Recommendations, essay, transcript.
Additional information: Applicant must be a current ASME student member in good standing, and must demonstrate a particular interest in the design, analysis, development, testing, operation, and maintenance of reactor systems and components, nuclear fusion, heat transport, nuclear fuels technology, and radioactive waste. Apply online.

Amount of award:	$5,000
Number of awards:	3
Application deadline:	March 1
Notification begins:	June 30
Total amount awarded:	$15,000

Contact:
ASME Centers Administrator
Attn: Beth Lefever
2 Park Avenue
New York, NY 10016-5990
Phone: 800-843-2763
Web: www.asme.org/about-asme/scholarship-and-loans/about-asme-scholarships

Stephen T. Kugle Scholarship

Type of award: Scholarship.
Intended use: For full-time junior or senior study at 4-year institution in United States. Designated institutions: Public colleges or universities in District E (Arizona, Arkansas, Colorado, Louisiana, New Mexico, Oklahoma, Texas, Utah, and Wyoming).
Eligibility: Applicant must be U.S. citizen.
Basis for selection: Major/career interest in engineering, mechanical. Applicant must demonstrate high academic achievement.
Application requirements: Recommendations, essay, transcript.
Additional information: Applicant must be American Society of Mechanical Engineers student member in good standing and U.S. citizen by birth. Minimum 3.0 GPA. Students from University of Texas at Arlington not eligible. Apply online.

Amount of award:	$2,500
Number of awards:	1
Application deadline:	March 1
Notification begins:	June 30

Contact:
ASME
Attn: Beth Lefever
2 Park Avenue
New York, NY 10016-5990
Phone: 800-843-2763
Web: www.asme.org/about-asme/scholarship-and-loans/about-asme-scholarships

William J. and Marijane E. Adams, Jr. Scholarship

Type of award: Scholarship.
Intended use: For full-time sophomore, junior or senior study at accredited 4-year institution in United States. Designated institutions: Schools with ABET-accredited programs in California, Nevada, and Hawaii.
Eligibility: Applicant must be residing in California, Hawaii or Nevada.
Basis for selection: Major/career interest in engineering, mechanical. Applicant must demonstrate financial need and high academic achievement.
Application requirements: Recommendations, essay, transcript.
Additional information: Minimum 2.5 GPA. Applicant must be member of American Society of Mechanical Engineers. Award designated for student with special interest in product development and design. Apply online.

Amount of award:	$3,500
Number of awards:	1
Application deadline:	March 1
Notification begins:	June 30
Total amount awarded:	$3,500

Contact:
ASME
Attn: Beth Lefever
2 Park Avenue
New York, NY 10016-5990
Phone: 800-843-2763
Web: www.asme.org/about-asme/scholarship-and-loans/about-asme-scholarships

Willis F. Thompson Memorial Scholarship

Type of award: Scholarship.
Intended use: For full-time sophomore, junior, senior or graduate study at accredited 4-year institution. Designated institutions: Schools with ABET-accredited programs.
Basis for selection: Major/career interest in engineering, mechanical. Applicant must demonstrate high academic achievement.
Application requirements: Recommendations, essay, transcript.
Additional information: Applicant must be American Society of Mechanical Engineers student member in good standing. Preference given to students who demonstrate interest in advancing field of power generation. Apply online.

Amount of award:	$5,000
Number of awards:	3
Application deadline:	March 1
Notification begins:	June 30
Total amount awarded:	$15,000

Contact:
ASME
Attn: Beth Lefever
2 Park Avenue
New York, NY 10016-5990
Phone: 800-843-2763
Web: www.asme.org/about-asme/scholarship-and-loans/about-asme-scholarships

Associated General Contractors Education and Research Foundation

AGC Education and Research Undergraduate Scholarship

Type of award: Scholarship, renewable.
Intended use: For full-time sophomore, junior or senior study at accredited 4-year institution. Designated institutions: ABET- or ACCE-accredited institutions.
Eligibility: Applicant must be U.S. citizen or permanent resident.
Basis for selection: Major/career interest in engineering, civil; engineering, construction or construction.
Application requirements: Recommendations, essay, transcript.
Additional information: Must be enrolled in or planning to enroll in an ABET- or ACCE-accredited full-time, four- or five-year university program of construction or civil engineering. Applications are available July 1 from AGC Website. Seniors with one full academic year of coursework remaining are eligible. Number of awards varies.

Amount of award:	$2,500-$7,500
Number of awards:	100
Number of applicants:	380
Application deadline:	November 1
Notification begins:	February 1
Total amount awarded:	$350,000

Contact:
Association of General Contractors Education and Research Foundation
Attn: Melinda Patrician, Director
2300 Wilson Boulevard, Suite 400
Arlington, VA 22201
Phone: 703-837-5342
Fax: 703-837-5451
Web: www.agcfoundation.org

James L. Allhands Essay Competition

Type of award: Scholarship, renewable.
Intended use: For full-time senior study at accredited 4-year institution. Designated institutions: ABET- or ACCE-accredited universities with construction or construction-related engineering programs.
Basis for selection: Competition/talent/interest in research paper, based on advancement of technological, educational, or vocational expertise in the construction industry. Major/career interest in engineering, civil; engineering, construction or construction.
Application requirements: Proof of eligibility. Essay abstract, letter from faculty sponsor.
Additional information: First prize is $1,000, plus all-expenses-paid trip to AGC convention; winner's faculty sponsor receives $500 and all-expenses-paid trip to convention. Second prize is $500. Third prize is $300. Application material must be emailed. Only five submittals from each college/university are accepted. See Website for essay topic and guidelines.

Amount of award:	$300-$1,000
Number of awards:	3
Number of applicants:	50
Application deadline:	November 15
Total amount awarded:	$2,300

Contact:
AGC Education and Research Foundation
Attn: Melinda Patrician, Director of Programs
2300 Wilson Boulevard, Suite 400
Arlington, VA 22201
Phone: 703-837-5342
Fax: 703-837-5451
Web: www.agc.org

Associated General Contractors of Maine Education Foundation

AGC of Maine Scholarship Program

Type of award: Scholarship.
Intended use: For full-time undergraduate study at accredited postsecondary institution in United States. Designated institutions: Schools in Maine.
Eligibility: Applicant must be U.S. citizen residing in Maine.
Basis for selection: Major/career interest in construction. Applicant must demonstrate financial need and high academic achievement.
Application requirements: Interview, recommendations, essay, transcript.
Additional information: Number of awards varies.

Amount of award:	$1,500-$5,000
Number of applicants:	30
Application deadline:	March 31
Total amount awarded:	$24,000

Contact:
AGC Maine
188 Whitten Road
Augusta, ME 04330
Phone: 207-622-4741
Web: www.agcmaine.org

The Associated Press Television and Radio Association

APTRA-Clete Roberts/Kathryn Dettman Memorial Journalism Scholarship

Type of award: Scholarship.
Intended use: For sophomore, junior, senior or graduate study at 4-year or graduate institution in United States. Designated institutions: Colleges and universities in California, Nevada, Hawaii, Arizona, New Mexico, Idaho, Washington, Colorado, Utah, Montana, Wyoming and Alaska.
Basis for selection: Major/career interest in journalism or radio/television/film. Applicant must demonstrate financial need, high academic achievement and seriousness of purpose.
Application requirements: Essay. May submit examples of broadcast-related work.
Additional information: Open to students pursuing career in broadcast journalism. Applications must be typed and mailed; no emailed or faxed submissions accepted. Visit Website for more information.

Amount of award:	$1,500
Number of awards:	1
Application deadline:	February 21

Contact:
AP West
Chris Havlik
1850 N. Central Avenue, Suite 640
Phoenix, AZ 85004
Web: www.aptra.com

Association for Library and Information Science Education

ALISE Bohdan S. Wynar Research Paper Competition

Type of award: Scholarship.
Intended use: For undergraduate or graduate study.

Basis for selection: Competition/talent/interest in research paper, based on any aspect of library and information science using any methodology. Major/career interest in library science.
Application requirements: Paper must not exceed 35 double-spaced pages with one-inch margins and 12-point font. Two title pages, one with and one without author name(s) and institution.
Additional information: Research papers prepared by joint investigators eligible; at least one author must be member of Association for Library and Information Science Education. Winners expected to present papers at ALISE Annual Conference. Can submit only one paper per competition and may not submit same paper to other ALISE competitions. Paper cannot have been published, though may be accepted for publication. Papers completed in pursuit of master's and doctoral degrees not eligible, though data and spinoffs from such papers are eligible, as are papers generated through other grants and funding. Visit Website for detailed explanation of requirements.

Amount of award:	$2,500
Number of awards:	2
Number of applicants:	13
Application deadline:	July 15
Notification begins:	October 1
Total amount awarded:	$5,000

Contact:
ALISE
65 E. Wacker Place, Suite 1900
Chicago, IL 60601-7246
Phone: 312-795-0996
Fax: 312-419-8950
Web: www.alise.org

ALISE Research Grant

Type of award: Research grant.
Intended use: For non-degree study.
Basis for selection: Major/career interest in library science. Applicant must demonstrate high academic achievement.
Application requirements: Research proposal.
Additional information: Must be member of Association for Library and Information Science Education. Proposal must not exceed 20 double-spaced pages. Award to support research broadly related to education for library and information science. Visit Website for detailed explanation of proposal requirements. More than one grant may be awarded; however, total amount of funding for all grants not to exceed $5,000. Award cannot be used to support doctoral dissertation. Awardee(s) must present preliminary report at ALISE Annual Conference.

Amount of award:	$5,000
Application deadline:	October 1
Total amount awarded:	$5,000

Contact:
ALISE
65 E. Wacker Place, Suite 1900
Chicago, IL 60601-7246
Phone: 312-795-0996
Fax: 312-419-8950
Web: www.alise.org

ALISE/Dialog Methodology Paper Competition

Type of award: Scholarship.
Intended use: For undergraduate or graduate study.
Basis for selection: Competition/talent/interest in research paper, based on description and discussion of a research method or technique. Major/career interest in library science.
Application requirements: Paper must not exceed 25 double-spaced pages with one-inch margins and 12-point font. Two title pages, one with and one without author name and institution. 200-word abstract.
Additional information: Papers prepared by joint authors eligible; at least one author must be member of Association for Library and Information Science Education. Papers completed in pursuit of master's or doctoral degrees are eligible, as are papers generated as result of research grant or other source of funding. Papers that stress findings are ineligible. Winners expected to present papers at ALISE Annual Conference. May submit only one paper per competition and may not submit same paper to multiple ALISE competitions.

Amount of award:	$500
Number of awards:	1
Number of applicants:	5
Application deadline:	July 15
Notification begins:	October 1
Total amount awarded:	$500

Contact:
ALISE
65 E. Wacker Place, Suite 1900
Chicago, IL 60601-7246
Phone: 312-795-0996
Fax: 312-419-8950
Web: www.alise.org

Association for Women in Architecture Foundation

Women in Architecture Scholarship

Type of award: Scholarship, renewable.
Intended use: For full-time sophomore, junior, senior or graduate study at 4-year or graduate institution.
Eligibility: Applicant must be female.
Basis for selection: Major/career interest in architecture; interior design; landscape architecture; urban planning; engineering, structural; engineering, civil; engineering, electrical/electronic or engineering, mechanical. Applicant must demonstrate high academic achievement.
Application requirements: Portfolio, recommendations, essay, transcript. SASE.
Additional information: Must be California resident or attending accredited California school to qualify. Students may also be studying land planning or environmental design. Must have completed minimum of 18 units in major by application due date. Applications may be downloaded from Website. Applications due in mid-April; see Website for exact date.

Amount of award:	$1,000
Number of awards:	5
Application deadline:	April 15
Total amount awarded:	$5,000

Contact:
Association for Women in Architecture Foundation
AWAF Scholarship
22815 Frampton Avenue
Torrance, CA 90501-5034
Phone: 310-534-8466
Fax: 310-257-6885
Web: www.awa-la.org/scholarships

Association for Women in Communications

Seattle Professional Chapter Scholarship

Type of award: Scholarship.
Intended use: For junior, senior or graduate study at accredited 4-year or graduate institution in United States. Designated institutions: Washington state colleges.
Eligibility: Applicant must be residing in Washington.
Basis for selection: Major/career interest in communications; journalism; radio/television/film; film/video; graphic arts/design; advertising; public relations or marketing. Applicant must demonstrate financial need and high academic achievement.
Application requirements: Transcript. Cover letter, resume, two work samples.
Additional information: Additional majors may include multimedia design, photography, or technical communication. Selection based on demonstrated excellence in communications and positive contributions to communications on campus or in community. Application deadline March/April; check Website for exact date. Amount and number of awards varies.

Amount of award:	$1,500
Number of awards:	2

Contact:
AWC Seattle Professional Chapter
Attn: Tina Christiansen
P.O. Box 60262
Shoreline, WA 98160
Web: www.seattleawc.org

Association of American Geographers

Anne U. White Fund

Type of award: Research grant, renewable.
Intended use: For non-degree study.
Basis for selection: Major/career interest in geography.
Application requirements: Research proposal.
Additional information: Fund enables Association of American Geographers member to engage in useful field study jointly with his/her partner. Must have been member for at least two years at time of application. Report summarizing results and documenting expenses underwritten by grant must be submitted within 12 months of receiving award.

Amount of award:	$1,500
Number of awards:	2
Application deadline:	December 31
Notification begins:	March 1

Contact:
Association of American Geographers
Attn: Anne U. White Fund
1710 16th Street, NW
Washington, DC 20009-3198
Phone: 202-234-1450
Fax: 202-234-2744
Web: www.aag.org/grantsawards

Darrel Hess Community College Geography Scholarship

Type of award: Scholarship, renewable.
Intended use: For at 2-year institution in United States.
Basis for selection: Major/career interest in geography. Applicant must demonstrate financial need and high academic achievement.
Application requirements: Recommendations, essay, transcript.
Additional information: Applicants eligible if currently enrolled in a U.S. community college, junior college, city college, or similar two-year educational institution at the time of submission of application. Applicant must have completed at least two transfer courses in geography and plan to transfer to a four-year institution as a geography major during the coming academic year. AAG membership strongly encouraged, but not required.

Amount of award:	$1,000
Number of awards:	4
Application deadline:	December 31

Contact:
Association of American Geographers
1710 16th Street NW
Washington, DC 20009-3198
Phone: 202-234-1450
Fax: 202-234-2744
Web: www.aag.org/grantsawards

Marble-Boyle Award

Type of award: Scholarship, renewable.
Intended use: For full-time senior study at accredited postsecondary institution in United States or Canada.
Basis for selection: Major/career interest in computer/information sciences or geography.
Application requirements: Recommendations, essay, transcript. Cover letter.
Additional information: Applicant must demonstrate reasonable intent to embark upon a career or further education that will make use of joint geographic science and computer science knowledge. AAG membership strongly encouraged, but not required. Award consists of $700 cash prize and $200 credit for books published by the ESRI Press. ESRI will provide priority consideration to awardees interested in participating in ESRI Summer Intern Program. Awardees also eligible to compete for an additional research fellowship award offered biannually by MicroGIS Foundation for Spatial Analysis (MFSA).

Amount of award:	$700
Number of awards:	3
Application deadline:	October 15

Contact:
Association of American Geographers
1710 16th Street NW
Washington, DC 20009-3198
Phone: 202-234-1450
Fax: 202-234-2744
Web: www.aag.org/grantsawards

Association of Insurance Compliance Professionals

AICP Heartland Chapter Jim Latteman Scholarship

Type of award: Scholarship, renewable.
Intended use: For full-time undergraduate or graduate study at postsecondary institution.
Eligibility: Applicant must be residing in Iowa, South Dakota, Minnesota, Nebraska, Kansas, North Dakota or Missouri.
Basis for selection: Major/career interest in accounting; business; business/management/administration; economics; finance/banking; mathematics or statistics. Applicant must demonstrate high academic achievement.
Application requirements: Recommendations, transcript. Resume, short narrative describing current and future interest to pursue education/career in the insurance field.
Additional information: Must be a Heartland member in good standing; a spouse (including domestic partner or civil union partner), son, daughter, grandson, granddaughter (including step or custodial) of a Heartland member in good standing; or be sponsored by current Heartland AICP member in good standing. Must be a permanent resident in the Heartland territory region. Minimum 2.75 GPA. Applicants with major/career interest in risk management also eligible. Part-time enrollment allowed only for Heartland members; must be enrolled for at least six hours or half-time as defined by the institution. Graduate students working towards an MBA in insurance, risk management, or mathematics, with an actuarial emphasis, are also eligible. Mathematics majors' studies should have emphasis in actuarial science. Visit Website for more details.

Amount of award:	$500
Number of awards:	1
Application deadline:	May 15
Notification begins:	May 31
Total amount awarded:	$500

Contact:
Association of Insurance Compliance Professionals
12100 Sunset Hills Road, Suite 130
Reston, VA 20190
Web: www.aicp.net

AICP Scholarship

Type of award: Scholarship, renewable.
Intended use: For full-time sophomore, junior, senior or master's study.
Basis for selection: Major/career interest in business; business/management/administration; economics; finance/banking; insurance/actuarial science; mathematics or statistics. Applicant must demonstrate high academic achievement.
Application requirements: Recommendations, transcript. Resume, short narrative describing current and future interest to pursue education/career in the insurance field.
Additional information: Minimum 3.0 GPA. Applicant must be at least a second-semester sophomore. Applicants with major/career interest in risk management also eligible.

Amount of award:	$1,000
Number of awards:	3
Number of applicants:	32
Application deadline:	June 1
Notification begins:	July 15
Total amount awarded:	$3,000

Contact:
Association of Insurance Compliance Professionals
12100 Sunset Hills Road, Suite 130
Reston, VA 20190
Phone: 703-234-4074
Fax: 703-435-4390
Web: www.aicp.net

Association of State Dam Safety Officials

ASDSO Undergraduate Scholarship

Type of award: Scholarship.
Intended use: For full-time senior study in United States.
Eligibility: Applicant must be U.S. citizen.
Basis for selection: Major/career interest in engineering, civil. Applicant must demonstrate financial need and high academic achievement.
Application requirements: Recommendations, essay, transcript.
Additional information: Must be planning to pursue career related to dam or levee safety. Minimum 2.5 GPA for first three years of college. Winners will also receive travel stipend to attend National Dam Safety Conference in Providence, Rhode Island.

Amount of award:	$10,000
Number of awards:	3
Number of applicants:	35
Application deadline:	March 31
Notification begins:	July 1
Total amount awarded:	$10,000

Contact:
Association of State Dam Safety Officials
450 Old Vine Street, 2nd Floor
Lexington, KY 40507
Phone: 859-257-5140
Fax: 859-323-1958
Web: www.damsafety.org

AXA Achievement Scholarship

AXA Achievement Scholarship in Association with U.S. News & World Report

Type of award: Scholarship.
Intended use: For full-time undergraduate study at accredited 2-year or 4-year institution in United States.
Eligibility: Applicant must be high school senior. Applicant must be U.S. citizen.
Application requirements: Recommendations.
Additional information: Fifty-two students, to be known as AXA Achievers, will be selected to receive $10,000 scholarships, one from each state, the District of Columbia and Puerto Rico. From among the state recipients, ten students will be named national AXA Achievers. They will be selected to receive national awards at $15,000 each for a total of $25,000

Scholarships

per national recipient. Must demonstrate achievement in a non-academic activity or project. Consideration will also be given to other extracurricular activities in school and community, work experience, and the applicant's academic record over the past four years. Visit Website for more information, application, and deadline date. Questions about the application process may be directed to Scholarship America's toll-free number or by e-mail to axaachievement@scholarshipamerica.org.

Amount of award: $10,000-$25,000
Number of awards: 52
Application deadline: December 1
Total amount awarded: $670,000

Contact:
AXA Achievement Scholarship
Scholarship America
One Scholarship Way
Saint Peter, MN 56082
Phone: 800-537-4180
Web: www.axa-achievement.com

Ayn Rand Institute

Atlas Shrugged Essay Contest

Type of award: Scholarship.
Intended use: For undergraduate study.
Basis for selection: Competition/talent/interest in writing/journalism, based on an outstanding grasp of the philosophic meaning of "Atlas Shrugged."
Application requirements: Essay between 800 and 1,600 words, typewritten and double-spaced.
Additional information: Student must be enrolled in full-time college degree program or 12th grade at time of entry. See Website for rules, guidelines, and topic questions.

Amount of award: $50-$10,000
Number of awards: 49
Number of applicants: 1,917
Application deadline: September 17
Notification begins: November 27
Total amount awarded: $24,000

Contact:
The Ayn Rand Institute
Atlas Shrugged Essay Contest
P.O. Box 57044
Irvine, CA 92619-7044
Phone: 949-222-6550
Fax: 949-222-6558
Web: www.aynrand.org/contests

The Fountainhead Essay Contest

Type of award: Scholarship.
Intended use: For undergraduate study.
Eligibility: Applicant must be high school junior or senior.
Basis for selection: Competition/talent/interest in writing/journalism, based on an outstanding grasp of the philosophic meaning of "The Fountainhead."
Application requirements: Essay between 800 and 1,600 words, typewritten and double-spaced.
Additional information: Rules, guidelines, and topic questions on Website.

Amount of award: $50-$10,000
Number of awards: 236
Number of applicants: 5,399
Application deadline: April 26
Notification begins: July 26
Total amount awarded: $43,250

Contact:
Ayn Rand Institute
"The Fountainhead" Essay Contest
P.O. Box 57044
Irvine, CA 92619-7044
Phone: 949-222-6550
Fax: 949-222-6558
Web: www.aynrand.org/contests

"Anthem" Essay Contest

Type of award: Scholarship.
Intended use: For undergraduate study.
Eligibility: Applicant must be high school freshman or sophomore.
Basis for selection: Competition/talent/interest in writing/journalism, based on outstanding grasp of the philosophic meaning of "Anthem."
Application requirements: Essay between 600 and 1,200 words, typewritten and double-spaced.
Additional information: Eighth-grade students may also apply. Rules, guidelines, and topic questions on Website.

Amount of award: $30-$2,000
Number of awards: 236
Number of applicants: 13,420
Application deadline: March 20
Notification begins: July 26
Total amount awarded: $14,000

Contact:
Ayn Rand Institute
"Anthem" Essay Contest
P.O. Box 57044
Irvine, CA 92619-7044
Phone: 949-222-6550
Fax: 949-222-6558
Web: www.aynrand.org/contests

"We the Living" Essay Contest

Type of award: Scholarship.
Intended use: For undergraduate study.
Eligibility: Applicant must be high school sophomore, junior or senior.
Basis for selection: Competition/talent/interest in writing/journalism, based on outstanding grasp of the philosophic meaning of "We the Living."
Application requirements: Essay between 700 and 1,500 words, typewritten and double-spaced.
Additional information: Rules, guidelines, and topic questions on Website. Deadline in early May.

Amount of award: $25-$3,000
Number of awards: 111

Contact:
Ayn Rand Institute
"We the Living" Essay Contest
P.O. Box 57044
Irvine, CA 92619-7044
Phone: 949-222-6550
Fax: 949-222-6558
Web: www.aynrandnovels.com/contests

Barry M. Goldwater Scholarship and Excellence In Education Foundation

Barry M. Goldwater Scholarship

Type of award: Scholarship, renewable.
Intended use: For full-time junior or senior study at accredited 2-year or 4-year institution in United States.
Eligibility: Applicant must be U.S. citizen, permanent resident or U.S. national.
Basis for selection: Major/career interest in engineering; mathematics; natural sciences or engineering, computer. Applicant must demonstrate high academic achievement and seriousness of purpose.
Application requirements: Recommendations, essay, transcript, nomination by Goldwater faculty representative. Permanent resident nominees must include letter of intent to obtain U.S. citizenship and photocopy of Permanent Resident Card.
Additional information: Bulletin of information, nomination materials, application, and list of faculty representatives available on Website. Applicants must be legal residents of state in which they are candidates. Residents of District of Columbia, Puerto Rico, Guam, American Samoa, Virgin Islands, and Commonwealth of Northern Mariana Islands also eligible. Must have minimum 3.0 GPA and rank in top 25 percent of class. Application deadline in late January; check Website for exact date.

Amount of award:	$7,500
Number of awards:	300
Number of applicants:	1,097
Application deadline:	January 31
Notification begins:	April 1
Total amount awarded:	$2,407,500

Contact:
Barry M. Goldwater Scholarship and Excellence in Education Foundation
6225 Brandon Avenue
Suite 315
Springfield, VA 22150-2519
Phone: 703-756-6012
Fax: 703-756-6015
Web: www.act.org/goldwater

Best Buy

Best Buy Scholarship Program

Type of award: Scholarship.
Intended use: For full-time undergraduate study at accredited postsecondary institution in United States.
Eligibility: Applicant must be enrolled in high school. Applicant must be U.S. citizen or permanent resident.
Basis for selection: Applicant must demonstrate high academic achievement and service orientation.
Additional information: Open to high school students in grades 9-12. Applicants planning to attend a college, university, or vocational school in Puerto Rico also eligible. Apply online. See Website for more information.

Amount of award:	$1,000
Number of awards:	1,100
Application deadline:	February 15
Total amount awarded:	$1,200,000

Contact:
Web: pr.bby.com/community-relations/programs/best-buy-scholarship-program

Bethesda Lutheran Communities

Lutheran Student Scholastic and Service Scholarship

Type of award: Scholarship.
Intended use: For full-time freshman, junior or senior study at accredited 4-year institution in United States.
Eligibility: Applicant must be Lutheran.
Basis for selection: Major/career interest in social work; education; psychology; mental health/therapy; education, special; education, early childhood; education, teacher; speech pathology/audiology; occupational therapy or health-related professions. Applicant must demonstrate high academic achievement, seriousness of purpose and service orientation.
Application requirements: Recommendations, essay, transcript, proof of eligibility. Community service hours in support of people with intellectual and developmental disabilities.
Additional information: Applicant must be active member of Lutheran congregation with career objectives in the field of intellectual and developmental disabilities. Minimum 3.0 GPA. Seminary students also eligible to apply.

Amount of award:	$500-$3,000
Number of awards:	2
Number of applicants:	40
Application deadline:	April 16
Notification begins:	June 1
Total amount awarded:	$10,000

Contact:
Bethesda Lutheran Communities
Attn: Pam Bergen
600 Hoffmann Drive
Watertown, WI 53094
Phone: 920-206-4410
Fax: 920-206-7706
Web: www.bethesdalutherancommunities.org

BioCommunications Association, Inc.

Endowment Fund For Education (EFFE)

Type of award: Scholarship.
Intended use: For full-time sophomore, junior, senior or graduate study at accredited vocational or 4-year institution.
Basis for selection: Major/career interest in arts, general; biomedical; communications or science, general.

Scholarships

Application requirements: Portfolio, recommendations, essay, transcript, proof of eligibility.
Additional information: For students pursuing careers in scientific/biomedical visual communications and scientific/biomedical photography.

Amount of award:	$500
Number of awards:	2
Application deadline:	April 30
Notification begins:	June 1

Contact:
BioCommunications Association, Inc.
220 Southwind Lane
Hillsborough, NC 27278-7907
Phone: 919-245-0906
Fax: 919-245-0906
Web: www.bca.org

Blinded Veterans Association

Kathern F. Gruber Scholarship Program

Type of award: Scholarship, renewable.
Intended use: For full-time undergraduate or graduate study at accredited postsecondary institution in United States.
Eligibility: Applicant must be U.S. citizen. Applicant must be dependent of disabled veteran; or spouse of disabled veteran who served in the Army, Air Force, Marines, Navy or Coast Guard.
Application requirements: Recommendations, essay, transcript.
Additional information: Dependent children, spouses, and grandchildren of blinded U.S. Armed Forces veterans are eligible, as well as blinded active duty members of the U.S. Armed Forces. Veteran must meet definition of blindness used by Blinded Veterans Association; blindness may be service-connected or non-service-connected. Katherine Gruber scholarships are awarded for one year only. The number of scholarships a recipient may receive under this program is limited to four. Notification begins in late June.

Amount of award:	$2,000
Number of awards:	6
Number of applicants:	18
Application deadline:	April 18
Total amount awarded:	$12,000

Contact:
Kathern F. Gruber Scholarship Program
Blinded Veterans Association
477 H Street NW
Washington, DC 20001-2694
Phone: 202-371-8880
Fax: 202-371-8258
Web: www.bva.org

Thomas H. Miller Scholarship

Type of award: Scholarship.
Intended use: For full-time undergraduate or graduate study at accredited postsecondary institution in United States.
Eligibility: Applicant must be U.S. citizen. Applicant must be dependent of disabled veteran; or spouse of disabled veteran who served in the Army, Air Force, Marines, Navy or Coast Guard.
Application requirements: Recommendations, essay, transcript.
Additional information: Dependent children, spouses, and grandchildren of blinded U.S. Armed Forces veterans are eligible, as well as blinded active duty members of the U.S. Armed Forces. Veteran must meet definition of blindness used by Blinded Veterans Association; blindness may be service-connected or non-service-connected. Preference given to applicants focusing on the arts. The number of scholarships recipient may receive under this program is limited to four. Notification begins in late June.

Amount of award:	$1,000
Number of awards:	1
Number of applicants:	18
Application deadline:	April 18
Total amount awarded:	$1,000

Contact:
Thomas H. Miller Scholarship Program
Blinded Veterans Association
477 H Street NW
Washington, DC 20001-2694
Phone: 202-371-8880
Fax: 202-371-8258
Web: www.bva.org

BlueScope Foundation, N.A.

Bluescope Foundation Scholarship

Type of award: Scholarship, renewable.
Intended use: For full-time undergraduate study at accredited 4-year institution.
Eligibility: Applicant must be high school senior.
Basis for selection: Applicant must demonstrate financial need, high academic achievement, depth of character, leadership and service orientation.
Application requirements: Recommendations, essay, transcript. SAT/ACT scores, financial report.
Additional information: Applicant's parent must be employed by BlueScope Steel. Contact human resources office at workplace for information and application. Renewable up to four years.

Amount of award:	$3,000
Number of awards:	12
Number of applicants:	46
Application deadline:	February 15
Notification begins:	April 30
Total amount awarded:	$104,000

Contact:
BlueScope Foundation, N.A.
P.O. Box 419917
Kansas City, MO 64141-6917
Phone: 816-968-3208
Fax: 816-627-8993

BMI Foundation, Inc.

BMI Student Composer Awards

Type of award: Scholarship.
Intended use: For undergraduate or graduate study at accredited postsecondary institution.

Eligibility: Applicant must be no older than 28. Applicant must be Citizen of a Western hemisphere country.
Basis for selection: Competition/talent/interest in music performance/composition, based on composition of classical music. Major/career interest in music.
Application requirements: Manuscript/recording of score, which must be submitted under a pseudonym. SASE.
Additional information: Application deadline in early February. Check Website for exact date and application. Must be enrolled in accredited public, private, or parochial secondary schools; accredited colleges or conservatories of music; or engaged in private study of music with recognized and established teachers (other than relatives). Visit Website for additional information.

Amount of award:	$500-$5,000
Notification begins:	July 1
Total amount awarded:	$20,000

Contact:
Deirdre Chadwick
BMI Student Composer Awards
7 World Trade Center, 250 Greenwich St.
New York, NY 10007-0030
Web: www.bmifoundation.org

John Lennon Scholarships

Type of award: Scholarship.
Intended use: For undergraduate or graduate study.
Eligibility: Applicant must be at least 17, no older than 25.
Basis for selection: Competition/talent/interest in music performance/composition, based on best song of any genre with original music and lyrics. Major/career interest in music or performing arts.
Application requirements: Music and lyrics of original song on CD or MP3 and three typed lyric sheets.
Additional information: Current students and alumnae at select schools may apply directly to Foundation; others must contact the National Association for Music Education chapter advisor at their college. Visit Website for deadlines, application, and more information.

Amount of award:	$5,000-$10,000
Number of awards:	3
Total amount awarded:	$20,000

Contact:
BMI Foundation, Inc.
John Lennon Scholarship Competition
7 World Trade Center, 250 Greenwich St.
New York, NY 10007-0030
Web: www.bmifoundation.org

peermusic Latin Scholarship

Type of award: Scholarship.
Intended use: For undergraduate or graduate study at postsecondary institution in or outside United States.
Eligibility: Applicant must be at least 16, no older than 24.
Basis for selection: Competition/talent/interest in music performance/composition, based on best song or instrumental work in any Latin genre with original music and lyrics. Major/career interest in music.
Application requirements: CD or MP3 of original song and typed lyric sheet. Should not include name of student or school.
Additional information: Applicants studying in Puerto Rico also eligible. Application deadline in early February. Check Website for exact date and application.

Amount of award:	$5,000
Number of awards:	1

Contact:
BMI Foundation, Inc.
peermusic Latin Scholarship Competition
7 World Trade Center, 250 Greenwich St.
New York, NY 10007-0030
Web: www.bmifoundation.org

Boy Scouts of America Patriots' Path Council

Frank D. Visceglia Memorial Scholarship

Type of award: Scholarship, renewable.
Intended use: For full-time freshman study at accredited 4-year institution.
Eligibility: Applicant must be male, high school senior. Applicant must be U.S. citizen or permanent resident residing in New Jersey.
Additional information: Applicant must be an Eagle Scout. Preference given to Scouts whose service projects relate to the environment or economy. Application available online.

Amount of award:	$1,000
Number of awards:	1
Number of applicants:	35
Application deadline:	June 1
Notification begins:	August 1
Total amount awarded:	$1,000

Contact:
The Frank D. Visceglia Memorial Scholarship Program
Attn: Dennis Kohl
222 Columbia Turnpike
Florham Park, NJ 07932
Phone: 973-765-9322
Fax: 973-765-9142
Web: www.advancement.ppbsa.org/scholarship.htm

Boys and Girls Clubs of Greater San Diego

Spence Reese Scholarship

Type of award: Scholarship, renewable.
Intended use: For full-time undergraduate study at accredited 4-year institution in United States.
Eligibility: Applicant must be male, high school senior.
Basis for selection: Major/career interest in engineering; law; medicine or political science/government. Applicant must demonstrate financial need and high academic achievement.
Application requirements: Recommendations, transcript. SAT/ACT scores, college acceptance letter.
Additional information: One award in each of four eligible majors. Award is renewable for four years of study. Application available on Website.

Amount of award:	$4,000
Number of awards:	4
Number of applicants:	40
Application deadline:	April 1
Notification begins:	May 15
Total amount awarded:	$32,000

Contact:
Boys and Girls Clubs of Greater San Diego
Attn: Spence Reese Scholarship Committee
115 W. Woodward Avenue
Escondido, CA 92025
Phone: 858-866-0591 ext. 201
Web: www.sdyouth.org/scholarships.aspx

Brandon Goodman Scholarship

BG Scholarship

Type of award: Scholarship.
Intended use: For undergraduate or graduate study at vocational, 2-year, 4-year or graduate institution.
Eligibility: Applicant must be U.S. citizen or permanent resident.
Basis for selection: Applicant must demonstrate financial need, high academic achievement and service orientation.
Application requirements: Essay.
Additional information: 2.0 minimum GPA. Twelve awards given monthly. Deadline is the last day of the month. Visit Website for application.

Amount of award:	$300
Number of awards:	144
Number of applicants:	7,200
Total amount awarded:	$4,200

Contact:
Brandon Goodman Scholarship
Phone: 949-547-9427
Web: www.bgscholarship.com/scholarship

Bridgestone

Teens Drive Smart Video Contest

Type of award: Scholarship.
Intended use: For full-time undergraduate study at accredited postsecondary institution in United States.
Eligibility: Applicant must be at least 16, no older than 21.
Additional information: Must submit original video 25-55 seconds long addressing automotive safety. Must have valid driver's license. Top 10 contest winners receive a free set of four Bridgestone- or Firestone-brand tires, maximum retail value of $1000. First place scholarship prize: $25,000; Second place: $15,000; Third place: $10,000. Top three finalists will be chosen by public vote. Deadline varies. Visit Website for more information.

Amount of award:	$10,000-$25,000
Number of awards:	10
Number of applicants:	2,322
Total amount awarded:	$52,500

Contact:
Bridgestone
Web: www.teensdrivesmart.com

Broadcast Education Association

Abe Voron Scholarship

Type of award: Scholarship.
Intended use: For full-time junior, senior or graduate study at 4-year or graduate institution. Designated institutions: BEA Institutional Member schools.
Basis for selection: Major/career interest in radio/television/film. Applicant must demonstrate high academic achievement, depth of character and seriousness of purpose.
Application requirements: Recommendations, essay, transcript.
Additional information: Award intended for study in radio only. Should be able to show evidence of potential to be outstanding electronic media professional. Application available from campus faculty or online.

Amount of award:	$5,000
Number of awards:	1
Application deadline:	October 10
Total amount awarded:	$5,000

Contact:
Broadcast Education Association (BEA)
1771 N Street, N.W.
Washington, DC 20036-2891
Phone: 202-429-3935
Web: www.beaweb.org

Alexander M. Tanger Scholarship

Type of award: Scholarship.
Intended use: For full-time junior, senior or graduate study at 4-year or graduate institution. Designated institutions: BEA Institutional Member schools.
Basis for selection: Major/career interest in radio/television/film. Applicant must demonstrate high academic achievement, depth of character and seriousness of purpose.
Application requirements: Recommendations, essay, transcript.
Additional information: Must show evidence of potential in electronic media. Application available from campus faculty or on Website.

Amount of award:	$5,000
Number of awards:	1
Application deadline:	October 10
Total amount awarded:	$5,000

Contact:
Broadcast Education Association (BEA)
1771 N Street, N.W.
Washington, DC 20036-2891
Phone: 202-429-3935
Web: www.beaweb.org

BEA Founders Award

Type of award: Scholarship.
Intended use: For full-time undergraduate study at 2-year or 4-year institution. Designated institutions: BEA Institutional Member schools.
Basis for selection: Major/career interest in radio/television/film. Applicant must demonstrate high academic achievement, depth of character and seriousness of purpose.
Application requirements: Recommendations, essay, transcript.

Additional information: Preference given to students enrolled in BEA 2-Year/Small College Member Institution or graduates of these programs now enrolled in BEA 4-Year Institution. Should show evidence of potential in electronic media. Application available from campus faculty or on Website.

Amount of award:	$1,500
Number of awards:	2
Application deadline:	October 10
Total amount awarded:	$3,000

Contact:
Broadcast Education Association (BEA)
1771 N Street, N.W.
Washington, DC 20036-2891
Phone: 202-429-3935
Web: www.beaweb.org

John Bayliss Scholarship Award

Type of award: Scholarship.
Intended use: For full-time junior, senior or graduate study at 4-year or graduate institution. Designated institutions: BEA Member Institutions.
Basis for selection: Major/career interest in radio/television/film. Applicant must demonstrate high academic achievement, depth of character and seriousness of purpose.
Application requirements: Recommendations, essay, transcript.
Additional information: Award intended for study in radio only. Should be able to show evidence of potential to be outstanding electronic media professional. Application available from campus faculty or online.

Amount of award:	$1,500
Number of awards:	1
Application deadline:	October 10
Total amount awarded:	$1,500

Contact:
Broadcast Education Association (BEA)
1771 N Street, N.W.
Washington, DC 20036-2891
Phone: 202-429-3935
Web: www.beaweb.org

Richard Eaton Foundation Award

Type of award: Scholarship.
Intended use: For full-time junior, senior or graduate study at 4-year or graduate institution. Designated institutions: BEA Institutional Member schools.
Basis for selection: Major/career interest in radio/television/film. Applicant must demonstrate high academic achievement, depth of character and seriousness of purpose.
Application requirements: Recommendations, essay, transcript.
Additional information: Must show evidence of potential in electronic media. Application available from campus faculty or on Website.

Amount of award:	$1,500
Number of awards:	1
Application deadline:	October 10

Contact:
Broadcast Education Association (BEA)
1771 N Street, NW
Washington, DC 20036-2891
Phone: 202-429-3935
Web: www.beaweb.org

Walter S. Patterson Scholarship

Type of award: Scholarship.
Intended use: For full-time junior, senior or graduate study at 4-year or graduate institution. Designated institutions: BEA Institutional Member schools.
Basis for selection: Major/career interest in radio/television/film. Applicant must demonstrate high academic achievement, depth of character and seriousness of purpose.
Application requirements: Recommendations, essay, transcript.
Additional information: Award intended for study in radio only. Should be able to show evidence of potential in electronic media. Application available from campus faculty or on Website.

Amount of award:	$1,750
Number of awards:	2
Application deadline:	October 10
Total amount awarded:	$3,500

Contact:
Broadcast Education Association (BEA)
1771 N Street, N.W.
Washington, DC 20036-2891
Phone: 202-429-3935
Web: www.beaweb.org

Brown and Caldwell

Brown and Caldwell Minority Scholarship Program

Type of award: Scholarship.
Intended use: For full-time junior, senior or graduate study at accredited 4-year or graduate institution.
Eligibility: Applicant must be Alaskan native, Asian American, African American, Mexican American, Hispanic American, Puerto Rican, American Indian or Native Hawaiian/Pacific Islander. Applicant must be U.S. citizen or permanent resident.
Basis for selection: Major/career interest in engineering, civil; engineering, chemical; engineering, environmental; environmental science; ecology or geology/earth sciences. Applicant must demonstrate high academic achievement.
Application requirements: Recommendations, essay, transcript. Resume.
Additional information: Award includes optional paid summer internship at Brown and Caldwell office. Minimum cumulative 3.0 GPA.

Amount of award:	$5,000
Number of awards:	4
Number of applicants:	71
Application deadline:	April 15
Notification begins:	May 15
Total amount awarded:	$20,000

Contact:
Brown and Caldwell
Attn: HR/Scholarship Program
P.O. Box 8045
Walnut Creek, CA 94596
Phone: 800-727-2224
Web: www.brownandcaldwell.com/scholarships

Dr. W. Wes Eckenfelder Jr. Scholarship

Type of award: Scholarship.
Intended use: For full-time junior, senior or graduate study at accredited postsecondary institution.
Eligibility: Applicant must be U.S. citizen or permanent resident.
Basis for selection: Major/career interest in engineering, civil; engineering, chemical; engineering, environmental; environmental science; environmental science or ecology. Applicant must demonstrate high academic achievement and seriousness of purpose.
Application requirements: Recommendations, essay, transcript. Resume.
Additional information: Minimum 3.0 GPA. Visit Website for additional information.

Amount of award:	$5,000
Number of awards:	1
Number of applicants:	98
Application deadline:	April 15
Notification begins:	May 15
Total amount awarded:	$5,000

Contact:
Brown and Caldwell
Attn: HR/Scholarship Program
P.O. Box 8045
Walnut Creek, CA 94596
Phone: 800-727-2224
Web: www.brownandcaldwell.com/scholarships

Building Industry Association

BIA Cares of San Diego Scholarship

Type of award: Scholarship.
Intended use: For full-time sophomore, junior or senior study at postsecondary institution.
Eligibility: Applicant must be residing in California.
Basis for selection: Major/career interest in engineering, civil; real estate; construction; finance/banking; landscape architecture; engineering, construction; advertising; accounting; architecture or engineering, structural. Applicant must demonstrate financial need, high academic achievement and seriousness of purpose.
Application requirements: Interview, essay, transcript, proof of eligibility.
Additional information: For residents of San Diego who have either graduated from a San Diego County high school or are attending college in San Diego and are interested in careers in the building industry. Also open to students pursuing major/career as developer, contractor, soils engineer, designer, land planner, framer, plumber, electrician, carpenter, city planner, or other related profession. Number and amount of awards varies. See Website for application and deadline.
Contact:
Building Industry Association of San Diego
c/o Nancy Diamond
9201 Spectrum Center Blvd., Suite 110
San Diego, CA 92123
Phone: 858-450-1221
Web: www.biasandiego.org/bia-cares

Bureau of Indian Education

Bureau of Indian Education Higher Education Grant Program

Type of award: Scholarship, renewable.
Intended use: For full-time undergraduate study at accredited 2-year or 4-year institution in United States.
Eligibility: Applicant must be American Indian. Member or at least one-quarter degree descendent of member of federally recognized tribe.
Basis for selection: Applicant must demonstrate financial need.
Application requirements: Proof of eligibility.
Additional information: Contacts or inquiries for these funds should be directed to the person's tribal headquarters. The Higher Education scholarships are not awarded through the D.C. offices. Award amount based on student's financial need. No application deadline.

Number of awards:	12,000
Total amount awarded:	$25,000,000

Contact:
Bureau of Indian Education
Division of Post Secondary Education
215 Dean A McGee, Suite 610
Oklahoma City, OK 73102
Phone: 405-605-6001
Fax: 405-605-6010
Web: www.bie.edu

Bureau of Indian Education-Oklahoma Area Education Office

Osage Tribal Education Committee Award

Type of award: Scholarship.
Intended use: For undergraduate or graduate study at accredited postsecondary institution in United States.
Eligibility: Applicant must be American Indian. Must be member of Osage Tribe.
Basis for selection: Applicant must demonstrate high academic achievement.
Application requirements: Transcript, proof of eligibility. Signed statement of privacy.
Additional information: Minimum 2.0 GPA. Part-time students funded at half rate. Application deadlines: July 1 for fall semester, December 31 for spring semester, and May 1 for summer semester (funds permitting). Contact Oklahoma Area Education Office for application and additional information.

Number of applicants:	204
Application deadline:	July 1, December 31

Contact:
Bureau of Indian Affairs - Oklahoma Area Education Office
200 N.W. 4th Street
Suite 4049
Oklahoma City, OK 73102
Phone: 405-605-6051 ext. 304
Web: www.osagetribe.com/education

California Association of Realtors Scholarship Foundation

C.A.R. Scholarship

Type of award: Scholarship, renewable.
Intended use: For undergraduate or graduate study at 2-year or 4-year institution. Designated institutions: California colleges/universities.
Eligibility: Applicant must be U.S. citizen residing in California.
Basis for selection: Major/career interest in real estate. Applicant must demonstrate financial need and high academic achievement.
Application requirements: Recommendations, essay, transcript, proof of eligibility. Photocopy of valid CA driver's license or ID card.
Additional information: Must be California resident of at least one year before applying. Awarded to all eligible applicants. Students attending two-year colleges receive up to $2,000; four-year college/university students receive up to $4,000. Application deadlines are April 1, September 1, and December 1, with notification about six weeks later. May receive one award per year, maximum two years. Minimum 2.6 GPA. Must have completed minimum 12 college-level course units within last four years; at least two courses in real estate or real-estate related. Must be enrolled in one real estate course at the time of submission of application. Visit Website for application, exact deadlines, and other information.

Amount of award:	$2,000-$4,000
Number of applicants:	26
Total amount awarded:	$42,000

Contact:
California Association of Realtors Scholarship Foundation
525 South Virgil Avenue
Los Angeles, CA 90020
Phone: 213-739-8243
Fax: 213-739-7286
Web: www.car.org/aboutus

California Farm Bureau Federation

California Farm Bureau Scholarship

Type of award: Scholarship, renewable.
Intended use: For full-time undergraduate study at accredited 4-year institution. Designated institutions: Colleges/universities in California.
Eligibility: Applicant must be U.S. citizen residing in California.
Basis for selection: Major/career interest in agriculture; agribusiness; engineering, agricultural or veterinary medicine. Applicant must demonstrate high academic achievement, leadership and seriousness of purpose.
Application requirements: Recommendations, transcript.
Additional information: Must be preparing for career in agricultural industry and a member of the Collegiate Farm Bureau in California. Visit Website for application. Number and amount of awards vary. Notification begins late May/early June.

Number of applicants:	250
Application deadline:	March 1
Total amount awarded:	$165,750

Contact:
California Farm Bureau Scholarship Foundation
2300 River Plaza Drive
Sacramento, CA 95833
Phone: 916-561-5500
Web: www.cfbf.com/scholarship

California Student Aid Commission

Cal Grant A & B Entitlement Award Program

Type of award: Scholarship, renewable.
Intended use: For undergraduate study at postsecondary institution. Designated institutions: Qualifying California postsecondary schools.
Eligibility: Applicant must be high school senior. Applicant must be U.S. citizen or permanent resident residing in California.
Basis for selection: Applicant must demonstrate financial need and high academic achievement.
Application requirements: FAFSA, GPA verification form.
Additional information: Applicants who graduated in the last year and high school graduates transferring from a California community college with a minimum 2.4 GPA are also eligible. Awards given to all eligible applicants. Minimum 3.0 GPA for Cal Grant A; minimum 2.0 GPA for Cal Grant B. Cal Grant A provides tuition and fees. Cal Grant B awards up to $1,473 the first year and $1,473 plus tuition and fees for years two through four. Visit Website or contact CSAC for more details.

Amount of award:	$1,473-$13,665
Number of applicants:	321,000
Application deadline:	March 2
Notification begins:	February 15
Total amount awarded:	$1,361,000,000

Contact:
California Student Aid Commission
Student Support Services Branch
P.O. Box 419027
Rancho Cordova, CA 95741-9027
Phone: 888-224-7268
Fax: 916-464-8002
Web: www.calgrants.org

Cal Grant A and B Competitive Awards

Type of award: Scholarship, renewable.
Intended use: For undergraduate study at postsecondary institution. Designated institutions: Qualifying California postsecondary schools.
Eligibility: Applicant must be U.S. citizen or permanent resident residing in California.
Basis for selection: Applicant must demonstrate financial need and high academic achievement.
Application requirements: FAFSA, GPA verification form.

Additional information: Minimum 3.0 GPA for Cal Grant A; minimum 2.0 GPA for Cal Grant B. Cal Grant A pays tuition and fees. Cal Grant B awards up to $1,473 first year and $1,473 plus tuition and fees for years two through four. Students with no available GPA can submit SAT, ACT, or GED scores. Visit Website or contact CSAC for more details.

Amount of award:	$1,473-$13,665
Number of awards:	22,500
Number of applicants:	524,600
Application deadline:	March 2, September 2
Notification begins:	April 30, October 15
Total amount awarded:	$126,000,000

Contact:
California Student Aid Commission
Student Support Services Branch
P.O. Box 419027
Rancho Cordova, CA 95741-9027
Phone: 888-224-7268
Fax: 916-464-8002
Web: www.calgrants.org

Cal Grant C Award

Type of award: Scholarship, renewable.
Intended use: For undergraduate study at vocational or 2-year institution. Designated institutions: Qualifying California postsecondary institutions.
Eligibility: Applicant must be U.S. citizen or permanent resident residing in California.
Basis for selection: Applicant must demonstrate financial need.
Application requirements: FAFSA, GPA verification form.
Additional information: Funding is available for up to two years, and vocational program must be at least four months in length. Visit Website or contact CSAC for more details.

Amount of award:	$547-$3,009
Number of awards:	7,761
Number of applicants:	18,800
Application deadline:	March 2
Notification begins:	May 30
Total amount awarded:	$8,986,000

Contact:
California Student Aid Commission
Student Support Services Branch
P.O. Box 419027
Rancho Cordova, CA 95741-9027
Phone: 888-224-7268
Fax: 916-464-8002
Web: www.calgrants.org

California Chafee Grant Program

Type of award: Scholarship, renewable.
Intended use: For undergraduate or graduate study at accredited postsecondary institution.
Eligibility: Applicant must be no older than 21.
Basis for selection: Applicant must demonstrate financial need.
Application requirements: FAFSA, Chafee Need Analysis Report.
Additional information: Must be current or former foster youth from any state attending a California college or current foster youth from California attending any college. Foster youth dependency of the court must have been established between the ages of 16 to 18. Students must maintain satisfactory academic progress. School must report financial need on the Chafee Need Analysis Report. Must not have reached 22nd birthday by July 1st of award year. Must be enrolled at least half-time in course of study lasting at least one academic year. Renewable through 23rd birthday. Apply early.

Amount of award:	$5,000
Number of awards:	3,143
Number of applicants:	6,048
Notification begins:	July 1
Total amount awarded:	$11,630,579

Contact:
California Student Aid Commission
Attn: Specialized Programs Operations Branch
P.O. Box 419029
Rancho Cordova, CA 95741-9029
Phone: 888-224-7268
Fax: 916-464-7977
Web: www.chafee.csac.ca.gov

California Child Development Grant Program

Type of award: Scholarship.
Intended use: For undergraduate study at accredited 2-year or 4-year institution. Designated institutions: California postsecondary institutions.
Eligibility: Applicant must be U.S. citizen or permanent resident residing in California.
Basis for selection: Major/career interest in education, early childhood. Applicant must demonstrate financial need.
Application requirements: Recommendations, nomination by postsecondary institution or employing agency. FAFSA.
Additional information: Recipients attending two-year institutions receive up to $1,000 annually; those attending four-year institutions receive up to $2,000 annually. Recipients must maintain at least half-time enrollment in approved course of study leading to Child Development Permit in one of following levels: Teacher, Master Teacher, Site Supervisor or Program Director. Must maintain satisfactory academic progress, meet federal Selective Service filing requirements, and commit to one year of full-time employment in licensed child care center for every year they receive the grant. Deadlines and notification dates vary. Visit Website for application and more information.

Amount of award:	$1,000-$2,000
Number of awards:	100
Number of applicants:	894
Application deadline:	June 15
Notification begins:	February 1
Total amount awarded:	$277,000

Contact:
California Student Aid Commission
Attn: Child Development Grant Program
P.O. Box 419029
Rancho Cordova, CA 95741-9029
Phone: 888-224-7268 opt. 3
Fax: 916-464-7977
Web: www.csac.ca.gov

California Law Enforcement Personnel Dependents (LEPD) Grant Program

Type of award: Scholarship, renewable.
Intended use: For undergraduate study at accredited 2-year or 4-year institution. Designated institutions: California postsecondary institutions.
Eligibility: Applicant must be U.S. citizen residing in California. Applicant's parent must have been killed or

disabled in work-related accident as firefighter, police officer or public safety officer.
Basis for selection: Applicant must demonstrate financial need.
Application requirements: SAR, birth certificate (not required for spouse), death certificate, findings of Workers' Compensation Appeals Board.
Additional information: Applicant must be dependent or spouse of California peace or law enforcement officer, officer or employee of Department of Corrections or Division of Juvenile Justice in California, or California firefighter, who was killed or 100 percent disabled in performance of duty. Number of awards varies.

Amount of award:	$1,551-$13,401
Number of applicants:	7
Notification begins:	February 1
Total amount awarded:	$21,460

Contact:
California Student Aid Commission
LEPD Program
P.O. Box 419029
Rancho Cordova, CA 95741-9029
Phone: 888-224-7268 opt. 3
Fax: 916-464-7977
Web: www.csac.ca.gov

California Teachers Association

California Teachers Association Martin Luther King, Jr., Memorial Scholarship

Type of award: Scholarship.
Intended use: For undergraduate or graduate study at accredited postsecondary institution.
Eligibility: Applicant must be Alaskan native, Asian American, African American, Mexican American, Hispanic American, Puerto Rican, American Indian or Native Hawaiian/Pacific Islander. Applicant must be residing in California.
Basis for selection: Major/career interest in education; education, early childhood; education, special or education, teacher. Applicant must demonstrate financial need.
Application requirements: Recommendations, essay, transcript, proof of eligibility.
Additional information: Must be active California Teachers Association (CTA) member, active Student CTA member, or dependent child of an active, retired, or deceased CTA member. Amount of award and number of awards varies. To receive funds, must show proof of registration in approved credential or degree program. Must pursue teaching-related career in public education. Application must be typed and mailed. Check Website for deadline and additional information.
Contact:
CTA Scholarship Committee Human Rights Department
c/o Janeya Dawson
P.O. Box 921
Burlingame, CA 94011-0921
Phone: 650-552-5446
Fax: 650-552-5001
Web: www.cta.org

CTA Scholarship for Dependent Children

Type of award: Scholarship, renewable.
Intended use: For full-time undergraduate or graduate study at accredited postsecondary institution.
Eligibility: Applicant must be residing in California.
Basis for selection: Major/career interest in education. Applicant must demonstrate high academic achievement, depth of character, leadership, seriousness of purpose and service orientation.
Application requirements: Recommendations, essay, transcript, proof of eligibility.
Additional information: Applicant must be dependent child of active, retired, or deceased member of California Teachers Association. Awards based on overall achievement in four categories: 1) involvement in and sensitivity to human, social, and civic issues; 2) characteristics such as responsibility, reliability, and integrity; 3) academic and vocational potential; and 4) special and personal achievements. Application deadline between end of January and beginning of February; visit Website for exact date and the most current information. Number of awards varies.

Amount of award:	$3,000-$5,000

Contact:
CTA Scholarship Committee Human Rights Department
c/o Janeya Dawson
P.O. Box 921
Burlingame, CA 94011-0921
Phone: 650-552-5446
Fax: 650-552-5001
Web: www.cta.org

CTA Scholarships for Members

Type of award: Scholarship, renewable.
Intended use: For full-time undergraduate or graduate study at accredited postsecondary institution.
Eligibility: Applicant must be residing in California.
Basis for selection: Major/career interest in education; education, early childhood; education, special or education, teacher. Applicant must demonstrate high academic achievement, depth of character, leadership, seriousness of purpose and service orientation.
Application requirements: Recommendations, essay, transcript, proof of eligibility.
Additional information: Scholarships awarded based on overall achievement in four categories: 1) involvement in and sensitivity to human, social, and civic issues; 2) characteristics such as responsibility, reliability, and integrity; 3) academic and vocational potential; and 4) special and personal achievements. Applicant must be active member of California Teachers Association (including members working on emergency credential). Application deadline is between end of January and beginning of February; visit Website for exact date and the most up-to-date information. Number of awards varies.

Amount of award:	$3,000
Number of awards:	5

Contact:
CTA Scholarship Committee Human Rights Department
c/o Janeya Dawson
P.O. Box 921
Burlingame, CA 94011-0921
Phone: 650-552-5446
Fax: 650-552-5001
Web: www.cta.org

GLBT "Guy DeRosa" Safety in Schools Grant and Scholarship Program

Type of award: Scholarship.
Intended use: For undergraduate or graduate study at 2-year, 4-year or graduate institution.
Application requirements: Essay, proof of eligibility.
Additional information: Awards support projects and presentations that promote understanding and respect for GLBT persons and GLBT educators. Must be active California Teachers Association (CTA) member, active Student CTA member, or a public school student or district nominated by a CTA or SCTA member. Number of awards varies. Both grants and scholarships available. Check Website for deadline and additional information. Application must be typed and mailed.

Amount of award:	$2,000

Contact:
California Teachers Association
Human Rights Department
1705 Murchison Drive
Burlingame, CA 94011-0921
Phone: 650-552-5446
Fax: 650-552-5001
Web: www.cta.org

L. Gordon Bittle Memorial Scholarship for SCTA

Type of award: Scholarship, renewable.
Intended use: For full-time undergraduate, graduate or non-degree study at accredited postsecondary institution.
Basis for selection: Major/career interest in education; education, early childhood; education, special or education, teacher. Applicant must demonstrate high academic achievement, depth of character and service orientation.
Application requirements: Recommendations, essay, transcript.
Additional information: Applicant must be active member of Student CTA. Must pursue career in public education. Not available to CTA members currently working in schools. May be enrolled in teacher credential program. Application deadline is between end of January and beginning of February; visit Website for exact date and more information.

Amount of award:	$3,000
Number of awards:	3
Number of applicants:	20

Contact:
CTA Scholarship Committee Human Rights Department
c/o Janeya Dawson
P.O. Box 921
Burlingame, CA 94011-0921
Phone: 650-552-5446
Fax: 650-552-5001
Web: www.cta.org

Carl's Jr. Restaurants

Carl N. & Margaret Karcher Founders' Scholarship

Type of award: Scholarship.
Intended use: For full-time freshman study at accredited vocational, 2-year or 4-year institution.
Eligibility: Applicant must be no older than 21, high school senior. Applicant must be residing in Utah, Texas, Alaska, Washington, Arizona, Nevada, Oklahoma, California, Oregon, Idaho, New Mexico, Colorado or Hawaii.
Application requirements: Transcript.
Additional information: High school graduates also eligible. Employees, affiliates, and franchisees of Carl Karcher Enterprises, Inc., Scholarship America, affiliated agencies and their immediate families are ineligible. Application available on Website beginning in January.

Amount of award:	$1,000
Number of awards:	60
Number of applicants:	1,000
Application deadline:	February 1
Total amount awarded:	$60,000

Contact:
Carl N. & Margaret Karcher Founders' Scholarship
c/o Scholarship America
One Scholarship Way, P.O. Box 297
St. Peter, MN 56082
Phone: 507-931-1682
Web: www.carlsjr.com/scholarship

Catching the Dream

MESBEC Scholarships

Type of award: Scholarship, renewable.
Intended use: For full-time undergraduate or graduate study at accredited postsecondary institution in United States.
Eligibility: Applicant must be Alaskan native or American Indian. Must be at least one-quarter Native American and enrolled member of federally recognized, state recognized, or terminated tribe. Applicant must be U.S. citizen or permanent resident.
Basis for selection: Major/career interest in mathematics; engineering; science, general; business; education; computer/information sciences; health sciences or medicine. Applicant must demonstrate high academic achievement, depth of character, leadership, seriousness of purpose and service orientation.
Application requirements: Recommendations, essay, transcript, proof of eligibility.
Additional information: Deadlines are March 15 for summer funding, April 15 for fall, September 15 for spring.

Amount of award:	$500-$5,000
Number of awards:	180
Number of applicants:	150
Application deadline:	April 15, September 15
Total amount awarded:	$300,000

Contact:
Catching the Dream
8200 Mountain Road NE
Suite 203
Albuquerque, NM 87110
Phone: 505-262-2351
Fax: 505-262-0534
Web: www.catchingthedream.org

Native American Leadership in Education Scholarship

Type of award: Scholarship, renewable.
Intended use: For full-time undergraduate or graduate study at accredited postsecondary institution in United States.
Eligibility: Applicant must be American Indian. Must be at least one-quarter Native American and enrolled member of federally recognized, state recognized, or terminated tribe. Applicant must be U.S. citizen or permanent resident.
Basis for selection: Major/career interest in education. Applicant must demonstrate high academic achievement, depth of character, leadership, seriousness of purpose and service orientation.
Application requirements: Recommendations, essay, transcript, proof of eligibility.
Additional information: Deadlines are March 15 for summer funding, April 15 for fall, September 15 for spring.

Amount of award:	$500-$5,000
Number of awards:	30
Number of applicants:	40
Application deadline:	April 15, September 15
Total amount awarded:	$100,000

Contact:
Catching the Dream
8200 Mountain Road NE
Suite 203
Albuquerque, NM 87110
Phone: 505-262-2351
Fax: 505-262-0534
Web: www.catchingthedream.org

Tribal Business Management Scholarship

Type of award: Scholarship, renewable.
Intended use: For full-time undergraduate, graduate or postgraduate study at accredited postsecondary institution in United States.
Eligibility: Applicant must be Alaskan native or American Indian. Must be at least one-quarter Native American and enrolled member of federally recognized, state recognized, or terminated tribe. Applicant must be U.S. citizen or permanent resident.
Basis for selection: Major/career interest in business; economics; finance/banking; hotel/restaurant management; accounting; marketing or business/management/administration. Applicant must demonstrate high academic achievement, depth of character, leadership, seriousness of purpose and service orientation.
Application requirements: Recommendations, essay, transcript, proof of eligibility.
Additional information: Scholarships are for fields of study directly related to tribal business development and management. Application deadlines are March 15 for summer semester, April 15 for fall semester, September 15 for spring semester.

Amount of award:	$500-$5,000
Number of awards:	15
Number of applicants:	30
Application deadline:	April 15, September 15
Total amount awarded:	$50,000

Contact:
Catching the Dream
8200 Mountain Road NE
Suite 203
Albuquerque, NM 87110
Phone: 505-262-2351
Fax: 505-262-0534
Web: www.catchingthedream.org

Catholic United Financial

Catholic United Financial Post-High School Tuition Scholarship

Type of award: Scholarship.
Intended use: For full-time freshman or sophomore study at accredited vocational, 2-year or 4-year institution in United States.
Basis for selection: Applicant must demonstrate leadership and service orientation.
Application requirements: Essay, proof of eligibility.
Additional information: Must have been member of Catholic United Financial for two years prior to application deadline. Award is $300 for students attending non-Catholic schools and $500 for those attending Catholic colleges. Visit Website for application. Number of awards varies.

Amount of award:	$300-$500
Number of awards:	520
Number of applicants:	565
Application deadline:	February 15
Notification begins:	April 1
Total amount awarded:	$160,700

Contact:
Catholic United Financial Scholarship Program
3499 Lexington Avenue North
St. Paul, MN 55126
Phone: 651-490-0170
Fax: 651-765-6556
Web: www.catholicunitedfinancial.org

CCNMA: Latino Journalists of California

CCNMA Scholarships

Type of award: Scholarship, renewable.
Intended use: For full-time undergraduate or graduate study at accredited postsecondary institution.
Eligibility: Applicant must be Mexican American, Hispanic American or Puerto Rican.
Basis for selection: Competition/talent/interest in writing/journalism. Major/career interest in journalism. Applicant must demonstrate financial need, high academic achievement, seriousness of purpose and service orientation.
Application requirements: Interview, recommendations, essay, transcript. Proof of full-time enrollment. Samples of work: newspaper clips, photographs, audio or television tapes.
Additional information: Must be a Latino resident of California attending school in or out of state, or nonresident attending school in California. Number of awards varies.

Amount of award: $500-$2,000
Number of awards: 6
Number of applicants: 100
Application deadline: April 1
Notification begins: June 1
Total amount awarded: $6,400

Contact:
CCNMA: Latino Journalists of California
725 Arizona Avenue
Suite 206
Santa Monica, CA 90401-1734
Phone: 310-458-8040
Fax: 310-576-0502
Web: www.ccnma.org

Center for Architecture

Center for Architecture Design Scholarship

Type of award: Scholarship.
Intended use: For undergraduate study at accredited postsecondary institution in United States. Designated institutions: New York State institutions.
Basis for selection: Major/career interest in architecture; design or engineering. Applicant must demonstrate financial need and high academic achievement.
Application requirements: Recommendations by dean or chair of school attended. Portfolio.
Additional information: Number of awards varies. Applicant may also study related disciplines, including planning, architectural engineering, civil engineering, electrical engineering, environmental engineering, mechanical engineering, structural engineering, architectural design, environmental design, furniture design, industrial design, interior design, landscape design, sustainable design, and urban design. Graduate students eligible if undergraduate degree is in a field other than architecture.

Amount of award: $5,000
Number of applicants: 20
Application deadline: March 15
Notification begins: May 31
Total amount awarded: $5,000

Contact:
Center for Architecture Foundation
Attn: CFA Design Scholarship
536 LaGuardia Place
New York, NY 10012
Phone: 212-358-6133
Web: www.cfafoundation.org/cfadesign

Eleanor Allwork Scholarship

Type of award: Scholarship.
Intended use: For undergraduate or graduate study at accredited postsecondary institution. Designated institutions: NAAB-accredited schools in the State of New York.
Eligibility: Applicant must be U.S. citizen, permanent resident or international student residing in New York.
Basis for selection: Major/career interest in architecture. Applicant must demonstrate financial need and high academic achievement.
Application requirements: Portfolio, recommendations, nomination by Dean of architecture school. Cover page with full contact information, SASE required for return of work samples. Must apply both online and hard copy and can be hand-delivered.
Additional information: Applicants must be nominated by the dean or chair of the school of architecture in which they are currently studying in order to apply. Awards and amounts may vary. Single or multiple awards up to $10,000. Graduate students eligible if from a different undergraduate background and currently completing their first architectural degree.

Amount of award: $7,500-$10,000
Number of applicants: 30
Application deadline: March 15
Notification begins: May 31
Total amount awarded: $15,000

Contact:
Center for Architecture Foundation
Attn: Eleanor Allwork Scholarship
536 LaGuardia Place
New York, NY 10012
Phone: 212-358-6133
Web: www.cfafoundation.org/allwork

The Center for Reintegration

Lilly Reintegration Scholarship

Type of award: Scholarship.
Intended use: For undergraduate or graduate study at accredited 2-year, 4-year or graduate institution in United States.
Eligibility: Applicant must be at least 18. Applicant must be U.S. citizen.
Basis for selection: Applicant must demonstrate financial need, high academic achievement, seriousness of purpose and service orientation.
Application requirements: Recommendations, essay, transcript. FAFSA. A copy of desired school's statement of standard costs for tuition, books, lab supplies, and mandatory fees. Signed Personal Consent & Release Form. Self-addressed stamped envelope.
Additional information: Must be diagnosed with bipolar, schizophrenia, schizophreniform disorder, or schizoaffective disorder. Must be currently receiving medical treatment for the disease, including medication and psychiatric follow-up. Must be actively involved in rehabilitative or reintegration efforts, such as clubhouse membership, part-time work, volunteer efforts, or school enrollment. Must have success in dealing with the disease.

Number of awards: 70
Number of applicants: 600
Application deadline: January 31
Notification begins: July 1

Contact:
Lilly Reintegration Scholarship
PMB 327
310 Busse Highway
Park Ridge, IL 60068-3251
Phone: 800-809-8202
Web: www.reintegration.com

Central Intelligence Agency

CIA Undergraduate Scholarship Program

Type of award: Scholarship, renewable.
Intended use: For full-time freshman or sophomore study at accredited 4-year institution in United States.
Eligibility: Applicant must be at least 18, high school senior. Applicant must be U.S. citizen.
Basis for selection: Major/career interest in engineering; computer/information sciences; foreign languages; international relations; human resources or finance/banking. Applicant must demonstrate financial need, high academic achievement, depth of character, patriotism and seriousness of purpose.
Application requirements: Recommendations, transcript. SAT/ACT scores, FAFSA or SAR.
Additional information: Applicant may have wide range of majors in addition to those listed. High school applicants must be 18 by April 1 of senior year. Minimum 3.0 GPA; 1500 SAT (1000 Math and Reading, 500 Writing), or 21 ACT required. Household income must not exceed $70,000 for family of four or $80,000 for family of five or more. Scholars work at CIA offices in Washington, D.C. metro area during summer breaks and receive annual salary in addition to up to $18,000 per school year for tuition, fees, books, and supplies. Must commit to employment with Agency after college graduation for period 1.5 times length of scholarship. Number of awards varies. Apply online. Deadline may vary; check site for exact date.

Amount of award:	$18,000
Application deadline:	October 15

Contact:
Phone: 800-368-3886
Fax: 703-374-2281
Web: www.cia.gov

C.G. Fuller Foundation c/o Bank of America

C.G. Fuller Foundation Scholarship

Type of award: Scholarship, renewable.
Intended use: For full-time undergraduate study at 4-year institution. Designated institutions: Colleges and universities in South Carolina.
Eligibility: Applicant must be high school senior. Applicant must be residing in South Carolina.
Basis for selection: Applicant must demonstrate financial need, high academic achievement and leadership.
Application requirements: Essay, transcript. Financial statement, copy of parents' most recent 1040 tax return, SAT or ACT scores, high school guidance form.
Additional information: Contact Bank of America office for application. 3.0 GPA and 1100 SAT or 24 ACT required. Number of awards varies with changes in funding. Parents' adjusted gross income must be $60,000 or less. Award is $1,250 per semester, renewable for four years if 3.0 GPA is maintained.

Amount of award:	$2,500
Number of applicants:	25
Application deadline:	March 15
Notification begins:	August 1

Contact:
C.G. Fuller Foundation Scholarship c/o Bank of America
#SC3-240-04-17
P.O. Box 448
Columbia, SC 29202-0448

ChairScholars Foundation, Inc.

National ChairScholars Scholarship

Type of award: Scholarship, renewable.
Intended use: For full-time undergraduate study at postsecondary institution.
Eligibility: Applicant must be physically challenged. Applicant must be no older than 21. Applicant must be U.S. citizen or permanent resident.
Basis for selection: Applicant must demonstrate financial need, high academic achievement and service orientation.
Application requirements: Recommendations, essay, transcript. Photograph, parent's IRS Form 1040 from last year, SAT and ACT scores.
Additional information: Applicant must have a serious physical disability but does not have to be confined to a wheelchair. Applicant must be unable to attend college without financial aid; no household income above $85,000. Applicant must have at least a B+ average. If applicant has obtained any other scholarships already, he or she must inform ChairScholars. Award is renewable up to four years, for maximum $20,000.

Amount of award:	$1,000-$5,000
Number of awards:	15
Number of applicants:	85
Application deadline:	April 15
Notification begins:	May 15
Total amount awarded:	$320,000

Contact:
ChairScholars Foundation, Inc.
16101 Carencia Lane
Odessa, FL 33556
Phone: 813-926-0544
Fax: 813-920-7661
Web: www.chairscholars.org

New York Metropolitan Area Scholarship Program

Type of award: Scholarship, renewable.
Eligibility: Applicant must be physically challenged. Applicant must be high school senior.
Basis for selection: Applicant must demonstrate financial need and high academic achievement.
Application requirements: Recommendations, essay, transcript. Recent photograph. Parent's or guardian's federal income tax return. Physician's documentation of disability. Notification of receipt of other scholarships.
Additional information: College freshmen also eligible. Minimum "C" average. Available to physically disabled students in the New York Metropolitan area: five boroughs of New York City, parts of Long Island, northern and central New Jersey. Visit Website for details and application.

Amount of award: $2,000-$5,000
Number of awards: 6
Number of applicants: 4
Application deadline: April 15
Notification begins: May 15
Total amount awarded: $32,000

Contact:
ChairScholars Foundation, Inc.
16101 Carencia Lane
Odessa, FL 33556
Phone: 813-926-0544
Fax: 813-920-7661
Web: www.chairscholars.org

Charles & Lucille King Family Foundation, Inc.

Charles & Lucille King Family Foundation Scholarships

Type of award: Scholarship, renewable.
Intended use: For full-time junior or senior study at accredited 4-year institution in United States.
Basis for selection: Major/career interest in communications or radio/television/film. Applicant must demonstrate financial need and high academic achievement.
Application requirements: Recommendations, transcript. Personal statement. Application form with financial information.
Additional information: Download application from Website.

Amount of award: $3,500
Application deadline: March 15

Contact:
Charles & Lucille King Family Foundation, Inc.
1212 Avenue of the Americas
7th Floor
New York, NY 10036
Phone: 212-682-2913
Web: www.kingfoundation.org

The Charles A. and Anne Morrow Lindbergh Foundation

Lindbergh Grant

Type of award: Research grant.
Intended use: For undergraduate or non-degree study at postsecondary institution.
Basis for selection: Major/career interest in agriculture; aviation; biomedical; education; environmental science; health sciences or natural resources/conservation.
Application requirements: Research proposal.
Additional information: Applicant research or educational project should address balance between technological advancement and environmental preservation. Citizens of all countries are eligible. Deadline is second Thursday in June.

Amount of award: $1,000-$10,580
Number of awards: 10
Number of applicants: 200
Notification begins: April 15

Contact:
The Charles A. and Anne Morrow Lindbergh Foundation
2150 Third Avenue North
Suite 310
Anoka, MN 55303-2200
Phone: 763-576-1596
Fax: 763-576-1664
Web: www.lindberghfoundation.org

Charleston Women in International Trade

Charleston Women in International Trade Scholarship

Type of award: Scholarship.
Intended use: For undergraduate study at accredited postsecondary institution in United States.
Eligibility: Applicant must be U.S. citizen residing in South Carolina.
Basis for selection: Applicant must demonstrate financial need and seriousness of purpose.
Application requirements: Recommendations, transcript, proof of eligibility. Two-page (minimum length), double-spaced essay explaining the importance of international trade and state your goals for working in the international business environment. Must also explain why you believe you should be awarded this scholarship. Listing of courses/work experience relevant to interest in international trade; extracurricular activities, civic and community involvement. List of relevant courses/work experience. Financial aid/tuition information.
Additional information: Applicant must be pursuing degree specific to international trade or related course of study. To apply, complete application on Website.

Amount of award: $1,500-$3,000
Number of awards: 4
Application deadline: February 28
Notification begins: January 1
Total amount awarded: $6,000

Contact:
Ashley Kutz Kelley, CWIT Awards Chairperson
P.O. Box 31258
Charleston, SC 29417
Phone: 843-577-8678
Web: www.cwitsc.org

Choctaw Nation of Oklahoma

Choctaw Nation Higher Education Program

Type of award: Scholarship, renewable.
Intended use: For undergraduate or graduate study at accredited 2-year, 4-year or graduate institution in United States.

Eligibility: Applicant must be American Indian. Must be enrolled member of Choctaw Tribe and have Certificate of Degree of Indian Blood (CDIB) and tribal membership card.
Basis for selection: Applicant must demonstrate high academic achievement.
Application requirements: Transcript. Proof of Choctaw descent. FAFSA. School enrollment verification via submission of class schedule.
Additional information: Program made up of two awards: a grant or a scholarship. Grant is based on financial need; minimum 2.0 GPA required. The scholarship is for applicants with minimum 2.5 GPA. Grant will assist with any unmet need up to award amount. Must reapply for renewal. Number of awards varies. May only receive either grant or scholarship.

Amount of award:	$1,000-$2,000
Number of awards:	5,000
Number of applicants:	5,200
Application deadline:	October 1, March 1
Notification begins:	July 15

Contact:
Choctaw Nation of Oklahoma
Higher Education Department
P.O. Box 1210
Durant, OK 74702-1210
Phone: 800-522-6170
Fax: 580-924-1267
Web: www.choctawnation.com

Christian Record Services

Christian Record Services Scholarship

Type of award: Scholarship, renewable.
Intended use: For full-time undergraduate study at postsecondary institution in United States.
Eligibility: Applicant must be visually impaired.
Basis for selection: Applicant must demonstrate financial need and high academic achievement.
Application requirements: Recommendations. Photo and bio.
Additional information: Applicants must be totally or legally blind. Awardees must reapply yearly.

Amount of award:	$500
Number of awards:	10
Application deadline:	April 1
Notification begins:	May 15
Total amount awarded:	$5,000

Contact:
Christian Record Services
4444 South 52 Street
Lincoln, NE 68516
Phone: 402-488-0981
Fax: 402-488-7582
Web: www.christianrecord.org

The Coca-Cola Foundation

Coca-Cola All-State Community Colleges Academic Team Scholarship

Type of award: Scholarship.
Intended use: For undergraduate study at 2-year institution in United States. Designated institutions: Community colleges.
Eligibility: Applicant must be U.S. citizen or permanent resident.
Basis for selection: Applicant must demonstrate high academic achievement, depth of character and service orientation.
Application requirements: Nomination by college at which student is enrolled or is planning to enroll.
Additional information: Applicant/nominee must have done community service within past 12 months. Minimum 3.5 GPA for all coursework completed in last five years. Minimum 30 credit hours at community college in past five years. Must be planning to enroll in at least two courses during next term. Children and grandchildren of Coca-Cola employees not eligible. Program administered by Phi Theta Kappa Honor Society. Award notification begins in March. Visit Website for college credit requirements and nomination information.

Amount of award:	$1,000-$2,000
Number of awards:	150
Number of applicants:	1,600
Application deadline:	December 1
Total amount awarded:	$187,500

Contact:
Scholarship Programs Department
Phi Theta Kappa Honor Society
1625 Eastover Drive
Jackson, MS 39211
Phone: 800-946-9995
Web: www.coca-colascholars.org

Coca-Cola Scholars Program

Type of award: Scholarship, renewable.
Intended use: For full-time undergraduate study at accredited 4-year institution in United States.
Eligibility: Applicant must be high school senior. Applicant must be U.S. citizen or permanent resident.
Basis for selection: Applicant must demonstrate high academic achievement, depth of character, leadership, seriousness of purpose and service orientation.
Additional information: Applicant may also be temporary resident in legalization program, refugee, asylee, Cuban/Haitian entrant, or Humanitarian Parole. Must be attending high school in United States or territories. Minimum 3.0 GPA required at the end of junior year high school. Award is for four years, $2,500 or $5,000 per year. Notification begins December 1 for semifinalists; mid-February for finalists. Children and grandchildren of Coca-Cola employees not eligible.

Amount of award:	$10,000-$20,000
Number of awards:	250
Number of applicants:	75,000
Application deadline:	October 31
Notification begins:	December 5
Total amount awarded:	$3,000,000

Contact:
Coca-Cola Scholars Foundation
Phone: 800-306-2653
Web: www.coca-colascholars.org

College Foundation of North Carolina

North Carolina Education Lottery Scholarship

Type of award: Scholarship.
Intended use: For undergraduate certificate study at vocational, 2-year or 4-year institution in United States. Designated institutions: Eligible North Carolina institutions (UNC campuses, community college campuses, independent college campuses and certain private colleges).
Eligibility: Applicant must be U.S. citizen or permanent resident residing in North Carolina.
Application requirements: FAFSA.
Additional information: Must meet Satisfactory Academic Progress requirements of institution. Eligibility based on same criteria as Federal Pell Grant with one exception: students not eligible for Federal Pell Grant with estimated family contribution of $5,000 or less are eligible for Education Lottery Scholarship. Go to fafsa.gov to fill out application.
Amount of award: $100-$3,400
Contact:
College Foundation of North Carolina
Phone: 866-866-2362
Web: www.cfnc.org and www.fafsa.org

Colorado Commission on Higher Education

Colorado Student Grant

Type of award: Scholarship.
Intended use: For undergraduate study at postsecondary institution. Designated institutions: Eligible Colorado institutions.
Eligibility: Applicant must be residing in Colorado.
Basis for selection: Applicant must demonstrate financial need.
Application requirements: FAFSA.
Additional information: Contact college financial aid office or visit Website for additional information. International students must be working toward becoming permanent resident of U.S.
Amount of award: $850-$5,000
Total amount awarded: $68,958,376
Contact:
Colorado Commission on Higher Education
1560 Broadway
Suite 1600
Denver, CO 80202
Phone: 303-866-2723
Web: highered.colorado.gov

Colorado Work-Study Program

Type of award: Scholarship.
Intended use: For undergraduate study at postsecondary institution. Designated institutions: Eligible postsecondary institutions in Colorado.
Eligibility: Applicant must be residing in Colorado.
Additional information: Part-time employment program for students who need work experience or who can prove financial need. International students must be working toward becoming permanent resident of U.S. Amount of award cannot exceed need. Institutions must award 70% of work-study allocations to students with documented need; remaining 30% may be awarded to students without need. Contact college financial aid office or visit Website for additional information.
Total amount awarded: $17,691,519
Contact:
Colorado Commission on Higher Education
1560 Broadway
Suite 1600
Denver, CO 80202
Phone: 303-866-2723
Web: highered.colorado.gov

Colorado Council on High School and College Relations

Colorado Council Volunteerism and Community Service Scholarship

Type of award: Scholarship.
Intended use: For full-time freshman study at 2-year or 4-year institution in United States. Designated institutions: Colorado Council member institutions.
Eligibility: Applicant must be high school senior. Applicant must be U.S. citizen or permanent resident residing in Colorado.
Basis for selection: Applicant must demonstrate high academic achievement and service orientation.
Application requirements: Recommendations, essay, transcript.
Additional information: Minimum 2.5 GPA. Must be enrolled full-time at Colorado Council member institution within six months of graduating from high school. Visit Website for full list of Colorado Council member institutions.
Amount of award: $1,500
Number of awards: 16
Number of applicants: 221
Application deadline: January 30
Total amount awarded: $21,000
Contact:
CCHS/CR Scholarship Committee
P.O. Box 3383
Pagosa Springs, CO 81147
Phone: 970-264-2231, ext.226
Web: www.coloradocouncil.org/resources/scholarship.php

Colorado Masons' Benevolent Fund Association

Colorado Masons Scholarship

Type of award: Scholarship, renewable.
Intended use: For full-time undergraduate study at accredited vocational, 2-year or 4-year institution. Designated institutions: Institutions of higher learning in Colorado.

Eligibility: Applicant must be high school senior. Applicant must be U.S. citizen residing in Colorado.
Basis for selection: Applicant must demonstrate financial need, high academic achievement and depth of character.
Application requirements: Interview, recommendations, essay, transcript, proof of eligibility. Letter of acceptance and FAFSA or SAR.
Additional information: Applicant must be graduating senior at public high school in Colorado. Scholarship is renewable for up to four years. Number of awards varies. Visit Website for application and details.

Amount of award:	$7,000
Number of applicants:	456
Application deadline:	March 15
Total amount awarded:	$279,000

Contact:
Colorado Masons' Benevolent Fund Association
Scholarship Administrator
2400 Consistory Court
Grand Junction, CO 81501
Phone: 303-290-8544
Web: www.cmbfa.org

Colorado Society of CPAs Educational Foundation

Colorado Society of CPAs General Scholarship

Type of award: Scholarship, renewable.
Intended use: For undergraduate or graduate study at accredited 4-year or graduate institution in United States. Designated institutions: Colorado colleges/universities with accredited accounting programs.
Eligibility: Applicant must be U.S. citizen or permanent resident residing in Colorado.
Basis for selection: Major/career interest in accounting. Applicant must demonstrate high academic achievement.
Application requirements: Essay, transcript.
Additional information: Must have completed six semester/eight quarter hours in accounting. Must be at least half-time student. Applicants should intend to practice the profession of accounting in Colorado. Minimum 3.0 GPA. International students must have work visa. Visit Website for application.

Amount of award:	$2,500
Application deadline:	June 1

Contact:
COCPA
7887 E. Belleview Avenue
Suite 200
Englewood, CO 80111-6076
Phone: 800-523-9082 or 303-773-2877
Web: www.want2bcpa.com

Mark J. Smith Scholarship

Type of award: Scholarship.
Intended use: For undergraduate or graduate study at accredited 4-year or graduate institution in United States. Designated institutions: Colorado colleges and universities with accredited accounting programs.
Eligibility: Applicant must be U.S. citizen or permanent resident residing in Colorado.
Basis for selection: Major/career interest in accounting. Applicant must demonstrate financial need and high academic achievement.
Application requirements: Essay, transcript.
Additional information: Special consideration for students from single-parent background or attending college as a single parent. Must have completed six semester/eight quarter hours in accounting. Must be at least half-time student. Applicants should intend to practice the profession of accounting in Colorado. Minimum 3.0 GPA. International students must have work visa. Visit Website for application.

Amount of award:	$2,500
Number of awards:	1
Application deadline:	June 1

Contact:
COCPA
7887 E. Belleview Avenue
Suite 200
Englewood, CO 80111-6076
Phone: 800-523-9082 or 303-773-2877
Web: www.want2bcpa.com

Columbus Citizens Foundation

College Scholarship Program

Type of award: Scholarship, renewable.
Intended use: For full-time undergraduate study at accredited 4-year institution in United States or Canada.
Eligibility: Applicant must be high school senior. Applicant must be Italian.
Basis for selection: Applicant must demonstrate financial need, high academic achievement and service orientation.
Application requirements: $30 application fee. Interview, recommendations, essay, transcript. Parent/guardian's most recent state and federal income tax returns, family tree.
Additional information: Applicant must be Italian American. Minimum 3.0 GPA. Family's taxable income must not exceed $25,000 per household dependent. Applicants who reach semifinalist round must travel to New York City for interview at own expense. Applications available on Website in first week of December each year; deadline is in February. Number and amount of awards varies. Special attention given to students pursuing a degree in culinary arts or engineering. Special attention given to students attending Boston College, Bowling Green State University, Brooklyn College, Brown University, Colgate University, Culinary Institute of America, Georgetown University, Harvard University, Hobert & William Smith Colleges, Rhode Island School of Design, University of Rhode Island, Villanova University, and Wagner College.

Amount of award:	$500-$6,250
Number of awards:	40
Number of applicants:	125
Application deadline:	February 14
Notification begins:	May 1
Total amount awarded:	$185,000

Contact:
Columbus Citizens Foundation College Scholarship Program
8 East 69th Street
New York, NY 10021-4906
Phone: 212-249-9923
Fax: 212-517-7619
Web: www.columbuscitizensfd.org

Scholarships

Congressional Black Caucus Foundation, Inc.

The CBC General Mills Health Scholarship

Type of award: Scholarship, renewable.
Intended use: For full-time undergraduate or graduate study at accredited vocational, 2-year, 4-year or graduate institution.
Eligibility: Applicant must be U.S. citizen or permanent resident.
Basis for selection: Major/career interest in engineering; health-related professions; medicine or technology. Applicant must demonstrate financial need, high academic achievement, leadership and service orientation.
Application requirements: Recommendations, essay, transcript, proof of eligibility. Copy of Student Aid Report (SAR).
Additional information: Minimum 2.75 GPA. Awards and amounts may vary. Preference given to CBC constituents and African-American students. Deadline in late March. Visit Website for application and details.

Amount of award:	$2,500
Number of awards:	43

Contact:
CBCF General Mills Health Scholarship Program
Scholarship Management Services
One Scholarship Way
Saint Peter, MN 56082
Phone: 507-931-1682
Web: www.cbcfinc.org

The CBC Spouses Education Scholarship

Type of award: Scholarship, renewable.
Intended use: For full-time undergraduate or graduate study at accredited 4-year or graduate institution in United States.
Eligibility: Applicant must be U.S. citizen or permanent resident.
Basis for selection: Applicant must demonstrate financial need, high academic achievement, leadership and service orientation.
Application requirements: Recommendations, essay, transcript. Resume, recent photo, copy of Student Aid Report (SAR).
Additional information: Minimum 2.5 GPA. Award amount varies. Selection made at district level. Preference given to CBC member constituents. Deadline in late May or early June. Visit Website for application and details.
Contact:
Congressional Black Caucus Foundation
1720 Massachusetts Avenue, NW
Washington, DC 20036
Phone: 202-263-2800
Fax: 202-775-0773
Web: www.cbcfinc.org

The CBC Spouses Heineken USA Performing Arts Scholarship Program

Type of award: Scholarship, renewable.
Intended use: For full-time undergraduate study at accredited 4-year institution.
Basis for selection: Major/career interest in performing arts or music. Applicant must demonstrate financial need, high academic achievement, leadership and service orientation.
Application requirements: Recommendations, essay, transcript, proof of eligibility. Resume, recent photograph, copy of Student Aid Report (SAR), two-minute performance sample.
Additional information: Minimum 2.5 GPA. Check Website for application and details. Deadline in late April or early May.

Amount of award:	$3,000
Number of awards:	10

Contact:
Congressional Black Caucus Foundation
1720 Massachusetts Avenue, NW
Washington, DC 20036
Phone: 202-263-2800
Fax: 202-775-0773
Web: www.cbcfinc.org

The CBC Spouses Visual Arts Scholarship

Type of award: Scholarship.
Intended use: For full-time undergraduate study at accredited 4-year institution in United States.
Basis for selection: Major/career interest in arts, general. Applicant must demonstrate financial need, high academic achievement, leadership and service orientation.
Application requirements: Recommendations, essay, transcript. Recent photo of applicant, resume, copy of Student Aid Report (SAR), up to five artwork samples. High school seniors must submit college acceptance letter.
Additional information: Minimum 2.5 GPA. Deadline in late April or early May. Check Website for application and details.

Amount of award:	$3,000
Number of awards:	10

Contact:
Congressional Black Caucus Foundation
1720 Massachusetts Avenue, NW
Washington, DC 20036
Phone: 202-263-2800
Fax: 202-775-0773
Web: www.cbcfinc.org

Louis Stokes Health Scholars

Type of award: Scholarship.
Intended use: For full-time undergraduate study at vocational, 2-year or 4-year institution.
Eligibility: Applicant must be U.S. citizen or permanent resident.
Basis for selection: Major/career interest in health-related professions. Applicant must demonstrate financial need and high academic achievement.
Application requirements: Recommendations, essay, transcript. Resume, photograph. Student Aid Report.
Additional information: High school seniors also eligible to apply. Minimum 3.0 GPA. For students entering the health workforce. Preference given to students demonstrating an interest in underserved communities. Students currently attending two-year institutions strongly encouraged to apply.

Deadline and number of awards may vary. Notification begins six to eight weeks after deadline.

Amount of award:	$4,000-$8,000
Number of awards:	10
Number of applicants:	130
Total amount awarded:	$90,000

Contact:
Congressional Black Caucus Foundation, Inc.
1720 Massachusetts Avenue, NW
Washington, DC 20036
Phone: 202-263-2800
Fax: 202-775-0773
Web: www.cbcfinc.org/scholarships

Congressional Hispanic Caucus Institute

Congressional Hispanic Caucus Institute Scholarship Awards

Type of award: Scholarship.
Intended use: For full-time undergraduate or graduate study at 2-year, 4-year or graduate institution.
Eligibility: Applicant must be U.S. citizen or permanent resident.
Basis for selection: Applicant must demonstrate financial need, leadership and service orientation.
Application requirements: Recommendations, essay. One-page resume, SAR.
Additional information: Community college students receive $1,000; students enrolled at four-year colleges or universities receive $2,500; students enrolled in graduate programs receive $5,000. Apply online.

Amount of award:	$1,000-$5,000
Number of awards:	150
Application deadline:	April 16

Contact:
Congressional Hispanic Caucus Institute Scholarship
911 2nd Street NE
Washington, DC 20002
Phone: 202-543-1771
Fax: 202-546-2143
Web: www.chci.org/scholarships

Connecticut Building Congress, Inc.

CBC Scholarship

Type of award: Scholarship, renewable.
Intended use: For undergraduate or master's study at 4-year institution in United States.
Eligibility: Applicant must be residing in Connecticut.
Basis for selection: Major/career interest in engineering, construction; architecture; construction management; surveying/mapping or construction. Applicant must demonstrate financial need and high academic achievement.
Application requirements: Essay, transcript. Student Aid Report or FAFSA.
Additional information: Must be involved in extracurricular activities and exhibit potential. Applicant may attend school outside of Connecticut. Open to high school seniors or enrolled college students studying eligible majors. Number of awards and amount at discretion of Board of Directors. Renewable based on academic performance, available funds, and continued study in construction-related major.

Amount of award:	$500-$2,000
Number of awards:	4
Number of applicants:	50
Application deadline:	March 30
Notification begins:	May 1
Total amount awarded:	$4,500

Contact:
Connecticut Building Congress
c/o DiBlasi Associates
500 Purdy Hill Road Suite 10
Monroe, CT 06468
Web: www.cbc-ct.org/CBC_Scholarship

Connecticut Office of Higher Education

Connecticut Aid for Public College Students

Type of award: Scholarship, renewable.
Intended use: For undergraduate study at 2-year or 4-year institution. Designated institutions: Connecticut public colleges and universities.
Eligibility: Applicant must be U.S. citizen residing in Connecticut.
Basis for selection: Applicant must demonstrate financial need.
Application requirements: FAFSA.
Additional information: Awards up to amount of unmet financial need, determined by the college. Deadline based on college financial aid deadline. Apply at financial aid office at Connecticut public college.

Number of awards:	20,349
Total amount awarded:	$29,808,460

Contact:
Connecticut Office of Higher Education
61 Woodland Street
Hartford, CT 06105-2391
Phone: 800-842-0229
Fax: 860-947-1311
Web: www.ctohe.org

Connecticut Aid to Dependents of Deceased/POW/MIA Veterans

Type of award: Scholarship.
Intended use: For undergraduate or graduate study. Designated institutions: Connecticut public colleges and universities.
Eligibility: Applicant must be U.S. citizen residing in Connecticut. Applicant must be dependent of deceased veteran or POW/MIA; or spouse of deceased veteran or POW/MIA. Death must be service-related. Parent/spouse must have been Connecticut resident prior to enlistment.
Application requirements: Proof of eligibility.
Additional information: Visit Website for more information.

Scholarships

Amount of award:	$800
Number of awards:	5

Contact:
Connecticut Office of Higher Education
61 Woodland Street
Hartford, CT 06105-2391
Phone: 800-842-0229
Fax: 860-947-1310
Web: www.ctohe.org

Connecticut Capitol Scholarship Program

Type of award: Scholarship, renewable.
Intended use: For undergraduate study at 2-year or 4-year institution. Designated institutions: Connecticut colleges and universities; eligible institutions in Massachusetts, Pennsylvania, Rhode Island, Vermont, and Washington, D.C.
Eligibility: Applicant must be high school senior. Applicant must be U.S. citizen or permanent resident residing in Connecticut.
Basis for selection: Applicant must demonstrate financial need and high academic achievement.
Application requirements: FAFSA.
Additional information: Must rank in top 20 percent of class, or have minimum 1800 SAT score or minimum 27 ACT score. May be used at institutions in Connecticut or at institutions in states with reciprocity agreements with Connecticut.

Amount of award:	$375-$2,000
Number of awards:	3,500
Number of applicants:	3,362
Application deadline:	February 15
Total amount awarded:	$4,321,965

Contact:
Connecticut Office of Higher Education
61 Woodland Street
Hartford, CT 06105-2391
Phone: 800-842-0229
Fax: 860-947-1313
Web: www.ctohe.org

Connecticut Independent College Student Grant

Type of award: Scholarship, renewable.
Intended use: For undergraduate study in United States. Designated institutions: Private institutions in Connecticut.
Eligibility: Applicant must be U.S. citizen residing in Connecticut.
Basis for selection: Applicant must demonstrate financial need.
Application requirements: FAFSA and any other financial aid forms required by the college.
Additional information: Award based on financial need. Deadline determined by financial aid deadline at each college.

Amount of award:	$8,166
Number of awards:	4,983
Total amount awarded:	$18,080,692

Contact:
Connecticut Office of Higher Education
61 Woodland Street
Hartford, CT 06105-2391
Phone: 800-842-0229
Fax: 860-947-1311
Web: www.ctohe.org

Connecticut Minority Teacher Incentive Grant

Type of award: Scholarship.
Intended use: For full-time junior or senior study. Designated institutions: Eligible Connecticut colleges and universities.
Eligibility: Applicant must be Alaskan native, Asian American, African American, Mexican American, Hispanic American, Puerto Rican, American Indian or Native Hawaiian/Pacific Islander. Applicant must be residing in Connecticut.
Basis for selection: Major/career interest in education; education, special or education, teacher.
Application requirements: Nomination by college or university's Education Dean, or other appropriate official.
Additional information: Must be enrolled in Connecticut college or university teacher preparation program. Grants up to $5,000/year for two years; loan reimbursement of $2,500/year for up to four years of teaching in Connecticut public school. Visit Website for more information.

Amount of award:	$2,500-$5,000
Number of awards:	45
Number of applicants:	36
Application deadline:	October 1
Total amount awarded:	$150,000

Contact:
Connecticut Office of Higher Education
61 Woodland Street
Hartford, CT 06105-2326
Phone: 860-947-1857
Fax: 860-947-1838
Web: www.ctohe.org

Connecticut Tuition Waiver for Senior Citizens

Type of award: Scholarship.
Intended use: For undergraduate study at 2-year or 4-year institution. Designated institutions: Connecticut public colleges and universities.
Eligibility: Applicant must be returning adult student. Applicant must be U.S. citizen residing in Connecticut.
Application requirements: Proof of eligibility.
Additional information: Waivers approved on space available basis. Apply through financial aid office of institution.

Amount of award:	Full tuition
Number of awards:	1,683
Total amount awarded:	$874,080

Contact:
Connecticut Office of Higher Education
61 Woodland Street
Hartford, CT 06105-2391
Phone: 800-842-0229
Fax: 860-947-1310
Web: www.ctohe.org

Connecticut Tuition Waiver for Veterans

Type of award: Scholarship, renewable.
Intended use: For undergraduate or graduate study. Designated institutions: Connecticut public colleges and universities.
Eligibility: Applicant must be U.S. citizen residing in Connecticut. Applicant must be veteran. Must have been Connecticut resident at time of enlistment. Active members of Connecticut Army or Air National Guard also eligible.
Application requirements: Proof of eligibility.
Additional information: Visit Website for more information.

Amount of award: Full tuition
Number of awards: 3,228
Total amount awarded: $4,365,411

Contact:
Connecticut Office of Higher Ed.
61 Woodland Street
Hartford, CT 06105-2326
Phone: 800-842-0229
Fax: 860-947-1310
Web: www.ctohe.org

Connecticut Tuition Waiver for Vietnam MIA/POW Dependents

Type of award: Scholarship.
Intended use: For undergraduate study. Designated institutions: Connecticut public colleges and universities.
Eligibility: Applicant must be U.S. citizen residing in Connecticut. Applicant must be dependent of POW/MIA; or spouse of POW/MIA. Open to spouse or dependent of veteran who is POW/MIA after 1/1/60.
Application requirements: Proof of eligibility.
Additional information: Apply at financial aid office of institution. Awarded through Connecticut public colleges. Visit Website for more information.

Amount of award: Full tuition

Contact:
Connecticut Office of Higher Ed.
61 Woodland Street
Hartford, CT 06105-2326
Phone: 800-842-0229
Fax: 860-947-1310
Web: www.ctohe.org

Weisman Scholarship

Type of award: Scholarship, renewable.
Intended use: For full-time junior or senior study. Designated institutions: Eligible Connecticut colleges and universities.
Eligibility: Applicant must be Alaskan native, Asian American, African American, Mexican American, Hispanic American, Puerto Rican, American Indian or Native Hawaiian/Pacific Islander. Applicant must be residing in Connecticut.
Basis for selection: Major/career interest in education or education, teacher.
Application requirements: Nomination by college or university's Education Dean, or other appropriate official.
Additional information: Must be enrolled in Connecticut teacher preparation program and intend to teach math or science in middle or high school. Loan reimbursement up to $2,500 per year for up to four years of teaching science or math in Connecticut public middle or high school. Visit Website for more information and deadline.

Amount of award: $2,500-$5,000
Number of awards: 2
Number of applicants: 47
Total amount awarded: $10,000

Contact:
Connecticut Office of Higher Ed.
61 Woodland Street
Hartford, CT 06105-2326
Phone: 800-842-0229
Fax: 860-947-1838
Web: www.ctohe.org

ConocoPhillips

ConocoPhillips Scholarships

Type of award: Scholarship, renewable.
Intended use: For undergraduate or graduate study at postsecondary institution in United States. Designated institutions: Colorado School of Mines, Kansas State University, Oklahoma State University, Texas A&M University, Texas Tech University, University of Oklahoma, University of Texas at Austin, University of Tulsa, University of Colorado.
Basis for selection: Major/career interest in business; engineering or geology/earth sciences. Applicant must demonstrate high academic achievement.
Additional information: Information and applications can only be obtained from the university directly.

Contact:
ConocoPhillips
Web: www.conocophillips.com/EN/careers/univrecruit/careerdev/scholarships/Pages/index.aspx

Consortium of Information and Telecommunication Executives

Traditional CITE Scholarship

Type of award: Scholarship.
Intended use: For full-time undergraduate study at accredited 4-year institution in United States.
Eligibility: Applicant must be African American. Applicant must be high school senior. Applicant must be U.S. citizen.
Basis for selection: Major/career interest in accounting; advertising; business; communications; computer/information sciences; engineering, electrical/electronic; engineering, industrial; finance/banking; marketing or mathematics. Applicant must demonstrate financial need and high academic achievement.
Application requirements: Recommendations, essay, transcript. College acceptance letter, proof of parents' income.
Additional information: Minimum 3.0 GPA. Applicant must reside in area where there is a CITE chapter. Family income must be $75,000 or less. Recipient must attend a scholarship event to accept award. Deadline in spring; see Website for date and details.

Amount of award: $3,000
Number of awards: 1
Total amount awarded: $3,000

Contact:
Web: www.forcite.org

Construction Institute of ASCE

CI Construction Engineering Student Scholarship

Type of award: Scholarship.
Intended use: For undergraduate study at 4-year institution.

Basis for selection: Major/career interest in engineering, civil or construction management. Applicant must demonstrate leadership.
Application requirements: Recommendations, transcript. Statement of professional goals, resume.
Additional information: Must be American Society of Civil Engineers member and/or Construction Institute student member in good standing and be enrolled in civil engineering program with concentration in construction engineering or construction management. Preference given to applicants enrolled in programs with an accredited Construction Management program. Award to be paid up to three years until graduation; amount determined by award committee.

Number of awards:	1
Application deadline:	April 1

Contact:
Construction Institute of ASCE
Attn: Construction Scholarship
1801 Alexander Bell Drive
Reston, VA 20191-4400
Phone: 703-295-6390
Fax: 703-295-6222
Web: www.asce.org

Costume Society of America

Adele Filene Student Presenter Grant

Type of award: Scholarship.
Intended use: For full-time undergraduate or graduate study in United States.
Eligibility: Applicant must be U.S. citizen or international student.
Basis for selection: Major/career interest in ethnic/cultural studies; art/art history; arts, general; history or fashion/fashion design/modeling.
Application requirements: One faculty recommendation. Must submit additional essay.
Additional information: Award only for those who have paper or research poster accepted for presentation at National Symposium. Award is for travel expenses to the meeting. Applicant must reside outside 200 mile radius of Symposium site. Must be student member of Costume Society of America. Major/career interests may include apparel design, historic costume, and fashion merchandising. Number of awards varies.

Amount of award:	$500
Application deadline:	March 1

Contact:
Chair, CSA Adele Filene Student Presenter Grant Committee
Attn: Dennita Sewell
1625 North Central Avenue
Phoenix, AZ 85004-1685
Phone: 602-257-1880
Web: www.costumesocietyamerica.com/GrantsAwards/adelefilene.html

Stella Blum Student Research Grant

Type of award: Research grant.
Intended use: For undergraduate or graduate study at accredited vocational, 2-year, 4-year or graduate institution in United States.
Eligibility: Applicant must be U.S. citizen, permanent resident or international student.
Basis for selection: Major/career interest in art/art history; arts, general; history; museum studies or performing arts.
Application requirements: Recommendations, transcript, proof of eligibility. References and written research proposal. The proposal should be typed, double-spaced, no more than 1,000 words. Must also submit a brief abstract, no more than 50 words. Must provide seven copies of all documents. Must also include letters of permission from any research site, museum or library applicant intends to visit for research.
Additional information: Must be member of Costume Society of America. Award is $2,000 for research and $500 for expenses to present at national meeting.

Amount of award:	$2,500
Number of awards:	1
Application deadline:	May 1
Notification begins:	August 1
Total amount awarded:	$2,500

Contact:
Costume Society of America
Attn: Ann Wass, Committee Chair
5903 60th Ave
Riverdale, MD 20737
Phone: 800-CSA-9447 or 908-359-1471
Fax: 908-450-1118
Web: www.costumesocietyamerica.com/GrantsAwards/stellablum.html

Council on International Educational Exchange

CIEE International Study Programs Scholarships

Type of award: Scholarship.
Intended use: For full-time undergraduate study at accredited 4-year institution. Designated institutions: CIEE Member or CIEE Academic Consortium Member institutions.
Basis for selection: Competition/talent/interest in study abroad. Applicant must demonstrate financial need and high academic achievement.
Application requirements: Essay, transcript.
Additional information: Available to CIEE Study Center program applicants only. Program application is used in consideration of scholarship applicants. Award is $2000 for winter, $1000 for summer. Visit Website for details and application.

Amount of award:	$1,000-$2,000
Application deadline:	April 1, November 1
Notification begins:	May 1, December 1

Contact:
CIEE
Attn: Scholarship Committee
300 Fore Street
Portland, ME 04101
Phone: 800-40-STUDY
Fax: 207-221-4299
Web: www.ciee.org/study/scholarships.aspx

Jennifer Ritzmann Scholarship for Studies in Tropical Biology

Type of award: Scholarship.
Intended use: For full-time undergraduate study at accredited 4-year institution. Designated institutions: CIEE Study Center program in Monteverde, Costa Rica.
Basis for selection: Competition/talent/interest in study abroad. Major/career interest in biology or ecology. Applicant must demonstrate financial need and high academic achievement.
Application requirements: Essay, transcript.
Additional information: Award is for students applying to the Monteverde, Costa Rica Tropical Ecology and Conservation or the Sustainability and Environment semester programs only. Visit Website for more information.

Amount of award:	$1,000
Number of awards:	2
Application deadline:	April 1, November 1
Notification begins:	May 1, December 1

Contact:
CIEE
Attn: Scholarship Committee
300 Fore Street
Portland, ME 04101
Phone: 800-40-STUDY
Fax: 207-221-4299
Web: www.ciee.org/study/scholarships.aspx

John E. Bowman Travel Grants

Type of award: Scholarship.
Intended use: For full-time undergraduate study at accredited 4-year institution. Designated institutions: CIEE Member or CIEE Academic Consortium member institutions.
Basis for selection: Competition/talent/interest in study abroad. Applicant must demonstrate financial need and high academic achievement.
Application requirements: Essay, transcript.
Additional information: Applicant must participate in CIEE study abroad program in Africa, Asia, Europe, or Latin America. Visit Website for details and application.

Amount of award:	$1,000
Application deadline:	April 1, November 1
Notification begins:	May 1, December 1

Contact:
CIEE
Attn: Scholarship Committee
300 Fore Street
Portland, ME 04101
Phone: 800-40-STUDY
Fax: 207-221-4299
Web: www.ciee.org/study/scholarships.aspx

Kathleen McDermott Scholarship

Type of award: Scholarship.
Intended use: For undergraduate study at postsecondary institution outside United States.
Basis for selection: Competition/talent/interest in study abroad. Major/career interest in public health or nursing. Applicant must demonstrate financial need.
Application requirements: Essay.
Additional information: Applicant must be a public health or nursing major and/or participating in a community public health study abroad program. Award amount varies depending on duration of study and financial need.

Amount of award:	$1,000-$2,500
Application deadline:	April 1, November 1

Contact:
CIEE
Attn: Scholarship Committee
300 Fore Street
Portland, ME 04101
Phone: 800-40-STUDY
Fax: 207-221-4299
Web: www.ciee.org/study-abroad/scholarships/

Michael Stohl Scholarship

Type of award: Scholarship.
Intended use: For undergraduate study at postsecondary institution outside United States. Designated institutions: CIEE Member or CIEE Academic Consortium member institutions.
Basis for selection: Competition/talent/interest in study abroad. Applicant must demonstrate financial need.
Application requirements: Essay.
Additional information: Applicant must be non-traditionally aged, first-generation college student from non-traditional background. Must plan to conduct research as part of a study abroad program.

Amount of award:	$1,000-$5,000
Application deadline:	April 1, November 1

Contact:
CIEE
Attn: Scholarship Committee
300 Fore Street
Portland, ME 04101
Phone: 800-40-STUDY
Fax: 207-221-4299
Web: www.ciee.org/study-abroad/scholarships/

Peter Wollitzer Scholarships for Study in Asia

Type of award: Scholarship.
Intended use: For full-time undergraduate study at accredited 4-year institution. Designated institutions: CIEE Academic Consortium Board Member institutions.
Basis for selection: Competition/talent/interest in study abroad. Applicant must demonstrate financial need and high academic achievement.
Application requirements: Essay, transcript.
Additional information: Applicant must participate in a CIEE Study Center program in Asia (includes Cambodia, China, India, Japan, Korea, Taiwan, Thailand, and Vietnam). Applicants also eligible if studying through the University of California Education Abroad Program (EAP) Office. Award amounts vary based on program duration and financial need.

Amount of award:	$1,000-$5,000
Number of awards:	3
Application deadline:	April 1, November 1
Notification begins:	May 1, December 1

Contact:
CIEE
Attn: Scholarship Committee
300 Fore Street
Portland, ME 04101
Phone: 800-40-STUDY
Fax: 207-221-4299
Web: www.ciee.org/study/scholarships.aspx

Robert B. Bailey Scholarship

Type of award: Scholarship.
Intended use: For full-time undergraduate or graduate study at accredited 4-year institution. Designated institutions: CIEE Member or CIEE Academic Consortium member institutions.
Basis for selection: Competition/talent/interest in study abroad. Applicant must demonstrate financial need and high academic achievement.
Application requirements: Essay, transcript.
Additional information: Available to CIEE Study Center applicants only. Must be self-identified as belonging to underrepresented group. Award amounts vary based on program duration and financial need. Program application is used in consideration of scholarship applicants. Visit Website for details and application.

Amount of award:	$1,000-$5,000
Application deadline:	April 1, November 1
Notification begins:	May 1, December 1

Contact:
CIEE
Attn: Scholarship Committee
300 Fore Street
Portland, ME 04101
Phone: 800-40-STUDY
Fax: 207-221-4299
Web: www.ciee.org/study/scholarships.aspx

Courage Center

Courage Center Scholarship for People with Disabilities

Type of award: Scholarship.
Intended use: For full-time undergraduate study at accredited vocational, 2-year or 4-year institution.
Eligibility: Applicant must be visually impaired, hearing impaired or physically challenged. Applicant must be U.S. citizen residing in Minnesota.
Basis for selection: Applicant must demonstrate financial need.
Application requirements: Interview, essay.
Additional information: If not Minnesota resident, student must be participant in Courage Center services.

Amount of award:	$500-$1,000
Number of awards:	20
Number of applicants:	20
Application deadline:	May 31
Notification begins:	July 31
Total amount awarded:	$10,500

Contact:
Courage Center Vocational Services
Attn: Administrative Assistant
3915 Golden Valley Road
Minneapolis, MN 55422
Phone: 763-520-0553
Fax: 763-520-0861
Web: www.couragecenter.org/ContentPages/Resources.aspx

Courage to Grow

Courage to Grow Scholarship

Type of award: Scholarship.
Intended use: For undergraduate or graduate study at vocational, 2-year, 4-year or graduate institution in United States.
Eligibility: Applicant must be U.S. citizen.
Basis for selection: Applicant must demonstrate financial need and high academic achievement.
Application requirements: Essay.
Additional information: High school seniors may also apply. Minimum 2.5 GPA. Program awards one $500 scholarship every month; deadline date is last day of each month. Visit Website for application and details.

Amount of award:	$6,000
Number of awards:	12
Number of applicants:	1,000
Total amount awarded:	$6,000

Contact:
Courage to Grow Scholarship
P.O. Box 2507
Chelan, WA 98816
Phone: 509-731-3056
Web: www.couragetogrowscholarship.com

The Cynthia E. Morgan Memorial Scholarship Fund

The Cynthia E. Morgan Memorial Scholarship Fund

Type of award: Scholarship.
Intended use: For undergraduate or graduate study at accredited vocational, 2-year or 4-year institution. Designated institutions: Maryland vocational school, college, or university.
Eligibility: Applicant must be high school junior or senior. Applicant must be residing in Maryland.
Basis for selection: Major/career interest in medicine; nursing; pharmacy/pharmaceutics/pharmacology; dietetics/nutrition; occupational therapy; physical therapy; physician assistant or speech pathology/audiology. Applicant must demonstrate financial need and high academic achievement.
Application requirements: Essay, transcript, proof of eligibility.
Additional information: Must be first person in immediate family to attend college. Must be entering or planning on entering medical or medical-related field.

Amount of award:	$1,000
Application deadline:	February 25
Notification begins:	March 15

Contact:
The Cynthia E. Morgan Memorial Scholarship Fund
5516 Maudes Way
White Marsh, MD 21162
Web: www.cemsfund.com

Cystic Fibrosis Foundation

Cystic Fibrosis Student Traineeship

Type of award: Research grant, renewable.
Intended use: For full-time senior, master's or doctoral study at accredited 4-year or graduate institution in United States.
Basis for selection: Major/career interest in medical specialties/research.
Application requirements: Recommendations, research proposal.
Additional information: Trainees must work with faculty sponsor on research project related to cystic fibrosis. Applications accepted throughout the year, but should be submitted at least two months prior to anticipated start date of project.

Amount of award:	$1,500

Contact:
Cystic Fibrosis Foundation
Grants & Contracts Office
6931 Arlington Road
Bethesda, MD 20814
Phone: 301-951-4422
Fax: 301-841-2605
Web: www.cff.org

The Dallas Foundation

The Chesapeake Energy Scholarship

Type of award: Scholarship, renewable.
Intended use: For undergraduate study at accredited vocational, 2-year or 4-year institution.
Eligibility: Applicant must be Alaskan native, Asian American, African American, Mexican American, Hispanic American, Puerto Rican, American Indian or Native Hawaiian/Pacific Islander. Applicant must be high school senior. Applicant must be U.S. citizen or permanent resident residing in Texas.
Basis for selection: Applicant must demonstrate high academic achievement and service orientation.
Application requirements: Recommendations, essay, transcript. FAFSA or SAR.
Additional information: Must be a graduating senior of eligible high schools in Dallas Independent School District. Must be active member of Education is Freedom (EIF Dallas). Must be female or member of minority group. Minimum 3.0 GPA. Must have taken SAT or ACT. Children and grandchildren of Chesapeake Energy employees not eligible. Visit Website for application. Deadline in mid-April.

Amount of award:	$20,000
Application deadline:	April 11

Contact:
The Dallas Foundation
3963 Maple Ave. Ste. 390
Dallas, TX 75219
Phone: 214-741-9898
Web: www.dallasfoundation.org

Dallas Architectural Foundation - Swank Travelling Fellowship

Type of award: Scholarship.
Intended use: For senior or graduate study at accredited postsecondary institution.
Eligibility: Applicant must be U.S. citizen or permanent resident residing in Texas.
Basis for selection: Major/career interest in architecture.
Application requirements: Portfolio, recommendations, essay, transcript. Resume, budget statement.
Additional information: Applicant must be permanent resident of the Dallas-Fort Worth area. Fellowship established to assist architecture students or recent graduates in broadening their architectural knowledge through travel. Funds must be used for travel and study costs, and within the same calendar year. Recipient must agree to present program of results to the Dallas Architectural Foundation board. Visit Website for application.

Amount of award:	$2,000
Number of awards:	1
Number of applicants:	5
Application deadline:	March 28
Total amount awarded:	$2,000

Contact:
Dallas Architectural Foundation
1909 Woodall Rodgers Freeway
Suite 100
Dallas, TX 75201
Phone: 214-742-3242
Web: www.dallascfa.com

The Dallas Morning New Journalism Scholarship

Type of award: Scholarship.
Intended use: For freshman study at 4-year institution.
Eligibility: Applicant must be high school senior. Applicant must be U.S. citizen or permanent resident residing in Texas.
Basis for selection: Major/career interest in journalism. Applicant must demonstrate high academic achievement, leadership and service orientation.
Application requirements: Recommendations, essay, transcript. Two samples demonstrating aptitude for print journalism. Description of community service experience.
Additional information: Must live within Collin, Dallas, Denton, Ellis, Kaufman, Rockwall, or Tarrant counties. Minimum 3.0 GPA. Must show aptitude for print journalism. Visit Website for application and deadline.

Amount of award:	$1,500
Number of awards:	3
Application deadline:	April 11

Contact:
The Dallas Morning News Journalism Scholarship
c/o The Dallas Foundation
3963 Maple Ave., Suite 390
Dallas, TX 75219
Phone: 214-741-9898
Web: www.dallasfoundation.org

Dr. Dan J. and Patricia S. Pickard Scholarship

Type of award: Scholarship, renewable.
Intended use: For freshman study at 2-year or 4-year institution.

Eligibility: Applicant must be African American. Applicant must be male. Applicant must be residing in Texas.
Basis for selection: Applicant must demonstrate financial need, high academic achievement and service orientation.
Application requirements: Recommendations, essay, transcript. FAFSA or SAR.
Additional information: Must be graduating from high school in Dallas County. Minimum 2.5 GPA. Visit Website for application.

Amount of award:	$1,000
Application deadline:	April 1

Contact:
The Dallas Foundation
3963 Maple Ave., Ste. 390
Dallas, TX 75219
Phone: 214-741-9898
Web: www.dallasfoundation.org

Dr. Don and Rose Marie Benton Scholarship

Type of award: Scholarship, renewable.
Intended use: For undergraduate or graduate study at accredited postsecondary institution in United States.
Eligibility: Applicant must be residing in Texas.
Application requirements: Nomination by member of the Scholarship Committee at Trinity River Mission.
Additional information: Award amount varies; maximum is $1,500. Number of awards varies. Applicant or parent must be affiliated with Trinity River Mission. Must reside in Dallas county.

Amount of award:	$1,500
Number of awards:	3
Application deadline:	April 1

Contact:
Trinity River Mission
Marie Rivera, Trinity River Mission
2060 Singleton Blvd., Suite 104
Dallas, TX 75212
Phone: 214-744-6774
Web: www.dallasfoundation.org

Hirsch Family Scholarship

Type of award: Scholarship.
Intended use: For freshman study at accredited vocational, 2-year or 4-year institution in United States.
Eligibility: Applicant must be high school senior.
Basis for selection: Applicant must demonstrate financial need and high academic achievement.
Application requirements: Recommendations, essay, transcript. List of extracurricular activities, community service, and work experience; FAFSA.
Additional information: Applicant must be the dependent child of an active employee of Eagle Materials, Performance Chemicals and Ingredients, Martin Fletcher, Hadlock Plastics, Highlander Partners and any of their majority-owned subsidiaries. Past recipients are encouraged to apply each year.

Amount of award:	$1,000-$6,000
Application deadline:	April 15

Contact:
The Dallas Foundation
3963 Maple Ave., Ste. 390
Dallas, TX 75219
Phone: 214-741-9898
Web: www.dallasfoundation.org

Jere W. Thompson, Jr. Scholarship Fund

Type of award: Scholarship, renewable.
Intended use: For full-time junior or senior study at accredited 4-year institution in United States. Designated institutions: Texas institutions.
Eligibility: Applicant must be U.S. citizen or permanent resident residing in Texas.
Basis for selection: Major/career interest in engineering, civil or engineering, construction. Applicant must demonstrate financial need, high academic achievement and seriousness of purpose.
Application requirements: Recommendations, essay, transcript, proof of eligibility. FAFSA or SAR.
Additional information: Applicant must be college sophomore. Award amount varies; maximum is $2,000 per semester, renewable for three additional semesters if student maintains 3.0 GPA and submits grade report within 45 days after the end of the semester. Recipients will be given opportunity for paid internship with one of scholarship's sponsors between junior and senior year. Preference may be given to residents of Collin, Dallas, Denton, or Tarrant counties. Visit Website for program profile and application.

Amount of award:	$2,000
Number of awards:	1
Application deadline:	April 11

Contact:
The Dallas Foundation
3963 Maple Ave., Ste. 390
Dallas, TX 75219
Phone: 214-741-9898
Web: www.dallasfoundation.org

The Tommy Tranchin Award

Type of award: Scholarship.
Intended use: For non-degree study at postsecondary institution.
Eligibility: Applicant must be physically challenged or learning disabled. Applicant must be high school freshman, sophomore, junior or senior. Applicant must be residing in Texas.
Application requirements: Recommendations, essay. Description and budget for proposed activity.
Additional information: Award for student with physical, emotional, or intellectual disability who wants to participate in an activity that furthers development in an area in which he/she excels or shows promise. Funds may be used for program expenses, travel, other related expenses. Must be high school student in North Texas. Award is up to $1,500. Visit Website for application.

Application deadline:	March 7

Contact:
The Dallas Foundation
3963 Maple Ave., Ste. 390
Dallas, TX 75219
Phone: 214-741-9898
Web: www.dallasfoundation.org

Daniels Fund

The Daniels Scholarship

Type of award: Scholarship, renewable.
Intended use: For freshman study at accredited 2-year or 4-year institution in United States. Designated institutions: Not-for-profit institutions.
Eligibility: Applicant must be high school senior. Applicant must be U.S. citizen or permanent resident residing in Wyoming, Utah, New Mexico or Colorado.
Basis for selection: Applicant must demonstrate financial need, high academic achievement, depth of character, seriousness of purpose and service orientation.
Application requirements: Interview, recommendations, essay, transcript, nomination. ACT/SAT scores, copies of income tax information, proof of U.S. citizenship.
Additional information: Minimum ACT score: 17. Minimum SAT score: 830. Daniels Scholarship covers unmet needs of the student. Amount is determined after all other financial aid sources and Expected Family Contribution have been applied. Amounts vary. Scholarship can only be used at one of the schools listed on student's application. Apply online. Semifinalists must submit additional materials and go through interview process. Amount of award varies. Notification begins April. Visit Website for more information.

Amount of award:	$49,000
Number of awards:	1,000
Number of applicants:	3,400
Application deadline:	November 29
Total amount awarded:	$13,815,064

Contact:
Daniels Fund
101 Monroe Street
Denver, CO 80206
Phone: 303-393-7220
Web: www.danielsfund.org

Data Processing Management Association/ Portland Chapter

DPMA/PC Scholarship

Type of award: Scholarship, renewable.
Intended use: For undergraduate study in United States. Designated institutions: Institutions in Oregon or Washington.
Eligibility: Applicant must be high school senior. Applicant must be residing in Oregon or Washington.
Basis for selection: Major/career interest in computer/ information sciences. Applicant must demonstrate financial need, high academic achievement and seriousness of purpose.
Application requirements: Recommendations, transcript. List and description of past and current IT-related activities, and of IT career goals. Explanation of reasons for applying for scholarship.
Additional information: Applicants must graduate from high school in Oregon or Clark County in Washington. Renewable for $500 each year if awardee maintains a minimum "B" GPA and remains in a technology-related program. Check Website for application deadline.

Amount of award:	$1,000
Number of awards:	1
Number of applicants:	17
Application deadline:	May 31
Notification begins:	June 15
Total amount awarded:	$4,000

Contact:
DPMA/PC Scholarship
Attn: Scholarship Chair
P.O. Box 61493
Vancouver, WA 98666
Fax: 360-816-0235
Web: www.dpmapc.com/scholarship.htm

Daughters of Union Veterans of the Civil War 1861-1865

Grand Army of the Republic Living Memorial Scholarship

Type of award: Scholarship.
Intended use: For sophomore, junior or senior study at accredited 4-year institution in United States.
Eligibility: Applicant must be descendant of veteran during Civil War. Must be lineal descendant of Union Veteran of Civil War of 1861-1865.
Basis for selection: Applicant must demonstrate depth of character, leadership, patriotism, seriousness of purpose and service orientation.
Application requirements: Transcript. Two letters of reference, ancestor's military record.
Additional information: Must be of good moral character and have firm belief in US Government. Must have satisfactory scholastic standing. Request for information and application honored only with SASE. Number of awards varies.

Amount of award:	$200-$500
Application deadline:	April 30
Notification begins:	August 30
Total amount awarded:	$1,500

Contact:
Daughters of Union Veterans of the Civil War 1861-1865
Sandra Millin
8004 Kingwood Road
Confluence, PA 15424

Davidson Institute

Davidson Fellows Scholarship

Type of award: Scholarship.
Intended use: For undergraduate study at accredited postsecondary institution in United States.
Eligibility: Applicant must be U.S. citizen or permanent resident.
Basis for selection: Major/career interest in literature; music; philosophy; mathematics; science, general; technology or engineering.
Application requirements: Three nominator forms. Signed statement of commitment that, if named a Davidson Fellow, the

Scholarships

applicant and a parent or guardian will attend the award reception in Washington, D.C.
Additional information: Applicants awarded for accomplishment that is recognized as significant by experts in that field and has a positive contribution to society. Applicant must be 18 or under as of October 4th of the year of application. Applications are accepted in the following categories: science, technology, engineering, mathematics, music, literature, philosophy, and outside the box. Work may be exceptionally creative application of existing knowledge, new idea with high impact, innovative solution with broad-range implications, important advancement that can be replicated and built upon, interdisciplinary discovery, prodigious performance, or another demonstration of extraordinary accomplishment. Application deadline is first Wednesday in February.

Amount of award:	$10,000-$50,000
Number of awards:	20
Notification begins:	July 1
Total amount awarded:	$500,000

Contact:
Davidson Institute for Talent Development
9665 Gateway Drive
Suite B
Reno, NV 89521
Phone: 775-852-3483 ext. 423
Fax: 775-852-2184
Web: www.davidsongifted.org/fellows

Davis-Roberts Scholarship Fund

Davis-Roberts Scholarship

Type of award: Scholarship, renewable.
Intended use: For full-time undergraduate study at 2-year or 4-year institution.
Eligibility: Applicant must be U.S. citizen residing in Wyoming.
Basis for selection: Applicant must demonstrate financial need.
Application requirements: Recommendations, essay, transcript. Applicant's photograph.
Additional information: Applicant must be member of Job's Daughters or DeMolay.

Amount of award:	$300-$1,000
Number of awards:	10
Number of applicants:	12
Application deadline:	June 15
Notification begins:	August 31
Total amount awarded:	$5,000

Contact:
Davis-Roberts Scholarship Fund
c/o Gary D. Skillern
P.O. Box 20645
Cheyenne, WY 82003
Phone: 307-632-0491

Delaware Higher Education Office

B. Bradford Barnes Scholarship

Type of award: Scholarship, renewable.
Intended use: For full-time freshman study at 4-year institution. Designated institutions: University of Delaware.
Eligibility: Applicant must be high school senior. Applicant must be U.S. citizen or permanent resident residing in Delaware.
Basis for selection: Applicant must demonstrate high academic achievement.
Application requirements: Essay, transcript. FAFSA.
Additional information: Must rank in top 25 percent of high school class. Combined score of 1800 on the SAT. Awards full tuition, fees, room, board, and books. Visit Website for deadline.

Amount of award:	Full tuition
Number of awards:	1
Number of applicants:	35

Contact:
Delaware Higher Education Office
John G. Townsend Building
401 Federal Street
Dover, DE 19901
Phone: 302-735-4120
Fax: 302-739-5894
Web: www.doe.k12.de.us/high-ed

Charles L. Hebner Memorial Scholarship

Type of award: Scholarship, renewable.
Intended use: For full-time undergraduate study at 4-year institution. Designated institutions: University of Delaware, Delaware State University.
Eligibility: Applicant must be high school senior. Applicant must be U.S. citizen or permanent resident residing in Delaware.
Basis for selection: Major/career interest in humanities/liberal arts; social/behavioral sciences or political science/government. Applicant must demonstrate high academic achievement.
Application requirements: Essay, transcript. FAFSA.
Additional information: Applicant must rank in top half of graduating class. Minimum combined score of 1350 on SAT. Preference given to political science majors. Award covers tuition, fees, room, board, and books. Visit Website for deadline information.

Amount of award:	Full tuition
Number of awards:	2
Number of applicants:	35

Contact:
Delaware Higher Education Office
John G. Townsend Building
401 Federal Street
Dover, DE 19901
Phone: 302-735-4120
Fax: 302-739-5894
Web: www.doe.k12.de.us/high-ed

Delaware Educational Benefits for Children of Deceased Veterans and Others

Type of award: Scholarship, renewable.
Intended use: For undergraduate study at postsecondary institution.
Eligibility: Applicant must be at least 16, no older than 24. Applicant must be U.S. citizen or permanent resident residing in Delaware.
Additional information: Must live in Delaware for at least three years before applying. Must apply at least four weeks before classes begin. Award prorated when major not available at a Delaware public college. Award for maximum of four years. Must be child of one of the following: member of armed forces whose death was service-related, who is or was a POW, or is officially MIA; state police officer whose death was service-related; or state employee of the Department of Transportation routinely employed in job-related activities on the state highway system whose death was job-related. Visit Website for deadline.

Amount of award:	Full tuition
Number of applicants:	2

Contact:
Delaware Higher Education Office
John G. Townsend Building
401 Federal Street
Dover, DE 19901
Phone: 302-735-4120
Fax: 302-739-5894
Web: www.doe.k12.de.us/high-ed

Delaware Scholarship Incentive Program

Type of award: Scholarship.
Intended use: For full-time undergraduate study at accredited 2-year or 4-year institution. Designated institutions: Nonprofit, regionally accredited institutions in Delaware or Pennsylvania.
Eligibility: Applicant must be U.S. citizen or permanent resident residing in Delaware.
Basis for selection: Applicant must demonstrate financial need and high academic achievement.
Application requirements: Transcript. FAFSA.
Additional information: Minimum 2.5 GPA. Full-time undergraduate and graduate students whose majors are not offered at a Delaware public college will be considered. Visit Website for deadline.

Amount of award:	$700-$2,200
Number of awards:	1,010
Number of applicants:	11,000
Total amount awarded:	$1,369,400

Contact:
Delaware Higher Education Office
John G. Townsend Buillding
401 Federal Street
Dover, DE 19901
Phone: 302-735-4120
Fax: 302-739-5894
Web: www.doe.k12.de.us/high-ed

Diamond State Scholarship

Type of award: Scholarship, renewable.
Intended use: For full-time freshman study at accredited vocational, 2-year or 4-year institution in United States. Designated institutions: Nonprofit, regionally accredited institutions.
Eligibility: Applicant must be high school senior. Applicant must be U.S. citizen or permanent resident residing in Delaware.
Basis for selection: Applicant must demonstrate high academic achievement.
Application requirements: Essay, transcript. SAT scores.
Additional information: Must rank in top 25 percent of high school class. Minimum combined score of 1800 on SAT. Visit Website for deadline.

Amount of award:	$1,250
Number of awards:	54
Number of applicants:	124
Total amount awarded:	$67,500

Contact:
Delaware Higher Education Office
John G. Townsend Building
401 Federal Street
Dover, DE 19901
Phone: 302-735-4120
Fax: 302-739-5894
Web: www.doe.k12.de.us/high-ed

Herman M. Holloway, Sr. Memorial Scholarship

Type of award: Scholarship, renewable.
Intended use: For full-time freshman study at 4-year institution. Designated institutions: Delaware State University.
Eligibility: Applicant must be high school senior. Applicant must be U.S. citizen or permanent resident residing in Delaware.
Basis for selection: Applicant must demonstrate high academic achievement.
Application requirements: Essay, transcript. FAFSA.
Additional information: Applicants must rank in upper half of class and have combined score of at least 1350 on SAT. Awards full tuition, fees, room, board, and books. Visit Website for deadline information.

Amount of award:	Full tuition
Number of awards:	1
Number of applicants:	60

Contact:
Delaware Higher Education Office
John G. Townsend Building
401 Federal Street
Dover, DE 19901
Phone: 302-735-4120
Fax: 302-739-5894
Web: www.doe.k12.de.us/high-ed

Distinguished Young Women

California's Distinguished Young Woman Competition

Type of award: Scholarship.
Intended use: For undergraduate study at accredited 2-year or 4-year institution in United States.
Eligibility: Applicant must be single, female, high school junior. Applicant must be U.S. citizen residing in California.

Basis for selection: Competition/talent/interest in poise/talent/fitness. Applicant must demonstrate high academic achievement.
Additional information: Local competitions held from January to May; state competition held in late July or early August. Awards not limited to state Junior Miss finalists; winners of various judged categories also receive awards. Participants must never have been pregnant or married. Minimum 3.0 GPA. Check Website for details.
Contact:
Distinguished Young Women (Formerly California's Junior Miss)
P.O. Box 2719
Bakersfield, CA 93303
Web: www.distinguishedyw.org/ca

Distinguished Young Women Scholarship

Type of award: Scholarship.
Intended use: For undergraduate or graduate study.
Eligibility: Applicant must be single, female, high school junior or senior. Applicant must be U.S. citizen.
Basis for selection: Competition/talent/interest in poise/talent/fitness, based on scholastic evaluation, skill in creative and performing arts, physical fitness, presence and composure, and panel interview.
Additional information: Must compete in state of legal residence. State winners expected to compete at higher levels. Must never have been married or pregnant. Only high school seniors can compete in national finals but students are encouraged to begin application process during sophomore year. Scholarship funds can be used for undergraduate work or deferred for graduate and professional studies. Evaluation categories: scholastic (20%), interview (25%), talent (25%), fitness (15%), self expression (15%). Visit Website for application and deadline information, as it varies from state to state.

Amount of award:	$100-$50,000
Number of applicants:	4,000
Total amount awarded:	$2,051,293

Contact:
Distinguished Young Women
Participant Inquiry
751 Government Street
Mobile, AL 36602
Phone: 800-256-5435
Fax: 251-431-0063
Web: www.distinguishedyw.org

District of Columbia Higher Education Financial Services

DC Tuition Assistance Grant Program (DCTAG)

Type of award: Scholarship, renewable.
Intended use: For undergraduate study at 2-year or 4-year institution in United States. Designated institutions: DCTAG-eligible institutions that can participate in Title IV programs.
Eligibility: Applicant must be no older than 24. Applicant must be U.S. citizen or permanent resident residing in District of Columbia.
Application requirements: Transcript, proof of eligibility. Student Aid Report, FAFSA, current utility bill, certified DC Income Tax Report (D-40) or a twelve month income/benefit history statement.
Additional information: Parents or guardian of applicant must be DC resident for 12 months prior to enrollment and throughout college. Award may not be used at proprietary institutions. Awards and deadlines vary. Visit Website for details.

Amount of award:	$2,500-$10,000

Contact:
Higher Education Financial Services
810 First St. NE
Third Floor
Washington, DC 20002
Phone: 202-727-2824
Web: www.osse.dc.gov/service/higher-education-financial-services

Do Something Scholarships

Do Something Awards

Type of award: Scholarship.
Intended use: For undergraduate study at postsecondary institution. Designated institutions: 501(c)3 non-profit organizations.
Eligibility: Applicant must be no older than 25, enrolled in high school.
Basis for selection: Applicant must demonstrate leadership and service orientation.
Application requirements: Recommendations, essay.
Additional information: Grant towards a youth driven community project. Five finalists receive $10,000. Grand prize winner will receive $100,000, $5,000 of which can be used as educational scholarship. Interview required for finalists (at Do Something's expense). Deadline is in spring. Visit Website for additional details.

Amount of award:	$10,000-$100,000
Number of awards:	5
Number of applicants:	518
Total amount awarded:	$140,000

Contact:
Do Something Scholarships
24-32 Union Square East
4th Floor
New York, NY 10003
Phone: 212-254-2390
Web: www.dosomething.org/programs/awards

Dolphin Scholarship Foundation

Dolphin Scholarship

Type of award: Scholarship, renewable.
Intended use: For full-time undergraduate study at accredited 4-year institution.

Eligibility: Applicant must be single, no older than 24. Applicant must be U.S. citizen. Must be child/stepchild of member or former member of U.S. Navy who served in, or in support of, Submarine Force.
Basis for selection: Applicant must demonstrate financial need, high academic achievement and service orientation.
Application requirements: Recommendations, essay, transcript, proof of eligibility. SAT/ACT scores.
Additional information: Applicant must be high school senior or college student. Applicant must demonstrate commitment to extracurricular activities and community service.

Amount of award:	$3,400
Number of awards:	116
Number of applicants:	380
Application deadline:	March 15
Notification begins:	May 1
Total amount awarded:	$391,000

Contact:
Dolphin Scholarship Foundation
4966 Euclid Road
Suite 109
Virginia Beach, VA 23462
Phone: 757-671-3200 ext. 112
Fax: 757-671-3330
Web: www.dolphinscholarship.org

Laura W. Bush Scholarship

Type of award: Scholarship, renewable.
Intended use: For undergraduate study at accredited 4-year institution.
Eligibility: Applicant must be no older than 24. Must be child/stepchild of member or former member of U.S. Navy submarine force who served on the USS Texas (SSN775).
Basis for selection: Applicant must demonstrate financial need, high academic achievement, depth of character, leadership, seriousness of purpose and service orientation.
Application requirements: SAT/ACT scores.
Additional information: Applicant must be unmarried high school senior or college student. Sponsor must be qualified in submarines and have served on active duty in the Submarine Force for a minimum of 8 years or must have served on active duty in direct submarine support activities for a minimum of 10 years. Visit Website for application and details.

Amount of award:	$3,400
Number of awards:	3
Number of applicants:	3
Application deadline:	March 15
Notification begins:	May 15
Total amount awarded:	$10,200

Contact:
Dolphin Scholarship Foundation
4966 Euclid Road, Suite 109
Virginia Beach, VA 23462
Phone: 757-671-3200 ext. 112
Fax: 757-671-3330
Web: www.dolphinscholarship.org

Eastern Orthodox Committee on Scouting

Boy and Girl Scouts Scholarship

Type of award: Scholarship.
Intended use: For full-time freshman study at accredited 4-year institution in United States.
Eligibility: Applicant must be high school senior. Applicant must be Eastern Orthodox. Applicant must be U.S. citizen.
Basis for selection: Applicant must demonstrate depth of character and service orientation.
Application requirements: Four letters of recommendation with application, one from each of following groups: religious institution, school, community leader, and head of Scouting unit.
Additional information: Eligible applicant must be registered member of Boy or Girl Scouts unit; Eagle Scout or Gold Award recipient; active member of Eastern Orthodox Church; have received Alpha Omega Religious Scout Award; have demonstrated practical citizenship in his or her church, school, Scouting unit, and community. Offers one $1,000 scholarship and one $500 scholarship upon acceptance to four-year accredited college or university.

Amount of award:	$500-$1,000
Number of awards:	2
Number of applicants:	120
Application deadline:	May 1
Total amount awarded:	$1,500

Contact:
EOCS Scholarship Committee
862 Guy Lombardo Avenue
Freeport, NY 11520
Phone: 516-868-4050
Web: www.eocs.org

Edmund F. Maxwell Foundation

Edmund F. Maxwell Foundation Scholarship

Type of award: Scholarship, renewable.
Intended use: For full-time freshman study. Designated institutions: Private colleges and universities.
Eligibility: Applicant must be U.S. citizen or permanent resident residing in Washington.
Basis for selection: Applicant must demonstrate financial need, high academic achievement, depth of character, leadership, seriousness of purpose and service orientation.
Application requirements: Essay, transcript. Financial aid worksheet.
Additional information: Must be resident of western Washington. Combined reading and math SAT scores must be greater than 1200. Equivalent ACT scores also accepted. Applicants encouraged to apply early in year. Awards and amounts may vary. Visit Website for application and more information.

Amount of award:	$5,000
Application deadline:	April 30
Notification begins:	June 1
Total amount awarded:	$255,000

Contact:
The Edmund F. Maxwell Foundation
4111 East Madison Street
#450
Seattle, WA 98112
Web: www.maxwell.org

Scholarships

Elie Wiesel Foundation for Humanity

Elie Wiesel Prize in Ethics

Type of award: Scholarship.
Intended use: For full-time junior or senior study at accredited 4-year institution in United States.
Basis for selection: Competition/talent/interest in writing/journalism.
Application requirements: Proof of eligibility. Letter from college/university verifying full-time junior or senior status. Sponsorship by faculty member. Submit essay concerning an ethical dilemma, issue, or question related to the contest's annual topic. In 3,000 to 4,000 words, students are encouraged to raise questions, single out issues, and identify dilemmas.
Additional information: First prize is $5,000; second prize is $2,500; third prize is $1,500; two honorable mentions are $500 each. Deadline is late December; Notification begins in May. See Website for more information and application.

Amount of award:	$500-$5,000
Number of awards:	5
Number of applicants:	300
Application deadline:	December 7
Notification begins:	May 31
Total amount awarded:	$10,000

Contact:
Elie Wiesel Prize in Ethics
The Elie Wiesel Foundation for Humanity
555 Madison Avenue, 20th Floor
New York, NY 10022
Phone: 212-490-7788
Fax: 212-490-6006
Web: apply.ethicsprize.org

Elizabeth Greenshields Foundation

The Elizabeth Greenshields Grant

Type of award: Scholarship, renewable.
Intended use: For undergraduate, graduate or non-degree study at postsecondary institution.
Basis for selection: Major/career interest in arts, general.
Application requirements: Jpeg on CD.
Additional information: For artists (fine arts) in early stages of careers creating representational or figurative works through painting, drawing, printmaking, or sculpture. Must make a commitment to making art a lifetime career. Applications are welcome throughout the year. All award amounts are in Canadian dollars. Funds may be used for any art-related purpose.

Amount of award:	$15,000
Number of awards:	50
Number of applicants:	1,000

Contact:
Elizabeth Greenshields Foundation
1814 Sherbrooke Street West, Suite 1
Montreal
Quebec, Canada, H3H 1E4
Phone: 514-937-9225
Web: www.elizabethgreenshieldsfoundation.ca

Elks National Foundation

Elks Most Valuable Student Scholarship

Type of award: Scholarship.
Intended use: For full-time undergraduate study at accredited postsecondary institution in United States.
Eligibility: Applicant must be high school senior. Applicant must be U.S. citizen.
Basis for selection: Applicant must demonstrate financial need, high academic achievement and leadership.
Application requirements: Essay, transcript. Counselor report, SAT/ACT scores, income range.
Additional information: Applications available starting September 1 from local Benevolent and Protective Order of Elks Lodge; also available on Website or by sending SASE to foundation. Application deadline is in December. Award is distributed over four years. Membership in Elks not required, but application must be endorsed by and submitted to local Elks Lodge for entry into competition. Judging occurs at lodge, district, and state level before reaching national competition.

Amount of award:	$4,000-$60,000
Number of awards:	500
Number of applicants:	20,000
Notification begins:	April 30
Total amount awarded:	$2,296,000

Contact:
Elks National Foundation
2750 North Lakeview Avenue
Chicago, IL 60614-2256
Phone: 773-755-4732
Fax: 773-755-4733
Web: www.elks.org/enf/scholars

Elks National Foundation Legacy Awards

Type of award: Scholarship.
Intended use: For full-time undergraduate study at accredited postsecondary institution in United States.
Eligibility: Applicant must be high school senior. Applicant must be U.S. citizen.
Basis for selection: Applicant must demonstrate high academic achievement and leadership.
Application requirements: Essay, transcript. SAT/ACT scores.
Additional information: Applicant must be child or grandchild of a current Elks member who has been paid-up and in good standing for two consecutive years. Application available September 1 from Website. Eligible applicants from Guam, Panama, Puerto Rico, and the Philippines may attend schools in those countries. Visit Website for additional information.

Amount of award:	$4,000
Number of awards:	250
Number of applicants:	1,800
Application deadline:	February 1
Notification begins:	April 30
Total amount awarded:	$1,000,000

Contact:
Elks National Foundation
2750 North Lakeview Avenue
Chicago, IL 60614-2256
Phone: 773-755-4732
Fax: 773-755-4733
Web: www.elks.org/enf/scholars

Engineers Foundation of Ohio

Engineers Foundation of Ohio Scholarships

Type of award: Scholarship.
Intended use: For freshman study at accredited 4-year institution in United States. Designated institutions: ABET-accredited schools in Ohio and University of Notre Dame.
Eligibility: Applicant must be high school senior. Applicant must be U.S. citizen residing in Ohio.
Basis for selection: Major/career interest in engineering. Applicant must demonstrate high academic achievement.
Application requirements: Essay, transcript.
Additional information: Minimum 3.0 GPA. Must have minimum 600 SAT (Math) and 500 SAT (Reading or Composition) or 29 ACT Math and 25 ACT English. EFO offers scholarships per year with various requirements; see Website for specifics. Some awards renewable.

Amount of award:	$500-$2,500
Application deadline:	December 15

Contact:
Engineers Foundation of Ohio
400 South Fifth Street
Suite 300
Columbus, OH 43215-5430
Phone: 614-223-1177
Fax: 614-223-1131
Web: www.ohioengineer.com

The Entomological Foundation

The Entomological Foundation BioQuip Undergraduate Scholarship

Type of award: Scholarship.
Intended use: For full-time junior or senior study at 4-year institution. Designated institutions: Institutions in United States, Canada, or Mexico.
Basis for selection: Competition/talent/interest in study abroad. Major/career interest in entomology; zoology; biology or science, general. Applicant must demonstrate financial need.
Application requirements: Recommendations, essay, transcript. Letter of nomination, three statements from school officials attesting to entomological interests, character, aptitude, financial need.
Additional information: Applicant must have been enrolled as undergraduate student in entomology in the fall prior to application deadline. If student's college or university does not offer a degree in entomology, student must be preparing to become an entomologist through his/her studies. By September 1 following application deadline, student must accumulate at least 90 credit hours and either complete two junior-level entomology courses or a research project in entomology. See Website for more information.

Amount of award:	$2,000
Number of awards:	1
Number of applicants:	72
Application deadline:	July 1
Notification begins:	September 30
Total amount awarded:	$2,000

Contact:
The Entomological Foundation
9332 Annapolis Road, Suite 210
Lanham, MD 20706
Phone: 301-731-4535
Web: www.entfdn.org

Stan Beck Fellowship

Type of award: Scholarship, renewable.
Intended use: For undergraduate or graduate study at 4-year or graduate institution. Designated institutions: Colleges or universities in the United States, Mexico, or Canada.
Basis for selection: Major/career interest in entomology; biology or zoology. Applicant must demonstrate financial need.
Application requirements: Recommendations, essay, transcript, proof of eligibility. Letter of nomination, letters of support demonstrating applicant's need or challenge.
Additional information: Award amount varies. Need is based on physical limitations or economic, minority, or environmental conditions. Applications must be submitted electronically. See Website for additional information.

Application deadline:	July 1

Contact:
The Entomological Foundation
9332 Annapolis Road, Suite 210
Lanham, MD 20706
Phone: 301-731-4535
Web: www.entfdn.org

The Environmental Institute for Golf

GCSAA Legacy Awards

Type of award: Scholarship.
Intended use: For full-time undergraduate or graduate study at accredited postsecondary institution.
Basis for selection: Applicant must demonstrate high academic achievement, leadership and service orientation.
Application requirements: Essay, transcript, proof of eligibility. Letter of acceptance from college or university (high school seniors).
Additional information: Applicant's parent or grandparent must have been a Golf Course Superintendents Association of

America (GCSAA) member for five or more consecutive years and must be current active member in one of the following classifications: A, Superintendent Member, C, Retired-A, Retired-B, or AA Life. Children or grandchildren of deceased members also eligible if member was active at time of death. Award limited to one student per family. Children of Syngenta Professional Products employees, The Environmental Institute for Golf's Board of Trustees, and GCSAA staff not eligible. Past winners are ineligible to apply the following year. They may re-apply after a one-year hiatus.

Amount of award: $1,500
Application deadline: April 15
Notification begins: June 15

Contact:
Golf Course Superintendents Association of America
Scholarship Program
1421 Research Park Drive
Lawrence, KS 66049-3859
Phone: 785-832-4445 or 800-472-7878 ext. 4445
Web: www.gcsaa.org

GCSAA Scholars Competition

Type of award: Scholarship.
Intended use: For sophomore, junior or senior study at accredited 2-year or 4-year institution.
Basis for selection: Major/career interest in turf management. Applicant must demonstrate high academic achievement and leadership.
Application requirements: Recommendations, essay, transcript, proof of eligibility.
Additional information: Must be member of Golf Course Superintendents Association of America. Must have completed at least 24 credit hours or the equivalent of one year of full-time study in the appropriate major. Must be planning career in golf course management or closely related profession. First and second place winners receive all-expense paid trip to GCSAA-sponsored Golf Industry Show. Children of GCSAA Environmental Institute for Golf's Board of Trustees, GCSAA Board of Directors, and GCSAA staff not eligible. Visit Website for details and application.

Amount of award: $500-$6,000
Number of awards: 28
Application deadline: June 1
Notification begins: August 1

Contact:
Golf Course Superintendents Association of America
Scholarship Program
1421 Research Park Drive
Lawrence, KS 66049-3859
Phone: 785-832-4445 or 800-472-7878 ext. 4445
Web: www.gcsaa.org

GCSAA Student Essay Contest

Type of award: Scholarship.
Intended use: For undergraduate or graduate study at postsecondary institution.
Basis for selection: Competition/talent/interest in writing/journalism, based on essay focusing on golf course management. Major/career interest in turf management.
Application requirements: Essay, proof of eligibility.
Additional information: Must be member of Golf Course Superintendents Association of America. Must be pursuing degree in turf grass science, agronomy, or any other field related to golf course management. First prize is $2000; second prize, $1500; third prize, $1000. Visit Website for details.

Amount of award: $1,000-$2,000
Number of awards: 3
Application deadline: March 31

Contact:
Golf Course Superintendents Association of America
Student Essay Contest
1421 Research Park Drive
Lawrence, KS 66049-3859
Phone: 800-472-7878 ext. 4445
Web: www.gcsaa.org

Epilepsy Foundation

Behavioral Sciences Student Fellowship

Type of award: Research grant.
Intended use: For undergraduate or graduate study in United States.
Basis for selection: Major/career interest in social/behavioral sciences; sociology; social work; psychology; anthropology; nursing; economics; rehabilitation/therapeutic services or political science/government.
Application requirements: Recommendations, research proposal.
Additional information: Three-month fellowship for epilepsy study project. Professor or advisor must supervise student's project. Other appropriate fields include vocational rehabilitation, counseling, and subjects relevant to epilepsy research or practice. Women and minorities are especially encouraged to apply. Deadline in March. Visit Website for application instructions and for more information.

Amount of award: $3,000
Number of applicants: 9
Notification begins: May 31

Contact:
Epilepsy Foundation
8301 Professional Place
Landover, MD 20785-2267
Phone: 301-459-3700
Fax: 301-577-2684
Web: www.epilepsyfoundation.org/research/grant-and-fellowship-opportunities.cfm

Epilepsy Foundation of San Diego County

Epilepsy Foundation of San Diego County Scholarship

Type of award: Scholarship.
Intended use: For undergraduate study at vocational, 2-year or 4-year institution.
Eligibility: Applicant must be residing in California.
Basis for selection: Applicant must demonstrate financial need and high academic achievement.
Additional information: Two categories of eligibility: 1) Student being treated for epilepsy who is or will be enrolled in a college, university, or trade school in the Fall. 2) Full-time college or university student involved in an epilepsy research

project in health or social science with minimum 3.0 GPA. All applicants must be residents of San Diego or Imperial counties, but may be attending school outside the area.

Amount of award:	$250-$3,000
Number of awards:	6
Number of applicants:	19
Application deadline:	May 1
Total amount awarded:	$9,750

Contact:
Epilepsy Foundation of San Diego County
2055 El Cajon Boulevard
San Diego, CA 92104
Phone: 619-296-0161
Fax: 619-296-0802
Web: www.epilepsysandiego.org

EqualityMaine Foundation

The Joel Abromson Memorial Scholarship

Type of award: Scholarship.
Intended use: For freshman study at postsecondary institution.
Eligibility: Applicant must be high school senior. Applicant must be U.S. citizen or permanent resident residing in Maine.
Basis for selection: Competition/talent/interest in gay/lesbian, based on involvement and leadership in promoting equality for lesbian, gay, bisexual, and transgender people in schools and community. Applicant must demonstrate depth of character and service orientation.
Application requirements: Recommendations, essay. Cover letter. Acceptance letter from chosen higher education institution.
Additional information: Visit Website for essay question and additional information.

Amount of award:	$1,000
Application deadline:	April 15

Contact:
EqualityMaine
P.O. Box 1951
Portland, ME 04104
Phone: 207-761-3732
Fax: 207-761-3752
Web: www.equalitymaine.org

ESA Foundation

ESA Foundation Scholarship Program

Type of award: Scholarship, renewable.
Intended use: For undergraduate or graduate study at vocational, 2-year, 4-year or graduate institution.
Basis for selection: Applicant must demonstrate financial need, high academic achievement, leadership and service orientation.
Application requirements: $5 application fee. Recommendations, essay, transcript.
Additional information: Individual scholarships have specific requirements; visit Website for details and application form.

Amount of award:	$500-$7,500
Number of awards:	196
Number of applicants:	9,000
Application deadline:	February 1
Notification begins:	June 1
Total amount awarded:	$195,000

Contact:
ESA Foundation
Kathy Loyd
1222 NW 651
Blairstown, MO 64726
Phone: 660-678-2611
Fax: 660-441-3310
Web: www.epsilonsigmaalpha.org/scholarships-and-grants

Executive Women International

Executive Women International Scholarship

Type of award: Scholarship, renewable.
Intended use: For full-time undergraduate study at accredited 4-year institution in United States.
Eligibility: Applicant must be high school senior.
Basis for selection: Applicant must demonstrate high academic achievement, depth of character, leadership, seriousness of purpose and service orientation.
Application requirements: Interview, recommendations, essay, transcript. Biographical Questionnaire, FAFSA, most recent Federal tax form(s) (Form 1040, pages 1 & 2; Form 1040A, pages 1 & 2; Form 1040EZ, page 1) from person who claims applicant on their income tax return.
Additional information: Applicant must reside within boundaries of participating Executive Women International chapter. Minimum 3.0 GPA. Scholarship awarded each academic year, for up to five consecutive years, until student completes degree. Applicants must have sponsoring teacher at their school. Must have a major/career interest in a professional field.

Amount of award:	$1,000-$5,000
Number of awards:	6
Application deadline:	April 30
Notification begins:	May 30
Total amount awarded:	$15,000

Contact:
Executive Women International
7414 South State St.
Midvale, UT 84047
Phone: 801-355-2800
Fax: 801-355-2852
Web: www.ewiconnect.com

Experimental Aircraft Association

David Alan Quick Scholarship

Type of award: Scholarship.
Intended use: For junior or senior study at accredited 4-year institution.

Basis for selection: Major/career interest in aerospace or engineering. Applicant must demonstrate financial need.
Application requirements: Recommendations, essay. Resume, financial information.
Additional information: Must be Experimental Aircraft Association member or recommended by EAA member. Awarded to student pursuing degree in aerospace or aeronautical engineering. Awards dependent on funding. Apply online.

Amount of award:	$500
Number of awards:	1
Application deadline:	February 28

Contact:
EAA Scholarship Department
P.O. 3086
Oshkosh, WI 54903-3086
Phone: 920-426-6823
Web: www.youngeagles.org/programs/scholarships

David Mineck Memorial Scholarship

Type of award: Scholarship.
Intended use: For undergraduate study at postsecondary institution.
Basis for selection: Major/career interest in aerospace.
Additional information: Must be an Experimental Aircraft Association member or recommended by an EAA member.

Amount of award:	$500
Application deadline:	February 28

Contact:
EAA Scholarship Department
P.O. 3086
Oshkosh, WI 54903-3086
Phone: 920-426-6823
Web: www.youngeagles.org/programs/scholarships

Hansen Scholarship

Type of award: Scholarship, renewable.
Intended use: For undergraduate study at accredited vocational, 2-year or 4-year institution.
Basis for selection: Major/career interest in aerospace; aviation or engineering. Applicant must demonstrate financial need, high academic achievement, depth of character, leadership and service orientation.
Application requirements: Recommendations, essay. Resume, financial information.
Additional information: Must be Experimental Aircraft Association member or recommended by EAA member. Student should be pursuing degree in aerospace engineering or aeronautical engineering. Awards dependent on funding. Visit Website for details and application.

Amount of award:	$1,000
Number of awards:	1
Application deadline:	February 28

Contact:
EAA Scholarship Department
P.O. 3086
Oshkosh, WI 54903-3086
Phone: 920-426-6823
Web: www.youngeagles.org/programs/scholarships

Harry E. Arcamuzi Aviation Scholarship

Type of award: Scholarship, renewable.
Intended use: For undergraduate study at postsecondary institution.
Basis for selection: Major/career interest in aviation.
Additional information: Must be an Experimental Aircraft Association member or recommended by EAA member. Must be inner city student with a 2.0 minimum GPA.

Amount of award:	$500
Application deadline:	February 28

Contact:
EAA Scholarship Department
P.O. 3086
Oshkosh, WI 54903-3086
Phone: 920-426-6823
Web: www.youngeagles.org/programs/scholarships

H.P. "Bud" Milligan Aviation Scholarship

Type of award: Scholarship, renewable.
Intended use: For undergraduate study at accredited vocational, 2-year or 4-year institution.
Basis for selection: Major/career interest in aviation. Applicant must demonstrate financial need, depth of character, leadership and service orientation.
Application requirements: Recommendations, essay. Resume, financial information.
Additional information: Must be Experimental Aircraft Association member or recommended by EAA member. Awards dependent on funding. Complete application online.

Amount of award:	$500
Number of awards:	1
Application deadline:	February 28

Contact:
EAA Scholarship Department
P.O. 3086
Oshkosh, WI 54903-3086
Phone: 920-426-6823
Web: www.youngeagles.org/programs/scholarships

Hudner Medal of Honor Scholarship

Type of award: Scholarship.
Intended use: For undergraduate study at postsecondary institution.
Basis for selection: Major/career interest in aviation; military science or public administration/service. Applicant must demonstrate financial need, leadership and service orientation.
Application requirements: Recommendations, essay. Resume, financial information.
Additional information: Must be an Experimental Aircraft Association member or recommended by EAA member and have strong record of involvement with Experimental Aircraft Association. Must express intent to serve the country through military or public service. Winner must attend award presentation dinner. Special consideration given to Wisconsin or nearby resident. Recommendation from Experimental Aircraft Association member strongly desired. Awards dependent on funding. Visit Website for additional information and application.

Amount of award:	$500
Number of awards:	1
Application deadline:	February 28

Contact:
EAA Scholarship Department
P.O. 3086
Oshkosh, WI 54903-3086
Phone: 920-426-6823
Web: www.youngeagles.org/programs/scholarships

Payzer Scholarship

Type of award: Scholarship.
Intended use: For undergraduate study at accredited postsecondary institution.
Basis for selection: Major/career interest in engineering; mathematics; physical sciences; biology or aviation. Applicant must demonstrate financial need, depth of character, leadership and service orientation.
Application requirements: Recommendations, essay. Resume, financial information.
Additional information: Must be current Experimental Aircraft Association member or recommended by EAA member. Applicant must intend to pursue career in engineering, mathematics, or physical/biological sciences. Awards dependent on funding. Complete application online.

Amount of award:	$5,000
Number of awards:	1
Application deadline:	February 28

Contact:
EAA Scholarship Department
P.O. 3086
Oshkosh, WI 54903-3086
Phone: 920-426-6823
Web: www.youngeagles.org/programs/scholarships

Richard Lee Vernon Aviation Scholarship

Type of award: Scholarship.
Intended use: For undergraduate study at postsecondary institution.
Basis for selection: Major/career interest in aviation. Applicant must demonstrate financial need and high academic achievement.
Application requirements: Recommendations, essay. Resume, financial information.
Additional information: Must be Experimental Aircraft Association member or recommended by EAA member. Awarded to a student pursuing training leading to professional aviation occupation. Awards dependent on funding. Apply online.

Amount of award:	$500
Number of awards:	1
Application deadline:	February 28

Contact:
EAA Scholarship Department
P.O. 3086
Oshkosh, WI 54903-3086
Phone: 920-426-6823
Web: www.youngeagles.org/programs/scholarships

Women Soar Scholarship for Innovation

Type of award: Scholarship.
Intended use: For undergraduate study at postsecondary institution.
Eligibility: Applicant must be high school junior or senior.
Basis for selection: Major/career interest in science, general; engineering or technology.
Application requirements: Fact-based technical paper, brief synopsis of current accomplishments, and written description of future plans.
Additional information: Must be an Experimental Aircraft Association member or recommended by an EAA member.

Amount of award:	$1,000
Application deadline:	February 28

Contact:
EAA Scholarship Department
P.O. 3086
Oshkosh, WI 54903-3086
Phone: 920-426-6823
Web: www.youngeagles.org/programs/scholarships

Explorers Club

Explorers Club Youth Activity Fund

Type of award: Research grant.
Intended use: For full-time undergraduate study at postsecondary institution.
Basis for selection: Competition/talent/interest in research paper, based on proposal's scientific and practical merit, investigator's competence, and budget's appropriateness. Major/career interest in natural sciences. Applicant must demonstrate seriousness of purpose.
Application requirements: Recommendations, proof of eligibility, research proposal. One-page description of project, budget, copy of student ID.
Additional information: For research project in the natural sciences under supervision of qualified scientist or institution. For high school students or undergraduates only. Recipients of grants must provide one- to two-page report on their exploration or research within year of receiving the grant. Request application form from club. Notifications begin April. See Website for more details and deadline.

Amount of award:	$500-$1,500
Number of applicants:	79
Application deadline:	November 1
Total amount awarded:	$125,200

Contact:
The Explorers Club
Attn: Coleen Castillo
46 East 70th Street
New York, NY 10021
Phone: 212-628-8383
Fax: 212-288-4449
Web: www.explorers.org

Federal Employee Education and Assistance Fund

Federal Employee Education and Assistance Fund Scholarship

Type of award: Scholarship.
Intended use: For undergraduate, master's or doctoral study at accredited 2-year, 4-year or graduate institution.

Eligibility: Applicant or parent must be employed by Federal/ U.S. Government.
Basis for selection: Applicant must demonstrate high academic achievement.
Application requirements: Recommendations, essay, transcript. List of community service/extracurricular activities.
Additional information: Current civilian federal and postal employees with minimum three years' service by the end of August of the application year and their dependents are eligible. Applicant must have completed community service activities. Minimum 3.0 GPA. Employee applicants eligible for part-time study; dependents must enroll full-time. Visit Website for application materials beginning in January.

Amount of award:	$500-$2,000
Number of applicants:	4,168
Application deadline:	March 28
Notification begins:	September 30
Total amount awarded:	$435,800

Contact:
Federal Employee Education and Assistance Fund
3333 S. Wadsworth Blvd.
Suite 300
Lakewood, CO 80227
Phone: 800-323-4140
Web: www.feea.org

Financial Service Centers of New York

Rewarding Young Leaders in Our Community Scholarship

Type of award: Scholarship.
Intended use: For freshman study at postsecondary institution.
Eligibility: Applicant must be U.S. citizen or permanent resident.
Basis for selection: Applicant must demonstrate high academic achievement, leadership and service orientation.
Application requirements: Essay, transcript. Written verification of community involvement.
Additional information: Applicant must have contributed at least 50 hours of volunteer service per year in high school.

Amount of award:	$500-$7,500
Number of awards:	16
Total amount awarded:	$40,000

Contact:
Financial Service Centers of New York
Mr. Sanford Herman, Chairman
21 Main Street, Suite 101, P.O. Box 647
Hackensack, NJ 07601-0647
Phone: 201-964-2442
Fax: 201-964-2369
Web: www.fscny.org/?controller=scholarshipprogram

First Catholic Slovak Ladies Association

First Catholic Slovak Ladies Association Scholarship Program

Type of award: Scholarship.
Intended use: For full-time undergraduate or graduate study at accredited postsecondary institution in United States or Canada.
Eligibility: Applicant or parent must be member/participant of First Catholic Slovak Ladies Association.
Basis for selection: Applicant must demonstrate high academic achievement, leadership and service orientation.
Application requirements: Recommendations, essay, transcript, proof of eligibility. SAT/ACT scores. Photograph.
Additional information: Applicant must be member of First Catholic Slovak Ladies Association for at least three years prior to date of application, and on a $1,000 legal reserve certificate, a $5,000 term certificate, or have an annuity certificate. Visit Website for more information.

Amount of award:	$1,250-$1,750
Number of awards:	133
Number of applicants:	396
Application deadline:	March 1
Notification begins:	June 15
Total amount awarded:	$248,250

Contact:
First Catholic Slovak Ladies Association
Director of Fraternal Scholarship Aid
24950 Chagrin Boulevard
Beachwood, OH 44122
Phone: 800-464-4642
Web: www.fcsla.org

Fisher Communications, Inc.

Fisher Broadcasting Company Scholarship for Minorities

Type of award: Scholarship.
Intended use: For full-time sophomore, junior or senior study at accredited vocational, 2-year or 4-year institution in United States.
Eligibility: Applicant must be Alaskan native, Asian American, African American, Mexican American, Hispanic American, Puerto Rican, American Indian or Native Hawaiian/Pacific Islander. Applicant must be U.S. citizen.
Basis for selection: Major/career interest in radio/television/ film; journalism or marketing. Applicant must demonstrate financial need, high academic achievement and depth of character.
Application requirements: Recommendations, essay, transcript, proof of eligibility. Estimated expense/income worksheet.
Additional information: Must have career interest in broadcast communications. Amount of award varies depending on need. Minimum 2.5 GPA. For use at schools in Washington, California, Oregon, and Idaho, or for students with permanent addresses in those states who attend school out of state. Must apply online.

Number of applicants:	25
Application deadline:	May 31
Notification begins:	July 30
Total amount awarded:	$18,000

Contact:
Fisher Communications Inc. Minority Scholarship
Attn: Human Resources
140 4th Ave. N.
Seattle, WA 98109
Web: www.fsci.com/careers/scholarships-for-minorities

Florida Department of Education

Access to Better Learning and Education (ABLE) Grant Program

Type of award: Scholarship, renewable.
Intended use: For full-time undergraduate study at accredited postsecondary institution in United States. Designated institutions: Eligible private Florida colleges and universities.
Eligibility: Applicant must be U.S. citizen or permanent resident residing in Florida.
Basis for selection: Applicant must demonstrate financial need.
Application requirements: FAFSA.
Additional information: Each participating institution determines application procedures, deadlines, and student eligibility. The amount of ABLE award plus all other scholarships and grants specifically designated for payment of tuition and fees cannot exceed the total amount of tuition and fees charged by the institution. Applications available from financial aid offices at participating institutions. May not be enrolled in program of study leading to degree in theology or divinity.

Amount of award: $803

Contact:
Office of Student Financial Assistance
325 West Gaines Street
Suite 1314
Tallahassee, FL 32399-0400
Phone: 888-827-2004
Web: www.floridastudentfinancialaid.org

Florida Academic Scholars Award

Type of award: Scholarship, renewable.
Intended use: For undergraduate study at postsecondary institution in United States. Designated institutions: Eligible Florida postsecondary institutions.
Eligibility: Applicant must be high school senior. Applicant must be U.S. citizen or permanent resident residing in Florida.
Basis for selection: Applicant must demonstrate high academic achievement and service orientation.
Additional information: Applicant must have minimum 3.5 GPA, taken 16 credits of college preparatory academic courses, completed 100 hours of community service, and scored at least 1290 on SAT or 29 on ACT (excluding writing sections). Applicant with highest academic ranking in each district will receive Academic Top Scholars award. Application available online, and must be completed before high school graduation. Check Website for additional information and requirements.

Amount of award: Full tuition

Contact:
Office of Student Financial Assistance
325 West Gaines Street
Suite 1314
Tallahassee, FL 32399-0400
Phone: 888-827-2004
Web: www.floridastudentfinancialaid.org

Florida Bright Futures Scholarship Program

Type of award: Scholarship.
Intended use: For freshman study at vocational, 2-year or 4-year institution in United States. Designated institutions: Eligible Florida institutions.
Eligibility: Applicant must be high school senior. Applicant must be U.S. citizen or permanent resident residing in Florida.
Basis for selection: Applicant must demonstrate high academic achievement.
Application requirements: Transcript. Must complete the Initial Student Florida Financial Aid Application. FAFSA.
Additional information: Must be a Florida resident and U.S. citizen or eligible non-citizen as determined by student's postsecondary institution. Must apply during senior year, after December 1 and prior to graduation. Must not have been found guilty of or have plead nolo contendere to a felony charge. Must meet academic requirements and hourly requirements. Award amount varies. Visit Website for more details.

Contact:
Florida Department of Education
325 West Gaines Street
Suite 1314
Tallahassee, FL 32399-0400
Phone: 888-827-2004
Fax: 850-487-1809
Web: www.floridastudentfinancialaid.org/SSFAD/home/uamain.htm

Florida First Generation Matching Grant Program

Type of award: Scholarship.
Intended use: For undergraduate study at postsecondary institution in United States. Designated institutions: Florida state universities and colleges.
Eligibility: Applicant must be U.S. citizen or permanent resident residing in Florida.
Basis for selection: Applicant must demonstrate financial need.
Application requirements: FAFSA.
Additional information: Open to currently enrolled first generation college students whose parents have not earned baccalaureate degrees or higher. Funding may vary. Each participating institution determines application procedures, deadlines, and student eligibility. Applications available from participating schools' financial aid offices.

Contact:
Office of Student Financial Assistance
325 West Gaines Street
Suite 1314
Tallahassee, FL 32399-0400
Phone: 888-827-2004
Web: www.floridastudentfinancialaid.org

Florida Gold Seal Vocational Scholars Award

Type of award: Scholarship, renewable.
Intended use: For undergraduate study at vocational, 2-year or 4-year institution. Designated institutions: Eligible Florida postsecondary institutions..
Eligibility: Applicant must be high school senior. Applicant must be U.S. citizen or permanent resident residing in Florida.
Basis for selection: Applicant must demonstrate high academic achievement and service orientation.

Additional information: Minimum 3.0 GPA in core credits, 3.5 GPA in minimum of three vocational credits. Specific CPT, SAT, or ACT test scores required. Must have completed 30 hours of community service. Check Website for additional information and requirements. Applications available online and must be completed before high school graduation.
Contact:
Office of Student Financial Assistance
325 West Gaines Street
Suite 1314
Tallahassee, FL 32399-0400
Phone: 888-827-2004
Web: www.floridastudentfinancialaid.org

Florida Medallion Scholars Award

Type of award: Scholarship, renewable.
Intended use: For undergraduate study at 2-year or 4-year institution. Designated institutions: Eligible Florida postsecondary institutions.
Eligibility: Applicant must be high school senior. Applicant must be U.S. citizen or permanent resident residing in Florida.
Basis for selection: Applicant must demonstrate high academic achievement and service orientation.
Additional information: Minimum 3.0 GPA. Minimum composite score of 1170 on SAT or 26 on ACT (excluding writing sections). Must have taken 16 credits of college preparatory academic courses and completed 75 hours of community service. Applications available online, and must be completed before high school graduation. Check Website for additional information and requirements.
Contact:
Office of Student Financial Assistance
325 West Gaines Street
Suite 1314
Tallahassee, FL 32399-0400
Phone: 888-827-2004
Web: www.floridastudentfinancialaid.org

Florida Public Postsecondary Career Education Student Assistance Grant Program

Type of award: Scholarship.
Intended use: For undergraduate study at postsecondary institution in United States. Designated institutions: Eligible Florida postsecondary institutions.
Eligibility: Applicant must be U.S. citizen or permanent resident residing in Florida.
Basis for selection: Applicant must demonstrate financial need.
Application requirements: FAFSA.
Additional information: Must be enrolled in certificate programs of 450 or more clock hours at participating Florida colleges (public community colleges) or career centers operated by district school boards. Each participating institution determines application procedures, deadlines, and student eligibility. Applications available from participating schools' financial aid offices.

Amount of award: $200-$2,534

Contact:
Office of Student Financial Assistance
325 West Gaines Street
Suite 1314
Tallahassee, FL 32399-0400
Phone: 888-827-2004
Web: www.floridastudentfinancialaid.org

Florida Scholarships for Children and Spouses of Deceased or Disabled Veterans

Type of award: Scholarship, renewable.
Intended use: For undergraduate study at postsecondary institution. Designated institutions: Eligible Florida postsecondary institutions.
Eligibility: Applicant must be at least 16, no older than 22. Applicant must be U.S. citizen or permanent resident residing in Florida. Applicant must be dependent of disabled veteran, deceased veteran or POW/MIA; or spouse of disabled veteran or deceased veteran.
Application requirements: Proof of eligibility.
Additional information: Child applicant must be between ages of 16 and 22. Spouse of deceased service member must not be remarried. Service members must be certified by Florida Department of Veterans Affairs. Award for students of eligible private schools based on average cost of Florida public tuition/ fees. Award amount varies. Visit Website for additional information.

Application deadline: April 1

Contact:
Office of Student Financial Assistance
325 West Gaines Street
Suite 1314
Tallahassee, FL 32399-0400
Phone: 888-827-2004
Web: www.floridastudentfinancialaid.org

Florida Student Assistance Grant (FSAG) Program

Type of award: Scholarship, renewable.
Intended use: For undergraduate study at 2-year or 4-year institution. Designated institutions: Eligible Florida postsecondary institutions.
Eligibility: Applicant must be U.S. citizen or permanent resident residing in Florida.
Basis for selection: Applicant must demonstrate financial need.
Application requirements: Proof of eligibility. FAFSA.
Additional information: Each participating institution determines application procedures, deadlines, student eligibility, and award amounts. Applications available from participating schools' financial aid offices. Visit Website for more information.

Amount of award: $2,534

Contact:
Office of Student Financial Assistance
325 West Gaines Street
Suite 1314
Tallahassee, FL 32399-0400
Phone: 888-827-2004
Web: www.floridastudentfinancialaid.org

Jose Marti Scholarship Challenge Grant Fund

Type of award: Scholarship, renewable.
Intended use: For full-time freshman or graduate study at 2-year, 4-year or graduate institution in United States. Designated institutions: Florida public or eligible private institutions.
Eligibility: Applicant must be Mexican American, Hispanic American or Puerto Rican. Applicant must be U.S. citizen or permanent resident residing in Florida.

Scholarships

Basis for selection: Applicant must demonstrate financial need and high academic achievement.
Application requirements: FAFSA.
Additional information: Minimum 3.0 GPA. Must be of Spanish culture, born in Mexico or Hispanic country of the Caribbean, Central America, or South America regardless of race, or child of same. Award number is limited to the amount of available funds. First priority to graduating high school seniors, second priority to graduate students. Applications available from high school guidance office or college financial aid office. Visit Website for more information.

Amount of award:	$2,000
Application deadline:	April 1

Contact:
Office of Student Financial Assistance
325 West Gaines Street
Suite 1314
Tallahassee, FL 32399-0400
Phone: 888-827-2004
Web: www.floridastudentfinancialaid.org

Mary McLeod Bethune Scholarship

Type of award: Scholarship, renewable.
Intended use: For full-time undergraduate study at 4-year institution in United States. Designated institutions: Bethune-Cookman University, Edward Waters College, Florida A&M University, and Florida Memorial University.
Eligibility: Applicant must be U.S. citizen or permanent resident residing in Florida.
Basis for selection: Applicant must demonstrate financial need and high academic achievement.
Additional information: Minimum 3.0 high school GPA. Deadlines established by participating institutions. Award funds contingent upon matching contributions raised by the eligible institutions. Applications can be obtained from any of four designated institutions' financial aid offices. Visit Website for more information.

Amount of award:	$3,000

Contact:
Office of Student Financial Assistance
325 West Gaines Street
Suite 1314
Tallahassee, FL 32399-0400
Phone: 888-827-2004
Web: www.floridastudentfinancialaid.org

Minority Teacher Education Scholarship Program/Florida Fund for Minority Teachers, Inc.

Type of award: Scholarship.
Intended use: For junior study at 4-year institution in United States. Designated institutions: Eligible Florida postsecondary institutions.
Eligibility: Applicant must be Alaskan native, Asian American, African American, Mexican American, Hispanic American, Puerto Rican, American Indian or Native Hawaiian/Pacific Islander. Applicant must be U.S. citizen or permanent resident residing in Florida.
Basis for selection: Major/career interest in education. Applicant must demonstrate high academic achievement.
Additional information: Must have earned 60 credit hours or Associate of Arts degree. Must not have exceeded 18 hours of upper division education courses, and be newly admitted into a teacher education program. Minimum 2.5 GPA. Special consideration given to Florida college (public community college) graduates.

Amount of award:	$4,000
Application deadline:	August 1, November 15

Contact:
Office of Student Financial Assistance
325 West Gaines Street
Suite 1314
Tallahassee, FL 32399-0400
Phone: 352-392-9196
Web: www.floridastudentfinancialaid.org

Rosewood Family Scholarship Program

Type of award: Scholarship, renewable.
Intended use: For full-time undergraduate study at vocational, 2-year or 4-year institution in United States. Designated institutions: Public postsecondary institutions.
Eligibility: Applicant must be U.S. citizen or permanent resident.
Basis for selection: Applicant must demonstrate financial need.
Application requirements: Transcript, proof of eligibility. FAFSA. If not Florida resident, copy of Student Aid Report (SAR) must be sent to OSFA and postmarked by May 15th.
Additional information: Applicant must be direct descendent of Rosewood families affected by the incidents of January, 1923; renewal applicants given priority. Award covers annual cost of tuition and fees up to $4,000 per semester for up to eight semesters. Visit Website for more information.

Amount of award:	$4,000
Number of awards:	25
Application deadline:	April 1

Contact:
Office of Student Financial Assistance
325 West Gaines Street
Suite 1314
Tallahassee, FL 32399-0400
Phone: 888-827-2004
Web: www.floridastudentfinancialaid.org

William L. Boyd, IV, Florida Resident Access Grant (FRAG) Program

Type of award: Scholarship, renewable.
Intended use: For full-time undergraduate study at accredited 4-year institution. Designated institutions: Eligible private, nonprofit Florida colleges and universities.
Eligibility: Applicant must be U.S. citizen or permanent resident residing in Florida.
Application requirements: Proof of eligibility. FAFSA.
Additional information: Applicant must not have previously received bachelor's degree and may not use award for study of divinity or theology. Amount of award plus all other scholarships and grants may not exceed total amount of tuition. Award amount may vary depending on institution. Contact financial aid office of eligible institutions for application and more information.

Amount of award:	$2,150

Contact:
Office of Student Financial Assistance
325 West Gaines Street
Suite 1314
Tallahassee, FL 32399-0400
Phone: 888-827-2004
Web: www.floridastudentfinancialaid.org

Folds of Honor Foundation

Folds of Honor Foundation Scholaships

Type of award: Scholarship, renewable.
Intended use: For undergraduate study at postsecondary institution.
Eligibility: Applicant must be dependent of disabled veteran, deceased veteran or POW/MIA; or spouse of disabled veteran, deceased veteran or POW/MIA.
Application requirements: Proof of eligibility. Proof of enrollment.
Additional information: Scholarships available through the Immediate Use Scholarship program. Applicants are also eligible if they are a spouse or dependent of one or more of the following: a veteran who with an established MEB/PEB or VA rating for service-connected disability; service member missing in action or captured in line of duty; service member who received a Purple Heart Medal.

Amount of award:	$1-$5,000
Number of awards:	1,200
Number of applicants:	1,400
Application deadline:	April 30
Total amount awarded:	$4,500,000

Contact:
Folds of Honor
Phone: 918-272-5307
Web: www.foldsofhonor.org/scholarships

Foreclosure.com

Foreclosure.com Scholarship Contest

Type of award: Scholarship.
Intended use: For undergraduate study at 4-year institution.
Additional information: Must be a currently enrolled undergraduate student. First place: $5,000; second through fifth place: $1,000 each. See Website for essay topic.

Amount of award:	$1,000-$5,000
Number of awards:	5
Number of applicants:	10,000
Application deadline:	December 1
Notification begins:	February 1
Total amount awarded:	$9,000

Contact:
Foreclosure.com
Phone: 561-988-9669 ext. 7387
Web: www.foreclosure.com/scholarship

Foundation for Surgical Technology

Foundation for Surgical Technology Student Scholarship

Type of award: Scholarship.
Intended use: For undergraduate study in United States.
Basis for selection: Major/career interest in surgical technology. Applicant must demonstrate financial need and high academic achievement.
Application requirements: Recommendations, transcript, proof of eligibility.
Additional information: Applicant must be enrolled in surgical technology program accredited by CAAHEP or ABHES and be eligible to sit for the NBSTSA national surgical technologist certifying examination. Award amount varies. Visit Website for application.

Number of applicants:	200
Application deadline:	March 1
Notification begins:	June 15

Contact:
The Foundation for Surgical Technology
Attn: Scholarship Department
6 West Dry Creek Circle, Suite 200
Littleton, CO 80120
Phone: 303-694-9130
Fax: 303-694-9169
Web: www.ast.org/educators/scholarships.aspx

Foundation of the National Student Nurses Association, Inc.

National Student Nurses Association Scholarship

Type of award: Scholarship.
Intended use: For full-time undergraduate study at accredited 2-year or 4-year institution. Designated institutions: State-approved schools of nursing or pre-nursing.
Eligibility: Applicant must be U.S. citizen or permanent resident.
Basis for selection: Major/career interest in nursing. Applicant must demonstrate financial need, high academic achievement and service orientation.
Application requirements: $10 application fee. Essay, transcript, proof of eligibility. National Student Nurses Association members must submit proof of membership.
Additional information: All applicants considered for following scholarships: General Scholarships, Career Mobility Scholarships, Breakthrough to Nursing Scholarships, Specialty Scholarships, and Promise of Nursing Scholarships. Applicants must be enrolled in nursing or pre-nursing program, and may hold alien registration. Awards granted for use in summer, fall of the same year and only spring of following academic year. Number of awards varies. Applications available from May through January. See Website for deadline and application.

Amount of award: $1,000-$2,500
Number of applicants: 109
Application deadline: January 14
Total amount awarded: $400,000

Contact:
Foundation of the National Student Nurses Association, Inc.
45 Main Street
Suite 606
Brooklyn, NY 11201
Phone: 718-210-0705
Fax: 718-797-1186
Web: www.nsna.org

Francis Ouimet Scholarship Fund

The Ouimet Scholarship

Type of award: Scholarship, renewable.
Intended use: For full-time undergraduate study at accredited postsecondary institution.
Basis for selection: Competition/talent/interest in athletics/sports. Applicant must demonstrate financial need, high academic achievement and leadership.
Application requirements: Interview, recommendations, essay, transcript. FAFSA and CSS Profile, SAT scores. Photo.
Additional information: Applicants must have worked on golf course in Massachusetts for at least two years in a golf-related position. Contact the Ouimet Fund office in June to be put on application mailing list for awards for following school year, or sign up for application online.

Amount of award: $1,500-$8,000
Number of awards: 260
Number of applicants: 364
Application deadline: December 1
Notification begins: August 31
Total amount awarded: $1,500,000

Contact:
Francis Ouimet Scholarship Fund
William F. Connell Golf House & Museum
300 Arnold Palmer Blvd.
Norton, MA 02766
Phone: 774-430-9095
Fax: 774-430-9091
Web: www.ouimet.org

Fred G. Zahn Foundation

Fred G. Zahn Scholarship Fund

Type of award: Scholarship, renewable.
Intended use: For undergraduate study at accredited 2-year or 4-year institution in United States. Designated institutions: Institutions in Washington state.
Eligibility: Applicant must be residing in Washington.
Basis for selection: Applicant must demonstrate financial need, high academic achievement and depth of character.
Application requirements: Essay, transcript. Student Aid Report.
Additional information: Must have graduated from Washington state high school. Preference to juniors and seniors with minimum 3.75 GPA. May obtain application and more information at eligible Washington state institutions.

Amount of award: $1,500
Application deadline: April 15
Notification begins: June 15

Contact:
Fred G. Zahn Scholarship Fund
c/o US Trust/Bank of America
P.O. Box 830259
Dallas, TX 75283-0259
Phone: 866-461-7282
Fax: 800-658-6507

Freedom From Religion Foundation

Michael Hakeem Memorial Award

Type of award: Scholarship.
Intended use: For full-time undergraduate or graduate study at postsecondary institution. Designated institutions: North American institutions.
Eligibility: Applicant must be no older than 25.
Basis for selection: Competition/talent/interest in writing/journalism, based on best-written essays.
Application requirements: Essay. Essay should be 750-900 words, typed, stapled, double-spaced with standard margins. Include autobiographical paragraph giving both campus and permanent addresses, phone numbers, and e-mail. Identify college/university, major, and interests. Essay on free thought concerning religion; essay most suitable for atheistic and agnostic student.
Additional information: Applicant must be currently enrolled college student. Essay topics and requirements change annually and are announced in February. Check Website for current topic. Students are requested not to inquire before then. Visit Website for more information. First place receives $3,000; second place, $2,000; third place, $1000; fourth place, $500; fifth place, $300; honorable mention(s), $200. Essays must be submitted via postal mail and email.

Amount of award: $200-$3,000
Application deadline: June 15
Notification begins: September 1

Contact:
Freedom From Religion Foundation
College Essay Competition
P.O. Box 750
Madison, WI 53701
Phone: 608-256-8900
Web: www.ffrf.org

William J. Schulz High School Essay Contest

Type of award: Scholarship.
Intended use: For freshman study at postsecondary institution.
Eligibility: Applicant must be high school senior.
Basis for selection: Competition/talent/interest in writing/journalism, based on best-written essays.
Application requirements: Essay, proof of eligibility. Essay should be 500-700 words, stapled, typed, double-spaced with standard margins. Include autobiographical paragraph giving

both campus and permanent address, phone numbers, and e-mail. Identify high school and college/university to be attended. Include intended major and other interests.
Additional information: Applicant must be college-bound high school senior. Essay topics and requirements change annually and are announced in February. Students are requested not to inquire before then. Visit Website for more information. First place receives $3,000; second place, $2,000; third place, $1000; fourth place, $500; fifth place, $300; honorable mention(s), $200. Essays must be submitted via postal mail and email.

Amount of award:	$200-$3,000
Application deadline:	June 1
Notification begins:	August 1

Contact:
Freedom From Religion Foundation
High School Essay Contest
P.O. Box 750
Madison, WI 53701
Phone: 608-256-8900
Web: www.ffrf.org

Future Farmers of America

AGCO Scholarships

Type of award: Scholarship.
Intended use: For full-time undergraduate study at 2-year or 4-year institution in United States.
Eligibility: Applicant must be no older than 22.
Basis for selection: Major/career interest in agriculture; agribusiness; marketing; engineering; education; journalism; public relations; business/management/administration; economics or food production/management/services. Applicant must demonstrate financial need, high academic achievement and service orientation.
Application requirements: Essay. High school ranking, GPA, SAT/ACT scores.
Additional information: Additional majors also eligible. Must be FFA member. Must obtain FFA advisor's electronic approval on Signature Page. Signature Page must be mailed and postmarked by February 22. Must have valid mailing address in the U.S. Eligibility requirements vary. Visit Website for additional details.

Amount of award:	$1,000-$2,000
Number of awards:	136
Application deadline:	February 15
Notification begins:	May 7

Contact:
National FFA Organization Scholarship Office
P.O. Box 68960
Indianapolis, IN 46268-0960
Phone: 317-802-6099
Web: www.ffa.org/programs/grantsandscholarships/Scholarships/Pages/default.aspx

Agricredit Acceptance LLC Scholarship

Type of award: Scholarship.
Intended use: For full-time undergraduate study at postsecondary institution in United States. Designated institutions: Iowa institutions.
Eligibility: Applicant must be no older than 22. Applicant must be residing in Iowa.
Basis for selection: Major/career interest in agriculture. Applicant must demonstrate financial need.
Application requirements: High school ranking, GPA, ACT/SAT test scores.
Additional information: Minimum 3.0 GPA. Must not be studying social services. Applicant or family must be involved in corn, dairy cattle, beef cattle, grain sorghum, irrigation, production agriculture, sheep, soybean, swine or vegetable production. Must live on a family farm. Must be a member of FFA. Must have valid mailing address in the U.S. Must obtain FFA advisor's electronic approval on Signature Page. Apply online.

Amount of award:	$2,500
Number of awards:	2
Application deadline:	February 15

Contact:
National FFA Organization Scholarship Office
P.O. Box 68960
Indianapolis, IN 46268-0960
Phone: 317-802-6099
Web: www.ffa.org/programs/grantsandscholarships/Scholarships/Pages/default.aspx

Agrium U.S. Inc. Scholarship

Type of award: Scholarship.
Intended use: For full-time undergraduate study at 4-year institution in United States.
Eligibility: Applicant must be no older than 22.
Basis for selection: Major/career interest in agriculture; agricultural education; engineering; business/management/administration; marketing or engineering.
Application requirements: High school ranking, GPA, SAT/ACT scores.
Additional information: Other agriculture-related fields also eligible. Must be a member of FFA. Must have valid mailing address in the U.S. Must obtain FFA advisor's electronic approval on Signature Page. Apply online.

Amount of award:	$1,000
Number of awards:	5
Application deadline:	February 15
Total amount awarded:	$5,000

Contact:
National FFA Organization Scholarship Office
P.O. Box 68960
Indianapolis, IN 46268-0960
Phone: 317-802-6099
Web: www.ffa.org/programs/grantsandscholarships/Scholarships/Pages/default.aspx

Alpha Gamma Rho Educational Foundation Scholarship

Type of award: Scholarship.
Intended use: For full-time undergraduate study at 4-year institution in United States. Designated institutions: Universities with Alpha Gamma Rho chapter.
Eligibility: Applicant must be male, no older than 22.
Basis for selection: Major/career interest in agriculture. Applicant must demonstrate leadership.
Application requirements: High school ranking, GPA, SAT/ACT scores.
Additional information: Must be a member of FFA. Must have valid mailing address in the U.S. Must obtain FFA advisor's electronic approval on Signature Page. Apply online.

Visit www.agrs.org for a list of universities with Alpha Gamma Rho chapters.

Amount of award: $1,000
Number of awards: 1
Application deadline: February 15

Contact:
National FFA Organization Scholarship Office
P.O. Box 68960
Indianapolis, IN 46268-0960
Phone: 317-802-6099
Web: www.ffa.org/programs/grantsandscholarships/Scholarships/Pages/default.aspx

American Family Insurance Scholarship

Type of award: Scholarship.
Intended use: For full-time undergraduate study at 4-year institution in United States.
Eligibility: Applicant must be no older than 22. Applicant must be residing in Wisconsin, Minnesota or Missouri.
Application requirements: High school ranking, GPA, SAT/ACT scores.
Additional information: Must be a member of FFA. Must have valid mailing address in the U.S. Must obtain FFA advisor's electronic approval on Signature Page. Apply online.

Amount of award: $1,000
Number of awards: 3
Application deadline: February 15
Total amount awarded: $3,000

Contact:
National FFA Scholarship Office
P.O. Box 68960
Indianapolis, IN 46268-0960
Phone: 317-802-6099
Web: www.ffa.org/programs/grantsandscholarships/Scholarships/Pages/default.aspx

American Veterinary Medical Association Scholarship

Type of award: Scholarship.
Intended use: For full-time undergraduate study at 4-year institution in United States.
Eligibility: Applicant must be no older than 22.
Basis for selection: Major/career interest in animal sciences; dairy; equestrian/equine studies; biology or veterinary medicine.
Application requirements: High school ranking, GPA, SAT/ACT scores.
Additional information: Preference to applicants planning a career in veterinary medicine or veterinary food supply/public health. Must be a member of FFA. Must have valid mailing address in the U.S. Must obtain FFA advisor's electronic approval on Signature Page. Apply online.

Amount of award: $1,000
Number of awards: 3
Application deadline: February 15
Total amount awarded: $3,000

Contact:
National FFA Organization Scholarship Office
P.O. Box 68960
Indianapolis, IN 46268-0960
Phone: 317-802-6099
Web: www.ffa.org/programs/grantsandscholarships/Scholarships/Pages/default.aspx

Ameriprise Financial and AGSTAR Financial Services, Inc. Scholarship

Type of award: Scholarship.
Intended use: For full-time undergraduate study at 4-year institution in United States.
Eligibility: Applicant must be no older than 22.
Basis for selection: Major/career interest in agriculture.
Application requirements: High school ranking, GPA, SAT/ACT scores.
Additional information: Must be a member of one of the following Minnesota FFA chapters: Fillmore Central, Kingsland, Lanesboro, Lewiston, Mabel-Canton, Rushford-Peterson, St. Charles, Winona. Family must be involved in production agriculture. Must live on family farm. Must be a member of FFA. Must have valid mailing address in the U.S. Must obtain FFA advisor's electronic approval on Signature Page. Apply online.

Amount of award: $1,000
Number of awards: 1
Application deadline: February 15

Contact:
National FFA Organization Scholarship Office
P.O. Box 68960
Indianapolis, IN 68960-0960
Phone: 317-802-6099
Web: www.ffa.org/programs/grantsandscholarships/Scholarships/Pages/default.aspx

The Andersons, Inc. Scholarship

Type of award: Scholarship.
Intended use: For full-time undergraduate study at 4-year institution in United States. Designated institutions: Illinois, Indiana, Michigan, Ohio institutions.
Eligibility: Applicant must be no older than 22. Applicant must be residing in Wisconsin, Iowa, Michigan, Ohio, Minnesota, Florida, Indiana, Nebraska, Illinois or Alabama.
Basis for selection: Major/career interest in agriculture. Applicant must demonstrate service orientation.
Application requirements: High school ranking, GPA, SAT/ACT scores.
Additional information: Social services concentrations not eligible. Must be a resident of one of the following counties: Montgomery in Alabama; Collier, Hendry, Highlands, Lee or Orange in Florida; Champaign, Fulton or Platt in Illinois; Carroll, Cass, Champaign, DeKalb, Delaware, Jay, Wabash or Wells in Indiana; Crawford in Iowa; Calhoun, Eaton, Hillsdale, Ingham, Ionia or Saint Joseph in Michigan; Winona in Minnesota; Buffalo, Keith, Fillmore in Nebraska; Dark, Fulton, Hamilton, Lucas, Sandusky, Seneca, Trumbuss, Wood or Wyandot in Ohio; Dane, Iowa, Outagamie or Wood in Wisconsin. Must be a member of FFA. Must have valid mailing address in the U.S. Must obtain FFA advisor's electronic approval on Signature Page. Apply online.

Amount of award: $1,250
Number of awards: 2
Application deadline: February 15
Total amount awarded: $2,500

Contact:
National FFA Organization Scholarship Office
P.O. Box 68960
Indianapolis, IN 46268-0960
Phone: 317-802-6099
Web: www.ffa.org/programs/grantsandscholarships/Scholarships/Pages/default.aspx

Animal Health International Scholarship

Type of award: Scholarship.
Intended use: For full-time undergraduate study at 4-year institution in United States.
Eligibility: Applicant must be no older than 22. Applicant must be residing in South Dakota, Kansas, Louisiana, Nevada, California, Mississippi, Montana, Nebraska, Alabama, Missouri, Iowa, Utah, Texas, Minnesota, Arkansas, Washington, Arizona, Florida, Georgia, Wyoming, Oklahoma, Oregon, New Mexico, Idaho, Colorado or North Dakota.
Basis for selection: Major/career interest in animal sciences or dairy.
Application requirements: High school ranking, GPA, SAT/ACT scores.
Additional information: Must be a member of FFA. Must have valid mailing address in the U.S. Must obtain FFA advisor's electronic approval on Signature Page. Apply online.

Amount of award:	$1,000
Number of awards:	1
Application deadline:	February 15

Contact:
National FFA Organization Scholarship Office
P.O. Box 68960
Indianapolis, IN 46268-0960
Phone: 317-802-6099
Web: www.ffa.org/programs/grantsandscholarships/Scholarships/Pages/default.aspx

Arabian Horse Association (Region 14) Scholarship

Type of award: Scholarship.
Intended use: For full-time undergraduate study at 4-year institution in United States.
Eligibility: Applicant must be no older than 22.
Basis for selection: Major/career interest in agriculture; dietetics/nutrition; communications; forestry; business/management/administration; finance/banking; marketing; engineering; public administration/service or education. Applicant must demonstrate leadership and service orientation.
Application requirements: High school ranking, GPA, SAT/ACT scores.
Additional information: Must be a member of FFA. Must have valid mailing address in the U.S. Must obtain FFA advisor's electronic approval on Signature Page. Apply online.

Amount of award:	$1,000
Number of awards:	1
Application deadline:	February 15

Contact:
National FFA Organization Scholarship Office
P.O. Box 68960
Indianapolis, IN 46268-0960
Phone: 317-802-6099
Web: www.ffa.org/programs/grantsandscholarships/Scholarships/Pages/default.aspx

Archer Daniels Midland Company Scholarships

Type of award: Scholarship.
Intended use: For full-time undergraduate study at 2-year or 4-year institution in United States.
Eligibility: Applicant must be no older than 22.
Basis for selection: Major/career interest in agriculture. Applicant must demonstrate high academic achievement, leadership and service orientation.
Application requirements: Essay. High school ranking, GPA, SAT/ACT scores.
Additional information: Must be current FFA member. Minimum 2.8 GPA. Some residency requirements may apply. FDA chapter of each recipient will also receive a $250 FFA grant from ADM to assist in continued education excellence. Must have valid mailing address in the U.S. Must obtain FFA advisor's electronic approval on Signature Page. Signature Page must be mailed and postmarked by February 22. Apply online at www.ffa.org.

Amount of award:	$1,000
Number of awards:	80
Application deadline:	February 15
Notification begins:	May 7
Total amount awarded:	$80,000

Contact:
National FFA Organization Scholarship Office
P.O. Box 68960
Indianapolis, IN 46268-0960
Phone: 317-802-6099
Web: www.ffa.org/programs/grantsandscholarships/Scholarships/Pages/default.aspx

Arysta LifeScience North America Scholarship

Type of award: Scholarship.
Intended use: For full-time undergraduate study at 4-year institution in United States.
Eligibility: Applicant must be no older than 22. Applicant must be residing in Iowa, South Dakota, Washington, Kansas, Arizona, California, Oregon, New Mexico, Illinois or North Dakota.
Basis for selection: Major/career interest in public relations; agriculture; marketing or entomology. Applicant must demonstrate high academic achievement.
Application requirements: High school ranking, GPA, SAT/ACT scores.
Additional information: Must be a member of FFA. Must have valid mailing address in the U.S. Must obtain FFA advisor's electronic approval on Signature Page. Minimum 3.0 GPA. Other majors also eligible. Apply online.

Amount of award:	$1,275
Number of awards:	5
Application deadline:	February 15

Contact:
National FFA Organization Scholarship Office
P.O. Box 68960
Indianapolis, IN 46268-0960
Phone: 317-802-6099
Web: www.ffa.org/programs/grantsandscholarships/Scholarships/Pages/default.aspx

Beck's Hybrids Scholarship

Type of award: Scholarship.
Intended use: For full-time undergraduate study at 4-year institution in United States.
Eligibility: Applicant must be no older than 22. Applicant must be residing in Michigan, Ohio, Indiana, Kentucky or Illinois.
Basis for selection: Major/career interest in agriculture.
Application requirements: High school ranking, GPA, ACT/SAT test scores.

Additional information: One scholarship awarded per state (Illinois, Indiana, Kentucky, Michigan, Ohio). Family must be a Beck's Hybrids Seed customer. Must be a member of FFA. Must have valid mailing address in the U.S. Must obtain FFA advisor's electronic approval on Signature Page. Apply online.

Amount of award: $2,000
Number of awards: 5
Application deadline: February 15

Contact:
National FFA Organization Scholarship Office
P.O. Box 68960
Indianapolis, IN 46268-0960
Phone: 317-802-6099
Web: www.ffa.org/programs/grantsandscholarships/Scholarships/Pages/default.aspx

Behlen Mfg. Co./Walter and Ruby Behlen Memorial Scholarship

Type of award: Scholarship.
Intended use: For full-time undergraduate study at 2-year or 4-year institution in United States.
Eligibility: Applicant must be no older than 22. Applicant must be residing in Nebraska.
Basis for selection: Major/career interest in agriculture or science, general.
Application requirements: High school ranking, GPA, SAT/ACT scores.
Additional information: Social services majors not eligible. Must be a member of FFA. Must have valid mailing address in the U.S. Must obtain FFA advisor's electronic approval on Signature Page. Apply online.

Amount of award: $1,000
Number of awards: 1
Application deadline: February 15

Contact:
National FFA Organization Scholarship Office
P.O. Box 68960
Indianapolis, IN 46268-0960
Phone: 317-802-6099
Web: www.ffa.org/programs/grantsandscholarships/Scholarships/Pages/default.aspx

Birdsong Peanuts Scholarship

Type of award: Scholarship.
Intended use: For full-time undergraduate study at 4-year institution in United States.
Eligibility: Applicant must be no older than 22. Applicant must be residing in Alabama, Georgia or Florida.
Basis for selection: Major/career interest in agriculture or agribusiness.
Application requirements: High school ranking, GPA, SAT/ACT scores.
Additional information: Applicant or applicant's family must be peanut producers. Must be a member of FFA. Must have valid mailing address in the U.S. Must obtain FFA advisor's electronic approval on Signature Page. Apply online.

Amount of award: $1,000
Number of awards: 1
Application deadline: February 15

Contact:
National FFA Organization Scholarship Office
P.O. Box 68960
Indianapolis, IN 46268-0960
Phone: 317-802-6099
Web: www.ffa.org/programs/grantsandscholarships/Scholarships/Pages/default.aspx

Blain's Farm & Feet Scholarship

Type of award: Scholarship.
Intended use: For full-time undergraduate study at 4-year institution in United States.
Eligibility: Applicant must be no older than 22. Applicant must be residing in Iowa or Illinois.
Basis for selection: Major/career interest in agricultural economics or agribusiness. Applicant must demonstrate financial need.
Application requirements: High school ranking, GPA, ACT/SAT test scores.
Additional information: Agricultural finance or international agriculture majors also eligible. Consideration first given to Blain's Farm & Fleet employees. Financial need given secondary consideration. Must be a resident of one of the following cities: Belvidere, Bloomington, Bourbonnais, Decatur, Freeport, Geneseo, Loves Park, Moline, Montgomery, Morton, Ottawa, Rockford, Sterling, Sycamore, Urbana or Woodstock in Illinois; Cedar Falls, Clinton, Davenport, or Muscatine in Iowa. Must be a member of FFA. Must have valid mailing address in the U.S. Must obtain FFA advisor's electronic approval on Signature Page. Apply online.

Amount of award: $2,000
Number of awards: 2
Application deadline: February 15

Contact:
National FFA Organization Scholarship Office
P.O. Box 68960
Indianapolis, IN 46268-0960
Phone: 317-802-6099
Web: www.ffa.org/programs/grantsandscholarships/Scholarships/Pages/default.aspx

BNSF Railway Company Scholarship

Type of award: Scholarship, renewable.
Intended use: For full-time undergraduate study at accredited 4-year institution in United States.
Eligibility: Applicant must be no older than 22. Applicant must be residing in Iowa, South Dakota, Texas, Minnesota, Kansas, California, Montana, Nebraska, Illinois or North Dakota.
Basis for selection: Major/career interest in agriculture; agricultural economics; agribusiness; marketing or finance/banking. Applicant must demonstrate high academic achievement.
Application requirements: Essay. High school ranking, GPA, SAT/ACT scores.
Additional information: Must be FFA member. Minimum 3.0 GPA. Marketing and finance majors must be related to agriculture. One scholarship will be awarded to an applicant from each eligible state. Award paid in yearly increments of $1250. Must maintain a 3.0 GPA and full-time status to renew scholarship. Must have valid mailing address in the U.S. Must obtain FFA advisor's electronic approval on Signature Page. Signature Page must be mailed and postmarked by February 22. Apply online at www.ffa.org.

Amount of award: $1,250-$5,000
Number of awards: 10
Application deadline: February 15
Notification begins: May 7

Scholarships

Contact:
National FFA Organization Scholarship Office
P.O. Box 68960
Indianapolis, IN 46268-0960
Phone: 317-802-6099
Web: www.ffa.org/programs/grantsandscholarships/Scholarships/Pages/default.aspx

Booker T. Washington Scholarship

Type of award: Scholarship.
Intended use: For full-time undergraduate study at 4-year institution in United States.
Eligibility: Applicant must be Alaskan native, Asian American, African American, Mexican American, Hispanic American, Puerto Rican, American Indian or Native Hawaiian/Pacific Islander. Applicant must be no older than 22.
Basis for selection: Major/career interest in agriculture.
Application requirements: High school ranking, GPA, SAT/ACT scores.
Additional information: Must be a member of FFA. Must have valid mailing address in the U.S. Must obtain FFA advisor's electronic approval on Signature Page. Apply online.

Amount of award:	$1,000
Number of awards:	5
Application deadline:	February 15
Total amount awarded:	$25,000

Contact:
National FFA Organization Scholarship Office
P.O. Box 68960
Indianapolis, IN 46268-0960
Phone: 317-802-6099
Web: www.ffa.org/programs/grantsandscholarships/Scholarships/Pages/default.aspx

Bridgestone Scholarship

Type of award: Scholarship.
Intended use: For full-time undergraduate study at 4-year institution in United States.
Eligibility: Applicant must be no older than 22.
Basis for selection: Major/career interest in agriculture. Applicant must demonstrate financial need, leadership and service orientation.
Application requirements: High school ranking, GPA, SAT/ACT scores.
Additional information: Must reside on a family farm. Must be a member of FFA. Must have valid mailing address in the U.S. Must obtain FFA advisor's electronic approval on Signature Page. Other majors also eligible. Apply online.

Amount of award:	$2,500
Number of awards:	5
Application deadline:	February 15

Contact:
National FFA Organization Scholarship Office
P.O. Box 68960
Indianapolis, IN 46268-0960
Phone: 317-802-6099
Web: www.ffa.org/programs/grantsandscholarships/Scholarships/Pages/default.aspx

Bunge North America Scholarship

Type of award: Scholarship.
Intended use: For full-time undergraduate study at 2-year or 4-year institution in United States.
Eligibility: Applicant must be no older than 22.
Basis for selection: Major/career interest in agribusiness; agricultural economics; agricultural education; agriculture; communications; science, general or engineering. Applicant must demonstrate high academic achievement and leadership.
Application requirements: High school ranking, GPA, SAT/ACT scores.
Additional information: Must be a member of FFA. Must have valid mailing address in the U.S. and reside in one of the 48 contiguous states. Must obtain FFA advisor's electronic approval on Signature Page. Minimum 2.5 GPA. Other majors also eligible. Apply online.

Amount of award:	$1,000
Number of awards:	8
Application deadline:	February 15

Contact:
National FFA Organization Scholarship Office
P.O. Box 68960
Indianapolis, IN 46268-0960
Phone: 317-802-6099
Web: www.ffa.org/programs/grantsandscholarships/Scholarships/Pages/default.aspx

Casey's General Stores, Inc. Scholarship

Type of award: Scholarship.
Intended use: For full-time undergraduate study at 2-year or 4-year institution in United States.
Eligibility: Applicant must be no older than 22. Applicant must be residing in Wisconsin, Iowa, South Dakota, Minnesota, Kansas, Indiana, Nebraska, Illinois or Missouri.
Basis for selection: Major/career interest in agribusiness; wildlife/fisheries; agriculture; food production/management/services; engineering; economics; finance/banking or entomology. Applicant must demonstrate leadership.
Application requirements: High school ranking, GPA, ACT/SAT test scores.
Additional information: Other eligible majors include: agricultural farm/food service/landscape/nursery/ranch or wildlife management, communications, sales, marketing, mechanization, power & equipment, conservation, plant or soil science, agricultural computer systems, agricultural public service or general agriculture with career path in agriculture or agribusiness. Must be a member of FFA. Must have valid mailing address in the U.S. Must obtain FFA advisor's electronic approval on Signature Page. Apply online.

Amount of award:	$1,000
Number of awards:	3
Application deadline:	February 15

Contact:
National FFA Organization Scholarship Office
P.O. Box 68960
Indianapolis, IN 46268-0960
Phone: 317-802-6099
Web: www.ffa.org/programs/grantsandscholarships/Scholarships/Pages/default.aspx

Charles P. Lake - Rain For Rent Scholarship

Type of award: Scholarship.
Intended use: For full-time sophomore, junior or senior study at 4-year institution in United States.
Eligibility: Applicant must be no older than 22. Applicant must be residing in California, Idaho or Arizona.
Basis for selection: Major/career interest in agriculture; agribusiness or engineering, agricultural. Applicant must

demonstrate financial need, high academic achievement, leadership and service orientation.
Application requirements: High school ranking, GPA, SAT/ACT scores.
Additional information: Minimum 3.0 GPA. Those majoring in agriculture power and equipment or soil and water conservation also eligible. Preference given to those specializing in irrigation and soil technology. Must be a member of FFA. Must have valid mailing address in the U.S. Must obtain FFA advisor's electronic approval on Signature Page. Apply online.

Amount of award:	$1,000
Number of awards:	2
Application deadline:	February 15
Total amount awarded:	$2,000

Contact:
National FFA Organization Scholarship Office
P.O. Box 68960
Indianapolis, IN 46268-0960
Phone: 317-802-6099
Web: www.ffa.org/programs/grantsandscholarships/Scholarships/Pages/default.aspx

Chief Industries Scholarship

Type of award: Scholarship.
Intended use: For full-time undergraduate study at 4-year institution in United States.
Eligibility: Applicant must be no older than 22. Applicant must be residing in Nebraska or Indiana.
Basis for selection: Major/career interest in agriculture.
Application requirements: High school ranking, GPA, SAT/ACT scores.
Additional information: Must be a member of FFA. Must have valid mailing address in the U.S. Must obtain FFA advisor's electronic approval on Signature Page. Apply online.

Amount of award:	$1,000
Number of awards:	1
Application deadline:	February 15

Contact:
National FFA Organization Scholarship Office
P.O. Box 68960
Indianapolis, IN 46268-0960
Phone: 317-802-6099
Web: www.ffa.org/programs/grantsandscholarships/Scholarships/Pages/default.aspx

Church & Dwight Company, Inc. Scholarship

Type of award: Scholarship.
Intended use: For full-time undergraduate study at 4-year institution in United States.
Eligibility: Applicant must be no older than 22. Applicant must be U.S. citizen.
Basis for selection: Major/career interest in animal sciences; dairy; agribusiness; engineering, agricultural or agriculture. Applicant must demonstrate high academic achievement.
Application requirements: High school ranking, GPA, SAT/ACT scores.
Additional information: Preference given to applicants with a demonstrated interest in a dairy-related career. Must be a member of FFA. Minimum 3.0 GPA. Must have valid mailing address in the U.S. Must obtain FFA advisor's electronic approval on Signature Page. Apply online.

Amount of award:	$1,000
Number of awards:	3
Application deadline:	February 15
Total amount awarded:	$3,000

Contact:
National FFA Organization Scholarship Office
P.O. Box 68960
Indianapolis, IN 46268-0960
Phone: 317-802-6099
Web: www.ffa.org/programs/grantsandscholarships/Scholarships/Pages/default.aspx

CNH Capital Scholarship

Type of award: Scholarship.
Intended use: For full-time undergraduate study at 4-year institution in United States. Designated institutions: Penn State University, Purdue University, University of Illinois at Urbana-Champaign, or University of Wisconsin-Madison.
Eligibility: Applicant must be no older than 22.
Basis for selection: Major/career interest in agribusiness; agriculture; agricultural economics; education; journalism; public relations; business; economics; finance/banking or marketing. Applicant must demonstrate high academic achievement, leadership and service orientation.
Application requirements: High school ranking, GPA, SAT/ACT scores.
Additional information: Must be a member of FFA. Must have valid mailing address in the U.S. Must obtain FFA advisor's electronic approval on Signature Page. Minimum 3.5 GPA. Other majors also eligible. Apply online.

Amount of award:	$8,000
Number of awards:	4
Application deadline:	February 15

Contact:
National FFA Organization Scholarship Office
P.O. Box 68960
Indianapolis, IN 46268-0960
Phone: 317-802-6099
Web: www.ffa.org/programs/grantsandscholarships/Scholarships/Pages/default.aspx

Cooperative Resources International Scholarship

Type of award: Scholarship.
Intended use: For full-time undergraduate study at 4-year institution in United States.
Eligibility: Applicant must be no older than 22.
Basis for selection: Major/career interest in animal sciences; dairy; agricultural education; journalism; public relations; marketing or veterinary medicine.
Application requirements: High school ranking, GPA, ACT/SAT test scores.
Additional information: Must be a member of FFA. Must have valid mailing address in the U.S. Must obtain FFA advisor's electronic approval on Signature Page. Apply online.

Amount of award:	$1,000
Number of awards:	2
Application deadline:	February 15

Contact:
National FFA Organization Scholarship Office
P.O. Box 68960
Indianapolis, IN 46268-0960
Phone: 317-802-6099 317-802-6099
Web: www.ffa.org/programs/grantsandscholarships/Scholarships/Pages/default.aspx

CSX Scholarship

Type of award: Scholarship, renewable.
Intended use: For full-time undergraduate study at 4-year institution in United States.
Eligibility: Applicant must be no older than 22. Applicant must be residing in Ohio, New York, Tennessee, South Carolina, Georgia, Florida, West Virginia, Illinois, Kentucky or Missouri.
Basis for selection: Major/career interest in agriculture; agribusiness; agricultural economics; communications or transportation. Applicant must demonstrate high academic achievement and leadership.
Application requirements: High school ranking, GPA, ACT/SAT test scores.
Additional information: Minimum 3.0 GPA. Award is renewable if minimum 3.0 GPA is maintained. Must be a member of FFA. Must have valid mailing address in the U.S. Must obtain FFA advisor's electronic approval on Signature Page. Apply online.

Amount of award:	$1,000
Number of awards:	10
Application deadline:	February 15

Contact:
National FFA Organization Scholarship Office
P.O. Box 68960
Indianapolis, IN 46268-0960
Phone: 317-802-6099
Web: www.ffa.org/programs/grantsandscholarships/Scholarships/Pages/default.aspx

Darling International, Inc. Scholarship

Type of award: Scholarship.
Intended use: For full-time undergraduate study at 4-year institution in United States. Designated institutions: Land grant colleges in Colorado, Illinois, Indiana, Iowa, Kansas, Nebraska, Wisconsin.
Eligibility: Applicant must be no older than 22.
Basis for selection: Major/career interest in agribusiness or agriculture.
Application requirements: High school ranking, GPA, ACT/SAT test scores.
Additional information: Must be a member of FFA. Must have valid mailing address in the U.S. Must obtain FFA advisor's electronic approval on Signature Page. Apply online.

Amount of award:	$2,000
Number of awards:	1
Application deadline:	February 15

Contact:
National FFA Organization Scholarship Office
P.O. Box 68960
Indianapolis, IN 46268-0960
Phone: 317-802-6099
Web: www.ffa.org/programs/grantsandscholarships/Scholarships/Pages/default.aspx

Dean Foods Company Scholarship

Type of award: Scholarship.
Intended use: For full-time undergraduate study at 4-year institution in United States.
Eligibility: Applicant must be no older than 22.
Basis for selection: Major/career interest in dairy; agriculture; food science/technology or veterinary medicine. Applicant must demonstrate financial need, leadership and service orientation.
Application requirements: High school ranking, GPA, SAT/ACT scores.
Additional information: Open to FFA members and non-members. Must have valid mailing address in the U.S. Other majors also eligible. Apply online.

Amount of award:	$1,000
Number of awards:	18
Application deadline:	February 15

Contact:
National FFA Organization Scholarship Office
P.O. Box 68960
Indianapolis, IN 46268-0960
Phone: 317-802-6099
Web: www.ffa.org/programs/grantsandscholarships/Scholarships/Pages/default.aspx

Dupont Pioneer Scholarships

Type of award: Scholarship.
Intended use: For full-time undergraduate study at 2-year or 4-year institution in United States.
Eligibility: Applicant must be no older than 22.
Basis for selection: Major/career interest in agribusiness; agricultural economics; agriculture or entomology.
Application requirements: High school ranking, GPA, ACT/SAT test scores.
Additional information: Minimum 3.0 GPA. Other eligible majors include: agronomy; crop, plant or soil science; farm and ranch management; horticulture; general agriculture/agricultural sciences; sustainable agriculture, agricultural communications, journalism, extension or public relations; agricultural business management, economics, finance, policy and management, systems management or international agriculture; sales and marketing; agricultural engineering, mechanization, power and equipment; Agriscience technician; biochemistry; biotechnology; plant breeding and genetics and plant pathology. Must be a member of FFA. Must have valid mailing address in the U.S. Must obtain FFA advisor's electronic approval on Signature Page. Apply online.

Amount of award:	$1,500
Number of awards:	10
Application deadline:	February 15

Contact:
National FFA Organization Scholarship Office
P.O. Box 68960
Indianapolis, IN 46268-0960
Phone: 317-802-6099
Web: www.ffa.org/programs/grantsandscholarships/Scholarships/Pages/default.aspx

Earl R. Sorensen Memorial Scholarships

Type of award: Scholarship.
Intended use: For full-time undergraduate study at 4-year institution in United States.
Eligibility: Applicant must be no older than 22. Applicant must be residing in Michigan or Iowa.
Basis for selection: Major/career interest in agriculture. Applicant must demonstrate service orientation.
Application requirements: High school ranking, GPA, SAT/ACT scores.
Additional information: Must not be pursuing degree in area of food service, parks and recreation studies or dietetics. Must be a member of FFA. Must have valid mailing address in the U.S. Must obtain FFA advisor's electronic approval on Signature Page. Apply online.

Amount of award: $1,000
Number of awards: 2
Application deadline: February 15
Total amount awarded: $2,000

Contact:
National FFA Organization Scholarship Office
P.O. Box 68960
Indianapolis, IN 46268-0960
Phone: 317-802-6099
Web: www.ffa.org/programs/grantsandscholarships/Scholarships/Pages/default.aspx

Farm Credit Services of Mid-America Scholarship

Type of award: Scholarship.
Intended use: For full-time undergraduate study at 4-year institution in United States.
Eligibility: Applicant must be no older than 22. Applicant must be residing in Ohio or Kentucky.
Basis for selection: Major/career interest in agribusiness; economics; finance/banking or accounting.
Application requirements: High school ranking, GPA, SAT/ACT scores.
Additional information: Must be a member of FFA. Must have valid mailing address in the U.S. Must obtain FFA advisor's electronic approval on Signature Page. Apply online.

Amount of award: $2,000
Number of awards: 2
Application deadline: February 15
Total amount awarded: $4,000

Contact:
National FFA Organization Scholarship Office
P.O. Box 68960
Indianapolis, IN 46268-0960
Phone: 317-802-6099
Web: www.ffa.org/programs/grantsandscholarships/Scholarships/Pages/default.aspx

Farmers Mutual Hail Insurance Company of Iowa Scholarship

Type of award: Scholarship.
Intended use: For full-time undergraduate study at 2-year or 4-year institution in United States.
Eligibility: Applicant must be no older than 22. Applicant must be residing in Iowa, Wisconsin, Michigan, South Dakota, Ohio, Minnesota, Arkansas, Kansas, Oklahoma, Nebraska, Indiana, Colorado, Illinois, Missouri or North Dakota.
Basis for selection: Major/career interest in agribusiness; agriculture or agricultural economics. Applicant must demonstrate high academic achievement.
Application requirements: High school ranking, GPA, SAT/ACT scores.
Additional information: Must be a member of FFA. One scholarship will be awarded to resident of Arkansas, Colorado, Illinois, Indiana, Kansas, Michigan, Minnesota, Missouri, North Dakota, Ohio, Oklahoma, South Dakota, and Wisconsin. Two scholarships will be awarded to residents of Iowa and Nebraska. Must have valid mailing address in the U.S. Must obtain FFA advisor's electronic approval on Signature Page. Minimum 2.5 GPA. Other majors also eligible. Apply online.

Amount of award: $1,500
Number of awards: 17
Application deadline: February 15

Contact:
National FFA Organization Scholarship Office
P.O. Box 68960
Indianapolis, IN 46268-0960
Phone: 317-802-6099
Web: www.ffa.org/programs/grantsandscholarships/Scholarships/Pages/default.aspx

Fastline Publications Scholarship

Type of award: Scholarship.
Intended use: For full-time undergraduate study at vocational, 2-year or 4-year institution in United States.
Eligibility: Applicant must be no older than 22. Applicant must be residing in Wisconsin, South Dakota, New York, Ohio, Tennessee, Kansas, Louisiana, Virginia, Mississippi, Nebraska, Alabama, Illinois, Kentucky, Missouri, Iowa, Michigan, Minnesota, Texas, Arkansas, Pennsylvania, South Carolina, Georgia, Florida, Oklahoma, West Virginia, Oregon, Idaho, Indiana, North Carolina or North Dakota.
Basis for selection: Major/career interest in agribusiness.
Application requirements: High school ranking, GPA, ACT/SAT test scores.
Additional information: Other eligible majors include farm & ranch management, livestock management of agricultural sales and marketing. Must live on a family farm and demonstrate interest in managing a farm. Must be a member of FFA. Must have valid mailing address in the U.S. Must obtain FFA advisor's electronic approval on Signature Page. Apply online.

Amount of award: $1,000
Number of awards: 26
Application deadline: February 15

Contact:
National FFA Organization Scholarship Office
P.O. Box 68960
Indianapolis, IN 46268-0960
Phone: 317-802-6099
Web: www.ffa.org/programs/grantsandscholarships/Scholarships/Pages/default.aspx

Fifth Third Bank of Central Indiana Scholarship

Type of award: Scholarship.
Intended use: For full-time undergraduate study at 2-year or 4-year institution in United States. Designated institutions: Indiana institutions.
Eligibility: Applicant must be Alaskan native, Asian American, African American, Mexican American, Hispanic American, Puerto Rican, American Indian or Native Hawaiian/Pacific Islander. Applicant must be no older than 22. Applicant must be residing in Indiana.
Basis for selection: Applicant must demonstrate financial need, high academic achievement, leadership and service orientation.
Application requirements: High school ranking, GPA, ACT/SAT test scores.
Additional information: Minimum 3.0 GPA. Must be a resident of Adams, Allen, Bartholomew, Benton, Brown, Clay, Dearborn, Decatur, Fayette, Hamilton, Hancock, Hendricks, Johnson, Marion, Monroe, Morgan, Orange, Parke, Ripley, Shelby, Sullivan, Tippecanoe, Vermillion or Vigo counties in Indiana. Must be a member of FFA. Must have valid mailing address in the U.S. Must obtain FFA advisor's electronic approval on Signature Page. Apply online.

Amount of award: $1,000
Number of awards: 2
Application deadline: February 15

Contact:
National FFA Organization Scholarship Office
P.O. Box 68960
Indianapolis, IN 46268-0960
Phone: 317-802-6099
Web: www.ffa.org/programs/grantsandscholarships/Scholarships/Pages/default.aspx

Ford Fund and Ford Trucks Built Ford Tough FFA Scholarship Program

Type of award: Scholarship.
Intended use: For full-time undergraduate study at 2-year or 4-year institution in United States.
Eligibility: Applicant must be no older than 22.
Basis for selection: Applicant must demonstrate high academic achievement.
Application requirements: Essay. High school ranking, GPA, SAT/ACT scores.
Additional information: Must be FFA member. Must have a Ford dealer signature and dealer code on the required Signature Page. To find participating dealers, visit FFA Website. 500 scholarships available at $1,000 each awarded on behalf of participating Ford dealers. Five additional scholarships at $1,000 available to students without participating Ford Truck dealer in the area that obtain signature and dealer code from local Ford dealer. Must obtain FFA advisor's electronic approval on Signature Page. Signature Page must be mailed and postmarked by February 22. Must have a valid mailing address in the U.S. Apply online at www.ffa.org.

Amount of award:	$1,000
Number of awards:	505
Application deadline:	February 15
Notification begins:	May 7
Total amount awarded:	$505,000

Contact:
National FFA Organization Scholarship Office
P.O. Box 68960
Indianapolis, IN 46268-0960
Phone: 317-802-6099
Web: www.ffa.org/programs/grantsandscholarships/Scholarships/Pages/default.aspx

Foth Production Solutions, LLC Scholarship

Type of award: Scholarship.
Intended use: For full-time undergraduate study at 2-year or 4-year institution in United States.
Eligibility: Applicant must be no older than 22. Applicant must be residing in Wisconsin.
Basis for selection: Major/career interest in biochemistry; engineering, agricultural; computer/information sciences; engineering, environmental; food science/technology or biology. Applicant must demonstrate high academic achievement.
Application requirements: High school ranking, GPA, SAT/ACT scores.
Additional information: Must be a member of FFA. Must have valid mailing address in the U.S. Must obtain FFA advisor's electronic approval on Signature Page. Minimum 3.0 GPA. Other majors also eligible. Must be Wisconsin resident, preferably in following counties: Brown, Calumet, Dane, Dodge, Door, Kewaunee, Marinette, Oconto, or Outagamie. Preference given to applicants planning to attend University of Wisconsin-Madison, University of Wisconsin-Platteville, University of Wisconsin-Milwaukee School of Engineering, Madison Area Technical College, or Northeast Wisconsin Technical College. Apply online.

Amount of award:	$1,000
Number of awards:	2
Application deadline:	February 15

Contact:
National FFA Organization Scholarship Office
P.O. Box 68960
Indianapolis, IN 46268-0960
Phone: 317-802-6099
Web: www.ffa.org/programs/grantsandscholarships/Scholarships/Pages/default.aspx

Foundation for Environmental Agriculture Scholarship

Type of award: Scholarship.
Intended use: For full-time undergraduate study at postsecondary institution in United States.
Eligibility: Applicant must be no older than 22.
Basis for selection: Major/career interest in agriculture; agricultural education; agribusiness; entomology or food science/technology. Applicant must demonstrate high academic achievement, leadership and service orientation.
Application requirements: High school ranking, GPA, SAT/ACT scores.
Additional information: Non-members of FFA eligible. Must have valid mailing address in the U.S. Other majors also eligible. Minimum 2.75 GPA. Apply online.

Amount of award:	$1,000
Number of awards:	2
Application deadline:	February 15

Contact:
National FFA Organization Scholarship Office
P.O. Box 68960
Indianapolis, IN 46268-0960
Phone: 317-802-6099
Web: www.ffa.org/programs/grantsandscholarships/Scholarships/Pages/default.aspx

Hoard's Dairyman Scholarship

Type of award: Scholarship.
Intended use: For full-time undergraduate study at 4-year institution in United States.
Eligibility: Applicant must be no older than 22.
Basis for selection: Major/career interest in dairy or agriculture.
Application requirements: High school ranking, GPA, SAT/ACT scores.
Additional information: Must be a member of FFA. Must have valid mailing address in the U.S. Must obtain FFA advisor's electronic approval on Signature Page. Applicants must be pursuing a degree in dairy science or agricultural journalism. Preference given to applicants with agricultural communications emphasis. Apply online.

Amount of award:	$1,000
Number of awards:	1
Application deadline:	February 15

Contact:
National FFA Organization Scholarship Office
P.O. Box 68960
Indianapolis, IN 46268-0960
Phone: 317-802-6099
Web: www.ffa.org/programs/grantsandscholarships/Scholarships/Pages/default.aspx

Hormel Foods Corporation Scholarship

Type of award: Scholarship.
Intended use: For full-time undergraduate study at 4-year institution in United States.
Eligibility: Applicant must be no older than 22. Applicant must be residing in Wisconsin, Michigan, Iowa, South Dakota, Minnesota, Kansas, Indiana, Nebraska, Illinois, North Dakota or Missouri.
Basis for selection: Major/career interest in agriculture; animal sciences; business/management/administration; economics; food production/management/services; food science/technology or hospitality administration/management. Applicant must demonstrate high academic achievement and leadership.
Application requirements: High school ranking, GPA, SAT/ACT scores.
Additional information: Minimum 3.0 GPA. Agronomy, animal nutrition, agricultural communications, agriculture policy/systems management/sales/marketing/engineering, food packaging majors also eligible. Must be a member of FFA. Must have valid mailing address in the U.S. Must obtain FFA advisor's electronic approval on Signature Page. Apply online.

Amount of award:	$1,500
Number of awards:	6
Application deadline:	February 15
Total amount awarded:	$9,000

Contact:
National FFA Organization Scholarship Office
P.O. Box 68960
Indianapolis, IN 46268-0960
Phone: 317-802-6099
Web: www.ffa.org/programs/grantsandscholarships/Scholarships/Pages/default.aspx

ILC Resources Scholarship

Type of award: Scholarship.
Intended use: For full-time undergraduate study at 4-year institution in United States. Designated institutions: Iowa State University, University of Nebraska, University of Minnesota, University of Missouri, Kansas State University, University of Illinois (Urbana), or South Dakota State University.
Eligibility: Applicant must be no older than 22. Applicant must be residing in Iowa, South Dakota, Minnesota, Kansas, Nebraska, Illinois, North Dakota or Missouri.
Basis for selection: Major/career interest in animal sciences or dairy. Applicant must demonstrate high academic achievement.
Application requirements: High school ranking, GPA, SAT/ACT scores.
Additional information: Must be a member of FFA pursuing a degree in animal, dairy, or poultry science with a preference in poultry. Must have valid mailing address in the U.S. Must obtain FFA advisor's electronic approval on Signature Page. Minimum 2.75 GPA. Apply online.

Amount of award:	$1,500
Number of awards:	1
Application deadline:	February 15

Contact:
National FFA Organization Scholarship Office
P.O. Box 68960
Indianapolis, IN 46268-0960
Phone: 317-802-6099
Web: www.ffa.org/programs/grantsandscholarships/Scholarships/Pages/default.aspx

Iowa Interstate Railroad, Ltd. Scholarship

Type of award: Scholarship.
Intended use: For full-time undergraduate study at 4-year institution in United States. Designated institutions: Institutions in Iowa and Illinois.
Eligibility: Applicant must be no older than 22. Applicant must be residing in Iowa.
Basis for selection: Major/career interest in agriculture; agribusiness or agricultural economics. Applicant must demonstrate high academic achievement.
Application requirements: High school ranking, GPA, SAT/ACT scores.
Additional information: Open to FFA members and non-members. Must have valid mailing address in the U.S. Other majors also eligible. Preference given to applicants with expressed interest in transportation. Minimum 3.0 GPA. Apply online.

Amount of award:	$1,000
Number of awards:	1
Application deadline:	February 15

Contact:
National FFA Organization Scholarship Office
P.O. Box 68960
Indianapolis, IN 46268-0960
Phone: 317-802-6099
Web: www.ffa.org/programs/grantsandscholarships/Scholarships/Pages/default.aspx

Irrigation Foundation Scholarship

Type of award: Scholarship.
Intended use: For full-time undergraduate study at 4-year institution in United States.
Eligibility: Applicant must be no older than 22.
Basis for selection: Major/career interest in horticulture; landscape architecture; agriculture; natural resources/conservation or agricultural education. Applicant must demonstrate high academic achievement.
Application requirements: High school ranking, GPA, SAT/ACT scores.
Additional information: Must be a member of FFA with an interest in irrigation. Must have valid mailing address in the U.S. Must obtain FFA advisor's electronic approval on Signature Page. Minimum 3.5 GPA. Other majors also eligible. Apply online.

Amount of award:	$1,000
Number of awards:	1
Application deadline:	February 15

Contact:
National FFA Organization Scholarship Office
P.O. Box 68960
Indianapolis, IN 46268-0960
Phone: 317-802-6099
Web: www.ffa.org/programs/grantsandscholarships/Scholarships/Pages/default.aspx

John and Amy Rakestraw Scholarship

Type of award: Scholarship.
Intended use: For full-time undergraduate study at 2-year or 4-year institution in United States.
Eligibility: Applicant must be no older than 22. Applicant must be residing in Mississippi or Colorado.

Scholarships

Basis for selection: Major/career interest in agriculture. Applicant must demonstrate leadership and service orientation.
Application requirements: High school ranking, GPA, SAT/ACT scores.
Additional information: Must have preference in animal nutrition, animal science, farm/livestock or ranch management. Must be involved in beef cattle. Must be a member of FFA. Must have valid mailing address in the U.S. Must obtain FFA advisor's electronic approval on Signature Page. Apply online.

Amount of award:	$1,000
Number of awards:	2
Application deadline:	February 15
Total amount awarded:	$2,000

Contact:
National FFA Organization Scholarship Office
P.O. Box 68960
Indianapolis, IN 46268-0960
Phone: 317-802-6099
Web: www.ffa.org/programs/grantsandscholarships/Scholarships/Pages/default.aspx

KenAG Scholarship

Type of award: Scholarship.
Intended use: For full-time undergraduate study at 4-year institution in United States.
Eligibility: Applicant must be no older than 22.
Basis for selection: Major/career interest in dairy.
Application requirements: High school ranking, GPA, SAT/ACT scores.
Additional information: Must be a member of FFA and pursuing a degree in dairy science. Must have valid mailing address in the U.S. Must obtain FFA advisor's electronic approval on Signature Page. Other majors also eligible. Apply online.

Amount of award:	$1,000
Number of awards:	1
Application deadline:	February 15

Contact:
National FFA Organization Scholarship Office
P.O. Box 68960
Indianapolis, IN 46268-0960
Phone: 317-802-6099
Web: www.ffa.org/programs/grantsandscholarships/Scholarships/Pages/default.aspx

Kent Nutrition Group, Inc. Scholarship

Type of award: Scholarship.
Intended use: For full-time undergraduate study at 4-year institution in United States. Designated institutions: Eligible institutions in Connecticut, Delaware, Illinois, Indiana, Iowa, Kansas, Kentucky, Maine, Maryland, Massachusetts, Michigan, Missouri, Nebraska, New Hampshire, New Jersey, New York, Ohio, Pennsylvania, Rhode Island, Vermont, Virginia, or West Virginia.
Eligibility: Applicant must be no older than 22. Applicant must be residing in Ohio, New York, Delaware, Kansas, Massachusetts, Virginia, Connecticut, Nebraska, Illinois, Kentucky, Missouri, Vermont, Iowa, Michigan, Maine, Maryland, Pennsylvania, New Hampshire, West Virginia, Indiana, New Jersey or Rhode Island.
Basis for selection: Major/career interest in animal sciences; dairy; agriculture or agribusiness.
Application requirements: High school ranking, GPA, SAT/ACT scores.
Additional information: Must be a member of FFA. Must have valid mailing address in the U.S. Must obtain FFA advisor's electronic approval on Signature Page. Other majors also eligible. Apply online.

Amount of award:	$1,000
Number of awards:	2
Application deadline:	February 15

Contact:
National FFA Organization Scholarship Office
P.O. Box 68960
Indianapolis, IN 46268-0960
Phone: 317-802-6099
Web: www.ffa.org/programs/grantsandscholarships/Scholarships/Pages/default.aspx

KeyBank Scholarship

Type of award: Scholarship.
Intended use: For full-time undergraduate study at accredited 2-year or 4-year institution in United States. Designated institutions: Idaho institutions.
Eligibility: Applicant must be no older than 22. Applicant must be residing in Idaho.
Basis for selection: Major/career interest in agriculture; communications; education; finance/banking; engineering; marketing; science, general; agricultural economics or business/management/administration. Applicant must demonstrate financial need and service orientation.
Application requirements: High school ranking, GPA, SAT/ACT scores.
Additional information: Must be a resident of Bannock, Bingham, Bonneville, Cassia, Fremont, Madison, Minidoka, Power, Teton, or Twin Falls counties in Idaho. Must be a member of FFA. Must have valid mailing address in the U.S. Must obtain FFA advisor's electronic approval on Signature Page. Apply online.

Amount of award:	$1,000
Number of awards:	1
Application deadline:	February 15

Contact:
National FFA Organization Scholarship Office
P.O. Box 68960
Indianapolis, IN 46268-0960
Phone: 317-802-6099
Web: www.ffa.org/programs/grantsandscholarships/Scholarships/Pages/default.aspx

Kikkoman Foods, Inc. Scholarship

Type of award: Scholarship.
Intended use: For full-time undergraduate study at 2-year or 4-year institution in United States. Designated institutions: Wisconsin institutions.
Eligibility: Applicant must be no older than 22. Applicant must be residing in Wisconsin.
Basis for selection: Major/career interest in agribusiness; food science/technology; dietetics/nutrition or food production/management/services.
Application requirements: High school ranking, GPA, SAT/ACT scores.
Additional information: Must be a member of FFA. Must have valid mailing address in the U.S. Must obtain FFA advisor's electronic approval on Signature Page. Other majors also eligible. Apply online.

Amount of award:	$1,000
Number of awards:	1
Application deadline:	February 15

Contact:
National FFA Organization Scholarship Office
P.O. Box 68960
Indianapolis, IN 46268-0960
Phone: 317-802-6099
Web: www.ffa.org/programs/grantsandscholarships/Scholarships/Pages/default.aspx

King Ranch Scholarship

Type of award: Scholarship.
Intended use: For full-time undergraduate study at 4-year institution in United States. Designated institutions: Texas A&M University-Kingsville, Texas Tech University, Texas A&M University-College Station, or University of Florida.
Eligibility: Applicant must be no older than 22.
Basis for selection: Major/career interest in agriculture or wildlife/fisheries. Applicant must demonstrate high academic achievement, leadership and service orientation.
Application requirements: High school ranking, GPA, SAT/ACT scores.
Additional information: Must be a member of FFA. For students pursuing a degree in agronomy, animal/crop or range science, or wildlife management. Preference given to residents of Texas, Florida, or New Mexico. Minimum 2.8 GPA. Must have valid mailing address in the U.S. Must obtain FFA advisor's electronic approval on Signature Page. Other majors also eligible. Apply online.

Amount of award:	$1,000
Number of awards:	1
Application deadline:	February 15

Contact:
National FFA Organization Scholarship Office
P.O. Box 68960
Indianapolis, IN 46268-0960
Phone: 317-802-6099
Web: www.ffa.org/programs/grantsandscholarships/Scholarships/Pages/default.aspx

Kohler Company Scholarship

Type of award: Scholarship.
Intended use: For full-time undergraduate study at vocational or 4-year institution in United States.
Eligibility: Applicant must be no older than 22.
Basis for selection: Major/career interest in turf management. Applicant must demonstrate high academic achievement and leadership.
Application requirements: High school ranking, GPA, ACT/SAT test scores.
Additional information: Minimum 3.0 GPA. Three scholarships for FFA members pursuing degree/certification in turf management, agriculture power and equipment or diesel mechanics. Two scholarships for FFA or non-FFA members pursuing degree/certification in diesel mechanics or agriculture power and equipment. Must have valid mailing address in the U.S. Must obtain FFA advisor's electronic approval on Signature Page. Apply online.

Amount of award:	$1,000
Number of awards:	5
Application deadline:	February 15

Contact:
National FFA Organization Scholarship Office
P.O. Box 68960
Indianapolis, IN 46268-0960
Phone: 317-802-6099
Web: www.ffa.org/programs/grantsandscholarships/Scholarships/Pages/default.aspx

Mahindra USA Women in Ag Scholarship

Type of award: Scholarship.
Intended use: For full-time undergraduate study at 2-year or 4-year institution in United States.
Eligibility: Applicant must be female, no older than 22. Applicant must be residing in Ohio, Tennessee, Kansas, Massachusetts, Louisiana, Connecticut, Mississippi, Kentucky, Michigan, Iowa, South Carolina, Florida, Oregon, New Jersey, Wisconsin, New York, Nevada, California, Virginia, Illinois, Alabama, Missouri, Vermont, Utah, Texas, Maine, Arkansas, Washington, Maryland, Arizona, Pennsylvania, Georgia, Oklahoma, New Hampshire, West Virginia, Idaho, New Mexico or North Carolina.
Basis for selection: Major/career interest in agriculture. Applicant must demonstrate financial need, high academic achievement, leadership and service orientation.
Application requirements: Essay. High school ranking, GPA, SAT/ACT scores.
Additional information: Must be member of FFA. Minimum 3.0 GPA. Food service, packaging, biosciences and/or technology, engineering, marine biology, natural resource management, parks and recreation studies, public service, and dietetics majors not eligible. Must have valid mailing address in the U.S. Must obtain FFA advisor's electronic approval on Signature Page. Signature Page must be mailed and postmarked by February 22. Apply online at www.ffa.org.

Amount of award:	$2,500
Number of awards:	4
Application deadline:	February 15
Notification begins:	May 7
Total amount awarded:	$10,000

Contact:
National FFA Organization Scholarship Office
P.O. Box 68960
Indianapolis, IN 46268-0960
Phone: 317-802-6099
Web: www.ffa.org/programs/grantsandscholarships/Scholarships/Pages/default.aspx

MetLife Foundation Scholarship

Type of award: Scholarship.
Intended use: For full-time undergraduate study at 4-year institution in United States.
Eligibility: Applicant must be no older than 22. Applicant must be residing in Wisconsin, South Dakota, Ohio, Tennessee, Kansas, Louisiana, California, Mississippi, Montana, Nebraska, Kentucky, Alabama, Illinois, Missouri, Iowa, Michigan, Texas, Minnesota, Arkansas, Washington, South Carolina, Florida, Georgia, Wyoming, Oklahoma, Idaho, Indiana, North Carolina, Colorado or North Dakota.
Basis for selection: Major/career interest in agribusiness; agriculture; communications; education; journalism; public relations; finance/banking; economics; marketing or engineering.
Application requirements: High school ranking, GPA, SAT/ACT scores.
Additional information: Must be a member of FFA. Must have valid mailing address in the U.S. Must obtain FFA advisor's electronic approval on Signature Page. Other majors also eligible. Apply online.

Amount of award:	$2,000
Number of awards:	10
Application deadline:	February 15

Contact:
National FFA Organization Scholarship Office
P.O. Box 68960
Indianapolis, IN 46268-0960
Phone: 317-802-6099
Web: www.ffa.org/programs/grantsandscholarships/Scholarships/Pages/default.aspx

Mills Fleet Farm Scholarship

Type of award: Scholarship.
Intended use: For full-time undergraduate study at 2-year or 4-year institution in United States.
Eligibility: Applicant must be no older than 22. Applicant must be residing in Iowa, Wisconsin, Minnesota or North Dakota.
Basis for selection: Major/career interest in agriculture; agribusiness; business/management/administration or engineering. Applicant must demonstrate high academic achievement.
Application requirements: High school ranking, GPA, ACT/SAT test scores.
Additional information: Minimum 3.0 GPA. Other eligible majors include: agricultural sciences, breeding, genetics, pathology, biotechnology. Visit Website for full listing of eligible counties of residence. Must be a member of FFA. Must have valid mailing address in the U.S. Must obtain FFA advisor's electronic approval on Signature Page. Apply online.

Amount of award:	$1,000
Number of awards:	6
Application deadline:	February 15

Contact:
National FFA Organization Scholarship Office
P.O. Box 68960
Indianapolis, IN 46268-0960
Phone: 317-802-6099
Web: www.ffa.org/programs/grantsandscholarships/Scholarships/Pages/default.aspx

NAPA Auto Parts Scholarship

Type of award: Scholarship.
Intended use: For full-time undergraduate study at 2-year or 4-year institution in United States.
Eligibility: Applicant must be no older than 22.
Basis for selection: Major/career interest in agribusiness; agricultural economics or agriculture.
Application requirements: High school ranking, GPA, SAT/ACT scores.
Additional information: Must be a member of FFA. Must have valid mailing address in the U.S. Must obtain FFA advisor's electronic approval on Signature Page. Preference given to applicants with interest in agricultural parts/aftermarket. Other majors also eligible. Apply online.

Amount of award:	$1,000
Number of awards:	18
Application deadline:	February 15

Contact:
National FFA Organization Scholarship Office
P.O. Box 68960
Indianapolis, IN 46268-0960
Phone: 317-802-6099
Web: www.ffa.org/programs/grantsandscholarships/Scholarships/Pages/default.aspx

The National FFA Alumni Association Scholarship

Type of award: Scholarship.
Intended use: For full-time undergraduate study at 4-year institution in United States.
Eligibility: Applicant must be no older than 22.
Basis for selection: Major/career interest in agricultural education.
Application requirements: High school ranking, GPA, SAT/ACT scores.
Additional information: Must be an alumni member or from an FFA chapter with an active alumni affiliate. Must be planning career as an agriculture teacher. Must be a member of FFA. Must have valid mailing address in the U.S. Must obtain FFA advisor's electronic approval on Signature Page. Apply online.

Amount of award:	$1,000
Number of awards:	1
Application deadline:	February 15

Contact:
National FFA Organization Scholarship Office
P.O. Box 68960
Indianapolis, IN 46268-0960
Phone: 317-802-6099
Web: www.ffa.org/programs/grantsandscholarships/Scholarships/Pages/default.aspx

The National FFA Scholarship Funded by National FFA Staff, Board and Individual Contributors

Type of award: Scholarship.
Intended use: For full-time undergraduate study at 4-year institution in United States.
Eligibility: Applicant must be no older than 22.
Basis for selection: Major/career interest in agricultural education.
Application requirements: High school ranking, GPA, SAT/ACT scores.
Additional information: Must be a member of FFA. Must have valid mailing address in the U.S. Must obtain FFA advisor's electronic approval on Signature Page. Apply online.

Amount of award:	$1,000
Number of awards:	1
Application deadline:	February 15

Contact:
National FFA Organization Scholarship Office
P.O. Box 68960
Indianapolis, IN 46268-0960
Phone: 317-802-6099
Web: www.ffa.org/programs/grantsandscholarships/Scholarships/Pages/default.aspx

National Mastis Council Scholarship

Type of award: Scholarship.
Intended use: For full-time undergraduate study at 2-year or 4-year institution in United States.
Eligibility: Applicant must be no older than 22.
Basis for selection: Major/career interest in animal sciences; dairy; education; journalism; marketing or veterinary medicine. Applicant must demonstrate service orientation.
Application requirements: High school ranking, GPA, ACT/SAT test scores.

Additional information: Available for FFA and non-FFA members. Must have a dairy background or plan to pursue a career related to dairy and have participated in community service. Must have valid mailing address in the U.S. Apply online.

Amount of award: $1,000
Number of awards: 1
Application deadline: February 15

Contact:
National FFA Organization Scholarship Office
P.O. Box 68960
Indianapolis, IN 46268-0960
Phone: 317-802-6099
Web: www.ffa.org/programs/grantsandscholarships/Scholarships/Pages/default.aspx

National Wild Turkey Federation Scholarship

Type of award: Scholarship.
Intended use: For full-time undergraduate study at 2-year or 4-year institution in United States.
Eligibility: Applicant must be no older than 22.
Basis for selection: Major/career interest in wildlife/fisheries. Applicant must demonstrate financial need, high academic achievement, leadership and service orientation.
Application requirements: High school ranking, GPA, SAT/ACT scores.
Additional information: Minimum 3.0 GPA. Must be pursuing degree in wildlife management. Must support preservation of the hunting tradition, demonstrate a commitment to conservation, actively participate in hunting sports, and have work or volunteer-related experience in the hunting sport. Must be a member of FFA. Must have valid mailing address in the U.S. Must obtain FFA advisor's electronic approval on Signature Page. Apply online.

Amount of award: $5,000
Number of awards: 1
Application deadline: February 15

Contact:
National FFA Organization Scholarship Office
P.O. Box 68960
Indianapolis, IN 46268-0960
Phone: 317-802-6099
Web: www.ffa.org/programs/grantsandscholarships/Scholarships/Pages/default.aspx

Norfolk Southern Foundation Scholarship

Type of award: Scholarship.
Intended use: For full-time undergraduate study at 4-year institution in United States. Designated institutions: Institutions in Alabama, Delaware, Georgia, Illinois, Indiana, Louisiana, Maryland, Michigan, Mississippi, Missouri, New York, North Carolina, Ohio, Pennsylvania, South Carolina, Tennessee, and Virginia.
Eligibility: Applicant must be no older than 22.
Basis for selection: Major/career interest in agriculture; communications; forestry; education; business/management/administration; finance/banking; marketing; science, general or engineering.
Application requirements: High school ranking, GPA, SAT/ACT scores.
Additional information: Must be a member of FFA. Must have valid mailing address in the U.S. Must obtain FFA advisor's electronic approval on Signature Page. Apply online.

Amount of award: $1,000
Number of awards: 3
Application deadline: February 15
Total amount awarded: $3,000

Contact:
National FFA Organization Scholarship Office
P.O. Box 68960
Indianapolis, IN 46268-0960
Phone: 317-802-6099
Web: www.ffa.org/programs/grantsandscholarships/Scholarships/Pages/default.aspx

Paradise Tomato Kitchens Scholarship

Type of award: Scholarship.
Intended use: For full-time undergraduate study at 4-year institution in United States. Designated institutions: Institutions in Indiana, Kentucky, or Ohio.
Eligibility: Applicant must be no older than 22. Applicant must be residing in Ohio, Indiana or Kentucky.
Basis for selection: Major/career interest in food science/technology. Applicant must demonstrate leadership.
Application requirements: High school ranking, GPA, ACT/SAT test scores.
Additional information: Preference given to applicants competing in state or national FFA sponsored events. Must be a member of FFA. Must have valid mailing address in the U.S. Must obtain FFA advisor's electronic approval on Signature Page. Apply online.

Amount of award: $2,000
Number of awards: 3
Application deadline: February 15

Contact:
National FFA Organization Scholarship Office
P.O. Box 68960
Indianapolis, IN 46268-0960
Phone: 317-802-6099
Web: www.ffa.org/programs/grantsandscholarships/Scholarships/Pages/default.aspx

Penton Media Scholarship

Type of award: Scholarship.
Intended use: For full-time undergraduate study at 4-year institution in United States.
Eligibility: Applicant must be no older than 22.
Basis for selection: Major/career interest in agriculture; communications; journalism or marketing. Applicant must demonstrate financial need.
Application requirements: High school ranking, GPA, SAT/ACT scores.
Additional information: Must live on a family-owned farm. Minimum 50% of family income must come from production agriculture. Must be a member of FFA. Must have valid mailing address in the U.S. Must obtain FFA advisor's electronic approval on Signature Page. Apply online.

Amount of award: $1,000
Number of awards: 1
Application deadline: February 15

Contact:
National FFA Organization Scholarship Office
P.O. Box 68960
Indianapolis, IN 46268-0960
Phone: 317-802-6099
Web: www.ffa.org/programs/grantsandscholarships/Scholarships/Pages/default.aspx

Pepsi-Cola Bottling of Eastern Oregon Scholarship

Type of award: Scholarship.
Intended use: For full-time undergraduate study at 2-year or 4-year institution in United States.
Eligibility: Applicant must be no older than 22. Applicant must be residing in Oregon.
Basis for selection: Applicant must demonstrate high academic achievement and service orientation.
Application requirements: High school ranking, GPA, ACT/SAT test scores.
Additional information: Minimum 3.5 GPA. Must not be pursuing major in agricultural education, hospitality, or other non-ag related majors. Must be a resident of Baker, Malhuer, Union, or Wallowa counties in Oregon. Must be a member of FFA. Must have valid mailing address in the U.S. Must obtain FFA advisor's electronic approval on Signature Page. Apply online.

Amount of award:	$1,000
Number of awards:	1
Application deadline:	February 15

Contact:
National FFA Organization Scholarship Office
P.O. Box 68960
Indianapolis, IN 46268-0960
Phone: 317-802-6099
Web: www.ffa.org/programs/grantsandscholarships/Scholarships/Pages/default.aspx

Peterson Family Scholarship

Type of award: Scholarship.
Intended use: For full-time undergraduate study at 4-year institution in United States.
Eligibility: Applicant must be no older than 22. Applicant must be residing in Montana.
Basis for selection: Major/career interest in agriculture; communications; education; business/management/administration; finance/banking; marketing; science, general or engineering.
Application requirements: High school ranking, GPA, SAT/ACT scores.
Additional information: Must be a member of the Shields Valley FFA chapter (MT0017). Must be a member of FFA. Must have valid mailing address in the U.S. Must obtain FFA advisor's electronic approval on Signature Page. Apply online.

Amount of award:	$1,000
Number of awards:	1
Application deadline:	February 15

Contact:
National FFA Organization Scholarship Office
P.O. Box 68960
Indianapolis, IN 46268-0960
Phone: 317-802-6099
Web: www.ffa.org/programs/grantsandscholarships/Scholarships/Pages/default.aspx

PLANET Academic Excellence Foundation Scholarship

Type of award: Scholarship.
Intended use: For full-time undergraduate study at 2-year or 4-year institution in United States.
Eligibility: Applicant must be no older than 22.
Basis for selection: Major/career interest in horticulture; landscape architecture; environmental science or turf management. Applicant must demonstrate leadership and service orientation.
Application requirements: High school ranking, GPA, SAT/ACT scores.
Additional information: Must be a member of FFA. Must have valid mailing address in the U.S. Must obtain FFA advisor's electronic approval on Signature Page. Other majors also eligible. Apply online.

Amount of award:	$1,500
Number of awards:	1
Application deadline:	February 15

Contact:
National FFA Organization Scholarship Office
P.O. Box 68960
Indianapolis, IN 46268-0960
Phone: 317-802-6099
Web: www.ffa.org/programs/grantsandscholarships/Scholarships/Pages/default.aspx

Rabo Agrifinance Scholarship

Type of award: Scholarship.
Intended use: For full-time undergraduate study at 2-year or 4-year institution in United States.
Eligibility: Applicant must be no older than 22.
Basis for selection: Major/career interest in agriculture; communications; education; business/management/administration; science, general or technology. Applicant must demonstrate high academic achievement and leadership.
Application requirements: High school ranking, GPA, ACT/SAT test scores.
Additional information: Minimum 3.0 GPA. Must be in top 50% of class. Preference given to applicants whose families are Rabo AgriFinance customers residing within the contiguous 48 states excluding California. Must live on family farm with interest in farm management. Must be a member of FFA. Must have valid mailing address in the U.S. Must obtain FFA advisor's electronic approval on Signature Page. Apply online.

Amount of award:	$3,500
Number of awards:	8
Application deadline:	February 15

Contact:
National FFA Organization Scholarship Office
P.O. Box 68960
Indianapolis, IN 46268-0960
Phone: 317-802-6099
Web: www.ffa.org/programs/grantsandscholarships/Scholarships/Pages/default.aspx

Ram Trucks Scholarship

Type of award: Scholarship.
Intended use: For full-time undergraduate study at 2-year or 4-year institution in United States.
Eligibility: Applicant must be no older than 22.
Basis for selection: Applicant must demonstrate financial need and high academic achievement.
Application requirements: Essay. High school ranking, GPA, SAT/ACT scores.
Additional information: Must be FFA member. Must have documented a strong supervised agricultural experience program (SAE). Must have valid mailing address in the U.S. Must obtain FFA advisor's electronic approval on Signature Page. Signature Page must be mailed and postmarked by February 22. Apply online.

Amount of award: $1,000-$2,500
Number of awards: 82
Application deadline: February 15
Notification begins: May 7
Total amount awarded: $50,000

Contact:
National FFA Organization Scholarship Office
P.O. Box 68960
Indianapolis, IN 46268-0960
Phone: 317-802-6099
Web: www.ffa.org/programs/grantsandscholarships/Scholarships/Pages/default.aspx

Red Barn Media Group Scholarship

Type of award: Scholarship.
Intended use: For full-time undergraduate study at postsecondary institution in United States.
Eligibility: Applicant must be no older than 22.
Application requirements: High school ranking, GPA, ACT/SAT test scores.
Additional information: Must be a member of FFA. Must have valid mailing address in the U.S. Must obtain FFA advisor's electronic approval on Signature Page. Apply online.

Amount of award: $1,000
Number of awards: 1
Application deadline: February 15

Contact:
National FFA Organization Scholarship Office
P.O. Box 68960
Indianapolis, IN 46268-0960
Phone: 317-802-6099
Web: www.ffa.org/programs/grantsandscholarships/Scholarships/Pages/default.aspx

Rose Acre Farms Scholarship

Type of award: Scholarship.
Intended use: For full-time undergraduate study at 4-year institution in United States.
Eligibility: Applicant must be no older than 22. Applicant must be residing in Iowa, Indiana, North Carolina, Illinois, Missouri or Georgia.
Basis for selection: Major/career interest in agriculture; animal sciences; food production/management/services or food science/technology.
Application requirements: High school ranking, GPA, SAT/ACT scores.
Additional information: FFA and non-FFA members eligible. Applicants majoring in nutrition, livestock management, breeding, genetics, pathology also eligible. Preference given to applicants majoring in food science or animal/poultry science. Must be resident of Clinton or Iroquois counties in Illinois; Adair, Guthrie, or Madison counties in Iowa; Johnson or Lincoln counties in Missouri; Clinton, Jackson, Jennings, Newton, Pulaski, or White counties in Indiana; Hart, Morgan, or Putnam counties in Georgia; and Hyde country in North Carolina. Must have valid mailing address in the U.S. Apply online.

Amount of award: $1,000
Number of awards: 16
Application deadline: February 15
Total amount awarded: $12,000

Contact:
National FFA Organization Scholarship Office
P.O. Box 68960
Indianapolis, IN 46268-0960
Phone: 317-802-6099
Web: www.ffa.org/programs/grantsandscholarships/Scholarships/Pages/default.aspx

Seneca Foods Corporation Scholarship

Type of award: Scholarship.
Intended use: For undergraduate study at 2-year or 4-year institution.
Basis for selection: Major/career interest in agriculture; science, general; horticulture; business/management/administration; education; engineering; finance/banking; entomology; food production/management/services or technology. Applicant must demonstrate high academic achievement and leadership.
Application requirements: High school ranking, GPA, ACT/SAT test scores.
Additional information: Minimum 2.0 GPA. Must be involved in fruit or vegetable production or processing. Must be a member of FFA. Must have valid mailing address in the U.S. Must obtain FFA advisor's electronic approval on Signature Page. Apply online.

Amount of award: $1,000
Number of awards: 11
Application deadline: February 15

Contact:
National FFA Organization Scholarship Office
P.O. Box 68960
Indianapolis, IN 46268-0960
Phone: 317-802-6099
Web: www.ffa.org/programs/grantsandscholarships/Scholarships/Pages/default.aspx

TeeJet Technologies Scholarship

Type of award: Scholarship.
Intended use: For full-time undergraduate study at 4-year institution in United States.
Eligibility: Applicant must be no older than 22.
Basis for selection: Major/career interest in engineering, agricultural.
Application requirements: High school ranking, GPA, SAT/ACT scores.
Additional information: Agricultural mechanization and agriculture power and equipment majors also eligible. Must be a member of FFA. Must have valid mailing address in the U.S. Must obtain FFA advisor's electronic approval on Signature Page. Apply online.

Amount of award: $1,000
Number of awards: 1
Application deadline: February 15

Contact:
National FFA Organization Scholarship Office
P.O. Box 68960
Indianapolis, IN 46268-0960
Phone: 317-802-6099
Web: www.ffa.org/programs/grantsandscholarships/Scholarships/Pages/default.aspx

Scholarships

Theisen's Home Farm Auto Scholarship

Type of award: Scholarship.
Intended use: For full-time undergraduate study at 2-year or 4-year institution in United States.
Eligibility: Applicant must be no older than 22. Applicant must be residing in Iowa.
Basis for selection: Major/career interest in animal sciences; dairy; agriculture; business/management/administration; economics; marketing or engineering.
Application requirements: High school ranking, GPA, SAT/ ACT scores.
Additional information: Some other majors also eligible. Must be resident of Benton, Cedar, Chickasaw, Clinton, Delaware, Dubuque, Floyd, Hardin, Jackson, Jasper, Johnson, Jones, Linn, Marion, Marshall, Poweshiek, Story, or Warren counties. Must be a member of FFA. Must have valid mailing address in the U.S. Must obtain FFA advisor's electronic approval on Signature Page. Apply online.

Amount of award:	$1,000
Number of awards:	4
Application deadline:	February 15
Total amount awarded:	$4,000

Contact:
National FFA Organization Scholarship Office
P.O. Box 68960
Indianapolis, IN 46268-0960
Phone: 317-802-6099
Web: www.ffa.org/programs/grantsandscholarships/Scholarships/ Pages/default.aspx

Toyota Motor Sales, U.S.A. Inc. Scholarship

Type of award: Scholarship.
Intended use: For full-time undergraduate study at 4-year institution in United States.
Eligibility: Applicant must be no older than 22. Applicant must be residing in Michigan, Texas, California, West Virginia, Mississippi, Indiana, Alabama, Kentucky or Missouri.
Basis for selection: Major/career interest in engineering, agricultural. Applicant must demonstrate financial need.
Application requirements: High school ranking, GPA, SAT/ ACT scores.
Additional information: Agricultural science/technology majors also eligible. Must have been active in extracurricular activities. Must be a member of FFA. Must have valid mailing address in the U.S. Must obtain FFA advisor's electronic approval on Signature Page. Apply online.

Amount of award:	$2,500
Number of awards:	10
Application deadline:	February 15
Total amount awarded:	$25,000

Contact:
National FFA Organization Scholarship Office
P.O. Box 68960
Indianapolis, IN 46268-0960
Phone: 317-802-6099
Web: www.ffa.org/programs/grantsandscholarships/Scholarships/ Pages/default.aspx

Tyrholm Big R Stores Scholarship

Type of award: Scholarship.
Intended use: For full-time undergraduate study at 4-year institution in United States.
Eligibility: Applicant must be no older than 22.
Basis for selection: Major/career interest in agriculture. Applicant must demonstrate financial need, high academic achievement, leadership and service orientation.
Application requirements: High school ranking, GPA, SAT/ ACT scores.
Additional information: Minimum 3.0 GPA. FFA chapter must be located in Modoc or Siskiyou counties in California, or in Crook, Deschutes, Jackson, Jefferson, Klamath, or Josephine counties in Oregon. Must be a member of FFA. Must have valid mailing address in the U.S. Must obtain FFA advisor's electronic approval on Signature Page. Apply online.

Amount of award:	$1,000
Number of awards:	3
Application deadline:	February 15
Total amount awarded:	$3,000

Contact:
National FFA Organization Scholarship Office
P.O. Box 68960
Indianapolis, IN 46268-0960
Phone: 317-802-6099
Web: www.ffa.org/programs/grantsandscholarships/Scholarships/ Pages/default.aspx

Tyson Foods Inc. Scholarship

Type of award: Scholarship.
Intended use: For full-time undergraduate study at 2-year or 4-year institution in United States.
Eligibility: Applicant must be no older than 22.
Basis for selection: Major/career interest in agriculture or animal sciences.
Application requirements: High school ranking, GPA, SAT/ ACT scores.
Additional information: Must be resident of a community in which a Tyson Foods processing facility is located. Other majors relating to agriculture also eligible. Must be a member of FFA. Must have valid mailing address in the U.S. Must obtain FFA advisor's electronic approval on Signature Page. Apply online.

Amount of award:	$1,000
Number of awards:	10
Application deadline:	February 15
Total amount awarded:	$10,000

Contact:
National FFA Organization Scholarship Office
P.O. Box 68960
Indianapolis, IN 46268-0960
Phone: 317-802-6099
Web: www.ffa.org/programs/grantsandscholarships/Scholarships/ Pages/default.aspx

United Dairymen of Idaho Scholarship

Type of award: Scholarship.
Intended use: For full-time undergraduate study at 2-year or 4-year institution in United States.
Eligibility: Applicant must be no older than 22. Applicant must be residing in Idaho.
Basis for selection: Major/career interest in dairy or agricultural education.
Application requirements: High school ranking, GPA, SAT/ ACT scores.
Additional information: Must have dairy cattle background. Must live on family farm and have dairy ownership/experience in supervised agricultural experience (SAE). Must be pursuing degree in dairy science, animal science as it relates to the dairy

industry, agricultural education or extension, animal breeding and genetics, large animal nutrition or large animal veterinarian. Must be a member of FFA. Must have valid mailing address in the U.S. Must obtain FFA advisor's electronic approval on Signature Page. Apply online.

Amount of award: $1,600
Number of awards: 3
Application deadline: February 15
Total amount awarded: $4,800

Contact:
National FFA Organization Scholarship Office
P.O. Box 68960
Indianapolis, IN 46268-0960
Phone: 317-802-6099
Web: www.ffa.org/programs/grantsandscholarships/Scholarships/Pages/default.aspx

Universal Lubricants Scholarship

Type of award: Scholarship.
Intended use: For full-time undergraduate study at 2-year or 4-year institution in United States.
Eligibility: Applicant must be no older than 22. Applicant must be residing in Kansas.
Basis for selection: Major/career interest in agriculture or agribusiness. Applicant must demonstrate high academic achievement, leadership and service orientation.
Application requirements: High school ranking, GPA, ACT/SAT test scores.
Additional information: Minimum 3.0 GPA. Must be pursuing degree in farm and ranch management, sustainable agriculture, agricultural business or agricultural system management, agriculture policy and management or power and equipment, conservation or diesel mechanics. Must be a member of FFA. Must have valid mailing address in the U.S. Must obtain FFA advisor's electronic approval on Signature Page. Apply online.

Amount of award: $5,000
Number of awards: 1
Application deadline: February 15

Contact:
National FFA Organization Scholarship Office
P.O. Box 68960
Indianapolis, IN 46268-0960
Phone: 317-802-6099
Web: www.ffa.org/programs/grantsandscholarships/Scholarships/Pages/default.aspx

Virgil Eihusen Foundation Scholarship

Type of award: Scholarship.
Intended use: For full-time undergraduate study at 2-year or 4-year institution in United States.
Eligibility: Applicant must be no older than 22. Applicant must be residing in Nebraska.
Basis for selection: Major/career interest in agriculture.
Application requirements: High school ranking, GPA, SAT/ACT scores.
Additional information: Must be a member of FFA. Must have valid mailing address in the U.S. Must obtain FFA advisor's electronic approval on Signature Page. Apply online.

Amount of award: $1,400
Number of awards: 1
Application deadline: February 15

Contact:
National FFA Organization Scholarship Office
P.O. Box 68960
Indianapolis, IN 46268-0960
Phone: 317-802-6099
Web: www.ffa.org/programs/grantsandscholarships/Scholarships/Pages/default.aspx

Wells Fargo Scholarship

Type of award: Scholarship.
Intended use: For full-time sophomore, junior or senior study at 4-year institution in United States. Designated institutions: University of California-Davis, California Polytechnic State University-San Luis Obispo, University of California-Fresno.
Eligibility: Applicant must be no older than 22. Applicant must be residing in California.
Basis for selection: Major/career interest in agriculture; animal sciences; dairy; business; business/management/administration; economics or food science/technology. Applicant must demonstrate financial need, high academic achievement and leadership.
Application requirements: High school ranking, GPA, SAT/ACT scores.
Additional information: Minimum 3.25 GPA. Must be a member of FFA. Must have valid mailing address in the U.S. Must obtain FFA advisor's electronic approval on Signature Page. Apply online.

Amount of award: $1,000
Number of awards: 2
Application deadline: February 15
Total amount awarded: $2,000

Contact:
National FFA Organization Scholarship Office
P.O. Box 68960
Indianapolis, IN 46268-0960
Phone: 317-802-6099
Web: www.ffa.org/programs/grantsandscholarships/Scholarships/Pages/default.aspx

Wilbur-Ellis Company High School Scholarship

Type of award: Scholarship.
Intended use: For full-time undergraduate study at 4-year institution in United States.
Eligibility: Applicant must be no older than 22. Applicant must be residing in South Dakota, New York, Ohio, Kansas, California, Montana, Nebraska, Michigan, Minnesota, Texas, , Washington, Arizona, Oregon, Idaho, New Mexico, Colorado or North Dakota.
Basis for selection: Major/career interest in agriculture; turf management; horticulture; entomology or biology. Applicant must demonstrate high academic achievement.
Application requirements: High school ranking, GPA, SAT/ACT scores.
Additional information: Minimum 3.25 GPA. Minimum SAT of 1000 out of 1600 or ACT of 20. Must live on family farm. Other majors also eligible. Must be a member of FFA. Must have valid mailing address in the U.S. Must obtain FFA advisor's electronic approval on Signature Page. Apply online.

Amount of award: $1,000-$5,000
Number of awards: 13
Application deadline: February 15
Total amount awarded: $19,000

Contact:
National FFA Organization Scholarship Office
P.O. Box 68960
Indianapolis, IN 46268-0960
Phone: 317-802-6099
Web: www.ffa.org/programs/grantsandscholarships/Scholarships/Pages/default.aspx

Wix Filters Scholarship

Type of award: Scholarship.
Intended use: For full-time undergraduate study at 2-year or 4-year institution in United States.
Eligibility: Applicant must be no older than 22.
Basis for selection: Major/career interest in engineering, agricultural. Applicant must demonstrate financial need, high academic achievement and service orientation.
Application requirements: High school ranking, GPA, SAT/ACT scores.
Additional information: Minimum 3.0 GPA. Must live on a family farm. Two scholarships for students pursuing a four-year degree in agricultural engineering. Four scholarships for students pursuing a two-year degree in agricultural mechanization or agriculture power and equipment. Must be a member of FFA. Must have valid mailing address in the U.S. Must obtain FFA advisor's electronic approval on Signature Page. Apply online.

Amount of award:	$1,000-$2,000
Number of awards:	6
Application deadline:	February 15
Total amount awarded:	$8,000

Contact:
National FFA Organization Scholarship Office
P.O. Box 68960
Indianapolis, IN 46268-0960
Phone: 317-802-6099
Web: www.ffa.org/programs/grantsandscholarships/Scholarships/Pages/default.aspx

Garden Club Federation of Massachusetts Scholarships

Garden Club Federation of Massachusetts

Type of award: Scholarship, renewable.
Intended use: For undergraduate or graduate study at accredited 2-year, 4-year or graduate institution. Designated institutions: For three of the eleven scholarships: one of the five campuses in the University of Massachusetts system.
Eligibility: Applicant must be U.S. citizen or permanent resident residing in Massachusetts.
Basis for selection: Major/career interest in horticulture; landscape architecture; forestry; environmental science; botany or biology. Applicant must demonstrate financial need, high academic achievement and depth of character.
Application requirements: Recommendations, essay, transcript. List of activities, GCFM Financial Aid form.
Additional information: Must be legal resident of Massachusetts for at least one year. Minimum 3.0 GPA. Floriculture, landscape design, agronomy, city planning, land management, and allied subjects are also eligible majors.

Amount of award:	$1,000
Number of awards:	11
Number of applicants:	27
Application deadline:	March 1
Total amount awarded:	$11,000

Contact:
Garden Club Federation of Massachusetts
Attn: Scholarship Secretary
219 Washington Street
Wellesley Hills, MA 02481
Phone: 781-237-0336
Web: www.gcfm.org

Garden Club of America

Caroline Thorn Kissel Summer Environmental Studies Scholarship

Type of award: Scholarship.
Intended use: For undergraduate or graduate study at postsecondary institution.
Eligibility: Applicant must be U.S. citizen residing in New Jersey.
Basis for selection: Major/career interest in environmental science.
Application requirements: Recommendations, essay.
Additional information: Must be either New Jersey resident or non-resident studying in New Jersey. All application elements must be mailed together in one envelope. Visit Website for application and deadline.

Amount of award:	$2,000
Number of awards:	1
Application deadline:	February 10

Contact:
Garden Club of America
Connie Yates
14 East 60th Street
New York, NY 10022-1002
Phone: 212-753-8287
Fax: 212-753-0134
Web: www.gcamerica.org

Clara Carter Higgins Scholarship and GCA Awards for Summer Environmental Studies

Type of award: Scholarship.
Intended use: For freshman, sophomore or junior study at 4-year institution.
Basis for selection: Major/career interest in environmental science or ecology.
Application requirements: Recommendations, essay, transcript.
Additional information: Awards for summer study in field of ecology and environmental studies. Application must be sent via mail.

Amount of award:	$2,000
Number of awards:	2
Application deadline:	February 10

Contact:
Garden Club of America Awards for Summer Environmental Studies
Connie Yates
14 East 60th Street
New York, NY 10022-1002
Phone: 212-753-8287
Fax: 212-753-0134
Web: www.gcamerica.org

Corliss Knapp Engle Scholarship in Horticulture

Type of award: Scholarship.
Intended use: For undergraduate, graduate, postgraduate or non-degree study at accredited postsecondary institution in United States.
Basis for selection: Major/career interest in horticulture.
Application requirements: Recommendations, essay.
Additional information: Award for research and documentation in the field of horticulture. Non-degree seeking applicants also eligible.

Amount of award:	$2,500
Application deadline:	February 10

Contact:
Garden Club of America
Connie Yates
14 East 60th Street
New York, NY 10022-1006
Phone: 212-753-8287
Fax: 212-753-0134
Web: www.gcamerica.org

Elizabeth Gardner Norweb Summer Environmental Studies Scholarship

Type of award: Scholarship.
Intended use: For sophomore, junior or senior study at 4-year institution in United States.
Basis for selection: Major/career interest in environmental science.
Application requirements: Recommendations, essay, transcript.
Additional information: Award funds summer studies in environmental field.

Amount of award:	$2,000
Application deadline:	February 10

Contact:
Garden Club of America
Connie Yates
14 East 60th Street
New York, NY 10022-1006
Phone: 212-753-8287
Fax: 212-753-0134
Web: www.gcamerica.org

Frances M. Peacock Native Bird Habitat Scholarship

Type of award: Scholarship.
Intended use: For senior or graduate study at postsecondary institution.
Basis for selection: Major/career interest in ornithology.
Application requirements: Project proposal of no more than five pages.
Additional information: Grant for advanced study of U.S. winter/summer habitat of threatened or endangered native birds. Awarded in cooperation with the Cornell Lab of Ornithology. Second semester juniors may apply for senior year. No phone calls. To apply, contact: www.birds.cornell.edu/about/jobs.html.

Amount of award:	$4,500
Number of awards:	1
Application deadline:	January 15
Notification begins:	March 31
Total amount awarded:	$4,500

Contact:
Cornell Lab of Ornithology
Scott Sutcliffe
159 Sapsucker Woods Road
Ithaca, NY 14850-1999
Fax: 212-753-8287
Web: www.gcamerica.org

GCA Award in Desert Studies

Type of award: Scholarship.
Intended use: For junior, senior or graduate study at accredited postsecondary institution in United States.
Basis for selection: Major/career interest in horticulture; botany; environmental science or landscape architecture.
Application requirements: Recommendations, essay. Resume, research/project proposal.
Additional information: Projects must pertain to arid environment, preference given to projects that generate scientifically sound water and plant management. Visit www.dbg.org for application information.

Amount of award:	$4,000
Application deadline:	January 15
Notification begins:	March 31

Contact:
Desert Botanical Garden
Kenny Zelov
1201 N. Galvin Parkway
Phoenix, AZ 85008
Phone: 480-481-8162
Web: www.gcamerica.org or www.dbg.org/educational-programs/scholarships

GCA Summer Scholarship in Field Botany

Type of award: Scholarship.
Intended use: For undergraduate or graduate study at accredited 4-year or graduate institution in United States.
Basis for selection: Major/career interest in botany.
Application requirements: Recommendations, essay, transcript.
Additional information: Award for summer study in field botany.

Amount of award:	$2,000
Number of awards:	1
Application deadline:	February 1

Contact:
Garden Club of America
Connie Yates
14 East 60th Street
New York, NY 10022-1006
Phone: 212-753-8287
Fax: 212-753-0134
Web: www.gcamerica.org

GCA Zone VI Fellowship in Urban Forestry

Type of award: Scholarship.
Intended use: For junior, senior or graduate study at 4-year institution.
Basis for selection: Major/career interest in horticulture; environmental science or forestry.
Additional information: Award funds research in urban forestry.

Amount of award:	$4,000
Application deadline:	January 31

Contact:
Department of Forest Resources and Environmental Conservation
Virginia Tech
310 Cheatham Hall
Blacksburg, VA 24061-0324
Phone: 540-231-7264
Fax: 212-753-8287
Web: www.urbanforestry.frec.vt.edu/scholarship/index.htm

Joan K. Hunt and Rachel M. Hunt Summer Scholarship in Field Botany

Type of award: Scholarship.
Intended use: For undergraduate or graduate study at accredited postsecondary institution in United States.
Basis for selection: Major/career interest in botany or horticulture.
Application requirements: Recommendations, essay, transcript.
Additional information: Submit application via U.S. Mail. Preference given to undergraduate students. Visit Website for application.

Amount of award:	$2,000
Application deadline:	February 1

Contact:
Garden Club of America
Connie Yates
14 East 60th Street
New York, NY 10022-1006
Phone: 212-753-8287
Fax: 212-753-0134
Web: www.gcamerica.org

Katharine M. Grosscup Scholarships in Horticulture

Type of award: Scholarship.
Intended use: For junior, senior or graduate study at accredited 4-year or graduate institution in United States.
Basis for selection: Major/career interest in horticulture. Applicant must demonstrate financial need and high academic achievement.
Application requirements: Interview, recommendations, essay, transcript.
Additional information: Minimum 3.5 GPA. Several scholarships available. Preference given to students who are residents of Pennsylvania, Ohio, West Virginia, Michigan, Indiana, and Kentucky. Major can be in related field. Please do not contact by phone. Application available on Website, and must be submitted via mail.

Amount of award:	$3,500
Application deadline:	January 10

Contact:
Katharine M. Grosscup Scholarship Committee
Cleveland Botanical Garden
11030 East Boulevard
Cleveland, OH 44106
Fax: 216-721-2056
Web: www.gcamerica.org

The Loy McCandless Marks Scholarship in Tropical Horticulture

Type of award: Scholarship.
Intended use: For sophomore, junior, senior or graduate study at accredited 4-year or graduate institution in United States.
Eligibility: Applicant must be U.S. citizen.
Basis for selection: Major/career interest in botany; horticulture or landscape architecture.
Application requirements: Recommendations, essay, transcript. Budget.
Additional information: For study and research at appropriate foreign institution specializing in study of tropical plants. Provides $5,000 each even-numbered year to student specializing in tropical horticulture, botany, or landscape architecture. Visit Website for application. Award only given in even-numbered years.

Amount of award:	$5,000
Number of awards:	1
Application deadline:	January 15

Contact:
Garden Club of America
Connie Yates
14 East 60th Street
New York, NY 10022-1002
Phone: 212-753-8287
Fax: 212-753-0134
Web: www.gcamerica.org

Mary T. Carothers Environmental Studies Scholarship

Type of award: Scholarship.
Intended use: For sophomore, junior or senior study at 4-year institution.
Basis for selection: Major/career interest in environmental science.
Additional information: Funds summer studies in environmental field.

Amount of award:	$2,000
Application deadline:	February 10

Contact:
Garden Club of America
Connie Yates
14 East 60th Street
New York, NY 10022-1006
Phone: 212-753-8287
Fax: 212-753-0134
Web: www.gcamerica.org

Sara Shallenberger Brown GCA National Parks Conservation Scholarship

Type of award: Scholarship.
Intended use: For undergraduate study in United States.
Eligibility: Applicant must be at least 19, no older than 20. Applicant must be U.S. citizen.

Application requirements: Recommendations, essay. Resume.
Additional information: Provides training, transportation, and $750 stipend to SCA apprentice crew leaders working under experienced leaders in three-week summer trail crew in one of America's national parks. Preference given to those with SCA experience. Application available on Website, and must be submitted via mail.

Amount of award:	$750
Application deadline:	February 15

Contact:
Garden Club of America
Connie Yates
14 East 60th Street
New York, NY 10022-1006
Phone: 212-753-8287
Fax: 212-753-0134
Web: www.gcamerica.org

Zeller Summer Scholarship in Medicinal Botany

Type of award: Scholarship.
Intended use: For undergraduate study at accredited postsecondary institution in United States.
Basis for selection: Major/career interest in botany.
Application requirements: Recommendations, essay, transcript.
Additional information: Mail all application materials together in one envelope.

Amount of award:	$2,000
Number of awards:	1
Application deadline:	February 1

Contact:
Garden Club of America
Connie Yates
14 East 60th Street
New York, NY 10022-1006
Phone: 212-753-8287
Fax: 212-753-0134
Web: www.gcamerica.org

The Gates Millennium Scholars

Gates Millennium Scholars Program

Type of award: Scholarship, renewable.
Intended use: For full-time freshman study at accredited 4-year institution in United States.
Eligibility: Applicant must be Alaskan native, Asian American, African American, Mexican American, Hispanic American, Puerto Rican, American Indian or Native Hawaiian/Pacific Islander. Applicant must be U.S. citizen or permanent resident.
Basis for selection: Applicant must demonstrate financial need, high academic achievement, leadership and service orientation.
Application requirements: Recommendations, transcript, nomination by high school principal, teacher, counselor, college president, professor, or dean. Nominee Personal Information Form, FAFSA, GMS information sheet, admission letter.
Additional information: Must be eligible for Pell Grant. Must participate in community service, volunteer work, or extracurricular activities. Minimum 3.3 GPA. Scholarship provides tuition, room, materials, and board not covered by existing financial aid. Eliminates loans, work-study, and outside jobs for scholarship recipients. Funded by Bill and Melinda Gates Foundation. Visit Website for application and deadline.

Number of awards:	1,000
Number of applicants:	13,350
Total amount awarded:	$61,415,141

Contact:
Gates Millenium Scholars
P.O. Box 10500
Fairfax, VA 22031
Phone: 877-690-4677
Web: www.gmsp.org

General Motors Foundation

Buick Achievers Scholarship Program

Type of award: Scholarship, renewable.
Intended use: For full-time undergraduate study at accredited 4-year institution in United States.
Eligibility: Applicant must be U.S. citizen.
Basis for selection: Major/career interest in automotive technology; engineering or technology. Applicant must demonstrate financial need, high academic achievement and leadership.
Additional information: Must demonstrate an interest in automotive career or career in related industries. Employees of General Motors are not eligible. Also open to residents of Puerto Rico. Select design and business majors may also qualify.

Amount of award:	$2,000-$25,000
Number of awards:	1,100
Application deadline:	February 28
Total amount awarded:	$4,500,000

Contact:
General Motors Foundation
One Scholarship Way
St. Peter, MN 56082
Phone: 800-537-4180
Fax: 507-931-2103
Web: buickachievers.scholarshipamerica.org

Georgia Student Finance Commission

Accel Program Grant

Type of award: Scholarship.
Intended use: For undergraduate study at accredited vocational, 2-year or 4-year institution.
Eligibility: Applicant must be high school junior or senior. Applicant must be U.S. citizen or permanent resident residing in Georgia.
Application requirements: Must submit completed application to high school for each participating term.
Additional information: Assistance for high school students to take college level coursework for credit in both high school and college. Must be approved by both high school and college as a dual credit enrollment student. Awards are pro-rated for

students taking less than 12 hours per semester. Students must apply on or before the last day of school term or student's withdrawal date, whichever is first. Visit Website for application, deadline, amount of award, and number of awards available.

Number of applicants: 5,185
Total amount awarded: $9,053,785

Contact:
Georgia Student Finance Commission
2082 East Exchange Place
Suite 100
Tucker, GA 30084
Phone: 800-505-4732
Fax: 770-724-9004
Web: www.gacollege411.org

Georgia Hope Grant - GED Recipient

Type of award: Scholarship.
Intended use: For undergraduate study at accredited vocational, 2-year or 4-year institution. Designated institutions: HOPE-eligible colleges and universities in Georgia.
Eligibility: Applicant must be U.S. citizen or permanent resident residing in Georgia.
Application requirements: Proof of eligibility.
Additional information: Must have received GED from Georgia Department of Technical and Adult Education after June 30, 1993. Submit HOPE voucher upon enrollment. Students receiving GED from DTAE receive voucher automatically. Visit Website for application, deadline, amount of award, and number of awards available.

Number of applicants: 3,877
Total amount awarded: $1,900,000

Contact:
Georgia Student Finance Commission
2082 East Exchange Place
Suite 100
Tucker, GA 30084
Phone: 800-505-4732
Fax: 770-724-9004
Web: www.gacollege411.org

Georgia Hope Grant - Public Technical Institution

Type of award: Scholarship, renewable.
Intended use: For undergraduate study at accredited vocational, 2-year or 4-year institution. Designated institutions: Branches and affiliates of the Georgia Department of Technical and Adult Education and branches of the University System of Georgia.
Eligibility: Applicant must be U.S. citizen or permanent resident residing in Georgia. Applicant may also be dependent child of military personnel stationed in Georgia.
Additional information: Must be enrolled, matriculated technical certificate or diploma student. Visit Website for application, deadline, amount of award, and number of awards available.

Number of applicants: 98,790
Total amount awarded: $92,200,000

Contact:
Georgia Student Finance Commission
2082 East Exchange Place
Suite 100
Tucker, GA 30084
Phone: 800-505-4732
Fax: 770-724-9004
Web: www.gacollege411.org

Georgia Hope Scholarship - Private Institution

Type of award: Scholarship, renewable.
Intended use: For undergraduate study at accredited 2-year or 4-year institution. Designated institutions: Eligible Georgia private colleges and universities.
Eligibility: Applicant must be U.S. citizen or permanent resident residing in Georgia.
Basis for selection: Applicant must demonstrate high academic achievement.
Additional information: Visit Website for application, deadline, amount of award, and number of awards available.

Number of applicants: 12,705
Total amount awarded: $39,400,000

Contact:
Georgia Student Finance Commission
2082 East Exchange Place
Suite 100
Tucker, GA 30084
Phone: 800-505-4732
Fax: 770-724-9004
Web: www.gacollege411.org

Georgia Hope Scholarship - Public College or University

Type of award: Scholarship, renewable.
Intended use: For undergraduate study at accredited 2-year or 4-year institution. Designated institutions: Eligible Georgia public colleges and universities.
Eligibility: Applicant must be U.S. citizen or permanent resident residing in Georgia.
Basis for selection: Applicant must demonstrate high academic achievement.
Application requirements: Proof of eligibility.
Additional information: Minimum 3.0 GPA. Must be designated HOPE scholar. Visit Website for application, deadline, amount of award, and number of awards available.

Number of applicants: 91,827
Total amount awarded: $327,200,000

Contact:
Georgia Student Finance Commission
2082 East Exchange Place
Suite 100
Tucker, GA 30084
Phone: 800-505-4732
Fax: 770-724-9004
Web: www.gacollege411.org

Georgia Student Finance Commission Public Safety Memorial Grant

Type of award: Scholarship, renewable.
Intended use: For full-time undergraduate study at accredited vocational, 2-year or 4-year institution. Designated institutions: Georgia colleges and public technical institutions.
Eligibility: Applicant must be U.S. citizen or permanent resident residing in Georgia. Applicant's parent must have been killed or disabled in work-related accident as firefighter, police officer or public safety officer.
Application requirements: Proof of eligibility.
Additional information: Must complete preliminary document that verifies claim with parent's former employer and doctors. Parent must have been permanently disabled or killed in the line of duty as Georgia police officer, firefighter, emergency medical technician, or corrections officer. Visit Website for application, deadline, amount of award, and number of awards available.

Amount of award:	$18,000
Number of applicants:	33
Total amount awarded:	$37,821

Contact:
Georgia Student Finance Commission
2082 East Exchange Place
Suite 100
Tucker, GA 30084
Phone: 800-505-4732
Fax: 770-724-9004
Web: www.gacollege411.org

Georgia Tuition Equalization Grant

Type of award: Scholarship, renewable.
Intended use: For full-time undergraduate study at accredited 2-year or 4-year institution. Designated institutions: GSFC approved institutions.
Eligibility: Applicant must be U.S. citizen or permanent resident residing in Georgia.
Application requirements: Proof of eligibility. Mileage affidavit (for out-of-state schools only).
Additional information: Must be enrolled at eligible private college or university in Georgia. Amount of award determined by Georgia General Assembly appropriations. Application deadlines set by schools. Visit Website for list of approved institutions, application, amount of award, and number of awards available.

Number of applicants:	34,903
Total amount awarded:	$20,541,490

Contact:
Georgia Student Finance Commission
2082 East Exchange Place
Suite 100
Tucker, GA 30084
Phone: 800-505-4732
Fax: 770-724-9004
Web: www.gacollege411.org

Glamour Magazine

Top 10 College Women Competition

Type of award: Scholarship.
Intended use: For full-time junior study at accredited 4-year institution in United States or Canada.
Eligibility: Applicant must be female.
Basis for selection: Applicant must demonstrate high academic achievement, leadership and service orientation.
Application requirements: Recommendations, essay, transcript. List of activities and awards, GPA, black-and-white or color photograph.
Additional information: See Website for deadline, application, and details. Not applicable in Quebec. Early application deadline is July 15th.

Amount of award:	$3,000-$20,000
Number of awards:	10

Contact:
Glamour's Top 10 College Women Competition
4 Times Square
16th Floor
New York, NY 10036-6593
Fax: 212-286-6922
Web: www.glamour.com/about/top-10-college-women

Golden Apple

Golden Apple Scholars of Illinois Program

Type of award: Scholarship.
Intended use: For undergraduate study at 4-year institution in United States. Designated institutions: Participating Illinois universities.
Eligibility: Applicant must be high school senior. Applicant must be U.S. citizen residing in Illinois.
Basis for selection: Major/career interest in education; education, early childhood; education, special or education, teacher. Applicant must demonstrate high academic achievement.
Application requirements: Transcript. SAT/ACT scores, eight essays.
Additional information: Must obtain teacher's certification and teach for five years in Illinois school of need. Must participate in Summer Institutes. Must be high school senior or college sophomore. Scholars receive $2,000 stipend for attending Summer Institute program. Recipients may receive a maximum of $23,000 over four years. Must demonstrate a passion for teaching. Visit Website for application, nomination forms and list of Golden Apple's partner universities.

Number of awards:	135
Number of applicants:	135
Application deadline:	November 1
Notification begins:	April 1
Total amount awarded:	$3,105,000

Scholarships

Contact:
Golden Apple
8 South Michigan Avenue
Suite 700
Chicago, IL 60603
Phone: 312-407-0006
Fax: 312-407-0344
Web: www.goldenapple.org

Golden Key International Honour Society

Golden Key Community Service Award

Type of award: Scholarship.
Intended use: For undergraduate or graduate study at accredited postsecondary institution.
Basis for selection: Applicant must demonstrate service orientation.
Application requirements: Recommendations, essay. List of extracurricular activities.
Additional information: Only Golden Key members who were enrolled as students during previous academic year eligible to apply. Winner and charity of winner's choice will each receive $1,000. Visit Website for application. Number of awards varies.

Amount of award:	$2,000
Number of awards:	5
Application deadline:	March 1

Contact:
Phone: 800-377-2401
Web: www.goldenkey.org

Golden Key Emerging Scholar Award

Type of award: Scholarship.
Intended use: For full-time sophomore study.
Basis for selection: Applicant must demonstrate high academic achievement.
Application requirements: Recommendations, essay, transcript. Resume. Letter from Golden Key chapter advisor stating your contributions.
Additional information: Open to Golden Key members only. Applicant must be active member in good standing. Visit Website for details and application.

Amount of award:	$1,000
Number of awards:	5
Application deadline:	April 1

Contact:
Golden Key International Honour Society
Phone: 800-377-2401
Web: www.goldenkey.org

Golden Key GEICO Life Award

Type of award: Scholarship.
Intended use: For undergraduate study at postsecondary institution.
Basis for selection: Applicant must demonstrate high academic achievement.
Application requirements: Recommendations, essay, transcript. Resume.
Additional information: Open to Golden Key members only. Must be balancing academic achievement and other commitments such as work or family. Applicant must be active undergraduate member in good standing who has completed at least 12 credit hours since returning to university. Visit Website for details and application.

Amount of award:	$1,000
Number of awards:	10
Application deadline:	April 1

Contact:
Golden Key International Honour Society
Phone: 800-377-2401
Web: www.goldenkey.org

Golden Key Outstanding Alumni Award

Type of award: Scholarship.
Intended use: For undergraduate study at postsecondary institution.
Application requirements: Recommendations, essay. Resume. Letters from both Golden Key chapter advisor and community official stating how you have promoted Golden Key on campus and in the community.
Additional information: Open to Golden Key alumni. Applicant must be active member in good standing. Visit Website for details and application.

Amount of award:	$1,000
Number of awards:	3
Application deadline:	April 1

Contact:
Phone: 800-377-2401
Web: www.goldenkey.org

Golden Key Outstanding Alumni Member Award

Type of award: Scholarship.
Intended use: For undergraduate study at postsecondary institution.
Application requirements: Recommendations, essay, transcript. Resume. Letters from both Golden Key chapter advisor and community official stating how you have promoted Golden Key on campus and in the community.
Additional information: Open to Golden Key members only. Applicant must be active member in good standing. Visit Website for details and application.

Amount of award:	$1,000
Number of awards:	3
Application deadline:	April 1

Contact:
Golden Key International Honour Society
Phone: 800-377-2401
Web: www.goldenkey.org

Golden Key Regional Student Leader of the Year Award

Type of award: Scholarship.
Intended use: For undergraduate or graduate study at accredited postsecondary institution in United States.
Basis for selection: Applicant must demonstrate high academic achievement and leadership.

Application requirements: Recommendations, essay, transcript. List of personal Golden Key involvement and other extracurricular activities.
Additional information: Open to Golden Key members only. Applicant must be active member in good standing. Winners at regional level will be considered for International Student Leader Award. Visit Website for details and application.

Amount of award:	$1,000
Number of awards:	1
Application deadline:	April 1

Contact:
Phone: 800-377-2401
Web: www.goldenkey.org

Golden Key Research Grants

Type of award: Research grant.
Intended use: For undergraduate or graduate study.
Basis for selection: Applicant must demonstrate high academic achievement.
Application requirements: Transcript. Budget summary and description of proposed research.
Additional information: Only Golden Key members eligible to apply. Grant for members to travel to professional conferences and student research symposia, or to conduct thesis research. Visit Website for details and application.

Amount of award:	$1,000
Number of awards:	10
Application deadline:	March 1

Contact:
Phone: 800-377-2401
Web: www.goldenkey.org

Golden Key Undergraduate Achievement Scholarship

Type of award: Scholarship.
Intended use: For undergraduate or graduate study at accredited postsecondary institution.
Basis for selection: Major/career interest in education. Applicant must demonstrate high academic achievement.
Application requirements: Recommendations, essay, transcript. Resume, essay detailing how you exemplify the Society's commitment to academics, leadership, and service.
Additional information: Open to Golden Key members only. Visit Website for application.

Amount of award:	$5,000
Number of awards:	25
Application deadline:	March 1

Contact:
Phone: 800-377-2401
Web: www.goldenkey.org

Golden Key Visual and Performing Arts Achievement Award

Type of award: Scholarship.
Intended use: For undergraduate or graduate study at accredited postsecondary institution.
Basis for selection: Competition/talent/interest in visual arts, based on quality of work submitted.
Application requirements: Digital images of visual work; digital file of performance (ten minute maximum).
Additional information: Open to Golden Key members only. At least one award in each of ten categories: painting, drawing, mixed media, sculpture, photography, computer-generated art/illustration/graphic design, instrumental performance, vocal performance, acting, and dance. One entry per member per category. Visit Website for details and application.

Amount of award:	$1,000
Number of awards:	10
Application deadline:	March 1

Contact:
Phone: 800-377-2401
Web: www.goldenkey.org

Study Abroad Scholarships

Type of award: Scholarship.
Intended use: For undergraduate, graduate or postgraduate study at postsecondary institution.
Basis for selection: Competition/talent/interest in study abroad, based on relevance of study abroad program to major field of study. Applicant must demonstrate high academic achievement.
Application requirements: Transcript, proof of eligibility. Description of planned academic program at host university. One-page statement of relevance of program to degree.
Additional information: Only Golden Key members eligible to apply. Number of awards varies. Visit Website for details and application.

Amount of award:	$1,000
Number of awards:	10
Application deadline:	March 1

Contact:
Phone: 800-377-2401
Web: www.goldenkey.org

Grange Insurance Association

Grange Insurance Scholarship

Type of award: Scholarship.
Intended use: For full-time undergraduate or graduate study at accredited vocational, 2-year, 4-year or graduate institution.
Eligibility: Applicant must be U.S. citizen or permanent resident residing in Wyoming, California, Oregon, Idaho, Washington or Colorado.
Basis for selection: Applicant must demonstrate financial need, high academic achievement, depth of character, leadership, patriotism, seriousness of purpose and service orientation.
Application requirements: Essay, transcript. Cover letter.
Additional information: Applicant must be one of the following: current GIA policyholder (or child of GIA policyholder) or child of current GIA company employee. Previous recipients also eligible to apply. Application must be postmarked by deadline.

Amount of award:	$1,000-$1,500
Number of awards:	26
Number of applicants:	72
Application deadline:	March 1
Notification begins:	April 15
Total amount awarded:	$26,000

Contact:
Grange Insurance Association
Scholarship Committee
P.O. Box 21089
Seattle, WA 98111-3089
Phone: 800-247-2643 ext. 2200
Web: www.grange.com

Great Minds in STEM

HENAAC Scholars Program

Type of award: Scholarship, renewable.
Intended use: For full-time undergraduate or graduate study at 2-year, 4-year or graduate institution.
Eligibility: Applicant must be Hispanic American.
Basis for selection: Major/career interest in engineering; mathematics; science, general or technology. Applicant must demonstrate high academic achievement and leadership.
Application requirements: Recommendations, essay, transcript. Resume.
Additional information: Minimum 3.0 GPA. Include SASE with application request, or download application from Website. Amount of award varies.

Amount of award:	$500-$10,000
Number of awards:	108
Application deadline:	April 30
Notification begins:	August 1
Total amount awarded:	$250,000

Contact:
Great Minds in STEM
Attn: HENAAC Scholars
602 Monterey Pass Road
Monterey Park, CA 91754
Phone: 323-262-0997
Fax: 323-262-0946
Web: www.greatmindsinstem.org

Greater Kanawha Valley Foundation

Greater Kanawha Valley Scholarship Program

Type of award: Scholarship, renewable.
Intended use: For full-time undergraduate or graduate study at 4-year or graduate institution.
Eligibility: Applicant must be residing in West Virginia.
Basis for selection: Applicant must demonstrate high academic achievement and depth of character.
Application requirements: Recommendations, transcript. First page of parents' federal income tax return.
Additional information: Minimum 20 ACT score and 2.5 GPA. Foundation offers more than 80 scholarships, each with specific eligibility criteria. Visit Website for complete listing, and to apply.

Amount of award:	$1,000
Number of awards:	450
Number of applicants:	719
Application deadline:	January 15
Notification begins:	May 15
Total amount awarded:	$475,000

Contact:
The Greater Kanawha Valley Foundation
900 Lee Street East
16th Floor
Charleston, WV 25301
Phone: 304-346-3620
Fax: 304-346-3640
Web: www.tgkvf.org

Greenhouse Scholars

Greenhouse Scholars Program

Type of award: Scholarship, renewable.
Intended use: For full-time undergraduate study at 4-year institution.
Eligibility: Applicant must be high school senior. Applicant must be U.S. citizen or permanent resident residing in Illinois or Colorado.
Basis for selection: Based on commitment to community, ability to persevere through difficult circumstances, strong sense of accountability. Applicant must demonstrate financial need, high academic achievement and leadership.
Application requirements: Transcript. Three letters of recommendation, ACT scores.
Additional information: The Greenhouse Scholars Program is a scholarship and mentorship program for under-resourced, high-achieving students. The program uses a 'Whole Person' approach to address the intellectual, academic, professional, and financial needs of students. Minimum 3.5 GPA. Renewable for four years. Visit Website for application and more information.

Amount of award:	$1,000-$5,000
Number of awards:	15
Number of applicants:	150
Application deadline:	January 20
Notification begins:	April 23
Total amount awarded:	$90,000

Contact:
Greenhouse Scholars
1881 9th Street
Suite 200
Boulder, CO 80302
Phone: 303-460-1735
Web: www.greenhousescholars.org

Harness Tracks of America

Harness Tracks of America Scholarship Fund

Type of award: Scholarship.
Intended use: For full-time undergraduate or graduate study at accredited postsecondary institution.
Eligibility: Applicant or parent must be member/participant of Harness Racing Industry.
Basis for selection: Applicant must demonstrate financial need and high academic achievement.
Application requirements: Essay, transcript, proof of eligibility. FAFSA and U.S. or Canadian tax return.
Additional information: Must be child of licensed driver, trainer, breeder, owner or caretaker of harness horses or be personally active in harness racing industry. Children of deceased industry members also eligible. Recommendations not required but considered if included with application. Awards based on financial need, academic excellence, and active harness racing involvement. Visit Website for more information.

Amount of award: $5,000
Number of awards: 3
Number of applicants: 23
Application deadline: May 15
Notification begins: September 15
Total amount awarded: $15,000
Contact:
Harness Tracks of America
12025 East Dry Gulch Place
Tucson, AZ 85749
Phone: 520-529-2525
Fax: 520-529-3235
Web: www.harnesstracks.com

Havana National Bank

McFarland Charitable Foundation Scholarship

Type of award: Scholarship, renewable.
Intended use: For full-time undergraduate study at accredited vocational, 2-year or 4-year institution in United States.
Basis for selection: Major/career interest in nursing. Applicant must demonstrate seriousness of purpose.
Application requirements: Interview, recommendations, transcript, proof of eligibility. Letter of acceptance to RN program.
Additional information: Award recipients must contractually obligate themselves to return to Havana, Illinois, and work as registered nurses for two years for each year of funding. Reverts to loan if work obligation is not met. Two co-signers are required. To fund RN programs only. Number of awards and amounts varies.
Application deadline: May 15
Notification begins: June 15
Contact:
Havana National Bank
112 South Orange
P.O. Box 200
Havana, IL 62644-0200
Phone: 309-543-3361
Web: www.havanabank.com

Hawaii Community Foundation

100th Infantry Battalion Memorial Scholarship Fund

Type of award: Scholarship.
Intended use: For full-time undergraduate or graduate study at 2-year or 4-year institution in United States.
Eligibility: Applicant must be U.S. citizen or permanent resident. Applicant must be descendant of veteran. Must be direct descendant of a 100th Infantry Battalion World War II veteran.
Basis for selection: Applicant must demonstrate financial need, high academic achievement, depth of character and service orientation.
Application requirements: Recommendations, essay, transcript, proof of eligibility. SAR, FAFSA, Personal Statement. Essay on topic: "What is the legacy of the 100th Infantry Battalion of WWII and how will you contribute to forwarding this legacy?" Name of World War II 100th Battalion member you are descended from and your relationship to individual.
Additional information: Must be direct descendant of a 100th Infantry Battalion World War II veteran and be willing to promote its legacy. Minimum 3.5 GPA. Applicant does not have to be resident of Hawaii.
Application deadline: February 15
Contact:
Hawaii Community Foundation Scholarships
827 Fort Street Mall
Honolulu, HI 96813
Phone: 888-731-3863
Fax: 808-521-6286
Web: www.hawaiicommunityfoundation.org

A & B Ohana Scholarship

Type of award: Scholarship, renewable.
Intended use: For full-time undergraduate study at 2-year or 4-year institution in United States.
Eligibility: Applicant must be residing in Hawaii.
Basis for selection: Applicant must demonstrate financial need and high academic achievement.
Application requirements: Recommendations, essay, transcript. FAFSA. Name and title of parent who is Alexander & Baldwin employee, SAR.
Additional information: Minimum 2.7 GPA. Must be dependent child of full-time employee of Alexander & Baldwin, Inc. Employee must have completed one year of full-time continuous service by application deadline. Must attend college or university with 501c3 status. If attending community college, award amount will be lower.
Application deadline: February 15
Contact:
Hawaii Community Foundation
827 Fort Street Mall
Honolulu, HI 96813
Phone: 888-731-3863
Fax: 808-521-6286
Web: www.hawaiicommunityfoundation.org

ABC Stores Jumpstart Scholarship

Type of award: Scholarship.
Intended use: For undergraduate or graduate study at accredited 2-year, 4-year or graduate institution in United States.
Eligibility: Applicant must be residing in Hawaii or Nevada.
Basis for selection: Applicant must demonstrate financial need, high academic achievement and depth of character.
Application requirements: Recommendations, essay, transcript. SAR, FAFSA, Personal Statement. Name of ABC Stores Employee and relationship (i.e., mother).
Additional information: Must be resident of Hawaii, Nevada, Guam, or Saipan. Minimum 2.7 GPA. Applicants must have permanent address in Hawaii. Amount of award may change yearly. Applicant must be employee or dependent of ABC Stores or Company Island Gourmet Markets employee.
Application deadline: February 15

Contact:
Hawaii Community Foundation Scholarships
827 Fort Street Mall
Honolulu, HI 96813
Phone: 888-731-3863
Fax: 808-521-6286
Web: www.hawaiicommunityfoundation.org

Aiea General Hospital Association Scholarship

Type of award: Scholarship, renewable.
Intended use: For full-time undergraduate study at accredited 2-year, 4-year or graduate institution in United States.
Eligibility: Applicant must be U.S. citizen or permanent resident residing in Hawaii.
Basis for selection: Major/career interest in health-related professions. Applicant must demonstrate financial need, high academic achievement and depth of character.
Application requirements: Recommendations, essay, transcript. FAFSA and SAR.
Additional information: Minimum 2.7 GPA. Applicant must be resident of Leeward Oahu ZIP Codes: 96701, 96706, 96707, 96782, 96792, or 96797. Amount and number of awards vary.
Application deadline: February 15
Contact:
Hawaii Community Foundation Scholarships
827 Fort Street Mall
Honolulu, HI 96813
Phone: 888-731-3863
Fax: 808-521-6286
Web: www.hawaiicommunityfoundation.org

Allan Eldin & Agnes Sutorik Geiger Scholarship Fund

Type of award: Scholarship.
Intended use: For full-time undergraduate or graduate study at accredited 2-year or 4-year institution in United States.
Eligibility: Applicant must be U.S. citizen residing in Hawaii.
Basis for selection: Major/career interest in veterinary medicine. Applicant must demonstrate financial need, high academic achievement and depth of character.
Application requirements: Recommendations, essay, transcript. SAR, FAFSA, Personal Statement.
Additional information: Minimum 3.0 GPA. Applicants must have permanent address in Hawaii. Applicants taking up mainland residency must have relatives living in Hawaii. Amount of award may change yearly.
Application deadline: February 15
Contact:
Hawaii Community Foundation Scholarships
827 Fort Street Mall
Honolulu, HI 96813
Phone: 888-731-3863
Fax: 808-521-6286
Web: www.hawaiicommunityfoundation.org

Alma White-Delta Kappa Gamma Scholarship

Type of award: Scholarship.
Intended use: For full-time junior, senior or graduate study at accredited postsecondary institution in United States.
Eligibility: Applicant must be U.S. citizen or permanent resident residing in Hawaii.
Basis for selection: Major/career interest in education. Applicant must demonstrate financial need, high academic achievement and depth of character.
Application requirements: Recommendations, essay, transcript. FAFSA and SAR. Official letter confirming enrollment in education program.
Additional information: Minimum 2.7 GPA. Applicants must have permanent address in Hawaii. Applicants taking up mainland residency must have relatives living in Hawaii. Amount and number of awards vary and may change yearly.
Application deadline: February 15
Contact:
Hawaii Community Foundation Scholarships
827 Fort Street Mall
Honolulu, HI 96813
Phone: 888-731-3863
Fax: 808-521-6286
Web: www.hawaiicommunityfoundation.org

Ambassador Minerva Jean Falcon Hawaii Scholarship

Type of award: Scholarship.
Intended use: For full-time undergraduate study at 2-year or 4-year institution. Designated institutions: 2-year or 4-year colleges in Hawaii.
Eligibility: Applicant must be Native Hawaiian/Pacific Islander. Applicant must be residing in Hawaii.
Basis for selection: Applicant must demonstrate financial need and high academic achievement.
Application requirements: Recommendations, essay, transcript. SAR.
Additional information: Minimum 2.7 GPA. Must be graduate of Hawaii high school. Must be of Filipino ancestry.
Application deadline: February 15
Contact:
Hawaii Community Foundation
827 Fort Street Mall
Honolulu, HI 96813
Phone: 888-731-3863
Fax: 808-521-6286
Web: www.hawaiicommunityfoundation.org

American Institute of Graphic Arts (AIGA) Honolulu Chapter Scholarship Fund

Type of award: Scholarship.
Intended use: For full-time undergraduate study at 2-year, 4-year or graduate institution.
Eligibility: Applicant must be residing in Hawaii.
Basis for selection: Major/career interest in arts, general or graphic arts/design. Applicant must demonstrate financial need and high academic achievement.
Application requirements: Recommendations, essay, transcript. SAR, FAFSA.
Additional information: Minimum 2.7 GPA. Must major in graphic design, visual communication, or commercial arts.
Application deadline: February 15
Contact:
Hawaii Community Foundation
827 Fort Street Mall
Honolulu, HI 96813
Phone: 888-731-3863
Fax: 808-521-6286
Web: www.hawaiicommunityfoundation.org

Arthur Jackman Memorial Scholarship

Type of award: Scholarship.
Intended use: For full-time undergraduate study at vocational institution in United States. Designated institutions: Hawaii community colleges.
Eligibility: Applicant must be residing in Hawaii.
Basis for selection: Applicant must demonstrate financial need and high academic achievement.
Application requirements: Recommendations, essay, transcript. SAR, FAFSA.
Additional information: Minimum 2.7 GPA. Must be enrolled in AS or AAS career technical degree program at Hawaii community college. Must be resident of island of Hawaii.
Application deadline: February 15
Contact:
Hawaii Community Foundation
827 Fort Street Mall
Honolulu, HI 96813
Phone: 888-731-3863
Fax: 808-521-6286
Web: www.hawaiicommunityfoundation.org

Bal Dasa Scholarship Fund

Type of award: Scholarship.
Intended use: For full-time undergraduate study at accredited 2-year or 4-year institution in United States.
Eligibility: Applicant must be U.S. citizen or permanent resident residing in Hawaii.
Basis for selection: Applicant must demonstrate financial need, high academic achievement and depth of character.
Application requirements: Essay, transcript. FAFSA and SAR.
Additional information: Minimum 2.7 GPA. Must be graduate of Waipahu High School. Award amount varies yearly. Applicants taking up mainland residency must have relatives living in Hawaii.
Application deadline: February 15
Contact:
Hawaii Community Foundation Scholarships
827 Fort Street Mall
Honolulu, HI 96813
Phone: 888-731-3863
Fax: 808-521-6286
Web: www.hawaiicommunityfoundation.org

Bick Bickson Scholarship

Type of award: Scholarship, renewable.
Intended use: For full-time undergraduate or graduate study at accredited 2-year or 4-year institution in United States.
Eligibility: Applicant must be U.S. citizen residing in Hawaii.
Basis for selection: Major/career interest in marketing; law or tourism/travel. Applicant must demonstrate financial need, high academic achievement and depth of character.
Application requirements: Essay, transcript. FAFSA.
Additional information: Minimum 3.0 GPA.
Application deadline: February 15
Contact:
Hawaii Community Foundation
827 Fort Street Mall
Honolulu, HI 96813
Phone: 888-731-3863
Fax: 808-521-6286
Web: www.hawaiicommunityfoundation.org

Blossom Kalama Evans Memorial Scholarship

Type of award: Scholarship, renewable.
Intended use: For full-time junior, senior or graduate study at accredited 4-year or graduate institution in United States.
Eligibility: Applicant must be Native Hawaiian/Pacific Islander. Applicant must be U.S. citizen or permanent resident residing in Hawaii.
Basis for selection: Major/career interest in Hawaiian studies. Applicant must demonstrate financial need, high academic achievement and depth of character.
Application requirements: Transcript. FAFSA and SAR. Personal essay stating how applicant's knowledge will be used to serve the needs of the Native Hawaiian community.
Additional information: Minimum 2.7 GPA. Students must be of Hawaiian ancestry. Preference given to students studying Hawaiian studies or language. Applicants must have permanent address in Hawaii. Applicants who take up mainland residency must have relatives living in Hawaii. Amount and number of awards vary.
Application deadline: February 15
Contact:
Hawaii Community Foundation Scholarships
827 Fort Street Mall
Honolulu, HI 96813
Phone: 888-731-3863
Fax: 808-521-6286
Web: www.hawaiicommunityfoundation.org

Booz Allen Scholarship

Type of award: Scholarship.
Intended use: For full-time undergraduate study at accredited 4-year institution.
Eligibility: Applicant must be residing in Hawaii.
Basis for selection: Applicant must demonstrate financial need and high academic achievement.
Application requirements: Recommendations, essay, transcript. SAR, FAFSA.
Additional information: Minimum 3.0 GPA.
Application deadline: February 15
Contact:
Hawaii Community Foundation
827 Fort Street Mall
Honolulu, HI 96813
Phone: 888-731-3863
Fax: 808-521-6286
Web: www.hawaiicommunityfoundation.org

Camille C. Chidiac Fund

Type of award: Scholarship.
Intended use: For full-time undergraduate study at accredited 2-year or 4-year institution in United States.
Eligibility: Applicant must be high school senior. Applicant must be U.S. citizen or permanent resident residing in Hawaii.
Basis for selection: Applicant must demonstrate financial need, high academic achievement and depth of character.
Application requirements: Essay, transcript. FAFSA and SAR. Essay must state why it is important for Hawaii students to be internationally aware.
Additional information: Minimum 2.7 GPA. Applicant must be student at Ka'u High School. Amount of scholarship varies yearly. Applicants taking up mainland residency must have relatives living in Hawaii.
Application deadline: February 15

Contact:
Hawaii Community Foundation Scholarships
827 Fort Street Mall
Honolulu, HI 96813
Phone: 888-731-3863
Fax: 808-521-6286
Web: www.hawaiicommunityfoundation.org

Candon, Todd, & Seabolt Scholarship Fund

Type of award: Scholarship.
Intended use: For junior or senior study at 4-year institution in United States.
Eligibility: Applicant must be U.S. citizen residing in Hawaii.
Basis for selection: Major/career interest in accounting or finance/banking. Applicant must demonstrate high academic achievement.
Application requirements: Recommendations, essay, transcript. SAR, FAFSA.
Additional information: Minimum 3.2 GPA.
Application deadline: February 15
Contact:
Hawaii Community Foundation Scholarships
827 Fort Street Mall
Honolulu, HI 96813
Phone: 888-731-3863
Fax: 808-521-6286
Web: www.hawaiicommunityfoundation.org

Castle & Cooke Mililani Technology Park Scholarship Fund

Type of award: Scholarship.
Intended use: For full-time freshman study at accredited 2-year or 4-year institution in United States.
Eligibility: Applicant must be high school senior. Applicant must be U.S. citizen or permanent resident residing in Hawaii.
Basis for selection: Major/career interest in science, general; engineering or computer/information sciences. Applicant must demonstrate financial need and high academic achievement.
Application requirements: Essay, transcript. FAFSA and SAR.
Additional information: Minimum 2.7 GPA. Applicants must be graduating senior from Leilehua, Mililani, or Waialua high schools. Preference given to majors in technology fields. Applicants must have permanent address in Hawaii. Applicants taking up mainland residency must have relatives living in Hawaii. Amount and number of awards vary and may change yearly.
Application deadline: February 15
Contact:
Hawaii Community Foundation Scholarships
827 Fort Street Mall
Honolulu, HI 96813
Phone: 888-731-3863
Fax: 808-521-6286
Web: www.hawaiicommunityfoundation.org

Castle & Cooke W. Y. Yim Scholarship Fund

Type of award: Scholarship.
Intended use: For full-time undergraduate or graduate study at accredited 2-year or 4-year institution in United States.
Eligibility: Applicant must be U.S. citizen residing in Hawaii.
Basis for selection: Applicant must demonstrate financial need, high academic achievement and depth of character.
Application requirements: Recommendations, essay, transcript. SAR, FAFSA, Personal Statement. Castle & Cooke employee name, position, and relationship to applicant.
Additional information: Minimum 3.0 GPA. Must be a dependent of current employee with at least one year of service with Castle & Cooke Hawaii affiliated company. Applicants must have permanent address in Hawaii. Applicants taking up mainland residency must have relatives living in Hawaii. Amount of award may change yearly.
Application deadline: February 15
Contact:
Hawaii Community Foundation Scholarships
827 Fort Street Mall
Honolulu, HI 96813
Phone: 888-731-3863
Fax: 808-521-6286
Web: www.hawaiicommunityfoundation.org

Cora Aguda Manayan Fund

Type of award: Scholarship, renewable.
Intended use: For full-time undergraduate or graduate study in United States.
Eligibility: Applicant must be of Filipino ancestry. Applicant must be U.S. citizen or permanent resident residing in Hawaii.
Basis for selection: Major/career interest in health-related professions. Applicant must demonstrate financial need, high academic achievement and depth of character.
Application requirements: Essay, transcript. FAFSA and SAR.
Additional information: Minimum 3.0 GPA. Preference given to students studying in Hawaii. Applicants must have permanent address in Hawaii. Applicants who take up mainland residency must have relatives living in Hawaii. Amount and number of awards vary.
Application deadline: February 15
Contact:
Hawaii Community Foundation Scholarships
827 Fort Street Mall
Honolulu, HI 96813
Phone: 888-731-3863
Fax: 808-521-6286
Web: www.hawaiicommunityfoundation.org

CPB Works For You Scholarship

Type of award: Scholarship.
Intended use: For undergraduate study at 2-year or 4-year institution.
Eligibility: Applicant must be residing in Hawaii.
Basis for selection: Applicant must demonstrate financial need and high academic achievement.
Application requirements: Recommendations, essay, transcript. SAR, FAFSA, name and position of CPB employee.
Additional information: Minimum 2.7 GPA. Must be active status employee or dependent child (no older than 25) of active status employee of CPB or CPHL with minimum one year of service by application deadline. Part-time awards will be less than full-time awards.
Application deadline: February 15

Contact:
Hawaii Community Foundation
827 Fort Street Mall
Honolulu, HI 96813
Phone: 888-731-3863
Fax: 808-521-6286
Web: www.hawaiicommunityfoundation.org

Dan & Pauline Lutkenhouse & Hawaii Tropical Botanical Garden Scholarship

Type of award: Scholarship.
Intended use: For full-time undergraduate study at accredited postsecondary institution.
Eligibility: Applicant must be residing in Hawaii.
Basis for selection: Major/career interest in agriculture; science, general; medicine or nursing. Applicant must demonstrate financial need and high academic achievement.
Application requirements: Recommendations, essay, transcript. SAR, FAFSA.
Additional information: Minimum 2.7 GPA. Must be resident of Hilo Coast and Hamakua Coast, north of Wailuki River.
Application deadline: February 15
Contact:
Hawaii Community Foundation
827 Fort Street Mall
Honolulu, HI 96813
Phone: 888-731-3863
Fax: 808-521-6286
Web: www.hawaiicommunityfoundation.org

David L. Irons Memorial Scholarship Fund

Type of award: Scholarship.
Intended use: For full-time freshman study at accredited 2-year or 4-year institution in United States.
Eligibility: Applicant must be high school senior. Applicant must be U.S. citizen or permanent resident residing in Hawaii.
Basis for selection: Applicant must demonstrate financial need, high academic achievement and depth of character.
Application requirements: Essay, transcript. FAFSA and SAR.
Additional information: Minimum 2.7 GPA. Applicant must be graduating senior at Punahou School. Applicants taking up mainland residency must have relatives living in Hawaii. Amount of award may change yearly.
Application deadline: February 15
Contact:
Hawaii Community Foundation Scholarships
827 Fort Street Mall
Honolulu, HI 96813
Phone: 888-731-3863
Fax: 808-521-6286
Web: www.hawaiicommunityfoundation.org

Dolly Ching Scholarship Fund

Type of award: Scholarship.
Intended use: For full-time undergraduate study at accredited postsecondary institution in United States. Designated institutions: Institutions in University of Hawaii system.
Eligibility: Applicant must be high school senior. Applicant must be U.S. citizen or permanent resident residing in Hawaii.
Basis for selection: Applicant must demonstrate financial need, high academic achievement, depth of character and service orientation.
Application requirements: Recommendations, essay, transcript. FAFSA and SAR.
Additional information: Minimum 2.7 GPA. Must be graduating senior from a high school on Kauai. Must be resident of Kauai. Amount and number of awards vary.
Application deadline: February 15
Contact:
Hawaii Community Foundation Scholarships
827 Fort Street Mall
Honolulu, HI 96813
Phone: 888-731-3863
Fax: 808-521-6286
Web: www.hawaiicommunityfoundation.org

Doris & Clarence Glick Classical Music Scholarship

Type of award: Scholarship.
Intended use: For full-time undergraduate study at accredited 2-year or 4-year institution in United States.
Eligibility: Applicant must be residing in Hawaii.
Basis for selection: Major/career interest in music. Applicant must demonstrate financial need, high academic achievement and depth of character.
Application requirements: Essay, transcript. FAFSA and SAR. Describe in personal statement how program of study relates to classical music.
Additional information: Minimum 2.7 GPA. Must major in music, with emphasis on classical music. Applicants must have permanent address in Hawaii. Applicants taking up mainland residency must have relatives living in Hawaii. Amount and number of awards vary and may change yearly.
Application deadline: February 15
Contact:
Hawaii Community Foundation Scholarships
827 Fort Street Mall
Honolulu, HI 96813
Phone: 888-731-3863
Fax: 808-521-6286
Web: www.hawaiicommunityfoundation.org

Dr. Alvin and Monica Saake Scholarship

Type of award: Scholarship.
Intended use: For full-time junior, senior or graduate study at accredited 2-year, 4-year or graduate institution.
Eligibility: Applicant must be residing in Hawaii.
Basis for selection: Major/career interest in physical education; athletic training; sports/sports administration; physical therapy or occupational therapy. Applicant must demonstrate financial need, high academic achievement and depth of character.
Application requirements: Essay, transcript. FAFSA and SAR.
Additional information: Minimum 2.7 GPA. Must be majoring in kinesiology, leisure science, physical education, athletic training, exercise science, sports medicine, physical therapy, or occupational therapy. Applicant must have permanent Hawaii address. Applicants taking up mainland residency must have relatives living in Hawaii.
Application deadline: February 15

Contact:
Hawaii Community Foundation Scholarships
827 Fort Street Mall
Honolulu, HI 96813
Phone: 888-731-3863
Fax: 808-521-6286
Web: www.hawaiicommunityfoundation.org

Dr. and Mrs. Moon Park Scholarship

Type of award: Scholarship.
Intended use: For full-time undergraduate or graduate study at accredited 2-year or 4-year institution in United States.
Eligibility: Applicant must be U.S. citizen residing in Hawaii.
Basis for selection: Applicant must demonstrate financial need and high academic achievement.
Application requirements: Recommendations, essay, transcript. SAR, FAFSA, Personal Statement. Clinical Laboratories of Hawaii, LLC employee name and relationship to applicant.
Additional information: Minimum 3.0 GPA. Must be an employee or child dependent with minimum one year of service of Clinical Laboratories of Hawaii, LLP and/or Pan Pacific Pathologies, LLC. Applicants must have permanent address in Hawaii. Applicants taking up mainland residency must have relatives living in Hawaii. Amount of award may change yearly.
Application deadline: February 15
Contact:
Hawaii Community Foundation Scholarships
827 Fort Street Mall
Honolulu, HI 96813
Phone: 888-731-3863
Fax: 808-521-6286
Web: www.hawaiicommunityfoundation.org

Dr. Edison and Sallie Miyawaki Scholarship

Type of award: Scholarship.
Intended use: For undergraduate study at accredited 2-year or 4-year institution.
Eligibility: Applicant must be residing in Hawaii.
Basis for selection: Applicant must demonstrate financial need and high academic achievement.
Application requirements: Recommendations, essay, transcript. FAFSA and SAR.
Additional information: GPA between 2.5 and 3.0. Must participate in extracurricular sports program. Amount and number of awards vary and may change yearly.
Application deadline: February 15
Contact:
Hawaii Community Foundation
827 Fort Street Mall
Honolulu, HI 96813
Phone: 888-731-3863
Fax: 808-521-6286
Web: www.hawaiicommunityfoundation.org

Dr. Hans & Clara Zimmerman Foundation Education Scholarship

Type of award: Scholarship.
Intended use: For full-time undergraduate or graduate study at accredited 2-year or 4-year institution in United States.
Eligibility: Applicant must be U.S. citizen or permanent resident residing in Hawaii.
Basis for selection: Major/career interest in education or education, teacher. Applicant must demonstrate financial need, high academic achievement, depth of character and leadership.
Application requirements: Recommendations, essay, transcript. FAFSA and SAR. Recommendations must include an evaluation of applicant's "classroom teaching effectiveness." Personal statement describing applicant's community service projects or activities. Essay must also answer question "What is your teaching philosophy and how is it applied in classroom today?" (with one example). Applicants disqualified if they fail to address essay topic in personal statement.
Additional information: Minimum 2.8 GPA. Must major in education with an emphasis on classroom teaching. Preference given to nontraditional students with at least two years of teaching experience. Preference given to students of Hawaiian ethnicity. Applicants must have permanent address in Hawaii. Amount and number of awards vary and may change yearly.
Application deadline: February 15
Contact:
Hawaii Community Foundation Scholarships
827 Fort Street Mall
Honolulu, HI 96813
Phone: 888-731-3863
Fax: 808-521-6286
Web: www.hawaiicommunityfoundation.org

Dr. Hans and Clara Zimmerman Foundation Health Scholarship

Type of award: Scholarship, renewable.
Intended use: For full-time junior, senior or graduate study at accredited postsecondary institution in United States.
Eligibility: Applicant must be U.S. citizen or permanent resident residing in Hawaii.
Basis for selection: Major/career interest in health sciences; health-related professions or medicine. Applicant must demonstrate financial need, high academic achievement and depth of character.
Application requirements: Transcript. FAFSA and SAR. Personal statement including description of applicant's community service projects or activities.
Additional information: Minimum 3.0 GPA. Applicants must have permanent address in Hawaii. Applicants who take up mainland residency must have relatives living in Hawaii. Sports medicine and some psychology majors ineligible. Amount and number of awards vary.
Application deadline: February 15
Contact:
Hawaii Community Foundation Scholarships
827 Fort Street Mall
Honolulu, HI 96813
Phone: 888-731-3863
Fax: 808-521-6286
Web: www.hawaiicommunityfoundation.org

Eastside & Northshore Kauai Scholarship Fund

Type of award: Scholarship.
Intended use: For full-time undergraduate or graduate study at accredited 2-year or 4-year institution in United States.
Eligibility: Applicant must be U.S. citizen residing in Hawaii.
Basis for selection: Applicant must demonstrate financial need, high academic achievement and depth of character.

Application requirements: Recommendations, essay, transcript. SAR, FAFSA, Personal Statement.
Additional information: Minimum 2.5 GPA. Must be resident of one of the following East and Northshore Kaua'i areas: Anahola (96703), Kapa'a (96746), Kilauea (96754), Hanalei (96714), Princeville (96722), Kealia (96751), Wailua (96746).
Application deadline: February 15
Contact:
Hawaii Community Foundation Scholarships
827 Fort Street Mall
Honolulu, HI 96813
Phone: 888-731-3863
Fax: 808-521-6286
Web: www.hawaiicommunityfoundation.org

Edward J. and Norma Doty Scholarship

Type of award: Scholarship.
Intended use: For full-time junior, senior or graduate study at accredited 2-year or 4-year institution in United States.
Eligibility: Applicant must be U.S. citizen or permanent resident residing in Hawaii.
Basis for selection: Major/career interest in medicine. Applicant must demonstrate financial need, high academic achievement and depth of character.
Application requirements: Essay, transcript. FAFSA and SAR.
Additional information: Minimum 2.7 GPA. Preference given to students specializing in geriatric medicine or Alzheimer's care. Applicants must have permanent address in Hawaii. Applicants taking up mainland residency must have relatives living in Hawaii. Amount of award may change yearly.
Application deadline: March 1
Contact:
Hawaii Community Foundation Scholarships
827 Fort Street Mall
Honolulu, HI 96813
Phone: 888-731-3863
Fax: 808-521-6286
Web: www.hawaiicommunityfoundation.org

Edward Payson and Bernice Pi'ilani Irwin Scholarship Trust Fund

Type of award: Scholarship.
Intended use: For full-time junior, senior or graduate study at accredited 4-year institution in United States.
Eligibility: Applicant must be U.S. citizen or permanent resident residing in Hawaii.
Basis for selection: Major/career interest in journalism or communications. Applicant must demonstrate financial need, high academic achievement and depth of character.
Application requirements: Essay, transcript. FAFSA and SAR.
Additional information: Minimum 2.7 GPA. Must have permanent address in Hawaii. Applicants who take up mainland residency must have relatives living in Hawaii. Amount and number of awards vary and may change yearly.
Application deadline: February 15
Contact:
Hawaii Community Foundation Scholarships
827 Fort Street Mall
Honolulu, HI 96813
Phone: 888-731-3863
Fax: 808-521-6286
Web: www.hawaiicommunityfoundation.org

E.E. Black Scholarship

Type of award: Scholarship, renewable.
Intended use: For full-time undergraduate study at accredited postsecondary institution in United States.
Eligibility: Applicant must be U.S. citizen or permanent resident residing in Hawaii.
Basis for selection: Applicant must demonstrate financial need, high academic achievement and depth of character.
Application requirements: Essay, transcript. FAFSA and SAR. Name of Tesoro employee and relationship.
Additional information: Minimum 3.0 GPA. Must be dependent of an employee of Tesoro Hawaii or its subsidiaries. Applicants must have permanent address in Hawaii. Applicants who take up mainland residency must have relatives living in Hawaii. Amount and number of awards vary.
Application deadline: February 15
Contact:
Hawaii Community Foundation Scholarships
827 Fort Street Mall
Honolulu, HI 96813
Phone: 888-731-3863
Fax: 808-521-6286
Web: www.hawaiicommunityfoundation.org

Elena Albano "Maka'alohilohi" Scholarship Fund

Type of award: Scholarship.
Intended use: For full-time undergraduate or graduate study at 2-year or 4-year institution in United States.
Eligibility: Applicant must be U.S. citizen residing in Hawaii.
Basis for selection: Applicant must demonstrate financial need, high academic achievement and depth of character.
Application requirements: Recommendations, essay, transcript. SAR, FAFSA, personal statement. Two letters of recommendation from mentors, teachers, counselors, or other mental health professionals.
Additional information: Minimum 2.7 GPA. Must be in recovery from mental health/behavioral/psychological disability. Must be resident of Maui county. Preference given to students of Hawaiian ancestry and renewal applicants. Applicants must have permanent address in Hawaii. Applicants taking up mainland residency must have relatives living in Hawaii. Amount of award may change yearly.
Application deadline: February 15
Contact:
Hawaii Community Foundation Scholarships
827 Fort Street Mall
Honolulu, HI 96813
Phone: 888-731-3863
Fax: 808-521-6286
Web: www.hawaiicommunityfoundation.org

Ellen Hamada Fashion Design Scholarship

Type of award: Scholarship.
Intended use: For full-time undergraduate study at 2-year institution in United States. Designated institutions: University of Hawaii community colleges.
Eligibility: Applicant must be residing in Hawaii.
Basis for selection: Major/career interest in fashion/fashion design/modeling. Applicant must demonstrate financial need and high academic achievement.
Application requirements: Recommendations, essay, transcript. SAR, FAFSA.

Additional information: Minimum 2.7 GPA.
Application deadline: February 15
Contact:
Hawaii Community Foundation
827 Fort Street Mall
Honolulu, HI 96813
Phone: 888-731-3863
Fax: 808-521-6286
Web: www.hawaiicommunityfoundation.org

Ellison Onizuka Memorial Scholarship

Type of award: Scholarship.
Intended use: For full-time undergraduate study at accredited 4-year institution in United States.
Eligibility: Applicant must be high school senior. Applicant must be U.S. citizen or permanent resident residing in Hawaii.
Basis for selection: Major/career interest in aerospace. Applicant must demonstrate financial need and depth of character.
Application requirements: Recommendations, transcript. SAT scores, FAFSA, SAR and personal statement describing extracurricular activities, club affiliations, and community service projects.
Additional information: Minimum 3.0 GPA. Applicants must have permanent address in Hawaii. Applicants who take up mainland residency must have relatives living in Hawaii. Amount and number of awards vary.
Application deadline: February 15
Contact:
Hawaii Community Foundation Scholarships
827 Fort Street Mall
Honolulu, HI 96813
Phone: 888-731-3863
Fax: 808-521-6286
Web: www.hawaiicommunityfoundation.org

Esther Kanagawa Memorial Art Scholarship

Type of award: Scholarship.
Intended use: For full-time undergraduate or graduate study at accredited 2-year or 4-year institution in United States.
Eligibility: Applicant must be high school senior. Applicant must be U.S. citizen or permanent resident residing in Hawaii.
Basis for selection: Major/career interest in arts, general. Applicant must demonstrate financial need, high academic achievement and depth of character.
Application requirements: Essay, transcript. FAFSA and SAR.
Additional information: Minimum 2.7 GPA. Must major in fine art, drawing, painting, sculpture, ceramics, or photography. Applicants must have permanent address in Hawaii. Applicants taking up mainland residency must have relatives living in Hawaii. Amount of award varies yearly.
Application deadline: February 15
Contact:
Hawaii Community Foundation Scholarships
827 Fort Street Mall
Honolulu, HI 96813
Phone: 888-731-3863
Fax: 808-521-6286
Web: www.hawaiicommunityfoundation.org

F. Koehnen Ltd. Scholarship Fund

Type of award: Scholarship.
Intended use: For full-time undergraduate or graduate study at accredited 4-year institution in United States.
Eligibility: Applicant must be U.S. citizen residing in Hawaii.
Basis for selection: Applicant must demonstrate financial need, high academic achievement and depth of character.
Application requirements: Recommendations, essay, transcript. SAR, FAFSA, Personal Statement. Name of employee, retail establishment and phone number of human resources department of retail establishment.
Additional information: Minimum 2.5 GPA. Must be graduate of high school on island of Hawaii. Must be son, daughter, or grandchild of employee of retail establishment on island of Hawaii.
Application deadline: February 15
Contact:
Hawaii Community Foundation Scholarships
827 Fort Street Mall
Honolulu, HI 96813
Phone: 888-731-3863
Fax: 808-521-6286
Web: www.hawaiicommunityfoundation.org

Filipino Nurses' Organization of Hawaii Scholarship

Type of award: Scholarship.
Intended use: For full-time undergraduate study at accredited 2-year or 4-year institution in United States.
Eligibility: Applicant must be of Filipino ancestry. Applicant must be U.S. citizen or permanent resident residing in Hawaii.
Basis for selection: Major/career interest in nursing. Applicant must demonstrate financial need, high academic achievement, depth of character and service orientation.
Application requirements: Essay, transcript. FAFSA and SAR.
Additional information: Minimum 2.7 GPA. Must have permanent address in Hawaii. Applicants taking up mainland residency must have relatives living in Hawaii. Amount of award may vary yearly.
Application deadline: February 15
Contact:
Hawaii Community Foundation Scholarships
827 Fort Street Mall
Honolulu, HI 96813
Phone: 888-731-3863
Fax: 808-521-6286
Web: www.hawaiicommunityfoundation.org

Financial Women International Scholarship

Type of award: Scholarship.
Intended use: For full-time junior, senior or graduate study at accredited 2-year or 4-year institution in United States.
Eligibility: Applicant must be female. Applicant must be U.S. citizen or permanent resident residing in Hawaii.
Basis for selection: Major/career interest in business. Applicant must demonstrate financial need, high academic achievement and depth of character.
Application requirements: Essay, transcript. FAFSA and SAR.
Additional information: Minimum 3.5 GPA. Applicant must have permanent address in Hawaii. Applicants taking up

mainland residency must have relatives living in Hawaii. Amount of award may change yearly.

Application deadline: February 15

Contact:
Hawaii Community Foundation Scholarships
827 Fort Street Mall
Honolulu, HI 96813
Phone: 888-731-3863
Fax: 808-521-6286
Web: www.hawaiicommunityfoundation.org

Fletcher & Fritzi Hoffmann Education Fund

Type of award: Scholarship.
Intended use: For full-time undergraduate study at accredited vocational, 2-year or 4-year institution. Designated institutions: Community colleges on island of Hawaii.
Eligibility: Applicant must be U.S. citizen or permanent resident residing in Hawaii.
Basis for selection: Applicant must demonstrate financial need, high academic achievement and depth of character.
Application requirements: Essay, transcript. FAFSA and SAR. Personal statement must include information on family's history and roots in the Hamakua area.
Additional information: Minimum 2.7 GPA. Preference given to Honoka'a high school graduates. Must be longtime resident of Hamakua Coast in 96727 zip code in Hawaii. Amount of award may change yearly.

Application deadline: February 15

Contact:
Hawaii Community Foundation Scholarships
827 Fort Street Mall
Suite 80
Honolulu, HI 96813
Phone: 888-731-3863
Fax: 808-521-6286
Web: www.hawaiicommunityfoundation.org

Frances S. Watanabe Memorial Scholarship

Type of award: Scholarship.
Intended use: For full-time undergraduate or graduate study at accredited 2-year institution in United States. Designated institutions: University of Hawaii community colleges.
Eligibility: Applicant must be U.S. citizen or permanent resident residing in Hawaii.
Basis for selection: Applicant must demonstrate financial need, high academic achievement and depth of character.
Application requirements: Essay, transcript. FAFSA, SAR.
Additional information: Minimum 2.7 GPA required. Must be member of Hawaii USA Federal Credit Union. Must be enrolled in AS or AAS career and technical degree in University of Hawaii community college system. Applicants must have permanent address in Hawaii. Applicants who take up mainland residency must have relatives living in Hawaii.

Application deadline: February 15

Contact:
Hawaii Community Foundation Scholarships
827 Fort Street Mall
Honolulu, HI 96813
Phone: 888-731-3863
Fax: 808-521-6286
Web: www.hawaiicommunityfoundation.org

George & Augusta Rapozo Kama'aina Scholarship Fund

Type of award: Scholarship.
Intended use: For undergraduate study at 2-year or 4-year institution.
Eligibility: Applicant must be residing in Hawaii.
Basis for selection: Applicant must demonstrate high academic achievement.
Application requirements: Recommendations, essay, transcript. FAFSA and SAR. Essay about family ties to Kauai or Ni'ihau and work, family and other commitments.
Additional information: Minimum 2.7 GPA. Must be graduate of Kauai or Ni'ihau high school or charter school. Preference given to Ni'ihau residents. Amount and number of awards vary and may change yearly.

Application deadline: February 15

Contact:
Hawaii Community Foundation
827 Fort Street Mall
Honolulu, HI 96813
Phone: 888-731-3863
Fax: 808-521-6286
Web: www.hawaiicommunityfoundation.org

George & Lucille Cushnie Scholarship

Type of award: Scholarship, renewable.
Intended use: For full-time undergraduate or graduate study at accredited 2-year, 4-year or graduate institution in United States.
Eligibility: Applicant must be U.S. citizen or permanent resident residing in Hawaii.
Basis for selection: Major/career interest in medicine. Applicant must demonstrate financial need, high academic achievement and depth of character.
Application requirements: Essay, transcript. FAFSA.
Additional information: Preference given to residents of the island of Hawaii. Minimum 2.7 GPA.

Application deadline: February 15

Contact:
Hawaii Community Foundation
827 Fort Street Mall
Honolulu, HI 96813
Phone: 888-731-3863
Fax: 808-521-6286
Web: www.hawaiicommunityfoundation.org

George Mason Business Scholarship Fund

Type of award: Scholarship.
Intended use: For full-time senior study at accredited 4-year institution. Designated institutions: Universities and colleges in Hawaii.
Eligibility: Applicant must be residing in Hawaii.
Basis for selection: Major/career interest in business or business/management/administration. Applicant must demonstrate financial need, high academic achievement and depth of character.
Application requirements: Essay, transcript. FAFSA and SAR. Essay must state why you have chosen business as an intended career and how you expect to make a difference in the business world.
Additional information: Minimum 3.0 GPA. Applicant must have permanent Hawaii address.

Application deadline: February 15
Contact:
Hawaii Community Foundation Scholarships
827 Fort Street Mall
Honolulu, HA 96813
Phone: 888-731-3863
Fax: 808-521-6286
Web: www.hawaiicommunityfoundation.org

George S. Ishiyama Unicold Scholarship

Type of award: Scholarship, renewable.
Intended use: For full-time undergraduate or graduate study at accredited 2-year, 4-year or graduate institution in United States.
Eligibility: Applicant must be at least 17, no older than 24.
Basis for selection: Applicant must demonstrate financial need, high academic achievement and depth of character.
Application requirements: Essay, transcript. FAFSA.
Additional information: Must be child of Unicold Employee from the Oakland, Honolulu & Los Angeles offices with minimum one year of service by application deadline. Must maintain 2.7-3.5 GPA. Preference given to first-generation college students and renewal applicants.
Application deadline: February 15
Contact:
Hawaii Community Foundation
827 Fort Street Mall
Honolulu, HI 96813
Phone: 888-731-3863
Fax: 808-521-6286
Web: www.hawaiicommunityfoundation.org

Gerrit R. Ludwig Scholarship

Type of award: Scholarship.
Intended use: For full-time undergraduate or graduate study at accredited 2-year, 4-year or graduate institution.
Eligibility: Applicant must be residing in Hawaii.
Basis for selection: Major/career interest in classics or arts, general. Applicant must demonstrate financial need, high academic achievement and depth of character.
Application requirements: Essay, transcript. FAFSA and SAR.
Additional information: Minimum 2.5 GPA. Preference given to applicants pursuing a degree in fine arts or classics. Must be graduate from East Hawaii public school: Hilo, Honoka'a, Ka'u, Kea'au, Laupahoehoe, Pahoa, Waiakea and Hawaii Academy of Arts and Science. Applicants taking up mainland residency must have relatives living in Hawaii.
Application deadline: February 15
Contact:
Hawaii Community Foundation Scholarships
827 Fort Street Mall
Honolulu, HI 96813
Phone: 888-731-3863
Fax: 808-521-6286
Web: www.hawaiicommunityfoundation.org

Good Eats Scholarship Fund

Type of award: Scholarship.
Intended use: For full-time undergraduate or graduate study at accredited vocational, 2-year or 4-year institution in United States.
Eligibility: Applicant must be U.S. citizen residing in Hawaii.
Basis for selection: Major/career interest in culinary arts; agriculture or food production/management/services. Applicant must demonstrate high academic achievement and depth of character.
Application requirements: Recommendations, essay, transcript. SAR, FAFSA, personal statement discussing activities that demonstrate interest in food production and preparation.
Additional information: Minimum 2.7 GPA. Must pursue post high school studies in culinary arts or agriculture. Must demonstrate interest in food production and preparation through participation in related classes, clubs, and activities.
Application deadline: February 15
Contact:
Hawaii Community Foundation Scholarships
827 Fort Street Mall
Honolulu, HI 96813
Phone: 888-731-3863
Fax: 808-521-6286
Web: www.hawaiicommunityfoundation.org

Grace Pacific Outstanding Scholars Fund

Type of award: Scholarship.
Intended use: For full-time undergraduate or graduate study at accredited 2-year or 4-year institution in United States.
Eligibility: Applicant must be high school senior. Applicant must be U.S. citizen residing in Hawaii.
Basis for selection: Applicant must demonstrate financial need, high academic achievement and depth of character.
Application requirements: Recommendations, essay, transcript. SAR, FAFSA, personal statement.
Additional information: Minimum 2.7 GPA. Must be former participant of Grace Pacific Outstanding Keiki Scholars Program. Applicants must have permanent address in Hawaii. Applicants taking up mainland residency must have relatives living in Hawaii. Amount of award may change yearly.
Application deadline: February 15
Contact:
Hawaii Community Foundation Scholarships
827 Fort Street Mall
Honolulu, HI 96813
Phone: 888-731-3863
Fax: 808-521-6286
Web: www.hawaiicommunityfoundation.org

Guy Marshall Scholarship Fund

Type of award: Scholarship.
Intended use: For full-time freshman study at accredited 2-year or 4-year institution in United States.
Eligibility: Applicant must be high school senior. Applicant must be U.S. citizen residing in Hawaii.
Basis for selection: Applicant must demonstrate financial need, high academic achievement and depth of character.
Application requirements: Recommendations, essay, transcript. SAR, FAFSA, personal statement.
Additional information: Must have 3.3 to 3.5 GPA. Must plan to attend college in continental United States. Must be graduate of Hawaii high school.
Application deadline: February 15

Contact:
Hawaii Community Foundation Scholarships
827 Fort Street Mall
Honolulu, HI 96813
Phone: 888-731-3863
Fax: 808-521-6286
Web: www.hawaiicommunityfoundation.org

Haseko Training Fund

Type of award: Scholarship.
Intended use: For full-time undergraduate study at accredited 2-year institution. Designated institutions: University of Hawaii community colleges.
Eligibility: Applicant must be residing in Hawaii.
Basis for selection: Applicant must demonstrate financial need and high academic achievement.
Application requirements: Recommendations, essay, transcript. SAR, FAFSA.
Additional information: Minimum 2.7 GPA. Must be Ewa Beach resident. Must enroll in AS or AAS career and technical degree program within University of Hawaii community college system. Preference given to student in marine-related program.
Application deadline: February 15
Contact:
Hawaii Community Foundation
827 Fort Street Mall
Honolulu, HI 96813
Phone: 888-731-3863
Fax: 808-521-6286
Web: www.hawaiicommunityfoundation.org

Hawaii Community Scholarship Fund

Type of award: Scholarship, renewable.
Intended use: For full-time undergraduate or graduate study at accredited 4-year institution in United States.
Eligibility: Applicant must be U.S. citizen or permanent resident residing in Hawaii.
Basis for selection: Major/career interest in arts, general; architecture; education; humanities/liberal arts or social/behavioral sciences. Applicant must demonstrate financial need, high academic achievement, depth of character and service orientation.
Application requirements: Essay, transcript. FAFSA and SAR.
Additional information: Must have 3.3 to 3.8 GPA. Must show commitment to community in Hawaii. Must be first-generation college student. Preference given to sophomores. Must have permanent address in Hawaii. Applicants taking up mainland residency must have relatives living in Hawaii. Amount and number of awards vary and may change yearly.
Application deadline: February 15
Contact:
Hawaii Community Foundation Scholarships
827 Fort Street Mall
Honolulu, HI 96813
Phone: 888-731-3863
Fax: 808-521-6286
Web: www.hawaiicommunityfoundation.org

Hawaii GEAR UP Scholars Program

Type of award: Scholarship.
Intended use: For full-time undergraduate study at accredited postsecondary institution.
Eligibility: Applicant must be residing in Hawaii.
Basis for selection: Applicant must demonstrate financial need and high academic achievement.
Application requirements: Recommendations, essay, transcript. SAR, FAFSA.
Additional information: Minimum 3.0 GPA. Must have graduated high school between 2007 and 2009. Must be Gear Up scholar and earn State of Hawaii Board of Education Recognition Diploma. Must be eligible for Pell Grant.
Application deadline: February 15
Contact:
Hawaii Community Foundation
827 Fort Street Mall
Honolulu, HI 96813
Phone: 888-731-3863
Fax: 808-521-6286
Web: www.hawaiicommunityfoundation.org

Hawaii Pacific Gerontological Society Nursing Scholarship Fund

Type of award: Scholarship.
Intended use: For full-time undergraduate or graduate study at accredited 2-year or 4-year institution in United States. Designated institutions: Two- or four-year colleges in Hawaii.
Eligibility: Applicant must be U.S. citizen residing in Hawaii.
Basis for selection: Major/career interest in nursing. Applicant must demonstrate financial need, high academic achievement and depth of character.
Application requirements: Recommendations, essay, transcript. SAR, FAFSA, essay explaining interest in geriatric nursing.
Additional information: Minimum 2.7 GPA. Must pursue an LN or RN degree with interest in geriatric nursing.
Application deadline: February 15
Contact:
Hawaii Community Foundation Scholarships
827 Fort Street Mall
Honolulu, HI 96813
Phone: 888-731-3863
Fax: 808-521-6286
Web: www.hawaiicommunityfoundation.org

Hawaii Pizza Hut Scholarship Fund

Type of award: Scholarship.
Intended use: For full-time undergraduate study at accredited 2-year or 4-year institution in United States.
Eligibility: Applicant must be U.S. citizen residing in Hawaii.
Basis for selection: Applicant must demonstrate financial need, high academic achievement and depth of character.
Application requirements: Recommendations, essay, transcript. SAR, FAFSA, personal statement.
Additional information: GPA must be between 3.0 and 3.5. Preference given to renewals.
Application deadline: February 15
Contact:
Hawaii Community Foundation Scholarships
827 Fort Street Mall
Honolulu, HI 96813
Phone: 888-731-3863
Fax: 808-521-6286
Web: www.hawaiicommunityfoundation.org

Hawaii Society of Certified Public Accountants Scholarship Fund

Type of award: Scholarship.
Intended use: For full-time junior, senior or graduate study at 4-year institution in United States. Designated institutions: Four-year colleges and universities in Hawaii.
Eligibility: Applicant must be U.S. citizen residing in Hawaii.
Basis for selection: Major/career interest in accounting. Applicant must demonstrate financial need, high academic achievement and depth of character.
Application requirements: Recommendations, essay, transcript. SAR, FAFSA, personal statement should include description of extracurricular activities, involvement in professional, civic and social organizations, and employment history.
Additional information: Minimum 3.0 GPA. Must have already completed two or more 300-level accounting courses. Preference given to students involved in Accounting Club.
Application deadline: February 15
Contact:
Hawaii Community Foundation Scholarships
827 Fort Street Mall
Honolulu, HI 96813
Phone: 888-731-3863
Fax: 808-521-6286
Web: www.hawaiicommunityfoundation.org

H.C. Shipman Vocational Scholarship Fund

Type of award: Scholarship.
Intended use: For full-time undergraduate study at accredited vocational or 2-year institution in United States. Designated institutions: University of Hawaii community colleges.
Eligibility: Applicant must be residing in Hawaii.
Basis for selection: Applicant must demonstrate high academic achievement.
Application requirements: Recommendations, essay, transcript. FAFSA and SAR.
Additional information: Minimum 2.0 GPA. Must be graduate of Kea'au High School or KeKula 'O Nawahiokalani'opu'u, Iki Laboratory Public Charter School. Must enroll in AS or AA career and technical degree program in University of Hawaii Community College system. Amount and number of awards vary and may change yearly.
Application deadline: February 15
Contact:
Hawaii Community Foundation
827 Fort Street Mall
Honolulu, HI 96813
Phone: 888-731-3863
Fax: 808-521-6286
Web: www.hawaiicommunityfoundation.org

Henry A. Zuberano Scholarship

Type of award: Scholarship.
Intended use: For full-time undergraduate study at accredited 2-year or 4-year institution.
Eligibility: Applicant must be residing in Hawaii.
Basis for selection: Major/career interest in political science/ government; international relations; business, international or public administration/service. Applicant must demonstrate financial need, high academic achievement and depth of character.
Application requirements: Essay, transcript. FAFSA and SAR.
Additional information: Minimum 2.7 GPA. Applicant must have permanent Hawaii address. Applicants taking up mainland residency must have relatives living in Hawaii.
Application deadline: February 15
Contact:
Hawaii Community Foundation Scholarships
827 Fort Street Mall
Honolulu, HI 96813
Phone: 888-731-3863
Fax: 808-521-6286
Web: www.hawaiicommunityfoundation.org

Henry and Dorothy Castle Memorial Scholarship

Type of award: Scholarship, renewable.
Intended use: For full-time undergraduate or graduate study at accredited 2-year, 4-year or graduate institution in United States.
Eligibility: Applicant must be U.S. citizen or permanent resident residing in Hawaii.
Basis for selection: Major/career interest in education, early childhood. Applicant must demonstrate financial need, high academic achievement and depth of character.
Application requirements: Essay, transcript. FAFSA and SAR. Essay stating interests and goals in early childhood education, and plans to contribute to field.
Additional information: Minimum 2.7 GPA required. Applicants must have permanent address in Hawaii. Applicants who take up mainland residency must have relatives living in Hawaii. Amount and number of awards vary and may change yearly.
Application deadline: February 15
Contact:
Hawaii Community Foundation Scholarships
827 Fort Street Mall
Honolulu, HI 96813
Phone: 888-731-3863
Fax: 808-521-6286
Web: www.hawaiicommunityfoundation.org

Herbert & Ollie Brook Fund

Type of award: Scholarship.
Intended use: For full-time undergraduate study at accredited 2-year or 4-year institution in United States.
Eligibility: Applicant must be high school senior. Applicant must be U.S. citizen residing in Hawaii.
Basis for selection: Applicant must demonstrate financial need, high academic achievement and depth of character.
Application requirements: Recommendations, essay, transcript. SAR, FAFSA, personal statement.
Additional information: Minimum 2.7 GPA. Must be high school senior in Maui County. Preference given to those who plan to return to Maui County after completing education to contribute to community.
Application deadline: February 15
Contact:
Hawaii Community Foundation Scholarships
827 Fort Street Mall
Honolulu, HI 96813
Phone: 888-731-3863
Fax: 808-521-6286
Web: www.hawaiicommunityfoundation.org

Hew-Shinn Scholarship Fund

Type of award: Scholarship.
Intended use: For full-time undergraduate study at accredited vocational or 2-year institution in United States. Designated institutions: University of Hawaii community colleges.
Eligibility: Applicant must be residing in Hawaii.
Basis for selection: Applicant must demonstrate financial need and high academic achievement.
Application requirements: Recommendations, essay, transcript. SAR, FAFSA.
Additional information: Minimum 2.7 GPA. Must be Maui county resident enrolled in vocational program in the University of Hawaii Community College system.
Application deadline: February 15
Contact:
Hawaii Community Foundation Scholarships
827 Fort Street Mall
Honolulu, HI 96813
Phone: 888-731-3863
Fax: 808-521-6286
Web: www.hawaiicommunityfoundation.org

Hideko & Zenzo Matsuyama Scholarship Fund

Type of award: Scholarship.
Intended use: For full-time undergraduate or graduate study at 2-year or 4-year institution in United States.
Eligibility: Applicant must be U.S. citizen residing in Hawaii.
Basis for selection: Applicant must demonstrate financial need, high academic achievement and depth of character.
Application requirements: Recommendations, essay, transcript. SAR, FAFSA, personal statement.
Additional information: Minimum 3.0 GPA. Must be graduate of high school in Hawaii or have received GED in Hawaii. Preference given to students of Japanese ancestry born in Hawaii.
Application deadline: February 15
Contact:
Hawaii Community Foundation Scholarships
827 Fort Street Mall
Honolulu, HI 96813
Phone: 888-731-3863
Fax: 808-521-6286
Web: www.hawaiicommunityfoundation.org

Hilo Chinese School Scholarship

Type of award: Scholarship.
Intended use: For full-time undergraduate or graduate study at accredited 2-year or 4-year institution in United States.
Eligibility: Applicant must be U.S. citizen residing in Hawaii.
Basis for selection: Applicant must demonstrate financial need, high academic achievement and depth of character.
Application requirements: Recommendations, essay, transcript. SAR, FAFSA, personal statement.
Additional information: Minimum 2.5 GPA. Must be resident of Hawaii island. Preference given to descendants of Hilo Chinese School alumni and students of Chinese ancestry.
Application deadline: February 15
Contact:
Hawaii Community Foundation Scholarships
827 Fort Street Mall
Honolulu, HI 96813
Phone: 888-731-3863
Fax: 808-521-6286
Web: www.hawaiicommunityfoundation.org

Hoku Scholarship Fund

Type of award: Scholarship.
Intended use: For full-time undergraduate or graduate study at accredited 2-year or 4-year institution.
Eligibility: Applicant must be residing in Hawaii.
Basis for selection: Major/career interest in physics; astronomy; mathematics; engineering; technology or computer/information sciences. Applicant must demonstrate high academic achievement.
Application requirements: Recommendations, essay, transcript. FAFSA and SAR.
Additional information: Minimum 3.0 GPA. Must have stated interest in observatory career. Amount and number of awards vary and may change yearly.
Application deadline: February 15
Contact:
Hawaii Community Foundation
827 Fort Street Mall
Honolulu, HI 96813
Phone: 888-731-3863
Fax: 808-521-6286
Web: www.hawaiicommunityfoundation.org

Hokulani Hawaii Fund

Type of award: Scholarship.
Intended use: For full-time at 4-year institution in United States. Designated institutions: Private institutions on U.S. mainland.
Eligibility: Applicant must be U.S. citizen residing in Hawaii.
Basis for selection: Applicant must demonstrate financial need and high academic achievement.
Application requirements: Recommendations, essay, transcript. FAFSA and SAR.
Additional information: GPA must be between 2.9 and 3.4. Must be graduate of private high school in Hawaii within last three years. Preference given to first generation college students. Amount and number of awards vary and may change yearly.
Application deadline: February 15
Contact:
Hawaii Community Foundation
827 Fort Street Mall
Honolulu, HI 96813
Phone: 888-731-3863
Fax: 808-521-6286
Web: www.hawaiicommunityfoundation.org

Hokuli'a Foundation Scholarship Fund

Type of award: Scholarship.
Intended use: For full-time undergraduate or graduate study at accredited 2-year or 4-year institution in United States.
Eligibility: Applicant must be U.S. citizen residing in Hawaii.
Basis for selection: Major/career interest in health-related professions; education or social work. Applicant must demonstrate financial need, high academic achievement, depth of character and service orientation.
Application requirements: Recommendations, essay, transcript. SAR, FAFSA, personal statement should include record of community service and how future career will benefit Hawaii residents and state intentions to stay or return to Hawaii after graduation.
Additional information: Minimum 2.7 GPA. Must be resident of South or North Kona. Preference given to students demonstrating emphasis in advancing native Hawaiian culture.

Application deadline: February 15
Contact:
Hawaii Community Foundation Scholarships
827 Fort Street Mall
Honolulu, HI 96813
Phone: 888-731-3863
Fax: 808-521-6286
Web: www.hawaiicommunityfoundation.org

Hon Chew Hee Scholarship Fund

Type of award: Scholarship.
Intended use: For full-time undergraduate or graduate study at accredited 2-year or 4-year institution in United States.
Eligibility: Applicant must be U.S. citizen residing in Hawaii.
Basis for selection: Major/career interest in art/art history. Applicant must demonstrate financial need, high academic achievement and depth of character.
Application requirements: Recommendations, essay, transcript. SAR, FAFSA, personal statement. Two letters of recommendation required. One must be from an art instructor.
Additional information: Minimum 2.7 GPA. Major in fine arts with preference given to students focusing on painting, drawing, sculpting, ceramics, printmaking, and textiles.
Application deadline: February 15
Contact:
Hawaii Community Foundation Scholarships
827 Fort Street Mall
Honolulu, HI 96813
Phone: 888-731-3863
Fax: 808-521-6286
Web: www.hawaiicommunityfoundation.org

Ho'omaka Hou - A New Beginning Fund

Type of award: Scholarship.
Intended use: For full-time undergraduate or graduate study at accredited 2-year or 4-year institution in United States.
Eligibility: Applicant must be U.S. citizen residing in Hawaii.
Basis for selection: Applicant must demonstrate financial need, high academic achievement and depth of character.
Application requirements: Recommendations, essay, transcript. SAR, FAFSA, personal statement should describe substance abuse problems and how they were overcome.
Additional information: Minimum 2.7 GPA. Applicant must have overcome substance abuse.
Application deadline: February 15
Contact:
Hawaii Community Foundation Scholarships
827 Fort Street Mall
Honolulu, HI 96813
Phone: 888-731-3863
Fax: 808-521-6286
Web: www.hawaiicommunityfoundation.org

Ian Doane Smith Scholarship Fund

Type of award: Scholarship.
Intended use: For full-time undergraduate or graduate study at accredited 2-year or 4-year institution in United States.
Eligibility: Applicant must be high school senior. Applicant must be U.S. citizen residing in Hawaii.
Basis for selection: Applicant must demonstrate financial need, high academic achievement, depth of character and service orientation.
Application requirements: Recommendations, essay, transcript. SAR, FAFSA, personal statement must detail community service and experiences with surfing or soccer.
Additional information: Minimum 2.7 GPA. Must be resident of island of Maui. Must be active in soccer and/or surfing.
Application deadline: February 15
Contact:
Hawaii Community Foundation Scholarships
827 Fort Street Mall
Honolulu, HI 96813
Phone: 888-731-3863
Fax: 808-521-6286
Web: www.hawaiicommunityfoundation.org

Ichiro & Masako Hirata Scholarship

Type of award: Scholarship.
Intended use: For full-time junior, senior or graduate study at accredited postsecondary institution.
Eligibility: Applicant must be residing in Hawaii.
Basis for selection: Major/career interest in education. Applicant must demonstrate financial need and high academic achievement.
Application requirements: Recommendations, essay, transcript. SAR, FAFSA.
Additional information: Minimum 3.0 GPA.
Application deadline: February 15
Contact:
Hawaii Community Foundation
827 Fort Street Mall
Honolulu, HI 96813
Phone: 888-731-3863
Fax: 808-521-6286
Web: www.hawaiicommunityfoundation.org

Ida M. Pope Memorial Scholarship

Type of award: Scholarship.
Intended use: For full-time undergraduate or graduate study at accredited 2-year or 4-year institution in United States.
Eligibility: Applicant must be Native Hawaiian/Pacific Islander. Applicant must be female. Applicant must be U.S. citizen residing in Hawaii.
Basis for selection: Major/career interest in health-related professions; science, general or education. Applicant must demonstrate high academic achievement and depth of character.
Application requirements: Recommendations, essay, transcript. SAR, FAFSA, personal statement. Birth certificate.
Additional information: Minimum 3.5 GPA. Must be of Hawaiian descent.
Application deadline: February 15
Contact:
Hawaii Community Foundation Scholarships
827 Fort Street Mall
Honolulu, HI 96813
Phone: 888-731-3863
Fax: 808-521-6286
Web: www.hawaiicommunityfoundation.org

Isemoto Contracting Co., Ltd. Scholarship Fund

Type of award: Scholarship.
Intended use: For full-time sophomore, junior, senior or graduate study at accredited 2-year or 4-year institution in United States.
Eligibility: Applicant must be U.S. citizen residing in Hawaii.

Basis for selection: Major/career interest in engineering; nursing or education. Applicant must demonstrate financial need, high academic achievement and depth of character.
Application requirements: Recommendations, essay, transcript. SAR, FAFSA, personal statement.
Additional information: Minimum 2.7 GPA. Must be graduate of high school on island of Hawaii. Must be accepted as upper classman to a school of engineering, teacher education program, or nursing program.
Application deadline: February 15
Contact:
Hawaii Community Foundation Scholarships
827 Fort Street Mall
Honolulu, HI 96813
Phone: 888-731-3863
Fax: 808-521-6286
Web: www.hawaiicommunityfoundation.org

Iwamoto Family Scholarship

Type of award: Scholarship, renewable.
Intended use: For full-time undergraduate or graduate study at accredited 2-year or 4-year institution in United States.
Eligibility: Applicant must be U.S. citizen or permanent resident residing in Hawaii.
Basis for selection: Applicant must demonstrate financial need, high academic achievement and depth of character.
Application requirements: Essay, transcript. FAFSA.
Additional information: Must be recent graduate of a Kauai high school. Minimum 3.0 GPA.
Application deadline: February 15
Contact:
Hawaii Community Foundation
827 Fort Street Mall
Honolulu, HI 96813
Phone: 888-731-3863
Fax: 808-521-6286
Web: www.hawaiicommunityfoundation.org

Iwamoto Family Vocational Scholarship

Type of award: Scholarship, renewable.
Intended use: For full-time undergraduate study at accredited 2-year institution in United States. Designated institutions: University of Hawaii community colleges.
Eligibility: Applicant must be U.S. citizen or permanent resident residing in Hawaii.
Basis for selection: Applicant must demonstrate financial need, high academic achievement and depth of character.
Application requirements: Essay, transcript. FAFSA.
Additional information: Minimum 2.8 GPA. Must be recent graduate of Kauai high school. Must be enrolled in vocational program in University of Hawaii community college system.
Application deadline: February 15
Contact:
Hawaii Community Foundation
827 Fort Street Mall
Honolulu, HI 96813
Phone: 888-731-3863
Fax: 808-521-6286
Web: www.hawaiicommunityfoundation.org

Jean Estes Epstein Charitable Foundation Scholarship

Type of award: Scholarship, renewable.
Intended use: For full-time freshman study at accredited postsecondary institution in United States. Designated institutions: Schools in the continental United States.
Eligibility: Applicant must be residing in Hawaii.
Basis for selection: Applicant must demonstrate financial need and high academic achievement.
Application requirements: Recommendations, essay, transcript. SAR, FAFSA, SAT/ACT scores. Personal statement must include personal and career goals.
Additional information: Minimum 3.7 GPA. Must be graduate of Hawaii public high school. Must attend college in the continental United States.
Application deadline: February 15
Contact:
Hawaii Community Foundation
827 Fort Street Mall
Honolulu, HI 96813
Phone: 888-731-3863
Fax: 808-521-6286
Web: www.hawaiicommunityfoundation.org

Jean Fitzgerald Scholarship Fund

Type of award: Scholarship, renewable.
Intended use: For full-time freshman study at accredited 2-year or 4-year institution in United States.
Eligibility: Applicant must be female, high school senior. Applicant must be U.S. citizen or permanent resident residing in Hawaii.
Basis for selection: Applicant must demonstrate financial need, high academic achievement and depth of character.
Application requirements: Essay, transcript. FAFSA and SAR.
Additional information: Minimum 2.7 GPA. Applicant must be active tennis player; preference may be given to USTA/ Hawaii Pacific Section members. Applicants must have permanent address in Hawaii. Applicants who take up mainland residency must have relatives living in Hawaii. Amount and number of awards vary.
Application deadline: February 15
Total amount awarded: $7,000
Contact:
Hawaii Community Foundation Scholarships
827 Fort Street Mall
Honolulu, HI 96813
Phone: 888-731-3863
Fax: 808-521-6286
Web: www.hawaiicommunityfoundation.org

Jean Ileialoha Beniamina Scholarship for Ni'ihau Students Fund

Type of award: Scholarship.
Intended use: For full-time undergraduate or graduate study at accredited postsecondary institution.
Eligibility: Applicant must be residing in Hawaii.
Basis for selection: Applicant must demonstrate financial need and high academic achievement.
Application requirements: Recommendations, essay, transcript. SAR, FAFSA. Essay describing family descent and connection to Ni'ihau and addressing proficiency in Hawaiian language and listing courses taken in Hawaiian.

Additional information: Minimum 2.7 GPA. Must be resident of Kauai or Ni'ihau Island. Preference given to current Ni'ihau residents or Kauai residents who are one or two generations removed from Ni'ihau Island. Preference given to students fluent in Hawaiian language.
Application deadline: February 15
Contact:
Hawaii Community Foundation
827 Fort Street Mall
Honolulu, HI 96813
Phone: 888-731-3863
Fax: 808-521-6286
Web: www.hawaiicommunityfoundation.org

Johanna Drew Cluney Scholarship

Type of award: Scholarship.
Intended use: For undergraduate study at accredited vocational or 2-year institution in United States. Designated institutions: Community colleges in the University of Hawaii system.
Eligibility: Applicant must be residing in Hawaii.
Basis for selection: Applicant must demonstrate financial need and high academic achievement.
Application requirements: Recommendations, essay, transcript. SAR, FAFSA.
Additional information: Minimum 2.7 GPA. Must be enrolled in University of Hawaii Community College system.
Application deadline: February 15
Contact:
Hawaii Community Foundation
827 Fort Street Mall
Honolulu, HI 96813
Phone: 888-731-3863
Fax: 808-521-6286
Web: www.hawaiicommunityfoundation.org

John & Anne Clifton Scholarship Fund

Type of award: Scholarship.
Intended use: For full-time undergraduate study at accredited 2-year or 4-year institution in United States. Designated institutions: Community colleges in the University of Hawaii system.
Eligibility: Applicant must be residing in Hawaii.
Basis for selection: Applicant must demonstrate financial need and high academic achievement.
Application requirements: Recommendations, essay, transcript. SAR, FAFSA.
Additional information: Minimum 2.7 GPA. Must be enrolled in a vocational educational program in the University of Hawaii Community College system.
Application deadline: February 15
Contact:
Hawaii Community Foundation
827 Fort Street Mall
Honolulu, HI 96813
Phone: 888-731-3863
Fax: 808-521-6286
Web: www.hawaiicommunityfoundation.org

John Dawe Dental Education Fund

Type of award: Scholarship, renewable.
Intended use: For full-time undergraduate or graduate study at accredited postsecondary institution in United States.
Eligibility: Applicant must be U.S. citizen or permanent resident residing in Hawaii.
Basis for selection: Major/career interest in dentistry; dental hygiene or dental assistant. Applicant must demonstrate financial need, high academic achievement and depth of character.
Application requirements: Recommendations, essay, transcript, proof of eligibility. FAFSA and SAR. Letter from school confirming enrollment in the dental hygiene or dentistry program.
Additional information: Minimum 2.7 GPA. Applicants must have permanent address in Hawaii. Applicants taking up mainland residency must have relatives living in Hawaii. Amount and number of awards vary.
Application deadline: February 15
Contact:
Hawaii Community Foundation Scholarships
827 Fort Street Mall
Honolulu, HI 96813
Phone: 888-731-3863
Fax: 808-521-6286
Web: www.hawaiicommunityfoundation.org

John M. Ross Foundation Scholarship

Type of award: Scholarship.
Intended use: For undergraduate study at 2-year or 4-year institution.
Eligibility: Applicant must be residing in Hawaii.
Basis for selection: Applicant must demonstrate financial need and high academic achievement.
Application requirements: Recommendations, essay, transcript. FAFSA and SAR.
Additional information: Minimum 2.7 GPA. Amount and number of awards vary and may change yearly.
Application deadline: February 15
Contact:
Hawaii Community Foundation
827 Fort Street Mall
Honolulu, HI 96813
Phone: 888-731-3863
Fax: 808-521-6286
Web: www.hawaiicommunityfoundation.org

Joseph & Alice Duarte Memorial Fund

Type of award: Scholarship.
Intended use: For full-time undergraduate or graduate study at accredited 2-year or 4-year institution in United States.
Eligibility: Applicant must be U.S. citizen residing in Hawaii.
Basis for selection: Applicant must demonstrate financial need, high academic achievement and depth of character.
Application requirements: Recommendations, essay, transcript. SAR, FAFSA, personal statement.
Additional information: Minimum 2.7 GPA. Must be from North or South Kona districts of Hawaii. Preference given to graduates of Holualoa Elementary School.
Application deadline: February 15
Contact:
Hawaii Community Foundation Scholarships
827 Fort Street Mall
Honolulu, HI 96813
Phone: 888-731-3863
Fax: 808-521-6286
Web: www.hawaiicommunityfoundation.org

Juliette M. Atherton Scholarship - Minister's Sons and Daughters

Type of award: Scholarship.
Intended use: For full-time undergraduate study at accredited postsecondary institution.
Eligibility: Applicant must be Protestant. Applicant must be residing in Hawaii.
Basis for selection: Applicant must demonstrate financial need and high academic achievement.
Application requirements: Recommendations, essay, transcript. SAR, FAFSA. Personal statement must include minister's current position, name of church/parish, denomination, place/date of ordination, name of seminary attended.
Additional information: Minimum 2.7 GPA. Must be dependent son or daughter of ordained and active Protestant minister in established denomination in Hawaii.
Application deadline: February 15
Contact:
Hawaii Community Foundation
827 Fort Street Mall
Honolulu, HI 96813
Phone: 888-731-3863
Fax: 808-521-6286
Web: www.hawaiicommunityfoundation.org

Ka'iulani Home for Girls Trust Scholarship

Type of award: Scholarship, renewable.
Intended use: For full-time freshman or sophomore study at accredited postsecondary institution in United States.
Eligibility: Applicant must be Native Hawaiian/Pacific Islander. Applicant must be female. Applicant must be U.S. citizen or permanent resident residing in Hawaii.
Basis for selection: Applicant must demonstrate financial need, high academic achievement and depth of character.
Application requirements: Essay, transcript, proof of eligibility. FAFSA and SAR, birth certificate.
Additional information: Minimum 3.3 GPA. Must be of Hawaiian ancestry. First time applicants must be freshmen or sophomores. Juniors and seniors who are past recipients also eligible. Must have permanent address in Hawaii. Applicants taking up mainland residency must have relatives living in Hawaii. Amount and number of awards vary and may change yearly.
Application deadline: February 15
Contact:
Hawaii Community Foundation Scholarships
827 Fort Street Mall
Honolulu, HI 96813
Phone: 888-731-3863
Fax: 808-521-6286
Web: www.hawaiicommunityfoundation.org

Ka'a'awa Community Fund

Type of award: Scholarship.
Intended use: For full-time undergraduate or graduate study at accredited 2-year or 4-year institution in United States.
Eligibility: Applicant must be U.S. citizen or permanent resident residing in Hawaii.
Basis for selection: Applicant must demonstrate financial need, high academic achievement and depth of character.
Application requirements: Essay, transcript. FAFSA and SAR.
Additional information: Minimum 2.7 GPA. Must be resident of the Ka'a'awa area on Windward O'ahu. Preference given to long-time residents. Amount and number of awards vary and may change yearly.
Application deadline: February 15
Contact:
Hawaii Community Foundation Scholarships
827 Fort Street Mall
Honolulu, HI 96813
Phone: 888-731-3863
Fax: 808-521-6286
Web: www.hawaiicommunityfoundation.org

Kahala Nui Residents Scholarship Fund

Type of award: Scholarship.
Intended use: For full-time undergraduate or graduate study at accredited 2-year or 4-year institution.
Eligibility: Applicant must be U.S. citizen residing in Hawaii.
Basis for selection: Applicant must demonstrate financial need, high academic achievement and depth of character.
Application requirements: Recommendations, essay, transcript. SAR, FAFSA, personal statement.
Additional information: Minimum 2.7 GPA. Applicant must be an employee or a dependent of an employee of Kahala Senior Living Community, Inc. for at least 6 months prior to application deadline. Amount of award varies.
Application deadline: February 15
Contact:
Hawaii Community Foundation Scholarships
827 Fort Street Mall
Honolulu, HI 96813
Phone: 888-731-3863
Fax: 808-521-6286
Web: www.hawaiicommunityfoundation.org

Kalihi Education Coalition Scholarship Fund

Type of award: Scholarship.
Intended use: For full-time undergraduate or graduate study at accredited postsecondary institution.
Eligibility: Applicant must be residing in Hawaii.
Basis for selection: Applicant must demonstrate financial need and high academic achievement.
Application requirements: Recommendations, essay, transcript. SAR, FAFSA.
Additional information: Minimum 3.0 GPA. Must either be a graduate or undergraduate student who is a resident of Kalihi-Palama with one of following zip codes: 96817, 96819.
Application deadline: February 15
Contact:
Hawaii Community Foundation
827 Fort Street Mall
Honolulu, HI 96813
Phone: 888-731-3863
Fax: 808-521-6286
Web: www.hawaiicommunityfoundation.org

Kapolei Business & Community Scholarship

Type of award: Scholarship.
Intended use: For full-time undergraduate study at accredited 2-year or 4-year institution in United States.

Eligibility: Applicant must be high school senior. Applicant must be U.S. citizen or permanent resident residing in Hawaii.
Basis for selection: Applicant must demonstrate financial need, high academic achievement and depth of character.
Application requirements: Essay, transcript. FAFSA and SAR.
Additional information: Minimum 2.7 GPA. Applicant must be a senior from Campbell, Nanakuli, or Waianae high schools. Applicants taking up mainland residency must have relatives living in Hawaii. Amount of award may vary yearly.
Application deadline: February 15
Contact:
Hawaii Community Foundation Scholarships
827 Fort Street Mall
Honolulu, HI 96813
Phone: 888-731-3863
Fax: 808-521-6286
Web: www.hawaiicommunityfoundation.org

Kawasaki-McGaha Scholarship Fund

Type of award: Scholarship.
Intended use: For full-time undergraduate study at postsecondary institution. Designated institutions: Hawaii Pacific University.
Eligibility: Applicant must be permanent resident residing in Hawaii.
Basis for selection: Major/career interest in computer/information sciences or international studies. Applicant must demonstrate financial need, high academic achievement and depth of character.
Application requirements: Essay, transcript. FAFSA and SAR.
Additional information: Minimum 2.7 GPA. Applicants must have permanent address in Hawaii. Applicants taking up mainland residency must have relatives living in Hawaii. Amount and number of awards vary and may change yearly.
Application deadline: February 15
Contact:
Hawaii Community Foundation Scholarships
827 Fort Street Mall
Honolulu, HI 96813
Phone: 888-731-3863
Fax: 808-521-6286
Web: www.hawaiicommunityfoundation.org

Kazuma and Ichiko Hisanaga Scholarship Fund

Type of award: Scholarship.
Intended use: For full-time undergraduate study at accredited 2-year or 4-year institution in United States. Designated institutions: NAIA or Division III school in the contiguous United States.
Eligibility: Applicant must be high school senior. Applicant must be U.S. citizen residing in Hawaii.
Basis for selection: Applicant must demonstrate financial need, high academic achievement, depth of character, leadership and service orientation.
Application requirements: Recommendations, essay, transcript. SAR, FAFSA, Personal statement detailing sports involvement, leadership experience and community service. One recommendation letter must be from high school athletic director, or post-secondary counselor or administrator.
Additional information: Minimum 3.0 GPA. Amount of award varies. Applicant must be a graduating senior at Hilo High School; if Hilo has no eligible applicants from Hilo High School, seniors from other Hawai'i Island high schools will be considered in the following order: Waiakea High School, St. Joseph High School, other Hawai'i Island high schools. Applicant must be an athlete that participated in a varsity high school sport. Preference given to those participating in more than one varsity sport. Must have served as the captain of a varsity sports team, a student government leader, or an officer of an extracurricular program.
Application deadline: February 15
Contact:
Hawaii Community Foundation Scholarships
827 Fort Street Mall
Honolulu, HI 96813
Phone: 888-731-3863
Fax: 808-521-6286
Web: www.hawaiicommunityfoundation.org

Kenneth Makinney & David T. Pietsch Familes Scholarship Fund

Type of award: Scholarship.
Intended use: For full-time undergraduate or graduate study at accredited postsecondary institution.
Eligibility: Applicant must be residing in Hawaii.
Basis for selection: Applicant must demonstrate financial need and high academic achievement.
Application requirements: Recommendations, essay, transcript. SAR, FAFSA, name and job title of Guaranty employee.
Additional information: Minimum 2.7 GPA. Must be full-time employee of at least one year or qualified dependent of Title Guaranty of Hawaii, Incorporated or Title Guaranty Escrow Services, Inc.
Application deadline: February 15
Contact:
Hawaii Community Foundation
827 Fort Street Mall
Honolulu, HI 96813
Phone: 888-731-3863
Fax: 808-521-6286
Web: www.hawaiicommunityfoundation.org

King Kekaulike High School Scholarship

Type of award: Scholarship.
Intended use: For full-time undergraduate study at accredited 2-year or 4-year institution in United States.
Eligibility: Applicant must be high school senior. Applicant must be U.S. citizen or permanent resident residing in Hawaii.
Basis for selection: Applicant must demonstrate financial need, high academic achievement, depth of character and service orientation.
Application requirements: Essay, transcript. FAFSA and SAR. Additional 500-word essay on how well Na Ali'i 3 R's (Respect, Relevance, and Rigor) relate to your future goals.
Additional information: Minimum 2.8 GPA and three or more hours of community service required. Applicant must be graduating senior at King Kekaulike High School. Children of KKHS staff members not eligible. Amount of award may change yearly. Applicants taking up mainland residency must have relatives living in Hawaii.
Application deadline: February 15

Contact:
Hawaii Community Foundation Scholarships
827 Fort Street Mall
Honolulu, HI 96813
Phone: 888-731-3863
Fax: 808-521-6286
Web: www.hawaiicommunityfoundation.org

K.M. Hatano Scholarship

Type of award: Scholarship, renewable.
Intended use: For full-time undergraduate study at accredited 4-year institution in United States. Designated institutions: Institutions in Hawaii.
Eligibility: Applicant must be high school senior. Applicant must be U.S. citizen or permanent resident residing in Hawaii.
Basis for selection: Applicant must demonstrate financial need, high academic achievement and depth of character.
Application requirements: Essay, transcript. FAFSA and SAR.
Additional information: Minimum 2.7 GPA. Applicant must be high school graduate of Maui, including Lanai or Molokai counties. Must attend college in Hawaii. Applicant must have permanent address in Hawaii. Applicants taking up mainland residency must have relatives living in Hawaii. Amount and number of awards vary and may change yearly.
Application deadline: February 15
Contact:
Hawaii Community Foundation Scholarships
827 Fort Street Mall
Honolulu, HI 96813
Phone: 888-731-3863
Fax: 808-521-6286
Web: www.hawaiicommunityfoundation.org

Kohala Ditch Education Fund

Type of award: Scholarship.
Intended use: For full-time undergraduate study at accredited 2-year or 4-year institution in United States.
Eligibility: Applicant must be high school senior. Applicant must be U.S. citizen or permanent resident residing in Hawaii.
Basis for selection: Applicant must demonstrate financial need, high academic achievement and depth of character.
Application requirements: Essay, transcript. FAFSA and SAR.
Additional information: Minimum 2.7 GPA. Applicant must be student at Kohala High School. Amount of award may change yearly. Applicants taking up mainland residency must have relatives living in Hawaii.
Application deadline: February 15
Contact:
Hawaii Community Foundation Scholarships
827 Fort Street Mall
Honolulu, HI 96813
Phone: 888-731-3863
Fax: 808-521-6286
Web: www.hawaiicommunityfoundation.org

Koloa Scholarship

Type of award: Scholarship, renewable.
Intended use: For full-time undergraduate or graduate study at accredited vocational, 2-year or 4-year institution in United States.
Eligibility: Applicant must be U.S. citizen or permanent resident residing in Hawaii.
Basis for selection: Applicant must demonstrate financial need, high academic achievement and depth of character.
Application requirements: Recommendations, transcript. FAFSA and SAR. Personal essay explaining personal understanding of meaning of "aloha," how it has played a part in personal development and how applicant hopes to use chosen field to further this meaning among family and community. Must include how long applicant has lived in Koloa area, list of books or other publications read on Hawaii's history, and list of relatives born in Koloa District, including relationship to applicant, and place and approximate year of birth.
Additional information: Minimum 2.0 GPA. Applicant must be resident of one of the following Kauai areas in Hawaii: Koloa, including Omao and Poipu (96756), Lawai (96765), or Kalaheo (96741). Applicants taking up mainland residency must have relatives living in Hawaii. Amount of award varies and may change yearly.
Application deadline: February 15
Contact:
Hawaii Community Foundation Scholarships
827 Fort Street Mall
Honolulu, HI 96813
Phone: 888-731-3863
Fax: 808-521-6286
Web: www.hawaiicommunityfoundation.org

Korean University Club Scholarship Fund

Type of award: Scholarship.
Intended use: For full-time undergraduate or graduate study at accredited 2-year or 4-year institution in United States.
Eligibility: Applicant must be U.S. citizen residing in Hawaii.
Basis for selection: Applicant must demonstrate financial need, high academic achievement and depth of character.
Application requirements: Recommendations, essay, transcript. SAR, FAFSA, Personal Statement.
Additional information: Minimum 2.7 GPA. Must be of Korean ancestry.
Application deadline: February 15
Contact:
Hawaii Community Foundation Scholarships
827 Fort Street Mall
Honolulu, HI 96813
Phone: 888-731-3863
Fax: 808-521-6286
Web: www.hawaiicommunityfoundation.org

Korean War Veteran's Children's Scholarship

Type of award: Scholarship.
Intended use: For full-time undergraduate study at 2-year or 4-year institution.
Eligibility: Applicant must be residing in Hawaii. Applicant must be descendant of veteran who served in the Army, Air Force, Marines or Navy.
Basis for selection: Applicant must demonstrate financial need and high academic achievement.
Application requirements: Recommendations, essay, transcript. FAFSA and SAR.
Additional information: Minimum 3.0 GPA. Must be direct descendant of Korean War veteran or soldier who served in foreign war. First preference given to descendants of those who died in combat, second preference to those who served in

Scholarships

Korea. Amount and number of awards vary and may change yearly.

Application deadline: February 15

Contact:
Hawaii Community Foundation
827 Fort Street Mall
Honolulu, HI 96813
Phone: 888-731-3863
Fax: 808-521-6286
Web: www.hawaiicommunityfoundation.org

Kurt W. Schneider Memorial Scholarship Fund

Type of award: Scholarship.
Intended use: For full-time undergraduate study at accredited 2-year or 4-year institution in United States.
Eligibility: Applicant must be high school senior. Applicant must be U.S. citizen or permanent resident residing in Hawaii.
Basis for selection: Major/career interest in tourism/travel. Applicant must demonstrate financial need, high academic achievement and depth of character.
Application requirements: Essay, transcript. FAFSA and SAR.
Additional information: Minimum 2.7 GPA. Applicant must be student at Lana'i High School. Preference given to travel industry management majors. Applicants taking up mainland residency must have relatives living in Hawaii. Amount of award may change yearly.

Application deadline: February 15

Contact:
Hawaii Community Foundation Scholarships
827 Fort Street Mall
Honolulu, HI 96813
Phone: 888-731-3863
Fax: 808-521-6286
Web: www.hawaiicommunityfoundation.org

Laura N. Dowsett Fund

Type of award: Scholarship, renewable.
Intended use: For full-time junior, senior or graduate study at accredited 2-year, 4-year or graduate institution in United States.
Eligibility: Applicant must be U.S. citizen or permanent resident residing in Hawaii.
Basis for selection: Major/career interest in occupational therapy. Applicant must demonstrate financial need, high academic achievement and depth of character.
Application requirements: Essay, transcript. FAFSA and SAR.
Additional information: Minimum 2.7 GPA. Applicants must have permanent address in Hawaii. Applicants who take up mainland residency must have relatives living in Hawaii. Amount and number of awards vary.

Application deadline: February 15

Contact:
Hawaii Community Foundation Scholarships
827 Fort Street Mall
Honolulu, HI 96813
Phone: 888-731-3863
Fax: 808-521-6286
Web: www.hawaiicommunityfoundation.org

Laura Rowe Burdick Scholarship Fund

Type of award: Scholarship.
Intended use: For full-time undergraduate study at accredited 2-year or 4-year institution in United States.
Eligibility: Applicant must be high school senior. Applicant must be U.S. citizen residing in Hawaii.
Basis for selection: Applicant must demonstrate financial need, high academic achievement, depth of character and service orientation.
Application requirements: Recommendations, essay, transcript. SAR, FAFSA, personal statement.
Additional information: Minimum 2.7 GPA. Amount of award varies. Applicant must be a high school senior in Maui County. Preference given to applicants who want to return to Maui County after completing their education or training in order to contribute to the community that formed them.

Application deadline: February 15

Contact:
Hawaii Community Foundation Scholarships
827 Fort Street Mall
Honolulu, HI 96813
Phone: 888-731-3863
Fax: 808-521-6286
Web: www.hawaiicommunityfoundation.org

Lillian B. Reynolds Scholarship

Type of award: Scholarship, renewable.
Intended use: For full-time undergraduate or graduate study at accredited 2-year, 4-year or graduate institution in United States.
Eligibility: Applicant must be U.S. citizen or permanent resident residing in Hawaii.
Basis for selection: Major/career interest in medicine or nursing. Applicant must demonstrate depth of character.
Application requirements: Essay, transcript. FAFSA.
Additional information: Minimum 2.7 GPA. Must be medical or nursing student.

Application deadline: February 15

Contact:
Hawaii Community Foundation
827 Fort Street Mall
Honolulu, HI 96813
Phone: 888-731-3863
Fax: 808-521-6286
Web: www.hawaiicommunityfoundation.org

Logan Nainoa Fujimoto Memorial Scholarship

Type of award: Scholarship.
Intended use: For full-time undergraduate study at accredited vocational institution in United States. Designated institutions: Vocational schools with automotive technology programs.
Eligibility: Applicant must be residing in Hawaii.
Basis for selection: Applicant must demonstrate financial need and high academic achievement.
Application requirements: Recommendations, essay, transcript. SAR, FAFSA.
Additional information: Minimum 2.7 GPA. Preference given to students attending Universal Technical Institute. Must be concentrating in Automotive Technology.

Application deadline: February 15

Contact:
Hawaii Community Foundation
827 Fort Street Mall
Honolulu, HI 96813
Phone: 888-731-3863
Fax: 808-521-6286
Web: www.hawaiicommunityfoundation.org

March Taylor Educational Fund Scholarship

Type of award: Scholarship, renewable.
Intended use: For full-time undergraduate study at accredited vocational institution in United States.
Eligibility: Applicant must be U.S. citizen or permanent resident residing in Hawaii.
Basis for selection: Applicant must demonstrate financial need, high academic achievement and depth of character.
Application requirements: Essay, transcript. FAFSA.
Additional information: Minimum 2.7 GPA. Must be from island of Hawaii, with preference given to residents of West Hawaii. Must be enrolled in auto body repair and painting program.

Application deadline: February 15

Contact:
Hawaii Community Foundation
827 Fort Street Mall
Honolulu 96813-HI
Phone: 888-731-3863
Fax: 808-521-6286
Web: www.hawaiicommunityfoundation.org

Margaret Follett Haskins (Maui) Scholarship

Type of award: Scholarship.
Intended use: For full-time junior or senior study at accredited 4-year institution in United States. Designated institutions: Schools in the University of Hawaii system.
Eligibility: Applicant must be residing in Hawaii.
Basis for selection: Applicant must demonstrate financial need and high academic achievement.
Application requirements: Recommendations, essay, transcript. FAFSA and SAR.
Additional information: Minimum 3.0 GPA. Must be graduate of Maui Community College attending 4-year University of Hawaii school. Amount and number of awards vary and may change yearly.

Application deadline: February 15

Contact:
Hawaii Community Foundation
827 Fort Street Mall
Honolulu, HI 96813
Phone: 888-731-3863
Fax: 808-521-6286
Web: www.hawaiicommunityfoundation.org

Margaret Follett Haskins Hawaii Scholarship

Type of award: Scholarship.
Intended use: For full-time junior or senior study at accredited 4-year institution in United States. Designated institutions: UH-Manoa, UH-Hilo, or UH-West Oahu.
Eligibility: Applicant must be residing in Hawaii.
Basis for selection: Applicant must demonstrate financial need and high academic achievement.
Application requirements: Recommendations, essay, transcript. FAFSA and SAR.
Additional information: Minimum 3.5 GPA. Must be current graduate of community college in University of Hawaii system transferring to UH-Manoa, UH-Hilo, or UH-West Oahu. Amount and number of awards vary and may change yearly.

Application deadline: February 15

Contact:
Hawaii Community Foundation
827 Fort Street Mall
Honolulu, HI 96813
Phone: 888-731-3863
Fax: 808-521-6286
Web: www.hawaiicommunityfoundation.org

Margaret Jones Memorial Nursing Scholarship

Type of award: Scholarship, renewable.
Intended use: For full-time junior, senior or graduate study at accredited 4-year or graduate institution in United States. Designated institutions: University of Hawaii, Manoa; University of Hawaii, Hilo; Hawaii Pacific University; or PhD programs in Hawaii or mainland U.S.
Eligibility: Applicant must be U.S. citizen or permanent resident residing in Hawaii.
Basis for selection: Major/career interest in nursing. Applicant must demonstrate financial need, high academic achievement and depth of character.
Application requirements: Essay, transcript. FAFSA and SAR.
Additional information: Minimum 3.0 GPA. Applicants must be enrolled in BSN, MSN, or doctoral nursing program. Preference may be given to members of Hawaii Nurses Association. Applicants must have permanent address in Hawaii. Applicant taking up mainland residency must have relatives living in Hawaii. Amount and number of awards vary and change yearly.

Number of awards: 13
Application deadline: February 15

Contact:
Hawaii Community Foundation Scholarships
827 Fort Street Mall
Honolulu, HI 96813
Phone: 888-731-3863
Fax: 808-521-6286
Web: www.hawaiicommunityfoundation.org

Marion Maccarrell Scott Scholarship

Type of award: Scholarship, renewable.
Intended use: For full-time undergraduate or graduate study at accredited postsecondary institution in United States. Designated institutions: Institutions on U.S. mainland.
Eligibility: Applicant must be U.S. citizen or permanent resident residing in Hawaii.
Basis for selection: Applicant must demonstrate financial need, high academic achievement and depth of character.
Application requirements: Essay, transcript. FAFSA and SAR. Essay (2-3 typed pages, double-spaced) must demonstrate commitment to international understanding and world peace.
Additional information: Minimum 2.8 GPA. Must be graduate of Hawaii public high school and attend accredited mainland U.S. college or university. Applicant must have permanent address in Hawaii. Applicants taking up mainland residency must have relatives living in Hawaii. Amount and number of awards vary and may change yearly.

Application deadline: February 15

Contact:
Hawaii Community Foundation Scholarships
827 Fort Street Mall
Honolulu, HI 96813
Phone: 888-731-3863
Fax: 808-521-6286
Web: www.hawaiicommunityfoundation.org

Mary Josephine Bloder Scholarship

Type of award: Scholarship.
Intended use: For full-time undergraduate study at accredited 2-year or 4-year institution in United States.
Eligibility: Applicant must be high school senior. Applicant must be U.S. citizen or permanent resident residing in Hawaii.
Basis for selection: Applicant must demonstrate financial need, high academic achievement and depth of character.
Application requirements: Recommendations, essay, transcript. FAFSA and SAR. One of the two letters of recommendation must be from Lahainaluna High School science teacher.
Additional information: Must be graduating senior at Lahainaluna High School. Preference given to boarding students. Must have high GPA in sciences. Applicants taking up mainland residency must have relatives living in Hawaii. Amount and number of awards vary and may change yearly.

Application deadline: February 15

Contact:
Hawaii Community Foundation Scholarships
827 Fort Street Mall
Honolulu, HI 96813
Phone: 888-731-3863
Fax: 808-521-6286
Web: www.hawaiicommunityfoundation.org

Mildred Towle Scholarship - Study Abroad

Type of award: Scholarship, renewable.
Intended use: For full-time junior, senior or graduate study at accredited postsecondary institution outside United States.
Eligibility: Applicant must be residing in Hawaii.
Basis for selection: Applicant must demonstrate financial need, high academic achievement and depth of character.
Application requirements: Essay, transcript. FAFSA and SAR. Essay must include intended country and semester of study.
Additional information: Minimum 3.0 GPA. Award for Hawaii residents studying abroad during regular academic year while enrolled at U.S. institution. Summer semester not included. Amount and number of awards vary and may change yearly.

Application deadline: February 15

Contact:
Hawaii Community Foundation Scholarships
827 Fort Street Mall
Honolulu, HI 96813
Phone: 888-731-3863
Fax: 808-521-6286
Web: www.hawaiicommunityfoundation.org

Mildred Towle Scholarship for African-Americans

Type of award: Scholarship.
Intended use: For undergraduate study at postsecondary institution. Designated institutions: Hawaii postsecondary institutions.
Eligibility: Applicant must be African American. Applicant must be U.S. citizen.
Basis for selection: Applicant must demonstrate high academic achievement.
Application requirements: Recommendations, essay, transcript. SAR.
Additional information: Minimum 3.0 GPA. Must attend school in Hawaii. Hawaii residency not required.

Application deadline: February 15
Total amount awarded: $11,000

Contact:
Hawaii Community Foundation Scholarships
827 Fort Street Mall
Honolulu, HI 96813
Phone: 888-731-3863
Fax: 808-521-6286
Web: www.hawaiicommunityfoundation.org

Mitsuo Shito Public Housing Scholarship

Type of award: Scholarship, renewable.
Intended use: For full-time undergraduate or graduate study at accredited 2-year or 4-year institution in United States.
Eligibility: Applicant must be U.S. citizen or permanent resident residing in Hawaii.
Basis for selection: Applicant must demonstrate financial need, high academic achievement and depth of character.
Application requirements: Essay, transcript. Must include name of public housing unit in personal statement. FAFSA.
Additional information: Preference given to residents of public housing in Hawaii. Minimum 2.7 GPA.

Application deadline: February 15

Contact:
Hawaii Community Foundation
827 Fort Street Mall
Honolulu 96813
Phone: 888-731-3863
Fax: 808-521-6286
Web: www.hawaiicommunityfoundation.org

Nick Van Pernis Scholarship

Type of award: Scholarship.
Intended use: For full-time undergraduate study at accredited 2-year or 4-year institution in United States.
Eligibility: Applicant must be U.S. citizen or permanent resident residing in Hawaii.
Basis for selection: Major/career interest in oceanography/marine studies; bioengineering; health sciences or education, early childhood. Applicant must demonstrate financial need, high academic achievement, depth of character and service orientation.
Application requirements: Essay, transcript. FAFSA and SAR. Essay must include record of community service and description of how student's education and career will benefit Hawaii residents.
Additional information: Minimum 2.7 GPA. Must be graduate of public or private school in the North Kona, South Kona, North Kohala, South Kohala, or Ka'u districts. Applicants

taking up mainland residency must have relatives living in Hawaii. Amount and number of awards may vary yearly.

Application deadline: February 15

Contact:
Hawaii Community Foundation Scholarships
827 Fort Street Mall
Honolulu, HI 96813
Phone: 888-731-3863
Fax: 808-521-6286
Web: www.hawaiicommunityfoundation.org

Office of Hawaiian Affairs Scholarship Fund

Type of award: Scholarship.
Intended use: For undergraduate or graduate study at accredited 2-year or 4-year institution in United States.
Eligibility: Applicant must be Native Hawaiian/Pacific Islander. Applicant must be U.S. citizen.
Basis for selection: Applicant must demonstrate financial need, high academic achievement and depth of character.
Application requirements: Recommendations, essay, transcript, proof of eligibility. SAR, FAFSA, personal statement.
Additional information: Minimum 2.0 GPA for undergraduate students, 3.0 GPA for graduate students. Applicant must be of Hawaiian ancestry; ancestry must be verified through OHA's Hawaiian Registry Program. Does not have to be resident of Hawaii. Amount of award varies.

Application deadline: February 15

Contact:
Hawaii Community Foundation Scholarships
827 Fort Street Mall
Honolulu, HI 96813
Phone: 888-731-3863
Fax: 808-521-6286
Web: www.hawaiicommunityfoundation.org

Oscar and Rosetta Fish Fund

Type of award: Scholarship.
Intended use: For full-time undergraduate or graduate study at 2-year or 4-year institution. Designated institutions: Any University of Hawaii campus, excluding Manoa.
Eligibility: Applicant must be U.S. citizen or permanent resident residing in Hawaii.
Basis for selection: Major/career interest in business. Applicant must demonstrate financial need, high academic achievement and depth of character.
Application requirements: Essay, transcript. FAFSA and SAR.
Additional information: Minimum 2.7 GPA. Must have permanent address in Hawaii. Amount and number of awards vary and may change yearly.

Application deadline: February 15

Contact:
Hawaii Community Foundation Scholarships
827 Fort Street Mall
Honolulu, HI 96813
Phone: 888-731-3863
Fax: 808-521-6286
Web: www.hawaiicommunityfoundation.org

Ouida Mundy Hill Memorial Fund

Type of award: Scholarship.
Intended use: For full-time undergraduate study at accredited vocational or 2-year institution in United States. Designated institutions: Community colleges in the University of Hawaii system.
Eligibility: Applicant must be residing in Hawaii.
Basis for selection: Applicant must demonstrate financial need and high academic achievement.
Application requirements: Recommendations, essay, transcript. SAR. FAFSA.
Additional information: Minimum 2.7 GPA. Must be enrolled in AS or AAS degree program.

Application deadline: February 15

Contact:
Hawaii Community Foundation
827 Fort Street Mall
Honolulu, HI 96813
Phone: 888-731-3863
Fax: 808-521-6286
Web: www.hawaiicommunityfoundation.org

Paulina L. Sorg Scholarship

Type of award: Scholarship.
Intended use: For full-time junior, senior or graduate study at accredited 4-year institution in United States.
Eligibility: Applicant must be U.S. citizen residing in Hawaii.
Basis for selection: Major/career interest in physical therapy or nursing. Applicant must demonstrate financial need, high academic achievement and depth of character.
Application requirements: Recommendations, essay, transcript. SAR, FAFSA, personal statement.
Additional information: Minimum 2.7 GPA. Amount of award varies.

Application deadline: February 15

Contact:
Hawaii Community Foundation Scholarships
827 Fort Street Mall
Honolulu, HI 96813
Phone: 888-731-3863
Fax: 808-521-6286
Web: www.hawaiicommunityfoundation.org

Perry & Sally Sorenson Scholarship for Dependents of Hospitality Workers

Type of award: Scholarship.
Intended use: For full-time undergraduate or graduate study at accredited 2-year or 4-year institution in United States.
Eligibility: Applicant must be U.S. citizen residing in Hawaii.
Basis for selection: Applicant must demonstrate financial need, high academic achievement and depth of character.
Application requirements: Recommendations, essay, transcript, proof of eligibility. SAR, FAFSA, personal statement, name of Outrigger employee/position at company.
Additional information: Minimum 2.7 GPA. Amount of award varies. Applicant must be a dependent of an employee currently employed by Outrigger Enterprises in Hawaii working in a hospitality industry position.

Application deadline: February 15

Contact:
Hawaii Community Foundation Scholarships
827 Fort Street Mall
Honolulu, HI 96813
Phone: 888-731-3863
Fax: 808-521-6286
Web: www.hawaiicommunityfoundation.org

Perry & Sally Sorenson Scholarship for Foster Youth

Type of award: Scholarship.
Intended use: For full-time undergraduate or graduate study at accredited 4-year or graduate institution in United States.
Eligibility: Applicant must be at least 18, no older than 25. Applicant must be U.S. citizen residing in Hawaii.
Basis for selection: Applicant must demonstrate financial need, high academic achievement and depth of character.
Application requirements: Recommendations, essay, transcript. SAR, FAFSA, personal statement.
Additional information: Minimum 2.0 GPA. Amount of award varies. Applicant must be permanently or temporarily separated from birth parent(s) and aged out of the foster care system in the state of Hawaii.
Application deadline: February 15
Contact:
Hawaii Community Foundation Scholarships
827 Fort Street Mall
Honolulu, HI 96813
Phone: 888-731-3863
Fax: 808-521-6286
Web: www.hawaiicommunityfoundation.org

Peter R. Papworth Scholarship

Type of award: Scholarship.
Intended use: For full-time sophomore, junior, senior or graduate study at accredited 2-year or 4-year institution in United States.
Eligibility: Applicant must be U.S. citizen residing in Hawaii.
Basis for selection: Applicant must demonstrate financial need, high academic achievement and depth of character.
Application requirements: Recommendations, essay, transcript. SAR, FAFSA, personal statement.
Additional information: Applicant must be a graduate of Campbell High School. Minimum 2.7 GPA. Amount of award varies.
Application deadline: February 15
Contact:
Hawaii Community Foundation Scholarships
827 Fort Street Mall
Honolulu, HI 96813
Phone: 888-731-3863
Fax: 808-521-6286
Web: www.hawaiicommunityfoundation.org

Philippine Nurses' Association Scholarship

Type of award: Scholarship.
Intended use: For full-time undergraduate or graduate study at accredited 4-year or graduate institution in United States.
Eligibility: Applicant must be Native Hawaiian/Pacific Islander. Applicant must be residing in Hawaii.
Basis for selection: Major/career interest in nursing. Applicant must demonstrate financial need and high academic achievement.
Application requirements: Recommendations, essay, transcript. FAFSA and SAR.
Additional information: Minimum 2.7 GPA. Must be of Filipino ancestry. Amount and number of awards vary and may change yearly.
Application deadline: February 15
Contact:
Hawaii Community Foundation
827 Fort Street Mall
Honolulu, HI 96813
Phone: 888-731-3863
Fax: 808-521-6286
Web: www.hawaiicommunityfoundation.org

PRSA-Hawaii/Roy Leffingwell Public Relations Scholarship

Type of award: Scholarship.
Intended use: For full-time junior, senior or graduate study at accredited 2-year or 4-year institution in United States.
Eligibility: Applicant must be U.S. citizen or permanent resident residing in Hawaii.
Basis for selection: Major/career interest in public relations; communications or journalism. Applicant must demonstrate financial need, high academic achievement and depth of character.
Application requirements: Essay, transcript. FAFSA and SAR.
Additional information: Minimum 2.7 GPA. Must intend to pursue career in public relations. Award amount varies.
Application deadline: February 15
Contact:
Hawaii Community Foundation Scholarships
827 Fort Street Mall
Honolulu, HI 96813
Phone: 888-731-3863
Fax: 808-521-6286
Web: www.hawaiicommunityfoundation.org

Ray Yoshida Kauai Fine Arts Scholarship

Type of award: Scholarship.
Intended use: For full-time undergraduate study at accredited 2-year or 4-year institution in United States.
Eligibility: Applicant must be high school senior. Applicant must be U.S. citizen residing in Hawaii.
Basis for selection: Major/career interest in arts, general. Applicant must demonstrate financial need, high academic achievement and depth of character.
Application requirements: Recommendations, essay, transcript. SAR, FAFSA, personal statement.
Additional information: Minimum 2.7 GPA. Amount of award varies. Applicant must be a high school senior from a school on the island of Kauai, and must pursue studies in Fine Arts.
Application deadline: February 15
Contact:
Hawaii Community Foundation Scholarships
827 Fort Street Mall
Honolulu, HI 96813
Phone: 888-731-3863
Fax: 808-521-6286
Web: www.hawaiicommunityfoundation.org

Raymond F. Cain Scholarship Fund

Type of award: Scholarship.
Intended use: For full-time undergraduate or graduate study at accredited 2-year or 4-year institution in United States.
Eligibility: Applicant must be U.S. citizen residing in Hawaii.

Basis for selection: Major/career interest in landscape architecture. Applicant must demonstrate financial need, high academic achievement and depth of character.
Application requirements: Recommendations, essay, transcript. SAR, FAFSA, personal statement.
Additional information: Minimum 2.7 GPA. Amount of award varies.
Application deadline: February 15
Contact:
Hawaii Community Foundation Scholarships
827 Fort Street Mall
Honolulu, HI 96813
Phone: 888-731-3863
Fax: 808-521-6286
Web: www.hawaiicommunityfoundation.org

Rich Meiers Health Administration Fund

Type of award: Scholarship.
Intended use: For full-time junior, senior or graduate study at accredited 2-year or 4-year institution in United States. Designated institutions: Hawaii institutions.
Eligibility: Applicant must be U.S. citizen residing in Hawaii.
Basis for selection: Major/career interest in health services administration. Applicant must demonstrate financial need, high academic achievement and depth of character.
Application requirements: Recommendations, essay, transcript. SAR, FAFSA, personal statement.
Additional information: Minimum 2.7 GPA. Amount of award varies. Majors may also include hospital administration, health care administration, and long-term care administration.
Application deadline: February 15
Contact:
Hawaii Community Foundation Scholarships
827 Fort Street Mall
Honolulu, HI 96813
Phone: 888-731-3863
Fax: 808-521-6286
Web: www.hawaiicommunityfoundation.org

Richard Smart Scholarship

Type of award: Scholarship, renewable.
Intended use: For full-time undergraduate or graduate study at accredited 2-year or 4-year institution in United States.
Eligibility: Applicant must be U.S. citizen or permanent resident residing in Hawaii.
Basis for selection: Applicant must demonstrate financial need, high academic achievement and depth of character.
Application requirements: Essay, transcript. FAFSA.
Additional information: Minimum 2.7 GPA. Must be first-generation college student. Must be from Waimea area (zip code 96743). Vocational programs not eligible.
Application deadline: February 15
Contact:
Hawaii Community Foundation
827 Fort Street Mall
Honolulu, HI 96813
Phone: 888-731-3863
Fax: 808-521-6286
Web: www.hawaiicommunityfoundation.org

Richie M. Gregory Fund

Type of award: Scholarship.
Intended use: For full-time undergraduate or graduate study at accredited 2-year or 4-year institution in United States.
Eligibility: Applicant must be U.S. citizen residing in Hawaii.
Basis for selection: Major/career interest in arts, general. Applicant must demonstrate financial need, high academic achievement and depth of character.
Application requirements: Recommendations, essay, transcript. SAR, FAFSA, personal statement.
Additional information: Minimum 2.7 GPA. Amount of award varies. Applicant must major in Art.
Application deadline: February 15
Contact:
Hawaii Community Foundation Scholarships
827 Fort Street Mall
Honolulu, HI 96813
Phone: 888-731-3863
Fax: 808-521-6286
Web: www.hawaiicommunityfoundation.org

Rise Up Scholarship

Type of award: Scholarship.
Intended use: For undergraduate study at accredited 2-year or 4-year institution in United States.
Eligibility: Applicant must be residing in Hawaii.
Basis for selection: Applicant must demonstrate financial need.
Application requirements: Recommendations, essay, transcript. FAFSA and SAR.
Additional information: Minimum 2.7 GPA. Must be resident of Kauai. Preference given to children of divorced parents. Amount and number of awards vary and may change yearly.
Application deadline: February 15
Contact:
Hawaii Community Foundation
827 Fort Street Mall
Honolulu, HI 96813
Phone: 888-731-3863
Fax: 808-521-6286
Web: www.hawaiicommunityfoundation.org

Robanna Fund

Type of award: Scholarship.
Intended use: For full-time undergraduate study at accredited 2-year or 4-year institution in United States.
Eligibility: Applicant must be U.S. citizen residing in Hawaii.
Basis for selection: Major/career interest in health-related professions. Applicant must demonstrate financial need, high academic achievement and depth of character.
Application requirements: Recommendations, essay, transcript. SAR, FAFSA, personal statement.
Additional information: Minimum 2.7 GPA. Amount of award varies.
Application deadline: February 15
Contact:
Hawaii Community Foundation Scholarships
827 Fort Street Mall
Honolulu, HI 96813
Phone: 888-731-3863
Fax: 808-521-6286
Web: www.hawaiicommunityfoundation.org

Ron Bright Scholarship

Type of award: Scholarship.
Intended use: For full-time undergraduate study at accredited 2-year or 4-year institution in United States.
Eligibility: Applicant must be high school senior. Applicant must be U.S. citizen or permanent resident residing in Hawaii.

Basis for selection: Major/career interest in education. Applicant must demonstrate financial need, high academic achievement and depth of character.
Application requirements: Essay, transcript. FAFSA and SAR. Grades from first semester of 12th grade.
Additional information: Minimum 2.7 GPA. Must attend one of the following Windward Oahu high schools: Castle, Kahuku, Kailua, Kalaheo, or Olomana. Preference given to students with extracurricular activities in the performing arts. Must have permanent address in Hawaii. Applicants taking up mainland residency must have relatives living in Hawaii. Amount and number of awards vary and may change yearly.
Application deadline: February 15
Contact:
Hawaii Community Foundation Scholarships
827 Fort Street Mall
Honolulu, HI 96813
Phone: 888-731-3863
Fax: 808-521-6286
Web: www.hawaiicommunityfoundation.org

Rosemary & Nellie Ebrie Fund

Type of award: Scholarship.
Intended use: For full-time undergraduate or graduate study at accredited 2-year or 4-year institution in United States.
Eligibility: Applicant must be Native Hawaiian/Pacific Islander. Applicant must be U.S. citizen or permanent resident residing in Hawaii.
Basis for selection: Applicant must demonstrate financial need, high academic achievement and depth of character.
Application requirements: Essay, transcript. FAFSA and SAR.
Additional information: Minimum 2.7 GPA. Must be of Hawaiian ancestry. Must be long-term resident born and currently living on the island of Hawaii. Applicants taking up mainland residency must have relatives living in Hawaii. Amount of award may change yearly.
Application deadline: February 15
Contact:
Hawaii Community Foundation Scholarships
827 Fort Street Mall
Honolulu, HI 96813
Phone: 888-731-3863
Fax: 808-521-6286
Web: www.hawaiicommunityfoundation.org

Safeway Foundation Hawaii Scholarship Fund

Type of award: Scholarship.
Intended use: For full-time undergraduate or graduate study at accredited 2-year or 4-year institution in United States. Designated institutions: Hawaii institutions.
Eligibility: Applicant must be U.S. citizen residing in Hawaii.
Basis for selection: Applicant must demonstrate financial need, high academic achievement and depth of character.
Application requirements: Recommendations, essay, transcript. SAR, FAFSA, personal statement.
Additional information: Minimum 3.0 GPA. Amount of award varies. Preference for current and past employees of Safeway Hawaii and their dependents.
Application deadline: February 15
Contact:
Hawaii Community Foundation Scholarships
827 Fort Street Mall
Honolulu, HI 96813
Phone: 888-731-3863
Fax: 808-521-6286
Web: www.hawaiicommunityfoundation.org

Sarah Rosenberg Teacher Education Scholarship

Type of award: Scholarship.
Intended use: For full-time senior study at accredited postsecondary institution.
Eligibility: Applicant must be residing in Hawaii.
Basis for selection: Major/career interest in education. Applicant must demonstrate financial need and high academic achievement.
Application requirements: Recommendations, essay, transcript. SAR, FAFSA.
Additional information: Minimum 2.7 GPA.
Application deadline: February 15
Contact:
Hawaii Community Foundation
827 Fort Street Mall
Honolulu, HI 96813
Phone: 888-731-3863
Fax: 808-521-6286
Web: www.hawaiicommunityfoundation.org

Senator Richard M. & Dr. Ruth Matsuura Scholarship Fund

Type of award: Scholarship.
Intended use: For full-time undergraduate or graduate study at accredited 2-year or 4-year institution in United States.
Eligibility: Applicant must be U.S. citizen residing in Hawaii.
Basis for selection: Applicant must demonstrate financial need, high academic achievement and depth of character.
Application requirements: Recommendations, essay, transcript. SAR, FAFSA, personal statement.
Additional information: Applicant must be a graduate of Hilo High School or Waiakea High School and a resident of the island of Hawaii. Minimum 2.7 GPA. Amount of award varies.
Application deadline: February 15
Contact:
Hawaii Community Foundation Scholarships
827 Fort Street Mall
Honolulu, HI 96813
Phone: 888-731-3863
Fax: 808-521-6286
Web: www.hawaiicommunityfoundation.org

Shirley McKown Scholarship Fund

Type of award: Scholarship.
Intended use: For full-time junior, senior or graduate study at accredited 4-year institution in United States.
Eligibility: Applicant must be U.S. citizen or permanent resident residing in Hawaii.
Basis for selection: Major/career interest in advertising; journalism or public relations. Applicant must demonstrate high academic achievement and depth of character.
Application requirements: Essay, transcript. FAFSA and SAR.

Additional information: Minimum 3.0 GPA. Applicants must have permanent address in Hawaii. Applicants taking up mainland residency must have relatives living in Hawaii.

Application deadline: February 15

Contact:
Hawaii Community Foundation Scholarships
827 Fort Street Mall
Honolulu, HI 96813
Phone: 888-731-3863
Fax: 808-521-6286
Web: www.hawaiicommunityfoundation.org

Shuichi, Katsu and Itsuyo Suga Scholarship

Type of award: Scholarship.
Intended use: For full-time undergraduate or graduate study at accredited 2-year or 4-year institution in United States.
Eligibility: Applicant must be U.S. citizen or permanent resident residing in Hawaii.
Basis for selection: Major/career interest in mathematics; physics; science, general; computer/information sciences or technology. Applicant must demonstrate financial need, high academic achievement and depth of character.
Application requirements: Essay, transcript. FAFSA and SAR.
Additional information: Minimum 3.0 GPA. Applicants must have permanent address in Hawaii. Applicants taking up mainland residency must have relatives living in Hawaii. Amount of award may change yearly.

Application deadline: February 15

Contact:
Hawaii Community Foundation Scholarships
827 Fort Street Mall
Honolulu, HI 96813
Phone: 888-731-3863
Fax: 808-521-6286
Web: www.hawaiicommunityfoundation.org

Takehiko Hasegawa Academic Scholarship

Type of award: Scholarship.
Intended use: For full-time undergraduate or graduate study at accredited 2-year or 4-year institution in United States.
Eligibility: Applicant must be U.S. citizen residing in Hawaii.
Basis for selection: Applicant must demonstrate financial need, high academic achievement and depth of character.
Application requirements: Recommendations, essay, transcript. SAR, FAFSA, personal statement.
Additional information: Minimum GPA of 3.5. Must be a resident of the Island of Kaua'i. Amount of award varies.

Application deadline: February 15

Contact:
Hawaii Community Foundation Scholarships
827 Fort Street Mall
Honolulu, HI 96813
Phone: 888-731-3863
Fax: 808-521-6286
Web: www.hawaiicommunityfoundation.org

Takehiko Hasegawa Kaua'i Community College Scholarship

Type of award: Scholarship, renewable.
Intended use: For full-time undergraduate study at accredited 2-year institution in United States. Designated institutions: Community college on island of Kauai.
Eligibility: Applicant must be U.S. citizen or permanent resident residing in Hawaii.
Basis for selection: Applicant must demonstrate financial need, high academic achievement and depth of character.
Application requirements: Essay, transcript. FAFSA.
Additional information: Minimum 2.7 GPA. Must be resident of Kauai and attend Kauai community college.

Application deadline: February 15

Contact:
Hawaii Community Foundation
827 Fort Street Mall
Honolulu, HI 96813
Phone: 888-731-3863
Fax: 808-521-6286
Web: www.hawaiicommunityfoundation.org

Thz Fo Farm Fund

Type of award: Scholarship.
Intended use: For full-time undergraduate or graduate study at accredited postsecondary institution in United States.
Eligibility: Applicant must be Chinese. Applicant must be U.S. citizen or permanent resident residing in Hawaii.
Basis for selection: Major/career interest in gerontology. Applicant must demonstrate financial need, high academic achievement and depth of character.
Application requirements: FAFSA and SAR.
Additional information: Minimum 2.7 GPA. Must be of Chinese ancestry. Applicants must have permanent address in Hawaii. Applicants who take up mainland residency must have relatives living in Hawaii. Amount of award varies.

Application deadline: February 15

Contact:
Hawaii Community Foundation Scholarships
827 Fort Street Mall
Honolulu, HI 96813
Phone: 888-731-3863
Fax: 808-521-6286
Web: www.hawaiicommunityfoundation.org

Times Supermarket Shop & Score Scholarship

Type of award: Scholarship.
Intended use: For full-time undergraduate study at accredited postsecondary institution in United States.
Eligibility: Applicant must be high school senior. Applicant must be residing in Hawaii.
Basis for selection: Applicant must demonstrate financial need and high academic achievement.
Application requirements: Recommendations, essay, transcript. SAR, FAFSA.
Additional information: Minimum 2.7 GPA. Must be graduating senior of any high school on Oahu participating in Times Shop and Score program.

Application deadline: February 15

Contact:
Hawaii Community Foundation
827 Fort Street Mall
Honolulu, HI 96813
Phone: 888-731-3863
Fax: 808-521-6286
Web: www.hawaiicommunityfoundation.org

Tommy Lee Memorial Scholarship Fund

Type of award: Scholarship.
Intended use: For full-time undergraduate study at accredited 2-year or 4-year institution in United States.
Eligibility: Applicant must be high school senior. Applicant must be U.S. citizen or permanent resident residing in Hawaii.
Basis for selection: Applicant must demonstrate financial need, high academic achievement and depth of character.
Application requirements: Recommendations, essay, transcript. FAFSA and SAR.
Additional information: Minimum 2.7 GPA. Must be high school senior residing in the Waialua or Haleiwa area. Applicants taking up mainland residency must have relatives living in Hawaii. Amount of award may change yearly.
Application deadline: February 15
Contact:
Hawaii Community Foundation Scholarships
827 Fort Street Mall
Honolulu, HI 96813
Phone: 888-731-3863
Fax: 808-521-6286
Web: www.hawaiicommunityfoundation.org

Tongan Cultural Society Scholarship

Type of award: Scholarship.
Intended use: For full-time undergraduate or graduate study at accredited 2-year or 4-year institution in United States. Designated institutions: Hawaii institutions.
Eligibility: Applicant must be U.S. citizen residing in Hawaii.
Basis for selection: Applicant must demonstrate financial need, high academic achievement and depth of character.
Application requirements: Recommendations, essay, transcript. SAR, FAFSA, personal statement.
Additional information: Must be of primarily Tongan ancestry. Must attend school in Hawaii. Minimum 2.7 GPA. Amount of awards varies.
Application deadline: February 15
Contact:
Hawaii Community Foundation Scholarships
827 Fort Street Mall
Honolulu, HI 96813
Phone: 888-731-3863
Fax: 808-521-6286
Web: www.hawaiicommunityfoundation.org

Toraji & Toki Yoshinaga Scholarship

Type of award: Scholarship.
Intended use: For full-time sophomore study at accredited 2-year or 4-year institution. Designated institutions: Brigham Young University-Hawaii, Chaminade University, Hawaii Pacific University, Heald College.
Eligibility: Applicant must be U.S. citizen or permanent resident residing in Hawaii.
Basis for selection: Applicant must demonstrate financial need, high academic achievement and depth of character.
Application requirements: Essay, transcript. FAFSA and SAR.
Additional information: Minimum 2.7 GPA. Applicants must have permanent address in Hawaii. Applicants taking up mainland residency must have relatives living in Hawaii. Amount of award may change yearly.
Application deadline: February 15
Contact:
Hawaii Community Foundation Scholarships
827 Fort Street Mall
Honolulu, HI 96813
Phone: 888-731-3863
Fax: 808-521-6286
Web: www.hawaiicommunityfoundation.org

Troy Barboza Educational Fund Scholarship

Type of award: Scholarship.
Intended use: For full-time undergraduate or graduate study at accredited postsecondary institution in United States.
Eligibility: Applicant must be residing in Hawaii. Applicant's parent must have been killed or disabled in work-related accident as firefighter, police officer or public safety officer.
Basis for selection: Applicant must demonstrate financial need and high academic achievement.
Application requirements: Recommendations, essay, transcript. SAR, FAFSA.
Additional information: Minimum 2.7 GPA. Must be public employee or dependent of public employee injured in line of duty.
Application deadline: February 15
Contact:
Hawaii Community Foundation
827 Fort Street Mall
Honolulu, HI 96813
Phone: 888-731-3863
Fax: 808-521-6286
Web: www.hawaiicommunityfoundation.org

Vicki Willder Scholarship Fund

Type of award: Scholarship.
Intended use: For full-time undergraduate study at accredited 2-year or 4-year institution in United States.
Eligibility: Applicant must be U.S. citizen or permanent resident residing in Hawaii.
Basis for selection: Major/career interest in culinary arts or tourism/travel. Applicant must demonstrate financial need, high academic achievement and depth of character.
Application requirements: Essay, transcript. FAFSA and SAR.
Additional information: Minimum 2.7 GPA. Applicant must graduate of Kamehameha Schools (Kapalama, Maui, or Kea'au). Preference given to students majoring in culinary arts or travel industry management. Applicants taking up mainland residency must have relatives living in Hawaii. Amount and number of awards vary and may change yearly.
Application deadline: February 15
Contact:
Hawaii Community Foundation Scholarships
827 Fort Street Mall
Honolulu, HI 96813
Phone: 888-731-3863
Fax: 808-521-6286
Web: www.hawaiicommunityfoundation.org

Victoria S. and Bradley L. Geist Foundation Scholarship

Type of award: Scholarship.
Intended use: For full-time undergraduate or graduate study at accredited postsecondary institution.
Eligibility: Applicant must be residing in Hawaii.
Basis for selection: Applicant must demonstrate financial need and high academic achievement.
Application requirements: Recommendations, essay, transcript, proof of eligibility. SAR, FAFSA, confirmation letter from DHS or Family Foster program case worker.
Additional information: Minimum 2.7 GPA. Must be currently or formerly placed in foster care in Hawaii. Deadlines are February 22nd for fall and spring; September 20th for spring only.

Application deadline:	February 22, September 20

Contact:
Hawaii Community Foundation
827 Fort Street Mall
Honolulu, HI 96813
Phone: 888-731-3863
Fax: 808-521-6286
Web: www.hawaiicommunityfoundation.org

Will J. Henderson Scholarship Fund in Hawaii

Type of award: Scholarship.
Intended use: For full-time undergraduate or graduate study at accredited vocational, 2-year or 4-year institution in United States. Designated institutions: Community colleges in Hawaii.
Eligibility: Applicant must be U.S. citizen residing in Hawaii.
Basis for selection: Applicant must demonstrate financial need, high academic achievement and depth of character.
Application requirements: Recommendations, essay, transcript. SAR, FAFSA, personal statement, name/job title of parent employed by Queen's Medical Center.
Additional information: Minimum 2.0 GPA. Amount of award varies. Applicant must be a child dependent of a current employee at Queen's Medical Center, and must attend community college in Hawaii.

Application deadline:	February 15

Contact:
Hawaii Community Foundation Scholarships
827 Fort Street Mall
Honolulu, HI 96813
Phone: 888-731-3863
Fax: 808-521-6286
Web: www.hawaiicommunityfoundation.org

William James & Dorothy Bading Lanquist Fund

Type of award: Scholarship.
Intended use: For full-time undergraduate or graduate study at accredited 2-year or 4-year institution in United States.
Eligibility: Applicant must be U.S. citizen or permanent resident residing in Hawaii.
Basis for selection: Major/career interest in physical sciences. Applicant must demonstrate financial need, high academic achievement and depth of character.
Application requirements: Essay, transcript. FAFSA and SAR.
Additional information: Minimum 3.0 GPA. Must major in the physical sciences or related fields, excluding biological and social sciences. Must have permanent address in Hawaii. Applicants taking up mainland residency must have relatives living in Hawaii. Amount and number of awards vary and may change yearly.

Application deadline:	February 15

Contact:
Hawaii Community Foundation Scholarships
827 Fort Street Mall
Honolulu, HI 96813
Phone: 888-731-3863
Fax: 808-521-6286
Web: www.hawaiicommunityfoundation.org

The Heart of America Foundation

The Christopher Reeve Award

Type of award: Scholarship.
Intended use: For freshman study at postsecondary institution.
Eligibility: Applicant must be enrolled in high school.
Basis for selection: Applicant must demonstrate depth of character and service orientation.
Application requirements: Recommendations, nomination by a person in the community not related to student.
Additional information: Student must have demonstrated compassion and caring service to community. Application must include information about nominee's service efforts, what sets nominee apart from peers, why nominee should be considered for award, and any supporting documentation. Apply online. Upon request, award is mailed to awardee's institution of choice.

Amount of award:	$1,000
Number of awards:	1
Application deadline:	October 31
Notification begins:	March 1
Total amount awarded:	$1,000

Contact:
The Heart of America Foundation
c/o Sara Muehlbauer
401 F Street NW, Suite 325
Washington, DC 20001
Phone: 202-347-6278
Web: www.heartofamerica.org/scholarships.htm

Helicopter Association International

Bill Sanderson Aviation Maintenance Technician Scholarship Award

Type of award: Scholarship.
Intended use: For undergraduate or non-degree study at vocational institution. Designated institutions: U.S. helicopter airframe and engine manufacturers; aviation maintenance schools.
Basis for selection: Major/career interest in aviation repair.
Application requirements: Recommendations.

Additional information: For students who wish to study helicopter maintenance. Award includes full tuition to aviation maintenance program and stipend of $650-1600. Applicant must be about to graduate from FAA-approved Part 147 Aviation Maintenance Technician School, or a recent recipient of Airframe and Powerplant (A&P) certificate or international equivalent. Applications and deadline information available on Website.

Amount of award:	$650-$1,600
Number of awards:	8
Number of applicants:	45
Application deadline:	December 31

Contact:
Bill Sanderson Aviation Maintenance Technician Scholarship
Helicopter Association International
1635 Prince Street
Alexandria, VA 22314-2818
Phone: 703-683-4646
Fax: 703-683-4745
Web: www.rotor.com

Helicopter Association International Commercial Helicopter Rating Scholarship

Type of award: Scholarship.
Intended use: For full-time undergraduate or non-degree study at vocational institution in or outside United States. Designated institutions: Certified FAA Part 147 training program.
Eligibility: Applicant must be U.S. citizen or international student.
Basis for selection: Major/career interest in aviation.
Application requirements: Recommendations, essay. Proof of enrollment in FAA Part 141 school helicopter pilot training program or international equivalent, copy of FAA or International Equivalent Certificate, resume, essay describing why you want to be a helicopter pilot, letter from school certifying they are FAA certified Part 141.
Additional information: Must be enrolled in certified FAA Part 141 school. Foreign students must prove foreign citizenship.

Amount of award:	$5,000
Number of awards:	4
Application deadline:	November 30

Contact:
Helicopter Association International
1635 Prince Street
Alexandria, VA 22314
Phone: 703-683-4646
Fax: 703-683-4745
Web: www.rotor.com

Helicopter Association International Maintenance Technician Certificate Scholarship

Type of award: Scholarship.
Intended use: For full-time undergraduate or non-degree study at vocational institution in or outside United States. Designated institutions: Certified FAA Part 147 training program.
Eligibility: Applicant must be U.S. citizen or international student.
Basis for selection: Major/career interest in aviation repair.
Application requirements: Recommendations, essay. Proof of enrollment in certified FAA Part 147 training program or international equivalent, resume, essay describing why you want to be a helicopter maintenance technician.
Additional information: Must be enrolled in FAA Part 147 program or international equivalent. Foreign students must provide proof of foreign citizenship.

Amount of award:	$2,500
Number of awards:	6
Application deadline:	December 31

Contact:
Helicopter Association International
1635 Prince Street
Alexandria, VA 22314
Phone: 703-683-4646
Fax: 703-683-4745
Web: www.rotor.com

Herschel C. Price Educational Foundation

Herschel C. Price Educational Scholarship

Type of award: Scholarship, renewable.
Intended use: For undergraduate or graduate study at accredited 2-year, 4-year or graduate institution in United States.
Eligibility: Applicant must be U.S. citizen.
Basis for selection: Applicant must demonstrate financial need and high academic achievement.
Application requirements: Interview, transcript.
Additional information: Applicant must reside in West Virginia or attend West Virginia college or university. Achievement in community activities also considered. Preference given to undergraduates. Limited number of applications available by written request in January and February for fall term or August and early September for spring term. Limited number of applications available.

Application deadline:	April 1, October 1
Notification begins:	May 15, November 15

Contact:
Herschel C. Price Educational Foundation
P.O. Box 412
Huntington, WV 25708-0412
Phone: 304-529-3852

Hispanic Association of Colleges and Universities

AETNA Nursing Scholarship

Type of award: Scholarship.
Intended use: For undergraduate or graduate study at 2-year or 4-year institution in United States. Designated institutions: HACU member institutions.
Basis for selection: Major/career interest in nursing. Applicant must demonstrate financial need.
Application requirements: Essay, transcript. FAFSA, resume.
Additional information: Minimum 3.0 GPA.

Amount of award:	$2,500

Contact:
Hispanic Association of Colleges and Universities
8415 Datapoint Drive, Suite 400
San Antonio, TX 78229
Phone: 202-833-8361
Fax: 202-261-5082
Web: www.hacu.net

NASCAR/Wendell Scott Sr. Award

Type of award: Scholarship.
Intended use: For full-time undergraduate or graduate study at 2-year, 4-year or graduate institution. Designated institutions: HACU member institutions.
Basis for selection: Major/career interest in engineering; business; public relations; marketing or technology.
Application requirements: Essay, transcript. FAFSA, resume.
Additional information: Minimum 3.0 GPA.
Amount of award: $3,300
Contact:
Hispanic Association of Colleges and Universities
8415 Datapoint Drive, Suite 400
San Antonio, TX 78229
Phone: 202-833-8361
Fax: 202-261-5082
Web: www.hacu.net

Travelers Scholarship

Type of award: Scholarship.
Intended use: For full-time undergraduate study at 2-year or 4-year institution. Designated institutions: HACU member institutions.
Basis for selection: Major/career interest in accounting; engineering, computer; computer/information sciences; finance/banking; business or human resources. Applicant must demonstrate high academic achievement.
Application requirements: Essay, transcript. FAFSA, resume.
Additional information: Minimum 3.0 GPA.
Amount of award: $5,000
Contact:
Hispanic Association of Colleges and Universities
8415 Datapoint Drive, Suite 400
San Antonio, TX 78229
Phone: 202-833-8361
Fax: 202-261-5082
Web: www.hacu.net

United Health/Hispanic Association of Colleges and Universities Scholarship

Type of award: Scholarship.
Intended use: For full-time undergraduate or graduate study at 2-year, 4-year or graduate institution.
Basis for selection: Major/career interest in psychology; dental assistant; dentistry; nursing; optometry/ophthalmology; medicine; pharmacy/pharmaceutics/pharmacology; public health or mental health/therapy. Applicant must demonstrate high academic achievement.
Application requirements: Essay, transcript. FAFSA, resume.
Additional information: Minimum 3.0 GPA.
Amount of award: $2,000
Contact:
Hispanic Association of Colleges and Universities
8415 Datapoint Drive, Suite 400
San Antonio, TX 78229
Phone: 202-833-8361
Fax: 202-261-5082
Web: www.hacu.net

Hispanic College Fund

Ford Blue Oval Scholarship

Type of award: Scholarship.
Intended use: For full-time undergraduate or graduate study at accredited 4-year or graduate institution. Designated institutions: Colleges in U.S. and Puerto Rico.
Eligibility: Applicant must be Mexican American, Hispanic American or Puerto Rican. Applicant must be U.S. citizen or international student.
Basis for selection: Applicant must demonstrate financial need and high academic achievement.
Application requirements: Resume, proof of family income, proof of citizenship status, financial aid verification.
Additional information: Minimum 3.0 GPA. Visit Website for deadline.
Amount of award: $500-$5,000
Contact:
Hispanic College Fund
1300 L Street NW, Suite 975
Washington, DC 20005
Phone: 800-644-4223
Fax: 202-296-3774
Web: www.hispanicfund.org

Google Hispanic College Fund Scholarship Program

Type of award: Scholarship.
Intended use: For full-time junior, senior, master's or doctoral study at postsecondary institution in or outside United States. Designated institutions: Institutions in the United States or Puerto Rico.
Eligibility: Applicant must be Hispanic American. Applicant must be U.S. citizen or permanent resident.
Basis for selection: Major/career interest in computer/information sciences or engineering, computer. Applicant must demonstrate financial need and high academic achievement.
Application requirements: Recommendations, essay, transcript. Proof of family income, proof of citizenship status, resume.
Additional information: Minimum 3.0 GPA. Visit Website for application and more information.
Amount of award: $10,000
Number of awards: 20
Number of applicants: 18
Application deadline: March 1
Total amount awarded: $180,000
Contact:
Hispanic College Fund
1300 L Street NW, Suite 975
Washington, DC 20005
Phone: 800-644-4223
Fax: 202-296-3774
Web: www.hispanicfund.org

Marriott Scholars Program

Type of award: Scholarship.
Intended use: For full-time undergraduate study at accredited postsecondary institution in United States. Designated institutions: Colleges in U.S. and Puerto Rico.
Eligibility: Applicant must be Mexican American, Hispanic American or Puerto Rican. Applicant must be U.S. citizen or permanent resident.
Basis for selection: Major/career interest in culinary arts; food production/management/services; hospitality administration/management or hotel/restaurant management. Applicant must demonstrate financial need and high academic achievement.
Application requirements: Recommendations, essay, transcript. Resume, proof of family income, proof of citizenship status, financial aid verification.
Additional information: Must plan to pursue a degree in hospitality management or related field. Minimum 3.0 GPA. Visit Website for deadline.

Amount of award:	$9,000
Application deadline:	March 1

Contact:
Hispanic College Fund
1300 L Street NW, Suite 975
Washington, DC 20005
Phone: 800-644-4223
Fax: 202-296-3774
Web: www.hispanicfund.org

Hispanic Heritage Foundation

Hispanic Heritage Youth Awards Program

Type of award: Scholarship.
Intended use: For full-time undergraduate study at postsecondary institution.
Eligibility: Applicant must be Hispanic American. Applicant must be high school junior. Applicant must be U.S. citizen or permanent resident.
Basis for selection: Applicant must demonstrate high academic achievement, depth of character, leadership and service orientation.
Application requirements: Recommendations, essay, transcript, proof of eligibility.
Additional information: Applicant must have at least one parent of Hispanic/Latino ancestry. Foundation offers regional and national awards in a number of categories; amount of award and application deadlines vary by year. Awards may also be used for education related expenses, or to establish a community service effort in the student's community. Applications due in June or July. Visit Website for application and updates regarding Youth Awards Program.

Amount of award:	$1,000
Number of awards:	160
Number of applicants:	10,000
Application deadline:	June 15
Notification begins:	March 1
Total amount awarded:	$210,000

Contact:
Hispanic Heritage Foundation
Hispanic Heritage Youth Awards
1444 Duke Street
Alexandria, VA 22314
Phone: 202-861-9797
Web: www.hispanicheritage.org

Hispanic Scholarship Fund

ALPFA Scholarship

Type of award: Scholarship.
Intended use: For full-time junior, senior or graduate study at accredited 4-year institution in United States.
Eligibility: Applicant must be Mexican American, Hispanic American or Puerto Rican. Applicant must be U.S. citizen or permanent resident.
Basis for selection: Major/career interest in accounting; business; economics; finance/banking; hospitality administration/management; human resources; international relations; technology or marketing. Applicant must demonstrate financial need and high academic achievement.
Application requirements: Recommendations, transcript. FAFSA, resume.
Additional information: Minimum 3.0 GPA. Open to community college students who intend to transfer to four-year college during award year.

Amount of award:	$2,000-$10,000
Application deadline:	January 31

Contact:
Hispanic Scholarship Fund
1411 West 190th Street
Suite 325
Gardena, CA 90248
Phone: 877-473-4636
Web: www.hsf.net

AT&T Foundation Scholarship

Type of award: Scholarship.
Intended use: For full-time undergraduate study at accredited 2-year or 4-year institution in United States.
Eligibility: Applicant must be Mexican American, Hispanic American or Puerto Rican. Applicant must be no older than 26. Applicant must be U.S. citizen or permanent resident.
Basis for selection: Applicant must demonstrate high academic achievement.
Application requirements: Recommendations, transcript. FAFSA.
Additional information: Minimum 3.0 GPA. Must be dependent of AT&T employee (minimum one year employment). Grandchildren of employees and children or stepchildren of senior managers and officers not eligible.

Amount of award:	$1,500-$2,500
Application deadline:	February 15

Contact:
Hispanic Scholarship Fund
1411 West 190th Street
Suite 325
Gardena, CA 90248
Phone: 877-473-4636
Web: www.hsf.net

Clorox Suena Sin Limites Mother Scholarship

Type of award: Scholarship.
Intended use: For at accredited 4-year institution in United States.
Eligibility: Applicant must be Mexican American, Hispanic American or Puerto Rican. Applicant must be female, at least 25, no older than 45, high school senior. Applicant must be U.S. citizen or permanent resident.
Basis for selection: Applicant must demonstrate financial need and high academic achievement.
Application requirements: Essay. FAFSA, essay detailing how scholarship will make their dreams a reality.
Additional information: Minimum 3.0 GPA. Must be a Latino mother between the ages of 25 and 45. Must have completed at least six transferable units.

Amount of award:	$10,000
Number of awards:	6
Application deadline:	December 21

Contact:
Hispanic Scholarship Fund
1411 West 190th Street
Suite 325
Gardena, CA 90248
Phone: 877-473-4636
Web: www.hsf.net

Coca-Cola Live Positively Publix Supermarkets Scholarship

Type of award: Scholarship.
Intended use: For full-time freshman study at accredited 2-year or 4-year institution in United States.
Eligibility: Applicant must be Mexican American, Hispanic American or Puerto Rican. Applicant must be at least 16, high school freshman. Applicant must be U.S. citizen or permanent resident residing in Florida.
Basis for selection: Applicant must demonstrate high academic achievement.
Application requirements: Recommendations, essay, transcript. FAFSA.
Additional information: Minimum 3.0 GPA. Open to Florida residents who are 16 and older.

Amount of award:	$1,000-$2,000
Number of awards:	20
Application deadline:	December 31

Contact:
Hispanic Scholarship Fund
1411 West 190th Street
Suite 325
Gardena, CA 90248
Phone: 877-473-4636
Web: www.hsf.net

Discover Scholarship

Type of award: Scholarship.
Intended use: For full-time undergraduate study at accredited 4-year institution in United States.
Eligibility: Applicant must be Mexican American, Hispanic American or Puerto Rican. Applicant must be U.S. citizen or permanent resident.
Basis for selection: Major/career interest in business; finance/banking; technology or marketing. Applicant must demonstrate financial need and high academic achievement.
Application requirements: Recommendations, transcript. Resume, FAFSA.
Additional information: Minimum 3.0 GPA. Must permanently reside or attend an institution in one of the following states: Arizona, California, Delaware, Illinois, Kentucky, New York, Ohio, Texas, Utah.

Amount of award:	$5,000
Application deadline:	February 1

Contact:
Hispanic Scholarship Fund
1411 West 190th Street
Suite 325
Gardena, CA 90248
Phone: 877-473-4636
Web: www.hsf.net

ExxonMobil Scholarship

Type of award: Scholarship.
Intended use: For full-time sophomore, junior or senior study at accredited 4-year institution in United States.
Eligibility: Applicant must be Mexican American, Hispanic American or Puerto Rican. Applicant must be U.S. citizen or international student.
Basis for selection: Major/career interest in engineering. Applicant must demonstrate financial need and high academic achievement.
Application requirements: Recommendations, transcript. FAFSA, resume.
Additional information: Minimum 3.2 GPA. Preference given to students at following universities: Colorado School of Mines, Lamar University, Louisiana State University and Agricultural & Mechanical College, Stanford University, Texas A&M - College Station, Texas Tech University, University of Florida, University of Houston - Main Campus, University of Oklahoma, University of Texas (at Austin, El Paso, or Pan American), Worcester Polytechnic Institute.

Amount of award:	$2,500
Application deadline:	April 30

Contact:
Hispanic Scholarship Fund
1411 West 190th Street
Suite 325
Gardena, CA 90248
Phone: 877-473-4636
Web: www.hsf.net

GE Hispanic Forum Scholarship

Type of award: Scholarship.
Intended use: For full-time sophomore, junior, senior or graduate study at accredited 4-year institution in United States. Designated institutions: Schools in Arizona, New Mexico, Puerto Rico and approved metro areas in U.S.
Eligibility: Applicant must be Mexican American, Hispanic American or Puerto Rican. Applicant must be U.S. citizen or international student.
Basis for selection: Major/career interest in accounting; aerospace; science, general; engineering; computer/information sciences; finance/banking; technology; manufacturing; mathematics or social work. Applicant must demonstrate financial need and high academic achievement.
Application requirements: Recommendations, transcript. FAFSA.
Additional information: Minimum 3.0 GPA. Must major in approved area. Must have permanent address and attend school in Arizona, New Mexico, Puerto Rico, or approved metro areas. See Website for details.

Amount of award: $1,500
Application deadline: December 15
Contact:
Hispanic Scholarship Fund
1411 West 190th Street
Suite 325
Gardena, CA 90248
Phone: 877-473-4636
Web: www.hsf.net

Goya Scholarship

Type of award: Scholarship.
Intended use: For full-time freshman study at accredited 2-year or 4-year institution in United States.
Eligibility: Applicant must be Mexican American, Hispanic American or Puerto Rican. Applicant must be high school senior. Applicant must be U.S. citizen or permanent resident.
Basis for selection: Applicant must demonstrate financial need and high academic achievement.
Application requirements: Recommendations, transcript. FAFSA.
Additional information: Minimum 3.0 GPA. Must be obtaining first undergraduate degree. Must be child of Goya employee, broker, or independent driver with at least one year employment. Parent must remain employed and in good standing for duration of child's participation in Goya program. Recipients must complete ten hours of community service per month during program.
Amount of award: $5,000
Application deadline: February 25
Contact:
Hispanic Scholarship Fund
1411 West 190th Street
Suite 325
Gardena, CA 90248
Phone: 877-473-4636
Web: www.hsf.net

Greater Houston Retailers and Coca-Cola Live Positively Scholarship

Type of award: Scholarship.
Intended use: For full-time undergraduate study at accredited 2-year or 4-year institution in United States.
Eligibility: Applicant must be at least 16, high school senior. Applicant must be U.S. citizen or permanent resident residing in Texas.
Application requirements: Essay. FAFSA.
Additional information: Minimum 3.0 GPA. Must have permanent address in Texas. Employees and relatives of employees of Hispanic Scholarship Fund, Coca-Cola Company and its promotional partners are ineligible.
Amount of award: $2,000-$5,000
Number of awards: 22
Application deadline: December 31
Contact:
Hispanic Scholarship Fund
1411 West 190th Street
Suite 325
Gardena, CA 90248
Phone: 877-473-4636
Web: www.hsf.net

HACEMOS Scholarship

Type of award: Scholarship.
Intended use: For full-time undergraduate study at accredited 2-year or 4-year institution in United States.
Eligibility: Applicant must be Mexican American, Hispanic American or Puerto Rican. Applicant must be no older than 25. Applicant must be U.S. citizen or international student residing in New York, Puerto Rico, Tennessee, California, Connecticut, Illinois, Missouri, Michigan, Texas, Arizona, Pennsylvania, Georgia, Florida, District of Columbia, Oklahoma, North Carolina or New Jersey.
Basis for selection: Applicant must demonstrate financial need and high academic achievement.
Application requirements: FAFSA.
Additional information: Minimum 3.0 GPA. Must be dependent of HAMECOS member. Must live in one of the following metro areas: Fresno, Los Angeles, Orange County, San Diego, San Ramon or San Francisco Bay Area in California; Arizona (entire state); Austin, Corpus Christi, Dallas/Plano/Irving, El Paso, Forth Worth/Arlington, Houston, Lubbock, or San Antonio in Texas; Joplin, Kansas City, or St. Louis in Missouri; Oklahoma (entire state); Chicago, IL; Michigan (entire state), Florida (entire state); North Carolina (entire state); Puerto Rico; Atlanta, GA; Nashville, TN; Hartford or New Haven in Connecticut; New Jersey (entire state), New York, NY; Pennsylvania (entire state); Washington, D.C.
Amount of award: $1,500-$2,500
Application deadline: February 28
Contact:
Hispanic Scholarship Fund
1411 West 190th Street
Suite 325
Gardena, CA 90248
Phone: 877-473-4636
Web: www.hsf.net

Honda Scholarship

Type of award: Scholarship.
Intended use: For junior or senior study at accredited 4-year institution in United States.
Eligibility: Applicant must be Mexican American, Hispanic American or Puerto Rican.
Basis for selection: Major/career interest in engineering or business. Applicant must demonstrate financial need and high academic achievement.
Application requirements: Recommendations, transcript. FAFSA, resume.
Additional information: Minimum 3.0 GPA. Must have interest in automotive industry.
Amount of award: $5,000
Application deadline: December 15
Contact:
Hispanic Scholarship Fund
1411 West 190th Street
Suite 325
Gardena, CA 90248
Phone: 877-473-4636
Web: www.hsf.net

HSF Achievement Scholarship

Type of award: Scholarship.
Intended use: For full-time freshman study at accredited 2-year institution in United States. Designated institutions:

Community College of Aurora (Colorado), Community College of Denver (Colorado), Austin Community College (Texas).
Eligibility: Applicant must be Mexican American, Hispanic American or Puerto Rican. Applicant must be high school senior. Applicant must be U.S. citizen or permanent resident residing in Texas or Colorado.
Basis for selection: Applicant must demonstrate financial need and high academic achievement.
Application requirements: Recommendations, transcript. FAFSA, SAT/ACT scores, Accuplacer scores, STAAR scores.
Additional information: Minimum 2.5 GPA. Must have permanent address in Denver, CO or Texas. Must be first-year student at community college who intends to transfer to four-year school. Must meet minimum test score requirements which differ by state. Preference given to Pell-eligible and first generation students. Must have completed certain courses to be eligible. Check Website for details.

Amount of award:	$1,250
Application deadline:	February 15

Contact:
Hispanic Scholarship Fund
1411 West 190th Street
Suite 325
Gardena, CA 90248
Phone: 877-473-4636
Web: www.hsf.net

HSF General College Scholarship

Type of award: Scholarship.
Intended use: For full-time undergraduate or graduate study at 2-year, 4-year or graduate institution in or outside United States. Designated institutions: Colleges in United States, Puerto Rico, U.S. Virgin Islands, and Guam.
Eligibility: Applicant must be Mexican American, Hispanic American or Puerto Rican. Applicant must be U.S. citizen or permanent resident.
Basis for selection: Applicant must demonstrate financial need, high academic achievement, seriousness of purpose and service orientation.
Application requirements: Recommendations, essay, transcript, proof of eligibility. FAFSA and SAR. Copy of permanent resident card or passport stamped I-551 (if applicable).
Additional information: Minimum 3.0 GPA. Must be pursuing first undergraduate or graduate degree. Visit Website or contact via e-mail for application deadlines and tips on how to apply.

Amount of award:	$1,000-$5,000
Application deadline:	December 15

Contact:
General Selection Committee Hispanic Scholarship Fund
1411 West 190th Street
Suite 325
Gardena, CA 90248
Phone: 877-473-4636
Web: www.hsf.net

Lockheed Martin American Heroes Scholarship

Type of award: Scholarship.
Intended use: For full-time junior or senior study at accredited 4-year institution in United States.
Eligibility: Applicant must be Mexican American, Hispanic American or Puerto Rican. Applicant must be U.S. citizen or permanent resident. Applicant must be veteran who served in the Army, Air Force, Marines or Navy. Must be military veteran or member of ROTC program.
Basis for selection: Major/career interest in science, general; mathematics; engineering; technology; engineering, computer; computer/information sciences or engineering, electrical/electronic.
Application requirements: FAFSA.
Additional information: Minimum 3.2 GPA. Must be military veteran or member of ROTC program.

Amount of award:	$5,400
Application deadline:	December 15

Contact:
Hispanic Scholarship Fund
1411 West 190th Street
Suite 325
Gardena, CA 90248
Phone: 877-473-4636
Web: www.hsf.net

Macy's College Scholarship Program

Type of award: Scholarship.
Intended use: For full-time undergraduate study at accredited 4-year institution in United States. Designated institutions: Baruch College, Columbia University, Miami Dade College, New York University, Pennsylvania State University, Syracuse University, Texas A&M University, Ohio State University, University of Arizona, University of California - Berkeley, University of Florida, University of Georgia, University of Maryland - College Park, University of Southern California, University of Texas - Austin, University of Washington.
Eligibility: Applicant must be Mexican American, Hispanic American or Puerto Rican. Applicant must be U.S. citizen or permanent resident.
Basis for selection: Applicant must demonstrate financial need and high academic achievement.
Application requirements: Recommendations, transcript. FAFSA.
Additional information: Minimum 3.0 GPA.

Amount of award:	$2,500
Application deadline:	December 15

Contact:
Hispanic Scholarship Fund
1411 West 190th Street
Suite 325
Gardena, CA 90248
Phone: 877-473-4636
Web: www.hsf.net

Marathon Oil Corporation College Scholarship

Type of award: Scholarship, renewable.
Intended use: For junior or master's study at 4-year institution.
Eligibility: Applicant must be Alaskan native, African American, Hispanic American, American Indian or Native Hawaiian/Pacific Islander. Applicant must be U.S. citizen or permanent resident.
Basis for selection: Major/career interest in engineering, chemical; engineering, civil; engineering, electrical/electronic; engineering, mechanical; engineering, petroleum; geology/earth sciences; geophysics; accounting or marketing. Applicant must demonstrate high academic achievement, leadership and seriousness of purpose.

Application requirements: Recommendations, essay, transcript. Resume and FAFSA.
Additional information: Other acceptable fields of study are global procurement or supply chain management, environmental health and safety, energy management, petroleum land management, transportation and logistics, and geotechnical engineering. Must be sophomore, or be graduating senior enrolling in master's program in geology or geophysics. Must agree to participate in a possible paid summer internship. Minimum 3.0 GPA. See Website for application and further requirements.

Amount of award:	$15,000
Number of awards:	20
Application deadline:	November 1

Contact:
HSF/Marathon Oil Corporation Scholarship Committee
1411 West 190th Street
Suite 325
Gardena, CA 90248
Phone: 877-473-4636
Web: www.hsf.net

Marathon Petroleum Corporation College Scholarship

Type of award: Scholarship.
Intended use: For full-time junior, senior or master's study at accredited 4-year institution in United States.
Eligibility: Applicant must be Mexican American, Hispanic American or Puerto Rican. Applicant must be U.S. citizen or permanent resident.
Basis for selection: Major/career interest in accounting; engineering, chemical; engineering, civil; computer/information sciences; engineering, electrical/electronic; engineering, environmental; finance/banking; engineering, industrial; technology or marketing. Applicant must demonstrate financial need and high academic achievement.
Application requirements: FAFSA.
Additional information: Minimum 3.0 GPA. Military veterans and ROTC members encouraged to apply. Preference given to those attending the following institutions: Bowling Green State University, Ohio Northern University, Purdue University, University of Findlay, Michigan State University, Ohio State University, University of Cincinnati, University of Toledo, Central Michigan University, Tiffin University, University of Michigan, Indiana University, University of Dayton, West Virginia University, Miami University (Ohio), University of Illinois-Urbana Champaign, Western Michigan University, Louisiana State University, North Carolina A&T, and University of Louisville. First year Master's students majoring in human resources management and first year law students also eligible.

Amount of award:	$7,500
Application deadline:	January 31

Contact:
Hispanic Scholarship Fund
1411 West 190th Street
Suite 325
Gardena, CA 90248
Phone: 877-473-4636
Web: www.hsf.net

Mary R. Molina Scholarship

Type of award: Scholarship.
Intended use: For full-time undergraduate or graduate study at accredited 2-year, 4-year or graduate institution in United States.
Eligibility: Applicant must be U.S. citizen or permanent resident.
Application requirements: FAFSA.
Additional information: Minimum 2.5 GPA. Must be employee or dependent of employee of Molina Healthcare.

Amount of award:	$2,500
Application deadline:	January 15

Contact:
Hispanic Scholarship Fund
1411 West 190th Street
Suite 325
Gardena, CA 90248
Phone: 877-473-4636
Web: www.hsf.net

Morgan Stanley Foundation Scholarship

Type of award: Scholarship.
Intended use: For full-time junior, senior or graduate study at accredited postsecondary institution in United States.
Eligibility: Applicant must be Mexican American, Hispanic American or Puerto Rican. Applicant must be high school junior or senior. Applicant must be U.S. citizen or permanent resident.
Basis for selection: Major/career interest in accounting; science, general; economics; finance/banking; technology; mathematics; computer/information sciences; engineering; English or literature.
Application requirements: Recommendations, transcript. FAFSA, resume. Essay: Are you interested in a career in financial services? What unique perspective will you bring to Morgan Stanley?
Additional information: Minimum 3.0 GPA. Possible internship opportunity at Morgan Stanley.

Amount of award:	$3,200
Number of awards:	20
Application deadline:	December 15

Contact:
Hispanic Scholarship Fund
1411 West 190th Street
Suite 325
Gardena, CA 90248
Phone: 877-473-4636
Web: www.hsf.net

Nissan North America, Inc. Scholarship Program

Type of award: Scholarship.
Intended use: For full-time sophomore, junior, senior or graduate study at accredited postsecondary institution in United States. Designated institutions: Accredited four-year postsecondary institutions in United States, Puerto Rico, U.S. Virgin Islands, and Guam.
Eligibility: Applicant must be Mexican American, Hispanic American or Puerto Rican. Applicant must be U.S. citizen or permanent resident residing in California, Michigan, Tennessee, Texas, Mississippi or Arizona.
Basis for selection: Major/career interest in business; engineering; advertising; human resources; international relations; marketing or public relations. Applicant must demonstrate financial need and high academic achievement.
Application requirements: Recommendations, essay, transcript, proof of eligibility. FAFSA and copy of permanent resident card or passport stamped I-551 (if applicable).

Additional information: Must have permanent address or attend school in one of the following locations: Arizona (state); Dallas/Fort Worth, Texas (metro); Michigan (state); Mississippi (state); San Diego, California (metro); Tennessee (state). Must be enrolled part-time or full-time at community college and plan to transfer to four-year institution in fall or spring of next academic year. Minimum 3.0 GPA. Visit Website or contact via e-mail for more information.

Amount of award: $5,000
Application deadline: March 31

Contact:
Community College Transfer Program Hispanic Scholarship Fund
1411 West 190th Street
Suite 325
Gardena, CA 90248
Phone: 877-473-4636
Web: www.hsf.net

Northwest Arkansas Bilingual Teacher Scholarship

Type of award: Scholarship.
Intended use: For full-time undergraduate study at accredited 2-year or 4-year institution in United States. Designated institutions: Northwest Arkansas Community College, Bentonville; University of Arkansas, Fayetteville.
Eligibility: Applicant must be Mexican American, Hispanic American or Puerto Rican. Applicant must be U.S. citizen or permanent resident.
Basis for selection: Applicant must demonstrate financial need and high academic achievement.
Application requirements: FAFSA.
Additional information: Minimum 3.0 GPA. All majors eligible, but must intend to become K-12 teacher in Northwest Arkansas. Preference given to graduates of Springdale school district, those eligible for Pell grant funding, and first-generation college students.

Application deadline: February 8

Contact:
Hispanic Scholarship Fund
1411 West 190th Street
Suite 325
Gardena, CA 90248
Phone: 877-473-4636
Web: www.hsf.net

Procter & Gamble - Orgullosa Scholarship

Type of award: Scholarship.
Intended use: For full-time undergraduate study at accredited 4-year institution in United States. Designated institutions: Universities in the United States, Puerto Rico, Guam, and the U.S. Virgin Islands.
Eligibility: Applicant must be Mexican American, Hispanic American or Puerto Rican. Applicant must be U.S. citizen or permanent resident.
Basis for selection: Major/career interest in engineering; mathematics; science, general or technology. Applicant must demonstrate high academic achievement.
Application requirements: FAFSA.
Additional information: Minimum 3.0 GPA.

Amount of award: $2,500
Application deadline: February 28

Contact:
Hispanic Scholarship Fund
1411 West 190th Street
Suite 325
Gardena, CA 90248
Phone: 877-473-4636
Web: www.hsf.net

USHCC-Wells Fargo Scholarship

Type of award: Scholarship.
Intended use: For full-time undergraduate or graduate study at accredited 4-year or graduate institution in United States.
Eligibility: Applicant must be Mexican American, Hispanic American or Puerto Rican.
Basis for selection: Applicant must demonstrate financial need and high academic achievement.
Application requirements: FAFSA.
Additional information: Minimum 3.0 GPA. Must be dependent or relative of U.S. Hispanic Chamber of Commerce members or employees or past participants of USHCC BizFest Program.

Amount of award: $2,500
Number of awards: 40
Application deadline: May 31

Contact:
Hispanic Scholarship Fund
1411 West 190th Street
Suite 325
Gardena, CA 90248
Phone: 877-473-4636
Web: www.hsf.net

VAMOS Scholarship

Type of award: Scholarship.
Intended use: For full-time freshman study at accredited 4-year institution in United States.
Eligibility: Applicant must be Mexican American, Hispanic American or Puerto Rican. Applicant must be high school senior. Applicant must be U.S. citizen or permanent resident.
Basis for selection: Applicant must demonstrate financial need and high academic achievement.
Application requirements: Recommendations, transcript. FAFSA.
Additional information: Minimum 3.0 GPA. Must be high school senior graduating from high school in Hidalgo, Cameron, or Starr counties in Texas.

Application deadline: February 28

Contact:
Hispanic Scholarship Fund
1411 West 190th Street
Suite 325
Gardena, CA 90248
Phone: 877-473-4636
Web: www.hsf.net

Hopi Tribe Grants and Scholarship Program

Hopi BIA Higher Education Grant

Type of award: Scholarship, renewable.
Intended use: For full-time undergraduate or graduate study at accredited 2-year, 4-year or graduate institution.

Eligibility: Applicant must be American Indian. Must be enrolled member of the Hopi Tribe.
Basis for selection: Applicant must demonstrate financial need and high academic achievement.
Additional information: Entering freshmen must have minimum 2.0 GPA for high school coursework or minimum composite score of 45% on GED Exam. Continuing students must have minimum 2.0 GPA for all graduate coursework. Four deadlines per year: November 1st (for winter quarter), December 1st (for spring), May 1st (for summer), and July 1st (for fall). Must reapply each academic year or semester. Number and amount of awards vary.

Number of applicants:	140
Application deadline:	December 1, July 1

Contact:
Hopi Tribe Grants and Scholarship Program
P.O. Box 123
Kykotsmovi, AZ 86039
Phone: 800-762-9630
Fax: 928-734-9575

Hopi Education Award

Type of award: Scholarship, renewable.
Intended use: For undergraduate or graduate study at accredited 2-year, 4-year or graduate institution.
Eligibility: Applicant must be American Indian. Must be enrolled member of the Hopi Tribe.
Basis for selection: Applicant must demonstrate financial need and high academic achievement.
Additional information: Entering freshmen must have minimum 2.5 GPA for high school coursework or minimum composite score of 45 percent on the GED Exam. Continuing students must have minimum 2.5 GPA for all college work. Four deadlines per year: November 1st (for winter quarter), December 1st (for spring), May 1st (for summer), and July 1st (for fall). Must reapply each academic year or semester.

Number of applicants:	140
Application deadline:	December 1, July 1

Contact:
Hopi Tribe Grants and Scholarship Program
P.O. Box 123
Kykotsmovi, AZ 86039
Phone: 800-762-9630
Fax: 928-734-9575

Hopi Tribal Priority Award

Type of award: Scholarship, renewable.
Intended use: For full-time junior, senior or graduate study at accredited 4-year or graduate institution.
Eligibility: Applicant must be American Indian. Must be enrolled member of the Hopi Tribe.
Basis for selection: Applicant must demonstrate high academic achievement, depth of character, leadership and seriousness of purpose.
Application requirements: Recommendations, transcript, proof of eligibility.
Additional information: Award is based on amount of college cost. Preference given to those majoring in fields considered to be of tribal priority. Applicant must have college submit financial needs analysis to determine amount of award.

Amount of award:	Full tuition
Number of applicants:	3

Contact:
Hopi Tribe Grants and Scholarship Program
P.O. Box 123
Kykotsmovi, AZ 86039
Phone: 800-762-9630
Fax: 928-734-9575

Horatio Alger Association

Horatio Alger Ak-Sar-Ben Scholarship Program

Type of award: Scholarship.
Intended use: For full-time undergraduate study at accredited 2-year or 4-year institution in United States.
Eligibility: Applicant must be high school senior. Applicant must be U.S. citizen residing in Iowa or Nebraska.
Basis for selection: Applicant must demonstrate financial need, high academic achievement, seriousness of purpose and service orientation.
Application requirements: Essay, transcript. Letter of support, income statement.
Additional information: Minimum 2.0 GPA. Program assists high school seniors who have faced and overcome great obstacles and have participated in co-curricular and community activities. Must plan to pursue bachelor's degree. See Website for application and list of eligible Iowa counties.

Amount of award:	$6,000
Number of awards:	50
Application deadline:	October 30

Contact:
Horatio Alger Association
99 Canal Center Plaza, Suite 320
Alexandria, VA 22314
Phone: 703-684-9444
Fax: 703-548-3822
Web: www.horatioalger.org/scholarships

Horatio Alger Arizona Scholarship

Type of award: Scholarship.
Intended use: For full-time freshman study at 2-year or 4-year institution in United States.
Eligibility: Applicant must be high school senior. Applicant must be U.S. citizen residing in Arizona.
Basis for selection: Applicant must demonstrate financial need, high academic achievement, seriousness of purpose and service orientation.
Application requirements: Essay, transcript. Letter of support, income statement.
Additional information: Minimum 2.0 GPA. Program assists high school seniors who have faced and overcome great obstacles and have participated in co-curricular and community activities. Must plan to pursue bachelor's degree.

Amount of award:	$5,000
Number of awards:	10
Application deadline:	October 30

Contact:
Horatio Alger Association
99 Canal Center Plaza, Suite 320
Alexandria, VA 22314
Phone: 703-684-9444
Fax: 703-548-3822
Web: www.horatioalger.org/scholarships

Horatio Alger California (Northern) Scholarship Program

Type of award: Scholarship.
Intended use: For full-time undergraduate study at accredited 2-year or 4-year institution in United States.
Eligibility: Applicant must be high school senior. Applicant must be U.S. citizen residing in California.
Basis for selection: Applicant must demonstrate financial need, high academic achievement, seriousness of purpose and service orientation.
Application requirements: Essay, transcript. Letter of support, income statement.
Additional information: Minimum 2.0 GPA. Program assists high school seniors who have faced and overcome great obstacles and have participated in co-curricular and community activities. Applicant should have strong commitment to use college degree in service to others. Must plan to pursue bachelor's degree. See Website for application.

Amount of award:	$5,000
Number of awards:	38
Application deadline:	October 30

Contact:
Horatio Alger Association
99 Canal Center Plaza, Suite 320
Alexandria, VA 22314
Phone: 703-684-9444
Fax: 703-548-3822
Web: www.horatioalger.org/scholarships

Horatio Alger Delaware Scholarship Program

Type of award: Scholarship.
Intended use: For full-time undergraduate study at accredited 2-year or 4-year institution in United States.
Eligibility: Applicant must be high school senior. Applicant must be U.S. citizen residing in Delaware.
Basis for selection: Applicant must demonstrate financial need, high academic achievement and service orientation.
Application requirements: Essay, transcript. Letter of support, income statement.
Additional information: Minimum 2.0 GPA. Program assists high school seniors who have faced and overcome great obstacles and have participated in co-curricular and community activities. Must plan to pursue bachelor's degree. See Website for application.

Amount of award:	$5,000
Number of awards:	5
Application deadline:	October 30

Contact:
Horatio Alger Association
99 Canal Center Drive, Suite 320
Alexandria, VA 22314
Phone: 703-684-9444
Fax: 703-548-3822
Web: www.horatioalger.org/scholarships

Horatio Alger District of Columbia, Maryland and Virginia Scholarship Program

Type of award: Scholarship.
Intended use: For full-time undergraduate study at accredited 2-year or 4-year institution in United States.
Eligibility: Applicant must be high school senior. Applicant must be U.S. citizen residing in Virginia, District of Columbia or Maryland.
Basis for selection: Applicant must demonstrate financial need, high academic achievement, seriousness of purpose and service orientation.
Application requirements: Essay, transcript. Letter of support, income statement.
Additional information: Program assists high school seniors who have faced and overcome great obstacles and have participated in co-curricular and community activities. See Website for list of eligible counties. Must plan to pursue bachelor's degree. See Website for application.

Amount of award:	$5,000
Number of awards:	20
Application deadline:	October 30

Contact:
Horatio Alger Association
99 Canal Center Plaza, Suite 320
Alexandria, VA 22314
Phone: 703-684-9444
Fax: 703-548-3822
Web: www.horatioalger.com/scholarships

Horatio Alger Georgia Scholarship Program

Type of award: Scholarship.
Intended use: For full-time undergraduate study at accredited 2-year or 4-year institution in United States.
Eligibility: Applicant must be high school senior. Applicant must be U.S. citizen residing in Georgia.
Basis for selection: Applicant must demonstrate financial need, high academic achievement, seriousness of purpose and service orientation.
Application requirements: Essay, transcript. Letter of support, income statement.
Additional information: Minimum 2.0 GPA. Program assists high school seniors who have faced and overcome great obstacles and have participated in co-curricular and community activities. Must plan to pursue bachelor's degree. Visit Website for application.

Amount of award:	$5,000
Number of awards:	50
Application deadline:	October 30

Contact:
Horatio Alger Assocation
99 Canal Center Plaza, Suite 320
Alexandria, VA 22314
Phone: 703-684-9444
Fax: 703-548-3822
Web: www.horatioalger.org/scholarships

Horatio Alger Illinois Scholarship Program

Type of award: Scholarship.
Intended use: For full-time undergraduate study at accredited 2-year or 4-year institution in United States.
Eligibility: Applicant must be high school senior. Applicant must be U.S. citizen residing in Illinois.
Basis for selection: Applicant must demonstrate financial need, high academic achievement and service orientation.
Application requirements: Essay, transcript. Letter of support, income statement.
Additional information: Minimum 2.0 GPA. Program assists high school seniors who have faced and overcome great

obstacles and have participated in co-curricular and community activities. Must plan to pursue bachelor's degree. Visit Website for application.

Amount of award: $5,000
Number of awards: 20
Application deadline: October 30

Contact:
Horatio Alger Association
99 Canal Center Plaza, Suite 320
Alexandria, VA 22314
Phone: 703-684-9444
Fax: 703-548-3822
Web: www.horatioalger.org/scholarships

Horatio Alger John Hardin Hudiburg Scholarship Program

Type of award: Scholarship.
Intended use: For in United States.
Eligibility: Applicant must be residing in Texas.
Basis for selection: Applicant must demonstrate financial need and high academic achievement.
Additional information: Minimum 2.0 GPA. Program assists high school seniors who have faced and overcome great obstacles and have participated in co-curricular and community activities. Must plan to pursue bachelor's degree. Visit Website for application. Must be Texas resident who attends school in one of the following districts: Grapevine-Colleyville, Hurst-Euless-Bedford, Keller, and Birdville ISD's.

Amount of award: $5,000
Number of awards: 1

Contact:
Horatio Alger Association
99 Canal Center Plaza, Suite 320
Alexandria, VA 22314
Phone: 703-684-9444
Fax: 703-548-3822
Web: www.horatioalger.org/scholarships

Horatio Alger Louisiana Scholarship Program

Type of award: Scholarship.
Intended use: For full-time undergraduate study at accredited 2-year or 4-year institution in United States. Designated institutions: Louisiana colleges and universities.
Eligibility: Applicant must be high school senior. Applicant must be U.S. citizen residing in Louisiana.
Basis for selection: Applicant must demonstrate financial need, high academic achievement, seriousness of purpose and service orientation.
Application requirements: Essay, transcript. Letter of support, income statement.
Additional information: Minimum 2.0 GPA. Program assists high school seniors who have faced and overcome great obstacles and have participated in co-curricular and community activities. Must plan to pursue bachelor's degree. See Website for application.

Amount of award: $10,500
Number of awards: 50
Application deadline: October 30

Contact:
Horatio Alger Association
99 Canal Center Plaza, Suite 320
Alexandria, VA 22314
Phone: 703-684-9444
Fax: 703-548-3822
Web: www.horatioalger.org/scholarships

Horatio Alger Missouri Scholarship Program

Type of award: Scholarship.
Intended use: For full-time undergraduate study at accredited 2-year or 4-year institution in United States.
Eligibility: Applicant must be high school senior. Applicant must be U.S. citizen residing in Missouri.
Basis for selection: Applicant must demonstrate financial need, high academic achievement, seriousness of purpose and service orientation.
Application requirements: Essay, transcript. Letter of support, income statement.
Additional information: Minimum 2.0 GPA. Program assists high school seniors who have faced and overcome great obstacles and have participated in co-curricular and community activities. Must plan to pursue bachelor's degree. See Website for application.

Amount of award: $5,000
Number of awards: 10
Application deadline: October 30

Contact:
Horatio Alger Association
99 Canal Center Plaza, Suite 320
Alexandria, VA 22314
Phone: 703-684-9444
Fax: 703-548-3822
Web: www.horatioalger.org/scholarships

Horatio Alger Montana Scholarship Program

Type of award: Scholarship.
Intended use: For full-time undergraduate study in United States. Designated institutions: University of Montana institutions.
Eligibility: Applicant must be high school senior. Applicant must be U.S. citizen residing in Montana.
Basis for selection: Applicant must demonstrate financial need, high academic achievement and service orientation.
Application requirements: Essay, transcript. Letter of support, income statement.
Additional information: Minimum 2.0 GPA. Program assists high school seniors who have faced and overcome great obstacles and have participated in co-curricular and community activities. Must plan to pursue bachelor's degree. See Website for application.

Amount of award: $5,000
Number of awards: 50
Application deadline: October 30

Contact:
Horatio Alger Association
99 Canal Center Plaza, Suite 320
Alexandria, VA 22314
Phone: 703-684-9444
Fax: 703-548-3822
Web: www.horatioalger.org/scholarships

Horatio Alger National Scholarship

Type of award: Scholarship.
Intended use: For full-time undergraduate study at accredited 2-year or 4-year institution in United States.
Eligibility: Applicant must be high school senior. Applicant must be U.S. citizen.
Basis for selection: Based on co-curricular and community activities. Applicant must demonstrate financial need, high academic achievement, seriousness of purpose and service orientation.
Application requirements: Essay, transcript. Letter of support, income statement.
Additional information: Minimum 2.0 GPA. Program assists high school seniors who have faced and overcome great obstacles and have participated in co-curricular and community activities. Must plan to pursue bachelor's degree. Visit Website for application.

Amount of award:	$20,000
Number of awards:	106
Application deadline:	October 30

Contact:
Horatio Alger Association
99 Canal Center Plaza, Suite 320
Alexandria, VA 22314
Phone: 703-684-9444
Fax: 703-548-3822
Web: www.horatioalger.org/scholarships

Horatio Alger North Dakota Scholarship Program

Type of award: Scholarship.
Intended use: For full-time undergraduate study at accredited 2-year or 4-year institution in United States.
Eligibility: Applicant must be high school senior. Applicant must be U.S. citizen residing in North Dakota.
Basis for selection: Applicant must demonstrate financial need, high academic achievement, seriousness of purpose and service orientation.
Application requirements: Essay, transcript. Letter of support, income statement.
Additional information: Minimum 2.0 GPA. Program assists high school seniors who have faced and overcome great obstacles and have participated in co-curricular and community activities. Must plan to pursue bachelor's degree. Visit Website for application.

Amount of award:	$5,000
Number of awards:	21
Application deadline:	October 30

Contact:
Horatio Alger Association
99 Canal Center Plaza, Suite 320
Alexandria, VA 22314
Phone: 703-684-9444
Fax: 703-548-3822
Web: www.horatioalger.org/scholarships

Horatio Alger Pennsylvania Scholarship Program

Type of award: Scholarship.
Intended use: For full-time undergraduate study at accredited 2-year or 4-year institution in United States.
Eligibility: Applicant must be high school senior. Applicant must be U.S. citizen residing in Pennsylvania.
Basis for selection: Applicant must demonstrate financial need, high academic achievement and service orientation.
Application requirements: Essay, transcript. Letter of support, income statement.
Additional information: Minimum 2.0 GPA. Program assists high school seniors who have faced and overcome great obstacles and have participated in co-curricular and community activities. Must plan to pursue bachelor's degree. See Website for application.

Amount of award:	$5,000
Number of awards:	50
Application deadline:	October 30

Contact:
Horatio Alger Association
99 Canal Center Drive, Suite 320
Alexandria, VA 22314
Phone: 703-684-9444
Fax: 703-548-3822
Web: www.horatioalger.org/scholarships

Horatio Alger Ronald C. Waranch Scholarship Program

Type of award: Scholarship.
Intended use: For at accredited 2-year or 4-year institution in United States.
Eligibility: Applicant must be high school senior. Applicant must be U.S. citizen residing in Georgia.
Basis for selection: Applicant must demonstrate financial need, high academic achievement, depth of character and seriousness of purpose.
Additional information: Minimum 2.0 GPA. Program assists high school seniors who have faced and overcome great obstacles and have participated in co-curricular and community activities. Must plan to pursue bachelor's degree. Visit Website for application.

Amount of award:	$5,000
Number of awards:	4

Contact:
Horatio Alger Association
99 Canal Center Plaza, Suite 320
Alexandria, VA 22314
Phone: 703-684-9444
Fax: 703-548-3822
Web: www.horatioalger.org/scholarships

Horatio Alger South Dakota Scholarship Program

Type of award: Scholarship.
Intended use: For full-time undergraduate study at accredited 2-year or 4-year institution in United States.
Eligibility: Applicant must be high school senior. Applicant must be U.S. citizen residing in South Dakota.
Basis for selection: Applicant must demonstrate financial need, high academic achievement, seriousness of purpose and service orientation.
Application requirements: Essay, transcript. Letter of support, income statement.
Additional information: Minimum 2.0 GPA. Program assists high school seniors who have faced and overcome great obstacles and have participated in co-curricular and community activities. Must plan to pursue bachelor's degree. See Website for application and more information.

Amount of award:	$5,000
Number of awards:	25
Application deadline:	October 30

Contact:
The Horatio Alger Association
99 Canal Center Plaza, Suite 320
Alexandria, VA 22314
Phone: 703-684-9444
Fax: 703-548-3822
Web: www.horatioalger.org/scholarships

Horatio Alger Texas Scholarship Program

Type of award: Scholarship.
Intended use: For full-time undergraduate study at accredited 2-year or 4-year institution in United States.
Eligibility: Applicant must be high school senior. Applicant must be U.S. citizen residing in Texas.
Basis for selection: Applicant must demonstrate financial need, high academic achievement, depth of character and service orientation.
Application requirements: Essay, transcript. Letter of support, income statement.
Additional information: Minimum 2.0 GPA required. Program assists high school seniors who have faced and overcome great obstacles and have participated in co-curricular and community activities. Must plan to pursue bachelor's degree. See Website for application.

Amount of award:	$5,000
Number of awards:	7
Application deadline:	October 30

Contact:
Horatio Alger Association
99 Canal Center Plaza, Suite 320
Alexandria, VA 22314
Phone: 703-684-9444
Fax: 703-548-3822
Web: www.horatioalger.org/scholarships

Horatio Alger Utah Scholarship Program

Type of award: Scholarship.
Intended use: For full-time undergraduate study at accredited 2-year or 4-year institution in United States.
Eligibility: Applicant must be high school senior. Applicant must be U.S. citizen residing in Utah.
Basis for selection: Applicant must demonstrate financial need, high academic achievement, seriousness of purpose and service orientation.
Application requirements: Essay, transcript. Letter of support, income statement.
Additional information: Minimum 2.0 GPA. Program assists high school seniors who have faced and overcome great obstacles and have participated in co-curricular and community activities. Must plan to pursue bachelor's degree. Visit Website for application.

Amount of award:	$5,000
Number of awards:	15
Application deadline:	October 30

Contact:
Horatio Alger Association
99 Canal Center Plaza, Suite 320
Alexandria, VA 22314
Phone: 703-684-9444
Fax: 703-548-3822
Web: www.horatioalger.org/scholarships

Horatio Alger Wyoming Scholarship Program

Type of award: Scholarship.
Intended use: For full-time undergraduate study at accredited 2-year or 4-year institution in United States.
Eligibility: Applicant must be high school senior. Applicant must be U.S. citizen residing in Wyoming.
Basis for selection: Applicant must demonstrate financial need, high academic achievement, seriousness of purpose and service orientation.
Application requirements: Essay, transcript. Letter of support, income statement.
Additional information: Minimum 2.0 GPA. Program assists high school seniors who have faced and overcome great obstacles and have participated in co-curricular and community activities. Must plan to pursue bachelor's degree. Visit Website for application.

Amount of award:	$5,000
Number of awards:	15
Application deadline:	October 30

Contact:
Horatio Alger Association
99 Canal Center Plaza, Suite 320
Alexandria, VA 22314
Phone: 703-684-9444
Fax: 703-548-3822
Web: www.horatioalger.org/scholarships

Horticultural Research Institute

Bryan A. Champion Scholarship

Type of award: Scholarship.
Intended use: For full-time sophomore, junior, senior or graduate study at accredited 2-year or 4-year institution in United States. Designated institutions: Institutions in Ohio.
Basis for selection: Major/career interest in horticulture or landscape architecture.
Application requirements: Recommendations, transcript. Resume, cover letter.
Additional information: Minimum 2.25 overall GPA and minimum 2.7 in major. Must have at least sophomore standing in four-year curriculum or senior standing in two-year curriculum. Preference given to applicants who plan to work within green industry following graduation. Previous winners eligible for additional funding. Visit Website for application and more information.

Amount of award:	$1,000
Application deadline:	May 31

Contact:
Horticultural Research Institute
1200 G Street NW
Suite 800
Washington, DC 20005
Phone: 202-695-2474
Fax: 888-761-7883
Web: www.hriresearch.org

Carville M. Akehurst Memorial Scholarship

Type of award: Scholarship.
Intended use: For full-time junior, senior or graduate study at accredited 2-year, 4-year or graduate institution.
Eligibility: Applicant must be residing in Virginia, West Virginia or Maryland.
Basis for selection: Major/career interest in horticulture or landscape architecture. Applicant must demonstrate high academic achievement.
Application requirements: Recommendations, essay, transcript. Resume, cover letter.
Additional information: Minimum 2.7 overall GPA and minimum 3.0 in major. Must have junior standing in four-year curriculum, or senior standing in two-year curriculum. Preference given to applicants who plan to work within industry following graduation. Previous winners eligible for additional funding. Visit Website for application and more information.

Amount of award:	$2,000
Number of awards:	2
Number of applicants:	10
Application deadline:	May 31
Total amount awarded:	$4,000

Contact:
Horticultural Research Institute
1200 G Street NW
Suite 800
Washington, DC 20005
Phone: 202-695-2474
Fax: 888-761-7883
Web: www.hriresearch.org

Horticultural Research Institute Spring Meadow Scholarship

Type of award: Scholarship.
Intended use: For full-time undergraduate or graduate study at accredited vocational, 2-year, 4-year or graduate institution.
Basis for selection: Major/career interest in horticulture or landscape architecture. Applicant must demonstrate high academic achievement.
Application requirements: Recommendations, essay, transcript. Resume, cover letter.
Additional information: Must have minimum 2.25 overall GPA, and minimum 2.7 in major. Must have at least sophomore standing in 4-year program or senior standing in 2-year program. Must be enrolled in accredited landscape, horticulture or related program. Must be interested in woody plant production, propagation, and breeding or horticulture sales and marketing. Preference given to those who plan to work in industry following graduation. Visit Website for application and more information.

Amount of award:	$3,000
Number of awards:	3
Number of applicants:	69
Application deadline:	May 31
Total amount awarded:	$1,500

Contact:
Horticultural Research Institute
1200 G Street NW
Suite 800
Washington, DC 20005
Phone: 202-695-2474
Fax: 888-761-7883
Web: www.hriresearch.org

Muggets Scholarship

Type of award: Scholarship, renewable.
Intended use: For full-time undergraduate or graduate study at vocational, 2-year, 4-year or graduate institution in United States. Designated institutions: California state colleges and universities.
Eligibility: Applicant must be residing in California.
Basis for selection: Major/career interest in landscape architecture or horticulture. Applicant must demonstrate high academic achievement.
Application requirements: Recommendations, essay, transcript. Cover letter and resume.
Additional information: Students enrolled in vocational agricultural programs also eligible. Must be a sophomore or above in 4-year program, or senior in 2-year program. Preference given to applicants who plan to work within the industry after graduation. Minimum 2.25 GPA overall; minimum 2.7 GPA in major. Visit Website for application.

Amount of award:	$1,500
Number of awards:	1
Application deadline:	May 31

Contact:
Endowment Program Administrator, Horticultural Research Institute
1200 G Street NW
Suite 800
Washington, DC 20005
Phone: 202-695-2474
Fax: 888-761-7883
Web: www.hriresearch.org

Susie & Bruce Usrey Scholarship

Type of award: Scholarship.
Intended use: For full-time undergraduate or graduate study at accredited 4-year or graduate institution in United States. Designated institutions: Institutions in California.
Basis for selection: Major/career interest in horticulture or landscape architecture.
Application requirements: Recommendations, transcript. Resume, cover letter.
Additional information: Minimum 2.25 overall GPA and minimum 2.7 in major. Preference given to applicants who plan to work within industry following graduation. Previous winners eligible for additional funding. Visit Website for application and more information.

Amount of award:	$500
Application deadline:	May 31

Contact:
Horticultural Research Institute
1200 G Street NW
Suite 800
Washington, DC 20005
Phone: 202-695-2474
Fax: 888-761-7883
Web: www.hriresearch.org

Timothy and Palmer W. Bigelow, Jr. Scholarship

Type of award: Scholarship.
Intended use: For full-time undergraduate or graduate study at accredited 2-year, 4-year or graduate institution.
Eligibility: Applicant must be residing in Vermont, New Hampshire, Connecticut, Maine, Massachusetts or Rhode Island.

Basis for selection: Major/career interest in landscape architecture or horticulture. Applicant must demonstrate financial need, high academic achievement, depth of character and seriousness of purpose.
Application requirements: Recommendations, essay, transcript. Resume and cover letter.
Additional information: Minimum 2.25 GPA for undergraduates and 3.0 GPA for graduate students. Must be enrolled in accredited landscape or horticulture program. Applicant must have senior standing in two-year program, junior standing in four-year program, or graduate standing. Applicant must be resident of one of the six New England states, but need not attend institution there. Preference given to applicants who plan to work in nursery industry after graduation. Preference also given to applicants who demonstrate financial need. Visit Website for application.

Amount of award:	$2,000
Number of awards:	1
Number of applicants:	8
Application deadline:	May 31
Notification begins:	July 1
Total amount awarded:	$3,000

Contact:
Horticultural Research Institute
1200 G Street NW
Suite 800
Washington, DC 20005
Phone: 202-695-2474
Fax: 888-761-7883
Web: www.hriresearch.org

Houston Livestock Show and Rodeo

Area Go Texan Scholarships

Type of award: Scholarship.
Intended use: For undergraduate study at postsecondary institution. Designated institutions: Texas colleges and universities.
Eligibility: Applicant must be high school senior. Applicant must be U.S. citizen residing in Texas.
Basis for selection: Applicant must demonstrate financial need, high academic achievement, depth of character, leadership and service orientation.
Application requirements: Recommendations, essay, transcript, proof of eligibility. Class standing and photograph. SAT/ACT scores. FAFSA.
Additional information: Scholarships awarded to one eligible public high school student from each of 62 Area Go Texan counties. Minimum 1350 SAT combined score (reading and math), or minimum 19 ACT score. Applicant must attend public high school and be in top third of graduating class. Applicant cannot receive more than $40,000 from financial aid or other scholarships. Contact sponsor or visit Website for eligible counties, deadline, and application.

Amount of award:	$18,000
Number of awards:	72
Application deadline:	March 1
Total amount awarded:	$1,050,000

Contact:
Houston Livestock Show and Rodeo
Office of Education Programs
P.O. Box 20070
Houston, TX 77225-0070
Phone: 832-667-1113
Web: www.hlsr.com

Houston Livestock Show and Rodeo Metropolitan Scholarships

Type of award: Scholarship, renewable.
Intended use: For undergraduate study at accredited 4-year institution in United States. Designated institutions: Colleges and universities in Texas.
Eligibility: Applicant must be high school senior. Applicant must be U.S. citizen residing in Texas.
Basis for selection: Applicant must demonstrate financial need, high academic achievement, depth of character and leadership.
Application requirements: Recommendations, essay, transcript. SAT/ACT Scores. FAFSA.
Additional information: Must be graduating from Houston-area public school districts in Brazoria, Chambers, Fort Bend, Galveston, Harris, Liberty, Montgomery, and Waller Counties. Must be in top quarter of graduating class and have minimum 1350 SAT (reading and math) or 19 ACT score.

Amount of award:	$18,000
Number of awards:	238
Application deadline:	March 1

Contact:
Houston Livestock Show and Rodeo
Office of Education Programs
P.O. Box 20070
Houston, TX 77225-0070
Phone: 832-667-1113
Web: www.hlsr.com

Houston Livestock Show and Rodeo Opportunity Scholarship

Type of award: Scholarship, renewable.
Intended use: For full-time undergraduate study at 4-year institution. Designated institutions: Texas colleges and universities.
Eligibility: Applicant must be high school senior. Applicant must be U.S. citizen residing in Texas.
Basis for selection: Applicant must demonstrate financial need, high academic achievement, depth of character, leadership and service orientation.
Application requirements: Recommendations, transcript, proof of eligibility. Up to three references. FAFSA. Two-page essay must describe importance of college and career goals. Class standing and photograph. SAT/ACT scores.
Additional information: Must have minimum 1300 SAT (reading and math) or 18 ACT. Must be graduating in top half of class from specified Texas school districts in Brazoria, Chambers, Fort Bend, Galveston, Harris, Liberty, Montgomery, or Waller counties. Visit Website for list of eligible districts, application, and more information. For applications, contact guidance counselor or Office of Education Programs.

Amount of award:	$18,000
Number of awards:	114
Application deadline:	March 1
Total amount awarded:	$1,500,000

Contact:
Houston Livestock Show and Rodeo
Office of Education Programs
P.O. Box 20070
Houston, TX 77225-0070
Phone: 832-667-1113
Web: www.hlsr.com

Houston Livestock Show and Rodeo School Art Scholarships

Type of award: Scholarship, renewable.
Intended use: For undergraduate study at accredited 4-year institution in United States. Designated institutions: Colleges and universities in Texas.
Eligibility: Applicant must be high school senior. Applicant must be U.S. citizen or international student residing in Texas.
Basis for selection: Applicant must demonstrate financial need, high academic achievement, depth of character and leadership.
Application requirements: Recommendations, essay, transcript, proof of eligibility. SAT/ACT scores. FAFSA.
Additional information: Must be high school senior who was judged by School Art Committee judges or who was selected to compete in Quick Draw competition. Must be in top quarter of class and have minimum 1350 SAT (reading and math) or 19 ACT score. Visit Website for deadline.

Amount of award: $18,000
Number of awards: 15
Application deadline: March 1

Contact:
Houston Livestock Show and Rodeo
Office of Education Programs
P.O. Box 20070
Houston, TX 77225-0070
Phone: 832-667-1113
Web: www.hlsr.com

ICMA Retirement Corporation

Vantagepoint Public Employee Memorial Scholarship Fund

Type of award: Scholarship.
Intended use: For full-time undergraduate or graduate study at accredited postsecondary institution.
Basis for selection: Applicant must demonstrate financial need, high academic achievement, leadership and service orientation.
Application requirements: Recommendations, essay, transcript, proof of eligibility. Statement of goals and aspirations, official letter from deceased employee's place of work certifying employee died in line of duty.
Additional information: High school seniors and graduates, as well as current undergraduate or graduate students eligible. Must be child or spouse of deceased local or state government employee who has died in the line of duty. Work experience, goals and aspirations, and unusual personal or family circumstances also factored into selection. Award amount varies; maximum is $10,000 (tuition and fees only). Visit Website for complete information and application.

Amount of award: $10,000
Application deadline: March 15
Notification begins: June 1

Contact:
Vantagepoint Public Employee Memorial Scholarship Program
c/o Scholarship America
One Scholarship Way
St. Peter, MN 56082
Phone: 202-962-8085
Web: www.vantagescholar.org

Idaho State Board of Education

Grow Your Own Teacher Scholarship Program

Type of award: Scholarship.
Intended use: For undergraduate study at 2-year or 4-year institution. Designated institutions: Boise State University, Idaho State University, Lewis-Clark State College, College of Southern Idaho.
Eligibility: Applicant must be residing in Idaho.
Basis for selection: Major/career interest in education. Applicant must demonstrate high academic achievement.
Application requirements: FAFSA.
Additional information: Program established to place bilingual education, ESL and Native American teachers in Idaho schools. Award for part-time students based on credit hours. Contact college of education at intended institution of matriculation for more information.

Amount of award: $3,000

Contact:
Idaho State Board of Education
650 West State Street
P.O. Box 83720
Boise, ID 83720-0037
Phone: 208-334-2270
Web: www.boardofed.idaho.gov/scholarship/gyo.asp

Idaho Freedom Scholarship

Type of award: Scholarship.
Intended use: For full-time undergraduate study at accredited 4-year institution in United States. Designated institutions: Eligible Idaho public universities and colleges.
Eligibility: Applicant must be U.S. citizen or permanent resident residing in Idaho. Applicant must be dependent of disabled veteran, deceased veteran or POW/MIA; or spouse of disabled veteran, deceased veteran or POW/MIA.
Additional information: Provides tuition waiver and on-campus housing plus up to $500 for books per semester. Must be child or spouse of Idaho citizen who was prisoner of war, missing in action, or became disabled or was killed in action.

Amount of award: Full tuition
Application deadline: February 15

Contact:
Idaho State Board of Education
650 West State Street
P.O. Box 83720
Boise, ID 83720-0037
Phone: 208-334-2270
Web: www.boardofed.idaho.gov/scholarship/freedom.asp

Idaho GEAR UP Scholarship

Type of award: Scholarship, renewable.
Intended use: For full-time undergraduate study at accredited 2-year or 4-year institution in United States. Designated institutions: North Idaho College, Lewis-Clark State College, College of Southern Idaho, Eastern Idaho Technical College, University of Idaho, Boise State University, Idaho State University, BYU Idaho, Northwest Nazarene University, College of Idaho, College of Western Idaho.
Eligibility: Applicant must be no older than 21. Applicant must be U.S. citizen or permanent resident.
Basis for selection: Applicant must demonstrate financial need.
Application requirements: FAFSA.
Additional information: Must be graduating senior from Idaho high school who participated in GEAR UP early intervention component (7th-10th grade).

Application deadline: February 15

Contact:
Idaho State Board of Education
650 West State Street
P.O. Box 83720
Boise, ID 83720-0037
Phone: 208-334-2270
Web: www.boardofed.idaho.gov/scholarship/gear_up.asp

Idaho Governor's Cup Scholarship

Type of award: Scholarship, renewable.
Intended use: For full-time undergraduate study at postsecondary institution. Designated institutions: Idaho state-funded colleges and universities.
Eligibility: Applicant must be high school senior. Applicant must be residing in Idaho.
Basis for selection: Applicant must demonstrate high academic achievement, leadership and service orientation.
Application requirements: Recommendations, essay, transcript. SAT/ACT scores. Documentation of volunteer work, leadership, and public service.
Additional information: Minimum 2.8 GPA. Must be graduating senior from Idaho high school who has demonstrated commitment to public service. For more information, contact high school guidance counselor or Idaho State Board of Education.

Amount of award: $3,000
Application deadline: February 15

Contact:
Idaho State Board of Education
650 West State Street
P.O. Box 83720
Boise, ID 83720-0037
Phone: 208-334-2270
Web: www.boardofed.idaho.gov/scholarship/gov_cup.asp

Idaho Opportunity Scholarship

Type of award: Scholarship.
Intended use: For full-time undergraduate study at 2-year or 4-year institution in United States. Designated institutions: Eligible Idaho colleges and universities.
Eligibility: Applicant must be U.S. citizen or permanent resident residing in Idaho.
Basis for selection: Applicant must demonstrate financial need.
Application requirements: FAFSA.
Additional information: Must be graduate of Idaho high school or received GED in Idaho.

Amount of award: $3,000
Application deadline: February 15

Contact:
Idaho State Board of Education
650 West State Street
P.O. Box 83720
Boise, ID 83720-0037
Phone: 208-334-2270
Web: www.boardofed.idaho.gov/scholarship/opportunity.asp

Idaho State Board of Education Public Safety Officer Dependent Scholarship

Type of award: Scholarship.
Intended use: For full-time undergraduate study at accredited 4-year institution in United States. Designated institutions: Idaho postsecondary institutions.
Eligibility: Applicant must be U.S. citizen or permanent resident residing in Idaho. Applicant's parent must have been killed or disabled in work-related accident as public safety officer.
Additional information: Must be graduate of Idaho high school or have taken GED in Idaho. Must be dependent of full-time Idaho public safety officer employed in Idaho that was killed or disabled in line of duty. Provides tuition waiver and on-campus housing plus up to $500 for books per semester.

Amount of award: Full tuition
Application deadline: February 15

Contact:
Idaho State Board of Education
650 West State Street
P.O. Box 83720
Boise, ID 83720-0037
Phone: 208-334-2270
Web: www.boardofed.idaho.gov/scholarship/pub_safety.asp

Robert R. Lee Promise Category A Scholarship

Type of award: Scholarship, renewable.
Intended use: For full-time freshman study at postsecondary institution. Designated institutions: Idaho state-funded colleges and universities.
Eligibility: Applicant must be high school senior. Applicant must be residing in Idaho.
Basis for selection: Applicant must demonstrate high academic achievement.
Application requirements: FAFSA.
Additional information: Applicant must be graduating senior of Idaho high school or equivalent. Academic applicants must have minimum 28 ACT and 3.5 GPA, and be in top ten percent of graduating class. Applicants for professional-technical programs must have minimum 2.8 GPA and take COMPASS exam. Apply online or contact Idaho State Board of Education for application.

Amount of award: $3,000
Number of awards: 25
Number of applicants: 3,000
Application deadline: February 15
Total amount awarded: $75,000

Contact:
Dana Kelly, Idaho State Board of Education
650 West State Street
P.O. Box 83720
Boise, ID 83720-0037
Phone: 208-334-2270
Web: www.boardofed.idaho.gov/scholarship/promise_a.asp

Robert R. Lee Promise Category B Scholarship

Type of award: Scholarship, renewable.
Intended use: For full-time freshman study at postsecondary institution. Designated institutions: Boise State University, College of Southern Idaho, Eastern Idaho Technical College, Idaho State University, Lewis-Clark State College, North Idaho College, University of Idaho, Northwest Nazarene University, BYU-Idaho, The College of Idaho, College of Western Idaho.
Eligibility: Applicant must be no older than 21. Applicant must be residing in Idaho.
Basis for selection: Applicant must demonstrate high academic achievement.
Additional information: Minimum 3.0 GPA or ACT score of 20. Must be younger than 22 on July 1 of academic term of award. Must have completed high school, or equivalent, in Idaho. For more information, contact college or university.

Amount of award:	$600
Application deadline:	February 15

Contact:
Dana Kelly, Idaho State Board of Education
650 West State Street
P.O. Box 83720
Boise, ID 83720-0037
Phone: 208-334-2270
Web: www.boardofed.idaho.gov/scholarship/promiseb.asp

Illinois Department of Veterans' Affairs

Illinois MIA/POW Scholarship

Type of award: Scholarship, renewable.
Intended use: For full-time undergraduate study at accredited postsecondary institution in United States. Designated institutions: Illinois state-supported schools.
Eligibility: Applicant must be U.S. citizen. Applicant must be dependent of disabled veteran, deceased veteran or POW/MIA; or spouse of disabled veteran, deceased veteran or POW/MIA.
Application requirements: Proof of eligibility.
Additional information: Available to dependents of veterans who have been declared prisoners of war, missing in action, become permanently disabled, or have died due to service related disability. Veteran must have been Illinois resident within six months of entering service.

Amount of award:	Full tuition

Contact:
Illinois Department of Veterans' Affairs
833 South Spring Street
P.O. Box 19432
Springfield, IL 62794-9432
Phone: 217-782-6641
Web: www.veterans.illinois.gov/benefits

Illinois Student Assistance Commission

Illinois Grant Program for Dependents of Correctional Officers

Type of award: Scholarship, renewable.
Intended use: For freshman study at 2-year or 4-year institution in United States. Designated institutions: ISAC-approved institutions in Illinois.
Eligibility: Applicant must be U.S. citizen or permanent resident. Applicant's parent must have been killed or disabled in work-related accident as public safety officer.
Application requirements: Proof of eligibility.
Additional information: Must be child or spouse of Illinois corrections officer killed or at least 90 percent disabled in line of duty. Award is equal to full tuition and mandatory fees at public Illinois institutions; at private schools a corresponding amount is awarded. Applicant need not be Illinois resident at time of enrollment. Beneficiaries may receive the equivalent of eight semesters or 12 quarters of assistance. Contact ISAC or visit Website for additional information.

Amount of award:	Full tuition
Application deadline:	October 1

Contact:
Illinois Student Assistance Commission
ISAC College Zone Counselor
1755 Lake Cook Road
Deerfield, IL 60015
Phone: 800-899-ISAC
Web: www.isac.org/students/during-college www.isac.org/students/during-college

Illinois Grant Program for Dependents of Police or Fire Officers

Type of award: Scholarship, renewable.
Intended use: For undergraduate or graduate study at 2-year, 4-year or graduate institution. Designated institutions: ISAC-approved institutions in Illinois.
Eligibility: Applicant must be U.S. citizen or permanent resident. Applicant's parent must have been killed or disabled in work-related accident as firefighter or police officer.
Application requirements: Proof of eligibility.
Additional information: Grant for tuition and fees for spouses and children of Illinois policemen or firemen killed or at least 90 percent disabled in line of duty. Award amount adjusted annually. Applicant need not be Illinois resident at time of enrollment. Beneficiaries may receive the equivalent of eight semesters or 12 quarters of assistance. Contact ISAC or visit Website for additional information.

Amount of award:	Full tuition
Application deadline:	October 1, March 1
Total amount awarded:	$710,192

Contact:
Illinois Student Assistance Commission
ISAC College Zone Counselor
1755 Lake Cook Road
Deerfield, IL 60015
Phone: 800-899-ISAC
Web: www.isac.org/students/during-college

Scholarships

Illinois Higher Education License Plate (HELP) Program

Type of award: Scholarship.
Intended use: For undergraduate study at accredited postsecondary institution in United States. Designated institutions: Participating Illinois universities.
Eligibility: Applicant must be U.S. citizen.
Application requirements: FAFSA.
Additional information: Provides grants to students who attend Illinois colleges for which collegiate license plates are available. Contact your college to determine if it participates in the HELP program. Number and amount of awards contingent on number of license plates sold.
Contact:
Illinois Student Assistance Commission
1755 Lake Cook Road
Deerfield, IL 60015
Phone: 800-899-ISAC
Web: www.isac.org/students/during-college www.isac.org/students/during-college

Illinois Monetary Award Program (MAP)

Type of award: Scholarship, renewable.
Intended use: For undergraduate study at 2-year or 4-year institution. Designated institutions: ISAC/MAP-approved institutions in Illinois.
Eligibility: Applicant must be U.S. citizen or permanent resident residing in Illinois.
Basis for selection: Applicant must demonstrate financial need.
Application requirements: FAFSA.
Additional information: Must not have received bachelor's degree. Must reapply every year for renewal. Contact ISAC or visit Website for application, deadlines, and additional information. Amount of award dependent on legislative action and available funding in any given year.
Contact:
Illinois Student Assistance Commission
ISAC College Zone Counselor
1755 Lake Cook Road
Deerfield, IL 60015
Phone: 800-899-ISAC
Web: www.isac.org/students/during-college

Illinois National Guard Grant

Type of award: Scholarship, renewable.
Intended use: For undergraduate or graduate study at 2-year or 4-year institution. Designated institutions: Approved Illinois institutions.
Eligibility: Applicant must be residing in Illinois. Applicant must be in military service in the Reserves/National Guard. Must have served at least one year of active duty in Illinois National Guard or Naval Militia.
Application requirements: Proof of eligibility.
Additional information: Available to enlisted and company grade officers up to rank of captain who have either served one year active duty; are currently on active duty status; or have been active for at least five consecutive years and have been called to federal active duty for at least six months and be within 12 months after discharge date. Applied toward tuition and certain fees. Recipients may use award for eight semesters or 12 quarters (or the equivalent). Award amount varies. Deadlines: 10/1 for full year, 3/1 for second/third term, 6/15 for summer term. Applications available from ISAC or National Guard units. Contact ISAC or National Guard units or visit Website for additional information.

Application deadline:	October 1

Contact:
Illinois Student Assistance Commission
ISAC College Zone Counselor
1755 Lake Cook Road
Deerfield, IL 60015
Phone: 800-899-ISAC
Web: www.isac.org/students/during-college

Illinois Special Education Teacher Tuition Waiver

Type of award: Scholarship, renewable.
Intended use: For undergraduate or graduate study at postsecondary institution in United States. Designated institutions: Eligible four-year institutions in Illinois: Chicago State University, Eastern Illinois University, Governors State University, Illinois State University, Northeastern Illinois University, Northern Illinois University, Southern Illinois University (Carbondale and Edwardsville), University of Illinois (Chicago, Springfield, Urbana), and Western Illinois University.
Eligibility: Applicant must be U.S. citizen or permanent resident residing in Illinois.
Basis for selection: Major/career interest in education, special.
Additional information: Must be Illinois high school graduate and rank in upper half of graduating class. Must not already hold valid teaching certificate in special education. Recipients must teach in Illinois for two years, or scholarship becomes loan. See Website for application and more details.

Amount of award:	Full tuition
Number of awards:	250
Application deadline:	March 1
Notification begins:	July 1

Contact:
Illinois Student Assistance Commission
1755 Lake Cook Road
Deerfield, IL 60015
Phone: 800-899-ISAC
Web: www.isac.org/students/during-college

Illinois Veteran Grant (IVG) Program

Type of award: Scholarship, renewable.
Intended use: For undergraduate or graduate study at postsecondary institution.
Eligibility: Applicant must be U.S. citizen or permanent resident residing in Illinois. Applicant must be veteran. Must have been Illinois resident or Illinois college student six months prior to entering service and must have returned to Illinois to reside within six months of leaving service. Must have served one year of federal active duty or have served in a foreign country in a time of hostilities in that country.
Application requirements: Proof of eligibility.
Additional information: Provides payment of tuition and mandatory fees to qualified Illinois veterans or military service members. Grant is available for equivalent of four academic years of full-time enrollment for undergraduate and graduate study. Recipient not required to enroll for minimum number of credit hours each term. One-time application only. See Website for additional information and application.

Amount of award:	Full tuition

Contact:
Illinois Student Assistance Commission
ISAC College Zone Counselor
1755 Lake Cook Road
Deerfield, IL 60015
Phone: 800-899-ISAC
Web: www.isac.org/students/during-college

Minority Teachers of Illinois Scholarship

Type of award: Scholarship, renewable.
Intended use: For undergraduate or graduate study at postsecondary institution. Designated institutions: ISAC-approved institutions in Illinois.
Eligibility: Applicant must be Alaskan native, Asian American, African American, Mexican American, Hispanic American, Puerto Rican, American Indian or Native Hawaiian/Pacific Islander. Applicant must be U.S. citizen or permanent resident residing in Illinois.
Basis for selection: Major/career interest in education, teacher or education. Applicant must demonstrate high academic achievement.
Application requirements: Teacher Education Program application.
Additional information: Minimum 2.5 GPA. Applicant should be in course of study leading to teacher certification. Recipient must sign commitment to teach one year in Illinois for each year assistance is received. Must teach at nonprofit Illinois preschool, elementary school, or secondary school with at least 30 percent minority enrollment. If teaching commitment is not fulfilled, scholarship converts to loan, and entire amount, plus interest, must be paid. Contact ISAC or visit Website for additional information.

Amount of award:	$5,000
Application deadline:	March 1

Contact:
Illinois Student Assistance Commission
ISAC College Zone Counselor
1755 Lake Cook Road
Deerfield, IL 60015
Phone: 800-899-ISAC
Web: www.isac.org/students/during-college

Immune Deficiency Foundation

Eric Marder Scholarship Program

Type of award: Scholarship.
Intended use: For undergraduate study at 2-year or 4-year institution.
Basis for selection: Applicant must demonstrate high academic achievement.
Application requirements: Recommendations, essay, proof of eligibility. Must have doctor's letter documenting the diagnosis of applicant's immunodeficiency disease. FAFSA or Federal Student Aid Report. Documentation of student's college/training school enrollment in coming or current semester.
Additional information: Scholarship open to patients with a primary immunodeficiency disease as classified by the World Health Organization.

Application deadline:	March 31
Notification begins:	June 1

Contact:
Immune Deficiency Foundation
40 West Chesapeake Ave.
Suite 308
Towson, MD 21204
Phone: 800-296-4433
Fax: 443-632-2566
Web: www.primaryimmune.org

Varun Bhaskaran Scholarship

Type of award: Scholarship.
Intended use: For undergraduate or graduate study at 2-year or 4-year institution.
Application requirements: Proof of eligibility.
Additional information: Applicant must be living with Wiskott-Aldrich Syndrome.

Application deadline:	March 31

Contact:
Immune Deficiency Foundation
40 W. Chesapeake Avenue
Suite 308
Towson, MD 21204
Web: www.primaryimmune.org/patients-and-families/idf-scholarship-programs

Institute of Food Technologists

Institute of Food Technologists Freshman Scholarship

Type of award: Scholarship, renewable.
Intended use: For full-time freshman study at 4-year institution in United States or Canada. Designated institutions: Educational institutions with approved programs in food science/technology.
Eligibility: Applicant must be high school senior.
Basis for selection: Major/career interest in food science/technology. Applicant must demonstrate high academic achievement.
Application requirements: Recommendations, essay, transcript. SAT/ACT report. Essay should be one page statement regarding applicant's desire to become food scientist/technologist.
Additional information: IFT Scholarship recipients must join IFT student association. Applicant must be high school senior or high school graduate entering college for first time. Minimum 3.0 GPA required. Must have a well-rounded personality. Must enroll in IFT-approved program. Program descriptions and application available on Website. All inquiries and completed applications should be directed to department head of approved school.

Amount of award:	$1,000
Application deadline:	March 15
Notification begins:	April 15

Contact:
Scholarship Department Institute of Food Technologists
Attn: Lisa Radachi
525 W. Van Buren, Suite 1000
Chicago, IL 60607
Phone: 312-782-8424
Fax: 312-782-8348
Web: www.ift.org

Institute of Food Technologists Undergraduate Scholarship

Type of award: Scholarship, renewable.
Intended use: For full-time sophomore, junior or senior study at 4-year institution in United States or Canada. Designated institutions: Educational institutions with approved programs in food science/technology.
Basis for selection: Major/career interest in food science/technology. Applicant must demonstrate high academic achievement.
Application requirements: Recommendations, transcript.
Additional information: Applicant must have minimum 3.0 GPA and must be enrolled in IFT-approved program. Program description and application available through Website or via fax. All other inquiries and completed applications should be directed to department head of approved school. Previous scholarship recipients must be IFT members to reapply.

Amount of award:	$500-$3,000
Application deadline:	April 1
Notification begins:	April 15

Contact:
Scholarship Department
Institute of Food Technologists
525 W. Van Buren, Suite 1000
Chicago, IL 60601
Phone: 312-782-8424
Fax: 312-782-8348
Web: www.ift.org

Insurance Scholarship Foundation of America

Award of Excellence Scholarship

Type of award: Scholarship.
Intended use: For full-time sophomore, junior or senior study at 4-year or graduate institution.
Basis for selection: Major/career interest in insurance/actuarial science. Applicant must demonstrate high academic achievement.
Additional information: Applicant must have major or minor in insurance, risk management, or actuarial science with a minimum 3.0 GPA. Must have completed or be currently enrolled in two insurance, actuarial science, or risk-management-related courses, a minimum of three credit hours each. Visit Website for application.

Amount of award:	$1,000
Application deadline:	May 15

Contact:
Insurance Scholarship Foundation of America
P.O. Box 866
Hendersonville, NC 28793-0866
Phone: 866-379-4732
Web: www.inssfa.org

ISFA Education Foundation College Scholarship

Type of award: Scholarship.
Intended use: For junior, senior or graduate study at accredited 4-year or graduate institution.
Basis for selection: Major/career interest in insurance/actuarial science. Applicant must demonstrate high academic achievement.
Application requirements: Recommendations, essay, transcript.
Additional information: Applicant must have major or minor in insurance, risk management, or actuarial science with a minimum 3.0 GPA. Must have completed or be currently enrolled in two insurance, actuarial science, or risk-management-related courses, a minimum of three credit hours each. Postmark dates have no bearing on application deadline. Visit Website for application.

Amount of award:	$500-$5,000
Number of awards:	175
Number of applicants:	433
Application deadline:	May 15, October 1
Total amount awarded:	$220,595

Contact:
Insurance Scholarship Foundation of America
P.O. Box 866
Hendersonville, NC 28793-0866
Phone: 866-379-4732
Web: www.inssfa.org

Marsh Scholarship

Type of award: Scholarship.
Intended use: For sophomore, junior or senior study at 4-year institution.
Basis for selection: Major/career interest in insurance/actuarial science. Applicant must demonstrate high academic achievement.
Additional information: Applicant must have major or minor in insurance, risk management, or actuarial science with a minimum 3.0 GPA. Must have completed or be currently enrolled in two insurance, actuarial science, or risk-management-related courses, a minimum of three credit hours each. Must not be receiving reimbursement for tuition or books from any outside source. Visit Website for application.

Amount of award:	$500-$5,000
Application deadline:	May 15

Contact:
Insurance Scholarship Foundation of America
P.O. Box 866
Hendersonville, NC 28793-0866
Phone: 866-379-4732
Web: www.inssfa.org

International Association of Fire Fighters

W.H. McClennan Scholarship

Type of award: Scholarship, renewable.
Intended use: For full-time undergraduate study at accredited vocational, 2-year or 4-year institution.
Eligibility: Applicant's parent must have been killed or disabled in work-related accident as firefighter.
Basis for selection: Applicant must demonstrate financial need, depth of character, seriousness of purpose and service orientation.
Application requirements: Recommendations, essay, transcript, proof of eligibility. IA77 McClennan application.

Additional information: Open to children of firefighters who were killed in the line of duty and were members in good standing of IAFF at the time of deaths.

Amount of award:	$2,500
Number of applicants:	50
Application deadline:	February 1
Notification begins:	August 1
Total amount awarded:	$127,500

Contact:
W. H. McClennan Scholarship/International Association of Fire Fighters
1750 New York Ave., NW
3rd Floor, Dept. of Education
Washington, DC 20006
Phone: 202-737-8484
Fax: 202-737-8418
Web: www.iaff.org/scholarships

International Buckskin Horse Association, Inc.

Buckskin Horse Association Scholarship

Type of award: Scholarship, renewable.
Intended use: For full-time undergraduate study at accredited postsecondary institution in United States.
Eligibility: Applicant must be high school senior. Applicant must be U.S. citizen.
Basis for selection: Applicant must demonstrate financial need, high academic achievement, depth of character, leadership and seriousness of purpose.
Application requirements: Portfolio, recommendations, proof of eligibility.
Additional information: Available to children of association members. Parent must have been member for at least 2 years.

Amount of award:	$500-$1,000
Number of awards:	12
Number of applicants:	8
Application deadline:	March 15
Notification begins:	September 15
Total amount awarded:	$7,500

Contact:
International Buckskin Horse Association, Inc.
P.O. Box 268
Shelby, IN 46377
Phone: 219-552-1013
Fax: 219-552-1013
Web: www.ibha.net

International Executive Housekeepers Association

IEHA Educational Foundation Scholarship

Type of award: Scholarship.
Intended use: For undergraduate or non-degree study at accredited postsecondary institution.
Basis for selection: Major/career interest in hospitality administration/management.
Application requirements: Essay, transcript. Letter from school official verifying enrollment. Class schedule and coursework curriculum. Original and three copies of prepared manuscript on housekeeping (maximum 2,000 words, double-spaced).
Additional information: Applicant must be member of International Executive Housekeepers Association. Scholarship will be awarded to student submitting best original manuscript on housekeeping within any industry segment (e.g., hospitality, healthcare, education, rehabilitation centers, government buildings). Other major/career interest: facilities management. Can be used for IEHA certification program. No set limit on number of awards granted.

Amount of award:	$800
Number of awards:	15
Application deadline:	January 10
Notification begins:	June 1
Total amount awarded:	$8,000

Contact:
International Executive Housekeepers Association
Educational Foundation Scholarships
1001 Eastwind Drive, Suite 301
Westerville, OH 43081-3361
Phone: 800-200-6342
Fax: 614-895-1248
Web: www.ieha.org

International Foodservice Editorial Council

Scholarship for Foodservice Communication Careers

Type of award: Scholarship.
Intended use: For full-time undergraduate or master's study at accredited postsecondary institution in United States.
Basis for selection: Major/career interest in food science/technology; food production/management/services; culinary arts; communications; public relations or journalism. Applicant must demonstrate financial need, high academic achievement, depth of character, leadership, seriousness of purpose and service orientation.
Application requirements: Recommendations, essay, transcript, proof of eligibility.
Additional information: Applicant must pursue academic study in editorial or public relations within the food service industry. Writing ability considered. Applications may be requested by e-mail or downloaded from Website.

Amount of award:	$500-$4,000
Number of awards:	8
Number of applicants:	85
Application deadline:	March 15
Notification begins:	July 1
Total amount awarded:	$17,000

Contact:
International Foodservice Editorial Council (IFEC)
P.O. Box 491
Hyde Park, NY 12538
Phone: 845-229-6973
Fax: 845-229-6973
Web: www.ifeconline.com

International Furnishings and Design Association Educational Foundation

Green/Sustainable Design Scholarship

Type of award: Scholarship.
Intended use: For undergraduate study in United States.
Basis for selection: Major/career interest in interior design.
Application requirements: Portfolio, recommendations, essay, transcript. Copies of original works featuring one or more aspects of green/sustainable design with detailed explanations, letter of recommendation from instructor on official school stationery.
Additional information: Student must be planning to seek LEED accreditation. See Website for further requirements and application.

Amount of award:	$1,500
Number of awards:	1
Number of applicants:	12
Application deadline:	March 31
Notification begins:	July 31
Total amount awarded:	$1,500

Contact:
IFDA Educational Foundation, Director of Grants/Scholarships
Sue Williams
Colleagues, 2700 East Grace Street
Richmond, VA 23223
Web: www.ifdaef.org

IFDA Leaders Commemorative Scholarship

Type of award: Scholarship.
Intended use: For undergraduate study at postsecondary institution in United States.
Eligibility: Applicant must be U.S. citizen or permanent resident.
Basis for selection: Major/career interest in design or interior design. Applicant must demonstrate depth of character, leadership and service orientation.
Application requirements: Portfolio, recommendations, essay, transcript. Copies of two examples of original design work, recommendation from professor on official school stationery.
Additional information: Must have completed four courses in interior design (or related field) at post-secondary level. Student must be involved with volunteer or community service and held leadership positions during past five years. See Website for further requirements and application.

Amount of award:	$1,500
Number of awards:	1
Number of applicants:	15
Application deadline:	March 31
Notification begins:	July 31
Total amount awarded:	$1,500

Contact:
IFDA Educational Foundation, Director of Grants/Scholarships
Sue Williams
Colleagues, 2700 East Grace Street
Richmond, VA 23223
Web: www.ifdaef.org

International Furnishings and Design Association Educational Foundation Part-Time Student Scholarship

Type of award: Scholarship.
Intended use: For half-time undergraduate study at postsecondary institution in United States.
Basis for selection: Major/career interest in interior design.
Application requirements: Portfolio, recommendations, essay, transcript. Two examples of the student's original work. Resume. Four copies of all application materials.
Additional information: Applicants must have completed four courses in interior design or related field. Must be currently enrolled in at least two courses as part-time student. Visit Website for application and additional information.

Amount of award:	$1,500
Number of awards:	1
Number of applicants:	9
Application deadline:	March 31
Notification begins:	July 31
Total amount awarded:	$1,500

Contact:
IFDA Educational Foundation, Director of Grants/Scholarships
Sue Williams
Colleagues, 2700 East Grace Street
Richmond, VA 23223
Web: www.ifdaef.org

International Furnishings and Design Association Student Member Scholarships

Type of award: Scholarship.
Intended use: For full-time undergraduate study at accredited postsecondary institution in United States.
Basis for selection: Major/career interest in interior design. Applicant must demonstrate high academic achievement, depth of character, seriousness of purpose and service orientation.
Application requirements: Recommendations, essay, transcript. Two to three examples of student work, four copies of each element of application. Recommendation from IFDA member. Recommendation from professor or instructor on official school stationery.
Additional information: Must be member of IFDA. Must have completed four courses in interior design (or related field) at post-secondary level. Must have completed at least one semester of postsecondary school. Furniture design majors also eligible. See Website for further requirements and application.

Amount of award:	$2,000
Number of awards:	1
Number of applicants:	2
Application deadline:	March 31
Notification begins:	July 31
Total amount awarded:	$2,000

Contact:
IFDA Educational Foundation, Director of Grants/Scholarships
Sue Williams
Colleagues, 2700 East Grace Street
Richmond, VA 23223
Web: www.ifdaef.org

Ruth Clark Furniture Design Scholarship

Type of award: Scholarship.
Intended use: For full-time undergraduate or graduate study at postsecondary institution in United States.
Eligibility: Applicant must be U.S. citizen or permanent resident.
Basis for selection: Major/career interest in design.
Application requirements: Portfolio, recommendations, essay, transcript. Letter from instructor on official school stationery. Five examples of original furniture designs.
Additional information: Must have completed four courses in interior design (or related field) at post-secondary level. Must be major in design with focus on residential upholstered and/or wood furniture design. See Website for further requirements and application.

Amount of award:	$3,000
Number of awards:	1
Number of applicants:	5
Application deadline:	March 31
Notification begins:	July 31
Total amount awarded:	$3,000

Contact:
IFDA Educational Foundation, Director of Grants/Scholarships
Sue Williams
Colleagues, 2700 East Grace Street
Richmond, VA 23223
Web: www.ifdaef.org

International Order of the King's Daughters and Sons

Health Career Scholarship

Type of award: Scholarship, renewable.
Intended use: For full-time junior, senior, master's or first professional study at accredited 4-year or graduate institution in United States or Canada.
Eligibility: Applicant must be U.S. citizen or Canadian citizen.
Basis for selection: Major/career interest in medicine; dentistry; pharmacy/pharmaceutics/pharmacology; nursing; health sciences; health-related professions; physical therapy or occupational therapy. Applicant must demonstrate financial need, high academic achievement, depth of character, leadership, seriousness of purpose and service orientation.
Application requirements: Recommendations, essay, transcript, proof of eligibility.
Additional information: To request application, student must write to director stating field and present level of study and include business-size SASE. Pre-med students not eligible. R.N., M.D. and D.D.S. students must have completed first year. Number of scholarships varies year to year.

Amount of award:	$1,000
Application deadline:	April 1

Contact:
International Order of the King's Daughters and Sons
Director, Health Careers Department
P.O. Box 1040
Chautauqua, NY 14722-1040
Phone: 716-357-4951
Fax: 716-357-3762
Web: www.iokds.org

North American Indian Scholarship

Type of award: Scholarship, renewable.
Intended use: For full-time undergraduate study at accredited 2-year or 4-year institution in United States.
Eligibility: Applicant must be American Indian. Applicant must be U.S. citizen.
Basis for selection: Applicant must demonstrate financial need, depth of character, leadership, seriousness of purpose and service orientation.
Application requirements: Recommendations, essay, transcript, proof of eligibility. Written documentation of tribal registration and other requirements. Photo.
Additional information: Offers scholarships with no restrictions as to tribal affiliations or Indian blood quantum. For more information, send SASE to director of North American Indian Department.

Amount of award:	$650
Application deadline:	April 1
Notification begins:	July 1

Contact:
International Order of the King's Daughters and Sons
Director, North American Indian Dept.
P.O. Box 1040
Chautauqua, NY 14722-1040
Phone: 716-357-4951
Fax: 716-357-3762
Web: www.iokds.org

Intertribal Timber Council

Truman D. Picard Scholarship

Type of award: Scholarship, renewable.
Intended use: For full-time undergraduate or graduate study at accredited 2-year, 4-year or graduate institution in United States.
Eligibility: Applicant must be Alaskan native or American Indian. Must be enrolled member of a federally recognized tribe. Applicant must be U.S. citizen.
Basis for selection: Major/career interest in natural resources/ conservation; forestry; wildlife/fisheries or agriculture. Applicant must demonstrate financial need, high academic achievement, depth of character, leadership, seriousness of purpose and service orientation.
Application requirements: Recommendations, transcript, proof of eligibility. Resume, and two-page (maximum) letter of application.
Additional information: Applicants must be Native American and pursuing higher education in natural resources. Check Website for application deadline dates.

Amount of award:	$1,500-$2,000
Number of applicants:	64
Application deadline:	January 18
Notification begins:	November 1
Total amount awarded:	$53,500

Contact:
Intertribal Timber Council
Education Committee
1112 NE 21st Avenue, Ste. 4
Portland, OR 97232-2114
Phone: 503-282-4296
Fax: 503-282-1274
Web: www.itcnet.org

Iowa College Student Aid Commission

All Iowa Opportunity Scholarship

Type of award: Scholarship.
Intended use: For undergraduate study at accredited 2-year or 4-year institution in United States. Designated institutions: Eligible Iowa colleges and universities.
Eligibility: Applicant must be high school senior. Applicant must be U.S. citizen residing in Iowa.
Basis for selection: Applicant must demonstrate high academic achievement.
Application requirements: FAFSA.
Additional information: Minimum 2.5 GPA. Awards of up to average tuition and fee rate of Regents University for current academic year. Priority given to students who participated in federal TRIO programs, students who graduated from alternative high schools, and homeless youth.

Amount of award:	$7,806
Application deadline:	March 1

Contact:
Iowa College Student Aid Commission
603 East 12th Street, 5th Floor
Des Moines, IA 50319
Phone: 877-272-4456
Fax: 515-725-3401
Web: www.iowacollegeaid.gov

Governor Terry E. Branstad Iowa State Fair Scholarship

Type of award: Scholarship.
Intended use: For undergraduate study at postsecondary institution in United States. Designated institutions: Iowa colleges and universities.
Eligibility: Applicant must be high school senior. Applicant must be U.S. citizen residing in Iowa.
Basis for selection: Applicant must demonstrate financial need.
Application requirements: Recommendations, essay. FAFSA, proof of involvement in Iowa State Fair.
Additional information: Must be graduating senior from Iowa state high school who has been actively involved with the Iowa State Fair. Visit Website for application.

Amount of award:	$500-$1,000
Number of awards:	4
Application deadline:	March 1

Contact:
Iowa College Student Aid Commission
603 East 12th Street, 5th Floor
Des Moines, IA 50319
Phone: 877-272-4456
Fax: 515-725-3401
Web: www.iowacollegeaid.gov

Iowa Grant

Type of award: Scholarship, renewable.
Intended use: For undergraduate study at vocational, 2-year or 4-year institution. Designated institutions: Iowa colleges and universities.
Eligibility: Applicant must be U.S. citizen or permanent resident residing in Iowa.
Basis for selection: Applicant must demonstrate financial need.
Application requirements: FAFSA.
Additional information: Award amount adjusted for part-time study. Eligible colleges and universities receive Iowa grant allocations and award grants to students with greatest financial need.

Amount of award:	$1,000
Application deadline:	July 1
Notification begins:	March 20
Total amount awarded:	$1,029,784

Contact:
Iowa College Student Aid Commission
603 East 12th Street, 5th Floor
Des Moines, IA 50319
Phone: 877-272-4456
Fax: 515-725-3401
Web: www.iowacollegeaid.gov

Iowa National Guard Educational Assistance Program

Type of award: Scholarship, renewable.
Intended use: For undergraduate study at accredited postsecondary institution. Designated institutions: Eligible Iowa colleges and universities.
Eligibility: Applicant must be U.S. citizen residing in Iowa. Applicant must be in military service in the Reserves/National Guard.
Application requirements: Iowa financial aid application.
Additional information: Applicant must be in military service in the Iowa Reserves/National Guard. Selection is based on National Guard designation. Award varies yearly. Maximum award is 80 percent of tuition for students at public institutions; for students at private institutions, award is equal to average tuition rate at Iowa Regents Universities.

Amount of award:	$6,658
Application deadline:	July 1

Contact:
Iowa College Student Aid Commission
603 East 12th Street, 5th Floor
Des Moines, IA 50139
Phone: 877-272-4456
Fax: 515-275-3401
Web: www.iowacollegeaid.gov

Iowa Tuition Grant

Type of award: Scholarship, renewable.
Intended use: For undergraduate study at accredited 2-year or 4-year institution. Designated institutions: Private colleges in Iowa.
Eligibility: Applicant must be U.S. citizen or permanent resident residing in Iowa.
Basis for selection: Applicant must demonstrate financial need.
Application requirements: Proof of eligibility. FAFSA.

Amount of award:	$4,000
Application deadline:	July 1

Contact:
Iowa College Student Aid Commission
603 East 12th Street, 5th Floor
Des Moines, IA 50319
Phone: 877-272-4456
Fax: 515-725-3401
Web: www.iowacollegeaid.gov

Iowa Vocational-Technical Tuition Grant

Type of award: Scholarship, renewable.
Intended use: For undergraduate study at vocational or 2-year institution. Designated institutions: Iowa community colleges.
Eligibility: Applicant must be U.S. citizen or permanent resident residing in Iowa.
Basis for selection: Applicant must demonstrate financial need.
Application requirements: Proof of eligibility. FAFSA.
Additional information: Only vocational-technical career majors considered.

Amount of award:	$1,200
Application deadline:	July 1

Contact:
Iowa College Student Aid Commission
603 East 12th Street, 5th Floor
Des Moines, IA 50319
Phone: 877-272-4456
Fax: 515-725-3401
Web: www.iowacollegeaid.gov

Robert D. Blue Scholarship

Type of award: Scholarship.
Intended use: For undergraduate study at postsecondary institution in United States. Designated institutions: Iowa colleges and universities.
Eligibility: Applicant must be U.S. citizen residing in Iowa.
Basis for selection: Applicant must demonstrate financial need, high academic achievement, depth of character, leadership and seriousness of purpose.
Application requirements: Recommendations, essay, transcript. GPA.
Additional information: Visit Website for application.

Amount of award:	$500-$1,000
Application deadline:	May 10

Contact:
Robert D. Blue Scholarship
Michael L. Fitzgerald, Treasurer of State
State Capitol Building
Des Moines, IA 50309-3609
Phone: 515-242-5270
Web: www.iowacollegeaid.gov

Italian Catholic Federation

Italian Catholic Federation Scholarship

Type of award: Scholarship, renewable.
Intended use: For full-time freshman study at accredited 2-year or 4-year institution.
Eligibility: Applicant must be high school senior. Applicant must be Italian. Applicant must be Roman Catholic. Applicant must be U.S. citizen residing in California, Illinois, Arizona or Nevada.
Basis for selection: Applicant must demonstrate financial need and high academic achievement.
Application requirements: Recommendations, essay, transcript.
Additional information: Minimum 3.2 GPA. Residency restrictions do not apply if parent or grandparent is member of Federation. Also open to non-Italian students whose parents or grandparents are members of Federation. First year's scholarship award is $400. Larger amounts available for advanced scholarships.

Amount of award:	$400
Number of awards:	450
Number of applicants:	491
Application deadline:	March 15
Notification begins:	May 1
Total amount awarded:	$77,600

Contact:
Italian Catholic Federation
8393 Capwell Drive
Suite 110
Oakland, CA 94621
Phone: 510-633-9058
Fax: 510-633-9758
Web: www.icf.org

IUE-CWA

Bruce van Ess Scholarship

Type of award: Scholarship.
Intended use: For full-time undergraduate study at accredited vocational, 2-year or 4-year institution.
Eligibility: Applicant or parent must be member/participant of International Union of EESMF Workers, AFL-CIO.
Basis for selection: Applicant must demonstrate depth of character, leadership, seriousness of purpose and service orientation.
Application requirements: Proof of GPA, short statement on civic contributions. 500-word essay on importance of labor movement.
Additional information: Available to all IUE-CWA members and employees (including retired or deceased members and employees) and their children and grandchildren. Apply online.

Amount of award:	$2,500
Number of awards:	1
Application deadline:	March 31
Total amount awarded:	$2,500

Contact:
IUE Department of Education
Web: www.iue-cwa.org

James B. Carey Scholarship

Type of award: Scholarship.
Intended use: For full-time undergraduate study at accredited postsecondary institution in United States.
Eligibility: Applicant or parent must be member/participant of International Union of EESMF Workers, AFL-CIO.
Basis for selection: Applicant must demonstrate depth of character, leadership, seriousness of purpose and service orientation.
Application requirements: Recommendations, transcript, proof of eligibility. 150-word essay on civic contributions, 500-word essay on importance of labor movement.
Additional information: Available to children and grandchildren of all IUE-CWA members and employees (including retired or deceased members and employees) and their children and grandchildren. Must be accepted or enrolled in college, university, nursing school, or technical school. Apply online.

Amount of award: $1,000
Number of awards: 9
Application deadline: March 31
Total amount awarded: $9,000
Contact:
IUE Department of Education
Web: www.iue-cwa.org

Paul Jennings Scholarship

Type of award: Scholarship.
Intended use: For full-time undergraduate study in United States.
Eligibility: Applicant must be high school senior.
Basis for selection: Applicant must demonstrate depth of character, leadership and service orientation.
Application requirements: Transcript, proof of eligibility. 150-word essay on civic contributions, 500-word essay on importance of labor movement.
Additional information: Award available to children and grandchildren of IUE-CWA members who are now or have been local union elected officials. Families of full-time union officers or employees not eligible. Must be accepted or enrolled in college, university, nursing school, or technical school. Apply online.
Amount of award: $3,000
Number of awards: 1
Application deadline: March 31
Total amount awarded: $3,000
Contact:
IUE Department of Education
Web: www.iue-cwa.org

Robert L. Livingston Scholarship

Type of award: Scholarship.
Intended use: For full-time undergraduate study at accredited vocational, 2-year or 4-year institution.
Basis for selection: Applicant must demonstrate depth of character, leadership, seriousness of purpose and service orientation.
Application requirements: Proof of GPA, short statement which includes applicant's civic contributions, career objectives, and extracurricular activities.
Additional information: Open to dependents of IUE-CWA members or retired members. Dependents of IUE-CWA Division employees ineligible. Apply online.
Amount of award: $1,500
Number of awards: 2
Application deadline: March 31
Total amount awarded: $3,000
Contact:
IUE Department of Education
Web: www.iue-cwa.org

Sal Ingrassia Scholarship

Type of award: Scholarship.
Intended use: For full-time undergraduate study at accredited vocational, 2-year or 4-year institution.
Eligibility: Applicant or parent must be member/participant of International Union of EESMF Workers, AFL-CIO.
Basis for selection: Applicant must demonstrate depth of character, leadership, seriousness of purpose and service orientation.
Application requirements: Proof of GPA, 150-word essay on civic contributions, 500-word essay on relationship to labor movement.
Additional information: Available to all IUE-CWA members and employees (including retired or deceased members and employees) and their children and grandchildren. Apply online.
Amount of award: $2,500
Number of awards: 1
Application deadline: March 31
Total amount awarded: $2,500
Contact:
IUE Department of Education
Web: www.iue-cwa.org

Willie Rudd Scholarship

Type of award: Scholarship.
Intended use: For full-time undergraduate study at accredited vocational, 2-year or 4-year institution.
Eligibility: Applicant or parent must be member/participant of International Union of EESMF Workers, AFL-CIO.
Basis for selection: Applicant must demonstrate depth of character, leadership, seriousness of purpose and service orientation.
Application requirements: Proof of GPA, 150-word essay on civic contributions, 500-word essay on importance of labor movement.
Additional information: Available to all IUE-CWA members and employees and their children and grandchildren (including retired or deceased members and employees). Apply online.
Amount of award: $1,000
Number of awards: 1
Application deadline: March 31
Total amount awarded: $1,000
Contact:
IUE Department of Education
Web: www.iue-cwa.org

Jack Kent Cooke Foundation

Jack Kent Cooke Foundation College Scholarship

Type of award: Scholarship.
Intended use: For full-time freshman study at 4-year institution.
Basis for selection: Applicant must demonstrate financial need, leadership and service orientation.
Application requirements: Recommendations, essay.
Additional information: Minimum 3.5 GPA. Standardized test scores must be in top 15 percent. Minimum SAT score 1200 (reading and math) or ACT score 26 or above. Must be graduate of U.S. high school. Applications due in November.
Amount of award: $30,000
Number of awards: 40
Contact:
Jack Kent Cooke Foundation
44325 Woodridge Parkway
Lansdowne, VA 20176
Phone: 703-723-8000
Fax: 703-554-6777
Web: www.jkcf.org

Jackie Robinson Foundation

Jackie Robinson Foundation Mentoring and Leadership Curriculum

Type of award: Scholarship, renewable.
Intended use: For full-time undergraduate study at accredited 4-year institution in United States.
Eligibility: Applicant must be Alaskan native, Asian American, African American, Mexican American, Hispanic American, Puerto Rican, American Indian or Native Hawaiian/Pacific Islander. Applicant must be high school senior. Applicant must be U.S. citizen.
Basis for selection: Applicant must demonstrate financial need, high academic achievement, leadership and service orientation.
Application requirements: Interview, recommendations, essay, transcript. SAT/ACT scores, list of extracurricular activities, parents' tax return, guidance counselor name and email address.
Additional information: Applicants must have minimum SAT score of 1000 or ACT score of 22. Award amount varies up to $7,500. Applications available online and must be submitted via website.

Amount of award:	$6,000
Number of awards:	60
Number of applicants:	3,000
Application deadline:	February 15
Notification begins:	June 15
Total amount awarded:	$1,800,000

Contact:
Jackie Robinson Foundation
Attn: Scholarship Programs
One Hudson Sq., 75 Varick Street, 2nd floor
New York, NY 10013-1917
Phone: 212-290-8600
Fax: 212-290-8081
Web: www.jackierobinson.org

James Beard Foundation

Allen Susser Scholarship

Type of award: Scholarship.
Intended use: For undergraduate study at postsecondary institution.
Basis for selection: Major/career interest in culinary arts.
Additional information: Must either be a resident of Florida or be enrolled or plan to enroll in a licensed or accredited culinary school in Florida.

Amount of award:	$5,500
Number of awards:	1
Application deadline:	May 15

Contact:
James Beard Foundation Scholarship Program
One Scholarship Way
Saint Peter, MN 56082
Phone: 507-931-1682
Web: www.jamesbeard.org

American Restaurant Scholarship

Type of award: Scholarship.
Intended use: For undergraduate study in United States. Designated institutions: Licensed or accredited culinary schools.
Basis for selection: Major/career interest in culinary arts. Applicant must demonstrate financial need.
Application requirements: Recommendations, transcript. Financial statement, resume.
Additional information: Must plan to enroll in licensed or accredited culinary school.

Amount of award:	$5,000
Number of awards:	1
Application deadline:	May 15

Contact:
Scholarship America
One Scholarship Way
St. Peter, MN 56082
Phone: 507-931-1682
Web: www.jamesbeard.org

Azurea at One Ocean Resort Hotel & Spa Scholarship

Type of award: Scholarship.
Intended use: For undergraduate study at postsecondary institution.
Additional information: Must be enrolled or plan to enroll in a licensed or accredited culinary or hospitality management program in Florida.

Amount of award:	$4,000
Number of awards:	1
Application deadline:	May 15

Contact:
James Beard Foundation Scholarship Program
One Scholarship Way
Saint Peter, MN 56082
Phone: 507-931-1682
Web: www.jamesbeard.org

Bern Laxer Memorial Scholarship

Type of award: Scholarship.
Intended use: For undergraduate study at accredited postsecondary institution. Designated institutions: Licensed or accredited culinary schools.
Eligibility: Applicant must be residing in Florida.
Basis for selection: Major/career interest in culinary arts; hospitality administration/management or food science/technology. Applicant must demonstrate financial need and high academic achievement.
Application requirements: Recommendations, essay, transcript, proof of eligibility. Proof of residency, financial statement, resume.
Additional information: Must have at least one year of culinary experience and have high school diploma or equivalent. One scholarship granted annually in one of the following categories: culinary studies, hospitality management, and viticulture/oenology. Recipients who reapply will be given priority consideration over new applicants. May be received for a maximum of four years, but applicant must maintain a B-GPA.

Amount of award:	$4,000
Number of awards:	2
Application deadline:	May 15
Total amount awarded:	$7,500

Scholarships

Contact:
Scholarship America
One Scholarship Way
St. Peter, MN 56082
Phone: 507-931-1682
Web: www.jamesbeard.org

Bill Ramsey/Craig Noone Memorial Scholarship

Type of award: Scholarship.
Intended use: For undergraduate study at postsecondary institution.
Basis for selection: Major/career interest in culinary arts.
Additional information: Must be enrolled or plan to enroll in a licensed or accredited culinary school.

Amount of award:	$5,000
Number of awards:	1
Application deadline:	May 15

Contact:
James Beard Foundation Scholarship Program
One Scholarship Way
Saint Peter, MN 56082
Phone: 507-931-1682
Web: www.jamesbeard.org

Bob Zappatelli Memorial Scholarship

Type of award: Scholarship.
Intended use: For undergraduate study at accredited postsecondary institution.
Basis for selection: Major/career interest in culinary arts; food production/management/services; food science/technology; hospitality administration/management or hotel/restaurant management.
Application requirements: Recommendations, essay, transcript.
Additional information: Must plan to enroll in culinary school. Preference given to Benchmark employees or relatives of employees. Must have experience in food and beverage industry.

Amount of award:	$3,000
Number of awards:	1
Application deadline:	May 15
Total amount awarded:	$5,000

Contact:
Scholarship America
One Scholarship Way
St. Peter, MN 56082
Phone: 504-931-1682
Web: www.jamesbeard.org

Chefs of Louisiana Cookery Scholarship

Type of award: Scholarship.
Intended use: For undergraduate study at postsecondary institution. Designated institutions: Culinary schools in Louisiana.
Eligibility: Applicant must be U.S. citizen residing in Louisiana.
Basis for selection: Major/career interest in culinary arts; food production/management/services; food science/technology; hospitality administration/management or hotel/restaurant management. Applicant must demonstrate financial need.
Application requirements: Recommendations, essay, transcript.
Additional information: Must plan to enroll in Louisiana culinary school.

Amount of award:	$5,000
Number of awards:	1
Application deadline:	May 15

Contact:
Scholarship America
One Scholarship Way
St. Peter, MN 56082
Phone: 504-931-1682
Web: www.jamesbeard.org

Christian Wolffer Scholarship

Type of award: Scholarship.
Intended use: For undergraduate study at accredited postsecondary institution. Designated institutions: Licensed or accredited culinary schools.
Eligibility: Applicant must be residing in New York.
Basis for selection: Major/career interest in culinary arts; food production/management/services or food science/technology. Applicant must demonstrate high academic achievement.
Application requirements: Recommendations, essay, transcript, proof of eligibility. Proof of residency, financial statement, resume.
Additional information: Minimum 3.0 GPA. Must be enrolled or planning to enroll in accredited culinary or wine studies program.

Amount of award:	$2,000
Number of awards:	1
Application deadline:	May 15
Total amount awarded:	$5,000

Contact:
Scholarship America
One Scholarship Way
St. Peter, MN 56082
Phone: 507-931-1682
Web: www.jamesbeard.org

Clay Triplette Scholarship

Type of award: Scholarship.
Intended use: For undergraduate study at accredited postsecondary institution.
Basis for selection: Major/career interest in culinary arts; food production/management/services or food science/technology. Applicant must demonstrate financial need.
Application requirements: Recommendations, transcript, proof of eligibility. Proof of residency, financial statement, resume, 250 word essay on James Beard.
Additional information: Applicants must be enrolled or planning to enroll in accredited baking or pastry studies program at licensed or accredited culinary school.

Amount of award:	$5,000
Number of awards:	1
Application deadline:	May 15
Total amount awarded:	$4,000

Contact:
Scholarship America
One Scholarship Way
St. Peter, MN 56082
Phone: 507-931-1682
Web: www.jamesbeard.org

Dana Campbell Memorial Scholarship

Type of award: Scholarship.
Intended use: For undergraduate study at 4-year institution in United States.
Eligibility: Applicant must be residing in Texas, Arkansas, Delaware, Maryland, Louisiana, South Carolina, Georgia, Florida, Oklahoma, Virginia, West Virginia, Mississippi, Kentucky, Alabama, North Carolina or Missouri.
Basis for selection: Major/career interest in food production/management/services; culinary arts or journalism.
Additional information: Must have career interest in food journalism. Must be in second or third year of study in journalism or food-related curriculum.

Amount of award:	$2,000
Number of awards:	1
Application deadline:	May 15

Contact:
James Beard Foundation Scholarship Program
One Scholarship Way
St. Peter, MN 56082
Phone: 507-931-1682
Web: www.jamesbeard.org

Deseo at the Westin Scholarship

Type of award: Scholarship.
Intended use: For undergraduate study at postsecondary institution.
Eligibility: Applicant must be residing in Arizona.
Basis for selection: Major/career interest in culinary arts; food production/management/services or food science/technology. Applicant must demonstrate financial need.
Application requirements: Recommendations, essay, transcript, proof of eligibility. Proof of residency, financial statement, resume.
Additional information: Applicants must have participated in Arizona Careers Through Culinary Arts program and be recommended by Arizona C-CAP.

Amount of award:	$3,750
Number of awards:	1
Application deadline:	May 15
Total amount awarded:	$6,250

Contact:
Scholarship America
One Scholarship Way
St. Peter, MN 56082
Phone: 507-931-1682
Web: www.jamesbeard.org

The Elkes Family Culinary Scholarship

Type of award: Scholarship.
Intended use: For undergraduate study at postsecondary institution.
Basis for selection: Major/career interest in culinary arts. Applicant must demonstrate financial need.
Application requirements: Recommendations, essay.
Additional information: Must be enrolled or plan to enroll in a licensed or accredited culinary school. Finalists must participate in an interview with JBF scholarship committee and Elkes Family Foundation.

Amount of award:	$42,500
Number of awards:	1
Application deadline:	May 15

Contact:
James Beard Foundation Scholarship Program
One Scholarship Way
Saint Peter, MN 56082
Phone: 507-931-1682
Web: www.jamesbeard.org

The Food Network Scholarship for Immigrants in the Kitchen

Type of award: Scholarship.
Intended use: For undergraduate study at accredited postsecondary institution. Designated institutions: Accredited culinary schools.
Eligibility: Applicant must be international student.
Basis for selection: Major/career interest in culinary arts.
Application requirements: Must substantiate immigrant status.
Additional information: Must be immigrant from country other than USA enrolled or planning to enroll in accredited culinary program.

Amount of award:	$5,000
Number of awards:	2
Application deadline:	May 15

Contact:
James Beard Foundation Scholarship Program
One Scholarship Way
St. Peter, MN 56082
Phone: 507-931-1682
Web: www.jamesbeard.org

James Beard Foundation School Scholarships

Type of award: Scholarship.
Intended use: For undergraduate study at postsecondary institution. Designated institutions: Participating culinary programs.
Basis for selection: Major/career interest in culinary arts.
Additional information: Scholarships are awarded as waivers to participating culinary programs. Eligibility and application requirements vary. Check Website for current list of participating programs and list of requirements.

Amount of award:	Full tuition
Application deadline:	May 15

Contact:
James Beard Foundation Scholarship Program
One Scholarship Way
Saint Peter, MN 56082
Phone: 507-931-1682
Web: www.jamesbeard.org

Jose and Victoria Martinez Maison Blanche Scholarship

Type of award: Scholarship.
Intended use: For undergraduate study at accredited postsecondary institution. Designated institutions: Accredited culinary schools.
Basis for selection: Major/career interest in culinary arts. Applicant must demonstrate financial need.
Additional information: Preference given to resident of the Gulf Coast of Florida. Must be enrolled or planning to enroll in accredited culinary program.

Amount of award:	$2,000
Number of awards:	1
Application deadline:	May 15

Contact:
James Beard Foundation Scholarship Program
One Scholarship Way
St. Peter, MN 56082
Phone: 507-931-1682
Web: www.jamesbeard.org

La Toque Scholarship in Wine Studies

Type of award: Scholarship.
Intended use: For undergraduate study at postsecondary institution. Designated institutions: Licensed or accredited culinary schools.
Basis for selection: Major/career interest in culinary arts or food production/management/services. Applicant must demonstrate financial need.
Application requirements: Recommendations, essay, transcript, proof of eligibility. Proof of residency, financial statement, resume.
Additional information: Applicants must be enrolled in or be planning to enroll in an accredited wine studies program.

Amount of award:	$3,000
Number of awards:	1
Application deadline:	May 15
Total amount awarded:	$6,000

Contact:
Scholarship America
One Scholarship Way
St. Peter, MN 56082
Phone: 507-931-1682
Web: www.jamesbeard.org

Lacroix at the Rittenhouse Scholarship

Type of award: Scholarship.
Intended use: For undergraduate study at postsecondary institution.
Eligibility: Applicant must be residing in Pennsylvania.
Basis for selection: Major/career interest in culinary arts.
Additional information: Must be enrolled or plan to enroll in a licensed or accredited culinary school.

Amount of award:	$2,500
Number of awards:	1
Application deadline:	May 15

Contact:
James Beard Foundation Scholarship Program
One Scholarship Way
Saint Peter, MN 56082
Phone: 507-931-1682
Web: www.jamesbeard.org

Lemaire Restaurant at the Jefferson Hotel Scholarship

Type of award: Scholarship.
Intended use: For undergraduate study at accredited postsecondary institution. Designated institutions: Accredited culinary schools.
Basis for selection: Major/career interest in culinary arts.
Additional information: Must be enrolled or planning to enroll in accredited culinary program.

Amount of award:	$4,500
Number of awards:	1
Application deadline:	May 15

Contact:
James Beard Foundation Scholarship Program
One Scholarship Way
St. Peter, MN 56082
Phone: 507-931-1682
Web: www.jamesbeard.org

New England Hadassah Scholarship

Type of award: Scholarship.
Intended use: For undergraduate study at postsecondary institution.
Eligibility: Applicant must be female.
Basis for selection: Major/career interest in culinary arts.
Additional information: Must be enrolled or plan to enroll in a licensed or accredited culinary school.

Amount of award:	$3,000
Number of awards:	1
Application deadline:	May 15

Contact:
James Beard Foundation Scholarship Program
One Scholarship Way
Saint Peter, MN 56082
Phone: 507-931-1682
Web: www.jamesbeard.org

Omaha Steaks Scholarship

Type of award: Scholarship.
Intended use: For undergraduate study at accredited postsecondary institution in United States. Designated institutions: Accredited culinary schools.
Basis for selection: Major/career interest in culinary arts.
Application requirements: Recommendations, transcript.
Additional information: Up to five scholarships will be awarded, with at least one scholarship awarded to applicant currently or planning to be enrolled in Culinary Arts Program of Omaha's Metropolitan Community College.

Amount of award:	$3,000
Number of awards:	5
Application deadline:	May 15

Contact:
James Beard Foundation Scholarship Program
One Scholarship Way
St. Peter, MN 56082
Phone: 507-931-1682
Web: www.jamesbeard.org

The Peter Cameron/Housewares Charity Foundation Scholarship

Type of award: Scholarship.
Intended use: For undergraduate study at accredited postsecondary institution. Designated institutions: Licensed or accredited culinary schools.
Eligibility: Applicant must be high school senior.
Basis for selection: Major/career interest in culinary arts; food production/management/services or food science/technology. Applicant must demonstrate financial need and high academic achievement.
Application requirements: Recommendations, essay, transcript, proof of eligibility. Financial statement, resume.
Additional information: Minimum 3.0 GPA. Must attend licensed or accredited culinary school.

Amount of award:	$4,000
Number of awards:	1
Application deadline:	May 15
Total amount awarded:	$4,000

Contact:
Scholarship America
One Scholarship Way
St. Peter, MN 56082
Phone: 507-931-1682
Web: www.jamesbeard.org

Peter Kump Memorial Scholarship

Type of award: Scholarship.
Intended use: For undergraduate study at accredited postsecondary institution. Designated institutions: Licensed or accredited culinary schools.
Eligibility: Applicant must be high school senior.
Basis for selection: Major/career interest in culinary arts; food production/management/services or food science/technology. Applicant must demonstrate financial need and high academic achievement.
Application requirements: Recommendations, essay, transcript, proof of eligibility. Proof of residency, financial statement, resume.
Additional information: Minimum 3.0 GPA. Minimum one year substantiated culinary experience.

Amount of award:	$5,000
Number of awards:	5
Application deadline:	May 15
Total amount awarded:	$12,000

Contact:
Scholarship America
One Scholarship Way
St. Peter, MN 56082
Phone: 507-931-1682
Web: www.jamesbeard.org

The Ranch House at Devil's Thumb Scholarship

Type of award: Scholarship.
Intended use: For undergraduate study at postsecondary institution.
Basis for selection: Major/career interest in culinary arts.
Additional information: Must be enrolled or plan to enroll in a licensed or accredited culinary school.

Amount of award:	$3,750
Number of awards:	1
Application deadline:	May 15

Contact:
James Beard Foundation Scholarship Program
One Scholarship Way
Saint Peter, MN 56082
Phone: 507-931-1682
Web: www.jamesbeard.org

Restaurant at Sunset Marquis Scholarship

Type of award: Scholarship.
Intended use: For undergraduate study at postsecondary institution.
Basis for selection: Major/career interest in culinary arts.
Additional information: Must be enrolled or plan to enroll in a licensed or accredited culinary school.

Amount of award:	$3,750
Number of awards:	1
Application deadline:	May 15

Contact:
James Beard Foundation Scholarship Program
One Scholarship Way
Saint Peter, MN 56082
Phone: 507-931-1682
Web: www.jamesbeard.org

Schnitzer Steel "Racing to Stop Hunger" Scholarship

Type of award: Scholarship.
Intended use: For undergraduate study at postsecondary institution.
Basis for selection: Major/career interest in culinary arts.
Application requirements: Essay on topic "Fighting Hunger in Oregon: What I've done or Would Like to Do to Make a Difference."
Additional information: Must be resident of Oregon or be enrolled or plan to enroll in a licensed or accredited culinary school in Oregon.

Amount of award:	$5,000
Number of awards:	2
Application deadline:	May 15

Contact:
James Beard Foundation Scholarship Program
One Scholarship Way
Saint Peter, MN 56082
Phone: 507-931-1682
Web: www.jamesbeard.org

Steven Scher Memorial Scholarship for Aspiring Restaurateurs

Type of award: Scholarship.
Intended use: For undergraduate study at accredited postsecondary institution.
Basis for selection: Major/career interest in culinary arts. Applicant must demonstrate financial need.
Application requirements: Essay. Detail work experience; list of top three favorite restaurants and explaining why they have earned that ranking. Essay detailing ideal restaurant/hospitality concept and reasons for entering the field.
Additional information: Must be enrolled in culinary or hospitality management program. Must be high school graduate. One scholarship will be granted for study in restaurant management at the French Culinary Institute in New York City; the other to an institution of the applicant's choice.

Amount of award:	$5,000
Number of awards:	2
Application deadline:	May 15
Total amount awarded:	$10,000

Contact:
James Beard Foundation Scholarship Program
One Scholarship Way
St. Peter, MN 56082
Phone: 507-931-1682
Web: www.jamesbeard.org

Studio at the Montage Resort & Spa Scholarship

Type of award: Scholarship.
Intended use: For undergraduate study at accredited postsecondary institution. Designated institutions: Licensed or accredited culinary schools.
Basis for selection: Major/career interest in culinary arts. Applicant must demonstrate financial need.

Application requirements: Recommendations, essay, transcript. Financial statement, resume.
Additional information: Must plan to attend licensed or accredited culinary school.

Amount of award:	$3,600
Number of awards:	1
Application deadline:	May 15
Total amount awarded:	$10,000

Contact:
Scholarship America
One Scholarship Way
St. Peter, MN 56082
Phone: 507-931-1682
Web: www.jamesbeard.org

Sunday Supper South Atlanta Scholarship

Type of award: Scholarship.
Intended use: For undergraduate study at accredited postsecondary institution.
Basis for selection: Major/career interest in culinary arts. Applicant must demonstrate financial need.
Additional information: Applicants must plan to enroll in accredited culinary school.

Amount of award:	$2,000-$5,000
Number of awards:	3
Application deadline:	May 15
Total amount awarded:	$11,500

Contact:
James Beard Foundation Scholarship Program
One Scholarship Way
St. Peter, MN 56082
Phone: 507-931-1682
Web: www.jamesbeard.org

Zov's Bistro Scholarship

Type of award: Scholarship.
Intended use: For undergraduate study at accredited postsecondary institution. Designated institutions: Licensed or accredited culinary schools.
Basis for selection: Major/career interest in culinary arts. Applicant must demonstrate financial need.
Application requirements: Recommendations, essay, transcript. Financial statement, resume.
Additional information: Must plan to enroll in licensed or accredited culinary school.

Amount of award:	$3,000
Number of awards:	1
Application deadline:	May 15

Contact:
Scholarship America
One Scholarship Way
St. Peter, MN 56082
Phone: 507-931-1682
Web: www.jamesbeard.org

James F. Byrnes Foundation

James F. Byrnes Scholarship

Type of award: Scholarship, renewable.
Intended use: For full-time at accredited 4-year institution.
Eligibility: Applicant must be high school senior. Applicant must be U.S. citizen residing in South Carolina.
Basis for selection: Applicant must demonstrate financial need, high academic achievement, depth of character, leadership, patriotism, seriousness of purpose and service orientation.
Application requirements: Interview, essay, transcript. SAT/ACT scores, photograph, autobiography (three typed pages maximum) describing home situation, death of parent/s, desire for college education, college ambitions, reasons financial assistance is needed, how college will be financed, etc. Two non-relative references (one from current guidance counselor or teacher).
Additional information: Applicant must be high school senior. Applicant must have minimum 2.5 GPA. One or both parents of applicant must be deceased. Visit Website for additional information.

Amount of award:	$3,250
Number of awards:	8
Number of applicants:	126
Application deadline:	February 15
Notification begins:	April 20
Total amount awarded:	$84,500

Contact:
James F. Byrnes Foundation
P.O. Box 6781
Columbia, SC 29260-6781
Phone: 803-254-9325
Fax: 803-254-9354
Web: www.byrnesscholars.org

Jaycee War Memorial Fund

Charles R. Ford Scholarship

Type of award: Scholarship.
Intended use: For undergraduate study at postsecondary institution.
Eligibility: Applicant or parent must be member/participant of Jaycees. Applicant must be returning adult student. Applicant must be U.S. citizen.
Basis for selection: Applicant must demonstrate financial need, high academic achievement and leadership.
Application requirements: $10 application fee.
Additional information: Must be active member of Jaycees who wishes to return to college or university to complete education. To receive application, send business-size SASE with application fee between July 1 and February 1. Make check or money order payable to the Jaycee War Memorial Fund. Visit Website for more information.

Amount of award:	$2,500
Number of awards:	1
Application deadline:	February 1
Notification begins:	May 15

Contact:
Jaycee War Memorial Fund
Ford Scholarship
P.O. Box 64
Jasper, IN 47547-0064
Phone: 812-309-3699
Web: www.usjaycees.org

Jaycee War Memorial Scholarship

Type of award: Scholarship.
Intended use: For full-time undergraduate study at accredited vocational, 2-year or 4-year institution.
Eligibility: Applicant or parent must be member/participant of Jaycees. Applicant must be U.S. citizen.
Basis for selection: Applicant must demonstrate financial need, high academic achievement and leadership.
Application requirements: $10 application fee.
Additional information: To receive application, send business-size SASE with application fee between July 1 and February 1. Make check or money order payable to the Jaycee War Memorial Fund. Visit Website for additional information.

Amount of award:	$1,000
Number of awards:	10
Application deadline:	February 1
Notification begins:	May 15
Total amount awarded:	$25,000

Contact:
Jaycee War Memorial Fund
Jaycee War Memorial Scholarship
P.O. Box 64
Jasper, IN 47547-0064
Phone: 812-309-3699
Web: www.usjaycees.org

Thomas Wood Baldridge Scholarship

Type of award: Scholarship.
Intended use: For full-time undergraduate study at accredited 2-year or 4-year institution.
Eligibility: Applicant or parent must be member/participant of Jaycees. Applicant must be U.S. citizen.
Basis for selection: Applicant must demonstrate financial need, high academic achievement and leadership.
Application requirements: $10 application fee.
Additional information: Applicant must be member or have immediate family who is Jaycee member. To receive application, send business-size SASE along with application fee between July 1 and February 1. Make check or money order payable to the Jaycee War Memorial Fund. Visit Website for additional information.

Amount of award:	$3,000
Number of awards:	1
Application deadline:	February 1
Notification begins:	May 15
Total amount awarded:	$3,000

Contact:
Jaycee War Memorial Fund
Baldridge Scholarship
P.O. Box 64
Jasper, IN 47547-0064
Phone: 812-309-3699
Web: www.usjaycees.org

Jeannette Rankin Foundation

Jeanette Rankin Foundation Scholarship

Type of award: Scholarship.
Intended use: For undergraduate study at accredited vocational, 2-year or 4-year institution in United States.
Eligibility: Applicant must be female, at least 35. Applicant must be U.S. citizen.
Basis for selection: Applicant must demonstrate financial need, depth of character and seriousness of purpose.
Application requirements: Recommendations, essay.
Additional information: Applicant must be 35+ as of March 1 and meet low-income guidelines. Must display courage and attainable goals. Download application from Website from November through mid-February, or send SASE with application request.

Amount of award:	$2,000
Number of applicants:	850
Application deadline:	March 1
Notification begins:	July 1
Total amount awarded:	$160,000

Contact:
Jeannette Rankin Foundation
1 Huntington Road, #701
Athens, GA 30606
Phone: 706-208-1211
Fax: 706-548-0202
Web: www.rankinfoundation.org

Scholarships

Jewish Guild Healthcare

Jewish Guild Scholar Program

Type of award: Scholarship.
Intended use: For freshman study at accredited 2-year or 4-year institution.
Eligibility: Applicant must be visually impaired. Applicant must be high school senior. Applicant must be U.S. citizen.
Basis for selection: Applicant must demonstrate high academic achievement.
Application requirements: Recommendations, essay, transcript, proof of eligibility. SAT/ACT scores, proof of legal blindness.
Additional information: Must be U.S. citizen who is legally blind. Students may apply at end of junior year.

Amount of award:	$10,000-$15,000
Number of awards:	16
Number of applicants:	52
Application deadline:	September 15
Notification begins:	December 15
Total amount awarded:	$160,000

Contact:
Jewish Guild Scholar Program
15 West 65th Street
New York, NY 10023
Phone: 212-769-7801
Web: www.guildhealth.org/guildscholar

Jewish Vocational Service

Jewish Vocational Service Scholarship Fund

Type of award: Scholarship, renewable.
Intended use: For full-time undergraduate or graduate study at accredited postsecondary institution in United States.

Eligibility: Applicant must be Jewish. Applicant must be U.S. citizen or permanent resident residing in California.
Basis for selection: Applicant must demonstrate financial need and high academic achievement.
Application requirements: Recommendations, essay, transcript. FAFSA and tax returns.
Additional information: Minimum 2.7 GPA. Must be Jewish and legal, permanent resident of Los Angeles County with verifiable financial need. Number of awards varies. Visit Website for electronic application.

Amount of award:	$2,000-$5,000
Number of applicants:	350
Application deadline:	March 29
Total amount awarded:	$458,000

Contact:
JVS Scholarship Fund
c/o Patricia Sills
6505 Wilshire Blvd., Suite 200
Los Angeles, CA 90048
Phone: 323-761-8888 ext. 8868
Fax: 323-761-8580
Web: www.jvsla.org

Jewish War Veterans of the United States of America

I. Rubinstein Memorial Grant

Type of award: Scholarship.
Intended use: For undergraduate study at accredited 4-year institution.
Eligibility: Applicant must be high school senior.
Basis for selection: Applicant must demonstrate high academic achievement, leadership and service orientation.
Application requirements: SAT/ACT scores.
Additional information: Applicant must be direct descendant of JWV member. Must be in upper 25 percent of high school class. Must have participated in extracurricular activities in school as well as in Jewish community. Visit Website for application and more information.

Amount of award:	$750
Number of awards:	1
Application deadline:	May 1

Contact:
Jewish War Veterans of the United States of America
National Scholarship Committee
1811 R Street NW
Washington, DC 20009
Phone: 202-265-6280
Fax: 202-234-5662
Web: www.jwv.org

Jewish War Veterans of the United States of America Bernard Rotberg Memorial Scholarship

Type of award: Scholarship.
Intended use: For freshman study at accredited 4-year institution.
Eligibility: Applicant must be high school senior. Applicant must be Jewish.
Basis for selection: Applicant must demonstrate financial need and high academic achievement.
Additional information: Applicant must be direct descendant of Jewish War Veterans member. Must be in upper 25 percent of high school class; must have participated in extracurricular activities in school as well as in Jewish community. SAT scores and recommendations encouraged. Visit Website for application and more information.

Amount of award:	$1,000
Number of awards:	1

Contact:
Jewish War Veterans of the United States of America
National Scholarship Committee
1811 R Street NW
Washington, DC 20009
Phone: 202-265-6280
Fax: 202-234-5662
Web: www.jwv.org

Robert and Rebecca Memorial Grant

Type of award: Research grant.
Intended use: For freshman study at accredited 4-year institution.
Eligibility: Applicant must be high school senior. Applicant must be Jewish.
Basis for selection: Applicant must demonstrate high academic achievement.
Application requirements: SAT/ACT scores.
Additional information: Applicant must be direct descendant of JWV member. Must be in upper 25 percent of high school class; must have participated in extracurricular activities in school as well as in Jewish community. Visit Website for application and more information.

Amount of award:	$1,250
Number of awards:	1
Application deadline:	May 1

Contact:
Jewish War Veterans of the United States of America
National Scholarship Committee
1811 R Street NW
Washington, DC 20009
Phone: 202-265-6280
Fax: 202-234-5662
Web: www.jwv.org

Seymour and Phyllis Shore Memorial Grant

Type of award: Research grant.
Intended use: For freshman study at accredited vocational or 4-year institution.
Eligibility: Applicant must be high school senior. Applicant must be Jewish.
Basis for selection: Applicant must demonstrate high academic achievement.
Application requirements: SAT/ACT scores.
Additional information: Applicant must be direct descendant of JWV member. Must be in upper 25 percent of high school class; must have participated in extracurricular activities in school as well as in Jewish community. Visit Website for application and more information.

Amount of award:	$1,500
Number of awards:	1
Application deadline:	May 1

Contact:
Jewish War Veterans of the United States of America
National Scholarship Committee
1811 R Street NW
Washington, DC 20009
Phone: 202-265-6280
Fax: 202-234-5662
Web: www.jwv.org

Johnson Scholarship Foundation

Children of Florida UPS Employees Scholarship

Type of award: Scholarship, renewable.
Intended use: For undergraduate study at accredited vocational, 2-year or 4-year institution in United States.
Eligibility: Applicant must be residing in Florida.
Basis for selection: Applicant must demonstrate financial need.
Application requirements: Recommendations, transcript, proof of eligibility. Parents' financial data.
Additional information: Must be a child of regular full-time or permanent part-time Florida UPS employee. UPS employee must currently reside in Florida. UPS employee must have a minimum of one year employment with the company as of application deadline and must be employed at UPS when awards are announced. Children of UPS retirees and deceased UPS employees who met the stated employee requirements at the time of retirement or death also eligible.

Amount of award:	$1,000-$10,000
Application deadline:	April 15
Notification begins:	January 1
Total amount awarded:	$1,040,000

Contact:
The Theodore R. and Vivian M. Johnson Scholarship Program
Scholarship Management Services
One Scholarship Way, P.O. Box 297
Saint Peter, MN 56082
Phone: 507-931-1682
Web: www.jsf.bz

State University System of Florida Theodore R. and Vivian M. Johnson Scholarship

Type of award: Scholarship, renewable.
Intended use: For undergraduate study at 4-year institution in United States. Designated institutions: State University System of Florida Institutions: Florida A&M University, University of Central Florida, Florida Atlantic University, University of Florida, Florida Gulf Coast University, University of North Florida, Florida International University, University of South Florida, Florida State University, University of West Florida, New College of Florida.
Eligibility: Applicant must be residing in Florida.
Basis for selection: Applicant must demonstrate financial need and high academic achievement.
Application requirements: Recommendations, essay, transcript, proof of eligibility. FAFSA. Must provide documentation of the nature and/or extent of disability. Must meet guidelines required by institution in which student is enrolled.
Additional information: Award is for students with disabilities. Minimum 2.0 GPA. Award amount varies and is dependent upon institution. Must meet specific qualifications to renew yearly. Apply directly to institution. Contact institution's financial aid office for more information.

Amount of award:	$1,500-$5,000
Application deadline:	May 15
Notification begins:	January 1
Total amount awarded:	$500,000

Contact:
Disability Resource Center of the pertinent state university.
Web: www.jsf.bz

Kansas Board of Regents

Career Technical Workforce Grant

Type of award: Scholarship.
Intended use: For undergraduate study at accredited vocational, 2-year or 4-year institution in United States. Designated institutions: Kansas schools offering technical or AAS degrees.
Eligibility: Applicant must be U.S. citizen residing in Kansas.
Application requirements: FAFSA.
Additional information: Applicant must be Kansas resident and graduate of Kansas accredited high school. Must be pursuing technical or Associate of Applied Science degree. Students pursuing baccalaureate degrees not eligible.

Amount of award:	$1,000

Contact:
Kansas Board of Regents
1000 SW Jackson Street
Suite 520
Topeka, KS 66612-1368
Phone: 785-296-3517
Fax: 785-296-0983
Web: www.kansasregents.org

Kansas Comprehensive Grant

Type of award: Scholarship, renewable.
Intended use: For full-time undergraduate study at accredited 4-year institution. Designated institutions: Kansas post-secondary institutions.
Eligibility: Applicant must be U.S. citizen or permanent resident.
Basis for selection: Applicant must demonstrate financial need.
Application requirements: Proof of eligibility. FAFSA.
Additional information: Up to $1,100 for those attending public institutions; up to $3,500 for those attending private institutions.

Number of awards:	9,423
Number of applicants:	27,255
Application deadline:	April 1
Notification begins:	May 1
Total amount awarded:	$16,143,305

Contact:
Kansas Board of Regents
1000 SW Jackson Street
Suite 520
Topeka, KS 66612-1368
Phone: 785-296-3517
Fax: 785-296-0983
Web: www.kansasregents.org

Kansas Ethnic Minority Scholarship

Type of award: Scholarship, renewable.
Intended use: For full-time undergraduate study at postsecondary institution. Designated institutions: Kansas post-secondary institutions.
Eligibility: Applicant must be Alaskan native, Asian American, African American, Mexican American, Hispanic American, Puerto Rican, American Indian or Native Hawaiian/Pacific Islander. Applicant must be U.S. citizen or permanent resident.
Basis for selection: Applicant must demonstrate financial need and high academic achievement.
Application requirements: $12 application fee. Proof of eligibility. State of Kansas Student Aid Application. FAFSA.
Additional information: Minimum 2.0 GPA.

Amount of award:	$1,850
Number of awards:	196
Number of applicants:	307
Application deadline:	May 1
Total amount awarded:	$347,230

Contact:
Kansas Board of Regents
1000 SW Jackson Street
Suite 520
Topeka, KS 66612-1368
Phone: 785-296-3517
Fax: 785-296-0983
Web: www.kansasregents.org

Kansas Military Service Scholarship

Type of award: Scholarship.
Intended use: For undergraduate study at accredited 2-year or 4-year institution in United States. Designated institutions: Institutions in Kansas.
Eligibility: Applicant must be U.S. citizen residing in Kansas. Applicant must be veteran who served in the Army, Air Force, Marines or Navy during Middle East War. Must be honorably discharged veteran who has served at least 90 days in suppport of conflict in Iraq or Afganistan or less than 90 days due to injury sustained in Iraq or Afghanistan.
Application requirements: Form DD-214, FAFSA.
Additional information: Applicant must be Kansas resident enrolled in Kansas school. Must be enrolled for minimum of 6 credit hours per semester.
Contact:
Kansas Board of Regents
1000 SW Jackson Street
Suite 520
Topeka, KS 66612-1368
Phone: 785-296-3517
Fax: 785-296-0983
Web: www.kansasregents.org

Kansas Nursing Service Scholarship

Type of award: Scholarship, renewable:
Intended use: For full-time undergraduate study at postsecondary institution. Designated institutions: Kansas postsecondary schools with approved nursing programs.
Eligibility: Applicant must be U.S. citizen or permanent resident.
Basis for selection: Major/career interest in nursing. Applicant must demonstrate financial need.
Application requirements: $12 application fee. State of Kansas Student Aid Application. FAFSA.
Additional information: Must obtain sponsorship from adult-care home licensed under the Adult Care Home Licensure Act; state agency that employs LPNs or RNs; or state-licensed medical care facility, psychiatric hospital, home health agency or local health department. Must agree to work in Kansas one year for each year that scholarship is received. If recipient does not meet obligation, award becomes loan.

Amount of award:	$2,500-$3,500
Number of awards:	140
Number of applicants:	339
Application deadline:	May 1
Total amount awarded:	$383,750

Contact:
Kansas Board of Regents
1000 SW Jackson Street
Suite 520
Topeka, KS 66612-1368
Phone: 785-296-3517
Fax: 785-296-0983
Web: www.kansasregents.org

Kansas ROTC Service Scholarship

Type of award: Scholarship.
Intended use: For full-time undergraduate study at postsecondary institution.
Eligibility: Applicant or parent must be member/participant of Reserve Officers Training Corps (ROTC). Applicant must be residing in Kansas.
Additional information: Applicant must be Kansas resident enrolled in Kansas ROTC program. Must be full-time undergraduate with at least 12 credit hours. Scholarship limited to eight semesters. Award amount may be up to tuition and costs of average four-year regents institution; average award is $1,650.

Number of awards:	20
Number of applicants:	17
Application deadline:	August 1
Total amount awarded:	$85,434

Contact:
Kansas Board of Regents, Director of Student Financial Assistance
1000 SW Jackson Street
Suite 520
Topeka, KS 66612-1368
Phone: 785-296-3517
Fax: 785-296-0983
Web: www.kansasregents.org

Kansas State Scholarship

Type of award: Scholarship, renewable.
Intended use: For full-time undergraduate study at postsecondary institution.
Eligibility: Applicant must be residing in Kansas.

Basis for selection: Applicant must demonstrate financial need and high academic achievement.
Application requirements: $12 application fee. Proof of eligibility. FAFSA.
Additional information: Applicant must be Kansas resident, high school senior or undergraduate, and must be designated State Scholar in senior year of high school. Must be enrolled in Kansas school. Must have high GPA (average: 3.9) and ACT scores (average: 30).

Amount of award:	$1,000
Number of awards:	1,112
Number of applicants:	2,155
Application deadline:	May 1
Total amount awarded:	$991,601

Contact:
Kansas Board of Regents
1000 SW Jackson Street
Suite 520
Topeka, KS 66612-1368
Phone: 785-296-3517
Fax: 785-296-0983
Web: www.kansasregents.org

Kansas Teacher Service Scholarship

Type of award: Scholarship, renewable.
Intended use: For full-time undergraduate or post-bachelor's certificate study at 4-year or graduate institution.
Basis for selection: Major/career interest in education, teacher or education, special. Applicant must demonstrate high academic achievement.
Application requirements: $12 application fee. Recommendations, transcript, proof of eligibility. FAFSA. Personal statement.
Additional information: Applicant must be Kansas resident enrolled in Kansas school that offers education degree. Must identify a "hard-to fill" or "underserved" area. Scholarships are competitive; selection based on ACT score, GPA, high school rank, transcript and recommendation. Preference given to juniors and seniors, or currently licensed teachers pursuing licensure or endorsement in hard-to-fill disciplines.

Amount of award:	$1,103-$5,574
Number of awards:	300
Number of applicants:	529
Application deadline:	May 1
Total amount awarded:	$1,057,923

Contact:
Kansas Board of Regents
1000 SW Jackson Street
Suite 520
Topeka, KS 66612-1368
Phone: 785-296-3517
Fax: 785-296-0983
Web: www.kansasregents.org

Kansas Vocational Education Scholarship

Type of award: Scholarship, renewable.
Intended use: For full-time undergraduate study at vocational or 2-year institution. Designated institutions: Kansas institutions.
Eligibility: Applicant must be U.S. citizen or permanent resident residing in Kansas.
Application requirements: $12 application fee. Essay, proof of eligibility.
Additional information: Applicant must be Kansas resident and graduate of Kansas high school. Must take vocational test given on first Saturday of November or March and complete Vocational Education application. Renewals awarded first; remaining scholarships offered to those with highest exam scores.

Amount of award:	$500
Number of awards:	237
Number of applicants:	288
Application deadline:	May 1, February 1
Notification begins:	May 15
Total amount awarded:	$118,500

Contact:
Kansas Board of Regents
1000 SW Jackson Street
Suite 520
Topeka, KS 66612-0983
Phone: 785-296-3517
Fax: 785-296-0983
Web: www.kansasregents.org

National Guard Educational Assistance Program

Type of award: Scholarship, renewable.
Intended use: For undergraduate study at postsecondary institution. Designated institutions: Kansas institutions.
Eligibility: Applicant must be U.S. citizen residing in Kansas.
Additional information: Award amount varies. Requires service obligation.

Amount of award:	Full tuition
Application deadline:	August 1

Contact:
Kansas Board of Regents, Attn: Diane Lindeman
1000 SW Jackson Street
Suite 520
Topeka, KS 66612-1368
Phone: 785-296-3517
Fax: 785-296-0983
Web: www.kansasregents.org/scholarships_and_grants

Kappa Kappa Gamma Foundation

Kappa Kappa Gamma Scholarship

Type of award: Scholarship, renewable.
Intended use: For full-time undergraduate or graduate study at 4-year or graduate institution in United States.
Basis for selection: Applicant must demonstrate financial need and high academic achievement.
Application requirements: Recommendations, transcript.
Additional information: Applicant must be active member in good standing of Kappa Kappa Gamma fraternity, with minimum 3.0 GPA. Recipients must reapply each year. Must be U.S. citizen or permanent resident from Canada. Number of awards varies.

Amount of award:	$500-$3,000
Number of applicants:	427
Application deadline:	February 1
Total amount awarded:	$448,529

Contact:
Kappa Kappa Gamma Foundation
P.O. Box 38
Columbus, OH 43216-0038
Phone: 614-228-6515
Fax: 614-228-6303
Web: www.kappa.org

KarMel Scholarship Committee

KarMel Scholarship

Type of award: Scholarship.
Intended use: For undergraduate or graduate study at postsecondary institution in United States.
Eligibility: Applicant must be U.S. citizen.
Basis for selection: Competition/talent/interest in gay/lesbian, based on artistic or written ability on Gay/Lesbian subject. Applicant must demonstrate depth of character, leadership and seriousness of purpose.
Application requirements: Artistic work or writing samples.
Additional information: Open to high school seniors, undergraduates, and graduate students. Applicant need not be gay/lesbian/bi to apply for scholarship, but must submit works that include gay/lesbian/bi content. Scholarship is divided into two categories: Best Written Gay/Lesbian/Bi Themed Work and Best Artistic Gay/Lesbian/Bi Themed Work. Applicant may submit up to three works in both categories. Written work of any length will be accepted. All applicants may submit work via e-mail or postal mail. Visit Website for more information.

Amount of award:	$300-$400
Number of awards:	35
Number of applicants:	1,300
Application deadline:	March 31
Notification begins:	July 31
Total amount awarded:	$3,000

Contact:
KarMel Scholarship Committee
P.O. Box 70382
Sunnyvale, CA 94086
Web: www.karenandmelody.com

Kentucky Higher Education Assistance Authority (KHEAA)

Kentucky College Access Program Grant (CAP)

Type of award: Scholarship, renewable.
Intended use: For undergraduate study at postsecondary institution. Designated institutions: Kentucky institutions.
Eligibility: Applicant must be U.S. citizen or permanent resident residing in Kentucky.
Basis for selection: Applicant must demonstrate financial need.
Application requirements: FAFSA.
Additional information: Applicant ineligible if family contribution exceeds the maximum Pell EFC. May be used at eligible schools. Visit Website for additional information.

Amount of award:	$50-$1,900
Number of awards:	37,300
Number of applicants:	305,000
Total amount awarded:	$58,600,000

Contact:
Kentucky Higher Education Assistance Authority (KHEAA)
Grant Programs
P.O. Box 798
Frankfort, KY 40602-0798
Phone: 800-928-8926
Fax: 502-696-7373
Web: www.kheaa.com

Kentucky Early Childhood Development Scholarship

Type of award: Scholarship.
Intended use: For half-time undergraduate study at 2-year or 4-year institution. Designated institutions: Approved Kentucky institutions.
Eligibility: Applicant must be U.S. citizen or permanent resident residing in Kentucky.
Basis for selection: Major/career interest in education, early childhood. Applicant must demonstrate financial need.
Application requirements: FAFSA and ECDS application.
Additional information: Part-time students working at least twenty hours in childcare facility eligible. Must agree to service commitment. To apply register through Zip Access on Website. Must reapply for each term. Deadlines: July 15 for fall, November 15 for spring, April 15 for summer.

Amount of award:	$1,800
Number of awards:	900
Number of applicants:	1,400
Application deadline:	July 15, November 15
Total amount awarded:	$1,200,000

Contact:
Kentucky Higher Education Assistance Authority
P.O. Box 798
Frankfort, KY 40602-0798
Phone: 800-928-8926
Fax: 502-696-7373
Web: www.kheaa.com

Kentucky Educational Excellence Scholarship (KEES)

Type of award: Scholarship, renewable.
Intended use: For undergraduate study at accredited vocational, 2-year or 4-year institution in United States. Designated institutions: Participating public and private postsecondary institutions in Kentucky and selected out-of-state institutions if program of study not offered in Kentucky.
Eligibility: Applicant must be enrolled in high school. Applicant must be U.S. citizen or permanent resident residing in Kentucky.
Basis for selection: Applicant must demonstrate high academic achievement.
Additional information: Scholarship is earned each year of high school. Minimum annual high school GPA of 2.5. Supplemental award is given for highest ACT score (or SAT equivalent) achieved by high school graduation, based on minimum ACT score of 15. Recipient must be enrolled in postsecondary program at least half-time. Visit Website or contact via e-mail for additional information.

Amount of award: $125-$2,500
Number of awards: 68,800
Number of applicants: 68,800
Total amount awarded: $98,600,000

Contact:
Kentucky Higher Education Assistance Authority (KHEAA)
P.O. Box 798
Frankfort, KY 40602-0798
Phone: 800-928-8926
Fax: 502-696-7373
Web: www.kheaa.com

Kentucky Go Higher Grant

Type of award: Scholarship.
Intended use: For undergraduate study at postsecondary institution in United States. Designated institutions: Kentucky colleges and universities.
Eligibility: Applicant must be at least 24. Applicant must be U.S. citizen or permanent resident residing in Kentucky.
Basis for selection: Applicant must demonstrate financial need.
Application requirements: FAFSA and Go Higher Grant application.
Additional information: For less than half-time adult students who are at least 24 years old.

Amount of award: $1,000
Number of awards: 190
Number of applicants: 610
Total amount awarded: $186,000

Contact:
Kentucky Higher Education Assistance Authority (KHEAA)
P.O. Box 798
Frankfort, KY 40602-0798
Phone: 800-928-8926
Web: www.kheaa.com

Kentucky Mary Jo Young Scholarship

Type of award: Scholarship.
Intended use: For non-degree study at postsecondary institution.
Eligibility: Applicant must be enrolled in high school. Applicant must be residing in Kentucky.
Basis for selection: Applicant must demonstrate financial need.
Additional information: Provides college tuition assistance to disadvantaged high school students taking dual credit college courses. Eligibility for free or reduced lunch through high school receive priority in selection process. Award amounts are: $420 per semester if taking one course; $840 per semester if taking two courses.

Number of applicants: 2,500
Application deadline: May 1
Notification begins: June 15
Total amount awarded: $335,000

Contact:
Kentucky Higher Education Assistance Authority (KHEAA)
P.O. Box 798
Frankfort, KY 40602-0798
Phone: 800-928-8926
Fax: 502-696-7373
Web: www.kheaa.com

Kentucky Teacher Scholarship

Type of award: Scholarship, renewable.
Intended use: For full-time undergraduate or graduate study at accredited 2-year, 4-year or graduate institution. Designated institutions: Participating Kentucky institutions.
Eligibility: Applicant must be U.S. citizen residing in Kentucky.
Basis for selection: Major/career interest in education, teacher; education, early childhood or education, special. Applicant must demonstrate financial need.
Application requirements: FAFSA and Kentucky teacher scholarship application.
Additional information: Must enroll in course of study leading to initial Kentucky teacher certification. Loan forgiveness for teaching in Kentucky schools: one semester for each semester of financial assistance, two semesters if service is in teacher shortage area. Scholarship becomes loan if recipient does not complete education program or fulfill teaching obligation. Visit Website for application (see ZipAccess) and additional information.

Amount of award: $300-$5,000
Number of awards: 10
Number of applicants: 1,400
Application deadline: May 1
Notification begins: May 30
Total amount awarded: $32,700

Contact:
Kentucky Higher Education Assistance Authority (KHEAA)
Teacher Scholarship Program
P.O. Box 798
Frankfort, KY 40602-0798
Phone: 800-928-8926
Fax: 502-696-7373
Web: www.kheaa.com

Kentucky Tuition Grant

Type of award: Scholarship, renewable.
Intended use: For full-time undergraduate study at 2-year or 4-year institution. Designated institutions: Eligible private institutions in Kentucky.
Eligibility: Applicant must be U.S. citizen residing in Kentucky.
Basis for selection: Applicant must demonstrate financial need.
Application requirements: FAFSA.
Additional information: Visit Website for additional information.

Amount of award: $200-$3,000
Number of awards: 11,900
Number of applicants: 53,400
Total amount awarded: $31,000,000

Contact:
Kentucky Higher Education Assistance Authority
Grant Programs
P.O. Box 798
Frankfort, KY 40602-0798
Phone: 800-928-8926
Fax: 502-696-7373
Web: www.kheaa.com

The Kim and Harold Louie Family Foundation

The Louie Foundation Scholarship

Type of award: Scholarship.
Intended use: For full-time undergraduate study at vocational, 2-year or 4-year institution.
Eligibility: Applicant must be U.S. citizen or permanent resident.
Basis for selection: Applicant must demonstrate financial need and high academic achievement.
Application requirements: Recommendations, transcript, proof of eligibility. Proof of acceptance to college, personal essays, SAR, proof of citizenship or legal residency.
Additional information: Minimum 3.2 GPA; SAT score of 1800 or ACT score of 25. Special consideration will be noted for applicants whose parents did not attend college, whose parents are United States veterans, who have overcome significant adversity, or who are first-generation immigrants to the United States.

Number of awards:	25
Number of applicants:	500
Application deadline:	March 15
Total amount awarded:	$100,000

Contact:
The Kim and Harold Louie Family Foundation - Scholarship
445 Pullman Rd.
Hillsborough, CA 94010
Phone: 650-491-3434
Fax: 650-490-3153
Web: www.louiefamilyfoundation.org

Kosciuszko Foundation

Kosciuszko Foundation Year Abroad Program

Type of award: Scholarship, renewable.
Intended use: For sophomore, junior, senior or graduate study at 4-year or graduate institution in Poland. Designated institutions: Jagiellonian University, Institute of Polish Diaspora and Ethnic Studies (formerly the Polonia Institute, Krakow).
Eligibility: Applicant must be U.S. citizen.
Basis for selection: Competition/talent/interest in study abroad. Major/career interest in Polish language/studies. Applicant must demonstrate high academic achievement.
Application requirements: $50 application fee. Recommendations, essay, transcript. Certificate of proficiency in Polish, two passport-sized photos with full name on reverse side of each. Graduates must submit copies of degree diplomas, Polish Ministry of Education application completed in English.
Additional information: Must have interest in Polish subjects and/or involvement in Polish-American community. Scholarship covers tuition and stipend for housing and living expenses for one academic year or semester. Airfare not included. Minimum 3.0 GPA. Visit Website for more information and application. Applications available from October 1 to December 30.

Amount of award:	Full tuition
Number of applicants:	12
Application deadline:	January 5
Total amount awarded:	$11,475

Contact:
Kosciuszko Foundation
Year Abroad Program
15 East 65th Street
New York, NY 10065
Phone: 212-734-2130 ext. 210
Fax: 212-628-4552
Web: www.thekf.org

Massachusetts Federation of Polish Women's Clubs Scholarships

Type of award: Scholarship.
Intended use: For full-time sophomore, junior or senior study at postsecondary institution in United States.
Eligibility: Applicant must be Polish. Applicant must be U.S. citizen or permanent resident.
Basis for selection: Applicant must demonstrate financial need and high academic achievement.
Application requirements: $35 application fee. Recommendations, essay, transcript, proof of eligibility. Proof of Polish ancestry. Two passport-sized photos with full name printed on reverse side of each. SASE.
Additional information: Applicant must be member of Massachusetts Federation of Polish Women's Clubs. Children and grandchildren of federation members also eligible. Minimum 3.0 GPA. Selection based on academic excellence, motivation, and interest in Polish subjects and involvement in Polish-American community. Only one member per immediate family may receive Massachusetts Federation of Polish Women's Scholarship during any given academic year. Visit Website for more information and application.

Amount of award:	$1,000
Number of awards:	1
Number of applicants:	3
Application deadline:	January 7
Notification begins:	May 1
Total amount awarded:	$7,000

Contact:
Kosciuszko Foundation
15 East 65th Street
New York, NY 10065
Phone: 212-734-2130 ext. 210
Fax: 212-628-4552
Web: www.thekf.org

The Polish American Club of North Jersey Scholarships

Type of award: Scholarship, renewable.
Intended use: For full-time undergraduate or graduate study at accredited postsecondary institution in United States.
Eligibility: Applicant must be Polish. Applicant must be U.S. citizen or permanent resident.
Basis for selection: Applicant must demonstrate financial need and high academic achievement.
Application requirements: $35 application fee. Recommendations, essay, transcript, proof of eligibility. Proof of Polish ancestry. Two passport-sized photos with full name printed on reverse side of each. SASE.
Additional information: Applicant must be an active member of Polish American Club of North Jersey. Children and grandchildren of Polish American Club of North Jersey

members also eligible. Minimum 3.0 GPA. Only one member per immediate family may receive a Polish American Club of North Jersey Scholarship during any given academic year. Selection based on academic excellence, motivation, and interest in Polish subjects and involvement in the Polish-American community. Number of awards varies. Applications available October 1 through December 30. Visit Website for application and more information.

Amount of award:	$500-$2,000
Number of applicants:	7
Application deadline:	January 15
Notification begins:	May 1
Total amount awarded:	$7,200

Contact:
Kosciuszko Foundation
15 East 65th Street
New York, NY 10065
Phone: 212-734-2130 ext. 210
Fax: 212-628-4552
Web: www.thekf.org

The Polish National Alliance of Brooklyn, USA, Inc. Scholarships

Type of award: Scholarship, renewable.
Intended use: For full-time undergraduate study at accredited postsecondary institution in United States.
Eligibility: Applicant or parent must be member/participant of Polish National Alliance of Brooklyn. Applicant must be Polish. Applicant must be U.S. citizen or permanent resident.
Basis for selection: Applicant must demonstrate financial need and high academic achievement.
Application requirements: $35 application fee. Recommendations, essay, transcript, proof of eligibility. Proof of Polish ancestry. Two passport-sized photos with full name printed on reverse side of each. SASE.
Additional information: Applicant must be member in good standing of Polish National Alliance of Brooklyn, USA, Inc. Minimum 3.0 GPA. Only one member per immediate family may receive scholarship during any given academic year. Selection based on academic excellence, motivation, and interest in Polish subjects and involvement in the Polish-American community. Applications available October 1 through December 30. Visit Website for application and more information.

Amount of award:	$2,000
Number of awards:	1
Number of applicants:	7
Application deadline:	January 7
Notification begins:	May 15
Total amount awarded:	$6,000

Contact:
Kosciuszko Foundation
15 East 65th Street
New York, NY 10065
Phone: 212-734-2130 ext. 210
Fax: 212-628-4552
Web: www.thekf.org

The Lagrant Foundation

Lagrant Scholarships

Type of award: Scholarship.
Intended use: For full-time sophomore, junior, senior or graduate study at accredited 4-year or graduate institution.
Eligibility: Applicant must be Alaskan native, African American, Mexican American, Hispanic American, Puerto Rican, American Indian or Native Hawaiian/Pacific Islander. Applicant must be U.S. citizen or permanent resident.
Basis for selection: Major/career interest in advertising; marketing or public relations. Applicant must demonstrate high academic achievement.
Application requirements: Recommendations, essay, transcript. Resume.
Additional information: Minimum 2.75 GPA for undergraduates; 3.2 GPA for graduate students. Scholarship winners must attend the career development workshop and the Annual Scholarship Recognition Reception and Award Program. Students attend welcome dinner and workshop with networking opportunities. Visit Website for application.

Amount of award:	$5,000-$10,000
Number of awards:	20
Number of applicants:	150
Application deadline:	February 28
Notification begins:	April 15
Total amount awarded:	$125,000

Contact:
The Lagrant Foundation
600 Wilshire Boulevard, Suite 1520
Los Angeles, CA 90017-3247
Phone: 323-469-8680
Fax: 323-469-8683
Web: www.lagrantfoundation.org

Lambda Alpha National Collegiate Honors Society for Anthropology

Lambda Alpha National Collegiate Honors Society Senior Scholarship

Type of award: Scholarship.
Intended use: For senior study in United States.
Eligibility: Applicant must be U.S. citizen or permanent resident.
Basis for selection: Major/career interest in anthropology. Applicant must demonstrate high academic achievement and seriousness of purpose.
Application requirements: Recommendations, transcript, nomination by faculty sponsor from department of anthropology. Curriculum vitae, writing sample.
Additional information: Applicant must be member of Lambda Alpha. Institution must have a chartered Lambda Alpha chapter. Apply in senior year.

Amount of award: $5,000
Number of awards: 1
Number of applicants: 16
Application deadline: March 1
Notification begins: May 1
Total amount awarded: $5,000

Contact:
Lambda Alpha National Collegiate Honors Society for Anthropology
Dept. of Anthropology, Attn: Mark Groover
Ball State University
Muncie, IN 47306-0435
Phone: 765-285-5297
Web: cms.bsu.edu/Academics/CollegesandDepartments/Anthropology/LambdaAlpha.aspx

Landscape Architecture Foundation

ASLA Council of Fellows Scholarship

Type of award: Scholarship.
Intended use: For junior or senior study at accredited 4-year institution in United States.
Eligibility: Applicant must be U.S. citizen or permanent resident.
Basis for selection: Applicant must demonstrate financial need.
Application requirements: Recommendations, essay. Resume, photo in jpg format; two letters of recommendation, at least one from a faculty member, 500-word essay about how applicant will contribute to the profession of landscape architecture; 250-word statement describing financial need; SAR.
Additional information: Two scholarships awarded; one specifically available to students of under-represented populations. Applicants seeking consideration for diversity scholarship should indicate specific cultural or ethnic group. Each winner will receive a one-year student ASLA membership and airfare to attend ASLA meeting where award is presented.

Amount of award: $4,000
Number of awards: 2
Application deadline: February 15
Total amount awarded: $8,000

Contact:
Landscape Architecture Foundation
818 18th Street
Suite 810
Washington, DC 20006
Phone: 202-331-7070
Fax: 202-331-7079
Web: www.lafoundation.org

Courtland Paul Scholarship

Type of award: Scholarship.
Intended use: For junior or senior study at accredited postsecondary institution. Designated institutions: Schools accredited by the Landscape Architecture Accreditation Board.
Eligibility: Applicant must be U.S. citizen.
Basis for selection: Major/career interest in landscape architecture. Applicant must demonstrate financial need, high academic achievement and seriousness of purpose.
Application requirements: Recommendations, essay. Cover sheet, personal profile, photo, resume.
Additional information: All application materials must be sent together in one email, except for the recommendation letters which must be sent by email from the author. Minimum 'C' GPA. Award must be used for tuition and/or books within the school year of the award.

Amount of award: $5,000
Number of awards: 1
Number of applicants: 37
Application deadline: February 15

Contact:
Landscape Architecture Foundation
818 18th Street
Suite 810
Washington, DC 20006
Phone: 202-331-7070
Fax: 202-331-7079
Web: www.lafoundation.org

The EDSA Minority Scholarship

Type of award: Scholarship.
Intended use: For junior, senior or graduate study at postsecondary institution.
Eligibility: Applicant must be Alaskan native, Asian American, African American, Mexican American, Hispanic American, Puerto Rican, American Indian or Native Hawaiian/Pacific Islander.
Basis for selection: Major/career interest in landscape architecture. Applicant must demonstrate financial need and seriousness of purpose.
Application requirements: Recommendations, transcript. Cover letter, photo, resume, personal profile, 500-word essay describing design effort you plan to pursue and its contribution to the advancement of the profession and your ethnic heritage, three work samples (jpg or pdf).
Additional information: Visit Website for more information.

Amount of award: $5,000
Number of awards: 1
Number of applicants: 7
Application deadline: February 15

Contact:
Landscape Architecture Foundation
818 18th Street
Suite 810
Washington, DC 20006
Phone: 202-331-7070
Fax: 202-331-7079
Web: www.lafoundation.org

Hawaii Chapter/David T. Woolsey Scholarship

Type of award: Scholarship.
Intended use: For full-time junior, senior or graduate study at accredited 4-year or graduate institution.
Eligibility: Applicant must be permanent resident residing in Hawaii.
Basis for selection: Major/career interest in landscape architecture. Applicant must demonstrate service orientation.
Application requirements: Recommendations, essay. Photo, cover letter, resume. Three 8.5 x 11 work samples as jpg or pdf. Personal profile, proof of Hawaii residency. One recommendation must be from design instructor.

Additional information: Applicant must be resident of Hawaii enrolled in landscape architecture program at accredited college or university. Visit Website for more information.

Amount of award:	$2,000
Number of awards:	1
Application deadline:	February 15

Contact:
Landscape Architecture Foundation
818 18th Street
Suite 810
Washington, DC 20006
Phone: 202-331-7070
Fax: 202-331-7079
Web: www.lafoundation.org

Landscape Forms Design for People Scholarship

Type of award: Scholarship.
Intended use: For full-time senior study at postsecondary institution. Designated institutions: Schools with LAAB-accredited program.
Basis for selection: Major/career interest in landscape architecture. Applicant must demonstrate financial need and seriousness of purpose.
Application requirements: Portfolio, recommendations, transcript. Cover sheet, photo, resume, personal profile, 300-word essay describing qualities essential to great and successful public spaces, three work samples (jpg or pdf).
Additional information: Must show proven contribution to design of public spaces that promote social interaction.

Amount of award:	$3,000
Number of awards:	1
Number of applicants:	17
Application deadline:	February 15

Contact:
Landscape Architecture Foundation
818 18th Street
Suite 810
Washington, DC 20006
Phone: 202-331-7070
Fax: 202-331-7079
Web: www.lafoundation.org

Peridian International Inc./Rae L. Price FASLA Scholarship

Type of award: Scholarship.
Intended use: For junior or senior study at postsecondary institution. Designated institutions: UCLA Extension or Cal Poly Pomona.
Eligibility: Applicant must be U.S. citizen.
Basis for selection: Major/career interest in landscape architecture. Applicant must demonstrate financial need and high academic achievement.
Application requirements: Recommendations, essay. Photo in jpg format, resume.
Additional information: Award restricted to tuition, books, and program required supplies. Minimum 'B' GPA.

Amount of award:	$5,000
Number of awards:	1
Application deadline:	February 15

Contact:
Landscape Architecture Foundation
818 18th Street
Suite 810
Washington, DC 20006
Phone: 202-331-7070
Fax: 202-331-7079
Web: www.lafoundation.org

Rain Bird Intelligent Use of Water Scholarship

Type of award: Scholarship.
Intended use: For full-time junior or senior study at accredited 4-year institution.
Basis for selection: Major/career interest in landscape architecture; horticulture; hydrology or urban planning. Applicant must demonstrate high academic achievement.
Application requirements: Essay. Photo, personal profile, resume. Cover letter explaining enclosures and interests. 300-word essay stating career goals and how applicant will continue advancement of landscape architecture.
Additional information: Visit Website for more information.

Amount of award:	$2,500
Number of awards:	1
Number of applicants:	30
Application deadline:	February 15

Contact:
Landscape Architecture Foundation
818 18th Street
Suite 810
Washington, DC 20006
Phone: 202-331-7070
Fax: 202-331-7079
Web: www.lafoundation.org

Steven G. King Play Environments Scholarship

Type of award: Scholarship.
Intended use: For full-time junior, senior or graduate study. Designated institutions: LAAB-accredited schools.
Basis for selection: Major/career interest in landscape architecture. Applicant must demonstrate financial need and seriousness of purpose.
Application requirements: Recommendations, transcript. Cover sheet, photo, resume, work samples, personal profile, 300- to 500-word essay explaining value of play and of integrating playgrounds into recreation environments, plan or details of play environment of applicant's design (jpg or pdf).
Additional information: Must have demonstrated interest in park and playground planning.

Amount of award:	$5,000
Number of awards:	1
Number of applicants:	9
Application deadline:	February 15

Contact:
Landscape Architecture Foundation
818 18th Street
Suite 810
Washington, DC 20006
Phone: 202-331-7070
Fax: 202-331-7079
Web: www.lafoundation.org

Latin American Educational Foundation

Latin American Educational Scholarship

Type of award: Scholarship, renewable.
Intended use: For full-time undergraduate or non-degree study at accredited postsecondary institution in United States.
Eligibility: Applicant must be Mexican American, Hispanic American or Puerto Rican. Applicant must be residing in Colorado.
Basis for selection: Applicant must demonstrate financial need, high academic achievement, leadership and service orientation.
Application requirements: Recommendations, essay, transcript. Previous year's tax return.
Additional information: Minimum 3.0 GPA. SAT/ACT scores required for high school seniors. Must be Hispanic American or actively involved in Hispanic American community. Recipients must fulfill ten hours of community service during the award year. Applicants must reapply each year.

Amount of award:	$750-$2,000
Number of awards:	100
Number of applicants:	350
Application deadline:	March 15
Notification begins:	June 15
Total amount awarded:	$200,000

Contact:
Latin American Education Foundation
561 Santa Fe Drive
Denver, CO 80204
Phone: 303-446-0541 ext. 12
Fax: 303-446-0526
Web: www.laef.org

League of United Latin American Citizens

GE Foundation/LULAC Scholarship Program

Type of award: Scholarship, renewable.
Intended use: For full-time sophomore study at accredited 2-year or 4-year institution in United States.
Eligibility: Applicant must be Alaskan native, Asian American, African American, Mexican American, Hispanic American, Puerto Rican, American Indian or Native Hawaiian/Pacific Islander. Applicant must be U.S. citizen or permanent resident.
Basis for selection: Major/career interest in business or engineering. Applicant must demonstrate high academic achievement, seriousness of purpose and service orientation.
Application requirements: Recommendations, essay, transcript, proof of eligibility.
Additional information: Must be minority student with minimum 3.25 GPA who is entering sophomore year in the fall. Recipients may be offered temporary summer or internship positions with GE businesses; however, the students are under no obligation to accept GE employment. Application available on Website.

Amount of award:	$5,000
Number of awards:	11
Notification begins:	August 15
Total amount awarded:	$55,000

Contact:
League of United Latin American Citizens
Attn: GE Scholarship
1133 19th Street NW, Suite 1000
Washington, DC 20036
Phone: 202-835-9646
Fax: 202-835-9685
Web: www.lnesc.org

LULAC General Awards

Type of award: Scholarship.
Intended use: For undergraduate or graduate study at accredited vocational, 2-year, 4-year or graduate institution in United States.
Eligibility: Applicant must be U.S. citizen or permanent resident.
Basis for selection: Applicant must demonstrate financial need, high academic achievement, depth of character, leadership and service orientation.
Application requirements: Verification of admittance to institution.
Additional information: Academic performance considered, however motivation, sincerity, and integrity will also be considered in selection process. Students are ineligible for scholarship if related to scholarship committee member, council president, or individual contributor to the local funds of the council. Submit application to local participating LULAC council. See Website for application and list of participating councils. Local council may require additional information and personal interview.

Amount of award:	$250-$1,000
Application deadline:	March 31
Notification begins:	May 15

Contact:
League of United Latin American Citizens
2000 L Street NW, Suite 610
Washington, DC 20036
Phone: 202-835-9646
Fax: 202-835-9685
Web: www.lnesc.org

LULAC Honors Awards

Type of award: Scholarship.
Intended use: For full-time undergraduate or graduate study at accredited vocational, 2-year, 4-year or graduate institution in United States.
Eligibility: Applicant must be U.S. citizen or permanent resident.
Basis for selection: Applicant must demonstrate high academic achievement.
Application requirements: Essay, transcript, proof of eligibility. Verification of admittance to institution. SAT/ACT scores.
Additional information: Students are ineligible for scholarship if related to scholarship committee member, council president, or individual contributor to the local funds of the council. Minimum 3.0 GPA. Entering freshmen must have scored at least 23 on ACT or 1100 (reading and math) on SAT. Submit application to local participating LULAC council. See Website for application and list of participating LULAC councils. Local LULAC council may require additional information and personal interview.

Amount of award: $500-$2,000
Application deadline: March 31
Notification begins: May 15

Contact:
League of United Latin American Citizens
2000 L Street NW, Suite 610
Washington, DC 20036
Phone: 202-835-9646
Fax: 202-835-9685
Web: www.lnesc.org

LULAC National Scholastic Achievement Awards

Type of award: Scholarship.
Intended use: For full-time undergraduate or graduate study at accredited 2-year, 4-year or graduate institution in United States.
Eligibility: Applicant must be U.S. citizen or permanent resident.
Basis for selection: Applicant must demonstrate high academic achievement.
Application requirements: Essay, transcript, proof of eligibility. Verification of admittance to institution. SAT/ACT scores.
Additional information: Students are ineligible for scholarship if related to scholarship committee member, council president, or individual contributor to the local funds of the council. Entering freshmen must have scored at least 29 on ACT or 1350 (reading and math) on SAT. Minimum 3.5 GPA. Minimum amount of award is $1,000. See Website for list of participating LULAC councils. Local LULAC council may require additional information and personal interview.

Amount of award: $2,000
Application deadline: March 31
Notification begins: May 15

Contact:
League of United Latin American Citizens
2000 L Street NW, Suite 610
Washington, DC 20036
Phone: 202-835-9646
Fax: 202-835-9685
Web: www.lnesc.org

Learning Ally

Marion Huber Learning Through Listening Award

Type of award: Scholarship.
Intended use: For undergraduate study at vocational, 2-year or 4-year institution.
Eligibility: Applicant must be learning disabled. Applicant must be high school senior.
Basis for selection: Applicant must demonstrate high academic achievement, leadership and service orientation.
Application requirements: Recommendations, essay, transcript. List of honors, achievements, and activities.
Additional information: Must be registered as a Learning Ally member for at least one year. Must not have previously received award from Learning Ally, formerly Recording for the Blind and Dyslexic. Family members of Learning Ally staff or volunteers serving on local or national board not eligible. Winners may be asked to represent Learning Ally as spokesperson and advocate at various events, with costs funded by Learning Ally. Winners must be present at celebratory event to receive award. Must have 3.0 GPA or better in grades 10-12. Applications due in March.

Amount of award: $2,000-$6,000
Number of awards: 6
Application deadline: March 15
Total amount awarded: $24,000

Contact:
NAA Awards
c/o Melissa Greenwald, Learning Ally
20 Roszel Road
Princeton, NJ 08540
Phone: 609-243-7087
Web: www.LearningAlly.org

Mary P. Oenslager Scholastic Achievement Award

Type of award: Scholarship.
Intended use: For senior, master's or doctoral study at accredited 4-year or graduate institution in United States.
Eligibility: Applicant must be visually impaired.
Basis for selection: Applicant must demonstrate high academic achievement, leadership and service orientation.
Application requirements: Recommendations, essay, transcript. List of honors, achievements, and community activities.
Additional information: Must be legally blind. Must have been registered as a Learning Ally member, formerly Recording for the Blind and Dyslexic, for at least one year. Must not have previously received an award from Learning Ally, formerly Recording for the Blind and Dyslexic. Must receive degree during the current year. Minimum 3.0 GPA on 4.0 scale or equivalent. Winners may be asked to represent Learning Ally as spokesperson and advocate at various events, with cost funded by Learning Ally. Winners must be present at celebratory event to receive award. Continuing education beyond bachelor's degree not required. Applications due in March.

Amount of award: $1,000-$6,000
Number of awards: 9
Application deadline: March 15
Total amount awarded: $30,000

Contact:
SAA Awards
c/o Melissa Greenwald, Learning Ally
20 Roszel Road
Princeton, NJ 08540
Phone: 609-243-7087
Web: www.LearningAlly.org

Learning for Life

Captain James J. Regan Memorial Scholarship

Type of award: Scholarship.
Intended use: For full-time undergraduate study at accredited postsecondary institution.
Eligibility: Applicant or parent must be member/participant of Learning for Life. Applicant must be U.S. citizen or permanent resident.

Basis for selection: Major/career interest in criminal justice/law enforcement. Applicant must demonstrate high academic achievement, leadership and seriousness of purpose.
Application requirements: Essay, transcript, proof of eligibility. Certification from post advisor, head of participating organization, Learning for Life representative. Three letters of recommendation (two from outside of law enforcement). Additional essay (minimum of 250 words) on "How Will Technology Affect Law Enforcement in the 21st Century?" Black-and-white photo (preferably in uniform). Must submit original and four copies of all materials.
Additional information: Program open to Learning for Life's Law Enforcement Explorers. Visit Website for application and more information.

Amount of award:	$500
Number of awards:	2
Application deadline:	March 31
Total amount awarded:	$1,000

Contact:
National Law Enforcement Scholarships and Awards
1325 West Walnut Hill Lane
P.O. Box 152079
Irving, TX 75015
Phone: 972-580-2433
Fax: 972-580-2502
Web: www.learning-for-life.org/exploring

Sheryl A. Horak Law Enforcement Explorer Scholarship

Type of award: Scholarship.
Intended use: For full-time undergraduate study at accredited 2-year or 4-year institution.
Eligibility: Applicant or parent must be member/participant of Learning for Life. Applicant must be high school senior. Applicant must be U.S. citizen or permanent resident.
Basis for selection: Major/career interest in criminal justice/law enforcement. Applicant must demonstrate high academic achievement, leadership and service orientation.
Application requirements: Transcript. Certification from post advisor, head of participating organization, Learning for Life representative. Three letters of recommendation (two from outside of law enforcement). Essay (500 words minimum) on "Why I Want to Pursue a Career in Law Enforcement." Black-and-white photo (preferably in uniform). Must submit original and two copies of all materials.
Additional information: Program open to Learning for Life's Law Enforcement Explorers. Number of awards granted varies. Visit Website for application and more information.

Amount of award:	$1,000
Application deadline:	March 31

Contact:
National Law Enforcement Scholarships and Awards
1325 West Walnut Hill Lane
P.O. Box 152079
Irving, TX 75015
Phone: 972-580-2433
Fax: 972-580-2502
Web: www.learning-for-life.org/exploring

Life and Health Insurance Foundation for Education

LIFE Lessons Scholarship Program

Type of award: Scholarship.
Intended use: For undergraduate study at postsecondary institution in United States.
Eligibility: Applicant must be at least 17, no older than 24. Applicant must be U.S. citizen or permanent resident.
Basis for selection: Competition/talent/interest in writing/journalism, based on 500-word essay or 3-minute video describing how applicant has experienced personal and financial challenges caused by death of parent or legal guardian.
Application requirements: Proof of eligibility. Essay of 500 words or 3-minute video describing personal and financial challenges caused by death of a parent and how lack of life insurance impacted their college funding plans.
Additional information: Applicant must have experienced the death of a parent or legal guardian. Apply online, or e-mail or call to receive paper application. Deadline dates vary. Visit Website for exact dates.

Amount of award:	$2,000-$15,000
Number of applicants:	2,000
Total amount awarded:	$125,000

Contact:
Life and Health Insurance Foundation for Education
Attn: Life Lessons Scholarship
1655 North Fort Meyer Drive, Suite 610
Arlington, VA 22209
Phone: 202-464-5000 ext. 4446
Fax: 202-464-5011
Web: www.lifehappens.org/lifelessons

Lighthouse International

Lighthouse College-Bound Award

Type of award: Scholarship.
Intended use: For full-time freshman study at accredited 2-year or 4-year institution in United States.
Eligibility: Applicant must be visually impaired. Applicant must be high school senior. Applicant must be U.S. citizen residing in New York, Delaware, Massachusetts, Virginia, Connecticut, Vermont, Maine, Maryland, Pennsylvania, South Carolina, Florida, Georgia, District of Columbia, New Hampshire, West Virginia, North Carolina, New Jersey or Rhode Island.
Basis for selection: Applicant must demonstrate high academic achievement.
Application requirements: Recommendations, essay, transcript, proof of eligibility. Official documentation of legal blindness. Recommendations required from two people other than family members. Personal essay should be 400-600 words. Letter of acceptance to college.
Additional information: Applicant must be legally blind. College-bound high school seniors or recent high school graduates now planning to begin college may apply. Previous SCA recipients and Lighthouse members and employees are ineligible. Application deadline in late February or early March; visit Website for exact dates.

Amount of award: $10,000
Number of awards: 1
Number of applicants: 65
Total amount awarded: $10,000
Contact:
Lighthouse International
Scholarship Awards Program
111 East 59 Street
New York, NY 10022-1202
Phone: 212-821-9200
Fax: 212-821-9707
Web: www.lighthouse.org/sca

Lighthouse Undergraduate Award

Type of award: Scholarship.
Intended use: For full-time undergraduate study at postsecondary institution in United States.
Eligibility: Applicant must be visually impaired. Applicant must be U.S. citizen residing in New York, Delaware, Massachusetts, Virginia, Connecticut, Vermont, Maine, Maryland, Pennsylvania, Florida, Georgia, South Carolina, District of Columbia, New Hampshire, West Virginia, North Carolina, New Jersey or Rhode Island.
Basis for selection: Applicant must demonstrate high academic achievement.
Application requirements: Recommendations, essay, transcript, proof of eligibility. Official documentation of legal blindness. Recommendations required from two people other than family members. Personal essay of 400-600 words.
Additional information: Applicant must be legally blind. Must reside in United States or U.S. territory. Previous SCA recipients and Lighthouse members and employees are ineligible. Application deadline in late February or early March; visit Website for exact dates.
Amount of award: $10,000
Number of awards: 1
Number of applicants: 65
Total amount awarded: $10,000
Contact:
Lighthouse International
Scholarship Awards Program
111 East 59 Street
New York, NY 10022-1202
Phone: 212-821-9200
Fax: 212-821-9707
Web: www.lighthouse.org

Los Padres Foundation

Los Padres Foundation College Tuition Assistance Program

Type of award: Scholarship, renewable.
Intended use: For full-time undergraduate or graduate study at 4-year or graduate institution in United States.
Eligibility: Applicant must be Mexican American, Hispanic American or Puerto Rican. Applicant must be high school senior. Applicant must be U.S. citizen or permanent resident residing in New York or New Jersey.
Basis for selection: Applicant must demonstrate financial need, high academic achievement, seriousness of purpose and service orientation.
Application requirements: Recommendations, essay, transcript. Proof of income.
Additional information: Primarily for Latin American or Puerto Rican students in New York or New Jersey metropolitan area. Applicant must have minimum 3.0 GPA and proof of low income. Applicant must be first generation in family to attend college. Award is renewable up to four years. Must complete 100 hours of community service by June 1st of first college year. Application available at financial aid office, high school counselor's office, and online.
Amount of award: $2,000
Number of applicants: 30
Application deadline: January 15
Contact:
Los Padres Foundation
CTA Program
P.O. Box 305
Nassau, DE 19969
Phone: 800-528-4105
Fax: 866-810-1361
Web: www.lospadresfoundation.org

Los Padres Foundation Second Chance Program

Type of award: Scholarship.
Intended use: For undergraduate study at accredited postsecondary institution.
Eligibility: Applicant must be Mexican American, Hispanic American or Puerto Rican. Applicant must be U.S. citizen or permanent resident residing in New York, Puerto Rico or New Jersey.
Basis for selection: Applicant must demonstrate financial need.
Application requirements: Transcript, proof of eligibility. Proof of low income.
Additional information: Minimum 3.0 GPA. Applicant must have high school diploma or GED and be out of high school for more than a year prior to submitting and never attended a postsecondary institution. Awardees must complete 100 hours of non-faith-based community service by June 1 of the first year in program. Must meet low-income federal guidelines.
Amount of award: $2,000
Application deadline: June 30
Contact:
Los Padres Foundation
Second Chance Program
P.O. Box 305
Nassau, DE 19969
Phone: 800-528-4105
Fax: 866-810-1361
Web: www.lospadresfoundation.org

Louisiana Department of Veterans Affairs

Louisiana Veterans Affairs Survivors and Dependents Education Program

Type of award: Scholarship, renewable.
Intended use: For full-time undergraduate, graduate or non-degree study at vocational, 2-year, 4-year or graduate

institution. Designated institutions: Louisiana public institutions.
Eligibility: Applicant must be residing in Louisiana. Applicant must be dependent of disabled veteran or deceased veteran. Deceased veteran must have died of wartime injuries.
Application requirements: Proof of eligibility. Certification of eligibility.
Additional information: Award is a tuition waiver at all Louisiana state-supported schools. Living veteran must be Louisiana resident for at least two years prior to child entering program. Deceased veteran must have been Louisiana resident for at least twelve months immediately preceding entry into service. Disability must be at least 90 percent as rated by U.S. Department of Veterans Affairs to qualify. Applicant also eligible if disability rating is 60 percent or more but employability rating is 100 percent unemployable. Waiver available for five year period before applicant turns 25. Award amounts vary.

Amount of award: Full tuition

Contact:
Louisiana Department of Veterans Affairs
P.O. Box 94095
Baton Rouge, LA 70804-9095
Phone: 225-219-5000
Web: www.vetaffairs.la.gov

Louisiana Office of Student Financial Assistance

Chafee Educational and Training Voucher

Type of award: Scholarship, renewable.
Intended use: For undergraduate study at postsecondary institution.
Eligibility: Applicant must be at least 15, no older than 21. Applicant must be residing in Louisiana.
Application requirements: FAFSA.
Additional information: Awards for students who have been in foster care system.

Amount of award: $5,000
Number of awards: 66
Number of applicants: 106
Total amount awarded: $332,565

Contact:
Louisiana Office of Student Financial Assistance
P.O. Box 91202
Baton Rouge, LA 70821-9202
Phone: 800-259-5626 ext. 1012
Fax: 255-922-0790
Web: www.osfa.la.gov

Louisiana Go Grants

Type of award: Scholarship, renewable.
Intended use: For undergraduate study at postsecondary institution.
Eligibility: Applicant must be residing in Louisiana.
Basis for selection: Applicant must demonstrate financial need.
Application requirements: FAFSA.
Additional information: Financial aid for nontraditional and low to moderate income students. Must receive Pell grant to qualify.

Amount of award: $1,000
Number of awards: 33,231
Total amount awarded: $25,982,911

Contact:
Louisiana Office of Student Financial Assistance
P.O. Box 91202
Baton Rouge, LA 70821-9202
Phone: 800-259-5626 ext 1012
Fax: 225-922-0790
Web: www.osfa.la.gov

Louisiana Rockefeller Wildlife Scholarship

Type of award: Scholarship, renewable.
Intended use: For full-time undergraduate or graduate study at 4-year or graduate institution. Designated institutions: Louisiana public colleges and universities.
Eligibility: Applicant must be U.S. citizen residing in Louisiana.
Basis for selection: Major/career interest in wildlife/fisheries; forestry or oceanography/marine studies. Applicant must demonstrate high academic achievement.
Application requirements: FAFSA, Rockefeller State Wildlife Application.
Additional information: Minimum 2.5 GPA for undergraduate students or 3.0 for graduate students. Undergraduate students must have earned at least 60 hours of college credit. Undergraduate award is $2,000; graduate award is $3,000.

Amount of award: $2,000-$3,000
Number of awards: 30
Number of applicants: 45
Application deadline: July 1
Total amount awarded: $60,000

Contact:
Louisiana Office of Student Financial Assistance
P.O. Box 91202
Baton Rouge, LA 70821-9202
Phone: 800-259-5626 ext. 1012
Fax: 225-922-0790
Web: www.osfa.la.gov

Louisiana Taylor Opportunity Program for Students (TOPS) Award

Type of award: Scholarship, renewable.
Intended use: For full-time undergraduate study at postsecondary institution. Designated institutions: Eligible Louisiana postsecondary institutions.
Eligibility: Applicant must be U.S. citizen or permanent resident residing in Louisiana.
Basis for selection: Applicant must demonstrate high academic achievement.
Application requirements: FAFSA. SAT or ACT scores.
Additional information: Open to Louisiana residents who will be first-time, full-time freshmen at Louisiana public or LAICU private postsecondary institutions no later than fall following first anniversary of high school graduation. Must have no criminal convictions. Must have completed 17.5 units college-prep TOPS core curriculum. Individual requirements for awards below; please send one inquiry, only, for all award levels: TOPS OPPORTUNITY AWARD: Equal to tuition at public institution (or weighted average tuition at LAICU member institution). Must have minimum 2.5 GPA, minimum ACT score based on state's prior year average (never below 20) or minimum SAT of 940. TOPS PERFORMANCE AWARDS:

Equal to tuition at public institution (or weighted average tuition at LAICU member institution) plus $400/yr stipend. Minimum 3.0 GPA, minimum ACT score of 23 or SAT score of 1050. TOPS HONORS AWARDS: Equal to tuition at public institution (or weighted average tuition at LAICU member institution) plus $800/yr stipend. Minimum 3.0 GPA, ACT score of 27 or SAT score of 1210. Contact Public Information Rep for more details.

Amount of award:	Full tuition
Number of applicants:	28,182
Application deadline:	July 1
Notification begins:	June 1
Total amount awarded:	$165,620,684

Contact:
Louisiana Office of Student Financial Assistance
P.O. Box 91202
Baton Rouge, LA 70821-9202
Phone: 800-259-5626 ext. 1012
Fax: 225-922-0790
Web: www.osfa.la.gov

Louisiana TOPS Tech Early Start Program

Type of award: Scholarship.
Intended use: For half-time undergraduate study at postsecondary institution in United States. Designated institutions: Louisiana public colleges.
Eligibility: Applicant must be high school junior or senior. Applicant must be U.S. citizen or permanent resident residing in Louisiana.
Additional information: Full tuition for six credit hours per semester for juniors and seniors in public Louisiana public high schools who are concurrently enrolled in public Louisiana college. Must be enrolled in vocational course leading to industry-based certification in a Top Demand Occupation. Minimum 2.0 GPA. Minimum 15 ACT score. Minimum passing score in English and math on GEE. Must have approved five-year education and career plan.

Amount of award:	$600

Contact:
Louisiana Office of Student Financial Assistance
P.O. Box 91202
Baton Rouge, LA 70821-9202
Phone: 800-259-5626 ext. 1012
Fax: 225-922-0790
Web: www.osfa.la.gov

Louisiana Tops Tech Program

Type of award: Scholarship, renewable.
Intended use: For full-time freshman study at postsecondary institution in United States. Designated institutions: Approved Louisiana institutions.
Eligibility: Applicant must be enrolled in high school. Applicant must be U.S. citizen or permanent resident residing in Louisiana.
Basis for selection: Applicant must demonstrate high academic achievement.
Application requirements: FAFSA.
Additional information: Minimum 2.5 GPA. Must have completed a certain number of Tech Core Units. Minimum 17 ACT score or SAT equivalent. Must enroll as first-time freshman. Full tuition to those attending community colleges and vocational schools. Partial tuition for students of schools where baccalaureate degrees are available.

Amount of award:	Full tuition
Application deadline:	July 1

Contact:
Louisiana Office of Student Financial Assistance
P.O. Box 91202
Baton Rouge, LA 70821
Phone: 800-259-5626 ext. 1012
Fax: 225-922-0790
Web: www.osfa.la.gov

Lowe's

The Carl Buchan Scholarship

Type of award: Scholarship.
Intended use: For full-time undergraduate study at accredited vocational, 2-year or 4-year institution in United States.
Eligibility: Applicant must be U.S. citizen.
Basis for selection: Applicant must demonstrate high academic achievement, leadership and service orientation.
Additional information: Minimum 3.25 GPA. Must be high school senior or current college undergraduate with at least one full semester completed. Must be full- or part-time Lowe's employee or qualified relative of employee with at least 90 days of service with Lowe's as of January 1 the year scholarship is awarded. Employee must still be employed at the time awards are announced. Must demonstrate history of commitment to community through leadership activities, community service, and/or work experience. Award not renewable, but students can reapply each year if eligibility requirements are met. Apply online.

Amount of award:	$5,000
Number of awards:	50
Application deadline:	February 28
Total amount awarded:	$250,000

Contact:
Lowe's
Web: www.lowes.com/scholarships

Lowe's Scholarship Program

Type of award: Scholarship.
Intended use: For full-time freshman study at accredited vocational, 2-year or 4-year institution in United States.
Eligibility: Applicant must be high school senior.
Basis for selection: Applicant must demonstrate high academic achievement, leadership and service orientation.
Additional information: Must maintain minimum 3.25 GPA. Must be residing in the United States. Lowe's employees and their children are also eligible. Must demonstrate a history of commitment to community through leadership activities, community service, and/or work experience. Award is not renewable, but students can reapply each year if they continue to meet eligibility requirements. Apply online.

Amount of award:	$2,500
Number of awards:	140
Application deadline:	February 28
Total amount awarded:	$350,000

Contact:
Lowe's
Web: www.lowes.com/scholarships

Maine Division of Veterans Services

Maine Veterans Services Dependents Educational Benefits

Type of award: Scholarship.
Intended use: For undergraduate or master's study at vocational, 2-year or 4-year institution. Designated institutions: Public universities in Maine.
Eligibility: Applicant must be at least 16, no older than 26. Applicant must be residing in Maine. Applicant must be dependent of disabled veteran; or spouse of disabled veteran. Must apply for program prior to 22nd birthday, or before 26th birthday if applicant was enrolled in the U.S. Armed Forces. Age limits apply to child applicants only, not spouses.
Basis for selection: Applicant must demonstrate high academic achievement.
Application requirements: Proof of eligibility. Proof of veteran's disability, birth certificate. Stepchildren must provide parent's marriage certificate. Adopted children must provide adoption certificate or proof of paternity to natural parent. Spouse must provide marriage certificate.
Additional information: Applicant must have graduated from high school and must be dependent of permanently and totally disabled veteran. Veteran must have been resident of Maine prior to enlistment or resident of Maine for five years preceding application for aid. Provides tuition at all branches of University of Maine system, all State of Maine vocational-technical colleges, and Maine Maritime Academy for eight semesters to be used within six years. Must maintain "C" average to continue receiving benefits. Award must be used within ten years.

Amount of award: Full tuition

Contact:
Maine Division of Veterans Services
117 State House Station
Augusta, ME 04333-0117
Phone: 207-430-6035
Fax: 207-626-4471
Web: www.mainebvs.org

Maine Innkeepers Association

Maine Innkeepers Association Scholarship

Type of award: Scholarship.
Intended use: For full-time undergraduate or graduate study at accredited vocational, 4-year or graduate institution in United States. Designated institutions: Institutions with fully accredited programs in hotel administration or culinary arts.
Eligibility: Applicant must be U.S. citizen or permanent resident residing in Maine.
Basis for selection: Major/career interest in culinary arts; hotel/restaurant management or hospitality administration/management. Applicant must demonstrate financial need and high academic achievement.
Application requirements: Recommendations, essay, transcript.
Additional information: Applicant must be Maine resident who is high school senior or college undergraduate. Deadline in early April; visit Website for exact date.

Amount of award:	$500-$2,500
Number of awards:	9
Number of applicants:	35
Application deadline:	April 4
Notification begins:	January 1
Total amount awarded:	$8,200

Contact:
Maine Innkeepers Association
Scholarship Chairperson
304 US Route 1
Freeport, ME 04032
Phone: 207-865-6100
Fax: 207-865-6120
Web: www.maineinns.com

Maine Metal Products Association Education Fund

Maine Metal Products Association Scholarship

Type of award: Scholarship.
Intended use: For undergraduate study at postsecondary institution.
Eligibility: Applicant must be residing in Maine.
Basis for selection: Major/career interest in engineering; welding or manufacturing. Applicant must demonstrate financial need, high academic achievement, depth of character, leadership, seriousness of purpose and service orientation.
Application requirements: Recommendations, essay, transcript, proof of eligibility.
Additional information: Applicant must have career interest in Maine precision machining technology or manufacturing technology industry or related majors. Amount of award varies based on need and fund account. Visit Website for more information.

Amount of award:	$250-$1,000
Number of applicants:	25
Application deadline:	April 30
Notification begins:	January 1
Total amount awarded:	$8,000

Contact:
Marion Sprague
Manufacturers Association of Maine
386 Bridgton Road
Westbrook, ME 04092
Phone: 207-854-2153
Fax: 207-854-3865
Web: www.mainemfg.com

Maine Society of Professional Engineers

Maine Society of Professional Engineers Scholarship Program

Type of award: Scholarship.
Intended use: For freshman study at 4-year institution in United States. Designated institutions: ABET-accredited engineering schools.
Eligibility: Applicant must be high school senior. Applicant must be permanent resident residing in Maine.
Basis for selection: Major/career interest in engineering or engineering, civil.
Application requirements: Interview, recommendations, essay, transcript. SAT/ACT scores.
Additional information: Applicant must intend to earn a degree in engineering and to enter the practice of engineering after graduation. Must go to ABET-accredited school. Money awarded only after successful completion of first semester. Must be resident of Maine but awardees do not have to attend school in Maine. Application available on Website.

Amount of award:	$1,500-$2,500
Number of awards:	2
Number of applicants:	40
Application deadline:	March 1
Notification begins:	May 30
Total amount awarded:	$5,000

Contact:
Colin C. Hewett
Maine Society of Professional Engineers
P.O. Box 318
Winthrop, ME 04364
Phone: 207-449-0339
Web: www.mespe.org

Maine State Society of Washington, D.C.

Maine State Society of Washington, D.C. Foundation Scholarship Program

Type of award: Scholarship.
Intended use: For full-time sophomore, junior or senior study at accredited 4-year institution. Designated institutions: Maine institutions.
Eligibility: Applicant must be no older than 25. Applicant must be U.S. citizen.
Basis for selection: Applicant must demonstrate high academic achievement and seriousness of purpose.
Application requirements: Portfolio, essay, transcript, proof of eligibility.
Additional information: Applicant must have been born in Maine or have been legal resident of Maine for at least four years or have at least one parent who was born in Maine or who has been legal resident of Maine for at least four years. Applicant must currently attend college in Maine, with a minimum GPA of 3.0 for latest academic year. Requests for applications must include SASE. Visit Website for application.

Amount of award:	$1,000
Number of applicants:	79
Application deadline:	April 1
Notification begins:	May 15
Total amount awarded:	$12,500

Contact:
Maine State Society of Washington, D.C. Foundation Scholarship
4718 Columbia Road
Annandale, VA 22003
Phone: 703-256-4524
Fax: 703-941-4674
Web: www.mainestatesociety.org/MSSFoundation.htm

Marine Corps Scholarship Foundation

Marine Corps Scholarship

Type of award: Scholarship, renewable.
Intended use: For undergraduate study at accredited vocational, 2-year or 4-year institution in United States.
Eligibility: Applicant must be U.S. citizen. Applicant must be **dependent of active service person or veteran in the Marines.** Must be child of active Marine, Marine reservist, or Marine who has received honorable discharge.
Basis for selection: Applicant must demonstrate financial need and high academic achievement.
Application requirements: Essay, transcript, proof of eligibility. FAFSA, tax return.
Additional information: Minimum 2.0 GPA. Gross family income must not exceed $91,000. Applications available online.

Amount of award:	$1,500-$10,000
Number of awards:	1,900
Application deadline:	March 1
Total amount awarded:	$3,500,000

Contact:
Marine Corps Scholarship Foundation
909 N. Washington Street
Suite 400
Alexandria, VA 22314
Phone: 866-496-5462
Web: www.mcsf.org

Maryland Higher Education Commission Office of Student Financial Assistance

Charles W. Riley Fire and Emergency Medical Services Tuition Reimbursement Program

Type of award: Scholarship, renewable.
Intended use: For undergraduate study at postsecondary institution.

Eligibility: Applicant must be U.S. citizen or permanent resident residing in Maryland.
Basis for selection: Major/career interest in fire science/technology or medical emergency. Applicant must demonstrate high academic achievement.
Application requirements: Transcript, proof of eligibility.
Additional information: Applicant must be active career/volunteer firefighter or ambulance/rescue squad member serving the Maryland community while taking courses, and must agree to continue to serve for one year after completing courses. Must maintain satisfactory academic progress and remain enrolled in eligible program to renew award. New applicants must apply through Website.

Amount of award:	Full tuition
Application deadline:	July 1

Contact:
Maryland Higher Ed. Commission Office of Student Financial Assistance
Reimbursement of Firefighters
6 North Liberty Street, Ground Suite
Annapolis, MD 21201
Phone: 800-974-0203
Web: mdcaps.mhec.state.md.us

Howard P. Rawlings Guaranteed Access Grant

Type of award: Scholarship, renewable.
Intended use: For full-time undergraduate study at accredited postsecondary institution.
Eligibility: Applicant must be high school senior. Applicant must be U.S. citizen or permanent resident residing in Maryland.
Basis for selection: Applicant must demonstrate financial need and high academic achievement.
Application requirements: Proof of eligibility. FAFSA.
Additional information: Applicant must be high school senior who has completed college preparatory program or has graduated prior to the academic year and provide written documentation explaining why he or she was unable to attend college within one year of graduation from high school. Minimum 2.5 GPA. Must meet Guaranteed Access Family Grant income requirements; award equals 100% of student's financial need. New applicants must apply through Website.

Amount of award:	$400-$15,500
Application deadline:	March 1

Contact:
Maryland Higher Ed. Commission Office of Student Financial Assistance
Guaranteed Access Grant
6 North Liberty Street, Ground Suite
Annapolis, MD 21201
Phone: 800-974-0203
Fax: 410-260-3200
Web: mdcaps.mhec.state.md.us

Maryland Delegate Scholarship

Type of award: Scholarship, renewable.
Intended use: For undergraduate or graduate study at vocational, 2-year, 4-year or graduate institution.
Eligibility: Applicant must be high school senior. Applicant must be U.S. citizen or permanent resident residing in Maryland.
Application requirements: Proof of eligibility, nomination by local state delegate. FAFSA.
Additional information: Applicant's parents (if applicant is dependent) must be Maryland residents. Rolling application deadline. Certain vocational programs eligible. Out-of-state institutions eligible only if major not offered in Maryland. Each state delegate makes awards to students. If OSFA makes awards for delegates, applicant must demonstrate financial need. Non-U.S. citizens living in Maryland may be eligible. Applicants must reapply yearly for renewal and maintain satisfactory academic progress.

Amount of award:	$200-$19,000
Application deadline:	March 1
Notification begins:	July 1

Contact:
Maryland Higher Ed. Commission Office of Student Financial Assistance
Delegate Scholarship
6 North Liberty Street, Ground Suite
Annapolis, MD 21201
Phone: 800-974-0203
Web: www.mhec.state.md.us/financialaid

Maryland Educational Assistance Grant

Type of award: Scholarship, renewable.
Intended use: For full-time undergraduate study at 2-year or 4-year institution. Designated institutions: Maryland institutions.
Eligibility: Applicant must be U.S. citizen or permanent resident residing in Maryland.
Basis for selection: Applicant must demonstrate financial need.
Application requirements: Proof of eligibility.
Additional information: Applicant's parents (if applicant is dependent) must be Maryland residents. Applicants are ranked by Expected Family Contribution (EFC); those with lowest EFC are awarded first. Award may be renewed if eligibility maintained and FAFSA is submitted by March 1 each year. Funds may not be available to award all eligible students each year.

Amount of award:	$400-$3,000
Application deadline:	March 1
Notification begins:	April 15

Contact:
Maryland Higher Ed. Commission Office of Student Financial Assistance
Educational Assistance Grant
6 North Liberty Street, Ground Suite
Annapolis, MD 21201
Phone: 800-974-0203
Web: www.mhec.state.md.us/financialaid

Maryland Edward T. Conroy Memorial Scholarship Program

Type of award: Scholarship, renewable.
Intended use: For undergraduate or graduate study at postsecondary institution. Designated institutions: Eligible Maryland institutions.
Eligibility: Applicant must be U.S. citizen residing in Maryland. Applicant must be veteran or disabled while on active duty; or dependent of veteran, disabled veteran or deceased veteran; or spouse of disabled veteran, deceased veteran or POW/MIA who served in the Army during Vietnam. If applicant is dependent of disabled US Armed Forces veteran, the veteran must be declared 100% disabled as direct result of military service. Applicant may also be dependent or surviving spouse of victim of September 11, 2001 attacks. Also open to dependent or surviving spouse (not remarried) of Maryland

resident who was public safety employee or volunteer who died or was 100% disabled in the line of duty.
Additional information: Must be Maryland resident unless spouse or child of Maryland state or local public safety employee killed in line of duty. Parent, veteran, POW, public safety employee, or volunteer specified above must have been resident of Maryland at time of death or when declared disabled. Amount of award may be equal to tuition and fees, but may not exceed $9,000. Visit Website for more information and application.

Amount of award: $9,000
Application deadline: July 15

Contact:
Contact financial aid office at individual institution
Web: www.mhec.state.md.us/financialaid

Maryland Jack F. Tolbert Memorial Grant

Type of award: Scholarship, renewable.
Intended use: For full-time undergraduate study at vocational institution. Designated institutions: Private career schools in Maryland.
Eligibility: Applicant must be U.S. citizen or permanent resident residing in Maryland.
Basis for selection: Applicant must demonstrate financial need.
Application requirements: Nomination by financial aid counselor at private career school. FAFSA.
Additional information: Applicant's parents (if applicant is dependent) must be Maryland residents. Applicant must enroll for minimum of 18 hours per week. Award amount varies; maximum is $500.

Amount of award: $500
Application deadline: March 1

Contact:
Contact financial aid office at individual institutions.
Phone: 800-974-0203
Web: www.mhec.state.md.us/financialaid

Maryland Part-Time Grant Program

Type of award: Scholarship, renewable.
Intended use: For half-time undergraduate study at accredited postsecondary institution. Designated institutions: Accredited institutions in Maryland.
Eligibility: Applicant must be enrolled in high school. Applicant must be residing in Maryland.
Basis for selection: Applicant must demonstrate financial need.
Application requirements: FAFSA.
Additional information: Applicant's parents (if applicant is dependent) must be Maryland residents. Must be taking 6 to 11 semester credit hours. Apply through financial aid office of Maryland institution. Applicants simultaneously enrolled in secondary school and an institution of higher education are also eligible. To renew award, student must maintain satisfactory academic progress and submit FAFSA by March 1 each year; may receive award up to eight years.

Amount of award: $200-$2,000
Application deadline: March 1

Contact:
Maryland Higher Ed. Commission Office of Student Financial Assistance
Part-Time Grant Program
6 North Liberty Street, Ground Suite
Annapolis, MD 21201
Phone: 800-974-0203
Web: www.mhec.state.md.us/financialaid

Maryland Senatorial Scholarship

Type of award: Scholarship, renewable.
Intended use: For undergraduate or graduate study at postsecondary institution. Designated institutions: Maryland colleges and universities.
Eligibility: Applicant must be residing in Maryland.
Basis for selection: Applicant must demonstrate financial need and high academic achievement.
Application requirements: Nomination by local state senator. FAFSA.
Additional information: Applicant and parents (if applicant is dependent) must be Maryland residents. SAT or ACT required for freshmen at four-year institutions unless applicant graduated from high school five years prior to aid application or has earned 24 college credit hours. Out-of-state institutions eligible only if major not offered in Maryland. Contact state senator's office for more information. Award automatically renewed if satisfactory academic progress is maintained. Full-time students may be awarded four years total, part-time students eight years total.

Amount of award: $400-$9,700
Application deadline: March 1

Contact:
Maryland Higher Ed. Commission Office of Student Financial Assistance
Senatorial Scholarship Program
6 North Liberty Street, Ground Suite
Annapolis, MD 21201
Phone: 800-974-0203
Web: www.mhec.state.md.us/financialaid

Maryland Tuition Reduction for Non-Resident Nursing Students

Type of award: Scholarship, renewable.
Intended use: For undergraduate study at postsecondary institution.
Eligibility: Applicant must be U.S. citizen.
Basis for selection: Major/career interest in nursing.
Additional information: Must be resident of state other than Maryland and accepted into Maryland degree-granting nursing program at two- or four-year public institution. Awardees fulfill service obligation in Maryland following graduation; two years for two-year program, four years for four-year program. Service must begin within six months of graduation. Award amount varies; college may reduce tuition so that non-residents pay tuition charged to Maryland resident. New applicants must apply through Website.

Number of applicants: 51

Contact:
Maryland Higher Ed. Commission Office of Student Financial Assistance
Out-of-State Nursing Program
6 North Liberty Street, Ground Suite
Annapolis, MD 21201
Phone: 800-974-0203
Web: mdcaps.mhec.state.md.us

Maryland Tuition Waiver for Foster Care Recipients

Type of award: Scholarship, renewable.
Intended use: For undergraduate study at 2-year or 4-year institution. Designated institutions: Eligible Maryland public institutions.
Eligibility: Applicant must be no older than 25. Applicant must be residing in Maryland.
Application requirements: FAFSA.
Additional information: Applicant must have resided in Maryland foster care home at time of high school graduation or completion of GED. Also open to applicants who resided in Maryland foster care home on 14th birthday and were subsequently adopted. The Department of Human Resources must confirm applicant's eligibility. Applicant must be enrolled as a degree-seeking student before age of 21. Award renewal possible if satisfactory academic progress and enrollment in eligible program maintained.

Amount of award:	Full tuition
Application deadline:	March 1

Contact:
Maryland Higher Ed. Commission Office of Student Financial Assistance
6 North Liberty Street, Ground Suite
Annapolis, MD 21201
Phone: 800-974-0203
Web: www.mhec.state.md.us/financialaid

Massachusetts Board of Higher Education

Adopted Child Tuition Waiver and Fee Assistance Program

Type of award: Scholarship.
Intended use: For undergraduate, post-bachelor's certificate or non-degree study at accredited vocational, 2-year or 4-year institution in United States. Designated institutions: Massachusetts public institutions.
Eligibility: Applicant must be no older than 24. Applicant must be U.S. citizen or permanent resident.
Application requirements: FAFSA.
Additional information: Must be in custody of Department of Children and Families and have been adopted by Massachusetts resident or eligible Massachusetts state employee.

Amount of award:	Full tuition

Contact:
Office of Student Financial Assistance
454 Broadway, Suite 200
Revere, MA 02151
Phone: 617-391-6070
Fax: 617-727-0667
Web: www.osfa.mass.edu

Agnes M. Lindsey Scholarship

Type of award: Scholarship.
Intended use: For full-time undergraduate study at 2-year or 4-year institution in United States. Designated institutions: Public institutions of higher education in Massachusetts.
Eligibility: Applicant must be U.S. citizen or permanent resident residing in Massachusetts.
Basis for selection: Applicant must demonstrate financial need.
Application requirements: FAFSA.
Additional information: Must be resident of rural Massachusetts.
Contact:
Office of Student Financial Assistance
454 Broadway, Suite 200
Revere, MA 02151
Phone: 617-391-6070
Fax: 617-727-0667
Web: www.osfa.mass.edu

Categorical Tuition Waiver

Type of award: Scholarship.
Intended use: For undergraduate study at accredited 2-year or 4-year institution in United States. Designated institutions: Massachusetts public institutions.
Eligibility: Applicant must be U.S. citizen or permanent resident residing in Massachusetts.
Additional information: Applicants must be in one of the following categories: military veteran, Native American, senior citizen, active member of armed forces, or clients of Massachusetts Rehabilitation Commission or Commission for the Blind.

Amount of award:	Full tuition

Contact:
Massachusetts Board of Higher Education
Office of Student Financial Assistance
454 Broadway, Suite 200
Revere, MA 02151
Phone: 617-391-6070
Fax: 617-727-0667
Web: www.osfa.mass.edu

DCF Foster Child Tuition Waiver and Fee Assistance Program

Type of award: Scholarship, renewable.
Intended use: For undergraduate or graduate study at postsecondary institution in United States.
Eligibility: Applicant must be no older than 24. Applicant must be U.S. citizen or permanent resident residing in Massachusetts.
Basis for selection: Applicant must demonstrate financial need.
Application requirements: FAFSA.
Additional information: Must be foster child who was placed in custody through a Care and Protection Petition. Must be child whose guardianship was sponsored by the Department of Children and Families through age 18. Must have been in custody for at least six months before age 18.

Amount of award:	Full tuition

Contact:
Office of Student Financial Assistance
454 Broadway, Suite 200
Revere, MA 02151
Phone: 617-391-6070
Fax: 617-727-0667
Web: www.osfa.mass.edu

Foster Child Grant Program

Type of award: Scholarship.
Intended use: For full-time undergraduate study at accredited 4-year institution in United States.

Eligibility: Applicant must be no older than 24. Applicant must be U.S. citizen or permanent resident residing in Massachusetts.
Application requirements: FAFSA.
Additional information: Must be Massachusetts resident who has been placed in custody of Department of Children and Families through a Care and Protection Petition.

Amount of award: $6,000

Contact:
Office of Student Financial Assistance
454 Broadway, Suite 200
Revere, MA 02151
Phone: 617-391-6070
Fax: 617-727-0667
Web: www.osfa.mass.edu

Gear Up Scholarship Program

Type of award: Scholarship.
Intended use: For undergraduate study at accredited 2-year or 4-year institution in United States. Designated institutions: Massachusetts public institutions.
Eligibility: Applicant must be no older than 21. Applicant must be U.S. citizen or permanent resident residing in Massachusetts.
Application requirements: FAFSA.
Additional information: Must be graduate of Massachusetts public high school. Must have participated in Early Intervention component of GEAR UP Massachusetts.

Contact:
Office of Student Financial Assistance
454 Broadway, Suite 200
Revere, MA 02151
Phone: 617-391-6070
Fax: 617-727-0667
Web: www.osfa.mass.edu

High Technology Scholar/Intern Tuition Waiver Program

Type of award: Scholarship.
Intended use: For undergraduate study at accredited 2-year or 4-year institution in United States. Designated institutions: Massachusetts public institutions.
Eligibility: Applicant must be U.S. citizen or permanent resident residing in Massachusetts.
Basis for selection: Major/career interest in engineering; technology or computer/information sciences.
Additional information: Student must be deemed eligible by participating company. Program encourages institutions to seek funding from business and industry for computer and information science, technology, and engineering scholarships that the Commonwealth will match with full waiver of student's annual tuition charges.

Amount of award: Full tuition

Contact:
Office of Student Financial Assistance
454 Broadway, Suite 200
Revere, MA 02151
Phone: 617-391-6070
Fax: 617-727-0667
Web: www.osfa.mass.edu

Incentive Program for Aspiring Teachers

Type of award: Scholarship.
Intended use: For junior or senior study at accredited 2-year or 4-year institution in United States. Designated institutions: Massachusetts public institutions.
Eligibility: Applicant must be U.S. citizen or permanent resident residing in Massachusetts.
Basis for selection: Major/career interest in education.
Additional information: Minimum 3.0 GPA. Must commit to teaching for two years in Massachusetts. If work commitment is not completed, waiver reverts to loan.

Amount of award: Full tuition

Contact:
Office of Student Financial Assistance
454 Broadway, Suite 200
Revere, MA 02151
Phone: 617-391-6070
Fax: 617-727-0667
Web: www.osfa.mass.edu

John and Abigail Adams Scholarship

Type of award: Scholarship.
Intended use: For full-time undergraduate study at 4-year institution in United States. Designated institutions: Massachusetts public colleges and universities.
Eligibility: Applicant must be U.S. citizen or permanent resident residing in Massachusetts.
Basis for selection: Applicant must demonstrate financial need and high academic achievement.
Application requirements: FAFSA.
Additional information: Students who are eligible will be notified in fall of senior year of high school. Must score in the Advanced Category in either the mathematics or language arts section of the grade 10 MCAS test and score in the proficient or advanced category on second subject. Must have MCAS score that ranks in top twenty-five percent of school district.

Contact:
Office of Student Financial Assistance
454 Broadway, Suite 200
Revere, MA 02151
Phone: 617-391-6070
Fax: 617-727-0667
Web: www.osfa.mass.edu

Joint Admissions Tuition Advantage Waiver Program

Type of award: Scholarship.
Intended use: For undergraduate study in United States. Designated institutions: Massachusetts institutions.
Additional information: Program provides tuition waiver equal to 33 percent of resident tuition at state college or participating university.

Contact:
Office of Student Financial Assistance
454 Broadway, Suite 200
Revere, MA 02151
Phone: 617-391-6070
Fax: 617-727-0667
Web: www.osfa.mass.edu

Scholarships

Massachusetts Cash Grant Program

Type of award: Scholarship.
Intended use: For undergraduate study at 2-year or 4-year institution in United States.
Eligibility: Applicant must be U.S. citizen or permanent resident residing in Massachusetts.
Basis for selection: Applicant must demonstrate financial need.
Additional information: Must be legal resident of Massachusetts for at least one year prior to application date. Those holding baccalaureate or professional degrees not eligible.
Contact:
Office of Student Financial Assistance
454 Broadway, Suite 200
Revere, MA 02151
Phone: 617-391-6070
Fax: 617-727-0667
Web: www.osfa.mass.edu

Massachusetts Christian A. Herter Memorial Scholarship Program

Type of award: Scholarship, renewable.
Intended use: For full-time undergraduate study at accredited vocational, 2-year or 4-year institution. Designated institutions: Massachusetts institutions.
Eligibility: Applicant must be high school sophomore or junior. Applicant must be U.S. citizen or permanent resident residing in Massachusetts.
Basis for selection: Applicant must demonstrate financial need, high academic achievement, depth of character and seriousness of purpose.
Application requirements: Interview, recommendations, essay, transcript, nomination by high school principal, counselor, teacher, or social service agency.
Additional information: Program provides grant assistance for students from low income or disadvantaged backgrounds who have had to overcome adverse circumstances. Selection made during sophomore and junior years in high school. Award amount is up to half of student's demonstrated financial need. Minimum 2.5 GPA.

Amount of award:	$15,000
Number of awards:	25
Number of applicants:	200
Application deadline:	February 1
Total amount awarded:	$900,000

Contact:
Office of Student Financial Assistance
Massachusetts Board of Higher Education
454 Broadway, Suite 200
Revere, MA 02151
Phone: 617-391-6070
Fax: 617-727-0667
Web: www.osfa.mass.edu

Massachusetts Early Childhood Educators Scholarship

Type of award: Scholarship.
Intended use: For undergraduate study at 4-year institution in United States. Designated institutions: Massachusetts public colleges and universities.
Eligibility: Applicant must be U.S. citizen or permanent resident residing in Massachusetts.
Basis for selection: Major/career interest in education, early childhood.
Additional information: Must be employed for at least one year as an educator or provider in early education and care program. Must continue employment in this field while pursuing degree. Those holding bachelor's degrees are ineligible.

Amount of award:	$4,500-$9,000

Contact:
Office of Student Financial Assistance
454 Broadway, Suite 200
Revere, MA 02151
Phone: 617-391-6070
Fax: 617-727-0667
Web: www.osfa.mass.edu

Massachusetts Educational Rewards Grant Program

Type of award: Scholarship.
Intended use: For undergraduate study at postsecondary institution in United States. Designated institutions: Massachusetts institutions offering post-secondary degrees or certificates.
Eligibility: Applicant must be U.S. citizen or permanent resident residing in Massachusetts.
Basis for selection: Applicant must demonstrate financial need.
Application requirements: FAFSA.
Additional information: Assistance for dislocated or incumbent workers whose income is at or below 200 percent of the federal poverty level. Up to thirty percent of the grant may be used for living expenses. Must be used for study in high-demand occupational fields.
Contact:
Office of Student Financial Assistance
454 Broadway, Suite 200
Revere, MA 02151
Phone: 617-391-6070
Fax: 617-727-0667
Web: www.osfa.mass.edu

Massachusetts Gilbert Matching Student Grant

Type of award: Scholarship, renewable.
Intended use: For full-time undergraduate study at accredited 2-year or 4-year institution. Designated institutions: Independent colleges or hospital schools of nursing in Massachusetts.
Eligibility: Applicant must be U.S. citizen or permanent resident residing in Massachusetts.
Basis for selection: Major/career interest in nursing. Applicant must demonstrate financial need.
Additional information: Deadline depends on institution. Applicant must be dependent of parent who has been a Massachusetts resident for at least 12 months prior to start of academic year. Must not have received prior bachelor's degree.

Amount of award:	$200-$2,500

Contact:
Apply to college financial aid office.
Phone: 617-391-6070
Fax: 617-727-0667
Web: www.osfa.mass.edu

Massachusetts High Demand Scholarship Program

Type of award: Scholarship.
Intended use: For undergraduate study at accredited 2-year or 4-year institution in United States. Designated institutions: Massachusetts public institutions.
Eligibility: Applicant must be U.S. citizen.
Application requirements: FAFSA.
Additional information: Must be enrolled in high need field.

Amount of award:	$2,000-$6,500
Application deadline:	January 15

Contact:
Office of Student Financial Assistance
454 Broadway, Suite 200
Revere, MA 02151
Phone: 617-391-6070
Fax: 617-727-0667
Web: www.osfa.mass.edu

Massachusetts MASSgrant Program

Type of award: Scholarship, renewable.
Intended use: For full-time undergraduate study at accredited vocational, 2-year or 4-year institution. Designated institutions: Schools in Massachusetts.
Eligibility: Applicant must be U.S. citizen or permanent resident or Massachusetts.
Basis for selection: Applicant must demonstrate financial need.
Application requirements: FAFSA.
Additional information: Applicant must have expected family contribution of $4,995 or less and be eligible for Title IV financial aid. Applicant must maintain satisfactory academic progress. Must not have received prior bachelor's degree. Award amount varies.

Number of awards:	28,553
Number of applicants:	250,000
Application deadline:	May 1
Notification begins:	June 15
Total amount awarded:	$24,000,000

Contact:
Office of Student Financial Assistance
Massachusetts Board of Higher Education
454 Broadway, Suite 200
Revere, MA 02151
Phone: 617-391-6070
Fax: 617-727-0667
Web: www.osfa.mass.edu

Massachusetts Math and Science Teachers Scholarship

Type of award: Scholarship.
Intended use: For undergraduate or graduate study at accredited 4-year or graduate institution in United States. Designated institutions: Public colleges or universities in Massachusetts that have approved educator preparation programs.
Eligibility: Applicant must be U.S. citizen or permanent resident residing in Massachusetts.
Basis for selection: Major/career interest in education; mathematics or science, general.
Application requirements: FAFSA.
Additional information: Must be employed as educator in Massachusetts public school or school that has publicly-funded special education. Must be teaching math or science. Must sign agreement to continue teaching in Massachusetts public school or repay funds. Teachers in high-need districts are eligible to receive one-hundred percent of costs.
Contact:
Office of Student Financial Assistance
454 Broadway, Suite 200
Revere, MA 02151
Phone: 617-391-6070
Fax: 617-727-0667
Web: www.osfa.mass.edu

Massachusetts Paraprofessional Teacher Preparation Grant Program

Type of award: Scholarship.
Intended use: For undergraduate study at 4-year institution in United States. Designated institutions: Massachusetts public colleges.
Eligibility: Applicant must be U.S. citizen or permanent resident residing in Massachusetts.
Basis for selection: Applicant must demonstrate financial need.
Application requirements: FAFSA.
Additional information: Must enroll in an undergraduate degree program leading to teacher certification in a Massachusetts Public College. Must be employed for at least two years as a paraprofessional in a Massachusetts public school, or if employed less than two years, student must study high need disciplines: math, science, special education, foreign language, and bilingual education. Those holding bachelor degrees not eligible.

Amount of award:	$4,000-$7,500

Contact:
Office of Student Financial Assistance
454 Broadway, Suite 200
Revere, MA 02151
Phone: 617-391-6070
Fax: 617-727-0667
Web: www.osfa.mass.edu

Massachusetts Part-Time Grant Program

Type of award: Scholarship.
Intended use: For half-time undergraduate study at 2-year or 4-year institution in United States. Designated institutions: Massachusetts colleges and universities.
Eligibility: Applicant must be U.S. citizen residing in Massachusetts.
Basis for selection: Applicant must demonstrate financial need.
Application requirements: FAFSA.
Additional information: Must be legal resident of Massachusetts for at least one year prior to application date. Those holding baccalaureate or professional degrees not eligible. Must be eligible for Title IV aid.
Contact:
Office of Student Financial Assistance
454 Broadway, Suite 200
Revere, MA 02151
Phone: 617-391-6070
Fax: 617-727-0667
Web: www.osfa.mass.edu

Massachusetts Public Service Grant Program

Type of award: Scholarship, renewable.
Intended use: For full-time undergraduate study at accredited 2-year or 4-year institution. Designated institutions: Massachusetts colleges and universities.
Eligibility: Applicant must be U.S. citizen or permanent resident residing in Massachusetts.
Application requirements: Proof of eligibility. FAFSA.
Additional information: Awards available for children or widowed spouse of deceased firefighters, police officers, or corrections officers who died from injuries received performing his or her duties. Children of veterans killed in action or Vietnam POWs also eligible. Award in form of entitlement grant. Applicant must be resident of Massachusetts at least one year prior to start of school. For recipients attending Massachusetts public college or university, award shall equal cost of tuition. Must not have received a prior bachelor's degree. Recipients attending Massachusetts independent college or university, award will be equivalent to highest tuition amount paid to public institution.

Amount of award:	Full tuition
Application deadline:	May 1
Notification begins:	June 1
Total amount awarded:	$22,665

Contact:
Office of Student Financial Assistance
Massachusetts Board of Higher Education
454 Broadway, Suite 200
Revere, MA 02151
Phone: 617-391-6070
Fax: 617-727-0667
Web: www.osfa.mass.edu

Paul Tsongas Scholarship Program

Type of award: Scholarship.
Intended use: For undergraduate study at postsecondary institution. Designated institutions: Massachusetts state colleges.
Eligibility: Applicant must be U.S. citizen or permanent resident residing in Massachusetts.
Basis for selection: Applicant must demonstrate financial need and high academic achievement.
Application requirements: SAT/ACT scores.
Additional information: Minimum 3.75 GPA. Tuition waiver for full tuition and related fees. For renewal, must maintain 3.3 GPA.

Amount of award:	Full tuition
Number of awards:	45

Contact:
Contact state college financial aid office.
Phone: 617-391-6070
Fax: 617-727-0667
Web: www.osfa.mass.edu

September 11, 2001 Tragedy Tuition Waiver Program

Type of award: Scholarship.
Intended use: For undergraduate study at accredited 2-year or 4-year institution in United States. Designated institutions: Massachusetts public institutions.
Eligibility: Applicant must be U.S. citizen residing in Massachusetts.
Application requirements: Student's birth certificate, official documentation of death related to September 11, 2001.
Additional information: Must be Massachusetts resident who is spouse or dependent of victim of events of September 11, 2001.

Amount of award:	Full tuition

Contact:
Office of Student Financial Assistance
454 Broadway, Suite 200
Revere, MA 02151
Phone: 617-391-6070
Fax: 617-727-0667
Web: www.osfa.mass.edu

Stanley Z. Koplik Certificate of Mastery Tuition Waiver Program

Type of award: Scholarship.
Intended use: For freshman study at accredited 2-year or 4-year institution in United States. Designated institutions: Massachusetts public institutions.
Eligibility: Applicant must be enrolled in high school. Applicant must be U.S. citizen residing in Massachusetts.
Additional information: Must be enrolled in Massachusetts public high school. Must score "Advanced" on at least one grade 10 MCAS test subject and score "Proficient" on remaining sections. Must fulfill one of the following criteria: two AP exams with a score of 3 or higher; 2 SAT II exams (minimum score dependent on subject area); SAT II exam and ACT I exam; SAT II exam and one other achievement; AP exam and one other achievement.

Amount of award:	Full tuition

Contact:
Office of Student Financial Assistance
454 Broadway, Suite 200
Revere, MA 02151
Phone: 617-391-6070
Fax: 617-727-0667
Web: www.osfa.mass.edu

Valedictorial Tuition Waiver Program

Type of award: Scholarship.
Intended use: For undergraduate study at accredited 2-year or 4-year institution in United States. Designated institutions: Massachusetts public institutions.
Eligibility: Applicant must be U.S. citizen or permanent resident residing in Massachusetts.
Additional information: Must be high school valedictorian.

Amount of award:	Full tuition

Contact:
Office of Student Financial Assistance
454 Broadway, Suite 200
Revere, MA 02151
Phone: 617-391-6070
Fax: 617-727-0667
Web: www.osfa.mass.edu

McKee Scholars

John McKee Scholarship

Type of award: Scholarship, renewable.
Intended use: For undergraduate study at vocational or 4-year institution.
Eligibility: Applicant must be male, no older than 19, enrolled in high school. Applicant must be U.S. citizen residing in Pennsylvania.
Basis for selection: Applicant must demonstrate financial need and high academic achievement.
Application requirements: Interview, transcript. SAT/ACT scores, SAR, application, evaluation.
Additional information: For male applicants whose fathers are dead, missing, permanently absent, or dysfunctional. Applicant must be a resident of Philadelphia, Bucks, Chester, Montgomery or Delaware counties. Award allotment after initial award year is based on upheld academic standards. Application available on Website.

Amount of award:	$1,000-$7,500
Number of awards:	70
Number of applicants:	56
Application deadline:	March 1
Notification begins:	May 1
Total amount awarded:	$225,250

Contact:
John McKee Scholarship Committee
Attn: Robert J. Stern, Executive Secretary
P.O. Box 144
Merion Station, PA 19066
Phone: 484-323-1348
Fax: 610-640-1965
Web: www.mckeescholars.org

Mendez Scholarships Non-Profit

Georgina S. Mendez Pharmacology Scholarship

Type of award: Scholarship.
Intended use: For undergraduate, graduate or postgraduate study at accredited postsecondary institution in United States.
Basis for selection: Major/career interest in pharmacy/pharmaceutics/pharmacology.
Application requirements: Recommendations, essay, transcript.
Additional information: Visit Website for application.

Amount of award:	$250-$1,000
Number of awards:	4
Number of applicants:	20
Total amount awarded:	$500

Contact:
Mendez Scholarships Non-Profit
40 Wai'Ohuli Street, #C
Kihei, HI 96753
Web: www.mendezscholars.org

John L. Mendez Business Scholarship

Type of award: Scholarship.
Intended use: For undergraduate, graduate or postgraduate study at accredited postsecondary institution in United States.
Basis for selection: Major/career interest in business.
Application requirements: Recommendations, essay, transcript.
Additional information: Visit Website for application.

Amount of award:	$250-$1,000
Number of awards:	4
Number of applicants:	20
Total amount awarded:	$500

Contact:
Mendez Scholarships Non-Profit
40 Wai'Ohuli Street, #C
Kihei, HI 96753
Web: www.mendezscholars.org

Julio C. Mendez Engineering Scholarship

Type of award: Scholarship.
Intended use: For undergraduate, graduate or postgraduate study at accredited postsecondary institution in United States.
Basis for selection: Major/career interest in engineering.
Application requirements: Recommendations, essay, transcript.
Additional information: Visit Website for application.

Amount of award:	$250-$1,000
Number of awards:	4
Number of applicants:	20
Total amount awarded:	$500

Contact:
Mendez Scholarships Non-Profit
40 Wai'Ohuli Street, #C
Kihei, HI 96753
Web: www.mendezscholars.org

Menominee Indian Tribe of Wisconsin

Menominee Adult Vocational Training Grant

Type of award: Scholarship, renewable.
Intended use: For undergraduate or non-degree study at accredited vocational, 2-year or 4-year institution in United States.
Eligibility: Applicant must be American Indian. Applicant must be enrolled member of Menominee Indian tribe of Wisconsin.
Basis for selection: Applicant must demonstrate financial need.
Application requirements: FAFSA and Menominee Tribal Grant Application.
Additional information: Award also applicable toward associate's degree. Must apply through college financial aid office.

Amount of award:	$550-$2,200
Number of applicants:	100
Application deadline:	October 30, March 1

Contact:
Menominee Indian Tribe of Wisconsin
P.O. Box 910
Keshena, WI 54135
Phone: 715-799-5118 or 715-799-5110
Fax: 715-799-5102
Web: www.menominee-nsn.gov

Menominee Higher Education Grant

Type of award: Scholarship, renewable.
Intended use: For undergraduate study at accredited 2-year or 4-year institution in United States.
Eligibility: Applicant must be American Indian. Applicant must be enrolled member of Menominee Indian tribe.
Basis for selection: Applicant must demonstrate financial need.
Application requirements: FAFSA and Menominee Tribal Grant Application.
Additional information: Applications and deadline dates available through Tribal Education office.

Amount of award:	$550-$2,200
Number of applicants:	200
Application deadline:	October 30, March 1

Contact:
Menominee Indian Tribe of Wisconsin
P.O. Box 910
Keshena, WI 54135
Phone: 715-799-5118 or 715-799-5110
Fax: 715-799-5102
Web: www.menominee-nsn.gov

The Merchants Exchange

The Merchants Exchange Scholarship Fund

Type of award: Scholarship, renewable.
Intended use: For junior, senior or graduate study at accredited postsecondary institution.
Basis for selection: Major/career interest in international relations. Applicant must demonstrate high academic achievement and depth of character.
Application requirements: Recommendations, transcript.
Additional information: Scholarship is for students studying maritime affairs/international trade. Minimum 2.5 GPA. Financial need may be considered if all other factors are equal. Visit Website for application.

Amount of award:	$1,500
Number of awards:	7
Number of applicants:	5
Application deadline:	May 31

Contact:
The Merchants Exchange
200 SW Market, Suite 190
Portland, OR 97201
Phone: 503-220-2092
Web: www.pdxmex.com

Michael and Susan Dell Foundation

Dell Scholars Program

Type of award: Scholarship.
Intended use: For freshman study at accredited 2-year or 4-year institution in United States.
Eligibility: Applicant must be high school senior. Applicant must be U.S. citizen or permanent resident.
Basis for selection: Applicant must demonstrate financial need, high academic achievement, depth of character and seriousness of purpose.
Application requirements: Recommendations, essay, transcript. Student Aid Report from FAFSA.
Additional information: Dell Scholars are students who demonstrate desire and ability to overcome barriers and to achieve their goals. Must have overcome obstacles to pursue education. Must have been participating in a Michael & Susan Dell Foundation approved college readiness program for a minimum of two years. Must be currently graduating from an accredited high school. Minimum 2.4 GPA. Must be entering into a bachelor's degree program in the fall directly after graduating high school. Recipients receive $20,000 over six years. Visit Website for more information.

Amount of award:	$5,000
Number of awards:	300
Application deadline:	January 15
Notification begins:	April 10

Contact:
Michael and Susan Dell Foundation
Phone: 800-294-2039
Web: www.dellscholars.org

Michigan Higher Education Assistance Authority

Children of Veterans Tuition Grant

Type of award: Scholarship, renewable.
Intended use: For undergraduate study at postsecondary institution. Designated institutions: Michigan institutions.
Eligibility: Applicant must be at least 16, no older than 25. Applicant must be U.S. citizen or permanent resident residing in Michigan. Applicant must be dependent of disabled veteran or deceased veteran.
Application requirements: Birth certificate, veteran's DD 214 certificate and casualty report.
Additional information: Veteran must have been killed in action, been listed as MIA, or been permanently disabled due to service-related injuries. Veteran must have been a Michigan resident before entering military service or must have established residency in Michigan after entering military service.

Amount of award:	$1,400-$2,800
Number of awards:	410
Total amount awarded:	$996,000

Contact:
Michigan Higher Education Assistance Authority
Office of Scholarships and Grants
P.O. Box 30462
Lansing, MI 48909-7962
Phone: 888-447-2687
Fax: 517-241-5835
Web: www.michigan.gov/osg

Michigan Competitive Scholarship

Type of award: Scholarship, renewable.
Intended use: For undergraduate study at postsecondary institution. Designated institutions: Michigan institutions.
Eligibility: Applicant must be U.S. citizen or permanent resident residing in Michigan.
Basis for selection: Applicant must demonstrate financial need and high academic achievement.
Application requirements: FAFSA and qualifying ACT score.

Amount of award:	$575-$1,512
Number of awards:	27,885
Application deadline:	March 1
Total amount awarded:	$37,071,451

Contact:
Michigan Higher Education Assistance Authority
Office of Scholarships and Grants
P.O. Box 30462
Lansing, MI 48909-7962
Phone: 888-447-2687
Fax: 517-241-5835
Web: www.michigan.gov/osg

Michigan Tuition Grant

Type of award: Scholarship, renewable.
Intended use: For undergraduate, master's or doctoral study at 2-year, 4-year or graduate institution. Designated institutions: Michigan institutions.
Eligibility: Applicant must be U.S. citizen or permanent resident residing in Michigan.
Basis for selection: Applicant must demonstrate financial need.
Application requirements: FAFSA.
Additional information: Theology or religious education students ineligible.

Number of awards:	22,000
Application deadline:	July 1
Total amount awarded:	$30,500,000

Contact:
Michigan Higher Education Assistance Authority
Office of Scholarships and Grants
P.O. Box 30462
Lansing, MI 48909-7962
Phone: 888-447-2687
Fax: 517-241-5835
Web: www.michigan.gov/osg

Michigan Tuition Incentive Program

Type of award: Scholarship, renewable.
Intended use: For undergraduate study at postsecondary institution. Designated institutions: Michigan institutions.
Eligibility: Applicant must be U.S. citizen or permanent resident residing in Michigan.
Basis for selection: Applicant must demonstrate financial need.
Application requirements: Proof of eligibility.
Additional information: Eligibility determined by Medicaid status. Provides tuition assistance for up to 24 semesters or 36 term credits for first two years. Up to $2,000 total assistance for third and fourth years.

Number of awards:	16,000
Total amount awarded:	$34,600,000

Contact:
Michigan Higher Education Assistance Authority
Office of Scholarships and Grants
P.O. Box 30462
Lansing, MI 48909-7962
Phone: 888-447-2687
Fax: 517-241-5835
Web: www.michigan.gov/osg

Michigan Society of Professional Engineers

Michigan Society of Professional Engineers Scholarships for High School Seniors

Type of award: Scholarship.
Intended use: For undergraduate study at accredited 4-year institution. Designated institutions: ABET-accredited schools in Michigan.
Eligibility: Applicant must be high school senior. Applicant must be U.S. citizen residing in Michigan.
Basis for selection: Major/career interest in engineering. Applicant must demonstrate high academic achievement, depth of character, leadership and service orientation.
Application requirements: Recommendations, essay, transcript. ACT scores.
Additional information: Minimum 3.0 GPA and 26 ACT score. Application must be postmarked by first Friday of February. Contact guidance counselor or local MSPE chapter for application and specific eligibility requirements. Applications must be submitted to local MSPE chapter.

Amount of award:	$750-$3,000
Number of awards:	23
Number of applicants:	120
Notification begins:	April 1
Total amount awarded:	$35,000

Contact:
Scholarship Coordinator Local MSPE Chapter
P.O. Box 15276
Lansing, MI 48901
Phone: 517-487-9388
Fax: 517-487-0635
Web: www.michiganspe.org

Microscopy Society of America

Microscopy Society of America Undergraduate Research Scholarship

Type of award: Research grant.
Intended use: For full-time junior or senior study at postsecondary institution.

Scholarships

Basis for selection: Major/career interest in science, general; biology; physics; chemistry; natural sciences or engineering, materials. Applicant must demonstrate seriousness of purpose.
Application requirements: Recommendations. Resume, budget, research proposal, letter from laboratory supervisor, letter from MSA member (may be same as supervisor or professor). Four hard copies of all application materials if not submitting electronically.
Additional information: Award for students interested in pursuing microscopy as career or major research tool. Applicant should be sponsored by MSA member. Must supply abstract of research project. Funds must be spent within year of award date, but in special cases may be extended to cover additional research during summer semester following graduation. Visit Website for more information and application.

Amount of award:	$3,000
Number of awards:	6
Number of applicants:	20
Application deadline:	December 31
Notification begins:	April 1
Total amount awarded:	$9,000

Contact:
Microscopy Society of America
Undergraduate Research Scholarship
12100 Sunset Hills Road, Suite 130
Reston, VA 20190
Phone: 800-538-3672
Fax: 703-435-4390
Web: www.microscopy.org

Microsoft Corporation

Microsoft General Scholarship

Type of award: Scholarship.
Intended use: For full-time undergraduate study at 4-year institution. Designated institutions: Colleges and universities in the United States, Canada, and Mexico.
Basis for selection: Major/career interest in computer/information sciences; engineering, computer; mathematics or physics. Applicant must demonstrate financial need and high academic achievement.
Application requirements: Recommendations, essay, transcript. Resume.
Additional information: Minimum 3.0 GPA. Scholarship will cover up to 100 percent of tuition for one academic year. All recipients required to complete salaried summer internship of 12 weeks or more at Microsoft in Redmond, Washington. Applicant must be enrolled in degree-granting program in computer science, computer engineering, or related technical discipline, with demonstrated interest in computer science. See Website for important dates, more information and application.

Amount of award:	Full tuition
Application deadline:	February 1
Notification begins:	March 20
Total amount awarded:	$500,000

Contact:
Microsoft Scholarship Program
Microsoft Corporation
One Microsoft Way
Redmond, WA 98052-8303
Web: www.microsoft.com/college/en/us/internships-scholarships.aspx

Midwestern Higher Education Compact

Midwest Student Exchange Program

Type of award: Scholarship, renewable.
Intended use: For full-time undergraduate, master's, doctoral or first professional study at accredited 2-year, 4-year or graduate institution in United States. Designated institutions: Participating institutions in Illinois, Indiana, Kansas, Michigan, Minnesota, Missouri, Nebraska, North Dakota, and Wisconsin.
Eligibility: Applicant must be residing in Wisconsin, Michigan, Minnesota, Kansas, Indiana, Nebraska, Illinois, Missouri or North Dakota.
Application requirements: Proof of eligibility.
Additional information: Reduced tuition rate for Illinois, Indiana, Kansas, Michigan, Minnesota, Missouri, Nebraska, North Dakota, and Wisconsin residents attending participating out-of-state institutions in one of eight other states in designated institutions or programs of study. For information, contact high school counselor or college admissions officer. For list of participating institutions and programs, and for individual state contact information, visit Website.

Number of applicants:	3,543
Total amount awarded:	$19,995,516

Contact:
Midwestern Higher Education Compact
105 Fifth Avenue S., Suite 450
Minneapolis, MN 55401
Phone: 612-677-2777
Fax: 612-767-3353
Web: msep.mhec.org

Military Officers Association of America

General John Paul Ratay Educational Fund Grants

Type of award: Scholarship.
Intended use: For undergraduate study at postsecondary institution.
Eligibility: Applicant must be U.S. citizen. Applicant must be dependent of veteran.
Additional information: Grants available to children of surviving spouse of retired officers. Must be seeking first undergraduate degree. Students cannot receive both an MOAA loan and Ratay grant.

Amount of award:	$5,500
Application deadline:	March 1
Notification begins:	May 1

Contact:
Military Officers Association of America
201 N. Washington Street
Alexandria, VA 22314
Phone: 703-549-2311
Web: www.moaa.org/education

MOAA American Patriot Scholarship Program

Type of award: Scholarship, renewable.
Intended use: For undergraduate study at postsecondary institution.
Eligibility: Applicant must be no older than 23. Applicant must be dependent of disabled veteran or deceased veteran.
Basis for selection: Applicant must demonstrate financial need and high academic achievement.
Additional information: Must be dependent of an active duty uniformed service member (including Drilling Reserve and National Guard). Minimum 3.0 GPA. Military academy cadets are ineligible. Must be seeking first undergraduate degree. Amount and number of awards given vary.

Amount of award:	$2,500
Number of awards:	50
Number of applicants:	60
Application deadline:	March 1
Notification begins:	May 1
Total amount awarded:	$300,000

Contact:
MOAA Scholarship Fun
American Patriot Scholarships
201 North Washington Street
Alexandria, VA 22314-2529
Phone: 800-234-6622
Web: www.moaa.org/education

Military Order of the Purple Heart

Military Order of the Purple Heart Scholarship

Type of award: Scholarship, renewable.
Intended use: For full-time undergraduate study at postsecondary institution.
Eligibility: Applicant must be U.S. citizen. Applicant must be descendant of veteran or disabled while on active duty; or dependent of disabled veteran or deceased veteran; or spouse of disabled veteran or deceased veteran. Applicant must be either a recipient of the Purple Heart or a descendent, spouse or widow of a recipient of the Purple Heart, a veteran killed in action, or a veteran who died of wounds incurred during service.
Basis for selection: Applicant must demonstrate high academic achievement.
Application requirements: $15 application fee. Recommendations, essay, transcript, proof of eligibility.
Additional information: Applicant must either be a recipient of the Purple Heart or spouse or descendant of recipient of the Purple Heart, or descendant or spouse of veteran killed in action or who died of wounds. Must have minimum unweighted 2.75 GPA. Deadline in mid February. Application package available on MOPH Website. Call MOPH for details.

Amount of award:	$3,000
Number of awards:	83
Number of applicants:	400
Application deadline:	February 15
Total amount awarded:	$250,000

Contact:
Military Order of the Purple Heart
Scholarship Coordinator
5413-B Backlick Road
Springfield, VA 22151
Phone: 703-642-5360
Fax: 703-642-2054
Web: www.purpleheart.org

Minnesota Department of Veterans Affairs

Minnesota Educational Assistance for Veterans

Type of award: Scholarship.
Intended use: For undergraduate or graduate study at postsecondary institution. Designated institutions: Approved Minnesota institutions.
Eligibility: Applicant must be U.S. citizen residing in Minnesota. Applicant must be veteran. Applicant must have been Minnesota resident at time of entry into active duty and for six months immediately preceding entry. Must have served 181 consecutive days of active duty.
Application requirements: Proof of eligibility. Military Service DD Form 214.
Additional information: Applicant must have exhausted eligible federal educational benefits prior to the delimiting date or within the eligibility period in which benefits were available. Grant is one-time award. Contact county veterans service officer or institution for more information.

Amount of award:	$750

Contact:
Minnesota Department of Veterans Affairs
Veterans Service Building, 2nd Floor
20 West 12 Street
St. Paul, MN 55155-2079
Phone: 651-296-2562
Fax: 651-296-3954
Web: www.mdva.state.mn.us/education

Minnesota Office of Higher Education

Minnesota GI Bill

Type of award: Scholarship, renewable.
Intended use: For undergraduate or graduate study at postsecondary institution. Designated institutions: Eligible Minnesota institutions.
Eligibility: Applicant must be in military service or veteran; or dependent of disabled veteran or deceased veteran; or spouse of disabled veteran or deceased veteran who serves or served in the Army, Air Force, Marines, Navy, Coast Guard or Reserves/National Guard.
Additional information: Applicant must be a veteran, or spouse or child of military personnel who died or became permanently disabled due to service on or after September 11, 2001. Applicant may also be non-veteran who has served a

total of five years in the United States military with any part of service occurring on or after September 11, 2001.

Amount of award:	$100-$3,000
Number of applicants:	1,281
Total amount awarded:	$812,605

Contact:
Minnesota Office of Higher Education
1450 Energy Park Drive, Suite 350
St. Paul, MN 55108-5227
Phone: 800-657-3866
Web: www.getreadyforcollege.org/military

Minnesota Indian Scholarship Program

Type of award: Scholarship.
Intended use: For undergraduate or graduate study in United States. Designated institutions: Eligible Minnesota institutions.
Eligibility: Applicant must be American Indian. Applicant must be residing in Minnesota.
Application requirements: Proof of one-fourth or more American Indian ancestry. FAFSA.
Additional information: Applicant must be at least one-quarter American Indian. Undergraduates must be enrolled at least three-quarters time and graduate students must be enrolled at least half-time. Undergraduates must be eligible for Pell grant or Minnesota state grant. Awards made on first-completed, first-served basis.

Amount of award:	$4,000-$6,000
Number of applicants:	2,360
Application deadline:	July 1
Notification begins:	February 1
Total amount awarded:	$1,736,794

Contact:
Minnesota Office of Higher Education
1450 Energy Park Drive, Suite 350
St. Paul, MN 55108-5227
Phone: 800-657-3866
Web: www.getreadyforcollege.org/indianscholarship

Minnesota Post-Secondary Child Care Grant

Type of award: Scholarship, renewable.
Intended use: For undergraduate study at accredited postsecondary institution. Designated institutions: Eligible Minnesota schools.
Eligibility: Applicant must be U.S. citizen or permanent resident residing in Minnesota.
Basis for selection: Applicant must demonstrate financial need.
Additional information: Apply at college's financial aid office. Award amount prorated upon enrollment. Award based on family income and size. Eligibility limited to applicants with children 12 years or younger; maximum of $2600 per eligible child per academic year. Applicant cannot be receiving Aid to Families With Dependent Children, Minnesota Family Investment Program, or tuition reciprocity, or be in default of loan. Those with bachelor's degree or eight semesters or 12 quarters of credit, or equivalent, are not eligible. Applicant must be enrolled at least half-time in nonsectarian program and must be in good academic standing. Deadlines established by individual institution.

Number of applicants:	2,863
Total amount awarded:	$5,828,199

Contact:
Minnesota Office of Higher Education
1450 Energy Park Drive, Suite 350
St. Paul, MN 55108-5227
Phone: 800-657-3866
Web: www.getreadyforcollege.org

Minnesota Public Safety Officers Survivors Program

Type of award: Scholarship.
Intended use: For undergraduate study at accredited 2-year or 4-year institution. Designated institutions: Eligible Minnesota schools.
Eligibility: Applicant must be residing in Minnesota. Applicant's parent must have been killed or disabled in work-related accident as firefighter, police officer or public safety officer.
Application requirements: Proof of eligibility. Eligibility certificate.
Additional information: Must be enrolled in degree or certificate program at institution participating in Minnesota State Grant Program. Applicant must be the surviving spouse or dependent child of a public safety officer killed in the line of duty. Also eligible if parent or spouse, not officially employed in public safety, was killed while assisting public safety officer or offering emergency medical assistance. Maximum age for dependent's child is 22 unless called for active military service, in which case maximum age is 29. Obtain eligibility certificate from Nancy Reissner, Department of Public Safety, 211 Transportation Building, St. Paul, MN 55155. Apply through financial aid office. Award covers tuition and fees up to $10,488 at four-year college and $5,808 at two-year college.

Number of applicants:	12
Total amount awarded:	$87,871

Contact:
Minnesota Office of Higher Education
1450 Energy Park Drive, Suite 350
St. Paul, MN 55108-5227
Phone: 800-657-3866
Web: www.getreadyforcollege.org

Minnesota State Grant Program

Type of award: Scholarship, renewable.
Intended use: For undergraduate study at accredited vocational, 2-year or 4-year institution.
Eligibility: Applicant must be U.S. citizen or permanent resident residing in Minnesota.
Basis for selection: Applicant must demonstrate financial need.
Application requirements: Proof of eligibility. FAFSA.
Additional information: Applicant must not have completed four years of college. If not Minnesota high school graduate and parents not residents of Minnesota, applicant must be resident of Minnesota for at least one year without being enrolled half-time or more. Cannot be in default on loans or delinquent on child-support payments. FAFSA used as application for Minnesota State Grant. Application deadline is 30 days from term start date.

Amount of award:	$100-$9,391
Number of awards:	103,509
Total amount awarded:	$142,766,992

Contact:
Minnesota Office of Higher Education
1450 Energy Park Drive, Suite 350
St. Paul, MN 55108-5227
Phone: 800-657-3866
Web: www.getreadyforcollege.org

Miss America Organization

Allman Medical Scholarships

Type of award: Scholarship, renewable.
Intended use: For undergraduate or graduate study at postsecondary institution.
Eligibility: Applicant must be female.
Basis for selection: Major/career interest in medicine. Applicant must demonstrate financial need and high academic achievement.
Application requirements: Recommendations, essay, transcript, proof of eligibility. MCAT scores.
Additional information: Must be pursuing a degree in medicine. Must have competed in Miss America system at local, state, or national level after 1998. Notification begins in August.

Application deadline: June 30

Contact:
Miss America Organization
222 New Road, Suite 700
Attn: Scholarships
Linwood, NJ 08221
Phone: 609-653-8700
Web: www.missamerica.org/scholarships

Eugenia Vellner Fischer Award for the Performing Arts

Type of award: Scholarship.
Intended use: For undergraduate or graduate study at postsecondary institution.
Eligibility: Applicant must be female.
Basis for selection: Major/career interest in performing arts. Applicant must demonstrate financial need and high academic achievement.
Application requirements: Recommendations, essay, transcript, proof of eligibility.
Additional information: Must be pursuing degree in the performing arts, such as dance or music. Must have competed in Miss America system in local, state, or national level after 1998. Visit Website for more information.

Application deadline: June 30
Notification begins: September 1

Contact:
Miss America Organization
Attn: Scholarships
222 New Road, Suite 700
Linwood, NJ 08221
Phone: 609-653-8700
Web: www.missamerica.org/scholarships

Miss America Competition Awards

Type of award: Scholarship.
Intended use: For undergraduate, graduate or non-degree study at accredited postsecondary institution.
Eligibility: Applicant must be single, female, at least 17, no older than 24. Applicant must be U.S. citizen.
Basis for selection: Competition/talent/interest in poise/talent/fitness. Applicant must demonstrate depth of character, leadership, patriotism, seriousness of purpose and service orientation.
Application requirements: Proof of eligibility.
Additional information: Local winners go on to compete at state level, and state winners compete for Miss America. Contestants will apply their talent, intelligence, and speaking ability, and demonstrate their commitment to community service. Cash and tuition-based scholarships available at every level of competition. Deadlines for local competitions vary. Contact the Miss America Organization for more information or visit Website.

Amount of award: $1,000-$50,000
Total amount awarded: $40,000,000

Contact:
Miss America Organization
Attn: Scholarships
222 New Road, Suite 700
Linwood, NJ 08221
Phone: 609-653-8700
Web: www.missamerica.org/scholarships

Mississippi Office of Student Financial Aid

Leveraging Educational Assistance Partnership Program (LEAP)

Type of award: Scholarship, renewable.
Intended use: For full-time undergraduate study at accredited 2-year or 4-year institution. Designated institutions: Mississippi institutions.
Eligibility: Applicant must be enrolled in high school. Applicant must be U.S. citizen or permanent resident residing in Mississippi.
Basis for selection: Applicant must demonstrate financial need and high academic achievement.
Application requirements: Recommendations, proof of eligibility. FAFSA.
Additional information: Must meet general requirements for participation in federal student aid program. Award amount varies. Apply to college financial aid office.

Contact:
Mississippi Student Financial Aid
3825 Ridgewood Road
Jackson, MS 39211-6453
Phone: 800-327-2980
Web: www.mississippi.edu/riseupms

Mississippi Eminent Scholars Grant

Type of award: Scholarship, renewable.
Intended use: For full-time undergraduate study at accredited vocational, 2-year or 4-year institution. Designated institutions: Eligible Mississippi institutions.
Eligibility: Applicant must be residing in Mississippi.
Basis for selection: Applicant must demonstrate high academic achievement.
Application requirements: Transcript. State of Mississippi tax return. ACT scores.

Scholarships

Additional information: Applicant may be high school senior. Must be Mississippi resident for at least one year. Minimum 3.5 GPA or rank in top 25 percent of class. Must have minimum ACT score of 29.

Amount of award: $2,500
Application deadline: September 15

Contact:
Mississippi Office of Student Financial Aid
3825 Ridgewood Road
Jackson, MS 39211-6453
Phone: 800-327-2980
Web: www.mississippi.edu/riseupms

Mississippi Higher Education Legislative Plan

Type of award: Scholarship, renewable.
Intended use: For full-time freshman or sophomore study at accredited 2-year or 4-year institution. Designated institutions: Eligible Mississippi institutions.
Eligibility: Applicant must be U.S. citizen residing in Mississippi.
Basis for selection: Applicant must demonstrate financial need and high academic achievement.
Application requirements: FAFSA. Household verification form.
Additional information: Minimum 2.5 GPA or must rank in top 50 percent of class. Must be legal resident of Mississippi for at least two years. Must have graduated from high school within two years of application. Preference given to early applicants. Covers tuition and fees up to ten semesters. Visit Website for application and more details.

Amount of award: Full tuition
Application deadline: March 31
Total amount awarded: $1,753,252

Contact:
Mississippi Office of Student Financial Aid
3825 Ridgewood Road
Jackson, MS 39211-6453
Phone: 800-327-2980
Web: www.mississippi.edu/riseupms

Mississippi Resident Tuition Assistance Grant

Type of award: Scholarship, renewable.
Intended use: For full-time undergraduate study at accredited vocational, 2-year or 4-year institution. Designated institutions: Eligible Mississippi institutions.
Eligibility: Applicant must be U.S. citizen residing in Mississippi.
Basis for selection: Applicant must demonstrate high academic achievement.
Application requirements: FAFSA and Student Aid Report.
Additional information: Applicant must be resident of Mississippi for at least one year. Must be receiving less than full Federal Pell Grant. Must have minimum 2.5 GPA or rank in top 50 percent of class. Award is up to $500 per year for freshmen and sophomores; up to $1,000 per year for juniors and seniors. Recipients must maintain minimum 2.5 GPA to reapply. Applicants must not be in default on an educational loan. Apply online.

Amount of award: $500-$1,000
Application deadline: September 15

Contact:
Mississippi Office of Student Financial Aid
3825 Ridgewood Road
Jackson, MS 39211-6453
Phone: 800-327-2980
Web: www.mississippi.edu/riseupms

Nissan Scholarship

Type of award: Scholarship, renewable.
Intended use: For full-time undergraduate study at 2-year or 4-year institution. Designated institutions: Mississippi public institutions.
Eligibility: Applicant must be high school senior. Applicant must be residing in Mississippi.
Basis for selection: Applicant must demonstrate financial need, high academic achievement, leadership, seriousness of purpose and service orientation.
Application requirements: Recommendations, transcript. FAFSA, 200-word essay. Resume. SAT/ACT scores.
Additional information: Must be graduating from Mississippi high school in current year. Must have 20 ACT score or 940 SAT score (reading and math). Minimum 2.0 GPA. Visit Website for more information and application. Number and amount of awards vary.

Amount of award: Full tuition
Application deadline: March 1

Contact:
Mississippi Office of Student Financial Aid
3825 Ridgewood Road
Jackson, MS 39211-6453
Phone: 800-327-2980
Web: www.mississippi.edu/riseupms

Missouri Department of Higher Education

A+ Scholarship Program

Type of award: Scholarship.
Intended use: For full-time undergraduate study at vocational or 2-year institution in United States. Designated institutions: Participating Missouri public community colleges or vocational/technical school or private 2-year vocational/technical schools.
Eligibility: Applicant must be U.S. citizen.
Basis for selection: Applicant must demonstrate high academic achievement.
Application requirements: FAFSA.
Additional information: Applicant must attend A+ high school for three consecutive years immediately prior to graduation. Minimum 2.5 GPA. Must have 95 percent attendance overall for grades 9-12. Must perform at least 50 hours unpaid tutoring or mentoring. Not applicable to theology or divinity studies.

Total amount awarded: $25,987,719

Contact:
Missouri Department of Higher Education
P.O. Box 1469
Jefferson City, MO 65102-1469
Phone: 800-473-6757, option 4
Fax: 573-751-6635
Web: www.dhe.mo.gov

Access Missouri Financial Assistance Program

Type of award: Scholarship, renewable.
Intended use: For full-time undergraduate study at vocational, 2-year or 4-year institution. Designated institutions: Approved Missouri institutions.
Eligibility: Applicant must be U.S. citizen or permanent resident residing in Missouri.
Basis for selection: Applicant must demonstrate financial need.
Application requirements: FAFSA.
Additional information: Must be used only toward first baccalaureate degree and may not be used towards theology or divinity studies. Eligibility based on Expected Family Contribution (EFC), with individuals with EFC of $12,000 or less eligible. Award amounts vary. No paper application. Students must apply for renewal each year.

Amount of award:	$300-$4,600
Application deadline:	April 1
Total amount awarded:	$59,585,406

Contact:
Missouri Department of Higher Education
P.O. Box 1469
Jefferson City, MO 65102-1469
Phone: 800-473-6757, option 4
Fax: 573-751-6635
Web: www.dhe.mo.gov

Advanced Placement Incentive Grant

Type of award: Scholarship.
Intended use: For full-time undergraduate study at vocational, 2-year or 4-year institution in United States. Designated institutions: Approved Missouri institutions.
Eligibility: Applicant must be U.S. citizen or permanent resident.
Basis for selection: Applicant must demonstrate high academic achievement.
Application requirements: Advanced Placement scores.
Additional information: Must achieve two grades of three or higher on Advanced Placement exams in math or science while attending a Missour public high school. Must receive an award under the Access Missouri Student Financial Assistance Program or A+ Scholarship program.

Amount of award:	$500
Application deadline:	June 1
Total amount awarded:	$29,500

Contact:
Missouri Department of Higher Education
P.O. Box 1469
Jefferson City, MO 65102-1469
Phone: 800-473-6757, option 4
Fax: 573-751-6635
Web: www.dhe.mo.gov

Marguerite Ross Barnett Memorial Scholarship

Type of award: Scholarship, renewable.
Intended use: For half-time undergraduate study at accredited vocational, 2-year or 4-year institution in United States. Designated institutions: Approved Missouri institutions.
Eligibility: Applicant must be at least 18. Applicant must be U.S. citizen or permanent resident residing in Missouri.
Basis for selection: Applicant must demonstrate financial need.
Application requirements: Proof of eligibility. FAFSA.
Additional information: May only be used for first baccalaureate degree. For students employed at least 20 hours per week while attending school part-time. Scholarship awarded on first-come, first-served basis. Maximum award is the lesser of the following: tuition charged at school of part-time enrollment or amount of tuition charged to Missouri undergraduate resident enrolled part-time in same class level at University of Missouri-Columbia. Employer must verify applicant's employment. Recipient may not be pursuing degree in theology or divinity.

Application deadline:	August 1
Total amount awarded:	$319,725

Contact:
Missouri Department of Higher Education
P.O. Box 1469
Jefferson City, MO 65102-1469
Phone: 800-473-6757, option 4
Fax: 573-751-6635
Web: www.dhe.mo.gov

Minority and Underrepresented Environmental Literacy Program

Type of award: Scholarship.
Intended use: For full-time undergraduate or master's study at accredited vocational, 2-year, 4-year or graduate institution in United States. Designated institutions: Missouri institutions with approved environmentally related programs.
Eligibility: Applicant must be U.S. citizen or permanent resident residing in Missouri.
Basis for selection: Major/career interest in wildlife/fisheries; engineering, environmental; engineering, chemical; engineering, agricultural; biology; geology/earth sciences; natural resources/conservation; environmental science; engineering, mechanical or engineering, civil. Applicant must demonstrate high academic achievement.
Application requirements: Recommendations, essay, transcript. Resume, ACT/SAT scores.
Additional information: Minimum 3.0 GPA. Preference given to African-American, Hispanic, Native American, Alaska Native, Hawaiian and Pacific Islander applicants.

Application deadline:	June 1
Total amount awarded:	$27,982

Contact:
Missouri Department of Higher Education
P.O. Box 1469
Jefferson City, MO 65102-1469
Phone: 800-473-6757, option 4
Fax: 573-751-6635
Web: www.dhe.mo.gov

Minority Teaching Scholarship

Type of award: Scholarship, renewable.
Intended use: For full-time undergraduate or master's study at accredited vocational, 2-year or 4-year institution in United States. Designated institutions: Approved Missouri institutions with approved teacher education programs.
Eligibility: Applicant must be Asian American, African American, Hispanic American or American Indian. Applicant must be returning adult student. Applicant must be U.S. citizen or permanent resident residing in Missouri.
Basis for selection: Major/career interest in education. Applicant must demonstrate high academic achievement.

Scholarships

Application requirements: Recommendations, essay, transcript, proof of eligibility.
Additional information: Must rank in top 25 percent of class and score in top 25 percent on ACT or SAT. If college graduate, may receive award if returning to a master's level math or science education program. Upon graduation, recipient must teach for five years in Missouri public schools or scholarship becomes loan. Applicant may be renewed for up to 4 years.

Amount of award:	$3,000
Number of awards:	100
Number of applicants:	20
Application deadline:	June 1
Total amount awarded:	$38,000

Contact:
Missouri Department of Higher Education
P.O. Box 1469
Jefferson City, MO 65102-1469
Phone: 800-473-6757, option 4
Fax: 573-751-6635
Web: www.dhe.mo.gov

Missouri Department of Higher Education Vietnam Veteran's Survivor Grant Program

Type of award: Scholarship, renewable.
Intended use: For full-time undergraduate study at accredited vocational, 2-year or 4-year institution in United States. Designated institutions: Approved Missouri institutions.
Eligibility: Applicant must be U.S. citizen or permanent resident. Applicant must be dependent of deceased veteran; or spouse of deceased veteran during Vietnam.
Application requirements: Proof of eligibility.
Additional information: May only be used for first baccalaureate degree. Veteran must have been resident of Missouri when entering service and at time of death. For children and spouses of Vietnam veterans whose death was attributed to or caused by exposure to toxic chemicals during Vietnam conflict. Applicant cannot pursue degree in theology or divinity. Applications accepted in January; end date based on fund availability. Amount of award varies. Maximum amount is the lesser of actual tuition charged for twelve credit hours at school where applicant is enrolled, or the average amount of tuition charged for twelve credit hours to undergraduate Missouri resident enrolled full-time in same class level and academic major at regional four-year public Missouri institutions.

Number of awards:	12
Number of applicants:	3
Total amount awarded:	$15,053

Contact:
Missouri Department of Higher Education
P.O. Box 1469
Jefferson City, MO 65102-1469
Phone: 800-473-6757, option 4
Fax: 573-751-6635
Web: www.dhe.mo.gov

Missouri Higher Education "Bright Flight" Academic Scholarship

Type of award: Scholarship, renewable.
Intended use: For full-time undergraduate study at accredited vocational, 2-year or 4-year institution in United States. Designated institutions: Approved Missouri institutions.
Eligibility: Applicant must be U.S. citizen or permanent resident residing in Missouri.
Basis for selection: Applicant must demonstrate high academic achievement.
Application requirements: Proof of eligibility. SAT/ACT scores.
Additional information: May only be used for first baccalaureate degree. May not be used for theology or divinity studies. SAT/ACT composite scores must be in top five percent of state students. Must achieve qualifying scores by June assessment date of senior year. GED and home-schooled students may also qualify. Application deadline is June assessment date of senior year. No paper application needed. Check with high school counselor or financial aid administrator for additional information or see Website. Deadline in June.

Amount of award:	$1,000-$3,000
Total amount awarded:	$10,856,464

Contact:
Missouri Department of Higher Education
P.O. Box 1469
Jefferson City, MO 65102-1469
Phone: 800-473-6757, option 4
Fax: 573-751-6635
Web: www.dhe.mo.gov

Public Safety Officer or Employee's Child Survivor Grant

Type of award: Scholarship, renewable.
Intended use: For full-time undergraduate study at accredited vocational, 2-year or 4-year institution in United States. Designated institutions: Approved Missouri public institutions.
Eligibility: Applicant must be U.S. citizen or permanent resident residing in Missouri.
Application requirements: Proof of eligibility.
Additional information: May only be used for first baccalaureate degree. For public safety officers who were permanently disabled in the line of duty or for children and spouses of Missouri public safety officers killed or permanently disabled in the line of duty. Children of Missouri Department of Highway and Transportation employees also eligible if parent died or was permanently disabled during performance of job. May not be used for theology or divinity studies. Award amounts vary; contact sponsor for information. Amount awarded is the lesser of 12 credit tuition hours at chosen institution or 12 credit tuition hours at University of Missouri. Applications accepted in January; end date based on fund availability.

Total amount awarded:	$74,488

Contact:
Missouri Department of Higher Education
P.O. Box 1469
Jefferson City, MO 65102-1469
Phone: 800-473-6757, option 4
Fax: 573-751-6635
Web: www.dhe.mo.gov

Missouri League for Nursing

Missouri League for Nursing Scholarship

Type of award: Scholarship, renewable.
Intended use: For full-time sophomore, junior, senior or master's study at accredited postsecondary institution. Designated institutions: Eligible institutions in Missouri.

Eligibility: Applicant must be U.S. citizen residing in Missouri.
Basis for selection: Major/career interest in nursing. Applicant must demonstrate financial need and high academic achievement.
Application requirements: Recommendations.
Additional information: Minimum 3.0 GPA. Scholarship must be used for study in Missouri. Amount of award varies. Applications can be obtained from dean of nationally recognized accredited schools of nursing in Missouri.

Amount of award:	$2,000
Number of awards:	2
Number of applicants:	30

Contact:
Contact deans at accredited nursing schools in Missouri.
Phone: 573-635-5355
Fax: 573-635-7908
Web: www.mlnmonursing.org

Montana Trappers Association

MTA Doug Slifka Memorial Scholarship

Type of award: Scholarship.
Intended use: For undergraduate study at postsecondary institution.
Eligibility: Applicant must be at least 15, no older than 25.
Basis for selection: Major/career interest in environmental science; life sciences; natural resources/conservation or wildlife/fisheries. Applicant must demonstrate depth of character and seriousness of purpose.
Application requirements: Interview, transcript. Essay or story on trapping or conservation. Recommendations by MTA members, teachers, or other pertinent individuals. Endorsement of MTA District Director (or sub-director) where applicant resides. Student involvement in activities that include MTA programs, trapping, school programs, and community service.
Additional information: Applicant must be member of MTA for at least one year or minor dependent of MTA member. Member must have been member of Association for one year prior to application. MTA members out of state and their families also eligible to apply. For application, complete request form on Website or contact local director, officer or committee member.

Amount of award:	$500
Number of awards:	2
Application deadline:	June 1
Total amount awarded:	$1,000

Contact:
Montana Trappers Association MTA Scholarship Committee
c/o Gary VanHaele
P.O. Box 264
Hysham, MT 59038
Phone: 406-342-5552
Web: www.montanatrappers.org/programs/scholarship.htm

Montana University System

Montana Governor's Best and Brightest Merit Scholarship

Type of award: Scholarship, renewable.
Intended use: For full-time undergraduate study at 2-year or 4-year institution. Designated institutions: Montana University system or tribal colleges.
Eligibility: Applicant must be residing in Montana.
Basis for selection: Applicant must demonstrate high academic achievement.
Application requirements: Transcript. SAT/ACT scores.
Additional information: Applications available on Website. Must have minimum 3.0 GPA or 20 ACT score or 1440 SAT score.

Amount of award:	$2,000
Application deadline:	March 15

Contact:
Governor's Best and Brightest Merit Scholarship
P.O. Box 203201
Helena, MT 59604-3101
Phone: 800-537-7508
Fax: 406-444-1469
Web: www.scholarship.mt.gov

Montana Governor's Best and Brightest Merit-at-Large Scholarship

Type of award: Scholarship, renewable.
Intended use: For full-time undergraduate study at 2-year or 4-year institution in United States. Designated institutions: Montana University System school or tribal college in Montana.
Eligibility: Applicant must be residing in Montana.
Basis for selection: Applicant must demonstrate high academic achievement.
Application requirements: Transcript. SAT/ACT score.
Additional information: Applications available on Website. Applicants must be Montana high school graduate. Must have minimum 3.0 GPA or 20 ACT score or 1440 SAT score.

Amount of award:	$2,000
Number of awards:	50
Application deadline:	March 15

Contact:
Montana University System
P.O. Box 203201
Helena, MT 59604-3101
Phone: 800-537-7508
Fax: 406-444-1469
Web: www.scholarship.mt.gov

Montana Governor's Best and Brightest Need Based Scholarship

Type of award: Scholarship.
Intended use: For undergraduate study at 2-year institution in United States. Designated institutions: Montana University System schools or Montana tribal colleges.
Eligibility: Applicant must be residing in Montana.
Basis for selection: Applicant must demonstrate financial need.
Application requirements: FAFSA.
Additional information: Applications available through college financial aid office.

Amount of award: $1,000
Application deadline: March 15
Contact:
Montana University System
P.O. Box 203201
Helena, MT 59604-3101
Phone: 800-537-7508
Fax: 406-444-1469
Web: www.scholarship.mt.gov

Montana Higher Education Grant

Type of award: Scholarship.
Intended use: For undergraduate study at postsecondary institution. Designated institutions: Eligible Montana institutions.
Eligibility: Applicant must be residing in Montana.
Basis for selection: Applicant must demonstrate financial need.
Application requirements: FAFSA.
Amount of award: $500-$600
Number of awards: 1,000
Total amount awarded: $600,000
Contact:
Contact college financial aid office for application information.
Phone: 800-537-7508
Fax: 406-444-1469
Web: www.scholarship.mt.gov

Montana Honorably Discharged Veteran Fee Waiver

Type of award: Scholarship.
Intended use: For undergraduate or graduate study at postsecondary institution. Designated institutions: Montana University system institutions.
Eligibility: Applicant must be permanent resident residing in Montana. Applicant must be veteran.
Application requirements: Proof of eligibility.
Additional information: Must have been honorably discharged person who served with the United States forces during wartime. Must be pursuing his or her initial undergraduate degree. Must have used up all federal veterans educational assistance benefits. Contact college financial aid office.
Amount of award: Full tuition
Contact:
Montana University System
P.O. Box 203201
Helena, MT 59620-3101
Phone: 800-537-7508
Fax: 406-444-1469
Web: www.scholarship.mt.gov

Montana University System Honor Scholarship

Type of award: Scholarship, renewable.
Intended use: For freshman study at 4-year institution. Designated institutions: Campuses in Montana University system, as well as Dawson, Flathead Valley, and Miles community colleges.
Eligibility: Applicant must be high school senior. Applicant must be U.S. citizen residing in Montana.
Basis for selection: Applicant must demonstrate high academic achievement.
Application requirements: Recommendations, transcript, proof of eligibility. College acceptance letter, SAT/ACT scores.
Additional information: Must be high school senior enrolled at accredited Montana high school for at least three years. Recipients ranked based on GPA and ACT or SAT score. Minimum 3.4 GPA. Must have met college preparatory requirements. Must submit completed application to high school guidance counselor. See Website for more details.
Amount of award: Full tuition
Application deadline: March 15
Contact:
Montana University System
P.O. Box 203201
Helena, MT 59620-3101
Phone: 800-537-7508
Fax: 406-444-1469
Web: www.scholarship.mt.gov

The Moody's Foundation

Moody's Mega Math "M3" Challenge

Type of award: Scholarship.
Intended use: For junior or senior study at 2-year or 4-year institution.
Eligibility: Applicant must be high school junior or senior. Applicant must be residing in Wisconsin, Ohio, New York, Tennessee, Delaware, Louisiana, Massachusetts, Virginia, Connecticut, Mississippi, Kentucky, Illinois, Alabama, Michigan, Vermont, Minnesota, Maine, Maryland, Pennsylvania, Florida, Georgia, South Carolina, District of Columbia, New Hampshire, West Virginia, Indiana, New Jersey, North Carolina or Rhode Island.
Basis for selection: Competition/talent/interest in academics, based on responses to the assigned modeling problem.
Application requirements: Must submit a viable solution paper by the deadline.
Additional information: Each school may enter up to two teams of three to five students. Team prizes range from $1,000 to $20,000. Visit Website for details and to register.
Amount of award: $1,000-$20,000
Number of awards: 55
Number of applicants: 4,500
Application deadline: February 21
Notification begins: April 8
Total amount awarded: $115,000
Contact:
Society for Industrial and Applied Mathematics
Attn: Frank Kunkle
3600 Market Street, 6th Floor
Philadelphia, PA 19104
Phone: 267-350-6388
Fax: 215-525-2756
Web: m3challenge.siam.org

Morgan Stanley

Morgan Stanley Richard B. Fisher Scholarship Program

Type of award: Scholarship.
Intended use: For sophomore or junior study at accredited 4-year institution.

Eligibility: Applicant must be African American, Mexican American, Hispanic American, Puerto Rican or American Indian.
Basis for selection: Major/career interest in finance/banking or technology. Applicant must demonstrate high academic achievement.
Application requirements: Interview.
Additional information: Program provides outstanding Black, Hispanic, Native American, and LGBT students with a financial award for exceptional academic achievement and a ten-week summer internship the summer prior to graduation. Must be currently enrolled as sophomore (for Institutional Securities, Investment Management, or Research Divisions) or junior (for the Finance, Operations, Technology, or Wealth Management Divisions). Applications due between December and February.
Contact:
Morgan Stanley
Web: www.morganstanley.com/about/careers/ischolarships_na.html

NAACP Legal Defense and Education Fund, Inc.

Herbert Lehman Educational Fund

Type of award: Scholarship, renewable.
Intended use: For full-time freshman or sophomore study at accredited 4-year institution in United States.
Eligibility: Applicant must be African American. Applicant must be high school senior. Applicant must be U.S. citizen.
Basis for selection: Applicant must demonstrate financial need, high academic achievement, depth of character, leadership, seriousness of purpose and service orientation.
Application requirements: Recommendations, essay, transcript. Standardized test scores.
Additional information: Apply online. See Website for additional information.

Amount of award:	$2,000
Application deadline:	March 31
Notification begins:	August 1

Contact:
The Herbert Lehman Fund
NAACP Legal Defense and Educational Fund, Inc
99 Hudson Street, Suite 1600
New York, NY 10013
Phone: 212-965-2200 or 212-965-2225
Fax: 212-219-1595
Web: www.naacpldf.org

NASA Alabama Space Grant Consortium

NASA Space Grant Undergraduate Scholarship

Type of award: Scholarship, renewable.
Intended use: For full-time junior or senior study at accredited 4-year institution. Designated institutions: Alabama Space Grant member universities: University of Alabama Huntsville, Alabama A&M, University of Alabama, University of Alabama Birmingham, University of South Alabama, Auburn University, Tuskegee University.
Eligibility: Applicant must be U.S. citizen residing in Alabama.
Basis for selection: Major/career interest in aerospace; engineering or science, general. Applicant must demonstrate high academic achievement.
Application requirements: Recommendations, essay, transcript, nomination by faculty advisor at Alabama Space Grant Consortium member institution. Resume.
Additional information: Applicants must have minimum 3.0 GPA and attend Alabama University. Must be in final term of sophomore year or later when applying. The Consortium actively encourages women, minority, and physically challenged students to apply, but others not excluded.

Amount of award:	$1,000
Number of awards:	40
Number of applicants:	32
Application deadline:	March 1
Notification begins:	May 15
Total amount awarded:	$31,500

Contact:
NASA Alabama Space Grant Consortium
University of Alabama in Huntsville
301 Sparkman Dr. Materials Science Bldg, 205
Huntsville, AL 35899
Phone: 256-824-6800
Fax: 256-824-6061
Web: www.uah.edu/ASGC

NASA Connecticut Space Grant Consortium

NASA Connecticut Space Grant Undergraduate Fellowship

Type of award: Research grant, renewable.
Intended use: For full-time undergraduate study at accredited 4-year institution in United States. Designated institutions: Connecticut Space Grant Consortium member institutions.
Eligibility: Applicant must be U.S. citizen.
Basis for selection: Major/career interest in aerospace; engineering or science, general. Applicant must demonstrate high academic achievement.
Application requirements: Recommendations, transcript, proof of eligibility, research proposal. Resume.
Additional information: Minimum 3.0 GPA. Consortium actively encourages women, minority, and disabled students to apply. Award amount varies; maximum is $5,000.

Amount of award:	$5,000
Number of awards:	9
Number of applicants:	20
Application deadline:	October 31
Total amount awarded:	$58,500

Contact:
NASA Connecticut Space Grant Consortium
University of Hartford
200 Bloomfield Ave.
West Hartford, CT 06117
Phone: 860-768-4813
Fax: 860-768-5073
Web: www.ctspacegrant.org

NASA Delaware Space Grant Consortium

Delaware Space Grant Undergraduate Tuition Scholarship

Type of award: Scholarship, renewable.
Intended use: For full-time sophomore, junior or senior study at postsecondary institution. Designated institutions: University of Delaware, Delaware Technical and Community College, Swarthmore College, Delaware State University at Dover, Villanova University, Wesley College, Wilmington University.
Eligibility: Applicant must be U.S. citizen.
Basis for selection: Major/career interest in aerospace; astronomy; mathematics; engineering; geography; geology/earth sciences; geophysics; physics; oceanography/marine studies or technology.
Application requirements: Recommendations, transcript, nomination by department chair, DESGC Consortium Representative, or advisor. Applicant statement; letter from Department Chairperson.
Additional information: Must have proven interest in space-related studies. Recipient must currently attend Delaware Space Grant Consortium member institution. Award amounts vary and are available pending funding. Contact Consortium office for deadlines and additional information.

Amount of award:	$2,500-$3,000
Number of awards:	12
Number of applicants:	10
Total amount awarded:	$28,500

Contact:
Delaware Space Grant Consortium Program Office
University of Delaware
212 Sharp Lab
Newark, DE 19716
Phone: 302-831-1094
Fax: 302-831-1843
Web: www.delspace.org

NASA Georgia Space Grant Consortium

NASA Space Grant Georgia Fellowship Program

Type of award: Scholarship, renewable.
Intended use: For full-time junior, senior, master's or doctoral study at accredited postsecondary institution in United States. Designated institutions: Albany State University, Clark Atlanta University, Columbus State University, Fort Valley State University, Georgia Institute of Technology, Georgia State University, Kennesaw State University, Mercer University, Morehouse College, Spelman College, State University of West Georgia, University of Georgia.
Eligibility: Applicant must be U.S. citizen residing in Georgia.
Basis for selection: Major/career interest in engineering; science, general; aerospace; physics; atmospheric sciences/meteorology; computer/information sciences; education or chemistry. Applicant must demonstrate seriousness of purpose and service orientation.
Application requirements: Interview, recommendations, essay, transcript.
Additional information: Funding available for students in all areas of engineering and science, and many areas of social science.
Contact:
Georgia Space Grant Consortium
Attn: Wanda G. Pierson
Aerospace Engineering
Atlanta, GA 30332-0150
Phone: 404-894-0521
Fax: 404-894-9313
Web: www.gasgc.org

NASA Hawaii Space Grant Consortium

NASA Space Grant Hawaii Undergraduate Fellowship Program

Type of award: Scholarship.
Intended use: For full-time undergraduate study at accredited postsecondary institution in United States. Designated institutions: Consortium member schools: University of Hawaii at Manoa, Hilo, and Maui, community colleges in Hawaii.
Eligibility: Applicant must be U.S. citizen.
Basis for selection: Major/career interest in astronomy; geology/earth sciences; oceanography/marine studies; physics; zoology; engineering or geography.
Application requirements: Recommendations, transcript. Abstract, research proposal, budget, resume. Three copies of all application materials.
Additional information: Must be resident of Hawaii or attend school at one of the designated institutions. Must be sponsored by a faculty member willing to act as the student's mentor during the award period. Field of study must be relevant to NASA's goals, e.g. areas of math, science, engineering, computer science (concerned with utilizing or exploring space), and air transportation. Full-time undergraduates at Manoa, Hilo with major declared can apply for two-semester fellowships. Stipend up to $4,000 per semester. Fellows may be eligible for up to $500 for supplies or travel. Recipients expected to work 10-15 hours per week on space-related projects. Women, under-represented minorities (specifically Native Hawaiians, other Pacific Islanders, Native Americans, Blacks, Hispanics), and physically challenged students who have interest in space-related fields are encouraged to apply. Visit Website for more information and application.

Amount of award:	$4,000
Number of applicants:	20
Application deadline:	June 15, December 1

Contact:
NASA Hawaii Space Grant Consortium
Phone: 808-956-3138
Fax: 808-956-6322
Web: www.spacegrant.hawaii.edu

NASA Idaho Space Grant Consortium

NASA Idaho Space Grant Undergraduate Scholarship

Type of award: Scholarship, renewable.
Intended use: For full-time undergraduate study at accredited 2-year or 4-year institution. Designated institutions: College of Idaho, Boise State University, College of Southern Idaho, Idaho State University, Lewis Clark State College, North Idaho College, Northwest Nazarene University, BYU-Idaho, and the University of Idaho.
Eligibility: Applicant must be U.S. citizen.
Basis for selection: Major/career interest in engineering; mathematics or science, general. Applicant must demonstrate high academic achievement.
Application requirements: Recommendations, essay. High school or college transcripts, SAT or ACT scores.
Additional information: Applicants must attend Idaho Space Grant Consortium member institution in Idaho and maintain a 3.0 GPA. Women, minority students, and disabled students encouraged to apply. Application essay should not exceed 500 words. Applications available on Website.

Amount of award:	$1,000-$2,500
Number of awards:	10
Number of applicants:	60
Application deadline:	March 4
Notification begins:	June 1
Total amount awarded:	$52,500

Contact:
NASA Idaho Space Grant Consortium
University of Idaho
875 Perimter Drive, Mail Stop 1026
Moscow, ID 83844-1026
Phone: 208-885-6438
Fax: 208-885-1399
Web: www.id.spacegrant.org

NASA Illinois Space Grant Consortium

NASA Space Grant Illinois Undergraduate Scholarship

Type of award: Scholarship, renewable.
Intended use: For full-time undergraduate study at postsecondary institution. Designated institutions: Illinois Space Grant Consortium member institutions.
Eligibility: Applicant must be U.S. citizen.
Basis for selection: Major/career interest in engineering; aerospace; astronomy or science, general. Applicant must demonstrate high academic achievement.
Application requirements: Recommendations, essay, transcript.
Additional information: Minimum 2.5 GPA. Contact sponsor for deadline information.

Amount of award:	$3,000
Number of applicants:	62
Total amount awarded:	$95,000

Contact:
Associate Director/Illinois Space Grant Consortium
U of Illinois-Urbana, 306 Talbot Lab
104 S. Wright Street
Urbana, IL 61801-2935
Phone: 217-244-8048
Fax: 217-244-0720
Web: www.ae.illinois.edu/ISGC

NASA Kentucky Space Grant Consortium

NASA Space Grant Kentucky Undergraduate Scholarship

Type of award: Scholarship, renewable.
Intended use: For full-time undergraduate study at accredited 4-year institution in United States. Designated institutions: Consortium member institutions.
Eligibility: Applicant must be U.S. citizen.
Basis for selection: Major/career interest in aerospace; astronomy; education; engineering or physics. Applicant must demonstrate high academic achievement.
Application requirements: Interview, recommendations, essay, transcript, nomination by professor/mentor at participating institution. Research proposal, written with mentor.
Additional information: Stipend for materials and travel up to $1500. Preference given to schools that waive tuition for recipient. Consortium actively encourages women, minority students, and physically challenged students to apply. Applicants doing work related to space exploration may qualify for funding, whatever their field of study may be.

Amount of award:	$6,000
Number of applicants:	10

Contact:
NASA/Kentucky Space Grant Consortium
University of Kentucky- Coll. Of Eng.
112 Robotics Building
Lexington, KY 40506-0108
Phone: 859-218-6272
Fax: 859-257-3304
Web: nasa.engr.uky.edu

NASA Maine Space Grant Consortium

NASA Space Grant Maine Consortium Annual Scholarship and Fellowship Program

Type of award: Research grant, renewable.
Intended use: For full-time undergraduate or graduate study at accredited 4-year or graduate institution. Designated institutions: University of Maine (Orono), University of Maine (Presque Isle), University of Southern Maine, University of New England, Maine Maritime Academy, College of the Atlantic, Bowdoin College, Colby College, Bates College.
Eligibility: Applicant must be U.S. citizen.

Scholarships

Basis for selection: Major/career interest in astronomy; geology/earth sciences; geophysics; engineering; aerospace; biology or medicine.
Additional information: Applicants from out of state who attend one of the designated institutions are eligible. Research project must be in an aerospace-related field. Applications from academic institutions in Maine other than those designated will be reviewed for consideration. Visit Website for additional details.

Amount of award:	$3,000-$6,000
Total amount awarded:	$135,000

Contact:
Maine Space Grant Consortium
87 Winthrop Street
Suite 200
Augusta, ME 04330
Phone: 877-397-7223
Fax: 207-622-4548
Web: www.msgc.org

NASA Michigan Space Grant Consortium

MSGC Undergraduate Underrepresented Minority Fellowship Program

Type of award: Research grant.
Intended use: For full-time undergraduate study at 4-year institution in United States. Designated institutions: Michigan Space Grant Consortium member institutions.
Eligibility: Applicant must be African American, Hispanic American, American Indian or Native Hawaiian/Pacific Islander. Applicant must be U.S. citizen residing in Michigan.
Basis for selection: Major/career interest in aerospace; engineering; science, general or mathematics. Applicant must demonstrate high academic achievement.
Application requirements: Recommendations, essay, transcript, research proposal. Description of project expectations and specifications; 150-word abstract.
Additional information: Offers support in form of undergraduate research and public service fellowships to students in aerospace, space science, Earth system science and other related science, engineering, or math fields. Students working on educational research topics in math, science, or technology also eligible to apply. Preference given to projects directly related to aerospace, space science, earth system science, and directly related educational efforts. Students required to identify a mentor with whom they intend to work. Underrepresented minority students who have a GPA below 3.0, but have strong mentorship, do qualify for an award. Visit Website for more information.

Amount of award:	$2,500
Application deadline:	November 20
Notification begins:	February 28
Total amount awarded:	$14,000

Contact:
NASA Michigan Space Grant Consortium
University of Michigan
1320 Beal Ave. - 1049 FXB
Ann Arbor, MI 48109-2140
Phone: 734-764-9508
Fax: 734-763-6904
Web: www.umich.edu/~msgc

NASA Space Grant Michigan Undergraduate Fellowship

Type of award: Research grant, renewable.
Intended use: For undergraduate study at accredited 4-year institution. Designated institutions: Michigan Space Grant Consortium member institutions.
Eligibility: Applicant must be U.S. citizen.
Basis for selection: Major/career interest in aerospace; engineering; science, general or mathematics. Applicant must demonstrate high academic achievement.
Application requirements: Essay, transcript. Two letters of recommendation; description of project expectations and specifications; 150-word abstract.
Additional information: Offers support in form of undergraduate research and public service fellowships to students in aerospace, space science, Earth system science and other related science, engineering, or math fields. Students working on educational research topics in math, science, or technology also eligible to apply. Preference given to projects directly related to aerospace, space science, Earth system science, and directly related educational efforts. Announcements for next funding interval can be found on Website.

Amount of award:	$2,500-$5,000
Application deadline:	November 20
Notification begins:	February 28
Total amount awarded:	$100,000

Contact:
NASA Space Grant Michigan Space Grant Consortium
University of Michigan
1320 Beal Ave. - 1049 FXB
Ann Arbor, MI 48109-2140
Phone: 734-764-9508
Fax: 734-763-6904
Web: www.umich.edu/~msgc

NASA Minnesota Space Grant Consortium

NASA Minnesota Space Grant Consortium Wide Scholarship

Type of award: Scholarship, renewable.
Intended use: For full-time undergraduate study at accredited 2-year or 4-year institution in United States. Designated institutions: Augsburg College, Bethel University, Bemidji State University, Carleton College, Concordia College, Fond du Lac Tribal and Community College, Leech Lake Tribal College, Macalester College, Southwest Minnesota State University, St. Catherine University, University of Minnesota - Duluth, University of Minnesota - Twin Cities, University of St. Thomas.
Eligibility: Applicant must be U.S. citizen.

Basis for selection: Major/career interest in aerospace; astronomy; atmospheric sciences/meteorology; mathematics; engineering; chemistry; physics or geology/earth sciences. Applicant must demonstrate high academic achievement.
Application requirements: Recommendations, essay, transcript. Letter of intent.
Additional information: Minimum 3.2 GPA. Women, minority, and physically challenged students encouraged to apply. Applicant must be attending a Minnesota Space Grant Consortium school but does not have to be a resident of the state. Must major in aerospace, astronomy, physics, geology, chemistry, mathematics, computer science, or engineering. Students should contact Space Grant representative at their school. Application deadlines vary by school.

Amount of award:	$500-$2,500
Number of awards:	15
Number of applicants:	40

Contact:
NASA Minnesota Space Grant Consortium
U of M: Dept of Aerospace Engineering
107 Akerman Hall, 110 Union St. SE
Minneapolis, MN 55455
Phone: 612-626-9295
Web: www.aem.umn.edu/mnsgc

NASA Missouri Space Grant Consortium

NASA Missouri State Space Grant Undergraduate Scholarship

Type of award: Scholarship, renewable.
Intended use: For full-time undergraduate study at accredited 4-year institution in United States. Designated institutions: Missouri State University, University of Missouri - Columbia, University of Missouri - Kansas City, Missouri University of Science and Technology, University of Missouri - St. Louis, and Washington University in St. Louis.
Eligibility: Applicant must be U.S. citizen residing in Missouri.
Basis for selection: Major/career interest in aerospace; astronomy; engineering; geology/earth sciences; physics; mathematics or engineering, mechanical.
Application requirements: Recommendations, essay, transcript.
Additional information: Program encourages applications from eligible space science students. Awardees must attend Missouri Space Grant Consortium affiliate institution. Women, minority students, and physically challenged students are actively encouraged to apply. Deadline varies but is usually the first week in April. Check sponsor for exact date. Awards normally granted sometime in May.

Amount of award:	$1,500-$3,500
Number of awards:	45
Number of applicants:	41
Total amount awarded:	$140,000

Contact:
NASA Missouri Space Grant Consortium
Missouri University of Science and Technology
137 Toomey Hall
Rolla, MO 65409-0050
Phone: 573-341-4887
Fax: 573-341-4607
Web: www.mst.edu/~spaceg

NASA Montana Space Grant Consortium

NASA Space Grant Montana Undergraduate Scholarship Program

Type of award: Scholarship, renewable.
Intended use: For full-time undergraduate study at accredited 2-year or 4-year institution in United States. Designated institutions: Montana Space Grant Consortium member institutions.
Eligibility: Applicant must be U.S. citizen.
Basis for selection: Major/career interest in aerospace; biology; chemistry; geology/earth sciences; physics; astronomy; computer/information sciences; engineering, chemical; engineering, civil or engineering, electrical/electronic. Applicant must demonstrate depth of character and leadership.
Application requirements: Recommendations, essay, transcript.
Additional information: Must attend Montana Space Grant Consortium member institution, but does not need to be Montana resident. Awards for one year, renewable on a competitive basis. Recipients must agree to provide MSGC with information about studies and employment beyond period of award. Visit Website for more information.

Amount of award:	$1,500
Number of awards:	24
Number of applicants:	45
Application deadline:	April 1
Total amount awarded:	$24,000

Contact:
NASA Space Grant Montana Space Grant Consortium
Montana State University
416 Cobleigh Hall, P.O. Box 173835
Bozeman, MT 59717-3835
Phone: 406-994-4223
Fax: 406-994-4452
Web: www.spacegrant.montana.edu

NASA Nevada Space Grant Consortium

NASA Space Grant Nevada Undergraduate Scholarship

Type of award: Scholarship.
Intended use: For full-time undergraduate or graduate study at accredited postsecondary institution in United States. Designated institutions: Nevada System of Higher Education institutions.

Scholarships

Eligibility: Applicant must be U.S. citizen.
Basis for selection: Major/career interest in aerospace; astronomy; biology; chemistry; computer/information sciences; geology/earth sciences; engineering; mathematics; science, general or physics.
Application requirements: Transcript. Resume. Career goal statement, including applicant's motivation toward aerospace career.
Additional information: Minimum 3.0 GPA. Applicant must attend school in Nevada. Math, science, engineering, or majors in relevant fields eligible to apply. Application available on Website. Contact institution of interest for more information. Application deadline usually in mid-April.
Contact:
Nevada Space Grant Consortium Program Coordinator
5550 West Flamingo Road
Suite A2
Las Vegas, NV 89103
Phone: 702-522-7081
Web: www.nvspacegrant.org

NASA New Mexico Space Grant Consortium

NASA Space Grant New Mexico Undergraduate Scholarship

Type of award: Research grant, renewable.
Intended use: For full-time sophomore, junior, senior or graduate study at accredited 4-year institution in United States. Designated institutions: New Mexico Space Grant Consortium institutions.
Eligibility: Applicant must be U.S. citizen.
Basis for selection: Major/career interest in astronomy; biology; chemistry; computer/information sciences; engineering, chemical; engineering, civil; engineering, electrical/electronic; engineering, mechanical; physics or mathematics. Applicant must demonstrate high academic achievement.
Application requirements: Transcript, research proposal, nomination by faculty mentor.
Additional information: Minimum 3.0 GPA. Geology, earth science, environmental science, agriculture, range science, and fishery and wildlife science majors also eligible. Preference given to applicants who can show nonfederal matching funds. Women, minority students, and physically challenged students encouraged to apply. Visit Website for application and more information.

Amount of award:	$5,000
Number of applicants:	50
Application deadline:	March 15
Notification begins:	April 15
Total amount awarded:	$150,000

Contact:
NASA New Mexico Space Grant Consortium
Box 30001 MSC SG
Las Cruces, NM 88003
Phone: 575-646-6414
Fax: 575-646-7791
Web: www.nmspacegrant.com

NASA North Carolina Space Grant Consortium

NASA North Carolina Space Grant Consortium Undergraduate Research Scholarship

Type of award: Scholarship.
Intended use: For full-time junior or senior study at postsecondary institution. Designated institutions: North Carolina Space Grant Consortium member institutions.
Eligibility: Applicant must be returning adult student. Applicant must be U.S. citizen.
Basis for selection: Major/career interest in science, general; engineering; aerospace; mathematics or technology. Applicant must demonstrate high academic achievement and leadership.
Application requirements: Recommendations, transcript, research proposal.
Additional information: Minimum 3.0 GPA. Visit Website for more information and application.

Amount of award:	$2,000-$5,000
Number of awards:	25
Number of applicants:	40
Application deadline:	February 15
Notification begins:	April 15
Total amount awarded:	$50,000

Contact:
NASA North Carolina Space Grant
NCSU Box 7515
Raleigh, NC 27695-7515
Phone: 919-515-4240
Fax: 919-515-5934
Web: www.ncspacegrant.org

NASA North Carolina Space Grant Consortium Undergraduate Scholarship Program

Type of award: Scholarship, renewable.
Intended use: For full-time freshman or sophomore study at 4-year institution. Designated institutions: North Carolina Space Grant Consortium Member Institutions.
Eligibility: Applicant must be U.S. citizen.
Basis for selection: Major/career interest in science, general; engineering; aerospace; technology or mathematics. Applicant must demonstrate high academic achievement and leadership.
Application requirements: Recommendations, essay, transcript.
Additional information: Minimum 3.0 GPA. May be new or returning adult student. Visit Website for application and more information.

Amount of award:	$2,000-$5,000
Number of awards:	10
Number of applicants:	20
Application deadline:	February 15
Notification begins:	April 15
Total amount awarded:	$20,000

Contact:
NASA North Carolina Space Grant
NCSU Box 7515
Raleigh, NC 27695-7515
Phone: 919-515-4240
Fax: 919-515-5934
Web: www.ncspacegrant.org

NASA North Dakota Space Grant Consortium

NASA Space Grant North Dakota Consortium Lillian Goettler Scholarship

Type of award: Scholarship.
Intended use: For full-time undergraduate study at accredited postsecondary institution in United States. Designated institutions: North Dakota State University.
Eligibility: Applicant must be female. Applicant must be U.S. citizen.
Basis for selection: Major/career interest in engineering; mathematics or science, general. Applicant must demonstrate high academic achievement.
Additional information: Must have minimum 3.5 GPA and ideally be involved in research project of interest to NASA. Must be enrolled on campus at NDSGC institution; long distance learning programs not eligible. Contact coordinator for deadline information.

Amount of award:	$2,500

Contact:
North Dakota Space Grant Consortium
U of North Dakota, Space Studies Dept.
P.O. Box 9008
Grand Forks, ND 58202-9008
Phone: 701-777-4856
Web: www.nd.spacegrant.org

NASA Space Grant North Dakota Undergraduate Scholarship

Type of award: Scholarship, renewable.
Intended use: For full-time undergraduate study at 2-year or 4-year institution. Designated institutions: Tribal or public NDSGC member institutions.
Eligibility: Applicant must be U.S. citizen.
Basis for selection: Major/career interest in biology; chemistry; engineering; geology/earth sciences; computer/information sciences or mathematics. Applicant must demonstrate high academic achievement.
Application requirements: Recommendations, transcript, nomination by participating North Dakota Space Grant Consortium member institution.
Additional information: Minimum 3.0 GPA. Must be enrolled on campus at NDSGC institution; long distance learning programs not eligible. Consortium actively encourages women, minority students, and physically challenged students to apply. Deadlines vary. Contact financial aid office at institutions directly.

Amount of award:	$500-$750

Contact:
Financial Aid Office at eligible institutions.
Web: www.nd.spacegrant.org

Pearl I. Young Scholarship

Type of award: Scholarship.
Intended use: For full-time undergraduate study at accredited postsecondary institution in United States. Designated institutions: University of North Dakota.
Eligibility: Applicant must be female. Applicant must be U.S. citizen or permanent resident.
Basis for selection: Major/career interest in biology; chemistry; engineering; geology/earth sciences; computer/information sciences or mathematics. Applicant must demonstrate high academic achievement.
Additional information: Applicants must have minimum 3.5 GPA and ideally be involved in research project of interest to NASA. Must be enrolled on campus at NDSGC institution; long distance learning programs not eligible. Contact coordinator for deadline information.

Amount of award:	$2,500
Number of awards:	1

Contact:
NASA Space Grant North Dakota Space Grant Consortium
U of North Dakota, Space Studies Dept.
P.O. Box 9008
Grand Forks, ND 58202-9008
Phone: 701-777-4856
Web: www.nd.spacegrant.org

NASA Ohio Space Grant Consortium

NASA Ohio Space Grant Junior/ Senior Scholarship Program

Type of award: Scholarship, renewable.
Intended use: For full-time junior or senior study at accredited 4-year institution. Designated institutions: Ohio Space Grant Consortium members.
Eligibility: Applicant must be U.S. citizen.
Basis for selection: Major/career interest in science, general; engineering; aerospace or mathematics.
Application requirements: Recommendations, essay, transcript. Proposal of research project.
Additional information: Applications available at OSGC office at Consortium member institutions. Awardees required to participate in research projects and present results at annual OSGC Research Symposium.

Amount of award:	$3,000-$4,000
Number of awards:	60
Number of applicants:	75
Application deadline:	March 1
Notification begins:	April 30
Total amount awarded:	$130,000

Contact:
OSGC campus representative.
Phone: 800-828-6742
Web: www.osgc.org/scholarship.html

Scholarships

NASA Oregon Space Grant Consortium

NASA Space Grant Oregon Undergraduate Scholarship

Type of award: Scholarship.
Intended use: For undergraduate or graduate study at accredited 2-year or 4-year institution in United States. Designated institutions: Oregon State University, University of Oregon, Portland State University, Eastern Oregon University, Southern Oregon University, Oregon Institute of Technology, Western Oregon University, George Fox University, Portland Community Colleges (Sylvania, Rock Creek and Cascades Campuses), Lane Community College, Pacific University, Linn Benton Community College, University of Portland.
Eligibility: Applicant must be U.S. citizen.
Basis for selection: Major/career interest in science, general; engineering; aerospace; mathematics; physical sciences; education or technology. Applicant must demonstrate high academic achievement.
Application requirements: Recommendations, essay, transcript.
Additional information: Contact Space Grant Consortium representative on campus or see Website for application deadlines and more information.
Contact:
Oregon NASA Space Grant Consortium
Oregon State University
92 Kerr Administration Bldg.
Corvallis, OR 97331-2103
Phone: 541-737-2414
Fax: 541-737-9946
Web: spacegrant.oregonstate.edu

NASA Pennsylvania Space Grant Consortium

NASA Pennsylvania Space Grant Undergraduate Scholarship

Type of award: Scholarship.
Intended use: For full-time junior or senior study at accredited 4-year institution in United States. Designated institutions: Pennsylvania universities and colleges.
Eligibility: Applicant must be U.S. citizen.
Basis for selection: Major/career interest in science, general; mathematics; engineering; education; aerospace or astronomy. Applicant must demonstrate high academic achievement.
Application requirements: Recommendations, essay, transcript. Resume, SAT scores, description of research project and plan of study.
Additional information: Contact campus Space Grant Consortium representative for details. Consortium actively encourages women, minority, and physically challenged students to apply.

Amount of award:	$4,000
Number of awards:	4
Number of applicants:	12
Application deadline:	April 1
Total amount awarded:	$8,000

Contact:
NASA Pennsylvania Space Grant Consortium
Penn State, University Park
2217 Earth-Engineering Sciences Building
University Park, PA 16802
Phone: 814-865-2535
Fax: 814-863-9563
Web: www.pa.spacegrant.org

NASA Rhode Island Space Grant Consortium

NASA Rhode Island Space Grant Summer Undergraduate Scholarship

Type of award: Scholarship, renewable.
Intended use: For sophomore, junior or senior study at postsecondary institution. Designated institutions: Rhode Island Space Grant Consortium member institutions: Brown University, Bryant University, Community College of Rhode Island, Providence College, Roger Williams University, Rhode Island College, Rhode Island School of Design, Salve Regina University, University of Rhode Island, Wheaton College.
Eligibility: Applicant must be U.S. citizen.
Basis for selection: Major/career interest in aerospace; biology; engineering; geology/earth sciences or physics. Applicant must demonstrate high academic achievement.
Application requirements: Interview, recommendations, essay, transcript. Research proposal, resume.
Additional information: Awardees expected to devote four hours per week to science education outreach. Application deadline in late February; call sponsor for exact dates. Number of awards may vary. Topics of study in space sciences also funded. Students should contact their campus representative or the Rhode Island Space Grant office.

Amount of award:	$3,000
Number of awards:	3
Number of applicants:	5
Application deadline:	February 8

Contact:
NASA Rhode Island Space Grant Consortium
Brown University
Box 1846
Providence, RI 02912
Phone: 401-863-1151
Fax: 401-863-3978
Web: www.brown.edu/initiatives/ri-space-grant

NASA Space Grant Rhode Island Undergraduate Research Scholarship

Type of award: Scholarship.
Intended use: For sophomore, junior or senior study at postsecondary institution. Designated institutions: Rhode Island Space Grant Consortium member institutions: Brown University, Bryant University, Community College of Rhode Island, Providence College, Roger Williams University, Rhode

Island College, Rhode Island School of Design, Salve Regina University, University of Rhode Island, Wheaton College.
Eligibility: Applicant must be U.S. citizen.
Basis for selection: Major/career interest in aerospace; biology; engineering; geology/earth sciences or physics. Applicant must demonstrate high academic achievement.
Application requirements: Interview, recommendations, essay, transcript. Research proposal, resume.
Additional information: Awardees expected to work full-time with 75 percent of time devoted to research and the other 25 percent to science education outreach. Applications due in February; call sponsor for exact dates. Number of awards may vary. Topics of study in space sciences also funded. Students should contact campus representative or the Rhode Island Space Grant office.

Amount of award:	$4,500
Number of awards:	4
Number of applicants:	15

Contact:
NASA Rhode Island Space Grant Consortium
Brown University
Box 1846
Providence, RI 02912
Phone: 401-863-1151
Fax: 401-863-3978
Web: www.brown.edu/initiatives/ri-space-grant

NASA South Carolina Space Grant Consortium

NASA Space Grant South Carolina Undergraduate Student Research Fellowship

Type of award: Research grant, renewable.
Intended use: For full-time sophomore, junior or senior study at accredited 4-year institution in United States. Designated institutions: SCSGC member institutions.
Eligibility: Applicant must be U.S. citizen.
Basis for selection: Major/career interest in aerospace; astronomy; atmospheric sciences/meteorology; engineering; environmental science; geophysics; mathematics or science, general. Applicant must demonstrate high academic achievement.
Application requirements: Recommendations, essay, transcript, research proposal. Faculty sponsorship. Resume.
Additional information: Applicants must attend South Carolina Space Grant Consortium member institution. Applicants must have sponsorship from a faculty advisor. Applicants may have a field of study or interest related to any NASA enterprise. Presentation and written report on project findings due within one year of completion. Consortium actively encourages women, minority, and disabled students to apply. See Website for application and more information.

Amount of award:	$5,000

Contact:
NASA South Carolina Space Grant Consortium, Tara B. Scozzaro, MPA
College of Charleston
66 George Street
Charleston, SC 29424
Phone: 843-953-5463
Fax: 843-953-5446
Web: www.cofc.edu/~scsgrant/scholar/overview.html

NASA Texas Space Grant Consortium

STEM Columbia Crew Memorial Scholarship

Type of award: Scholarship.
Intended use: For sophomore, junior or senior study at 2-year or 4-year institution in United States. Designated institutions: Texas Space Grant Consortium member institutions.
Eligibility: Applicant must be U.S. citizen.
Basis for selection: Major/career interest in science, general; technology; engineering or mathematics. Applicant must demonstrate high academic achievement.
Application requirements: Recommendations, transcript.
Additional information: First and second year medical students also eligible. Deadline in February or March. Check Website for details.

Amount of award:	$1,500
Number of awards:	30
Number of applicants:	100
Total amount awarded:	$45,000

Contact:
NASA Texas Space Grant Consortium
University of Texas at Austin
3925 West Braker Lane
Austin, TX 78759-5321
Phone: 800-248-8742
Web: www.tsgc.utexas.edu

NASA Utah Space Grant Consortium

NASA Utah Space Grant Consortium Undergraduate Scholarship

Type of award: Scholarship, renewable.
Intended use: For full-time undergraduate or graduate study at accredited postsecondary institution in United States. Designated institutions: Brigham Young University, Dixie State College, Salt Lake Community College, Snow College, Southern Utah University, Utah College of Applied Technology, The Leonardo, Utah State University, Utah Valley University, University of Utah, Weaver State University, Weber State University, and Westminster College.
Eligibility: Applicant must be U.S. citizen.

Basis for selection: Major/career interest in science, general; mathematics; engineering or technology. Applicant must demonstrate high academic achievement.
Application requirements: Recommendations, transcript, research proposal. Resume.
Additional information: Award varies from year to year. Contact sponsor for deadline information. Must be used at Utah Space Grant Consortium member institution. Award amounts are per month during academic year. Deadlines vary; check Website for details.

Amount of award:	$3,000-$9,000
Number of awards:	15
Number of applicants:	60
Total amount awarded:	$180,000

Contact:
Rocky Mountain NASA Space Grant Consortium
Utah State University
4120 Old Main Hill
Logan, UT 84322-4120
Phone: 435-797-0496
Fax: 435-797-3382
Web: www.utahspacegrant.com

NASA Vermont Space Grant Consortium

NASA Space Grant Vermont Consortium Undergraduate Scholarships

Type of award: Scholarship, renewable.
Intended use: For full-time undergraduate study at accredited postsecondary institution in United States. Designated institutions: Vermont institutions.
Eligibility: Applicant must be high school senior. Applicant must be U.S. citizen residing in Vermont.
Basis for selection: Major/career interest in science, general; engineering; mathematics; aerospace or physics. Applicant must demonstrate high academic achievement.
Application requirements: Recommendations, essay, transcript.
Additional information: Open to high school seniors in Vermont who intend to be enrolled full-time in the following year. Applicant must be enrolled in program relevant to NASA's goals at a Vermont institution. Minimum 3.0 GPA. Three awards designated for Native American applicants; three scholarships designated for Burlington Technical Center Aviation & Technical Center, Aerospace Work Force Development, and Aviation Technical School. Can be used at any accredited Vermont institution of higher education. Application deadline in April. Must attend awards ceremony and provide a report detailing impact of scholarship. Check website for details.

Amount of award:	$5,000
Number of awards:	10
Number of applicants:	15
Application deadline:	April 12
Notification begins:	May 17
Total amount awarded:	$18,000

Contact:
Vermont Space Grant Consortium
Votey Hall, College of Engineering and Math
University of Vermont
Burlington, VT 05405-0156
Phone: 802-656-1429
Web: www.cems.uvm.edu/VSGC

NASA Virginia Space Grant Consortium

Aerospace Undergraduate STEM Research Scholarship Program

Type of award: Scholarship.
Intended use: For full-time undergraduate study at accredited 4-year institution in United States. Designated institutions: Space Grant Consortium schools.
Eligibility: Applicant must be U.S. citizen.
Basis for selection: Major/career interest in aerospace; astronomy; chemistry; computer/information sciences; engineering; geology/earth sciences; mathematics or physics. Applicant must demonstrate high academic achievement.
Application requirements: Recommendations, essay, transcript, research proposal. Resume. Budget proposal.
Additional information: Any undergraduate major that includes coursework related to an understanding of aerospace is eligible. Must have completed at least two years of a STEM undergraduate program. Minimum 3.0 GPA. Awards can include $3,000 stipend plus $1,000 travel/research during the academic year, and $3,500 stipend plus $1,000 travel/research during the summer (ten weeks). Awardees must attend a Virginia Space Grant Consortium member institution and participate in USGC's Annual Student Research Conference. The consortium actively encourages women, minorities, and students with disabilities to apply.

Amount of award:	$1,000-$3,500
Application deadline:	February 10
Notification begins:	April 15

Contact:
Virginia Space Grant Consortium
600 Butler Farm Road, Suite 2253
Hampton, VA 23666
Phone: 757-766-5210
Fax: 757-766-5205
Web: www.vsgc.odu.edu

NASA Space Grant Virginia Community College STEM Scholarship

Type of award: Scholarship.
Intended use: For full-time sophomore study at accredited 2-year institution in United States. Designated institutions: Virginia community colleges.
Eligibility: Applicant must be U.S. citizen.
Basis for selection: Major/career interest in aerospace; computer/information sciences; electronics; engineering; mathematics; science, general or technology. Applicant must demonstrate high academic achievement.
Application requirements: Recommendations, essay, transcript. Resume, biographical information.

Additional information: Must apply during freshman year and be majoring in STEM program of study. Must have completed at least one semester of coursework. Minimum 3.0 GPA. Scholarship is open to students at all community colleges in Virginia. Application deadline may vary. Women, minorities, and students with disabilities are encouraged to apply. Visit Website for application.

Amount of award: $2,000
Application deadline: March 15
Notification begins: April 1

Contact:
Virginia Space Grant Consortium
600 Butler Farm Road, Suite 2253
Hampton, VA 23666
Phone: 757-766-5210
Fax: 757-766-5205
Web: www.vsgc.odu.edu

STEM Bridge Scholarship

Type of award: Scholarship, renewable.
Intended use: For full-time sophomore study at accredited 4-year institution in United States. Designated institutions: Virginia Space Grant Consortium member institutions.
Eligibility: Applicant must be Alaskan native, Asian American, African American, Mexican American, Hispanic American, Puerto Rican, American Indian or Native Hawaiian/Pacific Islander. Applicant must be U.S. citizen.
Basis for selection: Major/career interest in science, general; technology; engineering or mathematics.
Additional information: Minimum 3.0 GPA. Must be sophomore from federally recognized minority group with STEM major.

Amount of award: $1,000

Contact:
NASA Virginia Space Grant Consortium
600 Butler Farm Road, Suite 2253
Hampton, VA 23666
Phone: 757-766-5210
Fax: 757-766-5205
Web: www.vsgc.odu.edu

NASA West Virginia Space Grant Consortium

NASA West Virginia Space Grant Undergraduate Research Fellowship

Type of award: Scholarship.
Intended use: For full-time undergraduate study at accredited 4-year institution in United States. Designated institutions: West Virginia Space Grant Consortium member institutions.
Eligibility: Applicant must be U.S. citizen.
Basis for selection: Major/career interest in aerospace; science, general; engineering or mathematics. Applicant must demonstrate high academic achievement and seriousness of purpose.
Application requirements: Recommendations, essay, research proposal. Resume. One recommendation must be from research advisor. Proposal must include statement of purpose, methodology, expected results, and timeline.
Additional information: Visit Website for more information and application. Female and minority students encouraged to apply.

Amount of award: $4,500-$5,000
Application deadline: February 28
Notification begins: April 1

Contact:
NASA West Virginia Space Grant Consortium, West Virginia University
G-68 Engineering Sciences Building
P.O. Box 6070
Morgantown, WV 26506-6070
Phone: 304-293-4099 ext. 3738
Fax: 304-293-4970
Web: www.nasa.wvu.edu

NASA Wisconsin Space Grant Consortium

NASA Space Grant Wisconsin Consortium Undergraduate Research Program

Type of award: Research grant.
Intended use: For full-time undergraduate study at 2-year or 4-year institution. Designated institutions: WSGC colleges and universities.
Eligibility: Applicant must be U.S. citizen.
Basis for selection: Major/career interest in aerospace; astronomy; engineering; science, general; architecture; law; business or medicine. Applicant must demonstrate high academic achievement and seriousness of purpose.
Application requirements: Recommendations, transcript, research proposal. Project proposal with budget.
Additional information: Funding for qualified students to create and implement a research project related to aerospace, space science, or other interdisciplinary space-related studies. For academic year or summer term use. Minimum 3.0 GPA and above-average SAT/ACT scores required. Consortium encourages applications from women, minorities, and students with disabilities. For more information, see Website.

Amount of award: $3,500-$4,000
Number of awards: 8
Application deadline: February 1
Notification begins: March 30
Total amount awarded: $28,000

Contact:
Wisconsin Space Grant Consortium
University of Wisconsin, Green Bay
2420 Nicolet Drive
Green Bay, WI 54311-7001
Phone: 608-785-8431
Fax: 608-785-8403
Web: www.uwgb.edu/wsgc

NASA Space Grant Wisconsin Consortium Undergraduate Scholarship

Type of award: Scholarship, renewable.
Intended use: For full-time undergraduate study at accredited 4-year institution in United States. Designated institutions: WSGC colleges and universities.
Eligibility: Applicant must be U.S. citizen.

Basis for selection: Major/career interest in aerospace; astronomy; engineering; physics or science, general. Applicant must demonstrate high academic achievement.
Application requirements: Recommendations, essay, transcript.
Additional information: Applicant must attend Wisconsin Space Grant Consortium member institution and reside in Wisconsin during school year. Minimum 3.0 GPA and above-average SAT/ACT scores required. Qualified students may also apply for summer session's Undergraduate Research Award. Consortium actively encourages women, minorities, and students with disabilities to apply. See Website for application and details.

Amount of award:	$1,500
Application deadline:	February 1
Notification begins:	March 30

Contact:
Wisconsin Space Grant Consortium
University of Wisconsin, Green Bay
2420 Nicolet Drive
Green Bay, WI 54311-7001
Phone: 920-465-2108
Web: www.uwgb.edu/wsgc

National Academy for Nuclear Training

NANT Educational Assistance Program

Type of award: Scholarship, renewable.
Intended use: For full-time junior or senior study at accredited 4-year institution in United States.
Eligibility: Applicant must be U.S. citizen.
Basis for selection: Major/career interest in engineering, chemical; engineering, mechanical; engineering, electrical/electronic or engineering, nuclear. Applicant must demonstrate high academic achievement, depth of character, leadership, seriousness of purpose and service orientation.
Application requirements: Recommendations, transcript, proof of eligibility, nomination by INPO member utility.
Additional information: Minimum 3.0 GPA. Must have work experience at INPO member utility. Renewal for eligible students. Additional field of study: power generation health physics. Study of chemical engineering must include nuclear or power option. Applicant should be considering career in nuclear utility industry. For additional information and application deadline, contact by e-mail or visit Website. Application deadline in mid-June.

Amount of award:	$2,500
Number of awards:	125
Notification begins:	August 1

Contact:
National Academy for Nuclear Training Scholarship Program
101 ACT Drive
P.O. Box 4030
Iowa City, IA 52243-4030
Phone: 800-294-7492
Fax: 319-337-1204
Web: www.nei.org/careersandeducation

National Amateur Baseball Federation, Inc.

National Amateur Baseball Federation Scholarship

Type of award: Scholarship, renewable.
Intended use: For undergraduate study at accredited postsecondary institution in United States or Canada.
Basis for selection: Competition/talent/interest in athletics/sports. Major/career interest in athletic training. Applicant must demonstrate financial need and high academic achievement.
Application requirements: Recommendations, transcript, proof of eligibility, nomination by National Amateur Baseball Federation member association. Written statement. Documentation of previous awards received from sponsoring association, nomination by president or director of franchised member team.
Additional information: Amount of award determined annually. Applicant must have participated in National Amateur Baseball Federation event in the current season and be sponsored by National Amateur Baseball Federation member association. See Website for application.

Amount of award:	$500-$1,000
Number of awards:	10
Number of applicants:	11
Application deadline:	October 1
Notification begins:	January
Total amount awarded:	$3,000

Contact:
National Amateur Baseball Federation
Attn: Chairman Awards Committee
P.O. Box 705
Bowie, MD 20718
Phone: 410-721-4727
Fax: 410-721-4940
Web: www.nabf.com

National Association of Black Accountants Inc.

NABA National Scholarship Program

Type of award: Scholarship.
Intended use: For full-time undergraduate or master's study at 4-year or graduate institution.
Eligibility: Applicant must be Alaskan native, Asian American, African American, Mexican American, Hispanic American, Puerto Rican, American Indian or Native Hawaiian/Pacific Islander.
Basis for selection: Major/career interest in accounting; business; finance/banking or technology. Applicant must demonstrate high academic achievement, depth of character, leadership and service orientation.
Application requirements: Recommendations, essay, transcript, proof of eligibility. Resume.
Additional information: Must be active National Association of Black Accountants member. Applicants must have minimum

2.5 GPA for some awards, 3.3 GPA for others. Applicants must join association by December 31.

Amount of award: $1,000-$10,000
Number of awards: 40
Number of applicants: 350
Application deadline: January 31
Notification begins: April 30
Total amount awarded: $500,000

Contact:
National Association of Black Accountants Inc.
National Scholarship Program
7474 Greenway Center Drive, #1120
Greenbelt, MD 20770
Phone: 301-474-6222
Fax: 301-474-3114
Web: www.nabainc.org

National Association of Black Journalists

Allison E. Fisher Scholarship

Type of award: Scholarship.
Intended use: For undergraduate or graduate study at postsecondary institution.
Eligibility: Applicant must be U.S. citizen, permanent resident or international student.
Basis for selection: Major/career interest in journalism. Applicant must demonstrate high academic achievement and service orientation.
Application requirements: Recommendations, essay, transcript. Cover letter, resume. Applicants must submit minimum of five samples of published work in print, radio, television, photography, slideshows, website, or flash animation. Must send four copies of all application materials. Essay on topic: What are the top three reasons you would like to pursue a career in journalism and what do you hope your legacy as a journalist will be?"
Additional information: Minimum 3.0 GPA. Must be a print or broadcast journalism major and a member of NABJ. Deadline in March. Check Website for details.

Amount of award: $2,500
Number of awards: 1
Total amount awarded: $2,500

Contact:
National Association of Black Journalists
1100 Knight Hall, Suite 3100
College Park, MD 20742
Phone: 301-405-2573
Fax: 301-314-1714
Web: www.nabj.org

Carole Simpson Scholarship

Type of award: Scholarship.
Intended use: For undergraduate or graduate study at accredited 4-year or graduate institution.
Eligibility: Applicant must be African American. Applicant must be U.S. citizen, permanent resident or international student.
Basis for selection: Major/career interest in journalism or radio/television/film. Applicant must demonstrate high academic achievement.
Application requirements: Recommendations, essay, transcript. Resume, cover letter. Applicants must submit minimum of five samples of published work in print, radio, television, photography, slideshows, website, or flash animation. Essay topic: "How has Carole Simpson's career inspired you to pursue a career in broadcast journalism and what do you hope your legacy will be?"
Additional information: Minimum 2.5 GPA. Must be member of National Association of Black Journalists and major in broadcast journalism. Deadline in March. Check Website for details.

Amount of award: $2,500
Number of awards: 1
Total amount awarded: $2,500

Contact:
National Association of Black Journalists
1100 Knight Hall, Suite 3100
College Park, MD 20742
Phone: 301-405-2573
Fax: 301-314-1714
Web: www.nabj.org

DeWayne Wickham Founder's High School Scholarship

Type of award: Scholarship.
Intended use: For full-time freshman study at accredited 4-year institution in United States.
Eligibility: Applicant must be high school senior.
Basis for selection: Major/career interest in journalism or communications. Applicant must demonstrate financial need, high academic achievement and service orientation.
Application requirements: Portfolio, recommendations, essay, transcript. Resume, cover letter, work samples.
Additional information: GPA must be between 2.5 and 3.0 Must be high school senior and member of National Association of Black Journalists and major in broadcast journalism. Deadline in March. Check Website for details.

Amount of award: $2,500
Number of awards: 1

Contact:
National Association of Black Journalists
1100 Knight Hall, Suite 3100
College Park, MD 20742
Phone: 301-405-0248
Fax: 301-314-1714
Web: www.nabj.org

Larry Whiteside Scholarship

Type of award: Scholarship.
Intended use: For junior, senior or graduate study at accredited 4-year institution.
Eligibility: Applicant must be African American.
Basis for selection: Major/career interest in journalism. Applicant must demonstrate high academic achievement.
Application requirements: Portfolio, recommendations, essay, transcript. Resume, cover letter. Must submit three samples of work. Essay must profile sports journalist and why that person inspired you to pursue sports journalism as a career.
Additional information: Minimum 2.5 GPA in major and 2.0 major overall. Must be member of National Association of Black Journalists and be pursuing career in sports journalism. Recipient will receive free trip to NABJ Convention in Orlando, Florida. Deadline in March. Check Website for details.

Amount of award: $2,500
Number of awards: 1
Total amount awarded: $2,500
Contact:
National Association of Black Journalists
1100 Knight Hall, Suite 3100
College Park, MD 20742
Phone: 301-405-2573
Fax: 301-314-1714
Web: www.nabj.org

NABJ Scholarship

Type of award: Scholarship.
Intended use: For full-time undergraduate study at accredited 4-year institution in United States.
Basis for selection: Major/career interest in journalism or communications. Applicant must demonstrate high academic achievement and service orientation.
Application requirements: Portfolio, essay, transcript. Resume, cover letter, work samples.
Additional information: Minimum 2.5 GPA. Must be member of National Association of Black Journalists and major in journalism. Deadline in March. Check Website for details.
Amount of award: $2,500
Number of awards: 1
Contact:
National Association of Black Journalists
1100 Knight Hall, Suite 3100
College Park, MD 20742
Phone: 301-405-0248
Fax: 301-314-1714
Web: www.nabj.org

NABJ Visual Task Force (VTF) Scholarship

Type of award: Scholarship.
Intended use: For undergraduate or graduate study at 4-year or graduate institution.
Eligibility: Applicant must be African American.
Basis for selection: Major/career interest in journalism. Applicant must demonstrate high academic achievement.
Application requirements: Portfolio, recommendations, essay, transcript. Resume, cover letter. Applicants must submit minimum of five samples of published work in print, radio, television, photography, slideshows, Website, or flash animation. Essay should answer question: "What are the top three reasons you would like to pursue a career in visual journalism and how do you use your visual skills to effectively and creatively tell the story?"
Additional information: Minimum 2.75 GPA. Must be member of National Association of Black Journalists and have declared a concentration in visual journalism. Must have experience working on campus newspaper or TV studio and have had one internship. Deadline in March. Check Website for details.
Amount of award: $1,250
Number of awards: 2
Total amount awarded: $1,500
Contact:
National Association of Black Journalists
1100 Knight Hall, Suite 3100
College Park, MD 20742
Phone: 301-405-2573
Fax: 301-314-1714
Web: www.nabj.org

National Association of Letter Carriers

Costas G. Lemonopoulos Scholarship

Type of award: Scholarship, renewable.
Intended use: For full-time undergraduate study at accredited 4-year institution. Designated institutions: St. Petersburg Junior College or four-year public Florida university.
Basis for selection: Applicant must demonstrate high academic achievement.
Application requirements: Transcript. SAT/ACT scores and NALC form.
Additional information: Applicant must be child of National Association of Letter Carriers member in good standing (active, retired, or deceased). Preliminary application available on Website; required for further details and primary application form. Notification published in March issue of Postal Record magazine.
Number of awards: 20
Number of applicants: 150
Application deadline: June 1
Contact:
National Association of Letter Carriers
Costas G. Lemonopoulos Scholarship Trust
100 Indiana Avenue NW
Washington, DC 20001-2144
Phone: 202-393-4695
Fax: 202-737-1540
Web: www.nalc.org/nalc/members/scholarships.html

William C. Doherty Scholarships

Type of award: Scholarship, renewable.
Intended use: For full-time undergraduate study at accredited 4-year institution.
Eligibility: Applicant must be high school senior.
Basis for selection: Applicant must demonstrate financial need and high academic achievement.
Application requirements: Recommendations, essay, transcript, proof of eligibility. SAT/ACT scores.
Additional information: Applicant must be child of National Association of Letter Carriers member in good standing (active, retired, or deceased) for at least one year. Preliminary application on Website due December 31; supporting materials due March 31. Notification published in July issue of Postal Record magazine.
Amount of award: $4,000
Number of awards: 5
Number of applicants: 1,200
Application deadline: December 31
Total amount awarded: $21,000
Contact:
National Association of Letter Carriers
Scholarship Committee
100 Indiana Avenue NW
Washington, DC 20001-2144
Phone: 202-393-4695
Fax: 202-737-1540
Web: www.nalc.org/nalc/members/scholarships.html

National Association of Water Companies (NJ Chapter)

Water Companies (NJ Chapter) Scholarship

Type of award: Scholarship.
Intended use: For freshman, sophomore, junior, senior or graduate study at accredited 2-year, 4-year or graduate institution in United States. Designated institutions: New Jersey colleges and universities.
Eligibility: Applicant must be U.S. citizen residing in New Jersey.
Basis for selection: Major/career interest in hydrology; natural resources/conservation; science, general; engineering, environmental; finance/banking; communications; accounting; business; computer/information sciences or law. Applicant must demonstrate financial need, high academic achievement, depth of character, leadership, seriousness of purpose and service orientation.
Application requirements: Recommendations, essay, transcript. Essay must illustrate interest in water utility industry or related field.
Additional information: Applicant must have interest in fields of study related to water industry. Acceptable fields of study also include consumer affairs and human resources. At least five years residence in New Jersey required. Minimum 3.0 GPA.

Amount of award:	$2,500
Number of awards:	2
Number of applicants:	80
Application deadline:	April 1
Notification begins:	June 1
Total amount awarded:	$2,500

Contact:
Nat'l Assn. of Water Companies (NJ Chapter)
Gail P. Brady
49 Howell Drive
Verona, NJ 07044
Phone: 973-669-5807

National Association of Women in Construction

NAWIC Founders' Construction Trades Scholarship

Type of award: Scholarship.
Intended use: For undergraduate study at postsecondary institution.
Basis for selection: Major/career interest in construction or construction management. Applicant must demonstrate financial need.
Application requirements: Essay. Resume, list of extracurricular activities.
Additional information: Must be currently enrolled in construction-related training program approved by the Bureau of Apprenticeship Training or home state's Postsecondary Education Commission. Visit Website for application.

Amount of award:	$500-$2,500
Application deadline:	February 28
Total amount awarded:	$25,000

Contact:
National Association of Women in Construction
327 South Adams Street
Fort Worth, TX 76104
Phone: 800-552-3506
Web: www.nawic.org

NAWIC Founders' Undergraduate Scholarship

Type of award: Scholarship.
Intended use: For full-time undergraduate study at accredited 2-year or 4-year institution in United States or Canada.
Eligibility: Applicant must be U.S. citizen.
Basis for selection: Major/career interest in construction; construction management; engineering, construction or architecture. Applicant must demonstrate financial need and high academic achievement.
Application requirements: Interview, recommendations, essay, transcript. Resume.
Additional information: Number and amount of awards vary. Interest in construction, extracurricular activities, and employment experience also taken into consideration. Applicants must have completed three terms of study in construction-related field. Minimum 3.0 GPA. Only semifinalists will be interviewed. Visit Website for additional information and application.

Amount of award:	$500-$2,500
Application deadline:	February 28
Notification begins:	April 1
Total amount awarded:	$25,000

Contact:
National Association of Women in Construction
327 South Adams Street
Fort Worth, TX 76104
Phone: 800-552-3506
Web: www.nawic.org

National Athletic Trainers' Association Research & Education Foundation

Athletic Trainers' Entry Level Scholarship

Type of award: Scholarship.
Intended use: For full-time junior, senior, master's or doctoral study at 4-year or graduate institution.
Basis for selection: Major/career interest in athletic training. Applicant must demonstrate high academic achievement.
Application requirements: Recommendations, essay, transcript, proof of eligibility, nomination by BOC certified trainer.
Additional information: Must be National Athletic Trainers' Association member. Minimum 3.2 GPA. Intention to pursue the profession of athletic training as career required. Must be sponsored by a certified athletic trainer. Must be enrolled in Commission on Accreditation of Athletic Training Education

(CAATE)-accredited undergraduate or master's program. See complete guidelines on Website.

Amount of award:	$2,300
Application deadline:	February 4
Notification begins:	May 1

Contact:
National Athletic Trainers' Association
Research & Education Foundation
2952 Stemmons Freeway
Dallas, TX 75247
Phone: 800-879-6282 ext. 121
Fax: 214-637-2206
Web: www.natafoundation.org

National Black Nurses Association

Black Nurses Scholarship

Type of award: Scholarship.
Intended use: For undergraduate or graduate study at postsecondary institution.
Eligibility: Applicant must be African American.
Basis for selection: Major/career interest in nursing or nurse practitioner. Applicant must demonstrate leadership, seriousness of purpose and service orientation.
Application requirements: Recommendations, essay, transcript. Evidence of participation in both student nursing activities and the African-American community.
Additional information: Must be member of National Black Nurses Association and member of local chapter if one exists. Must be currently enrolled in a nursing program and have at least one full year of school left. Must be in good academic standing. Call association for current information on program.

Amount of award:	$500-$2,500
Number of awards:	12
Application deadline:	April 15
Notification begins:	July 1

Contact:
National Black Nurses Association
8630 Fenton Street
Room 330
Silver Spring, MD 20910
Phone: 301-589-3200
Fax: 301-589-3223
Web: www.nbna.org

National Commission for Cooperative Education

National Co-op Scholarship

Type of award: Scholarship, renewable.
Intended use: For undergraduate study at postsecondary institution. Designated institutions: Clarkson University, Drexel University, Johnson & Wales University, Kettering University, Rochester Institute of Technology, SUNY Oswego, University of Cincinnati, University of Massachusetts - Lowell, University of Toledo, Wentworth Institute of Technology.
Eligibility: Applicant must be high school senior. Applicant must be U.S. citizen.
Basis for selection: Applicant must demonstrate high academic achievement.
Application requirements: One-page essay on decision to pursue a college cooperative education program.
Additional information: Applicants must be accepted to and attend one of the twelve participating institutions. Application deadlines vary by institution. Minimum 3.5 GPA. Visit Website for more information and application.

Amount of award:	$6,000
Number of awards:	195
Total amount awarded:	$930,000

Contact:
National Commission for Cooperative Education
600 Suffolk Street
Suite 125
Lowell, MA 01854
Phone: 978-934-1870
Web: www.co-op.edu

National Dairy Shrine

Dairy Student Recognition Program

Type of award: Scholarship.
Intended use: For senior study at postsecondary institution.
Eligibility: Applicant must be U.S. citizen or Canadian citizen.
Basis for selection: Major/career interest in agriculture; business; dairy; environmental science; food production/management/services; food science/technology; law; manufacturing; marketing or veterinary medicine. Applicant must demonstrate leadership.
Application requirements: Recommendations, essay, transcript, nomination by college or university dairy-science department.
Additional information: Applicant must be recommended by university department. Must be U.S. or Canadian citizen. Cash awards for graduating seniors planning career in dairy cattle. Two candidates eligible per institution. First-place winner receives $2,000; second, $1,500; third through seventh, $1,000. National Dairy Shrine chooses final winners. Students who placed in top five in previous years not eligible for further competition.

Amount of award:	$1,000-$2,000
Number of awards:	9
Number of applicants:	22
Application deadline:	April 15
Notification begins:	August 1
Total amount awarded:	$9,500

Contact:
National Dairy Shrine
P.O. Box 725
Denmark, WI 54208
Phone: 920-863-6333
Fax: 920-863-6333
Web: www.dairyshrine.org

DMI Milk Marketing Scholarships

Type of award: Scholarship.
Intended use: For sophomore or junior study at postsecondary institution.
Eligibility: Applicant must be U.S. citizen.

Basis for selection: Major/career interest in agriculture; animal sciences; dairy; dietetics/nutrition or education. Applicant must demonstrate high academic achievement.
Application requirements: Recommendations, essay, transcript.
Additional information: For students interested in careers marketing milk or dairy products. Minimum 2.5 GPA. Visit Website for more details.

Amount of award:	$1,000-$1,500
Number of awards:	8
Number of applicants:	22
Application deadline:	April 15
Notification begins:	August 1
Total amount awarded:	$8,500

Contact:
National Dairy Shrine
P.O. Box 725
Denmark, WI 54208
Phone: 920-863-6333
Fax: 920-863-6333
Web: www.dairyshrine.org

Iager Dairy Scholarship

Type of award: Scholarship.
Intended use: For undergraduate study at 2-year institution.
Eligibility: Applicant must be U.S. citizen.
Basis for selection: Major/career interest in food production/management/services; food science/technology or dairy. Applicant must demonstrate high academic achievement and leadership.
Application requirements: Recommendations, essay, transcript.
Additional information: Must be second-year college student in two-year agricultural college. Minimum 2.5 GPA. May request application from Website or National Dairy Shrine.

Amount of award:	$1,000
Number of awards:	2
Number of applicants:	9
Application deadline:	April 15
Notification begins:	August 1
Total amount awarded:	$2,000

Contact:
National Dairy Shrine
P.O. Box 725
Denmark, WI 54208
Phone: 920-863-6333
Fax: 920-863-6333
Web: www.dairyshrine.org

Kildee Scholarship

Type of award: Scholarship.
Intended use: For junior, senior or graduate study at postsecondary institution.
Eligibility: Applicant must be U.S. citizen.
Basis for selection: Major/career interest in animal sciences; dairy; food production/management/services; food science/technology or veterinary medicine. Applicant must demonstrate high academic achievement and leadership.
Application requirements: Recommendations, essay, transcript.
Additional information: Applicant must have placed in top 25 in National 4-H, FFA or National Intercollegiate Judging Contests. First or second place winners from National Dairy Challenge are eligible to compete for graduate study scholarships. Up to two $3,000 scholarships for graduate study and one $2,000 scholarship for undergraduate study awarded. May request application from Website or National Dairy Shrine.

Amount of award:	$2,000-$3,000
Number of awards:	3
Number of applicants:	10
Application deadline:	April 15
Notification begins:	August 1
Total amount awarded:	$8,000

Contact:
National Dairy Shrine
P.O. Box 725
Denmark, WI 54208
Phone: 920-863-6333
Fax: 920-863-6333
Web: www.dairyshrine.org

Klussendorf Scholarship

Type of award: Scholarship.
Intended use: For sophomore, junior or senior study at 2-year or 4-year institution.
Eligibility: Applicant must be U.S. citizen.
Basis for selection: Major/career interest in animal sciences or dairy.
Application requirements: Recommendations, essay, transcript.
Additional information: For dairy or animal science majors in second, third, or fourth year of college. Must plan to become dairy cattle breeder, owner, herdsperson, or fitter. May request application from Website or National Dairy Shrine. Applicant must be U.S. or Canadian citizen.

Amount of award:	$2,000
Number of awards:	6
Number of applicants:	40
Application deadline:	April 15
Notification begins:	August 1
Total amount awarded:	$12,000

Contact:
National Dairy Shrine
P.O. Box 725
Denmark, WI 54208
Phone: 920-863-6333
Fax: 920-863-6333
Web: www.dairyshrine.org

Marshall E. McCullough Undergraduate Scholarship

Type of award: Scholarship.
Intended use: For full-time undergraduate study at accredited 4-year institution in United States.
Eligibility: Applicant must be high school senior. Applicant must be U.S. citizen.
Basis for selection: Major/career interest in animal sciences; dairy; communications or journalism.
Application requirements: Recommendations, essay, transcript.
Additional information: Finalists will be asked to submit video responding to specific questions about the dairy industry. Two awards: one for $2,500; one for $1,000. Must major in dairy/animal science with communications emphasis or agricultural journalism with dairy/animal science emphasis.

Amount of award:	$1,000-$2,500
Number of awards:	2
Number of applicants:	7
Application deadline:	April 15
Notification begins:	August 1
Total amount awarded:	$3,500

Contact:
National Dairy Shrine
P.O. Box 725
Denmark, WI 54208
Phone: 920-863-6333
Fax: 920-863-6333
Web: www.dairyshrine.org

National Dairy Shrine Maurice E. Core Scholarship

Type of award: Scholarship, renewable.
Intended use: For full-time freshman study at accredited 4-year institution.
Eligibility: Applicant must be U.S. citizen.
Basis for selection: Major/career interest in agriculture; animal sciences or dairy. Applicant must demonstrate high academic achievement, leadership and seriousness of purpose.
Application requirements: Recommendations, essay, transcript.
Additional information: Minimum 2.5 GPA. Student must have commitment to career in dairy.

Amount of award:	$1,000
Number of awards:	1
Number of applicants:	12
Application deadline:	April 15
Notification begins:	August 1
Total amount awarded:	$1,000

Contact:
National Dairy Shrine
P.O. Box 725
Denmark, WI 54208
Phone: 920-863-6333
Fax: 920-863-6333
Web: www.dairyshrine.org

National Eagle Scout Association

Hall/McElwain Merit Scholarship

Type of award: Scholarship.
Intended use: For undergraduate study at postsecondary institution.
Eligibility: Applicant must be male.
Basis for selection: Applicant must demonstrate leadership.
Application requirements: Recommendations, proof of eligibility.
Additional information: Applicant must be Eagle Scout. Must have strong record of participation in activities outside of scouting. Visit Website for more information and application.

Amount of award:	$1,000
Number of awards:	150
Number of applicants:	5,000
Application deadline:	December 31
Notification begins:	July 15
Total amount awarded:	$84,000

Contact:
NESA, Sum 322
1325 West Walnut Hill Lane
P.O. Box 152079
Irving, TX 75015-2079
Phone: 972-580-2183
Fax: 972-580-7870
Web: www.nesa.org

NESA Academic Scholarships

Type of award: Scholarship.
Intended use: For freshman study at accredited 4-year institution.
Eligibility: Applicant must be male, high school senior.
Basis for selection: Applicant must demonstrate financial need, high academic achievement and leadership.
Application requirements: Recommendations, transcript.
Additional information: Applicant must be Eagle Scout. Award may not be used at military institution. Minimum 1200 SAT or 28 ACT score.

Amount of award:	$2,500-$12,500
Number of awards:	66
Number of applicants:	2,500
Application deadline:	January 31
Notification begins:	July 15
Total amount awarded:	$300,000

Contact:
NESA, Sum 322
1325 West Walnut Hill Lane
P.O. Box 152079
Irving, TX 75015-2079
Phone: 972-580-2183
Fax: 972-580-7870
Web: www.nesa.org

National Environmental Health Association/ American Academy of Sanitarians

NEHA/AAS Scholarship

Type of award: Scholarship.
Intended use: For full-time junior, senior or graduate study at accredited 4-year or graduate institution.
Basis for selection: Major/career interest in environmental science or public health. Applicant must demonstrate financial need, high academic achievement and seriousness of purpose.
Application requirements: Transcript, proof of eligibility. Three letters of recommendation (one from active NEHA member, two from faculty members at applicant's school).
Additional information: Undergraduates must be enrolled in an Environmental Health Accreditation Council accredited school or National Environmental Health Association Institutional/Educational or sustaining member school (list available at sponsor Website). Graduates must be enrolled in environmental health science and/or public health program. Visit Website for further information and updates.

Amount of award:	$1,000-$1,500
Number of awards:	3
Number of applicants:	100
Application deadline:	February 1
Total amount awarded:	$3,500

Contact:
National Environmental Health Association
NEHA/AAS Scholarship, Att: Cindy Dimmitt
720 South Colorado Blvd., Suite 1000-N
Denver, CO 80246-1925
Phone: 303-756-9090
Fax: 303-691-9490
Web: www.neha.org

National Federation of the Blind

National Federation of the Blind Scholarships

Type of award: Scholarship, renewable.
Intended use: For full-time undergraduate or graduate study at postsecondary institution.
Eligibility: Applicant must be visually impaired. Applicant must be U.S. citizen.
Basis for selection: Major/career interest in humanities/liberal arts. Applicant must demonstrate financial need, high academic achievement and service orientation.
Application requirements: Recommendations, essay, transcript. Interview with NFB affiliate president, SAT/ACT scores (high school seniors only), proof of legal blindness.
Additional information: Applicant must be legally blind in both eyes. Recipients of Federation scholarships need not be members of National Federation of the Blind. Visit Website for application.

Amount of award:	$3,000-$12,000
Number of awards:	30
Application deadline:	March 31
Notification begins:	June 1

Contact:
National Federation of the Blind Scholarship Committee
NFB at Jernigan Place
200 East Wells Street
Baltimore, MD 21230
Phone: 410-659-9314 ext. 2415
Fax: 410-685-5653
Web: www.nfb.org/scholarships

National FFA

National FFA Collegiate Scholarship Program

Type of award: Scholarship.
Intended use: For undergraduate study at postsecondary institution.
Eligibility: Applicant must be no older than 22.
Basis for selection: Applicant must demonstrate financial need and high academic achievement.
Additional information: Must be FFA member. Visit Website for more information and application.

Amount of award:	$1,000-$10,000
Number of awards:	1,000
Number of applicants:	7,820
Application deadline:	February 15
Notification begins:	June 1
Total amount awarded:	$2,100,000

Contact:
National FFA
Attn: Scholarship Office
P.O. Box 68960
Indianapolis, IN 46268-0960
Phone: 317-802-6099
Web: www.ffa.org

National Genealogical Society

Rubincam Youth Award

Type of award: Scholarship.
Eligibility: Applicant must be at least 13, no older than 18, high school junior or senior. Applicant must be U.S. citizen, permanent resident or international student.
Application requirements: Essay. Supportive evidence and documentation.
Additional information: Submit a single-line genealogy in biographical format for five generations, starting with oneself. Must be in English and original unpublished work. Visit Website for exact specifications. NGS membership not required.

Amount of award:	$500
Number of awards:	2
Application deadline:	January 31
Total amount awarded:	$500

Contact:
National Genealogical Society Attn: NGS Rubincam Award
3108 Columbia Pike, Suite 300
Arlington, VA 22204-4370
Phone: 800-473-0050
Fax: 703-525-0052
Web: www.ngsgenealogy.org

National Ground Water Research and Education Foundation

NGWREF Len Assante Scholarship Fund

Type of award: Scholarship.
Intended use: For full-time undergraduate study at accredited 2-year or 4-year institution.
Basis for selection: Applicant must demonstrate financial need, high academic achievement, depth of character, leadership, patriotism, seriousness of purpose and service orientation.

Scholarships

Application requirements: Essay, transcript, proof of eligibility. Essay should be one-page biography.
Additional information: Applicant must be studying in a ground water-related field. Students in two-year well drilling associate degree program also eligible. Minimum 2.5 GPA. Amount and number of awards vary annually. Application available on Website.

Amount of award:	$1,000-$5,000
Number of awards:	10
Number of applicants:	80
Application deadline:	January 15
Total amount awarded:	$20,000

Contact:
NGWREF Len Assante Scholarship Fund
601 Dempsey Road
Westerville, OH 43081
Phone: 800-551-7379
Fax: 614-898-7786
Web: www.ngwa.org

National Inventors Hall of Fame

Collegiate Inventors Competition

Type of award: Scholarship.
Intended use: For full-time undergraduate or graduate study at postsecondary institution in United States or Canada.
Basis for selection: Competition/talent/interest in science project, based on invention's potential for society and scope of use.
Application requirements: Advisor letter; four copies of application and any supplementary material; personal essay describing invention, including a title page and one-paragraph overview of invention.
Additional information: Amount of awards varies. Entry must include summary of current literature and patent search, test data and invention's benefit. Entry must be original idea that has not been made available to public as a commercial product/ process. Must not have been patented or published more than one year prior to date of submission. Competition accepts individual and team entries. Students must be (or have been) enrolled full-time at least part of 12-month period prior to date entry submitted. For teams, at least one member must meet full-time eligibility criteria. Other team members must have been enrolled on part-time basis (at minimum) sometime during 24-month period prior to date entry submitted. Deadline varies. See Website for more information.

Amount of award:	$5,000-$15,000
Number of awards:	3
Application deadline:	June 15

Contact:
The Collegiate Inventors Competition
The National Inventors Hall of Fame
520 South Main Street, Suite 2423
Akron, OH 44311
Phone: 800-968-4332 ext. 5
Web: www.invent.org/collegiate

National Italian American Foundation

National Italian American Foundation Scholarship Program

Type of award: Scholarship.
Intended use: For full-time undergraduate or graduate study at accredited 4-year or graduate institution in United States.
Eligibility: Applicant must be U.S. citizen or permanent resident.
Basis for selection: Applicant must demonstrate high academic achievement, depth of character, leadership, seriousness of purpose and service orientation.
Application requirements: Recommendations, transcript. FAFSA (optional).
Additional information: Must be member of NIAF. Completed application and teacher evaluation submitted online. Awards in two categories. General Category I Awards: Open to Italian-American students who demonstrate outstanding potential and high academic achievement. General Category II Awards: Open to those students majoring or minoring in Italian Language, Italian studies, Italian American Studies, or related fields. Awards not applicable for summer study. Minimum 3.5 GPA.

Amount of award:	$2,000-$12,000
Number of awards:	150
Number of applicants:	5,500
Application deadline:	March 1
Notification begins:	May 17
Total amount awarded:	$340,000

Contact:
The National Italian American Foundation
1860 19th Street NW
Washington, DC 20009
Phone: 202-387-0600
Fax: 202-387-0800
Web: www.niaf.org/scholarships

National Jewish Committee on Scouting, Boy Scouts of America

Chester M. Vernon Memorial Eagle Scout Scholarship

Type of award: Scholarship, renewable.
Intended use: For full-time undergraduate study at accredited 2-year or 4-year institution.
Eligibility: Applicant must be male, high school senior. Applicant must be Jewish. Applicant must be U.S. citizen or permanent resident.
Basis for selection: Applicant must demonstrate financial need, depth of character, leadership and service orientation.
Application requirements: Recommendation from a volunteer or professional scout leader and from a religious leader. FAFSA.
Additional information: Applicant must be registered, active member of a Boy Scout troop, Varsity Scout team, or Venturing crew. Must have received Eagle Scout Award. Must

be active member of synagogue and have received Ner Tamid or Etz Chaim emblem. Award renewable for four years. Visit National Jewish Committee on Scouting Website for information and application. Recipients receive $1,000 per year for four years.

Amount of award: $4,000
Number of awards: 1
Number of applicants: 10
Application deadline: February 28
Notification begins: May 1
Total amount awarded: $1,000

Contact:
National Jewish Committee on Scouting, BSA
1325 West Walnut Hill Lane
P.O. Box 152079
Irving, TX 75015-2079
Phone: 972-580-2130
Fax: 972-580-2540
Web: www.jewishscouting.org

Frank L. Weil Memorial Eagle Scout Scholarship

Type of award: Scholarship.
Intended use: For full-time undergraduate study at accredited 2-year or 4-year institution.
Eligibility: Applicant must be male, high school senior. Applicant must be Jewish. Applicant must be U.S. citizen or permanent resident.
Basis for selection: Applicant must demonstrate depth of character, leadership and service orientation.
Application requirements: Recommendations from volunteer or professional scout leader and a religious leader. FAFSA.
Additional information: Recipient of scholarship receives $1,000. Two $500 second-place scholarship awards also given. Applicant must be registered, active member of a Boy Scout troop, Varsity Scout team, or Venturing crew. Must have received Eagle Scout Award. Must be active member of synagogue and have received Ner Tamid or Etz Chaim emblem. Visit National Jewish Committee on Scouting Website for more information and application.

Amount of award: $500-$1,000
Number of awards: 3
Number of applicants: 15
Application deadline: February 28
Notification begins: May 1
Total amount awarded: $2,000

Contact:
National Jewish Committee on Scouting, BSA
1325 West Walnut Hill Lane
P.O. Box 152079
Irving, TX 75015-2079
Phone: 972-580-2130
Fax: 972-580-2540
Web: www.jewishscouting.org

Rick Arkans Eagle Scout Scholarship

Type of award: Scholarship.
Intended use: For undergraduate study at postsecondary institution.
Eligibility: Applicant must be high school senior.
Basis for selection: Applicant must demonstrate financial need.
Application requirements: Recommendation from a volunteer or professional scout leader and from a religious leader. FAFSA.
Additional information: Applicant must be registered, active member of a Boy Scout troop, Varsity Scout team, or Venturing crew. Must have received Eagle Scout Award. Must be active member of synagogue and have received Ner Tamid or Etz Chaim emblem. Visit National Jewish Committee on Scouting Website for more information and application.

Amount of award: $1,000
Number of awards: 1
Number of applicants: 10
Application deadline: February 28
Notification begins: May 1
Total amount awarded: $1,000

Contact:
National Jewish Committee on Scouting, BSA
1325 West Walnut Hill Lane
P.O. Box 152079
Irving, TX 75015-2079
Phone: 972-580-2130
Fax: 972-580-2540
Web: www.jewishscouting.org

National Junior Classical League

Latin Honor Society Scholarship

Type of award: Scholarship.
Intended use: For full-time freshman study at 2-year or 4-year institution.
Eligibility: Applicant must be high school senior.
Basis for selection: Major/career interest in classics or education. Applicant must demonstrate high academic achievement.
Application requirements: Recommendations, essay, transcript.
Additional information: Must have been member in good standing of NJCL for at least three years and must be member of NJCL Latin Honor Society for current academic year and at least one preceding year. Must be planning to major in and teach Latin, Greek, or classics. Application available online.

Amount of award: $2,000
Number of awards: 1
Number of applicants: 7
Application deadline: May 1
Total amount awarded: $2,000

Contact:
National Junior Classical League, Attn: Scholarships
Miami University
422 Wells Mill Drive
Oxford, OH 45056
Phone: 513-529-7741
Web: www.njcl.org

National Junior Classical League Scholarship

Type of award: Scholarship.
Intended use: For full-time freshman study at 2-year or 4-year institution.
Eligibility: Applicant must be high school senior.

Scholarships

Basis for selection: Major/career interest in classics; education or humanities/liberal arts. Applicant must demonstrate financial need, high academic achievement, leadership, seriousness of purpose and service orientation.
Application requirements: Recommendations, essay, transcript. List of awards and activities.
Additional information: Must be NJCL member. Preference given to applicants who intend to teach Latin, Greek, or classical humanities.

Amount of award:	$1,200-$2,500
Number of awards:	11
Application deadline:	May 1

Contact:
National Junior Classical League, Attn: Scholarships
Miami University
422 Wells Mill Drive
Oxford, OH 45056
Phone: 513-529-7741
Web: www.njcl.org

National Merit Scholarship Corporation

National Achievement Scholarships

Type of award: Scholarship.
Intended use: For full-time undergraduate study at accredited postsecondary institution in United States.
Eligibility: Applicant must be African American. Applicant must be enrolled in high school. Applicant must be U.S. citizen or permanent resident.
Basis for selection: Applicant must demonstrate high academic achievement and leadership.
Application requirements: Recommendations, essay.
Additional information: A privately financed academic competition for Black American high school students. To enter, students must meet published participation requirements and request consideration in program when they take PSAT/NMSQT and enter National Merit Program. Entry requirements published each year in PSAT/NMSQT Official Student Guide, sent to schools for distribution to students before October test administration, and on NMSC's Website. Some 1,600 of highest scoring participants named Semifinalists on regional representation basis. Semifinalists must meet additional requirements and advance to Finalist standing to compete for about 800 National Achievement Scholarships offered annually. There are 700 National Achievement $2,500 Scholarships for which all Finalists compete and about 100 corporate-sponsored scholarships for Finalists who meet specified criteria of sponsoring organization.

Number of awards:	800
Number of applicants:	1,600
Notification begins:	February 15
Total amount awarded:	$2,400,000

Contact:
National Achievement Scholarship Program
1560 Sherman Avenue
Suite 200
Evanston, IL 60201-4897
Phone: 847-866-5100
Web: www.nationalmerit.org

National Merit Scholarships

Type of award: Scholarship.
Intended use: For full-time undergraduate study at accredited postsecondary institution in United States.
Eligibility: Applicant must be enrolled in high school. Applicant must be U.S. citizen or permanent resident.
Basis for selection: Applicant must demonstrate high academic achievement and leadership.
Application requirements: Recommendations, essay.
Additional information: Open to U.S. high school students who take PSAT/NMSQT in specified year in high school and meet other entry requirements. Entry requirements published each year in PSAT/NMSQT Official Student Guide, sent to schools for distribution to students before October test administration, and on NMSC's Website. Some 16,000 high-scoring participants designated Semifinalists on state representational basis. Applications sent to students through their schools. Semifinalists must meet additional requirements and advance to Finalist standing to be considered for National Merit Scholarships. About 8,000 awards of three types offered annually: 2,500 National Merit $2,500 Scholarships for which all Finalists compete; over 1,000 corporate-sponsored Merit Scholarship awards for Finalists who meet criteria of sponsoring corporate organization; and over 4,500 college-sponsored Merit Scholarship awards for Finalists who will attend sponsor college/university. Corporate organizations also provide about 1,300 Special Scholarships for other high performers in competition who are not Finalists. Permanent residents eligible if in process of becoming U.S. citizen.

Number of awards:	9,300
Number of applicants:	19,500
Notification begins:	March 1
Total amount awarded:	$47,500,000

Contact:
National Merit Scholarship Program
1560 Sherman Avenue
Suite 200
Evanston, IL 60201-4897
Phone: 847-866-5100
Web: www.nationalmerit.org

National Poultry & Food Distributors Association

NPFDA Scholarship

Type of award: Scholarship, renewable.
Intended use: For full-time junior or senior study at 4-year institution in United States.
Basis for selection: Major/career interest in dietetics/nutrition; agriculture; agricultural economics; agribusiness or food science/technology. Applicant must demonstrate high academic achievement.
Application requirements: Essay, transcript, proof of eligibility. Recommendation by dean.
Additional information: Poultry science, animal science, or related agricultural business majors also eligible.

Amount of award:	$1,500-$2,000
Number of awards:	4
Number of applicants:	80
Application deadline:	May 31
Notification begins:	January 1
Total amount awarded:	$6,500

Contact:
National Poultry & Food Distributors Association
2014 Osborne Road
St. Marys, GA 31558
Phone: 770-535-9901
Fax: 770-535-7385
Web: www.npfda.org

National Press Photographers Foundation

NPPF Scholarship

Type of award: Scholarship.
Intended use: For full-time undergraduate or graduate study at postsecondary institution in United States or Canada.
Basis for selection: Major/career interest in journalism. Applicant must demonstrate financial need.
Application requirements: Recommendations, essay. Portfolio of 6-12 slides (digital formats also accepted), statement of financial need, GPA.
Additional information: Applicants must be studying photojournalism. Visit Website for more information and application.

Amount of award:	$2,000
Number of awards:	1
Application deadline:	April 15

Contact:
National Press Photographers Foundation
James W. Brown, Ph.D.
10710 Pine Bluff Drive
Fishers, IN 46037
Web: www.nppf.org

National Restaurant Association Educational Foundation

Al Schulman Ecolab First-Time Freshmen Entrepeneurial Scholarship

Type of award: Scholarship.
Intended use: For undergraduate study at vocational, 2-year or 4-year institution.
Eligibility: Applicant must be U.S. citizen or permanent resident.
Basis for selection: Major/career interest in food science/technology; hotel/restaurant management; food science/technology; culinary arts or marketing.
Application requirements: Transcript. One to three letters of recommendation verifying work hours, on business or school letterhead, from current or previous employer in the restaurant or food service industry, paystubs, two essays: one stating food service background and career goals, the other discussing what person or experience influenced you to select food industry and how this will help you reach your career goals.
Additional information: Minimum 3.0 GPA. Must be first-time freshman accepted into accredited culinary school, or in college or university majoring in food service related major. Must plan to enroll in minimum of two terms for following school year. Must have minimum 250 hours of food-service-related work experience. Deadline in July or August. Visit Website for application.

Amount of award:	$3,000-$5,000
Application deadline:	July 24

Contact:
National Restaurant Association Educational Foundation
Scholarships and Mentoring Initiative
175 West Jackson Boulevard, Suite 1500
Chicago, IL 60604-2702
Phone: 800-765-2122 ext. 6738
Fax: 312-566-9733
Web: www.nraef.org/scholarships

Al Schuman Ecolab Undergraduate Entrepeneurial Scholarship

Type of award: Research grant.
Intended use: For undergraduate study at postsecondary institution. Designated institutions: California State Polytechnic University-Pomona, Cornell University, Culinary Institute of America, DePaul University, Johnson & Wales University, Kendall College, Lynn University, Michigan State University, New York University, Pennsylvania State University, Purdue University, University of Denver, University of Houston, University of Nevada-Las Vegas, University of Massachusetts-Amherst.
Eligibility: Applicant must be U.S. citizen or permanent resident.
Basis for selection: Major/career interest in culinary arts or food production/management/services. Applicant must demonstrate high academic achievement.
Application requirements: Recommendations, essay, transcript.
Additional information: Minimum 3.0 GPA. Targeted to students who show entrepreneurial spirit through written essay. Must be enrolled in food service related program. Must have completed at least one grading term of postsecondary program. Must be enrolled for at least two consecutive terms, but not entering last semester before graduating.

Amount of award:	$3,000-$5,500
Number of awards:	2
Application deadline:	March 15

Contact:
National Restaurant Educational Foundation
175 West Jackson Boulevard, Suite 1500
Attn: Scholarship Program
Chicago, IL 60604-2702
Phone: 800-756-2122, ext. 6738
Web: www.nraef.org

National Rifle Association

Jeanne E. Bray Law Enforcement Dependents Scholarship

Type of award: Scholarship.
Intended use: For full-time undergraduate or graduate study at accredited 2-year, 4-year or graduate institution in United States.

Eligibility: Applicant must be U.S. citizen. Applicant's parent must have been killed or disabled in work-related accident as police officer.
Basis for selection: Applicant must demonstrate high academic achievement and service orientation.
Application requirements: Recommendations, transcript, proof of eligibility. Letter from employing law enforcement agency; 500-700 word essay on the Second Amendment.
Additional information: Number of awards varies. Parent must be member of National Rifle Association. Parent must be active, disabled, deceased, discharged, or retired peace officer. Award given for up to four years or until applicable monetary cap is reached, as long as student maintains eligibility. Applications accepted on continuous basis.

Amount of award:	$500-$2,000
Number of applicants:	35
Application deadline:	November 15
Notification begins:	February 15

Contact:
National Rifle Association, Attn: Sandy S. Elkin
Jeanne E. Bray Memorial Scholarship
11250 Waples Mill Road
Fairfax, VA 22030
Phone: 800-554-9498
Fax: 703-267-1083
Web: www.le.nra.org/law-enforcement-benefits.aspx

National Science Teachers Association

Toshiba/NSTA ExploraVision Award

Type of award: Scholarship.
Intended use: For undergraduate or non-degree study at postsecondary institution in United States or Canada.
Eligibility: Applicant must be no older than 21, enrolled in high school.
Basis for selection: Competition/talent/interest in science project, based on scientific accuracy, creativity, communication and feasibility of vision. Major/career interest in science, general.
Application requirements: Essay. Abstract, written description of research and design project, five graphics simulating Web pages.
Additional information: Applicants must apply as teams of two, three, or four students and a coach. Applicant must attend public, private, or home school. Must be full-time student, no older than 21. Technology study project. Open to grades K-12. Members of first-place team receive $10,000 savings bond. Members of second-place team receive $5,000 savings bond. Regional winners receive Toshiba products. Contact sponsor for entry kit, and visit Website to download application.

Amount of award:	$5,000-$10,000
Number of applicants:	4,500
Application deadline:	January 31
Notification begins:	March 1
Total amount awarded:	$240,000

Contact:
Toshiba/NSTA ExploraVision Awards
1840 Wilson Boulevard
Arlington, VA 22201-3000
Phone: 800-EXPLOR9
Web: www.exploravision.org

National Sculpture Society

Sculpture Society Scholarship

Type of award: Scholarship.
Intended use: For undergraduate, master's or doctoral study at postsecondary institution in United States.
Eligibility: Applicant must be U.S. citizen or permanent resident.
Basis for selection: Competition/talent/interest in visual arts, based on images of figurative or representational sculpture created by applicant. Major/career interest in arts, general. Applicant must demonstrate financial need.
Application requirements: Recommendations, essay, proof of eligibility. Brief letter of application including biography and background in sculpture; ten to eighteen images of at least six sculptures submitted on CD; list of works shown on CD; proof of financial need; SASE.
Additional information: Must be studying figurative or representational sculpture. Work inspired by nature, or figurative or realistic sculpture, preferred.

Amount of award:	$2,000
Number of awards:	4
Number of applicants:	35
Application deadline:	June 1
Total amount awarded:	$8,000

Contact:
National Sculpture Society
c/o ANS
75 Varick Street, 11th Floor
New York, NY 10013
Phone: 212-764-5645
Fax: 212-764-5651
Web: www.nationalsculpture.org

National Security Agency

National Security Agency Stokes Educational Scholarship Program

Type of award: Scholarship, renewable.
Intended use: For full-time undergraduate study in United States.
Eligibility: Applicant must be high school senior. Applicant must be U.S. citizen.
Basis for selection: Major/career interest in computer/information sciences; engineering, computer or engineering, electrical/electronic. Applicant must demonstrate high academic achievement, depth of character, leadership, patriotism, seriousness of purpose and service orientation.
Application requirements: Recommendations, essay, transcript, proof of eligibility. Resume, SAT/ACT scores.
Additional information: Current applications available September 1st through November 15th of each year. Must submit online and hard copy applications. Preference given to those with minimum 3.0 GPA, 1600 SAT score (reading and math) and/or 25 ACT score. Must undergo polygraph and security screening. Freshmen must major in computer science or electrical or computer engineering. Awardees must work at NSA in area related to major for 12 weeks in summer and after graduation for at least one and a half times length of study. If work debt not repaid, scholarship reverts to debt. Tuition cap is $30,000 per year. See Website for current program information.

Amount of award: Full tuition
Number of awards: 20
Number of applicants: 800
Application deadline: November 15
Notification begins: May 1
Contact:
National Security Agency Stokes Scholars Program
9800 Savage Road
Suite 6779
Fort Meade, MD 20755-6779
Phone: 410-854-4725 or 866-NSA-HIRE
Fax: 410-854-3002
Web: www.nsa.gov

National Society of Accountants Scholarship Foundation

National Society of Accountants Scholarship

Type of award: Scholarship.
Intended use: For sophomore, junior or senior study at accredited vocational, 2-year or 4-year institution in United States.
Eligibility: Applicant must be U.S. citizen or Canadian citizen.
Basis for selection: Major/career interest in accounting. Applicant must demonstrate financial need, high academic achievement and leadership.
Application requirements: Transcript. Appraisal form.
Additional information: Minimum 3.0 GPA. Student must be enrolled in undergraduate accounting program at time of application. Visit Website for more information and application.
Amount of award: $500-$2,000
Number of awards: 32
Number of applicants: 1,200
Application deadline: March 10
Total amount awarded: $40,000
Contact:
National Society of Accountants Scholarship Program
c/o Scholarship Management Services
One Scholarship Way, P.O. Box 297
St. Peter, MN 56082
Phone: 507-931-1682
Web: www.nsacct.org

National Society of the Sons of the American Revolution

Arthur M. and Berdena King Eagle Scout Scholarship

Type of award: Scholarship.
Intended use: For undergraduate study at postsecondary institution.
Eligibility: Applicant must be male, no older than 18.
Basis for selection: Applicant must demonstrate depth of character, leadership and patriotism.
Application requirements: Essay, proof of eligibility. Essay should be 500 words on Revolutionary War, subject of applicant's choice. Four generation ancestor chart.
Additional information: Open to all Eagle Scouts currently registered in active unit who will not reach 19th birthday during year of application. Competition conducted in three phases: Chapter (local), Society (state), and National. Applicants need only apply at Chapter level. Winners at local level entered into state competition; state winners used in National contest. Number of awards varies. Awards may also be available at chapter and state level. See Website for more information and application.
Amount of award: $2,000-$8,000
Number of awards: 3
Application deadline: December 31
Total amount awarded: $14,000
Contact:
National Society of the Sons of the American Revolution
1000 South Fourth Street
Louisville, KY 40203
Phone: 502-589-1776
Web: www.sar.org/youth/eagle.html

National Speakers Association

National Speakers Association Scholarship

Type of award: Scholarship.
Intended use: For full-time junior, senior or graduate study at 4-year or graduate institution.
Basis for selection: Applicant must demonstrate financial need, high academic achievement, leadership and seriousness of purpose.
Application requirements: Recommendations, essay, transcript.
Additional information: Applicant must have above-average academic record and desire to be professional speaker. Application available on Website.
Amount of award: $5,000
Number of awards: 4
Number of applicants: 37
Application deadline: June 1
Notification begins: September 1
Total amount awarded: $20,000
Contact:
National Speakers Association
1500 South Priest Drive
Tempe, AZ 85281
Phone: 480-968-2552
Fax: 480-968-0911
Web: www.nsafoundation.org

National Stone, Sand & Gravel Association

Barry K. Wendt Commitment Award and Scholarship

Type of award: Scholarship.
Intended use: For full-time undergraduate study in United States. Designated institutions: Engineering schools.
Eligibility: Applicant must be U.S. citizen or permanent resident.
Basis for selection: Major/career interest in engineering. Applicant must demonstrate high academic achievement.
Application requirements: Recommendations, essay.
Additional information: Must be planning career in aggregate industry. Visit Website for details and application.

Number of awards:	1
Application deadline:	June 10

Contact:
Wendt Memorial Scholarship Committee
c/o NSSGA
1605 King Street
Alexandria, VA 22314
Phone: 703-525-8788
Fax: 703-525-7782
Web: www.nssga.org/careerscholarships/scholarships.cfm

Navy Supply Corps Foundation

Navy Supply Corps Foundation Scholarship

Type of award: Scholarship, renewable.
Intended use: For full-time undergraduate study at accredited 2-year or 4-year institution.
Eligibility: Applicant must be U.S. citizen. Applicant must be dependent of veteran who served in the Navy. Applicant must be family member of active duty or enlisted Navy Supply Corps Officer/Warrant Officer.
Basis for selection: Applicant must demonstrate financial need, high academic achievement, depth of character, leadership and service orientation.
Application requirements: Recommendations, transcript, proof of eligibility. FAFSA.
Additional information: Minimum 2.5 GPA. Any family member of Foundation member or enlisted member (active duty, reservist, or retired) is eligible for consideration. Number of awards varies. Visit Website for application and more information.

Amount of award:	$1,000-$10,000
Number of applicants:	225
Application deadline:	March 7
Notification begins:	May 23
Total amount awarded:	$203,500

Contact:
Navy Supply Corps Foundation
P.O. Box 6228
Athens, GA 30604
Phone: 706-354-4111
Fax: 706-354-0334
Web: www.usnscf.com

Navy-Marine Corps Relief Society

Gold Star Scholarship Program

Type of award: Scholarship, renewable.
Intended use: For full-time undergraduate study at postsecondary institution in United States.
Eligibility: Applicant must be dependent of deceased veteran; or spouse of deceased veteran who served in the Marines or Navy. Service member must have died on active duty, in combat situation, or after retirement.
Basis for selection: Applicant must demonstrate financial need and high academic achievement.
Application requirements: Transcript. Current military dependent ID card; DD214 and death certificate or DD1300, FAFSA.
Additional information: Minimum 2.0 GPA. Visit Website for more information and application. Must be child under 23 years of age or spouse of Navy or Marine Corps service member who died on active duty, in combat situation, or after retirement.

Amount of award:	$500-$2,500
Number of applicants:	50
Application deadline:	May 1
Total amount awarded:	$132,000

Contact:
Navy-Marine Corps Relief Society
875 North Randolph Street
Suite 225
Arlington, VA 22203-1977
Phone: 703-696-4960
Web: www.nmcrs.org/education

McAlinden Divers Scholarship

Type of award: Scholarship.
Intended use: For full-time undergraduate study at postsecondary institution.
Eligibility: Applicant must be dependent of active service person; or spouse of active service person. Must be child under 23 years of age or spouse of active duty or retired Navy-Marine Corp diver.
Basis for selection: Major/career interest in oceanography/ marine studies. Applicant must demonstrate financial need.
Application requirements: Transcript. FAFSA, Certificate DD 214.
Additional information: Must be studying oceanography, ocean agriculture, aqua culture, and must be completing or have completed dive certifications.

Amount of award:	$500-$3,000

Scholarships

Contact:
Navy-Marine Corps Relief Society
875 North Randolph Street
Suite 225
Arlington, VA 22203-1977
Phone: 703-696-4904
Web: www.nmcrs.org/education

Society of Sponsors Scholarship Program

Type of award: Scholarship.
Intended use: For full-time undergraduate study at accredited postsecondary institution.
Eligibility: Applicant must be dependent of disabled veteran who served in the Marines or Navy. Must have been wounded in combat during Iraq-Afghanistan conflict.
Basis for selection: Major/career interest in education.
Application requirements: Essay, transcript. Certificate DD214.
Additional information: Minimum 2.5 GPA. Applicants must be veteran wounded in combat during Iraq-Afghanistan conflict. Must be pursuing bachelor's degree leading to teacher licensure.

Amount of award:	$3,000
Number of awards:	5
Total amount awarded:	$3,000

Contact:
Navy-Marine Corps Relief Society
875 North Randolph Street
Suite 225
Arlington, VA 22203-1977
Phone: 703-696-4904
Fax: 703-696-0144
Web: www.nmcrs.org/education

Nebraska Coordinating Commission for Postsecondary Education

Nebraska Opportunity Grant

Type of award: Scholarship.
Intended use: For undergraduate study at postsecondary institution in United States. Designated institutions: Colleges and universities in Nebraska.
Eligibility: Applicant must be residing in Nebraska.
Basis for selection: Applicant must demonstrate financial need.
Application requirements: FAFSA.
Additional information: Award amount, application deadline, and requirements determined by individual institutions. Awards made on rolling basis. Notification begins in January preceding award year.

Number of applicants:	38,081
Total amount awarded:	$14,093,053

Contact:
Contact financial aid office at eligible institution
Phone: 402-471-2847
Fax: 402-471-2886
Web: www.ccpe.state.ne.us

New England Board of Higher Education

NEBHE's Tuition Break Regional Student Program

Type of award: Scholarship.
Intended use: For undergraduate or graduate study in United States. Designated institutions: New England public colleges and universities.
Eligibility: Applicant must be permanent resident residing in Vermont, New Hampshire, Connecticut, Maine, Massachusetts or Rhode Island.
Additional information: Regional Student Program provides tuition discount to New England residents who study majors not offered at public institutions in their own state at out-of-state public colleges in New England. See Website for program of approved majors.

Amount of award:	$7,000
Number of awards:	9,000
Total amount awarded:	$53,000,000

Contact:
New England Board of Higher Education
45 Temple Place
Boston, MA 02111
Phone: 617-357-9620
Web: www.nebhe.org/tuitionbreak

New England Employee Benefits Council

NEEBC Scholarship

Type of award: Scholarship, renewable.
Intended use: For undergraduate or graduate study at accredited postsecondary institution.
Basis for selection: Major/career interest in business/management/administration; human resources; insurance/actuarial science or health services administration. Applicant must demonstrate high academic achievement, depth of character, leadership, seriousness of purpose and service orientation.
Application requirements: Recommendations, transcript. 500-word essay; minimum of two references from college professors, NEEBC members or other benefits professionals.
Additional information: Applicants must aspire to career in employee benefits. Applicants must reside or attend college in New England.

Amount of award:	$2,500-$5,000
Number of applicants:	2
Application deadline:	April 1
Notification begins:	May 1
Total amount awarded:	$5,000

Contact:
New England Benefits Council
240 Bear Hill Road
Suite 102
Waltham, MA 02451
Phone: 781-684-8700
Web: www.neebc.org

New Jersey Commission on Higher Education

New Jersey Educational Opportunity Fund Grant

Type of award: Scholarship, renewable.
Intended use: For full-time undergraduate or graduate study at accredited 2-year or 4-year institution. Designated institutions: Participating New Jersey community colleges, four-year colleges and universities.
Eligibility: Applicant must be U.S. citizen or permanent resident residing in New Jersey.
Basis for selection: Applicant must demonstrate financial need.
Application requirements: FAFSA.
Additional information: For students from educationally disadvantaged backgrounds with demonstrated financial need. Must be New Jersey resident for at least 12 consecutive months prior to enrollment. Students are admitted into EOF program by college. Program includes summer sessions, tutoring, counseling, and student leadership development. Award amounts vary; undergraduate $200-$2,500, graduate $200-$4,350. Contact EOF director at institution for specific application requirements.

Amount of award:	$200-$2,500
Number of awards:	18,259
Application deadline:	October 1
Notification begins:	April 1
Total amount awarded:	$26,643,935

Contact:
New Jersey Commission on Higher Education
P.O. Box 542
Trenton, NJ 08625-0542
Phone: 609-984-2709
Fax: 609-633-5420
Web: www.nj.gov/highereducation/EOF

New Jersey Higher Education Student Assistance Authority

New Jersey Law Enforcement Officer Memorial Scholarship

Type of award: Scholarship.
Intended use: For full-time undergraduate study. Designated institutions: New Jersey institutions.
Eligibility: Applicant must be U.S. citizen residing in New Jersey. Applicant's parent must have been killed or disabled in work-related accident as police officer.
Application requirements: Proof of eligibility.
Additional information: Must be dependent of law enforcement officer killed in the line of duty. Award may cover up to the cost of attendance at any approved institution of higher education in New Jersey. Awards are renewable for up to four years.

Amount of award:	Full tuition
Application deadline:	October 1, March 1
Total amount awarded:	$118,600

Contact:
New Jersey Higher Education Student Assistance Authority
4 Quakerbridge Plaza
P.O. Box 540
Trenton, NJ 08625-0540
Phone: 800-792-8670
Fax: 609-588-2228
Web: www.hesaa.org

New Jersey Part-Time Tuition Aid Grant for County Colleges

Type of award: Scholarship, renewable.
Intended use: For half-time undergraduate study at postsecondary institution in United States. Designated institutions: Participating New Jersey county colleges.
Eligibility: Applicant must be U.S. citizen or permanent resident residing in New Jersey.
Basis for selection: Applicant must demonstrate financial need.
Application requirements: FAFSA.
Additional information: Must be enrolled part-time (6-11 credits). Must be legal New Jersey resident for at least 12 months prior to enrollment. Must maintain satisfactory academic progress. Renewals due June 1; new applications due October 1. Visit Website for application and additional information.

Number of applicants:	3,140
Application deadline:	June 1, October 1
Total amount awarded:	$6,659,976

Contact:
New Jersey Higher Education Student Assistance Authority
4 Quakerbridge Plaza
P.O. Box 540
Trenton, NJ 08625-0540
Phone: 800-792-8670
Fax: 609-588-2228
Web: www.hesaa.org

New Jersey STARS II

Type of award: Scholarship, renewable.
Intended use: For full-time undergraduate study at accredited 4-year institution in United States. Designated institutions: New Jersey public institutions.
Eligibility: Applicant must be U.S. citizen or permanent resident residing in New Jersey.
Basis for selection: Applicant must demonstrate financial need and high academic achievement.
Application requirements: FAFSA.
Additional information: Must be successful NJ STARS scholar receiving associate's degree with a minimum 3.25 GPA. Provides for tuition and approved fees for up to 18 credits per semester for four semesters at a New Jersey public four-year institution.

Amount of award:	$6,000-$7,000
Application deadline:	June 1, October 1
Total amount awarded:	$5,751,850

Contact:
New Jersey Higher Education Student Assistance Authority
4 Quakerbridge Plaza
P.O. Box 540
Trenton, NJ 08625-0540
Phone: 800-792-8670
Fax: 609-588-2228
Web: www.hesaa.org

New Jersey Student Tuition Assistance Reward Scholarship (NJSTARS)

Type of award: Scholarship, renewable.
Intended use: For full-time undergraduate study in United States. Designated institutions: New Jersey county colleges.
Eligibility: Applicant must be U.S. citizen or permanent resident residing in New Jersey.
Basis for selection: Applicant must demonstrate high academic achievement.
Application requirements: FAFSA.
Additional information: Must be resident of New Jersey for 12 months prior to high school graduation. Provides tuition and approved fees for up to 18 credits per semester for up to five semesters at a county college for students graduating in top 15 percent of high school class. To be eligible for renewal, students must have minimum 3.0 GPA.

Application deadline: March 1, October 1
Total amount awarded: $7,314,546

Contact:
New Jersey Higher Education Student Assistance Authority
4 Quakerbridge Plaza
P.O. Box 540
Trenton, NJ 08625-0540
Phone: 800-792-8670
Fax: 609-588-2228
Web: www.hesaa.org

New Jersey Tuition Aid Grants (TAG)

Type of award: Scholarship, renewable.
Intended use: For full-time undergraduate study in United States. Designated institutions: Approved New Jersey colleges, universities, and degree-granting proprietary institutions.
Eligibility: Applicant must be U.S. citizen or permanent resident residing in New Jersey.
Basis for selection: Applicant must demonstrate financial need.
Application requirements: FAFSA.
Additional information: Applicant must be legal New Jersey resident for at least 12 consecutive months immediately prior to enrollment. Students must maintain satisfactory academic progress. Deadline is June 1 for renewal students; October 1 for new applicants. Notification begins in March.

Number of applicants: 531,126
Application deadline: June 1, October 1
Total amount awarded: $281,995,208

Contact:
New Jersey Higher Education Student Assistance Authority
4 Quakerbridge Plaza
P.O. Box 540
Trenton, NJ 08625-0540
Phone: 800-792-8670
Fax: 609-558-2228
Web: www.hesaa.org

New Jersey World Trade Center Scholarship

Type of award: Scholarship, renewable.
Intended use: For full-time undergraduate study at postsecondary institution in United States.
Eligibility: Applicant must be residing in New Jersey.
Additional information: Must be spouse or dependent of New Jersey resident who was killed or is presumed dead as a result of the terrorist attacks of September 11, 2001. This includes first responders and rescue workers who died as a result of illness caused by attack sites.

Amount of award: $5,000
Number of applicants: 71
Application deadline: October 1, March 1
Total amount awarded: $279,971

Contact:
New Jersey Higher Education Student Assistance Authority
4 Quakerbridge Plaza
P.O. Box 540
Trenton, NJ 08625-0540
Phone: 800-792-8670
Fax: 609-588-2228
Web: www.hesaa.org

New Jersey State Golf Association

Caddie Scholarship

Type of award: Scholarship, renewable.
Intended use: For full-time undergraduate study at accredited 2-year or 4-year institution in United States. Designated institutions: Members of Association of American Colleges and Universities.
Basis for selection: Applicant must demonstrate financial need and high academic achievement.
Application requirements: Proof of eligibility. Recommendation from golf club.
Additional information: Applicants must have been a caddie for at least two seasons at a participating member club of New Jersey State Golf Association. Must be in top half of class and have minimum 900 SAT and 2.5 GPA. Awards renewable for up to four years. Foundation also offers one full scholarship award at Rutgers University.

Amount of award: $3,500-$7,500
Number of awards: 225
Number of applicants: 219
Application deadline: March 1
Notification begins: June 15
Total amount awarded: $713,600

Contact:
New Jersey State Golf Association
Caddie Scholarship Foundation
P.O. Box 6947
Freehold, NJ 07728
Phone: 848-863-6481
Web: www.njsga.org

New Mexico Commission on Higher Education

New Mexico Competitive Scholarships

Type of award: Scholarship.
Intended use: For full-time undergraduate study at 4-year institution in United States. Designated institutions: Public New Mexico institutions.

Scholarships

Basis for selection: Applicant must demonstrate high academic achievement.
Additional information: Minimum 3.5 GPA and 20 ACT score. Awards to encourage out-of-state students who have demonstrated high academic achievement in high school to enroll in public institutions in New Mexico. Recipients of at least $100 in competitive scholarships per semester eligible for resident tuition and fees. Applicants must meet GPA/ACT score requirements, which vary by institution. Contact financial aid office of any New Mexico public postsecondary institution or see Website.
Contact:
Contact financial aid office at institution.
Web: www.hed.state.nm.us

New Mexico Legislative Endowment Program

Type of award: Scholarship, renewable.
Intended use: For undergraduate study at accredited postsecondary institution. Designated institutions: Public institutions in New Mexico.
Eligibility: Applicant must be U.S. citizen or permanent resident residing in New Mexico.
Basis for selection: Applicant must demonstrate financial need.
Application requirements: FAFSA.
Additional information: Contact financial aid office of any public postsecondary institution in New Mexico. Four-year public institutions may award up to $2,500 per student per academic year. Two-year public institutions may award up to $1,000 per student per year. Part-time students eligible for prorated awards. Deadlines set by institutions.
Amount of award: $1,000-$2,500
Contact:
Contact financial aid office at institution.
Phone: 505-476-8400
Web: www.hed.state.nm.us

New Mexico Legislative Lottery Scholarship

Type of award: Scholarship.
Intended use: For full-time undergraduate study at postsecondary institution. Designated institutions: Eligible New Mexico public colleges and universities.
Eligibility: Applicant must be high school senior. Applicant must be residing in New Mexico.
Basis for selection: Applicant must demonstrate high academic achievement.
Additional information: Must complete 12 graded credit hours with 2.5 GPA in the first regular semester immediately following graduation from New Mexico high school. Deadlines vary according to institution; see Website or apply through financial aid office.
Amount of award: Full tuition
Contact:
Contact financial aid office at institution.
Phone: 505-476-8400
Web: www.hed.state.nm.us

New Mexico Scholars Program

Type of award: Scholarship, renewable.
Intended use: For full-time undergraduate study at accredited 2-year or 4-year institution. Designated institutions: Public institutions in New Mexico or the following private institutions: St. John's College, College of the Southwest.
Eligibility: Applicant must be no older than 21. Applicant must be U.S. citizen or permanent resident residing in New Mexico.
Basis for selection: Applicant must demonstrate financial need and high academic achievement.
Application requirements: FAFSA.
Additional information: Award includes books and required fees. Number of awards based on availability of funds. Must be graduate of New Mexico high school. Must have 25 ACT score or be in top five percent of class. Must attend eligible university by end of 21st birthday. Combined family income may not exceed $30,000 per year. Contact financial aid office of New Mexico postsecondary institution of choice for information and application. Application deadline set by institution.
Amount of award: Full tuition
Contact:
Contact financial aid office at institution
Phone: 505-476-8400
Web: www.hed.state.nm.us

New Mexico Student Choice Grant

Type of award: Scholarship, renewable.
Intended use: For undergraduate study at postsecondary institution. Designated institutions: St. John's College, College of the Southwest.
Eligibility: Applicant must be U.S. citizen or permanent resident residing in New Mexico.
Basis for selection: Applicant must demonstrate financial need.
Application requirements: FAFSA.
Additional information: Amount of award and application deadline determined by institution. Apply to financial aid office at one of designated colleges. Part-time students eligible for pro-rated awards.
Contact:
Contact financial aid office at institution.
Phone: 505-476-8400
Web: www.hed.state.nm.us

New Mexico Student Incentive Grant

Type of award: Scholarship, renewable.
Intended use: For undergraduate study at accredited postsecondary institution. Designated institutions: St. John's College, University of the Southwest, Institute of American Indian Art, Crownpoint Institute of Technology, Diné College, Southwestern Indian Polytechnic Institute.
Eligibility: Applicant must be U.S. citizen or permanent resident residing in New Mexico.
Basis for selection: Applicant must demonstrate financial need.
Application requirements: FAFSA.
Additional information: Must demonstrate exceptional financial need. Contact financial aid office of designated institutions for information, application, and deadline. Part-time students eligible for pro-rated awards.
Amount of award: $200-$2,500
Contact:
Contact financial aid office at institution.
Phone: 505-476-8400
Web: www.hed.state.nm.us

New York State Education Department

New York State Arthur O. Eve Higher Education Opportunity Program (HEOP)

Type of award: Scholarship.
Intended use: For undergraduate study at 2-year or 4-year institution. Designated institutions: Independent New York State colleges and universities.
Eligibility: Applicant must be residing in New York.
Basis for selection: Applicant must demonstrate financial need.
Additional information: Applicant must be resident of New York State for one year preceding entry into HEOP and be academically and economically disadvantaged. Contact college or university of interest for application and additional information, and apply at time of admission. Support services include pre-session summer program and tutoring, counseling, and special coursework during academic year. Award amounts vary; contact sponsor for information. For general information, contact New York State Education Department.

Number of applicants:	5,368

Contact:
New York State Education Department
Collegiate Development Prgms. Unit
89 Washington Avenue, Room 1071 EBA
Albany, NY 11234
Phone: 518-474-5313
Fax: 518-486-5221
Web: www.highered.nysed.gov/kiap/colldev/HEOP

New York State Grange

Caroline Kark Scholarship

Type of award: Scholarship.
Intended use: For undergraduate study at postsecondary institution.
Eligibility: Applicant or parent must be member/participant of New York State Grange. Applicant must be residing in New York.
Basis for selection: Major/career interest in deafness studies.
Additional information: Award available to Grange members preparing for a career working with the deaf or hearing impaired and to non-members who are deaf and want to further their education beyond high school. Hearing applicants must have been a Grange member for one year prior to applying. Deaf applicants must show sufficient hearing loss to receive full-time amplification.

Application deadline:	April 15
Notification begins:	June 15

Contact:
New York State Grange
100 Grange Place
Cortland, NY 13045
Phone: 607-756-7553
Fax: 607-756-7757
Web: www.nysgrange.org

Grange Denise Scholarship

Type of award: Scholarship, renewable.
Intended use: For full-time undergraduate study at 2-year or 4-year institution.
Eligibility: Applicant or parent must be member/participant of New York State Grange. Applicant must be residing in New York.
Basis for selection: Major/career interest in agriculture; agribusiness; agricultural education; agricultural economics or natural resources/conservation. Applicant must demonstrate financial need.
Application requirements: Recommendations, transcript.
Additional information: Send SASE for application.

Amount of award:	$1,000
Number of awards:	3
Number of applicants:	4
Application deadline:	April 15
Notification begins:	June 15
Total amount awarded:	$4,000

Contact:
New York State Grange
100 Grange Place
Cortland, NY 13045
Phone: 607-756-7553
Fax: 607-756-7757
Web: www.nysgrange.org

Grange Susan W. Freestone Education Award

Type of award: Scholarship, renewable.
Intended use: For full-time undergraduate or graduate study at 2-year or 4-year institution in United States. Designated institutions: Approved institutions in New York state.
Eligibility: Applicant or parent must be member/participant of New York State Grange. Applicant must be residing in New York.
Basis for selection: Applicant must demonstrate financial need, depth of character and service orientation.
Application requirements: Transcript.
Additional information: Applicant must be current New York State Grange member. Must have been Junior Grange member to qualify for maximum award. Send SASE for application. Activity in Grange work considered.

Amount of award:	$1,000
Number of awards:	2
Number of applicants:	4
Application deadline:	April 15
Notification begins:	June 15
Total amount awarded:	$4,000

Contact:
New York State Grange
100 Grange Place
Cortland, NY 13045
Phone: 607-756-7553
Fax: 607-756-7757
Web: www.nysgrange.org

June Gill Nursing Scholarship

Type of award: Scholarship, renewable.
Intended use: For undergraduate study at postsecondary institution.
Eligibility: Applicant or parent must be member/participant of New York State Grange. Applicant must be residing in New York.

Basis for selection: Major/career interest in nursing. Applicant must demonstrate financial need and high academic achievement.
Application requirements: Transcript, proof of eligibility. Career statement.
Additional information: Grandchild of member of the New York State Grange also eligible. Award amounts vary.

Amount of award:	$1,000
Number of awards:	2
Application deadline:	April 15
Notification begins:	June 1

Contact:
New York State Grange
100 Grange Place
Cortland, NY 13045
Phone: 607-756-7553
Fax: 607-756-7757
Web: www.nysgrange.org

New York State Higher Education Services Corporation

City University SEEK/College Discovery Program

Type of award: Scholarship.
Intended use: For undergraduate study at 2-year or 4-year institution. Designated institutions: City University of New York campuses.
Eligibility: Applicant must be U.S. citizen or permanent resident residing in New York.
Basis for selection: Applicant must demonstrate financial need.
Application requirements: Proof of eligibility. FAFSA, TAP.
Additional information: Applicant must be both academically and economically disadvantaged. Available at CUNY and community college campuses. Apply to CUNY financial aid office. For SEEK, student must have resided in New York State for at least one year; for College Discovery, student must have resided in New York City for at least one year.
Contact:
City University of New York
Office of Admission Services
1114 Avenue of the Americas
New York, NY 10036
Phone: 212-997-CUNY
Web: www.cuny.edu

Flight 587 Memorial Scholarships

Type of award: Scholarship, renewable.
Intended use: For full-time undergraduate study at postsecondary institution. Designated institutions: Approved New York state institutions.
Eligibility: Applicant must be residing in New York.
Application requirements: FAFSA. TAP. Scholarship supplement. Proof of applicant's relationship to the deceased (birth certificate, marriage license, etc.)
Additional information: Provides financial aid to children, spouses, and financial dependents of individuals killed as a direct result of American Airlines Flight 587's crash in the Belle Harbor neighborhood of Queens, New York, on the morning of November 12, 2001. Award is full tuition for students attending public colleges and universities in New York State, and the monetary equivalent for students attending private New York schools.

Amount of award:	Full tuition
Application deadline:	June 30

Contact:
New York State Higher Education Services Corporation
HESC Scholarship Unit
99 Washington Avenue, Room 1430A
Albany, NY 12255
Phone: 888-NYS-HESC
Web: www.hesc.com

New York Military Service Recognition Scholarship (MSRS)

Type of award: Scholarship, renewable.
Intended use: For full-time undergraduate study at 2-year or 4-year institution. Designated institutions: Approved New York State institutions.
Eligibility: Applicant must be residing in New York. Applicant must be disabled while on active duty; or dependent of disabled veteran, deceased veteran or POW/MIA; or spouse of disabled veteran, deceased veteran or POW/MIA. Must be child, spouse, or financial dependent of member of the U.S. armed forces or state-organized militia who, at any time after August 2, 1990, while New York State resident, (1) died or became permanently disabled as a result of injury or illness in a combat theater or combat zone or during military training operations in preparation for duty in a combat theater or (2) is classified as MIA in a combat theater or combat zone of operations.
Application requirements: FAFSA, TAP application.
Additional information: At public colleges and universities (CUNY or SUNY), award covers actual tuition and mandatory educational fees; actual room and board for living on campus (or an allowance for commuters); and allowances for books, supplies, and transportation. At private institutions, award amount equals SUNY four-year college tuition and fees and allowances for room and board, books, supplies, and transportation. New York State resident family members who were enrolled in undergraduate programs at U.S. colleges or universities outside of New York State on September 11, 2001, are also eligible. See Website for more details.

Amount of award:	Full tuition
Application deadline:	June 30

Contact:
New York State Higher Education Services Corporation
Scholarships and Grants
99 Washington Avenue
Albany, NY 12255
Phone: 888-NYS-HESC
Web: www.hesc.com

New York State Aid for Part-Time Study Program

Type of award: Scholarship, renewable.
Intended use: For half-time undergraduate study at postsecondary institution. Designated institutions: Participating New York state institutions.
Eligibility: Applicant must be U.S. citizen or permanent resident residing in New York.
Basis for selection: Applicant must demonstrate financial need and high academic achievement.
Application requirements: Proof of eligibility.

Additional information: Must fall within income limits. Campus-based program; recipients selected and award amount determined by school. Maximum award is $2,000. Must not have used up TAP eligibility or be in default on Federal Family Education Loan. Student must maintain minimum 2.0 GPA. Applications available from individual colleges.

Amount of award: $2,000

Contact:
New York State Higher Education Services Corporation
Scholarships and Grants
99 Washington Avenue
Albany, NY 12255
Phone: 888-NYS-HESC
Web: www.hesc.com

New York State Math and Science Teaching Incentive Program

Type of award: Scholarship.
Intended use: For full-time undergraduate or graduate study at 4-year or graduate institution in United States. Designated institutions: New York institutions.
Eligibility: Applicant must be U.S. citizen or permanent resident.
Basis for selection: Major/career interest in mathematics; education, teacher or science, general. Applicant must demonstrate high academic achievement.
Application requirements: FAFSA. Must apply for NYS Tuition Assistance Program.
Additional information: Award is for exchange of five years full-time employment as secondary education math or science teacher. Must be U.S. citizen or eligible non-citizen. Minimum 2.5 GPA. Must be matriculated in approved undergraduate or graduate program in New York State leading to career as secondary education math or science teacher. Program pays for student's annual tuition, up to the price of an undergraduate program at State University of New York, or actual tuition charged; whichever is less. Must retain 2.5 GPA, full-time attendance, and earn at least 27 credit hours yearly to retain award. May not have service obligation under another program. May not be in default on federally guaranteed student loan. Visit Website to apply.

Amount of award: $5,595
Application deadline: March 15

Contact:
New York State Higher Education Services Corporation
Phone: 888-697-4372
Web: www.hesc.com

New York State Memorial Scholarship for Families of Deceased Police/Volunteer Firefighters/Peace Officers and Emergency Medical Service Workers

Type of award: Scholarship, renewable.
Intended use: For full-time undergraduate study at 2-year or 4-year institution. Designated institutions: Approved New York institutions.
Eligibility: Applicant must be U.S. citizen residing in New York. Applicant's parent must have been killed or disabled in work-related accident as firefighter, police officer or public safety officer.
Application requirements: Proof of eligibility. Memorial Scholarship Supplement, FAFSA, and Express TAP Application.
Additional information: Spouse and/or children of police officer/firefighter/peace officer/EMS worker who died as result of injuries sustained in line of duty in service to New York State are eligible. Award will equal applicant's actual tuition cost or SUNY undergraduate tuition cost, whichever is less. Also provides funds to meet non-tuition costs, such as room and board, books, supplies, and transportation. Visit Website for additional information.

Amount of award: Full tuition
Application deadline: June 30

Contact:
New York State Higher Education Services Corporation
Scholarships and Grants
99 Washington Avenue
Albany, NY 12255
Phone: 888-NYS-HESC
Web: www.hesc.com

New York State Regents Awards for Children of Deceased and Disabled Veterans

Type of award: Scholarship.
Intended use: For full-time undergraduate or non-degree study at 2-year or 4-year institution.
Eligibility: Applicant must be residing in New York. Applicant must be dependent of veteran, disabled veteran or deceased veteran during Korean War, Persian Gulf War, WW I, WW II or Vietnam. Student's parent must have been disabled or deceased veteran or POW, or classified as MIA. Student whose parent is a veteran of Afghanistan conflict also eligible. Student whose parent has received Armed Forces, Navy, or Marine Corps expeditionary medal for participation in operations in Lebanon, Grenada, and Panama also eligible, as are students born with spina bifida whose parent(s) served in Vietnam between 12/22/61 and 5/7/75.
Application requirements: Proof of eligibility. FAFSA and Express TAP Application.
Additional information: Student must initially establish eligibility by submitting a Child of Veteran Award Supplement before applying. Veteran must be a resident of New York state. Visit Website for additional information.

Amount of award: $450
Application deadline: June 30

Contact:
New York State Higher Education Services Corporation
Scholarships and Grants
99 Washington Avenue
Albany, NY 12255
Phone: 888-NYS-HESC
Web: www.hesc.com

New York State Tuition Assistance Program

Type of award: Scholarship, renewable.
Intended use: For full-time undergraduate or graduate study at accredited postsecondary institution in United States. Designated institutions: TAP-eligible schools in New York.
Eligibility: Applicant must be U.S. citizen or permanent resident residing in New York.
Basis for selection: Applicant must demonstrate financial need.
Application requirements: Proof of eligibility. FAFSA.
Additional information: Must fall within income limits. Must be charged at least $200 tuition per year. Submit FAFSA to receive prefilled Express TAP Application (ETA) to review,

sign, and return. Award subject to budget appropriations. Must maintain at least C average. Must not be in default on a HESC-guaranteed loan. Part-time, first-time freshmen attending CUNY, SUNY, or not-for-profit independent degree-granting colleges also eligible. Visit Website for additional information.

Amount of award: $5,000
Application deadline: May 1

Contact:
New York State Higher Education Services Corporation
Grants and Scholarships
99 Washington Avenue
Albany, NY 12255
Phone: 888-NYS-HESC
Web: www.hesc.com

New York State Veterans Tuition Award

Type of award: Scholarship, renewable.
Intended use: For undergraduate or graduate study at accredited vocational, 2-year, 4-year or graduate institution in United States. Designated institutions: Approved postsecondary schools in New York.
Eligibility: Applicant must be returning adult student. Applicant must be U.S. citizen or permanent resident residing in New York. Applicant must be veteran during Persian Gulf War or Vietnam. Must have served in armed forces in hostilities in Indochina between December 1961 and May 1975, or in Persian Gulf on or after August 2, 1990. Veterans of the conflict in Afghanistan also eligible. Must not have been dishonorably discharged.
Application requirements: Proof of eligibility. FAFSA. Express Tap Application (ETA). Documentation of Indochina, Persian Gulf, or Afghanistan service.
Additional information: Students must have also applied for TAP and Federal Pell Grant awards. Visit Website for additional information.

Amount of award: $5,595
Application deadline: June 30

Contact:
New York State Higher Education Services Corporation
Scholarships and Grants
99 Washington Avenue
Albany, NY 12255
Phone: 888-NYS-HESC
Web: www.hesc.com

New York State World Trade Center Memorial Scholarship

Type of award: Scholarship, renewable.
Intended use: For full-time undergraduate study at 2-year or 4-year institution. Designated institutions: Approved New York colleges and universities.
Application requirements: Proof of eligibility. FAFSA, Express TAP Application.
Additional information: Must be child, spouse, or financial dependent of person who died or became severely and permanently disabled due to the September 11th attacks or rescue and recovery operation. At public colleges and universities (CUNY or SUNY), award covers actual tuition and mandatory educational fees; actual room and board for living on campus (or an allowance for commuters); and allowances for books, supplies, and transportation. At private institutions, award amount equals SUNY four-year college tuition and fees, and allowances for room and board, books, supplies, and transportation. New York State resident family members who were enrolled in undergraduate programs at U.S. colleges or universities outside of New York State on September 11, 2001, are also eligible. See Website for details.

Amount of award: Full tuition
Application deadline: June 30

Contact:
New York State Higher Education Services Corporation
Grants and Scholarships
99 Washington Avenue
Albany, NY 12255
Phone: 888-NYS-HESC
Web: www.hesc.com

New York State Office of Adult Career and Educational Services

New York State Readers Aid Program

Type of award: Scholarship, renewable.
Intended use: For undergraduate, master's or doctoral study at 2-year, 4-year or graduate institution.
Eligibility: Applicant must be visually impaired or hearing impaired. Applicant must be residing in New York.
Application requirements: Proof of eligibility.
Additional information: Applicant must be legally blind or deaf. Number of awards varies. Applications available at degree-granting institutions. Award provides funds for note-takers, readers, or interpreters. Applicant may be attending out-of-state institution.

Amount of award: $800
Number of applicants: 411
Application deadline: March 15, June 30
Total amount awarded: $300,000

Contact:
New York State Office of Adult Career and Educational Services
Readers Aid Program, Attn: Dennis Barlow
99 Washington Avenue, Room 1605
Albany, NY 12234
Phone: 518-474-7343
Fax: 518-473-6073
Web: www.acces.nysed.gov

New York Women in Communications Foundation

New York Women in Communications Foundation Scholarship

Type of award: Scholarship, renewable.
Intended use: For undergraduate or graduate study at accredited postsecondary institution.
Eligibility: Applicant must be U.S. citizen.

Basis for selection: Major/career interest in communications. Applicant must demonstrate financial need, high academic achievement, leadership and service orientation.
Application requirements: Interview, recommendations, essay, transcript, proof of eligibility. Resume.
Additional information: Minimum 3.2 GPA. Applicant must be majoring in a communications-related field or a high school senior intending to declare a major in a communications-related field. Must be attending school in New York City or be a resident of New York, New Jersey, Connecticut, or Pennsylvania. Finalists will be required to attend an in-person interview in New York City in March. Visit Website for application and additional requirements.

Amount of award:	$2,500-$10,000
Number of awards:	15
Number of applicants:	500
Application deadline:	January 24
Notification begins:	April 1
Total amount awarded:	$100,000

Contact:
New York Women in Communications Foundation Scholarship Program
355 Lexington Avenue, 15th Floor
New York, NY 10017-6603
Phone: 212-297-2133
Fax: 212-370-9047
Web: www.nywici.org

Nicodemus Wilderness Project

Apprentice Ecologist Initiative

Type of award: Scholarship.
Intended use: For at postsecondary institution.
Eligibility: Applicant must be at least 13, no older than 21.
Basis for selection: Applicant must demonstrate leadership, seriousness of purpose and service orientation.
Application requirements: Essay.
Additional information: Scholarships awarded annually to the authors of the top three Apprentice Ecologist essays. Applicants must be in primary (middle school), secondary (high school), or accredited post-secondary (undergraduate at college or university) educational institution. Visit Website for details.

Amount of award:	$100-$500
Number of awards:	3
Number of applicants:	112
Application deadline:	December 31
Notification begins:	April 1
Total amount awarded:	$850

Contact:
Nicodemus Wilderness Project
P.O. Box 40712
Albuquerque, NM 87196
Web: www.wildernessproject.org/volunteer_apprentice_ecologist

Nisei Student Relocation Commemorative Fund

Nisei Student Relocation Commemorative Fund Scholarship

Type of award: Scholarship.
Intended use: For freshman study at vocational, 2-year or 4-year institution in United States.
Eligibility: Applicant must be Southeast Asian (Vietnamese, Cambodian, Hmong, Laotian, Amerasian) refugee or immigrant. Applicant must be high school senior.
Basis for selection: Applicant must demonstrate financial need, high academic achievement and service orientation.
Application requirements: Recommendations, essay, transcript.
Additional information: Applicant must be high school senior living in city/area/region of the U.S. where scholarships are awarded, as determined annually by organization's board of directors. Location changes yearly; contact group for information. Number of awards varies.

Amount of award:	$250-$2,000
Number of awards:	60
Number of applicants:	175
Application deadline:	April 1
Total amount awarded:	$50,000

Contact:
Nisei Student Relocation Commemorative Fund Scholarship
Web: www.nsrcfund.org

NMIA Ohio

NMIA Ohio Scholarship Program

Type of award: Scholarship, renewable.
Intended use: For junior, senior or graduate study at accredited 4-year or graduate institution in United States.
Eligibility: Applicant must be U.S. citizen residing in Ohio.
Basis for selection: Applicant must demonstrate high academic achievement.
Additional information: Applicant must be interested in a career in Intelligence. Funds awarded may be used for tuition, room, board, and/or laboratory fees and will be payable to the student's institution. Size and number of awards depends on funding; one to six awards will be given each year. Scholarships for full-time students will be greater than scholarships for part-time students. Applicant must not be relative of NMIA or scholarship committee members. Preference is given to students attending Ohio colleges and universities. The decision of the Scholarship Committee is final and not subject to external review.

Amount of award:	$500-$2,000
Number of applicants:	7
Application deadline:	March 31
Notification begins:	April 1
Total amount awarded:	$3,000

Contact:
NMIA Ohio
c/o Deanne Otto
P.O. Box 341508
Beavercreek, OH 45434
Phone: 937-429-7601
Fax: 937-429-7602
Web: www.nmiaohio.org

Non Commissioned Officers Association

Non Commissioned Officers Association Scholarship for Children of Members

Type of award: Scholarship, renewable.
Intended use: For full-time undergraduate study in United States.
Application requirements: Transcript. Autobiography, ACT/SAT scores, and minimum 200-word essay on Americanism. Include two recommendation letters from school and one personal recommendation letter from adult who is not a relative.
Additional information: Applicant's parent must be member of Non Commissioned Officers Association.

Amount of award:	$900
Number of applicants:	127
Application deadline:	March 31
Notification begins:	June 1

Contact:
Non Commissioned Officers Association
P.O. Box 33790
San Antonio, TX 78265
Phone: 210-653-6161
Fax: 210-637-3337
Web: www.ncoausa.org

Non Commissioned Officers Association Scholarship for Spouses of Members

Type of award: Scholarship, renewable.
Intended use: For full-time undergraduate study in United States.
Application requirements: Transcript. Copy of high school diploma or GED, brief biographical background, and certificates for any training courses completed. Letter of intent describing degree course of study, plans for completion of program, and a closing paragraph on "What a College Degree Means to Me."
Additional information: Must be spouse of member of Non Commissioned Officers Association. Recipient must apply for auxiliary membership in Non Commissioned Officers Association.

Amount of award:	$900
Application deadline:	March 31
Notification begins:	June 1

Contact:
Non Commissioned Officers Association
P.O. Box 33790
San Antonio, TX 78265
Phone: 210-653-6161
Fax: 210-637-3337
Web: www.ncoausa.org

North American Limousin Foundation

Limi Boosters National Educational Grant

Type of award: Scholarship.
Intended use: For undergraduate study at vocational, 2-year or 4-year institution.
Basis for selection: Major/career interest in agriculture. Applicant must demonstrate financial need, high academic achievement, depth of character, leadership, patriotism, seriousness of purpose and service orientation.
Application requirements: Recommendations, proof of eligibility. Recent photo. One of the three recommendations must be from active NALF member other than relative or guardian, two must be from the following: school superintendent, school principal, minister, 4-H leader, FFA instructor, county agent, or teacher.
Additional information: Experience with Limousin cattle preferred. Proven excellence in Limousin activities as well as leadership skills demonstrated in NALJA, 4-H, and FFA. Must be NALF Junior member.

Amount of award:	$500-$750
Application deadline:	May 16

Contact:
Marci Hicks
P.O. Box 4253
Midway, KY 40347
Phone: 859-576-2602
Web: www.nalf.org

Limi Boosters Scholarship

Type of award: Scholarship.
Intended use: For undergraduate study at 4-year institution.
Basis for selection: Applicant must demonstrate financial need, high academic achievement, depth of character, leadership, patriotism, seriousness of purpose and service orientation.
Application requirements: Transcript, proof of eligibility. Three recommendations, one of which must be from active NALF member other than relative or guardian.
Additional information: Must be NALF member and be active in 4H and FFA work. Must rank in top third of class.

Amount of award:	$500-$750
Number of awards:	2
Application deadline:	May 16
Total amount awarded:	$3,000

Contact:
Marci Hicks
P.O. Box 4253
Midway, KY 40347
Phone: 859-576-2602
Web: www.nalf.org

North Carolina Community Colleges Foundation

North Carolina Community Colleges Wells Fargo Technical Scholarship

Type of award: Scholarship.
Intended use: For full-time sophomore study at vocational or 2-year institution.
Eligibility: Applicant must be residing in North Carolina.
Basis for selection: Applicant must demonstrate financial need and high academic achievement.
Additional information: Scholarships distributed through the 58 community colleges in the system; apply through financial aid office of institution where enrolled.

Amount of award:	$500

Contact:
North Carolina Community Colleges Foundation
5016 Mail Service Center
Raleigh, NC 27699
Phone: 919-807-7195
Fax: 919-807-7173
Web: www.nccommunitycolleges.edu

Rodney E. Powell Memorial Scholarship

Type of award: Scholarship.
Intended use: For full-time undergraduate study at 2-year institution. Designated institutions: Community colleges in Progress Energy's service area.
Eligibility: Applicant must be residing in North Carolina.
Basis for selection: Major/career interest in engineering, electrical/electronic; electronics or technology. Applicant must demonstrate financial need and high academic achievement.
Application requirements: Essay.
Additional information: Minimum 3.0 GPA. Scholarship for students of electronic technology. Applicant must be enrolled full-time or must intend to enroll as new student at designated institution. Number of awards varies.

Amount of award:	$1,000
Number of awards:	1

Contact:
North Carolina Department of Community Colleges
Attn: Lee McCollum
410 S. Wilmington Street PEB 7
Raleigh, NC 27601
Phone: 919-546-7585
Fax: 919-546-7652
Web: www.nccommunitycolleges.edu

North Carolina Division of Veterans Affairs

North Carolina Scholarships for Children of War Veterans

Type of award: Scholarship, renewable.
Intended use: For undergraduate or graduate study at accredited postsecondary institution.
Eligibility: Applicant must be no older than 24. Applicant must be residing in North Carolina. Applicant must be dependent of disabled veteran, deceased veteran or POW/MIA who served in the Army, Air Force, Marines, Navy or Coast Guard. Parent must have served during a period of war.
Basis for selection: Applicant must demonstrate financial need.
Application requirements: Interview, transcript, proof of eligibility. Birth certificate.
Additional information: Must be natural child or adopted child prior to age 15. For state schools, award is tuition waiver plus a room and board allowance for up to four years. For private schools, award is up to $4,500 per year. Parent must have been North Carolina resident at time of enlistment or child must have been born in and reside permanently in North Carolina. See Website for deadline information.

Amount of award:	Full tuition
Number of applicants:	555

Contact:
North Carolina Division of Veterans Affairs
1315 Mail Service Center
Raleigh, NC 27699-1315
Web: www.ncveterans.com

North Carolina Division of Vocational Rehabilitation Services

North Carolina Vocational Rehabilitation Award

Type of award: Scholarship, renewable.
Intended use: For full-time undergraduate study at accredited vocational, 2-year or 4-year institution.
Eligibility: Applicant must be physically challenged or learning disabled. Applicant must be residing in North Carolina.
Basis for selection: Applicant must demonstrate financial need.
Application requirements: Interview, proof of eligibility. Proof of mental, physical, or learning disability that is an impediment to employment.
Additional information: Award varies with need and eligibility. This program provides educational assistance for individuals who meet eligibility requirements and require training to reach their vocational goals. Visit Website for full eligibility requirements.
Contact:
North Carolina Division of Vocational Rehabilitation Services
2801 Mail Service Center
Raleigh, NC 27699-2801
Phone: 919-855-3500
Fax: 919-715-0616
Web: www.ncdhhs.gov/dvrs

North Carolina State Board of Refrigeration Examiners

North Carolina State Board of Refrigeration Examiners Scholarship

Type of award: Scholarship.
Intended use: For undergraduate study at 2-year institution.

Scholarships

Eligibility: Applicant must be residing in North Carolina.
Basis for selection: Major/career interest in air conditioning/heating/refrigeration technology. Applicant must demonstrate financial need and high academic achievement.
Application requirements: Essay.
Additional information: Number of awards varies. Must enroll in Associate of Applied Science degree of study in commercial refrigeration or HVAC/R technology. Must maintain GPA at or above level required for graduation. Must continue for duration of scholarship at the college where he or she was enrolled at the time of the scholarship award.

Number of awards: 2
Application deadline: January 1

Contact:
North Carolina State Board of Refrigeration Examiners
893 Highway 70 W
Garner, NC 27529
Phone: 919-779-4711
Fax: 919-779-4733
Web: www.refrigerationboard.org/wp

North Carolina State Education Assistance Authority

GlaxoSmithKline Opportunity Scholarship

Type of award: Scholarship.
Intended use: For undergraduate study at vocational, 2-year or 4-year institution in United States.
Eligibility: Applicant must be U.S. citizen or permanent resident residing in North Carolina.
Basis for selection: Applicant must demonstrate depth of character and seriousness of purpose.
Additional information: Applicant must have been a permanent resident of Durham, Orange, or Wake county for one year prior to application. GlaxoSmithKline and Triangle Community Foundation employees or their families not eligible. Visit Website for application.

Amount of award: $5,000
Number of awards: 5
Application deadline: March 15

Contact:
Triangle Community Foundation Scholarship Program
Attn: Gina Andersen
324 Blackwell Street, Suite 1220
Durham, NC 27701
Phone: 919-474-8370
Fax: 919-941-9208
Web: www.trianglecf.org

Golden LEAF Scholars Program - Two-Year Colleges

Type of award: Scholarship.
Intended use: For undergraduate study at 2-year institution. Designated institutions: Member institutions of North Carolina Community College system.
Eligibility: Applicant must be residing in North Carolina.
Basis for selection: Applicant must demonstrate financial need, high academic achievement, depth of character, leadership and service orientation.
Application requirements: Disclosure of other financial aid awards. FAFSA.
Additional information: Applicant must demonstrate need under federal TRIO formula. Award is up to $750 per semester (including summer) for curriculum students; up to $250 per semester for occupational education students. Finalist will undergo merit competition and be judged on academics, leadership, community service, and the effect of the economy's decline on his/her family. Must be permanent resident of one of 73 eligible counties. Visit Website for more information. Contact financial aid office for application.

Amount of award: $500-$1,500

Contact:
Contact financial aid office at local community college.
Phone: 888-684-8404
Fax: 919-549-8481
Web: www.cfnc.org

Golden LEAF Scholarship - Four-Year University Program

Type of award: Scholarship, renewable.
Intended use: For undergraduate study at 4-year institution. Designated institutions: Public universities.
Eligibility: Applicant must be residing in North Carolina.
Basis for selection: Applicant must demonstrate financial need.
Application requirements: FAFSA.
Additional information: Must be incoming freshman, transfer student from a North Carolina community college, or previous recipient applying for renewal. New applicants must be permanent resident of economically distressed and/or tobacco-dependent rural county. Recipients of other aid amounting to 75 percent or more of total education costs will be given low priority. Visit Website for application and more information.

Amount of award: $3,000
Number of awards: 215
Application deadline: March 15

Contact:
North Carolina State Education Assistance Authority
Phone: 888-684-8404
Web: www.cfnc.org

Jagannathan Scholarship

Type of award: Scholarship, renewable.
Intended use: For full-time freshman study at 4-year institution in United States. Designated institutions: Constituent institutions of the University of North Carolina.
Eligibility: Applicant must be high school senior. Applicant must be U.S. citizen or permanent resident residing in North Carolina.
Basis for selection: Applicant must demonstrate financial need, high academic achievement and leadership.
Application requirements: Proof of eligibility, nomination by high school guidance counselor, financial office of UNC institution, or Tolaram Polymers, Cookson Fibers, or related company. SAT scores, College Scholarship Service's PROFILE (register and file by February 8), and documented proof of financial need. FAFSA.
Additional information: Special consideration given to students whose parents are employees of Tolaram Polymers, Cookson Fibers, or related companies. Applications available at all North Carolina public high schools. Minimum SAT 1200

score (reading and math) or ACT equivalent. Check Website for specific details. Apply online.

Amount of award: $2,000
Number of awards: 4
Number of applicants: 4
Application deadline: February 15
Notification begins: May 1
Total amount awarded: $14,000

Contact:
North Carolina State Education Assistance Authority
Phone: 919-549-8614
Web: www.cfnc.org/jag

Latino Diamante Scholarship Fund

Type of award: Scholarship.
Intended use: For freshman or sophomore study at postsecondary institution. Designated institutions: North Carolina institutions.
Eligibility: Applicant must be Hispanic American. Applicant must be residing in North Carolina.
Basis for selection: Applicant must demonstrate high academic achievement.
Application requirements: Recommendations, essay, transcript.
Additional information: Minimum 2.5 GPA. Visit Website for application and more information.

Amount of award: $750
Number of awards: 2
Application deadline: August 15
Notification begins: September 15

Contact:
Diamante, Inc.
315 North Academy Street
Suite 256
Cary, NC 27513
Phone: 919-852-0075
Web: www.cfnc.org

NC Sheriff's Association Criminal Justice Scholarship

Type of award: Scholarship.
Intended use: For full-time undergraduate study in United States. Designated institutions: Appalachian State University, East Carolina University, Elizabeth City State University, Fayetteville State University, North Carolina Central University, North Carolina State University, University of North Carolina at Charlotte, University of North Carolina at Pembroke, University of North Carolina at Wilmington, Western Carolina University.
Eligibility: Applicant must be residing in North Carolina.
Basis for selection: Major/career interest in criminal justice/law enforcement. Applicant must demonstrate financial need.
Application requirements: Recommendations, essay, transcript.
Additional information: Application available at financial aid offices of eligible institutions. Application and supplemental material should be submitted to sheriff of county where applicant resides. First priority given to child of sheriff/law enforcement officer killed in the line of duty; second priority given to child of retired or deceased sheriff/law enforcement officer; third priority given to criminal justice students.

Amount of award: $2,000
Number of awards: 10
Number of applicants: 50
Total amount awarded: $20,000

Contact:
North Carolina State Education Assistance Authority
Phone: 919-549-8614
Web: www.ncseaa.edu

North Carolina Aubrey Lee Brooks Scholarship

Type of award: Scholarship, renewable.
Intended use: For full-time undergraduate study at 4-year institution in United States. Designated institutions: North Carolina State University, University of North Carolina at Chapel Hill, University of North Carolina at Greensboro.
Eligibility: Applicant must be high school senior. Applicant must be U.S. citizen residing in North Carolina.
Basis for selection: Applicant must demonstrate financial need, depth of character, leadership and seriousness of purpose.
Application requirements: Proof of eligibility. FAFSA.
Additional information: Award amount varies; maximum $11,100 per year, plus one-time computer award up to $2,500. Scholarship pays additional amounts for approved summer study or internships. Applications available through high school. Applicants must reside and attend high school in one of the following counties: Alamance, Bertie, Caswell, Durham, Forsyth, Granville, Guilford, Orange, Person, Rockingham, Stokes, Surry, Swain, or Warren. One additional scholarship awarded to student from cities of Greensboro and High Point and to eligible senior at North Carolina School of Science and Mathematics. Apply online.

Amount of award: $11,100
Number of awards: 17
Application deadline: January 31

Contact:
North Carolina State Education Assistance Authority
Phone: 919-549-8614
Web: www.cfnc.org

North Dakota University System

North Dakota Academic Scholarships

Type of award: Scholarship.
Intended use: For full-time freshman study at postsecondary institution. Designated institutions: North Dakota universities, colleges, and tribal colleges.
Eligibility: Applicant must be high school senior. Applicant must be residing in North Dakota.
Basis for selection: Applicant must demonstrate high academic achievement.
Additional information: Must be graduate of North Dakota high school. Minimum 3.0 GPA. Minimum 24 ACT score. Renewable for full-time students who maintain 2.75 GPA. Deadline in June. See Website for details.

Amount of award: $6,000
Application deadline: June 7
Notification begins: July 15

Contact:
North Dakota University System
1815 Schafer St., Ste. 202
Bismarck, ND 58501-1217
Phone: 701-224-2541
Fax: 701-224-5707
Web: www.ndus.edu

North Dakota Career & Technical Education Scholarships

Type of award: Scholarship, renewable.
Intended use: For full-time freshman study at postsecondary institution. Designated institutions: North Dakota universities, colleges, and tribal colleges.
Eligibility: Applicant must be high school senior. Applicant must be residing in North Dakota.
Basis for selection: Applicant must demonstrate high academic achievement.
Additional information: Must be graduate of North Dakota high school. Minimum 3.0 GPA. Minimum 24 ACT score or three 5s WorkKeys assessment. Renewable for full-time students who maintain 2.75 GPA. Deadline in June. See Website for details.

Amount of award:	$6,000
Application deadline:	June 7
Notification begins:	July 15

Contact:
North Dakota University System
1815 Schafer St., Ste. 202
Bismarck, ND 58501-1217
Phone: 701-224-2541
Fax: 701-224-5707
Web: www.ndus.edu

North Dakota Indian Scholarship Program

Type of award: Scholarship, renewable.
Intended use: For full-time undergraduate or graduate study at vocational, 2-year or 4-year institution.
Eligibility: Applicant must be American Indian. Must be enrolled member of Indian tribe. Applicant must be U.S. citizen residing in North Dakota.
Basis for selection: Applicant must demonstrate financial need and high academic achievement.
Application requirements: Transcript, proof of eligibility. Budget completed by financial aid officer at institution student is attending/will attend.
Additional information: Minimum 2.0 GPA. Priority given to undergraduates with cumulative 3.5 GPA or higher.

Amount of award:	$800-$2,000
Number of awards:	175
Number of applicants:	400
Application deadline:	July 15
Total amount awarded:	$102,000

Contact:
North Dakota University System
North Dakota Indian Scholarship Program
1815 Schafer St., Ste. 202
Bismarck, ND 58501
Phone: 701-224-2541
Web: www.ndus.edu

North Dakota Scholars Program

Type of award: Scholarship, renewable.
Intended use: For full-time undergraduate study at postsecondary institution.
Eligibility: Applicant must be high school junior. Applicant must be residing in North Dakota.
Basis for selection: Applicant must demonstrate high academic achievement.
Application requirements: Proof of eligibility.
Additional information: Applicant must take ACT between October and June of junior year and score in upper five percentile of all North Dakota ACT test-takers. Numeric sum of English, math, reading, and science reasoning scores may be considered. Award is full-tuition scholarship for students attending ND's public and tribal colleges; equal to NDSU/UND tuition for students attending private institutions. Recipients must maintain 3.5 GPA for renewal. Contact sponsor for more information and deadline.

Amount of award:	Full tuition
Number of awards:	60
Number of applicants:	400

Contact:
North Dakota University System Student Financial Assistance Program
600 East Boulevard
Dept. 215
Bismarck, ND 58505-0230
Phone: 701-224-2541
Web: www.ndus.edu

North Dakota State Student Incentive Grant

Type of award: Scholarship, renewable.
Intended use: For full-time undergraduate study at vocational, 2-year or 4-year institution. Designated institutions: North Dakota colleges.
Eligibility: Applicant must be U.S. citizen or permanent resident residing in North Dakota.
Basis for selection: Applicant must demonstrate financial need.
Application requirements: Proof of eligibility. FAFSA.
Additional information: Application automatic with FAFSA. Applicant must be first-time undergraduate student. Must not be in default on any federal loans or owe refund on any Title IV grants or loans.

Amount of award:	$800-$1,500
Number of awards:	8,200
Number of applicants:	28,000
Application deadline:	April 15
Total amount awarded:	$2,220,000

Contact:
North Dakota University System Student Financial Assistance Program
600 East Boulevard
Dept. 215
Bismarck, ND 58505-0230
Phone: 701-224-2541
Web: www.ndus.edu

Northern Cheyenne Tribal Education Department

Northern Cheyenne Higher Education Program

Type of award: Scholarship, renewable.
Intended use: For undergraduate study at postsecondary institution.
Eligibility: Applicant must be American Indian. Must be enrolled with Northern Cheyenne Tribe. Applicant must be U.S. citizen.
Basis for selection: Applicant must demonstrate financial need.
Application requirements: Recommendations, essay, transcript, proof of eligibility. FAFSA.
Additional information: Award amount varies, depends on unmet need. Deadlines: October 1 for spring, April 1 for summer, and March 1 for fall.

Amount of award:	$6,000
Number of awards:	80
Number of applicants:	68
Application deadline:	March 1, April 1
Notification begins:	January 1
Total amount awarded:	$186,299

Contact:
Northern Cheyenne Tribal Education Department
Attn: Norma Bixby
P.O. Box 307
Lame Deer, MT 59043
Phone: 406-477-6602
Fax: 406-477-8150
Web: www.cheyennenation.com

Northwest Danish Association

The Kaj Christensen Scholarship for Vocational Training

Type of award: Scholarship, renewable.
Intended use: For undergraduate or graduate study at postsecondary institution in or outside United States.
Eligibility: Applicant must be at least 17. Applicant must be U.S. citizen or permanent resident.
Basis for selection: Applicant must demonstrate depth of character and service orientation.
Application requirements: Recommendations, transcript. Personal essay on educational goals, two references.
Additional information: Must be member of Northwest Danish Association. Must demonstrate some connection to Denmark via life experience, travel, heritage, etc. Must be resident of Oregon or Washington. Must have interest in vocational training.

Amount of award:	$500
Number of awards:	1
Application deadline:	March 31
Notification begins:	June 1
Total amount awarded:	$500

Contact:
Northwest Danish Association
1833 North 105th Street
Suite 101
Seattle, WA 98133-8973
Phone: 800-564-7736 or 206-523-3263
Fax: 206-729-6997
Web: www.northwestdanishassociation.org

Northwest Danish Association Scholarship

Type of award: Scholarship.
Intended use: For undergraduate or graduate study at postsecondary institution in United States.
Eligibility: Applicant must be at least 17. Applicant must be U.S. citizen or permanent resident residing in Oregon or Washington.
Basis for selection: Applicant must demonstrate service orientation.
Application requirements: Recommendations, essay, transcript.
Additional information: Studies must be related to Danish community. Must be of Danish descent or married to someone of Danish descent, who actively participates in Danish community. Consideration given to those of non-Danish descent who show exceptional involvement with and service orientation related to Danish community. Must be resident of Oregon or Washington. Those training for artistic careers also considered.

Amount of award:	$500
Number of awards:	6
Application deadline:	March 31
Notification begins:	June 1
Total amount awarded:	$3,000

Contact:
Northwest Danish Association
1833 North 105th Street
Suite 101
Seattle, WA 98133-8973
Phone: 800-564-7736 or 206-523-3263
Fax: 206-729-6997
Web: www.northwestdanishassociation.org

OCA

OCA-AXA Achievement Scholarships

Type of award: Scholarship.
Intended use: For freshman study at postsecondary institution.
Eligibility: Applicant must be Asian American or Native Hawaiian/Pacific Islander. Applicant must be U.S. citizen or permanent resident.
Basis for selection: Applicant must demonstrate high academic achievement, leadership and service orientation.
Application requirements: Recommendations, essay. Resume.
Additional information: Minimum 3.0 GPA. Number of awards varies. Visit Website for more information and deadline.

Amount of award: $2,000
Number of awards: 10
Number of applicants: 250
Application deadline: January 15
Notification begins: May 1
Total amount awarded: $20,000

Contact:
OCA
1322 18th Street, NW
Washington, DC 20036
Phone: 202-223-5500
Fax: 202-296-0540
Web: www.ocanational.org

OCA/UPS Foundation Gold Mountain College Scholarship

Type of award: Scholarship.
Intended use: For full-time freshman study in United States.
Eligibility: Applicant must be Asian American or Native Hawaiian/Pacific Islander. Applicant must be U.S. citizen or permanent resident.
Basis for selection: Applicant must demonstrate financial need and high academic achievement.
Application requirements: Recommendations, essay. Resume, FAFSA.
Additional information: Minimum 3.0 GPA. Applicant must be Asian Pacific American and first person in family to go to college in the United States. Visit Website for deadline.

Amount of award: $2,000
Number of awards: 15
Number of applicants: 250
Application deadline: January 15
Notification begins: May 1
Total amount awarded: $30,000

Contact:
OCA
1322 18th Street, NW
Washington, DC 20036
Phone: 202-223-5500
Fax: 202-296-0540
Web: www.ocanational.org

Ohio Board of Regents

Ohio College Opportunity Grant

Type of award: Scholarship, renewable.
Intended use: For freshman study at accredited 2-year or 4-year institution. Designated institutions: Ohio and select Pennsylvania schools.
Eligibility: Applicant must be residing in Ohio.
Basis for selection: Applicant must demonstrate financial need.
Application requirements: FAFSA.
Additional information: Must be pursuing associates degree, bachelor's degree, or nursing diploma at an eligible institution. Amount of award varies. Visit Website for more information.

Number of applicants: 78,334
Application deadline: October 1
Total amount awarded: $74,077,823

Contact:
Ohio Board of Regents
Web: www.ohiohighered.org/ocog

Ohio Safety Officers College Memorial Fund

Type of award: Scholarship, renewable.
Intended use: For undergraduate study at accredited 2-year or 4-year institution. Designated institutions: Ohio institutions.
Eligibility: Applicant must be U.S. citizen or permanent resident residing in Ohio. Applicant's parent must have been killed or disabled in work-related accident as firefighter, police officer or public safety officer.
Application requirements: Proof of eligibility.
Additional information: Applicant whose spouse was killed in the line of duty as a firefighter, police officer, or public safety officer also eligible. Visit Website for more information. Award is for full instructional and general fee charges at public institutions and partial instructional and general fee charges at private institutions.

Number of applicants: 45
Total amount awarded: $304,142

Contact:
Ohio Board of Regents
Web: www.ohiohighered.org/safety-officers-college-fund

Ohio War Orphans Scholarship

Type of award: Scholarship, renewable.
Intended use: For full-time undergraduate study at accredited 2-year or 4-year institution. Designated institutions: Ohio institutions.
Eligibility: Applicant must be at least 16. Applicant must be U.S. citizen or permanent resident residing in Ohio. Applicant must be dependent of veteran, disabled veteran, deceased veteran or POW/MIA. Child of disabled veteran who has combined disability rating of 60% or more.
Application requirements: Proof of eligibility.
Additional information: Visit Website for more information. Minimum 2.0 GPA.

Number of applicants: 797
Application deadline: July 1
Notification begins: August 1
Total amount awarded: $4,157,552

Contact:
Ohio Board of Regents
Web: www.ohiohighered.org/ohio-war-orphans

Ohio National Guard

Ohio National Guard Scholarship Program

Type of award: Scholarship, renewable.
Intended use: For undergraduate study at accredited postsecondary institution. Designated institutions: Degree-granting institutions in Ohio approved by Ohio Board of Regents.
Eligibility: Applicant must be in military service in the Reserves/National Guard. Must enlist, re-enlist, or extend current enlistment to equal six years with Ohio National Guard. Must remain in good standing.
Application requirements: Proof of eligibility.
Additional information: Minimum three credit hours per semester or quarter. Award covers 100 percent of instructional and general fees for state-assisted institutions; average of state-assisted university fees for proprietary/private institutions.

Application deadlines: July 1 (fall), November 1 (winter quarter/spring semester), February 1 (spring quarter), April 1 (summer). Must not already possess bachelor's degree. Lifetime maximum of 12 full-time quarters or eight full-time semesters. Number of awards varies.

Amount of award:	Full tuition
Number of awards:	6,400
Number of applicants:	5,940
Total amount awarded:	$16,200,000

Contact:
Adjutant General's Department
Ohio National Guard Scholarship Program
2825 West Dublin Granville Road
Columbus, OH 43235
Phone: 888-400-6484 or 614-336-7053
Fax: 614-336-7318
Web: www.ongsp.org

Ohio Newspapers Foundation

Harold K. Douthit Scholarship

Type of award: Scholarship.
Intended use: For sophomore, junior or senior study at postsecondary institution. Designated institutions: Ohio institutions.
Eligibility: Applicant must be U.S. citizen residing in Ohio.
Basis for selection: Major/career interest in communications or journalism. Applicant must demonstrate financial need and high academic achievement.
Application requirements: Essay, transcript. Two letters of recommendation from faculty members. Writing samples.
Additional information: Applicant must be resident of one of the following Ohio counties: Cuyahoga, Lorain, Huron, Erie, Wood, Geauga, Sandusky, Ottawa, or Lucas. Minimum 3.0 GPA. Student may provide up to two published writing samples.

Amount of award:	$1,500
Number of awards:	1
Number of applicants:	14
Application deadline:	March 31
Notification begins:	May 15
Total amount awarded:	$1,500

Contact:
Ohio Newspapers Foundation Douthit Scholarship
1335 Dublin Road
Suite 216-B
Columbus, OH 43215
Phone: 614-486-6677
Web: www.ohionews.org

Ohio Newspapers Minority Scholarship

Type of award: Scholarship.
Intended use: For full-time freshman study at postsecondary institution. Designated institutions: Ohio institutions.
Eligibility: Applicant must be Asian American, African American, Hispanic American or American Indian. Applicant must be high school senior. Applicant must be residing in Ohio.
Basis for selection: Major/career interest in journalism. Applicant must demonstrate high academic achievement.
Application requirements: Recommendations, essay, transcript, proof of eligibility. Up to two writing samples or published articles.
Additional information: Minimum 2.5 GPA.

Amount of award:	$1,500
Number of awards:	1
Number of applicants:	8
Application deadline:	March 31
Notification begins:	May 15
Total amount awarded:	$1,500

Contact:
Ohio Newspapers Foundation Minority Scholarship
1335 Dublin Road
Suite 216-B
Columbus, OH 43215
Phone: 614-486-6677
Web: www.ohionews.org

Ohio Newspapers Women's Scholarship

Type of award: Scholarship.
Intended use: For junior or senior study at postsecondary institution. Designated institutions: Ohio institutions.
Eligibility: Applicant must be residing in Ohio.
Basis for selection: Major/career interest in communications or journalism.
Application requirements: Recommendations, transcript. Three or four newspaper clippings demonstrating applicant's writing skills. Answers to questions: Who or what was your inspiration to get involved in the field of journalism and why did you select print journalism as your area of interest? Why do you need a scholarship? What do you think qualifies you for a scholarship? What do you hope to accomplish during your career as a professional journalist?
Additional information: Applicants may be male or female.

Amount of award:	$1,500
Number of awards:	1
Application deadline:	March 31

Contact:
Ohio Newspapers Foundation Women's Scholarship
1335 Dublin Road
Suite 216-B
Columbus, OH 43215
Phone: 614-486-6677
Web: www.ohionews.org

University Journalism Scholarship

Type of award: Scholarship.
Intended use: For sophomore, junior or senior study at 2-year or 4-year institution. Designated institutions: Ohio institutions.
Eligibility: Applicant must be residing in Ohio.
Basis for selection: Major/career interest in communications or journalism. Applicant must demonstrate high academic achievement.
Application requirements: Essay, transcript. Two letters of recommendation from faculty members and published writing samples.
Additional information: Minimum 2.5 GPA. Preference given to applicants demonstrating career commitment to newspaper journalism.

Amount of award:	$1,500
Number of awards:	3
Number of applicants:	6
Application deadline:	March 31
Notification begins:	May 15

Contact:
Ohio Newspaper Foundation University Journalism Scholarship
1335 Dublin Road
Suite 216-B
Columbus, OH 43215
Phone: 614-486-6677
Web: www.ohionews.org

Oklahoma Engineering Foundation

Oklahoma Engineering Foundation Scholarship

Type of award: Scholarship, renewable.
Intended use: For undergraduate study at accredited 4-year institution in United States. Designated institutions: Oklahoma Christian University of Science & Arts, Oklahoma State University, University of Oklahoma, University of Central Oklahoma, Oral Roberts University, University of Tulsa.
Eligibility: Applicant must be high school senior. Applicant must be U.S. citizen residing in Oklahoma.
Basis for selection: Major/career interest in engineering. Applicant must demonstrate high academic achievement, depth of character, leadership and service orientation.
Application requirements: Interview, essay, transcript.
Additional information: Minimum 3.0 GPA, ACT composite score of 24-29, and ACT Math component score of 28 or above. Applicants eligible for National Merit or Oklahoma Regents Scholarships not eligible for this award. Visit Website for pre-qualification form. Award is $500/semester for a total of $4,000 per student.

Amount of award:	$1,000
Number of awards:	12
Number of applicants:	52
Application deadline:	February 15
Notification begins:	May 15
Total amount awarded:	$12,000

Contact:
Oklahoma Engineering Foundation Executive Director
201 Northeast 27th Street
Suite 125
Oklahoma City, OK 73105
Phone: 405-528-1435
Web: www.ospe.org

Oklahoma State Regents for Higher Education

George and Donna Nigh Public Service Scholarship

Type of award: Scholarship.
Intended use: For full-time undergraduate study at 4-year institution in United States.
Eligibility: Applicant must be U.S. citizen or permanent resident residing in Oklahoma.
Basis for selection: Major/career interest in public administration/service. Applicant must demonstrate high academic achievement.
Application requirements: Nomination by presidents of Oklahoma colleges and universities.
Additional information: Scholarship provides opportunities to outstanding students preparing for careers in public service. Winners must participate in seminars on public service offered by Nigh Institute. Eligible colleges may nominate one scholarship per year. For information, contact the Nigh Institute.

Amount of award:	$1,000

Contact:
Nigh Institute, Attn: Carl F. Reherman
Kilpatrick Bank
3001 E. Memorial Road
Edmond, OK 73013
Phone: 405-818-0414
Web: www.okcollegestart.org

Independent Living Act (Department of Human Services Tuition Waiver)

Type of award: Scholarship.
Intended use: For undergraduate study at vocational, 2-year or 4-year institution.
Eligibility: Applicant must be no older than 21. Applicant must be residing in Oklahoma.
Application requirements: Proof of eligibility.
Additional information: Awards tuition waivers to eligible individuals who have been or are in the Oklahoma Department of Human Services foster care program. Applicant must have been in DHS custody for at least nine months between the ages of 16 and 18. Within last three years, applicant must have graduated from State Board of Education-accredited high school, the Oklahoma School of Science and Mathematics, or approved school in a bordering state, or have attained GED. Tuition waivers available to eligible students up to age 26 or completion of baccalaureate degree or program certificate, whichever comes first.

Amount of award:	Full tuition

Contact:
Oklahoma State Regents for Higher Education
P.O. Box 108850
Oklahoma City, OK 73101-8850
Phone: 800-858-1840
Web: www.okhighered.org

National Guard Tuition Waiver

Type of award: Scholarship.
Intended use: For undergraduate study at 2-year or 4-year institution.
Eligibility: Applicant must be residing in Oklahoma. Applicant must be bona fide member in good standing of Oklahoma National Guard.
Application requirements: Proof of eligibility. Statement of Understanding and Certificate of Basic Eligibility.
Additional information: Applicant must be enrolled in degree-granting program. Applicant cannot currently have a bachelor's or graduate degree. Waivers not awarded for certificate-granting courses, continuing education courses, or career technology courses.

Amount of award:	Full tuition

Contact:
Oklahoma State Regents for Higher Education
P.O. Box 108850
Oklahoma City, OK 73101-8850
Phone: 800-858-1840 or 800-464-8273
Web: www.okhighered.org or www.ok.ngb.army.mil

Oklahoma Academic Scholars Program

Type of award: Scholarship, renewable.
Intended use: For full-time undergraduate study at postsecondary institution. Designated institutions: Oklahoma institutions.
Eligibility: Applicant must be residing in Oklahoma.
Basis for selection: Applicant must demonstrate high academic achievement.
Application requirements: Transcript, proof of eligibility.
Additional information: Applicant must be National Merit Scholar or Finalist; Presidential Scholar; have SAT/ACT in 99.5 percentile for Oklahoma residents. Out-of-state National Merit Scholars, National Merit Finalists, and United States Presidential Scholars may qualify. Application deadline varies.

Amount of award:	$1,800-$5,500

Contact:
Oklahoma State Regents for Higher Education
P.O. Box 108850
Oklahoma City, OK 73101-8850
Phone: 800-858-1840
Web: www.okhighered.org

Oklahoma Future Teachers Scholarship

Type of award: Scholarship, renewable.
Intended use: For undergraduate or graduate study at accredited 2-year or 4-year institution.
Eligibility: Applicant must be U.S. citizen or permanent resident residing in Oklahoma.
Basis for selection: Major/career interest in education, early childhood or education. Applicant must demonstrate high academic achievement.
Application requirements: Essay, transcript, proof of eligibility, nomination by college. SAT/ACT scores.
Additional information: Application deadline varies; visit Website for more information. Priority given to full-time students. Must maintain minimum 2.5 GPA. Recipient must agree to teach in shortage area in Oklahoma public schools for at least three years after graduation and licensure. Must apply for renewal. Visit Website for list of shortage areas.

Amount of award:	$500-$1,500
Number of awards:	85

Contact:
Oklahoma State Regents for Higher Education
P.O. Box 108850
Oklahoma City, OK 73101-8850
Phone: 800-858-1840
Web: www.okhighered.org

Oklahoma Tuition Aid Grant

Type of award: Scholarship, renewable.
Intended use: For undergraduate study at vocational, 2-year or 4-year institution. Designated institutions: Approved Oklahoma institutions.
Eligibility: Applicant must be residing in Oklahoma.
Basis for selection: Applicant must demonstrate financial need.
Application requirements: Proof of eligibility. FAFSA.
Additional information: Award is $1,000 for public schools and $1,300 for private non-profit institutions. For best consideration, apply as soon as possible after January 1.

Amount of award:	$1,000-$1,300
Number of awards:	26,000
Number of applicants:	50,000
Total amount awarded:	$19,750,576

Contact:
Oklahoma Tuition Aid Grant Program
P.O. Box 108850
Oklahoma City, OK 73101-8850
Phone: 800-858-1840
Web: www.okcollegestart.org

Oklahoma's Promise - Oklahoma Higher Learning Access Program

Type of award: Scholarship.
Intended use: For undergraduate study at 2-year or 4-year institution.
Eligibility: Applicant must be residing in Oklahoma.
Basis for selection: Applicant must demonstrate financial need, high academic achievement and seriousness of purpose.
Additional information: Scholarship for students in families earning less than $50,000 per year. Student must enroll in the program in eighth, ninth, or tenth grade and demonstrate commitment to academic success in high school; homeschooled students must be age 13, 14, or 15. Deadline for homeschooled students must occur before student's 16th birthday. Minimum 2.5 GPA. Award amount varies; full tuition at public institutions or portion of tuition at private institutions in OK. See counselor or visit Website for details.

Number of awards:	19,000
Number of applicants:	9,334
Application deadline:	June 30
Total amount awarded:	$54,000,000

Contact:
Oklahoma State Regents for Higher Education
P.O. Box 108850
Oklahoma City, OK 73101-8850
Phone: 800-858-1840
Web: www.okpromise.org

Regional University Baccalaureate Scholarship

Type of award: Scholarship.
Intended use: For full-time undergraduate study at postsecondary institution. Designated institutions: Participating Oklahoma regional universities.
Eligibility: Applicant must be residing in Oklahoma.
Basis for selection: Applicant must demonstrate high academic achievement.
Additional information: Must have ACT score of at least 30 or be National Merit Semifinalist or Commended Student. Award is $3,000 plus resident tuition waiver. Application deadlines vary by institution.

Amount of award:	$3,000

Contact:
Oklahoma State Regents for Higher Education
P.O. Box 108850
Oklahoma City, OK 73101-8850
Phone: 800-858-1840
Web: www.okhighered.org

SREB Academic Common Market

Type of award: Scholarship, renewable.
Intended use: For undergraduate or graduate study at 2-year, 4-year or graduate institution in United States.
Eligibility: Applicant must be U.S. citizen or permanent resident residing in Oklahoma.
Application requirements: Proof of eligibility. Copy of letter of acceptance into specific program, completed application and residency certification form, curricular information about the program.
Additional information: Academic Common Market allows Oklahoma residents to pay in-state tuition rates at a non-Oklahoma college or university in the South while studying in select programs not available at Oklahoma public institutions. Visit Website for eligible programs, application, more information.
Contact:
ACM State Coordinator for Oklahoma, Academic Common Market Program
Oklahoma State Regents for Higher Education
P.O. Box 108850
Oklahoma City, OK 73101-8850
Phone: 405-225-9170
Web: www.okcollegestart.org

OMNE/Nursing Leaders of Maine

OMNE/Nursing Leaders of Maine Scholarship

Type of award: Scholarship.
Intended use: For undergraduate or graduate study at accredited 4-year or graduate institution. Designated institutions: Maine institutions.
Eligibility: Applicant must be U.S. citizen residing in Maine.
Basis for selection: Major/career interest in nursing. Applicant must demonstrate high academic achievement, seriousness of purpose and service orientation.
Application requirements: Recommendations, transcript, proof of eligibility. Brief note explaining how scholarship would help applicant.
Additional information: Applicant must be enrolled in baccalaureate or graduate nursing program. Minimum 2.0 GPA. Applications must be sent to current OMNE chairperson. Visit Website for more information.

Amount of award:	$500
Number of awards:	2
Number of applicants:	30
Application deadline:	May 1
Notification begins:	June 30
Total amount awarded:	$1,000

Contact:
OMNE
Web: www.omne.org

One Family

One Family Scholars Program

Type of award: Scholarship.
Intended use: For undergraduate study at accredited 2-year or 4-year institution in United States.
Eligibility: Applicant must be U.S. citizen residing in Massachusetts.
Application requirements: Recommendations, transcript. Tax return, FAFSA, SAR.
Additional information: Applicants must be endorsed by partnering community organization. Must be single head of household with children under 18 with family income 200 percent below Federal Poverty Level.
Contact:
One Family
186 South Street
4th Floor
Boston, MA 02111
Fax: 617-588-0441
Web: www.onefamilyscholars.org

ONS Foundation

ONS Foundation Bachelor's Scholarships

Type of award: Scholarship.
Intended use: For undergraduate study at accredited 4-year institution in United States. Designated institutions: Schools accredited by National League for Nursing or Commission on Collegiate Nursing Education.
Basis for selection: Major/career interest in nursing or oncology. Applicant must demonstrate high academic achievement, depth of character, leadership and service orientation.
Application requirements: $5 application fee. Essay, transcript, proof of eligibility.
Additional information: Must be currently enrolled in bachelor's nursing degree program. At the end of each year of scholarship participation, recipient shall submit a summary of education activities in which he/she participated.

Amount of award:	$2,000
Number of applicants:	39
Application deadline:	February 1
Notification begins:	April 15
Total amount awarded:	$24,000

Contact:
ONS Foundation
125 Enterprise Drive
Pittsburgh, PA 15275-1214
Phone: 412-859-6100
Fax: 412-859-6163
Web: www.onsfoundation.org/apply/ed/Bachelors

Oregon Student Assistance Commission

Ahmad-Sehar Saleha Ahmad and Abrahim Ekramullah Zafar Foundation

Type of award: Scholarship, renewable.
Intended use: For undergraduate study at accredited 4-year institution in United States. Designated institutions: Public and nonprofit Oregon institutions.
Eligibility: Applicant must be female, high school senior. Applicant must be U.S. citizen or permanent resident residing in Oregon.
Basis for selection: Major/career interest in English. Applicant must demonstrate high academic achievement.
Application requirements: Essay, transcript. FAFSA.
Additional information: Must be graduating from Oregon high school. GED recipients and home-schooled seniors in Oregon are also eligible. Minimum 3.8 GPA. Visit Website for details and application.
Application deadline: March 1
Contact:
Oregon Student Assistance Commission
Grants and Scholarship Division
1500 Valley River Drive, Suite 100
Eugene, OR 97401
Phone: 800-452-8807
Web: www.osac.state.or.us

Albina Fuel Company Scholarship

Type of award: Scholarship.
Intended use: For undergraduate study in United States.
Application requirements: Essay, transcript.
Additional information: Applicant must be dependent child of current Albina Fuel Company employee who has been employed by Albina for at least one year by October 1 prior to application deadline. Early bird deadline mid-February. Visit Website for more details.
Application deadline: March 1
Contact:
Oregon Student Assistance Commission
Grants and Scholarship Division
1500 Valley River Drive, Suite 100
Eugene, OR 97401
Phone: 800-452-8807
Web: www.osac.state.or.us

Allcott/Hunt Share It Now II Scholarship

Type of award: Scholarship.
Intended use: For undergraduate study in United States.
Eligibility: Applicant must be residing in Oregon.
Basis for selection: Applicant must demonstrate financial need.
Application requirements: Essay, transcript. Names, addresses, and phone numbers of two community or school references. FAFSA strongly recommended.
Additional information: Preference given to first- or second-generation immigrants to the U.S. Early bird deadline mid-February. Visit Website for details.
Application deadline: March 1
Contact:
Oregon Student Assistance Commission
Grants and Scholarship Division
1500 Valley River Drive, Suite 100
Eugene, OR 97401
Phone: 800-452-8807
Web: www.osac.state.or.us

American Federation of State, County, and Municipal Employees (AFSCME) Oregon Council #75

Type of award: Scholarship, renewable.
Intended use: For undergraduate or graduate study at 4-year or graduate institution in United States.
Eligibility: Applicant must be U.S. citizen or permanent resident.
Application requirements: Transcript. FAFSA. Essay: What is the importance of organizing political action and contract bargaining for workers?
Additional information: Applicant, spouse (including life partner), parent, or grandparent must be member (active, laid-off, retired, or disabled) of Oregon AFSCME Council. Must have been member for at least one year prior to scholarship deadline or for one year prior to death, layoff, disability, or retirement. Part-time enrollment (minimum six credit hours) considered for active members and spouses or laid-off members. Early bird deadline mid-February. Visit Website for application and details.
Application deadline: March 1
Contact:
Oregon Student Assistance Commission
Grants and Scholarship Division
1500 Valley River Drive, Suite 100
Eugene, OR 97401
Phone: 800-452-8807
Web: www.osac.state.or.us

Bandon Submarine Cable Council Scholarship

Type of award: Scholarship, renewable.
Intended use: For undergraduate or graduate study at postsecondary institution in United States.
Eligibility: Applicant must be residing in Oregon.
Basis for selection: Applicant must demonstrate financial need.
Application requirements: Essay, transcript. FAFSA.
Additional information: First preference given to members of the Bandon Submarine Cable Council or their dependent children. Second preference given to commercial fishermen or their family members residing in Coos County. Third preference given to any commercial fishermen or family member. Fourth preference given to postsecondary students residing in Clatsop, Coos, Curry, Lane, Lincoln, or Tillamook counties. Fifth preference to any postsecondary student in Oregon. Early bird deadline mid-February. Visit Website for essay topic.
Application deadline: March 1
Contact:
Oregon Student Assistance Commission
Grants and Scholarship Division
1500 Valley River Drive, Suite 100
Eugene, OR 97401
Phone: 800-452-8807
Web: www.osac.state.or.us

Ben Selling Scholarship

Type of award: Scholarship, renewable.
Intended use: For sophomore, junior or senior study at postsecondary institution in United States. Designated institutions: Public and nonprofit institutions.
Eligibility: Applicant must be U.S. citizen or permanent resident residing in Oregon.
Basis for selection: Applicant must demonstrate financial need and high academic achievement.
Application requirements: Essay, transcript. FAFSA.
Additional information: Minimum 3.5 GPA. Early bird deadline in mid-February. Visit Website for details and application.

Amount of award: $500
Application deadline: March 1

Contact:
Oregon Student Assistance Commission
Grants and Scholarship Division
1500 Valley River Drive, Suite 100
Eugene, OR 97401
Phone: 800-452-8807
Web: www.osac.state.or.us

Scholarships

Benjamin Franklin/Edith Green Scholarship

Type of award: Scholarship.
Intended use: For full-time undergraduate study at accredited 4-year institution. Designated institutions: Oregon public colleges.
Eligibility: Applicant must be high school senior. Applicant must be U.S. citizen or permanent resident residing in Oregon.
Basis for selection: Applicant must demonstrate financial need and high academic achievement.
Application requirements: Essay, transcript. FAFSA.
Additional information: Minimum 3.45 GPA. Must show graduate from Oregon high school. Early bird deadline mid-February. Visit Website for details and application.

Application deadline: March 1

Contact:
Oregon Student Assistance Commission
Grants and Scholarship Division
1500 Valley River Drive, Suite 100
Eugene, OR 97401
Phone: 800-452-8807
Web: www.osac.state.or.us

Bertha P. Singer Scholarship

Type of award: Scholarship, renewable.
Intended use: For full-time sophomore, junior, senior or graduate study at accredited postsecondary institution. Designated institutions: Oregon institutions.
Eligibility: Applicant must be U.S. citizen or permanent resident residing in Oregon.
Basis for selection: Major/career interest in nursing. Applicant must demonstrate financial need and high academic achievement.
Application requirements: Essay, transcript, proof of eligibility. FAFSA.
Additional information: Employees of U.S. Bank, their children, or near relatives not eligible. Minimum 3.0 GPA. Must be a graduate of Oregon high school. Must be enrolling as a second-year student in two-year program or third-year student in a four-year program. Visit Website for details and application.

Application deadline: March 1

Contact:
Oregon Student Assistance Commission
Grants and Scholarship Division
1500 Valley River Drive, Suite 100
Eugene, OR 97401
Phone: 800-452-8807
Web: www.osac.state.or.us

Chafee Education and Training Grant

Type of award: Scholarship, renewable.
Intended use: For undergraduate or graduate study in United States.
Eligibility: Applicant must be at least 14, no older than 20. Applicant must be residing in Oregon.
Basis for selection: Applicant must demonstrate financial need and service orientation.
Application requirements: Transcript. Two essays, FAFSA.
Additional information: Applicant must currently be in or previously been in foster care placement with the Oregon Department of Human Services or federally recognized Oregon Tribes; be a former foster youth with 180 days of substitute care after age 14 with Oregon DHS or an Oregon Tribe; and exited substitute care at age 16 or older. Deadline for fall, August 1; spring, February 1; summer, May 1; winter, November 1. Students may continue receiving award until age 23, but first-time recipients must be no older than 20. May apply for fall after deadline, but all funds may already be allocated. Visit Website for details and supplemental information form.

Amount of award: $3,000
Application deadline: August 1, February 1

Contact:
Oregon Student Assistance Commission
Chafee Program
1500 Valley River Drive, Suite 100
Eugene, OR 97401
Phone: 800-452-8807
Fax: 541-687-7414
Web: www.osac.state.or.us/chafeetv.html

Clark-Phelps Scholarship

Type of award: Scholarship.
Intended use: For undergraduate or graduate study at 4-year or graduate institution. Designated institutions: Oregon public institutions.
Eligibility: Applicant must be U.S. citizen or permanent resident residing in Oregon or Alaska.
Basis for selection: Major/career interest in dentistry; medicine or nursing. Applicant must demonstrate financial need.
Application requirements: Essay, transcript. FAFSA.
Additional information: Preference given to Oregon Health and Science University students and graduates of Oregon and Alaskan high schools. Award amount varies. Early bird application deadline is mid-February. Visit Website for details and application.

Application deadline: March 1

Contact:
Oregon Student Assistance Commission
Grants and Scholarship Division
1500 Valley River Drive, Suite 100
Eugene, OR 97401
Phone: 800-452-8807
Web: www.osac.state.or.us

Darlene Hooley for Oregon Veterans Scholarship

Type of award: Scholarship.
Intended use: For undergraduate or graduate study at postsecondary institution in United States. Designated institutions: Oregon institutions.
Eligibility: Applicant must be U.S. citizen or permanent resident residing in Oregon. Applicant must be veteran who served in the Army, Air Force, Marines, Navy, Coast Guard or Reserves/National Guard. Must have served in armed services during Global War on Terror.
Basis for selection: Applicant must demonstrate financial need.
Application requirements: Essay, transcript, proof of eligibility. FAFSA.
Additional information: Award amount varies. Early bird application deadline is mid-February. Visit Website for details and application. Must have actively served in the military post 9/11/2001.
Application deadline: March 1
Contact:
Oregon Student Assistance Commission
Grants and Scholarship Division
1500 Valley River Drive, Suite 100
Eugene, OR 97401
Phone: 800-452-8807
Web: www.osac.state.or.us

David Family Scholarship

Type of award: Scholarship, renewable.
Intended use: For sophomore, junior, senior or graduate study at postsecondary institution in United States. Designated institutions: Public or nonprofit institutions.
Eligibility: Applicant must be U.S. citizen or permanent resident residing in Oregon.
Basis for selection: Major/career interest in health-related professions; health education; health sciences; education or health services administration. Applicant must demonstrate financial need and high academic achievement.
Application requirements: Essay, transcript. FAFSA.
Additional information: Minimum 2.5 GPA. Intended for residents of Benton, Clackamas, Lane, Multnomah, and Washington counties. Preference given to applicants enrolling at least half-time in upper-division or graduate health- or education-related programs at four-year colleges. Visit Website for details and application.
Application deadline: March 1
Contact:
Oregon Student Assistance Commission
Grants and Scholarship Division
1500 Valley River Drive, Suite 100
Eugene, OR 97401
Phone: 800-452-8807
Web: www.osac.state.or.us

Dorothy Campbell Memorial Scholarship

Type of award: Scholarship, renewable.
Intended use: For full-time undergraduate study at accredited 4-year institution. Designated institutions: Oregon institutions.
Eligibility: Applicant must be female, high school senior. Applicant must be U.S. citizen or permanent resident residing in Oregon.
Basis for selection: Applicant must demonstrate financial need and high academic achievement.
Application requirements: Transcript. FAFSA. Essay (one page): Describe strong continuing interest in golf and contribution the sport has made to applicant's development.
Additional information: Must have strong interest in golf. Preference given to applicants participating on high school golf team (including intramural team). Minimum 2.75 GPA. Early bird deadline in mid-February. Visit Website for details and application.
Application deadline: March 1
Contact:
Oregon Student Assistance Commission
Grants and Scholarship Division
1500 Valley River Drive, Suite 100
Eugene, OR 97401
Phone: 800-452-8807
Web: www.osac.state.or.us

Eugene Bennet Visual Arts Scholarship

Type of award: Scholarship.
Intended use: For undergraduate or graduate study in United States. Designated institutions: Public and nonprofit institutions.
Eligibility: Applicant must be residing in Oregon.
Basis for selection: Major/career interest in arts, general. Applicant must demonstrate financial need and high academic achievement.
Application requirements: Interview, essay, transcript. FAFSA.
Additional information: Applicants must be graduates of a Jackson County high school, or GED recipients or home-schooled graduates from Jackson County. Minimum 2.75 GPA. Career interest should be in fine/visual arts, not performing arts. Early bird deadline mid-February. Visit Website for details.
Application deadline: March 1
Contact:
Oregon Student Assistance Commission
Grants and Scholarship Division
1500 Valley River Drive, Suite 100
Eugene, OR 97401
Phone: 800-452-8807
Web: www.osac.state.or.us

Ford Opportunity Program

Type of award: Scholarship, renewable.
Intended use: For full-time undergraduate study at accredited 2-year or 4-year institution. Designated institutions: Public or nonprofit Oregon institutions.
Eligibility: Applicant must be single. Applicant must be U.S. citizen or permanent resident residing in Oregon.
Basis for selection: Applicant must demonstrate financial need and high academic achievement.
Application requirements: Interview, essay, transcript. FAFSA.
Additional information: Minimum 3.0 GPA or 2650 GED score, unless application is accompanied by special recommendation form from counselor or OSAC. Must be single head of household with custody of dependent child/children without the support of a domestic partner. Interviews required of all semifinalists. Visit Website for details and application.
Application deadline: March 1

Scholarships

Contact:
Oregon Student Assistance Commission
Grants and Scholarship Division
1500 Valley River Drive, Suite 100
Eugene, OR 97401
Phone: 800-452-8807
Web: www.osac.state.or.us

Ford Scholars Program

Type of award: Scholarship, renewable.
Intended use: For full-time undergraduate study at accredited 2-year or 4-year institution. Designated institutions: Public or nonprofit Oregon institutions.
Eligibility: Applicant must be U.S. citizen or permanent resident residing in Oregon.
Basis for selection: Applicant must demonstrate financial need and high academic achievement.
Application requirements: Interview, essay, transcript. FAFSA.
Additional information: Minimum 3.0 GPA or 2650 GED score, unless application accompanied by special recommendation form from counselor or OSAC. Intended for high school graduates who have not yet been full-time undergraduates, or for individuals who have completed two years at Oregon community college and are entering junior year at Oregon four-year college. Visit Website for details and application.
Application deadline: March 1
Contact:
Oregon Student Assistance Commission
Grants and Scholarship Division
1500 Valley River Drive, Suite 100
Eugene, OR 97401
Phone: 800-452-8807
Web: www.osac.state.or.us

Frank Stenzel M.D. and Kathryn Stenzel II Scholarship

Type of award: Scholarship, renewable.
Intended use: For undergraduate or graduate study at postsecondary institution in United States.
Eligibility: Applicant must be U.S. citizen or permanent resident residing in Oregon.
Basis for selection: Applicant must demonstrate financial need and high academic achievement.
Application requirements: Transcript. FAFSA.
Additional information: Not open to graduating high school seniors. Not open to medicine, nursing, or physician assistant majors. Preference given to nontraditional students, first-generation college students, and students approaching final year of program. Minimum GPA for first-time freshmen: 2.75. Minimum 2.5 GPA for current college students. Award amount varies. Early bird application deadline mid-February. Visit Website for details and application.
Application deadline: March 1
Contact:
Oregon Student Assistance Commission
Grants and Scholarship Division
1500 Valley River Drive, Suite 100
Eugene, OR 97401
Phone: 800-452-8807
Web: www.osac.state.or.us

Glenn Jackson Scholars

Type of award: Scholarship, renewable.
Intended use: For full-time undergraduate study at postsecondary institution in United States. Designated institutions: Public and nonprofit institutions.
Eligibility: Applicant must be high school senior. Applicant must be U.S. citizen or permanent resident residing in Oregon.
Basis for selection: Applicant must demonstrate financial need.
Application requirements: Essay, transcript. FAFSA.
Additional information: For dependents of employees/retirees of Oregon Department of Transportation or Parks and Recreation Department. Parent must have been employed by their department at least three years. Financial need not required, but considered. Early bird deadline mid-February. Visit Website for details and application.
Application deadline: March 1
Contact:
Oregon Student Assistance Commission
Grants and Scholarship Division
1500 Valley River Drive, Suite 100
Eugene, OR 97401
Phone: 800-452-8807
Web: www.osac.state.or.us

Ida M. Crawford Scholarship

Type of award: Scholarship, renewable.
Intended use: For full-time undergraduate study at accredited postsecondary institution in United States.
Eligibility: Applicant must be U.S. citizen or permanent resident residing in Oregon.
Basis for selection: Applicant must demonstrate financial need and high academic achievement.
Application requirements: Essay, transcript, proof of eligibility. FAFSA.
Additional information: Minimum 3.5 GPA. Must be graduate of accredited Oregon high school. Not available to students majoring in law, medicine, music, theology, or education. U.S. Bank employees, their children, and near relatives not eligible. Visit Website for details and application.
Application deadline: March 1
Contact:
Oregon Student Assistance Commission
Grants and Scholarship Division
1500 Valley River Drive, Suite 100
Eugene, OR 97401
Phone: 800-452-8807
Web: www.osac.state.or.us

Jackson Foundation Journalism Scholarship

Type of award: Scholarship, renewable.
Intended use: For full-time undergraduate study at postsecondary institution. Designated institutions: Public and nonprofit Oregon institutions.
Eligibility: Applicant must be U.S. citizen or permanent resident residing in Oregon.
Basis for selection: Major/career interest in journalism. Applicant must demonstrate financial need and high academic achievement.
Application requirements: Essay, transcript. FAFSA.
Additional information: Must be graduate of an Oregon high school. Preference given to applicants who have strong SAT writing scores. Early bird deadline mid-February. Visit Website for details and application.

Application deadline: March 1
Contact:
Oregon Student Assistance Commission
Grants and Scholarship Division
1500 Valley River Drive, Suite 100
Eugene, OR 97401
Phone: 800-452-8807
Web: www.osac.state.or.us

James Carlson Memorial Scholarship

Type of award: Scholarship.
Intended use: For full-time senior or graduate study at accredited 4-year institution in United States.
Eligibility: Applicant must be U.S. citizen or permanent resident residing in Oregon.
Basis for selection: Major/career interest in education; education, teacher; education, special or education, early childhood. Applicant must demonstrate financial need and high academic achievement.
Application requirements: Essay, transcript. FAFSA.
Additional information: Available to elementary or secondary education majors entering senior year or fifth year of study, or to graduate students in fifth year for elementary or secondary certificate. Preference given to students with experience living or working in diverse environments (250-350 word essay describing this experience required for applicants qualifying under this preference); dependents of Oregon Education Association members; and students committed to teaching autistic children. Early bird deadline in mid-February. Visit Website for details and application.
Application deadline: March 1
Contact:
Oregon Student Assistance Commission
Grants and Scholarship Division
1500 Valley River Drive, Suite 100
Eugene, OR 97401
Phone: 800-452-8807
Web: www.osac.state.or.us

Jeffrey Alan Scoggins Memorial Scholarship

Type of award: Scholarship.
Intended use: For junior or senior study at 4-year institution. Designated institutions: Oregon public and nonprofit institutions.
Eligibility: Applicant must be U.S. citizen or permanent resident residing in Oregon.
Basis for selection: Major/career interest in engineering. Applicant must demonstrate financial need and high academic achievement.
Application requirements: Essay, transcript. FAFSA.
Additional information: Minimum 3.0 GPA. Preference given to applicants attending Oregon State University and to members of Sigma Chi fraternity. Award amount varies. Early bird application deadline mid-February. Visit Website for details and application.
Application deadline: March 1
Contact:
Oregon Student Assistance Commission
Grants and Scholarship Division
1500 Valley River Drive, Suite 100
Eugene, OR 97401
Phone: 800-452-8807
Web: www.osac.state.or.us

Jerome B. Steinbach Scholarship

Type of award: Scholarship.
Intended use: For full-time sophomore, junior or senior study at accredited postsecondary institution in United States.
Eligibility: Applicant must be U.S. citizen residing in Oregon.
Basis for selection: Applicant must demonstrate financial need and high academic achievement.
Application requirements: Essay, transcript, proof of eligibility. FAFSA.
Additional information: Minimum 3.5 GPA. Must be U.S. citizen by birth. Must specify state of birth. U.S. Bank employees, their children, and near relatives not eligible. Early bird deadline in mid-February. Visit Website for details and application.
Application deadline: March 1
Contact:
Oregon Student Assistance Commission
Grants and Scholarship Division
1500 Valley River Drive, Suite 100
Eugene, OR 97401
Phone: 800-452-8807
Web: www.osac.state.or.us

Laurence R. Foster Memorial Scholarship

Type of award: Scholarship, renewable.
Intended use: For undergraduate or graduate study at accredited 4-year institution in United States. Designated institutions: Public and nonprofit institutions.
Eligibility: Applicant must be U.S. citizen or permanent resident residing in Oregon.
Basis for selection: Major/career interest in nursing; medical specialties/research; physician assistant; public health; medical assistant; health-related professions or nurse practitioner. Applicant must demonstrate financial need and service orientation.
Application requirements: Essay, transcript. FAFSA. Two additional essays.
Additional information: Applicant must be seeking career in public health, not private practice. General preference given to applicants of diverse cultures. Preference also given to persons working in (or graduate students majoring in) public health and to undergraduates entering junior/senior-year health programs. Early bird deadline in mid-February. Visit Website for essay topic and application.
Application deadline: March 1
Contact:
Oregon Student Assistance Commission
Grants and Scholarship Division
1500 Valley River Drive, Suite 100
Eugene, OR 97401
Phone: 800-452-8807
Web: www.osac.state.or.us

Maria C. Jackson-General George A. White Scholarship

Type of award: Scholarship, renewable.
Intended use: For full-time undergraduate or graduate study at postsecondary institution. Designated institutions: Oregon institutions.
Eligibility: Applicant must be U.S. citizen or permanent resident residing in Oregon. Applicant must be veteran; or dependent of active service person or veteran in the Army, Air

Force, Marines, Navy or Coast Guard. Must have been Oregon resident at time of enlistment.
Basis for selection: Applicant must demonstrate financial need and high academic achievement.
Application requirements: Essay, transcript, proof of eligibility. FAFSA.
Additional information: Minimum 3.75 GPA for undergraduates; no GPA requirement for graduate students or students at technical schools. U.S. Bank employees, children, and near relatives not eligible. Early bird deadline in mid-February. Visit Website for details and application.
Application deadline: March 1
Contact:
Oregon Student Assistance Commission
Grants and Scholarship Division
1500 Valley River Drive, Suite 100
Eugene, OR 97401
Phone: 800-452-8807
Web: www.osac.state.or.us

One World Scholarship Essay

Type of award: Scholarship.
Intended use: For undergraduate study in United States. Designated institutions: Public and nonprofit institutions.
Eligibility: Applicant must be no older than 21. Applicant must be residing in Oregon.
Basis for selection: Competition/talent/interest in writing/journalism, based on 500-word essay analyzing the inter-relationships of policy, programs, and personal responsibility on hunger and the stability of the food supply.
Application requirements: Transcript.
Additional information: Early bird deadline mid-February. Visit Website for more details.
Application deadline: March 1
Contact:
Oregon Student Assistance Commission
Grants and Scholarship Division
1500 Valley River Drive, Suite 100
Eugene, OR 97401
Phone: 800-452-8807
Web: www.osac.state.or.us

Oregon Alpha Delta Kappa Scholarship

Type of award: Scholarship, renewable.
Intended use: For full-time senior or graduate study at accredited postsecondary institution in United States. Designated institutions: Oregon institutions.
Eligibility: Applicant must be U.S. citizen or permanent resident residing in Oregon.
Basis for selection: Major/career interest in education. Applicant must demonstrate financial need and high academic achievement.
Application requirements: Transcript. FAFSA. Two essays.
Additional information: Applicants must be elementary or secondary education majors. Visit Website for details and application.
Application deadline: March 1
Contact:
Oregon Student Assistance Commission
Grants and Scholarship Division
1500 Valley River Drive, Suite 100
Eugene, OR 97401
Phone: 800-452-8807
Web: www.osac.state.or.us.

Oregon Dungeness Crab Commission

Type of award: Scholarship.
Intended use: For full-time undergraduate study at postsecondary institution in United States.
Eligibility: Applicant must be no older than 23. Applicant must be U.S. citizen or permanent resident residing in Oregon.
Basis for selection: Major/career interest in wildlife/fisheries or environmental science. Applicant must demonstrate high academic achievement.
Application requirements: Essay, transcript.
Additional information: Major/career interest restrictions do not apply to high school seniors. For dependents of licensed Oregon Dungeness Crab fishermen or crew. Early bird deadline in mid-February. Visit Website for details and application.
Application deadline: March 1
Contact:
Oregon Student Assistance Commission
Grants and Scholarship Division
1500 Valley River Drive, Suite 100
Eugene, OR 97401
Phone: 800-452-8807
Web: www.osac.state.or.us

Oregon Foundation for Blacktail Deer Scholarship

Type of award: Scholarship.
Intended use: For undergraduate study at postsecondary institution. Designated institutions: Oregon institutions.
Eligibility: Applicant must be residing in Oregon.
Basis for selection: Major/career interest in forestry; biology; wildlife/fisheries or zoology. Applicant must demonstrate financial need and seriousness of purpose.
Application requirements: Transcript. FAFSA. Essay (250 words) discussing the challenges of wildlife management in the coming ten years. Copy of previous year's hunting license.
Additional information: Must have serious commitment to career in wildlife management. Early bird deadline mid-February. Visit Website for details.
Application deadline: March 1
Contact:
Oregon Student Assistance Commission
Grants and Scholarship Division
1500 Valley River Drive, Suite 100
Eugene, OR 97401
Phone: 800-452-8807
Web: www.osac.state.or.us

Oregon Occupational Safety and Health Division Workers Memorial Scholarship

Type of award: Scholarship, renewable.
Intended use: For full-time undergraduate or graduate study at postsecondary institution in United States.
Eligibility: Applicant must be U.S. citizen or permanent resident residing in Oregon.
Basis for selection: Applicant must demonstrate financial need and high academic achievement.
Application requirements: Essay, transcript. FAFSA. Additional 500-word essay: "How has the injury or death of your parent or spouse affected or influenced your decision to further your education?" Must provide name, last four digits of social security number, or workers' compensation claim

number of worker permanently disabled or fatally injured; date of death or injury; location of incident; and exact relationship to applicant.
Additional information: Applicant must be dependent or spouse of Oregon worker permanently disabled on the job or be the recipient of fatality benefits as dependent or spouse of worker fatally injured in Oregon. Early bird deadline in mid-February. Visit Website for details and application.
Application deadline: March 1
Contact:
Oregon Student Assistance Commission
Grants and Scholarship Division
1500 Valley River Drive, Suite 100
Eugene, OR 97401
Phone: 800-452-8807
Web: www.osac.state.or.us

Oregon Scholarship Fund Community College Student Award Programs

Type of award: Scholarship, renewable.
Intended use: For undergraduate study at accredited 2-year institution. Designated institutions: Oregon community colleges.
Eligibility: Applicant must be high school senior. Applicant must be U.S. citizen or permanent resident residing in Oregon.
Basis for selection: Applicant must demonstrate financial need.
Application requirements: Essay, transcript. FAFSA.
Additional information: Early bird deadline in mid-February. Visit Website for details and application.
Application deadline: March 1
Contact:
Oregon Student Assistance Commission
Grants and Scholarship Division
1500 Valley River Drive, Suite 100
Eugene, OR 97401
Phone: 800-452-8807
Web: www.osac.state.or.us

Peter Connacher Memorial Scholarship

Type of award: Scholarship, renewable.
Intended use: For full-time undergraduate or graduate study at postsecondary institution in United States.
Eligibility: Applicant must be U.S. citizen or permanent resident. Must be former American prisoner of war or descendant.
Basis for selection: Applicant must demonstrate financial need and high academic achievement.
Application requirements: Transcript, proof of eligibility. FAFSA, two essays, copy of POW's military discharge papers and proof of POW status, if selected as a semifinalist. State relationship to POW on supporting documents.
Additional information: Preference given to Oregon residents and their dependents. Visit Website for details and application.
Application deadline: March 1
Contact:
Oregon Student Assistance Commission
Grants and Scholarship Division
1500 Valley River Drive, Suite 100
Eugene, OR 97401
Phone: 800-452-8807
Web: www.osac.state.or.us

Professional Land Surveyors of Oregon Scholarship

Type of award: Scholarship, renewable.
Intended use: For full-time undergraduate study at 2-year or 4-year institution. Designated institutions: Public and nonprofit Oregon institutions.
Eligibility: Applicant must be U.S. citizen or permanent resident residing in Oregon.
Basis for selection: Major/career interest in surveying/mapping. Applicant must demonstrate financial need.
Application requirements: Essay, transcript. FAFSA. Names, addresses, and phone numbers of two references (do not submit letters).
Additional information: Students must be enrolled in curricula leading to land-surveying career. Community college applicants must intend to transfer to eligible four-year schools. Four-year applicants must intend to take Fundamentals of Land Surveying (FLS) exam. Maximum award based on year in school. Early bird deadline mid-February. Visit Website for details and application.
Application deadline: March 1
Contact:
Oregon Student Assistance Commission
Grants and Scholarship Division
1500 Valley River Drive, Suite 100
Eugene, OR 97401
Phone: 800-452-8807
Web: www.osac.state.or.us

Richard F. Brentano Memorial Scholarship

Type of award: Scholarship, renewable.
Intended use: For full-time undergraduate study at postsecondary institution in United States.
Eligibility: Applicant must be U.S. citizen or permanent resident.
Basis for selection: Applicant must demonstrate high academic achievement.
Application requirements: Essay, transcript.
Additional information: Intended for children or IRS-legal dependents of employees of Waste Control Systems, Inc., and subsidiaries. Parent must have been employed by Waste Control Systems one year as of deadline. Early bird deadline mid-February. Visit Website for details and application.
Application deadline: March 1
Contact:
Oregon Student Assistance Commission
Grants and Scholarship Division
1500 Valley Drive, Suite 100
Eugene, OR 97401
Phone: 800-452-8807
Web: www.osac.state.or.us

Roger W. Emmons Memorial Scholarship

Type of award: Scholarship, renewable.
Intended use: For full-time undergraduate study at accredited postsecondary institution in United States. Designated institutions: Public and nonprofit institutions.
Eligibility: Applicant must be high school senior. Applicant must be U.S. citizen or permanent resident.
Basis for selection: Applicant must demonstrate high academic achievement.

Application requirements: Essay, transcript, proof of eligibility.
Additional information: Parent(s) or grandparent(s) must have been solid waste company owner(s) or employee(s) for at least three years and member(s) of Oregon Refuse & Recycling Association. Early bird deadline in mid-February. Visit Website for details and application.
Application deadline: March 1
Contact:
Oregon Student Assistance Commission
Grants and Scholarship Division
1500 Valley River Drive, Suite 100
Eugene, OR 97401
Phone: 800-452-8807
Web: www.osac.state.or.us

Teamsters Clyde C. Crosby/Joseph M. Edgar Memorial Scholarship

Type of award: Scholarship, renewable.
Intended use: For full-time undergraduate study at postsecondary institution in United States.
Eligibility: Applicant must be high school senior. Applicant must be U.S. citizen or permanent resident residing in Oregon.
Basis for selection: Applicant must demonstrate financial need and high academic achievement.
Application requirements: Essay, transcript. FAFSA.
Additional information: Minimum 3.0 cumulative GPA. Must be child or dependent stepchild of active, retired, disabled, or deceased member of local unions affiliated with Joint Council of Teamsters #37. Qualifying members must have been active at least one year. Early bird deadline in mid-February. Visit Website for details and application.
Application deadline: March 1
Contact:
Oregon Student Assistance Commission
Grants and Scholarship Division
1500 Valley River Drive, Suite 100
Eugene, OR 97401
Phone: 800-452-8807
Web: www.osac.state.or.us

Teamsters Council #37 Federal Credit Union Scholarship

Type of award: Scholarship.
Intended use: For undergraduate or graduate study at postsecondary institution in United States.
Eligibility: Applicant must be U.S. citizen or permanent resident residing in Oregon.
Basis for selection: Applicant must demonstrate financial need and high academic achievement.
Application requirements: Essay, transcript. FAFSA.
Additional information: For members (or dependents) of Council #37 credit union. Members must have been active in local affiliated with the Joint Council of Teamsters #37 for at least one year. Applicant must have cumulative GPA between 2.0 and 3.0. Early bird deadline mid-February. Visit Website for details and application.
Application deadline: March 1
Contact:
Oregon Student Assistance Commission
Grants and Scholarship Division
1500 Valley River Drive, Suite 100
Eugene, OR 97401
Phone: 800-452-8807
Web: www.osac.state.or.us

Teamsters Local 305 Scholarship

Type of award: Scholarship, renewable.
Intended use: For full-time undergraduate study at postsecondary institution in United States.
Eligibility: Applicant must be high school senior. Applicant must be U.S. citizen or permanent resident.
Basis for selection: Applicant must demonstrate high academic achievement.
Application requirements: Essay, transcript.
Additional information: Must be child or dependent stepchild of active, retired, disabled, or deceased member of Local 305 of the Joint Council of Teamsters #37. Member must have been active at least one year. Early bird deadline in mid-February. Visit Website for details and application.
Application deadline: March 1
Contact:
Oregon Student Assistance Commission
Grants and Scholarship Division
1500 Valley River Drive, Suite 100
Eugene, OR 97401
Phone: 800-452-8807
Web: www.osac.state.or.us

Walter and Marie Schmidt Scholarship

Type of award: Scholarship, renewable.
Intended use: For undergraduate study at postsecondary institution in United States.
Eligibility: Applicant must be U.S. citizen or permanent resident residing in Oregon.
Basis for selection: Major/career interest in nursing or gerontology. Applicant must demonstrate financial need and high academic achievement.
Application requirements: Essay, transcript. FAFSA. Additional essay describing desire to pursue nursing career in geriatric healthcare.
Additional information: Available to students enrolling in programs to become registered nurses and intending to pursue careers in geriatric healthcare. Priority given to students: 1) attending Lane Community College; 2) enrolled in another two-year nursing program. U.S. Bank employees, children, and near relatives not eligible. Early bird deadline in mid-February. Visit Website for details and application.
Application deadline: March 1
Contact:
Oregon Student Assistance Commission
Grants and Scholarship Division
1500 Valley River Drive, Suite 100
Eugene, OR 97401
Phone: 800-452-8807
Web: www.osac.state.or.us

Organization for Autism Research

Lisa Higgins Hussman Scholarship Program

Type of award: Scholarship.
Intended use: For undergraduate study at postsecondary institution.

Application requirements: Recommendations, essay. Documentation of autism diagnosis by physician.
Additional information: Award is for qualified individuals with more severe autism spectrum diagnoses (DSM-IV or later criteria). Awards given to students in 4 categories: 4-year undergraduate attendants; 2-year undergraduate attendants; trade, technical, or vocational school attendants; and post-secondary cooperative life skills or transition program attendants. Apply online. Visit Website for more information.

Amount of award:	$3,000
Number of awards:	4
Application deadline:	April 28
Total amount awarded:	$12,000

Contact:
Organization for Autism Research
2000 14th Street North
Suite 240
Arlington, VA 22201
Phone: 703-243-9710
Fax: 703-243-9751
Web: www.researchautism.org/news/otherevents/scholarship.asp

Schwallie Family Scholarship Program

Type of award: Scholarship.
Intended use: For full-time undergraduate study at accredited postsecondary institution in United States.
Eligibility: Applicant must be U.S. citizen or permanent resident.
Application requirements: Recommendations, essay, proof of eligibility. Documentation by physician of applicant's autism or Asperger's Syndrome.
Additional information: Award is for qualified individuals with autism or Asperger's Syndrome (DSM-IV or later criteria). One-time awards of $3,000 will be given to students in each of the following categories: 1) four-year undergraduate attendants; 2) two-year undergraduate attendants; and 3) trade, technical, or vocational school attendants. Apply online. Visit Website for more information.

Amount of award:	$3,000
Number of applicants:	725
Application deadline:	April 28
Notification begins:	July 6
Total amount awarded:	$73,000

Contact:
Organization for Autism Research
2000 14th Street North
Suite 240
Arlington, VA 22201
Phone: 703-243-9710
Fax: 703-243-9751
Web: www.researchautism.org/news/otherevents/scholarship.asp

The Orthotic and Prosthetic Education and Development Fund

Chester Haddan Scholarship Program

Type of award: Scholarship.
Intended use: For undergraduate or post-bachelor's certificate study at accredited 2-year or 4-year institution in United States.
Eligibility: Applicant must be U.S. citizen.
Basis for selection: Major/career interest in orthotics/prosthetics or medical specialties/research. Applicant must demonstrate financial need, depth of character, leadership, seriousness of purpose and service orientation.
Application requirements: Recommendations, transcript. A 200-word essay on why student wants to work in orthotics or prosthetics. Recent W-2 or letter from current employer.
Additional information: Students may apply directly or professors may nominate them. Applicants must be willing to financially contribute to their education.

Amount of award:	$1,000
Number of awards:	1
Application deadline:	January 31

Contact:
The Orthotic and Prosthetic Education and Development Fund
The Academy
1331 H Street, NW, Suite 501
Washington, DC 20005
Phone: 202-380-3663 ext. 212
Web: www.oandp.org/education

Dan McKeever Scholarship Program

Type of award: Scholarship.
Intended use: For senior or master's study at accredited 4-year institution in United States. Designated institutions: American Academy of Orthotists and Prosthetists-accredited institutions.
Eligibility: Applicant must be U.S. citizen.
Basis for selection: Major/career interest in orthotics/prosthetics or medical specialties/research. Applicant must demonstrate financial need, high academic achievement, leadership, seriousness of purpose and service orientation.
Application requirements: Recommendations, transcript. A 200-word essay on why student wants to work in orthotics or prosthetics. Recent W-2 or letter from current employer.
Additional information: Students may apply directly or professors may nominate them. Must maintain minimum 3.0 GPA. Applicants must be willing to financially contribute to their education.

Amount of award:	$1,000
Number of awards:	3
Application deadline:	May 30

Contact:
The Orthotic and Prosthetic Education and Development Fund
The Academy
1331 H Street, NW, Suite 501
Washington, DC 20005
Phone: 202-380-3663 ext. 212
Web: www.oandp.org/education

Ken Chagnon Scholarship

Type of award: Scholarship.
Intended use: For undergraduate study at accredited 2-year or 4-year institution in United States.
Eligibility: Applicant must be U.S. citizen.
Basis for selection: Major/career interest in orthotics/prosthetics or medical specialties/research. Applicant must demonstrate financial need, leadership and seriousness of purpose.
Application requirements: Recommendations, transcript. A 200-word essay on why student wants to work in orthotics or prosthetics. Recent W-2 or letter from current employer.
Additional information: Students may apply directly or professors may nominate them. Applicants must be willing to financially contribute to their education. Applicants must be

enrolled in technician program and show exceptional technical aptitude.

Amount of award: $500
Number of awards: 1
Application deadline: January 31

Contact:
The Orthotic and Prosthetic Education and Development Fund
The Academy
1331 H Street, NW, Suite 501
Washington, DC 20005
Phone: 202-380-3663 ext. 212
Web: www.oandp.org/education

Osage Tribal Education Committee

Osage Tribal Education Scholarship

Type of award: Scholarship, renewable.
Intended use: For undergraduate or graduate study at accredited postsecondary institution in United States.
Eligibility: Applicant must be American Indian. Must be a member of the Osage Nation. Applicant must be U.S. citizen.
Basis for selection: Applicant must demonstrate high academic achievement.
Application requirements: Proof of Osage Indian blood.
Additional information: Must maintain 2.0 GPA. Award amount varies.

Application deadline: July 1, December 31

Contact:
Osage Tribal Education Committee
Oklahoma Area Education Office
200 Northwest 4th, Suite 4049
Oklahoma City, OK 73102
Phone: 405-605-6051 ext. 304
Fax: 405-605-6057

Papercheck.com

Papercheck.com Charles Shafae' Scholarship Fund

Type of award: Scholarship.
Intended use: For undergraduate study at accredited 4-year institution in United States.
Eligibility: Applicant must be U.S. citizen or permanent resident.
Basis for selection: Competition/talent/interest in writing/journalism. Applicant must demonstrate high academic achievement.
Application requirements: Transcript. Minimum 1,000-word essay in MLA format. Include "works cited" page with at least two sources.
Additional information: Minimum 3.2 GPA. Applicant must be in good standing at institution. Visit Website for essay questions, guidelines, and deadline. Complete entry form online. Contact via e-mail.

Amount of award: $500
Number of awards: 2
Number of applicants: 200
Application deadline: January 1, June 1
Notification begins: June 1, January 1
Total amount awarded: $1,000

Contact:
Papercheck.com
Charles Shafae' Scholarship
12 Geary Street, Suite 808
San Francisco, CA 94108
Phone: 866-693-EDIT
Fax: 866-693-3348
Web: www.papercheck.com

Par Aide

Par Aide's Joseph S. Garske Collegiate Grant Program

Type of award: Scholarship, renewable.
Intended use: For undergraduate study at vocational, 2-year or 4-year institution.
Eligibility: Applicant must be high school senior.
Basis for selection: Applicant must demonstrate high academic achievement, leadership and service orientation.
Application requirements: Transcript. A 500-word essay evaluating a significant experience, achievement, or risk and its effect on the student.
Additional information: Minimum 2.0 GPA. Applicant's parent or stepparent must be Golf Course Superintendents Association of America member for five or more consecutive years in one of the following classifications: A, Superintendent Member, C, Retired-A, Retired-B, or AA life. Children or stepchildren of deceased members eligible if member was active for five years at time of death. Children of Par Aide employees, the Environmental Institute for Golf's Board of Trustees, the GCSAA Board of Directors, and GCSAA staff not eligible. First place award is $2,500; second place, $1,500; third place, $1,000. First-place awardees eligible for one-year renewal.

Amount of award: $1,000-$2,500
Number of awards: 3
Application deadline: March 15
Notification begins: May 15
Total amount awarded: $7,500

Contact:
Golf Course Superintendents Association of America
Garske Grant Program
1421 Research Park Drive
Lawrence, KS 66049-3859
Phone: 785-832-4445
Web: www.gcsaa.org

Patient Advocate Foundation

Patient Advocate Foundation Scholarships for Survivors

Type of award: Scholarship.
Intended use: For full-time undergraduate or graduate study at accredited 2-year, 4-year or graduate institution.

Eligibility: Applicant must be no older than 25.
Basis for selection: Applicant must demonstrate financial need, high academic achievement, depth of character, leadership and service orientation.
Application requirements: Recommendations, essay, transcript, proof of eligibility. Previous year's tax returns. Written documentation from physician stating medical history.
Additional information: Must be survivor of life-threatening, chronic, or debilitating disease. Must maintain 3.0 overall GPA. Must complete 20 hours of community service in year scholarship will be dispensed. Check Website for application deadline.

Amount of award:	$3,000
Number of awards:	12
Number of applicants:	150
Total amount awarded:	$36,000

Contact:
Patient Advocate Foundation
421 Butler Farm Rd.
Hampton, VA 23666
Web: www.patientadvocate.org

Peacock Productions, Inc.

Audria M. Edwards Scholarship Fund

Type of award: Scholarship, renewable.
Intended use: For full-time undergraduate study at accredited vocational, 2-year or 4-year institution in United States.
Eligibility: Applicant must be U.S. citizen residing in Oregon or Washington.
Basis for selection: Major/career interest in arts, general. Applicant must demonstrate financial need, depth of character and leadership.
Application requirements: Recommendations, essay, transcript, proof of eligibility.
Additional information: Applicant must be gay, lesbian, bisexual, or transgendered; or the child of gay, lesbian, bisexual, or transgendered parents. Applicant must be pursuing degree in academic field, trade, vocation, or the arts. Applicants living in Washington must reside in Clark, Cowlitz, Skamania, or Wahkiakum counties. Visit Website for application information.

Amount of award:	$1,000-$10,000
Application deadline:	May 1
Total amount awarded:	$5,000

Contact:
Peacock Productions, Inc.
Audria M. Edwards Scholarship Fund
P.O. Box 8854
Portland, OR 97207-8854
Web: www.peacockinthepark.com

Pearson Foundation

Pearson Prize for Higher Education

Type of award: Scholarship.
Intended use: For sophomore or junior study at accredited 2-year or 4-year institution.
Eligibility: Applicant must be U.S. citizen or permanent resident.
Basis for selection: Applicant must demonstrate high academic achievement, leadership and service orientation.
Application requirements: Recommendations.
Additional information: Minimum 2.5 GPA. Must have demonstrated leadership in community service. If applicant is graduating from a 2-year college, they must be transferring to 4-year program to be eligible. Must have at least 30 credits accumulated. Cannot have won Pearson Prize in the past. Cannot be related to someone from Pearson or Pearson Foundation. Apply online. Deadline in April. Semi-finalists notified in June. Winners notified in late July.

Amount of award:	$1,000
Number of awards:	100

Contact:
Pearson Foundation
Web: www.pearsonfoundation.org/pearsonprize

Penguin Putnam, Inc.

Signet Classic Student Scholarship Essay Contest

Type of award: Scholarship.
Intended use: For undergraduate study at postsecondary institution.
Eligibility: Applicant must be high school junior or senior. Applicant must be U.S. citizen or permanent resident.
Basis for selection: Competition/talent/interest in writing/journalism, based on style, content, grammar, and originality; judges look for clear, concise writing that is articulate, logically organized, and well-supported. Major/career interest in English or literature.
Application requirements: Proof of eligibility, nomination by high school English teacher. Entrant must read designated book and answer one of several book-related questions in two- to three-page essay. Cover letter on school letterhead from teacher. Only one junior and one senior essay may be submitted per teacher. Parent or legal guardian must submit essay for home-schooled students.
Additional information: Home-schooled entrants must be between ages of 16 and 18. Immediate relatives of employees of Penguin Group (USA) Inc. and its affiliates ineligible. Visit Website for details and application. Winner also receives Signet Classic library for school (or for public library in the case of home-schooled winner). Deadline in mid-April.

Amount of award:	$1,000
Number of awards:	5
Notification begins:	June 15
Total amount awarded:	$5,000

Contact:
Penguin Group Signet Classic Student Scholarship Essay Contest
Academic Marketing Department
375 Hudson Street
New York, NY 10014
Web: www.us.penguingroup.com/static/pages/services-academic/essayhome.html

Pennsylvania Higher Education Assistance Agency

Blind or Deaf Beneficiary Grant Program

Type of award: Scholarship, renewable.
Intended use: For at postsecondary institution.
Eligibility: Applicant must be visually impaired or hearing impaired. Applicant must be residing in Pennsylvania.
Basis for selection: Applicant must demonstrate high academic achievement.
Additional information: Award is up to $500. Student must be blind or deaf. Must qualify to receive benefits through the PA Office of Vocational Rehabilitation. Must maintain satisfactory academic progress. Award can replace student's EFC but cannot exceed cost of attendance. Awards are given on a first-come, first-served basis.

Amount of award: $500
Application deadline: December 31

Contact:
PHEAA State Grant and Special Programs
P.O. Box 8157
Harrisburg, PA 17105-8157
Phone: 800-692-7392
Web: www.pheaa.org

Chafee Education and Training Grant (ETG) Program

Type of award: Scholarship, renewable.
Intended use: For undergraduate study at accredited vocational, 2-year or 4-year institution. Designated institutions: Institutions approved by U.S. Department of Education for Title IV student assistance programs.
Eligibility: Applicant must be residing in Pennsylvania.
Basis for selection: Applicant must demonstrate financial need.
Application requirements: FAFSA.
Additional information: Must be eligible for services under the Commonwealth's Chafee Foster Care Independence Program. Must be in foster care or adopted from foster care after age 16. Must participate in ETG program on 21st birthday until age 23. Must maintain satisfactory academic progress. Visit Website for details and application.

Amount of award: $3,000

Contact:
PHEAA State Grant and Special Programs
P.O. Box 8157
Harrisburg, PA 17105-8157
Phone: 800-692-7392
Web: www.pheaa.org

Pennsylvania GEAR UP Scholarship

Type of award: Scholarship.
Intended use: For sophomore, junior or senior study at postsecondary institution in United States.
Eligibility: Applicant must be no older than 22. Applicant must be residing in Pennsylvania.
Application requirements: FAFSA.
Additional information: Must have graduated in 2008, 2009, 2010, or 2011 from one of the following high schools in the Philadelphia or Harrisburg school districts: Philadelphia high schools, Harrisburg University Science and Technology High School, Young Women's Leadership School at E.W. Rhodes High School, John Bartram Main High School, Martin Luther King High School, Strawberry Mansion High School, Harrisburg High School, William Penn High School, (ACTS and CTA). Must be deemed scholarship-eligible through participation in college readiness activities. Must be eligible for a Federal Pell Grant each year. Must meet all federal student aid requirements. Annual maximum GEAR UP scholarship is equal to the maximum Federal Pell Grant for the same academic year. GEAR UP scholarship may be reduced based on enrollment status, Expected Family Contribution (EFC), fund availability, or unmet cost as determined by the school's financial aid office. Awards contingent upon federal funding and are not guaranteed.

Contact:
PHEAA State Grant and Special Programs
P.O. Box 8157
Harrisburg, PA 17105-8157
Phone: 800-692-7392
Web: www.pheaa.org

Pennsylvania Higher Education Assistance Agency Partnership for Access to Higher Education (PATH)

Type of award: Scholarship, renewable.
Intended use: For undergraduate study at postsecondary institution in United States. Designated institutions: Pennsylvania State Grant-approved postsecondary institutions in Pennsylvania.
Eligibility: Applicant must be U.S. citizen residing in Pennsylvania.
Basis for selection: Applicant must demonstrate financial need and high academic achievement.
Application requirements: Nomination by participating PATH organization (visit PHEAA Website for list). FAFSA.
Additional information: Must receive a scholarship or grant from participating PHEAA PATH organization for the academic year that PATH aid is requested. Amount of award varies, and is up to $2,500 per academic year.

Amount of award: $2,500

Contact:
PHEAA State Grant and Special Programs
P.O. Box 8157
Harrisburg, PA 17105-8157
Phone: 800-443-0646
Web: www.pheaa.org

Pennsylvania Higher Education Assistance Agency Postsecondary Educational Gratuity Program

Type of award: Scholarship, renewable.
Intended use: For full-time undergraduate study at 2-year or 4-year institution. Designated institutions: Pennsylvania public institutions.
Eligibility: Applicant must be no older than 25. Applicant must be residing in Pennsylvania. Applicant must be dependent of deceased veteran. Applicant's parent must have been killed or disabled in work-related accident as firefighter, police officer or public safety officer.
Application requirements: Record of application for other financial aid. Certified copy of birth certificate. FAFSA.

Additional information: Applicant must be child by birth or adoption of deceased police officer, firefighter, rescue or ambulance squad member, corrections facility employee, or active National Guard member who died after January 1, 1976 as direct result of performing official duties; or child by birth or adoption of deceased sheriff, deputy sheriff, National Guard member, or certain other individual on federal or state active military duty who died since September 11, 2001 as direct result of performing official duties. Award may include waiver of tuition, fees, and room and board costs. Must apply for other available financial aid prior to application to this program. Visit Website for application.

Amount of award: Full tuition

Contact:
PHEAA State Grant and Special Programs
P.O. Box 8157
Harrisburg, PA 17105-8157
Phone: 800-692-7392
Web: www.pheaa.org

Pennsylvania State Grant Program

Type of award: Scholarship, renewable.
Intended use: For undergraduate study at accredited vocational, 2-year or 4-year institution in United States.
Eligibility: Applicant must be residing in Pennsylvania.
Basis for selection: Applicant must demonstrate financial need.
Application requirements: Proof of eligibility. FAFSA.
Additional information: Applicant must be high school graduate or GED recipient enrolled in PHEAA-approved program. Applicant must not already have four-year undergraduate degree. Grants are portable to approved institutions in other states. Number and amount of awards vary. Deadlines: May 1 for first-time applicants in business, trade, technical, or nursing schools or terminal two-year programs, first-time applicants planning to attend a community college and all renewal applicants; August 15 for summer-term applicants.

Application deadline: May 1, August 1

Contact:
PHEAA State Grant and Special Programs Division
P.O. Box 8157
Harrisburg, PA 17105-8157
Phone: 800-692-7392
Web: www.pheaa.org

Pennsylvania Targeted Industry Program (PA-TIP)

Type of award: Scholarship, renewable.
Intended use: For undergraduate study at postsecondary institution. Designated institutions: PHEAA approved institutions.
Basis for selection: Major/career interest in energy research; materials science or agriculture. Applicant must demonstrate financial need.
Application requirements: FAFSA.
Additional information: Must be domiciled in Pennsylvania. Provides need-based awards to students pursuing eligible courses of study that are greater than 10 weeks but less than 2 years in length (diploma or certificate programs) at approved schools. Awards for students enrolled in the following programs: Energy, Advanced Materials and Diversified Manufacturing, Agriculture and Food Production. Amount of award is up to equivalent maximum Pennsylvania State Grant award or 75 percent of the allowable program cost, whichever is less, per award year. Awards cover tuition, books, supplies, and specific living expenses.

Amount of award: $500-$4,348

Contact:
Pennsylvania Higher Education Assistance Agency
P.O. Box 8157
Harrisburg, PA 17105-8157
Phone: 800-692-7392
Fax: 717-720-3786
Web: www.pheaa.org/pa-tip

Pennsylvania Work-Study Program

Type of award: Scholarship, renewable.
Intended use: For undergraduate, master's, doctoral or first professional study at accredited postsecondary institution. Designated institutions: PHEAA-approved institutions.
Eligibility: Applicant must be U.S. citizen or permanent resident residing in Pennsylvania.
Basis for selection: Applicant must demonstrate financial need.
Application requirements: Interview, proof of eligibility. Proof of state grant or subsidized Stafford loan.
Additional information: Student must demonstrate ability to benefit from career-related high-tech or community service work experience. Applicant must be state grant or subsidized federal loan recipient and not owe state grant refund or be in default on student loan. Recipient must secure a job with PHEAA-approved on or off-campus SWSP employer. Amount and number of awards vary. Deadlines: Fall term only and academic year, October 1; spring term only, January 31; summer, May 31.

Application deadline: October 1, January 31

Contact:
PHEAA State Grant and Special Programs Division
P.O. Box 8157
Harrisburg, PA 17105-8157
Phone: 800-692-7392
Web: www.pheaa.org

Teacher Education Assistance for College and Higher Education (TEACH) Grant

Type of award: Scholarship, renewable.
Intended use: For undergraduate study at 4-year institution. Designated institutions: Participating institutions.
Basis for selection: Major/career interest in education.
Additional information: Award is for students who intend to teach in a public or private elementary or secondary school that serves low-income families. Award is up to $4,000 per year. Must agree to work full-time as a teacher in high-need field for at least 4 academic years within 8 calendar years from the date program of study is completed, for which TEACH Grant was received. If service is not completed, TEACH Grant will convert to Direct Unsubsidized Stafford Loan that must be repaid, charged interest from the date TEACH Grant is disbursed.

Amount of award: $4,000
Application deadline: April 1

Contact:
Pennsylvania Higher Education Assistance Agency
P.O. Box 8157
Harrisburg, PA 17105-8157
Phone: 800-692-7392
Fax: 717-720-3786
Web: www.studentaid.ed.gov

Pennsylvania State System of Higher Education Foundation, Inc.

Dr. & Mrs. Arthur William Phillips Scholarship

Type of award: Scholarship.
Intended use: For full-time freshman study at 4-year institution in United States. Designated institutions: Pennsylvania State System of Higher Education universities.
Eligibility: Applicant must be residing in Pennsylvania.
Basis for selection: Applicant must demonstrate financial need and high academic achievement.
Additional information: Must be resident of Butler, Clarion, Forest, Jefferson, Lawrence, Mercer, or Venango counties. Visit Website for deadline and other information. Universities select recipients.

Amount of award:	$500-$1,000
Total amount awarded:	$1,000

Contact:
Pennsylvania State System of Higher Education Foundation, Inc.
2896 N. 2nd Street
Harrisburg, PA 17110
Phone: 717-720-4065
Fax: 717-720-7082
Web: www.thepafoundation.org

Fitz Dixon Memorial Scholarship

Type of award: Scholarship.
Intended use: For undergraduate or graduate study at 4-year or graduate institution in United States. Designated institutions: Pennsylvania State System of Higher Education (PASSHE) universities.
Basis for selection: Applicant must demonstrate financial need, high academic achievement and service orientation.
Application requirements: Recommendations, essay. Community/University service form.
Additional information: Undergraduate applicants must have passed 45 credits at a PASSHE university with a minimum GPA of 3.0. Graduate students must have passed nine credits at a PASSHE university with a minimum GPA of 3.5.

Amount of award:	$500
Number of awards:	1
Number of applicants:	26
Application deadline:	May 31
Notification begins:	June 1
Total amount awarded:	$1,000

Contact:
Pennsylvania State System of Higher Education Foundation, Inc.
2896 N. 2nd Street
Harrisburg, PA 17110
Phone: 717-720-4065
Fax: 717-720-7082
Web: www.thepafoundation.org

Harry & Lorraine Ausprich Endowed Scholarship for the Arts

Type of award: Scholarship.
Intended use: For full-time undergraduate study at 4-year institution in United States. Designated institutions: Pennsylvania State System of Higher Education universities.
Basis for selection: Major/career interest in music; theater arts; arts, general or dance. Applicant must demonstrate high academic achievement.
Application requirements: Recommendations, essay.
Additional information: Pre-architecture students also eligible. Minimum 3.0 GPA. One to two scholarships are awarded yearly dependent on available funds. Amount of award varies. Visit Website for deadline.

Application deadline:	May 31
Notification begins:	June 30
Total amount awarded:	$1,000

Contact:
Pennsylvania State System of Higher Education Foundation, Inc.
2896 N. 2nd Street
Harrisburg, PA 17110
Phone: 717-720-4065
Fax: 717-720-7082
Web: www.thepafoundation.org

M & T Bank Scholarship

Type of award: Scholarship.
Intended use: For full-time freshman study at 4-year institution in United States. Designated institutions: Pennsylvania State System of Higher Education universities.
Eligibility: Applicant must be residing in Pennsylvania.
Basis for selection: Applicant must demonstrate financial need and high academic achievement.
Application requirements: Essay.
Additional information: Must be in top 25% of high school graduating class. Minimum 3.0 GPA. Must be residing in Cumberland, Dauphin, and Franklin counties in Pennsylvania.

Amount of award:	$1,000
Number of awards:	12
Number of applicants:	43
Application deadline:	May 31
Notification begins:	June 1
Total amount awarded:	$9,000

Contact:
Pennsylvania State System of Higher Education Foundation, Inc.
2896 N. 2nd Street
Harrisburg, PA 17110
Phone: 717-720-4065
Fax: 717-720-7082
Web: www.thepafoundation.org

Momentum, Inc. Healthcare Scholarship

Type of award: Scholarship.
Intended use: For full-time junior or senior study at 4-year institution in United States. Designated institutions: Pennsylvania State System of Higher Education universities.
Basis for selection: Major/career interest in health-related professions. Applicant must demonstrate high academic achievement.
Application requirements: Transcript. Powerpoint presentation, cover letter.

Additional information: Must reside in Cumberland, Dauphin, Franklin, Juniata, Mifflin, or Perry counties in Pennsylvania. Minimum 3.0 GPA. Must be majoring in a healthcare-related field.

Amount of award:	$1,000
Number of awards:	2
Application deadline:	May 31
Notification begins:	June 1

Contact:
Pennsylvania State System of Higher Education Foundation, Inc.
2896 N. 2nd Street
Harrisburg, PA 17110
Phone: 717-720-4086
Fax: 717-720-7082
Web: www.thepafoundation.org

PSECU International Education Scholarship

Type of award: Scholarship.
Intended use: For full-time undergraduate study at 4-year institution. Designated institutions: Pennsylvania State System of Higher Education institutions.
Additional information: Must be in good standing at university.

Amount of award:	$2,000
Number of awards:	10
Application deadline:	May 31
Notification begins:	June 1

Contact:
Pennsylvania State System of Higher Education Foundation, Inc.
2896 N. 2nd Street
Harrisburg, PA 17110
Phone: 717-720-4086
Fax: 717-720-7082
Web: www.thepafoundation.org

Quida and Anna Pichini Merit Scholarships

Type of award: Scholarship.
Intended use: For full-time undergraduate study at 4-year institution in United States. Designated institutions: Pennsylvania State System of Higher Education Foundation universities.
Eligibility: Applicant must be residing in Pennsylvania.
Basis for selection: Applicant must demonstrate high academic achievement and service orientation.
Application requirements: Recommendations, essay, transcript. Voluntary services verification form.
Additional information: Minimum 3.5 GPA. First preference given to Berks County residence of Polish or Italian descent. Preference given to PA residents of Polish or Italian descent.

Amount of award:	$1,000
Number of awards:	1
Application deadline:	May 31

Contact:
Pennsylvania State System of Higher Education Foundation, Inc.
2896 N. 2nd Street
Harrisburg, PA 17110
Phone: 717-720-4086
Fax: 717-720-7082
Web: www.thepafoundation.org

William D. Greenlee Scholarship

Type of award: Scholarship.
Intended use: For full-time junior or senior study at 4-year institution in United States. Designated institutions: Pennsylvania State System of Higher Education Foundation institutions.
Basis for selection: Major/career interest in political science/government; journalism or communications. Applicant must demonstrate high academic achievement.
Application requirements: Recommendations, essay, transcript.
Additional information: Must have a minimum of 60 credits and GPA of 3.0 or higher.

Amount of award:	$2,500
Number of awards:	2
Number of applicants:	12
Application deadline:	May 31
Notification begins:	June 1
Total amount awarded:	$10,000

Contact:
Pennsylvania State System of Higher Education Foundation, Inc.
2896 N. 2nd Street
Harrisburg, PA 17110
Web: www.thepafoundation.org

Pennsylvania State System of Higher Eduction, Inc.

Wells Fargo Endowed Scholarship for Academic Excellence

Type of award: Scholarship.
Intended use: For full-time freshman study at 4-year institution in United States. Designated institutions: Pennsylvania State System of Higher Education institutions.
Eligibility: Applicant must be high school senior.
Basis for selection: Applicant must demonstrate financial need and high academic achievement.
Additional information: Must reside in Allegheny, Berks, Bucks, Carbon, Chester, Cumberland, Dauphin, Delaware, Lackawanna, Lancaster, Lebanon, Lehigh, Luzerne, Monroe, Montgomery, Northampton, Philadelphia, Pike, or York counties in Pennsylvania. Must be in top 25% of high school graduating class with a GPA of 3.2 or better. Number of awards varies yearly.

Amount of award:	$1,000
Number of awards:	8
Application deadline:	May 31
Notification begins:	June 1

Contact:
Pennsylvania State System of Higher Eduction Foundation, Inc.
2896 N. 2nd Street
Harrisburg, PA 17110
Phone: 717-720-4086
Fax: 717-720-7082
Web: www.thepafoundation.org

Pennsylvania Women's Press Association

Pennsylvania Women's Press Association Scholarship

Type of award: Scholarship.
Intended use: For junior, senior or graduate study at 4-year or graduate institution in United States. Designated institutions: Pennsylvania institutions.
Eligibility: Applicant must be U.S. citizen or permanent resident residing in Pennsylvania.
Basis for selection: Major/career interest in journalism.
Application requirements: Essay, transcript. Clippings of published work from school newspapers or other publications; a list of siblings, including their ages and educational status; an optional statement of financial need.
Additional information: Winner is chosen on basis of proven journalistic ability, dedication to a newspaper career, and general merit. Men and women are eligible. Deadline in mid-April.

Amount of award:	$1,500
Number of awards:	1

Contact:
Pennsylvania Women's Press Association Scholarship Committee
c/o Teresa Spatara
P.O. Box 152
Sharpsville, PA 16150
Web: www.pwpa.us/scholarship

PFLAG National Office

PFLAG National Scholarship Program

Type of award: Scholarship.
Intended use: For full-time freshman study at 2-year or 4-year institution.
Eligibility: Applicant must be high school senior.
Basis for selection: Competition/talent/interest in gay/lesbian.
Additional information: Applicants who graduated within last year also eligible. Must self-identify as gay, lesbian, bisexual, transgender, or ally/supporter of LGBT people who has worked on behalf of the LGBT community or overcome odds because of identity. Applications and full details available online in December. Number of awards vary.

Amount of award:	$1,000-$5,000
Number of applicants:	300
Application deadline:	April 15
Notification begins:	May 17
Total amount awarded:	$35,000

Contact:
PFLAG National Office
1828 L. St. NW, Suite 660
Washington, DC 20036
Phone: 202-467-8180
Web: www.pflag.org

The Phillips Foundation

Ronald Reagan College Leaders Scholarship Program

Type of award: Scholarship, renewable.
Intended use: For full-time junior or senior study at accredited 4-year institution in United States.
Eligibility: Applicant must be U.S. citizen.
Basis for selection: Applicant must demonstrate high academic achievement, depth of character, leadership, patriotism, seriousness of purpose and service orientation.
Application requirements: Recommendations, essay. Proof of full-time enrollment in good standing; proof of leadership activities.
Additional information: Number of awards varies based on merit. Recipients will be notified in late March/early April. Visit Website for application and more information. Number of awards varies. Applications due in mid-January.

Amount of award:	$1,000-$10,000
Number of applicants:	430
Application deadline:	January 15
Notification begins:	April 15
Total amount awarded:	$217,000

Contact:
The Phillips Foundation
Attn: Jeff Hollingsworth
1 Massachusetts Avenue NW, Suite 620
Washington, DC 20001
Phone: 202-250-3887, ext. 628
Web: www.thephillipsfoundation.org

Plumbing-Heating-Cooling Contractors Educational Foundation

Delta Faucet Company Scholarship

Type of award: Scholarship.
Intended use: For full-time undergraduate study at accredited vocational, 2-year or 4-year institution in United States.
Eligibility: Applicant must be U.S. citizen or Canadian citizen.
Basis for selection: Major/career interest in air conditioning/heating/refrigeration technology; business/management/administration; construction management or engineering, mechanical. Applicant must demonstrate high academic achievement.
Application requirements: Recommendations, essay, transcript. SAT/ACT scores, list of extracurricular activities.
Additional information: Applicants must pursue studies in major related to plumbing-heating-cooling industry or apprentice in a PHCC-approved program. Must be sponsored by active member of PHCC National Association. Minimum 2.0 GPA. Visit Website for application.

Amount of award:	$2,500
Number of awards:	6
Number of applicants:	45
Application deadline:	May 1
Total amount awarded:	$15,000

Contact:
PHCC-EF Scholarships
180 South Washington St.
P.O. Box 6808
Falls Church, VA 22046
Phone: 800-533-7694
Fax: 703-237-7442
Web: www.phccfoundation.org

PHCC Auxiliary of Texas Scholarship

Type of award: Scholarship.
Intended use: For full-time undergraduate study at accredited 2-year or 4-year institution in United States.
Eligibility: Applicant must be high school senior. Applicant must be U.S. citizen residing in Texas.
Basis for selection: Applicant must demonstrate high academic achievement.
Application requirements: Recommendations, essay, transcript. SAT/ACT scores. List of extracurricular activities.
Additional information: Must be sponsored by active member of PHCC National Auxiliary residing in TX. Minimum 2.0 GPA. Visit Website for details and application.

Amount of award:	$1,500
Number of awards:	1
Application deadline:	May 1

Contact:
PHCC Educational Foundation
180 South Washington St.
P.O. Box 6808
Falls Church, VA 22046
Phone: 800-533-7694
Fax: 703-237-7442
Web: www.foundation.phccweb.org

PHCC Educational Foundation Scholarships

Type of award: Scholarship.
Intended use: For full-time undergraduate study at accredited vocational, 2-year or 4-year institution in United States.
Eligibility: Applicant must be U.S. citizen or Canadian citizen.
Basis for selection: Major/career interest in air conditioning/heating/refrigeration technology; business/management/administration; construction management or engineering, mechanical. Applicant must demonstrate financial need and high academic achievement.
Application requirements: Recommendations, essay, transcript. SAT/ACT scores. List of extracurricular activities.
Additional information: Students enrolled or planning to enroll in PHCC-approved apprenticeship program also eligible. Other eligible majors include mechanical CAD design, plumbing or HVACR installation, and others directly related to the plumbing-heating-cooling profession. Must be sponsored by active member of PHCC National Association. Minimum 2.0 GPA. Visit Website for details and application.

Amount of award:	$1,000-$4,000
Number of awards:	22
Application deadline:	May 1

Contact:
PHCC Educational Foundation
180 South Washington St.
P.O. Box 6808
Falls Church, VA 22040
Phone: 800-533-7694
Fax: 703-237-7442
Web: www.foundation.phccweb.org

PHCC of Massachusetts Auxiliary Scholarship

Type of award: Scholarship.
Intended use: For full-time undergraduate study at accredited vocational, 2-year or 4-year institution in United States.
Eligibility: Applicant must be high school senior. Applicant must be U.S. citizen residing in Massachusetts.
Basis for selection: Applicant must demonstrate high academic achievement.
Application requirements: Recommendations, essay, transcript. SAT/ACT scores. List of extracurricular activities.
Additional information: Students enrolled or planning to enroll in PHCC-approved apprenticeship program also eligible. Other eligible majors include mechanical CAD design, plumbing or HVACR installation, and others directly related to the plumbing-heating-cooling profession. Must be sponsored by active member of PHCC National Association. Minimum 2.0 GPA. Visit Website for details and application.

Amount of award:	$1,500
Number of awards:	1
Application deadline:	May 1

Contact:
PHCC Educational Foundation
180 South Washington St.
P.O. Box 6808
Falls Church, VA 22046
Phone: 800-533-7694
Fax: 703-237-7442
Web: www.phccfoundation.org

Point Foundation

Point Scholarship

Type of award: Scholarship.
Intended use: For undergraduate or graduate study at accredited 4-year institution in United States.
Basis for selection: Competition/talent/interest in gay/lesbian. Applicant must demonstrate financial need, high academic achievement, depth of character, leadership, seriousness of purpose and service orientation.
Application requirements: Essay, transcript. Two or three letters of recommendation, two of them from a teacher or professor. Applicants who have been out of school five years or more may substitute a reference from a supervisor for one letter.
Additional information: Applicants should have a history of leadership in the lesbian, gay, bisexual, and transgendered community and plan to be a LGBT leader in the future (not necessarily in a career). Award amount varies based on available funds; average award $10,000. Scholars must be willing to speak publicly at Foundation events, provide the Foundation with transcripts, remain in contact with Foundation, and do an individual community service project with the LGBT

community. Deadline occurs in February; visit Website for exact date and application.

Number of awards: 28

Contact:
Point Foundation
5757 Wilshire Blvd., Suite #370
Los Angeles, CA 90036
Phone: 323-933-1234
Web: www.pointfoundation.org

Presbyterian Church (USA)

National Presbyterian College Scholarship

Type of award: Scholarship, renewable.
Intended use: For full-time undergraduate study in United States. Designated institutions: Presbyterian-affiliated colleges.
Eligibility: Applicant must be high school senior. Applicant must be Presbyterian.
Basis for selection: Applicant must demonstrate financial need and high academic achievement.
Application requirements: Transcript. Recommendation from church pastor, biographical questionnaire, and record from high school guidance counselor.
Additional information: Must re-apply annually. Award is up to $1,500.

Number of awards:	30
Number of applicants:	30
Application deadline:	March 1
Notification begins:	May 1
Total amount awarded:	$45,000

Contact:
Presbyterian Church (USA)
Financial Aid for Studies
100 Witherspoon Street
Louisville, KY 40202-1396
Phone: 800-728-7228 ext. 5224
Fax: 502-569-8766
Web: www.pcusa.org/financialaid

Native American Education Grant

Type of award: Scholarship.
Intended use: For full-time undergraduate study at accredited postsecondary institution in United States.
Eligibility: Applicant must be Alaskan native or American Indian.
Basis for selection: Applicant must demonstrate financial need and high academic achievement.
Additional information: Minimum 2.5 GPA. Must demonstrate Cost of Attendance with preference given to students demonstrating financial need. Preference is given to members of Presbyterian Church (USA). Native American students from all faith traditions are encouraged to apply. Award is renewable up to first degree; after first degree dependent upon availability of funds. Award is up to $1,500. Visit Website to request application.

Number of awards:	30
Number of applicants:	20
Application deadline:	June 15
Total amount awarded:	$30,000

Contact:
Presbyterian Church (USA)
100 Witherspoon Street
Louisville, KY 40202-1396
Phone: 800-728-7228 ext. 5224
Fax: 502-569-8766
Web: www.pcusa.org/financialaid

Presbyterian Student Opportunity Scholarship

Type of award: Scholarship, renewable.
Intended use: For full-time sophomore, junior or senior study at accredited 4-year institution in United States.
Eligibility: Applicant must be Presbyterian. Applicant must be U.S. citizen or permanent resident.
Basis for selection: Applicant must demonstrate financial need and high academic achievement.
Application requirements: Recommendations, essay, transcript, proof of eligibility.
Additional information: Preference given to students of African American, Asian American, Hispanic American, Alaskan Native, and Native American descent. Minimum 2.5 GPA. Award is up to $2,000. Must reapply annually for renewal.

Number of awards:	80
Number of applicants:	42
Application deadline:	June 15
Notification begins:	August 1
Total amount awarded:	$99,100

Contact:
Presbyterian Church (USA)
Financial Aid for Studies
100 Witherspoon Street
Louisville, KY 40202-1396
Phone: 800-728-7228 ext. 5224
Fax: 502-569-8766
Web: www.pcusa.org/financialaid

Samuel Robinson Award

Type of award: Scholarship.
Intended use: For full-time junior or senior study at 4-year institution. Designated institutions: One of 69 colleges affiliated with Presbyterian Church (USA).
Eligibility: Applicant must be Presbyterian.
Application requirements: A 2,000-word essay on assigned topic related to the Catechism.
Additional information: Applicant must successfully recite answers of the Westminster Shorter Catechism. Award is up to $5,000. Amount of award based on annual funds.

Number of awards:	16
Number of applicants:	13
Application deadline:	April 1
Notification begins:	May 15
Total amount awarded:	$40,000

Contact:
Presbyterian Church (USA)
Financial Aid for Studies
100 Witherspoon Street
Louisville, KY 40202-1396
Phone: 800-728-7228 ext. 5224
Fax: 502-569-8766
Web: www.pcusa.org/financialaid

Pride of the Greater Lehigh Valley

Rainbow Scholarship and Queer Student of the Year Scholarship

Type of award: Scholarship.
Intended use: For undergraduate study at accredited postsecondary institution in United States.
Eligibility: Applicant must be residing in New Jersey or Pennsylvania.
Basis for selection: Applicant must demonstrate high academic achievement.
Application requirements: Recommendations, transcript.
Additional information: Rainbow Award Scholarship is awarded to GLBT (gay, lesbian, bisexual, transgender) student based on academic excellence. The GLBT Student of the Year Scholarship is awarded to GLBT student who is a leader in community activities. Applicant's high school or accredited institution or both must be located in: Berks, Bucks, Carbon, Lehigh, Monroe, Montgomery, Northampton, Schuylkill counties in Pennsylvania and Warren County in New Jersey. Students from diverse backgrounds encouraged to apply. Visit Website for more information and application.

Amount of award:	$500
Number of awards:	2
Number of applicants:	2
Application deadline:	July 31
Total amount awarded:	$1,200

Contact:
The Rainbow Scholarship
c/o Pride-GLV
1101 West Hamilton Street
Allentown, PA 18101-1043
Phone: 610-770-6200
Web: www.prideglv.org

The Princess Grace Foundation USA

Princess Grace Award for Dance

Type of award: Scholarship.
Intended use: For sophomore, junior or senior study in United States. Designated institutions: Non-profit institutions.
Eligibility: Applicant must be U.S. citizen or permanent resident.
Basis for selection: Major/career interest in dance.
Application requirements: Nomination by dean or department head. Resume, 1-page biography, 8 x 10 glossy photo, compilation of solos on DVD.
Additional information: Award amount varies.

Amount of award:	$7,500-$30,000
Number of awards:	6
Application deadline:	April 30
Notification begins:	July 31

Contact:
The Princess Grace Foundation USA
150 E. 58th Street
25th Floor
New York, NY 10155
Phone: 212-317-1470
Fax: 212-317-1473
Web: www.pgfusa.org

Princess Grace Award For Film

Type of award: Scholarship.
Intended use: For senior or graduate study at accredited 4-year or graduate institution. Designated institutions: Eligible film schools.
Eligibility: Applicant must be U.S. citizen or permanent resident.
Basis for selection: Major/career interest in film/video.
Application requirements: Nomination by dean or department head.
Additional information: Award amount varies. Scholarships to help produce thesis projects. Only students of invited film schools are eligible to apply.

Number of awards:	6
Application deadline:	June 1

Contact:
The Princess Grace Foundation USA
150 E. 58th Street
25th Floor
New York, NY 10155
Phone: 212-317-1470
Fax: 212-317-1473
Web: www.pgfusa.org

Princess Grace Award For Playwriting

Type of award: Scholarship.
Intended use: For undergraduate study in United States.
Eligibility: Applicant must be U.S. citizen or permanent resident.
Basis for selection: Competition/talent/interest in writing/journalism. Major/career interest in playwriting/screenwriting.
Application requirements: Recommendations, essay. Resume. One published, unproduced play.
Additional information: Award given directly to individual through residency at New Dramatists, Inc. in New York. Applicant must not have had any professional productions. Readings, workshops, and Equity showcases are admissible. See Website for application.

Amount of award:	$7,500
Number of awards:	1
Application deadline:	April 1

Contact:
The Princess Grace Playwriting Grant
c/o New Dramatists
424 W. 44th St.
New York, NY 10036
Phone: 212-757-6960
Web: www.pgfusa.org

Princess Grace Award For Theater

Type of award: Scholarship.
Intended use: For senior or master's study at accredited 4-year or graduate institution.
Eligibility: Applicant must be U.S. citizen or permanent resident.

Basis for selection: Major/career interest in theater arts or theater/production/technical.
Application requirements: Essay, nomination by dean or department head. Resume, 8 x 10 glossy photo, 1-page biography, DVD with 2-3 pieces of work.
Additional information: Scholarships awarded to students for their last year (undergraduate or graduate) of professional training in acting, directing, scenic, lighting, sound, costume design or projection design. Award amount varies.

Amount of award:	$7,500-$30,000
Number of awards:	6
Application deadline:	April 1

Contact:
The Princess Grace Foundation USA
150 E. 58th Street
25th Floor
New York, NY 10155
Phone: 212-317-1470
Fax: 212-317-1473
Web: www.pgfusa.org

Print and Graphics Scholarship Foundation

PGSF Annual Scholarship Competition

Type of award: Scholarship, renewable.
Intended use: For full-time undergraduate study at 2-year or 4-year institution in United States.
Eligibility: Applicant must be U.S. citizen.
Basis for selection: Major/career interest in graphic arts/design; printing or publishing. Applicant must demonstrate high academic achievement.
Application requirements: Recommendations, transcript. Biographical information including extracurricular activities and academic honors. Photocopy of intended course of study. High school students must submit SAT, PSAT/NMSQT, or ACT scores.
Additional information: To renew, recipients must maintain 3.0 GPA and continue as graphic arts/printing technology major. Application requirements and criteria may vary by trust fund member institution. Recipients must adhere to PGSF Facebook page activity specifications. Visit Website for application.

Amount of award:	$1,000-$5,000
Number of awards:	300
Number of applicants:	1,200
Application deadline:	April 1
Notification begins:	June 30
Total amount awarded:	$375,000

Contact:
Print and Graphics Scholarship Foundation
200 Deer Run Road
Sewickley, PA 15143-2600
Phone: 800-910-4283 or 412-259-1740
Web: www.pgsf.org

Professional Association of Georgia Educators Foundation, Inc.

PAGE Foundation Scholarships

Type of award: Scholarship.
Intended use: For junior, senior or post-bachelor's certificate study at accredited 4-year or graduate institution in United States.
Eligibility: Applicant must be U.S. citizen or permanent resident residing in Georgia.
Basis for selection: Major/career interest in education. Applicant must demonstrate high academic achievement and service orientation.
Application requirements: Recommendations, essay, transcript.
Additional information: Minimum 3.0 GPA. Must be PAGE or SPAGE member. Intended for future teachers and certified teachers seeking advanced degrees. Must agree to teach in Georgia for three years. Applications available from September to April. Visit Website for additional information, deadline, and application procedures.

Amount of award:	$1,000
Number of awards:	17
Number of applicants:	69
Application deadline:	April 30
Notification begins:	July 1
Total amount awarded:	$17,000

Contact:
PAGE Foundation
P.O. Box 942270
Atlanta, GA 31141-2270
Phone: 800-334-6861
Fax: 770-216-9672
Web: www.pagefoundation.org

Proof-Reading.com

Proof-Reading.com Scholarship Program

Type of award: Scholarship.
Intended use: For full-time at postsecondary institution in United States.
Eligibility: Applicant must be U.S. citizen or permanent resident.
Basis for selection: Applicant must demonstrate high academic achievement.
Application requirements: Minimum 1,500-word essay in MLA format answering topical question. Include work cited page with at least two sources.
Additional information: Must maintain a minimum 3.5 GPA. Visit Website for essay topic and online application.

Amount of award:	$1,500
Number of awards:	1
Number of applicants:	30
Application deadline:	June 1
Notification begins:	July 1
Total amount awarded:	$1,500

Contact:
Proof-Reading.com Scholarship Program
12 Geary Street
Suite #806
San Francisco, CA 91408-5720
Web: www.proof-reading.com/proof-reading_scholarship_program.asp

Quill and Scroll Foundation

Edward J. Nell Memorial Scholarship

Type of award: Scholarship.
Intended use: For full-time freshman study at accredited 2-year or 4-year institution in United States.
Eligibility: Applicant must be high school senior. Applicant must be U.S. citizen.
Basis for selection: Major/career interest in journalism. Applicant must demonstrate seriousness of purpose.
Application requirements: Recommendations, essay, transcript. Statement of intent to major in journalism. Three selections of student's journalistic work. One color photo of applicant.
Additional information: Open only to winners of Quill and Scroll's Annual National Yearbook Excellence or International Writing/Photo Contests at any time during high school career.

Amount of award:	$500-$1,500
Number of awards:	6
Number of applicants:	50
Application deadline:	May 10
Notification begins:	June 1
Total amount awarded:	$5,000

Contact:
Scholarship Committee Quill and Scroll Foundation
E346 Adler Journalism Building
University of Iowa
Iowa City, IA 52242-1401
Phone: 319-335-3457
Fax: 319-335-3989
Web: www.quillandscroll.org

Radio Television Digital News Association (RTDNA)

Carole Simpson Scholarship

Type of award: Scholarship.
Intended use: For full-time sophomore, junior or senior study at 4-year institution.
Basis for selection: Major/career interest in communications; film/video; journalism or radio/television/film. Applicant must demonstrate depth of character and seriousness of purpose.
Application requirements: Recommendations, essay, proof of eligibility. Cover letter. Three to five links to online work samples. Link to personal Website recommended.
Additional information: Must be preparing for career in electronic journalism. Preference given to minority students. Visit Website for deadline and application.

Amount of award:	$2,000
Number of awards:	1
Number of applicants:	20
Application deadline:	May 31
Total amount awarded:	$2,000

Contact:
RTDNA Scholarships
Phone: 202-725-8318
Web: www.rtdna.org

Ed Bradley Scholarship

Type of award: Scholarship.
Intended use: For full-time sophomore, junior or senior study at 4-year institution.
Basis for selection: Major/career interest in communications; film/video; journalism or radio/television/film. Applicant must demonstrate seriousness of purpose.
Application requirements: Recommendations, essay, proof of eligibility. Cover Letter. Three to five links of online relevant work samples. Link to personal Website recommended.
Additional information: Must have at least one full year of school remaining. Must be preparing for career in electronic journalism. Preference given to minority students. Visit Website for deadline and application.

Amount of award:	$10,000
Number of awards:	1
Number of applicants:	47
Application deadline:	May 31
Total amount awarded:	$10,000

Contact:
RTDNA Scholarships
Phone: 202-725-8318
Web: www.rtdna.org

The George Foreman Tribute to Lyndon B. Johnson Scholarship

Type of award: Scholarship.
Intended use: For full-time sophomore, junior or senior study at 4-year institution in United States. Designated institutions: University of Texas at Austin.
Eligibility: Applicant must be U.S. citizen or permanent resident residing in Texas.
Basis for selection: Major/career interest in communications; film/video; journalism or radio/television/film.
Application requirements: Recommendations, essay, proof of eligibility. Cover Letter. Three to five links to relevant online work samples. Link to personal website recommended.
Additional information: Must be preparing for career in electronic journalism. Visit Website for deadline and application.

Amount of award:	$6,000
Number of awards:	1
Number of applicants:	9
Application deadline:	May 31
Total amount awarded:	$6,000

Contact:
RTDNA Scholarships
Phone: 202-725-8318
Web: www.rtdna.org

Lou and Carole Prato Sports Reporting Scholarship

Type of award: Scholarship.
Intended use: For full-time sophomore, junior or senior study at postsecondary institution.
Basis for selection: Major/career interest in communications; film/video; journalism; radio/television/film or sports/sports administration.
Application requirements: Recommendations, essay, proof of eligibility. Cover Letter. Three to five links to relevant online work samples. Link to personal website recommended.
Additional information: Must be planning career as sports reporter in television or radio. Visit Website for deadline and application.

Amount of award:	$1,000
Number of awards:	1
Number of applicants:	15
Application deadline:	May 31
Total amount awarded:	$1,000

Contact:
RTDNA Scholarships
Phone: 202-725-8318
Web: www.rtdna.org

Mike Reynolds Scholarship

Type of award: Scholarship.
Intended use: For full-time sophomore, junior or senior study at 4-year institution in United States.
Basis for selection: Major/career interest in communications; film/video; journalism or radio/television/film. Applicant must demonstrate financial need and high academic achievement.
Application requirements: Recommendations, essay, proof of eligibility. FAFSA. Cover letter. Three to five links to relevant online work. Link to personal Website recommended.
Additional information: Applicant should indicate media-related jobs held and contribution made to funding of education. Must be preparing for career in electronic journalism. Visit Website for deadline and application.

Amount of award:	$1,000
Number of awards:	1
Application deadline:	May 31
Total amount awarded:	$1,000

Contact:
RTDNA Scholarships
Phone: 202-725-8318
Web: www.rtdna.org

Pete Wilson Journalism Scholarship

Type of award: Scholarship.
Intended use: For full-time sophomore, junior, senior or graduate study at accredited 4-year or graduate institution. Designated institutions: San Francisco Bay area institutions.
Eligibility: Applicant must be residing in California.
Basis for selection: Major/career interest in communications; film/video; journalism or radio/television/film.
Application requirements: Recommendations, essay, proof of eligibility. Cover Letter. Three to five links to relevant online work samples. Link to personal Website recommended.
Additional information: Must be preparing for career in electronic journalism. Must have one full year of school left to be eligible. Alternates yearly between graduate and undergraduate award winner. Visit Website for deadline and application.

Amount of award:	$2,000
Number of awards:	1
Application deadline:	May 31
Total amount awarded:	$2,000

Contact:
RTDNA Scholarships
Phone: 202-725-8318
Web: www.rtdna.org

Presidents Scholarships

Type of award: Scholarship.
Intended use: For full-time junior or senior study at 2-year or 4-year institution.
Basis for selection: Major/career interest in communications; film/video; journalism or radio/television/film. Applicant must demonstrate high academic achievement and seriousness of purpose.
Application requirements: Recommendations, essay, proof of eligibility. Cover letter. Three to five links to relevant online work samples. Link to personal website recommended.
Additional information: Must be preparing for career in electronic journalism. Visit Website for deadline and application.

Amount of award:	$1,000
Number of awards:	2
Number of applicants:	79
Application deadline:	May 31
Total amount awarded:	$2,000

Contact:
RTDNA Scholarships
Phone: 202-725-8318
Web: www.rtdna.org

Red River Valley Fighter Pilots Association

Red River Valley Fighter Pilots Association (RRVA) Scholarship Program

Type of award: Scholarship, renewable.
Intended use: For undergraduate or graduate study at accredited vocational, 2-year, 4-year or graduate institution in United States.
Eligibility: Applicant must be U.S. citizen.
Basis for selection: Applicant must demonstrate financial need, high academic achievement and service orientation.
Application requirements: Transcript, proof of eligibility. SAT/ACT scores.
Additional information: Kinship eligibility is as follows: Must be immediate dependent (legal son, daughter, or spouse) of 1) A U.S. aircrew member listed as Killed in Action (KIA) or Missing in Action (MIA) from any combat situation involving U.S. military from August 1964 (Vietnam Era) through the present; 2) a military aircrew member killed as the result of performing aircrew duties during a non-combat mission; 3) an RRVA member who is currently in good standing or was in good standing at the time of their death. Also eligible are those pursuing a career in field related to aviation/space (kinship not required). See Website for application and more information.

Amount of award: $500-$3,500
Number of awards: 32
Number of applicants: 42
Application deadline: May 15
Total amount awarded: $67,000

Contact:
Red River Valley Fighter Pilots Association
P.O. Box 1553
Front Royal, VA 22630
Phone: 540-636-9798
Fax: 540-636-9776
Web: www.river-rats.org

Renee B. Fisher Foundation

Milton Fisher Scholarship for Innovation and Creativity

Type of award: Scholarship, renewable.
Intended use: For undergraduate study.
Eligibility: Applicant must be high school junior or senior. Applicant must be residing in New York or Connecticut.
Application requirements: Recommendations, essay, transcript. Eight copies of additional materials to provide evidence supporting application. PSAT/ACT/SAT scores. Photocopy of letter of admission to college, photocopy of parents' IRS 1040 tax form.
Additional information: Must be a resident or attend/plan to attend college in Connecticut or the New York City Metropolitan area. Must have either come up with a distinctive solution to a problem faced by school, community or family; solved an artistic, scientific, or technical problem in new or unusual ways; or have developed an innovative way to save the environment or improve people's health. Financial need does not affect chances of winning; only the dollar amount of scholarship.

Amount of award: $1,000-$5,000
Number of awards: 6
Number of applicants: 131
Application deadline: April 30
Total amount awarded: $24,000

Contact:
Milton Fisher Scholarship
Community Foundation for Greater New Haven
70 Audubon Street
New Haven, CT 06510
Phone: 203-777-2386
Fax: 203-787-6584
Web: www.rbffoundation.org

Restaurant Association of Maryland Education Foundation

Letitia B. Carter Scholarship

Type of award: Scholarship.
Intended use: For undergraduate study in United States.
Eligibility: Applicant must be enrolled in high school. Applicant must be U.S. citizen residing in Maryland.
Basis for selection: Major/career interest in hospitality administration/management. Applicant must demonstrate high academic achievement.
Application requirements: Recommendations, essay. Paystub from most recent employer in industry-related work. Two typed and double-spaced essays: 1) Describe any personal skills and characteristics that will help you meet the future challenges of the food service/hospitality industry; 2) Which person was most influential in helping you choose a career in the food service/hospitality industry?
Additional information: Applicant must have applied to an RAMEF-recognized professional development program in hospitality or enrolled in a RAMEF-recognized food service/hospitality program. Any high school or college student applying for scholarship must have a minimum 3.0 cumulative GPA and a minimum of 400 hours documented industry experience. Any teachers or instructors applying must have a minimum of 1,500 hours documented industry experience. Visit Website for more information.

Amount of award: $500-$2,000
Number of applicants: 10
Application deadline: April 15
Notification begins: May 12
Total amount awarded: $5,000

Contact:
Restaurant Association of Maryland Education Foundation
6301 Hillside Court
Columbia, MD 21046
Phone: 410-290-6800
Fax: 410-290-6882
Web: www.ramef.org

Marcia S. Harris Legacy Fund Scholarship

Type of award: Scholarship.
Intended use: For undergraduate study at postsecondary institution.
Eligibility: Applicant must be residing in Maryland.
Basis for selection: Major/career interest in culinary arts; food production/management/services; food science/technology; hospitality administration/management or hotel/restaurant management. Applicant must demonstrate financial need and high academic achievement.
Application requirements: Interview. Proof of employment in culinary or hospitality industry. Three essays.
Additional information: Selection based on grades in food service coursework, essays, and work experience. Number and amount of award varies.

Number of applicants: 11
Application deadline: April 15
Notification begins: May 12
Total amount awarded: $2,000

Contact:
Restaurant Association of Maryland Education Foundation
6301 Hillside Court
Columbia, MD 21046
Phone: 410-290-6800 ext. 1015
Fax: 410-290-6882
Web: www.ramef.org

Scholarships

Rhode Island Higher Education Assistance Authority

College Bound Fund Academic Promise Scholarship

Type of award: Scholarship, renewable.
Intended use: For full-time undergraduate study at vocational, 2-year or 4-year institution. Designated institutions: Institutions participating in at least one Title IV financial aid program.
Eligibility: Applicant must be U.S. citizen or permanent resident residing in Rhode Island.
Basis for selection: Applicant must demonstrate financial need and high academic achievement.
Application requirements: FAFSA. SAT or ACT scores.
Additional information: Initial eligibility based on SAT/ACT scores and expected family contribution; renewal subject to maintenance of specified GPA. Dependent applicant's parent must reside in Rhode Island. Award notification begins in late spring.

Amount of award:	$2,500
Number of awards:	100
Number of applicants:	1,450
Application deadline:	March 1
Total amount awarded:	$1,000,000

Contact:
Rhode Island Higher Education Assistance Authority
560 Jefferson Boulevard
Warwick, RI 02886
Phone: 401-736-1170
Fax: 401-732-3541
Web: www.riheaa.org

Rhode Island State Grant

Type of award: Scholarship, renewable.
Intended use: For undergraduate study at vocational, 2-year or 4-year institution in or outside United States or Canada. Designated institutions: U.S., Canadian, or Mexican institutions that participate in at least one federal financial aid program.
Eligibility: Applicant must be U.S. citizen or permanent resident residing in Rhode Island.
Basis for selection: Applicant must demonstrate financial need.
Application requirements: FAFSA.
Additional information: Must meet all Title IV eligibility requirements. Dependent applicant's parent must reside in Rhode Island. Award notification begins in late spring.

Amount of award:	$250-$700
Number of awards:	21,000
Number of applicants:	63,066
Application deadline:	March 1
Total amount awarded:	$1,264,003

Contact:
Rhode Island Higher Education Assistance Authority
560 Jefferson Boulevard
Warwick, RI 02886
Phone: 401-736-1170
Fax: 401-736-1178
Web: www.riheaa.org

Rocky Mountain Coal Mining Institute

RCMI Technical/Trade School Scholarship

Type of award: Scholarship.
Intended use: For sophomore study at vocational or 2-year institution.
Eligibility: Applicant must be U.S. citizen residing in Wyoming, Utah, Texas, Montana, New Mexico, Colorado, North Dakota or Arizona.
Basis for selection: Major/career interest in engineering, mining or geology/earth sciences.
Additional information: Applicant must be first-year student at a two-year technical school in good standing. Must be studying an applicable trade and be interested in coal as a career path.

Amount of award:	$1,000
Number of awards:	8
Number of applicants:	7
Application deadline:	February 1
Notification begins:	March 1
Total amount awarded:	$7,000

Contact:
Rocky Mountain Coal Mining Institute
3500 S. Wadsworth Blvd., Ste. 211
Lakewood, CO 80235
Phone: 303-948-3300
Fax: 303-954-9004
Web: www.rmcmi.org

Rocky Mountain Coal Mining Institute Scholarship

Type of award: Scholarship, renewable.
Intended use: For full-time junior or senior study in United States. Designated institutions: Mining schools approved by Rocky Mountain Coal Mining Institute.
Eligibility: Applicant must be U.S. citizen residing in Wyoming, Utah, Texas, Montana, New Mexico, Colorado, Arizona or North Dakota.
Basis for selection: Major/career interest in engineering; engineering, mining or geology/earth sciences. Applicant must demonstrate high academic achievement.
Application requirements: Interview, recommendations.
Additional information: Must have career interest in western coal mining. Recommended 3.0 GPA or higher. One new award per Rocky Mountain Coal Mining Institute member state per year. Can be renewed as senior or post-graduate.

Amount of award:	$2,500
Number of awards:	8
Number of applicants:	32
Application deadline:	February 1
Notification begins:	March 1
Total amount awarded:	$40,000

Contact:
Rocky Mountain Coal Mining Institute
3500 S. Wadsworth Blvd., Ste. 211
Lakewood, CO 80235
Phone: 303-948-3300
Fax: 303-954-9004
Web: www.rmcmi.org

Roller Skating Foundation

Roller Skating Foundation College Scholarship

Type of award: Scholarship.
Intended use: For undergraduate study.
Basis for selection: Major/career interest in sports/sports administration; food production/management/services or hotel/restaurant management. Applicant must demonstrate high academic achievement and leadership.
Application requirements: Recommendations, essay, transcript. Copy of current Federal Income Tax return.
Additional information: Must have cumulative 3.4 GPA and 3.5 GPA in major. Contact Roller Skating Foundation for official application.

Amount of award:	$1,000
Number of awards:	1
Application deadline:	April 2
Total amount awarded:	$1,000

Contact:
Roller Skating Foundation
6905 Corporate Drive
Indianapolis, IN 46278
Phone: 317-347-2626
Fax: 317-347-2636
Web: www.rollerskating.org/about/foun.html

Roller Skating Foundation High School Senior Scholarship

Roller Skating Foundation

Type of award: Scholarship.
Intended use: For freshman study at 4-year institution.
Eligibility: Applicant must be high school senior.
Basis for selection: Applicant must demonstrate high academic achievement.
Additional information: Minimum 3.4 GPA. Student does not have to be a member of Roller Skating Foundation, but preferably has skated in a member rink. Contact RSF for official application.

Amount of award:	$4,000
Number of awards:	1
Application deadline:	April 2
Total amount awarded:	$4,000

Contact:
Roller Skating Foundation
6905 Corporate Drive
Indianapolis, IN 46278
Phone: 317-347-2626
Fax: 317-347-2636
Web: www.rollerskating.org/about/foun.html

Ron Brown Scholar Fund

Ron Brown Scholar Program

Type of award: Scholarship, renewable.
Intended use: For full-time undergraduate study at accredited 4-year institution in United States.
Eligibility: Applicant must be African American. Applicant must be high school senior. Applicant must be U.S. citizen or permanent resident.
Basis for selection: Applicant must demonstrate financial need, high academic achievement, depth of character, leadership, seriousness of purpose and service orientation.
Application requirements: Recommendations, essay, transcript.
Additional information: In addition to financial assistance, scholars get other benefits: summer internships, career guidance, placement opportunities, mentors, and leadership training. Scholarships may be used to pursue any academic discipline. Award is $10,000 per year for four years. 10 - 20 awards given yearly. Earlier deadline is for those who wish to have their information forwarded to select colleges and scholarship programs.

Amount of award:	$40,000
Number of awards:	20
Number of applicants:	6,300
Application deadline:	November 1, January 9
Notification begins:	April 1
Total amount awarded:	$480,000

Contact:
Ron Brown Scholar Program
1160 Pepsi Place, Suite 206
Charlottesville, VA 22901
Phone: 434-964-1588
Fax: 434-964-1589
Web: www.ronbrown.org

Ronald McDonald House Charities (RMHC)

RMHC U.S. Scholarship Programs

Type of award: Scholarship.
Intended use: For full-time undergraduate study at accredited vocational, 2-year or 4-year institution.
Eligibility: Applicant must be high school senior. Applicant must be U.S. citizen or permanent resident.
Basis for selection: Applicant must demonstrate financial need, high academic achievement, leadership and service orientation.
Application requirements: Recommendations, essay, transcript, proof of eligibility. IRS Form 1040, other valid financial documents.
Additional information: Must be a legal U.S. resident. Intended for those who live within geographic boundaries of RMHC chapter that offers scholarships. Geographic areas listed on Website. Some requirements include: RMHC/ASIA: Applicant must have at least one parent of Asian heritage; RMHC/Future African American Achievers: Applicant must have at least one parent of African American or Black/Caribbean heritage; RMHC/HACER: Applicant must have at least one parent of Hispanic heritage; RMHC/Scholars: All

Scholarships

students may apply regardless of ethnic heritage. Number of awards varies. Minimum award $1000. Award notification begins in May. See Website for contact information and application. Deadline in January.

Number of applicants:	15,000
Notification begins:	May 1
Total amount awarded:	$4,009,511

Contact:
Ronald McDonald House Charities Scholarship Program Administrators
One Kroc Drive
Oak Brook, IL 60523
Phone: 630-623-7048
Fax: 630-623-7488
Web: www.rmhc.org

Sachs Foundation

Sachs Foundation Undergraduate Grant

Type of award: Scholarship, renewable.
Intended use: For full-time undergraduate study at accredited 2-year or 4-year institution.
Eligibility: Applicant must be African American. Applicant must be high school senior. Applicant must be U.S. citizen or permanent resident residing in Colorado.
Basis for selection: Applicant must demonstrate financial need, high academic achievement, depth of character and leadership.
Application requirements: Interview, recommendations, transcript, proof of eligibility. Financial statement and parents' tax returns. Small recent photo. One-page personal biography. FAFSA. A copy of Colorado School Enrollment form.
Additional information: Must have been resident of Colorado for at least five years.

Amount of award:	$5,000
Number of awards:	35
Application deadline:	March 15

Contact:
Sachs Foundation
Phone: 719-633-2353
Web: www.sachsfoundation.org

SAE International

BMW/SAE Engineering Scholarships

Type of award: Scholarship, renewable.
Intended use: For full-time freshman study at accredited 4-year institution in United States. Designated institutions: ABET-accredited engineering schools.
Eligibility: Applicant must be high school senior. Applicant must be U.S. citizen.
Basis for selection: Major/career interest in engineering or computer/information sciences. Applicant must demonstrate high academic achievement, depth of character and leadership.
Application requirements: Transcript. SAT or ACT scores.
Additional information: Must have 3.75 GPA and rank in 90th percentile on ACT composite or SAT I (Math and Reading). Must maintain 3.0 GPA to renew scholarship. Renewable for four years. Visit Website for more information. For list of ABET-accredited schools, visit www.abet.org.

Amount of award:	$1,500
Number of awards:	1
Application deadline:	January 15
Notification begins:	June 30

Contact:
SAE International
SAE Engineering Scholarships
400 Commonwealth Drive
Warrendale, PA 15096-0001
Phone: 724-776-4841
Web: www.sae.org/scholarships

Edward D. Hendrickson/SAE Engineering Scholarship

Type of award: Scholarship, renewable.
Intended use: For undergraduate study at accredited postsecondary institution. Designated institutions: ABET-accredited institutions.
Eligibility: Applicant must be high school senior. Applicant must be U.S. citizen.
Basis for selection: Major/career interest in engineering. Applicant must demonstrate high academic achievement.
Application requirements: Essay, transcript. SAT or ACT scores.
Additional information: Minimum 3.75 GPA. Must rank in 90th percentile on SAT (Math and Reading) or composite ACT. Award renewable for three years if student maintains 3.0 GPA. Visit Website for application. For list of ABET-accredited schools, visit www.abet.org.

Amount of award:	$1,000
Number of awards:	1
Application deadline:	January 15
Notification begins:	June 30

Contact:
SAE International
SAE Engineering Scholarships
400 Commonwealth Drive
Warrendale, PA 15096-0001
Phone: 724-776-4841
Web: www.sae.org/scholarships

Fred M. Young, Sr./SAE Engineering Scholarship

Type of award: Scholarship, renewable.
Intended use: For undergraduate study at accredited postsecondary institution. Designated institutions: ABET-accredited institutions.
Eligibility: Applicant must be high school senior. Applicant must be U.S. citizen.
Basis for selection: Major/career interest in engineering. Applicant must demonstrate high academic achievement.
Application requirements: Transcript. SAT or ACT scores.
Additional information: Minimum 3.75 GPA. Applicants must rank in the 90th percentile on SAT (Math and Reading) or ACT. Award renewable for three years if student maintains 3.0 GPA. Visit Website for application. For list of ABET-accredited schools, visit www.abet.org.

Amount of award:	$1,000
Number of awards:	1
Application deadline:	January 15
Notification begins:	June 30

Contact:
SAE International
SAE Engineering Scholarships
400 Commonwealth Drive
Warrendale, PA 15096-0001
Phone: 724-776-4841
Web: www.sae.org/scholarships

Ralph K. Hillquist Honorary SAE Scholarship

Type of award: Scholarship.
Intended use: For full-time senior study at accredited 4-year institution in United States. Designated institutions: ABET-accredited engineering schools.
Eligibility: Applicant must be U.S. citizen.
Basis for selection: Major/career interest in engineering, mechanical. Applicant must demonstrate high academic achievement.
Application requirements: College transcript.
Additional information: Minimum 3.0 GPA. Any automotive-related engineering majors are eligible. Preference given to those with areas of expertise related to noise and vibration (statics, dynamic, physics, vibration). Award is given every other year at the SAE Noise & Vibration Conference. For list of ABET-accredited schools, visit www.abet.org.

Amount of award:	$1,000
Number of awards:	1
Application deadline:	January 15
Notification begins:	June 30

Contact:
SAE International
SAE Engineering Scholarships
400 Commonwealth Drive
Warrendale, PA 15096-0001
Phone: 724-776-4841
Web: www.sae.org/scholarships

SAE Detroit Section Technical Scholarship

Type of award: Scholarship, renewable.
Intended use: For freshman study at accredited 2-year or 4-year institution. Designated institutions: ABET-accredited schools.
Eligibility: Applicant must be high school senior. Applicant must be U.S. citizen.
Basis for selection: Major/career interest in engineering or computer/information sciences. Applicant must demonstrate financial need and high academic achievement.
Application requirements: Recommendations, transcript. FAFSA, SAT or ACT scores.
Additional information: Applicant must be child or grandchild of current SAE Detroit Section member. Minimum 3.0 GPA. Must maintain 2.5 GPA to renew scholarship. Renewable and transferable up to three consecutive years. Visit Website for application. For list of ABET-accredited schools, visit www.abet.org.

Amount of award:	$5,000
Number of awards:	2
Application deadline:	January 15
Notification begins:	June 30

Contact:
SAE International
SAE Engineering Scholarships
400 Commonwealth Drive
Warrendale, PA 15096-0001
Phone: 724-776-4841
Web: www.sae.org/scholarships

SAE Long-Term Member Sponsored Scholarship

Type of award: Scholarship.
Intended use: For full-time senior study at 4-year institution. Designated institutions: ABET-accredited engineering schools.
Basis for selection: Major/career interest in engineering. Applicant must demonstrate leadership.
Application requirements: Recommendations.
Additional information: Applicant must be active SAE student member. Must demonstrate support for SAE activities and programs. Must be junior in college at time of application. Number of awards varies. Apply online.

Amount of award:	$1,000
Application deadline:	February 15
Notification begins:	June 30

Contact:
SAE International
SAE Engineering Scholarships
400 Commonwealth Drive
Warrendale, PA 15096-0001
Phone: 724-776-4841
Web: www.sae.org/scholarships

SAE Women Engineers Committee Scholarship

Type of award: Scholarship.
Intended use: For freshman study. Designated institutions: ABET-accredited engineering schools.
Eligibility: Applicant must be female, high school senior. Applicant must be U.S. citizen.
Basis for selection: Major/career interest in engineering. Applicant must demonstrate high academic achievement.
Application requirements: Transcript. SAT or ACT scores.
Additional information: Minimum 3.0 GPA. Visit Website for application. For list of ABET-accredited schools, visit www.abet.org.

Amount of award:	$2,000
Number of awards:	1
Application deadline:	January 15
Notification begins:	June 30

Contact:
SAE International
SAE Engineering Scholarships
400 Commonwealth Drive
Warrendale, PA 15096-0001
Phone: 724-776-4841
Web: www.sae.org/scholarships

SAE/David Hermance Hybird Technologies Scholarship

Type of award: Scholarship.
Intended use: For junior study at accredited 2-year or 4-year institution in United States. Designated institutions: ABET-accredited engineering schools.
Eligibility: Applicant must be U.S. citizen.

Basis for selection: Major/career interest in engineering. Applicant must demonstrate high academic achievement.
Application requirements: High school and college transcripts. SAT/ACT scores.
Additional information: Minimum 3.5 GPA. For list of ABET-accredited schools, visit www.abet.org.

Amount of award:	$2,500
Number of awards:	1
Application deadline:	February 15
Notification begins:	June 30

Contact:
SAE International
SAE Engineering Scholarships
00 Commonwealth Drive
Warrendale, PA 15096-0001
Phone: 724-776-4841
Web: www.sae.org/scholarships

SAE/Ford Partnership for Advanced Studies Scholarship

Type of award: Scholarship.
Intended use: For full-time freshman study at accredited 4-year institution in United States. Designated institutions: ABET-accredited engineering schools.
Eligibility: Applicant must be high school senior. Applicant must be U.S. citizen.
Basis for selection: Major/career interest in engineering. Applicant must demonstrate high academic achievement.
Application requirements: Recommendations, transcript. SAT/ACT scores.
Additional information: Minimum 3.0 GPA. Must rank in the 90th percentile in both math and critical reading on SAT I or the composite ACT scores. Must be past or present student of Ford PAS program at their high school or in a Ford PAS afterschool/weekend/summer/college program. For list of ABET-accredited schools, visit www.abet.org.

Amount of award:	$5,000
Number of awards:	1
Application deadline:	January 15
Notification begins:	June 30

Contact:
SAE International
SAE Engineering Scholarships
400 Commonwealth Drive
Warrendale, PA 15096-0001
Phone: 724-776-4841
Web: www.sae.org/scholarships

Tau Beta Pi/SAE Engineering Scholarship

Type of award: Scholarship.
Intended use: For freshman study at accredited postsecondary institution. Designated institutions: ABET-accredited engineering schools.
Eligibility: Applicant must be high school senior. Applicant must be U.S. citizen.
Basis for selection: Major/career interest in engineering. Applicant must demonstrate high academic achievement.
Application requirements: Transcript. SAT or ACT scores.
Additional information: Minimum 3.75 GPA. Applicant must rank in 90th percentile on SAT (Math and Reading) or composite ACT. Visit Website for application. For list of ABET-accredited schools, visit www.abet.org.

Amount of award:	$1,000
Number of awards:	6
Application deadline:	January 15
Notification begins:	June 30
Total amount awarded:	$6,000

Contact:
SAE International
SAE Engineering Scholarships
400 Commonwealth Drive
Warrendale, PA 15096-0001
Phone: 724-776-4841
Web: www.sae.org/scholarships

TMC/SAE Donald D. Dawson Technical Scholarship

Type of award: Scholarship, renewable.
Intended use: For undergraduate study. Designated institutions: ABET-accredited engineering schools.
Eligibility: Applicant must be U.S. citizen.
Basis for selection: Major/career interest in engineering. Applicant must demonstrate high academic achievement.
Application requirements: Transcript. Essay showing evidence of hands-on automotive experience or activity, SAT or ACT scores.
Additional information: Graduating high school seniors must have minimum 3.25 GPA, 600 SAT (Math) and 550 SAT (Reading), 27 ACT. Transfer students from four-year schools with 3.0 GPA, and students/graduates of technical/vocational schools with 3.5 GPA also eligible. Award renewable for four years as long as a 3.0 GPA maintained. Visit Website for application. For list of ABET-accredited schools, visit www.abet.org.

Amount of award:	$1,500
Number of awards:	1
Application deadline:	January 15
Notification begins:	June 30

Contact:
SAE International
SAE Engineering Scholarships
400 Commonwealth Drive
Warrendale, PA 15096-0001
Phone: 724-776-4841
Web: www.sae.org/scholarships

Yanmar/SAE Scholarship

Type of award: Scholarship, renewable.
Intended use: For full-time senior or graduate study at accredited 4-year institution. Designated institutions: ABET-accredited engineering schools.
Eligibility: Applicant must be U.S. citizen or Canadian or Mexican citizen.
Basis for selection: Major/career interest in engineering. Applicant must demonstrate high academic achievement and leadership.
Application requirements: College transcript.
Additional information: Must pursue course of study or research related to conservation of energy in transportation, agriculture and construction, or power generation. Emphasis placed on research or study related to internal combustion engine. Must be junior in college or post-graduate at time of application. Scholarship renewable for one additional year if in good standing with university and minimum 2.5 GPA. Visit Website for application. For list of ABET-accredited schools, visit www.abet.org.

Amount of award: $1,000
Number of awards: 1
Application deadline: February 15
Notification begins: June 30
Contact:
SAE International
SAE Scholarship & Award Program
400 Commonwealth Drive
Warrendale, PA 15096-0001
Phone: 724-776-4841
Web: www.sae.org/scholarships

Salute to Education, Inc.

Salute to Education Scholarship

Type of award: Scholarship.
Intended use: For undergraduate study at postsecondary institution.
Eligibility: Applicant must be high school senior. Applicant must be U.S. citizen residing in Florida.
Basis for selection: Applicant must demonstrate financial need, high academic achievement, depth of character, leadership, seriousness of purpose and service orientation.
Additional information: Minimum 3.0 GPA. Number of total scholarships varies. Winners of this one-time grant also receive laptop computer. Applicant must be a resident of and attend an accredited public or private high school in Miami-Dade or Broward County. Scholarships in following categories: athletics, language arts and foreign languages, leadership/service, mathematics/computer science, natural science, and performing arts & visual arts. Visit Website for application and deadline. Application deadline in late January. Notification begins mid-April.
Amount of award: $1,500
Number of applicants: 1,500
Total amount awarded: $120,000
Contact:
Salute to Education, Inc.
P.O. Box 833425
Miami, FL 33283
Phone: 305-799-6726
Fax: 786-515-9864
Web: www.stescholarships.org

Scarlett Family Foundation Scholarship Program

Scarlett Family Foundation Scholarship

Type of award: Scholarship, renewable.
Intended use: For full-time undergraduate study at postsecondary institution. Designated institutions: Not-for-profit institutions.
Eligibility: Applicant must be residing in Tennessee.
Basis for selection: Major/career interest in accounting; business; business, international; business/management/administration or finance/banking. Applicant must demonstrate financial need and high academic achievement.
Application requirements: Essay, transcript. FAFSA.
Additional information: Minimum award is $2500. Amount of award varies based on need. Minimum of 2.5 GPA preferred. Must have demonstrated entrepreneurial interests or leadership. Applicant must be from one of 39 counties in Tennessee. Visit Website for details.
Amount of award: $2,500-$15,000
Number of awards: 18
Number of applicants: 770
Application deadline: December 15
Notification begins: March 15
Total amount awarded: $457,000
Contact:
Scarlett Family Foundation Scholarship Program
c/o ISTS, Inc.
1321 Murfreesboro Rd., Ste. 800
Nashville, TN 37217
Phone: 615-777-3750
Fax: 615-320-3151
Web: www.scarlettfoundation.org

Scholarship America

Scholarship America Scholarships

Type of award: Scholarship.
Intended use: For undergraduate or graduate study at postsecondary institution.
Additional information: Scholarship America awards scholarships through multiple national, regional, and local scholarship programs for various levels of study. Eligibility criteria, award amounts, and deadlines vary by scholarship and sponsor. Students who register with Scholarship America can be matched with scholarship for which they may be eligible.
Amount of award: $100-$30,000
Number of awards: 106,500
Number of applicants: 400,000
Total amount awarded: $203,000,000
Contact:
Scholarship America
1550 American Blvd E
Suite 155
Minneapolis, MN 55425
Phone: 952-830-7300
Web: www.scholarshipamerica.org

Screen Actors Guild Foundation

John L. Dales Standard Scholarship

Type of award: Scholarship, renewable.
Intended use: For full-time undergraduate or graduate study at accredited 2-year, 4-year or graduate institution in United States.
Eligibility: Applicant or parent must be member/participant of Screen Actor's Guild.
Basis for selection: Applicant must demonstrate financial need.

Application requirements: Recommendations, essay, transcript, proof of eligibility. Most recent federal income tax return and additional financial information. SAT/ACT scores.
Additional information: Member under the age of 22 must have been a member for five years and have lifetime earnings of $30,000. Parent of applicant must have ten vested years of pension credits or lifetime earnings of $150,000. Consult office or Website for more information. Number and amount of awards vary.

Number of awards:	81
Number of applicants:	135
Application deadline:	March 15
Notification begins:	July 7
Total amount awarded:	$282,000

Contact:
Screen Actors Guild Foundation
John L. Dales Scholarship Fund
5757 Wilshire Boulevard, Suite 124
Los Angeles, CA 90036
Phone: 323-549-6649
Fax: 323-549-6710
Web: www.sagfoundation.org

John L. Dales Transitional Scholarship

Type of award: Scholarship, renewable.
Intended use: For full-time undergraduate or graduate study at accredited postsecondary institution in United States.
Eligibility: Applicant or parent must be member/participant of Screen Actor's Guild.
Basis for selection: Applicant must demonstrate financial need.
Application requirements: Recommendations, essay, transcript, proof of eligibility. Most recent federal income tax return and additional financial information. SAT/ACT scores.
Additional information: Must be member of Screen Actors Guild. Applicant must have ten vested years of pension credits with SAG or lifetime earnings of $150,000. Consult office or visit Website for more information. Number and amount of awards vary.

Number of awards:	7
Number of applicants:	15
Application deadline:	March 15
Notification begins:	July 7
Total amount awarded:	$24,000

Contact:
Screen Actors Guild Foundation
John L. Dales Scholarship Fund
5757 Wilshire Boulevard, Suite 124
Los Angeles, CA 90036
Phone: 323-549-6649
Fax: 323-549-6710
Web: www.sagfoundation.org

Seabee Memorial Scholarship Association, Inc.

Seabee Memorial Scholarship

Type of award: Scholarship, renewable.
Intended use: For full-time undergraduate study at accredited 4-year institution in United States.
Eligibility: Applicant must be U.S. citizen. Applicant must be descendant of veteran who served in the Navy. Applicant must be child or grandchild of a currently enlisted, honorably discharged, or deceased member of Naval Construction FORCE (Seabees) or Navy CEC (Civil Engineer Corps).
Basis for selection: Applicant must demonstrate financial need, high academic achievement, depth of character, leadership, patriotism, seriousness of purpose and service orientation.
Application requirements: Essay, transcript, proof of eligibility. IRS Form 1040. Official document (DD214, reenlistment certificate, transfer orders, etc.) that verifies rate/rank of sponsor.
Additional information: Not available for part-time or graduate students. Not available for great-grandchildren of members of Seabees or Navy CEC. Award is renewable for up to four years. Download application from Website.

Amount of award:	$2,000
Number of awards:	100
Number of applicants:	415
Application deadline:	April 15
Notification begins:	June 15

Contact:
Scholarship Committee
P.O. Box 6574
Silver Spring, MD 20916
Phone: 301-570-2850
Fax: 301-570-2873
Web: www.seabee.org

Second Marine Division Association

Second Marine Division Association Scholarship Fund

Type of award: Scholarship, renewable.
Intended use: For full-time undergraduate study at accredited vocational, 2-year or 4-year institution.
Eligibility: Must be dependent child or grandchild of person who serves or served in Second Marine Division, U.S. Marine Corps, or unit attached to the division.
Basis for selection: Applicant must demonstrate financial need and high academic achievement.
Application requirements: Essay, transcript, proof of eligibility. Income verification.
Additional information: Family's adjusted gross income should not exceed $75,000 for the taxable year prior to application. Exceptions may be made for larger families. Minimum 2.5 GPA. Must reapply for renewal. Include SASE when requesting application. Parent or grandparent who served in the Second Marine Division must join SMDA, if not already a member, once scholarship is awarded.

Amount of award:	$1,200
Number of awards:	40
Number of applicants:	38
Application deadline:	April 1, July 1
Notification begins:	September 15
Total amount awarded:	$38,400

Contact:
Second Marine Division Association Memorial Scholarship Fund
Phone: 910-451-3167
Web: www.2Dmardiv.com

Senator George J. Mitchell Scholarship Research Institute

Senator George J. Mitchell Scholarship

Type of award: Scholarship, renewable.
Intended use: For freshman study at accredited 2-year or 4-year institution in United States.
Eligibility: Applicant must be high school senior. Applicant must be U.S. citizen residing in Maine.
Basis for selection: Applicant must demonstrate financial need, high academic achievement and service orientation.
Application requirements: Essay, transcript, proof of eligibility. Letter from guidance counselor, SAR, copy of financial aid award from college student plans to attend.
Additional information: One award made to graduating senior from every public high school in Maine. Renewable for up to four years. Award total is $6,000 ($1,500 per year for four years). Scholarship to be applied to spring semester bill. Application due April 1, supporting materials due May 1.

Amount of award:	$1,500-$6,000
Number of awards:	127
Number of applicants:	1,200
Application deadline:	April 1
Notification begins:	June 1
Total amount awarded:	$750,000

Contact:
Senator George J. Mitchell Scholarship Research Institute
22 Monument Square
Suite 200
Portland, ME 04101
Phone: 207-773-7700
Fax: 207-773-1133
Web: www.mitchellinstitute.org

Seneca Nation and BIA

Seneca Nation Higher Education Program

Type of award: Scholarship, renewable.
Intended use: For undergraduate or graduate study at accredited 2-year, 4-year or graduate institution.
Eligibility: Applicant must be American Indian. Must be an enrolled member of Seneca Nation of Indians. Applicant must be U.S. citizen.
Basis for selection: Applicant must demonstrate financial need.
Application requirements: Essay, transcript, proof of eligibility. Proof of tribal enrollment, letter of reference from non-relative. FAFSA. NYS Tuition Assistance Program Application, NYS Indian Aid Application (for NY residents).
Additional information: Amount and number of awards vary. Residency requirements: Level 1- New York State residents living on reservation; Level 2- New York State residents living in New York; Level 3- Enrolled members living outside New York. Application deadlines: fall, July 1; spring, December 1; summer, May 1. Contact sponsor or see Website for more information.

Application deadline:	July 1, December 1

Contact:
Seneca Nation of Indians
Higher Education Program
12861 Route 438
Irving, NY 14081
Phone: 716-532-3341
Fax: 716-532-3269
Web: www.sni.org/hep

Sertoma

Sertoma Scholarships for Students Who are Hard of Hearing or Deaf

Type of award: Scholarship, renewable.
Intended use: For full-time undergraduate study at 4-year institution in United States.
Eligibility: Applicant must be hearing impaired. Applicant must be U.S. citizen.
Basis for selection: Applicant must demonstrate high academic achievement, depth of character, seriousness of purpose and service orientation.
Application requirements: Transcript. Statement of purpose, two letters of recommendation, documentation of hearing impairment in form of recent audiogram or signed statement by hearing-health professional.
Additional information: Applicant must have minimum of 40 dB bilateral hearing loss as evidenced by an audiogram. Must demonstrate how their hearing loss has shaped their lives to become the person they are today. Must have minimum 3.2 GPA. Visit Website for application and more information.

Amount of award:	$1,000
Number of awards:	45
Number of applicants:	220
Application deadline:	May 1
Notification begins:	June 15
Total amount awarded:	$45,000

Contact:
Sertoma, Inc.
Attn: Scholarships
1912 East Meyer Boulevard
Kansas City, MO 64132-1174
Phone: 800-593-5646
Fax: 816-333-4320
Web: www.sertoma.org/scholarship

Scholarships

Shoshone Tribe

Shoshone Tribal Scholarship

Type of award: Scholarship, renewable.
Intended use: For undergraduate or graduate study at accredited vocational, 2-year or 4-year institution in United States.
Eligibility: Applicant must be American Indian. Must be enrolled member of Eastern Shoshone Tribe.
Basis for selection: Applicant must demonstrate financial need and high academic achievement.
Application requirements: Transcript, proof of eligibility. FAFSA. Letter of Acceptance from school attending. Formal personal letter. Certificate of Indian Blood from Shoshone Enrollment.
Additional information: Must first apply for Pell Grant and appropriate campus-based aid. Minimum 2.5 GPA. Award renewable for maximum ten semesters. Application deadlines: academic year, June 15; winter, November 15; spring, February 15; summer, April 15. Number of awards varies.

Amount of award:	$50-$15,000
Number of awards:	60
Number of applicants:	100
Application deadline:	June 15, November 15
Total amount awarded:	$300,000

Contact:
Eastern Shoshone Tribe
PL102-447 Program
104 Washakie Street, P.O. Box 628
Fort Washakie, WY 82514
Phone: 307-335-8000
Fax: 307-335-8004
Web: www.easternshoshoneeducation.com

Sid Richardson Memorial Fund

Sid Richardson Scholarship

Type of award: Scholarship, renewable.
Intended use: For full-time undergraduate or graduate study at accredited postsecondary institution.
Basis for selection: Applicant must demonstrate financial need and high academic achievement.
Application requirements: Essay, transcript, proof of eligibility. SAT or ACT scores.
Additional information: Those eligible to apply for a Sid Richardson Memorial Fund scholarship are direct descendants (children or grandchildren) of persons who qualified for Early Retirement, Normal Retirement, Disability Retirement, or Death Benefits from The Bass Retirement Plan (formerly The Retirement Plan For Employees of Bass Enterprises Production Co.), Retirement Plan for Employees of Barbnet / San Jose Cattle Co., Retirement Plan for Employees of City Center Development Co., City Club Retirement Plan, Retirement Plan for Employees of Richardson Aviation, G.P., Retirement Plan for Employees of Sid W. Richardson Foundation, or Retirement Plan for Employees of Sundance Square. Those eligible also include direct descendants (children or grandchildren) of persons presently employed with a minimum of three years' full-time service with any of the following employers: Barbnet Investment Co. (tax ID #75-2033355), BEPCO, L.P. (tax ID #75-1076930), BOPCO, L.P. (tax ID #37-1483123), City Club of Ft. Worth (tax ID #75-2035506), Richardson Aviation (tax ID #75-2125310), San Jose Cattle Co. (tax ID #75-1018369), Sid Richardson Carbon Co. (SRCE, L.P.) (tax ID #75-2468081), Sid W. Richardson Foundation (tax ID #75-6015828), and Sundance Square Management, L.P. (tax ID #20-1942332). Direct a written request for an application to Shanda Ranelle, Sid Richardson Memorial Fund, 309 Main Street, Fort Worth, Texas 76102 or sranelle@sidrichardson.org. The request may also be faxed to 817-332-2176. Include student name and address, qualifying employee name, Social Security Number of employee, qualifying company name, and dates of employment.

Amount of award:	$500-$7,000
Number of applicants:	87
Application deadline:	March 31
Notification begins:	May 22
Total amount awarded:	$252,000

Contact:
Sid Richardson Memorial Fund
309 Main Street
Fort Worth, TX 76102
Phone: 817-336-0494
Fax: 817-332-2176

Sidney B. Meadows Scholarship Endowment Fund

Southern Nursery Organization Sidney B. Meadows Scholarship

Type of award: Scholarship.
Intended use: For full-time junior, senior, master's or doctoral study at accredited 4-year or graduate institution.
Eligibility: Applicant must be U.S. citizen residing in Tennessee, Louisiana, Virginia, Mississippi, Alabama, Kentucky, Missouri, Texas, Arkansas, Maryland, Florida, Georgia, South Carolina, Oklahoma, West Virginia or North Carolina.
Basis for selection: Major/career interest in horticulture. Applicant must demonstrate high academic achievement.
Application requirements: Recommendations, transcript. Resume, cover letter.
Additional information: Must be enrolled in ornamental horticulture or related discipline in good standing. Minimum 2.75 GPA for undergraduates, 3.0 for graduates. Must be resident of one of 16 states in Southern Nursery Organization, but matriculation in these states is not mandatory. Preference given to applicants who plan to work in the horticulture industry after graduation, and for those who demonstrate financial need. Visit Website for application and additional information.

Amount of award:	$1,500
Number of awards:	12
Application deadline:	May 31
Notification begins:	July 1
Total amount awarded:	$18,000

Contact:
Sidney B. Meadows Scholarship Endowment Fund
P.O. Box 801513
Acworth, GA 30101
Phone: 678-813-1880
Fax: 678-813-1881
Web: www.sbmsef.org

Siemens Foundation

Siemens Awards for Advanced Placement

Type of award: Scholarship.
Intended use: For full-time freshman study at accredited 4-year institution.
Eligibility: Applicant must be enrolled in high school.
Basis for selection: Competition/talent/interest in academics, based on the most scores of "5" on AP tests in eight subjects: Calculus BC, Computer Science A, Statistics, Chemistry, Biology, Environmental Science, Physics C: Mechanics, and Physics C: Electricity. Applicant must demonstrate high academic achievement.
Additional information: A $2,000 college scholarship awarded each spring for up to one male and one female student from each of the 50 states. No application for award. Two additional national winners (one male, one female) will be awarded $5,000 college scholarship. Students must still be in high school in the spring when the award is announced. Must attain a score of 5 on at least two of the aforementioned exams. Composite exams used as tiebreaker if multiple students attain same number of 5's. All U.S. high school students who have taken an AP exam in year prior to applying are eligible, as well as homeschooled students. Students may be awarded state or national award only once, but state winners may be considered for national award in subsequent years. See Website for more details.

Amount of award:	$2,000-$5,000
Number of awards:	102
Notification begins:	January 1
Total amount awarded:	$20,800

Contact:
The College Board
Attn: Siemens Awards for AP
11955 Democracy Drive
Reston, VA 20190
Phone: 877-358-6777
Fax: 703-935-7795
Web: www.collegeboard.com/saap or www.siemens-foundation.org/en/advanced_placement.htm

Siemens Competition in Math, Science and Technology

Type of award: Scholarship.
Intended use: For full-time undergraduate or graduate study at accredited 4-year or graduate institution.
Eligibility: Applicant must be enrolled in high school. Applicant must be U.S. citizen or permanent resident.
Basis for selection: Competition/talent/interest in science project, based on originality, scientific importance, validity, creativity, academic rigor, clarity of expression, comprehensiveness, experimental work, field knowledge. Major/career interest in biology; chemistry; engineering; environmental science; materials science; mathematics; physics; computer/information sciences or medicine.
Application requirements: Proof of eligibility, research proposal. An 18-page (maximum) research report followed by poster and oral presentations for Regional Finalists. Confirmation page signed by school administrator. Completed supplemental form and project advisor or mentor comments form.
Additional information: Competition to encourage students to do research in math, science, or technology, giving young scientists the opportunity to present their research to leading scientists in their field. Regional Finalists awarded trip to compete at one of six regional competitions. At regional event, after presenting poster, oral presentation, and participating in Q&A session, student or team of students will qualify for $1,000 or $3,000 scholarship. National Finalists qualify for $10,000 to $100,000 scholarship. Individual applicants must be seniors; team applicants may be freshmen, sophomores, juniors, or seniors. Register at Website.

Amount of award:	$1,000-$100,000
Number of awards:	60
Number of applicants:	1,911
Application deadline:	September 30
Notification begins:	October 19
Total amount awarded:	$617,000

Contact:
The College Board
Attn: Siemens Competition
11955 Democracy Drive
Reston, VA 20190
Phone: 877-358-6777
Fax: 703-935-7795
Web: siemens.collegeboard.org

Siemens We Can Change the World Challenge

Type of award: Scholarship, renewable.
Intended use: For at postsecondary institution.
Eligibility: Applicant must be enrolled in high school.
Basis for selection: Competition/talent/interest in academics, based on identification of environmental issue or problem and research, scientific approach, sharing and replication to a larger audience, global impact, creativity and innovation.
Additional information: Competition to encourage K-12 students to develop innovative green solutions for environmental issues. High school 1st, 2nd, and 3rd place teams could win $50,000, $25,000, and $10,000 respectively, to be shared equally among team members. Deadline in March.

Amount of award:	$10,000-$50,000
Number of awards:	3
Number of applicants:	300
Total amount awarded:	$85,000

Contact:
Siemens Foundation
Web: www.wecanchange.com

Slovak Gymnastic Union Sokol, USA

Milan Getting Scholarship

Type of award: Scholarship, renewable.
Intended use: For full-time undergraduate study at accredited 4-year institution.

Scholarships

Eligibility: Applicant must be high school junior or senior. Applicant must be U.S. citizen.
Basis for selection: Applicant must demonstrate high academic achievement, depth of character, leadership, patriotism and seriousness of purpose.
Application requirements: Recommendations, transcript.
Additional information: Applicant must be member in good standing of Slovak Gymnastic Union Sokol, USA, for at least three years. Minimum scholastic average of C+ or equivalent required. Award renewable for four years. Number of awards varies. Deadline in March. Contact sponsor for application form and more information.

Amount of award:	$500
Number of applicants:	6
Total amount awarded:	$6,000

Contact:
Slovak Gymnastic Union Sokol, USA
P.O. Box 189
East Orange, NJ 07019
Phone: 888-253-0362
Web: www.sokolusa.org

Slovenian Women's Union of America

Slovenian Women's Union Scholarship Foundation

Type of award: Scholarship.
Intended use: For full-time undergraduate study at accredited 2-year or 4-year institution in United States.
Basis for selection: Applicant must demonstrate financial need, depth of character, leadership and service orientation.
Application requirements: Recommendations, essay, transcript. FAFSA, resume, and photograph.
Additional information: Applicant must be member of Slovenian Women's Union or active participant of organization's activities for three years. Open to women and men with interest in promoting Slovene culture. Recommendation must be from SWUA branch officer and instructor. Number of awards varies. Contact Mary Turvey at SWUA for more information.

Amount of award:	$1,000-$2,000
Number of awards:	8
Number of applicants:	18
Application deadline:	March 1
Notification begins:	April 1
Total amount awarded:	$10,000

Contact:
Slovenian Women's Union of America
Scholarship Director
4 Lawrence Drive
Marquette, MI 49855
Phone: 906-249-4288
Web: www.slovenianunion.org

SME Education Foundation

Albert E. Wischmeyer Memorial Scholarship Award

Type of award: Scholarship, renewable.
Intended use: For full-time undergraduate study at accredited 4-year institution. Designated institutions: Institutions located in the state of New York.
Eligibility: Applicant must be U.S. citizen or permanent resident residing in New York.
Basis for selection: Major/career interest in manufacturing; engineering or technology. Applicant must demonstrate high academic achievement.
Application requirements: Recommendations, essay, transcript. Resume, SAT or ACT scores for current high school students.
Additional information: Applicants must reside in New York State west of Interstate 81. Minimum 2.5 GPA. Must reapply for renewal. Application available on Website. Awards vary.

Application deadline:	February 1

Contact:
SME Education Foundation
One SME Drive, P.O. Box 930
Dearborn, MI 48121-0930
Phone: 313-425-3300
Web: www.smeef.org

Allen and Loureena Weber Scholarship

Type of award: Scholarship.
Intended use: For sophomore, junior or senior study at 2-year or 4-year institution in United States. Designated institutions: University of Cincinnati or Kentucky institutions.
Eligibility: Applicant must be U.S. citizen or permanent resident residing in Kentucky.
Basis for selection: Major/career interest in manufacturing; engineering, mechanical; engineering, industrial or technology. Applicant must demonstrate high academic achievement.
Application requirements: Recommendations, transcript. Resume.
Additional information: Minimum 3.0 GPA. First preference given to students who are graduates of Dayton High School (Dayton, KY). Second preference given to other high schools in Dayton, KY area. Must have technical aptitude and desire for education and practical learning. Scholarship may be used toward books, fees, or tuition.

Application deadline:	February 1

Contact:
SME Education Foundation
One SME Drive, P.O. Box 930
Dearborn, MI 48121-0930
Phone: 313-425-3300
Web: www.smeef.org

Alvin and June Sabroff Manufacturing Engineering Scholarship

Type of award: Scholarship.
Intended use: For undergraduate study at accredited 4-year institution in United States or Canada.
Eligibility: Applicant must be U.S. citizen.

Basis for selection: Major/career interest in manufacturing; engineering or technology. Applicant must demonstrate high academic achievement.
Application requirements: Recommendations, transcript. Resume.
Additional information: Minimum 3.0 GPA. Must be seeking degree in manufacturing engineering, technology, or closely related field. First preference given to applicants attending college or university in Ohio. Award amount varies.
Application deadline: February 1
Contact:
SME Education Foundation
One SME Drive, P.O. Box 930
Dearborn, MI 48121-0930
Phone: 313-425-3300
Web: www.smeef.org

Arthur and Gladys Cervenka Scholarship

Type of award: Scholarship, renewable.
Intended use: For full-time sophomore, junior or senior study at accredited 4-year institution in United States or Canada.
Basis for selection: Major/career interest in manufacturing; engineering or technology. Applicant must demonstrate high academic achievement.
Application requirements: Recommendations, essay, transcript. Resume.
Additional information: Must be residing in the U.S. or Canada. Applicant must have completed minimum of 30 college credit hours. Minimum 3.0 GPA. Preference given to students attending institutions in Florida. Awards vary.
Application deadline: February 1
Contact:
SME Education Foundation
One SME Drive, P.O. Box 930
Dearborn, MI 48121-0930
Phone: 313-425-3300
Web: www.smeef.org

Chapter 17 - St. Louis Scholarship

Type of award: Scholarship, renewable.
Intended use: For sophomore, junior or senior study at accredited 2-year or 4-year institution.
Basis for selection: Major/career interest in manufacturing; engineering; engineering, mechanical or technology. Applicant must demonstrate high academic achievement, depth of character and seriousness of purpose.
Application requirements: Recommendations, essay, transcript. Resume.
Additional information: Must be residing in the U.S. or Canada. Applicants must be enrolled in manufacturing engineering, industrial technology, or related degree program. Preference given to applicants residing in boundaries of St. Louis Chapter 17. Second preference given to applicants living in Missouri. Minimum 2.5 GPA. Must reapply for renewal. Application available on Website. Awards vary.
Application deadline: February 1
Contact:
SME Education Foundation
One SME Drive, P.O. Box 930
Dearborn, MI 48121-0930
Phone: 313-425-3300
Web: www.smeef.org

Chapter 198 - Downriver Detroit Scholarship

Type of award: Scholarship.
Intended use: For full-time undergraduate or graduate study at accredited 2-year, 4-year or graduate institution.
Basis for selection: Major/career interest in manufacturing; engineering, mechanical; engineering; technology or mathematics. Applicant must demonstrate high academic achievement.
Application requirements: Recommendations, essay, transcript. Resume, SAT or ACT scores for current high school students.
Additional information: Must be residing in the U.S. or Canada. First preference given to children or grandchildren of current SME Downriver Chapter 198 members. Second preference given to members of student SME chapters sponsored by Chapter 198 or Ann Arbor Area Chapter 079. Third preference given to residents of Michigan. Fourth preference given to applicants planning to attend college/ university in Michigan. Not restricted to Michigan. Minimum 2.5 GPA. Awards vary.
Application deadline: February 1
Contact:
SME Education Foundation
One SME Drive, P.O. Box 930
Dearborn, MI 48121-0930
Phone: 313-425-3300
Web: www.smeef.org

Chapter 23 - Quad Cities Iowa/ Illinois Scholarship

Type of award: Scholarship.
Intended use: For undergraduate study at accredited 4-year institution.
Basis for selection: Major/career interest in manufacturing. Applicant must demonstrate high academic achievement.
Application requirements: Recommendations, transcript. Resume.
Additional information: Minimum 2.5 GPA. Scholarship may be used toward books, fees, or tuition. First preference given to applicant who is a child, grandchild, or stepchild of registered SME member or student member. Second preference given to applicant who is resident of Iowa or Illinois and attending an Iowa or Illinois college or university. Third preference given to students who are residents of Iowa or Illinois. Fourth preference will be given to applicants who attend a college or university located in Iowa or Illinois. Award amount varies.
Application deadline: February 1
Contact:
SME Education Foundation
One SME Drive, P.O. Box 930
Dearborn, MI 48121-0930
Phone: 313-425-3300
Web: www.smeef.org

Chapter 311 - Tri City Scholarship

Type of award: Scholarship.
Intended use: For undergraduate study at accredited 4-year institution.
Basis for selection: Major/career interest in manufacturing; engineering or engineering, industrial. Applicant must demonstrate high academic achievement.
Application requirements: Recommendations, transcript. Resume.

Additional information: Manufacturing engineering technology or closely related majors also eligible. Minimum 3.0 GPA. First preference given to scholarship applicants who are residents of Michigan. Second preference given to applicants seeking education from college or university in Michigan. Award amount varies.

Application deadline: February 1

Contact:
SME Education Foundation
One SME Drive, P.O. Box 930
Dearborn, MI 48121-0930
Phone: 313-425-3300
Web: www.smeef.org

Chapter 4 - Lawrence A. Wacker Memorial Scholarship

Type of award: Scholarship, renewable.
Intended use: For undergraduate study at accredited 4-year institution in United States. Designated institutions: Wisconsin institutions.
Basis for selection: Major/career interest in manufacturing; engineering, industrial or engineering, mechanical. Applicant must demonstrate high academic achievement.
Application requirements: Recommendations, essay, transcript. Resume, SAT or ACT scores for current high school students.
Additional information: Applicants must be seeking bachelor's degree in manufacturing, mechanical, or industrial engineering. Minimum 3.0 GPA. One scholarship granted to graduating high school senior, one to current undergraduate. First preference given to SME Chapter 4 members or spouses, children, or grandchildren of members. Second preference given to residents of Milwaukee, Ozaukee, Washington, and Waukesha counties. Third preference given to Wisconsin residents. Application available on Website. Award amounts vary.

Number of awards: 2
Application deadline: February 1

Contact:
SME Education Foundation
One SME Drive, P.O. Box 930
Dearborn, MI 48121-0930
Phone: 313-425-3300
Web: www.smeef.org

Chapter 52 - Wichita Scholarship

Type of award: Scholarship.
Intended use: For sophomore, junior, senior or graduate study at accredited 2-year, 4-year or graduate institution in United States. Designated institutions: Kansas institutions.
Eligibility: Applicant must be residing in Kansas.
Basis for selection: Major/career interest in engineering; engineering, mechanical; engineering, industrial; manufacturing or technology. Applicant must demonstrate high academic achievement.
Application requirements: Recommendations, essay, transcript. Resume.
Additional information: Must be residing in the U.S. or Canada. First preference given to children, grandchildren, or other relatives of current SME Wichita Chapter 52 members. Second preference given to residents of Kansas, Oklahoma, and Missouri. Third preference given to applicants attending colleges or universities in Kansas. Minimum 2.5 GPA. Awards vary.

Application deadline: February 1

Contact:
SME Education Foundation
One SME Drive, P.O. Box 930
Dearborn, MI 48121-0930
Phone: 313-425-3300
Web: www.smeef.org

Chapter 56 - Fort Wayne Scholarship

Type of award: Scholarship.
Intended use: For undergraduate or graduate study at 2-year, 4-year or graduate institution. Designated institutions: Indiana institutions.
Eligibility: Applicant must be residing in Indiana.
Basis for selection: Major/career interest in engineering or engineering, mechanical. Applicant must demonstrate high academic achievement.
Application requirements: Recommendations, essay, transcript. Resume, SAT or ACT scores for high school students.
Additional information: Must be residing in the U.S. or Canada. First preference given to children or grandchildren of current members of SME Fort Wayne Chapter 56. Second preference given to members of SME student chapters sponsored by Chapter 56. Third preference given to residents of Indiana. Fourth preference given to applicants attending or planning to attend Indiana institutions. Minimum 2.5 GPA. Awards vary.

Application deadline: February 1

Contact:
SME Education Foundation
One SME Drive, P.O. Box 930
Dearborn, MI 48121-0930
Phone: 313-425-3300
Web: www.smeef.org

Chapter 6 - Fairfield County Scholarship

Type of award: Scholarship.
Intended use: For full-time undergraduate study in United States or Canada.
Basis for selection: Major/career interest in engineering; manufacturing or technology. Applicant must demonstrate high academic achievement.
Application requirements: Recommendations, essay, transcript. Resume, SAT or ACT scores for current high school students.
Additional information: Must be residing in the U.S. or Canada. Minimum 3.0 GPA. Preference given to residents of the eastern United States. Award amount varies.

Application deadline: February 1

Contact:
SME Education Foundation
One SME Drive, P.O. Box 930
Dearborn, MI 48121-0930
Phone: 313-425-3300
Web: www.smeef.org

Chapter 67 - Phoenix Scholarship

Type of award: Scholarship, renewable.
Intended use: For full-time undergraduate study. Designated institutions: Arizona institutions.
Eligibility: Applicant must be residing in Arizona.

Basis for selection: Major/career interest in engineering; manufacturing or technology. Applicant must demonstrate high academic achievement.
Application requirements: Recommendations, essay, transcript. Resume, SAT or ACT scores for current high school students.
Additional information: Minimum 2.5 overall GPA; maintain 3.0 in manufacturing courses to continue eligibility in future years. Awards vary.
Application deadline: February 1
Contact:
SME Education Foundation
One SME Drive, P.O. Box 930
Dearborn, MI 48121-0930
Phone: 313-425-3300
Web: www.smeef.org

Chapter 93 - Albuquerque Scholarship

Type of award: Scholarship.
Intended use: For undergraduate study at accredited 2-year or 4-year institution in United States. Designated institutions: Colleges and universities in New Mexico.
Basis for selection: Major/career interest in engineering. Applicant must demonstrate high academic achievement.
Application requirements: Recommendations, transcript. Resume.
Additional information: Minimum 2.5 GPA. Must be pursuing manufacturing engineering or manufacturing technology. Scholarship may be used toward books, fees, or tuition. First preference goes to applicant who is child/grandchild/stepchild of current Chapter 93 member. Second preference given to SME student member attending a New Mexico university. Third preference given to applicants residing in New Mexico. Fourth preference given to scholarship applicants planning to attend engineering college or university in New Mexico. Fifth preference given to applicants pursuing associate's degree. Award amount varies.
Application deadline: February 1
Contact:
SME Education Foundation
One SME Drive, P.O. Box 930
Dearborn, MI 48121-0930
Phone: 313-425-3300
Web: www.smeef.org

Chapter One - Detroit Founding Chapter Scholarship Award

Type of award: Scholarship, renewable.
Intended use: For undergraduate or graduate study at accredited 2-year, 4-year or graduate institution. Designated institutions: Wayne State University, Lawrence Technological University, University of Detroit Mercy, Focus: HOPE Center for Advanced Technologies, Henry Ford Community College, Macomb Community College, University of Michigan.
Basis for selection: Major/career interest in manufacturing or engineering. Applicant must demonstrate high academic achievement, depth of character and leadership.
Application requirements: Recommendations, essay, transcript. Resume.
Additional information: Awarded to one student each at associate, baccalaureate, and graduate levels. Applicants must be enrolled in manufacturing engineering, manufacturing engineering technology, or closely related degree or certificate program. Student must be member of SME student chapter sponsored by Detroit Chapter 1. Minimum 3.0 GPA. Applicants must reapply for renewal. Financial need considered only between two otherwise equal applicants. Application available on Website. Awards vary.
Application deadline: February 1
Contact:
SME Education Foundation
One SME Drive, P.O. Box 930
Dearborn, MI 48121-0930
Phone: 313-425-3300
Web: www.smeef.org

Clarence & Josephine Myers Scholarship

Type of award: Scholarship.
Intended use: For undergraduate or graduate study at 2-year, 4-year or graduate institution. Designated institutions: Indiana institutions.
Basis for selection: Major/career interest in engineering, mechanical; engineering; manufacturing or engineering, industrial. Applicant must demonstrate high academic achievement.
Application requirements: Recommendations, essay, transcript. Resume, SAT or ACT scores for current high school students.
Additional information: Preference given to students planning to attend or currently attending college or university in Indiana, students who attend Arsenal Technological High School in Indianapolis, members of SME student chapters sponsored by SME Chapter 37, and children or grandchildren of current SME Chapter 37 members. Minimum 3.0 GPA. Award varies.
Application deadline: February 1
Contact:
SME Education Foundation
One SME Drive, P.O. Box 930
Dearborn, MI 48121-0930
Phone: 313-425-3300
Web: www.smeef.org

Clinton J. Helton Manufacturing Scholarship Award

Type of award: Scholarship.
Intended use: For full-time sophomore, junior or senior study at accredited 4-year institution. Designated institutions: Colorado State University and all University of Colorado campuses.
Eligibility: Applicant must be residing in Colorado.
Basis for selection: Major/career interest in manufacturing; engineering or technology. Applicant must demonstrate high academic achievement and depth of character.
Application requirements: Recommendations, essay, transcript. Resume.
Additional information: Applicants must be enrolled in manufacturing engineering or technology degree program and must have completed at least 30 credit hours. Minimum 3.0 GPA. Applicants must reapply for renewal. Application available on Website. Awards vary.
Application deadline: February 1
Contact:
SME Education Foundation
One SME Drive, P.O. Box 930
Dearborn, MI 48121-0930
Phone: 313-425-3300
Web: www.smeef.org

Connie and Robert T. Gunter Scholarship

Type of award: Scholarship.
Intended use: For full-time sophomore, junior or senior study at accredited 4-year institution. Designated institutions: Georgia Institute of Technology, Georgia Southern College, Southern College of Technology.
Basis for selection: Major/career interest in manufacturing; engineering or technology. Applicant must demonstrate high academic achievement, depth of character and seriousness of purpose.
Application requirements: Recommendations, essay, transcript. Resume.
Additional information: Must be residing in the U.S. or Canada. Applicants must be enrolled in manufacturing engineering degree program and must have completed at least 30 credit hours. Minimum 3.5 GPA. Applicants must reapply for renewal. Application available on Website. Award amount varies.
Application deadline: February 1
Contact:
SME Education Foundation
One SME Drive, P.O. Box 930
Dearborn, MI 48121-0930
Phone: 313-425-3300
Web: www.smeef.org

E. Wayne Kay Co-op Scholarship

Type of award: Scholarship, renewable.
Intended use: For full-time sophomore, junior or senior study at accredited postsecondary institution in United States or Canada.
Basis for selection: Major/career interest in manufacturing; engineering or technology. Applicant must demonstrate high academic achievement.
Application requirements: Essay, transcript, proof of eligibility. Letter of recommendation from employer and letter of support from faculty member at college or university.
Additional information: Must be residing in the U.S. or Canada. Applicants must be enrolled in manufacturing engineering or technology degree program and working through co-op program in a manufacturing-related environment. Applicants must have completed minimum 30 college credit hours. Must provide evidence of demonstrated excellence related to manufacturing engineering or technology which may include project completed for employer. Minimum 3.0 GPA. Applicants must reapply for renewal. Application available on Website. Awards vary.
Application deadline: February 1
Contact:
SME Educational Foundation
One SME Drive, P.O. Box 930
Dearborn, MI 48121-0930
Phone: 313-425-3300
Web: www.smeef.org

E. Wayne Kay Community College Scholarship

Type of award: Scholarship, renewable.
Intended use: For full-time freshman or sophomore study at accredited vocational or 2-year institution in United States or Canada. Designated institutions: Community colleges and trade schools.
Basis for selection: Major/career interest in manufacturing or technology. Applicant must demonstrate high academic achievement.
Application requirements: Recommendations, essay, transcript. Resume, SAT or ACT scores.
Additional information: Must be residing in the U.S. or Canada. Applicants must be enrolled in manufacturing engineering or closely related degree program at a two-year community college or trade school in the U.S. or Canada. Entering freshman or sophomore students with 60 or fewer college credits are also eligible. Minimum 3.0 GPA. Must reapply for renewal. Application available on Website. Awards vary.
Application deadline: February 1
Contact:
SME Education Foundation
One SME Drive, P.O. Box 930
Dearborn, MI 48121-0930
Phone: 313-425-3300
Web: www.smeef.org

E. Wayne Kay High School Scholarship

Type of award: Scholarship, renewable.
Intended use: For full-time freshman study at accredited 4-year institution in United States or Canada.
Eligibility: Applicant must be high school senior.
Basis for selection: Major/career interest in manufacturing; engineering or technology. Applicant must demonstrate high academic achievement.
Application requirements: Recommendations, essay, transcript. Resume, SAT or ACT scores.
Additional information: Must be residing in the U.S. or Canada. Applicant must commit to enrolling in manufacturing engineering or technology degree program. Minimum 3.0 GPA. Application available on Website. Awards vary.
Application deadline: February 1
Contact:
SME Foundation
One SME Drive, P.O. Box 930
Dearborn, MI 48121-0930
Phone: 313-425-3300
Web: www.smeef.org

E. Wayne Kay Scholarship

Type of award: Scholarship, renewable.
Intended use: For full-time undergraduate study at accredited 4-year institution in United States or Canada.
Basis for selection: Major/career interest in manufacturing or engineering. Applicant must demonstrate high academic achievement.
Application requirements: Recommendations, essay, transcript. Resume.
Additional information: Must be residing in the U.S. or Canada. Applicants must be enrolled in manufacturing engineering or technology degree program or closely related field. Minimum 3.0 GPA. Must reapply for renewal. Application available on Website. Awards vary.
Application deadline: February 1
Contact:
SME Education Foundaiton
One SME Drive, P.O. Box 930
Dearborn, MI 48121-0930
Phone: 313-425-3300
Web: www.smeef.org

Edward S. Roth Manufacturing Engineering Scholarship

Type of award: Scholarship, renewable.
Intended use: For full-time undergraduate or graduate study at accredited 4-year institution in United States. Designated institutions: California State Polytechnic University; University of Miami, FL; Bradley University, IL; Central State University, OH; Miami University, OH; Boston University; Worcester Polytechnic Institute, MA; University of Massachusetts; St. Cloud State University, MN; University of Texas-Pan American; Brigham Young University, UT; Utah State University.
Eligibility: Applicant must be U.S. citizen.
Basis for selection: Major/career interest in manufacturing or engineering. Applicant must demonstrate high academic achievement, depth of character and seriousness of purpose.
Application requirements: Recommendations, essay, transcript. Resume.
Additional information: Applicants must be enrolled in manufacturing engineering degree program. Minimum 3.0 GPA. Preference given to students demonstrating financial need, minority students, and students participating in co-op program. Some preferences given to graduating high school seniors and graduate students. Must reapply for renewal. Application available on Website. Award amount varies.
Application deadline: February 1
Contact:
SME Education Foundation
One SME Drive, P.O. Box 930
Dearborn, MI 48121-0930
Phone: 313-425-3300
Web: www.smeef.org

Giuliano Mazzetti Scholarship

Type of award: Scholarship, renewable.
Intended use: For full-time sophomore, junior or senior study at accredited 4-year institution in United States or Canada.
Basis for selection: Major/career interest in manufacturing; engineering or technology. Applicant must demonstrate high academic achievement.
Application requirements: Recommendations, essay, transcript. Resume.
Additional information: Must be residing in the U.S. or Canada. Applicants must be enrolled in manufacturing engineering, technology, or closely related degree program and must have completed minimum 30 college credit hours. Minimum 3.0 GPA. Must reapply for renewal. Application available on Website. Awards vary.
Application deadline: February 1
Contact:
SME Education Foundation
One SME Drive, P.O. Box 930
Dearborn, MI 48121-0930
Phone: 313-425-3300
Web: www.smeef.org

Lucile B. Kaufman Women's Scholarship

Type of award: Scholarship, renewable.
Intended use: For full-time sophomore, junior or senior study at 4-year institution in United States or Canada.
Eligibility: Applicant must be female.
Basis for selection: Major/career interest in manufacturing or engineering. Applicant must demonstrate high academic achievement.
Application requirements: Recommendations, essay, transcript. Resume.
Additional information: Must be residing in the U.S. or Canada. Applicants must be enrolled in manufacturing engineering or manufacturing engineering technology degree program and must have completed minimum 30 credits. Minimum 3.0 GPA. Must reapply for renewal. Application available on Website. Awards vary.
Application deadline: February 1
Contact:
SME Education Foundation
One SME Drive, P.O. Box 930
Dearborn, MI 48121-0930
Phone: 313-425-3300
Web: www.smeef.org

Myrtle and Earl Walker Scholarship

Type of award: Scholarship, renewable.
Intended use: For full-time undergraduate study at accredited 4-year institution in United States or Canada.
Basis for selection: Major/career interest in manufacturing or engineering. Applicant must demonstrate high academic achievement.
Application requirements: Recommendations, essay, transcript. Resume.
Additional information: Must be residing in the U.S. or Canada. Applicants must be enrolled in manufacturing engineering degree or technology program and must have completed minimum 15 credits. Minimum 3.0 GPA. Must reapply for renewal. Application available on Website. Awards vary.
Application deadline: February 1
Contact:
SME Education Foundation
One SME Drive, P.O. Box 930
Dearborn, MI 48121-0930
Phone: 313-425-3300
Web: www.smeef.org

North Central Region Scholarship

Type of award: Scholarship.
Intended use: For full-time undergraduate study at 2-year or 4-year institution. Designated institutions: Institutions in Iowa, Minnesota, Nebraska, North Dakota, South Dakota, Wisconsin, or the upper peninsula of Michigan.
Eligibility: Applicant must be residing in Michigan, Wisconsin, Iowa, South Dakota, Minnesota, Nebraska or North Dakota.
Basis for selection: Major/career interest in manufacturing; engineering or engineering, mechanical. Applicant must demonstrate high academic achievement.
Application requirements: Recommendations, essay, transcript. Resume, SAT or ACT scores for current high school students.
Additional information: Must be residing in the U.S. or Canada. First preference given to applicants from the North Central Region who are SME members, spouses of members, or children or grandchildren of members. Second preference given to residents of Iowa, Minnesota, Nebraska, North Dakota, South Dakota, Wisconsin, and the upper peninsula of Michigan. Minimum 3.0 GPA. Awards vary.
Application deadline: February 1

Contact:
SME Education Foundation
One SME Drive, P.O. Box 930
Dearborn, MI 48121-0930
Phone: 313-425-3300
Web: www.smeef.org

SME Directors Scholarship

Type of award: Scholarship, renewable.
Intended use: For full-time sophomore, junior or senior study at accredited 4-year institution in United States or Canada.
Basis for selection: Major/career interest in manufacturing. Applicant must demonstrate high academic achievement and leadership.
Application requirements: Recommendations, essay, transcript. Resume.
Additional information: Must be residing in the U.S. or Canada. Applicants must have completed minimum 30 college credit hours. Minimum 3.5 GPA. Applicants must reapply for renewal. Preference given to applicants who demonstrate leadership skills in a community, academic, or professional environment. Application available on Website. Awards vary.
Application deadline: February 1
Contact:
SME Education Foundation
One SME Drive, P.O. Box 930
Dearborn, MI 48121-0930
Phone: 313-425-3300
Web: www.smeef.org

SME Education Foundation Family Scholarship

Type of award: Scholarship.
Intended use: For full-time undergraduate study in United States or Canada.
Basis for selection: Major/career interest in engineering or manufacturing. Applicant must demonstrate high academic achievement.
Application requirements: Recommendations, essay, transcript. Resume. High school seniors must submit SAT/ACT scores.
Additional information: Must be residing in the U.S. or Canada. Applicant must have parent or grandparent who has been SME member in good standing for at least two years. Graduating high school seniors and current undergraduates with fewer than 30 credit hours are eligible. Minimum 3.0 GPA. Minimum 1000 SAT or 21 ACT. Awards vary.
Application deadline: February 1
Contact:
SME Education Foundation
One SME Drive, P.O. Box 930
Dearborn, MI 48121-0930
Phone: 313-425-3300
Web: www.smeef.org

SME-FF Future Leaders of Manufacturing Scholarships

Type of award: Scholarship.
Intended use: For full-time undergraduate or graduate study at accredited postsecondary institution in United States.
Basis for selection: Major/career interest in manufacturing; engineering or technology.
Application requirements: Recommendations, transcript, nomination by SME student chapter faculty advisor. Resume.
Additional information: Must be residing in the U.S. or Canada. Applicant must be current SME student member. Faculty advisors may only nominate one student from the chapter. Visit Website for nomination form and application. Awards vary.
Application deadline: February 1
Contact:
SME Education Foundation
One SME Drive, P.O. Box 930
Dearborn, MI 48121-0930
Phone: 313-425-3300
Web: www.smeef.org

Walt Bartram Memorial Education Award (Region 12 and Chapter 119)

Type of award: Scholarship, renewable.
Intended use: For full-time undergraduate study at accredited 2-year or 4-year institution. Designated institutions: Schools with manufacturing engineering programs within the areas of Arizona, New Mexico, or Southern California.
Eligibility: Applicant must be high school senior.
Basis for selection: Major/career interest in manufacturing or engineering. Applicant must demonstrate high academic achievement, depth of character and seriousness of purpose.
Application requirements: Recommendations, essay, transcript. Resume, SAT or ACT scores for current high school students.
Additional information: Applicant must be enrolled in manufacturing engineering or closely related degree program. Minimum 3.5 GPA. Application available on Website. Award varies.
Application deadline: February 1
Contact:
SME Foundation
One SME Drive, P.O. Box 930
Dearborn, MI 48121-0930
Phone: 313-425-3300
Web: www.smeef.org

William E. Weisel Scholarship

Type of award: Scholarship, renewable.
Intended use: For full-time sophomore, junior or senior study at 4-year institution in United States or Canada.
Basis for selection: Major/career interest in manufacturing; engineering; robotics or technology. Applicant must demonstrate high academic achievement.
Application requirements: Recommendations, essay, transcript. Resume.
Additional information: Must be residing in the U.S. or Canada. Applicant must be enrolled in manufacturing engineering degree program and must have completed minimum 30 credits. Preference given to applicants seeking career in robotics or automated systems used in manufacturing. Consideration given to students who intend to apply knowledge to career in medical robotics. Minimum 3.0 GPA. Applicants must reapply for renewal. Financial need considered only between two otherwise equal applicants. Application available on Website. Awards vary.
Application deadline: February 1
Contact:
SME Education Foundation
One SME Drive, P.O. Box 930
Dearborn, MI 48121-0930
Phone: 313-425-3300
Web: www.smeef.org

Sociedad Honoraria Hispanica

Joseph S. Adams Senior Scholarship

Type of award: Scholarship.
Intended use: For full-time freshman study in United States.
Eligibility: Applicant must be high school senior.
Basis for selection: Major/career interest in Latin American studies or foreign languages. Applicant must demonstrate high academic achievement, depth of character, leadership, patriotism, seriousness of purpose and service orientation.
Application requirements: Recommendations, essay, transcript, proof of eligibility, nomination by local high school chapter sponsor. 5-minute video clip in Spanish meeting criteria listed on Website.
Additional information: Applicant must be active senior member of Sociedad Honoraria Hispanica. Applicant must be presently enrolled in high school Spanish or Portuguese class. SHH members should contact their sponsor, not the national director, regarding application before December 31. All majors eligible; strong interest in Latin American Studies, Spanish, Portuguese preferred. Only one member per chapter may apply. Visit Website for application.

Amount of award:	$1,000-$2,000
Number of awards:	56
Number of applicants:	200
Application deadline:	December 15
Notification begins:	April 30
Total amount awarded:	$68,000

Contact:
Sociedad Honoraria Hispanica
Phone: 847-550-0455
Web: www.sociedadhonorariahispanica.org

Society for Range Management

Masonic Range Science Scholarship

Type of award: Scholarship, renewable.
Intended use: For full-time freshman or sophomore study at postsecondary institution. Designated institutions: Colleges or universities with range science programs.
Basis for selection: Major/career interest in range science. Applicant must demonstrate high academic achievement and leadership.
Application requirements: Recommendations, essay, transcript, nomination by member of Society for Range Management, National Association of Conservation Districts, or Soil and Water Conservation Society. SAT/ACT scores.
Additional information: Home-schooled applicants also welcome to apply. Award amount varies. Renewable for maximum of eight semesters. Student must maintain 2.5 GPA first two semesters, 3.0 GPA any subsequent semesters. Visit Website for more information and application.

Number of awards:	1
Number of applicants:	16
Application deadline:	January 6
Notification begins:	March 1
Total amount awarded:	$5,000

Contact:
Society for Range Management
Paul Loeffler
P.O. Box 1407
Alpine, TX 79831-1407
Phone: 303-986-3309
Fax: 303-986-3892
Web: www.rangelands.org

Society of Daughters of the United States Army

Society of Daughters of United States Army Scholarship Program

Type of award: Scholarship, renewable.
Intended use: For full-time undergraduate study at accredited postsecondary institution.
Eligibility: Applicant must be female. Applicant must be daughter or granddaughter (including step or adopted) of a career warrant (WO 1-5) or commissioned officer (2nd & 1st LT, CPT, MAJ, LTC, COL, or General) of U.S. Army who (1) is currently on active duty; (2) retired from active duty after at least 20 years of service; (3) was medically retired before 20 years of active service; (4) died while on active duty; or (5) died after retiring from active duty with 20 or more years of service.
Basis for selection: Applicant must demonstrate high academic achievement, depth of character, leadership, patriotism and seriousness of purpose.
Additional information: Minimum 3.0 GPA. Scholarships cover academic expenses only. Request for application must include parent or grandparent's name, rank, component (Active, Regular, Reserve), inclusive dates of active service, and relationship to applicant. Number of awards varies annually. Send business-size SASE and one letter of request only. Do not send birth certificate or original documents. Do not use registered/certified mail. All application submissions become property of DUSA. Application request deadline is March 1. Completed applications due from March 15 to March 31.

Amount of award:	$1,000
Number of applicants:	100
Application deadline:	March 31
Notification begins:	June 1
Total amount awarded:	$8,000

Contact:
Society of Daughters of the United States Army
Mary P. Maroney, Scholarship Chairman
11804 Grey Birch Place
Reston, VA 20191-4223

Society of Exploraiton Geophysicists

SEG/Denver Geophysical Society Scholarship

Type of award: Scholarship.
Intended use: For full-time junior, senior or graduate study at accredited 4-year or graduate institution. Designated

Scholarships

institutions: Colorado, Wyoming, Utah, New Mexico institutions.
Basis for selection: Major/career interest in geophysics; geology/earth sciences; physics or environmental science.
Application requirements: Recommendations, essay, transcript. SAT or ACT scores for high school and undergraduate students, GRE or TOEFL scores for graduate students.
Additional information: Must have a declared major in the geosciences. Applicants must intend to pursue career in exploration geophysics (graduate students in operations, teaching, or research). Visit Website for more information. Apply online.

Amount of award:	$500-$14,000
Application deadline:	March 1
Notification begins:	September 1

Contact:
SEG Foundation
Phone: 918-497-5500
Web: www.seg.org

Society of Exploration Geophysicists

Anadarko/SEG Scholarship

Type of award: Scholarship.
Intended use: For full-time undergraduate or graduate study at accredited 4-year or graduate institution in United States.
Basis for selection: Major/career interest in geophysics; geology/earth sciences; physics or environmental science.
Application requirements: Recommendations, essay, transcript. SAT or ACT scores for high school and undergraduate students, GRE or TOEFL scores for graduate students.
Additional information: Must be willing to pursue career in U.S. after graduation. Applicants must intend to pursue career in exploration geophysics (graduate students in operations, teaching, or research). Visit Website for more information. Apply online.

Amount of award:	$500-$14,000
Application deadline:	March 1
Notification begins:	September 1

Contact:
SEG Foundation
Phone: 918-497-5500
Web: www.seg.org

Dallas Geophysical Society Scholarship

Type of award: Scholarship.
Intended use: For full-time undergraduate or graduate study at accredited 4-year or graduate institution. Designated institutions: Texas institutions (not necessary for Texas residents).
Eligibility: Applicant must be residing in Texas.
Basis for selection: Major/career interest in geophysics; geology/earth sciences; physics or environmental science.
Application requirements: Recommendations, essay, transcript. SAT or ACT scores for high school and undergraduate students, GRE or TOEFL scores for graduate students.
Additional information: Must be attending Texas institution or consider Texas home. Applicants must intend to pursue career in exploration geophysics (graduate students in operations, teaching, or research). Visit Website for more information. Apply online.

Amount of award:	$500-$14,000
Application deadline:	March 1
Notification begins:	September 1

Contact:
SEG Foundation
Phone: 918-497-5500
Web: www.seg.org

DGS/Karen Kellogg Shaw Memorial Scholarship

Type of award: Scholarship.
Intended use: For full-time undergraduate or graduate study at accredited 4-year or graduate institution. Designated institutions: Texas institutions.
Basis for selection: Major/career interest in geophysics; physics; geology/earth sciences or environmental science.
Application requirements: Recommendations, essay, transcript. SAT or ACT scores for high school and undergraduate students, GRE or TOEFL scores for graduate students.
Additional information: First preference: Student at Southern Methodist University. Second preference: Student attending a North Texas school or a student at any accredited university who received their H.S. diploma from a school in the Dallas metroplex area. Third preference: Student attending any accredited university in Texas. Applicants must intend to pursue career in exploration geophysics (graduate students in operations, teaching, or research). Visit Website for more information. Apply online.

Amount of award:	$500-$14,000
Application deadline:	March 1
Notification begins:	September 1

Contact:
SEG Foundation
Phone: 918-497-5500
Web: www.seg.org

Donald and Nancy Frye Scholarship

Type of award: Scholarship.
Intended use: For full-time undergraduate study at accredited 4-year institution in United States.
Basis for selection: Major/career interest in geophysics; geology/earth sciences; physics or environmental science.
Application requirements: Recommendations, essay, transcript. SAT or ACT scores for high school and undergraduate students, GRE or TOEFL scores for graduate students.
Additional information: Applicants must intend to pursue career in exploration geophysics. Visit Website for more information. Apply online.

Amount of award:	$500-$14,000
Application deadline:	March 1
Notification begins:	September 1

Contact:
SEG Foundation
Phone: 918-497-5500
Web: www.seg.org

Excel Geophysical Services Scholarship

Type of award: Scholarship.
Intended use: For full-time undergraduate or graduate study at accredited 4-year or graduate institution in United States or Canada.
Basis for selection: Major/career interest in geophysics; geology/earth sciences; physics or environmental science.
Application requirements: Recommendations, essay, transcript. SAT or ACT scores for high school and undergraduate students, GRE or TOEFL scores for graduate students.
Additional information: Applicants must intend to pursue career in exploration geophysics (graduate students in operations, teaching, or research). Visit Website for more information. Apply online.

Amount of award:	$500-$14,000
Application deadline:	March 1
Notification begins:	September 1

Contact:
SEG Foundation
Phone: 918-497-5500
Web: www.seg.org

Geophysical Society of Alaska Scholarship

Type of award: Scholarship.
Intended use: For full-time undergraduate or graduate study at accredited 4-year or graduate institution. Designated institutions: Alaska institutions (unless an Alaskan resident).
Eligibility: Applicant must be residing in Alaska.
Basis for selection: Major/career interest in geophysics; geology/earth sciences; physics or environmental science.
Application requirements: Recommendations, essay, transcript. SAT or ACT scores for high school and undergraduate students, GRE or TOEFL scores for graduate students.
Additional information: Must be a resident or attending school in Alaska. Applicants must intend to pursue career in exploration geophysics (graduate students in operations, teaching, or research). Visit Website for more information. Apply online.

Amount of award:	$500-$14,000
Application deadline:	March 1
Notification begins:	September 1

Contact:
SEG Foundation
Phone: 918-497-5500
Web: www.seg.org

Geophysical Society of Tulsa Scholarship

Type of award: Scholarship.
Intended use: For full-time undergraduate or graduate study at accredited 4-year or graduate institution.
Basis for selection: Major/career interest in geophysics. Applicant must demonstrate high academic achievement.
Application requirements: Recommendations, essay, transcript. SAT or ACT scores for high school and undergraduate students, GRE or TOEFL scores for graduate students.
Additional information: Must be resident of Oklahoma or be attending school in Oklahoma. Must be undergraduate or graduate student majoring in geophysics. If no one meets criteria, then physical science and math majors will be considered. Apply online.

Amount of award:	$500-$14,000
Application deadline:	March 1
Notification begins:	September 1

Contact:
SEG Foundation
Phone: 918-497-5500
Web: www.seg.org

GSH/Hugh Hardy Scholarship

Type of award: Scholarship.
Intended use: For full-time undergraduate or graduate study at accredited 4-year or graduate institution. Designated institutions: Institutions in Houston, TX.
Eligibility: Applicant must be U.S. citizen.
Basis for selection: Major/career interest in geophysics; geology/earth sciences; physics or environmental science.
Application requirements: Recommendations, essay, transcript. SAT or ACT scores for high school and undergraduate students, GRE or TOEFL scores for graduate students.
Additional information: Must have a declared major in Geophysics or related Earth Science field. If no applicants are enrolled at an institution in Houston, TX, the SEGF Scholarship Committee may select a qualified student enrolled at a college or university in Texas. If unavailable, a qualified student attending an institution in the U.S. will be chosen. Applicants must intend to pursue career in exploration geophysics (graduate students in operations, teaching, or research). Visit Website for more information. Apply online.

Amount of award:	$500-$14,000
Application deadline:	March 1
Notification begins:	September 1

Contact:
SEG Foundation
Phone: 918-497-5500
Web: www.seg.org

G.W. Hohmann Memorial Scholarship

Type of award: Scholarship.
Intended use: For full-time undergraduate or graduate study at accredited 4-year or graduate institution.
Basis for selection: Major/career interest in geophysics; geology/earth sciences; physics or environmental science. Applicant must demonstrate high academic achievement.
Application requirements: Recommendations, essay, transcript. SAT or ACT scores for high school and undergraduate students, GRE or TOEFL scores for graduate student.
Additional information: Applicants must intend to pursue career in exploration geophysics (graduate students in operations, teaching, or research). Visit Website for more information. Apply online.

Amount of award:	$500-$14,000
Application deadline:	March 1
Notification begins:	September 1

Contact:
SEG Foundation
Phone: 918-497-5500
Web: www.seg.org

Paradigm Scholarship

Type of award: Scholarship.
Intended use: For full-time undergraduate or graduate study at accredited 4-year or graduate institution in United States. Designated institutions: Louisiana institutions.
Basis for selection: Major/career interest in geophysics; geology/earth sciences; physics or environmental science.
Application requirements: Recommendations, essay, transcript. SAT or ACT scores for high school and undergraduate students, GRE or TOEFL scores for graduate students.
Additional information: Applicants must intend to pursue career in exploration geophysics (graduate students in operations, teaching, or research). Visit Website for more information. Apply online.

Amount of award:	$500-$14,000
Application deadline:	March 1
Notification begins:	September 1

Contact:
SEG Foundation
Phone: 918-497-5500
Web: www.seg.org

Rodney Cottrell Scholarship

Type of award: Scholarship.
Intended use: For full-time undergraduate or graduate study at accredited 4-year or graduate institution.
Eligibility: Applicant must be U.S. citizen.
Basis for selection: Major/career interest in geophysics.
Application requirements: Recommendations, essay, transcript. SAT or ACT scores for high school and undergraduate students, GRE or TOEFL scores for graduate students.
Additional information: Applicants must intend to pursue career in exploration geophysics (graduate students in operations, teaching, or research). Visit Website for more information. Apply online.

Amount of award:	$500-$14,000
Application deadline:	March 1
Notification begins:	September 1

Contact:
SEG Foundation
Phone: 918-497-5500
Web: www.seg.org

SEG Foundation/Apache Scholarship

Type of award: Scholarship.
Intended use: For full-time undergraduate or graduate study at accredited 4-year or graduate institution.
Basis for selection: Major/career interest in geophysics; geology/earth sciences; physics or environmental science.
Application requirements: Recommendations, essay, transcript. SAT or ACT scores for high school and undergraduate students, GRE or TOEFL scores for graduate students.
Additional information: Award is for students studying in countries where Apache operates: U.S., Canada, U.K., Australia, Argentina, and Egypt. Applicants must intend to pursue career in exploration geophysics (graduate students in operations, teaching, or research). Visit Website for more information. Apply online.

Amount of award:	$500-$14,000
Application deadline:	March 1
Notification begins:	September 1

Contact:
SEG Foundation
Phone: 918-497-5500
Web: www.seg.org

SEG/Gary and Lorene Servos Scholarship

Type of award: Scholarship.
Intended use: For full-time junior, senior or graduate study at accredited 4-year or graduate institution.
Basis for selection: Major/career interest in geology/earth sciences; geophysics; physics or environmental science.
Application requirements: Recommendations, essay, transcript. SAT or ACT scores for high school and undergraduate students, GRE or TOEFL scores for graduate students.
Additional information: Must be focusing on applied groundwater exploration. Award may be used as a scholarship or study grant. Applicants must intend to pursue career in exploration geophysics (graduate students in operations, teaching, or research). Visit Website for more information. Apply online.

Amount of award:	$500-$14,000
Application deadline:	March 1
Notification begins:	September 1

Contact:
SEG Foundation
Phone: 918-497-5500
Web: www.seg.org

SEG/Marvin and Jene Hewitt Scholarship

Type of award: Scholarship.
Intended use: For full-time undergraduate or graduate study at accredited 4-year or graduate institution.
Basis for selection: Major/career interest in geophysics.
Application requirements: Recommendations, essay, transcript. SAT or ACT scores for high school and undergraduate students, GRE or TOEFL scores for graduate students.
Additional information: Must major in Exploration Geophysics or related field. Applicants must intend to pursue career in exploration geophysics (graduate students in operations, teaching, or research). Visit Website for more information. Apply online.

Amount of award:	$500-$14,000
Application deadline:	March 1
Notification begins:	September 1

Contact:
SEG Foundation
Phone: 918-497-5500
Web: www.seg.org

SEG/P.C. Havens/Seismic Exchange Inc. Scholarship

Type of award: Scholarship.
Intended use: For full-time undergraduate study at accredited 4-year institution in United States.
Basis for selection: Major/career interest in geophysics or geology/earth sciences.
Application requirements: Recommendations, essay, transcript. SAT or ACT scores for high school and undergraduate students, GRE or TOEFL scores for graduate students.

Additional information: Applicants must intend to pursue career in exploration geophysics. Visit Website for more information. Apply online.

Amount of award:	$500-$14,000
Application deadline:	March 1
Notification begins:	September 1

Contact:
SEG Foundation
Phone: 918-497-5500
Web: www.seg.org

Society of Exploration Geophysicists Scholarship

Type of award: Scholarship, renewable.
Intended use: For full-time undergraduate or graduate study at accredited 4-year or graduate institution.
Basis for selection: Major/career interest in geophysics; geology/earth sciences; physics or environmental science. Applicant must demonstrate high academic achievement.
Application requirements: Recommendations, essay, transcript. SAT or ACT scores for high school and undergraduate students, GRE or TOEFL scores for graduate students.
Additional information: Number of scholarships available yearly depends on the number of sponsors and the amount they contribute. Applicants must intend to pursue career in exploration geophysics (graduate students in operations, teaching, or research). Visit Website for more information.

Amount of award:	$500-$14,000
Number of applicants:	120
Application deadline:	March 1
Notification begins:	September 1
Total amount awarded:	$369,430

Contact:
SEG Foundation
Scholarship Committee
P.O. Box 702740
Tulsa, OK 74170-2740
Phone: 918-497-5500
Web: www.seg.org

Society of Physics Students

Herbert Levy Memorial Endowment Fund Scholarship

Type of award: Scholarship.
Intended use: For full-time junior or senior study at 4-year institution.
Eligibility: Applicant or parent must be member/participant of Society of Physics Students.
Basis for selection: Major/career interest in physics. Applicant must demonstrate financial need.
Application requirements: Recommendations, transcript. Statement of financial need. Completed W-9 Federal Tax Form.
Additional information: Must be active in SPS programs.

Amount of award:	$2,000
Application deadline:	February 15

Contact:
Society of Physics Students
One Physics Ellipse
College Park, MD 20740
Phone: 301-209-3007
Fax: 301-209-0839
Web: www.spsnational.org

Peggy Dixon Two-Year Scholarship

Type of award: Scholarship.
Intended use: For full-time junior or senior study at 4-year institution.
Eligibility: Applicant or parent must be member/participant of Society of Physics Students.
Basis for selection: Major/career interest in physics. Applicant must demonstrate high academic achievement.
Application requirements: Recommendations, transcript. Completed W-9 Federal Tax Form.
Additional information: Award is for students transitioning from two-year college into a physics bachelor's degree program. Must have completed at least one semester or quarter of introductory physics sequence and be registered in appropriate subsequent physics courses. Must be active in SPS programs.

Amount of award:	$2,000
Application deadline:	February 15

Contact:
Society of Physics Students
One Physics Ellipse
College Park, MD 20740
Phone: 301-209-3007
Fax: 301-209-0839
Web: www.spsnational.org

Society of Physics Students Future Teacher Scholarship

Type of award: Scholarship.
Intended use: For full-time junior or senior study at 4-year institution.
Eligibility: Applicant or parent must be member/participant of Society of Physics Students.
Basis for selection: Major/career interest in physics or education.
Application requirements: Recommendations, transcript. Statement from SPS Advisor certifying participation in teacher education program. W-9 Federal Tax Form.
Additional information: Must be participating in a teacher education program and planning to pursue a career in physics education. Must be active in SPS programs.

Amount of award:	$2,000
Application deadline:	February 15

Contact:
Society of Physics Students
One Physics Ellipse
College Park, MD 20740
Phone: 301-209-3007
Fax: 301-209-0839
Web: www.spsnational.org

Society of Physics Students Leadership Scholarship

Type of award: Scholarship.
Intended use: For full-time junior or senior study at 2-year or 4-year institution.

Scholarships

Eligibility: Applicant or parent must be member/participant of Society of Physics Students.
Basis for selection: Major/career interest in physics. Applicant must demonstrate high academic achievement and seriousness of purpose.
Application requirements: Transcript. Letters of recommendation from at least two full-time faculty members.
Additional information: Awards payable in equal installments at the beginning of each semester or quarter of full-time study in final year of baccalaureate degree. Applicants in two-year schools should apply after completing one semester of physics. Must be active participant in Society of Physics Students. Must show intention for continued scholastic development in physics. Number of awards varies. Obtain application from Website or SPS Chapter Adviser.

Amount of award:	$2,000-$5,000
Application deadline:	February 15
Notification begins:	April 1
Total amount awarded:	$39,500

Contact:
Society of Physics Students
One Physics Ellipse
College Park, MD 20740
Phone: 301-209-3007
Fax: 301-209-0839
Web: www.spsnational.org

Society of Plastics Engineers

Extrusion Division/Lew Erwin Memorial Scholarship

Type of award: Scholarship.
Intended use: For full-time senior or master's study at 4-year or graduate institution.
Basis for selection: Major/career interest in chemistry; engineering; engineering, chemical; engineering, materials; engineering, mechanical or physics. Applicant must demonstrate financial need.
Application requirements: Research proposal. One- to two-page typed statement explaining reasons for application, qualifications, and educational/career goals in the plastics industry. Recommendation letter from faculty adviser associated with project.
Additional information: All applicants must be in good academic standing and have a demonstrated interest in the plastics industry. Applicants must be Ph.D. candidate or working on senior or MS research project in polymer extrusion that the scholarship will help support. The project must be described in writing, including background, objective, and proposed experiments. Recipient will be expected to furnish final research summary report. Visit Website for more information.

Amount of award:	$2,500
Number of awards:	1
Application deadline:	March 1
Total amount awarded:	$2,500

Contact:
Society of Plastics Engineers
13 Church Hill Road
Newtown, CT 06470
Phone: 203-740-5447
Fax: 203-775-8490
Web: www.4spe.org/spe-foundation

Fleming/Blaszcak Scholarship

Type of award: Scholarship.
Intended use: For full-time undergraduate or graduate study at 4-year or graduate institution.
Eligibility: Applicant must be Mexican American. Applicant must be U.S. citizen or permanent resident.
Basis for selection: Major/career interest in chemistry; engineering; engineering, chemical; engineering, materials; engineering, mechanical or physics. Applicant must demonstrate financial need.
Application requirements: Transcript. One- to two-page typed statement explaining reasons for application, qualifications, and educational/career goals in the plastics industry. Three recommendation letters: two from teachers or school officials and one from an employer or non-relative.
Additional information: All applicants must be in good standing and have a demonstrated interest in the plastics industry. Visit Website for more information.

Amount of award:	$2,000
Number of awards:	1
Application deadline:	March 1
Total amount awarded:	$2,000

Contact:
Society of Plastics Engineers
13 Church Hill Road
Newtown, CT 06470
Phone: 203-740-5447
Fax: 203-775-8490
Web: www.4spe.org/spe-foundation

Gulf Coast Hurricane Scholarships

Type of award: Scholarship.
Intended use: For full-time undergraduate or graduate study at 2-year, 4-year or graduate institution in United States. Designated institutions: Florida, Alabama, Mississippi, Louisiana, Texas institutions.
Eligibility: Applicant must be residing in Texas, Mississippi, Alabama, Louisiana or Florida.
Basis for selection: Major/career interest in chemistry; engineering; engineering, chemical; engineering, materials; engineering, materials or physics. Applicant must demonstrate financial need and high academic achievement.
Application requirements: Recommendations, essay, transcript, proof of eligibility. A listing of employment history, including description of work with plastics/polymers. A list of current and past school activities and community activities and honors.
Additional information: Applicants must have a demonstrated or expressed interest in the plastics industry. Applicants must be majoring in or taking courses that are beneficial to a career in the plastics/polymer industry. One four-year university scholarship of $6,000 (funds distributed on a yearly basis) and one two-year junior or technical institute scholarships of $2,000 (funds distributed on a yearly basis) are available. Applicants must be a resident of, and attending college in, a Gulf Coast State (Florida, Alabama, Mississippi, Louisiana, and Texas).

Amount of award: $2,000-$6,000
Number of awards: 2
Application deadline: March 1
Contact:
Society of Plastics Engineers
13 Church Hill Road
Newtown, CT 06470
Phone: 203-740-5447
Fax: 203-775-8490
Web: www.4spe.org/spe-foundation

K. K. Wang Scholarship

Type of award: Scholarship.
Intended use: For full-time undergraduate or graduate study at 2-year, 4-year or graduate institution.
Basis for selection: Major/career interest in chemistry; engineering; engineering, chemical; engineering, materials; engineering, mechanical or physics. Applicant must demonstrate financial need and high academic achievement.
Application requirements: Recommendations, essay, transcript. A listing of employment history, including description of work in the plastics/polymers industry. A list of current and past school activities, community activities, and honors.
Additional information: Applicants must have a demonstrated or expressed interest in the plastics industry, and must be majoring or taking courses that are beneficial to a career in the plastics/polymer industry. Applicants must have experience in injection molding and computer-aided engineering (CAE), such as courses taken, research conducted, or jobs held.
Amount of award: $2,000
Number of awards: 1
Application deadline: March 1
Total amount awarded: $2,000
Contact:
Society of Plastics Engineers
13 Church Hill Road
Newtown, CT 06470
Phone: 203-740-5447
Fax: 203-775-8490
Web: www.4spe.org/spe-foundation

Pittsburgh Scholarship

Type of award: Scholarship, renewable.
Intended use: For full-time undergraduate or graduate study at 2-year, 4-year or graduate institution.
Eligibility: Applicant must be residing in Pennsylvania.
Basis for selection: Major/career interest in chemistry; engineering, chemical; engineering, mechanical; physics or engineering, industrial. Applicant must demonstrate financial need.
Application requirements: Recommendations, essay, transcript, proof of eligibility. List of current and past school and community activities and honors. List of employment history with detailed description of any involvement in plastics/polymers.
Additional information: All applicants must be in good standing with their colleges and must have a demonstrated or expressed interest in the plastics industry. Plastics engineering and polymer science majors also eligible. Must be resident of one of the following Pennsylvania counties: Allegheny, Armstrong, Beaver, Bedford, Blair, Brooke, Butler, Cambria, Clarion, Clearfield, Fayette, Greene, Hancock, Indiana, Jefferson, Lawrence, Mercer, Somerset, Venango, Washington, or Westmoreland. Visit Website for more information.
Amount of award: $2,000
Number of awards: 2
Application deadline: March 1
Total amount awarded: $4,000
Contact:
Society of Plastics Engineers
13 Church Hill Road
Newtown, CT 06470
Phone: 203-740-5447
Fax: 203-775-8490
Web: www.4spe.org/spe-foundation

Plastics Pioneers Scholarships

Type of award: Scholarship, renewable.
Intended use: For full-time undergraduate study at 2-year or 4-year institution.
Eligibility: Applicant must be U.S. citizen.
Basis for selection: Major/career interest in chemistry; engineering, chemical; engineering, mechanical; physics or engineering, industrial. Applicant must demonstrate financial need.
Application requirements: Recommendations, essay, transcript. List of current and past school activities and community activities and honors. List of employment history with detailed description of any involvement in plastics/polymers.
Additional information: All applicants must be in good standing with their colleges and must have a demonstrated or expressed interest in the plastics industry. Must be committed to becoming "hands-on" worker in the plastics industry as plastics technician or engineer. Plastics engineering and polymer science majors also eligible. Visit Website for more information.
Amount of award: $3,000
Number of awards: 10
Application deadline: March 1
Total amount awarded: $30,000
Contact:
Society of Plastics Engineers
13 Church Hill Road
Newtown, CT 06470
Phone: 203-740-5447
Fax: 203-775-8490
Web: www.4spe.org/spe-foundation

Society of Plastics Engineers General Scholarships

Type of award: Scholarship, renewable.
Intended use: For full-time undergraduate or graduate study at vocational, 2-year, 4-year or graduate institution.
Basis for selection: Major/career interest in chemistry; engineering; engineering, chemical; engineering, mechanical; engineering, materials or physics. Applicant must demonstrate financial need and seriousness of purpose.
Application requirements: Transcript. One- to two-page typed statement explaining reasons for application, qualifications, and educational/career goals in the plastics industry. Three recommendation letters: two from teachers or school officials and one from an employer or non-relative.
Additional information: All applicants must be in good standing with their colleges and must have a demonstrated interest in the plastics industry. Recipients must re-apply for renewal, for up to three additional years. Visit Website for more information.

Amount of award: $1,000-$4,000
Application deadline: March 1
Total amount awarded: $107,500

Contact:
Society of Plastics Engineers
13 Church Hill Road
Newtown, CT 06470
Phone: 203-740-5447
Fax: 203-775-8490
Web: www.4spe.org/spe-foundation

The SPE Foundation Blow Molding Division Memorial Scholarships

Type of award: Scholarship.
Intended use: For junior study at 4-year institution.
Basis for selection: Major/career interest in engineering. Applicant must demonstrate financial need.
Application requirements: Recommendations, transcript. Essay on the importance of blow molding to the technical parts and packing industries.
Additional information: Applicants must be members of a Society of Plastics Engineers Student Chapter and be in second year of four-year undergraduate plastics engineering program. Award is $6,000, payable over two years.

Amount of award: $6,000
Number of awards: 2
Application deadline: March 1
Total amount awarded: $12,000

Contact:
Society of Plastics Engineers
13 Church Hill Road
Newtown, CT 06470
Phone: 203-740-5447
Fax: 203-775-8490
Web: www.4spe.org/spe-foundation

Thermoforming Division Memorial Scholarship

Type of award: Scholarship.
Intended use: For full-time undergraduate or graduate study at vocational, 2-year, 4-year or graduate institution.
Basis for selection: Major/career interest in chemistry; engineering; engineering, chemical; engineering, materials; engineering, mechanical or physics. Applicant must demonstrate financial need.
Application requirements: Transcript. One- to two-page typed statement explaining reasons for application, qualifications, and educational/career goals. Statement detailing exposure to the thermostat industry, including courses, research conducted, or jobs held. Three recommendation letters: two from teachers or school officials, and one from an employer or other non-relative.
Additional information: All applicants must be in good standing and have a demonstrated interest in the plastics industry. Visit Website for more information.

Amount of award: $5,000
Number of awards: 2
Application deadline: March 1
Total amount awarded: $10,000

Contact:
Society of Plastics Engineers
13 Church Hill Road
Newtown, CT 06470
Phone: 203-740-5447
Fax: 203-775-8490
Web: www.4spe.org/spe-foundation

Thermoset Division/James I. MacKenzie Memorial Scholarship

Type of award: Scholarship.
Intended use: For full-time undergraduate or graduate study at vocational, 2-year or 4-year institution.
Basis for selection: Major/career interest in chemistry; engineering; engineering, chemical; engineering, materials; engineering, mechanical or physics. Applicant must demonstrate financial need.
Application requirements: Transcript. One- to two-page typed statement explaining reasons for application, qualifications, and educational/career goals. Statement detailing exposure to the thermoset industry. Three recommendation letters: two from teachers or school officials and one from an employer or non-relative.
Additional information: All applicants must be in good academic standing and have a demonstrated interest in the plastics industry. Must have experience in the thermoset industry, such as courses taken, research conducted, or jobs held. Visit Website for more information.

Amount of award: $2,500
Number of awards: 2
Application deadline: March 1
Total amount awarded: $5,000

Contact:
Society of Plastics Engineers
13 Church Hill Road
Newtown, CT 06470
Phone: 203-740-5447
Fax: 203-775-8490
Web: www.4spe.org/spe-foundation

Western Plastics Pioneers Scholarship

Type of award: Scholarship, renewable.
Intended use: For full-time undergraduate study at 2-year or 4-year institution. Designated institutions: Institutions in Arizona, California, Oregon, or Washington state.
Basis for selection: Major/career interest in chemistry; engineering, chemical; engineering, mechanical; physics or engineering, industrial. Applicant must demonstrate financial need.
Application requirements: Recommendations, essay, transcript. List of current and past school activities and community activities and honors. List of employment history with detailed description of any involvement in plastics/ polymers.
Additional information: All applicants must be in good standing with their colleges and must have a demonstrated or expressed interest in the plastics industry. Plastics engineering and polymer science majors also eligible. Visit Website for more information.

Amount of award: $1,000
Number of awards: 1
Application deadline: March
Total amount awarded: $1,000

Contact:
Society of Plastics Engineers
13 Church Hill Road
Newtown, CT 06470
Phone: 203-740-5447
Fax: 203-775-8490
Web: www.4spe.org/spe-foundation

The Society of the Descendants of the Signers of the Declaration of Independence

The Society of the Descendants of the Signers of the Declaration of Independence Annual Scholarship

Type of award: Scholarship, renewable.
Intended use: For full-time undergraduate or graduate study at accredited vocational, 2-year, 4-year or graduate institution in or outside United States.
Basis for selection: Applicant must demonstrate high academic achievement, depth of character, leadership, patriotism, seriousness of purpose and service orientation.
Application requirements: Recommendations, essay, transcript, proof of eligibility. Resume.
Additional information: Applicant must be member of the Society of the Descendants of the Signers of the Declaration of Independence. Applicant must reapply for renewal. Number and amount of awards vary. See Website for application deadline and more information.

Number of applicants:	56
Application deadline:	February 28
Notification begins:	July 4
Total amount awarded:	$200,000

Contact:
Descendants of the Signers of the Declaration of Independence
Web: www.dsdi1776.com

Society of Women Engineers

SWE Scholarships

Type of award: Scholarship.
Intended use: For full-time undergraduate or graduate study at accredited 4-year or graduate institution in United States.
Eligibility: Applicant or parent must be member/participant of Society of Women Engineers. Applicant must be female. Applicant must be U.S. citizen or permanent resident.
Basis for selection: Major/career interest in engineering or engineering, computer. Applicant must demonstrate high academic achievement.
Application requirements: Recommendations, essay, transcript, proof of eligibility.
Additional information: Must not be receiving full education funding from another organization. Applicants must be enrolled in ABET- or CSAB-accredited program or SWE-approved school. Preference given to computer-related engineering majors. Visit www.abet.org for list of ABET-accredited schools. Visit Website for application. Award amount varies.

Amount of award:	$1,000-$10,000
Number of awards:	198
Application deadline:	February 15, May 15
Notification begins:	September 15
Total amount awarded:	$577,000

Contact:
Society of Women Engineers
Phone: 877-793-4636
Web: www.societyofwomenengineers.swe.org

Sodexo Foundation

Stephen J. Brady STOP Hunger Scholarships

Type of award: Scholarship.
Intended use: For undergraduate, graduate, postgraduate or non-degree study at accredited postsecondary institution in United States.
Eligibility: Applicant must be U.S. citizen or permanent resident.
Basis for selection: Applicant must demonstrate service orientation.
Application requirements: Recommendations.
Additional information: Awards open to applicants who have performed unpaid, U.S. hunger-related volunteer services within the last 12 months. Added consideration for applicants fighting childhood hunger. Employees of Sodexo and previous recipients not eligible to apply, but previous regional STOP Hunger Honorees may apply. Award recipients will receive a $5,000 scholarship and a $5,000 grant to the local hunger-related charity of their choice. Visit Website for application and details.

Amount of award:	$5,000
Number of awards:	5
Number of applicants:	7,000
Application deadline:	December 3
Notification begins:	March 1
Total amount awarded:	$25,000

Contact:
Phone: 800-763-3946 ext. 44848
Web: www.sodexofoundation.org/hunger_us/scholarships/scholarships.asp

Soil and Water Conservation Society

Donald A. Williams Soil Conservation Scholarship

Type of award: Scholarship.
Intended use: For undergraduate study at postsecondary institution.
Eligibility: Applicant or parent must be member/participant of Soil and Water Conservation Society.

Basis for selection: Major/career interest in natural resources/ conservation. Applicant must demonstrate financial need, depth of character and seriousness of purpose.
Application requirements: Recommendations, essay.
Additional information: Applicant must have been member of Soil and Water Conservation Society for at least one year at time of application. Must demonstrate competence in line of work. Must have completed at least one year of full-time employment and be currently employed in a natural resource conservation endeavor. Number of awards varies. Visit Website for application and deadline.

Amount of award:	$1,000
Number of awards:	1

Contact:
SWCS-Scholarship
945 SW Ankeny Road
Ankeny, IA 50023
Phone: 515-289-2331
Fax: 515-289-1227
Web: www.swcs.org

Melville H. Cohee Student Leader Conservation Scholarship

Type of award: Scholarship.
Intended use: For full-time junior, senior or graduate study at accredited 4-year or graduate institution.
Eligibility: Applicant or parent must be member/participant of Soil and Water Conservation Society.
Basis for selection: Major/career interest in natural resources/ conservation.
Additional information: Must have been member of SWCS for at least 1 year. Family members of the Professional Development Committee not eligible. Visit Website for application and deadline.

Amount of award:	$500
Number of awards:	1

Contact:
SWCS-Scholarship
945 SW Ankeny Road
Ankeny, IA 50023
Phone: 515-289-2331
Fax: 515-289-1227
Web: www.swcs.org

Sons of Italy Foundation

Henry Salvatori Scholarship

Type of award: Scholarship.
Intended use: For full-time undergraduate study.
Eligibility: Applicant must be high school senior. Applicant must be Italian. Applicant must be U.S. citizen.
Basis for selection: Applicant must demonstrate high academic achievement, depth of character, leadership, patriotism, seriousness of purpose and service orientation.
Application requirements: $30 application fee. Essay, transcript, proof of eligibility. SAT/ACT scores. Cover letter, resume. Two letters of recommendation from public figures who have demonstrated the ideals of liberty, freedom, and equality in their work.
Additional information: Must have at least one Italian or Italian-American grandparent. Visit Website for application.

Amount of award:	$5,000
Number of awards:	1
Number of applicants:	200
Application deadline:	February 28
Notification begins:	April 15
Total amount awarded:	$5,000

Contact:
Sons of Italy Foundation
219 E Street NE
Washington, DC 20002
Phone: 202-547-2900
Web: www.osia.org

Sant'Anna Institute-Sorrento Lingue Scholarship

Type of award: Scholarship.
Intended use: For junior, senior or graduate study at accredited postsecondary institution outside United States.
Eligibility: Applicant must be Italian. Applicant must be U.S. citizen.
Basis for selection: Major/career interest in Italian.
Application requirements: $30 application fee. Recommendations, essay, transcript. Essay must be submitted in Italian. SAT/ACT scores. Resume, cover letter.
Additional information: Scholarship for study abroad in Sorrento, Italy from January to June. Must have at least one Italian or Italian-American grandparent. Basic knowledge of Italian language preferred. Visit Website for application and more information.

Application deadline:	February 28

Contact:
Sons of Italy Foundation
219 E Street NE
Washington, DC 20002
Phone: 202-547-2900
Web: www.osia.org

Sons of Italy General Scholarship

Type of award: Scholarship.
Intended use: For undergraduate or graduate study at accredited 4-year institution.
Eligibility: Applicant must be Italian. Applicant must be U.S. citizen.
Application requirements: $30 application fee. Recommendations, essay, transcript. Resume, cover letter. SAT/ ACT scores.
Additional information: Must have at least one Italian or Italian-American grandparent. Visit Website for application.

Application deadline:	February 28

Contact:
Sons of Italy Foundation
219 E Street NE
Washington, DC 20002
Phone: 202-547-2900
Web: www.osia.org

Sons of Italy Italian Language Scholarship

Type of award: Scholarship.
Intended use: For junior or senior study.
Eligibility: Applicant must be Italian. Applicant must be U.S. citizen.
Basis for selection: Major/career interest in Italian.

Application requirements: $30 application fee. Recommendations, essay, transcript. Resume, cover letter. SAT/ACT scores. Essay must be in Italian.
Additional information: Must have at least one Italian or Italian-American grandparent. Visit Website for application.

Application deadline:	February 28

Contact:
Sons of Italy Foundation
219 E Street NE
Washington, DC 20002
Phone: 202-547-2900
Web: www.osia.org

Sons of Italy National Leadership Grant

Type of award: Scholarship.
Intended use: For full-time undergraduate, master's, doctoral or first professional study at accredited 4-year or graduate institution in United States.
Eligibility: Applicant must be Italian. Applicant must be U.S. citizen.
Basis for selection: Applicant must demonstrate high academic achievement, depth of character, leadership, seriousness of purpose and service orientation.
Application requirements: $30 application fee. Recommendations, essay, transcript, proof of eligibility. SAT/ACT scores, resume.
Additional information: Must have at least one Italian or Italian-American grandparent. Amount and number of awards vary. Visit Website for application.

Amount of award:	$5,000-$25,000
Number of awards:	12
Number of applicants:	600
Application deadline:	February 28
Notification begins:	April 15

Contact:
Sons of Italy Foundation
219 E Street NE
Washington, DC 20002
Phone: 202-547-2900
Web: www.osia.org

Sons of Norway Foundation

Astrid G. Cates Scholarship Fund and Myrtle Beinhauer Scholarship

Type of award: Scholarship.
Intended use: For undergraduate study at postsecondary institution.
Eligibility: Applicant or parent must be member/participant of Sons of Norway. Applicant must be U.S. citizen.
Basis for selection: Applicant must demonstrate financial need, high academic achievement, depth of character and service orientation.
Application requirements: Recommendations, essay, transcript, proof of eligibility. Headshot.
Additional information: Applicant, parent, or grandparent must be current member of Sons of Norway District 1-6. Student must include the following information with application: GPA, what type of study is intended, where and when. Related fees must be specified, as well as long-term career goals, Sons of Norway involvement, extracurricular activities and financial need. The Cates Scholarship is $1,000; Beinhauer Scholarship awards $3,000 to the most qualified of all candidates. Student can be awarded maximum two scholarships within five-year period. Visit Website for application. Apply online.

Amount of award:	$1,000-$3,000
Number of awards:	8
Number of applicants:	99
Application deadline:	March 1
Notification begins:	May 1

Contact:
Sons of Norway Foundation
Phone: 800-945-8851
Web: www.sonsofnorway.com/foundation

King Olav V Norwegian-American Heritage Fund

Type of award: Scholarship.
Intended use: For full-time undergraduate or graduate study at accredited postsecondary institution in United States.
Eligibility: Applicant or parent must be member/participant of Sons of Norway. Applicant must be at least 18.
Basis for selection: Major/career interest in Scandinavian studies/research. Applicant must demonstrate financial need, high academic achievement, depth of character, leadership and service orientation.
Application requirements: Recommendations, transcript, proof of eligibility. SAT or ACT scores. Essay of maximum 500 words about reasons for application; course of study to be pursued; length of the course; name, tuition, and other costs of institution; amount of financial assistance desired; and how the applicant's course of study will benefit his or her community and accord with the goals and objectives of the Sons of Norway Foundation, headshot.
Additional information: Open to Americans who have demonstrated keen and sincere interest in Norwegian heritage or Norwegians who have demonstrated interest in American heritage and have desire to further study heritage (arts, crafts, literature, history, music, folklore, etc.) at recognized educational institution. Number and amount of awards varies. Visit Website for application.

Amount of award:	$1,000-$1,500
Number of applicants:	100
Application deadline:	March 1
Notification begins:	May 1

Contact:
Sons of Norway Foundation
Phone: 800-945-8851
Web: www.sonsofnorway.com/foundation

Nancy Lorraine Jensen Memorial Scholarship

Type of award: Scholarship, renewable.
Intended use: For full-time undergraduate study.
Eligibility: Applicant or parent must be member/participant of Sons of Norway. Applicant must be female, at least 17, no older than 35. Applicant must be U.S. citizen.
Basis for selection: Major/career interest in chemistry; physics; engineering, electrical/electronic; engineering, mechanical or engineering, chemical. Applicant must demonstrate high academic achievement, depth of character and seriousness of purpose.
Application requirements: Recommendations, essay, transcript, proof of eligibility. SAT/ACT scores, headshot.

Scholarships

Additional information: Applicant or applicant's parent or grandparent must have been a member of Sons of Norway for at least three years. Must have completed at least one semester of undergraduate study in current program. Award is no less than 50 percent of one semester's tuition and no more than full tuition for one year. Minimum 1800 SAT (or at least 600 Math) or 26 ACT. Must apply each year. Visit Website for application. Apply online.

Number of awards: 6
Application deadline: April 1

Contact:
Sons of Norway Foundation
Phone: 800-945-8851
Web: www.sonsofnorway.com/foundation

Sons of the Republic of Texas

Texas History Essay Contest

Type of award: Scholarship.
Intended use: For freshman study at 4-year institution.
Eligibility: Applicant must be high school senior.
Basis for selection: Competition/talent/interest in research paper, based on depth of research in Texas history, originality of thought and expression, and organization.
Application requirements: Four photocopies of essay (total of 5 copies) including a CD copy with contestant's name, address, phone number and year of contest.
Additional information: Graduating seniors of any high school or home school may enter. Must follow Chicago Manual of Style or Turabian's Manual for Writers. Visit Website for yearly topic and more information.

Amount of award: $1,000-$3,000
Number of awards: 3
Application deadline: January 31
Total amount awarded: $6,000

Contact:
Sons of the Republic of Texas
1717 8th Street
Bay City, TX 77414
Phone: 979-245-6644
Web: www.srttexas.org

South Carolina Commission on Higher Education

Palmetto Fellows Scholarship Program

Type of award: Scholarship, renewable.
Intended use: For full-time undergraduate study at 4-year institution. Designated institutions: Eligible South Carolina institutions.
Eligibility: Applicant must be high school senior. Applicant must be U.S. citizen or permanent resident residing in South Carolina.
Basis for selection: Applicant must demonstrate high academic achievement.
Application requirements: Transcript. ACT/SAT scores. Must apply through guidance counselor.
Additional information: Minimum 1200 SAT (Math and Reading) or 27 ACT, 3.5 GPA on the SC Uniform Grading Policy, and rank in top six percent of class. Class ranking requirement waived for students with 1400 SAT (Math and Reading) or 32 ACT and 4.0 GPA. High school graduates or students who have completed home-school program as prescribed by law may be eligible. For more information, contact guidance counselor or S.C. Commission.

Amount of award: $6,700-$7,500
Application deadline: December 15, June 15
Notification begins: February 15, August 15
Total amount awarded: $44,035,892

Contact:
South Carolina Commission on Higher Education
1122 Lady Street, Suite 300
Columbia, SC 29201
Phone: 877-349-7183 or 803-787-2286
Fax: 803-737-2297
Web: www.che.sc.gov

South Carolina Dayco Scholarship Program

Type of award: Scholarship, renewable.
Intended use: For full-time freshman study at 4-year institution in United States. Designated institutions: South Carolina institutions.
Eligibility: Applicant must be high school senior. Applicant must be U.S. citizen or permanent resident residing in South Carolina.
Basis for selection: Applicant must demonstrate financial need and high academic achievement.
Application requirements: Transcript, proof of eligibility. Need analysis, affidavit documenting that student has never been convicted of felonies or alcohol- or drug-related misdemeanor offenses.
Additional information: Must be either an employee or dependent of an employee of a branch of Dayco Products, Inc. in South Carolina. Employee must be employed by Dayco for at least four calendar years. In the event that there are no eligible dependents meeting above criteria, the award will be given to a resident of one of the counties of Walterboro, Williston, or Easley. Minimum 3.25 GPA. Must rank in top 20% of graduating high school class. Must have completed 12 credit hours at time of scholarship disbursement. Must not owe refund or repayment to a grant program or be under default on a loan. Must not have criminal record. Must reapply and meet eligibility requirements annually. Amount of award varies.

Contact:
South Carolina Commission on Higher Education
1122 Lady Street, Suite 300
Columbia, SC 29201
Phone: 803-737-2260
Fax: 803-737-2297
Web: www.che.sc.gov

South Carolina HOPE Scholarships

Type of award: Scholarship.
Intended use: For freshman study at 4-year institution. Designated institutions: Eligible South Carolina institutions.
Eligibility: Applicant must be U.S. citizen or permanent resident residing in South Carolina.
Basis for selection: Applicant must demonstrate high academic achievement.
Application requirements: Transcript, proof of eligibility.

Additional information: No application necessary. College or university will determine eligibility based on official high school transcript and will notify students directly. Minimum 3.0 cumulative GPA upon high school graduation. Student must certify that he/she has not been convicted of any felonies or any second drug/alcohol misdemeanors within past academic year. Contact institution's financial aid office for more information.

Amount of award:	$2,800
Number of awards:	2,724
Total amount awarded:	$7,037,260

Contact:
South Carolina Commission on Higher Education
1122 Lady Street, Suite 300
Columbia, SC 29201
Phone: 803-737-2260
Fax: 803-737-2297
Web: www.che.sc.gov

South Carolina LIFE Scholarship Program

Type of award: Scholarship, renewable.
Intended use: For full-time freshman study at vocational, 2-year or 4-year institution. Designated institutions: Eligible institutions in South Carolina.
Eligibility: Applicant must be U.S. citizen or permanent resident residing in South Carolina.
Basis for selection: Applicant must demonstrate high academic achievement.
Application requirements: Transcript. SAT/ACT scores.
Additional information: First-time entering freshmen at four-year institutions must meet two of three criteria: 3.0 high school GPA on Uniform Grading Policy (UGP); minimum 1100 SAT or 24 ACT; rank in top 30 percent of graduating class. First-time entering freshmen at two-year institution must have 3.0 high school GPA on UGP. Applicant must graduate from high school as South Carolina resident. No application required; college/university will determine eligibility based on transcript and will notify student directly. Maximum award $5,000 for four-year schools, average in-state tuition for two-year schools, and up to full in-state tuition at technical schools, not to exceed $5,000. Students in approved math and science programs could earn an additional $2,500.

Amount of award:	$5,000
Number of awards:	31,004
Total amount awarded:	$150,595,333

Contact:
South Carolina Commission on Higher Education
1122 Lady Street, Suite 300
Columbia, SC 29201
Phone: 803-737-2260
Fax: 803-737-2297
Web: www.che.sc.gov

South Carolina Lottery Tuition Assistance Program

Type of award: Scholarship, renewable.
Intended use: For undergraduate study at vocational or 2-year institution. Designated institutions: Eligible South Carolina institutions.
Eligibility: Applicant must be U.S. citizen or permanent resident residing in South Carolina.
Application requirements: FAFSA or FAFSA waiver.
Additional information: Award may not exceed cost of tuition. Award based on lottery revenue and number of applicants. Amount varies by semester. All federal grants and need-based grants must be awarded first before determining amount for which student is eligible. Student must be degree-seeking and enrolled in minimum six credit hours. Visit Website for more information.

Number of awards:	45,628
Number of applicants:	59,486
Total amount awarded:	$47,641,997

Contact:
South Carolina Commission on Higher Education
1122 Lady Street, Suite 300
Columbia, SC 29201
Phone: 803-737-2262
Fax: 803-737-2297
Web: www.che.sc.gov

South Carolina Need-Based Grants Program

Type of award: Scholarship.
Intended use: For undergraduate study at vocational, 2-year or 4-year institution. Designated institutions: Eligible South Carolina public institutions.
Eligibility: Applicant must be U.S. citizen or permanent resident residing in South Carolina.
Basis for selection: Applicant must demonstrate financial need.
Application requirements: FAFSA.
Additional information: May receive award for maximum eight full-time equivalent terms or until degree is earned, whichever is less. Must enroll in at least 12 credit hours per semester if full-time or six if part-time. Visit Website for more information.

Amount of award:	$1,250-$2,500
Number of awards:	28,051
Number of applicants:	28,507
Total amount awarded:	$26,989,583

Contact:
South Carolina Commission on Higher Education
1122 Lady Street, Suite 300
Columbia, SC 29201
Phone: 803-737-2262
Fax: 803-737-2297
Web: www.che.sc.gov

South Carolina Higher Education Tuition Grants Commission

South Carolina Tuition Grants

Type of award: Scholarship, renewable.
Intended use: For full-time undergraduate study at accredited 2-year or 4-year institution in United States. Designated institutions: Participating South Carolina private, nonprofit institutions (visit Website for list).
Eligibility: Applicant must be U.S. citizen residing in South Carolina.
Basis for selection: Applicant must demonstrate financial need and high academic achievement.
Application requirements: FAFSA.
Additional information: Award amount varies. Recipient may reapply for up to four years. Incoming freshmen must score

Scholarships

900 SAT (Math and Reading) or 19 ACT, graduate in top three-fourths of high school class, or graduate from South Carolina high school with 2.0 GPA. Upperclassmen must complete 24 semester hours and meet college's satisfactory progress requirements. Application is automatic with FAFSA; submit to federal processor and list eligible college in college choice section. All eligible applicants funded if deadline is met. Contact campus financial aid office for details.

Amount of award:	$2,550-$2,800
Number of awards:	14,200
Number of applicants:	27,206
Application deadline:	June 30
Total amount awarded:	$37,948,782

Contact:
South Carolina Higher Education Tuition Grants Commission
800 Dutch Square Blvd., Suite 260A
Columbia, SC 29210-7317
Phone: 803-896-1120
Fax: 803-896-1126
Web: www.sctuitiongrants.com

Scholarships

South Dakota Board of Regents

Dakota Corps Scholarship Program

Type of award: Scholarship.
Intended use: For freshman study at 4-year institution in United States. Designated institutions: Participating South Dakota institutions.
Eligibility: Applicant must be U.S. citizen or permanent resident.
Basis for selection: Applicant must demonstrate high academic achievement and service orientation.
Application requirements: Essay. Certification from high school counselor, principal, or other official.
Additional information: Must have graduated from accredited South Dakota high school with minimum 2.8 GPA. Minimum ACT score of 24 or SAT equivalent. Must agree in writing to stay in South Dakota and work in a critical need occupation after graduation for as many years as the scholarship was received plus one year. Must apply for Dakota Corps Scholarship for school period that begins within one year of high school graduation or within one year of release from active duty in armed forces.

Application deadline:	February 1

Contact:
South Dakota Board of Regents
Attn: Dakota Corps Scholarship Program
306 East Capitol Ave., Suite 200
Pierre, SD 57501
Phone: 800-874-9033
Web: www.sdbor.edu

Jump Start Scholarship Program

Type of award: Scholarship.
Intended use: For at postsecondary institution in United States. Designated institutions: Participating South Dakota institutions.
Eligibility: Applicant must be U.S. citizen residing in South Dakota.
Additional information: Award is for South Dakota students who meet high school graduation requirements in three years. Must have attended public high school full-time for at least two years, and must attend postsecondary institution within one year of high school graduation. All students that meet criteria are awarded.

Amount of award:	$1,812
Application deadline:	September 1
Total amount awarded:	$17,713

Contact:
South Dakota Board of Regents
306 E. Capitol Ave., Suite 200
Pierre, SD 57501-2545
Web: www.sdbor.edu

South Dakota Annis I. Fowler/ Kaden Scholarship

Type of award: Scholarship.
Intended use: For freshman study at postsecondary institution. Designated institutions: University of South Dakota, Black Hills State University, Dakota State University, and Northern State University.
Eligibility: Applicant must be high school senior. Applicant must be U.S. citizen residing in South Dakota.
Basis for selection: Major/career interest in education, early childhood. Applicant must demonstrate high academic achievement, depth of character, leadership, seriousness of purpose and service orientation.
Application requirements: Recommendations, essay, transcript, proof of eligibility. ACT scores.
Additional information: Open to high school seniors who have a cumulative GPA of 3.0 after three years. Applicants must select elementary education as major field. Special consideration given to applicants with demonstrated motivation or disability, or who are self-supporting. Transcript must include class rank, cumulative GPA, and list of courses to be taken during senior year. Deadline in late February.

Amount of award:	$1,000
Number of awards:	2
Number of applicants:	30
Notification begins:	April 15

Contact:
South Dakota Board of Regents
Scholarship Committee
306 E. Capitol Avenue, Suite 200
Pierre, SD 57501-3159
Phone: 605-773-3455
Web: www.sdbor.edu

South Dakota Ardell Bjugstad Scholarship

Type of award: Scholarship.
Intended use: For freshman study at postsecondary institution in United States.
Eligibility: Applicant must be American Indian. Must be member of federally recognized Indian tribe whose reservation is in North Dakota or South Dakota. Applicant must be high school senior. Applicant must be U.S. citizen residing in South Dakota or North Dakota.
Basis for selection: Major/career interest in agribusiness; agriculture; natural resources/conservation or environmental science. Applicant must demonstrate high academic achievement, depth of character, leadership and seriousness of purpose.
Application requirements: Recommendations, transcript. Verification of tribal enrollment.

Additional information: Transcript must include class rank and cumulative GPA.

Amount of award:	$500
Number of awards:	1
Number of applicants:	3
Notification begins:	April 15

Contact:
South Dakota Board of Regents
Scholarship Committee
306 E. Capitol Avenue, Suite 200
Pierre, SD 57501-3159
Phone: 605-773-3455
Web: www.sdbor.edu

South Dakota Haines Memorial Scholarship

Type of award: Scholarship.
Intended use: For full-time sophomore, junior or senior study at accredited 4-year institution in United States. Designated institutions: University of South Dakota, Black Hills State University, Dakota State University, Northern State University, South Dakota State University.
Eligibility: Applicant must be residing in South Dakota.
Basis for selection: Major/career interest in education; education, early childhood; education, special or education, teacher. Applicant must demonstrate high academic achievement, depth of character, leadership, seriousness of purpose and service orientation.
Application requirements: Proof of eligibility. Resume. Two two-page essays: one describing personal philosophy and another describing philosophy of education.
Additional information: Minimum 3.5 college GPA. Deadline in late February.

Amount of award:	$2,150
Number of awards:	1
Number of applicants:	20
Notification begins:	April 15

Contact:
South Dakota Board of Regents Scholarship Committee
306 E. Capitol, Suite 200
Pierre, SD 57501-3159
Phone: 605-773-3455
Web: www.sdbor.edu

South Dakota Marlin R. Scarborough Memorial Scholarship

Type of award: Scholarship.
Intended use: For full-time junior study at accredited 4-year institution in United States. Designated institutions: Public institutions in South Dakota.
Eligibility: Applicant must be residing in South Dakota.
Basis for selection: Applicant must demonstrate high academic achievement, depth of character, leadership, seriousness of purpose and service orientation.
Application requirements: Nomination by participating South Dakota public university. Essay explaining leadership and academic qualities, career plans, and educational interests.
Additional information: Students at all public universities in South Dakota eligible to apply. Applicants are to be of junior standing at public university in South Dakota when they receive funding. Submit application to school financial aid office. Minimum 3.5 GPA. Must have completed three full semesters at same university. Each South Dakota public university may nominate one student. Application deadlines vary by university; visit Website for dates and application.

Amount of award:	$1,500
Number of awards:	1
Notification begins:	April 15

Contact:
South Dakota Board of Regents Scholarship Committee
306 East Capitol, Suite 200
Pierre, SD 57501-3159
Phone: 605-773-3455
Web: www.sdbor.edu

South Dakota Opportunity Scholarship Program

Type of award: Scholarship.
Intended use: For undergraduate study at accredited vocational, 2-year or 4-year institution in United States. Designated institutions: Augustana College, Colorado Technical University, Dakota Wesleyan University, Lake Area Technical Institute, Mitchell Technical Institute, Northern State University, South Dakota School of Mines & Technology, Southeast Technical Institute, University of Sioux Falls, Black Hills State University, Dakota State University, Kilian Community College, Mount Mary College, National American University, Presentation College, South Dakota State University, University of South Dakota, Western Dakota Technical Institute.
Eligibility: Applicant must be U.S. citizen or permanent resident residing in South Dakota.
Basis for selection: Applicant must demonstrate high academic achievement.
Application requirements: Transcript. SAT/ACT scores.
Additional information: Award is distributed bi-annually over four academic years. Minimum 1090 SAT (Verbal and Math) and 24 ACT. Minimum 3.0 GPA. See Website for specific high school curriculum requirements, which must be completed with no final grade below a 2.0. Completed applications must be submitted directly to the institution to which applicant is applying. Visit Website for detailed credit hour requirements.

Amount of award:	$5,000
Number of applicants:	3,975
Application deadline:	September 1, January 15
Total amount awarded:	$4,000,000

Contact:
South Dakota Board of Regents c/o Dr. Paul D. Turman
306 E. Capitol Ave., Suite 200
Pierre, SD 57501-2545
Phone: 605-773-3455
Web: www.sdbor.edu

Southern Regional Education Board

Academic Common Market

Type of award: Scholarship.
Intended use: For undergraduate, master's, doctoral or first professional study at accredited 2-year, 4-year or graduate institution in United States. Designated institutions: Participating institutions in Alabama, Arkansas, Delaware, Georgia, Kentucky, Louisiana, Maryland, Mississippi, Oklahoma, South Carolina, Tennessee, Virginia, West Virginia.
Application requirements: Proof of eligibility.
Additional information: The Academic Common Market is a tuition-savings program for college students in the SREB

member states who want to pursue degrees that are not offered by their in-state institutions. The program is not competitive or merit-based, but applicants must meet state residency and college program requirements. For list of participating institutions and programs, and for individual state contact information, visit Website.
Contact:
Phone: 404-875-9211 ext. 261
Web: www.sreb.org/page/1304/academic_common_market.html

Southern Scholarship Foundation

Southern Scholarship Foundation Scholarships

Type of award: Scholarship, renewable.
Intended use: For undergraduate or graduate study in United States. Designated institutions: Florida State University, Florida A&M, University of Florida, Florida Gulf Coast University.
Basis for selection: Applicant must demonstrate financial need, high academic achievement, depth of character and service orientation.
Application requirements: Interview, recommendations, essay, transcript, proof of eligibility. Resume, FAFSA, SAR, recent color photograph.
Additional information: Number of awards varies. Minimum 3.0 GPA. Applicants encouraged to submit early in spring and fall semesters. Applications accepted year-round. Graduating high school students and students currently attending community college and universities are eligible to apply. Awards given in the form of housing at one of 26 Florida-based scholarship houses. The rent-free scholarship housing is equal to $7,000 to $10,000 per year. Awardees do not pay rent, but are responsible for basic household expenses. Each student contributes approximately $950/semester. Florida Gulf Coast University awards are for females only.

Number of awards:	80
Number of applicants:	500
Application deadline:	March 1, October 31

Contact:
Southern Scholarship Foundation
Attn: Barby Moro
322 Stadium Drive
Tallahassee, FL 32304
Phone: 850-222-3833
Fax: 850-222-6750
Web: www.southernscholarship.org

SPIE - The International Society for Optical Engineering

SPIE Optics and Photonics Education Scholarships

Type of award: Scholarship, renewable.
Intended use: For undergraduate, graduate or non-degree study at accredited postsecondary institution in or outside United States.
Basis for selection: Major/career interest in engineering or physics. Applicant must demonstrate seriousness of purpose.
Application requirements: Recommendations, essay.
Additional information: Open only to SPIE student members; nonmembers may submit SPIE student membership application and dues with scholarship application. High school and pre-university students may receive one-year complimentary membership. Applicant must be enrolled in optics, photonics, imaging, optoelectronics, or related program at accredited institution for year in which award will be used (unless high school student). Award amount and number of awards varies. Students must reapply for renewal. Visit Website for application and deadline.

Amount of award:	$2,000-$11,000
Number of applicants:	360
Application deadline:	February 15
Notification begins:	May 1

Contact:
SPIE Scholarship Committee
Web: www.spie.org/scholarships

Staples

Staples Associates Annual Scholarships Plan

Type of award: Scholarship, renewable.
Intended use: For undergraduate, graduate or non-degree study at vocational, 2-year, 4-year or graduate institution.
Application requirements: Proof of eligibility.
Additional information: Applicants must have worked at Staples for 90 days, averaging at least 18 hours per week. Contact Human Resources for complete details and application. Number of awards granted depends on funding.

Amount of award:	$750-$2,000
Number of applicants:	3,000
Application deadline:	September 30
Notification begins:	November 15
Total amount awarded:	$2,500,000

Contact:
Staples
500 Staples Drive
Framingham, MA 01702
Phone: 888-490-4747

State Council of Higher Education for Virginia

Virginia Academic Common Market

Type of award: Scholarship.
Intended use: For full-time undergraduate or graduate study at 4-year or graduate institution. Designated institutions: Participating public institutions in 15 southeastern states.
Eligibility: Applicant must be U.S. citizen or permanent resident residing in Virginia.
Application requirements: Institution acceptance letter, verification documents.
Additional information: Awards Virginia residents in-state tuition at participating out-of-state institutions in the South.

Institution must offer program unavailable at Virginia public institutions. Applicant must be domiciled in Virginia. Deadlines vary by institution.

Contact:
State Council of Higher Education for Virginia
Academic Common Market
101 N 14th Street, 10th Fl. Monroe Bldg.
Richmond, VA 23219
Phone: 804-225-2620
Fax: 804-225-2604
Web: www.schev.edu/students/AcademicCommonMkt.asp

Virginia Tuition Assistance Grant

Type of award: Scholarship, renewable.
Intended use: For full-time undergraduate, master's, doctoral or first professional study at accredited 4-year or graduate institution. Designated institutions: Participating private nonprofit institutions in Virginia.
Eligibility: Applicant must be residing in Virginia.
Basis for selection: Major/career interest in health-related professions.
Additional information: Must be in eligible degree program in participating Virginia private college. Graduate students must be enrolled in health-related major. Applicant must be domiciled in Virginia. Theology and divinity majors not eligible. Maximum award is $3200 for undergraduates. Awards depend on available funding. If funding is insufficient, priority given first to renewals, then to new applicants who apply prior to deadline. Interested students should contact financial aid office of qualifying postsecondary institution.

Amount of award:	$1,300-$2,800
Number of awards:	21,000
Application deadline:	July 31
Total amount awarded:	$60,000,000

Contact:
Contact representative at participating private institutions.
Web: www.schev.edu/forms/TAGApplication1314.pdf

State of Alabama

Alabama Scholarship for Dependents of Blind Parents

Type of award: Scholarship, renewable.
Intended use: For undergraduate study at vocational, 2-year or 4-year institution. Designated institutions: Alabama public institutions.
Eligibility: Parent must be visually impaired. Applicant must be U.S. citizen or permanent resident residing in Alabama.
Basis for selection: Applicant must demonstrate financial need.
Application requirements: Proof of eligibility.
Additional information: Award waives instructional fees and tuition costs and pays for portion of books. Parent must be head of household and legally blind, and family income must be at or below 1.3 times the federal poverty guidelines. Applicant must have been Alabama resident for five years prior to application. Must reapply for renewal. Award available for all eligible applicants.

Amount of award:	Full tuition
Application deadline:	June 30, September 30

Contact:
Alabama Department of Rehabilitation Services
Attn: Debra Culver
4 Medical Office Park
Talladega, AL 35160
Phone: 256-362-0638

State Student Assistance Commission of Indiana

Frank O'Bannon Grant

Type of award: Scholarship, renewable.
Intended use: For full-time undergraduate study at 2-year or 4-year institution. Designated institutions: Eligible Indiana schools.
Eligibility: Applicant must be U.S. citizen or permanent resident residing in Indiana.
Basis for selection: Applicant must demonstrate financial need.
Application requirements: FAFSA.
Additional information: Submitting FAFSA automatically fulfills application requirement. All eligible students offered an award. Amount of award varies. Visit Website for list of eligible schools.

Number of awards:	50,000
Number of applicants:	54,554
Application deadline:	March 10
Notification begins:	July 1
Total amount awarded:	$196,838,902

Contact:
State Student Assistance Commission of Indiana
W462 Indiana Government Center South
402 West Washington Street
Indianapolis, IN 46204
Phone: 888-528-4719
Web: www.in.gov/ssaci

Indiana Minority Teacher & Special Education Services Scholarship

Type of award: Scholarship, renewable.
Intended use: For full-time undergraduate or graduate study at accredited 4-year or graduate institution.
Eligibility: Applicant must be African American, Mexican American, Hispanic American or Puerto Rican. Applicant must be U.S. citizen or permanent resident residing in Indiana.
Basis for selection: Major/career interest in education; education, special; occupational therapy or physical therapy. Applicant must demonstrate financial need and high academic achievement.
Application requirements: Proof of eligibility. FAFSA.
Additional information: Minimum 2.0 GPA. Applicant must be black or Hispanic, unless applicant is entering field of special education, or occupational/physical therapy. Graduate students must be seeking a teaching certificate. Number of awards varies. Application deadline established by school. Schools responsible for selecting and notifying eligible applicants. Applications available online. Contact college financial aid office for more information.

Amount of award:	$1,000-$4,000
Number of applicants:	214
Total amount awarded:	$240,000

Contact:
State Student Assistance Commission of Indiana
Phone: 317-232-2350
Web: www.in.gov/ssaci

Indiana National Guard Supplemental Grant

Type of award: Scholarship, renewable.
Intended use: For undergraduate study at 2-year or 4-year institution. Designated institutions: Indiana state-funded colleges and universities.
Eligibility: Applicant must be residing in Indiana. Applicant must be member of Indiana Air and Army National Guard. Applicant must be in active drilling status and be certified by Indiana National Guard (ING).
Application requirements: FAFSA.
Additional information: Room, board, and textbooks not covered. Contact unit commander with eligibility and certification questions.

Amount of award:	Full tuition
Number of applicants:	726
Application deadline:	March 10
Notification begins:	September 1
Total amount awarded:	$2,509,489

Contact:
State Student Assistance Commission of Indiana
W462 Indiana Government Center
402 West Washington Street
Indianapolis, IN 46204
Phone: 888-528-4719
Web: www.in.gov/ssaci

Indiana Nursing Scholarship

Type of award: Scholarship, renewable.
Intended use: For undergraduate study at accredited vocational, 2-year or 4-year institution. Designated institutions: Eligible Indiana schools.
Eligibility: Applicant must be U.S. citizen residing in Indiana.
Basis for selection: Major/career interest in nursing. Applicant must demonstrate financial need and high academic achievement.
Application requirements: Proof of eligibility. FAFSA.
Additional information: Minimum 2.0 GPA. Must be admitted to eligible Indiana school. Must commit to work two years as nurse in specific Indiana health care settings. Application available online. Schools select eligible recipients. Number of awards varies. Deadline varies by institution.

Amount of award:	$50-$5,000
Number of applicants:	330
Total amount awarded:	$224,661

Contact:
State Student Assistance Commission of Indiana
Phone: 317-232-2355
Web: www.in.gov/ssaci

Indiana Twenty-First Century Scholars Program

Type of award: Scholarship.
Intended use: For full-time undergraduate study at accredited 2-year or 4-year institution. Designated institutions: Participating Indiana schools.
Eligibility: Applicant must be high school senior. Applicant must be U.S. citizen or permanent resident residing in Indiana.
Basis for selection: Applicant must demonstrate financial need and high academic achievement.
Application requirements: FAFSA.
Additional information: Minimum 2.0 high school GPA. Must enroll in 7th or 8th grade by taking pledge to remain drug, alcohol, and crime free. Must file affirmation that pledge was fulfilled in high school senior year. Full tuition waiver after other financial aid applied. Must meet income eligibility requirements. Number and amount of awards varies. Visit Website for details.

Number of awards:	9,875
Number of applicants:	9,875
Notification begins:	July 1
Total amount awarded:	$22,787,104

Contact:
State Student Assistance Commission of Indiana
Web: www.in.gov/ssaci

The Mitch Daniels Early Graduation Scholarship

Type of award: Scholarship.
Intended use: For freshman study at 4-year institution in United States. Designated institutions: SSACI-eligible Indiana colleges.
Eligibility: Applicant must be U.S. citizen residing in Indiana.
Application requirements: FAFSA. Application must be signed by principal or superintendent.
Additional information: Must graduate one year early from a publicly supported high school, after December 31, 2010. Must have attended publicly supported high school full-time for at least the last two semesters before graduating. See Website for additional criteria.

Amount of award:	$4,000

Contact:
State Student Assistance Commission of Indiana
Attn: Mitch Daniels Early Graduation
402 W. Washington Street W462
Indianapolis, IN 46204
Phone: 317-232-2350
Fax: 317-232-3260
Web: www.in.gov/ssaci

Stephen T. Marchello Scholarship Foundation

Legacy of Hope

Type of award: Scholarship.
Intended use: For undergraduate study at accredited vocational, 2-year or 4-year institution in United States.
Eligibility: Applicant must be high school senior. Applicant must be U.S. citizen residing in Montana or Colorado.
Application requirements: Interview, recommendations, essay, transcript, proof of eligibility. SAT/ACT scores (when available).
Additional information: Some awards renewable depending on fund availability; all others are one-time grants. Applicant must be survivor of childhood cancer. Visit Website for more information. Application available online. Number and amount of awards vary.

Amount of award: $400-$1,500
Number of awards: 6
Number of applicants: 20
Application deadline: March 15
Total amount awarded: $9,500

Contact:
Stephen T. Marchello Scholarship Foundation
1170 East Long Place
Centennial, CO 80122
Phone: 303-886-5018
Web: www.stmfoundation.org

Studio Art Centers International

Anna K. Meredith Fund Scholarship

Type of award: Scholarship.
Intended use: For undergraduate study in Florence, Italy. Designated institutions: Studio Art Centers International (SACI).
Basis for selection: Competition/talent/interest in study abroad. Major/career interest in arts, general or art/art history. Applicant must demonstrate financial need and high academic achievement.
Application requirements: Portfolio. SAR/FAFSA.
Additional information: Must demonstrate artistic talent. Must be accepted to study with Studio Art Centers International. Number of awards varies depending on budget.

Amount of award: $2,000
Application deadline: March 15, October 15
Notification begins: April 15, November 15

Contact:
Studio Art Centers International
50 Broad Street
Suite 1617
New York, NY 10004-2372
Phone: 212-248-7225
Web: www.saci-florence.org

Clare Brett Smith Scholarship

Type of award: Scholarship.
Intended use: For undergraduate or graduate study in Florence, Italy. Designated institutions: Studio Art Centers International (SACI).
Basis for selection: Competition/talent/interest in study abroad. Major/career interest in arts, general. Applicant must demonstrate financial need.
Application requirements: Portfolio. SAR/FAFSA.
Additional information: Must be accepted to study with Studio Art Centers International. Applicant must be studying photography.

Amount of award: $1,000
Number of awards: 2
Application deadline: March 15, October 15
Notification begins: April 15, November 15

Contact:
Studio Art Centers International
50 Broad Street
Suite 1617
New York, NY 10004-2372
Phone: 212-248-7225
Web: www.saci-florence.org

Elizabeth A. Sackler Museum Educational Trust

Type of award: Scholarship.
Intended use: For undergraduate study in Florence, Italy. Designated institutions: Studio Art Centers International (SACI).
Eligibility: Applicant must be female.
Basis for selection: Major/career interest in arts, general or art/art history. Applicant must demonstrate financial need and high academic achievement.
Application requirements: Portfolio, recommendations. FAFSA/SAR, statement of intent.
Additional information: Must be accepted to study with Studio Art Centers International. Must attend SACI for one full academic year. Must exhibit exceptional artistic talent in painting, drawing, printmaking, sculpture, ceramics, photography, art history, or art conservation. Must maintain a 3.0 to retain scholarship in the spring. Visit Website for application and more information.

Amount of award: $7,500
Number of awards: 1
Application deadline: March 15
Notification begins: May 1
Total amount awarded: $15,000

Contact:
Studio Art Centers International
50 Broad Street
Suite 1617
New York, NY 10004-2372
Phone: 212-248-7225
Web: www.saci-florence.org

Florence Travel Stipend

Type of award: Scholarship.
Intended use: For undergraduate study. Designated institutions: Studio Art Centers International (SACI) institutions.
Basis for selection: Major/career interest in arts, general or art/art history.
Application requirements: $60 application fee. Portfolio. FAFSA.
Additional information: Award is two free roundtrip tickets to SACI Florence, Italy. Must be attending SACI in the spring term. Valid only on SACI's spring term group flight from New York.

Number of awards: 2
Application deadline: October 15

Contact:
Studio Art Centers International
50 Broad Street
Suite 1617
New York, NY 10004-2372
Phone: 212-248-7225
Web: www.saci-florence.org

The Gillian Award

Type of award: Scholarship.
Intended use: For undergraduate study. Designated institutions: Studio Art Centers International (SACI).
Eligibility: Applicant must be female.
Basis for selection: Major/career interest in arts, general.
Application requirements: $60 application fee. Portfolio. FAFSA.
Additional information: Award is open to a female artist with demonstrated artistic achievement who will be attending in both fall and spring terms. Award offers opportunity for

aspiring fine artist to live and work in Florence, utilizing all the resources of SACI.

Amount of award: $3,000
Number of awards: 1
Application deadline: March 15, October 15

Contact:
Studio Art Centers International
50 Broad Street
Suite 1617
New York, NY 10004-2372
Phone: 212-248-7225
Web: www.saci-florence.org

International Incentive Awards

Type of award: Scholarship.
Intended use: For junior or senior study in Florence, Italy. Designated institutions: Studio Art Centers International (SACI).
Basis for selection: Competition/talent/interest in study abroad. Major/career interest in arts, general or art/art history. Applicant must demonstrate financial need and high academic achievement.
Application requirements: Portfolio. SAR/FAFSA.
Additional information: Must be accepted to study with Studio Art Centers International. Minimum 3.0 GPA. Special efforts made to encourage applications from minorities and underrepresented groups. Number of awards varies depending on budget.

Amount of award: $1,500
Application deadline: March 15, October 15
Notification begins: April 15, November 15

Contact:
Studio Art Centers International
50 Broad Street
Suite 1617
New York, NY 10004-2372
Phone: 212-248-7225
Web: www.saci-florence.org

Jules Maidoff Scholarship

Type of award: Scholarship.
Intended use: For undergraduate or graduate study in Florence, Italy. Designated institutions: Studio Art Centers International (SACI).
Basis for selection: Competition/talent/interest in study abroad. Major/career interest in arts, general or art/art history. Applicant must demonstrate financial need.
Application requirements: Portfolio. FAFSA/SAR.
Additional information: Must be accepted to study with Studio Art Centers International. Awarded to students exhibiting both exceptional artistic talent and financial need. Number of awards varies depending on budget.

Amount of award: $2,500
Application deadline: March 15, October 15
Notification begins: April 15, November 15

Contact:
Studio Art Centers International
50 Broad Street
Suite 1617
New York, NY 10004-2372
Phone: 212-248-7225
Web: www.saci-florence.org

Lele Cassin Scholarship

Type of award: Scholarship.
Intended use: For undergraduate or graduate study in Florence, Italy. Designated institutions: Studio Art Centers International (SACI).
Basis for selection: Competition/talent/interest in study abroad. Major/career interest in film/video. Applicant must demonstrate financial need.
Application requirements: Video (no longer than 15 minutes) of own work. SAR/FAFSA.
Additional information: Must be accepted to study with Studio Art Centers International. Number of awards offered varies yearly according to budget.

Amount of award: $1,000
Application deadline: March 15, October 15
Notification begins: April 15, November 15

Contact:
Studio Art Centers International
50 Broad Street
Suite 1617
New York, NY 10004-2372
Phone: 212-248-7225
Web: www.saci-florence.org

SACI Alumni Heritage Scholarship

Type of award: Scholarship.
Intended use: For undergraduate or graduate study at postsecondary institution in Florence, Italy. Designated institutions: Studio Art Centers International (SACI).
Basis for selection: Major/career interest in arts, general or art/art history. Applicant must demonstrate financial need and high academic achievement.
Application requirements: Portfolio. FAFSA/SAR. Statement indicating the name of parent who attended SACI and dates of attendance.
Additional information: Must be accepted to study with Studio Art Centers International and have a parent who attended SACI. Applicants for late spring or summer terms must submit materials by the admissions deadline of the term they wish to enroll. Number of awards varies depending on budget.

Amount of award: $1,500
Application deadline: March 15, October 15
Notification begins: April 15, November 15

Contact:
Studio Art Centers International
50 Broad Street
Suite 1617
New York, NY 10004-2372
Phone: 212-248-7225
Web: www.saci-florence.com

SACI Consortium Scholarship

Type of award: Scholarship.
Intended use: For undergraduate or graduate study in Florence, Italy. Designated institutions: Studio Art Centers International (SACI) consortium institutions.
Basis for selection: Competition/talent/interest in study abroad. Major/career interest in arts, general or art/art history. Applicant must demonstrate financial need.
Application requirements: Portfolio, nomination by SACI consortium school. FAFSA/SAR.
Additional information: Must be accepted to study with Studio Art Centers International. Each consortium school may submit one nominee. Award for one semester; one award

available per semester. See Website for list of eligible institutions.

Amount of award: Full tuition
Number of awards: 2
Application deadline: March 15, October 15
Notification begins: April 15, November 15

Contact:
Studio Art Centers International
50 Broad Street
Suite 1617
New York, NY 10004-2372
Phone: 212-248-7225
Web: www.saci-florence.org

Sunkist Growers

A.W. Bodine Sunkist Memorial Scholarship

Type of award: Scholarship, renewable.
Intended use: For full-time undergraduate study at accredited 2-year or 4-year institution.
Basis for selection: Applicant must demonstrate financial need, high academic achievement, depth of character, leadership, seriousness of purpose and service orientation.
Application requirements: Recommendations, essay, transcript, proof of eligibility. SAT or ACT scores, tax return (or parents' tax return for applicants younger than 21).
Additional information: Applicant or someone in immediate family must have derived majority of income from California- or Arizona-based agriculture. All majors eligible. Award renewable up to four years based on annual review. Must maintain 2.7 GPA and carry 12 credits per semester to qualify for renewal. Number of awards varies. Visit Website for application.

Amount of award: $2,000
Number of applicants: 300
Application deadline: April 30

Contact:
A.W. Bodine Sunkist Memorial Scholarship
Sunkist Growers
P.O. Box 7888
Van Nuys, CA 91409-7888
Web: www.sunkist.com/about/bodine_scholarship.aspx

Supreme Guardian Council, International Order of Job's Daughters

The Grotto Scholarships

Type of award: Scholarship.
Intended use: For full-time undergraduate study at 2-year or 4-year institution.
Eligibility: Applicant must be single, female, no older than 30.
Basis for selection: Major/career interest in dentistry. Applicant must demonstrate financial need, high academic achievement, depth of character, leadership and seriousness of purpose.
Application requirements: Recommendations, transcript, proof of eligibility. Personal letter.
Additional information: Applicant must be member of Job's Daughters. Job's Daughters activities, financial self-help, and achievements outside of Job's Daughters are also factors in awarding scholarships. Training in the handicapped field is preferred. Visit Website for more information.

Amount of award: $1,500
Application deadline: April 30

Contact:
International Order of Job's Daughters
Web: www.jobsdaughtersinternational.org

Supreme Guardian Council, International Order of Job's Daughters Scholarship

Type of award: Scholarship.
Intended use: For full-time undergraduate study at vocational, 2-year or 4-year institution.
Eligibility: Applicant must be single, female, no older than 30.
Basis for selection: Applicant must demonstrate financial need, high academic achievement, depth of character, leadership, seriousness of purpose and service orientation.
Application requirements: Recommendations, transcript, proof of eligibility. Personal letter.
Additional information: Applicant must be member of Job's Daughters. Job's Daughters activities, applicant's financial self-help, and achievements outside of Job's Daughters are also factors in awarding scholarships. Number of awards varies. Visit Website for more information.

Amount of award: $750
Number of applicants: 100
Application deadline: April 30

Contact:
Supreme Guardian Council
Web: www.jobsdaughtersinternational.org

Susie Holmes Memorial Scholarship

Type of award: Scholarship.
Intended use: For full-time undergraduate study at vocational, 2-year or 4-year institution.
Eligibility: Applicant must be single, female, no older than 30.
Basis for selection: Applicant must demonstrate financial need, high academic achievement, depth of character and seriousness of purpose.
Application requirements: Recommendations, transcript, proof of eligibility. Personal letter.
Additional information: Applicant must be member of Job's Daughters. Must be high school graduate with 2.5 GPA; show dedicated, continuous, joyful service to Job's Daughters; and regularly attend Grand and/or Supreme Session and participate in competitions. Job's Daughter's activities, applicant's financial self-help, and achievements outside of Job's Daughters are also factors in awarding scholarships. Visit Website for more details.

Amount of award: $1,000
Application deadline: April 30

Contact:
Supreme Guardian Council, International Order of Job's Daughters
Web: www.jobsdaughtersinternational.org

Swiss Benevolent Society of New York

Sonia Streuli Maguire Outstanding Scholastic Achievement Award

Type of award: Scholarship.
Intended use: For full-time senior, post-bachelor's certificate, master's, doctoral or first professional study at accredited 4-year or graduate institution in United States.
Eligibility: Applicant must be Swiss. Applicant must be permanent resident residing in New York, Connecticut, Delaware, New Jersey or Pennsylvania.
Basis for selection: Applicant must demonstrate high academic achievement.
Application requirements: Recommendations, transcript, proof of eligibility. SAT/GRE results.
Additional information: Applicant or parent must be Swiss national. Must have minimum 3.8 GPA. Visit Website for application.

Application deadline:	March 31
Notification begins:	June 1

Contact:
Swiss Benevolent Society Scholarship Committee
500 Fifth Avenue
Room 1800
New York, NY 10110
Phone: 212-246-0655
Fax: 212-246-1366
Web: www.sbsny.org/sbs_scholarships.html

Swiss Benevolent Society Medicus Student Exchange

Type of award: Scholarship.
Intended use: For full-time junior, senior or graduate study at accredited 4-year or graduate institution in universities and polytechnic institutes in Switzerland.
Eligibility: Applicant must be Swiss. Applicant must be U.S. citizen or permanent resident.
Basis for selection: Competition/talent/interest in study abroad. Applicant must demonstrate financial need and high academic achievement.
Application requirements: Recommendations, transcript, proof of eligibility. SAT or GRE scores. Letter of acceptance from Swiss institution. Statement of funding. Proof of fluency in language of instruction.
Additional information: Provides partial financial support for U.S. students accepted to Swiss post-secondary institutions. Applicant or parent must be Swiss national. Visit Website for application.

Application deadline:	March 31
Notification begins:	June 1

Contact:
Swiss Benevolent Society Scholarship Committee
500 Fifth Avenue
Room 1800
New York, NY 10110
Phone: 212-246-0655
Fax: 212-246-1366
Web: www.sbsny.org/sbs_scholarships.html

Swiss Benevolent Society Pellegrini Scholarship

Type of award: Scholarship, renewable.
Intended use: For undergraduate, graduate or non-degree study at accredited postsecondary institution in United States.
Eligibility: Applicant must be Swiss. Applicant must be permanent resident residing in New York, Connecticut, Delaware, New Jersey or Pennsylvania.
Basis for selection: Applicant must demonstrate financial need and high academic achievement.
Application requirements: Recommendations, transcript, proof of eligibility. SAT or GRE scores. Proof of Swiss parentage and tax return. Copy of bursar's bill. Incoming freshmen should provide figures of anticipated cost.
Additional information: Applicant or parent must be Swiss national. Minimum 3.0 GPA. Visit Website for application.

Application deadline:	March 31
Notification begins:	June 1

Contact:
Swiss Benevolent Society Scholarship Committee
500 Fifth Avenue
Room 1800
New York, NY 10110
Phone: 212-246-0655
Fax: 212-246-1366
Web: www.sbsny.org/sbs_scholarships.html

TAG Education Collaborative

TAG Education Collaborative Web Challenge Contest

Type of award: Scholarship.
Intended use: For full-time undergraduate study.
Eligibility: Applicant must be enrolled in high school. Applicant must be U.S. citizen or permanent resident residing in Georgia.
Basis for selection: Competition/talent/interest in web-site design, based on use of technology to create a theme-based project. Major/career interest in computer/information sciences or computer graphics. Applicant must demonstrate seriousness of purpose.
Application requirements: Proof of eligibility.
Additional information: Applicants work in teams of up to four members to create projects using free and/or open source technologies. Team must be sponsored by faculty adviser. Total amount awarded varies. Visit Website for registration information, deadline, and contest information and theme.

Number of awards:	25
Number of applicants:	100
Total amount awarded:	$21,100

Contact:
TAG Education Collaborative
Web: www.tagedonline.org

Taglit-Birthright Israel

Taglit-Birthright Israel Gift

Type of award: Scholarship.
Intended use: For undergraduate or graduate study at postsecondary institution.
Eligibility: Applicant must be at least 18, no older than 26. Applicant must be Jewish.
Application requirements: Proof of eligibility. Passport.
Additional information: Applicant must be out of high school. All eligible applicants receive free trip to Israel under the auspices of Aish HaTorah, Hillel, and other organizations. Round-trip airfare and ten days of program activity (including hotel, transportation, and most meals) are funded. Must not have visited Israel previously on an educational peer-group trip or study program. Must not have lived in Israel past age 12. Visit Website or contact sponsor for current offerings.

Number of awards:	20,000

Contact:
Phone: 888-994-7723
Web: www.birthrightisrael.com

Tall Clubs International

TCI Student Scholarships

Type of award: Scholarship.
Intended use: For freshman study at accredited 2-year or 4-year institution.
Eligibility: Applicant must be no older than 20.
Basis for selection: Applicant must demonstrate high academic achievement.
Application requirements: Recommendations, essay, transcript, nomination by local Tall Clubs. College entry test scores, photograph for publication, release form to publish essay and/or photo of applicant.
Additional information: Must meet height requirement: 5'10" for women and 6'2" for men. Number of awards available varies. Contact local TCI Member Club and request their sponsorship as candidate for scholarship.

Amount of award:	$1,000
Number of applicants:	400
Application deadline:	March 1
Notification begins:	July 15
Total amount awarded:	$4,000

Contact:
Tall Clubs International
Web: www.tall.org/scholarships.cfm

Tennessee Student Assistance Corporation

Helping Heroes Grant

Type of award: Scholarship, renewable.
Intended use: For undergraduate study at 2-year or 4-year institution.
Eligibility: Applicant must be residing in Tennessee. Applicant must be veteran who served in the Army, Air Force, Marines, Navy or Reserves/National Guard. Must be a veteran who was honorably discharged and was awarded the Iraq Campaign Medal, Afghanistan Campaign Medal, or Global War on Terrorism Expeditionary Medal.
Additional information: Award amount is up to $2,000. Fall application deadline is September 1; spring deadline is February 1; summer deadline is May 1. Scholarships are given on a first-come, first-served basis, with up to $750,000 awarded per academic year.

Amount of award:	$2,000
Number of awards:	510
Application deadline:	September 1, February 1
Total amount awarded:	$806,000

Contact:
Tennessee Student Assistance Corporation
Parkway Towers, Suite 1510
404 James Robertson Parkway
Nashville, TN 37243-0820
Phone: 800-342-1633
Fax: 615-741-6101
Web: www.tn.gov/collegepays

Hope Foster Child Tuition Grant

Type of award: Scholarship, renewable.
Intended use: For undergraduate study at 2-year or 4-year institution.
Eligibility: Applicant must be residing in Tennessee.
Application requirements: FAFSA.
Additional information: Must meet the academic requirements for the HOPE Scholarship or HOPE Access Grant. Must have been in custody of Tennessee Department of Children's Services for at least one year after age 14.

Amount of award:	Full tuition
Number of awards:	64
Application deadline:	September 1
Notification begins:	January 1
Total amount awarded:	$354,000

Contact:
Tennessee Student Assistance Corporation
Parkway Towers, Suite 1510
404 James Robertson Parkway
Nashville, TN 37243-0820
Phone: 800-342-1663
Fax: 615-741-6101
Web: www.tn.gov/collegepays

HOPE-Aspire Award

Type of award: Scholarship.
Intended use: For freshman or sophomore study at postsecondary institution. Designated institutions: Eligible Tennessee institutions.
Eligibility: Applicant must be residing in Tennessee.
Basis for selection: Applicant must demonstrate financial need and high academic achievement.
Application requirements: FAFSA.
Additional information: Applicant must be eligible for HOPE. Entering freshman must have a minimum 21 ACT or 980 SAT or 3.0 GPA. Parent's or student's income must be $36,000 or less. Applicant must be a Tennessee resident for one year prior to enrollment.

Amount of award: $2,250
Number of awards: 19,625
Application deadline: September 1
Notification begins: January 1
Total amount awarded: $94,600,000

Contact:
Tennessee Student Assistance Corporation
Parkway Towers, Suite 1510
404 James Robertson Parkway
Nashville, TN 37243-0820
Phone: 800-342-1663
Fax: 615-741-6101
Web: www.tn.gov/collegepays

Hope-General Assembly Merit Scholarship

Type of award: Scholarship, renewable.
Intended use: For undergraduate study at postsecondary institution. Designated institutions: Eligible Tennessee institutions.
Eligibility: Applicant must be residing in Tennessee.
Basis for selection: Applicant must demonstrate high academic achievement.
Application requirements: FAFSA.
Additional information: Supplement to HOPE Scholarship. Entering freshman must have minimum 3.75 weighted GPA and 29 ACT or 1280 SAT. Applicant must be a resident of Tennessee for one year prior to enrollment.

Amount of award: $1,500
Number of awards: 6,089
Application deadline: September 1
Notification begins: January 1
Total amount awarded: $30,200,000

Contact:
Tennessee Student Assistance Corporation
Parkway Towers, Suite 1510
404 James Robertson Parkway
Nashville, TN 37243-0820
Phone: 800-342-1663
Fax: 614-741-6101
Web: www.tn.gov/collegepays

Tennessee Dependent Children Scholarship Program

Type of award: Scholarship, renewable.
Intended use: For full-time undergraduate study at accredited postsecondary institution.
Eligibility: Applicant must be U.S. citizen residing in Tennessee. Applicant's parent must have been killed or disabled in work-related accident as firefighter or police officer.
Basis for selection: Applicant must demonstrate financial need.
Application requirements: Proof of eligibility. FAFSA.
Additional information: Applicant must be enrolled in a degree-granting program. Applicant's parent may also be emergency medical technician killed or disabled in work-related accident. Award based on student's financial aid package.

Amount of award: Full tuition
Number of awards: 22
Number of applicants: 56
Application deadline: July 15
Total amount awarded: $178,000

Contact:
Tennessee Student Assistance Corporation
Parkway Towers, Suite 1510
404 James Robertson Parkway
Nashville, TN 37243-0820
Phone: 800-342-1663
Fax: 615-741-6101
Web: www.tn.gov/collegepays

Tennessee Dual Enrollment Grant

Type of award: Scholarship, renewable.
Intended use: For undergraduate study at postsecondary institution.
Eligibility: Applicant must be high school junior or senior. Applicant must be residing in Tennessee.
Additional information: Award is up to $1,200. Student must meet dual enrollment requirements for high school and postsecondary institution. Must be a Tennessee resident for at least one year prior to enrollment. Visit Website for designated institutions. Application deadline is September 15 for fall; February 1 for spring; May 1 for summer. Apply online.

Amount of award: $1,200
Number of awards: 16,995
Application deadline: September 15, February 1
Total amount awarded: $8,700,000

Contact:
Tennessee Student Assistance Corporation
Parkway Towers, Suite 1510
404 James Robertson Parkway
Nashville, TN 37243-0820
Phone: 800-342-1663
Fax: 615-741-6101
Web: www.tn.gov/collegepays

Tennessee HOPE Access Grant

Type of award: Scholarship.
Intended use: For freshman study at 2-year or 4-year institution. Designated institutions: Eligible Tennessee institutions.
Eligibility: Applicant must be residing in Tennessee.
Basis for selection: Applicant must demonstrate financial need and high academic achievement.
Application requirements: FAFSA.
Additional information: Award amount is up to $4,125 for four-year institutions or up to $2,625 for two-year institutions. Minimum 2.75 GPA. Minimum 18 ACT, 860 SAT. Parents' or independent student and spouse's adjusted gross income must be $36,000 or less on IRS tax form. Applicant must be a Tennessee resident for one year prior to enrollment.

Amount of award: $2,625-$4,125
Number of awards: 468
Application deadline: September 1
Notification begins: January 1
Total amount awarded: $955,000

Contact:
Tennessee Student Assistance Corporation
Parkway Towers, Suite 1510
404 James Robertson Parkway
Nashville, TN 37243-0820
Phone: 800-342-1663
Fax: 615-741-6101
Web: www.tn.gov/collegepays

Tennessee HOPE Scholarship

Type of award: Scholarship.
Intended use: For undergraduate study at postsecondary institution. Designated institutions: Eligible Tennessee institutions.
Eligibility: Applicant must be residing in Tennessee.
Basis for selection: Applicant must demonstrate high academic achievement.
Application requirements: FAFSA.
Additional information: Applicant must be a Tennessee resident for one year prior to enrollment. Award amount is up to $6,000 for four-year institutions, up to $3,000 for two-year institutions. Minimum 3.0 GPA or 21 ACT/980 SAT.

Amount of award:	$3,000-$6,000
Number of awards:	43,814
Application deadline:	September 1
Notification begins:	January 1
Total amount awarded:	$152,900,000

Contact:
Tennessee Student Assistance Corporation
Parkway Towers, Suite 1510
404 James Robertson Parkway
Nashville, TN 37243-0820
Phone: 800-342-1663
Fax: 615-741-6101
Web: www.tn.gov/collegepays

Tennessee Ned McWherter Scholars Program

Type of award: Scholarship, renewable.
Intended use: For full-time freshman study at accredited 2-year or 4-year institution.
Eligibility: Applicant must be high school senior. Applicant must be U.S. citizen residing in Tennessee.
Basis for selection: Applicant must demonstrate high academic achievement and leadership.
Application requirements: Transcript, proof of eligibility. List of leadership activities.
Additional information: Applicant must score at 95th percentile on ACT/SAT. Minimum 3.5 cumulative GPA. Difficulty of high school courses considered.

Amount of award:	$6,000
Number of awards:	190
Number of applicants:	1,232
Application deadline:	February 15
Total amount awarded:	$555,000

Contact:
Tennessee Student Assistance Corporation
Parkway Towers, Suite 1510
404 James Robertson Parkway
Nashville, TN 37243-0820
Phone: 800-342-1663
Fax: 615-741-6101
Web: www.tn.gov/collegepays

Tennessee Student Assistance Award Program

Type of award: Scholarship, renewable.
Intended use: For undergraduate study at postsecondary institution.
Eligibility: Applicant must be U.S. citizen residing in Tennessee.
Basis for selection: Applicant must demonstrate financial need.
Application requirements: FAFSA.
Additional information: Applicant's expected family contribution must be $2,100 or less. Award is up to $4,000 for private institutions; up to $2,000 for public, based on funding.

Number of awards:	28,766
Number of applicants:	4,634,000
Total amount awarded:	$53,500,000

Contact:
Tennessee Student Assistance Corporation
Parkway Towers, Suite 1510
404 James Robertson Parkway
Nashville, TN 37243-0820
Phone: 800-342-1663
Fax: 615-741-6101
Web: www.tn.gov/collegepays

Wilder-Naifeh Technical Skills Grant

Type of award: Scholarship.
Intended use: For freshman or sophomore study at vocational institution. Designated institutions: Tennessee Technology Centers.
Eligibility: Applicant must be residing in Tennessee.
Application requirements: FAFSA.
Additional information: Applicant must be Tennessee resident for one year prior to enrollment. Application deadline varies. See Website for details.

Amount of award:	$2,000
Number of awards:	10,928
Application deadline:	July 1
Notification begins:	January 1
Total amount awarded:	$12,800,000

Contact:
Tennessee Student Assistance Corporation
Parkway Towers, Suite 1510
404 James Robertson Parkway
Nashville, TN 37243-0820
Phone: 800-342-1663
Fax: 615-741-6101
Web: www.tn.gov/collegepays

Texas 4-H Club

Texas 4-H Opportunity Scholarships

Type of award: Scholarship, renewable.
Intended use: For undergraduate study at accredited 4-year institution in United States. Designated institutions: Colleges and universities in Texas.
Eligibility: Applicant must be high school senior. Applicant must be U.S. citizen residing in Texas.
Basis for selection: Applicant must demonstrate financial need and high academic achievement.
Application requirements: Recommendations, essay, transcript. SAT/ACT scores.
Additional information: Must be current Texas 4-H member in good standing. Must graduate from Texas public/private high school or home school in top fourth of class or upper half of class, depending on scholarship. Must have minimum 1350 SAT or 19 ACT score. Cannot have applied for scholarship though state FFA or state FCCLA.

Amount of award: $1,000-$18,000
Number of awards: 225
Number of applicants: 350
Application deadline: January 31
Notification begins: June 1
Total amount awarded: $2,250,000

Contact:
Texas 4-H and Youth Development Foundation
Scholarship Selection Committee
4180 S Highway 6
College Station, TX 77845
Phone: 979-845-1212
Fax: 979-845-6495
Web: texas4-h.tamu.edu

Texas Association, Family Career and Community Leaders of America

Blue Bell Scholarship

Type of award: Scholarship.
Intended use: For full-time undergraduate study at accredited postsecondary institution in United States. Designated institutions: Colleges and universities in Texas.
Eligibility: Applicant must be high school senior. Applicant must be U.S. citizen residing in Texas.
Basis for selection: Applicant must demonstrate financial need, high academic achievement, depth of character and leadership.
Application requirements: Recommendations, essay, transcript. SAT/ACT scores.
Additional information: Must be active member of Family Career and Community Leaders of America in good standing. Must have passed TAKS Mastery/Exit Level exam and be in top fourth of graduating class.

Amount of award: $1,000
Number of awards: 5
Number of applicants: 123
Application deadline: March 1
Notification begins: April 1
Total amount awarded: $5,000

Contact:
Texas Association, Family Career and Community Leaders of America
1107 W. 45th St.
Austin, TX 78756
Phone: 512-306-0099
Fax: 512-442-7100
Web: www.texasfccla.org

C. J. Davidson Scholarship

Type of award: Scholarship, renewable.
Intended use: For undergraduate study at accredited postsecondary institution in United States. Designated institutions: Texas colleges with family and consumer sciences departments.
Eligibility: Applicant must be high school senior. Applicant must be U.S. citizen residing in Texas.
Basis for selection: Applicant must demonstrate financial need and high academic achievement.
Application requirements: Recommendations, essay, transcript. SAT/ACT scores.
Additional information: Must graduate from a Texas high school with 85 average. Must be active member of Family Career and Community Leaders of America for at least one year. Must major in family/consumer sciences.

Amount of award: $16,000
Number of awards: 10
Number of applicants: 25
Application deadline: March 1
Notification begins: April 1
Total amount awarded: $160,000

Contact:
Texas Association, Family Career and Community Leaders of America
1107 W. 45th St.
Austin, TX 78756
Phone: 512-306-0099
Fax: 512-442-7100
Web: www.texasfccla.org

Houston Livestock Show and Rodeo Scholarships

Type of award: Scholarship, renewable.
Intended use: For full-time undergraduate study at accredited 4-year institution in United States. Designated institutions: Colleges and universities in Texas.
Eligibility: Applicant must be high school senior. Applicant must be U.S. citizen residing in Texas.
Basis for selection: Applicant must demonstrate financial need, high academic achievement, depth of character and leadership.
Application requirements: Recommendations, essay, transcript. SAT/ACT scores.
Additional information: Must be current member of Family Career and Community Leaders of America in good standing. Must graduate from Texas public high school in top fourth of class and have minimum 1350 SAT or 19 ACT score. Cannot have applied for scholarship through Texas 4-H or FFA.

Amount of award: $16,000
Number of awards: 10
Number of applicants: 110
Application deadline: March 1
Notification begins: April 1
Total amount awarded: $160,000

Contact:
Texas Association, Family Career and Community Leaders of America
1107 W. 45th St.
Austin, TX 78756
Phone: 512-306-0099
Fax: 512-442-7100
Web: www.texasfccla.org

Texas Farm Bureau Scholarship

Type of award: Scholarship.
Intended use: For full-time undergraduate study at accredited postsecondary institution in United States. Designated institutions: Texas colleges and universities with family and consumer sciences departments.
Eligibility: Applicant must be high school senior. Applicant must be U.S. citizen residing in Texas.
Basis for selection: Applicant must demonstrate financial need, high academic achievement, depth of character and leadership.

Application requirements: Recommendations, essay, transcript. SAT/ACT scores, two copies of autobiography.
Additional information: Must be active Family Career and Community Leaders of America member in good standing for at least one year. Must be FFCLA regional or state officer. Must be a graduate of Texas high school with minimum 85 average. Must major in family/consumer sciences.

Amount of award:	$1,000
Number of awards:	1
Number of applicants:	5
Application deadline:	March 1
Notification begins:	April 1
Total amount awarded:	$1,000

Contact:
Texas Association, Family Career and Community Leaders of America
1107 W. 45th St.
Austin, TX 78756
Phone: 512-306-0099
Fax: 512-442-7100
Web: www.texasfccla.org

Texas Future Farmers of America

FFA Scholarships

Type of award: Scholarship, renewable.
Intended use: For undergraduate study at accredited 4-year institution in United States. Designated institutions: Colleges and universities in Texas.
Eligibility: Applicant must be high school senior. Applicant must be U.S. citizen residing in Texas.
Basis for selection: Applicant must demonstrate financial need, high academic achievement and leadership.
Application requirements: Interview, recommendations, essay, transcript. SAT/ACT scores.
Additional information: Must be current member of and have participation in Texas FFA and be in good standing. Must have graduated from Texas public high school in top half of class. Must have minimum 1350 SAT or 19 ACT score. Cannot have applied for scholarship through Texas 4-H or FCCLA. Preliminary deadlines vary based on area. Visit Website for more information.

Amount of award:	$2,000-$18,000
Number of awards:	135
Number of applicants:	700
Notification begins:	June 10
Total amount awarded:	$2,000,000

Contact:
Texas FFA Association
614 East 12th Street
Austin, TX 78701
Phone: 512-480-8045
Fax: 512-476-2894
Web: www.texasffa.org

Texas Higher Education Coordinating Board

Texas Armed Services Scholarship Program

Type of award: Scholarship.
Intended use: For freshman study at 4-year institution.
Eligibility: Applicant must be high school senior. Applicant must be U.S. citizen or permanent resident residing in Texas.
Basis for selection: Applicant must demonstrate high academic achievement.
Application requirements: Nomination by the governor, lieutenant governor, state senator, or state representative.
Additional information: Must meet two of four following criteria: Minimum 3.0 GPA. Minimum 1590 (SAT) or 23 (ACT). Must be ranked in top third of high school graduating class or be on track to graduate high school with the Distinguished Achievement Program (DAP) or the International Baccalaureate Program (IB). Must enroll in Reserve Officers' Training Corps, agree to four years of ROTC training, and graduate no later than five years after date first enrolled. After graduation, must enter into four-year commitment to Texas Army or Texas Air Force National Guard, contract to serve as commissioned officer in branch in the U.S., or repay scholarship if requirements not met. See Website for additional criteria.

Amount of award:	$10,000

Contact:
Texas Higher Education Coordinating Board
Phone: 800-242-3062
Web: www.collegeforalltexans.com

Texas Competitive Scholarship Waiver

Type of award: Scholarship.
Intended use: For undergraduate study at 4-year institution in United States. Designated institutions: Public institutions in Texas.
Eligibility: Applicant must be U.S. citizen, permanent resident or international student residing in Texas.
Additional information: Program enables public institutions to grant waiver of nonresident tuition charges to individuals who receive scholarships totaling at least $1,000 awarded by their institution in competition open both to residents and to nonresidents. Students must have competed with other students, including Texas residents, for the award. Student may receive a waiver of nonresident tuition for the period of time covered by the scholarship, not to exceed 12 months. Process for applying for waivers varies from college to college.
Contact:
Texas Higher Education Coordinating Board
Phone: 800-242-3062
Web: www.collegeforalltexans.com

Texas Concurrent Enrollment Waiver (Enrollment in Two Texas Community Colleges)

Type of award: Scholarship.
Intended use: For undergraduate study at 2-year or 4-year institution in United States. Designated institutions: Texas public colleges or universities.

Scholarships

Eligibility: Applicant must be residing in Texas.
Application requirements: Proof of eligibility. Proof of concurrent enrollment.
Additional information: Waiver provides a break in tuition charges to students enrolled at two public Texas community colleges at the same time. Award is reduced tuition at second institution of enrollment (student pays minimum tuition rate at second institution). No funds may be used to pay tuition for continuing education classes for which the college receives no state tax support. For more information, contact registrar at second college in which you are enrolled.
Contact:
Texas Higher Education Coordinating Board
Phone: 800-242-3062
Web: www.collegeforalltexans.com

Texas Exemption for Peace Officers Disabled in the Line of Duty

Type of award: Scholarship.
Intended use: For undergraduate study at postsecondary institution in United States. Designated institutions: Texas public colleges and universities.
Eligibility: Applicant must be residing in Texas.
Application requirements: Proof of eligibility. Satisfactory evidence of status as a disabled peace officer as required by institution.
Additional information: Award for persons injured in the line of duty while serving as peace officers in Texas. Must enroll in classes for which college receives tax support. Maximum award is exemption from payment of tuition and fees for not more than 12 semesters or sessions. Contact college for additional information.

Amount of award: Full tuition

Contact:
Texas Higher Education Coordinating Board
Phone: 800-242-3062
Web: www.collegeforalltexans.com

Texas Exemption for Students Under Conservatorship of the Dept. of Family & Protective Services

Type of award: Scholarship, renewable.
Intended use: For undergraduate or graduate study at accredited vocational, 2-year or 4-year institution in United States. Designated institutions: Texas public colleges and universities.
Eligibility: Applicant must be U.S. citizen or permanent resident residing in Texas.
Application requirements: Proof of eligibility from the Department of Family and Protective Services.
Additional information: Applicants must have been either in the care or conservatorship of Texas Department of Family and Protective Services on the day before their 18th birthday, the day of their graduation from high school, or the day of receipt of GED or the day preceding; or in the care or conservatorship of the TDFS on 14th birthday and then adopted. Must enroll in college before 25th birthday. Program awards tuition and fees; once student determined eligible for the benefit, it continues indefinitely. Contact college's financial aid office for application.

Amount of award: Full tuition

Contact:
Texas Higher Education Coordinating Board
Phone: 800-242-3062
Web: www.collegeforalltexans.com

Texas Exemption for the Surviving Spouse and Dependent Children of Certain Deceased Public Servants (Employees)

Type of award: Scholarship.
Intended use: For full-time undergraduate study at postsecondary institution in United States. Designated institutions: Texas public colleges and universities.
Eligibility: Applicant must be residing in Texas.
Application requirements: Proof of eligibility.
Additional information: Exemption for surviving spouse and/or minor dependent children of certain public employees (defined by Texas Government Code 615.003) killed in the line of duty. Public employee must have died on or after September 1, 2000. Program covers cost of tuition and fees, textbooks, and possibly room and board. Visit Website for link to list of eligible public servants. Contact registrar's office at college/university for information on claiming this exemption.

Amount of award: Full tuition

Contact:
Texas Higher Education Coordinating Board
Phone: 800-242-3062
Web: www.collegeforalltexans.com

Texas Exemptions for Texas Veterans (Hazelwood Exemption)

Type of award: Scholarship, renewable.
Intended use: For undergraduate or graduate study at accredited 2-year, 4-year or graduate institution. Designated institutions: Texas public colleges and universities.
Eligibility: Applicant must be U.S. citizen residing in Texas. Applicant must be veteran; or dependent of disabled veteran or deceased veteran. Must have served at least 181 days of active military duty, excluding basic training. Must have received honorable discharge or general discharge under honorable conditions. If dependent of disabled veteran, parent must be totally disabled for purposes of employability as result of service-related injury or illness.
Application requirements: Proof of eligibility.
Additional information: Must have tuition and fee charges that exceed all federal education benefits. Veteran must have been resident of Texas prior to enlistment. Award amount includes all dues, fees, and charges, excluding property deposit, student services, and lodging/board/clothing fees. Must be enrolled in courses receiving state tax support. For a child of eligible veteran to receive benefits, child must be 25 or younger on first day of semester that exemption is claimed, must make satisfactory progress, must be biological, stepchild, adopted or claimed as dependent in current or previous tax year. If a child whom hours have been delegated fails to use all of the assigned hours, a veteran may re-assign available unused hours to another dependent child. If the veteran has died prior to this transfer request, another legally designated caretaker may re-assign unused hours to an eligible child. Applicants should contact specific school's financial aid office for more information.

Amount of award: Full tuition

Contact:
Texas Higher Education Coordinating Board
Phone: 800-242-3062
Web: www.collegeforalltexans.com

Texas Federal Supplemental Educational Opportunity Grant

Type of award: Scholarship.
Intended use: For undergraduate study at vocational, 2-year, 4-year or graduate institution in United States.
Eligibility: Applicant must be U.S. citizen or permanent resident.
Basis for selection: Applicant must demonstrate financial need and high academic achievement.
Application requirements: FAFSA.
Additional information: Must have valid Social Security Number. Expected Family Contribution must be lower than the federal cut-off rate set each year. Must have high school diploma, GED Certificate, pass test approved by the U.S. Department of Education or meet other standards approved by U.S. Department of Education. Must register for the Selective Service.

Amount of award: $100-$4,000

Contact:
Texas Higher Education Coordinating Board
Phone: 800-242-3062
Web: www.collegeforalltexans.com

Texas Fifth-Year Accounting Student Scholarship Program

Type of award: Scholarship.
Intended use: For senior, post-bachelor's certificate or master's study at accredited postsecondary institution in United States. Designated institutions: Texas institutions.
Eligibility: Applicant must be residing in Texas.
Basis for selection: Major/career interest in accounting. Applicant must demonstrate financial need and high academic achievement.
Application requirements: Proof of eligibility. Signed statement of intent to take CPA exam in Texas. FAFSA.
Additional information: Must be enrolled as fifth-year accounting student who has completed at least 120 credit hours, including 15 hours of accounting. Must register for selective service or be exempt from this requirement. Contact college financial aid office for application.

Amount of award: $5,000

Contact:
Texas Higher Education Coordinating Board
Phone: 800-242-3062
Web: www.collegeforalltexans.com

Texas Good Neighbor Scholarship

Type of award: Scholarship.
Intended use: For undergraduate or graduate study at accredited 2-year, 4-year or graduate institution in United States. Designated institutions: Texas public colleges and universities.
Eligibility: Applicant must be native-born citizen of any Western Hemisphere country other than Cuba.
Application requirements: Proof of eligibility.
Additional information: Must plan to return to native country. Contact institution's financial aid office or the international student affairs office for application. Award covers one year of tuition.

Amount of award: Full tuition

Contact:
College For All Texans
Phone: 800-242-3062
Web: www.collegeforalltexans.com

TEXAS Grant (Toward Excellence, Access, and Success)

Type of award: Scholarship, renewable.
Intended use: For undergraduate study at vocational, 2-year or 4-year institution. Designated institutions: Texas public colleges or universities.
Eligibility: Applicant must be U.S. citizen or permanent resident residing in Texas.
Basis for selection: Applicant must demonstrate financial need and high academic achievement.
Application requirements: Selective Service registration or exemption from requirement. FAFSA.
Additional information: Applicant must have completed Recommended High School Program or Distinguished Achievement Program, enroll in college at least 3/4-time (unless granted hardship waiver) within 16 months of high school graduation, and must receive first award prior to completing 30 hours on campus. Also eligible are students with associate degrees from public technical or community colleges in Texas, who enroll in public Texas universities within 12 months of receiving associate's. Expected Family Contribution (EFC) to education must be less than $4,000. Minimum 2.5 GPA required to renew award. Applicant must not have been convicted of felony or crime involving controlled substance. Award not to exceed student's need or public institution tuition and fees. Must register for Selective Service or be exempt from this requirement. Contact financial aid office at specific college/university for application deadline and procedures.

Amount of award: Full tuition

Contact:
Texas Higher Education Coordinating Board
Phone: 800-242-3062
Web: www.collegeforalltexans.com

Texas Highest Ranking High School Graduate Tuition Exemption

Type of award: Scholarship.
Intended use: For freshman study at accredited postsecondary institution. Designated institutions: Texas public colleges and universities.
Basis for selection: Applicant must demonstrate high academic achievement.
Application requirements: Proof of eligibility. Valedictorian certificate issued by Texas Education Agency.
Additional information: Must be highest-ranking graduate of accredited public or private Texas high school. Award covers tuition during both semesters of first regular session immediately following the student's high school graduation; fees not included. Deadline varies. Contact college/university financial aid office to apply.

Amount of award: Full tuition

Contact:
College For All Texans
Phone: 800-242-3062
Web: www.collegeforalltexans.com

Texas National Guard Tuition Assistance Program

Type of award: Scholarship.
Intended use: For undergraduate or graduate study at postsecondary institution in United States. Designated institutions: Texas institutions.
Eligibility: Applicant must be residing in Texas.
Application requirements: Proof of eligibility.

Additional information: Program provides tuition exemption to active, drilling members of Texas National Guard, Texas Air Guard, or State Guard. Must be registered for Selective Service or exempt from this requirement. Awards at public colleges/universities are for student's tuition charges up to 12 credit hours per semester. Awards for private, non-profit institutions are based on public university amount. For more information, visit Texas National Guard Website at www.agd.state.tx.us. Applicants may also contact the commander of their National Guard, Air Guard, or State Guard unit, or the education officer via information below.

Amount of award: Full tuition

Contact:
State Adjutant General's Office
P.O. Box 5218/AGTX-PAE
Austin, TX 78763-5218
Phone: 512-782-5515
Web: www.collegeforalltexans.com

Texas Public Educational Grant

Type of award: Scholarship.
Intended use: For undergraduate or graduate study at accredited vocational, 2-year or 4-year institution. Designated institutions: Texas public colleges and universities.
Basis for selection: Applicant must demonstrate financial need.
Application requirements: FAFSA.
Additional information: Award amount varies; may not exceed student's financial need. Deadline varies. Applicant must register for Selective Service, unless exempt. Contact financial aid office at college/university for more information.
Contact:
Texas Higher Education Coordinating Board
Phone: 800-242-3062
Web: www.collegeforalltexans.com

Texas Reduction in Tuition Charges for Students Taking 15 or More Semester Credit Hours Per Term

Type of award: Scholarship.
Intended use: For full-time undergraduate study at postsecondary institution. Designated institutions: Texas public colleges and universities.
Eligibility: Applicant must be residing in Texas.
Application requirements: Proof of eligibility.
Additional information: Applicant must be enrolled in at least 15 credit hours at institution during semester/term for which reduction is offered. Must be making satisfactory progress toward completion of a degree program. Contact registrar's office at college/university to inquire whether they offer reduction.
Contact:
Texas Higher Education Coordinating Board
Phone: 800-242-3062
Web: www.collegeforalltexans.com

Texas Senior Citizen, 65 or Older, Free Tuition for Up to 6 Credit Hours

Type of award: Scholarship.
Intended use: For half-time undergraduate or graduate study at 2-year or 4-year institution in United States. Designated institutions: Participating Texas public colleges and universities.
Eligibility: Applicant must be at least 65, returning adult student. Applicant must be residing in Texas.
Application requirements: Proof of eligibility.
Additional information: Program allows senior citizens to take up to 6 credit hours per semester, tuition-free. Texas institutions not required to offer program; applicants should check with registrar. Classes must not already be filled with students paying at full price and must use tax support for some of their cost. Contact college for additional information.
Contact:
Texas Higher Education Coordinating Board
Phone: 800-242-3062
Web: www.collegeforalltexans.com

Texas Tuition Equalization Grant (TEG)

Type of award: Scholarship.
Intended use: For full-time undergraduate or graduate study at accredited 2-year or 4-year institution in United States. Designated institutions: Private, non-profit Texas colleges and universities.
Eligibility: Applicant must be U.S. citizen or permanent resident residing in Texas.
Basis for selection: Applicant must demonstrate financial need.
Application requirements: Proof of eligibility. Selective Service registration or exemption from requirement. FAFSA.
Additional information: Non-resident National Merit Finalists also eligible. Not open to athletic scholarship recipients. Must maintain 2.5 GPA and complete 24 credit hours per year. Award cannot exceed difference between applicant's tuition at private institution and what applicant would pay at public institution. Award amount varies; maximum is $3,518, but students with exceptional need may receive up to $5,277. Applicants should contact the financial aid office at the Texas private college/university they plan to attend for more information.

Number of awards: 28,000

Contact:
Texas Higher Education Coordinating Board
Phone: 800-242-3062
Web: www.collegeforalltexans.com

Texas Tuition Exemption for Blind or Deaf Students

Type of award: Scholarship, renewable.
Intended use: For undergraduate or graduate study at accredited 2-year or 4-year institution in United States. Designated institutions: Texas public colleges and universities.
Eligibility: Applicant must be visually impaired or hearing impaired. Applicant must be U.S. citizen or permanent resident residing in Texas.
Basis for selection: Applicant must demonstrate depth of character.
Application requirements: Recommendations, transcript, proof of eligibility. Certification of disability. Written statement indicating which certificate, degree program, or professional enhancement applicant intends to pursue.
Additional information: Must be certified by Texas Department of Assistive and Rehabilitative Services and have high school diploma or equivalent. Applicant must enroll in classes for which the college receives tax support. Award does not include fees or charges for lodging, board, or clothing.

Application deadline varies. Contact financial aid office at college/university for more information.

Amount of award: Full tuition

Contact:
Texas Higher Education Coordinating Board
Phone: 800-242-3062
Web: www.collegeforalltexans.com

Texas Tuition Exemption for Children of Disabled or Deceased Firefighters, Peace Officers, Game Wardens, and Employees of Correctional Institutions

Type of award: Scholarship, renewable.
Intended use: For undergraduate or graduate study at 2-year or 4-year institution in United States. Designated institutions: Texas public colleges and universities.
Eligibility: Applicant must be no older than 21. Applicant must be residing in Texas. Applicant's parent must have been killed or disabled in work-related accident as firefighter, police officer or public safety officer.
Application requirements: Proof of eligibility.
Additional information: Applicant must be child of paid or volunteer firefighter; paid municipal, county or state peace officer; custodial employee of Department of Corrections; or game warden disabled or killed in Texas in the line of duty. Persons eligible to participate in a school district's special education program under section 29.003 at age 22 may also apply. Applicant must enroll in courses that use tax support to cover some of their cost. Applicant must obtain certification form from Texas Higher Education Coordinating Board, have parent's former employer complete it, and submit to Texas Higher Education Coordinating Board. The Board will notify applicant's institution of eligibility. Students may be exempted from tuition and fees for the first 120 semester credits or until age 26, whichever comes first.

Amount of award: Full tuition

Contact:
Texas Higher Education Coordinating Board
Phone: 800-242-3062
Web: www.collegeforalltexans.com

Texas Tuition Rebate for Certain Undergraduates

Type of award: Scholarship.
Intended use: For full-time undergraduate study at postsecondary institution in United States. Designated institutions: Texas public colleges and universities.
Eligibility: Applicant must be residing in Texas.
Additional information: Program provides tuition rebates for students who efficiently acquire their bachelor's degrees. Students must graduate in a timely manner to receive rebate: within four years for four-year degree, five years for five-year degree. Student must have taken all coursework at Texas public institutions, and must have been entitled to pay in-state tuition at all times while pursuing degree. Student must complete bachelor's degree with no more than 3 hours in excess of degree plan, excluding up to 9 hours of credit by examination. Students must apply for tuition rebate prior to receiving bachelor's degree. Contact business office at college/university for more information.

Amount of award: $1,000

Contact:
Texas Higher Education Coordinating Board
Phone: 800-242-3062
Web: www.collegeforalltexans.com

Texas Tuition Reduction for Students Taking More Than 15 Hours

Type of award: Scholarship.
Intended use: For full-time undergraduate study at 4-year institution in United States. Designated institutions: Texas public colleges or universities.
Additional information: Award is reduced tuition. Must be enrolled in at least 15 semester credit hours at institution during semester or term for which reduction is offered. College governing board determines whether institution will offer reduction. Contact registrar's office to find out if college is offering this reduction.

Contact:
Texas Higher Education Coordinating Board
Phone: 800-242-3062
Web: www.collegeforalltexans.com

Tuition Exemption for Children of U.S. Military POW/MIAs from Texas

Type of award: Scholarship, renewable.
Intended use: For undergraduate study at accredited 2-year or 4-year institution. Designated institutions: Texas public colleges or universities.
Eligibility: Applicant must be no older than 25. Applicant must be U.S. citizen or permanent resident residing in Texas. Applicant must be dependent of POW/MIA.
Application requirements: Proof of eligibility. Documentation from Department of Defense that a parent, classified as Texas resident, is MIA or a POW. FAFSA.
Additional information: Applicants 22 to 25 years of age must receive most of their support from a parent. Applicant must enroll in courses that use tax support to cover some of their cost. Award does not include room, board, clothing, or property deposits. Applicants should contact the registrar at the college/university they plan to attend for more information.

Amount of award: Full tuition

Contact:
Texas Higher Education Coordinating Board
Phone: 800-242-3062
Web: www.collegeforalltexans.com

Third Marine Division Association

Third Marine Division Memorial Scholarship Fund

Type of award: Scholarship, renewable.
Intended use: For undergraduate study at accredited 2-year or 4-year institution in United States or Canada.
Eligibility: Applicant must be U.S. citizen. Must be dependent child of qualified member or deceased member (Marine or Navy Corpsman) of the Third Marine Division Association, or

Scholarships

dependent child of any military personnel who served in any Third Marine Division (Reinf) unit and who died as result of combat actions while serving in Vietnam between March 8, 1965 and November 27, 1969, or in operations Desert Shield, Desert Storm, or any other qualified Persian Gulf operations after August 2, 1990. Dependent children of deceased Third Marine Division personnel who served in above operations whose post-service deaths have been certified by the Department of Veterans Affairs to have been the result of combat-related wounds or other disabilities incurred during the period of eligible combat service, and were not the result of any misconduct by the veteran, are also eligible.
Basis for selection: Applicant must demonstrate financial need and high academic achievement.
Application requirements: Proof of eligibility. Financial aid form.
Additional information: Minimum 2.0 GPA. Number of awards varies. Eligible dependent children participating automatically receive renewal application forms.

Amount of award:	$500-$1,500
Number of applicants:	12
Application deadline:	April 15
Notification begins:	June 15
Total amount awarded:	$9,300

Contact:
MGySgt James G. Kyser USMC (Ret)
Secretary, Memorial Scholarship Fund
15727 Vista Drive
Dumfries, VA 22025-1810
Web: www.caltrap.com

Thurgood Marshall College Fund

Thurgood Marshall Scholarship Award

Type of award: Scholarship, renewable.
Intended use: For full-time undergraduate or graduate study at 4-year or graduate institution in United States. Designated institutions: One of 47 designated historically black public universities.
Eligibility: Applicant must be U.S. citizen or permanent resident.
Basis for selection: Applicant must demonstrate financial need, high academic achievement, leadership and service orientation.
Application requirements: Recommendations, essay, transcript. Resume, headshot or personal photograph. FAFSA.
Additional information: Must have high school or current GPA of 3.0 or higher, and must maintain throughout duration of scholarship. Contact university's Thurgood Marshall College Fund campus coordinator directly for more information, or visit Website.

Amount of award:	$3,100
Number of awards:	200
Number of applicants:	2,270
Application deadline:	August 15
Total amount awarded:	$1,200,000

Contact:
Thurgood Marshall College Fund
901 F Street
Suite 300
Washington, DC 20004
Phone: 202-507-4851
Fax: 202-652-2934
Web: www.thurgoodmarshallfund.net/scholarship/about-scholarships-program

Tourism Cares

ASTA Alaska Airlines Scholarship

Type of award: Scholarship.
Intended use: For sophomore, junior or senior study at accredited 2-year or 4-year institution in United States or Canada.
Eligibility: Applicant must be U.S. citizen, permanent resident or Canadian citizen or resident.
Basis for selection: Major/career interest in tourism/travel or hospitality administration/management. Applicant must demonstrate high academic achievement.
Application requirements: Essay, transcript. Resume, copy of U.S. or Canadian Passport or Alien Registration Card. Two evaluations and letters of recommendation (one from hospitality/tourism-related faculty member, one from hospitality/tourism professional).
Additional information: Minimum 3.0 GPA. Must be entering the second year of a two-year school, third year of a three-year school (for Quebec), junior or senior year of a four-year school, any year of graduate study. Check Website for deadline and additional criteria.

Amount of award:	$1,000
Number of awards:	1

Contact:
Tourism Cares
275 Turnpike Street
Suite 307
Canton, MA 02021
Phone: 781-821-5990
Fax: 781-821-8949
Web: www.tourismcares.org/student-programs

ASTA American Express Travel Scholarship

Type of award: Scholarship, renewable.
Intended use: For full-time freshman study at accredited 2-year or 4-year institution in United States or Canada.
Eligibility: Applicant must be high school senior. Applicant must be U.S. citizen or permanent resident.
Basis for selection: Major/career interest in hospitality administration/management or tourism/travel. Applicant must demonstrate high academic achievement.
Application requirements: Essay, transcript. Resume. U.S. Passport or U.S. Alien Registration Card. Two evaluations and letters of recommendation (one from hospitality/tourism-related faculty member, one from hospitality/tourism professional).
Additional information: Minimum 3.0 GPA. Applicant must be high school senior attending high school with the Academy of Hospitality & Tourism (AOHT) Program, graduating at end of semester or term. Visit Website for deadline, application, additional criteria.

Amount of award: $1,000
Number of awards: 1
Contact:
Tourism Cares
275 Turnpike Street
Suite 307
Canton, MA 02021
Phone: 781-821-5990
Fax: 781-821-8949
Web: www.tourismcares.org/student-programs

ASTA Arizona Scholarship

Type of award: Scholarship, renewable.
Intended use: For sophomore, junior or senior study at accredited 2-year or 4-year institution in United States. Designated institutions: Colleges and universities in Arizona.
Eligibility: Applicant must be U.S. citizen, permanent resident or Canadian citizen/resident.
Basis for selection: Major/career interest in tourism/travel. Applicant must demonstrate high academic achievement.
Application requirements: Essay, transcript. Resume. U.S. or Canadian passport or U.S. or Canadian Alien Registration Card. Two evaluations and letters of recommendation (one from hospitality/tourism-related faculty member, one from hospitality/tourism professional).
Additional information: Minimum 3.0 GPA. Applicants attending two-year schools must be entering second year of program; students attending four-year schools must be entering junior or senior years. Visit Website for application, deadline, additional criteria.
Amount of award: $2,000
Number of awards: 1
Contact:
Tourism Cares
275 Turnpike Street
Suite 307
Canton, MA 02021
Phone: 781-821-5990
Fax: 781-821-8949
Web: www.tourismcares.org/student-programs

ASTA Northern California Chapter - Richard Epping Scholarship

Type of award: Scholarship, renewable.
Intended use: For sophomore, junior or senior study at accredited 2-year or 4-year institution in United States. Designated institutions: Colleges and universities in California.
Eligibility: Applicant must be U.S. citizen or permanent resident residing in California.
Basis for selection: Major/career interest in hospitality administration/management or tourism/travel. Applicant must demonstrate high academic achievement.
Application requirements: Essay, transcript. Resume. U.S. passport or Alien Registration Card, California driver's license. Two evaluations and letters of recommendation (one from hospitality/tourism-related faculty member, one from hospitality/tourism professional).
Additional information: Minimum 3.0 GPA. Must be entering second year at two-year school, junior or senior year at four-year school. Visit Website for application, deadline, additional criteria.
Amount of award: $1,000
Number of awards: 1
Contact:
Tourism Cares
275 Turnpike Street
Suite 307
Canton, MA 02021
Phone: 781-821-5990
Fax: 781-821-8949
Web: www.tourismcares.org/student-programs

ASTA Pacific Northwest Chapter/ William Hunt Scholarship

Type of award: Scholarship.
Intended use: For sophomore, junior or senior study at accredited 2-year or 4-year institution in United States or Canada.
Eligibility: Applicant must be U.S. citizen or permanent resident residing in Oregon, Montana, Alaska, Idaho or Washington.
Basis for selection: Major/career interest in tourism/travel or hospitality administration/management. Applicant must demonstrate high academic achievement.
Application requirements: Essay, transcript. Resume. U.S. Passport or U.S. Alien Registration card. U.S. driver's license as proof of state residency. Two evaluations and letters of recommendation (one from hospitality/tourism-related faculty member, one from hospitality/tourism professional).
Additional information: Minimum 3.0 GPA. Must be entering the second year of a two-year school, or junior or senior year of a four-year school. Submit all items in electronic form except transcript, which should be sent directly from school. Visit Website for deadline and additional eligibility criteria.
Amount of award: $1,000
Number of awards: 1
Contact:
Tourism Cares
275 Turnpike Street
Suite 307
Canton, MA 02021
Phone: 781-821-5990
Fax: 781-821-8949
Web: www.tourismcares.org/student-programs

ASTA Princess Cruises Scholarship

Type of award: Scholarship, renewable.
Intended use: For sophomore, junior or senior study at accredited 2-year or 4-year institution in United States or Canada.
Eligibility: Applicant must be U.S. citizen, permanent resident or Canadian citizen/resident.
Basis for selection: Major/career interest in hospitality administration/management or tourism/travel. Applicant must demonstrate high academic achievement.
Application requirements: Recommendations, essay, transcript. Resume. U.S. or Canadian passport or U.S. or Canadian Alien Registration Card. Two evaluations and letters of recommendation (one from hospitality/tourism-related faculty member, one from hospitality/tourism professional).
Additional information: Minimum 3.0 GPA. Must be entering the second year of a two-year school, third year of a three-year school (Quebec), junior or senior year of a four-year school. Visit Website for application, deadline, additional criteria.
Amount of award: $2,500
Number of awards: 1

Contact:
Tourism Cares
275 Turnpike Street
Suite 307
Canton, MA 02021
Phone: 781-821-5990
Fax: 781-821-8949
Web: www.tourismcares.org/student-programs

IATAN Ronald A. Santana Memorial Scholarship

Type of award: Scholarship.
Intended use: For sophomore, junior or senior study at 2-year or 4-year institution in United States.
Eligibility: Applicant must be U.S. citizen, permanent resident or Guam or Puerto Rico citizens/residents.
Basis for selection: Major/career interest in tourism/travel or hospitality administration/management. Applicant must demonstrate high academic achievement.
Application requirements: Essay, transcript. Resume. U.S. passport or Alien Registration Card. Two evaluations and letters of recommendation (one from hospitality/tourism-related faculty member, one from hospitality/tourism professional).
Additional information: Minimum 3.0 GPA. Applicants attending two-year schools must be entering second year of program; students attending four-year schools must be entering junior or senior year. Visit Website for application, deadline, additional criteria.

Amount of award: $1,000
Number of awards: 5
Total amount awarded: $5,000

Contact:
Tourism Cares
275 Turnpike Street
Suite 307
Canton, MA 02021
Phone: 781-821-5990
Fax: 781-821-8949
Web: www.tourismcares.org/student-programs

NTA Canada Scholarship

Type of award: Scholarship.
Intended use: For full-time sophomore, junior, senior or graduate study at accredited 2-year or 4-year institution in United States or Canada.
Eligibility: Applicant must be permanent resident of Canada.
Basis for selection: Major/career interest in tourism/travel or hospitality administration/management. Applicant must demonstrate high academic achievement.
Application requirements: Essay, transcript. Resume. Canadian passport or Canadian Alien Registration Card. Two evaluations and letters of recommendation from hospitality/tourism-related faculty, one from a professional in the hospitality/tourism industry.
Additional information: Minimum 3.0 GPA. Must demonstrate focus and commitment to tourism. Must be entering the second year of a two-year school, third year of a three-year school (Quebec), senior year of a four-year school, any year of graduate school. Visit Website for application, deadline, additional criteria.

Amount of award: $1,000
Number of awards: 1

Contact:
Tourism Cares
275 Turnpike Street
Suite 307
Canton, MA 02021
Phone: 781-821-5990
Fax: 781-821-8949
Web: www.tourismcares.org/student-programs

NTA Connecticut Scholarship

Type of award: Scholarship.
Intended use: For junior or senior study at accredited 4-year institution in United States.
Eligibility: Applicant must be U.S. citizen or permanent resident residing in Connecticut.
Basis for selection: Major/career interest in hospitality administration/management or tourism/travel. Applicant must demonstrate high academic achievement.
Application requirements: Essay, transcript. Resume. U.S. passport or Alien Registration Card, Connecticut driver's license. Two evaluations and letters of recommendation (one from hospitality/tourism-related faculty member, one from hospitality/tourism professional).
Additional information: Minimum 3.0 GPA. Visit Website for application, deadline, additional criteria.

Amount of award: $1,000
Number of awards: 1

Contact:
Tourism Cares
275 Turnpike Street
Suite 307
Canton, MA 02021
Phone: 781-821-5990
Fax: 781-821-8949
Web: www.tourismcares.org/student-programs

NTA Florida Scholarship

Type of award: Scholarship.
Intended use: For sophomore, junior or senior study at accredited 2-year or 4-year institution in United States.
Eligibility: Applicant must be U.S. citizen or permanent resident residing in Florida.
Basis for selection: Major/career interest in hospitality administration/management or tourism/travel. Applicant must demonstrate high academic achievement.
Application requirements: Essay, transcript. Resume. U.S. passport or Alien Registration Card, Florida driver's license. Two evaluations and letters of recommendation (one from hospitality/tourism-related faculty member, one from hospitality/tourism professional).
Additional information: Minimum 3.0 GPA. Must be entering the second year of a two-year school, junior or senior year of a four-year school. Visit Website for application, deadline, additional criteria.

Amount of award: $1,500
Number of awards: 1

Contact:
Tourism Cares
275 Turnpike Street
Suite 307
Canton, MA 02021
Phone: 781-821-5990
Fax: 781-821-8949
Web: www.tourismcares.org/student-programs

NTA LaMacchia Family Scholarship

Type of award: Scholarship.
Intended use: For full-time junior or senior study at 4-year institution. Designated institutions: Wisconsin institutions.
Eligibility: Applicant must be U.S. citizen or permanent resident.
Basis for selection: Major/career interest in tourism/travel or hospitality administration/management. Applicant must demonstrate high academic achievement.
Application requirements: Essay, transcript. Resume. U.S. passport or Alien Registration Card. Two evaluations and letters of recommendation (one from hospitality/tourism-related faculty member, one from hospitality/tourism professional).
Additional information: Must have minimum 3.0 GPA. Visit Website for application, deadline, additional criteria.

Amount of award:	$1,000
Number of awards:	1

Contact:
Tourism Cares
275 Turnpike Street
Suite 307
Canton, MA 02021
Phone: 781-821-5990
Fax: 781-821-8949
Web: www.tourismcares.org/student-programs

NTA Massachusetts Scholarship

Type of award: Scholarship.
Intended use: For sophomore, junior or senior study at accredited 2-year or 4-year institution in United States. Designated institutions: .
Eligibility: Applicant must be U.S. citizen or permanent resident residing in Massachusetts.
Basis for selection: Major/career interest in hospitality administration/management or tourism/travel. Applicant must demonstrate high academic achievement.
Application requirements: Essay, transcript. Resume. U.S. passport or Alien Registration Card, Massachusetts driver's license. Two evaluations and letters of recommendation (one from hospitality/tourism-related faculty member, one from hospitality/tourism professional).
Additional information: Minimum 3.0 GPA. Applicants attending two-year schools must be entering second year of program; students attending four-year schools must be entering junior or senior years. Visit Website for application, deadline, additional criteria.

Amount of award:	$1,000
Number of awards:	1

Contact:
Tourism Cares
275 Turnpike Street
Suite 307
Canton, MA 02021
Phone: 781-821-5990
Fax: 781-821-8949
Web: www.tourismcares.org/student-programs

NTA New Horizons - Kathy LeTarte Scholarship

Type of award: Scholarship.
Intended use: For junior or senior study at accredited 4-year institution in United States or Canada.
Eligibility: Applicant must be U.S. citizen or permanent resident residing in Michigan.
Basis for selection: Major/career interest in tourism/travel or hospitality administration/management. Applicant must demonstrate high academic achievement.
Application requirements: Essay, transcript. Resume. U.S. passport or U.S. Alien Registration Card. Michigan driver's license. Two evaluations and letters of recommendation (one from hospitality/tourism-related faculty and one from a professional in hospitality/tourism industry).
Additional information: Minimum 3.0 GPA. Must be entering third year of three-year school (Quebec), or junior, senior year of four-year school. Visit Website for application, deadline, additional criteria.

Amount of award:	$1,000
Number of awards:	1

Contact:
Tourism Cares
275 Turnpike Street
Suite 307
Canton, MA 02021
Phone: 781-821-5990
Fax: 781-821-8949
Web: www.tourismcares.org/student-programs

NTA New Jersey Scholarship

Type of award: Scholarship.
Intended use: For sophomore, junior or senior study at accredited 2-year or 4-year institution in United States.
Eligibility: Applicant must be U.S. citizen or permanent resident residing in New Jersey.
Basis for selection: Major/career interest in hospitality administration/management or tourism/travel. Applicant must demonstrate high academic achievement.
Application requirements: Essay, transcript. Resume. U.S. passport or U.S. Alien Registration Card. New Jersey driver's license. Two evaluations and letters of recommendation (one from hospitality/tourism-related faculty member, one from hospitality/tourism professional).
Additional information: Minimum 3.0 GPA. Applicant must be entering the second year of a two-year school, or junior or senior year of a four-year school. Visit Website for application, deadline, additional criteria.

Amount of award:	$1,000
Number of awards:	1

Contact:
Tourism Cares
275 Turnpike Street
Suite 307
Canton, MA 02021
Phone: 781-821-5990
Fax: 781-821-8949
Web: www.tourismcares.org/student-programs

NTA New York Scholarship

Type of award: Scholarship.
Intended use: For full-time sophomore, junior or senior study at accredited 2-year or 4-year institution in United States.
Eligibility: Applicant must be U.S. citizen or permanent resident residing in New York.
Basis for selection: Major/career interest in hospitality administration/management or tourism/travel. Applicant must demonstrate high academic achievement.
Application requirements: Essay, transcript. Resume. U.S. passport or U.S. Alien Registration Card. New York driver's license. Two evaluations and letters of recommendation (one from hospitality/tourism-related faculty member, one from hospitality/tourism professional).

Additional information: Minimum 3.0 GPA. Applicants attending two-year schools must be entering second year of program; students at four-year schools must be entering junior or senior years. Visit Website for application, deadline, additional criteria.

Amount of award: $1,000
Number of awards: 1

Contact:
Tourism Cares
275 Turnpike Street
Suite 307
Canton, MA 02021
Phone: 781-821-5990
Fax: 781-821-8949
Web: www.tourismcares.org/student-programs

NTA North America Scholarship

Type of award: Scholarship.
Intended use: For sophomore, junior, senior or graduate study at 2-year, 4-year or graduate institution in United States or Canada.
Eligibility: Applicant must be U.S. citizen, permanent resident or Canadian citizen/resident.
Basis for selection: Major/career interest in tourism/travel or hospitality administration/management. Applicant must demonstrate high academic achievement.
Application requirements: Essay, transcript. Resume. U.S. or Canadian passport or U.S. or Canadian Alien Registration Card. Two evaluations and letters of recommendation (one from hospitality/tourism-related faculty member, one from hospitality/tourism professional).
Additional information: Minimum 3.0 GPA. Applicants attending two-year schools must be entering second year of program; students attending four-year schools must be entering junior or senior year. Visit Website for application, deadline, additional criteria.

Amount of award: $1,000
Number of awards: 13
Total amount awarded: $13,000

Contact:
Tourism Cares
275 Turnpike Street
Suite 307
Canton, MA 02021
Phone: 781-821-5990
Fax: 781-821-8949
Web: www.tourismcares.org/student-programs

NTA Ohio Scholarship

Type of award: Scholarship.
Intended use: For sophomore, junior or senior study at accredited 2-year or 4-year institution in United States.
Eligibility: Applicant must be U.S. citizen or permanent resident residing in Ohio.
Basis for selection: Major/career interest in hospitality administration/management or tourism/travel. Applicant must demonstrate high academic achievement.
Application requirements: Essay, transcript. Resume. U.S. passport or Alien Registration Card, Ohio driver's license. Two evaluations and letters of recommendation (one from hospitality/tourism-related faculty member, one from hospitality/tourism professional).
Additional information: Minimum 3.0 GPA. Applicants attending two-year schools must be entering second year of program; students at four-year schools must be entering junior or senior years. Visit Website for application, deadline, additional criteria.

Amount of award: $1,000
Number of awards: 1

Contact:
Tourism Cares
275 Turnpike Street
Suite 307
Canton, MA 02021
Phone: 781-821-5990
Fax: 781-821-8949
Web: www.tourismcares.org/student-programs

NTA Pat & Jim Host Scholarship

Type of award: Scholarship.
Intended use: For full-time sophomore, junior, senior or graduate study at accredited 4-year institution in United States.
Eligibility: Applicant must be U.S. citizen or permanent resident residing in Kentucky.
Basis for selection: Major/career interest in tourism/travel or hospitality administration/management. Applicant must demonstrate high academic achievement.
Application requirements: Essay, transcript. Resume. U.S. passport or U.S. Alien Registration Card. Copy of Kentucky driver's license. Two evaluations and letters of recommendation (one from hospitality/tourism-related faculty member; other from hospitality/tourism industry professional).
Additional information: Minimum 3.0 GPA. Must demonstrate a clear focus on and commitment to tourism. Visit Website for application, deadline, additional criteria.

Amount of award: $1,000
Number of awards: 1

Contact:
Tourism Cares
275 Turnpike Street
Suite 307
Canton, MA 02021
Phone: 781-821-5990
Fax: 781-821-8949
Web: www.tourismcares.org/student-programs

NTA Rene Campbell - Ruth McKinney Scholarship

Type of award: Scholarship.
Intended use: For sophomore, junior or senior study at accredited 4-year institution in United States or Canada.
Eligibility: Applicant must be U.S. citizen or permanent resident residing in North Carolina.
Basis for selection: Major/career interest in tourism/travel or hospitality administration/management. Applicant must demonstrate high academic achievement.
Application requirements: Essay, transcript. Resume. U.S. Passport or U.S. Alien Registration Card, North Carolina driver's license. Two evaluations and letters of recommendation (one from hospitality/tourism-related faculty member, one from hospitality/tourism professional).
Additional information: Minimum 3.0 GPA. Must be entering the second year of a two-year school, third year of a three-year school (Quebec), junior or senior year of a four-year school. Visit Website for application, deadline, additional criteria.

Amount of award: $1,000
Number of awards: 1

Contact:
Tourism Cares
275 Turnpike Street
Suite 307
Canton, MA 02021
Phone: 781-821-5990
Fax: 781-821-8949
Web: www.tourismcares.org/student-programs

NTA Utah Keith Griffall Scholarship

Type of award: Scholarship.
Intended use: For sophomore, junior or senior study at accredited 2-year or 4-year institution in United States.
Eligibility: Applicant must be U.S. citizen or permanent resident residing in Utah.
Basis for selection: Major/career interest in hospitality administration/management or tourism/travel. Applicant must demonstrate high academic achievement.
Application requirements: Essay, transcript. Resume. U.S. Passport or Alien Registration Card, Utah driver's license. Two evaluations and letters of recommendation (one from hospitality/tourism-related faculty member, one from hospitality/tourism professional).
Additional information: Minimum 3.0 GPA. Must be entering the second year of a two-year school, junior or senior year of a four-year school. Visit Website for application, deadline, additional criteria.

Amount of award:	$1,000
Number of awards:	1

Contact:
Tourism Cares
275 Turnpike Street
Suite 307
Canton, MA 02021
Phone: 781-821-5900
Fax: 781-821-8949
Web: www.tourismcares.org/student-programs

Transportation Clubs International

Alice Glaisyer Warfield Memorial Scholarship

Type of award: Scholarship.
Intended use: For undergraduate or graduate study at accredited postsecondary institution.
Eligibility: Applicant or parent must be member/participant of Transportation Clubs International.
Basis for selection: Major/career interest in transportation. Applicant must demonstrate financial need, high academic achievement, depth of character and service orientation.
Application requirements: Recommendations, essay, transcript. Small current photograph (for publication).
Additional information: Minimum 3.0 GPA.

Amount of award:	$1,500
Number of awards:	1
Application deadline:	May 31
Total amount awarded:	$1,500

Contact:
Transportation Clubs International Scholarships
Ms. Lynn Donovick, Martin Midstream Partners
Three Riverway, Ste. 400
Houston, TX 77056
Web: www.transportationclubsinternational.com

Charlotte Woods Memorial Scholarship

Type of award: Scholarship.
Intended use: For undergraduate study.
Eligibility: Applicant or parent must be member/participant of Transportation Clubs International.
Basis for selection: Major/career interest in transportation. Applicant must demonstrate financial need, high academic achievement, depth of character and service orientation.
Application requirements: Recommendations, essay, transcript. Small current photograph (for publication).
Additional information: Minimum 3.0 GPA.

Amount of award:	$1,500
Number of awards:	1
Application deadline:	May 31
Total amount awarded:	$1,500

Contact:
Transportation Clubs International Scholarships
Ms. Lynn Donovick, Martin Midstream Partners
Three Riverway, Ste. 400
Houston, TX 77056
Web: www.transportationclubsinternational.com

Denny Lydic Scholarship

Type of award: Scholarship.
Intended use: For undergraduate or graduate study at accredited vocational, 4-year or graduate institution.
Eligibility: Applicant or parent must be member/participant of Transportation Clubs International.
Basis for selection: Major/career interest in transportation. Applicant must demonstrate financial need, high academic achievement, depth of character and service orientation.
Application requirements: Recommendations, essay, transcript. Small current photograph (for publication).
Additional information: Minimum 3.0 GPA. Award amount varies; up to $1,000.

Amount of award:	$1,000
Number of awards:	1
Application deadline:	May 31
Total amount awarded:	$1,000

Contact:
Transportation Clubs International Scholarships
Ms. Lynn Donovick, Martin Midstream Partners
Three Riverway, Ste. 400
Houston, TX 77056
Web: www.transportationclubsinternational.com

Ginger and Fred Deines Canada Scholarship

Type of award: Scholarship.
Intended use: For undergraduate or graduate study in United States or Canada.
Eligibility: Applicant or parent must be member/participant of Transportation Clubs International. Applicant must be Canadian citizen.

Basis for selection: Major/career interest in transportation. Applicant must demonstrate financial need, high academic achievement, depth of character and service orientation.
Application requirements: Recommendations, essay, transcript. Small current photograph (for publication).
Additional information: Minimum 3.0 GPA.

Amount of award:	$2,000
Number of awards:	1
Application deadline:	May 31
Total amount awarded:	$2,000

Contact:
Transportation Clubs International Scholarships
Ms. Lynn Donovick, Martin Midstream Partners
Three Riverway, Ste. 400
Houston, TX 77056
Web: www.transportationclubsinternational.com

Ginger and Fred Deines Mexico Scholarship

Type of award: Scholarship.
Intended use: For undergraduate or graduate study. Designated institutions: Institutions in U.S. or Mexico.
Eligibility: Applicant or parent must be member/participant of Transportation Clubs International. Applicant must be Mexican citizen.
Basis for selection: Major/career interest in transportation. Applicant must demonstrate financial need, high academic achievement, depth of character and service orientation.
Application requirements: Recommendations, essay, transcript. Small current photograph (for publication).
Additional information: Minimum 3.0 GPA.

Amount of award:	$2,000
Number of awards:	1
Application deadline:	May 31
Total amount awarded:	$2,000

Contact:
Transportation Clubs International Scholarships
Ms. Lynn Donovick, Martin Midstream Partners
Three Riverway, Ste. 400
Houston, TX 77056
Web: www.transportationclubsinternational.com

Hooper Memorial Scholarship

Type of award: Scholarship.
Intended use: For undergraduate or graduate study.
Eligibility: Applicant or parent must be member/participant of Transportation Clubs International.
Basis for selection: Major/career interest in transportation. Applicant must demonstrate financial need, high academic achievement, depth of character and service orientation.
Application requirements: Recommendations, essay, transcript. Small current photograph (for publication).
Additional information: Minimum 3.0 GPA.

Amount of award:	$2,000
Number of awards:	1
Application deadline:	May 31
Total amount awarded:	$2,000

Contact:
Transportation Clubs International Scholarships
Ms. Lynn Donovick, Martin Midstream Partners
Three Riverway, Ste. 400
Houston, TX 77056
Web: www.transportationclubsinternational.com

Texas Transportation Scholarship

Type of award: Scholarship.
Intended use: For undergraduate or graduate study.
Eligibility: Applicant or parent must be member/participant of Transportation Clubs International.
Basis for selection: Major/career interest in transportation. Applicant must demonstrate financial need, high academic achievement, depth of character and service orientation.
Application requirements: Recommendations, essay, transcript. Small current photograph (for publication).
Additional information: Applicant must have been enrolled in a Texas school for some phase of elementary through high school education. Minimum 3.0 GPA.

Amount of award:	$1,500
Number of awards:	1
Application deadline:	May 31
Total amount awarded:	$1,500

Contact:
Transportation Clubs International Scholarships
Ms. Lynn Donovick, Martin Midstream Partners
Three Riverway, Ste. 400
Houston, TX 77056
Web: www.transportationclubsinternational.com

Treacy Foundation

Treacy Foundation Scholarship

Type of award: Scholarship, renewable.
Intended use: For full-time freshman or sophomore study at postsecondary institution.
Eligibility: Applicant must be residing in Montana, Idaho or North Dakota.
Basis for selection: Applicant must demonstrate financial need, leadership, seriousness of purpose and service orientation.
Application requirements: Transcript. Letter stating reason for applying, including personal information.
Additional information: Student may attend school outside of ND, ID, and MT. Applications available online from January to end of April.

Amount of award:	$2,000
Number of awards:	22
Number of applicants:	50
Application deadline:	May 1
Notification begins:	May 15
Total amount awarded:	$101,000

Contact:
Treacy Foundation
P.O. Box 1479
Helena, MT 59624
Phone: 406-443-3549
Fax: 406-443-6183
Web: www.treacyfoundation.org

Trinity Episcopal Church

Shannon Scholarship

Type of award: Scholarship, renewable.
Intended use: For undergraduate study at postsecondary institution.
Eligibility: Applicant must be female. Applicant must be Episcopal. Applicant must be residing in Pennsylvania.
Basis for selection: Applicant must demonstrate financial need.
Application requirements: Proof of eligibility.
Additional information: Only open to daughters of Episcopal clergy who are canonical residents in the state of Pennsylvania. Must apply for state and federal financial assistance first. Previous recipients may reapply. Number of awards varies. For more information, contact church office.

Amount of award:	$500-$6,000
Application deadline:	April 30
Notification begins:	June 30
Total amount awarded:	$20,000

Contact:
Trinity Episcopal Church
200 South Second Street
Pottsville, PA 17901
Phone: 570-622-8720

Two Ten Footwear Foundation

Two Ten Footwear Design Scholarship

Type of award: Scholarship, renewable.
Intended use: For undergraduate or graduate study in or outside United States.
Eligibility: Applicant must be U.S. citizen or permanent resident.
Basis for selection: Based on design talent. Major/career interest in design. Applicant must demonstrate financial need.
Application requirements: Portfolio, recommendations, essay, transcript.
Additional information: Individual must be attending recognized design program. Must be interested in pursuing career in footwear design.

Amount of award:	$1,000-$5,000
Application deadline:	February 28

Contact:
ISTS
Phone: 855-670-4787
Web: www.twoten.org

Two Ten Footwear Foundation Scholarship

Type of award: Scholarship, renewable.
Intended use: For undergraduate study at accredited vocational, 2-year or 4-year institution.
Eligibility: Applicant or parent must be employed by Footwear/Leather Industry. Applicant must be U.S. citizen or permanent resident.
Basis for selection: Applicant must demonstrate financial need and high academic achievement.
Application requirements: Recommendations, essay, transcript, proof of eligibility.
Additional information: Must have two years and 1,000 hours of work experience in footwear/leather industry. Additional information and application available on Website.

Amount of award:	$210-$3,000
Application deadline:	February 28
Notification begins:	June 15
Total amount awarded:	$700,000

Contact:
ISTS
Phone: 855-670-4787
Web: www.twoten.org

UCB Pharma Inc.

Keppra Family Epilepsy Scholarship Program

Type of award: Scholarship.
Intended use: For undergraduate or graduate study at vocational, 2-year, 4-year or graduate institution in United States.
Eligibility: Applicant must be U.S. citizen or permanent resident.
Basis for selection: Applicant must demonstrate high academic achievement, leadership and service orientation.
Application requirements: Transcript. Essay or artistic presentation explaining why applicant should be selected for scholarship (awards received, community involvement, etc.) and how epilepsy has impacted his or her life. Photograph. Three letters of recommendation: one from a school official, one from a community member, and one from applicant's epilepsy healthcare team.
Additional information: Scholarships are awarded to people with epilepsy, and to caregivers and family members of epilepsy patients. Visit Website for deadline and application.

Amount of award:	$5,000
Number of awards:	25
Application deadline:	May 15
Total amount awarded:	$200,000

Contact:
UCB Family Epilepsy Scholarship Program
c/o Summit Medical Communications
1421 E. Broad St., Suite 340
Furquay-Varina, NC 27526
Phone: 866-825-1920
Web: www.ucbepilepsyscholarship.com

The Ulman Cancer Fund

The Ulman Cancer Fund Scholarship

Type of award: Scholarship.
Intended use: For undergraduate study at 4-year institution.
Eligibility: Applicant must be U.S. citizen.
Basis for selection: Applicant must demonstrate financial need, leadership and service orientation.

Application requirements: Recommendations, essay, proof of eligibility. Physician verification form or copy of death certificate (if applicable), signed agreement to complete 40 hours of community service.
Additional information: Must be a young adult cancer survivor or patient diagnosed between the ages of 15-35 or a young adult who has lost a parent/guardian to cancer or must have a parent/guardian diagnosed or undergoing treatment for cancer or must have sibling diagnosed or undergoing treatment or must have lost a sibling due to cancer. Award recipient must complete 40 hours of community service.

Amount of award:	$2,500
Application deadline:	April 1

Contact:
The Ulman Cancer Fund, Attn: Scholarship
921 East Fort Avenue, Suite 325
Baltimore, MD 21230
Web: www.ulmanfund.org

Unico Foundation, Inc.

Alphonse A. Miele Scholarship

Type of award: Scholarship.
Intended use: For undergraduate study at postsecondary institution.
Eligibility: Applicant must be high school senior. Applicant must be Italian.
Basis for selection: Applicant must demonstrate financial need, high academic achievement, depth of character and leadership.
Application requirements: Recommendations, essay, transcript, proof of eligibility. SAT/ACT scores.
Additional information: Applications must be acquired from and submitted through a participating local UNICO chapter. Must be of Italian heritage. Award is $1,500 per year for four years.

Amount of award:	$6,000
Number of awards:	1
Application deadline:	April 15

Contact:
Unico Foundation, Inc.
271 US Highway, 46 #F-103
Fairfield, NJ 07004
Phone: 973-808-0035
Web: www.unico.org

Major Don S. Gentile Scholarship

Type of award: Scholarship.
Intended use: For undergraduate study at postsecondary institution.
Eligibility: Applicant must be high school senior. Applicant must be Italian.
Basis for selection: Applicant must demonstrate financial need, high academic achievement, depth of character and leadership.
Application requirements: Recommendations, essay, transcript, proof of eligibility. SAT/ACT scores.
Additional information: Applications must be acquired from and submitted through a participating local UNICO chapter. Must be of Italian heritage. Award is $1,500 per year for four years.

Amount of award:	$6,000
Number of awards:	1
Application deadline:	April 15

Contact:
Unico Foundation, Inc.
271 US Highway 46 #F-103
Fairfield, NJ 07004-2458
Phone: 973-808-0035
Web: www.unico.org

Theodore Mazza Scholarship

Type of award: Scholarship.
Intended use: For undergraduate study at postsecondary institution.
Eligibility: Applicant must be high school senior. Applicant must be Italian.
Basis for selection: Applicant must demonstrate financial need, high academic achievement, depth of character and leadership.
Application requirements: Recommendations, essay, transcript, proof of eligibility. SAT/ACT scores.
Additional information: Applications must be acquired from and submitted through a participating local UNICO chapter. Must be of Italian heritage. Award is $1,500 per year for four years.

Amount of award:	$6,000
Number of awards:	1
Application deadline:	April 15

Contact:
Unico Foundation, Inc.
271 US Highway 46 #F-103
Fairfield, NJ 07004-2458
Web: www.unico.org

William C. Davini Scholarship

Type of award: Scholarship.
Intended use: For undergraduate study at postsecondary institution.
Eligibility: Applicant must be high school senior. Applicant must be Italian.
Basis for selection: Applicant must demonstrate financial need, high academic achievement, depth of character and leadership.
Application requirements: Recommendations, essay, transcript, proof of eligibility. SAT/ACT scores.
Additional information: Applications must be acquired from and submitted through a participating local UNICO chapter. Must be of Italian heritage. Award is $1,500 per year for four years.

Amount of award:	$6,000
Number of awards:	1
Application deadline:	April 15

Contact:
Unico Foundation, Inc.
271 US Highway 46 #F-103
Fairfield, NJ 07004-2458
Web: www.unico.org

Union Plus

Union Plus Scholarship

Type of award: Scholarship.
Intended use: For undergraduate or graduate study at accredited vocational, 2-year, 4-year or graduate institution.
Basis for selection: Applicant must demonstrate financial need, high academic achievement, depth of character and leadership.
Application requirements: Recommendations, essay, proof of eligibility.
Additional information: Open to current or retired members, and dependents and spouses of current or retired members, of unions that participate in Union Plus programs. Minimum 3.0 GPA preferred.

Amount of award:	$500-$4,000
Number of awards:	108
Number of applicants:	4,237
Application deadline:	January 31
Notification begins:	May 31
Total amount awarded:	$150,000

Contact:
Union Plus Education Foundation c/o Union Privilege
1100 1st St. NE, Ste. 850
Washington, DC 20002
Web: www.unionplus.org

Unitarian Universalist Association

Children of Unitarian Universalist Ministers College Stipend

Type of award: Scholarship.
Intended use: For undergraduate study at 4-year institution.
Application requirements: Proof of college enrollment.
Additional information: Must be child of Unitarian Universalist Minister. Priority given to applicants whose family income does not exceed $50,000. Visit Website for deadlines.
Contact:
UUA Office of Church Staff Finances
c/o Joyce Stewart
25 Beacon Street
Boston, MA 02108-2800
Phone: 617-742-2100
Fax: 617-742-2875
Web: www.uua.org

Stanfield and D'Orlando Art Scholarships

Type of award: Scholarship.
Intended use: For full-time undergraduate or graduate study in United States.
Eligibility: Applicant must be Unitarian Universalist.
Basis for selection: Major/career interest in arts, general. Applicant must demonstrate financial need, depth of character and service orientation.
Application requirements: Portfolio, recommendations, essay, transcript, proof of eligibility.
Additional information: Number of awards varies; on average, five are given. Applicant must be preparing for fine arts career in fields such as painting, drawing, sculpture, or photography. Art therapy and performing arts majors not eligible. Returning adult students also eligible. See Website for application and more information.

Amount of award:	$1,000-$5,000
Number of awards:	5
Number of applicants:	15
Application deadline:	February 15
Notification begins:	May 1
Total amount awarded:	$20,000

Contact:
Unitarian Universalist Funding Program
P.O. Box 301149
Jamaica Plain, MA 02130
Phone: 617-971-9600
Fax: 617-971-0029
Web: www.uua.org/giving/awardsscholarships/

United Federation of Teachers

Albert Shanker College Scholarship Fund

Type of award: Scholarship.
Intended use: For freshman study.
Eligibility: Applicant must be high school senior. Applicant must be residing in New York.
Basis for selection: Applicant must demonstrate financial need, high academic achievement, leadership and service orientation.
Application requirements: Recommendations, essay, transcript, proof of eligibility. Valid proof of family income.
Additional information: Award is for New York City public high school seniors who will graduate from vocational, academic, or alternative school, night school, or New York City Board of Education alternative educational program. Must apply for and be eligible to receive federal financial aid. Must submit official documentation of income from all sources. Visit Website to determine financial eligibility and for more information.

Amount of award:	$5,000
Number of awards:	1
Application deadline:	January 31

Contact:
United Federation of Teachers
Web: www.uft.org/scholarship-fund

United Food and Commercial Workers International Union

United Food and Commercial Workers International Union Plus Scholarship Program

Type of award: Scholarship.
Intended use: For undergraduate or graduate study at accredited postsecondary institution in United States.

Eligibility: Applicant or parent must be member/participant of United Food and Commerical Workers.
Basis for selection: Applicant must demonstrate high academic achievement and service orientation.
Application requirements: Essay, transcript. Complete biographical questionnaire.
Additional information: Minimum 3.0 GPA. Applicant or applicant's parent must be member of United Food and Commercial Workers International Union for one year prior to application. Dependents of members must be under age 20.

Amount of award:	$500-$4,000
Number of awards:	14
Number of applicants:	3,500
Application deadline:	January 31
Notification begins:	July 1
Total amount awarded:	$56,000

Contact:
United Food and Commercial Workers International Union
Web: www.ufcw.org/scholarship

United Methodist Church General Board of Higher Education and Ministry

United Methodist Scholarships

Type of award: Scholarship, renewable.
Intended use: For full-time undergraduate or graduate study at accredited 2-year, 4-year or graduate institution in United States.
Eligibility: Applicant must be United Methodist.
Basis for selection: Applicant must demonstrate high academic achievement and seriousness of purpose.
Application requirements: Recommendations, essay, transcript. Online application.
Additional information: All recipients must be full active members of United Methodist Church for minimum of one year prior to application and maintain minimum 2.5 GPA. Awards vary. Some scholarships are renewable. Visit Website for more information. Deadline in March.

Notification begins:	June 1

Contact:
United Methodist Church General Board of Higher Education and Ministry
Office of Loans and Scholarships
P.O. Box 340007
Nashville, TN 37203-0007
Phone: 615-340-7344
Web: www.gbhem.org

United Methodist Communications

Leonard M. Perryman Communications Scholarship for Ethnic Minority Students

Type of award: Scholarship.
Intended use: For full-time junior or senior study at accredited 4-year institution in United States.
Eligibility: Applicant must be Alaskan native, Asian American, African American, Mexican American, Hispanic American, Puerto Rican, American Indian or Native Hawaiian/Pacific Islander. Applicant must be United Methodist.
Basis for selection: Major/career interest in journalism; communications; radio/television/film or religion/theology. Applicant must demonstrate seriousness of purpose.
Application requirements: Recommendations, essay, transcript. Three examples of journalistic work in any medium; photograph (appropriate for publicity purposes).
Additional information: Must plan to pursue career in religious journalism or religious communication. Application forms may be downloaded from Website.

Amount of award:	$2,500
Number of awards:	1
Number of applicants:	6
Application deadline:	March 15
Total amount awarded:	$2,500

Contact:
United Methodist Communications
Communications Ministry Team
P.O. Box 320, 810 12th Avenue South
Nashville, TN 37202-0320
Phone: 888-278-4862
Web: www.umcom.org

United Methodist Higher Education Foundation

Hoover-Lee Scholars Program

Type of award: Scholarship.
Intended use: For full-time undergraduate study at accredited 4-year or graduate institution in United States. Designated institutions: United Methodist-related institutions.
Eligibility: Applicant must be United Methodist. Applicant must be Southeast Asia and Fukien Province.
Basis for selection: Applicant must demonstrate high academic achievement and service orientation.
Application requirements: Recommendations, essay, transcript. A copy of TOEFL score report, a recent photograph.
Additional information: Priority also given to students who wish to dedicate their lives to serving humankind as demonstrated by scholarship benefactors. Must agree to return to native country following graduation. Must be starting school in Fall semester. Must be comfortable with English language. Minimum TOEFL scores: 500 paper or 173 computer for undergraduates; 600 paper or 250 for graduates. Minimum 3.0 GPA.

Amount of award:	$15,000
Application deadline:	March 1

Contact:
United Methodist Higher Education Foundation
Phone: 800-811-8110
Web: www.umhef.org

September 11 Memorial Scholarship

Type of award: Scholarship.
Intended use: For full-time undergraduate or graduate study at 4-year or graduate institution in United States.
Eligibility: Applicant must be United Methodist. Applicant must be U.S. citizen or permanent resident.

Basis for selection: Applicant must demonstrate high academic achievement.
Application requirements: Transcript, proof of eligibility. A letter from pastor of United Methodist Church verifying membership in that church if attending non-United Methodist school. Copy of institution's billing statement for period applicant is requesting assistance. Physician's letter attesting to applicant's disability or disability of applicant's parent/guardian as a result of 9/11 terrorist attacks. Birth certificate if applicant is dependent of a direct victim of 9/11 terrorist attacks. Financial Statement.
Additional information: Must have lost a parent or guardian or have had a parent or guardian disabled as a result of the September 11, 2001 terrorist attacks or be a direct victim disabled as a result of the September 11, 2001 terrorist attacks. Must be attending one of the 123 United Methodist-related institutions in the United States or be United Methodist student attending higher-education institution in the United States. Visit Website for more information.
Contact:
United Methodist Higher Education Foundation
60 Music Square East
Suite 350
Nashville, TN 37203
Phone: 800-811-8110
Web: www.umhef.org

United Negro College Fund

UNCF Merck Science Initiative

Type of award: Scholarship.
Intended use: For full-time junior study at 4-year institution in United States.
Eligibility: Applicant must be African American. Applicant must be U.S. citizen or permanent resident.
Basis for selection: Major/career interest in life sciences; physical sciences or engineering. Applicant must demonstrate high academic achievement.
Additional information: Minimum 3.3 GPA. Must be committed to and eligible for 10- to 12-week summer internship at a Merck facility. Summer internship includes stipend of at least $5,000. Apply online.

Amount of award:	$25,000-$30,000
Number of awards:	15
Application deadline:	December 1

Contact:
United Negro College Fund
Web: umsi.uncf.org

United States Army/ROTC

United States Army/ROTC Four-Year Scholarship

Type of award: Scholarship, renewable.
Intended use: For freshman study at accredited 4-year institution in United States.
Eligibility: Applicant must be at least 17, no older than 26. Applicant must be U.S. citizen. Must enlist in Army on active duty or in Army Reserve or Army National Guard for minimum eight years.
Basis for selection: Major/career interest in military science. Applicant must demonstrate high academic achievement and depth of character.
Application requirements: Interview, recommendations, transcript. SAT/ACT scores. Proof of high school class rank.
Additional information: Recipient receives living allowance (increasing each year) for each year of scholarship, plus allowance for books and other educational items. Minimum 920 SAT (Math and Reading) or 19 ACT. Minimum 2.5 GPA. Limited number of three- and two-year scholarships available once student is on campus; check with professor of military science once enrolled. Contact local Army ROTC recruiter or visit Website for application.

Amount of award:	Full tuition

Contact:
U.S. Army ROTC
Phone: 888-550-ARMY
Web: www.goarmy.com/rotc/high-school-students/four-year-scholarship.html

U.S. Army/ROTC Nursing Scholarship

Type of award: Scholarship.
Intended use: For undergraduate study at accredited 4-year institution in United States.
Eligibility: Applicant must be at least 17, no older than 26. Applicant must be U.S. citizen.
Basis for selection: Major/career interest in military science or nursing. Applicant must demonstrate high academic achievement and depth of character.
Application requirements: Interview, transcript.
Additional information: Must enlist to serve in the Army on Active Duty or in a Reserve Component for eight years. Minimum 920 SAT (Math and Reading) or 19 ACT. Must maintain minimum 2.5 GPA in college. Scholarships offered at different levels, providing college tuition and educational fees. All applicants considered for each level. Includes living allowance (increasing each year) for each year of scholarship, plus allowance for books and other educational items. Travel expenses not included. Limited number of three- and two-year scholarships available once student is on campus; check with school's professor of military science or contact local Army ROTC recruiter.

Amount of award:	Full tuition

Contact:
U.S. Army ROTC
Phone: 888-550-ARMY
Web: www.goarmy.com/rotc/nurse_program.jsp

United States Association of Blind Athletes

Arthur and Helen Copeland Scholarship

Type of award: Scholarship.
Intended use: For full-time undergraduate study at 2-year or 4-year institution.
Eligibility: Applicant must be visually impaired. Applicant must be female. Applicant must be U.S. citizen.

Scholarships

Basis for selection: Applicant must demonstrate high academic achievement and service orientation.
Application requirements: Transcript, proof of eligibility. Autobiographical sketch outlining community service, USABA involvement, academic goals, and objective for which scholarship funds will be used.
Additional information: Applicants must be legally blind. Preference given to applicants who are members of the United States Association of Blind Athletes. Must be a high school senior or in college. $500 award may be split into two $250 scholarships if there are two qualified applicants.

Amount of award:	$500
Number of awards:	2
Application deadline:	August 15
Notification begins:	November 1
Total amount awarded:	$500

Contact:
United States Association of Blind Athletes
c/o Mark Lucas
1 Olympic Plaza
Colorado Springs, CO 80909
Phone: 719-866-3220
Fax: 719-866-3400
Web: www.usaba.org

Arthur E. Copeland Scholarship

Type of award: Scholarship.
Intended use: For full-time undergraduate study at 2-year or 4-year institution.
Eligibility: Applicant must be visually impaired. Applicant must be male. Applicant must be U.S. citizen.
Basis for selection: Applicant must demonstrate high academic achievement and service orientation.
Application requirements: Transcript, proof of eligibility. Autobiographical sketch outlining community service, USABA involvement, academic goals, and objective for use of scholarship funds. References.
Additional information: Applicants must be legally blind. Preference given to applicants who are members of the United States Association of Blind Athletes. Must be high school senior or in college. Must have participated in USABA sports programs or plan on participating in future programs. Preference given to athletes. $500 award may be split into two $250 scholarships if there are two qualified applicants.

Amount of award:	$500
Number of awards:	1
Application deadline:	August 15
Notification begins:	November 1
Total amount awarded:	$500

Contact:
United States Association of Blind Athletes
c/o Mark Lucas
1 Olympic Plaza
Colorado Springs, CO 80909
Phone: 719-866-3220
Fax: 719-866-3400
Web: www.usaba.org

United States Institute of Peace

National Peace Essay Contest

Type of award: Scholarship.
Intended use: For undergraduate study at postsecondary institution.
Eligibility: Applicant must be enrolled in high school. Applicant must be U.S. citizen or permanent resident.
Basis for selection: Competition/talent/interest in writing/journalism.
Application requirements: 1500-word essay on topic chosen by the Institute. Student form and coordinator form.
Additional information: All high school students, including home-schooled students, foreign exchange students, or those enrolled in correspondence programs are eligible. All information regarding essay topic and online submission process can be found on Website. State-level winners receive $1,000 and will compete for national awards of $10,000, $5,000, and $2,500 (national amount includes state award). Also invited to attend awards program in Washington, DC. Visit Website for more information, including essay topic and study guide.

Amount of award:	$1,000-$10,000
Number of awards:	53
Number of applicants:	1,200
Application deadline:	February 1
Notification begins:	May 1
Total amount awarded:	$67,500

Contact:
United States Institute of Peace
2301 Constitution Ave. NW
Washington, DC 20037
Phone: 202-457-1700
Fax: 202-429-6063
Web: www.usip.org/npec

United Transportation Union Insurance Association

United Transportation Union Insurance Association Scholarship

Type of award: Scholarship, renewable.
Intended use: For full-time undergraduate study at accredited vocational, 2-year or 4-year institution in or outside United States.
Eligibility: Applicant or parent must be member/participant of United Transportation Union. Applicant must be no older than 25. Applicant must be permanent resident.
Application requirements: Proof of eligibility.
Additional information: Must own a UTUIA policy. Scholarships awarded by lottery. Applicant must be accepted to or enrolled in an eligible institution. Members and direct descendants of living or deceased members eligible. Notification takes place prior to fall enrollment. Deadline is last business day in March.

Amount of award:	$500
Number of awards:	50
Number of applicants:	900

Contact:
United Transportation Union Insurance Association
24950 Country Club Blvd., Ste. 340
North Olmsted, OH 44070-5333
Phone: 216-228-9400
Web: www.utuia.org/scholarship/utuiasch.htm

University Film and Video Association

Carole Fielding Video Grant

Type of award: Research grant.
Intended use: For undergraduate or graduate study at accredited 2-year or 4-year institution.
Basis for selection: Major/career interest in film/video.
Application requirements: Resume, budget, research/production proposal.
Additional information: Project categories include narrative, documentary, experimental, multimedia/installation, animation, and research. Applicant must be sponsored by faculty member who is active member of University Film and Video Association. Number of awards varies. Visit Website for application.

Amount of award:	$500-$1,000
Application deadline:	December 15
Notification begins:	March 31
Total amount awarded:	$4,000

Contact:
Prof. Adrianne Carageorge, UFVA Carole Fielding Student Grants Chair
Rochester Inst. Of Tech., Bldg. 7B, Rm. 2270
70 Lomb Memorial Dr.
Rochester, NY 14623-5604
Web: www.ufva.org

Upakar

Indian American Scholarship

Type of award: Scholarship, renewable.
Intended use: For freshman study.
Eligibility: Applicant must be Asian American. Applicant must be U.S. citizen or permanent resident.
Basis for selection: Applicant must demonstrate financial need and high academic achievement.
Application requirements: Recommendations, essay.
Additional information: Applicant must have either been born or have one grandparent/parent who was born in the Republic of India. Applicant must have cumulative, unadjusted GPA over 3.6. Applicant's family must have Adjusted Gross Income of less than $75,000. Must have green card or be American citizen.

Amount of award:	$2,000
Number of awards:	20
Number of applicants:	250
Application deadline:	April 30
Notification begins:	June 1
Total amount awarded:	$60,000

Contact:
Upakar c/o M. Mukunda
10237 Nolan Drive
Rockville, MD 20850
Web: www.upakarfoundation.org

U.S. Army Recruiting Command

Montgomery GI Bill (MGIB)

Type of award: Scholarship.
Intended use: For undergraduate or graduate study at accredited postsecondary institution in United States.
Eligibility: Applicant must be at least 17, no older than 35. Applicant must be U.S. citizen. Applicant must be in military service in the Army.
Basis for selection: Applicant must demonstrate depth of character, leadership, patriotism, seriousness of purpose and service orientation.
Application requirements: Interview. Armed Services Vocational Aptitude Battery.
Additional information: Award amount varies depending on type of service. Contact local recruiter or Army job counselor for more information.
Contact:
U.S. Army Recruiting Command
Phone: 888-550-ARMY
Web: www.goarmy.com

Montgomery GI Bill (MGIB) "Kicker"

Type of award: Scholarship.
Intended use: For full-time at 2-year or 4-year institution.
Eligibility: Applicant must be at least 17, no older than 35. Applicant must be U.S. citizen or permanent resident.
Basis for selection: Applicant must demonstrate high academic achievement and depth of character.
Additional information: Student can add up to $695/month to Montgomery GI Bill for up to 36 months (total up to $25,020) with the GI Bill Kicker. Amounts vary according to job and rank. Visit Website to request more information.
Contact:
U.S. Army Recruiting Command
Phone: 888-550-ARMY
Web: www.goarmy.com

Selected Reserve Montgomery GI Bill

Type of award: Scholarship.
Intended use: For undergraduate or graduate study at accredited postsecondary institution.
Eligibility: Applicant must be at least 17, no older than 35. Applicant must be U.S. citizen. Applicant must be veteran who served in the Army or Reserves/National Guard.

Scholarships

Basis for selection: Applicant must demonstrate depth of character, leadership, patriotism, seriousness of purpose and service orientation.
Application requirements: Interview. Armed Services Vocational Aptitude Battery.
Additional information: Award amount varies. Contact local recruiter or Army job counselor for more information.
Contact:
U.S. Army Recruiting Command
Phone: 888-550-ARMY
Web: www.goarmy.com

U.S. Army Recruiting Command Student Loan Repayment Program

Type of award: Scholarship.
Intended use: For at 2-year or 4-year institution.
Eligibility: Applicant must be at least 17, no older than 35. Applicant must be U.S. citizen or permanent resident.
Basis for selection: Applicant must demonstrate high academic achievement and depth of character.
Additional information: Offered to qualified applicants at the time of enlistment. Visit Website for more information.
Contact:
U.S. Army Recruiting Command
Phone: 888-550-ARMY
Web: www.goarmy.com

U.S. Department of Agriculture

USDA/1890 National Scholars Program

Type of award: Scholarship, renewable.
Intended use: For full-time freshman, sophomore or junior study at 4-year institution in United States. Designated institutions: One of the 1890 Historically Black Land-Grant Institutions: Alabama A&M University, Alcorn State University (MS), Delaware State University, Florida A&M University, Fort Valley State University (GA), Kentucky State University, Lincoln University (MO), Langston University (OK), North Carolina A&T University, Prairie View A&M University (TX), South Carolina State University, Southern University (LA), Tennessee State University, Tuskegee University (AL), University of Arkansas at Pine Bluff, University of Maryland at Eastern Shore, Virginia State University, and West Virginia State University.
Eligibility: Applicant must be U.S. citizen.
Basis for selection: Major/career interest in agriculture; agribusiness; agricultural education; agricultural economics; animal sciences; botany; food science/technology; wildlife/fisheries; forestry or horticulture. Applicant must demonstrate high academic achievement, leadership and service orientation.
Application requirements: Transcript. SAT/ACT scores. Current high school seniors: One recommendation from school counselor and one recommendation from high school teacher. Current college students: Recommendation from Department Head, Dean of College, or University Vice President and recommendation from college professor. 500- to 800-word essay.
Additional information: Must be seeking bachelor's degree in agriculture, food, natural resource sciences, or related disciplines. Scholarship covers full tuition and fees, plus room and board, for four years, up to $120,000. Upon completion of academic degree program, recipient has obligation of one year of service to USDA for each year of financial support. Number of awards varies depending on funding. Minimum 1000 SAT (Math and Reading; 1500 Math/Reading/Writing) or minimum 21 ACT and 3.0 GPA. Program includes summer employment. Upon successful completion of summer program, students are eligible for non-competitive transition as permanent employees. Contact designated institutions for more information and application.

Amount of award:	Full tuition
Number of applicants:	421
Application deadline:	February 1
Notification begins:	May 1
Total amount awarded:	$2,280,000

Contact:
U.S. Department of Agriculture
Web: www.outreach.usda.gov/education/1890/index.htm

U.S. Department of Education

Federal Pell Grant Program

Type of award: Scholarship, renewable.
Intended use: For undergraduate study at 2-year or 4-year institution.
Eligibility: Applicant must be U.S. citizen or permanent resident.
Basis for selection: Applicant must demonstrate financial need.
Application requirements: Proof of eligibility. FAFSA.
Additional information: Grant based on financial need, costs to attend school, and enrollment status. Must not have previously earned baccalaureate or professional degree. Amount of award varies; the maximum amount is $5,550. Visit Website for more information.

Application deadline:	June 30

Contact:
Federal Student Aid Information Center
Phone: 800-4-FED-AID
Web: www.studentaid.ed.gov

Federal Supplemental Educational Opportunity Grant Program

Type of award: Scholarship, renewable.
Intended use: For undergraduate study at accredited vocational, 2-year or 4-year institution in United States.
Eligibility: Applicant must be U.S. citizen or permanent resident.
Basis for selection: Applicant must demonstrate financial need.
Application requirements: Proof of eligibility. FAFSA.
Additional information: Priority given to Federal Pell Grant recipients with exceptional financial need. Must not have defaulted on federal grant or educational loan. Awards not generally made to students enrolled less than half-time. Check with institution's financial aid office for deadline.

Amount of award:	$100-$4,000

Contact:
Federal Student Aid Information Center
Phone: 800-4-FED-AID
Web: www.studentaid.ed.gov

Federal Work-Study Program

Type of award: Scholarship.
Intended use: For undergraduate or graduate study at accredited postsecondary institution in United States.
Eligibility: Applicant must be U.S. citizen or permanent resident.
Basis for selection: Applicant must demonstrate financial need.
Application requirements: Proof of eligibility. FAFSA.
Additional information: Part-time on-campus and off-campus jobs based on class schedule and academic progress. Students earn at least federal minimum wage. Visit Website for more information.

Application deadline: June 30

Contact:
Federal Student Aid Information Center
Phone: 800-4-FED-AID
Web: www.studentaid.ed.gov

Iraq and Afghanistan Service Grant

Type of award: Scholarship.
Intended use: For undergraduate study at 4-year institution in United States.
Eligibility: Applicant must be no older than 24. Applicant must be U.S. citizen or permanent resident. Applicant must be dependent of deceased veteran.
Additional information: Grant is for students whose parent or guardian was a member of the U.S. Armed Forces and died as a result of service performed in Iraq or Afghanistan after September 11, 2001. Must not be eligible for Pell Grant on the basis of Expected Family Contribution but meet the remaining Federal Pell Grant eligibility requirements. Must be enrolled in college at least part-time at time of parent's or guardian's death.
Contact:
Federal Student Aid Information Center
Phone: 800-4-FED-AID
Web: www.studentaid.ed.gov

U.S. Department of Education Rehabilitation Services Administration

U.S. Department of Education Rehabilitation Vocational Rehabilitation Assistance

Type of award: Scholarship, renewable.
Intended use: For undergraduate or graduate study at postsecondary institution in United States.
Additional information: Number of awards varies; amount varies depending on institution. Applicant must have a disability. Award applicable to many fields/majors, but must be consistent with applicant's abilities, interest, and informed choice. Must contact state vocational rehabilitation agency to become eligible. See Website for more information.

Contact:
U.S. Dept. of Education, OSERS, Rehabilitation Services Administration
Potomac Center Plaza
500 12th St. S.W., Rm. 5032
Washington, DC 20202-2800
Phone: 202-245-7325
Web: www.ed.gov

U.S. Department of Health and Human Services

National Health Service Corps Scholarship

Type of award: Scholarship.
Intended use: For full-time undergraduate or graduate study at accredited 4-year or graduate institution in United States.
Eligibility: Applicant must be U.S. citizen.
Basis for selection: Major/career interest in dentistry; nursing; nurse practitioner; physician assistant or midwifery. Applicant must demonstrate depth of character, seriousness of purpose and service orientation.
Application requirements: Interview, recommendations, essay, transcript, proof of eligibility. Resume, tuition bill, W-4.
Additional information: Students pursuing degree in allopathic or osteopathic medicine also eligible. Doctorate nurse training and "pre-professional" students ineligible. Awardees commit to providing health-care services in a National Health Service Corps approved site. One year of service owed for every year of scholarship support. Minimum service commitment two years; maximum four years. Award includes monthly stipend. Must be in training program. Number of awards varies. Visit Website for deadline and application.

Amount of award: Full tuition
Number of applicants: 1,400

Contact:
Web: www.nhsc.hrsa.gov

U.S. Environmental Protection Agency

EPA Greater Research Opportunities Undergraduate Student Fellowships

Type of award: Scholarship.
Intended use: For full-time junior or senior study at accredited 4-year institution in United States.
Eligibility: Applicant must be U.S. citizen or permanent resident.
Basis for selection: Major/career interest in life sciences; environmental science; engineering; social/behavioral sciences; physical sciences; mathematics; computer/information sciences or economics. Applicant must demonstrate financial need, high academic achievement and seriousness of purpose.
Application requirements: Recommendations, essay, transcript, proof of eligibility. Pre-application form. Resident

Aliens must include green card number. EPA may verify number with the Immigration and Naturalization Service.
Additional information: Award provides funding for last two years of four-year education. Students must apply before beginning of junior year. Applicant must attend a four-year institution or be in the second year at a two-year school at the time of applying, with the intent of transferring to a four-year institution. Minimum 3.0 GPA. Fellowship provides up to $19,700 per year for two years to cover tuition and fees as well as $9,500 of internship support for a three month period. Stipends and expense allowance also provided. Recipient must complete summer internship at EPA facility between funded junior and senior years. Preference given to applicants attending academic institutions that are not highly funded for development of environmental research. See Website for link to list. Applicants must submit preapplication form first; following a merit review, top-ranked applicants will be asked to submit formal application. See Website for application and deadline.

Amount of award: $50,000
Number of awards: 40
Total amount awarded: $2,000,000

Contact:
U.S. Environmental Protection Agency
Peer Review Division (8725F)
1200 Pennsylvania Avenue, NW
Washington, DC 20460
Phone: 800-490-9194
Web: www.epa.gov/ncer/fellow

EPA National Network for Environmental Management Studies Fellowship

Type of award: Research grant.
Intended use: For undergraduate or graduate study.
Eligibility: Applicant must be U.S. citizen or permanent resident.
Basis for selection: Major/career interest in environmental science; public relations; communications; computer/information sciences or law. Applicant must demonstrate high academic achievement, leadership and seriousness of purpose.
Application requirements: Transcript. Resume. One-page work-plan proposal. Letter of reference from faculty member or department head familiar with student's work and qualifications; letter must discuss student's aptitude and/or experience for project.
Additional information: Program provides students with research opportunities and experience at EPA locations nationwide. NNEMS develops and distributes annual catalog listing available research opportunities for coming year. Selected students receive stipend for performing research project. Projects also available in environmental management/administration and environmental policy, regulation, and law. Undergraduate applicants must: 1) be enrolled in program directly related to pollution control or environmental protection; 2) have 3.0 GPA; 3) have already completed four courses related to environmental field. Seniors who graduate prior to completion of advertised NNEMS fellowship period ineligible unless admitted to graduate school with submittable verification. Visit Website for award information and deadline. Catalog of available research opportunities available at www.epa.gov/education/students.html.

Number of awards: 32
Number of applicants: 345
Total amount awarded: $316,087

Contact:
U.S. Environmental Protection Agency
Web: www.epa.gov/enviroed/students.html

U.S. Navy/Marine NROTC College Scholarship Program

ROTC/Navy Nurse Corps Scholarship Program

Type of award: Scholarship.
Intended use: For full-time freshman study at accredited 4-year institution in United States. Designated institutions: NROTC-approved nursing schools.
Eligibility: Applicant must be at least 17, no older than 23. Applicant must be U.S. citizen.
Basis for selection: Major/career interest in nursing. Applicant must demonstrate high academic achievement and leadership.
Application requirements: Interview, recommendations, transcript, proof of eligibility.
Additional information: Scholarships are highly competitive and based on individual merit. Scholarships pay for college tuition, fees, books, uniforms, and offer $250 monthly allowance, which increases yearly. Electronic application is first step in application process. Number of awards varies. Applicant must be medically qualified for the NROTC Scholarship Program. Minimum 530 SAT (Reading), 520 (Math); minimum 22 ACT (English), 21 (Math). For Nurse and Navy applicants: If in top 10% of class, test scores may be below the stated minimum. Participation in extracurricular activities and work experience required. Applicants must have fewer than 30 hours college credit. Obligation of eight years commissioned service, four of which must be active duty. Contact local recruiter for more details.

Amount of award: Full tuition
Number of applicants: 500
Application deadline: January 31

Contact:
Contact local recruitment officer.
Phone: 800-NAV-ROTC
Web: www.nrotc.navy.mil

ROTC/Navy/Marine Four-Year Scholarship

Type of award: Scholarship.
Intended use: For full-time freshman study at accredited 4-year institution in United States. Designated institutions: Colleges and universities hosting NROTC program.
Eligibility: Applicant must be at least 17, no older than 23. Applicant must be U.S. citizen.
Basis for selection: Applicant must demonstrate high academic achievement and leadership.
Application requirements: Interview, recommendations, transcript, proof of eligibility.
Additional information: Scholarships are highly competitive and based on individual merit. Provide full tuition, fees, book allowance, and $250 monthly allowance, which increases annually. Number of awards varies. Applicant must be medically qualified for NROTC Scholarship. Minimum 530 SAT (Reading), 520 (Math); minimum 22 ACT (English), 21

(Math). Participation in extracurricular activities and work experience required. Applicant must have fewer than 30 hours college credit. Obligation of eight years commissioned service, five of which must be active duty. Contact nearest NROTC unit for more information. Visit Website to fill out electronic application.

Amount of award: Full tuition
Number of applicants: 5,500
Application deadline: January 31

Contact:
Contact local recruitment officer.
Phone: 800-NAV-ROTC
Web: www.nrotc.navy.mil

ROTC/Navy/Marine Two-Year Scholarship

Type of award: Scholarship.
Intended use: For full-time junior or senior study at 4-year institution in United States. Designated institutions: Colleges and universities hosting NROTC programs.
Eligibility: Applicant must be at least 17, no older than 23. Applicant must be U.S. citizen.
Basis for selection: Applicant must demonstrate high academic achievement and leadership.
Application requirements: Interview, recommendations, transcript, proof of eligibility.
Additional information: Scholarships are highly competitive and based on individual merit. Scholarships open to students who have completed sophomore year, or third year in a five-year curriculum. NROTC scholarships pay for college tuition, fees, book allowance, uniforms, and $250 monthly allowance, which increases annually. Minimum 530 SAT (Reading), 520 (Math); minimum 22 ACT (English), 21 ACT (Math). Participation in extracurricular activities and work experience required. Total military service obligation is eight years, five of which must be active duty. Contact local NROTC unit of university you wish to attend for more information.

Amount of award: Full tuition
Number of applicants: 50
Application deadline: March 15

Contact:
Contact local recruitment officer.
Phone: 800-NAV-ROTC
Web: www.nrotc.navy.mil

USTA Tennis and Education Foundation

USTA Scholarships

Type of award: Scholarship, renewable.
Intended use: For full-time undergraduate study at accredited 2-year or 4-year institution.
Eligibility: Applicant must be high school senior.
Basis for selection: Applicant must demonstrate financial need, high academic achievement, leadership and seriousness of purpose.
Application requirements: Interview, recommendations, essay, transcript. Photograph, FAFSA or SAR, ACT/SAT scores.
Additional information: Minimum 3.0 GPA. Applicant must have participated in USTA or other organized youth tennis program. The USTA offers seven scholarship programs. Amount and number of awards vary. Applications available online and must be mailed to local USTA Section office. Visit Website for application, deadline, and individual scholarship requirements. Deadline in February.

Amount of award: $1,000-$15,000
Number of awards: 76
Total amount awarded: $379,000

Contact:
United States Tennis Association
Phone: 914-696-7000
Web: www.ustaserves.com/grants_scholarships/college_scholarships_/

Utah Higher Education Assistance Authority (UHEAA)

Higher Education Success Stipend Program

Type of award: Scholarship, renewable.
Intended use: For undergraduate study at postsecondary institution.
Eligibility: Applicant must be residing in Utah.
Basis for selection: Applicant must demonstrate financial need.
Application requirements: FAFSA.
Additional information: Allocations are made to participating Utah institutions. Contact participating institution's financial aid office.

Amount of award: $300-$5,000
Number of awards: 7,028
Number of applicants: 2,365
Total amount awarded: $2,108,570

Contact:
Utah Higher Education Assistance Authority (UHEAA)
Web: www.uheaa.org

Utilities Employees Credit Union

UECU Student Scholarship Program

Type of award: Scholarship.
Intended use: For undergraduate or graduate study at accredited postsecondary institution.
Basis for selection: Applicant must demonstrate high academic achievement.
Application requirements: Essay or video on current year's scholarship contest topic. GPA, list of honors and activities.
Additional information: Award is for students with family in the utility/energy industry and students pursuing energy career who have joined EnergyPeopleConnect.com. Must be a UECU member in good standing with a UECU Share Savings Account in his/her own name. Cannot be an employee of UECU, its affiliates, a UECU board member, a supervisory committee member, or family member and/or living in the same household. Must be pursuing employment in energy-related fields or be family members of workers in the energy or utility industries. Minimum 3.0 GPA.

Amount of award:	$1,000
Number of awards:	2
Number of applicants:	30
Application deadline:	April 30
Notification begins:	June 1
Total amount awarded:	$2,000

Contact:
Utilities Employees Credit Union, Attn: Marketing Department
P.O. Box 14864
Reading, PA 19612
Phone: 800-288-6423
Web: www.uecu.org/scholarship

The Vegetarian Resource Group

The Vegetarian Resource Group College Scholarships

Type of award: Scholarship.
Intended use: For freshman study at postsecondary institution in United States.
Eligibility: Applicant must be high school senior. Applicant must be U.S. citizen.
Application requirements: Recommendations, essay, transcript.
Additional information: Award for graduating high school students who have promoted vegetarianism or veganism in their schools or communities. Students will be judged on having shown compassion, courage and a strong commitment to promoting a peaceful world through a vegetarian or vegan diet/lifestyle. Visit Website for application information.

Amount of award:	$5,000
Number of awards:	2
Number of applicants:	200
Application deadline:	February 20
Notification begins:	May 1
Total amount awarded:	$10,000

Contact:
The Vegetarian Resource Group
P.O. Box 1463
Baltimore, MD 21203
Phone: 410-366-8343
Fax: 410-366-8804
Web: www.vrg.org

Vegetarian Video Scholarship

Type of award: Scholarship.
Intended use: For undergraduate study.
Eligibility: Applicant must be U.S. citizen.
Additional information: Create and submit a video about what you want others to know about vegetarianism and/or veganism. Use of humor and feelings encouraged. See Website for full video submission guidelines.

Amount of award:	$250-$500
Number of awards:	3
Application deadline:	April 20

Contact:
The Vegetarian Resource Group
P.O. Box 1463
Baltimore, MD 21203
Phone: 410-336-8343
Fax: 410-366-8804
Web: www.vrg.org/videoscholarship.php

Ventura County Japanese-American Citizens League

Ventura County Japanese-American Citizens League Scholarships

Type of award: Scholarship.
Intended use: For freshman study at vocational, 2-year, 4-year or graduate institution in United States.
Eligibility: Applicant must be high school senior. Applicant must be Japanese. Applicant must be U.S. citizen residing in California.
Application requirements: Recommendations, essay, transcript, proof of eligibility. SAT scores.
Additional information: Applicant must be a Ventura County high school senior and a member of the Japanese American Citizens League. Amount and number of awards depend on available funding. Visit Website for application.

Application deadline:	April 1
Total amount awarded:	$10,000

Contact:
Ventura County JACL Scholarship Committee
P.O. Box 1092
Camarillo, CA 93011
Phone: 805-498-0764
Web: www.vcjacl.org

Vermont Golf Association Scholarship Fund, Inc.

Vermont Golf Association Scholarship

Type of award: Scholarship, renewable.
Intended use: For full-time undergraduate study at 2-year or 4-year institution.
Eligibility: Applicant must be high school senior. Applicant must be permanent resident residing in Vermont.
Basis for selection: Applicant must demonstrate high academic achievement.
Application requirements: Interview, recommendations, transcript. FAFSA.
Additional information: Must be graduate of Vermont high school and in top 40 percent of class or have GPA of 3.0 and 1500 SAT. Students of Hanover High School, NH, Riverdell Interstate School District, NH, and Grandville High School, NY, are also eligible. Applicant must have valid connection to golf.

Amount of award: $1,000
Number of awards: 10
Number of applicants: 38
Application deadline: April 20
Total amount awarded: $10,000

Contact:
Vermont Golf Association Scholarship Fund
P.O. Box 1612
Station A
Rutland, VT 05701
Phone: 802-775-7837
Fax: 802-773-7182
Web: www.vtga.org

Vermont Student Assistance Corporation

AIWF Culinary Scholarship

Type of award: Scholarship.
Intended use: For undergraduate study at accredited postsecondary institution. Designated institutions: Institutions approved for federal Title IV funding.
Eligibility: Applicant must be U.S. citizen or permanent resident residing in Vermont.
Basis for selection: Major/career interest in culinary arts. Applicant must demonstrate financial need.
Application requirements: Recommendations, essay. Personal interview (if necessary).
Additional information: Must attend school at least three-quarters time. Must have been Vermont resident for at least ten years. Deadline in early March.

Amount of award: $2,500
Number of awards: 1
Number of applicants: 18

Contact:
VSAC Scholarships Program
10 East Allen Street
P.O. Box 2000
Winooski, VT 05404
Phone: 888-253-4819
Web: www.vsac.org/scholarships

Alfred T. Granger Student Art Fund Scholarship

Type of award: Scholarship.
Intended use: For undergraduate or graduate study at accredited postsecondary institution. Designated institutions: Institutions approved for federal Title IV funding.
Eligibility: Applicant must be U.S. citizen or permanent resident residing in Vermont.
Basis for selection: Major/career interest in architecture; interior design; arts, general or design. Applicant must demonstrate financial need and high academic achievement.
Application requirements: Portfolio, recommendations.
Additional information: Minimum 3.1 GPA. Architectural engineering, lighting design, and mechanical drawing (CAD) majors also eligible. Four awards of $2,500 each for undergraduates and two $5,000 awards for graduate students. Deadline in early March.

Amount of award: $2,500-$5,000
Number of awards: 6
Number of applicants: 57

Contact:
VSAC Scholarships Program
10 East Allen Street
P.O. Box 2000
Winooski, VT 05404
Phone: 888-253-4819
Web: www.vsac.org/scholarships

Calvin Coolidge Memorial Foundation Scholarship

Type of award: Scholarship.
Intended use: For undergraduate study at accredited postsecondary institution. Designated institutions: Institutions approved for federal Title IV funding.
Eligibility: Applicant must be U.S. citizen or permanent resident residing in Vermont.
Basis for selection: Major/career interest in archaeology; anthropology; criminal justice/law enforcement; economics; geography; history; international relations; philosophy; political science/government or psychology. Applicant must demonstrate high academic achievement and service orientation.
Application requirements: Recommendations, essay.
Additional information: Must be enrolled at least three-quarters time. Social work, sociology, urban studies, and other social science majors also eligible. Deadline in early March.

Amount of award: $1,000
Number of awards: 1
Number of applicants: 195

Contact:
VSAC Scholarships Program
10 East Allen Street
P.O. Box 2000
Winooski, VT 05404
Phone: 888-253-4819
Web: www.vsac.org/scholarships

Champlain Valley Street Rodders Scholarship

Type of award: Scholarship.
Intended use: For undergraduate study at accredited postsecondary institution. Designated institutions: Institutions approved for federal Title IV funding.
Eligibility: Applicant must be enrolled in high school. Applicant must be residing in Vermont.
Basis for selection: Major/career interest in automotive technology. Applicant must demonstrate financial need and high academic achievement.
Application requirements: Recommendations, essay, transcript. FAFSA, tax return.
Additional information: Minimum 7.75 GPA on a 10.0 scale or 3.0 GPA on a 4.0 scale. Must be in the automotive field, mechanics, or repair. Applicant must have been Vermont resident for at least five years at time of application.

Amount of award: $500
Number of awards: 1
Number of applicants: 10

Contact:
VSAC Scholarships Program
10 East Allen Street
P.O. Box 2000
Winooski, VT 05404
Phone: 888-253-4819
Web: www.vsac.org/scholarships

Charles E. Leonard Memorial Scholarship

Type of award: Scholarship.
Intended use: For undergraduate or graduate study at accredited postsecondary institution. Designated institutions: Institutions approved for federal Title IV funding.
Eligibility: Applicant of parent must be visually impaired. Applicant must be U.S. citizen or permanent resident residing in Vermont.
Basis for selection: Applicant must demonstrate financial need and high academic achievement.
Application requirements: Essay.
Additional information: Applicants pursuing career in education/rehabilitation of blind or visually impaired people also eligible. Deadline in early March.

Amount of award:	$500
Number of awards:	3
Number of applicants:	8

Contact:
VSAC Scholarships Program
10 East Allen Street
P.O. Box 2000
Winooski, VT 05404
Phone: 888-253-4819
Web: www.vsac.org/scholarships

Emily Lester Vermont Opportunity Scholarship

Type of award: Scholarship, renewable.
Intended use: For undergraduate study at accredited postsecondary institution. Designated institutions: Vermont schools approved for federal Title IV funding.
Eligibility: Applicant must be residing in Vermont.
Basis for selection: Applicant must demonstrate financial need.
Application requirements: Proof of eligibility.
Additional information: Applicant must be under the custody of the Vermont commissioner of social and rehabilitation services or be between the ages of 18 and 24 and have been under the custody of the commissioner for at least six months between ages 16 and 18. Graduating high school seniors also eligible. Deadline in early March.

Amount of award:	$1,000-$3,000
Total amount awarded:	$22,500

Contact:
VSAC Scholarship Program
10 East Allen Street
P.O. Box 2000
Winooski, VT 05404
Phone: 888-253-4819
Web: www.vsac.org/scholarships

Jedidiah Zabrosky Scholarship

Type of award: Scholarship.
Intended use: For full-time undergraduate study at 2-year or 4-year institution in United States. Designated institutions: Castleton State College, Lyndon State College, Johnson State College, Community College of Vermont, Vermont Technical College, University of Vermont.
Eligibility: Applicant must be residing in Vermont.
Basis for selection: Major/career interest in business or education. Applicant must demonstrate financial need, high academic achievement and service orientation.
Application requirements: Recommendations, essay.
Additional information: Minimum 2.5 GPA. Applicant must be employed at time of application working minimum ten hours per week. Deadline in early March.

Amount of award:	$2,000
Number of awards:	1
Number of applicants:	40

Contact:
VSAC Scholarships Progam
10 East Allen Street
P.O. Box 2000
Winooski, VT 05404
Phone: 888-253-4819
Web: www.vsac.org/scholarships

Kittredge Coddington Memorial Scholarship

Type of award: Scholarship.
Intended use: For undergraduate study at accredited postsecondary institution. Designated institutions: Vermont institutions approved for federal Title IV funding.
Eligibility: Applicant must be enrolled in high school. Applicant must be U.S. citizen or permanent resident residing in Vermont.
Basis for selection: Major/career interest in business; business, international or business/management/administration.
Application requirements: Recommendations, essay.
Additional information: Must be planning career in business or industry. Deadline in early March.

Amount of award:	$500
Number of awards:	1
Number of applicants:	55

Contact:
VSAC Scholarships Program
10 East Allen Street
P.O. Box 2000
Winooski, VT 05404
Phone: 888-253-4819
Web: www.vsac.org/scholarships

Lee A. Lyman Memorial Music Scholarship

Type of award: Scholarship.
Intended use: For undergraduate or graduate study at accredited postsecondary institution. Designated institutions: Institutions approved for federal Title IV funding.
Eligibility: Applicant must be U.S. citizen or permanent resident residing in Vermont.
Basis for selection: Major/career interest in music. Applicant must demonstrate financial need and high academic achievement.
Application requirements: Recommendations, essay.
Additional information: Must demonstrate participation in music-related activities, performances, or groups. Deadline in early March.

Amount of award:	$1,000
Number of awards:	4
Number of applicants:	34
Total amount awarded:	$4,000

Contact:
VSAC Scholarships Program
10 East Allen Street
P.O. Box 2000
Winooski, VT 05404
Phone: 888-253-4819
Web: www.vsac.org/scholarships

Patrick and Judith McHugh Scholarship

Type of award: Scholarship.
Intended use: For undergraduate or graduate study at accredited postsecondary institution. Designated institutions: Institutions approved for federal Title IV funding.
Eligibility: Applicant must be U.S. citizen or permanent resident residing in Vermont.
Basis for selection: Major/career interest in health-related professions; dentistry; medicine; mental health/therapy; nursing; pharmacy/pharmaceutics/pharmacology or psychology. Applicant must demonstrate financial need.
Application requirements: Recommendations, essay.
Additional information: Must be enrolled at least three-quarters time. Deadline in early March.

Amount of award:	$1,000
Number of awards:	1
Number of applicants:	260

Contact:
VSAC Scholarships Program
10 East Allen Street
P.O. Box 2000
Winooski, VT 05404
Phone: 888-253-4819
Web: www.vsac.org/scholarships

People's United Bank Scholarship

Type of award: Scholarship, renewable.
Intended use: For full-time freshman study at accredited 2-year or 4-year institution in United States. Designated institutions: Vermont postsecondary schools approved for federal Title IV funding.
Eligibility: Applicant must be high school senior. Applicant must be residing in Vermont.
Basis for selection: Applicant must demonstrate financial need, high academic achievement and service orientation.
Application requirements: Recommendations, essay.
Additional information: Minimum 3.5 GPA. Deadline in early March.

Amount of award:	$2,500
Number of awards:	2
Number of applicants:	305

Contact:
VSAC Scholarships Program
10 East Allen Street
P.O. Box 2000
Winooski, VT 05404
Phone: 888-253-4819
Web: www.vsac.org/scholarships

Philip and Alice Angell Eastern Star Scholarship

Type of award: Scholarship.
Intended use: For undergraduate study at accredited 2-year or 4-year institution. Designated institutions: Postsecondary institutions approved for federal Title IV funding.
Eligibility: Applicant must be residing in Vermont.
Basis for selection: Major/career interest in business or education. Applicant must demonstrate financial need and high academic achievement.
Application requirements: Recommendations, essay.
Additional information: Minimum 3.5 GPA. Graduating high school seniors eligible. Deadline in early March.

Amount of award:	$500
Number of awards:	1
Number of applicants:	118

Contact:
VSAC Scholarships Program
10 East Allen Street
P.O. Box 2000
Winooski, VT 05404
Phone: 888-253-4819
Web: www.vsac.org/scholarships

RehabGYM Scholarship

Type of award: Scholarship.
Intended use: For undergraduate study at accredited postsecondary institution. Designated institutions: Institutions approved for federal Title IV funding.
Eligibility: Applicant must be physically challenged. Applicant must be U.S. citizen or permanent resident residing in Vermont.
Basis for selection: Applicant must demonstrate financial need.
Application requirements: Essay.
Additional information: Must be enrolled at least three-quarters time. Must have overcome significant physical challenge or illness. Deadline in early March.

Amount of award:	$1,000
Number of awards:	1
Number of applicants:	47

Contact:
VSAC Scholarships Program
10 East Allen Street
P.O. Box 2000
Winooski, VT 05404
Phone: 888-253-4819
Web: www.vsac.org/scholarships

Samara Foundation of Vermont Scholarship

Type of award: Scholarship.
Intended use: For undergraduate study at vocational, 2-year or 4-year institution.
Eligibility: Applicant must be high school senior. Applicant must be residing in Vermont.
Basis for selection: Competition/talent/interest in gay/lesbian.
Application requirements: Recommendations, essay.
Additional information: Applicant must demonstrate, through personal experience and/or public commitment, dedication to the interests of the gay, lesbian, bisexual, transgendered, and questioning community. Up to $5,000 is awarded annually. Deadline in early March.

Number of awards:	3
Number of applicants:	15

Contact:
VSAC Scholarships Programs
10 East Allen Street
P.O. Box 2000
Winooski, VT 05404
Phone: 888-253-4819
Web: www.vsac.org/scholarships

Students With Disabilities Endowed Scholarship Honoring Elizabeth Daley Jeffords

Type of award: Scholarship.
Intended use: For undergraduate study at accredited postsecondary institution. Designated institutions: Institutions approved for federal Title IV funding.
Eligibility: Applicant must be visually impaired, hearing impaired, physically challenged or learning disabled. Applicant must be U.S. citizen or permanent resident residing in Vermont.
Basis for selection: Applicant must demonstrate financial need and seriousness of purpose.
Application requirements: Recommendations, essay, proof of eligibility. Personal interview (if necessary).
Additional information: Number of awards varies. Deadline in early March.

Amount of award:	$1,500
Number of awards:	1
Number of applicants:	58

Contact:
VSAC Scholarships Program
10 East Allen Street
P.O. Box 2000
Winooski, VT 05404
Phone: 888-253-4819
Web: www.vsac.org/scholarships

Vermont Incentive Grant

Type of award: Scholarship.
Intended use: For full-time undergraduate study in United States.
Eligibility: Applicant must be U.S. citizen or permanent resident residing in Vermont.
Basis for selection: Applicant must demonstrate financial need.
Application requirements: Proof of eligibility. FAFSA.
Additional information: Must not yet have bachelor's degree. Vermont residents who attend Vermont College of Medicine or who are enrolled in Doctor of Veterinary Science program also eligible. Application may be completed online. Grant applications considered on first-come, first-served basis while funding is available.
Contact:
VSAC Scholarships Program
10 East Allen Street
P.O. Box 2000
Winooski, VT 05404
Phone: 800-882-4166 or 802-654-3750
Web: www.vsac.org

Vermont John H. Chafee Education and Training Scholarship

Type of award: Scholarship.
Intended use: For undergraduate study at accredited vocational, 2-year or 4-year institution. Designated institutions: Institutions approved for federal Title IV funding.
Eligibility: Applicant must be no older than 21. Applicant must be U.S. citizen or permanent resident residing in Vermont.
Basis for selection: Applicant must demonstrate financial need.
Additional information: Must be under custody of Vermont Commissioner of the Department for Children and Families (DCF) through eighteenth birthday or be adopted after age 16. Deadline in early March.

Amount of award:	$1,000-$5,000

Contact:
VSAC Scholarships Program
10 East Allen Street
P.O. Box 2000
Winooski, VT 05404
Phone: 888-253-4819
Web: www.vsac.org/scholarships

Vermont Non-Degree Program

Type of award: Scholarship.
Intended use: For non-degree study at postsecondary institution in United States.
Eligibility: Applicant must be permanent resident residing in Vermont.
Basis for selection: Applicant must demonstrate financial need.
Application requirements: Proof of eligibility.
Additional information: Award amount varies. Applicants must be enrolled in non-degree course that will improve employability or encourage further study. Applications available at Vermont Department of Employment and Training offices, schools and vocation centers, and VSAC. Grant applications considered on a first-come, first-served basis as long as funding is available.

Number of applicants:	1,290
Total amount awarded:	$645,732

Contact:
VSAC Scholarships Program
10 East Allen Street
P.O. Box 2000
Winooski, VT 05404
Phone: 800-882-4166 or 802-654-3750
Web: www.vsac.org

Vermont Part-Time Grant

Type of award: Scholarship.
Intended use: For half-time undergraduate study at vocational, 2-year or 4-year institution in United States.
Eligibility: Applicant must be permanent resident residing in Vermont.
Basis for selection: Applicant must demonstrate financial need.
Application requirements: Proof of eligibility. FAFSA.
Additional information: Must be taking fewer than 12 credits and not yet received bachelor's degree unless they are attending the University of Vermont College of Medicine or are enrolled in a doctor of veterinary medicine program. Award amounts vary according to number of credits.

Number of applicants:	3,743
Total amount awarded:	$1,016,909

Contact:
VSAC Scholarships Program
10 East Allen Street
P.O. Box 2000
Winooski, VT 05404
Phone: 800-882-4166 or 802-654-3750
Web: www.vsac.org

Veterans of Foreign Wars

Voice of Democracy Scholarship

Type of award: Scholarship.
Intended use: For undergraduate or graduate study at postsecondary institution in United States.
Eligibility: Applicant must be no older than 19, enrolled in high school.
Application requirements: Audiotape or CD of essay. Participants are judged by tape or CD, not written essay script.
Additional information: Student must be 19 or younger to apply. Must apply through high school or local Veterans of Foreign Wars post. Not all VFW posts participate in program. Any entry submitted to VFW National Headquarters will be returned to sender. Selection based on interpretation of assigned patriotic theme, content, and presentation of recorded 3-5 minute audio-essay. Visit Website for additional information and application form. Award is non-renewable.

Amount of award:	$1,000-$30,000
Number of awards:	54
Number of applicants:	50,000
Application deadline:	November 1
Total amount awarded:	$151,000

Contact:
Veterans of Foreign Wars National Headquarters
Voice of Democracy Program
406 West 34 Street
Kansas City, MO 64111
Phone: 816-968-1117
Fax: 816-968-1149
Web: www.vfw.org/Community/Programs

Virgin Islands Board of Education

Virgin Islands Music Scholarship

Type of award: Scholarship, renewable.
Intended use: For full-time undergraduate study at accredited 2-year or 4-year institution in United States.
Eligibility: Applicant must be U.S. citizen or permanent resident residing in Virgin Islands.
Basis for selection: Major/career interest in music. Applicant must demonstrate high academic achievement.
Application requirements: Transcript. Acceptance letter from college or university if first-time applicant.
Additional information: Minimum 2.0 GPA. Deadline in early May.

Amount of award:	$2,000

Contact:
Virgin Islands Board of Education Financial Aid Office
P.O. Box 11900
St. Thomas, VI 00801
Phone: 340-774-4546
Web: www.myviboe.com

Virginia Department of Education

Virginia Lee-Jackson Scholarship

Type of award: Scholarship.
Intended use: For full-time freshman study at accredited 2-year or 4-year institution in United States.
Eligibility: Applicant must be high school junior or senior. Applicant must be residing in Virginia.
Basis for selection: Competition/talent/interest in writing/journalism.
Application requirements: Essay demonstrating appreciation for virtues exemplified by General Robert E. Lee or General "Stonewall" Jackson.
Additional information: Award amount varies depending on essay. Additional awards for exceptional essays. Students must submit essay and application form to high school principal or guidance counselor. Application deadline is generally in mid-February. Community college awardees must plan to enroll in their college's transfer program. See Website for more information.

Amount of award:	$1,000-$10,000
Number of awards:	18
Total amount awarded:	$44,000

Contact:
The Lee-Jackson Foundation
P.O. Box 8121
Charlottesville, VA 22906
Web: www.lee-jackson.org

Virginia Department of Health

Mary Marshall Nursing RN Scholarship

Type of award: Scholarship.
Intended use: For undergraduate study at postsecondary institution in United States. Designated institutions: Virginia institutions.
Eligibility: Applicant must be residing in Virginia.
Basis for selection: Major/career interest in nursing.
Additional information: Award amount varies. Provides awards to students who agree to work in nursing profession in Virginia at rate of one month for every $100 of aid received. Must be eligible for in-state tuition at the time award is distributed. Recipient may reapply for up to four succeeding years. Applications and guidelines available from dean or financial aid office at applicant's nursing school, or from address listed.

Amount of award:	$300-$2,000
Number of awards:	73
Application deadline:	June 30

Contact:
Virginia Department of Health
109 Governor Street
Suite 1016-E
Richmond, VA 23219
Phone: 804-864-7435
Fax: 804-864-7440
Web: www.vdh.virginia.gov

Mary Marshall Nursing Scholarship Program (LPN)

Type of award: Scholarship.
Intended use: For undergraduate study. Designated institutions: Virginia nursing schools.
Basis for selection: Major/career interest in nursing. Applicant must demonstrate financial need.
Application requirements: Recommendations, transcript. FAFSA.
Additional information: Applicant must be eligible for Virginia in-state tuition at the time of award distribution. Award amount varies. Provides awards to students who agree to work in nursing practice in Virginia at rate of one month for every $100 of aid received. Recipient may reapply for up to four succeeding years. Applications and guidelines available from dean or financial aid office at applicant's nursing school, or from address listed.

Amount of award:	$400-$600
Number of awards:	48
Number of applicants:	79
Application deadline:	June 30
Total amount awarded:	$25,800

Contact:
Virginia Department of Health
109 Governor Street
Suite 1016-E
Richmond, VA 23219
Phone: 804-864-7435
Fax: 804-864-7440
Web: www.vdh.virginia.gov

Virginia's Nurse Practitioner Nurse Midwife Scholarship

Type of award: Scholarship.
Intended use: For full-time undergraduate study at postsecondary institution. Designated institutions: Institutions in Virginia.
Basis for selection: Major/career interest in nurse practitioner. Applicant must demonstrate high academic achievement and depth of character.
Application requirements: Recommendations, transcript.
Additional information: Virginia resident preferred. Applicant must commit to post-graduate employment in a medically underserved area of Virginia, in a setting that provides services to persons unable to pay and participates in all government-sponsored insurance programs. Employment must last for number of years equal to the number of annual scholarships received. If work commitment is not fulfilled or student does not complete studies, the award amount converts to loan. 3.0 GPA minimum preferred. Award amount and number of awards varies.

Amount of award:	$5,000
Number of applicants:	5
Application deadline:	June 30
Notification begins:	September 15
Total amount awarded:	$25,000

Contact:
Virginia Department of Health
109 Governor Street
Suite 1016-E
Richmond, VA 23219
Phone: 804-864-7435
Fax: 804-864-7440
Web: www.vdh.virginia.gov

Virginia Museum of Fine Arts

Virginia Museum of Fine Arts Visual Arts and Art History Fellowship

Type of award: Scholarship, renewable.
Intended use: For full-time undergraduate or graduate study at accredited 4-year or graduate institution.
Eligibility: Applicant must be U.S. citizen or permanent resident residing in Virginia.
Basis for selection: Major/career interest in arts, general; film/video or art/art history. Applicant must demonstrate financial need.
Application requirements: Portfolio, transcript. Eight images on CD representing recent work or three of the following: 16mm or video format films, videos, DVD, research papers, or published articles. References.
Additional information: May apply in one of the following categories on the undergraduate or graduate level: crafts, drawing, sculpture, filmmaking, painting, photography, printmaking. Candidates in art history may apply on the graduate level only. Visit Website for guidelines and application.

Amount of award:	$2,000-$8,000
Number of awards:	28
Number of applicants:	771
Application deadline:	November 8
Notification begins:	February 1
Total amount awarded:	$168,000

Contact:
Virginia Museum of Fine Arts Fellowships
Art and Education Division
200 N. Boulevard
Richmond, VA 23220-4007
Phone: 804-204-2685 or 804-204-2685
Fax: 804-204-2675
Web: www.vmfa.museum/fellowships

Wal-Mart Foundation

Wal-Mart Dependent Scholarship

Type of award: Scholarship, renewable.
Intended use: For full-time undergraduate study at accredited 2-year or 4-year institution in United States.
Eligibility: Applicant or parent must be employed by Wal-Mart Stores, Inc. Applicant must be high school senior. Applicant must be U.S. citizen or permanent resident.

Basis for selection: Applicant must demonstrate financial need and high academic achievement.
Application requirements: Transcript, proof of eligibility. SAT/ACT scores and financial data.
Additional information: Award for dependents of Wal-Mart associates. Employee must have been working at Wal-Mart for at least six consecutive months. Visit Website for application and deadline information. Minimum 2.0 GPA.

Amount of award:	$3,250
Number of awards:	26
Number of applicants:	2,600
Application deadline:	March 15

Contact:
Wal-Mart Dependent Scholarship
301 ACT Drive
P.O. Box 4030
Iowa City, IA 52243-4030
Phone: 877-333-0284
Web: www.walmartstores.com/communitygiving

Washington Crossing Foundation

Washington Crossing Foundation Scholarship

Type of award: Scholarship.
Intended use: For full-time undergraduate study at accredited 4-year institution.
Eligibility: Applicant must be high school senior. Applicant must be U.S. citizen.
Basis for selection: Major/career interest in political science/government or public administration/service. Applicant must demonstrate high academic achievement, depth of character, leadership, patriotism, seriousness of purpose and service orientation.
Application requirements: Recommendations, transcript. Essay on why student is planning a career in government service, including any inspiration derived from Washington's famous crossing of the Delaware. SAT/ACT scores.
Additional information: Number of awards varies. Visit Website for more information.

Amount of award:	$1,000-$5,000
Application deadline:	January 15
Notification begins:	June 30
Total amount awarded:	$42,000

Contact:
Washington Crossing Foundation
Attn: Vice Chairman
P.O. Box 503
Levittown, PA 19058
Phone: 215-949-8841
Web: www.gwcf.org

Washington Media Scholars Foundation

Media Plan Case Competition

Type of award: Scholarship.
Intended use: For undergraduate study at 4-year institution in United States.
Eligibility: Applicant must be at least 18.
Basis for selection: Competition/talent/interest in academics, based on creation of an in-depth media plan.
Additional information: The Media Plan Case Competition is made up of three rounds. The Qualification Round, the Case Competition semi-finals, and the Case Competition finals. Teams who reach the finals earn an all-expense-paid trip to Washington, D.C. to compete in the presentation round and network with media industry professionals. See Website for details. Deadline in February.

Amount of award:	$2,000-$3,000
Number of awards:	4
Number of applicants:	200
Total amount awarded:	$10,000

Contact:
Washington Media Scholars Foundation
815 Slaters Lane
Alexandria, VA 22314
Web: www.mediascholars.org/case-competition

Washington Media Scholars Media Fellows Program

Type of award: Scholarship.
Intended use: For junior or senior study at 4-year institution.
Eligibility: Applicant must be U.S. citizen.
Basis for selection: Applicant must demonstrate high academic achievement.
Application requirements: Recommendations, essay. Must submit written proposal in which student articulates career goals, course load, and financial need in 600 words or less. Proposal should include biographical information, statement of financial need, planned course load, career goals.
Additional information: Minimum 3.0 GPA in major concentration. Letter of recommendation may be from a professor, adviser, other home university official, a mentor, or previous employer.

Amount of award:	$1,000-$5,000
Number of awards:	10
Number of applicants:	1,000
Application deadline:	July 17
Notification begins:	August 17
Total amount awarded:	$30,000

Contact:
Washington Media Scholars Foundation
815 Slaters Lane
Alexandria, VA 22314
Phone: 703-299-4399
Web: www.mediascholars.org

Washington State Higher Education Coordinating Board

Washington State Need Grant

Type of award: Scholarship, renewable.
Intended use: For undergraduate study at accredited vocational, 2-year or 4-year institution. Designated institutions: Eligible postsecondary institutions in Washington.
Eligibility: Applicant must be U.S. citizen or permanent resident residing in Washington.

Basis for selection: Applicant must demonstrate financial need.
Application requirements: Proof of eligibility. FAFSA.
Additional information: Grants are given only to students from low-income families. Family income must be equal to or less than 70 percent of the state median. Must meet qualifications every year for renewal, up to five years. Contact institution's financial aid office for additional requirements and deadlines. Must not be pursuing a degree in theology. Number of awards varies. Visit Website for family income requirements and more information.

Amount of award:	$1,412-$10,868
Total amount awarded:	$182,735,778

Contact:
Washington State Higher Education Coordinating Board
917 Lakeridge Way
P.O. Box 43430
Olympia, WA 98504-3430
Phone: 360-753-7850
Web: www.hecb.wa.gov

Washington State PTA

Washington State Scholarship Program

Type of award: Scholarship.
Intended use: For full-time freshman study at accredited vocational, 2-year or 4-year institution.
Eligibility: Applicant must be residing in Washington.
Basis for selection: Applicant must demonstrate financial need, high academic achievement, depth of character, leadership, seriousness of purpose and service orientation.
Application requirements: Recommendations, essay, transcript, proof of eligibility.
Additional information: Minimum 3.0 GPA. Must be graduate of a Washington State public high school. Grant administered according to college's determination. Not transferable to another institution if already enrolled in classes. Visit Website for additional information and application.

Amount of award:	$1,000-$2,000
Number of awards:	60
Number of applicants:	2,000
Application deadline:	March 1
Total amount awarded:	$65,000

Contact:
Washington State Scholarship Program
2003 65 Avenue West
Tacoma, WA 98466-6215
Phone: 800-562-3804
Web: www.wastatepta.org

Wells Fargo

CollegeSTEPS

Type of award: Scholarship.
Intended use: For undergraduate study at postsecondary institution.
Eligibility: Applicant must be enrolled in high school. Applicant must be U.S. citizen or permanent resident.
Additional information: Awardees selected via random drawing. High school and college students eligible. Visit Wellsfargo.com/collegesteps to apply. Employees of Wells Fargo and immediate family members not eligible.

Amount of award:	$1,000
Number of awards:	40
Total amount awarded:	$40,000

Contact:
Education Financial Services
Wells Fargo
P.O. Box 5185
Sioux Falls, SD 57117-5185
Phone: 888-511-7302
Web: www.wellsfargo.com/collegesteps

Welsh Society of Philadelphia

Welsh Heritage Scholarship

Type of award: Scholarship, renewable.
Intended use: For full-time undergraduate study at accredited 2-year or 4-year institution.
Eligibility: Applicant must be Welsh.
Basis for selection: Applicant must demonstrate high academic achievement and seriousness of purpose.
Application requirements: Recommendations, essay, transcript. Statement of purpose.
Additional information: Applicant must be of Welsh descent. Applicant must live or attend college within 100 miles of Philadelphia. Participation in Welsh/Welsh-American organizations or events preferred.

Amount of award:	$500-$1,000
Number of awards:	5
Number of applicants:	50
Application deadline:	May 1
Total amount awarded:	$5,000

Contact:
Welsh Society of Philadelphia Scholarship Committee
Sc/o Dr. Donald Marcus
P.O. Box 7287
St. David's, PA 19087-7287
Web: www.philadelphiawelsh.org

Welsh Society of Philadelphia Undergraduate Scholarship

Type of award: Scholarship.
Intended use: For full-time undergraduate study at accredited 2-year or 4-year institution in United States.
Eligibility: Applicant must be Welsh. Applicant must be residing in Delaware, New Jersey, Maryland or Pennsylvania.
Basis for selection: Applicant must demonstrate high academic achievement, leadership, seriousness of purpose and service orientation.
Application requirements: Recommendations, essay, transcript, proof of eligibility.
Additional information: Applicant must be of Welsh descent. Must live or attend school within 100 miles of Philadelphia. Applicants studying in Wales with a primary residence within 100 miles of Philadelphia also eligible. Must rank in top third of class.

Amount of award:	$500-$1,000
Number of awards:	7
Number of applicants:	40
Application deadline:	May 1
Total amount awarded:	$5,000

Contact:
Welsh Society of Philadelphia Scholarship Committee
c/o Dr. Donald Marcus
P.O. Box 7287
St. Davids, PA 19087-7287
Web: www.philadelphiawelsh.org

West Pharmaceutical Services, Inc.

Herman O. West Foundation Scholarship Program

Type of award: Scholarship, renewable.
Intended use: For full-time undergraduate study at accredited 2-year or 4-year institution.
Eligibility: Applicant or parent must be employed by West Pharmaceutical Services, Inc. Applicant must be high school senior. Applicant must be U.S. citizen.
Basis for selection: Applicant must demonstrate high academic achievement.
Application requirements: Recommendations, essay, transcript, proof of eligibility. List of extracurricular activities.
Additional information: Parent must be employee of West Pharmaceutical Services, Inc. Award is renewable annually for maximum of four years.

Amount of award:	$2,500
Number of awards:	7
Number of applicants:	26
Application deadline:	February 28
Notification begins:	May 1
Total amount awarded:	$70,000

Contact:
H.O. West Foundation
560 Herman O. West Drive
Exton, PA 19341
Phone: 610-594-2945

West Virginia Department of Veterans Assistance

West Virginia War Orphans Educational Assistance

Type of award: Scholarship, renewable.
Intended use: For undergraduate, graduate or non-degree study in United States.
Eligibility: Applicant must be at least 16, no older than 25. Applicant must be U.S. citizen residing in West Virginia. Applicant must be dependent of deceased veteran who served in the Army, Air Force, Marines, Navy, Coast Guard or Reserves/National Guard. Applicant's parent must be veteran who was killed while on active duty during wartime or who died of injury or illness resulting from wartime service.
Application requirements: Proof of eligibility.
Additional information: Award is waiver of tuition and registration fees for West Virginia residents attending a West Virginia school. If attending a private school in West Virginia or out of state college, may only receive a maximum of $2,000 for academic year. Non-West Virginia residents exempt.

Amount of award:	Full tuition
Number of applicants:	5
Application deadline:	August 1, December 1
Notification begins:	July 15, December 15
Total amount awarded:	$11,000

Contact:
West Virginia Department of Veterans Assistance
Attn: Angela S. Meadows
1514 B. Kanawha Blvd. East
Charleston, WV 25311
Phone: 304-558-3661 or 866-984-8387
Fax: 304-558-3662
Web: www.veterans.wv.gov

Scholarships

West Virginia Higher Education Policy Commission

PROMISE Scholarship

Type of award: Scholarship, renewable.
Intended use: For undergraduate study at 2-year or 4-year institution.
Eligibility: Applicant must be U.S. citizen or permanent resident residing in West Virginia.
Basis for selection: Applicant must demonstrate high academic achievement.
Application requirements: FAFSA.
Additional information: Merit-based scholarship; all eligible applicants will receive award up to $4,750. Minimum 22 composite ACT, with scores of at least 20 in math, science, English, and reading, or 1020 SAT (Math and Reading) with minimum 480 Math and 490 Reading. Minimum 3.0 GPA. GED/home-schooled students must maintain a 2500 minimum score on the GED. Tuition waiver only for public institutions. Students attending private institutions will receive tuition assistance based on average cost of public college tuition and fees. See Website for more information.

Amount of award:	$4,750
Number of awards:	10,000
Number of applicants:	8,000
Application deadline:	March 1
Notification begins:	April 1
Total amount awarded:	$30,000,000

Contact:
West Virginia Higher Education Policy Commission
PROMISE Scholarship Program Staff
1018 Kanawha Boulevard East, Suite 700
Charleston, WV 25301-2800
Phone: 877-987-7664 or 304-558-4618
Web: www.cfwv.com

West Virginia Engineering, Science, and Technology Scholarship

Type of award: Scholarship, renewable.
Intended use: For full-time undergraduate study at 2-year or 4-year institution in United States. Designated institutions: Eligible West Virginia institutions.
Eligibility: Applicant must be U.S. citizen or permanent resident residing in West Virginia.
Basis for selection: Major/career interest in science, general; engineering; engineering, civil; engineering, computer; engineering, electrical/electronic; engineering, mechanical; computer/information sciences; life sciences; physical sciences or natural sciences. Applicant must demonstrate high academic achievement and seriousness of purpose.
Application requirements: Essay, transcript.
Additional information: Recipients should obtain degree/certificate in engineering, science, or technology and pursue career in West Virginia. Recipient must, within one year after ceasing to be a full-time student, work full-time in engineering, science, or technology field in West Virginia, or begin a program of community service relating to these fields in West Virginia for a duration of one year for each year scholarship was received. If work requirement fails to be met, recipient must repay scholarship plus interest and any required collection fees. Interested high school students should apply through high school counselor; currently enrolled college/university students should apply through their institution. Minimum 3.0 GPA. Application available on Website.

Amount of award:	$3,000
Number of awards:	100
Number of applicants:	400
Application deadline:	March 1
Total amount awarded:	$395,802

Contact:
West Virginia Higher Education Policy Commission
Financial Aid Program Staff
1018 Kanawha Boulevard East, Suite 700
Charleston, WV 25301-2800
Phone: 304-558-4618 or 877-987-7664
Web: www.cfwv.com

West Virginia Higher Education Adult Part-time Student (HEAPS) Grant Program

Type of award: Scholarship, renewable.
Intended use: For half-time undergraduate certificate, freshman, sophomore, junior or senior study at postsecondary institution. Designated institutions: West Virginia institutions.
Eligibility: Applicant must be returning adult student. Applicant must be U.S. citizen or permanent resident residing in West Virginia.
Basis for selection: Applicant must demonstrate financial need and high academic achievement.
Application requirements: FAFSA and any supplemental materials required by individual institutions.
Additional information: Applicant must be out of high school for at least two years and plan to continue education on part-time basis. Must either be enrolled in college with cumulative 2.0 GPA (for renewal applicants), or be accepted for enrollment by intended institution (for first-time applicants); must have complied with Military Selective Service Act; must qualify as independent student according to federal financial aid criteria; must not be in default on higher education loan; and must not be incarcerated in correctional facility. At public colleges/universities, award is actual amount of tuition and fees. At independent colleges/universities and vocational/technical schools, award is based upon average per credit/term hours tuition and fee charges assessed by all public undergraduate institutions. Contact school's financial aid office, or visit Website for additional information.
Contact:
West Virginia Higher Education Policy Commission
1018 Kanawha Boulevard East, Suite 700
Charleston, WV 25301-2800
Phone: 304-558-4618 or 877-987-7664
Web: www.cfwv.com

West Virginia Higher Education Grant

Type of award: Scholarship, renewable.
Intended use: For full-time undergraduate study at accredited 2-year or 4-year institution. Designated institutions: West Virginia or Pennsylvania institutions.
Eligibility: Applicant must be U.S. citizen or permanent resident residing in West Virginia.
Basis for selection: Applicant must demonstrate financial need and high academic achievement.
Application requirements: Transcript. FAFSA. ACT/SAT scores.
Additional information: Applicants must fill out common application for state-level financial aid programs. Visit Website for application.

Amount of award:	$350-$2,500
Number of awards:	9,800
Number of applicants:	34,000
Application deadline:	April 15
Total amount awarded:	$34,600,000

Contact:
West Virginia Higher Education Grant Program
Office of Financial Aid and Outreach Services
1018 Kanawha Boulevard East, Suite 700
Charleston, WV 25301-2800
Phone: 304-558-4618 or 877-987-7664
Fax: 304-558-5719
Web: www.cfwv.com

West Virginia Underwood-Smith Teacher Scholarship

Type of award: Scholarship, renewable.
Intended use: For full-time undergraduate or graduate study at 4-year or graduate institution.
Eligibility: Applicant must be U.S. citizen or permanent resident residing in West Virginia.
Basis for selection: Major/career interest in education; education, early childhood; education, special or education, teacher. Applicant must demonstrate high academic achievement.
Application requirements: Essay, proof of eligibility.
Additional information: Recipients must agree to teach at the public school level in West Virginia for two years for each year the scholarship is received or be willing to repay the scholarship on a pro rata basis. Visit Website for details and application.

Amount of award:	$5,000
Number of awards:	54
Number of applicants:	100
Total amount awarded:	$235,000

Contact:
West Virginia Higher Education Policy Commission
Underwood-Smith Teacher Scholarship Program
1018 Kanawha Boulevard East, Suite 700
Charleston, WV 25301-2800
Phone: 304-558-4614 or 877-987-7664
Web: www.cfwv.com

Western European Architecture Foundation

Gabriel Prize

Type of award: Research grant.
Intended use: For non-degree study at postsecondary institution.
Eligibility: Applicant must be U.S. citizen.
Basis for selection: Major/career interest in architecture. Applicant must demonstrate seriousness of purpose.
Application requirements: Portfolio, recommendations, research proposal. Resume.
Additional information: Award to encourage personal investigative and critical studies of French architectural compositions completed between 1630 and 1930. Work is expected to be executed in France under supervision of foundation's European representative. Winner is required to begin studies in France by May 1, keep a traveling sketchbook, and prepare three large colored drawings within three months. Must use stipend for travel and study. Send SASE for return of materials. Visit Website for application and deadline.

Amount of award:	$20,000
Number of awards:	1
Number of applicants:	24
Total amount awarded:	$20,000

Contact:
Western European Architecture Foundation
306 West Sunset, Suite 115
San Antonio, TX 78209
Phone: 210-829-4040
Fax: 210-829-4049
Web: www.gabrielprize.org

Western Golf Association/ Evans Scholars Foundation

Chick Evans Caddie Scholarship

Type of award: Scholarship, renewable.
Intended use: For full-time undergraduate study at accredited 4-year institution in United States. Designated institutions: Visit Website for comprehensive list of designated institutions.
Eligibility: Applicant must be high school senior.
Basis for selection: Competition/talent/interest in athletics/ sports, based on consistent caddie record at Western Golf Association-affiliated club. Applicant must demonstrate financial need, high academic achievement, depth of character and leadership.
Application requirements: Recommendations, essay, transcript, proof of eligibility. Tax returns, financial aid profile.
Additional information: Scholarship for full tuition, plus housing. Must have caddied minimum two years at Western Golf Association-affiliated club and maintain at least B average in college prep classes. Must have strong caddie record and work at sponsoring club during summer of application. Most recipients attend one of 14 universities where Evans Scholars Foundation owns and operates chapter house. Approximately 200 new Evans Scholarships awarded each year. Renewable up to four years. See Website for designated institutions.

Amount of award:	Full tuition
Number of awards:	200
Number of applicants:	678
Application deadline:	September 30
Notification begins:	March 1
Total amount awarded:	$8,000,000

Contact:
Scholarship Committee
Western Golf Assoc./Evans Scholars Foundation
1 Briar Road
Golf, IL 60029
Phone: 847-724-4600
Fax: 847-724-7133
Web: www.evansscholarsfoundation.com

Western Interstate Commission for Higher Education

Western Undergraduate Exchange

Type of award: Scholarship.
Intended use: For full-time undergraduate study at accredited 2-year or 4-year institution in United States. Designated institutions: Participating institutions in Alaska, Arizona, California, Colorado, Hawaii, Idaho, Montana, Nevada, New Mexico, North Dakota, Oregon, South Dakota, Utah, Washington, Wyoming.
Application requirements: Proof of eligibility.
Additional information: Students who are residents of Western Interstate Commission for Higher Education states are eligible to request a reduced tuition rate of 150% of resident tuition at participating two- and four-year college programs outside of their home state. The WUE reduced tuition rate is not automatically awarded to all eligible candidates. For list of participating institutions and programs, and for individual state contact information, visit Website.
Contact:
Student Exchange Programs - WICHE
3035 Center Green Drive
Boulder, CO 80301
Phone: 303-541-0270
Web: www.wiche.edu/wue

William Randolph Hearst Foundation

Hearst Journalism Award

Type of award: Scholarship.
Intended use: For undergraduate study at accredited 4-year institution. Designated institutions: Institutions accredited by

Scholarships

Accrediting Council on Education in Journalism and Mass Communication.
Basis for selection: Competition/talent/interest in writing/journalism, based on newsworthiness, research, excellence of journalistic writing, photojournalism, or broadcast news. Major/career interest in journalism; radio/television/film or communications.
Additional information: Field of study may also include photojournalism or broadcast news. Applicants must be actively involved in campus media and submit work that has been published or aired. Competition consists of monthly contests and one championship. Scholarships awarded to student winners with matching grants awarded to their departments of journalism. Entries must be submitted by journalism department. For additional information and deadlines, applicants should contact journalism department chair or visit Website. Only two applicants per competition per school.

Amount of award:	$1,000-$2,600
Number of awards:	14
Total amount awarded:	$500,000

Contact:
Heart Journalism Awards Program
90 New Montgomery Street
Suite 1212
San Francisco, CA 94105-4504
Phone: 415-908-4565 or 800-841-7048 ext. 4565
Web: www.hearstfdn.org

United States Senate Youth Program

Type of award: Scholarship.
Intended use: For undergraduate study at accredited 2-year or 4-year institution in United States.
Eligibility: Applicant must be high school junior or senior. Applicant must be U.S. citizen or permanent resident.
Basis for selection: Applicant must demonstrate leadership and service orientation.
Application requirements: Nomination by high school principal or teacher.
Additional information: Applicant must be permanent resident of and currently enrolled in public or private secondary school located in the state (including District of Columbia) in which parent or guardian legally resides. Must be currently serving in elected capacity as student body officer, class officer, student council representative, or student representative to district, regional, or state-level civic or educational organization. Selection process managed by state-level department of education. Scholarship includes all-expenses-paid week in Washington, D.C., in March. Application deadline is in early fall for most states; application available from high school principal or teacher. Visit Website for more information.

Amount of award:	$5,000
Number of awards:	104
Notification begins:	December 1
Total amount awarded:	$520,000

Contact:
Rayne Guilford, Program Director
William Randolph Hearst Foundation
90 New Montgomery Street, Suite 1212
San Francisco, CA 94105-4504
Phone: 800-841-7048 ext. 4540
Fax: 415-243-0760
Web: www.ussenateyouth.org

Wilson Ornithological Society

George A. Hall/Harold F. Mayfield Award

Type of award: Research grant.
Intended use: For non-degree study at postsecondary institution.
Basis for selection: Major/career interest in ornithology.
Application requirements: Recommendations, research proposal. Budget. Research proposal must be no longer than three pages.
Additional information: Research proposal must not exceed three pages. Award restricted to amateur researchers, including high school students, without access to funds and facilities of academic institutions or governmental agencies. Willingness to report research results as oral or poster paper is condition of award. Award should be used for equipment, supplies, travel, or living expenses. Visit Website for contact information and application.

Amount of award:	$1,000
Number of awards:	1
Number of applicants:	4
Application deadline:	February 1
Total amount awarded:	$1,000

Contact:
Wilson Ornithological Society
Web: www.wilsonsociety.org/awards

Paul A. Stewart Award

Type of award: Research grant.
Intended use: For undergraduate, master's, doctoral, postgraduate or non-degree study at postsecondary institution.
Basis for selection: Major/career interest in ornithology.
Application requirements: Recommendations, research proposal. Research budget.
Additional information: Research proposal should not exceed three pages. Preference given to proposals studying bird movements based on banding, analysis of recoveries, and returns of banded birds, with an emphasis on economic ornithology. Willingness to report research results as oral or poster paper is condition of award. Visit Website for contact information and application.

Amount of award:	$1,000
Number of awards:	8
Number of applicants:	18
Application deadline:	February 1
Total amount awarded:	$8,000

Contact:
Wilson Ornithological Society
Web: www.wilsonsociety.org/awards

Wisconsin Department of Veterans Affairs

Wisconsin Veterans Affairs Retraining Grant

Type of award: Scholarship.
Intended use: For undergraduate study at accredited vocational institution. Designated institutions: Wisconsin technical

colleges; occupational/technical schools approved by the Wisconsin Educational Approval Board; Wisconsin on-the-job training programs.
Eligibility: Applicant must be residing in Wisconsin. Applicant must be veteran. Must have served two years of continuous active duty during peacetime or 90 days of active duty during designated wartime period.
Basis for selection: Applicant must demonstrate financial need.
Additional information: Applicant must be recently unemployed or underemployed and registered for or enrolled in education program that will lead to re-employment and be completed within two years. Must have been involuntarily laid off within a period beginning one year before WDVA receives application. Must have been employed for six consecutive months with same employer or in the same or similar occupation. Must have been a resident of Wisconsin on entry into military service or a continuous resident of Wisconsin for at least five years after separation from military service. Apply year-round at local county Veterans Service Office to establish eligibility.

Amount of award:	$3,000

Contact:
Wisconsin Department of Veterans Affairs
201 W. Washington Ave.
P.O. Box 7843
Madison, WI 53707-7843
Phone: 800-947-8387
Web: www.WisVets.com/RetrainingGrants

Wisconsin Veterans Education GI Bill Tuition Remission Program

Type of award: Scholarship, renewable.
Intended use: For undergraduate study at vocational, 2-year or 4-year institution. Designated institutions: University of Wisconsin system schools, Wisconsin Technical College system schools.
Eligibility: Applicant must be residing in Wisconsin. Applicant must be veteran; or dependent of veteran, disabled veteran or deceased veteran; or spouse of veteran, disabled veteran or deceased veteran.
Basis for selection: Applicant must demonstrate financial need.
Application requirements: Proof of eligibility. Federal tax return or proof of annual income.
Additional information: Veteran must have been Wisconsin resident at time of entry into active duty; children of veterans must be between ages 17-25; widowed spouse of veteran must not be remarried. Veterans and spouses of veterans rated by the federal VA with a combined service-connected disability rating of 30% or greater are also eligible. Family income limit of $50,000; limit increases by $1,000 for each independent child. Veterans may receive up to 100 percent reimbursement of cost of tuition and fees. May receive reimbursement for up to eight semesters of full-time study. Visit Website for list of eligible schools, further requirements, and deadlines.
Contact:
Wisconsin Department of Veterans Affairs
201 W. Washington Ave.
P.O. Box 7843
Madison, WI 53707-7843
Phone: 800-947-8387
Web: www.WisVets.com/WisGIBill

Wisconsin Higher Educational Aids Board

Wisconsin Academic Excellence Scholarship

Type of award: Scholarship, renewable.
Intended use: For full-time undergraduate study at vocational, 2-year or 4-year institution. Designated institutions: Wisconsin non-profit colleges or universities.
Eligibility: Applicant must be high school senior. Applicant must be residing in Wisconsin.
Basis for selection: Applicant must demonstrate high academic achievement.
Application requirements: Nomination by high school guidance counselor.
Additional information: Awarded to Wisconsin high school seniors who have the highest grade point average in each public and private high school throughout Wisconsin. Must be registered with Selective Service, unless exempt. 3.0 GPA must be maintained for renewal.

Amount of award:	$2,250
Number of awards:	2,670
Application deadline:	March 1
Total amount awarded:	$2,894,469

Contact:
Higher Educational Aids Board
Attn: Nancy Wilkison
P.O. Box 7885
Madison, WI 53707-7885
Phone: 608-267-2213
Web: www.heab.state.wi.us

Wisconsin Hearing & Visually Handicapped Student Grant

Type of award: Scholarship, renewable.
Intended use: For undergraduate study at postsecondary institution. Designated institutions: Non-profit Wisconsin institutions; some out-of-state schools.
Eligibility: Applicant must be visually impaired or hearing impaired. Applicant must be residing in Wisconsin.
Basis for selection: Applicant must demonstrate financial need.
Application requirements: Proof of eligibility. FAFSA.

Amount of award:	$250-$1,800
Number of awards:	54
Total amount awarded:	$85,910

Contact:
Higher Educational Aids Board
Attn: Cindy Cooley
P.O. Box 7885
Madison, WI 53707-7885
Phone: 608-266-0888
Web: www.heab.state.wi.us

Wisconsin Higher Education Grant

Type of award: Scholarship, renewable.
Intended use: For undergraduate study at vocational or 4-year institution. Designated institutions: University of Wisconsin, Wisconsin Technical College, tribal institutions.
Eligibility: Applicant must be residing in Wisconsin.
Basis for selection: Applicant must demonstrate financial need.

Scholarships

Application requirements: Proof of eligibility. FAFSA.
Additional information: Apply with FAFSA through high school guidance counselor or financial aid office of institution. Must be registered with Selective Service, unless exempt. Rolling deadline.

Amount of award:	$250-$3,000
Number of awards:	37,172
Total amount awarded:	$35,060,586

Contact:
Higher Educational Aids Board
Attn: Cindy Cooley
P.O. Box 7885
Madison, WI 53707-7885
Phone: 608-266-0888
Web: www.heab.state.wi.us

Scholarships

Wisconsin Indian Student Assistance Grant

Type of award: Scholarship, renewable.
Intended use: For undergraduate or graduate study at postsecondary institution. Designated institutions: University of Wisconsin, Wisconsin Technical College, independent colleges and universities, tribal colleges, proprietary institutions in Wisconsin.
Eligibility: Applicant must be American Indian. Must be at least one-quarter Native American. Applicant must be residing in Wisconsin.
Basis for selection: Applicant must demonstrate financial need.
Application requirements: Proof of eligibility. FAFSA.
Additional information: Must be at least 25% Native American. Must be registered with Selective Service, unless exempt.

Amount of award:	$250-$1,100
Number of awards:	837
Total amount awarded:	$784,857

Contact:
Higher Educational Aids Board
Attn: Cindy Cooley
P.O. Box 7885
Madison, WI 53707-7885
Phone: 608-266-0888
Web: www.heab.state.wi.us

Wisconsin Minority Undergraduate Retention Grant

Type of award: Scholarship, renewable.
Intended use: For sophomore, junior or senior study at vocational, 2-year or 4-year institution. Designated institutions: Wisconsin technical colleges, independent colleges and universities, or tribal colleges.
Eligibility: Applicant must be Asian American, African American, Mexican American, Hispanic American, Puerto Rican or American Indian. Asian American applicants must be former citizens or children of former citizens of Laos, Vietnam, or Cambodia admitted to United States after 12/31/75. Applicant must be U.S. citizen or permanent resident residing in Wisconsin.
Basis for selection: Applicant must demonstrate financial need.
Application requirements: FAFSA and nomination by Financial Aid Office.

Amount of award:	$250-$2,500
Number of awards:	913
Number of applicants:	915
Total amount awarded:	$687,596

Contact:
Higher Educational Aids Board
Attn: Deanna Schulz
P.O. Box 7885
Wisconsin, WI 53707-7885
Phone: 608-267-2212
Web: www.heab.state.wi.us

Wisconsin Talent Incentive Program Grant

Type of award: Scholarship, renewable.
Intended use: For freshman study at postsecondary institution. Designated institutions: Non-profit Wisconsin institutions.
Eligibility: Applicant must be residing in Wisconsin.
Basis for selection: Applicant must demonstrate financial need.
Application requirements: Nomination by financial aid department or Wisconsin Educational Opportunity Programs. FAFSA.
Additional information: Applicant must meet at least one of non-traditional/economically disadvantaged criteria. Visit Website for list. Eligibility cannot exceed ten semesters.

Amount of award:	$250-$1,800
Number of awards:	4,146
Total amount awarded:	$5,489,498

Contact:
Higher Educational Aids Board
Attn: Colette Brown
P.O. Box 7885
Madison, WI 53707-7885
Phone: 608-266-1665
Web: www.heab.state.wi.us

Wisconsin Tuition Grant

Type of award: Scholarship, renewable.
Intended use: For undergraduate study at postsecondary institution. Designated institutions: Independent, nonprofit institutions in Wisconsin.
Eligibility: Applicant must be residing in Wisconsin.
Basis for selection: Applicant must demonstrate financial need.
Application requirements: FAFSA.
Additional information: Minimum award $250; maximum award amount set annually by HEAB. Must be registered for Selective Service, unless exempt.

Number of awards:	12,343
Total amount awarded:	$23,247,820

Contact:
Higher Educational Aids Board
Attn: Deanna Schulz
P.O. Box 7885
Madison, WI 53707-7885
Phone: 608-267-2212
Web: www.heab.state.wi.us

Women Grocers of America

Mary Macey Scholarship

Type of award: Scholarship, renewable.
Intended use: For sophomore, junior, senior or graduate study at accredited 2-year, 4-year or graduate institution in United States.
Basis for selection: Major/career interest in food production/management/services. Applicant must demonstrate high academic achievement.
Application requirements: Recommendations, essay, transcript.
Additional information: Must plan on a career in the independent sector of the grocery industry. Majors in public health and hotel management are not eligible. Minimum 2.0 GPA. Minimum of two $1500 awards each year. Deadline in mid-April.

Amount of award:	$1,500
Number of awards:	5
Number of applicants:	15
Application deadline:	April 19
Notification begins:	May 14
Total amount awarded:	$3,000

Contact:
Women Grocers of America
1005 North Glebe Road
Suite 250
Arlington, VA 22201-5758
Phone: 703-516-0700
Fax: 703-516-0115
Web: www.nationalgrocers.org

Women in Defense, A National Security Organization

Horizons Scholarship

Type of award: Scholarship.
Intended use: For junior, senior or graduate study at accredited 4-year institution in United States.
Eligibility: Applicant must be female. Applicant must be U.S. citizen.
Basis for selection: Major/career interest in science, general; engineering; mathematics; computer/information sciences; physics; business; law; international relations or political science/government. Applicant must demonstrate financial need and high academic achievement.
Application requirements: Recommendations, essay, transcript. Proof of citizenship.
Additional information: Scholarship intended to provide financial assistance to women either employed or planning careers in defense or national security areas. Minimum 3.25 GPA. Studies must be aimed at national defense/national security. Visit Website for details and application (no phone calls). Award amount varies.

Number of awards:	5
Number of applicants:	40
Application deadline:	July 1
Total amount awarded:	$31,000

Contact:
Women in Defense
2111 Wilson Blvd., Suite 400
Arlington, VA 22201-3061
Phone: 703-522-1820
Fax: 703-522-1885
Web: www.wid.ndia.org

Women's Western Golf Foundation

Women's Western Golf Foundation Scholarship

Type of award: Scholarship, renewable.
Intended use: For full-time freshman study at accredited 4-year institution in United States.
Eligibility: Applicant must be female, high school senior. Applicant must be U.S. citizen.
Basis for selection: Competition/talent/interest in athletics/sports. Applicant must demonstrate financial need, high academic achievement, depth of character, leadership and seriousness of purpose.
Application requirements: Essay, transcript, proof of eligibility. SAT/ACT scores, FAFSA. Personal recommendation required from high school teacher or counselor. List of high school activities.
Additional information: Must be in top 15 percent of class. 3.5 GPA is recommended. Must demonstrate involvement in golf, but skill not criterion. Deadline to request application is March 1; SASE required. Awards renew for each of four years, assuming scholarship terms are fulfilled (financial need, GPA above 3.0). About 20 new awards each year, plus 50 renewals.

Amount of award:	$2,000
Number of awards:	22
Number of applicants:	500
Application deadline:	April 5
Notification begins:	May 20
Total amount awarded:	$150,000

Contact:
Director of Scholarship
Women's Western Golf Foundation
393 Ramsay Road
Deerfield, IL 60015

Woodrow Wilson National Fellowship Foundation

Thomas R. Pickering Foreign Affairs Fellowship

Type of award: Scholarship.
Intended use: For full-time senior or graduate study at accredited 4-year or graduate institution in United States. Designated institutions: Institutions affiliated with Association of Professional Schools of International Affairs (graduate portion of fellowship).
Eligibility: Applicant must be U.S. citizen.

Scholarships

Basis for selection: Major/career interest in international relations; communications; history; economics; political science/government; foreign languages or business/management/administration. Applicant must demonstrate financial need, high academic achievement, depth of character, leadership, seriousness of purpose and service orientation.
Application requirements: Recommendations, essay, transcript, proof of eligibility. Resume, SAT or ACT scores, SAR, if applicable.
Additional information: Award is up to $40,000 toward tuition, mandatory fees, books, travel, and living stipend. Undergraduates must apply as juniors; applicants for graduate fellowship must be seeking admission to graduate school for the following academic year. Must have interest in career as Foreign Service officer. Number of fellowships determined by available funding. Finalists will attend interview session in Washington, D.C.; transportation to interview site paid. Orientation in Washington, D.C. Medical and security clearances required for program participation. Applicants must have minimum 3.2 GPA at time of application and maintain GPA throughout fellowship. Women and members of minority groups historically underrepresented in the Foreign Service encouraged to apply. Successful applicants obligated to a minimum of three years as a Foreign Service officer. Must register and apply online. Deadline varies; visit Website for details.
Contact:
Dr. Caryl Loney-McFarlane, Pickering Foreign Affairs Fellowship
Woodrow Wilson National Fellowship Foundation
P.O. Box 2437
Princeton, NJ 08543-2437
Phone: 609-452-7007
Web: www.woodrow.org

Worldstudio Foundation

Worldstudio AIGA Scholarship

Type of award: Scholarship.
Intended use: For full-time undergraduate or graduate study at accredited 2-year or 4-year institution in United States.
Eligibility: Applicant must be U.S. citizen or permanent resident.
Basis for selection: Major/career interest in graphic arts/design or arts, general. Applicant must demonstrate financial need, high academic achievement, seriousness of purpose and service orientation.
Application requirements: Portfolio, recommendations, transcript. Statement of purpose and self-portrait.
Additional information: Illustration, art direction for advertising, interactive design/motion graphics, and photography majors also eligible. The foundation's primary aim is to increase diversity in the creative professions and to foster social and environmental responsibility in the artists, designers, and studios of tomorrow. Applicants must be enrolled in courses related to or planning a career in design arts professions, and must demonstrate a social agenda in their work. Students with minority status given preference. Minimum 2.0 GPA. Visit Website for guidelines and application. Awards not offered for performing arts.

Amount of award:	$500-$5,000
Number of awards:	20
Number of applicants:	400
Application deadline:	March 28

Contact:
Worldstudio Foundation AIGA Scholarships
164 Fifth Avenue
New York, NY 10010
Phone: 212-807-1990
Web: www.scholarships.worldstudioinc.com

Wyzant Tutoring

Wyzant College Scholarship

Type of award: Scholarship.
Intended use: For undergraduate study at 4-year institution.
Basis for selection: Competition/talent/interest in writing/journalism.
Application requirements: 300-word essay on assigned topic. Topic available on Wyzant website.
Additional information: First place winner receives $10,000 to school of choice; second place, $3,000; third place, $2,000. See Website for application and details.

Amount of award:	$2,000-$10,000
Number of awards:	3
Application deadline:	May 1
Total amount awarded:	$15,000

Contact:
Wyzant College Scholarship
1714 N. Damen Ave
Suite 3N
Chicago, IL 60647
Phone: 877-999-2681
Fax: 773-345-5525
Web: www.wyzant.com/scholarships

Xerox

Technical Minority Scholarship

Type of award: Scholarship.
Intended use: For full-time undergraduate or graduate study in United States.
Eligibility: Applicant must be Alaskan native, Asian American, African American, Mexican American, Hispanic American, Puerto Rican, American Indian or Native Hawaiian/Pacific Islander. Applicant must be U.S. citizen or permanent resident.
Basis for selection: Major/career interest in chemistry; engineering; science, general; information systems; physics or computer/information sciences. Applicant must demonstrate high academic achievement, leadership, patriotism and seriousness of purpose.
Application requirements: Resume and cover letter.
Additional information: Minimum 3.0 GPA. Spouses and children of Xerox employees not eligible. Visit Website for application and more information.

Amount of award:	$1,000-$10,000
Number of awards:	99
Number of applicants:	1,524
Application deadline:	September 30
Notification begins:	December 31
Total amount awarded:	$160,000

Contact:
Xerox
Technical Minority Scholarship Program
150 State Street, 4th Floor
Rochester, NY 14614
Web: www.xeroxstudentcareers.com

Yakama Nation Higher Education Program

Yakama Nation Tribal Scholarship

Type of award: Scholarship.
Intended use: For undergraduate, master's or doctoral study at accredited 2-year, 4-year or graduate institution.
Eligibility: Must be enrolled member of Yakama Nation.
Application requirements: Transcript. High school or GED score sheet. Tribal ID card copy. Enrollment verification, FAFSA, college acceptance letter.
Additional information: Maximum $3,000 awarded to undergraduate students; maximum $6,000 awarded to graduate students. Recipients notified two weeks prior to the start of semester to which aid will be applied.

Amount of award:	$3,000-$6,000
Number of awards:	300
Number of applicants:	299
Application deadline:	July 1
Notification begins:	July 10
Total amount awarded:	$200,000

Contact:
Yakama Nation Higher Education Program
P.O. Box 151
Toppenish, WA 98948
Phone: 509-865-5121
Fax: 509-865-6994

Internships

Academy of Television Arts & Sciences Foundation

Academy of Television Arts & Sciences Student Internship Program

Type of award: Internship.
Intended use: For full-time undergraduate or graduate study in United States.
Eligibility: Applicant must be U.S. citizen, permanent resident or international student.
Basis for selection: Major/career interest in film/video or radio/television/film.
Application requirements: Recommendations, essay, transcript. Resume.
Additional information: Designed to expose students to professional TV production, techniques, and practices. Opportunities available in many fields; see Website for categories and special requirements. Internships are full-time for eight weeks. Interns responsible for housing, transportation, and living expenses. Interns must have car for transportation in Los Angeles. International students must be authorized to work in the United States. Apply online.

Amount of award:	$4,000
Number of awards:	41
Number of applicants:	1,200
Application deadline:	March 15
Notification begins:	May 15

Contact:
Academy of Television Arts & Sciences Foundation
Nancy Robinson, Student Internship Program
5220 Lankershim Boulevard
North Hollywood, CA 91601-3109
Phone: 818-754-2800
Web: www.emmysfoundationintern.org

Allstate

Allstate Internships

Type of award: Internship, renewable.
Intended use: For full-time undergraduate study at accredited 4-year institution.
Basis for selection: Major/career interest in insurance/actuarial science; accounting; marketing; business; business/management/administration; computer/information sciences; finance/banking; mathematics or statistics. Applicant must demonstrate high academic achievement.
Application requirements: Resume and cover letter.
Additional information: In addition to salary, eligible interns may receive subsidized transportation to and from Allstate Home Office in Northbrook, IL, at beginning and end of internship; daily transportation; and subsidized housing. Please respond directly to position posted on Website.
Contact:
Allstate Insurance Company
2775 Sanders Road
Northbrook, IL 60062
Web: www.allstate.jobs

American Association of Advertising Agencies

American Association of Advertising Agencies Multicultural Advertising Intern Program

Type of award: Internship, renewable.
Intended use: For full-time senior or graduate study at accredited 4-year or graduate institution.
Eligibility: Applicant must be Asian American, African American, Mexican American, Hispanic American, Puerto Rican, American Indian or Native Hawaiian/Pacific Islander. Applicant must be U.S. citizen or permanent resident.
Basis for selection: Major/career interest in advertising. Applicant must demonstrate high academic achievement and seriousness of purpose.
Application requirements: Recommendations, essay, transcript. Resume, work samples (if applying for creative internship).
Additional information: Applicants must have completed at least junior year of college and have strong interest in advertising. Minimum 3.0 GPA. Students are placed in member agency offices for ten weeks during the summer. $10/hour. MAIP interns requesting travel/housing assistance will be responsible for paying $1,000 to the 4A's toward summer housing and transportation cost. Can apply for following departments: account management, digital/interactive design, media planning/buying, broadcast production, traffic, art direction, copywriting, public relations, internet marketing, project management, social media, or strategic/account planning. Agency professionals interview semifinalists before selection. Application deadline is second Friday in November; notification in late December. Number of awards varies. See Website for more information.

Number of applicants:	325

Contact:
American Association of Advertising Agencies
1065 Avenue of the Americas
16th Floor
New York, NY 10018
Phone: 212-850-0731
Fax: 212-682-8391
Web: maipmatters.aaaa.org

American Bar Foundation

American Bar Foundation Summer Research Diversity Fellowships in Law and Social Sciences for Undergraduate Students

Type of award: Internship.
Intended use: For junior or senior study at 4-year institution.
Eligibility: Applicant must be U.S. citizen or permanent resident.
Basis for selection: Major/career interest in law; social/behavioral sciences; criminal justice/law enforcement; public administration/service or humanities/liberal arts. Applicant must demonstrate high academic achievement.
Application requirements: Recommendations, essay, transcript.
Additional information: Interns work eight 35-hour weeks as research assistants at American Bar Foundation in Chicago. Fellowships are intended for, but not limited to, persons who are African American, Hispanic/Latino, Native American, Asian, or Puerto Rican. Applicants must have minimum 3.0 GPA and intend to pursue academic major in social sciences or humanities. See Website for program specifics.

Amount of award:	$3,600
Number of awards:	4
Number of applicants:	200
Application deadline:	February 15
Notification begins:	April 1

Contact:
American Bar Foundation - Summer Diversity Fellowships
750 North Lake Shore Drive, Fourth Floor
Chicago, IL 60611
Phone: 312-988-6560
Fax: 312-988-6579
Web: www.americanbarfoundation.org/fellowships/Call_for_Summer_Research_Diversity_Fellows.html

American Conservatory Theater

American Conservatory Theater Production Fellowships

Type of award: Internship.
Intended use: For undergraduate, graduate or non-degree study.
Eligibility: Applicant must be U.S. citizen or permanent resident.
Basis for selection: Major/career interest in performing arts; theater arts or theater/production/technical.
Application requirements: Recommendations, essay. Resume. Writing sample and/or portfolio, if required by specific fellowship.
Additional information: Provides fellow with practical experience in many areas of theater production. Departments include costume rentals, costume shop, properties, stage management, and production. Fellowships are full-time for duration of entire season (September to June). A weekly stipend is available. Visit Website for more information.

Number of awards:	6
Number of applicants:	120
Application deadline:	March 31
Notification begins:	May 10

Contact:
American Conservatory Theater
Fellowship Coordinator
30 Grant Avenue, 6th Floor
San Francisco, CA 94108-5834
Phone: 415-834-3200
Web: www.act-sf.org/fellowships

Artistic and Administrative Fellowships

Type of award: Internship.
Intended use: For undergraduate, graduate or non-degree study.
Eligibility: Applicant must be U.S. citizen or permanent resident.
Basis for selection: Major/career interest in theater arts; theater/production/technical; arts management; performing arts; public relations; marketing; English or literature.
Application requirements: Recommendations, essay. Resume. Writing sample and/or portfolio if required by specific fellowship.
Additional information: Provides fellow with opportunity to work in artistic, development, dramaturgy, general management, graphic design, marketing/public relations, education/publications, or web development departments. Fellowship is full-time for duration of entire season (September to June). A weekly stipend is available. Visit Website for more information.

Number of awards:	8
Number of applicants:	120
Application deadline:	March 31
Notification begins:	May 10

Contact:
American Conservatory Theater
Fellowship Coordinator
30 Grant Avenue, 6th Floor
San Francisco, CA 94108-5834
Phone: 415-834-3200
Web: www.act-sf.org/fellowships

American Federation of State, County and Municipal Employees

AFSCMA/UNCF Union Scholars Program

Type of award: Internship.
Intended use: For sophomore or junior study at 4-year institution.
Eligibility: Applicant must be Alaskan native, Asian American, African American, Mexican American, Hispanic American, Puerto Rican, American Indian or Native Hawaiian/Pacific Islander.
Basis for selection: Major/career interest in ethnic/cultural studies; women's studies; sociology; anthropology; history; political science/government; psychology; social work;

economics or public administration/service. Applicant must demonstrate high academic achievement.
Application requirements: Recommendations, essay, transcript.
Additional information: Labor studies and American studies majors also eligible. Minimum 2.5 GPA. Must demonstrate interest in working for social and economic justice through the labor movement. Must have a driver's license. Award is a ten-week summer field placement to participate in union organizing campaign in one of several U.S. locations. Includes on-site housing and week-long orientation and training. Scholars receive up to $4,000 stipend and up to $5,000 academic scholarship for upcoming school year.

Amount of award:	$4,000-$9,000
Application deadline:	February 28

Contact:
AFSCME
Attn: Department of Education
1625 L Street, NW
Washington, DC 20036-5687
Phone: 866-671-7237
Web: www.afscme.org or www.uncf.org

American Museum of Natural History

Anthropology Internship Program

Type of award: Internship.
Intended use: For undergraduate or graduate study.
Basis for selection: Major/career interest in anthropology; archaeology or museum studies.
Application requirements: Essay, transcript. Resume, contact information of academic advisor.
Additional information: Must specify whether applying for paid, academic credit, or unpaid internship. Deadlines: April 1 for summer; August 27 for fall; December 1 for spring. Recent graduates also eligible. Number of awards varies.

Application deadline:	April 1, December 1

Contact:
American Museum of Natural History
Attn: Anita Caltabiano
Central Park West at 79th Street
New York, NY 10024-5192
Phone: 212-769-5375
Web: www.research.amnh.org/anthropology/about/internship

Research Experiences for Undergraduates in the Physical Sciences

Type of award: Internship.
Intended use: For undergraduate study at accredited postsecondary institution in United States.
Eligibility: Applicant must be U.S. citizen or permanent resident.
Basis for selection: Major/career interest in physical sciences; astronomy or geophysics. Applicant must demonstrate high academic achievement and seriousness of purpose.
Application requirements: Essay, transcript. List of courses. List of references. Ranking of first two choices among summer projects listed on Website and explanation of why applicant chose them.
Additional information: Nearby university dormitory housing or housing stipend provided, as well as travel to and from New York City, as per need. Visit Website for updated list of projects offered and application. Application must be submitted electronically. Contact Dr. James Webster (jdw@amnh.org) for more information on the Earth and Planetary Science program or Dr. Charles Liu (cliu@amnh.org) for the Astrophysics program. Amount and number of awards vary. Deadline may vary. Visit Website for exact date.

Amount of award:	$5,100
Application deadline:	February 1

Contact:
Richard Gilder Graduate School, REU Program in Physical Sciences
American Museum of Natural History
Central Park West at 79th Street
New York, NY 10024-5192
Phone: 212-769-5055
Web: www.research.amnh.org/physsci/reu.html

American Society of International Law

American Society of International Law Internships

Type of award: Internship.
Intended use: For undergraduate or graduate study at accredited postsecondary institution.
Basis for selection: Major/career interest in accounting; communications; international relations; law; public administration/service or public relations.
Application requirements: Cover letter, resume.
Additional information: Positions are based in Washington, D.C. and require a minimum commitment of 15 hours per week during fall and spring semesters. Summer semester positions may require a commitment of more than 15 hours per week. All internships unpaid; students may arrange academic credit. Visit Website for application requirements. Applications accepted on rolling basis.
Contact:
American Society of International Law
Internship Coordinator
2223 Massachusetts Avenue, NW
Washington, DC 20008
Phone: 202-939-6000
Fax: 202-797-7133
Web: www.asil.org/asil-internships.cfm

Americans for the Arts

Americans for the Arts Arts & Business Council of New York Internship

Type of award: Internship.
Intended use: For undergraduate or graduate study.
Basis for selection: Major/career interest in nonprofit administration; arts, general or arts management.

Application requirements: Cover letter, resume.
Additional information: Ten-week internship available on part-time basis for winter/spring and fall terms, and full-time basis for summer. $500 stipend for winter/spring, $1000 stipend for summer. Recent college graduates also eligible. Application deadlines are in March for summer, July for fall, and October for winter/spring. Visit Website for details and deadlines. Internship takes place in New York City. Candidates should have a passion for the arts, knowledge of Microsoft Office, and be able to multi-task and work with minimal supervision. Internship not always available for all seasons.

Amount of award: $500-$1,000
Number of awards: 1

Contact:
Americans for the Arts
Internship Coordinator
1000 Vermont Avenue, NW, 6th Floor
Washington, DC 20005
Phone: 202-371-0424
Web: www.americansforthearts.org

Americans for the Arts Arts Action Fund Internship

Type of award: Internship.
Intended use: For undergraduate or graduate study at postsecondary institution.
Basis for selection: Major/career interest in arts management; nonprofit administration or political science/government.
Application requirements: Cover letter, resume.
Additional information: Applicant may also be recent college graduate. Ten-week positions available part-time for winter/spring and fall and full-time for summer. Application deadlines are March for summer, July for fall, and October for winter/spring. Internship not always available for all seasons. Check Website for more details and deadlines. $500 stipend for winter/spring, $1000 stipend for summer. Must have excellent written and organizational skills, some experience in campaigns or political activities, strong computer skills (including proficiency in Microsoft Office and Adobe Creative Suite), and interest in basic Website management. Download application from Website or apply online.

Amount of award: $500-$1,000
Number of awards: 1

Contact:
Americans for the Arts
Internship Coordinator
1000 Vermont Avenue, NW, 6th Floor
Washington, DC 20005
Phone: 202-371-0424
Web: www.americansforthearts.org

Americans for the Arts Arts Marketing Internship

Type of award: Internship.
Intended use: For undergraduate or graduate study at postsecondary institution.
Basis for selection: Major/career interest in arts management; marketing; arts, general or nonprofit administration.
Application requirements: Cover letter, resume.
Additional information: Internship available on part-time basis for winter/spring and fall terms, and full-time basis for summer. $500 stipend for winter/spring, $1000 stipend for summer. Lasts ten to twelve weeks. Recent college graduates also eligible. Application deadlines are in March for summer, July for fall, and October for winter/spring. Internship takes place in New York City. Candidates should have a passion for the arts, knowledge of social media and Microsoft Office, Photoshop, and InDesign, and be able to multi-task and work with minimal supervision. Internship not always available for all seasons. Visit Website for details and deadlines.

Amount of award: $500-$1,000

Contact:
Americans for the Arts
Internship Coordinator
1000 Vermont Avenue, NW, 6th Floor
Washington, DC 20005
Phone: 202-371-0424
Web: www.americansforthearts.org

Americans for the Arts Arts Policy Internship

Type of award: Internship.
Intended use: For undergraduate or graduate study.
Basis for selection: Major/career interest in arts management; arts, general or nonprofit administration.
Application requirements: Cover letter, resume.
Additional information: Internship takes place in New York City office. Recent college graduates may apply. Positions available part-time for winter/spring and fall and full-time for summer. Application deadlines are March for summer, July for fall, and October for winter/spring. Internship not always available for all seasons. Check Website for details and deadlines. $500 stipend for winter/spring, $1000 stipend for summer. Must know MS office (especially Excel), be able to work independently, have good communication skills, and an interest in arts and culture policy.

Amount of award: $500-$1,000
Number of awards: 1

Contact:
Americans for the Arts
Internship Coordinator
1000 Vermont Avenue, NW, 6th Floor
Washington, DC 20005
Phone: 202-371-0424
Web: www.americansforthearts.org

Americans for the Arts Development Internship

Type of award: Internship.
Intended use: For undergraduate or graduate study at postsecondary institution.
Basis for selection: Major/career interest in arts management; arts, general or nonprofit administration.
Application requirements: Cover letter, resume.
Additional information: Internship available on part-time basis for winter/spring and fall terms, and full-time basis for summer. $500 stipend for winter/spring, $1000 stipend for summer. Lasts ten to twelve weeks. Recent college graduates also eligible. Application deadlines are in March for summer, July for fall, and October for winter/spring. Internship takes place in Washington, D.C. Candidates should have a passion for the arts, knowledge of Microsoft Office, and be able to multi-task and work with minimal supervision. Internship not always available for all seasons. Visit Website for details and deadlines.

Amount of award: $500-$1,000

Contact:
Americans for the Arts
Internship Coordinator
1000 Vermont Avenue, NW, 6th Floor
Washington, DC 20005
Phone: 202-371-0424
Web: www.americansforthearts.org

Americans for the Arts Government and Public Affairs Internship

Type of award: Internship.
Intended use: For undergraduate or graduate study at postsecondary institution.
Basis for selection: Major/career interest in arts management; arts, general; education; governmental public relations; public administration/service or nonprofit administration.
Application requirements: Cover letter, resume.
Additional information: Recent college graduates may apply. Ten-week positions available part-time for winter/spring and fall and full-time for summer. Application deadlines are March for summer, July for fall, and October for winter/spring. Internship not always available for all seasons. Check Website for details and deadlines. $500 stipend for winter/spring, $1000 stipend for summer. Must know MS Office and have good communication skills. Download application from Website or apply online.

Amount of award:	$500-$1,000
Number of awards:	1

Contact:
Americans for the Arts
Internship Coordinator
1000 Vermont Avenue, NW, 6th Floor
Washington, DC 20005
Phone: 202-371-0424
Web: www.americansforthearts.org

Americans for the Arts Leadership Alliances Internship

Type of award: Internship.
Intended use: For undergraduate or graduate study at postsecondary institution.
Basis for selection: Major/career interest in arts, general or nonprofit administration.
Application requirements: Cover letter, resume.
Additional information: Recent college graduates may apply. Ten-week positions available part-time for winter/spring and fall and full-time for summer. Application deadlines are March for summer, July for fall, and October for winter/spring. Internship not always available for all seasons. Check Website for details and deadlines. $500 stipend for winter/spring, $1000 stipend for summer. Must know MS Office and have good communication skills. Must know Word and Excel, especially mail merge and data sorting. Good communication skills and gregarious personality preferred. Download application from Website or apply online.

Amount of award:	$500-$1,000
Number of awards:	1

Contact:
Americans for the Arts
Internship Coordinator
1000 Vermont Avenue, NW, 6th Floor
Washington, DC 20005
Phone: 202-371-0424
Web: www.americansforthearts.org

Americans for the Arts Local Arts Advancement Services Internship

Type of award: Internship.
Intended use: For undergraduate or graduate study at postsecondary institution.
Basis for selection: Major/career interest in arts management; arts, general; communications or nonprofit administration.
Application requirements: Cover letter, resume.
Additional information: Recent college graduates may apply. Ten-week position available part-time for winter/spring and fall and full-time for summer. Application deadlines are March for summer, July for fall, and October for winter/spring. Internship not always available for all seasons. $500 stipend for fall/spring, $1000 stipend for summer. Must know Microsoft Office and Outlook, and have exceptional written and verbal communication skills. Check Website for details, deadlines and application.

Amount of award:	$500-$1,000
Number of awards:	1

Contact:
Americans for the Arts
Internship Coordinator
1000 Vermont Avenue, NW, 6th Floor
Washington, DC 20005
Phone: 202-371-0424
Web: www.americansforthearts.org

Americans for the Arts Marketing and Communications Internship

Type of award: Internship.
Intended use: For undergraduate or graduate study at postsecondary institution.
Basis for selection: Major/career interest in public relations; marketing; communications or nonprofit administration.
Application requirements: Cover letter, resume.
Additional information: Recent college graduates may apply. Ten-week positions available part-time for winter/spring and fall and full-time for summer. Application deadlines are March for summer, July for fall, and October for winter/spring. Internship not always available for all seasons. Check Website for details and deadlines. $500 stipend for winter/spring, $1000 stipend for summer. Must know MS Office and have good phone manner. Experience with database software, HTML, and proofreading/editing a plus. Download application from Website or apply online.

Amount of award:	$500-$1,000
Number of awards:	1

Contact:
Americans for the Arts
Internship Coordinator
1000 Vermont Avenue, NW, 6th Floor
Washington, DC 20005
Phone: 202-371-0424
Web: www.americansforthearts.org

Americans for the Arts Meetings and Events/Executive Office Internship

Type of award: Internship.
Intended use: For undergraduate or graduate study at 4-year or graduate institution.

Basis for selection: Major/career interest in hospitality administration/management; hotel/restaurant management; communications; public relations or nonprofit administration.
Application requirements: Cover letter, resume.
Additional information: Recent college graduates also eligible. Ten-week internship available in Washington, D.C. on part-time basis for winter/spring and fall terms and full-time for summer. $500 stipend for fall/spring, $1000 stipend for summer. Application deadlines are in March for summer, July for fall, and October for winter/spring. Internship not always available for all seasons. Must have strong knowledge of Microsoft Office. Candidate should have interest in event planning and/or nonprofit sector. Visit Website for details and deadlines.

Amount of award: $500-$1,000
Number of awards: 1

Contact:
Americans for the Arts
Internship Coordinator
1000 Vermont Avenue, NW, 6th Floor
Washington, DC 20005
Phone: 202-371-0424
Web: www.americansforthearts.org

Americans for the Arts Membership Internship

Type of award: Internship.
Intended use: For undergraduate or graduate study at 4-year or graduate institution.
Basis for selection: Major/career interest in nonprofit administration; arts management; arts, general or marketing.
Application requirements: Cover letter, resume.
Additional information: Recent college graduates also eligible. Ten-week internship in Washington, D.C.; available part-time for winter/spring and fall and full-time for summer. $500 stipend for winter/spring, $1000 stipend for summer. Application deadlines are in March for summer, July for fall, and October for winter/spring. Internship not always available for all seasons. Check Website for details and deadlines. Must have knowledge of Microsoft Office; experience using database software a plus. Ideal candidate has interest and experience in marketing, membership, or arts administration.

Amount of award: $500-$1,000
Number of awards: 1

Contact:
Americans for the Arts
Internship Coordinator
1000 Vermont Avenue, NW, 6th Floor
Washington, DC 20005
Phone: 202-371-0424
Web: www.americansforthearts.org

Americans for the Arts Private-Sector Initiatives Internship

Type of award: Internship.
Intended use: For undergraduate or graduate study at postsecondary institution.
Basis for selection: Major/career interest in business; arts, general; arts management or nonprofit administration.
Application requirements: Cover letter, resume.
Additional information: Recent college graduates may apply. Position is based in New York, NY. Major/career interest in program management, research, and development. Ten-week internship available part-time for winter/spring and fall and full-time for summer. Application deadlines are in March for summer, July for fall, and October for winter/spring. Internship not always available for all seasons. Check Website for details and deadlines. $500 stipend for winter/spring, $1000 stipend for summer. Must have excellent writing and research skills, know MS Office (especially Excel), and have interest in the business value of the arts. Download application from Website or apply online.

Amount of award: $500-$1,000
Number of awards: 1

Contact:
Americans for the Arts
Internship Coordinator
1000 Vermont Avenue, NW, 6th Floor
Washington, DC 20005
Phone: 202-371-0424
Web: www.americansforthearts.org

Americans for the Arts Research Services Internship

Type of award: Internship.
Intended use: For undergraduate or graduate study.
Basis for selection: Major/career interest in nonprofit administration; arts management or arts, general.
Application requirements: Cover letter, resume.
Additional information: Recent college graduates also eligible. Ten-week positions available part-time for winter/spring and fall and full-time for summer. Application deadlines are March for summer, July for fall, and October for winter/spring. $500 stipend for fall/spring, $1000 stipend for summer. Must have knowledge of Microsoft Office and be able to work independently. Commitment to serve the nonprofit arts field required. Internship may not be available every year, check Website for details and deadlines.

Amount of award: $500-$1,000
Number of awards: 1

Contact:
Americans for the Arts
Internship Coordinator
1000 Vermont Avenue, NW, 6th Floor
Washington, DC 20005
Phone: 202-371-0424
Web: www.americansforthearts.org

Applied Arts

Applied Arts Internships

Type of award: Internship.
Intended use: For undergraduate or graduate study at postsecondary institution.
Basis for selection: Major/career interest in arts, general; public administration/service; marketing; education or arts management.
Application requirements: Resume, cover letter.
Additional information: Internships are for college credit and are open to all high school/college/international students or graduates. Available in the following fields: education TA in fine arts (painting, drawing, sculpture, digital media, and photography); arts management; events management; office assistant; public service; youth program assistant; marketing/promotion. Discounted classes may be available. Rolling application deadline and open duration. E-mail applications preferred.

Number of awards: 10
Number of applicants: 100
Contact:
Applied Arts
Attn: Internship Coordinator
P.O. Box 1336
Amagansett, NY 11930
Phone: 631-267-2787
Fax: 631-267-3428
Web: www.appliedartsschool.com/internships.html

Elizabeth Dow Ltd. Internships

Type of award: Internship.
Intended use: For undergraduate or graduate study.
Basis for selection: Major/career interest in arts, general; interior design; marketing; design or arts management.
Application requirements: Recommendations. Resume, cover letter.
Additional information: High school students and recent college graduates also eligible to apply. Internship is unpaid, but college credit available. Program has rolling admission; duration of internship is flexible. Number of internships may vary.
Number of awards: 30
Number of applicants: 100
Contact:
Elizabeth Dow Ltd.
Attn: Internship Coordinator
P.O. Box 2310
Amagansett, NY 11930
Phone: 631-267-3401
Fax: 631-267-3428
Web: www.appliedartsschool.com/internships.html

Applied Materials

Applied Materials Internship and Co-op Program

Type of award: Internship.
Intended use: For undergraduate or graduate study at accredited postsecondary institution.
Basis for selection: Major/career interest in accounting; business; business/management/administration; computer/information sciences; engineering, chemical; engineering, electrical/electronic; engineering, mechanical; finance/banking; materials science or physics. Applicant must demonstrate high academic achievement.
Application requirements: Resume.
Additional information: Applicant should have interest in semi-conductor industry. Summer and year-round internships and co-op positions based in Texas and California. Visit Website to submit resume and to find out when internship interviews will be held at college campuses. Internships are paid and may also include relocation assistance, medical insurance, and additional benefits.
Contact:
Applied Materials, Attn: Global College Programs
3050 Bowers Avenue
P.O. Box 58039
Santa Clara, CA 95054-3299
Web: www.appliedmaterials.com/careers

Arts and Business Council of New York

Arts and Business Council of New York Multicultural Arts Management Internship Program

Type of award: Internship.
Intended use: For sophomore, junior or senior study at 2-year or 4-year institution.
Basis for selection: Major/career interest in arts management.
Application requirements: Interview, recommendations, essay, transcript. Resume, cover letter.
Additional information: Interns spend ten weeks (June-August) working full-time at a New York City arts organization. Preference given to African-American, Asian-American, Latino/a, and Native American students. Must have taken arts, business, or marketing courses, or been involved in similar extracurricular activities. Interviews take place February/March; phone interviews may be arranged. Deadline in February. Visit Website for exact date and application.
Amount of award: $2,500
Contact:
Americans for the Arts
Attn: Internship Program
One East 53rd Street, 3rd Floor
New York, NY 10022
Phone: 212-279-5910
Fax: 212-279-5915
Web: www.artsandbusiness-ny.org

Asian American Journalists Association

AAJA/NBC Summer Partnership

Type of award: Internship.
Intended use: For sophomore, junior, senior or graduate study at 4-year or graduate institution in United States.
Eligibility: Applicant must be at least 18.
Basis for selection: Major/career interest in journalism.
Application requirements: Recommendations, essay, transcript. Resume, work samples, and photo copy of ID or drivers' license.
Additional information: Internship lasts 10 weeks in New York City and includes $5000 stipend and AAJA mentor. AAJA membership is encouraged for applicants and required for recipients. Preference given to applicants with production experience.
Amount of award: $5,000
Number of awards: 3
Application deadline: March 1
Contact:
Asian American Journalists Association
AAJA/NBC Summer Partnership
5 Third Street, Suite 1108
San Francisco, CA 94103
Phone: 415-346-2051 ext. 102
Fax: 415-346-6343
Web: www.aaja.org

Bernstein-Rein Advertising

Advertising Internship

Type of award: Internship.
Intended use: For junior study.
Basis for selection: Major/career interest in advertising; communications or marketing.
Application requirements: Interview. Resume, cover letter, three reference names.
Additional information: Internship runs for eight weeks in summer. Applicant must have one or two semesters left before graduation. Pay is $10 per hour. Two positions each in account management, media, and creative. One position available in social media. Application available online.

Number of awards:	7
Number of applicants:	250
Application deadline:	March 30
Notification begins:	May 1

Contact:
Bernstein-Rein
Human Resources
4600 Madison, Suite 1500
Kansas City, MO 64112
Phone: 816-756-0640
Fax: 816-399-6000
Web: internships.bernstein-rein.com

Black & Veatch Corporation

Black & Veatch Summer Internship Program

Type of award: Internship.
Intended use: For full-time junior or senior study in United States.
Eligibility: Applicant must be U.S. citizen or permanent resident.
Basis for selection: Major/career interest in architecture; engineering, nuclear; engineering, civil; engineering, electrical/electronic; engineering, mechanical; technology or construction management. Applicant must demonstrate high academic achievement.
Application requirements: Resume.
Additional information: Internship compensation varies by discipline. Additional acceptable majors/career interests include construction management and mechanical, electrical or civil technicians. Minimum 2.75 GPA. Positions offered across the U.S. Positions will be posted online until filled.
Contact:
Web: www.bv.com/collegecareers

Board of Governors of the Federal Reserve System

Economic Research Division Project Internships

Type of award: Internship, renewable.
Intended use: For undergraduate or graduate study at postsecondary institution.
Eligibility: Applicant must be U.S. citizen or permanent resident.
Basis for selection: Major/career interest in economics; statistics; computer/information sciences; mathematics or finance/banking. Applicant must demonstrate high academic achievement.
Application requirements: Recommendations, transcript. Resume, cover letter.
Additional information: Paid internship lasts from June to September. Submit application by e-mail.

Application deadline:	April 1

Contact:
Board of Governors of the Federal Reserve System
20th Street and Constitution Avenue NW
Washington, DC 20551
Phone: 202-452-3880
Web: www.federalreserve.gov/careers/intern_research.htm

Boeing Company

Boeing Internships

Type of award: Internship.
Intended use: For undergraduate or graduate study in United States.
Eligibility: Applicant must be U.S. citizen or permanent resident.
Basis for selection: Major/career interest in aerospace; computer/information sciences; statistics; human resources; manufacturing; economics; science, general; engineering; mathematics or business.
Application requirements: Resume.
Additional information: Internships available in Alabama, Arizona, California, Illinois, Missouri, Oklahoma, Oregon, Pennsylvania, South Carolina, Texas, Washington, D.C. (Metro) and Washington state. Deadlines, eligibility requirements, and compensation vary depending on position. See Website for detailed information on available positions and to submit resume.

Number of awards:	1,200

Contact:
Web: www.boeing.com/careers

Boston Globe

Boston Globe Summer Internship

Type of award: Internship.
Intended use: For junior, senior or graduate study at 4-year or graduate institution.
Basis for selection: Major/career interest in journalism.
Application requirements: Interview, recommendations. Writing samples/clips, resume.
Additional information: Full-time, paid 12-week summer internship. Current undergraduate students in any major may apply, as well as journalism graduate students without professional experience as newspaper reporter. Applicants must have had at least one previous internship at daily newspaper. Application available online in September.

Number of awards: 10
Number of applicants: 500
Application deadline: November 1
Notification begins: December 31
Contact:
The Boston Globe
Attn: Paula Bouknight
P.O. Box 55819
Boston, MA 02205-5819
Phone: 617-929-3120
Web: www.bostonglobe.com/newsintern

Citizens for Global Solutions

Citizens for Global Solutions Internship

Type of award: Internship, renewable.
Intended use: For undergraduate or graduate study at postsecondary institution.
Basis for selection: Major/career interest in international relations; international studies; information systems; journalism; nonprofit administration; political science/government or web design.
Application requirements: Resume, cover letter, three- to five- page writing sample.
Additional information: Recent graduates also eligible. Internship includes $10 per day stipend. Application deadlines are April 1 for summer, July 15 for fall, and November 15 for spring. Visit Website for more information.
Application deadline: April 1, July 15
Contact:
Citizens for Global Solutions
420 7th Street SE
Washington, DC 20003-2796
Phone: 202-546-3950 ext. 100
Fax: 202-546-3749
Web: www.globalsolutions.org/jobs

Congressional Hispanic Caucus Institute

CHCI Congressional Internship

Type of award: Internship.
Intended use: For full-time undergraduate study at accredited 2-year or 4-year institution.
Eligibility: Applicant must be U.S. citizen or permanent resident.
Basis for selection: Applicant must demonstrate high academic achievement, leadership and service orientation.
Application requirements: Recommendations, transcript. Three personal essays, resume.
Additional information: Spring (12 week), fall (12 week) and summer (eight week) internship in Washington, D.C. congressional offices. Transportation, housing, and stipend provided; $2,500 for eight week program, and $3,750 for 12 week program. Must have excellent writing and analytical skills and active participation in community service activities. Work experience is complemented by leadership development sessions. Minimum 3.0 GPA preferred. Deadlines: November 2 (spring), February 1 (summer), April 26 (fall). Visit Website for deadline information and application.
Amount of award: $2,500-$3,750
Number of awards: 60
Number of applicants: 1,000
Application deadline: November 2, January 25
Contact:
CHCI Internship Program
911 Second Street, NE
Washington, DC 20002
Phone: 202-543-1771
Fax: 202-546-2143
Web: www.chci.org/internships

Congressional Institute, Inc.

Congressional Institute Internships

Type of award: Internship.
Intended use: For undergraduate study at accredited 2-year or 4-year institution in United States.
Eligibility: Applicant must be U.S. citizen.
Basis for selection: Major/career interest in political science/government; public administration/service; law or communications. Applicant must demonstrate high academic achievement.
Application requirements: Recommendations. Resume and writing samples.
Additional information: Paid internships available throughout the year on flexible terms. Must have interest in public policy or legislative policy issues. Visit Website for application and additional information.
Contact:
Congressional Institute, Inc.
1700 Diagonal Road
Suite 730
Alexandria, VA 22314
Phone: 703-837-8812
Fax: 703-837-8817
Web: www.conginst.org

Cushman School

Cushman School Internship

Type of award: Internship, renewable.
Intended use: For undergraduate or graduate study.
Basis for selection: Major/career interest in education.
Application requirements: Resume, cover letter.
Additional information: Internship is 17 weeks on Cushman School campus for fall and spring semesters. Interns assist staff in grading papers, supervising students, and performing administrative work. Internships are full-time, 8 a.m. to 4 p.m., Monday to Friday. Stipend of $2,000 for U.S. students and $3,000 for international students awarded each semester. International students must have J1 visa. Rolling application deadline. Number of internships varies.
Amount of award: $2,000-$3,000

Contact:
Cushman School
Arvi Balseiro
592 Northeast 60th Street
Miami, FL 33137
Phone: 305-757-1966
Fax: 305-757-1632
Web: www.cushmanschool.org

Denver Rescue Mission

Denver Rescue Mission Center for Mission Studies Internships

Type of award: Internship.
Intended use: For junior, senior or graduate study at postsecondary institution in United States.
Basis for selection: Major/career interest in social work; religion/theology; ministry; nonprofit administration; health services administration; public relations; marketing or information systems. Applicant must demonstrate service orientation.
Application requirements: Interview. Background check.
Additional information: Denver Rescue Mission is a nondenominational Christian charity offering internships in the following areas: child development, family studies, human services, management information systems, medical office administration, public relations/marketing, social work, volunteer relations, counseling, family therapy, shelter management, and nonprofit administration. Internships vary in length, and some may have gender, age, level-of-study, or other requirements. Full-time interns qualify for a $250 tuition remuneration and a $50 monthly stipend. Housing included. See Website for details and to apply.
Contact:
Denver Rescue Mission
3501 E. 46th Ave.
Denver, CO 80216
Phone: 303-953-3951
Web: www.denverrescuemission.org

Dow Jones News Fund

Dow Jones Business Reporting Intern Program

Type of award: Internship.
Intended use: For full-time junior, senior or graduate study.
Eligibility: Applicant must be U.S. citizen, permanent resident or international student.
Basis for selection: Major/career interest in journalism or business. Applicant must demonstrate high academic achievement and seriousness of purpose.
Application requirements: Interview, essay, transcript. Resume, three to five recently published clips, reporting test.
Additional information: May have any major, but must plan to pursue journalism career. Special interest in business a plus. Applications available online August to November 1. All applicants notified by January 31. Applicants must take reporting test administered by designated professor on applicant's campus. Telephone interview required for finalists. Paid summer internships as business reporters at news media companies last at least 10 weeks. Interns returning to school receive scholarship at end of summer to apply toward following year. All interns attend pre-internship training that lasts one week. International students must have work visa.

Amount of award:	$1,000
Number of awards:	12
Number of applicants:	100
Application deadline:	November 1
Notification begins:	January 15
Total amount awarded:	$12,000

Contact:
Dow Jones News Fund
Business Reporting Intern Program
P.O. Box 300
Princeton, NJ 08543-0300
Phone: 609-452-2820
Web: www.newsfund.org

Dow Jones Digital Intern Program

Type of award: Internship.
Intended use: For full-time junior, senior or graduate study in United States.
Eligibility: Applicant must be U.S. citizen, permanent resident or international student.
Basis for selection: Major/career interest in journalism. Applicant must demonstrate high academic achievement and seriousness of purpose.
Application requirements: Essay, transcript. Resume, exam.
Additional information: May have any major but must intend to pursue journalism career. Common application form for all editing programs available online starting in August. Must take editing test administered by designated professor on applicant's campus. Finalists undergo telephone interview. Paid 10 to 12-week summer internships as editors at daily newspapers, online newspapers, or news services. Must attend one-week pre-internship training at Arizona State University. Interns returning to school receive scholarship. International students must have work visa.

Amount of award:	$1,000
Number of awards:	12
Number of applicants:	600
Application deadline:	November 1
Notification begins:	December 15
Total amount awarded:	$12,000

Contact:
Dow Jones News Fund
Digital Editing Intern Program
P.O. Box 300
Princeton, NJ 08543-0300
Phone: 609-452-2820
Web: www.newsfund.org

Dow Jones News Editing Intern Program

Type of award: Internship.
Intended use: For full-time junior, senior or graduate study in United States.
Eligibility: Applicant must be U.S. citizen, permanent resident or international student.
Basis for selection: Major/career interest in journalism. Applicant must demonstrate high academic achievement and seriousness of purpose.
Application requirements: Essay, transcript. Resume, editing test.

Additional information: May have any major but must plan to pursue journalism career. Common application form for all editing programs available online starting in August. All applicants notified by December 31. Editing test administered by designated professor on applicant's campus. Telephone interview required for finalists. Paid summer internships, as editors at daily newspapers, online newspapers, or real-time financial news services, last 10 to 12 weeks. Interns returning to school receive scholarship at end of summer to apply toward following year. All interns attend pre-internship training that lasts one week. International students must have work visa.

Amount of award:	$1,000
Number of awards:	50
Number of applicants:	600
Application deadline:	November 1
Notification begins:	December 15
Total amount awarded:	$40,000

Contact:
Dow Jones News Fund
News Editing Intern Program
P.O. Box 300
Princeton, NJ 08543-0300
Phone: 609-452-2820
Web: www.newsfund.org

Dow Jones Sports Editing Intern Program

Type of award: Internship.
Intended use: For full-time junior, senior or graduate study.
Eligibility: Applicant must be U.S. citizen, permanent resident or international student.
Basis for selection: Major/career interest in journalism.
Application requirements: Essay, transcript. Editing exam, resume.
Additional information: Applicants may have any major but must plan to pursue career in journalism. Interns will work on sports copy desks at daily newspapers and attend training at the University of Nebraska at Lincoln, taught by Dr. Charlyne Berens. Seminars last two weeks. Applicants may apply for sports, online, and/or news copy editing programs using common application form beginning in August. International students must have work visa.

Amount of award:	$1,000
Number of awards:	12
Number of applicants:	600
Application deadline:	November 1
Notification begins:	December 15
Total amount awarded:	$12,000

Contact:
Dow Jones News Fund
Sports Editing Intern Program
P.O. Box 300
Princeton, NJ 08543-0300
Phone: 609-452-2820
Web: www.newsfund.org

DuPont Company

DuPont Co-ops

Type of award: Internship.
Intended use: For full-time sophomore, junior or senior study at accredited 4-year institution in United States.
Eligibility: Applicant must be U.S. citizen or permanent resident.
Basis for selection: Major/career interest in accounting; engineering, chemical; engineering, electrical/electronic; engineering, mechanical; finance/banking; marketing or science, general. Applicant must demonstrate high academic achievement.
Application requirements: Resume and cover letter.
Additional information: Co-ops available at DuPont company sites throughout U.S. Participants alternate work assignments and academic terms. Applicants can start no earlier than after completion of freshman year and work a minimum of three industrial work periods. Preference given to juniors and seniors. Must be registered with school's co-op office. Competitive compensation. Minimum 3.0 GPA. Must apply through Website.
Contact:
Phone: 302-774-1000
Web: www.dupont.com/careers

DuPont Internships

Type of award: Internship.
Intended use: For full-time sophomore, junior, senior or master's study at accredited 4-year institution in United States.
Eligibility: Applicant must be U.S. citizen or permanent resident.
Basis for selection: Major/career interest in accounting; finance/banking; marketing or information systems. Applicant must demonstrate high academic achievement.
Application requirements: Resume and cover letter.
Additional information: Interns normally work in summer between junior and senior years at DuPont company sites throughout U.S. May apply for extended internship. Minimum 3.0 GPA. Number and amount of awards vary. Must apply through Website.
Contact:
Phone: 302-774-1000
Web: www.dupont.com/careers

Eastman Kodak Company

Eastman Kodak Cooperative Internship Programs

Type of award: Internship.
Intended use: For full-time sophomore, junior, senior or graduate study.
Basis for selection: Major/career interest in accounting; business; chemistry; computer/information sciences; engineering; finance/banking; manufacturing; marketing; physics or graphic arts/design. Applicant must demonstrate high academic achievement.
Application requirements: Resume and cover letter.
Additional information: Internship must be minimum ten consecutive weeks during summer. Positions offered in Rochester, NY, Windsor, CO, and Dayton, OH. Internship includes competitive salary based upon discipline and education level, travel expenses, assistance locating housing, mentoring, and student activities. Applicant must be drug-screened as condition of employment. Apply online. Number of available internships varies.
Contact:
Web: www.kodak.com/go/careers

Entergy

Entergy Jumpstart Co-ops and Internships

Type of award: Internship, renewable.
Intended use: For full-time undergraduate or graduate study at accredited 4-year or graduate institution in United States.
Eligibility: Applicant must be U.S. citizen or permanent resident.
Basis for selection: Major/career interest in engineering, civil; business; accounting; human resources; finance/banking; engineering, electrical/electronic; engineering, mechanical; engineering, nuclear or information systems. Applicant must demonstrate high academic achievement and depth of character.
Additional information: Paid co-ops and internships available. Minimum 3.0 GPA. Apply online. Visit Website for application deadline and current openings. Must have work experience and give graduation date.
Contact:
Phone: 504-576-4000
Web: www.entergy.com/careers

Entertainment Weekly

Entertainment Weekly Internship Program

Type of award: Internship.
Intended use: For junior, senior or postgraduate study at postsecondary institution.
Application requirements: Resume, cover letter, and five clips/writing samples.
Additional information: Internships in editorial department last 12-18 weeks and pay $10 per hour. Summer internships open to rising seniors and recent graduates. Fall and spring internships for recent college graduates only. Application deadlines are Feb. 15 for summer, Jun. 15 for fall, and Oct. 15 for winter. Number of internships varies.

Number of applicants:	200
Application deadline:	February 15, June 15
Notification begins:	March 1, July 1

Contact:
Entertainment Weekly Internship Program
Attn: Tina Jordan
135 W. 50th Street, 3rd Floor
New York, NY 10020
Phone: 212-522-4098
Fax: 212-522-6104
Web: www.ew.com

ESPN Inc.

ESPN Internship

Type of award: Internship.
Intended use: For full-time junior study.
Eligibility: Applicant must be U.S. citizen or permanent resident.
Basis for selection: Major/career interest in sports/sports administration; communications; computer/information sciences; statistics; graphic arts/design; journalism; marketing or radio/television/film.
Application requirements: Resume and cover letter.
Additional information: Applicants should be current students within 12 months of graduation during the internship. Other majors welcome to apply. Internships last ten weeks at 40 hours per week. Most positions based in Bristol, CT or New York, NY, with limited opportunities at other locations. CT and NY interns may qualify for subsidized housing. Previous internship experience a plus. Competitive pay. Course credit offered based on college requirements. Limited internships offered in spring and fall; majority of internships offered in summer. Applications processed on rolling basis; apply online. Check Website for available positions and deadline.

Number of applicants:	10,000

Contact:
ESPN Inc.
Web: www.espncareers.com/campus

Essence Magazine

Essence Summer Internship

Type of award: Internship, renewable.
Intended use: For undergraduate or graduate study at accredited 4-year institution in United States.
Basis for selection: Major/career interest in advertising; business; fashion/fashion design/modeling; graphic arts/design; journalism; marketing; public relations or publishing.
Application requirements: Resume and writing sample or digital portfolio.
Additional information: Must be authorized to work in U.S. Nine-week summer internships available in several departments: sales and marketing, Essence.com, fashion and beauty, art/photo, public relations, business office, and editorial. Interns responsible for finding their own housing. Receive bi-weekly paycheck. Must have appreciation for magazine industry; be self-motivated and detail-oriented. Visit Website for application and more information. Number of internships varies.

Number of applicants:	300
Application deadline:	January 31
Notification begins:	March 31

Contact:
Essence Internship Program, Attn: Human Resources
1271 Avenue of the Americas
7th Floor
New York, NY 10020
Phone: 212-522-1212
Fax: 212-467-2357
Web: www.essence.com/internships

Federal Reserve Bank of New York

Federal Reserve Bank of New York Undergraduate Summer Internship

Type of award: Internship.
Intended use: For full-time junior or senior study at postsecondary institution.

Basis for selection: Major/career interest in finance/banking; economics; business; computer/information sciences; accounting or public administration/service. Applicant must demonstrate high academic achievement.
Application requirements: Interview, transcript. Cover letter, resume.
Additional information: Paid internships begin in late May/ early June. Applicants must have completed sophomore year of college before beginning internship. Applicants must be available for in-person interviews in March/April. Housing not provided. International students must be legally authorized to work in U.S. on a multi-year basis for other than practical training purposes. Submit resume online. Deadline varies. Visit Website for exact date.
Contact:
Federal Reserve Bank of New York
Summer Internship Coordinator
33 Liberty Street
New York, NY 10045
Phone: 212-720-5000
Web: www.ny.frb.org/careers/summerintern.html

Feminist Majority Foundation

Feminism & Leadership Internship

Type of award: Internship.
Intended use: For undergraduate study at accredited 4-year institution.
Basis for selection: Major/career interest in women's studies or political science/government. Applicant must demonstrate high academic achievement and leadership.
Application requirements: Resume, cover letter, writing sample.
Additional information: Recent graduates may also apply. Full-time or part-time internships for a minimum of two months available year-round in the Washington, DC, area and Los Angeles. Interns have various responsibilities, such as monitoring press conferences and coalition meetings, researching, attending rallies, and organizing events. Internships unpaid, but students may be able to earn small stipend in exchange for administrative work. Applicants with experience working on women's issues preferred. People of color, people with disabilities, and math/science majors encouraged to apply. Application deadlines for DC office are March 31 for summer, July 15 for fall, and October 15 for spring. Applications processed on rolling basis for LA office. See Website for more information.

Application deadline:	March 31, July 15

Contact:
Feminist Majority Foundation
Attn: Internship Coordinator
1600 Wilson Boulevard, Suite 801
Arlington, VA 22209
Phone: 703-522-2214
Fax: 703-522-2219
Web: www.feminist.org/intern

Filoli

Filoli Garden Internships and Apprenticeships

Type of award: Internship.
Intended use: For undergraduate, graduate or non-degree study at postsecondary institution. Designated institutions: Filoli.
Basis for selection: Major/career interest in horticulture; landscape architecture or botany. Applicant must demonstrate high academic achievement, depth of character, leadership and seriousness of purpose.
Application requirements: Recommendations, transcript. Resume and cover letter outlining interests.
Additional information: Also for students pursuing careers in public garden management and landscape maintenance. Students paid $8 per hour and may earn college credit for ten-week internship program or six-month apprenticeship program. Applicants must have at least 12 units of horticulture classes and 3.0 GPA. Ability to work well with public and work teams essential. Maximum five students per internship. Visit Website for deadlines and application.

Amount of award:	$3,200-$8,320
Number of awards:	20
Number of applicants:	21
Total amount awarded:	$36,480

Contact:
Filoli
Jim Salyards/Filoli Garden Internships
86 Canada Road
Woodside, CA 94062
Phone: 650-364-8300 ext. 223
Fax: 650-366-7836
Web: www.filoli.org/education/garden-internships.html

Florida Department of Education

Florida Work Experience Program

Type of award: Internship, renewable.
Intended use: For undergraduate study at vocational, 2-year or 4-year institution. Designated institutions: Eligible Florida postsecondary institutions,
Eligibility: Applicant must be U.S. citizen or permanent resident residing in Florida.
Basis for selection: Applicant must demonstrate financial need and high academic achievement.
Application requirements: Proof of eligibility. FAFSA.
Additional information: Minimum 2.0 GPA. Provides students with opportunity to be employed off-campus in jobs related to their academic major or area of career interest. Applications available from participating schools' financial aid offices. Amount of award determined by institution and may not exceed student's financial need.
Contact:
Office of Student Financial Assistance
325 West Gaines Street
Suite 1314
Tallahassee, FL 32399-0400
Phone: 888-827-2004
Web: www.floridastudentfinancialaid.org

Fox Group

Fox Internship

Type of award: Internship.
Intended use: For junior, senior or graduate study at accredited 4-year or graduate institution.
Eligibility: Applicant must be International student eligible to work in United States.
Application requirements: Resume.
Additional information: Paid internships are available in all departments within Film, Television and Digital Media. Applicants must be current students. College credit available. Apply via Website.
Contact:
Web: www.foxcareers.com

Franklin D. Roosevelt Library

Roosevelt Archival Internships

Type of award: Internship.
Intended use: For undergraduate or graduate study at postsecondary institution.
Basis for selection: Major/career interest in library science; computer/information sciences; museum studies; history; political science/government or education.
Application requirements: Transcript.
Additional information: Interns work at FDR library with other interns and staff organizing and automating archival materials, making indices, finding aids and databases, digitizing documents and photographs, and assisting with other projects. Internship can last up to eight weeks and must take place during summer break (mid-May through end of August). Housing not provided. Work Monday through Friday, 9 a.m. to 5 p.m. Stipend of $3200 for eight weeks (two payments; first payment after Week 1 and second after Week 8). Number of awards depends on funding. Familiarity with FDR presidency helpful. Visit Website for application.

Number of awards:	3
Number of applicants:	75
Application deadline:	April 1
Notification begins:	April 15

Contact:
Franklin D. Roosevelt Library
Roosevelt Archival Internship Program
4079 Albany Post Road
Hyde Park, NY 12538
Phone: 845-486-7745
Fax: 845-486-1147
Web: www.fdrlibrary.marist.edu/getinvolved.html

Garden Club of America

GCA Internship in Garden History and Design

Type of award: Internship.
Intended use: For undergraduate or graduate study at postsecondary institution.
Basis for selection: Major/career interest in botany; horticulture; landscape architecture or museum studies.
Application requirements: Recommendations, essay, transcript. Two letters of recommendation (one from professor in major, one from adviser).
Additional information: May apply to Archives of American Gardens in Washington, D.C., or at other eligible institutions (contact sponsor to verify). Stipend provided; GCA funds act as supplement.

Amount of award:	$2,000
Number of awards:	1
Application deadline:	February 15

Contact:
Garden Club of America
Connie Yates
14 East 60th Street
New York, NY 10022-1002
Phone: 212-753-8287
Fax: 212-753-0134
Web: www.gcamerica.org

Genentech, Inc.

Genentech, Inc. Internship Program

Type of award: Internship, renewable.
Intended use: For full-time undergraduate or graduate study at accredited 4-year or graduate institution.
Basis for selection: Major/career interest in biology; business; chemistry; computer/information sciences; engineering; engineering, biomedical; engineering, chemical; law; life sciences or medicine. Applicant must demonstrate high academic achievement.
Application requirements: Resume and cover letter.
Additional information: Paid summer internships last 9-12 weeks and are available in various research and business areas. Must have already completed one year of study. International students must have work authorization. Applications accepted January through April. Internships take place in South San Francisco, Vacaville, and Oceanside, California and Hillsboro, Oregon. Apply online or check Website for campus recruiting schedule.
Contact:
Genentech, Inc.
1 DNA Way
South San Francisco, CA 94080-4990
Phone: 650-225-1000
Fax: 650-225-6000
Web: www.gene.com/careers/academic-programs

Hannaford Bros. Co.

Hannaford Internships

Type of award: Internship.
Intended use: For undergraduate or master's study at postsecondary institution.
Eligibility: Applicant must be U.S. citizen, permanent resident or international student.
Basis for selection: Major/career interest in pharmacy/ pharmaceutics/pharmacology. Applicant must demonstrate high academic achievement.

Application requirements: Cover letter and resume.
Additional information: Twelve week paid summer internship, beginning early June. Interns at Hannaford are exposed to a multicultural organization with support systems and training opportunities. Internships available at Hannaford's corporate office, distribution centers, and retail locations. Pharmacy internships also available. Inquire at campus placement office to schedule recruiting interview or e-mail for additional information. Minimum 3.0 GPA. Must be legally authorized to work in United States. Amount of payment or course credit awarded varies. International students must have work authorization. Visit Website for more information. Applications accepted online only.
Application deadline: February 15
Contact:
Hannaford Brothers Company Employment Department
Phone: 800-442-6049
Fax: 207-885-2859
Web: www.hannaford.com

Hispanic Association of Colleges and Universities

HACU National Internship Program

Type of award: Internship.
Intended use: For sophomore, junior, senior or graduate study at 2-year, 4-year or graduate institution. Designated institutions: Institutions with significant number of Hispanic students.
Eligibility: Applicant must be U.S. citizen or permanent resident.
Basis for selection: Applicant must demonstrate high academic achievement and service orientation.
Application requirements: Essay, transcript. Resume.
Additional information: Paid internships provide opportunities for students from institutions with significant numbers of Hispanic students to explore potential careers with federal agencies and private corporations. Interns work in Washington, DC, area and field sites throughout country. Some internships require U.S. citizenship to participate. Applicants must have 3.0 GPA and have completed freshman year of college before internship begins. Weekly pay varies according to class level: $470 for sophomores and juniors, $500 for seniors and $570 for graduates. Must be active in college and community service. Fall and spring internships last 15 weeks; summer internships last ten weeks. Deadlines: November for spring, February for summer, June for fall. Visit Website for more information.
Contact:
Hispanic Association of Colleges and Universities
One Dupont Circle, NW
Suite 430
Washington, DC 20036
Phone: 202-467-0893
Web: www.hacu.net

Hoffman-La Roche Inc.

Hoffman-La Roche Inc. Student Internship

Type of award: Internship.
Intended use: For full-time freshman, sophomore, junior or graduate study at postsecondary institution.
Basis for selection: Major/career interest in pharmacy/pharmaceutics/pharmacology; engineering; computer/information sciences; science, general; business; business/management/administration; biology; chemistry or biochemistry.
Application requirements: Interview. Cover letter, resume.
Additional information: Applicant must be authorized to work in the United States. Internship fields, topics, and amount of compensation vary. Send materials to address provided. If deadline is missed, application will be considered after those students who have met deadline. Visit Website for more information and internship descriptions.
Contact:
University Relations Department
Hoffman-La Roche, Inc.
340 Kingsland Street
Nutley, NJ 07110-1199
Phone: 973-235-4035 or 973-235-5000
Web: www.rocheusa.com

IBM

IBM Co-op and Intern Program

Type of award: Internship.
Intended use: For full-time sophomore, junior, senior or graduate study at accredited 4-year or graduate institution in United States.
Basis for selection: Major/career interest in computer/information sciences; engineering, computer; engineering, electrical/electronic; information systems; accounting or finance/banking. Applicant must demonstrate high academic achievement and leadership.
Application requirements: Interview.
Additional information: Applicants chosen on competitive basis, based on relevant work or research experience, communication, team skills, and high evaluation during interview process. Most awardees are undergraduate juniors or first year master's students. Competitive salary based on number of credits completed towards degree. Applicants hired on semester basis. Must submit resume via IBM Website.
Contact:
IBM Co-op and Intern Program
Web: www-03.ibm.com/employment/students.html

The Indianapolis Star

Pulliam Journalism Fellowship

Type of award: Internship.
Intended use: For junior, senior, graduate or postgraduate study at postsecondary institution.
Basis for selection: Competition/talent/interest in writing/journalism. Major/career interest in humanities/liberal arts or journalism. Applicant must demonstrate high academic achievement, depth of character, leadership and seriousness of purpose.
Application requirements: Recommendations, transcript, proof of eligibility. Writing samples. Recent photograph.
Additional information: Paid fellowship lasts ten weeks during summer. Ten recipients work for The Indianapolis Star, ten for The Arizona Republic in Phoenix. Early deadline in

November. Some candidates may be accepted post-deadline. Visit Website for application and more information.

Amount of award:	$6,500
Number of awards:	20
Number of applicants:	175
Application deadline:	November 1

Contact:
Russell B. Pulliam, Director
The Pulliam Fellowship
P.O. Box 145
Indianapolis, IN 46206-0145
Phone: 317-444-6001
Web: www.indystar.com/pjf

INROADS, Inc.

INROADS Internship

Type of award: Internship, renewable.
Intended use: For full-time freshman or sophomore study.
Eligibility: Applicant must be Alaskan native, Asian American, African American, Mexican American, Hispanic American, Puerto Rican, American Indian or Native Hawaiian/Pacific Islander. Applicant must be high school senior. Applicant must be U.S. citizen or permanent resident.
Basis for selection: Major/career interest in engineering; business; computer/information sciences; communications; retailing/merchandising; health-related professions or accounting. Applicant must demonstrate high academic achievement, leadership and service orientation.
Application requirements: Interview, transcript. Resume. National College Component Application.
Additional information: Applicant must have minimum 3.0 GPA or college 2.8 GPA. Must be full-time undergraduate with at least two summers or 54 credit hours remaining. Internship duration and compensation varies, and deadlines vary according to local affiliate office. Visit Website for additional information.

Number of awards:	4,000
Number of applicants:	20,000
Application deadline:	May 31

Contact:
INROADS, Inc.
10 S. Broadway
Suite 300
St. Louis, MO 63102
Phone: 314-241-7488
Fax: 314-241-9325
Web: www.inroads.org

Institute of Human Studies

Harper Internship Program

Type of award: Internship.
Intended use: For undergraduate or graduate study at postsecondary institution.
Additional information: Internships available in all departments. Competitive daily stipend offered. Available to all ages and experience levels.

Contact:
Institute of Human Studies
3351 Fairfax Drive, MSN IC5
Arlington, VA 22201
Phone: 703-993-4880
Web: www.theihs.org

International Radio and Television Society Foundation

International Radio and Television Society Foundation Summer Fellowship Program

Type of award: Internship.
Intended use: For junior, senior or graduate study at postsecondary institution.
Basis for selection: Major/career interest in communications.
Additional information: Nine week internship. Applicants must have prior internship experience and demonstrated interest in the field of communications. Fellows are awarded travel and housing expenses as well as an allowance. Visit Website for deadlines, information, and application.

Number of awards:	25
Application deadline:	December 1

Contact:
International Radio and Television Society Foundation
420 Lexington Avenue, Suite 1601
New York, NY 10170
Phone: 212-867-6650 ext. 303
Fax: 212-867-6653
Web: www.irts.org

J. Paul Getty Trust

J. Paul Getty Multicultural Undergraduate Summer Internships at the Getty Center

Type of award: Internship.
Intended use: For full-time undergraduate study at 4-year institution.
Eligibility: Applicant must be Asian American, African American, Mexican American, Hispanic American, Puerto Rican, American Indian or Native Hawaiian/Pacific Islander. Applicant must be U.S. citizen.
Basis for selection: Major/career interest in arts management; communications; humanities/liberal arts; architecture; museum studies/administration or art/art history.
Application requirements: Interview, recommendations. Supplemental application (plus three copies), all official transcripts (plus three copies), and SASE.
Additional information: Ten-week internship in specific departments of Getty Museum and other programs located at the Getty Center in Los Angeles. Interns receive $3500 stipend. Limited to students attending school in or residing in Los Angeles County. Intended for outstanding students who are

members of groups currently underrepresented in museum professions and fields related to visual arts and humanities. Applicants must have completed at least one semester of college by June and not be graduating before December. Housing and transportation not included. Applications accepted in December, and applicants notified of acceptance in early May.

Amount of award: $3,500
Number of awards: 100
Number of applicants: 124
Application deadline: February 1

Contact:
Multicultural Undergraduate Internships at the Getty Center
The Getty Foundation
1200 Getty Center Dr., Suite 800
Los Angeles, CA 90049-1685
Phone: 310-440-7320
Fax: 310-440-7703
Web: www.getty.edu/grants/education

The John F. Kennedy Center for the Performing Arts

Kennedy Center Arts Management Internship

Type of award: Internship.
Intended use: For junior, senior or post-bachelor's certificate study at accredited 4-year or graduate institution.
Basis for selection: Major/career interest in arts management.
Application requirements: Interview, transcript. Cover letter stating career goals. Two letters of recommendation. Resume and writing sample.
Additional information: Arts education majors also eligible. Three- to four-month part-time or full-time internship in many Kennedy Center departments. College credit may be available. Interns attend weekly sessions led by executives of Kennedy Center and other major arts institutions in Washington, D.C. Interns may attend performances, workshops, classes, and courses presented by center, free of charge (space available), during their internship. Visit Website for application, deadline, and more information.

Number of awards: 60
Number of applicants: 800

Contact:
Vilar Institute for Arts Management/Internships
2700 F Street NW
Washington, DC 20566
Phone: 202-416-8800
Web: www.kennedy-center.org/education/artsmanagement/internships

John F. Kennedy Library Foundation

Kennedy Library Archival Internship

Type of award: Internship.
Intended use: For undergraduate or graduate study at postsecondary institution. Designated institutions: John F. Kennedy Presidential Library.
Eligibility: Applicant must be U.S. citizen or permanent resident.
Basis for selection: Major/career interest in history; political science/government; library science; English; journalism; communications or museum studies. Applicant must demonstrate high academic achievement.
Application requirements: Interview, recommendations, transcript.
Additional information: Minimum 12 hours per week, $12.50 per hour. Provides intern with opportunity to work on projects such as digitizing papers of Kennedy and his administration. Interns given career-relevant archival experience. Internships open up as vacancies occur. Library considers proposals for unpaid internships, independent study, work-study, and internships undertaken for academic credit. See Website for application and more information.

Contact:
Archival Internships c/o Intern Coordinator
John F. Kennedy Presidential Library & Museum
Columbia Point
Boston, MA 02125-3313
Phone: 617-514-1629
Fax: 617-514-1625
Web: www.jfklibrary.org

John Wiley and Sons, Inc.

John Wiley and Sons, Inc. Internship Program

Type of award: Internship.
Intended use: For full-time junior or senior study at 4-year institution.
Basis for selection: Major/career interest in marketing; publishing; information systems or public relations.
Application requirements: Resume. Letter addressing why applicant would like to be selected for the program and listing areas of interest.
Additional information: Summer internship programs available for students who have completed junior year; program runs from mid-June through mid-August. Internships available in marketing, editorial, production, information technology, new media, and publicity; based at corporate offices in Hoboken and Somerset in NJ, Indianapolis, San Francisco, and Malden, MA. Interns receive weekly stipend. Those interested in interning in Hoboken, NJ, Somerset, NJ, San Francisco, CA, Indianapolis, IN, and Malden, MA should visit www.wiley.com for more information. Application address varies by city. See Website for details.

Application deadline: April 1

Contact:
John Wiley and Sons, Inc. Attn: Internship Program
Human Resources Department
111 River Street
Hoboken, NJ 07030-5774
Fax: 201-748-6049
Web: www.wiley.com

Johnson Controls

Johnson Controls Co-op and Internship Programs

Type of award: Internship, renewable.
Intended use: For full-time undergraduate or graduate study at accredited 4-year institution in United States.
Basis for selection: Major/career interest in engineering; law; business/management/administration; manufacturing or automotive technology. Applicant must demonstrate high academic achievement.
Application requirements: Proof of eligibility. Resume, cover letter.
Additional information: Johnson Controls offers several co-op and internship programs in locations throughout the U.S. and abroad. The Engineering Co-op Program develops and trains students in all aspects of the Automotive Systems Group at Johnson Controls. Over a period of two to five years, mechanical and design engineering students alternate between work terms at Johnson Controls and school terms at college or university. Paid summer internships and positions in most other company divisions also available. Visit Website for complete program descriptions and application.
Contact:
Johnson Controls
Human Resources
5757 N. Green Bay Ave.
Milwaukee, WI 53209
Phone: 414-524-1200
Web: www.johnsoncontrols.com

Kentucky Higher Education Assistance Authority (KHEAA)

Kentucky Work-Study Program

Type of award: Internship, renewable.
Intended use: For undergraduate, master's, doctoral, first professional or postgraduate study at vocational, 2-year, 4-year or graduate institution. Designated institutions: Approved Kentucky institutions.
Eligibility: Applicant must be U.S. citizen residing in Kentucky.
Application requirements: Interview, proof of eligibility.
Additional information: Job must be related to major course of study. Work-study wage is at least federal minimum wage. May also be enrolled in technical schools. Visit Website for additional information.

Number of awards:	690
Number of applicants:	690
Total amount awarded:	$507,200

Contact:
Kentucky Higher Education Assistance Authority (KHEAA)
KHEAA Work-Study Program
P.O. Box 798
Frankfort, KY 40602-0798
Phone: 800-928-8926
Fax: 502-696-7373
Web: www.kheaa.com

Louis Carr Internship Foundation (LCIF)

Louis Carr Summer Internship

Type of award: Internship.
Intended use: For full-time freshman, sophomore or junior study in United States.
Eligibility: Applicant must be Asian American, African American, Mexican American, Hispanic American, Puerto Rican, American Indian or Native Hawaiian/Pacific Islander. Applicant must be U.S. citizen.
Basis for selection: Major/career interest in advertising; marketing or communications. Applicant must demonstrate high academic achievement, depth of character, leadership and seriousness of purpose.
Application requirements: Recommendations, essay, transcript. Resume.
Additional information: Paid, ten-week summer internship in New York, Chicago, Detroit, or Washington D.C.

Amount of award:	$4,000
Number of awards:	10
Number of applicants:	16
Application deadline:	March 1
Notification begins:	April 15
Total amount awarded:	$84,000

Contact:
Louis Carr Internship Foundation
P.O. Box 81859
Chicago, IL 60681-0589
Phone: 312-819-8617
Fax: 312-540-1109
Web: www.louiscarrfoundation.org

Macy's, Inc.

Internships at Macy's and Bloomingdale's

Type of award: Internship, renewable.
Intended use: For full-time undergraduate study.
Basis for selection: Applicant must demonstrate high academic achievement.
Application requirements: Resume.
Additional information: Eight- to ten-week paid internships offered in buying, planning, store management, product development, design, and macys.com. Apply online or visit Website for campus recruiting schedule.

Number of awards:	350

Contact:
Macy's, Inc.
Web: www.macysjobs.com/college/internships

Makovsky & Company Inc.

Makovsky & Company Inc. Public Relations Internship

Type of award: Internship.
Intended use: For senior study at 4-year institution in United States or Canada.
Basis for selection: Major/career interest in public relations; communications; English or political science/government. Applicant must demonstrate high academic achievement.
Application requirements: Interview. Resume, cover letter, writing sample.
Additional information: Two to four full- or part-time (20 hours minimum) paid positions offered in summer. Compensation $10/hr. Must major in public relations or related subject. Applicant must be responsible, diligent, and energetic. Provides opportunity to receive hands-on experience in all facets of public relations under direction of forums staff.

Number of awards:	4
Number of applicants:	200
Application deadline:	March 15

Contact:
Makovsky & Company, Inc. Internship Coordinator
16 East 34th Street
15th Floor
New York, NY 10016
Phone: 212-508-9670
Fax: 212-751-9710
Web: www.makovsky.com

MCC Theater

MCC Theater Internships

Type of award: Internship.
Intended use: For undergraduate study at vocational institution.
Eligibility: Applicant must be residing in New York.
Basis for selection: Major/career interest in theater arts; theater/production/technical; performing arts; design; business/management/administration or arts management.
Application requirements: Resume.
Additional information: Rolling application deadlines, negotiable schedule. Internships available in general management/theater administration, development, marketing, production, and literary and arts education. College credit available. E-mail resume to apply.
Contact:
MCC Theater
311 West 43rd Street, Suite 302
New York, NY 10036
Phone: 212-727-7722
Fax: 212-727-7780
Web: www.mcctheater.org/jobs

Metropolitan Museum of Art

The Cloisters Summer Internship Program

Type of award: Internship.
Intended use: For sophomore, junior or senior study at postsecondary institution.
Basis for selection: Major/career interest in art/art history; history; museum studies or museum studies/administration.
Application requirements: $50 application fee. Recommendations, essay, transcript. Resume and list of art history courses taken.
Additional information: Must be currently enrolled college student at time of internship. First- and second-year students especially encouraged to apply. Interns receive $2,925 stipend. Interest in medieval history appreciated. Nine-week full-time internship from mid-June to mid-August. Five-day, 35-hour work week.

Amount of award:	$2,925
Number of awards:	8
Application deadline:	January 15
Notification begins:	April 10

Contact:
The Cloisters
College Internship Program
Fort Tryon Park
New York, NY 10040
Phone: 212-650-2280
Web: www.metmuseum.org/education

Metropolitan Museum of Art Mentoring Program for College Juniors

Type of award: Internship.
Intended use: For sophomore or junior study at postsecondary institution.
Application requirements: $35 application fee. Recommendations, transcript.
Additional information: Interns work full-time for 6 weeks over the summer. Designed to encourage college juniors from diverse backgrounds to pursue museum careers. Participants work in one of the Museum's departments (curatorial, administrative, or educational). Includes a two-week orientation of the Museum, meetings with Museum professionals, a Museum mentor, and field trips to other institutions. Visit Website for deadline and application details.

Amount of award:	$3,250

Contact:
Metropolitan Museum of Art
1000 Fifth Avenue
New York, NY 10028-0198
Phone: 212-570-3710
Web: www.metmuseum.org/education

Metropolitan Museum of Art Six-Month Internship

Type of award: Internship.
Intended use: For senior, graduate or non-degree study at 4-year or graduate institution.

Internships

Eligibility: Applicant must be U.S. citizen or international student.
Basis for selection: Major/career interest in art/art history; museum studies or history.
Application requirements: $50 application fee. Recommendations, transcript, proof of eligibility. Resume. List of art history and other relevant courses taken and foreign languages spoken. 500-word essay describing career goals, interest in museum work, specific areas of interest within the museum, and reasons for applying to the program.
Additional information: Interns work full-time from early June to early December and participate in summer orientation program. Interns receive $11,000 stipend. International students must have permission to earn stipend in U.S. Visit Website for more information.

Amount of award:	$11,000
Number of awards:	2

Contact:
Metropolitan Museum of Art
1000 Fifth Avenue
New York, NY 10028-0198
Phone: 212-570-3710
Web: www.metmuseum.org/education

Metropolitan Museum of Art Summer Internship Program

Type of award: Internship.
Intended use: For senior, graduate or non-degree study at postsecondary institution.
Eligibility: Applicant must be U.S. citizen or international student.
Basis for selection: Major/career interest in art/art history; arts management or museum studies/administration. Applicant must demonstrate seriousness of purpose.
Application requirements: $50 application fee. Typed paper indicating desired internship, including name, home and school addresses and phone numbers. Resume. Two academic recommendations. Transcripts. Separate list with art history or relevant courses taken and knowledge of foreign languages. 500-word (maximum) essay describing career goals, interest in museum work, specific areas of interest within the museum, and reason for applying.
Additional information: Ten-week program for college students, recent college graduates who have not yet entered graduate school, and graduate students who have completed at least one year of graduate work in art history or related field. Interns work full-time. International students must have permission to work in U.S. Applicants should have broad background in art history. Program begins in June with two-week orientation, ends in August, and includes $3,250 honorarium for college interns and recent graduates and $3,500 for graduate interns. Visit Website for more information.

Amount of award:	$3,250
Number of awards:	40

Contact:
Attn: Internship Programs
Metropolitan Museum of Art
1000 Fifth Avenue
New York, NY 10028-0198
Phone: 212-570-3710
Web: www.metmuseum.org/education

Minnesota Office of Higher Education

Minnesota Work-Study Program

Type of award: Internship.
Intended use: For undergraduate or graduate study.
Eligibility: Applicant must be U.S. citizen or permanent resident residing in Minnesota.
Basis for selection: Applicant must demonstrate financial need.
Application requirements: Interview.
Additional information: This is a work-study program, but it may be applied to internships. Work placement must be approved by school or nonprofit agency. Must be used at Minnesota college or for internship with nonprofit or private sector employer located in Minnesota. Must be enrolled for at least six credit hours. Apply to financial aid office of school. Award maximum set at cost of attendance minus EFC and other financial aid.

Number of applicants:	11,073
Total amount awarded:	$14,379,530

Contact:
Minnesota Office of Higher Education
1450 Energy Park Drive, Suite 350
St. Paul, MN 55108-5227
Phone: 800-657-3866
Web: www.getreadyforcollege.org

Morris Arboretum of the University of Pennsylvania

Arboriculture Internship

Type of award: Internship.
Intended use: For undergraduate or graduate study at postsecondary institution.
Basis for selection: Major/career interest in horticulture; forestry or landscape architecture.
Application requirements: Recommendations, transcript. Letter of intent, resume.
Additional information: Applicant should have interest in arboriculture. Internships train students in most up-to-date tree care techniques. Interns work 40 hours per week at hourly rate of $10.60 for full year. Intern works with Chief Arborist in all aspects of tree care, including tree assessment, pruning, cabling, and removal. Safety-conscious techniques are emphasized, and recent innovations in climbing and rigging are demonstrated and put into practice. Other opportunities include assisting with outreach activities including workshops and off-site consulting. Benefits include health, vision, and dental plan. Must have solid academic background in arboriculture and horticulture. Tree climbing ability helpful. Driver's license required. Academic credit given.

Application deadline:	February 15

Contact:
Morris Arboretum of the University of Pennsylvania
Jan McFarlan, Education Coordinator
100 Northwestern Avenue
Philadelphia, PA 19118
Phone: 215-247-5777 ext. 156
Web: www.business-services.upenn.edu/arboretum

Morris Arboretum Education Internship

Type of award: Internship.
Intended use: For undergraduate or graduate study at postsecondary institution.
Basis for selection: Major/career interest in education; botany; horticulture; ecology or education, teacher.
Application requirements: Recommendations, transcript. Letter of intent, resume.
Additional information: Interns work 40 hours/week at hourly wage of $10.60 for full year. Interns develop workshops for experienced guides, training sessions for new guides, occasionally lead tours. Other responsibilities include supervising the school tour program, running special programs for the public, helping to prepare the adult education course brochure, and writing promotional copy including a newsletter for volunteer guides. Benefits include health, vision, and dental plan, and tuition benefits. Academic background or experience in education or educational programming preferred. Knowledge of plant-related subjects helpful. Strong writing and interpersonal skills essential. Academic credit given.

Application deadline: February 15

Contact:
Morris Arboretum of the University of Pennsylvania
Jan McFarlan, Education Coordinator
100 Northwestern Avenue
Philadelphia, PA 19118
Phone: 215-247-5777 ext. 156
Web: www.business-services.upenn.edu/arboretum

Morris Arboretum Horticulture Internship

Type of award: Internship.
Intended use: For undergraduate or graduate study at postsecondary institution.
Basis for selection: Major/career interest in horticulture.
Application requirements: Recommendations, transcript. Letter of intent, resume.
Additional information: Intern assists in all phases of garden development and care of collections. Specific emphasis on refining practical horticultural skills. Supervisory skills are developed by directing activities of volunteers and part-time staff. Other activities include developing Integrated Pest Management skills, arboricultural techniques, and the operation and maintenance of garden machinery. Special projects will be assigned to develop individual skills in garden planning and management. Must have strong academic background in horticulture or closely related field. Interns work 40 hours per week at hourly wage of $10.60 for full year. Benefits include health, vision, and dental plan, and tuition benefits. Some internships require travel. Driver's license required. Academic credit given.

Application deadline: February 15

Contact:
Morris Arboretum of the University of Pennsylvania
Jan McFarlan, Education Coordinator
100 Northwestern Avenue
Philadelphia, PA 19118
Phone: 215-247-5777 ext. 156
Web: www.business-services.upenn.edu/arboretum

Plant Propagation Internship

Type of award: Internship.
Intended use: For undergraduate or graduate study at postsecondary institution.
Basis for selection: Major/career interest in botany or horticulture.
Application requirements: Recommendations, transcript. Letter of intent, resume.
Additional information: Strong background in woody landscape plants, plant propagation, nursery management, and plant physiology required. Interns work 40 hours/week at hourly rate of $10.60 for full year. Benefits include health, vision, and dental plan and tuition benefits. Academic credit given. Intern assists propagator in the development of plant propagation and production schemes for arboretum. Emphasis is placed on the refinement of skills in traditional methods of plant propagation, nursery production, and greenhouse management. Other duties include management of the field nursery and data collection for ongoing research projects.

Application deadline: February 15

Contact:
Morris Arboretum of the University of Pennsylvania
Jan McFarlan, Education Coordinator
100 Northwestern Avenue
Philadelphia, PA 19118
Phone: 215-247-5777 ext. 156
Web: www.business-services.upenn.edu/arboretum

Plant Protection Internship

Type of award: Internship.
Intended use: For undergraduate or graduate study at postsecondary institution.
Basis for selection: Major/career interest in horticulture; entomology or botany.
Application requirements: Recommendations, transcript. Letter of intent, resume.
Additional information: Interns work 40 hours per week at hourly wage of $10.60 for full year. Course work in entomology or plant pathology required. Intern assists arboretum's plant pathologist with the Integrated Pest Management program, which includes regular monitoring of the living collection and communicating information on pests and diseases to staff members. Related projects include establishing threshold levels for specific plant pests and evaluating the effectiveness of control measures. Modern laboratory facilities are available for identifying plant pests and pathogens. Intern also participates in Plant Clinic's daily operations, providing diagnostic services to the public about horticultural problems. Benefits include health, vision, and dental plan and tuition benefits. Strong writing skills essential. Academic credit given.

Application deadline: February 15

Contact:
Morris Arboretum of the University of Pennsylvania
Jan McFarlan, Education Coordinator
100 Northwestern Avenue
Philadelphia, PA 19118
Phone: 215-247-5777 ext. 156
Web: www.business-services.upenn.edu/arboretum

Rose and Flower Garden Internship

Type of award: Internship.
Intended use: For undergraduate or graduate study at postsecondary institution.
Basis for selection: Major/career interest in horticulture. Applicant must demonstrate seriousness of purpose.
Application requirements: Recommendations, transcript. Letter of intent, resume.
Additional information: Intern assists Rosarian in garden development, management, and care of collections. Emphasis on mastering skills used in the culture of modern and antique roses, developing pest management skills, and refining horticulture skills including formal garden maintenance. Other duties include plant record keeping, support for volunteer gardeners, operation of garden machinery, and supervision of part-time staff. Interns work 40-hour week at hourly rate of $10.60 for full year. Benefits include health, vision, and dental plan, and tuition benefits. Applicant should have strong academic background in horticulture with course work in herbaceous and woody landscape plants. Driver's license required. Academic credit given.

Application deadline: February 15

Contact:
Morris Arboretum of the University of Pennsylvania
Jan McFarlan, Education Coordinator
100 Northwestern Avenue
Philadelphia, PA 19118
Phone: 215-247-5777 ext. 156
Web: www.business-services.upenn.edu/arboretum

Urban Forestry Internship

Type of award: Internship.
Intended use: For undergraduate study at postsecondary institution.
Basis for selection: Major/career interest in forestry; horticulture; landscape architecture or ecology.
Application requirements: Recommendations, transcript. Letter of intent, resume.
Additional information: Intern will engage in urban forestry and natural resources programs and strategies for public gardens, government agencies, and educational and community organizations; learn and teach stewardship concepts and practical applications through riparian and woodland restoration projects; develop community partnership, urban vegetation analysis, and management planning skills. Interns work 40 hours per week at hourly wage of $10.60 for full year. Benefits include health, vision, and dental plan and tuition benefits. Academic background in urban forestry, horticulture, landscape design, or related field. Communication skills essential. Car required; mileage reimbursed. Academic credit given.

Application deadline: February 15

Contact:
Morris Arboretum of the University of Pennsylvania
Jan McFarlan, Education Coordinator
100 Northwestern Avenue
Philadelphia, PA 19118
Phone: 215-247-5777 ext. 156
Web: www.business-services.upenn.edu/arboretum

Mother Jones

Mother Jones Ben Bagdikian Fellowship Program

Type of award: Internship.
Intended use: For junior, senior, graduate or non-degree study at postsecondary institution.
Basis for selection: Major/career interest in political science/government; communications; journalism or publishing. Applicant must demonstrate high academic achievement.
Application requirements: Interview, recommendations. Resume with cover letter; contact information for two references; writing samples.
Additional information: Deadlines are rolling. Internships are full-time and run six months with stipend of $1,000/month with seven-day vacation allowance. After six months, interns may apply for fellowship program which also runs six months with $1,400/month stipend. Hours vary according to magazine production schedule. No course credit offered. Reporting, writing, and research skills preferred. See Website for more information. Application deadlines occur twice a year: April 1st and October 1st.

Number of awards: 10
Application deadline: April 1, October 1

Contact:
Mother Jones
Attn: Ben Bagdikian Fellowship Program
222 Sutter Street, Suite 600
San Francisco, CA 94108
Web: www.motherjones.com

Museum of Modern Art

Museum of Modern Art Internship

Type of award: Internship.
Intended use: For junior, senior, graduate or non-degree study at postsecondary institution.
Eligibility: Applicant must be U.S. citizen, permanent resident or international student.
Application requirements: Interview, essay, transcript. Resume and one recommendation.
Additional information: Course credit available, but not required. Fall, spring, summer, and 12-month internships. Twelve-month internships are paid, full-time programs for recent college graduates. Fall, spring, and summer internships are part-time and unpaid. Fields of study encompass broad spectrum of topics. Visit Website for complete list of departments, applications, and deadline information.

Number of awards: 130
Number of applicants: 2,500

Contact:
The Museum of Modern Art
Internship Coordinator, Human Resources
11 W. 53rd Street
New York, NY 10019
Web: www.moma.org/learn/courses/internships

NASA Arizona Space Grant Consortium

NASA Space Grant Arizona Undergraduate Research Internship

Type of award: Internship, renewable.
Intended use: For full-time sophomore, junior or senior study at accredited 2-year or 4-year institution in United States. Designated institutions: Arizona Space Grant Consortium (AZSGC) colleges and universities.
Eligibility: Applicant must be U.S. citizen residing in Arizona.
Basis for selection: Major/career interest in aerospace; astronomy; engineering; physics; geology/earth sciences; science, general; journalism or education.
Additional information: Approximately 100 students will be employed for 10-20 hours per week for the academic year in research programs, working alongside upper-level graduate students and practicing scientists. Hourly wage offered. Awardees must attend Arizona Space Grant Consortium member institution. Availability of internships varies. Some internships are renewable. Current announcements/application posted on Website.

Number of applicants:	350

Contact:
NASA Space Grant Arizona Space Grant Consortium
Lunar and Planetary Laboratory, Room 349
U of Arizona, 1629 E. University Blvd.
Tucson, AZ 85721-0092
Phone: 520-621-8556
Web: spacegrant.arizona.edu

NASA Delaware Space Grant Consortium

Delaware Space Grant Undergraduate Summer Research Internship

Type of award: Internship, renewable.
Intended use: For full-time sophomore, junior or senior study at postsecondary institution. Designated institutions: University of Delaware, Delaware Technical and Community College, Swarthmore College, Delaware State University at Dover, Villanova University, Wesley College, Wilmington University.
Eligibility: Applicant must be U.S. citizen.
Basis for selection: Major/career interest in geography; mathematics; science, general; technology or engineering.
Application requirements: Recommendations, transcript. Description of proposed research project from faculty mentor.
Additional information: Must have proven interest in space-related studies. Recipient must attend a Delaware Space Grant Consortium member institution. Stipend offered. Contact Consortium office for deadlines and additional information.

Amount of award:	$3,500
Number of awards:	5
Number of applicants:	5
Total amount awarded:	$17,500

Contact:
Delaware Space Grant Consortium Program Office
University of Delaware
212 Sharp Lab
Newark, DE 19716
Phone: 302-831-1094
Fax: 302-831-1843
Web: www.delspace.org

NASA New Jersey Space Grant Consortium

NASA New Jersey Space Grant Consortium Undergraduate Summer Fellowships in Engineering and Science

Type of award: Internship, renewable.
Intended use: For junior or senior study at accredited 4-year institution in United States. Designated institutions: Georgian Court University, New Jersey Institute of Technology, Princeton University, Raritan Valley Community College, Rutgers University, Stevens Institute of Technology, University of Medicine and Dentistry of NJ, New Jersey City University, Rowan University, Seton Hall, College of New Jersey.
Eligibility: Applicant must be U.S. citizen.
Basis for selection: Major/career interest in aerospace; biology; computer/information sciences; engineering, computer; engineering, chemical; engineering, electrical/electronic; engineering, mechanical; materials science; natural sciences or physical sciences.
Application requirements: Recommendations, essay. Biographical sketch, statement that describes career goals and what applicant hopes to accomplish as Space Grant Fellow, plan for immediate future and reference letter from faculty adviser.
Additional information: Applicants must have completed at least two but preferably three years of college. Open to all science and engineering majors, but preference given to aerospace majors. Consortium actively encourages women, minority students, and physically challenged students to apply. Preference given to students attending NJSGC member institutions. Academic year ($2,000 stipend) and summer fellowships ($4,000 stipend) offered. Summer fellowship deadline in April. Academic year fellowship has ongoing deadline, although applications preferred by September. Visit Website for important dates and additional information.

Amount of award:	$2,000-$4,000
Number of awards:	37
Number of applicants:	75
Application deadline:	April 1
Total amount awarded:	$175,000

Contact:
Program Director, New Jersey Space Grant Consortium
Rutgers University, College of Engineering
Room B134, 98 Brett Road
Piscataway, NJ 08854
Phone: 201-216-8964
Web: njsgc.rutgers.edu

NASA Pennsylvania Space Grant Consortium

NASA Academy Internship

Type of award: Internship.
Intended use: For full-time junior, senior or graduate study at accredited 4-year or graduate institution in United States. Designated institutions: Pennsylvania colleges and universities.
Eligibility: Applicant must be U.S. citizen or permanent resident residing in Pennsylvania.
Basis for selection: Major/career interest in engineering; science, general; mathematics; aerospace or astronomy. Applicant must demonstrate high academic achievement and leadership.
Application requirements: Recommendations, essay, transcript.
Additional information: Minimum 3.0 GPA. Awards are for ten-week internships at participating NASA centers. Minimum B average required. Stipend, plus room and board and travel expenses. Earth science students also eligible. Awardees must attend Pennsylvania institution or be a full-time resident. Interns receive $5,000 stipend. Consortium actively encourages women, minority, and physically challenged students to apply. Visit the NASA Academy Website for application information.

Amount of award:	$5,000
Number of awards:	2
Number of applicants:	24
Application deadline:	March 15
Total amount awarded:	$15,000

Contact:
NASA Pennsylvania Space Grant Consortium
Penn State, University Park
2217 Earth-Engineering Sciences Building
University Park, PA 16802
Phone: 814-865-2535
Fax: 814-863-9563
Web: www.pa.spacegrant.org or www.academyapp.com

National Association of Black Journalists

NABJ Internships

Type of award: Internship.
Intended use: For full-time undergraduate study at postsecondary institution.
Eligibility: Applicant must be African American.
Basis for selection: Major/career interest in journalism or radio/television/film.
Application requirements: Portfolio, recommendations, essay. Resume, cover letter. Applicants must submit minimum of five samples of published work in print, radio, television, photography, slideshows, website, or flash animation.
Additional information: Ten-week paid internship in print, broadcast, or multimedia journalism. Must be current NABJ member. Must have prior experience in collegiate or professional media. Must be member of National Association of Black Journalists. Weekly stipend varies between $400 and $600. Some internships are unpaid. Visit Website for more information.

Contact:
National Association of Black Journalists
1100 Knight Hall, Suite 3100
College Park, MD 20742
Phone: 301-405-2573
Fax: 301-314-1714
Web: www.nabj.org

National Geographic Society

National Geographic Society Geography Students Internship

Type of award: Internship.
Intended use: For junior, senior or master's study at 4-year or graduate institution in United States.
Basis for selection: Major/career interest in geography or cartography.
Application requirements: Recommendations, essay, transcript. Resume.
Additional information: Spring, summer, and fall internships for 14 to 16 weeks in Washington, D.C., at $400 per week. Application deadline for all internships in the fall. Emphasis on editorial and cartographic research. Students should contact their school's geography department chair or call internship hotline for more information.

Number of awards:	30
Number of applicants:	100

Contact:
National Geographic Society
Robert E. Dulli
1145 17 Street, NW
Washington, DC 20036-4688
Phone: 202-857-7134
Web: www.nationalgeographic.com

National Museum of the American Indian

National Museum of the American Indian Internship

Type of award: Internship.
Intended use: For undergraduate, graduate or non-degree study at postsecondary institution.
Basis for selection: Major/career interest in museum studies. Applicant must demonstrate high academic achievement.
Application requirements: Recommendations, essay, transcript. Resume.
Additional information: Provides educational work/research experience for students in museum practice and related programming using resources of museum and other Smithsonian offices. Internships available at NMAI in Suitland, MD; Washington, DC; and New York City. Applicants must have minimum 3.0 GPA. Four 10-week internships, deadlines as follows: February 6 for summer; July 12 for fall; October 10 for winter; and November 20 for spring. Selection based on professional and educational goals of student; needs of

museum. Students receiving stipends must work full-time; other interns must work at least 20 hours per week. Museum will grant academic credit if student makes arrangements with school. Visit Website or contact via e-mail for more information and application.

Number of awards: 20
Number of applicants: 40
Application deadline: November 20, February 6

Contact:
Internship Program, National Museum of the American Indian
Cultural Resources Center-Community Services
4220 Silver Hill Road
Suitland, MD 20746-2863
Phone: 202-633-6645
Web: www.nmai.si.edu

National Museum of Women in the Arts

Museum Coca-Cola Internship

Type of award: Internship.
Intended use: For junior, senior, graduate or non-degree study in United States.
Basis for selection: Major/career interest in public relations; advertising; library science; journalism; museum studies; art/art history; museum studies/administration; accounting; education or retailing/merchandising. Applicant must demonstrate high academic achievement and seriousness of purpose.
Application requirements: Recommendations, transcript. Resume, cover letter, and one- to two-page writing sample.
Additional information: Internship available to students interested in pursuing careers in museum environments. Minimum 3.25 GPA. Interns receive $1500 stipend. Full-time internship lasts 12 weeks; application deadline for spring is October 15; summer is March 15; fall is June 15.

Amount of award: $1,500
Number of awards: 3
Number of applicants: 50
Application deadline: October 15, March 15
Total amount awarded: $1,500

Contact:
National Museum of Women in the Arts
Manager of Public Programs Education Dept.
1250 New York Avenue, NW
Washington, DC 20005-3970
Phone: 800-222-7270
Fax: 202-393-3234
Web: www.nmwa.org

Southern California Council Endowed Internship

Type of award: Internship, renewable.
Intended use: For junior, senior or graduate study at postsecondary institution. Designated institutions: Art and design institutions in Los Angeles County area.
Eligibility: Applicant must be residing in California.
Basis for selection: Major/career interest in art/art history; arts management; arts, general; museum studies or museum studies/administration. Applicant must demonstrate high academic achievement.
Application requirements: Recommendations, essay, transcript. Cover letter, brief writing sample, resume.
Additional information: Full-time, twelve-week internship. $2,000 stipend. Applicant must be resident of Los Angeles County. Minimum 3.25 GPA. Application deadline for spring is October 15; summer is March 15; fall is June 15.

Amount of award: $2,000
Number of awards: 1
Number of applicants: 1
Application deadline: March 15, June 15

Contact:
National Museum of Women in the Arts
Manager of Public Programs Education Dept.
1250 New York Avenue, NW
Washington, DC 20005-3970
Phone: 800-222-7270
Fax: 202-393-3234
Web: www.nmwa.org

National Science Foundation

Research Experiences for Undergraduates - Maria Mitchell Observatory

Type of award: Internship.
Intended use: For undergraduate study at 4-year institution. Designated institutions: Maria Mitchell Observatory, Nantucket, MA.
Eligibility: Applicant must be U.S. citizen or permanent resident.
Basis for selection: Major/career interest in astronomy. Applicant must demonstrate high academic achievement.
Application requirements: Recommendations, essay, transcript.
Additional information: Positions provide chance for students to conduct independent research and to participate in common project. Students expected to develop their ability to communicate with the public. Furnished housing is available at no cost. Partial travel funds available. Internship runs from June through August, with $1,700 monthly stipend. Applicant must demonstrate motivation in research. Minimum of one year undergraduate physics required.

Number of awards: 6
Number of applicants: 100
Application deadline: February 15
Notification begins: March 1

Contact:
Maria Mitchell Observatory
4 Vestal Street
Nantucket, MA 02554
Phone: 508-228-9273
Fax: 508-228-1031
Web: www.mariamitchell.org/get-involved/internships/reu

NCR Corporation

NCR Summer Internships

Type of award: Internship.
Intended use: For full-time undergraduate study at accredited 4-year institution.

Basis for selection: Major/career interest in accounting; computer/information sciences; engineering, computer; finance/banking; human resources; information systems or marketing. Applicant must demonstrate high academic achievement.
Application requirements: Interview, proof of eligibility. Resume.
Additional information: Minimum 3.0 GPA. Must have at least one semester or two quarters remaining before graduation. Interns paid hourly wage. Applicants must complete personal profile including resume on Website before applying for positions. Applicants encouraged to visit Website frequently during spring to review newly added offerings and important information.
Contact:
Visit Website for more information.
Web: www.ncr.com/careers

New Dramatists

Bernard B. Jacobs Internship Program

Type of award: Internship.
Intended use: For undergraduate or graduate study at postsecondary institution.
Basis for selection: Major/career interest in theater arts; performing arts or arts management.
Application requirements: Interview, recommendations, essay. Resume.
Additional information: Must have passion for new plays and playwrights. Twelve- to twenty-week internships, three to five days per week. Internships run September to December, January to May, and June to August. Stipend is $25 per week for three days, $50 per week for five days. College credit may be available. Computer and writing skills essential. Applications must be filled out online.

Application deadline: November 30, July 16

Contact:
New Dramatists
Internship Coordinator
424 West 44th Street
New York, NY 10036
Phone: 212-757-6960
Fax: 212-265-4738
Web: www.newdramatists.org

New Mexico Commission on Higher Education

New Mexico Work-Study Program

Type of award: Internship, renewable.
Intended use: For undergraduate or graduate study at postsecondary institution. Designated institutions: St. John's College, University of the Southwest, Institute of American Indian Art, Crownpoint Institute of Technology, Diné College, Southwestern Indian Polytechnic Institute.
Eligibility: Applicant must be U.S. citizen or permanent resident residing in New Mexico.
Basis for selection: Applicant must demonstrate financial need.
Application requirements: FAFSA.
Additional information: Awards vary. Limit of 20 hours per week, on-campus or off-campus in federal, state, or local public agency. New Mexico residents receive state portion of funding. Contact financial aid office of New Mexico public postsecondary institutions for information, deadlines, and application.
Contact:
Contact financial aid office at institution.
Phone: 505-476-8400
Web: www.hed.state.nm.us

The New Republic

The New Republic Internships

Type of award: Internship.
Intended use: For undergraduate, graduate or non-degree study at postsecondary institution.
Eligibility: Applicant must be U.S. citizen.
Basis for selection: Major/career interest in journalism. Applicant must demonstrate depth of character and seriousness of purpose.
Application requirements: Cover letter, resume.
Additional information: Visit Website for list of available internships. Past internships include social media, literary, reporter-researcher, editorial web, and business associate. Provides intern with opportunity to gain editorial experience at leading opinion magazine located in Washington, D.C.
Contact:
The New Republic
Web: www.tnr.com

New York State Assembly

New York State Assembly Session Internship Program

Type of award: Internship, renewable.
Intended use: For full-time junior, senior or graduate study at accredited postsecondary institution in United States.
Basis for selection: Applicant must demonstrate high academic achievement.
Application requirements: Recommendations, essay, transcript, proof of eligibility. Writing sample. Letter from college endorsing candidate and outlining course credit arrangements.
Additional information: All majors eligible. Interns assigned to work with assembly members or assembly staff. Program runs from January to May. Undergraduate interns receive $4,140 stipend. Graduate interns receive $11,500 stipend. Applications accepted on an ongoing basis until deadline. Extensions granted upon request. Housing not provided, but assistance offered in finding apartments and roommates. Visit Website for deadline information.

Amount of award:	$4,140-$11,500
Number of awards:	150
Number of applicants:	200
Application deadline:	November 1

Contact:
Kathleen McCarty, Director New York State Assembly
Assembly Intern Committee
Legislative Office Building, Room 104A
Albany, NY 12248
Phone: 518-455-4704
Fax: 518-455-4705
Web: www.assembly.state.ny.us/internship/

New York Times

David E. Rosenbaum Reporting Internship in Washington, D.C.

Type of award: Internship.
Intended use: For senior or graduate study at postsecondary institution.
Basis for selection: Major/career interest in journalism.
Application requirements: Essay. Cover letter, resume, 6 clips from daily professional or college media organizations, essay about interest in Washington reporting. Do not submit a Website link if it shows more than 6 clips.
Additional information: Ten-week summer internship at the Washington Bureau for aspiring reporters with interest in government and policy. Portion of first week spent in New York for orientation. Salary is $960/week. Applications via Website only. No telephone calls.

Number of awards:	1
Number of applicants:	150
Application deadline:	October 30

Contact:
New York Times
Web: www.nytimes-internship.com/internships/david-rosenbaum-reporting-fellow

New York Times James Reston Reporting Fellowships

Type of award: Internship.
Intended use: For senior, graduate or non-degree study at postsecondary institution.
Basis for selection: Major/career interest in journalism. Applicant must demonstrate seriousness of purpose.
Application requirements: Portfolio. Cover letter, resume, eight to ten writing samples.
Additional information: Ten-week summer internship available. Must be authorized to work in U.S. for duration of internship. All applicants must have had at least one previous internship, preferably on a daily newspaper. Visit Website for internship descriptions and more information.

Number of awards:	4
Application deadline:	November 15

Contact:
The New York Times
Web: www.nytco.com/careers/internships/summer.html

NY Times Internships

Type of award: Internship.
Intended use: For undergraduate study at postsecondary institution.
Additional information: Variety of internships offered for undergraduates. Visit Website for current offerings and to apply.
Contact:
New York Times
Web: www.nytco.com/careers

NextEra Energy

NextEra Energy Internship Program

Type of award: Internship, renewable.
Intended use: For full-time undergraduate study at accredited vocational, 2-year or 4-year institution in United States.
Eligibility: Applicant must be U.S. citizen or permanent resident.
Basis for selection: Major/career interest in engineering; engineering, nuclear; engineering, mechanical; engineering, electrical/electronic; engineering, civil; engineering, industrial; finance/banking; accounting; computer/information sciences or business. Applicant must demonstrate high academic achievement.
Application requirements: Resume.
Additional information: Positions are paid. Minimum 3.0 GPA. Apply online or check Website for campus recruiting calendar.
Contact:
NextEra Energy
Web: www.nexteraenergy.com/careers/college.shtml

Oak Ridge Institute for Science and Education

Air Force Research Laboratory, 711 Human Performance Wing

Type of award: Internship, renewable.
Intended use: For undergraduate, graduate or postgraduate study at 4-year or graduate institution.
Basis for selection: Major/career interest in mathematics; computer/information sciences; science, general; social/behavioral sciences or engineering.
Additional information: Research Participation program for 711 HPW provides opportunities to participate in on-going applied research and development projects. Located in Wright Patterson Air Force Base, Ohio. Appointments made up to one year, full- or part-time. Applications accepted year-round. Stipend based on research area and academic classification.
Contact:
Oak Ridge Institute for Science and Education
Web: see.orau.org

Department of Energy Community College Institute at Oak Ridge National Laboratory

Type of award: Internship.
Intended use: For full-time undergraduate study at accredited 2-year institution in United States.
Eligibility: Applicant must be at least 18. Applicant must be U.S. citizen or permanent resident.
Basis for selection: Major/career interest in computer/information sciences; science, general; engineering;

environmental science; life sciences; mathematics or physical sciences. Applicant must demonstrate high academic achievement.
Application requirements: Recommendations, transcript. Proof of health insurance. Proof of citizenship or resident alien status.
Additional information: Applicant must be student at community college. Provides opportunities to participate in research in a broad range of science and engineering activities related to basic sciences, energy, and the environment at the Oak Ridge National Laboratory in Oak Ridge, TN. Applicant must have passed at least 12 credit hours of coursework toward a degree (with at least six credit hours in science, math, engineering, or technology courses) at community college. Minimum 3.0 GPA. Ten-week summer internship. Bi-weekly stipend. Limited travel reimbursement and limited housing allowance. Visit Website for application and deadlines.
Contact:
Oak Ridge Institute for Science and Education
Web: see.orau.org

DHS HS-STEM Summer Internship Program

Type of award: Internship.
Intended use: For full-time junior or senior study at accredited 2-year or 4-year institution in United States.
Eligibility: Applicant must be at least 18. Applicant must be U.S. citizen.
Basis for selection: Major/career interest in science, general; computer/information sciences; technology; engineering or mathematics. Applicant must demonstrate high academic achievement.
Application requirements: Recommendations, essay, transcript. Birth certificate, citizenship information form.
Additional information: Minimum 3.3 GPA. United States Department of Homeland Security (DHS) HS-STEM Summer Internship Program provides 10-week summer research experience. Homeland security-related science majors also eligible. Must be covered under health insurance plan. Must be available for 10 consecutive weeks full-time. 40 hours per week required. $500 weekly stipend. Deadline in early January.

Amount of award: $5,000
Number of awards: 50

Contact:
Oak Ridge Institute for Science and Education
Web: see.orau.org

DHS Summer Faculty and Student Research Team Program for Minority Serving Institutions

Type of award: Internship.
Intended use: For undergraduate or graduate study at accredited 4-year or graduate institution in United States. Designated institutions: Minority serving institution.
Eligibility: Applicant must be U.S. citizen.
Basis for selection: Major/career interest in life sciences; health sciences; mathematics; computer/information sciences; physical sciences; environmental science; social/behavioral sciences or engineering.
Additional information: 10-week summer research appointment for faculty and student research teams. Applications accepted in winter. Approximately 10 teams each term. Locations across U.S. Undergraduates receive a stipend of $500/week. Graduates receive stipend of $600/week. If student lives more than 50 miles one-way from the summer research locations, a combined housing and travel expense of $1500 for the summer is given.

Amount of award: $5,000-$7,500

Contact:
Oak Ridge Institute for Science and Education
Web: see.orau.org

DOE Faculty and Student Teams Program at Oak Ridge National Laboratory

Type of award: Internship.
Intended use: For undergraduate study at 4-year institution.
Eligibility: Applicant must be U.S. citizen or permanent resident.
Basis for selection: Major/career interest in computer/information sciences; environmental science; engineering; life sciences; health sciences; mathematics or physical sciences.
Additional information: Program located at the Oak Ridge National Laboratory (Oak Ridge, TN). Undergraduates work with faculty members in science and engineering research. 10-week summer term with bi-weekly stipend; limited travel reimbursement and housing allowance.
Contact:
Oak Ridge Institute for Science and Education
Web: see.orau.org

DOE Scholars Program

Type of award: Internship.
Intended use: For undergraduate certificate, graduate or postgraduate study at accredited 4-year or graduate institution.
Eligibility: Applicant must be U.S. citizen.
Basis for selection: Major/career interest in business; communications; graphic arts/design; mathematics; computer graphics; physical sciences; science, general or engineering.
Application requirements: Recommendations, essay. Resume.
Additional information: DOE Scholars Program provides opportunities at various Department of Energy sites throughout the U.S. Up to $650 stipend per week depending on academic status. Travel to and from appointment site will be paid when distance is over 60 miles one-way.
Contact:
Oak Ridge Institute for Science and Education
Web: see.orau.org

DOE Science Undergraduate Laboratory Internships at Oak Ridge National Laboratory

Type of award: Internship.
Intended use: For undergraduate study at postsecondary institution.
Eligibility: Applicant must be U.S. citizen or permanent resident.
Basis for selection: Major/career interest in computer/information sciences; physical sciences; mathematics; life sciences; engineering; science, general or environmental science.
Application requirements: Recommendations, transcript. Proof of health insurance.
Additional information: Applicant must have intention to teach. Internship program provides opportunity to participate in research in a broad range of science and engineering activities related to basic sciences, energy, and the environment at the Oak Ridge National Laboratory (Oak Ridge, TN). Bi-weekly

stipend; limited travel reimbursement and housing allowance. Internship lasts ten weeks in the summer. See Website for more information and deadlines.
Contact:
Oak Ridge Institute for Science and Education
Web: see.orau.org

Environmental Management Participation at the U.S. Army Environmental Command (USAEC)

Type of award: Internship, renewable.
Intended use: For undergraduate or graduate study at 2-year, 4-year or graduate institution.
Eligibility: Applicant must be U.S. citizen.
Basis for selection: Major/career interest in archaeology; biology; chemistry; computer/information sciences; ecology; engineering; entomology; environmental science; forestry or zoology. Applicant must demonstrate high academic achievement.
Application requirements: Recommendations, transcript. Resume, proof of health insurance.
Additional information: Provides opportunities to participate in research in environmental programs involving cultural and natural resources, restoration, compliance, conservation, pollution prevention, validation, demonstration, technology transfer, quality assurance and quality control, training, information management and reporting, and related programs. Up to one year; full-time or part-time appointments. Stipend based on research area and academic classification. Minimum 2.5 GPA. Applications accepted year-round. Number of awards varies. Visit Website for application.
Contact:
Oak Ridge Institute for Science and Education
Web: see.orau.org

Higher Education Research Experiences at Oak Ridge National Laboratory for Students

Type of award: Internship.
Intended use: For undergraduate or graduate study in United States.
Eligibility: Applicant must be at least 18. Applicant must be U.S. citizen or permanent resident.
Basis for selection: Major/career interest in computer/information sciences; environmental science; engineering, environmental; health sciences; life sciences; medicine; physical sciences or mathematics. Applicant must demonstrate high academic achievement.
Application requirements: Recommendations, transcript. Two academic references.
Additional information: Provides opportunities to participate in research in a broad range of science and engineering activities related to basic sciences, energy, and the environment at the Oak Ridge National Laboratory (Oak Ridge, TN). Terms vary with academic level; full- or part-time positions available. Minimum 2.5 GPA. Weekly stipend varies with academic level. One round-trip travel reimbursement and housing allowance. Number of awards varies. Deadlines for undergraduates: February 1 for summer, June 1 for fall, and October 1 for spring. Deadline for freshmen is February 1. See Website for application and more information.
Application deadline: February 1, June 1
Contact:
Oak Ridge Institute for Science and Education
Web: see.orau.org

Laboratory Technology Program

Type of award: Internship, renewable.
Intended use: For undergraduate or graduate study at postsecondary institution.
Eligibility: Applicant must be U.S. citizen or permanent resident residing in Tennessee.
Basis for selection: Major/career interest in engineering or physical sciences. Applicant must demonstrate high academic achievement.
Application requirements: Recommendations, transcript.
Additional information: Applicant must be attending a regionally-accredited college or university. Provides opportunity to receive hands-on experience in technical areas via long-term assignment at the Oak Ridge National Laboratory (Oak Ridge, TN). Minimum 2.5 GPA. Internship duration varies with academic level; full-time or part-time appointments of up to one year, renewable up to two additional years. Applications accepted year-round. Stipend available; amount based on academic level or degree. Interns also receive benefits of full-time or part-time employees. Depending on fund availability, participants may be eligible for 100% tuition reimbursement.
Contact:
Oak Ridge Institute for Science and Education
Web: see.orau.org

Mickey Leland Energy Fellowship Program

Type of award: Internship.
Intended use: For full-time sophomore, junior or senior study at accredited 4-year institution.
Eligibility: Applicant must be U.S. citizen.
Basis for selection: Major/career interest in science, general; technology; engineering or mathematics.
Additional information: Minimum 3.0 GPA. Must be female or minority student. 10-week program runs during summer. Paid stipend and transportation expenses given. Recipients will work on focused research projects consistent with the mission of the Office of Fossil Energy. Awards vary. Visit Website for details.
Contact:
Oak Ridge Institute for Science and Education
Web: see.orau.org

National Energy Technology Laboratory Professional Internship Program

Type of award: Internship, renewable.
Intended use: For undergraduate or graduate study at accredited 2-year, 4-year or graduate institution in United States. Designated institutions: National Energy Technology Laboratory (Pittsburgh, PA, Albany, OR, and Morgantown, WV).
Eligibility: Applicant must be at least 18.
Basis for selection: Major/career interest in chemistry; computer/information sciences; engineering; environmental science; geology/earth sciences; mathematics; physics; physical sciences or statistics.
Application requirements: Transcript. Proof of health insurance. Two references; at least one academic reference.

Internships

Additional information: Provides opportunities to participate in energy-related research. 10 weeks to 3 months, full-time or part-time appointments. Weekly stipend. Limited travel reimbursement (round-trip transportation expenses between facility and home or campus). Off-campus tuition and fees may be paid. Deadline for summer is February 15. Number of awards varies. Visit Website for application. Applications accepted year-round.

Number of applicants: 80

Contact:
Oak Ridge Institute for Science and Education
Web: see.orau.org

Nuclear Regulatory Commission Historically Black Colleges and Universities Student Research Participation

Type of award: Internship.
Intended use: For undergraduate or graduate study at accredited postsecondary institution in United States. Designated institutions: Laboratories conducting NRC research; some appointments on HBCU campuses; some appointments at host universities under the guidance of principal investigators who have NRC research grants.
Eligibility: Applicant must be U.S. citizen or permanent resident.
Basis for selection: Major/career interest in computer/information sciences; engineering; biology; mathematics; geophysics; physics; materials science; physical sciences; health sciences or statistics. Applicant must demonstrate high academic achievement.
Application requirements: Recommendations, transcript. Resume.
Additional information: Provides opportunities for students from historically black colleges to participate in ongoing NRC research and development. Ten to twelve weeks during the summer; some part-time appointments of one year. Monthly stipend of $3,800 per month or normal salary rate, whichever is greater. Limited travel reimbursement (round-trip transportation expenses between facility and home or campus). Funded by U.S. Nuclear Regulatory Commission. Visit Website for application.
Contact:
Oak Ridge Institute for Science and Education
Web: see.orau.org

Oak Ridge National Laboratory Undergraduate Student Cooperative Education Program

Type of award: Internship.
Intended use: For sophomore, junior or senior study at accredited 4-year institution in United States.
Basis for selection: Major/career interest in computer/information sciences; science, general; engineering; life sciences; environmental science; physical sciences or mathematics.
Application requirements: Recommendations.
Additional information: Co-op program provides opportunities for qualified undergraduate students to receive hands-on experience in real-world setting. Must be available for more than one term at ORNL alternating with terms at academic institution. Fall, winter/spring, and summer terms available; apply three months before requested start date. Stipends vary by discipline and academic status and range from $530 to $900 per week. Students from outside area may qualify for $105/week housing allowance and travel reimbursement.
Contact:
Oak Ridge Institute for Science and Education
Phone: 865-576-2311
Web: see.orau.org

Oak Ridge Nuclear Engineering Science Laboratory Synthesis

Type of award: Internship.
Intended use: For undergraduate study at 4-year institution in United States.
Basis for selection: Major/career interest in engineering or physical sciences. Applicant must demonstrate high academic achievement.
Additional information: Program is a cooperative research initiative geared toward students in physics and nuclear engineering. Minimum 3.0 GPA. 2/1 deadline is for 10-week summer appointment. Limited number of fall and spring appointments. Weekly stipend varies with academic level. One round-trip travel reimbursement; housing allowance.

Application deadline: February 1

Contact:
Oak Ridge Institute for Science and Education
Web: see.orau.org

Oak Ridge Science Semester

Type of award: Internship.
Intended use: For full-time junior or senior study at accredited 4-year institution in United States.
Basis for selection: Major/career interest in astronomy; computer/information sciences; engineering; environmental science; health sciences; physics; biology; geology/earth sciences or mathematics. Applicant must demonstrate high academic achievement.
Application requirements: Recommendations, transcript.
Additional information: Provides opportunities to participate in research in a broad range of scientific research areas at the Oak Ridge National Laboratory in Oak Ridge, TN. Program is 16 weeks in the fall (late August through mid-December). Housing paid for by program. Academic credit offered for combination of research, coursework, and seminar series. Minimum 3.0 GPA. Visit Website for application deadline.

Amount of award: $6,800

Contact:
Oak Ridge Institute for Science and Education
Web: www.denison.edu/oakridge

Research Participation at the Centers for Disease Control and Prevention/Agency for Toxic Substances and Disease Registry

Type of award: Internship.
Intended use: For undergraduate or graduate study at accredited 2-year, 4-year or graduate institution in United States. Designated institutions: Centers for Disease Control and Prevention (Atlanta, GA and other domestic and international locations) and Agency for Toxic Substances and Disease Registry (Atlanta, GA).
Basis for selection: Major/career interest in economics; environmental science; epidemiology; health sciences; life sciences; medicine; physical sciences; science, general or

Internships

pharmacy/pharmaceutics/pharmacology. Applicant must demonstrate high academic achievement.
Application requirements: Recommendations, transcript. Resume, proof of health insurance.
Additional information: Provides opportunities to participate in research on infectious diseases, environmental health, epidemiology, or occupational safety and health. Minimum 2.5 GPA. One month to one year; full-time or part-time appointments. Stipend based on research area(s) and academic classification. Applications accepted year-round. See Website for application.
Contact:
Oak Ridge Institute for Science and Education
Web: see.orau.org or www.orau.gov/cdc

Research Participation at the National Center for Toxicological Research

Type of award: Internship, renewable.
Intended use: For undergraduate or graduate study at accredited 2-year, 4-year or graduate institution in United States.
Basis for selection: Major/career interest in biology; chemistry; computer/information sciences; mathematics; pharmacy/pharmaceutics/pharmacology; science, general or medicine.
Application requirements: Recommendations, transcript. Resume, proof of health insurance.
Additional information: Provides opportunities to participate in research on biological effects of potentially toxic chemicals and solutions to toxicology problems that have a major impact on human health and the environment at the National Center for Toxicological Research in Jefferson, AK. One month to one year; full-time or part-time appointments. Stipend based on research area and academic classification. Applications accepted year-round for academic year appointments. Number of awards varies. Visit Website for application.

Number of applicants: 100

Contact:
Oak Ridge Institute for Science and Education
Web: see.orau.org

Research Participation at the U.S. Food and Drug Administration

Type of award: Internship, renewable.
Intended use: For undergraduate or graduate study at accredited 4-year or graduate institution.
Basis for selection: Major/career interest in life sciences; health sciences; bioengineering; physical sciences; veterinary medicine; epidemiology; food science/technology; materials science or pharmacy/pharmaceutics/pharmacology.
Application requirements: Recommendations. Resume.
Additional information: Program provides opportunities to participate in research related to the mission of the U.S. Food and Drug Administration. Appointments available at the Center for Biologics Evaluation and Research, Center for Devices and Radiological Health, Center for Drug Evaluation and Research, Center for Food Safety and Applied Nutrition, Center for Veterinary Medicine, and Office of the Commissioner. Program is from one month to one year, up to five years maximum, full-time or part-time appointments available. Stipend based on research area(s) and educational level. Applications accepted year-round.
Contact:
Oak Ridge Institute for Science and Education
Phone: 865-576-9241
Web: see.orau.org

Research Participation Program for the Combat Casualty Care Research Program (CCCRP)

Type of award: Internship, renewable.
Intended use: For undergraduate, graduate or postgraduate study at 4-year or graduate institution.
Eligibility: Applicant must be U.S. citizen.
Basis for selection: Major/career interest in life sciences; health sciences; mathematics; computer/information sciences; physical sciences; social/behavioral sciences or engineering.
Additional information: Program located at Ft. Detrick, Maryland. Program is focused on leveraging cutting-edge research and knowledge from government and civilian research programs to fill existing and emerging gaps in combat casualty care. Appointments up to one year, full- or part-time. Stipend available. Visit Web site for more details.
Contact:
Oak Ridge Institute for Science and Education
Web: see.orau.org

Research Participation Program for the Johns Hopkins University Applied Physics Laboratory

Type of award: Internship, renewable.
Intended use: For undergraduate, graduate or postgraduate study at 4-year or graduate institution.
Eligibility: Applicant must be U.S. citizen.
Basis for selection: Major/career interest in mathematics; physical sciences; graphic arts/design; computer/information sciences; engineering or communications.
Application requirements: Recommendations, transcript. Resume.
Additional information: Program takes place at Johns Hopkins University in Laurel, Maryland. Appointments made up to one year, full-time or part-time. Stipend based on research area(s) and academic classification. Applications accepted year-round.
Contact:
Oak Ridge Institute for Science and Education
Web: see.orau.org

Research Participation Program for the Joint POW/MIA Accounting Command/Central Identification Laboratory (JPAC-CIL)

Type of award: Internship, renewable.
Intended use: For undergraduate, graduate or postgraduate study at 4-year or graduate institution.
Eligibility: Applicant must be U.S. citizen or permanent resident.
Basis for selection: Major/career interest in anthropology; archaeology; history; military science or international studies.
Additional information: Program located at Central Identification Laboratory, Hickam Air Force Base, Hawaii. Program's purpose is to achieve fullest possible accounting of all Americans missing as a result of nation's past conflicts and to locate, exhume, and identify remains of individuals killed

during military service. Applications accepted year-round. Stipend available.
Contact:
Oak Ridge Institute for Science and Education
Web: see.orau.org

Research Participation Program for the U.S. Air Force Research Laboratory (USAFRL), Wright Patterson Air Force Base

Type of award: Internship, renewable.
Intended use: For undergraduate, graduate or postgraduate study at 4-year or graduate institution.
Eligibility: Applicant must be U.S. citizen or permanent resident.
Basis for selection: Major/career interest in life sciences; health sciences; mathematics; physical sciences; environmental science; social/behavioral sciences or engineering.
Additional information: Program located at various locations across U.S. Wright Patterson Air Force Base, Ohio, and other approved locations. Appointments made up to one year, full-time or part-time. Negotiable stipend. Applications accepted year-round. Visit Website for details.
Contact:
Oak Ridge Institute for Science and Education
Web: see.orau.org

Research Participation Program for the U.S. Air Force Research Laboratory, Tyndall Air Force Base (AFRL-TYNDALL)

Type of award: Internship, renewable.
Intended use: For undergraduate, graduate or postgraduate study at 4-year or graduate institution.
Eligibility: Applicant must be U.S. citizen or permanent resident.
Basis for selection: Major/career interest in materials science; aerospace or electronics.
Additional information: Program located at the Air Force Research Laboratory in Florida. Other eligible disciplines include: thermal protect materials, metallic and non-metallic structural materials, aerospace propulsion, electromagnetic metal and ceramic composite, electro-optic, and electromagnetic materials. Program duration is up to one year for full- or part-time appointments. Applications accepted year-round. Stipend available. Visit Website for details.
Contact:
Oak Ridge Institute for Science and Education
Web: see.orau.org

Research Participation Program for the U.S. Air Force School of Aerospace Medicine (USAFSAM)

Type of award: Internship, renewable.
Intended use: For undergraduate, graduate or postgraduate study at 4-year or graduate institution.
Eligibility: Applicant must be U.S. citizen.
Basis for selection: Major/career interest in life sciences; public health; epidemiology; biomedical; computer/information sciences; engineering; environmental science or physical sciences.
Additional information: Program located at the Air Force Institute for Operational Health, Brooks Air Force Base, in San Antonio, Texas. Appointments up to one year, full- or part-time. Applications accepted year-round. Stipend and limited travel reimbursement available. Visit Website for details.
Contact:
Oak Ridge Institute for Science and Education
Web: see.orau.org

Research Participation Program for the U.S. Army Aeromedical Research Laboratory (USAARL)

Type of award: Internship, renewable.
Intended use: For undergraduate, graduate or postgraduate study at 4-year or graduate institution.
Eligibility: Applicant must be U.S. citizen.
Basis for selection: Major/career interest in life sciences; health sciences; communications; graphic arts/design; mathematics; computer/information sciences; physical sciences; social/behavioral sciences; engineering or biology.
Additional information: Research program's purpose is to prevent or minimize health hazards in military operations environment and sustain the aviator's individual performance. Program locations are across U.S. including Fort Rucker, Alabama. Duration is up to one year, full- or part-time. Applications accepted year-round. Stipend available.
Contact:
Oak Ridge Institute for Science and Education
Web: see.orau.org

Research Participation Program for the U.S. Army Medical Research Institute of Chemical Defense

Type of award: Internship, renewable.
Intended use: For undergraduate or graduate study at 2-year, 4-year or graduate institution in United States.
Eligibility: Applicant must be U.S. citizen.
Basis for selection: Major/career interest in biochemistry; biology; medicine or physical sciences. Applicant must demonstrate high academic achievement.
Application requirements: Recommendations, transcript. Resume.
Additional information: Provides opportunities to participate in development of medical countermeasures to chemical warfare agents at the U.S. Army Medical Research Institute of Chemical Defense (Aberdeen Proving Ground, MD). Internship lasts up to one year; full- and part-time appointments available. Stipend based on research area and academic classification. Number of awards varies. Minimum 2.5 GPA. Applications accepted year-round. Visit Website for application and details.
Contact:
Oak Ridge Institute for Science and Education
Web: see.orau.org

Research Participation Program for the U.S. Army Public Health Command

Type of award: Internship, renewable.
Intended use: For undergraduate, graduate or postgraduate study at 4-year or graduate institution.
Eligibility: Applicant must be U.S. citizen.

Basis for selection: Major/career interest in life sciences; health sciences; communications; graphic arts/design; mathematics; computer/information sciences; environmental science; social/behavioral sciences; biology or chemistry.
Additional information: Other eligible disciplines include: entomology, environmental/ civil/ mechanical/ chemical engineering, environmental sciences, industrial hygiene, medical sciences, physical sciences, toxicology, sociology, psychology. Program is various location across U.S.; Landstuhl, Germany; Camp Zana, Japan; and other locations. Appointments up to one year, full- or part-time. Applications accepted year-round. Stipend available.
Contact:
Oak Ridge Institute for Science and Education
Web: see.orau.org

Research Participation Program for the U.S. Army Research Institute for Environmental Medicine (USARIEM)

Type of award: Internship, renewable.
Intended use: For undergraduate, graduate or postgraduate study at 4-year or graduate institution.
Eligibility: Applicant must be U.S. citizen.
Basis for selection: Major/career interest in life sciences; health sciences; mathematics; computer/information sciences; physical sciences; social/behavioral sciences; engineering; chemistry; engineering, environmental or environmental science.
Additional information: Program is at the U.S. Army Center for Health Promotion and Preventive Medicine (Aberdeen Proving Ground, MD) and other approved locations. Opportunities exist in the areas of Performance Optimization, Preventive Medicine & Planning, Material Development, Monitoring Strategies and Predictive Algorithms, and Health Hazard Assessment.
Contact:
Oak Ridge Institute for Science and Education
Web: see.orau.org

Research Participation Program for the U.S. Army Research Laboratory

Type of award: Internship.
Intended use: For undergraduate or graduate study at 2-year, 4-year or graduate institution in United States.
Eligibility: Applicant must be U.S. citizen.
Basis for selection: Major/career interest in biology; medicine; physical sciences; computer/information sciences; materials science or engineering. Applicant must demonstrate high academic achievement.
Application requirements: Recommendations, transcript.
Additional information: Provides opportunities to participate in research and technology development in areas such as engineering, mechanics, chemistry, survivability & lethality analysis, sensors & electron devices, and weapons & materials research related to enhancing the technologies and analytical support to assure supremacy of America's ground forces at the U.S. Army Research Laboratory (Adelphi and Aberdeen Proving Ground, MD) and other approved locations. Internship lasts up to one year; up to a total of four years; full- or part-time appointments available. Stipend based on research area and classification. Number of awards varies. Minimum 2.5 GPA. Applications accepted year-round. Visit Website for application.
Contact:
Oak Ridge Institute for Science and Education
Web: see.orau.org

Student Internship Program at the U.S. Army Center for Health Promotion and Preventive Medicine

Type of award: Internship, renewable.
Intended use: For undergraduate or graduate study at postsecondary institution in United States.
Eligibility: Applicant must be U.S. citizen.
Basis for selection: Major/career interest in biology; chemistry; entomology; engineering; environmental science; physical sciences; science, general or health sciences. Applicant must demonstrate high academic achievement.
Application requirements: Recommendations, transcript. Resume, proof of insurance.
Additional information: Internship is at U.S. Army Center for Health Promotion and Preventive Medicine (Aberdeen Proving Ground, MD) and other approved locations. Provides opportunities to participate in applied clinical research in areas such as occupational and environmental health engineering, entomology, ionizing and non-ionizing radiation, health promotion, industrial hygiene and worksite hazards, ergonomics, environmental sanitation and hygiene, laboratory science, chemistry, biology, toxicology, health physics, environmental health risk assessment and risk communication, and related projects. Up to one year; full-time or part-time appointments. Minimum 2.5 GPA. Stipend based on research area and academic classification. Number of awards varies. Applications accepted year-round. Visit Website for application.
Contact:
Oak Ridge Institute for Science and Education
Web: see.orau.org

Student Research at the U.S. Army Edgewood Chemical Biological Center

Type of award: Internship, renewable.
Intended use: For undergraduate or graduate study at accredited 4-year or graduate institution in United States.
Eligibility: Applicant must be U.S. citizen.
Basis for selection: Major/career interest in biology; computer/ information sciences; engineering; environmental science; physical sciences; science, general or mathematics.
Application requirements: Transcript. Resume.
Additional information: Location: U.S. Army Edgewood Chemical Biological Center in Aberdeen Proving Ground, MD. Provides opportunities to participate in research and development in support of military missions. Three months to one year; full-time or part-time appointments. Stipend based on research area and academic classification. Applications accepted year-round. Award amount and number vary. Visit Website for application.
Contact:
Oak Ridge Institute for Science and Education
Web: see.orau.org

U.S. Air Force Medial Support Agency

Type of award: Internship, renewable.
Intended use: For undergraduate, graduate or postgraduate study at 4-year or graduate institution.

Eligibility: Applicant must be U.S. citizen.
Basis for selection: Major/career interest in life sciences; health sciences; mathematics; computer/information sciences or social/behavioral sciences.
Additional information: Program located in San Antonio, Texas and Virginia. Applications accepted year-round. Stipend available.
Contact:
Oak Ridge Institute for Science and Education
Web: see.orau.org

U.S. Army Natick Soldier Research Development & Engineering Center

Type of award: Internship, renewable.
Intended use: For undergraduate, graduate or postgraduate study at 4-year or graduate institution.
Eligibility: Applicant must be U.S. citizen.
Basis for selection: Major/career interest in life sciences; health sciences; mathematics; computer/information sciences; physical sciences or engineering.
Additional information: Program located at the U.S. Army Natick Soldier Systems Center in Natick, Massachusetts. Provides opportunities to participate in NSRDEC's ongoing and applied research and development projects. Appointments up to one-year, full- or part-time. Applications accepted year-round.
Contact:
Oak Ridge Institute for Science and Education
Web: see.orau.org

Ohio Newspapers Foundation

AdOhio Advertising Internship

Type of award: Internship.
Intended use: For junior or senior study at postsecondary institution. Designated institutions: Ohio institutions.
Eligibility: Applicant must be residing in Ohio.
Basis for selection: Major/career interest in journalism or advertising.
Application requirements: Resume, writing samples, and cover letter.
Additional information: Ten-week internship in Columbus office of this trade association, which represents 83 daily newspapers, more than 180 weekly newspapers, and more than 150 Websites in Ohio. Duties include writing and layout for sales presentation sheets and client mailings, assistance with newspaper ad bid sheets, newspaper tear sheets, and research. Internship lasts 10 weeks. Negotiable start date after June 1. Salary is $350 per week. Finalists will be contacted for interviews.

Application deadline:	March 31
Notification begins:	May 1

Contact:
Ohio Newspapers Foundation
Walt Dozier, AdOhio
1335 Dublin Road, Suite 216-B
Columbus, OH 43215
Web: www.ohionews.org

Ohio Newspaper Association Publications/Public Relations Internship

Type of award: Internship.
Intended use: For junior or senior study at postsecondary institution. Designated institutions: Ohio institutions.
Eligibility: Applicant must be residing in Ohio.
Basis for selection: Major/career interest in communications or journalism.
Application requirements: Resume, writing samples, and cover letter.
Additional information: Ten-week internship at trade association, which represents 83 daily newspapers, more than 180 weekly newspapers, and more than 150 Websites in Ohio. Duties include writing and assisting in production of newsletter, miscellaneous flyers and mailings, meeting planning, and research. Internship lasts ten weeks. Negotiable start date after June 1. Salary of $350 per week. Finalists will be contacted for interviews.

Application deadline:	March 31
Notification begins:	May 1

Contact:
Ohio Newspapers Foundation
Dennis Hetzel, Executive Director
1335 Dublin Road, Suite 216-B
Columbus, OH 43215
Web: www.ohionews.org

Oracle Corporation

Oracle Product Development Summer Internship Program

Type of award: Internship.
Intended use: For full-time sophomore, junior, senior or graduate study at accredited 4-year or graduate institution in United States.
Basis for selection: Major/career interest in computer/information sciences. Applicant must demonstrate high academic achievement.
Application requirements: Resume.
Additional information: Foreign student must have unrestricted permission to work in United States. Interns are offered excellent compensation and fully furnished corporate apartments are provided. Car/bike rentals and round-trip travel expenses are paid for, as well as a helicopter ride under the Golden Gate Bridge. Visit Website to submit resume and sign up to search for current openings.

Application deadline:	January 1
Notification begins:	February 28

Contact:
Oracle Corporation
500 Oracle Parkway
Redwood Shores, CA 94065
Phone: 800-633-0738
Web: www.oracle.com/us/corporate/careers/college/internships/index.html

Internships

Owens Corning

Owens Corning Internships

Type of award: Internship.
Intended use: For full-time junior, senior, master's or doctoral study at accredited 4-year institution.
Eligibility: Applicant must be U.S. citizen or permanent resident.
Basis for selection: Major/career interest in engineering; accounting; environmental science; information systems; marketing; materials science; technology or finance/banking. Applicant must demonstrate high academic achievement and leadership.
Application requirements: Proof of eligibility.
Additional information: Variety of internships offered with housing assistance, competitive salary. Summer programs last twelve weeks. Positions throughout the U.S. See Website for more information.
Contact:
Owens Corning
One Owens Corning Parkway
Toledo, OH 43659
Phone: 1-800-GET-PINK
Web: www.owenscorningcareers.com

Pacific Gas and Electric Company

Pacific Gas and Electric Summer Intern Program

Type of award: Internship.
Intended use: For full-time undergraduate or graduate study in United States.
Eligibility: Applicant must be U.S. citizen or permanent resident.
Basis for selection: Major/career interest in business; chemistry; statistics; computer/information sciences; economics; engineering; geology/earth sciences; marketing; engineering, mechanical or public administration/service. Applicant must demonstrate high academic achievement and seriousness of purpose.
Application requirements: Interview. Resume, cover letter.
Additional information: Paid internships available throughout northern and central California, including company headquarters in San Francisco. Deadline is rolling, but early applications are encouraged. Resume may be submitted online; format specifications available online. Visit Website or call sponsor for openings and campus recruitment dates. Must be eligible to work in the United States. Number and amount of awards vary. Most internships are summer only and typically last ten to twelve weeks. Internships include a competitive salary and paid company holidays.
Contact:
Pacific Gas and Electric Company
Web: www.pge.com/about/careers/college/intern

PBS

PBS Internships

Type of award: Internship.
Intended use: For undergraduate or graduate study at postsecondary institution.
Application requirements: Resume and cover letter.
Additional information: Various internships are available in different departments. All paid, except for internship in General Counsel's office. Internships also offered for graduate students seeking an MBA. Internships change on a semester basis. Recruitment starts in July for fall; November: winter and spring; February: summer. Visit Website for internship listings, application forms, and more information.
Contact:
PBS Internship Program
2100 Crystal Dr.
Arlington, VA 22202
Phone: 703-739-5088
Web: www.pbs.org/jobs

PGA Tour

PGA Tour Diversity Intern Program

Type of award: Internship.
Intended use: For sophomore, junior, senior or graduate study at postsecondary institution.
Eligibility: Applicant must be U.S. citizen.
Basis for selection: Major/career interest in marketing; business/management/administration; communications; information systems; journalism; radio/television/film; sports/sports administration or public relations. Applicant must demonstrate high academic achievement, depth of character, leadership, seriousness of purpose and service orientation.
Application requirements: Interview, recommendations, essay, transcript.
Additional information: Non-citizens eligible to work in U.S. may also apply. Internship lasts ten weeks and is paid. Internship sites located in Florida. Minimum 3.0 GPA. Visit Website to apply. Deadline in February.

Amount of award:	$4,400
Number of awards:	18
Number of applicants:	1,450
Notification begins:	May 1
Total amount awarded:	$132,000

Contact:
PGA Tour Diversity Intern Program
Web: www.pgatour.com

Phipps Conservatory and Botanical Gardens

Phipps Conservatory and Botanical Gardens Internships

Type of award: Internship.
Intended use: For junior, senior or graduate study at accredited 2-year or 4-year institution.

Eligibility: Applicant must be U.S. citizen.
Basis for selection: Major/career interest in horticulture; landscape architecture; environmental science or botany. Applicant must demonstrate high academic achievement.
Application requirements: Recommendations. Resume and cover letter.
Additional information: Interns paid $8 per hour. Related majors, such as environmental education, also eligible. Internships may be full- or part-time. Seven positions available in summer; one to two positions available during academic year. Application deadline is rolling. Contact sponsor or visit Website for more information.

Number of awards:	8
Number of applicants:	8
Application deadline:	January 31
Notification begins:	February 15

Contact:
Phipps Conservatory and Botanical Gardens Human Resources
One Schenley Park
Pittsburgh, PA 15213
Phone: 412-622-6915 x3229
Fax: 412-622-7363
Web: www.phipps.conservatory.org

Princeton Plasma Physics Laboratory

Plasma Physics National Undergraduate Fellowship Program

Type of award: Internship.
Intended use: For junior study at 4-year institution in United States.
Eligibility: Applicant must be U.S. citizen or permanent resident.
Basis for selection: Major/career interest in engineering; physics; mathematics or computer/information sciences. Applicant must demonstrate high academic achievement, depth of character, leadership, seriousness of purpose and service orientation.
Application requirements: Recommendations, essay, transcript.
Additional information: Minimum 3.5 GPA. Internship paid and lasts nine weeks in the summer. Housing and travel costs provided. Application due in February.

Amount of award:	$4,800
Number of awards:	25
Number of applicants:	100
Application deadline:	February 29
Notification begins:	March 15

Contact:
Princeton Plasma Physics Laboratory
P.O. Box 451
Princeton, NJ 08543-0451
Phone: 609-243-2116
Web: science-education.pppl.gov

Rhode Island State Government

Rhode Island State Government Internship Program

Type of award: Internship, renewable.
Intended use: For undergraduate or postgraduate study at postsecondary institution.
Eligibility: Applicant must be residing in Rhode Island.
Basis for selection: Major/career interest in governmental public relations or public administration/service. Applicant must demonstrate high academic achievement, depth of character, leadership, seriousness of purpose and service orientation.
Application requirements: Interview, recommendations, transcript, proof of eligibility. Writing sample (for law students only).
Additional information: Minimum 2.5 GPA. Summer program lasts eight weeks; spring and fall programs last entire semester. Fall application deadline is rolling. Compensation for summer interns only, at $100 per week. Spring and fall interns earn academic credit or work-study, if eligible. All placements in Rhode Island.

Number of awards:	243
Number of applicants:	450

Contact:
Rhode Island State Government
State Capitol, Room 8AA
Providence, RI 02903
Phone: 401-222-6782
Fax: 401-222-4447
Web: webserver.rilin.state.ri.us/internoffice

Simon and Schuster Inc.

Simon and Schuster Internship Program

Type of award: Internship, renewable.
Intended use: For full-time undergraduate or graduate study at accredited vocational, 4-year or graduate institution.
Basis for selection: Major/career interest in publishing. Applicant must demonstrate high academic achievement and leadership.
Application requirements: Interview. Resume. Cover letter.
Additional information: Internship program is designed to train and recruit a diverse group of students interested in exploring careers in publishing. Summer, spring, fall, and year-round programs are available. Student must register for academic credit with their college or university and provide official documentation confirming this information. During spring/fall semesters, intern works a minimum 16 hours to a maximum 20 hours per week. During summer semester, office hours are 9 to 5 p.m. Applicants must have well-rounded extracurricular interests and work experience. Visit Website for application.
Contact:
Simon and Schuster, Inc.
Web: www.simonandschuster.biz/careers/internships

Smithsonian Environmental Research Center

Smithsonian Environmental Research Center Internship Program

Type of award: Internship, renewable.
Intended use: For undergraduate or master's study at 4-year or graduate institution.
Basis for selection: Major/career interest in biology; chemistry; environmental science; physics; mathematics or education. Applicant must demonstrate seriousness of purpose.
Application requirements: Recommendations, essay, transcript. Resume.
Additional information: Internship provides professional training in the environmental sciences. Projects are 40 hours per week, lasting from twelve to sixteen weeks. Stipend is $500 per week and available winter/spring, summer, and fall. Dorm space is available for $105 per week on limited basis. Several application deadlines: spring, November 15; summer, February 1; fall, June 1. Applicants should demonstrate academic credentials, relevant experience, and the congruence of expressed goals with those of internship program. Open to all undergraduates, recent college graduates (within six months), and beginning Master's students.

Number of awards:	40
Number of applicants:	350
Application deadline:	November 15, February 1
Notification begins:	December 15, April 15
Total amount awarded:	$245,000

Contact:
Smithsonian Environmental Research Center
Professional Training Program
647 Contees Wharf Road
Edgewater, MD 21037
Phone: 443-428-2217
Fax: 443-428-2380
Web: www.serc.si.edu/internship/index.htm

Smithsonian Institution

James E. Webb Internship Program for Minority Undergraduate Seniors and Graduate Students in Business and Public Administration

Type of award: Internship.
Intended use: For senior or graduate study at 4-year or graduate institution. Designated institutions: Smithsonian Institution.
Eligibility: Applicant must be Alaskan native, Asian American, African American, Mexican American, Hispanic American, Puerto Rican, American Indian or Native Hawaiian/Pacific Islander. Applicant must be U.S. citizen or permanent resident.
Basis for selection: Major/career interest in business/management/administration or public administration/service. Applicant must demonstrate high academic achievement.
Application requirements: Recommendations, essay, transcript. Resume.
Additional information: Minimum 3.0 GPA. Applicant must be minority student enrolled as undergraduate senior or graduate student in business or public administration program. Selection based on relevance of internship at the Smithsonian to student's academic and career goals. Internships are full-time, 40 hours per week for ten weeks. Stipend is $550 per week, with additional travel allowances offered in some cases. Deadlines: February 1 for summer and fall; October 1 for spring. Contact sponsor or visit Website for more information and application.

Application deadline:	February 1, October 1

Contact:
Smithsonian Institution Office of Fellowships
470 L'Enfant Plaza, SW, Suite 7102, MRC 902
P.O. Box 37012
Washington, DC 20013-7012
Phone: 202-633-7070
Web: www.si.edu/ofi

Smithsonian Minority Internship

Type of award: Internship.
Intended use: For undergraduate or graduate study at postsecondary institution. Designated institutions: Smithsonian Institution.
Basis for selection: Major/career interest in anthropology; archaeology; ecology; environmental science; art/art history; museum studies; zoology or natural sciences. Applicant must demonstrate high academic achievement.
Application requirements: Recommendations, essay, transcript. Resume.
Additional information: Research internships at Smithsonian Institution in anthropology/archaeology; astrophysics and astronomy; earth sciences/paleontology; ecology; environmental, behavioral (tropical animals), evolutionary, and systematic biology; history of science and technology; history of art (including American contemporary, African, Asian); 20th-century American crafts; social and cultural history and folk life of America. Applicants must have major/career interest in research or museum-related activity pursued by the Smithsonian Institution. Stipend of $550 per week for ten weeks. February 1 deadline for summer session and for fall; October 1 deadline for spring. Intended for U.S. minority groups under-represented in Smithsonian scholarly programs. Contact sponsor for minority requirements. Minimum 3.0 GPA. Visit Website for more information.

Application deadline:	February 1, October 1

Contact:
Smithsonian Institution Office of Fellowships
470 L'Enfant Plaza, SW, Suite 7102, MRC 902
P.O. Box 37012
Washington, DC 20013-7012
Phone: 202-633-7070
Web: www.si.edu/ofi

Smithsonian Native American Internship

Type of award: Internship.
Intended use: For undergraduate or graduate study at postsecondary institution. Designated institutions: Smithsonian Institution.
Eligibility: Applicant must be Alaskan native or American Indian.
Basis for selection: Major/career interest in Native American studies.
Application requirements: Recommendations, essay, transcript. Resume.

Internships

Additional information: Internship at Smithsonian Institution in research or museum activities related to Native American studies. Stipend of $550 a week for ten weeks. Deadline for summer and fall is February 1; spring is October 1. American Indian students encouraged to apply. Contact Office of Fellowships for application procedures or visit Website.

Application deadline: February 1, October 1

Contact:
Smithsonian Institution Office of Fellowships
470 L'Enfant Plaza, SW, Suite 7102, MRC 902
P.O. Box 37012
Washington, DC 20013-7012
Phone: 202-633-7070
Web: www.si.edu/ofi

Society of Physics Students

Society of Physics Students Summer Internship Program

Type of award: Internship.
Intended use: For full-time undergraduate study.
Eligibility: Applicant or parent must be member/participant of Society of Physics Students.
Basis for selection: Major/career interest in physics. Applicant must demonstrate high academic achievement.
Application requirements: Transcript. Resume and cover letter. Two letters of recommendation (one should be written by SPS advisor).
Additional information: Offers nine-and-a-half-week internships in science policy and research for undergraduate physics majors. Internships include $4,500 stipend, paid housing, and transportation supplement. Internships are based in Washington, D.C. Applicants must be active SPS members with excellent scholastic record and experience in science outreach events or science research. See Website for application and deadline.

Amount of award:	$4,500
Number of awards:	12
Number of applicants:	483
Application deadline:	February 1
Notification begins:	March 15.
Total amount awarded:	$33,300

Contact:
SPS Summer Internship Program
One Physics Ellipse
College Park, MD 20740
Phone: 301-209-3007
Fax: 301-209-0839
Web: www.spsnational.org/programs/internships

Solomon R. Guggenheim Museum

Guggenheim Museum Internship

Type of award: Internship.
Intended use: For junior, senior or graduate study at postsecondary institution.
Basis for selection: Major/career interest in art/art history; arts, general; arts management; communications; education; finance/banking; graphic arts/design; library science; museum studies or museum studies/administration. Applicant must demonstrate high academic achievement.
Application requirements: Interview, recommendations. Cover letter, resume, writing sample.
Additional information: Potential internships available in Conservation, Curatorial, Education, Development, Director's Office, Exhibition Design, Exhibition Management, Finance, Graphic Design, Human Resources, Information Technology, Legal, Library Archives, Marketing, Photography, Public Affairs, Publications and Digital Media, Registration, Visitor Services, and more. International students must have J-1 visa. Internships during academic year are for college credit; some stipends available in summer. Application deadlines are January 18 for summer, May 1 for fall and academic year, October 18 for spring. Spring, fall, and academic year internships are full- or part-time, with minimum commitment of 16 hours/week for three months. Summer internships are full-time.

Number of awards:	40
Number of applicants:	300
Application deadline:	January 18, May 1

Contact:
Solomon R. Guggenheim Museum
Internship Program
1071 Fifth Avenue
New York, NY 10128-0173
Web: www.guggenheim.org

Peggy Guggenheim Internship

Type of award: Internship.
Intended use: For undergraduate or graduate study at postsecondary institution.
Basis for selection: Major/career interest in arts, general; art/art history; education; museum studies or museum studies/administration. Applicant must demonstrate high academic achievement, depth of character, leadership and seriousness of purpose.
Application requirements: Recommendations, essay, transcript. Resume.
Additional information: One- to three-month internship at Peggy Guggenheim Collection in Venice, Italy. Must be fluent in English with knowledge of spoken Italian. Interns receive a monthly stipend. Visit Website for details.

Number of applicants: 1,400

Contact:
Peggy Guggenheim Collection, Internship Coodinator
701 Dorsoduro
30123 Venice, Italy
Phone: 39-041-240-5401
Web: www.guggenheim.org or www.guggenheim-venice.it

Sony Music Entertainment

Sony Credited Internship

Type of award: Internship.
Intended use: For undergraduate or graduate study at accredited postsecondary institution.
Eligibility: Applicant must be U.S. citizen or permanent resident.

Basis for selection: Major/career interest in accounting; business; finance/banking; communications; computer/information sciences; law; music; music management or marketing.
Application requirements: Interview, transcript, proof of eligibility. Resume and cover letter.
Additional information: Unpaid internship. Applicant must be available to work at least 15 hours a week. Internships are available in various departments throughout company. Must possess excellent computer skills (Word, Excel and Outlook) and strong organizational skills. Applicant must be enrolled at accredited university and provide verification of course credit. Visit Website for available internship listings. Apply online.

Number of awards:	60
Number of applicants:	200

Contact:
Phone: 212-833-8000
Web: www.sonymusic.com

Southface Energy Institute

Southface Internship

Type of award: Internship.
Intended use: For undergraduate or graduate study at accredited 2-year, 4-year or graduate institution in United States.
Eligibility: Applicant must be U.S. citizen, permanent resident or international student.
Basis for selection: Major/career interest in architecture; business/management/administration; engineering, civil; engineering, environmental; engineering, mechanical; environmental science; graphic arts/design; landscape architecture; public relations or urban planning. Applicant must demonstrate high academic achievement.
Application requirements: Names of references with contact information. Resume and cover letter.
Additional information: Internships cover variety of interests: sustainable building, community design, water-efficient landscaping, smart growth, environmental event planning, energy policy and tech assistance, non-profit marketing, and public relations. Six- to twelve-month positions available. Students work 40 hours per week; weekly stipend of $100. Shared housing available if space permits. Transportation assistance available. Applications accepted year-round. International students must have work authorization.
Contact:
Web: www.southface.org

Spoleto Festival USA

Spoleto Festival USA Apprenticeship Program

Type of award: Internship, renewable.
Intended use: For undergraduate, graduate or non-degree study in United States.
Basis for selection: Major/career interest in arts management; arts, general; music; public relations or theater/production/technical. Applicant must demonstrate seriousness of purpose.
Application requirements: Recommendations. Writing sample (media applicants only). Resume, cover letter.
Additional information: Four-week full-time apprenticeship with arts professionals producing and operating international arts festival from May 13 to June 9. Posts available in media relations, development, box office, production, orchestra management, finance and accounting, artist services/facilities management, and office administration. Weekly stipend may be provided; housing and travel allowance provided. See Website for details and deadlines. Deadline in mid-February.

Number of awards:	50

Contact:
Spoleto Festival USA
Apprentice Program
14 George Street
Charleston, SC 29401
Web: www.spoletousa.org

Sports Journalism Institute

Aspiring Sports Journalist Internship

Type of award: Internship.
Intended use: For sophomore or junior study at postsecondary institution.
Basis for selection: Major/career interest in journalism; communications; publishing; English or sports/sports administration. Applicant must demonstrate high academic achievement and seriousness of purpose.
Application requirements: Recommendations, essay, transcript. Professional-style photo, up to seven writing samples.
Additional information: The Sports Journalism Institute is a nine-week, paid summer training and internship program for undergraduates interested in sports journalism. Applicants need not be journalism majors. A $500 scholarship is available for students returning to college upon successful completion of program. Visit Website for more information, application, and deadline.

Amount of award:	$500
Number of awards:	10

Contact:
Gregory Lee, Executive Sports Editor
South Florida Sun Sentinel
500 E. Broward Blvd.
Ft. Lauderdale, FL 33394
Web: www.sportsjournalisminstitute.org

Student Conservation Association

SCA Conservation Internships

Type of award: Internship, renewable.
Intended use: For undergraduate or graduate study at accredited postsecondary institution in United States.
Basis for selection: Major/career interest in archaeology; ecology; forestry; natural resources/conservation; history; education; wildlife/fisheries; biology or communications.

Application requirements: Resume.
Additional information: Travel and housing is provided, and a weekly stipend is given for food. Positions at various locations in United States. Applicants are advised to apply three months prior to position start date. Rolling admissions process—seven application deadlines per year. Applicants with interest in environmental education, interpretation, marine biology, and wilderness preservation also eligible. See Website for application.

Amount of award: $1,000-$4,725

Contact:
Admissions Department Student Conservation Association
P.O. Box 550
Charlestown, NH 03603
Phone: 603-543-1700
Fax: 603-543-1828
Web: www.thesca.org

Texas Historical Commission

Diversity Internship Program

Type of award: Internship.
Intended use: For sophomore, junior, senior or graduate study at 2-year, 4-year or graduate institution in United States.
Eligibility: Applicant must be Alaskan native, Asian American, African American, Mexican American, Hispanic American, Puerto Rican, American Indian or Native Hawaiian/Pacific Islander. Applicant must be U.S. citizen.
Basis for selection: Applicant must demonstrate high academic achievement.
Application requirements: Recommendations, transcript. Resume or CV, list of previous experience with the Texas Historical Commission, if any.
Additional information: Minimum 3.0 GPA. Applicants must either attend institutions in Texas, or be Texas residents attending school out-of-state. Preservation Fellows receive a $5,000 stipend for eight weeks of 40-hour-week employment under the supervision of the THC, either at its headquarters in Austin or "in the field" with an associated preservation organization. Apply online. Deadline in March.

Amount of award: $5,000
Number of awards: 2
Number of applicants: 5
Notification begins: September 1
Total amount awarded: $10,000

Contact:
Texas Historical Commission
Phone: 512-936-0857
Fax: 512-936-4872
Web: www.thc.state.tx.us

Time Inc.

Time Inc. Internship Program

Type of award: Internship.
Intended use: For undergraduate or graduate study at accredited 4-year or graduate institution.
Basis for selection: Major/career interest in finance/banking; advertising; communications; graphic arts/design; information systems; journalism or marketing. Applicant must demonstrate high academic achievement.
Application requirements: Essay. Cover letter and resume.
Additional information: Spring and fall academic year internships are offered on an as-needed basis, with available positions and magazines/Websites varying each semester. Most positions require a minimum of 14 hours per week and are based in NYC. Nine- to ten-week paid summer internship programs are also available.

Contact:
Time Inc.
1271 Avenue of the Americas
7th Floor
New York, NY 10020
Phone: 212-522-1212
Web: www.timeinc.com/careers

Tyson Foods, Inc.

Tyson Foods Intern Program

Type of award: Internship.
Intended use: For full-time undergraduate study at accredited vocational, 2-year or 4-year institution.
Basis for selection: Major/career interest in agribusiness; agriculture; computer/information sciences; engineering; food production/management/services; food science/technology; health-related professions; law; marketing or science, general. Applicant must demonstrate high academic achievement.
Application requirements: Proof of eligibility. Resume and cover letter.
Additional information: Various paid internships include but not limited to computer programming, industrial engineering, livestock procurement, quality assurance, carcass sales, and production. Program locations across the United States. Must be eligible to work in the U.S. Visit Website for job descriptions and list of campus recruiting events, or to submit resume and cover letter. Summer and academic-year internships available.

Number of awards: 50

Contact:
Tyson Foods, Inc.
Web: www.tysonfoodscareers.com

United States Holocaust Memorial Museum

United States Holocaust Memorial Museum Internship

Type of award: Internship, renewable.
Intended use: For freshman, sophomore, junior, senior or graduate study at postsecondary institution.
Eligibility: Applicant must be U.S. citizen, permanent resident or international student.
Basis for selection: Major/career interest in museum studies/ administration; history; English; foreign languages;

communications; geography; graphic arts/design or communications.
Additional information: Semester-long internships available during summer, fall, and spring in Holocaust research and museum studies. Phone interviews conducted with top qualified candidates. Most positions unpaid. Applicants interested in German or Eastern European studies also eligible. Application deadline is March 1 for summer; July 1 for fall; October 15 for winter/spring. Apply online. All applicants subject to criminal background check. International students must have work authorization. Award notification begins at the end of March.

Number of awards:	70
Number of applicants:	500
Application deadline:	March 1
Notification begins:	April 1

Contact:
Internship Coordinator, Office of Volunteer and Intern Services
United States Holocaust Memorial Museum
100 Raoul Wallenburg Place, SW
Washington, DC 20024-2150
Phone: 202-488-0400
Web: www.ushmm.org

United States Senate

U.S. Senate Member Internships

Type of award: Internship.
Intended use: For full-time undergraduate study at accredited 4-year institution.
Eligibility: Applicant must be U.S. citizen or permanent resident.
Basis for selection: Major/career interest in political science/government; law; communications; public relations; public administration/service or economics. Applicant must demonstrate high academic achievement.
Application requirements: Resume, cover letter, writing sample.
Additional information: Senate member interns generally reside or attend college in senator's state. Positions available in Washington, D.C., or member's state. Internships may be unpaid or paid (less common), but generally offer assistance obtaining college credit. Term of service, eligibility vary. Some internships restricted to upper-level undergraduates. Senators administer their own internship programs. Contact individual senator's office directly. Visit Website for links to member sites, e-mail addresses, and telephone numbers.
Contact:
Office of (name of senator)
United States Senate
Washington, DC 20510
Web: www.senate.gov

U.S. Department of State

U.S. Department of State Internship

Type of award: Internship.
Intended use: For junior, senior or graduate study at accredited 4-year or graduate institution.
Eligibility: Applicant must be U.S. citizen.
Basis for selection: Major/career interest in political science/government; foreign languages; governmental public relations; business; public administration/service; social work; economics; information systems; journalism or science, general. Applicant must demonstrate high academic achievement.
Application requirements: Transcript. Statement of interest.
Additional information: Must have a minimum of 60 credit hours. Undergraduate seniors must be intending to go to graduate school. Provides opportunities working in varied administrative branches of the Department of State, both abroad and in Washington, D.C. Internships are generally unpaid, but many institutions provide academic credit and/or financial assistance for overseas assignments. Paid internships primarily granted to students in financial need. Must be able to work a minimum of ten weeks. Selected students must undergo background investigation to receive security clearance. Random drug testing performed. Internships available year-round. Visit Website for more information.
Contact:
U.S. Department of State
Web: www.careers.state.gov/students

U.S. House of Representatives

House Member Internships

Type of award: Internship, renewable.
Intended use: For full-time undergraduate study.
Eligibility: Applicant must be U.S. citizen or permanent resident.
Basis for selection: Major/career interest in political science/government; public administration/service; public relations or communications. Applicant must demonstrate high academic achievement.
Additional information: Members of the United Stated House of Representatives use undergraduate interns for a variety of jobs including constituent contact, research, and correspondence. Positions are based in Congressional District Offices and in Washington, D.C. Internships generally facilitate course credit, but offer no stipend. Some paid internships are funded through private nonprofit organizations. Information about the individual House member intern programs can usually be found online. A complete set of links to representatives' sites is available at www.house.gov. In general, applicants residing in the member's home district and enrolled in the same political party are favored. Typically, many Washington, D.C.-based internships are filled by students from outside the member district. Applicants may also be interested in working for congressperson serving on committee (i.e. Agriculture, Financial Services) relevant to their major. Interested parties should contact the representative with whom they are interested in working.
Contact:
Contact individual congressman/congresswoman's office.
Phone: 202-224-3121
Web: www.house.gov

U.S. National Arboretum

U.S. National Arboretum Horticultural Internship

Type of award: Internship.
Intended use: For undergraduate or graduate study at postsecondary institution.
Basis for selection: Major/career interest in botany; horticulture or landscape architecture.
Application requirements: Transcript. Resume, cover letter.
Additional information: Interns work on independent projects supervised by arboretum staff. Pay is $11.91 per hour. Full-time and part-time positions available, usually between 7 a.m. and 3:30 p.m. College credit available. Must have completed course work or have acquired practical experience in horticulture or related field. Must have basic gardening or laboratory skills, interest in plants, and ability to work independently. Visit Website for more information and application.
Contact:
Internship Coordinator
U.S. National Arboretum
3501 New York Avenue, NE
Washington, DC 20002-1958
Phone: 202-245-4563
Fax: 202-245-4575
Web: www.usna.usda.gov

U.S. National Arboretum National Herb Garden Year-Long Internship

Type of award: Internship.
Intended use: For full-time undergraduate or graduate study at postsecondary institution.
Eligibility: Applicant must be U.S. citizen.
Basis for selection: Major/career interest in agriculture; botany; education; forestry; horticulture or public administration/service.
Application requirements: Transcript. Resume and cover letter.
Additional information: Internships pay stipend of $16.33 per hour. Average workday for most interns: Monday through Friday, 7 a.m. to 3:30 p.m. Provides opportunity to gain experience in plant research in premier horticultural collection. Basic gardening or laboratory skills, interest in plants, strong communication skills, and ability to work independently preferred. See Website for deadline, application, and more information.
Contact:
Internship Coordinator
U.S. National Arboretum
3501 New York Avenue, NE
Washington, DC 20002-1958
Phone: 202-245-4563
Fax: 202-245-4575
Web: www.usna.usda.gov

The Wall Street Journal

The Wall Street Journal Asia Internship

Type of award: Internship.
Intended use: For undergraduate or graduate study at postsecondary institution.
Basis for selection: Major/career interest in journalism.
Application requirements: Cover letter, resume and up to six writing samples.
Additional information: Internships available in the U.S., Europe, and Asia. Selection process strongly emphasizes submitted clips and journalistic experience. Roundtrip airfare allowance included. Pay is $700 per week. Candidate should be fluent in one or more Asian languages—preferably Mandarin, Japanese or Korean—a strong interest in business reporting in Asia, and experience living or working in the region.

Number of awards:	1
Application deadline:	November 1

Contact:
The Wall Street Journal Asia
Almar Latour, Editor-in-Chief
25/F Central Plaza, 18 Harbour Road
Wanchai, Hong Kong
Web: www.dowjones.com/djcom/careers/wsj-interns.asp

The Wall Street Journal Europe Internship

Type of award: Internship.
Intended use: For undergraduate or graduate study at postsecondary institution.
Basis for selection: Major/career interest in journalism.
Application requirements: Cover letter, resume and up to six writing samples. Proof of health insurance.
Additional information: Reporting interns will work in WSJ news bureau in Europe. Must be fluent in one or more of the following languages: French, German, Dutch, or Russian. Must demonstrate interest in Europe and willingness and ability to work in overseas environment. Selection process strongly emphasizes submitted clips and journalistic experience. Successful applicants must pay own roundtrip airfare. Pay is $700 per week. Include email address and expected month and year of graduation at top of cover letter.

Number of awards:	1
Application deadline:	November 1

Contact:
The Wall Street Journal Europe
Attn: Terence Roth, Managing Editor
10 Fleet Place
London, EC4M 7QN
Web: www.dowjones.com/djcom/careers/wsj-interns.asp

The Wall Street Journal Journalism Internship

Type of award: Internship.
Intended use: For undergraduate or graduate study at postsecondary institution.
Basis for selection: Major/career interest in journalism.
Application requirements: Cover letter, resume, and up to six writing samples.
Additional information: Interns work in one of news bureaus. Previous journalism or college newspaper experience required.

All majors encouraged to apply. Currently enrolled students only. Apply online.

Number of awards: 15
Number of applicants: 335
Application deadline: November 1
Notification begins: February 28

Contact:
The Wall Street Journal
Dep. Managing Editor
Web: www.dowjones.com/careers-interns.asp

The Walt Disney Company

Disney Theme Parks & Resorts Professional Internships

Type of award: Internship.
Intended use: For junior or senior study at 2-year or 4-year institution in United States.
Eligibility: Applicant must be U.S. citizen, permanent resident or currently studying in the U.S. under an F-1 visa.
Basis for selection: Major/career interest in animal sciences; architecture; construction management; engineering; finance/banking; communications; human resources; hospitality administration/management; marketing or computer/information sciences. Applicant must demonstrate high academic achievement, seriousness of purpose and service orientation.
Application requirements: Interview. Resume and cover letter.
Additional information: Internships available in a variety of fields. Offerings vary by season. Certain roles only open to alumni participants of the Disney College Program. For most positions, applicants must be enrolled in college/university during spring/fall semester prior to participation. Pay rates and schedules vary by location. Must have valid driver's license. Housing may be available, with the exception of management internships. Visit Website for more information, application deadline, and to search for openings.

Contact:
Disney Professional Recruiting
P.O. Box 10000
Lake Buena Vista, FL 32830
Phone: 800-722-2930
Web: www.disneyinterns.com

Walt Disney World and Disneyland

Disney College Program

Type of award: Internship.
Intended use: For undergraduate study at postsecondary institution.
Eligibility: Applicant must be U.S. citizen, permanent resident or students studying in the U.S. under an F-1 visa.
Application requirements: Interview. Online application and Web-based interview required.
Additional information: Disney College Program is a semester-long paid internship at the Walt Disney World® Resort near Orlando, FL or the Disneyland® Resort in Anaheim, CA, in which students work in a front-line role at theme parks and resorts, participate in college-level coursework, and live in company-sponsored housing with other students from around the globe. Applicant must be enrolled in a college/university during the spring/fall semester prior to participation. Work schedules and pay rates vary by role. College credit may be available. Must have strong communication skills, understanding of guest service principles, ability to work independently and/or with large team. Program terms vary; are at least one semester in length. See Website for application and more information.

Number of awards: 10,000

Contact:
Disney College Recruiting
Phone: 800-722-2930
Web: www.disneycollegeprogram.com

Washington Internships for Students of Engineering

Washington Internships for Students of Engineering

Type of award: Internship.
Intended use: For junior, senior or graduate study at postsecondary institution.
Eligibility: Applicant must be U.S. citizen or permanent resident.
Basis for selection: Major/career interest in computer/information sciences; engineering; engineering, chemical; engineering, electrical/electronic or engineering, mechanical.
Application requirements: Recommendations, essay, transcript. Reference forms.
Additional information: Nine-week summer internship learning about technological issues and public policy available to students who have completed three years of study. Internship located in Washington, D.C. Interns write required research paper as part of process. Lodging expenses covered. Must be member of and sponsored by ANS, ASCE, ASME, IEEE, or SAE. IEEE will sponsor computer science majors. Graduate students beginning Masters study in technology policy-related degree also eligible. $2,100 stipend provided to assist with intern's living and travel expenses. Apply directly to sponsoring organization; application forms and sponsor contact information available on Website.

Amount of award: $2,100
Number of awards: 13
Application deadline: December 31
Total amount awarded: $25,200

Contact:
Washington Internships for Students of Engineering
Phone: 202-785-0017
Fax: 202-785-0835
Web: www.wise-intern.org

Wells Fargo

Wells Fargo Undergraduate Internships

Type of award: Internship.
Intended use: For full-time junior or senior study at accredited 4-year institution.

Eligibility: Applicant must be U.S. citizen or permanent resident.
Basis for selection: Major/career interest in finance/banking; accounting; business/management/administration; economics or real estate. Applicant must demonstrate high academic achievement and leadership.
Application requirements: Resume and cover letter.
Additional information: Ten- to twelve-week program consists of work assignments and professional development opportunities related to corporate and investment banking. Number of awards varies. Locations in major cities throughout the U.S. Visit Website to search for internships and to create a profile and apply online.
Contact:
Wells Fargo
Web: www.wellsfargo.com

Wolf Trap Foundation for the Performing Arts

Wolf Trap Foundation for the Performing Arts Internship

Type of award: Internship.
Intended use: For sophomore, junior, senior or graduate study in United States.
Eligibility: Applicant must be U.S. citizen, permanent resident or international student.
Basis for selection: Major/career interest in performing arts or arts management. Applicant must demonstrate seriousness of purpose.
Application requirements: Recommendations. Resume. Cover letter outlining career goals and specifying internship desired. Two writing samples (except technical, scenic painting, costuming, stage management, accounting, graphic design, photography, or information systems applicants). Graphic Design, Web Communications, and Multimedia applicants must submit three design samples. Refer to individual internship descriptions for additional required materials.
Additional information: Deadline for summer is March 1, deadline for fall is July 1, deadline for spring is November 1. All positions paid. College credit available. Applicant must have own car. Public transit not available. Internships are offered in: Ticket Services, Planning and Initiatives, Accounting, Information Services, Technical Theater, Costuming, Scenic/prop painting, Stage Management, Administrative, Directing, Programming and Production, Photography, Marketing, Ad Sales/Group Sales, Graphic Design, Web Communications, Creative Copywriting, Public Relations, Multimedia, Special Events, Major Gifts, Annual Fund, Education. International students must have J-1 or F-1 visa. Also available to recent college graduates. Internships vary by season. Visit Website for more details.

Number of awards:	30
Number of applicants:	712
Application deadline:	March 1, July 1
Notification begins:	April 1, August 1

Contact:
Wolf Trap Foundation for the Performing Arts
Attn: Erin Perry
1645 Trap Road
Vienna, VA 22182
Phone: 703-255-1933
Fax: 703-255-1924
Web: www.wolftrap.org/internships

The World Food Prize

George Washington Carver Internship

Type of award: Internship.
Intended use: For undergraduate or graduate study at 4-year or graduate institution.
Basis for selection: Major/career interest in agriculture; science, general; business; education; political science/government; communications or graphic arts/design. Applicant must demonstrate high academic achievement, seriousness of purpose and service orientation.
Application requirements: Resume and cover letter. Reference letter and writing samples suggested but not required.
Additional information: Interns come from variety of academic disciplines, and roles are often specialized to individual's background or interest. Interns learn first-hand both public and private side of operating an international non-profit organization and increase their understanding of the international fight against hunger, malnutrition, and poverty. Unpaid internship; course credit available. Summer deadline: March 15. Fall deadline: May 1. Spring deadline: November 15. 15-hour/week minimum. Internships seasonal.

Number of awards:	7
Number of applicants:	65
Application deadline:	March 15, May 1

Contact:
The World Food Prize
666 Grand Ave.
Suite 1700
Des Moines, IA 50309
Phone: 515-245-3731
Web: www.worldfoodprize.org

Internships

Loans

American Legion Kentucky Auxiliary

Mary Barrett Marshall Student Loan Fund

Type of award: Loan, renewable.
Intended use: For undergraduate study at vocational, 2-year or 4-year institution. Designated institutions: Eligible postsecondary institutions in Kentucky.
Eligibility: Applicant or parent must be member/participant of American Legion Auxiliary. Applicant must be female. Applicant must be residing in Kentucky. Applicant must be descendant of veteran; or dependent of veteran; or spouse of veteran or deceased veteran during Grenada conflict, Korean War, Lebanon conflict, Panama conflict, Persian Gulf War, WW I, WW II or Vietnam.
Basis for selection: Applicant must demonstrate financial need.
Application requirements: SASE.
Additional information: Maximum $800 per year, payable monthly without interest after graduation or upon securing employment; 6% interest after five years.

Amount of award:	$800
Application deadline:	April 1

Contact:
American Legion Auxiliary, Department of Kentucky
P.O. Box 5435
Frankfort, KY 40602
Phone: 502-352-2380
Fax: 502-352-2381
Web: www.kyamlegionaux.org

American Legion South Dakota

American Legion South Dakota Educational Loan

Type of award: Loan, renewable.
Intended use: For undergraduate study at vocational, 2-year or 4-year institution. Designated institutions: South Dakota institutions.
Eligibility: Applicant must be residing in South Dakota. Applicant must be veteran or descendant of veteran; or dependent of veteran.
Additional information: Up to $1,500 per year; $3,000 maximum; 3% interest on unpaid balance.

Amount of award:	$1,500-$3,000
Application deadline:	November 1, May 1

Contact:
American Legion South Dakota
Department Adjutant
P.O. Box 67
Watertown, SD 57201-0067
Phone: 605-886-3604
Web: www.sdlegion.org

ASME Auxiliary, Inc.

ASME Auxiliary Student Loan Fund

Type of award: Loan.
Intended use: For junior, senior or graduate study at accredited 4-year or graduate institution in United States. Designated institutions: Schools with ABET-accredited mechanical engineering or engineering technology curricula.
Eligibility: Applicant must be U.S. citizen.
Basis for selection: Major/career interest in engineering, mechanical. Applicant must demonstrate financial need and high academic achievement.
Application requirements: Recommendations.
Additional information: Loans are interest-free until graduation. Applications accepted on a rolling basis. Must be American Society of Mechanical Engineers member. Number of loans available varies. Visit Website for more information application or send SASE to address.

Amount of award:	$5,000

Contact:
ASME Foundation - Susan Hawthorne
White Horse Village, S #121
535 Gradyville Road
Newtown Square, PA 19073-2814
Web: www.asme.org/about-asme/scholarship-and-loans/asme-foundation-student-loans

ASME Foundation

ASME Student Loan Program

Type of award: Loan, renewable.
Intended use: For full-time undergraduate or graduate study. Designated institutions: North American institutions.
Basis for selection: Major/career interest in engineering, mechanical. Applicant must demonstrate financial need and high academic achievement.
Additional information: Applicant must be student member of American Society of Mechanical Engineers in United States, Canada or Mexico, and enrolled in mechanical engineering or mechanical engineering technology program/courses. Minimum 2.2 GPA for undergraduates; minimum 3.2 GPA for graduates. Deadline is April 20 for summer term, July 20 for fall term, October 20 for winter term, and January 20 for spring term. Award is up to $3,000 per year with $9,000 maximum for

undergraduate degree and additional $3,000 for graduate students. Visit Website for application.

Amount of award: $3,000
Application deadline: April 20, July 20

Contact:
ASME
Roseann Picolli
22 Law Drive, MS: NO1
Fairfield, NJ 07007-2900
Phone: 973-244-2319
Web: www.asme.org/about-asme/scholarship-and-loans/about-asme-scholarships

Delaware Higher Education Office

Christa McAuliffe Teacher Incentive Program

Type of award: Loan, renewable.
Intended use: For undergraduate study at accredited 4-year institution.
Eligibility: Applicant must be U.S. citizen or permanent resident residing in Delaware.
Basis for selection: Major/career interest in education. Applicant must demonstrate high academic achievement.
Application requirements: Essay, transcript. SAT scores.
Additional information: Applicant must be high school senior with combined score of 1570 on the SAT and rank in top half of class, or undergraduate with minimum 2.75 GPA. Preference given to applicants planning to teach in critical need area as defined by DE Department of Education. Though award is for full-time students, it may be prorated for part-time students in a qualifying program. Loan not to exceed cost of tuition, fees, and other direct educational expenses. Loan forgiveness provision at rate of one year of teaching in a DE public school for one year of loan. Visit Website for deadline information.

Number of applicants: 69

Contact:
Delaware Higher Education Office
John G. Townsend Building
401 Federal Street
Dover, DE 19901
Phone: 302-735-4120
Fax: 302-739-5894
Web: www.doe.k12.de.us/high-ed

Delaware Nursing Incentive Program

Type of award: Loan, renewable.
Intended use: For undergraduate study at accredited vocational, 2-year or 4-year institution in United States. Designated institutions: Colleges with accredited nursing programs that lead to RN, LPN, or BSN certification.
Eligibility: Applicant must be U.S. citizen or permanent resident residing in Delaware.
Basis for selection: Major/career interest in nursing. Applicant must demonstrate high academic achievement.
Application requirements: Essay, transcript.
Additional information: Loan-forgiveness for practicing nursing at state-owned hospital or clinic, one year for each year of loan. High school seniors must rank in top half of class and have at least 2.5 GPA. Though award generally for full-time students who are residents of DE, current state employees do not have to be DE residents and may be considered for part-time enrollment. RNs with five or more years of state service may enroll in BSN program full or part time. Loan not to exceed cost of tuition, fees, and other direct educational expenses. Visit Website for deadline information.

Number of applicants: 84
Total amount awarded: $35,000

Contact:
Delaware Higher Education Office
John G. Townsend Building
401 Federal Street
Dover, DE 19901
Phone: 302-735-4120
Fax: 302-739-5894
Web: www.doe.k12.de.us/high-ed

Franklin Lindsay Student Aid Fund

Franklin Lindsay Student Aid Loan

Type of award: Loan, renewable.
Intended use: For full-time sophomore, junior, senior or graduate study at accredited 4-year or graduate institution in United States. Designated institutions: Texas colleges accredited by the Southern Association of Colleges and Schools Commission on Colleges.
Eligibility: Applicant must be U.S. citizen.
Basis for selection: Applicant must demonstrate financial need and high academic achievement.
Application requirements: Interview, recommendations, transcript. Copy of driver's license or ID and proof of school enrollment.
Additional information: Minimum 2.0 GPA for undergraduates and 3.0 for graduates. Must have co-signer who is U.S. citizen. Upon graduation or termination from school, loan goes to repayment structure at four percent, with maximum payment term of seven years. Visit Website for application and more information.

Amount of award: $7,000
Number of applicants: 97
Application deadline: June 1
Total amount awarded: $723,550

Contact:
The Franklin Lindsay Student Aid Fund
c/o JPMorgan Chase Bank, N.A.
P.O. Box 227237
Dallas, TX 75222-7237
Phone: 866-300-6222
Web: www.franklinlindsay.org

Grand Encampment of Knights Templar of the USA

Knights Templar Educational Foundation Loan

Type of award: Loan, renewable.
Intended use: For junior, senior or first professional study at accredited vocational, 4-year or graduate institution in United States.

Basis for selection: Applicant must demonstrate high academic achievement and depth of character.
Application requirements: Recommendations.
Additional information: Student should request application from Grand Encampment of Knights Templar in state of residence. Available loan amount varies by state division.
Contact:
Grand Encampment of Knights Templar of the USA
5909 West Loop South
Suite 495
Belaire, TX 77401-2402
Phone: 713-349-8700
Fax: 713-349-8710
Web: www.knightstemplar.org

Jewish Family and Children's Services (JFCS)

JFCS Scholarship Fund

Type of award: Scholarship.
Intended use: For undergraduate or graduate study at postsecondary institution.
Eligibility: Applicant must be Jewish. Applicant must be residing in California.
Basis for selection: Applicant must demonstrate financial need and high academic achievement.
Additional information: Minimum 2.75 GPA for grants. Applicants must demonstrate connection to Jewish community. High school seniors, undergraduates, and graduate students may apply. Applicants may also be high school students traveling to Israel. Grants available for residents of Sonoma, Marin, San Francisco, San Mateo, or Santa Clara counties; loans available for all nine Bay area counties. Deadline is for consideration for school year; applicants for Israel travel, Holocaust study, and vocational study may apply any time. Organization has several scholarships and loans; see Website for more details.

Amount of award:	$1,000-$1,500
Number of awards:	100
Application deadline:	August 1

Contact:
Jewish Family and Children's Services
Attn: Eric Singer
2150 Post Street
San Francisco, CA 94115
Phone: 415-359-2463
Web: www.jfcs.org

Maine Educational Loan Authority

The Maine Loan

Type of award: Loan.
Intended use: For undergraduate or graduate study at accredited vocational, 2-year, 4-year or graduate institution in United States or Canada.
Eligibility: Applicant must be residing in Maine.
Application requirements: Proof of eligibility. Income information/credit analysis.
Additional information: Loans available to Maine residents attending approved schools and out-of-state students attending Maine schools. May borrow full cost of education minus other financial aid. May be used to pay prior balance up to one academic year. Applicant has 5-15 years to repay, depending on amount owed. See Website for interest rates, payment options, and additional information. Applications accepted year round. Minimum loan amount is $1,000.

Number of applicants:	2,510
Total amount awarded:	$30,000,000

Contact:
Maine Educational Loan Authority
131 Presumpscot Street
Portland, ME 04103
Phone: 800-922-6352
Fax: 207-791-3616
Web: www.mela.net

Massachusetts Board of Higher Education

Massachusetts No Interest Loan

Type of award: Loan.
Intended use: For full-time undergraduate study at accredited vocational, 2-year or 4-year institution.
Eligibility: Applicant must be U.S. citizen or permanent resident residing in Massachusetts.
Basis for selection: Applicant must demonstrate financial need.
Application requirements: FAFSA.
Additional information: No Interest Loan (NIL) Program offers no interest loans to those who meet requirements; students have 10 years to repay NIL loans and a borrowing limit of $20,000 ($4,000/year). Must not have received prior bachelor's degree.

Amount of award:	$1,000-$4,000
Number of applicants:	2,200
Total amount awarded:	$6,000,000

Contact:
Office of Student Financial Assistance
Massachusetts Board of Higher Education
454 Broadway, Suite 200
Revere, MA 02151
Phone: 617-391-6070
Fax: 617-727-0667
Web: www.osfa.mass.edu

Military Officers Association of America

MOAA Interest-Free Loan and Grant Program

Type of award: Loan, renewable.
Intended use: For full-time undergraduate study at accredited 2-year or 4-year institution in United States.

Loans

Eligibility: Applicant must be no older than 23. Applicant must be U.S. citizen. Applicant must be dependent of active service person, veteran or deceased veteran who serves or served in the Army, Air Force, Marines, Navy, Coast Guard or Reserves/National Guard. Applicant must be child of MOAA member or active-duty, Reserve, National Guard, or retired enlisted military personnel.
Basis for selection: Applicant must demonstrate financial need, high academic achievement, depth of character, leadership, patriotism, seriousness of purpose and service orientation.
Application requirements: Essay, transcript, proof of eligibility. SAT/ACT score. Parent or sponsor's military status and/or MOAA number.
Additional information: Minimum 3.0 GPA. Applicant must be child of active-duty or retired officer or enlisted personnel. Must be under 24; however, if applicant served in Uniformed Service before completing college, maximum age for eligibility increases by number of years served, up to five years. Parent must sign promissory note before funds can be disbursed. Military academy cadets not eligible. Application available on Website.

Amount of award:	$5,500
Number of awards:	1,600
Number of applicants:	2,000
Application deadline:	March 1
Notification begins:	May 1
Total amount awarded:	$8,800,000

Contact:
MOAA Scholarship Fund
Educational Assistance Program
201 North Washington Street
Alexandria, VA 22314-2529
Phone: 800-234-6622
Web: www.moaa.org/education

Minnesota Office of Higher Education

Minnesota Student Educational Loan Fund (SELF)

Type of award: Loan.
Intended use: For undergraduate or graduate study at vocational, 2-year, 4-year or graduate institution. Designated institutions: Minnesota and eligible out-of-state institutions.
Additional information: Applicant must be enrolled at least half-time in eligible Minnesota school, or be Minnesota resident enrolled in eligible school outside Minnesota. Must seek aid from certain other sources before applying, except federal unsubsidized and subsidized Stafford loans, National Direct Student loans, HEAL loans, and other private loans. Institution must approve application. Must have a creditworthy cosigner.

Amount of award:	$500-$10,000
Number of applicants:	14,124
Total amount awarded:	$85,416,423

Contact:
Minnesota Office of Higher Education
1450 Energy Park Drive, Suite 350
St. Paul, MN 55108-5227
Phone: 800-657-3866
Web: www.selfloan.org

Mississippi Office of Student Financial Aid

Critical Needs Teacher Loan/ Scholarship

Type of award: Loan, renewable.
Intended use: For junior or senior study at 4-year institution in United States. Designated institutions: Mississippi institutions.
Eligibility: Applicant must be U.S. citizen residing in Mississippi.
Basis for selection: Major/career interest in education; education, early childhood; education, special or education, teacher. Applicant must demonstrate high academic achievement.
Application requirements: Signed CNTP Rules and Regulations.
Additional information: Minimum 2.5 GPA or must rank in top 50 percent of class. Must have ACT score of 21 or higher or Praxis 1 passing score. Must be enrolled in program of study leading to Class "A" teacher educator license. Must agree to full-time employment in Mississippi public school located in critical teacher shortage or subject area. Must participate in Entrance Counseling. Award covers tuition, fees, and housing plus book allowance. Students at private institutions receive award equivalent to costs at nearest comparable public institution. Interested non-Mississippi residents may apply if they have been accepted to Mississippi school. See Website for application and more information.

Application deadline:	March 31

Contact:
Mississippi Office of Student Financial Aid
3825 Ridgewood Road
Jackson, MS 39211-6453
Phone: 800-327-2980
Web: www.mississippi.edu/riseupms

Mississippi Health Care Professions Loan/Scholarship

Type of award: Loan, renewable.
Intended use: For full-time junior, senior or graduate study at accredited 4-year or graduate institution. Designated institutions: Mississippi institutions.
Eligibility: Applicant must be residing in Mississippi.
Basis for selection: Major/career interest in physical therapy; occupational therapy; speech pathology/audiology or psychology. Applicant must demonstrate high academic achievement.
Application requirements: Transcript, proof of eligibility. Mississippi tax return.
Additional information: Loan forgiveness for service in Mississippi health care institution: one year for each year of financial assistance, with a maximum of two years. Undergraduates must major in speech pathology/audiology, psychology, or occupational therapy; graduates must major in physical therapy or occupational therapy at University of Mississippi Medical Center. Visit Website for application and further information.

Amount of award:	$1,500-$6,000
Application deadline:	March 31
Notification begins:	August 1

Loans

Contact:
Susan Eckels, Program Manager
Mississippi Office of Student Financial Aid
3825 Ridgewood Road
Jackson, MS 39211-6453
Phone: 601-432-6997
Fax: 601-432-6527
Web: www.mississippi.edu/riseupms

Mississippi William Winter Teacher Scholar Loan Program

Type of award: Loan, renewable.
Intended use: For full-time junior or senior study at 4-year institution. Designated institutions: Mississippi institutions.
Eligibility: Applicant must be U.S. citizen residing in Mississippi.
Basis for selection: Major/career interest in education; education, early childhood; education, special or education, teacher. Applicant must demonstrate high academic achievement.
Application requirements: Proof of eligibility.
Additional information: Must be studying towards a Class A teacher educator license. Minimum 2.5 GPA or must rank in top 50 percent of class. Loan forgiveness for teaching service in Mississippi public school or public school district: one year for each year of financial assistance, for a maximum of two years. Apply online.

Amount of award:	$4,000
Application deadline:	March 31
Notification begins:	August 1
Total amount awarded:	$1,921,658

Contact:
Mississippi Office of Student Financial Aid
3825 Ridgewood Road
Jackson, MS 39211-6453
Phone: 800-327-2980
Fax: 601-432-6527
Web: www.mississippi.edu/riseupms

Navy-Marine Corps Relief Society

Vice Admiral E.P. Travers Loan

Type of award: Loan, renewable.
Intended use: For full-time undergraduate study in United States.
Eligibility: Applicant must be U.S. citizen. Applicant must be dependent of active service person; or spouse of active service person in the Marines or Navy.
Basis for selection: Applicant must demonstrate financial need and high academic achievement.
Application requirements: Proof of eligibility. Current military ID of service member, FAFSA.
Additional information: Minimum 2.0 GPA. Applicant must be dependent child of an active duty or retired service member of Navy or Marine Corp (including Reservists on active duty) or a spouse of active duty service member. Loan must be repaid in allotments over 24-month period (minimum monthly repayment is $50). Must reapply to renew.

Amount of award:	$500-$3,000
Number of applicants:	1,200
Application deadline:	May 1
Total amount awarded:	$800,000

Contact:
Navy-Marine Corps Relief Society
875 North Randolph Street, Suite 225
Arlington, VA 22203
Phone: 703-696-4960
Web: www.nmcrs.org/education

New Jersey Higher Education Student Assistance Authority

New Jersey Class Loan Program

Type of award: Loan.
Intended use: For undergraduate or graduate study at accredited vocational, 2-year, 4-year or graduate institution in United States. Designated institutions: Approved institutions. Proprietary institutions also eligible.
Eligibility: Applicant must be U.S. citizen or permanent resident.
Application requirements: Proof of eligibility. Income and credit history, FAFSA, school certification.
Additional information: All New Jersey residents may apply, as may out-of-state students attending school in New Jersey. Must demonstrate credit-worthiness or provide co-signer. Parent or other eligible family member may borrow on behalf of student. Maximum loan amount may not exceed education cost less all other financial aid. Minimum loan amount $500. Low fixed interest rate loans available for both undergraduate and graduate students. Two percent administrative fee deducted from approved loan amount. Apply online for instant credit approval.

Total amount awarded:	$337,147,137

Contact:
New Jersey Higher Education Student Assistance Authority
4 Quakerbridge Plaza
P.O. Box 540
Trenton, NJ 08625-0540
Phone: 800-792-8670
Fax: 609-588-2228
Web: www.hesaa.org

New Mexico Commission on Higher Education

New Mexico Allied Health Student Loan-for-Service Program

Type of award: Loan, renewable.
Intended use: For undergraduate or graduate study at accredited postsecondary institution. Designated institutions: Public postsecondary institutions in New Mexico.
Eligibility: Applicant must be U.S. citizen or permanent resident residing in New Mexico.

Basis for selection: Major/career interest in health-related professions; occupational therapy; mental health/therapy; physical therapy; pharmacy/pharmaceutics/pharmacology; dietetics/nutrition or speech pathology/audiology. Applicant must demonstrate financial need.
Application requirements: FAFSA.
Additional information: Loan forgiveness offered to those who practice in medically underserved areas in New Mexico. Must be accepted by or enrolled in approved programs at accredited New Mexico public postsecondary institution. Call sponsor number or visit Website for application and more information.

Amount of award:	$12,000
Application deadline:	July 1

Contact:
New Mexico Higher Education Department
Financial Aid and Student Services
2048 Galisteo Street
Santa Fe, NM 87505
Phone: 505-476-8400
Web: www.hed.state.nm.us

New Mexico Nursing Student Loan-for-Service

Type of award: Loan, renewable.
Intended use: For undergraduate or graduate study at accredited 2-year or 4-year institution. Designated institutions: New Mexico public colleges and universities.
Eligibility: Applicant must be U.S. citizen or permanent resident residing in New Mexico.
Basis for selection: Major/career interest in nursing. Applicant must demonstrate financial need.
Application requirements: FAFSA.
Additional information: Loan forgiveness for New Mexico resident to practice in medically underserved areas in New Mexico. Part-time students eligible for prorated awards.

Amount of award:	$12,000
Application deadline:	July 1

Contact:
New Mexico Commission on Higher Education
Financial Aid and Student Services
2048 Galisteo Street
Santa Fe, NM 87505
Phone: 505-476-8400
Web: www.hed.state.nm.us

New Mexico Teacher's Loan-for-Service

Type of award: Loan.
Intended use: For undergraduate or post-bachelor's certificate study at accredited postsecondary institution. Designated institutions: Public college or university.
Eligibility: Applicant must be physically challenged. Applicant must be U.S. citizen or permanent resident residing in New Mexico.
Basis for selection: Major/career interest in education, teacher. Applicant must demonstrate financial need.
Application requirements: FAFSA.
Additional information: Must be accepted by undergraduate, graduate, or alternative licensure teacher preparation program approved by State Board of Education. Must provide one year of teaching service for each year of award at a public school in New Mexico.

Amount of award:	$4,000
Application deadline:	July 1

Contact:
New Mexico Commission on Higher Education
Financial Aid and Student Services
2048 Galisteo Street
Santa Fe, NM 87505
Phone: 505-476-8400
Web: www.hed.state.nm.us

New York State Grange

Grange Student Loan Fund

Type of award: Loan, renewable.
Intended use: For full-time undergraduate or graduate study at postsecondary institution.
Eligibility: Applicant or parent must be member/participant of New York State Grange. Applicant must be residing in New York.
Basis for selection: Applicant must demonstrate financial need.
Additional information: Must have been member of New York State Grange for at least 6 months at time of application. Must send SASE for application. Loanee may borrow a maximum of $10,000. May apply for less than the maximum award. Loan repayment at five percent annual interest.

Amount of award:	$2,000
Number of awards:	11
Number of applicants:	11
Application deadline:	April 15
Notification begins:	June 15
Total amount awarded:	$22,000

Contact:
New York State Grange
100 Grange Place
Cortland, NY 13045
Phone: 607-756-7553
Fax: 607-756-7757
Web: www.nysgrange.org

Ohio Board of Regents

Ohio Nurse Education Assistance Loan Program

Type of award: Loan, renewable.
Intended use: For undergraduate, post-bachelor's certificate or master's study at 4-year or graduate institution. Designated institutions: Eligible Ohio institutions.
Eligibility: Applicant must be U.S. citizen or permanent resident residing in Ohio.
Basis for selection: Major/career interest in nursing. Applicant must demonstrate financial need.
Application requirements: Proof of eligibility. FAFSA.
Additional information: Future nurse applicants must demonstrate financial need. Future nurse instructor applicants awarded on first-come, first-served basis. Award amount varies; up to $3,000 for future nurses, and at least $5,000 for future nurse instructors. Must not be in default or owe refund to any federal financial aid programs. Number of awards varies. Visit Website for application and more information.

Number of applicants: 202
Application deadline: July 15
Notification begins: August 31
Total amount awarded: $364,476

Contact:
Ohio Board of Regents
Web: www.ohiohighered.org/nealp

Pickett and Hatcher Educational Fund, Inc.

Pickett and Hatcher Educational Loan

Type of award: Loan, renewable.
Intended use: For full-time undergraduate study at 4-year institution.
Eligibility: Applicant must be U.S. citizen.
Basis for selection: Applicant must demonstrate financial need and high academic achievement.
Additional information: Not available to law, medicine, or ministry students. Loans renewed up to $40,000. Applications accepted year-round.

Amount of award: $1,000-$10,000
Number of awards: 550
Number of applicants: 413
Total amount awarded: $3,855,885

Contact:
Pickett and Hatcher Educational Fund, Inc.
Loan Program
P.O. Box 8169
Columbus, GA 31908-8169
Phone: 706-327-6586
Fax: 706-324-6788
Web: www.phef.org

Presbyterian Church (USA)

Presbyterian Undergraduate and Graduate Loan

Type of award: Loan, renewable.
Intended use: For full-time undergraduate or graduate study at accredited 2-year, 4-year or graduate institution in United States.
Eligibility: Applicant must be Presbyterian. Applicant must be U.S. citizen or permanent resident.
Basis for selection: Applicant must demonstrate financial need and high academic achievement.
Additional information: Must establish and maintain minimum 2.0 GPA. Contact office for current interest rates and deferment policies. Must give evidence of financial reliability. Award is up to $3,000. Undergraduates and graduates can apply for up to $15,000, spread out over length of undergraduate and graduate studies.

Number of awards: 150
Number of applicants: 52
Application deadline: July 30
Notification begins: August 15
Total amount awarded: $153,500

Contact:
Presbyterian Church (USA)
Financial Aid for Studies
100 Witherspoon Street
Louisville, KY 40202-1396
Phone: 800-728-7228 ext. 5224
Fax: 502-569-8766
Web: www.pcusa.org/financialaid

South Carolina Student Loan Corporation

South Carolina Teacher Loans

Type of award: Loan, renewable.
Intended use: For undergraduate or graduate study at accredited 2-year, 4-year or graduate institution.
Eligibility: Applicant must be U.S. citizen or permanent resident residing in South Carolina.
Basis for selection: Major/career interest in education; education, early childhood; education, special or education, teacher. Applicant must demonstrate high academic achievement.
Additional information: Freshmen and sophomores may borrow up to $2,500 per year; juniors, seniors, and graduate students may borrow up to $5,000 per year. Graduate study eligible only if required for initial teacher certification. Entering freshmen must have SAT score equal to South Carolina state average for year of high school graduation, and rank in top 40 percent of high school class. Undergraduate and entering graduate applicants must have 2.75 GPA and have passed PRAXIS 1 Examination. Graduate applicants who have completed at least one semester must have 3.5 GPA. Applicants with SAT score of 1100 or greater (1650 or greater for exams taken on or after March 1, 2005) or ACT score of 24 or greater are exempt from PRAXIS 1 requirement. Loan forgiveness for service in teacher shortage area in South Carolina public schools: 20 percent or $3,000, whichever is greater, for each year of service, 33 percent or $5,000, whichever is greater, if service in geographic and subject shortage area. Apply early.

Amount of award: $2,500-$5,000
Application deadline: April 15
Notification begins: July 15
Total amount awarded: $5,000,000

Contact:
South Carolina Student Loan Corporation
P.O. Box 102405
Columbia, SC 29224
Phone: 803-798-0916 or 800-347-2752
Web: www.scstudentloan.org

Student Aid Foundation

Student Aid Foundation Loan

Type of award: Loan, renewable.
Intended use: For full-time undergraduate, master's, doctoral or first professional study at accredited vocational, 2-year, 4-year or graduate institution in United States.

Eligibility: Applicant must be female. Applicant must be U.S. citizen residing in Georgia.
Basis for selection: Applicant must demonstrate financial need, high academic achievement and seriousness of purpose.
Application requirements: Recommendations, essay, transcript.
Additional information: Non-Georgia residents attending Georgia institutions can qualify. Loan not forgivable. Must have financially responsible endorser. Minimum 2.5 GPA. Send SASE with request for application, or download it from Website.

Amount of award:	$3,500-$7,500
Number of awards:	40
Number of applicants:	89
Application deadline:	April 15
Notification begins:	June 1

Contact:
Student Aid Foundation
#312
2550 Sandy Plains Road, Suite 225
Marietta, GA 30066
Phone: 770-973-7077
Fax: 770-973-2220
Web: www.studentaidfoundation.org

Tennessee Student Assistance Corporation

Math And Science Teachers Loan Forgiveness Program

Type of award: Loan, renewable.
Intended use: For undergraduate certificate, graduate or postgraduate study at postsecondary institution.
Eligibility: Applicant must be residing in Tennessee.
Basis for selection: Major/career interest in mathematics; science, general or education.
Additional information: Must be admitted to post-secondary institution seeking advanced degree in math/science, or a certificate to teach math/science, and be a tenured Tennessee public school teacher. Application deadline is September 1 for students beginning the academic year in the fall, February 1 for spring, and May 1 for summer. Apply online.

Amount of award:	$2,000
Number of awards:	18
Application deadline:	September 1, February 1
Total amount awarded:	$36,000

Contact:
Tennessee Student Assistance Corporation
404 James Robertson Parkway
Parkway Towers, Suite 1510
Nashville, TN 37243-0820
Phone: 800-342-1663
Web: www.tn.gov/collegepays

Tennessee Minority Teaching Fellows Program

Type of award: Loan, renewable.
Intended use: For full-time undergraduate study at accredited 2-year or 4-year institution.
Eligibility: Applicant must be Alaskan native, Asian American, African American, Hispanic American, American Indian or Native Hawaiian/Pacific Islander. Applicant must be U.S. citizen residing in Tennessee.
Basis for selection: Major/career interest in education. Applicant must demonstrate high academic achievement.
Application requirements: Recommendations, essay, transcript. List of extracurricular activities.
Additional information: Entering freshmen applicants have priority and must have minimum 2.75 GPA, rank in top 25 percent of class, or score at least 18 on ACT (860 SAT). Undergraduate applicants must have minimum 2.5 GPA. Must make commitment to teaching. Loan can be forgiven by teaching in Tennessee public pre K-12 schools, one year for each year of funding.

Amount of award:	$5,000
Number of awards:	115
Number of applicants:	266
Application deadline:	April 15
Total amount awarded:	$543,000

Contact:
Tennessee Student Assistance Corporation
404 James Robertson Parkway
Parkway Towers, Suite 1510
Nashville, TN 37243-0820
Phone: 800-342-1663
Fax: 615-741-6101
Web: www.tn.gov/collegepays

Tennessee Teaching Scholars Program

Type of award: Loan, renewable.
Intended use: For junior, senior, post-bachelor's certificate or master's study at accredited 4-year or graduate institution.
Eligibility: Applicant must be U.S. citizen residing in Tennessee.
Basis for selection: Major/career interest in education; education, teacher; education, special or education, early childhood. Applicant must demonstrate high academic achievement.
Application requirements: Recommendations, transcript, proof of eligibility. Verification of standardized test score and acceptance into Teacher Licensure Program.
Additional information: Loan can be forgiven for teaching in Tennessee public schools, K-12. Minimum 2.75 cumulative GPA and a standardized test score adequate for admission to the Teacher Education Program in Tennessee schools. Amount of award based on funding.

Amount of award:	$5,000
Number of awards:	161
Number of applicants:	349
Application deadline:	April 15
Total amount awarded:	$647,000

Contact:
Tennessee Student Assistance Corporation
404 James Robertson Parkway
Parkway Towers, Suite 1510
Nashville, TN 37243-0820
Phone: 800-342-1663
Fax: 615-741-6101
Web: www.tn.gov/collegepays

Texas Higher Education Coordinating Board

Texas College Access Loan (CAL)

Type of award: Loan.
Intended use: For undergraduate or graduate study at 2-year, 4-year or graduate institution in United States. Designated institutions: Texas institutions.
Eligibility: Applicant must be U.S. citizen or permanent resident residing in Texas.
Additional information: Texas colleges and universities have a limited number of CAL loans. Applicants need not show financial need. The loan may be used to cover the family's expected contribution (EFC). Co-signers must have good credit and meet other program criteria. Loans will not be sold to another lender and will be serviced by the THECB until paid in full. Apply online.
Contact:
Texas Higher Education Coordinating Board
Phone: 800-242-3062
Web: www.collegeforalltexans.com and www.hhloans.com

William D. Ford Direct Student Loans

Type of award: Loan.
Intended use: For undergraduate study at vocational, 2-year or 4-year institution in United States.
Eligibility: Applicant must be U.S. citizen or permanent resident.
Basis for selection: Applicant must demonstrate financial need and high academic achievement.
Application requirements: FAFSA.
Additional information: Borrowers must not be in default or delinquent on any federal student loan. Contact college financial aid office for more information.
Amount of award: $2,625-$18,500
Contact:
Texas Higher Education Coordinating Board
Phone: 800-242-3062
Web: www.collegeforalltexans.com

United Methodist Church

United Methodist Loan Program

Type of award: Loan, renewable.
Intended use: For undergraduate or graduate study at accredited postsecondary institution in United States.
Eligibility: Applicant must be United Methodist.
Basis for selection: Applicant must demonstrate high academic achievement.
Additional information: Must be active member of United Methodist Church one year prior to application. Must maintain 2.5 GPA. May reapply for loan to maximum of $30,000. Interest rate 5 percent; cosigner required. Ten years permitted to repay loan after graduation or withdrawal from school. Qualified applicants are chosen on a first-come, first-served basis.
Amount of award: $5,000
Contact:
United Methodist Church/Board of Higher Education and Ministry
Office of Loans and Scholarships
P.O. Box 340007
Nashville, TN 37203-0007
Phone: 615-340-7346
Web: www.gbhem.org

UPS

United Parcel Service Earn & Learn Program Loans

Type of award: Loan.
Intended use: For undergraduate study at accredited vocational, 2-year or 4-year institution in United States.
Application requirements: Proof of eligibility.
Additional information: Must be UPS employee. Award for part-time employees is $3,000 per year in student loans with $15,000 lifetime maximum. Award for part-time management employees is $4,000 per year with a $20,000 lifetime maximum. Visit Website for participating locations and job listings.
Amount of award: $3,000-$20,000
Contact:
UPS
Phone: 888-WORK-UPS
Web: www.upsjobs.com

U.S. Department of Education

Federal Direct Loans

Type of award: Loan, renewable.
Intended use: For undergraduate or graduate study at postsecondary institution.
Eligibility: Applicant must be U.S. citizen or permanent resident.
Basis for selection: Applicant must demonstrate financial need.
Application requirements: Proof of eligibility. FAFSA and promissory note.
Additional information: Some loans subsidized, based on need eligibility. Loan amount depends on grade level in school and student type. Telecommunications Device for the Deaf at 800-730-8913. FAFSA available online. Visit Website for interest rates.
Amount of award: $5,500-$20,500
Contact:
Federal Student Aid Information Center
Phone: 800-4-FED-AID
Web: www.studentaid.ed.gov

Federal Perkins Loan

Type of award: Loan, renewable.
Intended use: For undergraduate or graduate study at accredited postsecondary institution in United States.

Loans

Eligibility: Applicant must be U.S. citizen or permanent resident.
Basis for selection: Applicant must demonstrate financial need.
Application requirements: Proof of eligibility. FAFSA.
Additional information: Maximum annual loan amount: $5,500 for undergraduates, $8,000 for graduates. Five percent interest rate. Applicant must demonstrate exceptional financial need. Repayment begins nine months after graduation, leaving school, or dropping below half-time status. Visit Website for more information.

Application deadline: June 30

Contact:
Federal Student Aid Information Center
Phone: 800-4-FED AID
Web: www.studentaid.ed.gov

Federal Plus Loan

Type of award: Loan.
Intended use: For undergraduate or graduate study at accredited postsecondary institution in or outside United States or Canada.
Eligibility: Applicant must be U.S. citizen or permanent resident.
Basis for selection: Applicant must demonstrate financial need.
Application requirements: PLUS loan application and promissory note. FAFSA.
Additional information: Unsubsidized loans for parents of undergraduate students, or for graduate students. Must pass credit check. Interest rate is 7.9 percent. Award amount varies. Loan is equal to cost of attendance minus any other financial aid. Generally, repayment must begin 60 days after the loan is fully disbursed. Visit Website for more information.

Application deadline: June 30

Contact:
Federal Student Aid Information Center
Phone: 800-4-FED-AID
Web: www.studentaid.ed.gov

Utah State Office of Education

Utah Career Teaching Scholarship/ T.H. Bell Teaching Incentive Loan

Type of award: Loan, renewable.
Intended use: For full-time undergraduate study at accredited 4-year institution. Designated institutions: Utah institutions.
Eligibility: Applicant must be high school junior or senior. Applicant must be U.S. citizen residing in Utah.
Basis for selection: Major/career interest in education, teacher; education; education, early childhood or education, special.
Application requirements: Transcript. SAT/ACT score sheet.
Additional information: Must have completed requirements for Early Graduation Program (including ACT). Awardees at public institutions receive a waiver for tuition and fees. Awardees at private institutions receive $995 per semester. Awardees must teach in Utah public school for term equal to number of years loan was received in order to have loans forgiven. Visit Website for application.

Amount of award: Full tuition
Number of applicants: 110
Application deadline: March 28

Contact:
Utah State Office of Education Teaching and Learning
Linda Alder, Teaching & Learning - Licensing
250 East 500 South/P.O. Box 144200
Salt Lake City, UT 84114-4200
Web: www.schools.utah.gov/cert/loans-and-scholarships.aspx

Virgin Islands Board of Education

Virgin Islands Territorial Grants/ Loans Program

Type of award: Loan, renewable.
Intended use: For full-time undergraduate or graduate study at accredited postsecondary institution.
Eligibility: Applicant must be U.S. citizen or permanent resident residing in Virgin Islands.
Basis for selection: Applicant must demonstrate high academic achievement.
Application requirements: Transcript. Acceptance letter from institution for first-time applicants or transfer students.
Additional information: Minimum 2.0 GPA. Six percent interest on repayment, additional 2 percent if delinquent. Number and amount of award varies. Deadline in early May.

Contact:
Virgin Islands Board of Education
Scholarship Committee
P.O. Box 11900
St. Thomas, VI 00801
Phone: 340-774-4546
Web: www.myviboe.com

Wisconsin Higher Educational Aids Board

Wisconsin Minority Teacher Loan Program

Type of award: Loan, renewable.
Intended use: For junior, senior or graduate study at accredited 4-year institution. Designated institutions: Wisconsin colleges and universities offering teaching degree.
Eligibility: Applicant must be Asian American, African American, Mexican American, Hispanic American, Puerto Rican or American Indian. Asian American applicants must be either former citizens or descendants of former citizens of Laos, Vietnam, or Cambodia admitted to the U.S. after 12/31/1975. Applicant must be residing in Wisconsin.
Basis for selection: Major/career interest in education; education, special or education, teacher. Applicant must demonstrate financial need.
Application requirements: Nomination by financial aid office. FAFSA.
Additional information: Recipient must agree to teach in Wisconsin school district where minority students constitute at

least 29 percent of enrollment or in school district participating in the inter-district pupil transfer (Chapter 220) program. For each year student teaches in eligible district, 25 percent of loan is forgiven; otherwise loan must be repaid at interest rate of 5 percent. Must be registered with Selective Service, unless exempt.

Amount of award: $250-$2,500
Number of awards: 109
Total amount awarded: $238,662

Contact:
Higher Educational Aids Board
Attn: Deanna Schulz
P.O. Box 7885
Madison, WI 53707-7885
Phone: 608-267-2212
Web: www.heab.state.wi.us

Sponsor Index

10,000 Degrees, 79
1199SEIU Benefit Funds, 79
1st Marine Division Association, 79
Abbie Sargent Memorial Scholarship Fund, 80
Academy of Interactive Arts & Sciences, 80
Academy of Nutrition and Dietetics, 80
Academy of Television Arts & Sciences Foundation, 81 , 549
ACFE Foundation, 81
The Actuarial Foundation, 81
ADHA Institute for Oral Health, 82
AFSA Scholarship Programs, 84
AfterCollege, 85
AHIMA Foundation, 87
Air Force Aid Society, 87
Air Force/ROTC, 87
Air Traffic Control Association, Inc., 88
Aircraft Electronics Association Educational Foundation, 88
Alabama Commission on Higher Education, 90
Alabama Department of Postsecondary Education, 91
Alabama Department of Veterans Affairs, 92
Alaska Commission on Postsecondary Education, 92
Alexander Graham Bell Association for the Deaf and Hard of Hearing, 92
Alexia Foundation, 93
Alliance for Young Artists and Writers, 93
Allstate, 549
Alpha Beta Gamma International Business Honor Society, 94
Alpha Mu Gamma, the National Collegiate Foreign Language Honor Society, 94
Alumnae Panhellenic Association of Washington, D.C., 94
Alzheimer's Foundation of America, 95
AMBUCS, 95
American Alpine Club, 95
American Association for Cancer Research, 96
American Association of Advertising Agencies, 549
American Association of University Women San Jose, 96
American Bar Foundation, 550
American Board of Funeral Service Education, 96
American Center of Oriental Research, 97
American Chemical Society, 97
American Classical League, 97
American College of Musicians, 98
American Congress on Surveying and Mapping, 98
American Conservatory Theater, 550
American Council of Engineering Companies, 101
American Council of the Blind, 101
American Dental Assistants Association, 101
American Federation of State, County and Municipal Employees, 101, 550
American Fire Sprinkler Association, 102
American Floral Endowment, 102
American Foundation for the Blind, 106
American Ground Water Trust, 108
American Helicopter Society, 108
American Hellenic Educational Progressive Association Educational Foundation, 109
American Hotel & Lodging Educational Foundation, 109
American Indian College Fund, 110
American Indian Endowed Scholarship Program, 114
American Indian Science & Engineering Society, 114
American Institute for Foreign Study, 115
American Institute of Aeronautics and Astronautics, 116
American Institute of Architects, 117
American Institute of Architects New Jersey, 117
American Institute of Certified Public Accountants, 117
American Institute of Polish Culture, 118
American Legacy Foundation, 118
American Legion, 119
American Legion Alabama, 119
American Legion Alabama Auxiliary, 119
American Legion Alaska, 120
American Legion Alaska Auxiliary, 120
American Legion Arizona, 120
American Legion Arizona Auxiliary, 121
American Legion Arkansas, 121
American Legion Arkansas Auxiliary, 122
American Legion California, 122
American Legion California Auxiliary, 123
American Legion Colorado, 123
American Legion Colorado Auxiliary, 123
American Legion Connecticut, 124
American Legion Connecticut Auxiliary, 124
American Legion Delaware Auxiliary, 125
American Legion District of Columbia, 125
American Legion Florida, 125
American Legion Florida Auxiliary, 126
American Legion Georgia, 127
American Legion Georgia Auxiliary, 127
American Legion Hawaii, 127
American Legion Idaho, 127
American Legion Idaho Auxiliary, 128
American Legion Illinois, 128
American Legion Illinois Auxiliary, 129
American Legion Indiana, 130
American Legion Indiana Auxiliary, 131
American Legion Iowa, 131
American Legion Iowa Auxiliary, 132
American Legion Kansas, 133
American Legion Kansas Auxiliary, 135
American Legion Kentucky, 135
American Legion Kentucky Auxiliary, 135, 593
American Legion Maine, 136
American Legion Maine Auxiliary, 136
American Legion Maryland, 137
American Legion Maryland Auxiliary, 138
American Legion Massachusetts, 138
American Legion Massachusetts Auxiliary, 139
American Legion Michigan, 139
American Legion Michigan Auxiliary, 140
American Legion Minnesota, 140
American Legion Minnesota Auxiliary, 141
American Legion Mississippi Auxiliary, 141
American Legion Missouri, 142
American Legion Missouri Auxiliary, 144
American Legion Montana Auxiliary, 144
American Legion National Headquarters, 145
American Legion Nebraska, 147
American Legion Nebraska Auxiliary, 148
American Legion Nevada, 149
American Legion Nevada Auxiliary, 149
American Legion New Hampshire, 150

American Legion New Hampshire Auxiliary, 152
American Legion New Jersey, 153
American Legion New Jersey Auxiliary, 153
American Legion New Mexico Auxiliary, 154
American Legion New York, 154
American Legion New York Auxiliary, 155
American Legion North Carolina, 155
American Legion North Carolina Auxiliary, 156
American Legion North Dakota, 156
American Legion North Dakota Auxiliary, 157
American Legion Ohio, 157
American Legion Ohio Auxiliary, 157
American Legion Oregon, 158
American Legion Oregon Auxiliary, 158
American Legion Pennsylvania, 159
American Legion Pennsylvania Auxiliary, 159
American Legion Puerto Rico Auxiliary, 160
American Legion Rhode Island, 160
American Legion Rhode Island Auxiliary, 160
American Legion South Carolina, 160
American Legion South Carolina Auxiliary, 161
American Legion South Dakota, 161, 593
American Legion South Dakota Auxiliary, 161
American Legion Tennessee, 162
American Legion Tennessee Auxiliary, 163
American Legion Texas, 163
American Legion Texas Auxiliary, 163
American Legion Utah Auxiliary, 164
American Legion Vermont, 164
American Legion Virginia, 164
American Legion Virginia Auxiliary, 165
American Legion Washington, 166
American Legion Washington Auxiliary, 166
American Legion West Virginia, 167
American Legion West Virginia Auxiliary, 168
American Legion Wisconsin, 168
American Legion Wisconsin Auxiliary, 169
American Legion Wyoming, 170
American Legion Wyoming Auxiliary, 170
American Medical Technologists, 171
American Meteorological Society, 171
American Military Retirees Association, 172
American Morgan Horse Institute, 172
American Museum of Natural History, 173, 551
American Nuclear Society, 173
American Physical Society, 177
American Public Power Association, 178
American Quarter Horse Foundation, 178
American Radio Relay League (ARRL) Foundation, Inc., 178
American Respiratory Care Foundation, 192
American Society for Enology and Viticulture, 193
American Society for Microbiology, 193
American Society of Civil Engineers, 194
American Society of Heating, Refrigerating, and Air-Conditioning Engineers, Inc., 195
American Society of Interior Designers Foundation, Inc., 198
American Society of International Law, 551
American Society of Naval Engineers, 199
American Water Ski Educational Foundation, 199
American Welding Society Foundation, Inc., 200
Americans for the Arts, 551
Angie Houtz Memorial Fund, 205
Annie's Homegrown, 205
Appaloosa Youth Foundation, 205
Applied Arts, 554
Applied Materials, 555
Arkansas Department of Higher Education, 205
Armed Forces Communications and Electronics Association, 207
Armenian General Benevolent Union (AGBU), 209
ARMY Emergency Relief, 209
The Art Institutes, 210
Arthur and Doreen Parrett Scholarship Trust Fund, 210
Arts and Business Council of New York, 555
The ASCAP Foundation, 210
ASCO Numatics, 211
Asian American Journalists Association, 211, 555
Asian American Journalists Association, Texas Chapter, 212
ASM Materials Education Foundation, 212
ASME Auxiliary, Inc., 214, 593
ASME Foundation, 215, 593
Associated General Contractors Education and Research Foundation, 219
Associated General Contractors of Maine Education Foundation, 220
The Associated Press Television and Radio Association, 220
Association for Library and Information Science Education, 220
Association for Women in Architecture Foundation, 221
Association for Women in Communications, 222
Association of American Geographers, 222
Association of Insurance Compliance Professionals, 223
Association of State Dam Safety Officials, 223
AXA Achievement Scholarship, 223
Ayn Rand Institute, 224
Barry M. Goldwater Scholarship and Excellence In Education Foundation, 225
Bernstein-Rein Advertising, 556
Best Buy, 225
Bethesda Lutheran Communities, 225
BioCommunications Association, Inc., 225
Black & Veatch Corporation, 556
Blinded Veterans Association, 226
BlueScope Foundation, N.A., 226
BMI Foundation, Inc., 226
Board of Governors of the Federal Reserve System, 556
Boeing Company, 556
Boston Globe, 556
Boy Scouts of America Patriots' Path Council, 227
Boys and Girls Clubs of Greater San Diego, 227
Brandon Goodman Scholarship, 228
Bridgestone, 228
Broadcast Education Association, 228
Brown and Caldwell, 229
Building Industry Association, 230
Bureau of Indian Education, 230
Bureau of Indian Education-Oklahoma Area Education Office, 230
California Association of Realtors Scholarship Foundation, 231
California Farm Bureau Federation, 231
California Student Aid Commission, 231
California Teachers Association, 233
Carl's Jr. Restaurants, 234
Catching the Dream, 234
Catholic United Financial, 235
CCNMA: Latino Journalists of California, 235
Center for Architecture, 236
The Center for Reintegration, 236
Central Intelligence Agency, 237
C.G. Fuller Foundation c/o Bank of America, 237
ChairScholars Foundation, Inc., 237
The Charles A. and Anne Morrow Lindbergh Foundation, 238
Charles & Lucille King Family Foundation, Inc., 238
Charleston Women in International Trade, 238
Choctaw Nation of Oklahoma, 238
Christian Record Services, 239
Citizens for Global Solutions, 557
The Coca-Cola Foundation, 239
College Foundation of North Carolina, 240
Colorado Commission on Higher Education, 240

Colorado Council on High School and College Relations, 240
Colorado Masons' Benevolent Fund Association, 240
Colorado Society of CPAs Educational Foundation, 241
Columbus Citizens Foundation, 241
Congressional Black Caucus Foundation, Inc., 242
Congressional Hispanic Caucus Institute, 243, 557
Congressional Institute, Inc., 557
Connecticut Building Congress, Inc., 243
Connecticut Office of Higher Education, 243
ConocoPhillips, 245
Consortium of Information and Telecommunication Executives, 245
Construction Institute of ASCE, 245
Costume Society of America, 246
Council on International Educational Exchange, 246
Courage Center, 248
Courage to Grow, 248
Cushman School, 557
The Cynthia E. Morgan Memorial Scholarship Fund, 248
Cystic Fibrosis Foundation, 249
The Dallas Foundation, 249
Daniels Fund, 251
Data Processing Management Association/Portland Chapter, 251
Daughters of Union Veterans of the Civil War 1861-1865, 251
Davidson Institute, 251
Davis-Roberts Scholarship Fund, 252
Delaware Higher Education Office, 252, 594
Denver Rescue Mission, 558
Distinguished Young Women, 253
District of Columbia Higher Education Financial Services, 254
Do Something Scholarships, 254
Dolphin Scholarship Foundation, 254
Dow Jones News Fund, 558
DuPont Company, 559
Eastern Orthodox Committee on Scouting, 255
Eastman Kodak Company, 559
Edmund F. Maxwell Foundation, 255
Elie Wiesel Foundation for Humanity, 256
Elizabeth Greenshields Foundation, 256
Elks National Foundation, 256
Engineers Foundation of Ohio, 257
Entergy, 560
Entertainment Weekly, 560
The Entomological Foundation, 257
The Environmental Institute for Golf, 257
Epilepsy Foundation, 258
Epilepsy Foundation of San Diego County, 258
EqualityMaine Foundation, 259
ESA Foundation, 259
ESPN Inc., 560
Essence Magazine, 560
Executive Women International, 259
Experimental Aircraft Association, 259
Explorers Club, 261
Federal Employee Education and Assistance Fund, 261
Federal Reserve Bank of New York, 560
Feminist Majority Foundation, 561
Filoli, 561
Financial Service Centers of New York, 262
First Catholic Slovak Ladies Association, 262
Fisher Communications, Inc., 262
Florida Department of Education, 263, 561
Folds of Honor Foundation, 266
Foreclosure.com, 266
Foundation for Surgical Technology, 266
Foundation of the National Student Nurses Association, Inc., 266
Fox Group, 562
Francis Ouimet Scholarship Fund, 267
Franklin D. Roosevelt Library, 562
Franklin Lindsay Student Aid Fund, 594
Fred G. Zahn Foundation, 267
Freedom From Religion Foundation, 267
Future Farmers of America, 268
Garden Club Federation of Massachusetts Scholarships, 286
Garden Club of America, 286, 562
The Gates Millennium Scholars, 289
Genentech, Inc., 562
General Motors Foundation, 289
Georgia Student Finance Commission, 289
Glamour Magazine, 291
Golden Apple, 291
Golden Key International Honour Society, 292
Grand Encampment of Knights Templar of the USA, 594
Grange Insurance Association, 293
Great Minds in STEM, 294
Greater Kanawha Valley Foundation, 294
Greenhouse Scholars, 294
Hannaford Bros. Co., 562
Harness Tracks of America, 294
Havana National Bank, 295
Hawaii Community Foundation, 295
The Heart of America Foundation, 323
Helicopter Association International, 323
Herschel C. Price Educational Foundation, 324
Hispanic Association of Colleges and Universities, 324, 563
Hispanic College Fund, 325
Hispanic Heritage Foundation, 326
Hispanic Scholarship Fund, 326
Hoffman-La Roche Inc., 563
Hopi Tribe Grants and Scholarship Program, 331
Horatio Alger Association, 332
Horticultural Research Institute, 336
Houston Livestock Show and Rodeo, 338
IBM, 563
ICMA Retirement Corporation, 339
Idaho State Board of Education, 339
Illinois Department of Veterans' Affairs, 341
Illinois Student Assistance Commission, 341
Immune Deficiency Foundation, 343
The Indianapolis Star, 563
INROADS, Inc., 564
Institute of Food Technologists, 343
Institute of Human Studies, 564
Insurance Scholarship Foundation of America, 344
International Association of Fire Fighters, 344
International Buckskin Horse Association, Inc., 345
International Executive Housekeepers Association, 345
International Foodservice Editorial Council, 345
International Furnishings and Design Association Educational Foundation, 346
International Order of the King's Daughters and Sons, 347
International Radio and Television Society Foundation, 564
Intertribal Timber Council, 347
Iowa College Student Aid Commission, 348
Italian Catholic Federation, 349
IUE-CWA, 349
J. Paul Getty Trust, 564
Jack Kent Cooke Foundation, 350
Jackie Robinson Foundation, 351
James Beard Foundation, 351
James F. Byrnes Foundation, 356
Jaycee War Memorial Fund, 356
Jeannette Rankin Foundation, 357
Jewish Family and Children's Services (JFCS), 595
Jewish Guild Healthcare, 357
Jewish Vocational Service, 357
Jewish War Veterans of the United States of America, 358
The John F. Kennedy Center for the Performing Arts, 565
John F. Kennedy Library Foundation, 565
John Wiley and Sons, Inc., 565
Johnson Controls, 566
Johnson Scholarship Foundation, 359
Kansas Board of Regents, 359
Kappa Kappa Gamma Foundation, 361
KarMel Scholarship Committee, 362
Kentucky Higher Education Assistance Authority (KHEAA), 362, 566
The Kim and Harold Louie Family Foundation, 364
Kosciuszko Foundation, 364
The Lagrant Foundation, 365

Lambda Alpha National Collegiate Honors Society for Anthropology, 365
Landscape Architecture Foundation, 366
Latin American Educational Foundation, 368
League of United Latin American Citizens, 368
Learning Ally, 369
Learning for Life, 369
Life and Health Insurance Foundation for Education, 370
Lighthouse International, 370
Los Padres Foundation, 371
Louis Carr Internship Foundation (LCIF), 566
Louisiana Department of Veterans Affairs, 371
Louisiana Office of Student Financial Assistance, 372
Lowe's, 373
Macy's, Inc., 566
Maine Division of Veterans Services, 374
Maine Educational Loan Authority, 595
Maine Innkeepers Association, 374
Maine Metal Products Association Education Fund, 374
Maine Society of Professional Engineers, 375
Maine State Society of Washington, D.C., 375
Makovsky & Company Inc., 567
Marine Corps Scholarship Foundation, 375
Maryland Higher Education Commission Office of Student Financial Assistance, 375
Massachusetts Board of Higher Education, 378, 595
MCC Theater, 567
McKee Scholars, 383
Mendez Scholarships Non-Profit, 383
Menominee Indian Tribe of Wisconsin, 383
The Merchants Exchange, 384
Metropolitan Museum of Art, 567
Michael and Susan Dell Foundation, 384
Michigan Higher Education Assistance Authority, 384
Michigan Society of Professional Engineers, 385
Microscopy Society of America, 385
Microsoft Corporation, 386
Midwestern Higher Education Compact, 386
Military Officers Association of America, 386, 595
Military Order of the Purple Heart, 387
Minnesota Department of Veterans Affairs, 387
Minnesota Office of Higher Education, 387, 568, 596
Miss America Organization, 389
Mississippi Office of Student Financial Aid, 389, 596
Missouri Department of Higher Education, 390
Missouri League for Nursing, 392
Montana Trappers Association, 393
Montana University System, 393
The Moody's Foundation, 394
Morgan Stanley, 394
Morris Arboretum of the University of Pennsylvania, 568
Mother Jones, 570
Museum of Modern Art, 570
NAACP Legal Defense and Education Fund, Inc., 395
NASA Alabama Space Grant Consortium, 395
NASA Arizona Space Grant Consortium, 571
NASA Connecticut Space Grant Consortium, 395
NASA Delaware Space Grant Consortium, 396, 571
NASA Georgia Space Grant Consortium, 396
NASA Hawaii Space Grant Consortium, 396
NASA Idaho Space Grant Consortium, 397
NASA Illinois Space Grant Consortium, 397
NASA Kentucky Space Grant Consortium, 397
NASA Maine Space Grant Consortium, 397
NASA Michigan Space Grant Consortium, 398
NASA Minnesota Space Grant Consortium, 398
NASA Missouri Space Grant Consortium, 399
NASA Montana Space Grant Consortium, 399
NASA Nevada Space Grant Consortium, 399
NASA New Jersey Space Grant Consortium, 571
NASA New Mexico Space Grant Consortium, 400
NASA North Carolina Space Grant Consortium, 400
NASA North Dakota Space Grant Consortium, 401
NASA Ohio Space Grant Consortium, 401
NASA Oregon Space Grant Consortium, 402
NASA Pennsylvania Space Grant Consortium, 402, 572
NASA Rhode Island Space Grant Consortium, 402
NASA South Carolina Space Grant Consortium, 403
NASA Texas Space Grant Consortium, 403
NASA Utah Space Grant Consortium, 403
NASA Vermont Space Grant Consortium, 404
NASA Virginia Space Grant Consortium, 404
NASA West Virginia Space Grant Consortium, 405
NASA Wisconsin Space Grant Consortium, 405
National Academy for Nuclear Training, 406
National Amateur Baseball Federation, Inc., 406
National Association of Black Accountants Inc., 406
National Association of Black Journalists, 407, 572
National Association of Letter Carriers, 408
National Association of Water Companies (NJ Chapter), 409
National Association of Women in Construction, 409
National Athletic Trainers' Association Research & Education Foundation, 409
National Black Nurses Association, 410
National Commission for Cooperative Education, 410
National Dairy Shrine, 410
National Eagle Scout Association, 412
National Environmental Health Association/American Academy of Sanitarians, 412
National Federation of the Blind, 413
National FFA, 413
National Genealogical Society, 413
National Geographic Society, 572
National Ground Water Research and Education Foundation, 413
National Inventors Hall of Fame, 414
National Italian American Foundation, 414
National Jewish Committee on Scouting, Boy Scouts of America, 414
National Junior Classical League, 415
National Merit Scholarship Corporation, 416
National Museum of the American Indian, 572
National Museum of Women in the Arts, 573
National Poultry & Food Distributors Association, 416
National Press Photographers Foundation, 417
National Restaurant Association Educational Foundation, 417
National Rifle Association, 417
National Science Foundation, 573
National Science Teachers Association, 418
National Sculpture Society, 418
National Security Agency, 418
National Society of Accountants Scholarship Foundation, 419
National Society of the Sons of the American Revolution, 419
National Speakers Association, 419

National Stone, Sand & Gravel Association, 420
Navy Supply Corps Foundation, 420
Navy-Marine Corps Relief Society, 420, 597
NCR Corporation, 573
Nebraska Coordinating Commission for Postsecondary Education, 421
New Dramatists, 574
New England Board of Higher Education, 421
New England Employee Benefits Council, 421
New Jersey Commission on Higher Education, 422
New Jersey Higher Education Student Assistance Authority, 422, 597
New Jersey State Golf Association, 423
New Mexico Commission on Higher Education, 423, 574, 597
The New Republic, 574
New York State Assembly, 574
New York State Education Department, 425
New York State Grange, 425, 598
New York State Higher Education Services Corporation, 426
New York State Office of Adult Career and Educational Services, 428
New York Times, 575
New York Women in Communications Foundation, 428
NextEra Energy, 575
Nicodemus Wilderness Project, 429
Nisei Student Relocation Commemorative Fund, 429
NMIA Ohio, 429
Non Commissioned Officers Association, 430
North American Limousin Foundation, 430
North Carolina Community Colleges Foundation, 431
North Carolina Division of Veterans Affairs, 431
North Carolina Division of Vocational Rehabilitation Services, 431
North Carolina State Board of Refrigeration Examiners, 431
North Carolina State Education Assistance Authority, 432
North Dakota University System, 433
Northern Cheyenne Tribal Education Department, 435
Northwest Danish Association, 435
Oak Ridge Institute for Science and Education, 575
OCA, 435
Ohio Board of Regents, 436, 598
Ohio National Guard, 436
Ohio Newspapers Foundation, 437, 582
Oklahoma Engineering Foundation, 438
Oklahoma State Regents for Higher Education, 438
OMNE/Nursing Leaders of Maine, 440
One Family, 440
ONS Foundation, 440
Oracle Corporation, 582
Oregon Student Assistance Commission, 441
Organization for Autism Research, 448
The Orthotic and Prosthetic Education and Development Fund, 449
Osage Tribal Education Committee, 450
Owens Corning, 583
Pacific Gas and Electric Company, 583
Papercheck.com, 450
Par Aide, 450
Patient Advocate Foundation, 450
PBS, 583
Peacock Productions, Inc., 451
Pearson Foundation, 451
Penguin Putnam, Inc., 451
Pennsylvania Higher Education Assistance Agency, 452
Pennsylvania State System of Higher Education Foundation, Inc., 454
Pennsylvania State System of Higher Eduction, Inc., 455
Pennsylvania Women's Press Association, 456
PFLAG National Office, 456
PGA Tour, 583
The Phillips Foundation, 456
Phipps Conservatory and Botanical Gardens, 583
Pickett and Hatcher Educational Fund, Inc., 599
Plumbing-Heating-Cooling Contractors Educational Foundation, 456
Point Foundation, 457
Presbyterian Church (USA), 458, 599
Pride of the Greater Lehigh Valley, 459
The Princess Grace Foundation USA, 459
Princeton Plasma Physics Laboratory, 584
Print and Graphics Scholarship Foundation, 460
Professional Association of Georgia Educators Foundation, Inc., 460
Proof-Reading.com, 460
Quill and Scroll Foundation, 461
Radio Television Digital News Association (RTDNA), 461
Red River Valley Fighter Pilots Association, 462
Renee B. Fisher Foundation, 463
Restaurant Association of Maryland Education Foundation, 463
Rhode Island Higher Education Assistance Authority, 464
Rhode Island State Government, 584
Rocky Mountain Coal Mining Institute, 464
Roller Skating Foundation, 465
Roller Skating Foundation High School Senior Scholarship, 465
Ron Brown Scholar Fund, 465
Ronald McDonald House Charities (RMHC), 465
Sachs Foundation, 466
SAE International, 466
Salute to Education, Inc., 469
Scarlett Family Foundation Scholarship Program, 469
Scholarship America, 469
Screen Actors Guild Foundation, 469
Seabee Memorial Scholarship Association, Inc., 470
Second Marine Division Association, 470
Senator George J. Mitchell Scholarship Research Institute, 471
Seneca Nation and BIA, 471
Sertoma, 471
Shoshone Tribe, 472
Sid Richardson Memorial Fund, 472
Sidney B. Meadows Scholarship Endowment Fund, 472
Siemens Foundation, 473
Simon and Schuster Inc., 584
Slovak Gymnastic Union Sokol, USA, 473
Slovenian Women's Union of America, 474
SME Education Foundation, 474
Smithsonian Environmental Research Center, 585
Smithsonian Institution, 585
Sociedad Honoraria Hispanica, 481
Society for Range Management, 481
Society of Daughters of the United States Army, 481
Society of Exploraiton Geophysicists, 481
Society of Exploration Geophysicists, 482
Society of Physics Students, 485, 586
Society of Plastics Engineers, 486
The Society of the Descendants of the Signers of the Declaration of Independence, 489
Society of Women Engineers, 489
Sodexo Foundation, 489
Soil and Water Conservation Society, 489
Solomon R. Guggenheim Museum, 586
Sons of Italy Foundation, 490
Sons of Norway Foundation, 491
Sons of the Republic of Texas, 492
Sony Music Entertainment, 586
South Carolina Commission on Higher Education, 492
South Carolina Higher Education Tuition Grants Commission, 493
South Carolina Student Loan Corporation, 599
South Dakota Board of Regents, 494
Southern Regional Education Board, 495
Southern Scholarship Foundation, 496
Southface Energy Institute, 587
SPIE - The International Society for Optical Engineering, 496
Spoleto Festival USA, 587
Sports Journalism Institute, 587
Staples, 496
State Council of Higher Education for Virginia, 496
State of Alabama, 497

State Student Assistance Commission of Indiana, 497
Stephen T. Marchello Scholarship Foundation, 498
Student Aid Foundation, 599
Student Conservation Association, 587
Studio Art Centers International, 499
Sunkist Growers, 501
Supreme Guardian Council, International Order of Job's Daughters, 501
Swiss Benevolent Society of New York, 502
TAG Education Collaborative, 502
Taglit-Birthright Israel, 503
Tall Clubs International, 503
Tennessee Student Assistance Corporation, 503, 600
Texas 4-H Club, 505
Texas Association, Family Career and Community Leaders of America, 506
Texas Future Farmers of America, 507
Texas Higher Education Coordinating Board, 507, 601
Texas Historical Commission, 588
Third Marine Division Association, 511
Thurgood Marshall College Fund, 512
Time Inc., 588
Tourism Cares, 512
Transportation Clubs International, 517
Treacy Foundation, 518
Trinity Episcopal Church, 519
Two Ten Footwear Foundation, 519
Tyson Foods, Inc., 588
UCB Pharma Inc., 519
The Ulman Cancer Fund, 519
Unico Foundation, Inc., 520
Union Plus, 521
Unitarian Universalist Association, 521
United Federation of Teachers, 521
United Food and Commercial Workers International Union, 521
United Methodist Church, 601
United Methodist Church General Board of Higher Education and Ministry, 522
United Methodist Communications, 522
United Methodist Higher Education Foundation, 522
United Negro College Fund, 523
United States Army/ROTC, 523
United States Association of Blind Athletes, 523
United States Holocaust Memorial Museum, 588
United States Institute of Peace, 524
United States Senate, 589
United Transportation Union Insurance Association, 524
University Film and Video Association, 525
Upakar, 525
UPS, 601
U.S. Army Recruiting Command, 525
U.S. Department of Agriculture, 526
U.S. Department of Education, 526, 601
U.S. Department of Education Rehabilitation Services Administration, 527
U.S. Department of Health and Human Services, 527
U.S. Department of State, 589
U.S. Environmental Protection Agency, 527
U.S. House of Representatives, 589
U.S. National Arboretum, 590
U.S. Navy/Marine NROTC College Scholarship Program, 528
USTA Tennis and Education Foundation, 529
Utah Higher Education Assistance Authority (UHEAA), 529
Utah State Office of Education, 602
Utilities Employees Credit Union, 529
The Vegetarian Resource Group, 530
Ventura County Japanese-American Citizens League, 530
Vermont Golf Association Scholarship Fund, Inc., 530
Vermont Student Assistance Corporation, 531
Veterans of Foreign Wars, 535
Virgin Islands Board of Education, 535, 602
Virginia Department of Education, 535
Virginia Department of Health, 535
Virginia Museum of Fine Arts, 536
The Wall Street Journal, 590
Wal-Mart Foundation, 536
The Walt Disney Company, 591
Walt Disney World and Disneyland, 591
Washington Crossing Foundation, 537
Washington Internships for Students of Engineering, 591
Washington Media Scholars Foundation, 537
Washington State Higher Education Coordinating Board, 537
Washington State PTA, 538
Wells Fargo, 538, 591
Welsh Society of Philadelphia, 538
West Pharmaceutical Services, Inc., 539
West Virginia Department of Veterans Assistance, 539
West Virginia Higher Education Policy Commission, 539
Western European Architecture Foundation, 541
Western Golf Association/Evans Scholars Foundation, 541
Western Interstate Commission for Higher Education, 541
William Randolph Hearst Foundation, 541
Wilson Ornithological Society, 542
Wisconsin Department of Veterans Affairs, 542
Wisconsin Higher Educational Aids Board, 543, 602
Wolf Trap Foundation for the Performing Arts, 592
Women Grocers of America, 545
Women in Defense, A National Security Organization, 545
Women's Western Golf Foundation, 545
Woodrow Wilson National Fellowship Foundation, 545
The World Food Prize, 592
Worldstudio Foundation, 546
Wyzant Tutoring, 546
Xerox, 546
Yakama Nation Higher Education Program, 547

Program Index

10,000 Degrees Undergraduate Scholarships, 79
100th Infantry Battalion Memorial Scholarship Fund, 295
1st Marine Division Association Scholarship, 79
A & B Ohana Scholarship, 295
A+ Scholarship Program, 390
AAGS Joseph F. Dracup Scholarship Award, 98
AAJA Texas Student Scholarship, 212
AAJA/NBC Summer Partnership, 555
Abbie Sargent Memorial Scholarship, 80
ABC Stores Jumpstart Scholarship, 295
Abe Voron Scholarship, 228
Academic Common Market, 495
Academy of Nutrition and Dietetics Graduate, Baccalaureate or Coordinated Program Scholarships, 80
Academy of Television Arts & Sciences Student Internship Program, 549
Accel Program Grant, 289
Accelerator Applications Division Scholarship, 173
Access Missouri Financial Assistance Program, 391
Access to Better Learning and Education (ABLE) Grant Program, 263
Accountemps Student Scholarship, 117
ACEC Scholarship, 101
ACSM Fellows Scholarship, 98
Actuarial Diversity Scholarships, 81
Actuary of Tomorrow Stuart A. Robertson Memorial Scholarship, 82
Adele Filene Student Presenter Grant, 246
ADHA Institute for Oral Health Scholarship for Academic Excellence, 82
Adler Science and Math Scholarship, 137
AdOhio Advertising Internship, 582
Adopted Child Tuition Waiver and Fee Assistance Program, 378
Adrienne Alix Scholarship, 152
Advanced Placement Incentive Grant, 391
Advertising Internship, 556
Aerospace Undergraduate STEM Research Scholarship Program, 404
AETNA Nursing Scholarship, 324
AFA Teens for Alzheimer's Awareness College Scholarship, 95
AFCEA Intelligence Scholarship, 207
AFCEA Military Personnel & Dependents Scholarship, 207
AFCEA ROTC Scholarship, 207
AFCEA Scholarship for Underserved Students (HBCU), 208
AFCEA War Veterans/Disabled War Veterans Scholarship, 208
AFSA $20,000 High School Scholarship Contest, 102
AFSA $5,000 Second Chance Scholarship Contest, 102
AFSCMA/UNCF Union Scholars Program, 550
AFSCME Family Scholarship, 101
AfterCollege Business Student Scholarship, 85
AfterCollege Computer Science & Engineering Student Scholarship, 85
AfterCollege Electrical Engineering Student Scholarship, 85
AfterCollege Engineering Scholarship, 85
AfterCollege Medical Technologist & Clinical Lab Scientist Student Scholarship, 86
AfterCollege Pharmacy Student Scholarship, 86
AfterCollege Science Student Scholarship, 86
AfterCollege Speech Language Pathology Student Scholarship, 86
AfterCollege/AACN Nursing Student Scholarships, 86
AG Bell College Scholarship Awards, 92
AGBU International Scholarships, 209
AGC Education and Research Undergraduate Scholarship, 219
AGC of Maine Scholarship Program, 220
AGCO Scholarships, 268
Agnes M. Lindsey Scholarship, 378
Agnes Malakate Kezios Scholarship, 214
Agricredit Acceptance LLC Scholarship, 268
Agrium U.S. Inc. Scholarship, 268
AHEPA Educational Foundation Scholarships, 109
AHIMA Student Merit Scholarships, 87
Ahmad-Sehar Saleha Ahmad and Abrahim Ekramullah Zafar Foundation, 441
AIA New Jersey Scholarship Foundation, 117
AIAA Foundation Undergraduate Scholarship, 116
AIA/AAF Minority/Disadvantaged Scholarship, 117
AICP Heartland Chapter Jim Latteman Scholarship, 223
AICP Scholarship, 223
Aiea General Hospital Association Scholarship, 296
Air Force Research Laboratory, 711 Human Performance Wing, 575
Air Force Sergeants Association Scholarship, Airmen Memorial Foundation, and Chief Master Sergeants of the Air Force Scholarship Programs, 84
Air Force/ROTC Four-Year Scholarship (Types 1, 2, and 7), 87
Air Traffic Control Full-Time Employee Student Scholarship, 88
Air Traffic Control Non-Employee Student Scholarship, 88
Airgas-Jerry Baker Scholarship, 200
Airgas-Terry Jarvis Memorial Scholarship, 200
AISES Google Scholarship, 114
AIWF Culinary Scholarship, 531
Al Schulman Ecolab First-Time Freshmen Entrepeneurial Scholarship, 417
Al Schuman Ecolab Undergraduate Entrepeneurial Scholarship, 417
Alabama G.I. Dependents' Scholarship Program, 92
Alabama Institutional Scholarship Waivers, 91
Alabama Junior/Community College Athletic Scholarship, 91
Alabama National Guard Educational Assistance Program, 90
Alabama Scholarship for Dependents of Blind Parents, 497
Alabama Student Assistance Program, 91
Alabama Student Grant Program, 91
Alaska Boys State Scholarship, 120
Alaska Performance Scholarship, 92
AlaskAdvantage Education Grant, 92
Albert E. Wischmeyer Memorial Scholarship Award, 474
The Albert H. Hix, W8AH, Memorial Scholarship, 178
Albert M. Lappin Scholarship, 133
Albert Shanker College Scholarship Fund, 521
Albert T. Marcoux Memorial Scholarship, 150
Albina Fuel Company Scholarship, 441
Alexander M. Tanger Scholarship, 228
Alexia Foundation Grant and Scholarship, 93
The Alfred E. Friend, Jr., W4CF Memorial Scholarship, 179

Alfred T. Granger Student Art Fund Scholarship, 531
Alice Glaisyer Warfield Memorial Scholarship, 517
ALISE Bohdan S. Wynar Research Paper Competition, 220
ALISE Research Grant, 221
ALISE/Dialog Methodology Paper Competition, 221
All Iowa Opportunity Scholarship, 348
Allan Eldin & Agnes Sutorik Geiger Scholarship Fund, 296
Allcott/Hunt Share It Now II Scholarship, 441
The Allen and Bertha Watson Memorial Scholarship, 179
Allen and Loureena Weber Scholarship, 474
Allen J. Baldwin Scholarship, 214
Allen Rhodes Memorial Scholarship, 215
Allen Susser Scholarship, 351
Allison E. Fisher Scholarship, 407
Allman Medical Scholarships, 389
Allstate Internships, 549
Alma White-Delta Kappa Gamma Scholarship, 296
Aloha Scholarship, 144
ALPFA Scholarship, 326
Alpha Beta Gamma National Scholarship, 94
Alpha Gamma Rho Educational Foundation Scholarship, 268
Alpha Mu Gamma Scholarships, 94
Alphonse A. Miele Scholarship, 520
Alumnae Panhellenic Association Women's Scholarship, 94
Alvin and June Sabroff Manufacturing Engineering Scholarship, 474
Alwin B. Newton Scholarship, 195
Ambassador Minerva Jean Falcon Hawaii Scholarship, 296
AMBUCS Scholars-Scholarship for Therapists, 95
American Association of Advertising Agencies Multicultural Advertising Intern Program, 549
American Bar Foundation Summer Research Diversity Fellowships in Law and Social Sciences for Undergraduate Students, 550
American Board of Funeral Service Education National Scholarship, 96
American Chemical Society Scholars Program, 97
American Conservatory Theater Production Fellowships, 550
American Electric Power Scholarship, 215
American Express Scholarship Competition, 109
American Family Insurance Scholarship, 269
American Federation of State, County, and Municipal Employees (AFSCME) Oregon Council #75, 441
American Florists' Exchange Scholarship, 102
American Hotel & Lodging Educational Foundation Incoming Freshman Scholarship Competition, 109
American Institute of Certified Public Accountants Scholarship for Minority Accounting Students, 118
American Institute of Graphic Arts (AIGA) Honolulu Chapter Scholarship Fund, 296
American Legion Alabama Auxiliary Scholarship, 119
American Legion Alabama Oratorical Contest, 119
American Legion Alabama Scholarship, 119
American Legion Alaska Auxiliary Scholarship, 120
American Legion Alaska Auxiliary Western District Scholarship, 120
American Legion Alaska Oratorical Contest, 120
American Legion Arizona Auxiliary Health Care Occupation Scholarship, 121
American Legion Arizona Auxiliary Nurses' Scholarship, 121
American Legion Arizona Oratorical Contest, 120
American Legion Arkansas Auxiliary Scholarships, 122
American Legion Arkansas Oratorical Contest, 121
American Legion Auxiliary National Presidents Scholarship, 145
American Legion Auxiliary Spirit of Youth Scholarship for Junior Members, 145
American Legion California Auxiliary General Scholarships, 123
American Legion California Oratorical Contest, 122
American Legion Colorado Auxiliary Department President's Scholarship, 123
American Legion Colorado Auxiliary Department President's Scholarship for Junior Auxiliary Members, 124
American Legion Colorado Auxiliary Past Presidents Parley Nurse's Scholarship, 124
American Legion Colorado National High School Oratorical Contest, 123
American Legion Connecticut Auxiliary Memorial Education Grant, 124
American Legion Connecticut Auxiliary Past Presidents Parley Education Grant, 125
American Legion Connecticut National High School Oratorical Contest, 124
American Legion Coudret Trust Scholarship, 122
American Legion Delaware Auxiliary Past Presidents Parley Nursing Scholarship, 125
American Legion Department of Iowa Scholarships, 132
American Legion Department of Massachusetts Oratorical Contest, 138
American Legion Department Oratorical Contest, 158
American Legion District of Columbia National High School Oratorical Contest, 125
American Legion Eagle Scout of the Year, 146
American Legion Florida Auxiliary Department Scholarships, 126
American Legion Florida Auxiliary Memorial Scholarship, 126
American Legion Florida Eagle Scout of the Year, 125
American Legion Florida General Scholarship, 126
American Legion Florida High School Oratorical Contest, 126
American Legion Georgia Auxiliary Past Presidents Parley Nurses Scholarship, 127
American Legion Georgia Oratorical Contest, 127
American Legion Georgia Scholarship, 127
American Legion Hawaii Oratorical Contest, 127
American Legion Idaho Auxiliary Nurse's Scholarship, 128
American Legion Idaho Oratorical Contest, 127
American Legion Idaho Scholarships, 128
American Legion Illinois Auxiliary Ada Mucklestone Memorial Scholarship, 129
American Legion Illinois Auxiliary Special Education Teaching Scholarships, 129
American Legion Illinois Auxiliary Student Nurse Scholarship, 129
American Legion Illinois Boy Scout Scholarship, 128
American Legion Illinois Oratorical Contest, 128
American Legion Illinois Scholarships, 128
American Legion Indiana Americanism and Government Test, 130
American Legion Indiana Auxiliary Past Presidents Parley Nursing Scholarship, 131
American Legion Indiana Eagle Scout of the Year Scholarship, 130
American Legion Indiana Family Scholarship, 130
American Legion Indiana Oratorical Contest, 130
American Legion Iowa Auxiliary Past President's Scholarship, 132
American Legion Iowa Boy Scout of the Year Scholarship, 131
American Legion Iowa Oratorical Contest, 131

American Legion Iowa Outstanding Citizen of Boys State Scholarship, 132
American Legion Kansas Auxiliary Department Scholarships, 135
American Legion Kansas Music Scholarship, 133
American Legion Kansas Oratorical Contest, 133
American Legion Kentucky Auxiliary Mary Barrett Marshall Scholarship, 135
American Legion Kentucky Department Oratorical Awards, 135
American Legion Legacy Scholarship, 146
American Legion Maine Auxiliary Presidents Parley Nursing Scholarship, 136
American Legion Maine Auxiliary Scholarship, 136
American Legion Maine Children and Youth Scholarship, 136
American Legion Maryland Auxiliary Past Presidents Parley Scholarship, 138
American Legion Maryland Auxiliary Scholarship, 138
American Legion Maryland Boys State Scholarship, 137
American Legion Maryland Oratorical Contest, 137
American Legion Maryland Scholarship, 137
American Legion Massachusetts Auxiliary Past Presidents Parley Scholarship, 139
American Legion Massachusetts Auxiliary Scholarship, 139
American Legion Massachusetts General and Nursing Scholarships, 138
American Legion Michigan Auxiliary Medical Career Scholarships, 140
American Legion Michigan Auxiliary Memorial Scholarship, 140
American Legion Michigan Auxiliary National President's Scholarship, 140
American Legion Michigan Oratorical Contest, 139
American Legion Minnesota Auxiliary Department Scholarship, 141
American Legion Minnesota Auxiliary Past Presidents Parley Health Care Scholarship, 141
American Legion Minnesota Legionnaire Insurance Trust Scholarship, 140
American Legion Minnesota Memorial Scholarship, 141
American Legion Minnesota Oratorical Contest, 141
American Legion Mississippi Auxiliary Scholarship, 141
American Legion Missouri Auxiliary National President's Scholarship, 144
American Legion Missouri Auxiliary Past Presidents Parley Scholarship, 144
American Legion Missouri Auxiliary Scholarship, 144
American Legion Missouri Commander's Scholarship Fund, 142
American Legion Missouri Oratorical Contest, 142
American Legion Montana Auxiliary Scholarships (1), 145
American Legion Montana Auxiliary Scholarships (2), 145
American Legion National High School Oratorical Contest, 146
American Legion Nebraska Auxiliary Graduate Scholarship, 148
American Legion Nebraska Auxiliary Junior Member Scholarship, 148
American Legion Nebraska Auxiliary Nurse Gift Tuition Scholarships, 148
American Legion Nebraska Auxiliary Practical Nursing Scholarship, 148
American Legion Nebraska Auxiliary Student Aid Grant or Vocational Technical Scholarship, 148
American Legion Nebraska Oratorical Contest, 147
American Legion Nebraska President's Scholarship, 148
American Legion Nevada Auxiliary Past Presidents Parley Nurses' Scholarship, 149
American Legion Nevada Auxiliary President's Scholarship, 150
American Legion Nevada Oratorical Contest, 149
American Legion New Hampshire Auxiliary Past Presidents Parley Nurses' Scholarship, 152
American Legion New Hampshire Boys State Scholarship, 150
American Legion New Hampshire Department Vocational Scholarship, 150
American Legion New Hampshire Oratorical Contest, 150
American Legion New Jersey Auxiliary Department Scholarships, 153
American Legion New Jersey Auxiliary Past Presidents Parley Nurses' Scholarship, 153
American Legion New Jersey Department of New Jersey Scholarship, 153
American Legion New Jersey Oratorical Contest, 153
American Legion New Mexico Auxiliary National Presidents Scholarship, 154
American Legion New Mexico Auxiliary Past President's Parley Scholarship for Nurses, 154
American Legion New York Auxiliary Past Presidents Parley Student Scholarship in Medical Field, 155
American Legion New York Auxiliary Scholarship, 155
American Legion New York Oratorical Contest, 154
American Legion North Carolina Oratorical Contest, 155
American Legion North Dakota Auxiliary Past Presidents Parley Scholarship, 157
American Legion North Dakota Auxiliary Scholarships, 157
American Legion North Dakota Oratorical Contest, 156
American Legion Ohio Auxiliary Department President's Scholarship, 157
American Legion Ohio Auxiliary Past Presidents Parley Nurse's Scholarship, 158
American Legion Ohio Department Oratorical Awards, 157
American Legion Ohio Scholarships, 157
American Legion Oregon Auxiliary Department Nurses Scholarship, 158
American Legion Oregon Auxiliary National President's Scholarship, 158
American Legion Pennsylvania High School Oratorical Contest, 119
American Legion Puerto Rico Auxiliary Nursing Scholarships, 160
American Legion Rhode Island Auxiliary Book Award, 160
American Legion Rhode Island Oratorical Contest, 160
American Legion Scholarship for Non-Traditional Students, 146
American Legion South Carolina Auxiliary Scholarship, 161
American Legion South Carolina Department Oratorical Contest, 160
American Legion South Dakota Auxiliary Scholarships, 161
American Legion South Dakota Auxiliary Senior Member Scholarship, 161
American Legion South Dakota Educational Loan, 593
American Legion South Dakota Oratorical Contest, 161
American Legion Tennessee Eagle Scout of the Year Scholarship, 162
American Legion Tennessee Oratorical Contest, 162
American Legion Texas Auxiliary General Education Scholarship, 163
American Legion Texas Oratorical Contest, 163
American Legion Texas Past Presidents Parley Scholarship, 163
American Legion Utah Auxiliary National President's Scholarship, 164
American Legion Vermont Eagle Scout of the Year, 164
American Legion Vermont National High School Oratorical Contest, 164
American Legion Vermont Scholarship, 164

American Legion Virginia Auxiliary Past Presidents Parley Nurse's Scholarship, 165
American Legion Virginia Oratorical Contest, 164
American Legion Washington Auxiliary Scholarships, 166
American Legion Washington Children and Youth Scholarship Fund, 166
American Legion Washington Department Oratorical Contest, 166
American Legion West Virginia Auxiliary Scholarship, 168
American Legion West Virginia Oratorical Contest, 167
American Legion Western District Postsecondary Scholarship, 120
American Legion Wisconsin Auxiliary Department President's Scholarship, 169
American Legion Wisconsin Auxiliary H.S. and Angeline Lewis Scholarships, 169
American Legion Wisconsin Auxiliary Merit and Memorial Scholarship, 169
American Legion Wisconsin Auxiliary Past Presidents Parley R.N. Scholarship, 169
American Legion Wisconsin Baseball Scholarship, 168
American Legion Wisconsin Eagle Scout of the Year Scholarship, 168
American Legion Wisconsin Oratorical Contest Scholarships, 168
American Legion Wyoming Auxiliary Past Presidents Parley Scholarship, 170
American Legion Wyoming E.A. Blackmore Memorial Scholarship, 170
American Legion Wyoming Oratorical Contest, 170
American Medical Technologists Student Scholarship, 171
American Meteorological Society Freshman Undergraduate Scholarship Program, 171
American Meteorological Society Named Undergraduate Scholarship, 171
American Meteorological Society/Industry Minority Scholarship, 172
American Nuclear Society Operations and Power Division Scholarship, 174
American Quarter Horse Foundation Scholarships, 178
American Restaurant Scholarship, 351
American Society for Enology and Viticulture Scholarship Program, 193
American Society for Microbiology Undergraduate Research Fellowship (URF), 193
American Society of Interior Designers Legacy Scholarship for Undergraduates, 198
American Society of International Law Internships, 551
American Veterinary Medical Association Scholarship, 269
American Water Ski Educational Foundation Scholarship, 199
American Welding Society District Scholarship Program, 200
Americanism Essay Contest Scholarship, 129
Americans for the Arts Arts Action Fund Internship, 552
Americans for the Arts Arts & Business Council of New York Internship, 551
Americans for the Arts Arts Marketing Internship, 552
Americans for the Arts Arts Policy Internship, 552
Americans for the Arts Development Internship, 552
Americans for the Arts Government and Public Affairs Internship, 553
Americans for the Arts Leadership Alliances Internship, 553
Americans for the Arts Local Arts Advancement Services Internship, 553
Americans for the Arts Marketing and Communications Internship, 553
Americans for the Arts Meetings and Events/Executive Office Internship, 553
Americans for the Arts Membership Internship, 554
Americans for the Arts Private-Sector Initiatives Internship, 554
Americans for the Arts Research Services Internship, 554
Ameriprise Financial and AGSTAR Financial Services, Inc. Scholarship, 269
AMHI Educational Scholarships, 172
AMHI van Schaik Dressage Scholarship, 173
Amtrol Scholarship, 108
Anadarko/SEG Scholarship, 482
The Andersons, Inc. Scholarship, 269
Androscoggin Amateur Radio Club Scholarship, 179
Angelo S. Bisesti Scholarship, 174
Angie Houtz Scholarship, 205
Animal Health International Scholarship, 270
Anna Gear Junior Scholarship, 165
Anna K. Meredith Fund Scholarship, 499
Anne U. White Fund, 222
Annie's Homegrown Sustainable Agriculture Scholarships, 205
Anonymous Foundation Scholarship, 110
ANS Decommissioning, Decontamination and Reutilization Scholarship, 174
ANS Incoming Freshman Scholarship, 174
ANS Undergraduate Scholarships, 174
ANS Washington, D.C. Section Undergraduate Scholarship, 175
Anthony A. Welmas Scholarship, 110
Anthropology Internship Program, 551
Appaloosa Youth Foundation Educational Scholarships, 205
Applied Arts Internships, 554
Applied Materials Internship and Co-op Program, 555
Apprentice Ecologist Initiative, 429
APTRA-Clete Roberts/Kathryn Dettman Memorial Journalism Scholarship, 220
Arabian Horse Association (Region 14) Scholarship, 270
Arboriculture Internship, 568
Archer Daniels Midland Company Scholarships, 270
Area Go Texan Scholarships, 338
Arizona Chapter Vertical Flight Engineering Scholarship, 108
Arizona Public Service Navajo Scholars Program, 111
Arkansas Academic Challenge Scholarship, 205
Arkansas Governor's Scholars Program, 206
Arkansas Law Enforcement Officers' Dependents Scholarship, 206
Arkansas Military Dependents Scholarship Program, 206
Arkansas Second Effort Scholarship, 206
Arkansas Workforce Improvement Grant, 207
Armenian General Benevolent Union Performing Arts Fellowships, 209
The ARRL Earl I. Anderson Scholarship, 179
ARRL Foundation General Fund Scholarship, 179
ARRL Foundation PHD Scholarship, 180
The ARRL Northwestern Division Scholarship Fund, 180
The ARRL Scholarship to Honor Barry Goldwater, K7UGA, 180
Arsham Amirikian Engineering Scholarship, 200
Arthur and Doreen Parrett Scholarship, 210
Arthur and Gladys Cervenka Scholarship, 475
Arthur and Helen Copeland Scholarship, 523
Arthur E. Copeland Scholarship, 524
Arthur Jackman Memorial Scholarship, 297
Arthur K. Gilkey Memorial/Bedayn Research Grants, 95
Arthur M. and Berdena King Eagle Scout Scholarship, 419
Arthur Patch McKinlay Scholarship, 97
Artistic and Administrative Fellowships, 550
Arts and Business Council of New York Multicultural Arts Management Internship Program, 555

Program Index

Arysta LifeScience North America Scholarship, 270
ASDSO Undergraduate Scholarship, 223
ASHRAE Engineering Technology Scholarships, 196
ASHRAE General Scholarships, 196
ASHRAE Memorial Scholarship, 196
ASHRAE Region IV Benny Bootle Scholarship, 196
ASHRAE Region VIII Scholarship, 196
Asian American Journalists Association Print & Online News Grants, 211
ASLA Council of Fellows Scholarship, 366
ASM Outstanding Scholars Awards, 212
ASME Auxiliary Student Loan Fund, 593
ASME Auxiliary/FIRST Clarke Scholarship, 216
The ASME Foundation Hanley Scholarship, 216
ASME Foundation Scholarships, 216
ASME Metropolitan Section John Rice Memorial Scholarship, 216
ASME Power Division Scholarship, 217
ASME Student Loan Program, 593
ASNE Scholarship, 199
Aspiring Sports Journalist Internship, 587
ASTA Alaska Airlines Scholarship, 512
ASTA American Express Travel Scholarship, 512
ASTA Arizona Scholarship, 513
ASTA Northern California Chapter - Richard Epping Scholarship, 513
ASTA Pacific Northwest Chapter/William Hunt Scholarship, 513
ASTA Princess Cruises Scholarship, 513
Astrid G. Cates Scholarship Fund and Myrtle Beinhauer Scholarship, 491
A.T. Anderson Memorial Scholarship, 114
AT&T Foundation Scholarship, 326
Athletic Trainers' Entry Level Scholarship, 409
Atlas Shrugged Essay Contest, 224
Audria M. Edwards Scholarship Fund, 451
Austin Family Scholarship Endowment, 111
Averyl Elaine Keriakedes Memorial Scholarship, 149
A.W. Bodine Sunkist Memorial Scholarship, 501
Award of Excellence Scholarship, 344
AXA Achievement Scholarship in Association with U.S. News & World Report, 223
Azurea at One Ocean Resort Hotel & Spa Scholarship, 351
B. Bradford Barnes Scholarship, 252
B. Charles Tiney Memorial ASCE Student Chapter Scholarship, 194
Bal Dasa Scholarship Fund, 297
Ball Horticultural Company Scholarship, 103
Bandon Submarine Cable Council Scholarship, 441
Baroid Scholarship, 108
Barry K. Wendt Commitment Award and Scholarship, 420
Barry M. Goldwater Scholarship, 225
BEA Founders Award, 228
Beck's Hybrids Scholarship, 270
Behavioral Sciences Student Fellowship, 258
Behlen Mfg. Co./Walter and Ruby Behlen Memorial Scholarship, 271
Ben Selling Scholarship, 442
Benjamin Franklin/Edith Green Scholarship, 442
Bern Laxer Memorial Scholarship, 351
Berna Lou Cartwright Scholarship, 215
Bernard B. Jacobs Internship Program, 574
Berntsen International Scholarship in Surveying, 99
Berntsen International Scholarship in Surveying Technology, 99
Bertha P. Singer Scholarship, 442
Best Buy Scholarship Program, 225
Best Teen Chef Culinary Scholarship Competition, 210
The Betty Weatherford, KQ6RE, Memorial Scholarship, 180
BG Scholarship, 228
BIA Cares of San Diego Scholarship, 230
Bick Bickson Scholarship, 297
Bill Ramsey/Craig Noone Memorial Scholarship, 352
Bill Sanderson Aviation Maintenance Technician Scholarship Award, 323
The Bill, W2ONV, and Ann Salerno Memorial Scholarship, 180
Bioworks/IPM Sustainable Practices Scholarship, 103
Birdsong Peanuts Scholarship, 271
Black & Veatch Summer Internship Program, 556
Black Nurses Scholarship, 410
Blain's Farm & Feet Scholarship, 271
Blind or Deaf Beneficiary Grant Program, 452
Blossom Kalama Evans Memorial Scholarship, 297
Blue Bell Scholarship, 506
Bluescope Foundation Scholarship, 226
BMI Student Composer Awards, 226
BMW/SAE Engineering Scholarships, 466
BNSF Railway Company Scholarship, 271
Bob Zappatelli Memorial Scholarship, 352
Boeing Internships, 556
Booker T. Washington Scholarship, 272
Booz Allen Scholarship, 297
Boston Globe Summer Internship, 556
Boy and Girl Scouts Scholarship, 255
Bridgestone Scholarship, 272
Broadcast News Grants, 211
Brown and Caldwell Minority Scholarship Program, 229
Bruce van Ess Scholarship, 349
Bryan A. Champion Scholarship, 336
Buckingham Memorial Scholarship, 88
Buckskin Horse Association Scholarship, 345
Bud Olman Memorial Scholarship, 103
Buick Achievers Scholarship Program, 289
Bunge North America Scholarship, 272
Bureau of Indian Education Higher Education Grant Program, 230
Burlington Northern Santa Fe Foundation Scholarship, 115
The Byron Blanchard, N1EKV Memorial Scholarship Fund, 181
C. J. Davidson Scholarship, 506
Caddie Scholarship, 423
Cady McDonnell Memorial Scholarship, 99
Cal Grant A & B Entitlement Award Program, 231
Cal Grant A and B Competitive Awards, 231
Cal Grant C Award, 232
California Chafee Grant Program, 232
California Child Development Grant Program, 232
California Farm Bureau Scholarship, 231
California Law Enforcement Personnel Dependents (LEPD) Grant Program, 232
California Teachers Association Martin Luther King, Jr., Memorial Scholarship, 233
California's Distinguished Young Woman Competition, 253
Calvin Coolidge Memorial Foundation Scholarship, 531
Camille C. Chidiac Fund, 297
Candon, Todd, & Seabolt Scholarship Fund, 298
Captain James J. Regan Memorial Scholarship, 369
C.A.R. Scholarship, 231
Career Technical Workforce Grant, 359
The Carl Buchan Scholarship, 373
Carl N. & Margaret Karcher Founders' Scholarship, 234
Carol Bauhs Benson Scholarship, 82
Carole Fielding Video Grant, 525
The Carole J. Streeter, KB9JBR, Scholarship, 181
Carole Simpson Scholarship, 407
Carole Simpson Scholarship, 461
Caroline Kark Scholarship, 425
Caroline Thorn Kissel Summer Environmental Studies Scholarship, 286
Carville M. Akehurst Memorial Scholarship, 337
Casey's General Stores, Inc. Scholarship, 272

Castle & Cooke Mililani Technology Park Scholarship Fund, 298
Castle & Cooke W. Y. Yim Scholarship Fund, 298
Categorical Tuition Waiver, 378
Catholic United Financial Post-High School Tuition Scholarship, 235
The CBC General Mills Health Scholarship, 242
CBC Scholarship, 243
The CBC Spouses Education Scholarship, 242
The CBC Spouses Heineken USA Performing Arts Scholarship Program, 242
The CBC Spouses Visual Arts Scholarship, 242
CCNMA Scholarships, 235
Center for Architecture Design Scholarship, 236
The Central Arizona DX Association Scholarship, 181
C.G. Fuller Foundation Scholarship, 237
Chafee Education and Training Grant, 442
Chafee Education and Training Grant (ETG) Program, 452
Chafee Educational and Training Voucher, 372
The Challenge Met Scholarship, 181
Champlain Valley Street Rodders Scholarship, 531
Chapter 17 - St. Louis Scholarship, 475
Chapter 198 - Downriver Detroit Scholarship, 475
Chapter 23 - Quad Cities Iowa/Illinois Scholarship, 475
Chapter 311 - Tri City Scholarship, 475
Chapter 4 - Lawrence A. Wacker Memorial Scholarship, 476
Chapter 52 - Wichita Scholarship, 476
Chapter 56 - Fort Wayne Scholarship, 476
Chapter 6 - Fairfield County Scholarship, 476
Chapter 67 - Phoenix Scholarship, 476
Chapter 93 - Albuquerque Scholarship, 477
Chapter One - Detroit Founding Chapter Scholarship Award, 477
Charles & Lucille King Family Foundation Scholarships, 238
Charles and Annette Hill Scholarship, 133
Charles B. Scharp Scholarship, 215
The Charles Clarke Cordle Memorial Scholarship, 181
Charles E. Leonard Memorial Scholarship, 532
Charles L. Bacon Memorial Scholarship, 142
Charles L. Hebner Memorial Scholarship, 252
The Charles N. Fisher Memorial Scholarship, 182
Charles P. Lake - Rain For Rent Scholarship, 272
Charles R. Ford Scholarship, 356
Charles (Tommy) Thomas Memorial Scholarship, 175
Charles W. Riley Fire and Emergency Medical Services Tuition Reimbursement Program, 375
Charleston Women in International Trade Scholarship, 238
Charlotte Woods Memorial Scholarship, 517
CHCI Congressional Internship, 557
Chefs of Louisiana Cookery Scholarship, 352
The Chesapeake Energy Scholarship, 249
Chester Haddan Scholarship Program, 449
Chester M. Vernon Memorial Eagle Scout Scholarship, 414
The Chicago FM Club Scholarship, 182
Chick Evans Caddie Scholarship, 541
Chief Industries Scholarship, 273
Children of Florida UPS Employees Scholarship, 359
Children of Unitarian Universalist Ministers College Stipend, 521
Children of Veterans Tuition Grant, 384
Children of Warriors National President's Scholarship, 165
Choctaw Nation Higher Education Program, 238
Christa McAuliffe Memorial Scholarship, 151
Christa McAuliffe Teacher Incentive Program, 594
Christian Record Services Scholarship, 239
Christian Wolffer Scholarship, 352
The Christopher Reeve Award, 323
Church & Dwight Company, Inc. Scholarship, 273
CI Construction Engineering Student Scholarship, 245
CIA Undergraduate Scholarship Program, 237
CIC/Anna Chennault Scholarship, 212
CIEE International Study Programs Scholarships, 246
CIGNA Foundation Tribal Scholars Healthcare, 111
Citizens for Global Solutions Internship, 557
City University SEEK/College Discovery Program, 426
Claire Oliphant Memorial Scholarship, 153
Clara Carter Higgins Scholarship and GCA Awards for Summer Environmental Studies, 286
Clare Brett Smith Scholarship, 499
Clarence & Josephine Myers Scholarship, 477
Clark-Phelps Scholarship, 442
Clay Triplette Scholarship, 352
Clinton J. Helton Manufacturing Scholarship Award, 477
The Cloisters Summer Internship Program, 567
Clorox Suena Sin Limites Mother Scholarship, 327
CNH Capital Scholarship, 273
Coca-Cola All-State Community Colleges Academic Team Scholarship, 239
Coca-Cola Live Positively Publix Supermarkets Scholarship, 327
Coca-Cola Scholars Program, 239
Colgate "Bright Smiles, Bright Futures" Minority Scholarships, 82
College Bound Fund Academic Promise Scholarship, 464
College Scholarship Program, 241
CollegeSTEPS, 538
Collegiate Inventors Competition, 414
Colon Furr Nursing Scholarship, 156
Colorado Council Volunteerism and Community Service Scholarship, 240
Colorado Masons Scholarship, 240
Colorado Society of CPAs General Scholarship, 241
Colorado Student Grant, 240
Colorado Work-Study Program, 240
Congressional Hispanic Caucus Institute Scholarship Awards, 243
Congressional Institute Internships, 557
Connecticut Aid for Public College Students, 243
Connecticut Aid to Dependents of Deceased/POW/MIA Veterans, 243
Connecticut Capitol Scholarship Program, 244
Connecticut Independent College Student Grant, 244
Connecticut Minority Teacher Incentive Grant, 244
Connecticut Tuition Waiver for Senior Citizens, 244
Connecticut Tuition Waiver for Veterans, 244
Connecticut Tuition Waiver for Vietnam MIA/POW Dependents, 245
Connie and Robert T. Gunter Scholarship, 478
ConocoPhillips Scholarships, 245
Cooperative Resources International Scholarship, 273
Cora Aguda Manayan Fund, 298
Corliss Knapp Engle Scholarship in Horticulture, 287
Costas G. Lemonopoulos Scholarship, 408
Courage Center Scholarship for People with Disabilities, 248
Courage to Grow Scholarship, 248
Courtland Paul Scholarship, 366
CPB Works For You Scholarship, 298
Crest Oral-B Dental Hygiene Scholarship, 83
Critical Needs Teacher Loan/Scholarship, 596
CSX Scholarship, 274
CTA Scholarship for Dependent Children, 233
CTA Scholarships for Members, 233
Cushman School Internship, 557
Cyber Security Scholarships, 208

The Cynthia E. Morgan Memorial Scholarship Fund, 248
Cystic Fibrosis Student Traineeship, 249
D. Fred and Mariam L. Bovie Scholarship, 201
D. Fred and Mariam L. Bovie Technical Scholarship, 201
Dairy Student Recognition Program, 410
Dakota Corps Scholarship Program, 494
Dallas Architectural Foundation - Swank Travelling Fellowship, 249
Dallas Geophysical Society Scholarship, 482
The Dallas Morning New Journalism Scholarship, 249
Dan & Pauline Lutkenhouse & Hawaii Tropical Botanical Garden Scholarship, 299
Dan McKeever Scholarship Program, 449
Dana Campbell Memorial Scholarship, 353
Daniel E. Lambert Memorial Scholarship, 136
The Daniels Scholarship, 251
Darlene Hooley for Oregon Veterans Scholarship, 443
Darling International, Inc. Scholarship, 274
Darrel Hess Community College Geography Scholarship, 222
David Alan Quick Scholarship, 259
David Arver Memorial Scholarship, 88
David Barrett Memorial Scholarship, 198
David E. Rosenbaum Reporting Internship in Washington, D.C., 575
David Family Scholarship, 443
The David Knaus Memorial Scholarship, 182
David L. Irons Memorial Scholarship Fund, 299
David Mineck Memorial Scholarship, 260
Davidson Fellows Scholarship, 251
Davis-Roberts Scholarship, 252
Dayle and Frances Pieper Scholarship, 166
The Dayton Amateur Radio Association Scholarships, 182
DC Tuition Assistance Grant Program (DCTAG), 254
DCF Foster Child Tuition Waiver and Fee Assistance Program, 378
Dean Foods Company Scholarship, 274
DEED Student Research Grants, 178
Delaware Educational Benefits for Children of Deceased Veterans and Others, 253
Delaware Nursing Incentive Program, 594
Delaware Scholarship Incentive Program, 253
Delaware Space Grant Undergraduate Summer Research Internship, 571
Delaware Space Grant Undergraduate Tuition Scholarship, 396
Delayed Education Scholarship for Women, 175
Dell Scholars Program, 384
Della Van Deuren Memorial Scholarship, 170
Delta Faucet Company Scholarship, 456
Delta Gamma Foundation Florence Margaret Harvey Memorial Scholarship, 106
Denny Lydic Scholarship, 517
Denver Rescue Mission Center for Mission Studies Internships, 558
Department of Energy Community College Institute at Oak Ridge National Laboratory, 575
Department of New Hampshire Scholarship, 151
Deseo at the Westin Scholarship, 353
DeWayne Wickham Founder's High School Scholarship, 407
DGS/Karen Kellogg Shaw Memorial Scholarship, 482
DHS HS-STEM Summer Internship Program, 576
DHS Summer Faculty and Student Research Team Program for Minority Serving Institutions, 576
Diamond State Scholarship, 253
Discover Scholarship, 327
Disney College Program, 591
Disney Theme Parks & Resorts Professional Internships, 591
Distinguished Young Women Scholarship, 254
Diversity Abroad Achievement Scholarship, 115
Diversity Internship Program, 588
DMI Milk Marketing Scholarships, 410
Do Something Awards, 254
DOE Faculty and Student Teams Program at Oak Ridge National Laboratory, 576
DOE Scholars Program, 576
DOE Science Undergraduate Laboratory Internships at Oak Ridge National Laboratory, 576
Dolly Ching Scholarship Fund, 299
Dolphin Scholarship, 254
The Don Riebhoff Memorial Scholarship, 182
Donald A. Williams Soil Conservation Scholarship, 489
Donald and Nancy Frye Scholarship, 482
Donald and Shirley Hastings National Scholarship, 201
Donald F. Hastings Scholarship, 201
Doris & Clarence Glick Classical Music Scholarship, 299
Dorothy Campbell Memorial Scholarship, 443
Dow Jones Business Reporting Intern Program, 558
Dow Jones Digital Intern Program, 558
Dow Jones News Editing Intern Program, 558
Dow Jones Sports Editing Intern Program, 559
DPMA/PC Scholarship, 251
Dr. Alma S. Adams Scholarship for Outreach and Health Communications to Reduce Tobacco Use Among Priority Populations, 118
Dr. Alvin and Monica Saake Scholarship, 299
Dr. & Mrs. Arthur William Phillips Scholarship, 454
Dr. and Mrs. Moon Park Scholarship, 300
Dr. Click Cowger Scholarship, 134
Dr. Dan J. and Patricia S. Pickard Scholarship, 249
Dr. Don and Rose Marie Benton Scholarship, 250
Dr. Edison and Sallie Miyawaki Scholarship, 300
Dr. Esther Wilkins Scholarship, 83
Dr. Hannah K. Vuolo Memorial Scholarship, 154
Dr. Hans & Clara Zimmerman Foundation Education Scholarship, 300
Dr. Hans and Clara Zimmerman Foundation Health Scholarship, 300
The Dr. James L. Lawson Memorial Scholarship, 183
Dr. Kate Waller Barrett Grant, 165
Dr. W. Wes Eckenfelder Jr. Scholarship, 230
Duane Hanson Scholarship, 197
DuPont Co-ops, 559
DuPont Internships, 559
Dupont Pioneer Scholarships, 274
Dutch and Ginger Arver Scholarship, 89
E. Wayne Kay Community College Scholarship, 478
E. Wayne Kay Co-op Scholarship, 478
E. Wayne Kay High School Scholarship, 478
E. Wayne Kay Scholarship, 478
Earl Dedman Memorial Scholarship, 103
Earl R. Sorensen Memorial Scholarships, 274
Eastman Kodak Cooperative Internship Programs, 559
Eastside & Northshore Kauai Scholarship Fund, 300
Ecolab Scholarship Competition, 110
Economic Research Division Project Internships, 556
Ecotrust Native American Scholarship, 111
Ed Bradley Scholarship, 461
Edgar J. Boschult Memorial Scholarship, 147
The Edmond A. Metzger Scholarship, 183
Edmund F. Maxwell Foundation Scholarship, 255

Edna M. Barcus Memorial Scholarship and Hoosier Scholarship, 131
The EDSA Minority Scholarship, 366
Edward D. Hendrickson/SAE Engineering Scholarship, 466
Edward J. and Norma Doty Scholarship, 301
Edward J. Brady Memorial Scholarship, 202
Edward J. Dulis Scholarship, 213
Edward J. Nell Memorial Scholarship, 461
Edward Payson and Bernice Pi'ilani Irwin Scholarship Trust Fund, 301
Edward S. Roth Manufacturing Engineering Scholarship, 479
E.E. Black Scholarship, 301
Eight and Forty Lung and Respiratory Disease Nursing Scholarship, 146
Eleanor Allwork Scholarship, 236
Elena Albano "Maka'alohilohi" Scholarship Fund, 301
Elie Wiesel Prize in Ethics, 256
Elizabeth A. Sackler Museum Educational Trust, 499
Elizabeth Dow Ltd. Internships, 555
Elizabeth Gardner Norweb Summer Environmental Studies Scholarship, 287
The Elizabeth Greenshields Grant, 256
The Elkes Family Culinary Scholarship, 353
Elks Most Valuable Student Scholarship, 256
Elks National Foundation Legacy Awards, 256
Ellen Hamada Fashion Design Scholarship, 301
Ellison Onizuka Memorial Scholarship, 302
Elsie B. Brown Scholarship Fund, 152
Emily Lester Vermont Opportunity Scholarship, 532
Endowment Fund For Education (EFFE), 225
Engineers Foundation of Ohio Scholarships, 257
Entergy Jumpstart Co-ops and Internships, 560
Entertainment Weekly Internship Program, 560
The Entomological Foundation BioQuip Undergraduate Scholarship, 257
Environmental Management Participation at the U.S. Army Environmental Command (USAEC), 577
EPA Greater Research Opportunities Undergraduate Student Fellowships, 527
EPA National Network for Environmental Management Studies Fellowship, 528
Epilepsy Foundation of San Diego County Scholarship, 258
Eric Marder Scholarship Program, 343
Erman W. Taylor Memorial Scholarship, 142
ESA Foundation Scholarship Program, 259
ESPN Internship, 560
Essence Summer Internship, 560
Esther Kanagawa Memorial Art Scholarship, 302
Eugene Bennet Visual Arts Scholarship, 443
Eugene C. Figg Jr. Civil Engineering Scholarship, 194
The Eugene "Gene" Sallee, W4YFR, Memorial Scholarship, 183
Eugenia Vellner Fischer Award for the Performing Arts, 389
Excel Geophysical Services Scholarship, 483
Executive Women International Scholarship, 259
Explorers Club Youth Activity Fund, 261
Extrusion Division/Lew Erwin Memorial Scholarship, 486
ExxonMobil Scholarship, 327
F. Koehnen Ltd. Scholarship Fund, 302
Farm Credit Services of Mid-America Scholarship, 275
Farmers Mutual Hail Insurance Company of Iowa Scholarship, 275
Fastline Publications Scholarship, 275
Father James B. Macelwane Annual Award, 172
Federal Direct Loans, 601
Federal Employee Education and Assistance Fund Scholarship, 261
Federal Pell Grant Program, 526
Federal Perkins Loan, 601
Federal Plus Loan, 602
Federal Reserve Bank of New York Undergraduate Summer Internship, 560
Federal Supplemental Educational Opportunity Grant Program, 526
Federal Work-Study Program, 527
Feminism & Leadership Internship, 561
Ferdinand Torres Scholarship, 107
FFA Scholarships, 507
Field Aviation Co. Inc. Scholarship, 89
Fifth Third Bank of Central Indiana Scholarship, 275
Filipino Nurses' Organization of Hawaii Scholarship, 302
Filoli Garden Internships and Apprenticeships, 561
Financial Women International Scholarship, 302
First Catholic Slovak Ladies Association Scholarship Program, 262
Fisher Broadcasting Company Scholarship for Minorities, 262
Fitz Dixon Memorial Scholarship, 454
Fleming/Blaszcak Scholarship, 486
Fletcher & Fritzi Hoffmann Education Fund, 303
Flight 587 Memorial Scholarships, 426
Florence Lemcke Memorial Scholarship, 166
Florence Travel Stipend, 499
Florida Academic Scholars Award, 263
Florida Bright Futures Scholarship Program, 263
Florida First Generation Matching Grant Program, 263
Florida Gold Seal Vocational Scholars Award, 263
Florida Medallion Scholars Award, 264
Florida Public Postsecondary Career Education Student Assistance Grant Program, 264
Florida Scholarships for Children and Spouses of Deceased or Disabled Veterans, 264
Florida Student Assistance Grant (FSAG) Program, 264
Florida Work Experience Program, 561
Floyd Qualls Memorial Scholarship, 101
Folds of Honor Foundation Scholaships, 266
The Food Network Scholarship for Immigrants in the Kitchen, 353
Ford Blue Oval Scholarship, 325
Ford Fund and Ford Trucks Built Ford Tough FFA Scholarship Program, 276
Ford Motor Company Tribal College Scholarship, 112
Ford Opportunity Program, 443
Ford Scholars Program, 444
Foreclosure.com Scholarship Contest, 266
Foster Child Grant Program, 378
Foth Production Solutions, LLC Scholarship, 276
Foundation for Environmental Agriculture Scholarship, 276
Foundation for Surgical Technology Student Scholarship, 266
The Fountainhead Essay Contest, 224
Fox Internship, 562
Fran Johnson Non-Traditional Scholarship, 104
Frances M. Peacock Native Bird Habitat Scholarship, 287
Frances S. Watanabe Memorial Scholarship, 303
The Francis Walton Memorial Scholarship, 183
Frank and Dorothy Miller ASME Auxiliary Scholarships, 217
Frank D. Visceglia Memorial Scholarship, 227
Frank L. Weil Memorial Eagle Scout Scholarship, 415
Frank M. Coda Scholarship, 197
Frank O'Bannon Grant, 497
Frank Stenzel M.D. and Kathryn Stenzel II Scholarship, 444
Franklin Lindsay Student Aid Loan, 594
Fred G. Zahn Scholarship Fund, 267
Fred M. Young, Sr./SAE Engineering Scholarship, 466
The Fred R. McDaniel Memorial Scholarship, 184

Freeman Fellowship, 194
F.W. "Beich" Beichley Scholarship, 217
Gabe A. Hartl Scholarship, 88
Gabriel Prize, 541
Garden Club Federation of Massachusetts, 286
Garland Duncan Scholarships, 217
Garmin Scholarship, 89
Gary J. Miller Undergraduate Prizes for Cancer and Cancer-Related Biomedical Research, 96
The Gary Wagner, K3OMI, Scholarship, 184
Gates Millennium Scholars Program, 289
GCA Award in Desert Studies, 287
GCA Internship in Garden History and Design, 562
GCA Summer Scholarship in Field Botany, 287
GCA Zone VI Fellowship in Urban Forestry, 288
GCSAA Legacy Awards, 257
GCSAA Scholars Competition, 258
GCSAA Student Essay Contest, 258
GE Foundation/LULAC Scholarship Program, 368
GE Hispanic Forum Scholarship, 327
Gear Up Scholarship Program, 379
Genentech, Inc. Internship Program, 562
General Henry H. Arnold Education Grant, 87
General John Paul Ratay Educational Fund Grants, 386
Geophysical Society of Alaska Scholarship, 483
Geophysical Society of Tulsa Scholarship, 483
George A. Hall/Harold F. Mayfield Award, 542
George A. Roberts Scholarships, 213
George & Augusta Rapozo Kama'aina Scholarship Fund, 303
George & Lucille Cushnie Scholarship, 303
George and Donna Nigh Public Service Scholarship, 438
The George Foreman Tribute to Lyndon B. Johnson Scholarship, 461
George Mason Business Scholarship Fund, 303
George S. Ishiyama Unicold Scholarship, 304
George Washington Carver Internship, 592
Georgia Hope Grant - GED Recipient, 290
Georgia Hope Grant - Public Technical Institution, 290
Georgia Hope Scholarship - Private Institution, 290
Georgia Hope Scholarship - Public College or University, 290
Georgia Student Finance Commission Public Safety Memorial Grant, 291
Georgia Tuition Equalization Grant, 291
Georgina S. Mendez Pharmacology Scholarship, 383
Gerrit R. Ludwig Scholarship, 304
The Gillian Award, 499
Ginger and Fred Deines Canada Scholarship, 517
Ginger and Fred Deines Mexico Scholarship, 518
Giuliano Mazzetti Scholarship, 479
The Gladys C. Anderson Memorial Scholarship, 107
GlaxoSmithKline Opportunity Scholarship, 432
GLBT "Guy DeRosa" Safety in Schools Grant and Scholarship Program, 234
Glenn Jackson Scholars, 444
Gold Star Scholarship Program, 420
Golden Apple Scholars of Illinois Program, 291
Golden Key Community Service Award, 292
Golden Key Emerging Scholar Award, 292
Golden Key GEICO Life Award, 292
Golden Key Outstanding Alumni Award, 292
Golden Key Outstanding Alumni Member Award, 292
Golden Key Regional Student Leader of the Year Award, 292
Golden Key Research Grants, 293
Golden Key Undergraduate Achievement Scholarship, 293
Golden Key Visual and Performing Arts Achievement Award, 293
Golden LEAF Scholars Program - Two-Year Colleges, 432
Golden LEAF Scholarship - Four-Year University Program, 432
Good Eats Scholarship Fund, 304
Google Hispanic College Fund Scholarship Program, 325
Governor Terry E. Branstad Iowa State Fair Scholarship, 348
Goya Scholarship, 328
Grace Pacific Outstanding Scholars Fund, 304
Grace S. High Memorial Child Welfare Scholarship Fund, 152
Grand Army of the Republic Living Memorial Scholarship, 251
Grange Denise Scholarship, 425
Grange Insurance Scholarship, 293
Grange Student Loan Fund, 598
Grange Susan W. Freestone Education Award, 425
Greater Houston Retailers and Coca-Cola Live Positively Scholarship, 328
Greater Kanawha Valley Scholarship Program, 294
Greenhouse Scholars Program, 294
Green/Sustainable Design Scholarship, 346
The Grotto Scholarships, 501
Grow Your Own Teacher Scholarship Program, 339
GSH/Hugh Hardy Scholarship, 483
Guggenheim Museum Internship, 586
Gulf Coast Hurricane Scholarships, 486
Guy M. Wilson Scholarship, 139
Guy Marshall Scholarship Fund, 304
G.W. Hohmann Memorial Scholarship, 483
The Gwinnett Amateur Radio Society Scholarship, 184
HACEMOS Scholarship, 328
HACU (Hispanic Association of Colleges and Universities) Scholarships, 115
HACU National Internship Program, 563
Hall/McElwain Merit Scholarship, 412
Hannaford Internships, 562
Hansen Scholarship, 260
Harness Tracks of America Scholarship Fund, 294
Harold Bettinger Memorial Scholarship, 104
Harold K. Douthit Scholarship, 437
Harper Internship Program, 564
Harriet Hoffman Memorial Scholarship, 132
Harriet Irsay Scholarship, 118
Harry & Lorraine Ausprich Endowed Scholarship for the Arts, 454
Harry E. Arcamuzi Aviation Scholarship, 260
Haseko Training Fund, 305
Hattie Tedrow Memorial Fund Scholarship, 156
Hawaii Chapter/David T. Woolsey Scholarship, 366
Hawaii Community Scholarship Fund, 305
Hawaii GEAR UP Scholars Program, 305
Hawaii Pacific Gerontological Society Nursing Scholarship Fund, 305
Hawaii Pizza Hut Scholarship Fund, 305
Hawaii Society of Certified Public Accountants Scholarship Fund, 306
H.C. Shipman Vocational Scholarship Fund, 306
Health Career Scholarship, 347
Hearst Journalism Award, 541
Helen K. and Arthur E. Johnson Foundation Scholarship, 112
Helicopter Association International Commercial Helicopter Rating Scholarship, 324
Helicopter Association International Maintenance Technician Certificate Scholarship, 324
Helping Heroes Grant, 503
HENAAC Scholars Program, 294
Henry A. Zuberano Scholarship, 306
Henry Adams Scholarship, 197
Henry and Dorothy Castle Memorial Scholarship, 306
The Henry Broughton, K2AE, Memorial Scholarship, 184
Henry Salvatori Scholarship, 490

The Herb Alpert Young Jazz Composer Awards, 210
Herbert & Ollie Brook Fund, 306
Herbert Lehman Educational Fund, 395
Herbert Levy Memorial Endowment Fund Scholarship, 485
Herman M. Holloway, Sr. Memorial Scholarship, 253
Herman O. West Foundation Scholarship Program, 539
Herschel C. Price Educational Scholarship, 324
Hershey Company Tribal Scholarship, 112
Hew-Shinn Scholarship Fund, 307
Hideko & Zenzo Matsuyama Scholarship Fund, 307
High Technology Scholar/Intern Tuition Waiver Program, 379
Higher Education Research Experiences at Oak Ridge National Laboratory for Students, 577
Higher Education Success Stipend Program, 529
Hilo Chinese School Scholarship, 307
Hirsch Family Scholarship, 250
Hispanic Heritage Youth Awards Program, 326
Hoard's Dairyman Scholarship, 276
Hoffman-La Roche Inc. Student Internship, 563
Hoku Scholarship Fund, 307
Hokulani Hawaii Fund, 307
Hokuli'a Foundation Scholarship Fund, 307
Hon Chew Hee Scholarship Fund, 308
Honda Scholarship, 328
Hooper Memorial Scholarship, 518
Hoover-Lee Scholars Program, 522
Hope Foster Child Tuition Grant, 503
HOPE-Aspire Award, 503
Hope-General Assembly Merit Scholarship, 504
Hopi BIA Higher Education Grant, 331
Hopi Education Award, 332
Hopi Tribal Priority Award, 332
Horatio Alger Ak-Sar-Ben Scholarship Program, 332
Horatio Alger Arizona Scholarship, 332
Horatio Alger California (Northern) Scholarship Program, 333
Horatio Alger Delaware Scholarship Program, 333
Horatio Alger District of Columbia, Maryland and Virginia Scholarship Program, 333
Horatio Alger Georgia Scholarship Program, 333
Horatio Alger Illinois Scholarship Program, 333
Horatio Alger John Hardin Hudiburg Scholarship Program, 334
Horatio Alger Louisiana Scholarship Program, 334
Horatio Alger Missouri Scholarship Program, 334
Horatio Alger Montana Scholarship Program, 334
Horatio Alger National Scholarship, 335
Horatio Alger North Dakota Scholarship Program, 335
Horatio Alger Pennsylvania Scholarship Program, 335
Horatio Alger Ronald C. Waranch Scholarship Program, 335
Horatio Alger South Dakota Scholarship Program, 335
Horatio Alger Texas Scholarship Program, 336
Horatio Alger Utah Scholarship Program, 336
Horatio Alger Wyoming Scholarship Program, 336
Horizons Scholarship, 545
Hormel Foods Corporation Scholarship, 277
Ho'omaka Hou - A New Beginning Fund, 308
Horticultural Research Institute Spring Meadow Scholarship, 337
House Member Internships, 589
Houston Livestock Show and Rodeo Metropolitan Scholarships, 338
Houston Livestock Show and Rodeo Opportunity Scholarship, 338
Houston Livestock Show and Rodeo Scholarships, 506
Houston Livestock Show and Rodeo School Art Scholarships, 339
Howard E. and Wilma J. Adkins Memorial Scholarship, 202
Howard P. Rawlings Guaranteed Access Grant, 376
H.P. "Bud" Milligan Aviation Scholarship, 260
HSF Achievement Scholarship, 328
HSF General College Scholarship, 329
Hudner Medal of Honor Scholarship, 260
Hu-Friedy/Esther Wilkins Instrument Scholarships, 83
Hugh A. Smith Scholarship, 134
Human Factors, Instrumentation and Controls Division (HFICD) Nuclear Power Scholarship, 175
The Hyatt Hotels Fund for Minority Lodging Management Students Competition, 110
I. Rubinstein Memorial Grant, 358
Iager Dairy Scholarship, 411
Ian Doane Smith Scholarship Fund, 308
IATAN Ronald A. Santana Memorial Scholarship, 514
IBM Co-op and Intern Program, 563
Ichiro & Masako Hirata Scholarship, 308
Ida M. Crawford Scholarship, 444
Ida M. Pope Memorial Scholarship, 308
Idaho Freedom Scholarship, 339
Idaho GEAR UP Scholarship, 340
Idaho Governor's Cup Scholarship, 340
Idaho Opportunity Scholarship, 340
Idaho State Board of Education Public Safety Officer Dependent Scholarship, 340
IEHA Educational Foundation Scholarship, 345
IFDA Leaders Commemorative Scholarship, 346
ILC Resources Scholarship, 277
Illinois Grant Program for Dependents of Correctional Officers, 341
Illinois Grant Program for Dependents of Police or Fire Officers, 341
Illinois Higher Education License Plate (HELP) Program, 342
Illinois MIA/POW Scholarship, 341
Illinois Monetary Award Program (MAP), 342
Illinois National Guard Grant, 342
Illinois Special Education Teacher Tuition Waiver, 342
Illinois Veteran Grant (IVG) Program, 342
Incentive Program for Aspiring Teachers, 379
Independent Living Act (Department of Human Services Tuition Waiver), 438
Indian American Scholarship, 525
Indiana Minority Teacher & Special Education Services Scholarship, 497
Indiana National Guard Supplemental Grant, 498
Indiana Nursing Scholarship, 498
Indiana Twenty-First Century Scholars Program, 498
The Indianapolis Amateur Radio Association Fund, 184
Industrial Automation Engineering College Scholarships, 211
INROADS Internship, 564
Institute of Food Technologists Freshman Scholarship, 343
Institute of Food Technologists Undergraduate Scholarship, 344
Intel Scholarship, 115
International Furnishings and Design Association Educational Foundation Part-Time Student Scholarship, 346
International Furnishings and Design Association Student Member Scholarships, 346
International Incentive Awards, 500
International Radio and Television Society Foundation Summer Fellowship Program, 564
International Semester Scholarship, 116
Internships at Macy's and Bloomingdale's, 566
Iowa Grant, 348
Iowa Interstate Railroad, Ltd. Scholarship, 277
Iowa National Guard Educational Assistance Program, 348
Iowa Tuition Grant, 348
Iowa Vocational-Technical Tuition Grant, 349
Iraq and Afghanistan Service Grant, 527

IRARC Memorial, Joseph P. Rubino, WA4MMD, Scholarship, 185
Irene Winifred Eno Grant, 198
Irrigation Foundation Scholarship, 277
The Irving W. Cook WA0CGS Scholarship, 185
Isemoto Contracting Co., Ltd. Scholarship Fund, 308
ISFA Education Foundation College Scholarship, 344
Italian Catholic Federation Scholarship, 349
Iwamoto Family Scholarship, 309
Iwamoto Family Vocational Scholarship, 309
J. Paul Getty Multicultural Undergraduate Summer Internships at the Getty Center, 564
J. Richard Mehalick Scholarship, 197
Jack Kent Cooke Foundation College Scholarship, 350
Jack R. Barckhoff Welding Management Scholarship, 202
Jackie Robinson Foundation Mentoring and Leadership Curriculum, 351
The Jackson County ARA Scholarship, 185
Jackson Foundation Journalism Scholarship, 444
Jacob Van Namen Marketing Scholarship, 104
Jagannathan Scholarship, 432
The Jake McClain Driver KC5WXA Scholarship Fund, 185
James A. Turner, Jr. Memorial Scholarship, 202
James B. Carey Scholarship, 349
James Beard Foundation School Scholarships, 353
James Bridenbaugh Memorial Scholarship, 104
James Carlson Memorial Scholarship, 445
James E. Webb Internship Program for Minority Undergraduate Seniors and Graduate Students in Business and Public Administration, 585
James F. Byrnes Scholarship, 356
James F. Mulholland American Legion Scholarship, 154
James K. Vogt Radiochemistry Scholarship, 176
James L. Allhands Essay Competition, 220
James V. Day Scholarship, 136
Jaycee War Memorial Scholarship, 357
Jean Estes Epstein Charitable Foundation Scholarship, 309
Jean Fitzgerald Scholarship Fund, 309
Jean Ileialoha Beniamina Scholarship for Ni'ihau Students Fund, 309
Jeanette Rankin Foundation Scholarship, 357
Jeanne E. Bray Law Enforcement Dependents Scholarship, 417
Jedidiah Zabrosky Scholarship, 532
Jeffrey Alan Scoggins Memorial Scholarship, 445
Jennifer C. Groot Fellowship, 97
Jennifer Ritzmann Scholarship for Studies in Tropical Biology, 247
Jere W. Thompson, Jr. Scholarship Fund, 250
Jerome B. Steinbach Scholarship, 445
Jerry Clark Memorial Scholarship, 102
Jewish Guild Scholar Program, 357
Jewish Vocational Service Scholarship Fund, 357
Jewish War Veterans of the United States of America Bernard Rotberg Memorial Scholarship, 358
JFCS Scholarship Fund, 595
Jimmy A. Young Memorial Education Recognition Award, 192
J.K. Rathmell, Jr. Memorial Scholarship for Work/Study Abroad, 104
Joan K. Hunt and Rachel M. Hunt Summer Scholarship in Field Botany, 288
The Joel Abromson Memorial Scholarship, 259
Joel Polsky Academic Achievement Award, 199
Joel Polsky Prize, 199
Johanna Drew Cluney Scholarship, 310
John A. High Child Welfare Scholarship, 151
John & Anne Clifton Scholarship Fund, 310
John & Elsa Gracik Scholarships, 217
John and Abigail Adams Scholarship, 379
John and Amy Rakestraw Scholarship, 277
John and Geraldine Hobble Licensed Practical Nursing Scholarship, 134
John and Muriel Landis Scholarship, 176
John Bayliss Scholarship Award, 229
John C. Lincoln Memorial Scholarship, 202
John Dawe Dental Education Fund, 310
John E. Bowman Travel Grants, 247
John L. Dales Standard Scholarship, 469
John L. Dales Transitional Scholarship, 470
John L. Mendez Business Scholarship, 383
John L. Tomasovic, Sr. Scholarship, 105
John Lenard Civil Engineering Scholarship, 194
John Lennon Scholarships, 227
John M. Haniak Scholarship, 213
John M. Ross Foundation Scholarship, 310
John McKee Scholarship, 383
John R. Lamarsh Scholarship, 176
John Wiley and Sons, Inc. Internship Program, 565
Johnny Davis Memorial Scholarship, 89
Johnson Controls Co-op and Internship Programs, 566
Joint Admissions Tuition Advantage Waiver Program, 379
Jose and Victoria Martinez Maison Blanche Scholarship, 353
Jose Marti Scholarship Challenge Grant Fund, 264
Joseph & Alice Duarte Memorial Fund, 310
Joseph J. Frank Scholarship, 143
Joseph P. Gavenonis Scholarship, 159
Joseph R. Dietrich Scholarship, 176
Joseph S. Adams Senior Scholarship, 481
Joseph Tauber Scholarship, 79
Josephine and Robert B.B. Moorman Scholarship, 195
Jules Maidoff Scholarship, 500
Juliette A. Southard/Oral-B Laboratories Scholarship, 101
Juliette M. Atherton Scholarship - Minister's Sons and Daughters, 311
Julio and Sarah Armellini Scholarship, 105
Julio C. Mendez Engineering Scholarship, 383
Jump Start Scholarship Program, 494
June Gill Nursing Scholarship, 425
K. K. Wang Scholarship, 487
The K2TEO Martin J. Green, Sr. Memorial Scholarship, 185
Kahala Nui Residents Scholarship Fund, 311
The Kaj Christensen Scholarship for Vocational Training, 435
Kalihi Education Coalition Scholarship Fund, 311
Ka'iulani Home for Girls Trust Scholarship, 311
Kansas Comprehensive Grant, 359
Kansas Ethnic Minority Scholarship, 360
Kansas Military Service Scholarship, 360
Kansas Nursing Service Scholarship, 360
Kansas ROTC Service Scholarship, 360
Kansas State Scholarship, 360
Kansas Teacher Service Scholarship, 361
Kansas Vocational Education Scholarship, 361
Kapolei Business & Community Scholarship, 311
Kappa Kappa Gamma Scholarship, 361
Karla Girts Memorial Community Outreach Scholarship, 83
KarMel Scholarship, 362
Ka'a'awa Community Fund, 311
Kate Gleason Scholarship, 218
Katharine M. Grosscup Scholarships in Horticulture, 288
Kathern F. Gruber Scholarship Program, 226
Kathleen McDermott Scholarship, 247
Kawasaki-McGaha Scholarship Fund, 312
Kazuma and Ichiko Hisanaga Scholarship Fund, 312

Ken Chagnon Scholarship, 449
KenAG Scholarship, 278
Kennedy Center Arts Management Internship, 565
Kennedy Library Archival Internship, 565
Kenneth Andrew Roe Mechanical Engineering Scholarship, 218
Kenneth Makinney & David T. Pietsch Familes Scholarship Fund, 312
Kent Nutrition Group, Inc. Scholarship, 278
Kentucky College Access Program Grant (CAP), 362
Kentucky Early Childhood Development Scholarship, 362
Kentucky Educational Excellence Scholarship (KEES), 362
Kentucky Go Higher Grant, 363
Kentucky Mary Jo Young Scholarship, 363
Kentucky Teacher Scholarship, 363
Kentucky Tuition Grant, 363
Kentucky Work-Study Program, 566
Keppra Family Epilepsy Scholarship Program, 519
KeyBank Scholarship, 278
Kikkoman Foods, Inc. Scholarship, 278
Kildee Scholarship, 411
King Kekaulike High School Scholarship, 312
King Olav V Norwegian-American Heritage Fund, 491
King Ranch Scholarship, 279
Kittredge Coddington Memorial Scholarship, 532
Klussendorf Scholarship, 411
K.M. Hatano Scholarship, 313
Knights Templar Educational Foundation Loan, 594
Kohala Ditch Education Fund, 313
Kohler Company Scholarship, 279
Koloa Scholarship, 313
Korean University Club Scholarship Fund, 313
Korean War Veteran's Children's Scholarship, 313
Kosciuszko Foundation Year Abroad Program, 364
Kurt W. Schneider Memorial Scholarship Fund, 314
L. Gordon Bittle Memorial Scholarship for SCTA, 234
The L. Phil and Alice J. Wicker Scholarship, 186
L-3 Avionics Systems Scholarship, 89
La Toque Scholarship in Wine Studies, 354
Laboratory Technology Program, 577
Lacroix at the Rittenhouse Scholarship, 354
Ladish Co. Foundation Scholarships, 213
Lagrant Scholarships, 365
Lambda Alpha National Collegiate Honors Society Senior Scholarship, 365
Landscape Forms Design for People Scholarship, 367
Larry Whiteside Scholarship, 407
Latin American Educational Scholarship, 368
Latin Honor Society Scholarship, 415
Latino Diamante Scholarship Fund, 433
Laura Blackburn Memorial Scholarship, 135
Laura N. Dowsett Fund, 314
Laura Rowe Burdick Scholarship Fund, 314
Laura W. Bush Scholarship, 255
Laurence R. Foster Memorial Scholarship, 445
Lawrence W. and Francis W. Cox Scholarship, 195
The L.B. Cebik, W4RNL, and Jean Cebik, N4TZP, Memorial Scholarship, 186
"Anthem" Essay Contest, 224
"We the Living" Essay Contest, 224
Lee A. Lyman Memorial Music Scholarship, 532
Lee Tarbox Memorial Scholarship, 90
Legacy of Hope, 498
Lele Cassin Scholarship, 500
Lemaire Restaurant at the Jefferson Hotel Scholarship, 354
Leonard M. Perryman Communications Scholarship for Ethnic Minority Students, 522
Letitia B. Carter Scholarship, 463
Leveraging Educational Assistance Partnership Program (LEAP), 389
LIFE Lessons Scholarship Program, 370
Lighthouse College-Bound Award, 370
Lighthouse Undergraduate Award, 371
Lillian B. Reynolds Scholarship, 314
Lillie Lois Ford Boys' Scholarship, 143
Lillie Lois Ford Girls' Scholarship, 143
Lilly Reintegration Scholarship, 236
Limi Boosters National Educational Grant, 430
Limi Boosters Scholarship, 430
Lindbergh Grant, 238
Lisa Higgins Hussman Scholarship Program, 448
Lockheed Martin American Heroes Scholarship, 329
Logan Nainoa Fujimoto Memorial Scholarship, 314
Long Island Flower Grower Association (LIFGA) Scholarship, 105
Los Padres Foundation College Tuition Assistance Program, 371
Los Padres Foundation Second Chance Program, 371
Lou and Carole Prato Sports Reporting Scholarship, 462
The Louie Foundation Scholarship, 364
Louis Carr Summer Internship, 566
Louis Stokes Health Scholars, 242
Louisiana Go Grants, 372
The Louisiana Memorial Scholarship, 186
Louisiana Rockefeller Wildlife Scholarship, 372
Louisiana Taylor Opportunity Program for Students (TOPS) Award, 372
Louisiana TOPS Tech Early Start Program, 373
Louisiana Tops Tech Program, 373
Louisiana Veterans Affairs Survivors and Dependents Education Program, 371
Lowell Gaylor Memorial Scholarship, 90
The Lowell H. and Dorothy Loving Undergraduate Scholarship, 99
Lowe's Scholarship Program, 373
The Loy McCandless Marks Scholarship in Tropical Horticulture, 288
Lucile B. Kaufman Women's Scholarship, 479
Lucille & Charles A. Wert Scholarship, 213
Lucille Ganey Memorial Scholarship, 123
LULAC General Awards, 368
LULAC Honors Awards, 368
LULAC National Scholastic Achievement Awards, 369
Lutheran Student Scholastic and Service Scholarship, 225
Lynn G. Bellenger Scholarship, 197
M & T Bank Scholarship, 454
Macy's College Scholarship Program, 329
The Magnolia DX Association Scholarship, 186
Mahindra USA Women in Ag Scholarship, 279
Maine Innkeepers Association Scholarship, 374
The Maine Loan, 595
Maine Metal Products Association Scholarship, 374
Maine Society of Professional Engineers Scholarship Program, 375
Maine State Society of Washington, D.C. Foundation Scholarship Program, 375
Maine Veterans Services Dependents Educational Benefits, 374
Major Don S. Gentile Scholarship, 520
Makovsky & Company Inc. Public Relations Internship, 567
Marathon Oil Corporation College Scholarship, 329
Marathon Petroleum Corporation College Scholarship, 330
Marble-Boyle Award, 222
March Taylor Educational Fund Scholarship, 315
Marcia S. Harris Legacy Fund Scholarship, 463
Margaret Follett Haskins Hawaii Scholarship, 315
Margaret Follett Haskins (Maui) Scholarship, 315
Margaret Jones Memorial Nursing Scholarship, 315

Marguerite McAlpin Nurse's Scholarship, 167
Marguerite Ross Barnett Memorial Scholarship, 391
Maria C. Jackson-General George A. White Scholarship, 445
Marie Sheehe Trade School Scholarship, 129
Marine Corps Scholarship, 375
Marion Huber Learning Through Listening Award, 369
Marion J. Bagley Scholarship, 152
Marion Maccarrell Scott Scholarship, 315
Mark Beaumont Scholarship Fund, 80
Mark J. Smith Scholarship, 241
Markham-Colegrave International Scholarship, 105
Marriott Scholars Program, 326
Marsh Scholarship, 344
Marshall E. McCullough Undergraduate Scholarship, 411
Mary Barrett Marshall Student Loan Fund, 593
Mary Josephine Bloder Scholarship, 316
The Mary Lou Brown Scholarship, 186
Mary Macey Scholarship, 545
Mary Marshall Nursing RN Scholarship, 535
Mary Marshall Nursing Scholarship Program (LPN), 536
Mary McLeod Bethune Scholarship, 265
Mary P. Oenslager Scholastic Achievement Award, 369
Mary R. Molina Scholarship, 330
Mary T. Carothers Environmental Studies Scholarship, 288
Mary Virginia Macrea Memorial Scholarship, 132
Maryland Delegate Scholarship, 376
Maryland Educational Assistance Grant, 376
Maryland Edward T. Conroy Memorial Scholarship Program, 376
Maryland Jack F. Tolbert Memorial Grant, 377
Maryland Part-Time Grant Program, 377
Maryland Senatorial Scholarship, 377
Maryland Tuition Reduction for Non-Resident Nursing Students, 377
Maryland Tuition Waiver for Foster Care Recipients, 378
Masonic Range Science Scholarship, 481
Massachusetts Cash Grant Program, 380
Massachusetts Christian A. Herter Memorial Scholarship Program, 380
Massachusetts Early Childhood Educators Scholarship, 380
Massachusetts Educational Rewards Grant Program, 380
Massachusetts Federation of Polish Women's Clubs Scholarships, 364
Massachusetts Gilbert Matching Student Grant, 380
Massachusetts High Demand Scholarship Program, 381
Massachusetts MASSgrant Program, 381
Massachusetts Math and Science Teachers Scholarship, 381
Massachusetts No Interest Loan, 595
Massachusetts Paraprofessional Teacher Preparation Grant Program, 381
Massachusetts Part-Time Grant Program, 381
Massachusetts Public Service Grant Program, 382
Math And Science Teachers Loan Forgiveness Program, 600
Matsuo Bridge Company Ltd. of Japan Scholarship, 203
Maureen V. O'Donnell/Eunice C. Kraft Teacher Training Scholarships, 97
Maynard Jensen American Legion Memorial Scholarship, 147
McAlinden Divers Scholarship, 420
MCC Theater Internships, 567
McFarland Charitable Foundation Scholarship, 295
M.D. Jack Murphy Memorial Nurses Training Fund, 143
Media Plan Case Competition, 537
Melville H. Cohee Student Leader Conservation Scholarship, 490
Melvin R. Green Scholarships, 218
Menominee Adult Vocational Training Grant, 383
Menominee Higher Education Grant, 384
The Merchants Exchange Scholarship Fund, 384
MESBEC Scholarships, 234
MetLife Foundation Scholarship, 279
Metropolitan Museum of Art Mentoring Program for College Juniors, 567
Metropolitan Museum of Art Six-Month Internship, 567
Metropolitan Museum of Art Summer Internship Program, 568
MG James Ursano Scholarship Program, 209
Michael Hakeem Memorial Award, 267
Michael Stohl Scholarship, 247
Michigan Competitive Scholarship, 385
Michigan Society of Professional Engineers Scholarships for High School Seniors, 385
Michigan Tuition Grant, 385
Michigan Tuition Incentive Program, 385
Mickey Leland Energy Fellowship Program, 577
Microscopy Society of America Undergraduate Research Scholarship, 385
Microsoft General Scholarship, 386
Mid-Continent Instrument Scholarship, 90
Midwest Student Exchange Program, 386
Mike and Flo Novovesky Scholarship, 106
Mike Reynolds Scholarship, 462
Milan Getting Scholarship, 473
Mildred R. Knoles Scholarship, 130
Mildred Towle Scholarship - Study Abroad, 316
Mildred Towle Scholarship for African-Americans, 316
Military Order of the Purple Heart Scholarship, 387
Miller Electric Manufacturing Company Ivic Scholarship, 203
Miller Electric Mfg. Co. Scholarship, 203
Mills Fleet Farm Scholarship, 280
Milton Fisher Scholarship for Innovation and Creativity, 463
Minnesota Educational Assistance for Veterans, 387
Minnesota GI Bill, 387
Minnesota Indian Scholarship Program, 388
Minnesota Post-Secondary Child Care Grant, 388
Minnesota Public Safety Officers Survivors Program, 388
Minnesota State Grant Program, 388
Minnesota Student Educational Loan Fund (SELF), 596
Minnesota Work-Study Program, 568
Minority and Underrepresented Environmental Literacy Program, 391
Minority Teacher Education Scholarship Program/Florida Fund for Minority Teachers, Inc., 265
Minority Teachers of Illinois Scholarship, 343
Minority Teaching Scholarship, 391
Miss America Competition Awards, 389
Mississippi Eminent Scholars Grant, 389
Mississippi Health Care Professions Loan/Scholarship, 596
Mississippi Higher Education Legislative Plan, 390
Mississippi Resident Tuition Assistance Grant, 390
The Mississippi Scholarship, 187
Mississippi William Winter Teacher Scholar Loan Program, 597
Missouri Department of Higher Education Vietnam Veteran's Survivor Grant Program, 392
Missouri Higher Education "Bright Flight" Academic Scholarship, 392
Missouri League for Nursing Scholarship, 392
Mister Rogers Memorial Scholarship, 81
The Mitch Daniels Early Graduation Scholarship, 498
Mitsuo Shito Public Housing Scholarship, 316
MOAA American Patriot Scholarship Program, 387

MOAA Interest-Free Loan and Grant Program, 595
Momentum, Inc. Healthcare Scholarship, 454
Montana Governor's Best and Brightest Merit Scholarship, 393
Montana Governor's Best and Brightest Merit-at-Large Scholarship, 393
Montana Governor's Best and Brightest Need Based Scholarship, 393
Montana Higher Education Grant, 394
Montana Honorably Discharged Veteran Fee Waiver, 394
Montana University System Honor Scholarship, 394
Montgomery GI Bill (MGIB), 525
Montgomery GI Bill (MGIB) "Kicker", 525
Moody's Mega Math "M3" Challenge, 394
Morgan Stanley Foundation Scholarship, 330
Morgan Stanley Richard B. Fisher Scholarship Program, 394
Morgan Stanley Scholars Program, 112
Morris Arboretum Education Internship, 569
Morris Arboretum Horticulture Internship, 569
Morton B. Duggan, Jr. Memorial Education Recognition Award, 192
Morton Gould Young Composer Awards, 210
Mother Jones Ben Bagdikian Fellowship Program, 570
MSGC Undergraduate Underrepresented Minority Fellowship Program, 398
MTA Doug Slifka Memorial Scholarship, 393
Muggets Scholarship, 337
Museum Coca-Cola Internship, 573
Museum of Modern Art Internship, 570
Myrtle and Earl Walker Scholarship, 479
NABA National Scholarship Program, 406
NABJ Internships, 572
NABJ Scholarship, 408
NABJ Visual Task Force (VTF) Scholarship, 408
NAFEO (National Association for Equal Opportunity in Higher Education) Scholarships, 116
Nancy Lorraine Jensen Memorial Scholarship, 491
Nannie W. Norfleet Scholarship, 156
NANT Educational Assistance Program, 406
NAPA Auto Parts Scholarship, 280
NASA Academy Internship, 572
NASA Connecticut Space Grant Undergraduate Fellowship, 395
NASA Idaho Space Grant Undergraduate Scholarship, 397
NASA Minnesota Space Grant Consortium Wide Scholarship, 398
NASA Missouri State Space Grant Undergraduate Scholarship, 399
NASA New Jersey Space Grant Consortium Undergraduate Summer Fellowships in Engineering and Science, 571
NASA North Carolina Space Grant Consortium Undergraduate Research Scholarship, 400
NASA North Carolina Space Grant Consortium Undergraduate Scholarship Program, 400
NASA Ohio Space Grant Junior/Senior Scholarship Program, 401
NASA Pennsylvania Space Grant Undergraduate Scholarship, 402
NASA Rhode Island Space Grant Summer Undergraduate Scholarship, 402
NASA Space Grant Arizona Undergraduate Research Internship, 571
NASA Space Grant Georgia Fellowship Program, 396
NASA Space Grant Hawaii Undergraduate Fellowship Program, 396
NASA Space Grant Illinois Undergraduate Scholarship, 397
NASA Space Grant Kentucky Undergraduate Scholarship, 397
NASA Space Grant Maine Consortium Annual Scholarship and Fellowship Program, 397
NASA Space Grant Michigan Undergraduate Fellowship, 398
NASA Space Grant Montana Undergraduate Scholarship Program, 399
NASA Space Grant Nevada Undergraduate Scholarship, 399
NASA Space Grant New Mexico Undergraduate Scholarship, 400
NASA Space Grant North Dakota Consortium Lillian Goettler Scholarship, 401
NASA Space Grant North Dakota Undergraduate Scholarship, 401
NASA Space Grant Oregon Undergraduate Scholarship, 402
NASA Space Grant Rhode Island Undergraduate Research Scholarship, 402
NASA Space Grant South Carolina Undergraduate Student Research Fellowship, 403
NASA Space Grant Undergraduate Scholarship, 395
NASA Space Grant Vermont Consortium Undergraduate Scholarships, 404
NASA Space Grant Virginia Community College STEM Scholarship, 404
NASA Space Grant Wisconsin Consortium Undergraduate Research Program, 405
NASA Space Grant Wisconsin Consortium Undergraduate Scholarship, 405
NASA Utah Space Grant Consortium Undergraduate Scholarship, 403
NASA West Virginia Space Grant Undergraduate Research Fellowship, 405
NASCAR/Wendell Scott Sr. Award, 325
National Achievement Scholarships, 416
National Amateur Baseball Federation Scholarship, 406
National ChairScholars Scholarship, 237
National Co-op Scholarship, 410
National Dairy Shrine Maurice E. Core Scholarship, 412
National Energy Technology Laboratory Professional Internship Program, 577
National Federation of the Blind Scholarships, 413
The National FFA Alumni Association Scholarship, 280
National FFA Collegiate Scholarship Program, 413
The National FFA Scholarship Funded by National FFA Staff, Board and Individual Contributors, 280
National Geographic Society Geography Students Internship, 572
National Greenhouse Manufacturing Association (NGMA) Scholarship, 106
National Guard Educational Assistance Program, 361
National Guard Tuition Waiver, 438
National Guild of Piano Teachers $200 Scholarship, 98
National Guild of Piano Teachers Composition Contest, 98
National Health Service Corps Scholarship, 527
National Italian American Foundation Scholarship Program, 414
National Junior Classical League Scholarship, 415
National Mastis Council Scholarship, 280
National Merit Scholarships, 416
National Museum of the American Indian Internship, 572
National Peace Essay Contest, 524
National Presbyterian College Scholarship, 458
National Security Agency Stokes Educational Scholarship Program, 418
National Society of Accountants Scholarship, 419
National Speakers Association Scholarship, 419
National Student Nurses Association Scholarship, 266
National Wild Turkey Federation Scholarship, 281

Native American Education Grant, 458
Native American Leadership in Education Scholarship, 235
Navy Supply Corps Foundation Scholarship, 420
NAWIC Founders' Construction Trades Scholarship, 409
NAWIC Founders' Undergraduate Scholarship, 409
NBRC/AMP Robert M. Lawrence, MD Education Recognition Award, 193
NBRC/AMP William W. Burgin, Jr. MD Education Recognition Award, 193
NC Sheriff's Association Criminal Justice Scholarship, 433
NCR Summer Internships, 573
NEBHE's Tuition Break Regional Student Program, 421
Nebraska Opportunity Grant, 421
NEEBC Scholarship, 421
NEHA/AAS Scholarship, 412
NESA Academic Scholarships, 412
Nettie Dracup Memorial Scholarship, 100
The New England FEMARA Scholarship, 187
New England Hadassah Scholarship, 354
New Jersey Class Loan Program, 597
New Jersey Educational Opportunity Fund Grant, 422
New Jersey Law Enforcement Officer Memorial Scholarship, 422
New Jersey Part-Time Tuition Aid Grant for County Colleges, 422
New Jersey STARS II, 422
New Jersey Student Tuition Assistance Reward Scholarship (NJSTARS), 423
New Jersey Tuition Aid Grants (TAG), 423
New Jersey World Trade Center Scholarship, 423
New Leader Scholarship, 79
New Mexico Allied Health Student Loan-for-Service Program, 597
New Mexico Competitive Scholarships, 423
New Mexico Legislative Endowment Program, 424
New Mexico Legislative Lottery Scholarship, 424
New Mexico Nursing Student Loan-for-Service, 598
New Mexico Scholars Program, 424
New Mexico Student Choice Grant, 424
New Mexico Student Incentive Grant, 424
New Mexico Teacher's Loan-for-Service, 598
New Mexico Work-Study Program, 574
The New Republic Internships, 574
New York American Legion Press Association Scholarship, 155
New York Metropolitan Area Scholarship Program, 237
New York Military Service Recognition Scholarship (MSRS), 426
New York State Aid for Part-Time Study Program, 426
New York State Arthur O. Eve Higher Education Opportunity Program (HEOP), 425
New York State Assembly Session Internship Program, 574
New York State Math and Science Teaching Incentive Program, 427
New York State Memorial Scholarship for Families of Deceased Police/Volunteer Firefighters/Peace Officers and Emergency Medical Service Workers, 427
New York State Readers Aid Program, 428
New York State Regents Awards for Children of Deceased and Disabled Veterans, 427
New York State Tuition Assistance Program, 427
New York State Veterans Tuition Award, 428
New York State World Trade Center Memorial Scholarship, 428
New York Times James Reston Reporting Fellowships, 575
New York Women in Communications Foundation Scholarship, 428
NextEra Energy Internship Program, 575
NGWREF Len Assante Scholarship Fund, 413
Nick Van Pernis Scholarship, 316
Nisei Student Relocation Commemorative Fund Scholarship, 429
Nissan North America, Inc. Scholarship, 112
Nissan North America, Inc. Scholarship Program, 330
Nissan Scholarship, 390
NMIA Ohio Scholarship Program, 429
Non Commissioned Officers Association Scholarship for Children of Members, 430
Non Commissioned Officers Association Scholarship for Spouses of Members, 430
Norfolk Southern Foundation Scholarship, 281
The Norman E. Strohmeier, W2VRS, Memorial Scholarship, 187
North American Indian Scholarship, 347
North Carolina Aubrey Lee Brooks Scholarship, 433
North Carolina Community Colleges Wells Fargo Technical Scholarship, 431
North Carolina Education Lottery Scholarship, 240
North Carolina Scholarships for Children of War Veterans, 431
North Carolina State Board of Refrigeration Examiners Scholarship, 431
North Carolina Vocational Rehabilitation Award, 431
North Central Region Scholarship, 479
North Dakota Academic Scholarships, 433
North Dakota Career & Technical Education Scholarships, 434
North Dakota Indian Scholarship Program, 434
North Dakota Scholars Program, 434
North Dakota State Student Incentive Grant, 434
The North Fulton Amateur Radio League Scholarship Fund, 187
The Northern California DX Foundation Scholarship, 187
Northern Cheyenne Higher Education Program, 435
Northwest Arkansas Bilingual Teacher Scholarship, 331
Northwest Danish Association Scholarship, 435
NPFDA Scholarship, 416
NPPF Scholarship, 417
NSPS Board of Governors Scholarship, 100
NSPS Scholarships, 100
NTA Canada Scholarship, 514
NTA Connecticut Scholarship, 514
NTA Florida Scholarship, 514
NTA LaMacchia Family Scholarship, 515
NTA Massachusetts Scholarship, 515
NTA New Horizons - Kathy LeTarte Scholarship, 515
NTA New Jersey Scholarship, 515
NTA New York Scholarship, 515
NTA North America Scholarship, 516
NTA Ohio Scholarship, 516
NTA Pat & Jim Host Scholarship, 516
NTA Rene Campbell - Ruth McKinney Scholarship, 516
NTA Utah Keith Griffall Scholarship, 517
Nuclear Engineering Division (NED) Scholarship, 218
Nuclear Regulatory Commission Historically Black Colleges and Universities Student Research Participation, 578
NY Times Internships, 575
Oak Ridge National Laboratory Undergraduate Student Cooperative Education Program, 578
Oak Ridge Nuclear Engineering Science Laboratory Synthesis, 578
Oak Ridge Science Semester, 578
OCA-AXA Achievement Scholarships, 435
OCA/UPS Foundation Gold Mountain College Scholarship, 436
Office of Hawaiian Affairs Scholarship Fund, 317
Ohio College Opportunity Grant, 436

Ohio National Guard Scholarship Program, 436
Ohio Newspaper Association Publications/Public Relations Internship, 582
Ohio Newspapers Minority Scholarship, 437
Ohio Newspapers Women's Scholarship, 437
Ohio Nurse Education Assistance Loan Program, 598
Ohio Safety Officers College Memorial Fund, 436
Ohio War Orphans Scholarship, 436
Oklahoma Academic Scholars Program, 439
Oklahoma Engineering Foundation Scholarship, 438
Oklahoma Future Teachers Scholarship, 439
Oklahoma Tuition Aid Grant, 439
Oklahoma's Promise - Oklahoma Higher Learning Access Program, 439
Omaha Steaks Scholarship, 354
OMNE/Nursing Leaders of Maine Scholarship, 440
One Family Scholars Program, 440
One World Scholarship Essay, 446
ONS Foundation Bachelor's Scholarships, 440
Oracle Product Development Summer Internship Program, 582
Oregon Alpha Delta Kappa Scholarship, 446
Oregon Dungeness Crab Commission, 446
Oregon Foundation for Blacktail Deer Scholarship, 446
Oregon Occupational Safety and Health Division Workers Memorial Scholarship, 446
Oregon Scholarship Fund Community College Student Award Programs, 447
The Orlando HamCation Scholarship, 188
Osage Tribal Education Committee Award, 230
Osage Tribal Education Scholarship, 450
Oscar and Rosetta Fish Fund, 317
Ouida Mundy Hill Memorial Fund, 317
The Ouimet Scholarship, 267
The Outdoor Hams Scholarship, 188
Owens Corning Internships, 583
Pacific Gas and Electric Summer Intern Program, 583
PAGE Foundation Scholarships, 460
Palmetto Fellows Scholarship Program, 492
Papercheck.com Charles Shafae' Scholarship Fund, 450
Par Aide's Joseph S. Garske Collegiate Grant Program, 450
Paradigm Scholarship, 484
Paradise Tomato Kitchens Scholarship, 281
Past Presidents Scholarship, 203
Patient Advocate Foundation Scholarships for Survivors, 450
Patrick and Judith McHugh Scholarship, 533
Paul A. Stewart Award, 542
The Paul and Helen L. Grauer Scholarship, 188
The Paul and Helen Ruckes Scholarship, 107
Paul Jennings Scholarship, 350
Paul Tsongas Scholarship Program, 382
Paulina L. Sorg Scholarship, 317
Payzer Scholarship, 261
PBS Internships, 583
Pearl I. Young Scholarship, 401
Pearson Prize for Higher Education, 451
peermusic Latin Scholarship, 227
Peggy Dixon Two-Year Scholarship, 485
Peggy Guggenheim Internship, 586
Pennsylvania GEAR UP Scholarship, 452
Pennsylvania Higher Education Assistance Agency Partnership for Access to Higher Education (PATH), 452
Pennsylvania Higher Education Assistance Agency Postsecondary Educational Gratuity Program, 452
Pennsylvania State Grant Program, 453
Pennsylvania Targeted Industry Program (PA-TIP), 453
Pennsylvania Women's Press Association Scholarship, 456
Pennsylvania Work-Study Program, 453
Penton Media Scholarship, 281
People's United Bank Scholarship, 533
The Peoria Area Amateur Radio Club Scholarship, 188
Pepsi-Cola Bottling of Eastern Oregon Scholarship, 282
Peridian International Inc./Rae L. Price FASLA Scholarship, 367
Perry & Sally Sorenson Scholarship for Dependents of Hospitality Workers, 317
Perry & Sally Sorenson Scholarship for Foster Youth, 318
Pete Wilson Journalism Scholarship, 462
The Peter Cameron/Housewares Charity Foundation Scholarship, 354
Peter Connacher Memorial Scholarship, 447
Peter Kump Memorial Scholarship, 355
Peter R. Papworth Scholarship, 318
Peter Wollitzer Scholarships for Study in Asia, 247
Peterson Family Scholarship, 282
PFLAG National Scholarship Program, 456
PGA Tour Diversity Intern Program, 583
PGSF Annual Scholarship Competition, 460
PHCC Auxiliary of Texas Scholarship, 457
PHCC Educational Foundation Scholarships, 457
PHCC of Massachusetts Auxiliary Scholarship, 457
Philip and Alice Angell Eastern Star Scholarship, 533
Philippine Nurses' Association Scholarship, 318
Phipps Conservatory and Botanical Gardens Internships, 583
Pickett and Hatcher Educational Loan, 599
Pittsburgh Local Section Scholarship, 176
Pittsburgh Scholarship, 487
PLANET Academic Excellence Foundation Scholarship, 282
Plant Propagation Internship, 569
Plant Protection Internship, 569
Plasma Physics National Undergraduate Fellowship Program, 584
Plastics Pioneers Scholarships, 487
Point Scholarship, 457
Police/Firefighters' Survivors Educational Assistance Program, 91
The Polish American Club of North Jersey Scholarships, 364
The Polish National Alliance of Brooklyn, USA, Inc. Scholarships, 365
Praxair International Scholarship, 203
Presbyterian Student Opportunity Scholarship, 458
Presbyterian Undergraduate and Graduate Loan, 599
Presidents Scholarships, 462
Princess Grace Award for Dance, 459
Princess Grace Award For Film, 459
Princess Grace Award For Playwriting, 459
Princess Grace Award For Theater, 459
Procter & Gamble - Orgullosa Scholarship, 331
Professional Land Surveyors of Oregon Scholarship, 447
PROMISE Scholarship, 539
Proof-Reading.com Scholarship Program, 460
PRSA-Hawaii/Roy Leffingwell Public Relations Scholarship, 318
PSECU International Education Scholarship, 455
Public Safety Officer or Employee's Child Survivor Grant, 392
Pulliam Journalism Fellowship, 563
Quida and Anna Pichini Merit Scholarships, 455
Rabo Agrifinance Scholarship, 282
Rain Bird Intelligent Use of Water Scholarship, 367
Rainbow Scholarship and Queer Student of the Year Scholarship, 459
Ralph K. Hillquist Honorary SAE Scholarship, 467
Ram Trucks Scholarship, 282

The Ranch House at Devil's Thumb Scholarship, 355
Randy Pausch Scholarship Fund, 80
The Ray, NØRP, & Katie, WØKTE, Pautz Scholarship, 189
Ray Yoshida Kauai Fine Arts Scholarship, 318
Raymond DiSalvo Scholarship, 177
Raymond F. Cain Scholarship Fund, 318
Raymond K. Conley Memorial Scholarship, 151
RCMI Technical/Trade School Scholarship, 464
Red Barn Media Group Scholarship, 283
Red River Valley Fighter Pilots Association (RRVA) Scholarship Program, 462
Regional University Baccalaureate Scholarship, 439
RehabGYM Scholarship, 533
Research Experiences for Undergraduates - Maria Mitchell Observatory, 573
Research Experiences for Undergraduates in the Physical Sciences, 551
Research Participation at the Centers for Disease Control and Prevention/Agency for Toxic Substances and Disease Registry, 578
Research Participation at the National Center for Toxicological Research, 579
Research Participation at the U.S. Food and Drug Administration, 579
Research Participation Program for the Combat Casualty Care Research Program (CCCRP), 579
Research Participation Program for the Johns Hopkins University Applied Physics Laboratory, 579
Research Participation Program for the Joint POW/MIA Accounting Command/Central Identification Laboratory (JPAC-CIL), 579
Research Participation Program for the U.S. Air Force Research Laboratory, Tyndall Air Force Base (AFRL-TYNDALL), 580
Research Participation Program for the U.S. Air Force Research Laboratory (USAFRL), Wright Patterson Air Force Base, 580
Research Participation Program for the U.S. Air Force School of Aerospace Medicine (USAFSAM), 580
Research Participation Program for the U.S. Army Aeromedical Research Laboratory (USAARL), 580
Research Participation Program for the U.S. Army Medical Research Institute of Chemical Defense, 580
Research Participation Program for the U.S. Army Public Health Command, 580
Research Participation Program for the U.S. Army Research Institute for Environmental Medicine (USARIEM), 581
Research Participation Program for the U.S. Army Research Laboratory, 581
Restaurant at Sunset Marquis Scholarship, 355
Reuben Trane Scholarship, 198
Rewarding Young Leaders in Our Community Scholarship, 262
Rhode Island State Government Internship Program, 584
Rhode Island State Grant, 464
Rich Meiers Health Administration Fund, 319
Richard Eaton Foundation Award, 229
Richard F. Brentano Memorial Scholarship, 447
Richard Lee Vernon Aviation Scholarship, 261
Richard Smart Scholarship, 319
The Richard W. Bendicksen, N7ZL, Memorial Scholarship, 189
Richie M. Gregory Fund, 319
Rick Arkans Eagle Scout Scholarship, 415
Rise Up Scholarship, 319
Ritchie-Jennings Memorial Scholarship, 81
R.L. Gillette Scholarship, 107
RMHC U.S. Scholarship Programs, 465
Robanna Fund, 319
Robert and Rebecca Memorial Grant, 358
Robert B. Bailey Scholarship, 248
Robert D. Blue Scholarship, 349
Robert G. Lacy Scholarship, 177
Robert L. Livingston Scholarship, 350
Robert L. Peaslee Brazing Scholarship, 204
Robert R. Lee Promise Category A Scholarship, 340
Robert R. Lee Promise Category B Scholarship, 341
Robert T. (Bob) Liner Scholarship, 177
Robert W. Valimont Endowment Fund Scholarship, 159
Roberta Marie Stretch Memorial Scholarship, 149
Rocky Mountain Coal Mining Institute Scholarship, 464
The Rocky Mountain Division Scholarship, 189
Rodney Cottrell Scholarship, 484
Rodney E. Powell Memorial Scholarship, 431
Roger W. Emmons Memorial Scholarship, 447
Roller Skating Foundation, 465
Roller Skating Foundation College Scholarship, 465
Ron Bright Scholarship, 319
Ron Brown Scholar Program, 465
Ronald Reagan College Leaders Scholarship Program, 456
Roosevelt Archival Internships, 562
Rose Acre Farms Scholarship, 283
Rose and Flower Garden Internship, 570
Rosedale Post 346 Scholarship, 134
Rosemary & Nellie Ebrie Fund, 320
Rosewood Family Scholarship Program, 265
ROTC/Navy Nurse Corps Scholarship Program, 528
ROTC/Navy/Marine Four-Year Scholarship, 528
ROTC/Navy/Marine Two-Year Scholarship, 529
Rubincam Youth Award, 413
Ruby Paul Campaign Fund Scholarship, 149
Rudolf Nissim Prize, 211
The Rudolph Dillman Memorial Scholarship, 107
Ruth Clark Furniture Design Scholarship, 347
RWMA Scholarship, 204
Sachs Foundation Undergraduate Grant, 466
SACI Alumni Heritage Scholarship, 500
SACI Consortium Scholarship, 500
SAE Detroit Section Technical Scholarship, 467
SAE Long-Term Member Sponsored Scholarship, 467
SAE Women Engineers Committee Scholarship, 467
SAE/David Hermance Hybird Technologies Scholarship, 467
SAE/Ford Partnership for Advanced Studies Scholarship, 468
Safeway Foundation Hawaii Scholarship Fund, 320
Sal Ingrassia Scholarship, 350
Salute to Education Scholarship, 469
Samara Foundation of Vermont Scholarship, 533
Samsung American Legion Scholarship, 147
Samuel Fletcher Tapman ASCE Student Chapter Scholarship, 195
Samuel Robinson Award, 458
San Jose Local Scholarships for Women, 96
San Manuel Band of Missions Indians Tribal Scholarship, 113
Sant'Anna Institute-Sorrento Lingue Scholarship, 490
Sara Shallenberger Brown GCA National Parks Conservation Scholarship, 288
Sarah Rosenberg Teacher Education Scholarship, 320
SCA Conservation Internships, 587
Scarlett Family Foundation Scholarship, 469
Schneider-Emanuel American Legion Scholarships, 168
Schnitzer Steel "Racing to Stop Hunger" Scholarship, 355
Scholarship America Scholarships, 469
Scholarship for Children of Deceased or Totally Disabled Veterans, 159

Program Index

Scholarship for Children of Living Veterans, 159
Scholarship for Foodservice Communication Careers, 345
Scholarship for Minority Undergraduate Physics Majors, 177
The Scholarship of the Morris Radio Club of New Jersey, 189
Scholastic Art Portfolio Gold Award, 93
Scholastic Art Portfolio Silver With Distinction Award, 93
Scholastic Photography Portfolio Silver Award, 93
Scholastic Writing Portfolio Gold Award, 94
Schonstedt Scholarships in Surveying, 100
Schwallie Family Scholarship Program, 449
Sculpture Society Scholarship, 418
Seabee Memorial Scholarship, 470
Seattle Professional Chapter Scholarship, 222
Second Marine Division Association Scholarship Fund, 470
Seed Companies Scholarship, 106
SEG Foundation/Apache Scholarship, 484
SEG/Denver Geophysical Society Scholarship, 481
SEG/Gary and Lorene Servos Scholarship, 484
SEG/Marvin and Jene Hewitt Scholarship, 484
SEG/P.C. Havens/Seismic Exchange Inc. Scholarship, 484
Selected Reserve Montgomery GI Bill, 525
Senator George J. Mitchell Scholarship, 471
Senator Richard M. & Dr. Ruth Matsuura Scholarship Fund, 320
Seneca Foods Corporation Scholarship, 283
Seneca Nation Higher Education Program, 471
September 11, 2001 Tragedy Tuition Waiver Program, 382
September 11 Memorial Scholarship, 522
Sergeant Major Douglas R. Drum Memorial Scholarship, 172
Sertoma Scholarships for Students Who are Hard of Hearing or Deaf, 471
Seymour and Phyllis Shore Memorial Grant, 358
Shane Dean Voyles Memorial Scholarship, 144
Shannon Scholarship, 519
Sheryl A. Horak Law Enforcement Explorer Scholarship, 370
Shirley McKown Scholarship Fund, 320
Shoshone Tribal Scholarship, 472
Shuichi, Katsu and Itsuyo Suga Scholarship, 321
Sid Richardson Scholarship, 472
Siemens Awards for Advanced Placement, 473
Siemens Competition in Math, Science and Technology, 473
Siemens We Can Change the World Challenge, 473
Sigma Phi Alpha Certificate/Associate Scholarship, 84
Sigma Phi Alpha Undergraduate Scholarship, 84
Signet Classic Student Scholarship Essay Contest, 451
Silver Eagle Indian Scholarship, 150
Simon and Schuster Internship Program, 584
The Six Meter Club of Chicago Scholarship, 189
Slovenian Women's Union Scholarship Foundation, 474
SME Directors Scholarship, 480
SME Education Foundation Family Scholarship, 480
SME-FF Future Leaders of Manufacturing Scholarships, 480
Smithsonian Environmental Research Center Internship Program, 585
Smithsonian Minority Internship, 585
Smithsonian Native American Internship, 585
Society of Daughters of United States Army Scholarship Program, 481
Society of Exploration Geophysicists Scholarship, 485
Society of Physics Students Future Teacher Scholarship, 485
Society of Physics Students Leadership Scholarship, 485
Society of Physics Students Summer Internship Program, 586
Society of Plastics Engineers General Scholarships, 487
Society of Sponsors Scholarship Program, 421
The Society of the Descendants of the Signers of the Declaration of Independence Annual Scholarship, 489
Sonia Streuli Maguire Outstanding Scholastic Achievement Award, 502
Sons of Italy General Scholarship, 490
Sons of Italy Italian Language Scholarship, 490
Sons of Italy National Leadership Grant, 491
Sons of the American Legion Scholarship, 167
Sony Credited Internship, 586
South Carolina Dayco Scholarship Program, 492
South Carolina HOPE Scholarships, 492
South Carolina LIFE Scholarship Program, 493
South Carolina Lottery Tuition Assistance Program, 493
South Carolina Need-Based Grants Program, 493
South Carolina Teacher Loans, 599
South Carolina Tuition Grants, 493
South Dakota Annis I. Fowler/Kaden Scholarship, 494
South Dakota Ardell Bjugstad Scholarship, 494
South Dakota Haines Memorial Scholarship, 495
South Dakota Marlin R. Scarborough Memorial Scholarship, 495
South Dakota Opportunity Scholarship Program, 495
The Southeastern DX Club Scholarship Fund, 190
Southern California Council Endowed Internship, 573
Southern Nursery Organization Sidney B. Meadows Scholarship, 472
Southern Scholarship Foundation Scholarships, 496
Southface Internship, 587
Sovereign Nations Scholarship, 113
The SPE Foundation Blow Molding Division Memorial Scholarships, 488
Spence Reese Scholarship, 227
SPIE Optics and Photonics Education Scholarships, 496
Spirit of Youth Scholarship, 159
Spoleto Festival USA Apprenticeship Program, 587
SREB Academic Common Market, 440
Stan Beck Fellowship, 257
Stanfield and D'Orlando Art Scholarships, 521
Stanford Chen Internship Grant, 212
Stanley Z. Koplik Certificate of Mastery Tuition Waiver Program, 382
Staples Associates Annual Scholarships Plan, 496
State University System of Florida Theodore R. and Vivian M. Johnson Scholarship, 359
Stella Blum Student Research Grant, 246
STEM Bridge Scholarship, 405
STEM Columbia Crew Memorial Scholarship, 403
STEM Majors Scholarship, 208
STEM Teacher Scholarships, 209
Stephen J. Brady STOP Hunger Scholarships, 489
Stephen T. Kugle Scholarship, 219
Steven G. King Play Environments Scholarship, 367
Steven Scher Memorial Scholarship for Aspiring Restaurateurs, 355
Student Aid Foundation Loan, 599
Student Internship Program at the U.S. Army Center for Health Promotion and Preventive Medicine, 581
Student Research at the U.S. Army Edgewood Chemical Biological Center, 581
Students With Disabilities Endowed Scholarship Honoring Elizabeth Daley Jeffords, 534
Studio at the Montage Resort & Spa Scholarship, 355

Study Abroad Scholarships, 293
Sunday Supper South Atlanta Scholarship, 356
Supreme Guardian Council, International Order of Job's Daughters Scholarship, 501
Susan Burdett Scholarship, 167
Susie & Bruce Usrey Scholarship, 337
Susie Holmes Memorial Scholarship, 501
SWE Scholarships, 489
Swiss Benevolent Society Medicus Student Exchange, 502
Swiss Benevolent Society Pellegrini Scholarship, 502
Sylvia W. Farny Scholarship, 215
TAG Education Collaborative Web Challenge Contest, 502
Taglit-Birthright Israel Gift, 503
Takehiko Hasegawa Academic Scholarship, 321
Takehiko Hasegawa Kaua'i Community College Scholarship, 321
Tau Beta Pi/SAE Engineering Scholarship, 468
TCI Student Scholarships, 503
Teacher Education Assistance for College and Higher Education (TEACH) Grant, 453
Teamsters Clyde C. Crosby/Joseph M. Edgar Memorial Scholarship, 448
Teamsters Council #37 Federal Credit Union Scholarship, 448
Teamsters Local 305 Scholarship, 448
Technical Minority Scholarship, 546
Ted and Nora Anderson Scholarship, 134
The Ted, W4VHF, and Itice, K4LVV, Goldthorpe Scholarship, 190
TeeJet Technologies Scholarship, 283
Teens Drive Smart Video Contest, 228
Tennessee Dependent Children Scholarship Program, 504
Tennessee Dual Enrollment Grant, 504
Tennessee HOPE Access Grant, 504
Tennessee HOPE Scholarship, 505
Tennessee Minority Teaching Fellows Program, 600
Tennessee Ned McWherter Scholars Program, 505
Tennessee Student Assistance Award Program, 505
Tennessee Teaching Scholars Program, 600
Texas 4-H Opportunity Scholarships, 505
Texas Armed Services Scholarship Program, 507
Texas College Access Loan (CAL), 601
Texas Competitive Scholarship Waiver, 507
Texas Concurrent Enrollment Waiver (Enrollment in Two Texas Community Colleges), 507
Texas Exemption for Peace Officers Disabled in the Line of Duty, 508
Texas Exemption for Students Under Conservatorship of the Dept. of Family & Protective Services, 508
Texas Exemption for the Surviving Spouse and Dependent Children of Certain Deceased Public Servants (Employees), 508
Texas Exemptions for Texas Veterans (Hazelwood Exemption), 508
Texas Farm Bureau Scholarship, 506
Texas Federal Supplemental Educational Opportunity Grant, 509
Texas Fifth-Year Accounting Student Scholarship Program, 509
Texas Good Neighbor Scholarship, 509
TEXAS Grant (Toward Excellence, Access, and Success), 509
Texas Highest Ranking High School Graduate Tuition Exemption, 509
Texas History Essay Contest, 492
Texas National Guard Tuition Assistance Program, 509
Texas Public Educational Grant, 510
Texas Reduction in Tuition Charges for Students Taking 15 or More Semester Credit Hours Per Term, 510
Texas Senior Citizen, 65 or Older, Free Tuition for Up to 6 Credit Hours, 510
Texas Transportation Scholarship, 518
Texas Tuition Equalization Grant (TEG), 510
Texas Tuition Exemption for Blind or Deaf Students, 510
Texas Tuition Exemption for Children of Disabled or Deceased Firefighters, Peace Officers, Game Wardens, and Employees of Correctional Institutions, 511
Texas Tuition Rebate for Certain Undergraduates, 511
Texas Tuition Reduction for Students Taking More Than 15 Hours, 511
Theisen's Home Farm Auto Scholarship, 284
Thelma Foster Junior American Legion Auxiliary Members Scholarship, 162
Thelma Foster Senior American Legion Auxiliary Member Scholarship, 162
Theodore Mazza Scholarship, 520
Thermoforming Division Memorial Scholarship, 488
Thermoset Division/James I. MacKenzie Memorial Scholarship, 488
Third Marine Division Memorial Scholarship Fund, 511
Thomas H. Miller Scholarship, 226
Thomas J. Bardos Science Education Awards for Undergraduate Students, 96
Thomas M. Stetson Scholarship, 108
Thomas R. Pickering Foreign Affairs Fellowship, 545
The Thomas W. Porter, W8KYZ, Scholarship Honoring Michael Daugherty, W8LSE, 190
Thomas Wood Baldridge Scholarship, 357
Thurgood Marshall Scholarship Award, 512
Thz Fo Farm Fund, 321
Time Inc. Internship Program, 588
Times Supermarket Shop & Score Scholarship, 321
Timothy and Palmer W. Bigelow, Jr. Scholarship, 337
TMC/SAE Donald D. Dawson Technical Scholarship, 468
The Tom and Judith Comstock Scholarship, 190
Tommy Lee Memorial Scholarship Fund, 322
The Tommy Tranchin Award, 250
Tongan Cultural Society Scholarship, 322
Top 10 College Women Competition, 291
Toraji & Toki Yoshinaga Scholarship, 322
Toshiba/NSTA ExploraVision Award, 418
Toyota Motor Sales, U.S.A. Inc. Scholarship, 284
Traditional CITE Scholarship, 245
Travelers Foundation Scholarship, 113
Travelers Scholarship, 325
Treacy Foundation Scholarship, 518
Tribal Business Management Scholarship, 235
Tri-State Surveying & Photogrammetry Kris M. Kunze Scholarship, 100
Troy Barboza Educational Fund Scholarship, 322
Truman D. Picard Scholarship, 347
Tuition Exemption for Children of U.S. Military POW/MIAs from Texas, 511
Two Ten Footwear Design Scholarship, 519
Two Ten Footwear Foundation Scholarship, 519
Tyrholm Big R Stores Scholarship, 284
Tyson Foods Inc. Scholarship, 284
Tyson Foods Intern Program, 588
UECU Student Scholarship Program, 529
The Ulman Cancer Fund Scholarship, 519
UNCF Merck Science Initiative, 523
Union Plus Scholarship, 521
United Dairymen of Idaho Scholarship, 284
United Food and Commercial Workers International Union Plus Scholarship Program, 521
United Health Foundation Scholarship, 113
United Health/Hispanic Association of Colleges and Universities Scholarship, 325
United Methodist Loan Program, 601
United Methodist Scholarships, 522
United Parcel Service Earn & Learn Program Loans, 601

United States Army/ROTC Four-Year Scholarship, 523
United States Holocaust Memorial Museum Internship, 588
United States Senate Youth Program, 542
United Transportation Union Insurance Association Scholarship, 524
Universal Lubricants Scholarship, 285
University Journalism Scholarship, 437
Urban Forestry Internship, 570
U.S. Air Force Medial Support Agency, 581
U.S. Army Natick Soldier Research Development & Engineering Center, 582
U.S. Army Recruiting Command Student Loan Repayment Program, 526
U.S. Army/ROTC Nursing Scholarship, 523
U.S. Department of Education Rehabilitation Vocational Rehabilitation Assistance, 527
U.S. Department of State Internship, 589
U.S. National Arboretum Horticultural Internship, 590
U.S. National Arboretum National Herb Garden Year-Long Internship, 590
U.S. Senate Member Internships, 589
USDA/1890 National Scholars Program, 526
USHCC-Wells Fargo Scholarship, 331
USTA Scholarships; 529
Utah Career Teaching Scholarship/T.H. Bell Teaching Incentive Loan, 602
Valedictorial Tuition Waiver Program, 382
VAMOS Scholarship, 331
Vantagepoint Public Employee Memorial Scholarship Fund, 339
Vara Gray Scholarship Fund, 163
Varun Bhaskaran Scholarship, 343
The Vegetarian Resource Group College Scholarships, 530
Vegetarian Video Scholarship, 530
Ventura County Japanese-American Citizens League Scholarships, 530
Vermont Golf Association Scholarship, 530
Vermont Incentive Grant, 534
Vermont John H. Chafee Education and Training Scholarship, 534
Vermont Non-Degree Program, 534
Vermont Part-Time Grant, 534
Vertical Flight Foundation Scholarship, 109
Vice Admiral E.P. Travers Loan, 597
Vicki Willder Scholarship Fund, 322
The Victor Poor W5SMM Memorial Scholarship Fund, 190
Victoria S. and Bradley L. Geist Foundation Scholarship, 323
Violet Morrow Education Scholarship, 124
Virgil Eihusen Foundation Scholarship, 285
Virgin Islands Music Scholarship, 535
Virgin Islands Territorial Grants/Loans Program, 602
Virginia Academic Common Market, 496
Virginia Lee-Jackson Scholarship, 535
Virginia Museum of Fine Arts Visual Arts and Art History Fellowship, 536
Virginia Tuition Assistance Grant, 497
Virginia's Nurse Practitioner Nurse Midwife Scholarship, 536
Vocational (Bettinger, Holden and Perry) Memorial Scholarship, 106
Voice of Democracy Scholarship, 535
The Wall Street Journal Asia Internship, 590
The Wall Street Journal Europe Internship, 590
The Wall Street Journal Journalism Internship, 590
Wal-Mart Dependent Scholarship, 536
Walt Bartram Memorial Education Award (Region 12 and Chapter 119), 480
Walter and Marie Schmidt Scholarship, 448
Walter S. Patterson Scholarship, 229
Washington Crossing Foundation Scholarship, 537
Washington Internships for Students of Engineering, 591
Washington Media Scholars Media Fellows Program, 537
Washington State American Indian Endowed Scholarship, 114
Washington State Need Grant, 537
Washington State Scholarship Program, 538
Water Companies (NJ Chapter) Scholarship, 409
The Wayne Nelson, KB4UT, Memorial Scholarship, 191
Weisman Scholarship, 245
Wells Fargo Endowed Scholarship for Academic Excellence, 455
Wells Fargo Scholarship, 285
Wells Fargo Undergraduate Internships, 591
Welsh Heritage Scholarship, 538
Welsh Society of Philadelphia Undergraduate Scholarship, 538
West Virginia Engineering, Science, and Technology Scholarship, 540
West Virginia Higher Education Adult Part-time Student (HEAPS) Grant Program, 540
West Virginia Higher Education Grant, 540
West Virginia Underwood-Smith Teacher Scholarship, 540
West Virginia War Orphans Educational Assistance, 539
Western Plastics Pioneers Scholarship, 488
Western Undergraduate Exchange, 541
W.H. McClennan Scholarship, 344
Wilbur-Ellis Company High School Scholarship, 285
Wilder-Naifeh Technical Skills Grant, 505
Will J. Henderson Scholarship Fund in Hawaii, 323
William A. and Ann M. Brothers Scholarship, 204
William & Mary Dyrkacz Scholarships, 214
William B. Howell Memorial Scholarship, 204
The William Bennett, W7PHO, Memorial Scholarship, 191
William C. Davini Scholarship, 520
William C. Doherty Scholarships, 408
William D. & Jewell W. Brewer Scholarship Trusts, 139
William D. Ford Direct Student Loans, 601
William D. Greenlee Scholarship, 455
William E. Weisel Scholarship, 480
William J. and Marijane E. Adams, Jr. Scholarship, 219
William J. Schulz High School Essay Contest, 267
William James & Dorothy Bading Lanquist Fund, 323
William L. Boyd, IV, Florida Resident Access Grant (FRAG) Program, 265
William Park Woodside Founder's Scholarship, 214
William R. and Mila Kimel Scholarship, 177
The William R. Goldfarb Memorial Scholarship, 191
Willie Rudd Scholarship, 350
Willis F. Thompson Memorial Scholarship, 219
Willis H. Carrier Scholarship, 198
Wilma D. Hoyal/Maxine Chilton Memorial Scholarship, 121
Wilma Motley Memorial California Merit Scholarship, 84
Wisconsin Academic Excellence Scholarship, 543
Wisconsin Hearing & Visually Handicapped Student Grant, 543
Wisconsin Higher Education Grant, 543
Wisconsin Indian Student Assistance Grant, 544
Wisconsin Minority Teacher Loan Program, 602
Wisconsin Minority Undergraduate Retention Grant, 544
Wisconsin Talent Incentive Program Grant, 544
Wisconsin Tuition Grant, 544
Wisconsin Veterans Affairs Retraining Grant, 542
Wisconsin Veterans Education GI Bill Tuition Remission Program, 543
Wix Filters Scholarship, 286
Wolf Trap Foundation for the Performing Arts Internship, 592
Women in Architecture Scholarship, 221
Women Soar Scholarship for Innovation, 261

Women's Self Worth Foundation
Scholarship, 114
Women's Western Golf Foundation
Scholarship, 545
Wooddy Scholarship, 82
Worldstudio AIGA Scholarship, 546
Wyzant College Scholarship, 546
Yakama Nation Tribal Scholarship, 547
Yankee Clipper Contest Club Youth
Scholarship, 191
Yanmar/SAE Scholarship, 468
The Yasme Foundation
Scholarship, 191
Y.C. Yang Civil Engineering
Scholarship, 195
Young Naturalist Awards, 173
The You've Got a Friend in
Pennsylvania Scholarship, 192
The Zachary Taylor Stevens
Scholarship, 192
Zeller Summer Scholarship in
Medicinal Botany, 289
Zov's Bistro Scholarship, 356

More College Planning Resources from the College Board

College Handbook 2014

The only guide listing all accredited universities, two-year and four-year colleges, and technical schools in the United States — more than 3,900 in total.

2,200 pages, paperback
ISBN: 978-1-4573-0018-9
$29.99

The Official SAT Study Guide™: Second Edition

The Official SAT Study Guide™ is the only book that features 10 official practice tests created by the test maker. The No. 1 best-selling guide is packed with valuable test-taking approaches and focused sets of practice questions — just like those on the actual SAT® — to help students get ready for the test.

998 pages, trade paper
ISBN: 978-0-87447-852-5
$21.99

Book of Majors 2014

Explore in-depth descriptions of 200 majors, and see where over 1,100 majors are offered at colleges nationwide.

1,350 pages, paperback
ISBN: 978-1-4573-0022-6
$27.99

Get It Together for College, 2nd Edition

Take advantage of expert tips that help students stay on top of the college admission process.

240 pages, paperback
ISBN: 978-0-87447-974-4
$15.99

PAYING FOR COLLEGE

Getting Financial Aid 2014

A must-have book in today's economy, this is the perfect resource for families managing the high cost of college. This easy step-by-step guide shows why, when and how to apply for financial aid.

1,050 pages, paperback
978-1-4573-0019-6
$22.99

Scholarship Handbook 2014

The most complete and comprehensive guide to help families tap into the more than 1.7 million scholarships, internships and loans available to students each year.

624 pages, paperback
ISBN: 978-1-4573-0020-2
$29.99

13b-7693

Available wherever books are sold. Distributed by Macmillan.

Visit the College Board on the Web: www.collegeboard.org.